AN OF GENETIC FACTORS

IN AUTISM

A HANDBOOK FOR PROFESSIONALS

by the same author:

An A–Z of the Genetic Factors in Autism
A Handbook for Parents and Carers
ISBN 978 1 84310 679 1

Dietary Interventions in Autism Spectrum Disorders
Why They Work When They Do, Why They Don't When They Don't
ISBN 978 1 84310 939 6

Diagnosis and Intervention to Meet Their Needs
2nd edition
Colwyn Trevarthen, Jacqueline Robarts, Despina Papoudi and Kenneth J. Aitken
ISBN 978 1 85302 555 6

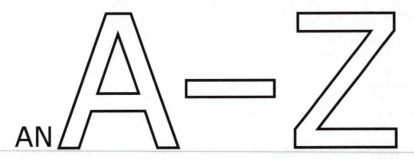

AN A–Z

OF GENETIC FACTORS

IN AUTISM

A HANDBOOK FOR PROFESSIONALS

KENNETH J. AITKEN

Jessica Kingsley *Publishers*
London and Philadelphia

First published in 2010
by Jessica Kingsley Publishers
116 Pentonville Road
London N1 9JB, UK
and
400 Market Street, Suite 400
Philadelphia, PA 19106, USA

www.jkp.com

Library of Congress Cataloging in Publication Data
Aitken, Kenneth J.
  An A-Z of genetic factors in autism : a handbook for professionals/Kenneth J. Aitken.
      p. ; cm.
  Includes bibliographical references and index.
  ISBN 978-1-84310-976-1 (alk. paper)
  1. Autism in children. 2. Autism spectrum disorders. 3. Mental illness – Genetic aspects. I. Title.
  [DNLM: 1. Autistic Disorder – genetics. 2. Autistic Disorder – complications. 3. Autistic
Disorder – therapy. 4. Genetic Diseases, Inborn – complications. WS 350.6 A311a 2010]
  RJ506.A9A39 2010
  618.92'85882-dc22
                                2010012797

British Library Cataloguing in Publication Data
A CIP catalogue record for this book is available from the British Library

ISBN 978 1 84310 976 1

Printed and bound in Great Britain by
MPG Books Group

#607319084

CONTENTS

SECTION B: *Genetic Conditions Seen in the Autistic Spectrum Disorders*

SECTION C: Some Conditions with Similarities to ASD 365

List of Tables

List of Figures

ACKNOWLEDGEMENTS

First and foremost, my thanks go to the very many individuals, families, staff and support groups I have talked to, worked with and learnt from over the past 30 years. They have enriched my knowledge of this fascinating area by allowing me to learn from and share with them.

I have been fortunate, over my career, to have learnt from and worked with a great many able clinicians and researchers who have taught me much about different relevant areas, such as infant and child development; developmental neurology; developmental psychopathology; neuroscience; genetics; and the field of autistic spectrum disorders. My thanks go to all of those mentioned below for helping me to my current level of understanding and for enabling me to convey, I hope, some of the rich complexity and excitement of work in this field. As always in such circumstances, any omissions and errors of fact or of interpretation are entirely my own.

My interest in the area of developmental psychology was stimulated by my long-time mentor and colleague Colwyn Trevarthen, whose dual interests and expertise in neuroscience and child development kindled my own. I was also fortunate in my early studies in psychology to have many excellent teachers, including John Beloff, Tom Bower, Margaret Donaldson, John Marshall, Lynne Murray, Jennifer Wishart and Peter Wright, who did much to channel and direct me. In philosophy, my thanks go particularly to Roy Bhaskar, Larry Briskman and Neil Tennant, all of whose views on philosophy of science and logic did much to sharpen my understanding of research method.

I have been fortunate to work with or under, and to be taught by, a number of leading clinicians in the area of ASD and developmental neuroscience, including Keith Brown; John Clements; Patricia Howlin; Marcel Kinsbourne; Robert Minns; Michael Rutter; Lorna Wing; Sula Wolff; and Bill Yule. I have also had the good fortune to attend taught courses by Henri Hecaen and Jean Aicardi, and to have worked on early neurobehavioural development with Heidelise Als, Berry Brazelton, Victor and Lilly Dubowitz and Kevin Nugent.

Over the years, I have discussed many of the issues raised here with a range of colleagues, including Simon Baron-Cohen; Tom Berney; Adrian Bird; B.J. Casey; Mary Coleman; John Corbett; Christopher Gillberg; James Harris; Bruce McEwen; John Menkes; Sid Shapiro; Walter Spitzer; Helen Tager-Flusberg; and Philip and Oznat Teitelbaum.

My interest in dietary and gastrointestinal factors has been stimulated by discussion with many clinicians and researchers, including Karoly Horvath; Simon Murch; Karl Reichelt; Bernie Rimland; Paul Shattock; and Paul Whiteley; in immunology through discussions with Paul Ashwood; Jonathan Brostoff; Jack Marchalonis; and Ivan Roitt; and in fatty acid metabolism by Gordon Bell; David Horrobin; Basant Puri; Alex Richardson; and Marion Ross.

My interest in genetics began many years ago through discussions with Conrad Waddington, and in behavioural genetics through contact with David Fulker, Robert Hinde and Aubrey Manning. This interest has extended steadily through my involvement in groups such as the Society for the Study of Behavioural Phenotypes, Sackler Foundation Neuroscience Think-tank meetings, the Scottish Autism Research Group and the International Society for Autism Research, and through discussions with clinical colleagues such as Martin Bax, Peter Baxter Greig and O'Brien.

I offer my greatest thanks for much of my longstanding and continuing interest in this fascinating area to Christopher Gillberg and Mary Coleman, whose early volume *The Biology of the Autistic Syndromes* (Coleman and Gillberg 1985) sparked what has become a lifelong fascination.

PRELUDE

The only real voyage of discovery consists not in seeking new
landscapes but in having new eyes.

Marcel Proust

Getting a diagnosis of autistic spectrum disorder (ASD) can be seen as a major hurdle – and also a major achievement – by families. Waiting lists can be lengthy and the number of clinicians adequately trained to use appropriate diagnostic assessments is still worryingly small. The development of the American Psychiatric Association's *DSM-V* and the World Health Organization's *ICD-11* is underway and changes in the criteria for ASD are likely on both systems. (Currently *ICD-10*, or the tenth revision of the *International Classification of Diseases*, is the World Health Organization's system for classifying medical conditions; *DSM-IV Tr* is the text revision of the fourth edition of the American Psychiatric Association's *Diagnostic and Statistical Manual*.) The *DSM-V* is due to be published in 2012 and *ICD-11* in 2014. As both systems are conducting field trials (which, for the ICD system, is a major change from their usual sapiential approach), we should soon have (one hopes, consistent) 'evidence-based' diagnostic criteria worldwide.

ASD diagnosis typically gives families access to a lot of very general information about the fact that the person may have a range of difficulties and/or differences which are part of what is talked about as 'the triad of impairments' – problems with social interaction; problems with communication; and restricted repetitive and stereotyped patterns of behaviour,

interests and activities. Diagnosis of ASD can also lead to help from a range of services and interventions aimed at improving communication, supporting families and improving quality of life.

Getting a diagnosis can also give access to specialist educational placements, practical help over educational and vocational issues, respite care and financial support. However, simply having an ASD diagnosis provides little information about the nature of the individual, why they are the way they are, or whether they will require such help and support.

The range of differences that can lead to a diagnosis mean that you can be tall, medium or short; slight, average or heavily built; have a large head, a regular-sized head or a small head; be learning disabled, of normal IQ or of high intelligence. You may or may not have epilepsy; you may or may not have immune abnormalities; you may or may not have sensory problems; you may or may not have gastrointestinal problems; you may or may not have any of a wide range of associated metabolic differences or difficulties. You might or might not benefit from any of a range of specific treatments, supplements, therapies or other interventions. There has been concern expressed over the broad range of presentations that come under the umbrella of ASD, and whether divisions into groupings based on cause, or into 'primary' and 'secondary' autism, might make things more manageable (Benaron 2003).

DSM-V seems likely to move to a broader ASD classification, including Asperger syndrome and Childhood Disintegrative Disorder and Pervasive Developmental Disorder Not Otherwise Specified under the same 'autistic spectrum disorder' umbrella diagnosis. It also seems likely that the updated criteria will recommend that genetic and metabolic screening are incorporated as a more routine part of clinical diagnostic assessment (Swedo 2009).

In this volume, we discuss the wide range of genetic conditions that have been reported in association with a diagnosis of autistic spectrum disorder. In doing so, we fully acknowledge that this 'blueprint' is likely to alter as larger and better studies clarify where such links are robust and where they are chance associations; where there is a specific behavioural phenotype and where there is a wide variation in presentation. (See Moss and Howlin 2009 for further discussion of these important issues.)

Individual differences are often due to differences in genetic make-up. Establishing the nature of the genetic basis in an individual can be just as important for effective care and management as obtaining the initial diagnosis of ASD itself (Robin 2006). Simply getting the diagnosis of an ASD does not clarify our understanding about the neurobiology; however, knowledge about neurobiological factors may be important or even critical to providing the best help for someone with an ASD, or in highlighting areas of additional need or difficulty. Often these differences within ASD are not adequately considered or properly assessed. Sometimes they are ignored on the basis that if they are not autism-specific, they are not relevant to management.

It is this gap in understanding, where increasing knowledge of the differences within autism are often as important as recognizing the commonalities across those with the diagnosis, that forms the focus of this book.

The constant media barrage of information on the latest craze in miracle cures, and the claims that this or that treatment can work for anyone with autism, do little to help. Many 'weird and wonderful' treatments can be found, some of which, no doubt, are effective for some people with ASD, and some of which do neither good nor ill to most, while some are dangerous to many, and a few can be tragically fatal (MMWR 2006).

All too often, alternative treatments are advocated because they are available rather than because they are effective. Sometimes, there is evidence that one person has changed dramatically (with the implicit inference that if it worked for them, it might work for another child with ASD).

In attempting to provide a fairly comprehensive coverage of the literature, some conditions are discussed in this book in significantly more detail than others – Down syndrome, for example, because it is relatively common and has been recognized for a considerable period, has a large amount of information, both on the condition and on interventions. In addition, there has been considerable controversy over the possible benefits of alternative therapies and a range of studies have been carried out on their merits and demerits. This literature is presented to enable the interested reader to access detailed information on what has been tried, rather than 'cherry-picking' information on successful approaches. There is also a large literature on the biology and genetics of various other conditions, such as the muscular dystrophies, neurofibromatosis and the Joubert and Williams syndromes.

For a number of other conditions, the literature is more sparse.

Many of the approaches that are discussed here in relation to specific genetic conditions are at an early stage in their evaluation. These are highlighted to raise awareness of developments which are beginning to have an effect on clinical management.

INTRODUCTION

Knowledge is of two kinds. We know a subject ourselves, or we know where we can find information on it.

Samuel Johnson (1709–1784)

For some, being on the autistic spectrum is how they are, it is how they always want to be, and it is something that carries no associated problems. For those fortunate people, this book may help to offer a clearer understanding of why they may be as they are, without having much further effect on their lives. This is just like taking a course in human biology or psychology that may help all of us to come to a different view of why we feel and act as we do.

Many famous able people may have had an ASD – Isaac Newton, the polymath; Charles Darwin, the 'father' of evolutionary theory; Ludwig Wittgenstein, the philosopher; Albert Einstein, the physicist, discoverer of relativity and 'father' of the atomic bomb; Paul Erdos, the mathematician; Samuel Beckett, the playwright and poet; Erik Satie, the jazz musician and L.S. Lowry, the 'matchstick-man' painter have all been thought, by some at least, to have ASDs. (For more detailed discussion of the putative association between creativity and ASD, see Brown 2010; Fitzgerald 2004, 2005; Treffert 2006, 2010; Walker and Fitzgerald 2006.) Similar arguments have been made for a link between creativity and various other conditions, such as schizophrenia (Horrobin 2001) and manic-depression/bipolar disorder (Jamison 1993).

The expanding panoply of gifted individuals who are thought to have been on the autistic spectrum seems somehow at odds with the fact that ASDs are usually seen as a set of conditions associated with communication difficulties, problems with social understanding, learning problems, and often with a host of associated medical issues. 'Savant skills' (isolated areas of extreme ability) are found in individuals with ASDs, but are by no means typical or even common in this group. This indicates the variation across those with ASDs rather than suggesting some key common factor.

Widespread public awareness of ASD is often dated to Dustin Hoffman's portrayal of an autistic savant in the film *Rainman* – a character based loosely on a real autistic 'mega-savant', Kim Peek (Peek 1997; Peek and Hanson 2007). This portrayal has led to the public expectation that anyone with an ASD will have some spectacular ability.

This book fills some of the gaps in basic knowledge – about whether genetic and epigenetic factors can cause or contribute to autistic conditions, and about how and why they should be assessed. Where there is sufficient evidence, it also suggests what can and could be done to help. I hope that, at the very least, this will make many people dealing with the ASDs stop and think.

For many with an ASD, rather than being exclusively an asset, their condition is associated with problems that they would much rather not have – problems such as epilepsy, anxiety, depression, gastrointestinal difficulties, immune sensitivities, learning problems, sleep problems and dietary sensitivities. For these people, and for their carers, this book may offer insight and help.

The past decade has seen a revolution in our ability to both detect and understand genetic and epigenetic conditions. Where it had previously been assumed that specific genetic disorders were rare in autism (perhaps seen at most in one to three per cent of cases), developing technologies allow the examination of DNA in ever finer detail. The focus for several years was on identifying the specific set of genes that were thought to be abnormal in most people with ASD. We now know that genetic abnormalities are relatively common in ASD, but there is little support from recent research for a common set of affected genes. Rather, there appear to be a large number of genetic factors, each sufficient to increase the risk. Equally, we are coming to realize that there are ethnic differences in the genetics of disease that may have important implications for screening and care:

> …the genetic variants predicted to underlie common disease are often not common across populations with different ancestry or differ significantly in frequency among such populations. (Bamshad and Guthery 2007)

As we shall see, a number of these conditions are much more common in certain ethnic groups than in others.

In the past, twin concordance levels were used to argue for a common genetic mechanism in autism. The reason for high levels of concordance in identical twins – where both twins are similarly affected – is typically that both share the same core genetic make-up (although for some things it could be due to having the same exposure, as we would see if both twins had been exposed to the same toxin or disease). If one pair of identical twins shares a genetic difference that predisposes both of them to develop ASD, it does not necessarily mean, however, that they will share this same make-up with the next pair of concordant identical twins. Because one pair of identical twins who both have fragile-X syndrome are both autistic, this does not mean that another pair of identical twins who are both autistic will both have fragile-X.

There is a flaw in the argument for common heritability that can be highlighted if we look at the following.

Most people would claim to follow the logic by which the statements A and B below lead to conclusion C:

A) All men are mortal.

B) Socrates is a man.

Therefore:

C) Socrates is mortal.

That A+B lead to C seems clear and logical, but it is not a necessary conclusion. By following the same line of argument, you could also reach the following conclusion:

Therefore:

C) All men are Socrates.

– which most of us would see as clearly false (although it would be true if Socrates was the only man). A similar logical error seems to be made with ASD. The reasoning typically runs as follows:

A) All ASD has a genetic cause.

B) Fragile-X is a genetic cause of ASD.

Therefore:

C) All ASD is caused by fragile-X.

This could only be correct if ASD were caused by fragile-X, *and* ASD had a single, genetic cause. The following conclusion would be more sensible:

Therefore:

C) Fragile-X can be one genetic cause of ASD.

Here the situation is further complicated by the fact that not all people with fragile-X are also autistic.

There are many syndromes and conditions that have been associated with ASDs – some are more common in the families of those with an autistic spectrum disorder; others are genetic conditions that have been found more often than expected in those who are on the spectrum. Some of these findings may turn out to be mere chance associations, reported because they looked significant at the time. Some people may have more than one genetic difference.

A single polygenic cause could lead to a high MZ, low DZ concordance rate; however, a number of independent but sufficient genetic causes could equally give rise to a high concordance rate if a number of genetic and/or environmental causes were independently sufficient, as both MZ twins will have the same genetic make-up, and are also more likely to be exposed to the same environment. (For example, sharing a chorion will increase the likelihood of common viral exposure.)

Twin studies bring further complexities. Being born a twin increases risks of a range of problems – you are typically born smaller and have a higher than normal risk of a range of perinatal difficulties. There has been considerable debate over whether being born a twin increases your risk of developing ASD. Betancur, Leboyer and Gillberg (2002) and Ho, Todd and Constantino (2005) both suggest it may, while Hallmayer *et al.* (2002) suggest that it does not. For certain conditions such as Goldenhar syndrome [38], there does appear to be an increased risk of being autistic associated with being an MZ twin (Wieczorek *et al.* 2007).

As we will discuss, conditions that a few years ago were seen as genetic and therefore unchangeable are now seen as genetic but modifiable, because we now have a better understanding of how they operate and how these factors can affect development. The major change in our understanding of genetics has come from our increasing understanding of how genetic mechanisms are affected by non-genetic factors like parental behaviour and diet.

Schizophrenia, a condition in which there have now been over 700 candidate genes proposed and some 1,300 association studies carried out, still seems far from any resolution of its genetic underpinnings (Collier 2008; Crow 2008; Need *et al.* 2009; O'Donovan, Craddock and Owen 2008; Sullivan 2008b).

There is a regular stream of new reports on possible associations between genetic conditions and ASD. (See Chugani *et al.* 2007; Kanavin *et al.* 2007; Mefford *et al.* 2008; Neves-Pereira *et al.* 2009; Zafeiriou *et al.* 2007; and Zannolli *et al.* 2003 for a number of examples.)

There are regular reports of new techniques that allow the detection and study of smaller and smaller differences in our genetic make-up, the latest being the use of 'cytogenetic arrays' (the Ledbetter Paper provided a good introduction to the technology) to detect small copy number variations resulting in microdeletions and duplications. The majority of these differences were virtually unknown even five years ago. A short, readable introduction to this issue can be found in a *New England Journal of Medicine* editorial (Ledbetter 2008).

It is important to understand that because something has a genetic basis, this does not necessarily mean that it is unchangeable; in much the same way that understanding the history of events that resulted in a fear or depression does not mean that it is untreatable. Understanding why is the first step to successful intervention (where this is needed), because knowledge of the mechanisms involved gives an idea of the ways in which they may be altered.

Several sufficient causes may operate in the same individual, and it is important that this possibility is explored, especially if the presenting phenotype is atypical (see, for example, Stevens, Tartaglia, Hagerman and Riley 2010).

Where to start?

Typically, families are beginning to ask questions about whether their child is developing normally by the middle of their second year (De Giacomo and Fombonne 1998). An Atlanta study (Wiggins, Baio and Rice 2006) found that, on average, diagnostic assessments were only begun when the child was around 48 months, with diagnoses typically being made when they were approximately 61 months – over a year later.

In England and Wales, the National Autism Plan for Children (NAP-C) gave a target of 8.5 months from initial concerns to diagnostic formulation and feedback to families (NIASA 2003). It has rapidly become apparent that achieving this target has been impossible in many areas (Preece and Mott 2006; Sharma, Chandrakantha and Mold 2007).

There is a palpable frustration in the lay literature, expressed by informed parents of affected children, some with basic medical qualifications, over the apparent lack of progress in identifying causal mechanisms and scientifically based approaches to treatment (Fitzpatrick 2008; Nadesan 2005). A simple fallacy in much of this literature is that ASD is a single, ill-understood condition, with the implicit assumption that there may be one approach that will be likely to help all, once the biological basis has been better understood. A corollary to this is that in the meantime anything that has been shown to be unhelpful in group studies will not be helpful to anyone on the autistic spectrum.

Particular 'behavioural phenotypes' present as ASD and can often be linked to particular genetic conditions, and many of those currently known are detailed in later sections of this book. Children with particular genetic differences predisposing to ASD can show worse reactions than others to natural infections or to particular treatments (Poling 2006; Towbin K.E., Fyre, Shofner and Zimmerman 2003b).

A wide range of clinical disorders are common in those with ASDs, more and more of which are being linked to specific genetic conditions, to previously undescribed genetic factors or metabolic differences (Aitken 2008; Caglayan 2010; Cohen 2003; Gillberg and Billstedt 2000; Gillberg and Coleman 1996; Spence 2004; Sykes and Lamb 2007).

It is important to understand that much of the progress being made in understanding the ASDs comes from approaches – for example, knock-in and knock-out animal genetic models, molecular epidemiology and studies of epigenetic factors – that are not part of the academic training of the majority of clinicians who work with ASD, most of whom will have a medical, clinical psychology or paramedical background. Progress requires a cross-disciplinary perspective that is lacking from much of the clinical literature, and not provided in the 'evidence-based medicine' (EBM) model that forms the basis for current health approaches. EBM has revolutionized our healthcare systems by focusing on the research evidence on what works. (For a basic introduction see Goldacre 2009, and for a proper discussion, see Straus,

Richardson, Glasziou and Haynes 2005.) Methods have been developed to evaluate what works, how well, and with whom. EBM relies on access to good, well-conducted research on agreed conditions. The approach is inherently sound, but can only be effective where there is research on an agreed condition. The major problem in much clinical practice is that there is poor agreement on the nature of the condition and/or little research evidence, but a need to do something (Horrobin 2003).

As ASDs can arise for a range of possible genetic reasons, some with treatment implications and some so far without, we need to develop much better research models to tease out what approaches might work with which conditions, and why (a point frequently made in Fitzpatrick 2008).

There are a number of ways in which ASDs can present with obvious physical and developmental differences that are probably genetic in origin, but for which we, as yet, have no knowledge of the likely genetic basis. For example, Snape and colleagues (Snape *et al.* 2006) described a nine-year-old child with intellectual disability and autism in combination with an unusual skull shape and long fingers with contracted ligaments, but without the gene defect in FBN2 typically seen in this type of skeletal problem. Harry Chugani's group in Detroit have reported on four children with autism and unilateral facial port-wine staining. (Such facial colouration is typically seen in Sturge-Weber syndrome accompanied by cortical damage to the opposite side of the brain.) None of these children showed evidence on MRI imaging of the brain atrophy typically seen in Sturge-Weber syndrome, and their metabolic profiles differed from other children with autism reported by the same group (Chugani *et al.* 2007; but see the discussion in section [59] below).

For several of the conditions included here the evidence to date suggests a link with ASD, but so far has only been described by one clinical or research group. Now that, in the USA at least, there is a network of research centres collaborating on collecting data – one such group being the CPEA (Collaborative Program for Excellence in Autism), another being the PARIS (Paris Autism International Sibpair Study group) – getting such replication of findings should become easier. So far, lack of replication often arises as certain centres pursue specific interests that are not researched in other centres, or use techniques that are not used elsewhere.

Some conditions such as congenital adrenal hyperplasia [25] have been included here because they have been frequently cited elsewhere as possible factors, and the biological reasoning behind this may be important, although the current evidence does not suggest that they are important in the pathogenesis of ASD.

Although confirmation of the same finding by other researchers is taken as a benchmark of the likely importance of any finding in clinical science, this convention has become blurred in ASD because:

1. interesting associations may be truly causally related, but if untested by other groups lack the 'independent replication' typically relied on in modern clinical science. This results in an apparent *'false negative'* – where there is lack of replication as replication has not been attempted, rather than because it has been attempted and not been achieved

2. as multicentre and multinational research collaborations have developed, data from several genetic and tissue databanks (such as the Autism Genetic Resource Exchange (AGRE), the Simons Foundation Simplex collection,

and the EuroBioBank network) are now commonly used by numbers of different researchers – and 'confirmation' of findings may now sometimes be based on analyses of samples taken or data submitted on the same individuals as were used in publications by those reporting the initial findings. Where part of the same material from the same subjects is looked at by several centres, or where several databanks have acquired material from the same subjects, this could lead to misleadingly impressive agreement – everyone finds the same thing because they are all looking at the same subset of people. This type of mistake can lead to *false positive* results – the conclusion *either* that an association is present where there is none, *or*, where an association is present, that it is stronger than it actually is.

We now have numerous examples of cases where a significant association found by one study or group cannot be replicated elsewhere. The paroxonase 1 (PON1) association with ASD seen in North America but not in Southern Europe is one such example (see D'Amelio *et al.* 2005).

Given the reported association between prematurity and subsequent ASD (Indredavik, Vik, Skranes and Brubakk 2008; Limperopoulos *et al.* 2008), it is interesting to note that, from the Norwegian MoBa cohort (den norske **Mor** and **Barn**-undersokelsen; the MoBa project is a large, detailed prospective study of development in 100,000 infants from consecutive Norwegian pregnancies), there appears to be an association between foetal PON1 and premature birth (Ryckman *et al.* 2010).

There are various problems with the current research framework.

1. There is a reluctance to fund independent replication of research – once a finding is already in the literature it loses novelty and is less attractive as a fundable research project; assuming that the right questions are addressed, the move to multi-centre studies should lessen the problems inherent in this. However, there is a concomitant increase in expense in such exercises.

2. Whether Government or charity funded, most research has been driven by a small number of individuals with particular views of what is sensible to pursue – as these tend to be more senior figures, their fondly held views often lag behind current scientific thinking and delay the investigation of less 'mainstream' hypotheses.

3. In some areas, such as the extent and nature of gastrointestinal involvement, for example, political expedience and potential effects on public health can be major factors in driving the research agenda rather than the clinical merit or otherwise of the ideas involved.

Terms used in this book

For simplicity, the term 'autistic spectrum disorder' (ASD) has been used throughout to indicate those who meet the criteria for an *ICD-10* or *DSM-IV* ASD diagnosis.

These two systems are the diagnostic classifications in use worldwide. They are the accepted standard for diagnosis; however we also have to accept that they have their limitations. In a recent interview when asked about the relative merits of the current DSM and ICD systems, Professor Sir Michael Rutter replied as follows:

> We have a system, in both cases where there are far too manydiagnoses; there is no way any psychiatrist can remember the algorithms for hundreds of diagnoses, so what do psychiatrists do? They opt out by diagnosing NOS, which means that the individual

psychiatrist is thinking "I don't believe in the differentiation" or "I couldn't be bothered with it". Either way, as a piece of scientific information, it is useless.

Rutter (2010) p216.

There are obviously limitations on the rigorous application of complex systems in clinical practice. In much of the research we go on to discuss we accept that the standard we are comparing against is typically diagnosis through the rigorous application of one or other of these systems.

The main genetic conditions that have been reported in association with ASD diagnoses are discussed. For a number of these, there is a clinical literature associated with a particular name. Where it appears that this may be synonymous with another condition (as we see, for example, with the various conditions linked to 22q11.2), more than one entry may appear. Each condition is given a separate section, with relevant information to link to any other possible names. It may be that, for a genetic condition identified several years ago, developments in our understanding have changed the way this is known to operate. Conditions are also discussed where, although there is little evidence to support their association with ASD, they have been frequently cited in the literature.

I have used UK spellings like 'paediatric', 'behaviour' and 'centre' rather than their more widely used American equivalents of 'pediatric', 'behavior' and 'center'.

The term 'learning disability' is used in the UK and European sense of a person with a global cognitive difficulty, rather than in the American sense of someone who has a more discrete impairment. In the UK the latter would be called a 'specific learning impairment'. The equivalent American term for learning disability would be 'intellectual disability' (Harris 2006).

Many of the conditions discussed are referred to by multiple terms used in the literature. Where a condition is mentioned which is treated in a separate section of the book, the number of the relevant section is given in square brackets for ease of cross-referencing (for example: 'Apert syndrome [12]').

A brief note on genetic terms

We will refer to the 'gene locus' for particular conditions. Genes, as we know them, are studied in a particular state of cell development known as 'metaphase', when DNA compacts into chromosomes. At this stage, the DNA is tightly wound around 'histones', almost like thread around a bobbin, and bound up inside 'scaffolding proteins' ready for cell division. At this point, the chromosomes can be seen under a light microscope. This is when chromosomes look the way most people expect to see them from biology textbooks at school or university. They can be photographed, and the pairs of chromosomes sorted into a karyogram as we see in Figure A1. An area called the 'centromere' can be seen on each chromosome (a narrower band of material seen some way along the chromosome), to which 'spindle fibres' attach during cell division itself, and along which each chromosome separates into two, usually identical, halves.

What do the numbers given as the gene locus tell us? Where we discuss adenylosuccinate lyase (ADSL) deficiency, for example, you will see that it is linked to a particular gene locus:

22q13.1

In humans, males have an X and a Y sex chromosome and females have two X chromosomes. The other 22 pairs of chromosomes are the same in both sexes and are called 'autosomes'. The autosomes are numbered in descending order of size, so chromosome 22 is the smallest autosome pair found in human DNA. This chromosome has over 800 genes. Genes are coding sequences of DNA that result in the production of proteins.

The letters **p** and **q** are used in the gene locus term when a more precise location on the chromosome is known. The **p**, standing for 'petit' (or small), signifies the shorter length of chromosome from the centromere and the **q** signifies the longer section. The numbers after **p** or **q** indicate how far from the centromere the region lies: the larger the number, the further from the centromere. **22q12** is closer to the centromere than **22q13** and **22q13.1** is closer than **22q13.2**.

This means that the gene difference identified as being present in those with ADSL deficiency is found on chromosome 22 (the autosomes are placed in descending order of size from 1 to 22, so in this case the difference is on the smallest autosome); further, it is on the **q** or longer section of chromosome 22, and at a site which is labelled **13.1**, which tells us how far along the section from the centromere the difference is found.

Schematically, chromosome 22 looks like the diagram below. The diagram shows a variety of clinical conditions and their approximate locations within chromosome 22.

This image is adapted, with permission, from one produced by the US Department of Energy Genome Program and, along with images for all of the nuclear chromosomes and similar lists of associated conditions, this can be accessed from their website (http://genomics.energy.gov).

The area where the defective gene that results in adenylosuccinate lyase (ADSL) deficiency [9] is found is close to the bottom horizontal band on the diagram, and the centromere is the narrow 'waist' signified by the two short bars between the ellipse and the main body of the chromosome, at the top of the diagram.

Animal models

Where possible, in discussing specific conditions, I have tried to include available animal research on genetic models. The development of many such models in different species has allowed investigation of many genetic factors, as these affect metabolism and neural development. (See Inlow and Restifo 2004 for a useful introduction to such comparative genetic approaches.) As with all other areas discussed, there are limitations and caveats (see, for example: Kozul *et al.* 2008), and ethical issues raised by animal studies, however, much has been learnt through such work and where this is relevant it has been discussed.

Kenneth J. Aitken
Edinburgh, March 2010

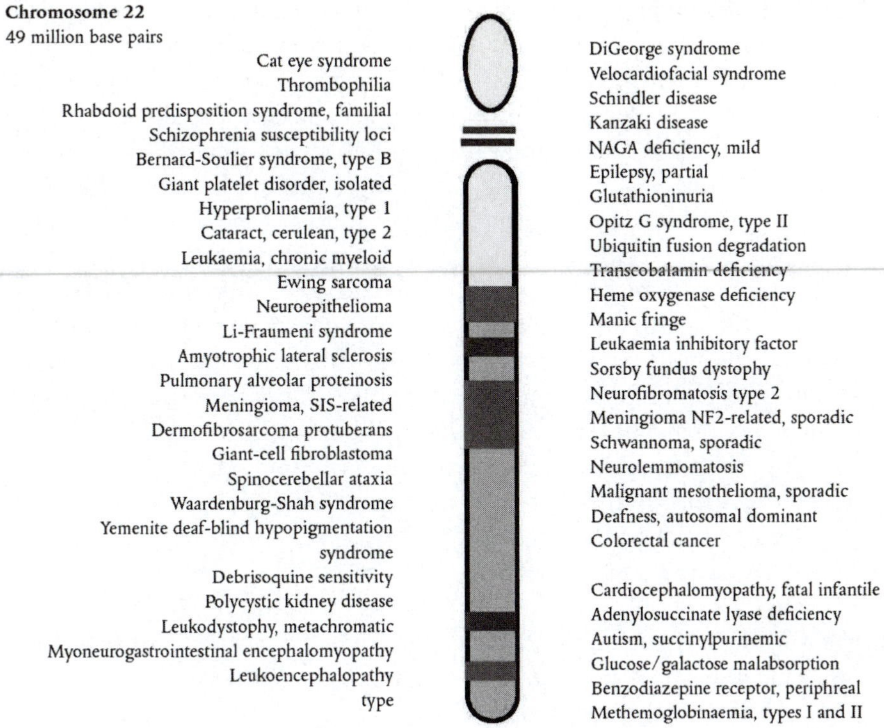

Chromosome 22

49 million base pairs

Cat eye syndrome
Thrombophilia
Rhabdoid predisposition syndrome, familial
Schizophrenia susceptibility loci
Bernard-Soulier syndrome, type B
Giant platelet disorder, isolated
Hyperprolinaemia, type 1
Cataract, cerulean, type 2
Leukaemia, chronic myeloid
Ewing sarcoma
Neuroepithelioma
Li-Fraumeni syndrome
Amyotrophic lateral sclerosis
Pulmonary alveolar proteinosis
Meningioma, SIS-related
Dermofibrosarcoma protuberans
Giant-cell fibroblastoma
Spinocerebellar ataxia
Waardenburg-Shah syndrome
Yemenite deaf-blind hypopigmentation
syndrome
Debrisoquine sensitivity
Polycystic kidney disease
Leukodystophy, metachromatic
Myoneurogastrointestinal encephalomyopathy
Leukoencephalopathy
type

DiGeorge syndrome
Velocardiofacial syndrome
Schindler disease
Kanzaki disease
NAGA deficiency, mild
Epilepsy, partial
Glutathioninuria
Opitz G syndrome, type II
Ubiquitin fusion degradation
Transcobalamin deficiency
Heme oxygenase deficiency
Manic fringe
Leukaemia inhibitory factor
Sorsby fundus dystophy
Neurofibromatosis type 2
Meningioma NF2-related, sporadic
Schwannoma, sporadic
Neurolemmomatosis
Malignant mesothelioma, sporadic
Deafness, autosomal dominant
Colorectal cancer

Cardiocephalomyopathy, fatal infantile
Adenylosuccinate lyase deficiency
Autism, succinylpurinemic
Glucose/galactose malabsorption
Benzodiazepine receptor, periphreal
Methemoglobinaemia, types I and II

Figure A1: Schematic of chromosome 22

SECTION A

Focus on the Autistic Spectrum Disorders

WHAT IS THE PURPOSE
OF A BOOK LIKE THIS?

> Improbable as it is, all other explanations are more improbable still.
>
> *Sherlock Holmes in Silver Blaze,*
> *Arthur Conan Doyle (1892)*

> The most incomprehensible thing about the world is that it is comprehensible.
>
> *Albert Einstein: 'Physics and Reality.'*
> *Journal of the Franklin Institute (March 1936)*

> A witty saying proves nothing.
>
> *Voltaire*
> *(alias François-Marie Arouet)*

There is often a mismatch of expectations between what parents are hoping for from clinical assessment coupled with the implied benefits they expect from publicized research, and the reality of what is provided in clinical practice. Headlines that proclaim "autism can be diagnosed in 15 minutes from a brain scan" or that tout the failsafe nature and dramatic effects of the latest autism 'cure' set high expectations that can rarely be matched.

A UK survey (Charman and Clare 2004) found that the research priorities that were identified by people with autism and their families diverged from those that

Identified Research Priority	As rated by Individuals and their families (N = 248) (%)	As rated by Researchers (N = 331) (%)	ISI* current activity (%)
Causes	42	29	19
Epidemiology	2	2	
Diagnosis	7	12	
Symptoms	13	27	51
Interventions	32	28	20
Family and Services	4	3	

*ISI = the Institute for Scientific Information (Data from: Charman and Clare 2004

were identified by researchers and from emphasis in current research:

'I don't want to know *that* I am autistic, I want to know *why* and what we can do about it!' is the issue many people raise or have risen on their behalf after receiving a diagnosis. Those affected and their families want to know about causes and potential treatments, while current research is largely focused on symptoms, and much current service provision is focused on catering to individual symptomology rather than improving function.

Why someone has an ASD is the question that often remains unanswered clinically, is largely a function of genetic makeup, and it is also the issue this book sets out to look into.

Much of the material addressed in this volume is complex, and outside the scope of clinical training for many 'front-line' professionals involved in assessment and diagnosis of ASD. I have attempted to convey my own view of its relevance, and to present it in as straightforward a way as I can, however, to paraphrase Einstein, it is as simple as I can make it, but not simpler. I hope what it can do is to provide some basic information to help the reader to a better understanding of some of what is known of the genetics and the biology of the autistic spectrum disorders (ASDs), how these relate to differences in the clinical phenotype and to the likelihood of particular problems, and how applying that knowledge can help to improve the quality of life and outcome for many of those on the autistic spectrum.

A little knowledge may be a dangerous thing, but for many of those with ASD, having no knowledge can be far worse. When the latest breakthrough approach is being touted by the media, or is recommended by a friend or covered by a documentary, understanding why it might (or might not) be of relevance for someone else can be crucial in weighing up either the possible benefit or the waste of time, energy and resources involved, and even in judging whether it might cause harm. A large proportion of those with an ASD – a best estimate at the moment would be at least 65 per cent – have conditions with a clear genetic basis. We now know that there are a large number of such conditions, and an increasing number are turning out to have major implications for management and treatment. The best help for someone with an ASD depends on understanding the basis to their condition, not merely in making generalizations from others with an ASD. Breakthroughs in autism treatment will inevitably come in many small steps, one condition at a time, rather than through discovery of *the* cause and *the* treatment for everyone.

Finding a genetic factor that has been linked to autism is not necessary – not all cases of autism can be shown to have a genetic difference, and most of the genes that have been implicated do not cause autism in all cases, but only increase its likelihood. To quote from a popular book by the parent of a child with ASD:

> The genes underlying diseases are generally just risk factors, not direct causes. Genetic predispositions interact with the lives we lead (the countries we live in, the families we form, the way we manage our bodies), and these interactions can affect illness expressions.

(Grinker 2007, pp.119–120)

Most books and guidelines on ASDs start by making the assumption that ASD is a single diagnosis, implying a single cause. Few, if any, approaches have been shown to be of much benefit to most/all of those with ASD, with the possible exception of behavioural interventions.

If autism were a single condition, little could be done, other than funding rapid diagnostic services and behavioural intervention programmes by appropriately trained therapists, and increasing the provision of long-term support services.

Approaches such as applied behavioural analysis (ABA) are helpful to a wide range of people, being based on generic behavioural principles and are not ASD-specific (Granpeesheh, Tarbox and Dixon 2009; Kasari and Lawton 2010). Opinions on the level of benefit from ABA vary (Ospina *et al.* 2008; Parsons *et al.* 2009). Behavioural approaches are just as likely to help others with behavioural issues or developmental disabilities. The beneficial effects are not reliant on accurate diagnosis, but on accurate functional analysis.

Most other ASD interventions, where they are effective, work only for subgroups. This book indicates some of the biological reasons why this is the case, and at the need to revise our views of ASD and of what we should be doing to systematically investigate and help.

In some cases, an apparent benefit may turn out to be little more than a placebo effect. This can happen where belief in something affects how successfully it works or appears to work. This is a factor in all treatments – there will be a proportion of cases where improvements result from factors other than the physiological effect of the treatment, even where the treatment had a real biological effect (Evans 2003; Goldacre 2009). In other cases, change may or may not occur, and may be the result of a critical difference between those individuals who did and those who did not benefit from treatment. This applies to many possible factors in ASD, from restriction diets in phenylketonuria [57] to likely benefits in tuberous sclerosis [73]. (For discussion, see Aitken 2009.) Although it is less often acknowledged,

such specificity applies as much too conventional pharmacotherapies as to alternative biobehavioural approaches.

Many simple tests may need to be done, often at particular times, or developmental stages to rule in or rule out different possible causes. For example various clinical possibilities should be investigated in children with accelerated head growth and ASD behaviour. These include PTEN (phosphatase and tensin homologue) gene defects (such as Bannayan-Riley-Ruvalcaba syndrome (BRRS) [15], basal cell naevus syndrome (BCNS) [16], Cowden syndrome [26], Proteus syndrome [62], and Sotos syndrome [68]) (Butler *et al.* 2005). To evaluate possible overgrowth, you have to have the information that the baby's head is growing too fast, you need to have serial head measurements to check how fast the head is growing, and you need to have robust comparison data. For North America and the UK, there is good data on head growth, but only over the first three years of life. Ideally, therefore, such measures should be taken early, because the correct diagnosis may be important for understanding the problem and for commencing appropriate therapy.

In general terms, we know that growth is different in many of those with ASD (Whiteley, Dodou, Todd and Shattock 2004; Xiong *et al.* 2007). A recently described but as yet unreplicated association with physical overgrowth is MOMO syndrome (where there is a combination of Macrosomia, Obesity, Macrocephaly and Ocular abnormalities – Giunco *et al.* 2008).

Many children with large heads are perfectly normal. The clinical term 'benign familial megalencephaly' described the situation where large heads run in the family and everyone in the family is developmentally normal (Day and Schutt 1979).

There is a group of other 'overgrowth' conditions which typically result in an enlarged head but which have not to date been linked to ASD: Beckwith-Wiedemann syndrome; hemihyperplasia [84]; Klippel-Trelaunay syndrome; Maffucci syndrome; Parkes Weber syndrome; PEHO syndrome [86]; Perlman syndrome; Simpson-Golabi-Behmel syndrome Type 1 [87]; Sturge-Weber syndrome [88]; and Weaver syndrome [89]. Some, such as Sturge-Weber (see section [59] on port-wine facial staining and autism) and Weaver (see sections on Rubinstein-Taybi [64] and Sotos [68] syndromes), appear to overlap with conditions with a known ASD association. These other overgrowth conditions also have particular developmental issues associated with them – epilepsy in Sturge-Weber, for example – so differentiating between such conditions can be important for providing the best care and support.

Some investigations, such as neurotransmitter imaging, may only be warranted where a specific genetic/metabolic diagnosis has been clarified. (For recent developments in this area, see Lee, Weng, Peng and Tzen 2009.) Many factors have different developmental trajectories in the ASDs when compared to controls – factors such as differences in the development and maturation of cortical serotonergic neurotransmitter pathways (Chandana *et al.* 2005).

Better understanding of the pathogenesis of behavioural phenotypes consistent with an ASD is revealing a complex of independent and overlapping factors, many of which are proving to be genetic (see, e.g. Thompson and Levitt 2010). This improved understanding of the basis to diagnosis will have major positive effects on clinical outcome.

THE NEED FOR BIOLOGICALLY FOCUSED INTERVENTIONS

An overview of medical intervention strategies in autism stated the following: 'There is a lack of clinically based evidence on which to universally recommend a rational clinical algorithm for treatment; we suggest that rational pharmacotherapy may offer symptomatic relief to core areas of dysfunction in the autistic population. Future research into rational medical treatment options is desperately needed.' (Chez, Memon and Hung 2004).

If the evidence suggested that the same approach was best for helping everyone with an ASD, whatever the cause, then teasing apart the various causes and conditions that can result in ASD might be of academic interest, but wouldn't be of much further clinical use. There are indeed some approaches that are broadly applicable and are starting to show positive results, such as intensive early behavioural intervention (Dawson *et al.* 2010), but these tend to be approaches that would potentially benefit any individual with developmental difficulties and are not 'ASD-specific'.

A number of clinical papers have reviewed the evidence on treatments from the perspective that ASD is a single condition. These have all come to the same general conclusion: the evidence for beneficial effects of most treatments is limited at best (Diggle and McConachie 2009; Green *et al.* 2010; Herbert, Sharp and Gaudiano 2002; Howlin 1998; Levy and Hyman 2005; Lilienfeld 2005; Ospina *et al.* 2008). This conclusion discounts those cases where improvement resulted from a clearly documented treatment, but where the findings could not be repeated with other people with an ASD. This is not because these results are being ignored, but because of the assumption that the same underlying cause affects everyone and therefore that the same treatment should be equally beneficial to all.

Differentiation within the autistic continuum is clearly possible based on biological factors such as genetics with clear implications for best management and treatment based on such biological differences. It seems Luddite and nonsensical for anyone to maintain the position that such differentiation would be neither relevant nor useful.

To illustrate this point, I will take a little time to discuss one 'alternative' treatment for autism that was popular in the late 1990s but that has largely fallen out of favour: secretin.

Secretin is a compound produced from S-cells near the top of the small intestine, usually in response to food leaving the stomach. It triggers the release of alkaline fluids from the pancreas to neutralize the hydrochloric acid produced by the lining of the stomach. If this did not happen, stomach acid would inflame, and then begin to digest, the walls of the intestine, and would imbalance the gut bacteria, leading to dysbiosis.

In 1998, three autistic children were reported to have made huge improvements in their development and social and communicative function after being given secretin infusions as part of a routine gastrointestinal assessment (Horvath *et al.* 1998).

Secretin has been used for many years as a test of pancreatic function – when secretin is infused, the pancreas should release more alkaline fluid into the small intestine. Prior to Horvath *et al.*'s report secretin had never been used as a treatment, and to date it has never been licensed for use as a treatment, but only for use in clinical investigation of pancreatic function.

In the US, media coverage of the 'wonder cure' led to a clamour for secretin infusions on the part of parents of autistic children and, very quickly, to a total exhaustion of the world supply. (At that time secretin was only produced in small amounts by the Scandinavian company Schering, which extracted secretin from pig pancreas. Synthetic secretin was not yet available.)

Since Horvath *et al.*'s initial paper there has been a massive amount of media coverage and research on the possible use of secretin in the treatment of autism, the final 'headline result' being that secretin is ineffective as a treatment for children with ASD. (See Esch and Carr 2004.) Systematic randomized controlled studies could not replicate the initial findings reported by Horvath's group in their three initial cases. (For a review see Sturmey 2005.) Is this the correct conclusion to draw?

A crucial premise for the conclusion that 'secretin does not help those with ASD' would be that the later trials had been carried out on children that were the same as those studied by Horvath's team – that they were comparing like with like. It may, however, be the case that some biological factor common to all the responders in the initial paper constituted a crucial difference in their biological make-up.

A small pharmaceutical company, the Repligen Corporation, had started to investigate the possible use of synthetic secretin as a treatment for ASD. Although their Phase II trial results were disappointing overall, as few of their treatment cases showed benefit, they did highlight that there might be specific biological differences in the few children they found to be secretin responders. They had carefully selected individuals with ASD, co-morbid learning disability and gastrointestinal problems, matching the descriptions of the children in the Horvath *et al.* paper. From their clinical presentation, these cases looked, on the face of it, to be the same as the original cases reported by Karoly Horvath *et al.* Despite this matching, only a small subgroup in the trial was secretin responsive. They differed from most of the Repligen ASD trial group in having low levels of two biomarkers called 'faecal calprotectin' and 'chymotripsyn', when compared to secretin non-responders. This finding suggests that only a minority within a small subgroup of those with ASD may benefit from treatment with secretin. It also suggests that this small minority could possibly be identified and treated, apparently to good effect.

Other research groups are also now reporting possible benefits from secretin, again in subgroups of those with ASD and not in the whole population (Pallanti *et al.* 2005).

It has also been found that a subgroup of people with ASDs have heterozygous sequence variants of the gene coding for secretin, which is found at 11p15.5 (Yamagata *et al.* 2002). To date, however, the two findings have not been put together – we don't know if it is those who show these secretin gene variants who also have low calprotectin and chymotrypsin and may respond to secretin treatment. If that turned out to be the case, we would have a genetic test that identified those children who could benefit from being given secretin therapeutically.

At the time that the research studies on secretin were attempting to replicate the initial findings by Horvath *et al.*, it was assumed that gastrointestinal problems were no more common in ASD populations than in the general population. More recent research has found that such problems are significantly more common in individuals with ASD.

The view that treatments can only be effective if they produce benefits across all or most of those with ASD has the potential drawback of discounting valuable treatments that help subgroups of those with ASD. This would be like giving the same strength of reading glasses to everyone with reading problems (those with differing degrees of poor vision, those with dyslexia and those with learning difficulties), and concluding that glasses do not help anyone read better, because for some glasses blurred their vision, or had no effect on their reading difficulty, and only a small subgroup – those whose poor eyesight happened to be corrected by the strength of glasses being trialled – could read better.

Mainstream medical/psychiatric approaches to ASD have set out in search of the 'Holy Grail' of a single effective treatment for ASD. Putting to one side the fact that many with an ASD do not want or need to be treated, this is based on a fundamental misconception about the nature of the ASDs.

There is a strong incentive for the pharmaceutical industry to find a 'one size fits all' treatment approach for ASD. There are now more 'patient years' of ASD than of Alzheimer's disease (Gerlai and Gerlai 2003). With a condition that is now thought to affect almost one per cent of the population, a 'single problem – single

treatment' view becomes tremendously appealing – always assuming, of course, that such a treatment could be found.

Let's assume a dimension on which we can plot models of autism, from monolithic views of autism as a single entity, to views that propose a number of independently sufficient causes. At the monolithic end of the spectrum is the *laissez faire* view that, whatever is learnt about their causes, the ASDs are unchanging and unchangeable. This gains some credence from reviews of therapeutic approaches that show scant evidence of benefit (see, for example, Howlin 1997; Scottish Intercollegiate Guideline Network 2007). At this same end of the scale, we also see views of autism as a consequence of some single factor (key genes, organophosphate exposure, vitamin B12 deficiency, excess TV, or whatever). Clinicians who adopt this view see autism as a single, treatable condition, working from the assumption that the neurobiological underpinnings of all ASDs are the same, and that a similar approach to treatment should help all people with ASDs.

These views are naïve and are based on conjecture and overgeneralization, and they have the potential drawback either of convincing people that nothing will be of benefit, or of raising the false hope that a particular treatment may help one person with ASD because it has helped another.

As is now abundantly clear, both the biological basis and the likely response to treatment often differ from one person to the next. Whether someone has a myosin defect like Duchenne, a cholesterol defect like Smith-Lemli-Opitz syndrome, a B12 defect like methylmalonic acidaemia or a glutamate abnormality like fragile-X can have major implications for how that person could be helped, if indeed help were needed.

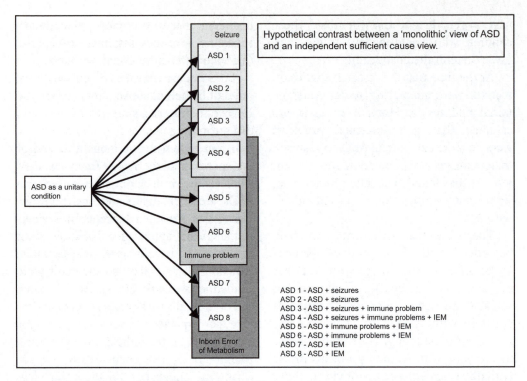

Figure A2: Single versus multiple sufficient causes for ASD

Much of the literature still speaks of 'autism', 'autistic disorder' or 'ASD' is if it were a single condition with a uniform pattern of symptomology and symptom evolution over time. There is a continuum from this 'lumping' view of a single condition (but with differing opinions on how changeable it is) to a 'splitter' view of ASD as having multiple sufficient causes that require different potential treatment strategies. For an early discussion of the lumper v splitter debate in genetics, see McKusick (1969). Figure A2 tries to contrast these views in a highly simplified differentiation based on three overlapping areas of possible symptomology.

Some 'alternative' medical practitioners (for example, Jepson and Johnson 2007; McCandless 2007) use a variety of metabolic assessments as a basis for their interventions and are looking at 'biochemical individuality' (Williams 1956). Where this type of approach can

be married to a knowledge of specific biological mechanisms underpinning such differences, it holds much promise.

At the present time, however, for many of the approaches that are being advocated, there is a weak evidence-base that links demonstrated biological differences either to a biologically plausible causal mechanism, or to evidence of benefit from specific interventions.

From a range of sources, it is now apparent that the 'monolithic' view of autism as caused by a single, core genetic mechanism is untenable: despite exhaustive research, no common gene or group of genes has emerged that accounts for a large proportion of those with an ASD. Instead, there are clearly a number of independently sufficient factors that increase the likelihood of developing an ASD.

'Alternative' approaches

It is important for clinicians to be aware of the extent to which complementary and alternative medicine approaches (CAMs) are currently employed by families with members who have ASD, and equally for such families to be aware that CAMs may interact with conventional treatments.

In one US survey of 284 children with ASD, approximately 30 per cent were using CAMs (Levy S.E. *et al.* 2003). A further survey of 479 families found a wide range of treatments being employed, including dietary interventions by 129 (approximately 27 per cent), and chelation (treatment for heavy metal toxicity which can take a variety of forms) by 32 (6.7 per cent), and many families had used multiple conventional medications (Goin-Kochel, Myers and Mackintosh 2007). The types of CAMs used by parents predict the types of CAMs they are likely to use with their children (Yussman, Ryan, Auinger and Weitzman 2004).

In mouse genetic research laboratory feed contamination can radically affect gene expression results (Kozul *et al.* 2008). The lack of clinician awareness of the extent to which dietary approaches are used, their interaction with conventional treatments, and their possible effects may be an important factor influencing current intervention research.

Many of the dietary approaches advocated both in mainstream medical and 'alternative/complementary' approaches (for example, casein-free–gluten-free; simple carbohydrate and Atkins diets) result in marked carbohydrate restriction. These may be markedly beneficial to some, but can lead to a variety of problems such as osteoporosis, copper imbalance, kidney and visual problems if not properly implemented and monitored (for further discussion, see Aitken 2009). In some individuals with already highly self-restricted diets these types of approach may be contra-indicated or impossible to implement. The extent, if any, to which such factors may influence the ontogeny of any of the genetic processes we go on to discuss has to date received only cursory examination.

Alternative treatments such as chelation could conceivably be beneficial in some cases if used appropriately and where clinically warranted. However, chelation can also be harmful if used in cases where not clinically indicated (Stangle *et al.* 2007), and can even prove fatal if used inadvisedly (MMWR 2006). There is only limited evidence on clinical benefits from mercury chelation where there are elevated mercury or lead levels from known exposure (Chisolm 2001; Liu *et al.* 2002; McFee and Caraccio 2001). Chelation will also bind biologically essential minerals (Guldager, Jørgensen and Grandjean 1996). Ensuring that essential minerals are not unduly depleted is therefore an important component of any such approach. The evidence on efficacy is limited at best (Rush, Hjelmhaug and Lobner 2008), and typical methods of challenge testing to justify treatment maintenance appear difficult to justify (Charlton and Wallace 2009). Based on the current evidence, chelation should only be adopted with caution, where there is clear evidence of toxic exposure and accumulation, and under competent medical supervision.

The issue of potential benefit from chelation has become confounded with the issue of mercury exposure and the mercury-based thiomersal/thimerosal preservative which has been used in certain 'killed' vaccines (see Bradstreet *et al.* 2003; Fombonne *et al.* 2006; and Holmes, Blaxill and Hayley 2003 for contrasting opinions on this area). This has politicized rather than clarified the issue, with many now viewing it from the standpoint of litigation and possible cover-up, rather than biology. It is possible that some children with ASD may have problems with the clearance of heavy metals, making them more vulnerable to the effects of toxic metal exposure. I fear that objectivity on this issue is likely to come only with 20/20 hindsight. As with the relationship between tobacco smoke and lung cancer, where decades of research were effectively ignored, thanks to the power of the tobacco lobby – or the developmental effects of exposure to lead in petrol fumes – it is instructive to look at the tentative conclusions in early reviews of research in this area (for example Rutter 1983).

A further word of caution is needed with respect to some of the tests that are argued to indicate the presence of problems requiring chelation (Austin and Shandley 2008; Nataf et al. 2006). It is true that urinary porphyrins can be elevated by acute and excessive exposure to heavy metal, but they are also elevated in treated epileptic patients, and coproporphyrin elevation may be caused by a renal problem that is common in those with epilepsy, rather than heavy metal retention. (For further discussion, see Tutor-Crespo, Hermida and Tutor 2005). As epilepsy is common in those with ASD (with epileptiform EEGs being reported in over 60 per cent of one large series of over 800 routinely screened ASD cases), this may be a highly important and relevant factor (Chez, Memon and Hung 2004). Although only two cases in the Nataf et al. (2006) series were diagnosed as epileptic, it is unclear how many had received EEGs. Elevated porphyrin levels occur in epileptics on active anti-epileptic medication, whether or not they have autism, and the results of such testing, taken in isolation, without screening for seizure activity, have the potential to be misleading, and possibly

followed by inappropriate and dangerous treatment.

As there is emerging evidence from animal research that chelation of animals that are not heavy metal toxic can result in lasting cognitive deficits, such approaches should on current evidence be treated with caution (Stangle et al. 2007). A second reason for caution is the evidence from primates that there is little correlation between blood and brain levels of heavy metals, or of reduction in brain levels in response to chelation (Cremin, Luck, Laughlin and Smith 1999).

In general in the ASD area, there is an urgent need for well-conducted clinical assessments of the various biologically plausible and clinically justifiable treatments and approaches that are being used (Bodfish 2004; Chez, Memon and Hung 2004; Levy and Hyman 2005). A critical point is the need to recognize that some treatments may be highly effective with some who have ASD, but ineffective, harmful or even fatal for others.

Increasing calls are being made for new approaches to evaluating treatments and interventions across the biomedical area. These calls are coming from both conventional and CAM clinicians. There is concern over the extent to which the 'evidence-based' approach to management has been skewed by the role of funding agencies and political pressures (Angell 2004; Smith M. 2006), and by the tight regulatory restrictions that discourage innovation in pharmaceutical development (Epstein 2006).

For matters to progress, it is important for us to understand the biological basis to ASD in the individual rather than the general population, and there is an urgent need to develop a research base for assessment and clinical intervention.

What is unrealistic, but far too often the case, is expecting families to accept the view that lack of peer-reviewed published evidence is sufficient reason to recommend doing nothing. The literature, and clinical experience, suggest that most families will 'vote with their feet', and that in the face of clinicians saying things like 'there are no randomized controlled trials of CF–GF diet/B12/secretin… – let's wait and see what the research shows before proceeding', they will go ahead anyway. This response is understandable for two main reasons:

1. there has been a surprising lack of funded research to look into the effects of many of the available treatments, so even where systematic research has been started we are still likely to be several years away from having clear answers

2. what we do know is that with effective treatments, whatever they may be, the later they are started, the less successful the outcome they seem to produce.

As a parent, I would not want to be told 'OK, we now have the evidence that this seems to work' five years too late to help my child. Unfortunately, this situation places vulnerable families in a position where they can far too easily be exploited by private clinics offering false hope without adequate knowledge or expertise.

I would not disagree that many people with ASDs show clinical benefit from approaches that are purely symptom-focused – helping with sleep/gastric discomfort/anxiety, for example. These sorts of problems are often present; and symptom-based management is the basis for most current conventional and CAM approaches. I would suggest, however, that a better biological understanding of why a given set of problems occurs in a particular individual is far more likely to generate a successful outcome.

We need to move away from a view of ASD where clinicians say something like 'I have found that this sometimes works, so why don't we try it' to one where we are able to say:

Treatment 1 is likely to help because he/she has A/B/C.

Treatment 2 is unlikely to work for him/her because…

Treatment 3 could cause problems because…

To develop an understanding of the causes of ASD at this level, we need a better understanding of the metabolic and, in many cases, the genetic factors involved.

ASD AND 'INBORN ERRORS OF METABOLISM'

A number of the conditions we will go on to consider are known as 'inborn errors of metabolism'. Sir Archibald E. Garrod pioneered work in this area with his early studies of alcaptonuria (Garrod 1902) and in his book *Inborn Errors of Metabolism* (1909).

Garrod is acknowledged as the first to establish a link between enzymes and behaviour. (For an excellent overview of Garrod's contributions, see Scriver 2001.)

Alkaptonuria is *not* known to be associated with ASD. It is a rare, easily recognized disorder and results in urine that quickly turns black through contact with the air, and in the production of red/black earwax. The nappies of affected infants usually horrify unsuspecting parents who assume that their baby is bleeding internally.

Before Garrod's work, alcaptonuria was thought to result from a bacterial infection. He demonstrated that it was an inherited disorder, more frequently seen in first-cousin marriages. It was found to result from the build-up of a chemical (alkaptonuric acid, aka homogentisic acid), and was due to lack of one specific enzyme (homogentisic acid oxidase).

One of Garrod's lasting contributions was his recognition of individual differences in metabolism and in susceptibility to disease:

Owing, as I believe, to their chemical individuality, different human beings differ widely in their liability to individual maladies, and to some extent in the signs and symptoms which they exhibit. (Garrod, quoted in Prasad and Galbraith 2005)

A number of inborn errors of metabolism are now known to be associated with ASDs (see Table A1).

As the biology underpinning these conditions becomes better understood, clinical approaches to management are becoming more sophisticated and outcomes are improving.

In addition, several organic acidurias (also known as acidaemias) have been described in association with ASDs. These are conditions in which there is a build-up of compounds resulting from fatty acid and deaminated amino acid degradation. Those described in association with ASD are detailed in Table A2.

Table A1: Inborn errors of metabolism associated with ASD

• Adenylosuccinate lyase (ADSL) deficiency	[9]
• Dihydropyrimidine dehydrogenase (DPYS) deficiency	[30]
• Guanidinoacetate methyltransferase (GAMT) deficiency	[37]
• Phenylketonuria (PKU)	[57]
• Smith-Lemli-Opitz syndrome (SLOS)	[66]
• Succinic semialdehyde dehydrogenase (SSADH) deficiency	[69]

Table A2: Organic acidurias associated with ASDs

• L-2-hydroxyglutaric aciduria	[40]
• 2-methylbutyryl-CoA dehydrogenase deficiency	[47]
• Methylmalonic acidaemia	

BIOCHEMICAL INDIVIDUALITY: THE IMPORTANCE OF BIOLOGICAL DIFFERENCES IN CLINICALLY HETEROGENOUS POPULATIONS

The idea that individual biological differences affect susceptibility to disorders is a key concept that underpins this book. Roger Williams (1956) coined the term in his book *Biochemical Individuality*, where he introduces the notion of individual biological vulnerabilities.

One of the most important aspects of refining this general approach is linking up our knowledge of several apparently disparate areas:

- *behavioural phenotyping* (clear description of the behaviours which can typify someone with an ASD)

- *metabolic medicine* (examining differences in biological processes which can be identified on biological testing)

- *molecular genetics* (study of the genetic and epigenetic mechanisms and individual differences which can result in metabolic abnormalities, and ultimately in the behaviours that give rise to the diagnosis, to suggest how we might be able to correct them).

Aymé (2000) discusses some of the resources that are allowing this type of integration to develop.

As the science develops, it is becoming more and more apparent that advances in this area will come out of multidisciplinary collaboration across clinical and academic areas which have previously had little common ground – something that requires a lot of new learning for people from any traditional discipline. (See discussions in Plomin and Davis 2009; Reiss 2009.)

Unless we can understand the processes involved, we will always be one step behind in helping, as otherwise we need to wait on the behaviour of the person being sufficiently different to establish diagnosis before we can do anything. *A biological level of understanding allows* **prediction** *of* likely behaviour on the basis of knowledge of the processes involved, and can lead to preventive rather than remediative intervention.

A good example of this is phenylketonuria (PKU) [57]. This condition was at one time commonly associated with ASD, and still is in some parts of the world (Vanli, Yilmaz, Tokatli and Anlar 2006). It is diagnosed in infancy by a heelstick blood test – the 'Guthrie test'. Today we would never say, 'the Guthrie test indicates this child has phenylketonuria, let's wait *until* we see if there are any developmental problems, then consider whether to use dietary intervention'. Because we understand, in part at least, the processes involved, we are confident that developmental problems will arise *unless* we intervene. Equally, a phenylalanine-restricted dietary intervention will only help those with PKU, and will not help those who may have a similar behavioural phenotype but without this physiological difference. In this instance we have an understanding of the biology and of the effect that it will have on development and behaviour if it is not addressed.

If an early attempt had been made to treat ASD with a phenylalanine-free diet, it would have been shown to be ineffective, as only a small proportion of those with ASD would have shown any positive treatment response. Identifying the small group who would respond, based on their disorder, has made their treatment both clinically useful and highly cost-effective.

Many similar examples now exist where we can link genetic differences to outcome – Smith-Lemli-Opitz syndrome (SLOS) [66] is a condition where the body fails to make adequate amounts of cholesterol. If we screened for SLOS and intervened with early cholesterol supplementation, the evidence suggests that we could markedly improve outcome and quality of life for those with this genetic basis to their developmental problems (Aneja and Tierney 2008). As SLOS may be the most common genetic factor in ASD, with a previously unrecognized high population prevalence (Ciara *et al.* 2006), the implications for individuals and families could be substantial, and at the level of the national economy the financial impact could be enormous (Knapp, Romeo and Beecham 2009; Ganz 2007).

The exciting developments in our understanding of fragile-X syndrome

[35] suggest that it may also soon present similar clinical opportunities for early intervention.

The study of 'behavioural phenotypes' is a relatively new field (see Aitken 1998; Goodey 2006; O'Brien and Yule 1996), and is still not well known to many clinicians working in the ASD field.

There are slightly different definitions in the clinical literature, but in essence the study of behavioural phenotypes is the study of syndrome-specific patterns of behaviour that characterize and help to differentiate between particular clinical conditions.

To quote from a review of the complexities of understanding the genetics of ASDs:

> The field of complex genetics is replete with many researchers and reviewers who want to promote their overly focused interest in one method at the exclusion of others. However, it is essential that the restricted interests of patients with autism not be reflected in overly restrictive genetic approaches if we are to better understand the genetics of autism. (Veenstra-Vanderweele, Christian and Cook 2004)

The concept of behavioural phenotypes has some parallels with the concept of 'endophenotypes' that has been gaining popularity in mental health research (Bearden and Freimer 2006; Cannon and Keller 2006; Castellanos and Tannock 2002) and of 'emotional endophenotypes' in ethology (Panksepp 2006; Burgdorf and Panksepp 2006).

I hope that careful reading of this book will help put paid to the view that any single treatment approach could be found which would help everyone with an ASD. ASD is not a single condition, and the wide range of sufficient mechanisms that can lead to ASD behaviour will not respond to a common approach to treatment. The take-home message is not that there is no treatment for ASD, but that the idea that there could ever be *one* treatment is wrong. There are many appropriate treatments for many of the conditions that result in ASD behaviour. It is also true to say that at the time of writing there are also many sufficient causes for which we do not as yet have any specific treatments. The issues here are complex, and so, for many of those affected, will be the solutions.

Environmental influences have major effects on human cognition, on development and on the likelihood of psychopathology (McGue and Bouchard 1998; Shonkoff and Phillips 2000). Environmental stressors may be important in predicting ASD symptomology.

ASD behaviours are more commonly reported in studies of children exposed to extreme environmental stresses. In adopted Romanian children from extremely stressed residential facilities, both ASD symptomology and autistic disorder have been found to be more common (Hoksbergen *et al.* 2005; Rutter *et al.* 1999). It is always possible, however, that the initial placement of these children was due, at least in part, to their own constitutional difficulties, and that expectations played a part in subsequent records of their behaviour.

Supporting the relevance of environmental factors, even where genetic aspects are known, there is emerging evidence for changes in DNA methylation and for changes in brain development resulting from differences in maternal behaviour. Maternal licking and grooming in rats markedly affects gene expression, which suggests a far more direct influence of social environment on genetics than had previously been suspected (Kaffman and Meaney 2007; Weaver, Meaney and Szyf

2006). Similarly, dietary factors can also have marked effects on gene expression (Dolinoy, Weidman and Jirtle 2007).

A 'single cause' view of autism led to the idea of a single mechanism, and the idea that there would possibly be a single treatment. It also led to studies of interventions with groups based on the assumption that all those treated were the same by virtue of having an ASD diagnosis. For some approaches, such as the use of structured, predictable, non-distracting environments, there is little doubt that they are helpful, but the effect of such factors is hardly autism-specific.

In a prescient paper, Michael Rutter provided a useful overview of 11 *mis-*conceptions about disorders that have a genetic component (Rutter 1991). Given how little the picture has changed in the intervening years, these false assumptions are worth reiterating here.

1. Strong genetic effects mean that environmental influences must be unimportant.

2. Genes provide a limit to potential.

3. Genetic strategies are of no value in studying environmental influences.

4. Nature and nurture are separate.

5. Genes for serious diseases are necessarily bad.

6. Diseases have nothing to do with normal variation.

7. Genetic findings won't help identify diseases.

8. Genetic influences diminish with age.

9. Disorders that run in families must be genetic.

10. Disorders that seem not to run in families cannot be genetic.

11. Single major genes lead only to specific rare diseases that follow a Mendelian pattern.

The essence of Rutter's argument, as I understand it, is that genes are always relevant but not always prescriptive, and that many of the models used to assess genetic effects do not necessarily allow us to conclude that what is being looked at is a genetic phenomenon.

Our understanding of how genetic mechanisms operate is constantly growing and changing. Identifying a genetic cause does not condemn someone's condition as unchangeable. Genetic factors can influence nutritional requirements (Stover 2006; Stover and Garza 2002). The same genetic difference can have hugely different effects on two individuals, in some cases due to a process which has been called 'synergistic heterozygosity' – an interaction with other, often also genetically driven, metabolic differences (Vockley *et al.* 2000).

As we broaden our assessments of individuals with a range of developmental disorders, we are finding that the variation in outcome is often far greater than reading about 'typical' or classic cases would lead anyone to believe. This is partly because the most obvious, most similar and sometimes most impaired cases are likely to be discovered first, and found to have some common underlying features, before less obvious and less severe cases come to light.

Here is a brief example of the same problem from a slightly different area. Aicardi syndrome is a complex developmental disorder (*not* said to be associated with ASD, so far at least). In this syndrome, there are a range of reported abnormalities in the structure of the brain and visual system, with early onset epilepsy and typically, in the published literature, with severe developmental delay. Despite this typical reported pattern of associations, there are now a number of case reports of Aicardi syndrome with normal cognitive development, despite the presence of all of the other features. (See Grosso, Lasorella *et al.* 2007 for a case report and literature review.)

In contrast to the polarized camps ('autism is genetic, therefore unchangeable' vs 'autism is biological but environmental, and therefore changeable'), which view ASD as a singular phenomenon, but with different emphases on what this implies, here we make a different initial assumption: *there is no single entity which we can call 'autistic spectrum disorder'*, so, at our current level of knowledge, for most situations we need to try to understand the causes in the individual case. This approach draws inspiration from various clinicians and researchers who have consistently argued that the ASDs are not caused by a single but as yet still nebulous mechanism, but can be caused by a range of independently sufficient processes. Better understanding of these processes should lead to better understanding of, and in some cases specific treatments for, those underlying conditions (Coleman 2005; Gillberg and Coleman 1996).

One important aspect of this viewpoint, which many of those who adopt the more polarized views of autism often seem to fail to grasp, is that, for some of the genetic factors at least, later intervention can be beneficial (Ehninger *et al.* 2008b). We are not merely talking about ways of reclassifying people who cannot be helped, but about ways of classifying that can enable help to be focused more effectively. This view also suggests that individualized approaches become relevant only after carrying out appropriate investigations that identify the specific nature of the difficulties in any given case.

This book provides information on a range of differences that can result in or increase the likelihood of ASDs. It discusses a wide range of conditions and a number of relevant genetic advances. We will examine how many of these conditions are currently thought to differ from each other, and what implications knowledge of these differences has, or may have, for the provision of more individualized treatment, and for a new agenda for, and perspective on, ASD research.

Some of these conditions (such as Timothy syndrome [70]) are rare and, although they may have implications for treatment of the affected individual, are unlikely causes within the broader scheme of things; others (like fragile-X syndrome [35]) are common genetic causes with practical implications for a significant ASD subgroup. Some differences, such as Potocki-Lupski syndrome [60], are of unknown prevalence – they may be common factors in ASD, but we do not currently have information on how common they are. Finally, there are other conditions still (such as Smith-Lemli-Opitz syndrome (SLOS) [66] and methylene/tetrahydrofolate reductase (MTHFR) deficiency) [85]) that are much more common than was previously appreciated, and which may account for a significant proportion of individuals with ASD, and have specific treatment implications.

We need to develop ways of assessing the bases of the differences in clinical pattern and response seen in clinical treatment across the spectrum of those with a diagnosis of ASD. A critical component of this process is to learn how to understand individual differences in terms of their genetic bases, and how this leads to specific clinical and behavioural phenotypes, and what consequences this may have for health and development. (For a general discussion of these ideas, see Valle 2004.)

Genetic factors are being implicated in a huge range of human faculties. There is a general assumption that differences from 'normal' will be problematic. This turns out to be far from the case. We have many examples where genetic differences from the 'typical' convey an advantage:

1. Over the history of the Olympic games, runners from Kalenjin tribal groups in Kenya have been by far the most successful in long-distance running events. Part of the reason for their pre-eminence is a genetic enzyme difference in metabolizing lactate (Moran et al. 2004; Vollind et al. 2004), which allows Kalenjin runners to exercise longer before lactate builds up in muscle and impairs performance.

2. Differences in creative dance performance ability seem to be linked to differences in a serotonin transporter and an arginine vasopressin receptor polymorphism (Bachner-Melman et al. 2005).

3. In humans and in many other species (Lee S-J. 2007), the myostatin gene controls muscle development, with a homozygous mutation resulting in a marked increase in muscle bulk. This type of mutation has been shown to significantly enhance the race performance of 'bully' whippets, which have larger, stronger muscles than their genetically normal competitors (Mosher et al. 2007). The same phenomenon is seen in Texel sheep and Belgian blue cattle (Lee S-J. 2007). In one German boy, homozygous mutation resulted in increased muscle bulk and strength, with him being dubbed 'the Strongest Boy in the World' (Reilley 2006; Schuelke et al. 2004).

4. To take a more extreme example, primates were, until recently, unique on earth in having the ability to discriminate red and green due to the presence of two types of cone cells in the retina. The development of 'knock-in' mice with equivalent receptors has

produced, for the first time, mice with an equivalent colour sense to primates (Onishi *et al.* 2005; Smallwood *et al.* 2003). Such mice are able to reliably make red–green choice distinctions (Conway 2007).

These findings do not mean that it is *necessarily* pointless entering a long-distance competition against a Kenyan running team; that you will *necessarily* be a hopeless dancer without the right genetic make-up; that you can never develop bigger muscles by working out in a gym; or even that colour-blindness, which is genetic and currently uncorrectable, is now understood and will be potentially correctable (developments from the methods that can produce colour vision *de novo* in mice may prove to be capable of correcting colour blindness in humans). In the same way, many of the conditions we go on to discuss in this book do not mean that someone will *necessarily* develop an ASD. These biological differences change the likelihood – they weight the dice, and better understanding of the mechanisms may, and in some cases does, provide the potential to bring about change.

With much in the history of clinical genetics, conclusions have been drawn, based on studies of clinical groups, before comparative data has been available from the rest of the population. With XYY [4], for example, initial conclusions that it was associated with aggressive behaviour and criminality were drawn after looking at prison populations and finding higher than expected rates – *before* the general population prevalence of having an additional Y chromosome was known (Jacobs *et al.* 1965). Subsequent research revealed that there was no such link, and that the slightly increased rate of XYY in prison populations was largely due to the increased chance of being caught for those with a mild learning disability in general (Witkin *et al.* 1976). It may prove to be the case that some of the associations suggested here will also turn out to be less clear-cut, as larger groups are studied.

In this volume, you will find a number of conditions that were thought to be distinct but that have the same genetic basis. You will find others which were thought to be the same, but that have proved to be caused by independent mechanisms. For many, we have not yet screened the general population. This stage is important, as a genetic difference might be benign in some, and without this information we may be assuming that the presence of a given deletion/inversion/transposition/difference will *necessarily* lead to a given outcome when it is just as likely not to – the mistake that was made in interpreting the prison population prevalence of XYY.

For most of the conditions we go on to discuss, the likelihood of ASD appears, on current evidence, to be higher than it is in the rest of the population, but it is not a one-to-one link. Equally, there is a proportion of cases who have none of the conditions discussed here, but who are autistic in any event. Some of the biological factors discussed here may turn out to be biological vulnerabilities which increase risk only when they are combined with some type of environmental exposure. An example of this type of mechanism seems to be the link between differences in the PON1 gene and the effects being seen in people exposed to organophosphates (D'Amelio *et al.* 2005). PON1 is a gene that codes for an arylesterase, one effect of which is the oxidation of the insecticide parathion. The genetic difference in PON1 is more common in American than Italian autistic children, as is the level of exposure to organophosphates. It is the combination of genetic risk and environmental exposure that seems to be the critical factor. Analysis of data from the MoBa (den norske **Mo**r and **Ba**rn-undersokelsen) study mentioned earlier has found that there is a link between PON1 in the foetus and an increased risk of premature birth (Ryckman *et al.* 2010). As other studies have also shown a link between premature birth and increased likelihood of ASD for example, Indredavik, Vik, Skranes and Brubakk 2008), these factors may be associated.

IS ASD GETTING MORE COMMON?

The issue of ASD prevalence has been a subject of much heated debate. Are there today really more people with ASD or is this just a combination of changing criteria, better public and professional awareness, and better recognition? After much research and argument we still do not know the answer to this critical question, despite strident arguments for (Blaxill 2004) and against (Fombonne 2005). Prevalence (the number of people identified as having ASD within any given community) is definitely up, but incidence (the numbers of new cases per head of population, using the same criteria) may or may not be. A further important point is that many of the prevalence studies to date were developed to address particular questions concerning specific, apparently high-prevalence communities, as with the Brick Township study (Bertrand *et al.* 2001).There is evidence for geographical clustering of autism cases. In California, geographical high-prevalence clusters seem to be stable over time and account for much of the rise in rates of cases (Mazumdar *et al.* 2010). This type of pattern could indicate local differences in environmental exposure or in diagnostic practice. Some further recent analyses by Peter Bearman's group at Columbia University suggest that a major factor in the Californian prevalence changes has been 'information diffusion' (Liu, King and Bearman 2010). Changing diagnostic practices have also been an important influence, particularly in the US

with a rise in acceptance of co-morbidity and individuals who had previously been diagnosed with mental retardation receiving an autistic disorder diagnosis (King and Bearman 2009), an issue refered to as diagnostic overshadowing. A further important factor that contributes to an actual rise in the numbers of number of new individuals is increasing parental age at childbirth as this is associated with an increased risk of relevant de novo genetic mutations (Liu, Zerubavel and Bearman 2010).

There is a need to develop comprehensive clinical databases of ASD cases, providing a picture across defined populations; however, these are proving challenging to implement (McConachie *et al.* 2009).

There will continue to be debate over the reasons behind the rise in prevalence of the ASDs – far more children are being identified and diagnosed with ASD today than was the case a decade ago, even when using the same criteria (Hertz-Picciotto and Delwiche 2009). Whether this ultimately proves to be a genuine rise in incidence, or simply a concatenation of factors reflecting increased rates of identification (such as better public and clinician awareness, an increase in numbers of appropriately trained clinicians, earlier diagnosis and better access to services), remains to be definitively addressed. It is clear that a complex network of factors is involved. Prevalence figures have risen markedly over time across all of the populations so far reported (Fombonne 2005, 2009; Sun and Allison 2010).

Whatever the reasons for the change, robust diagnostic tools are now employed and the population of individuals with ASD is far higher than had previously been thought. The implications of recognizing these numbers and adequately addressing the needs of those with ASD who are now agreed to exist, whatever the reasons, puts a huge strain on available resources.

Current figures suggest that ASD is as common as schizophrenia (Honda, Shimizu and Rutter 2006; MacDermott *et al.* 2007; Reading 2006), and that it has outstripped Alzheimer's disease in terms of number of client years (Gerlai and Gerlai 2003). ASD is also identified far earlier than either of these other groups, and carries a normal life expectancy (Shavelle,

Strauss and Pickett 2001). Those with ASD as a group place a higher financial burden on health resources for various reasons such as increased rates of immune, cardiac and CNS problems, while those at the more severe end of the spectrum in terms of physical or learning impairments can require permanent residential placement. When the needs of those with ASDs are adequately met, this is highly expensive to affected families, to clinical and support services, and to the community at large (Jarbrink and Knapp 2001; Knapp, Romeo and Beecham 2009). Recognizing the specific needs of subgroups within this population, improving their quality of life and degree of independence, reducing their chronic health support needs and improving their developmental outcome is an urgent priority.

A BRIEF HISTORY OF RESEARCH ON ASD

Learn from yesterday, live for today, hope for tomorrow. The important thing is to stop questioning.

Albert Einstein (1879–1955)
Relativity: The Special and the General Theory 1917

Dr Leo Kanner, a Viennese-born psychiatrist living in the USA and working in New York, is credited with penning the first accepted and clear description of autism (Kanner 1943). In his early writing we learn of a condition that he described as '*a biologically provided defect in affective contact*'. This description captures the essence of the condition – it is a biological difference in the individual that interferes with their ability to function socially.

In Kanner's time, genetics was virtually unknown as a clinical discipline; the 'double helix' structure of DNA was yet to be discovered, and although heritability was accepted – certain characteristics, like eye colour, skin colour and male pattern baldness, were known to be inherited, as were certain illness propensities (haemophilia, for example) – we had no understanding of the mechanisms by which developmental disorders came into being. It was no accident that when biological factors in psychiatry began to be studied in earnest, schizophrenia came to be viewed as 'the graveyard of the clinical geneticist'. The frequent contradictions and failures of replication in the psychiatric genetic literature continue to perplex many working in this field

(Persaud 2007). There are many reasons why genetic investigation of 'psychiatric' conditions is fraught with difficulty (Bearden, Reus and Freimer 2004), not least the difficulty in reaching agreement over the endophenotypes (key biological features) for many such disorders (Bearden and Freimer 2006). Recent developments, many thanks to the requirements of the Human Genome Project, have broadened the range of methods for addressing such issues through the use of powerful high-throughput, low-cost techniques (Ropers 2007).

Psychiatry and biomedical sciences have never proved to be easy bedfellows. (I would accept that this is far more the case in Europe, including the UK, than in the US, where biomedical assessment has assumed a much more prominent position within mainstream psychiatry.)

There has only ever been one Nobel Prize awarded to someone practising in psychiatry – this was awarded to an Austrian, Julius Wagner-Jauregg, in 1927. Wagner-Jauregg discovered, by chance, that after contracting malaria, individuals with the then common condition known as generalized paralysis of the insane (GPI) often improved dramatically. By deliberately infecting patients with malaria he found that he could effect clinical improvement in those with GPI who were under his care. GPI was caused, although this was not known at the time, by contracting syphilis. The mechanism by which these problems were related, and the way in which the cure worked, were unknown. The Nobel Prize, in this instance, was awarded for the inspired application of a chance observation.

It subsequently transpired that Wagner-Jauregg's treatment, which predated the sulphonamide drugs that replaced it, worked by causing a spike in body temperature. The change in body temperature made it too hot for the spirochetes that caused the syphilis to survive, thus bringing about the improvement. (For an excellent review of the history of syphilis, its apparent association with giftedness, and its sequelae, see Hayden 2003.)

Unfortunately, the last half-century has been largely devoid of such serendipitous psychiatric observations, and so the psychiatric trophy room has been devoid of any further serendipitous Nobels.

The intervening years have seen huge changes in factors like the diagnostic classifications in use, and the waxing and waning of enthusiasm in psychiatry for a huge range of treatments – from insulin coma to electroconvulsive therapy to psychosurgery to various forms of pharmacotherapy – without major strides being made in understanding of mechanism or in treatment effectiveness.

As an interesting aside, one study has found that the onset of autism can sometimes be seen after high fever and convulsions brought on by severe malaria (Mankoski et al. 2006), as can an acquired semantic-pragmatic communication disorder (Carter et al. 2006). One paper has speculated on differences in fever suppression being linked to autism aetiology (Torres 2003).

It can be seen how far things have progressed in some respects and how little in others by reading an early systematic review by Edward Ornitz of the state of play in the field of autism some 30 years ago (Ornitz 1973; a more recent historical account of the development of ideas on autism can be found in Wolff 2004). It is only since the focusing of biomedical sciences on ASD conditions in the first decade of the twenty-first century that significant advances are being made in our understanding of their biologies.

Reading the autobiography of Nobel laureate Eric Kandel (Kandel 2006), who grew up in the Vienna of Freudian psychoanalysis, and trained in psychiatry early in his career, but went on to excel in the experimental understanding of the neurobiology of memory in aplysia (a type of marine mollusc), you begin to grasp some of the massive changes in biological understanding that have taken place since the mid-twentieth century in the biological sciences. Kandel's classic paper 'Psychotherapy and the single synapse: The impact of psychiatric thought on neurobiological research' (Kandel 1979) stands out as an early call for biological and psychological levels of understanding to inform each other.

In the early post-war years, autism was described, within the framework of psychiatric disorders, as a condition in what at the time was the fledgeling area of child psychiatry. Once the nosological validity of the condition was accepted, it became a precious 'jewel in the crown' of this emerging specialism, apparently validating the notion of a psychiatric disorder resulting from extreme stress and/or deprivation. Coupling the characterization of the condition with an increasing belief that it was 'psychogenic' in origin (i.e. seen as due purely to psychological factors such as a cold, emotionless style of parenting), this led to various other notions:

1. that autism is a single condition, which will, in the fullness of time, have a single treatment

2. that, as a psychogenic condition, it is outside the areas of interest, knowledge and expertise of medical specialities other than psychiatry

3. that biological factors do not contribute either to its genesis or to its development

4. that it is mainly a concern of child psychiatry, and of limited interest to adult psychiatric services.

Let's now look at each of these ideas in turn.

CONSIDERATION OF SOME STRONGLY HELD VIEWS

1. 'Autism is a single condition'

> Autism is a common and heterogeneous childhood neurodevelopmental disorder. Analogous to broad syndromes such as mental retardation, autism has many etiologies and should be considered not as a single disorder but, rather, as 'the autisms'. (Geschwind and Levitt 2007)

Scarcely a week goes by without a claim to have discovered *the* cause of autism. A huge range of possibilities has been proposed, from 'refrigerator parenting' (Bettelheim 1955, 1967) to excessive TV watching (Waldman, Nicholson and Adilov 2006), and we are seeing attempts to provide general models that account for the similarities across disparate aetiologies in ASD such as the 'disconnection syndromes model' (Geschwind and Levitt 2007), disordered connectivity model (Rippon, Brock, Brown and Boucher 2007; Minshew and Keller 2010; Assaf *et al* 2010) and the 'foetal testosterone model' (Knickmeyer and Baron-Cohen 2006).

Working from the idea that autism is a single condition, a considerable effort has been expended in trying to ensure that subjects in research studies are 'phenotypically comparable'. Methods for selecting homogenous ASD populations for research are being developed (Gotham,

Pickles and Lord 2008; Kolevzon *et al.* 2004).

Age, IQ and autism severity are important variables which affect aspects of autistic presentation. Restricted, repetitive behaviours and resistance to change seem to vary independently of all other such aspects (Hus *et al.* 2007).

Much excellent and important work has been carried out based on the notion of homogeneity within the ASD population – that a common diagnosis means a common basis. For many things, such as schooling and social care, the similarities across ASD may be more important by far than the differences within this population.

A large amount of useful research has been generated using this paradigm. To take one example, there appear to be differences in auditory processing, particularly of human speech, which are characteristic of the autistic population (Boddaert *et al.* 2003, 2004; Ceponiene *et al.* 2003; Gage *et al.* 2003; Groen *et al.* 2009; Kuhl, Coffey-Corina, Padden and Dawson 2005; Samson *et al.* 2006). It is important to recognize that such common differences need not indicate a common genetic difference but could reflect something else, such as an effect of selective attention and exposure. The results found differ from those found in normal controls, but no systematic research has tried to compare those with an ASD diagnosis with other relevant clinical groups, or with non-affected sibling controls.

When we examine how the human brain processes birdsong, we find that experts on birds are different from other people in the way their brains process birdsong (Chartrand, Filon-Bilodeau and Belin 2007). Such differences could as easily be 'cause' as 'effect' – practice in birdsong discrimination may hone certain brain networks and prune others, as is thought to happen when infants learn to discriminate their own from other languages. (For an introduction to this literature, see Condon and Sander 1974; Feldman 2007; Kuhl 2000; Trevarthen and Aitken 2001.) Or maybe people whose brains have an innate facility for birdsong recognition are more likely to specialize in this area. The same may be true of the differences in auditory processing seen in ASD.

The issue of diagnostic validity – that the condition being studied is a 'real' phenomenon and not just an arbitrary set of signs and symptoms – has long plagued psychiatric assessments of ASD. Improvements in diagnostic *reliability* have not been paralleled by improvements in diagnostic *validity*:

> Diagnosis has confounded psychiatry for the past century, with the *DSM* approach enhancing diagnostic reliability but not validity. (Insel and Fenton 2005)

A huge amount of research funding has been poured into finding the genes that cause autism. The first biological 'hunch' – based on the high likelihood of identical twins both being affected, compared with non-identical twins, coupled with a steady reported rate of autism in the population (reported as around 4.5 in every 10,000 live births) – was that autism would turn out to be a single disorder caused by a small number of necessary and sufficient genes. This idea, although consistent with the literature at the time it was first put forward, seems less and less tenable. A paper published in the journal *Nature Neuroscience* (Happé, Ronald and Plomin 2006) concludes that the various behavioural components which make up the 'autistic triad of impairments' – if indeed they are coherent entities – at the very least vary independently and cannot be viewed as resulting from any common genetic basis. As these researchers come from a background that historically has emphasized the discrete and singular nature of autism, it is interesting to note that their scholarly review reaches very different conclusions:

> …if different features of autism are caused by different genes, associated with different brain regions and related to different core cognitive impairments, it seems likely they will respond to different types of treatment. Abandoning the search for a single cause for a single entity of autism may also mean abandoning the search for a single 'cure' or intervention. (Happé, Ronald and Plomin 2006)

It seems that, at best, people who argue for a common mechanism are now looking for three groups of partially co-occurring genes affecting systems which are sometimes all affected in the same individual, rather than for a single genetic mechanism. However, even this watered-down, single genetic mechanism view is poorly supported by the large number of screening studies that have attempted to find common genetic *differences* across people with a clinical diagnosis of autism.

In some respects it is worrying, given this variability within the clinical population, that attempts are being made to find methods by which more homogenous research populations can be selected within the range of ASD (Kolevzon *et al.* 2004). It is also worrying if this is the basis on which treatment trials are carried out and evaluated. If a subgroup that responds to a given treatment is differentiable from others with an ASD diagnosis, and the rest of the treatment group does not respond, this should not be grounds for dismissing a treatment as ineffective. On the contrary, it provides grounds to criticize the study as flawed in its design, dealing with a heterogeneous population but analysing it as if it were a homogenous one.

We now have strong evidence of a large number of genetic differences that occur in subgroups of those who meet the behavioural criteria for an ASD diagnosis (Autism Genome Project Consortium 2007; Freitag 2007; Sebat *et al.* 2007; Yang and Gill 2007). There is a steadily expanding group of identified genetic conditions that show different clinical phenotypes, but all of which, to a greater or lesser extent, fit or overlap with current criteria for ASD.

In some areas we are finding evidence suggesting an underlying genetic aetiology for a particular pattern of presentation, but as yet only in small numbers of reported cases. The possible link between 13q12–q13 abnormalities, autistic diagnosis, language deficits and auditory processing problems provides such an example (Bradford *et al.* 2001; Smith M. *et al.* 2002)

Clearly the underlying mechanisms are proving to be far more complex and elusive than was originally hoped, and are confounded by factors such as comorbidity with other developmental problems, leading to ascertainment bias and skewing of reported sex ratios (see Skuse 2007 for further discussion). ASD often presents as part of a complex picture along with other physical and behavioural features. Where other factors lead to closer monitoring, this can make diagnosis more likely in some circumstances (ascertainment bias), while in others it lowers likelihood of diagnosis, with ASD features being attributed to something else (such as developmetal delay or epilepsy) – this is known as 'diagnostic overshadowing'.

That said, much progress has been made in identifying biological mechanisms sufficient to cause ASD. In line with the conclusions reached by Happé, Ronald and Plomin (2006), we are now seeing the emergence of a number of discrete treatments that target the specific biological differences stemming from different genetic aetiologies.

2. 'Autism is psychogenic in origin and belongs within the realm of psychiatry'

The view that autism was a psychogenic disorder can be traced to early post-World War II developments in American psychotherapy. It was most heavily influenced by the writings and clinical work of Bruno Bettelheim, whose own experiences in a German concentration camp had strongly coloured his views of the extent to which behaviour and development could be affected by early emotional experience (Bettelheim 1955, 1967).

Many were convinced that the evidence, such as it was, was strongly against a genetic basis:

> Though claims have been made for genetic determinants in the causation of autism, it is unlikely that any are involved, for we have quite a number of records of identical twins, one of whom was autistic and the other was not. (Montagu 1986)

A useful early discussion of the psychogenic model of ASD can be found in Rutter (1968).

As we discover more sophisticated research methods, many autistic conditions are being shown to have genetic bases, both at the level of resolution, with subtelomeric deletions being shown to have effects (Barbosa-Gonçalves *et al.* 2008), and by using techniques that increase the probability of finding associated genes – such as 'homozygosity mapping' (looking in families where shared ancestry creates the likelihood of finding autosomal recessive genes, as is the case in certain cultural groups). (See Morrow *et al.* 2008.)

> Although genetic influences predominate in autism, it is clear that it is a multifactorial disorder, and it must be expected that some environmental factors will be implicated in the causal pathways. (Rutter 2006)

Historically it was clearly the case, during the period when autism was viewed as a psychogenic condition, that few clinical specialities other than psychiatry were interested in the ASDs, and more recently when the ASDs were viewed as a single genetic condition of unknown aetiology this view continued to hold true.

A seminal book by Bernard Rimland (1964) led to a change in view of the ASDs from psychogenic to biologically based, but this did not fundamentally change clinical practice at the time.

The second historical phase in our understanding of autism saw the condition viewed as genetic in origin, as predetermined (not 'experience-dependent'), and consequently as unaffected by environmental factors. This view led to the logical corollary that the emphasis was placed on finding the genes involved, as only by achieving this were we likely to be able to unravel the process and identify the

specific approach to treatment that this level of understanding would bring about. This has led to the current position, where we have a plethora of independently sufficient predisposing genetic factors that increase the risk of developing autism (Veenstra-Vanderweele, Christian and Cook 2004).

The third, most recent phase is based on the recognition that a single-cause view of ASD was becoming progressively less tenable, and that subgroups of people with a diagnosis of ASD have discrete and often treatable disorders. Various factors have contributed to this change of view, including the following:

1. *Recognizing that aspects of the social environment can act as mediating variables* – in more stressful situations it may be more likely that an ASD will manifest in a manner which brings it to clinical attention (as in the Romanian adoptee studies). Here, removing the psychological stressors can bring about improvement.

2. *Understanding the role of epigenetic factors* – a whole range of mechanisms that may influence whether a genetic difference has an effect or not.

   Here I am using the term 'epigenetic' in the more restricted sense used in current cell biology (see Bird A. 2007; Jaenisch and Bird 2003), rather than in the broader sense popularized earlier by Conrad Waddington (see Slack 2002 for discussion). A brief historical discussion of epigenetics can be found in Holliday (2006).

   The principal epigenetic mechanisms currently known are telomere modification (Blasco 2007); chromatin remodelling through histone modification (Ausio *et al.* 2003); RNA-associated gene silencing (an important defect in fragile-X syndrome [35, 36]); and genomic imprinting (seen in

Prader-Willi syndrome [61]). Hendrich and Bickmore (2001) usefully review chromatin defects and chromatin re-modelling as involved in ATR-X [81], Rett syndrome [63a], Rubinstein-Taybi syndrome [64] and Coffin-Lowry syndrome [21].

For a simple introduction to these mechanisms as applied to psychiatric disorders, including Rett syndrome [63a], see Tsankova, Renthal, Kumar and Nestler (2007); for a discussion of how diets, nutrient differences and medication can affect epigenetic processes, see Junien (2006); for a discussion of genomic imprinting, see Butler (2010); and for more general overviews of how these epigenetic factors influence the expression of DNA and can alter the course of brain development, see Dolinoy, Weidman and Jirtle (2007); Jiang, Bressler and Beaudet (2004); McClung and Nestler (2007); and MacDonald and Roskams (2009).

There is considerable interest in the ways in which epigenetic mechanisms can affect disease susceptibility (Jirtle, Sander and Barrett 2000; Jirtle and Skinner 2007).

The conditions we go on to discuss in which such epigenetic processes are known to be particularly important include ATR-X [81]; Rett syndrome [63a, 63b]; Rubinstein-Taybi syndrome [64]; Angelman syndrome [11]; Prader-Willi syndrome [61]; and Coffin-Lowry syndrome [21]. Several of these are conditions that arise from defects in chromatin structure and modification (Hendrich and Bickmore 2001).

The importance of epigenetic factors for the development of clinical conditions is becoming far better understood and appreciated (Falls, Pulford, Wylie and Jirtle 1999; Gosden and Feinberg 2007; Jiang, Bressler and Beaudet 2004; Jirtle and Skinner 2007; Rodenhiser and Mann 2006; Waggoner 2007). The concept of imbalanced genomic imprinting as a specific risk factor for ASD has been advanced (Badcock and Crespi 2006). Other mechanisms, such as preferential X inactivation in females and its role in epigenetic control, are only beginning to be understood (Agrelo and Wutz 2010).

There are significant improvements in the technologies available to enable rapid profiling of epigenetic mechanisms in the individual case, such as DNA methylation profiling (Schumacher et al. 2006). These are not commonly available as clinical tools, but should become so as their utility and validity become better known and established.

Inheritance of epigenetic factors has become an important area for both research and clinical understanding, and the complexities of what is inherited over and above nuclear DNA are only now becoming apparent.

In the nuclei of sperm, protamines are found in place of histones. These are displaced, after the egg is fertilized, by histones derived from the egg. Some epigenetic factors are therefore inherited almost entirely from the mother, as are mitochondria in most cases. This gives a whole new Darwinian spin to sociobiology – female preference for a mate may be 'warts and all' partly on the basis that for her offspring the 'warts' are less likely to be part of the procreational deal, as a range of epigenetic factors are far less likely to be passed on from the father than from the mother, and so need not affect partner choice.

A recent genome-wide linkage analysis of data from 1216 families using cases from the AGRE database and NIMH autism repository examined 16,311 SNPs for evidence of potential parent-of-origin effects (Fradin *et al.* 2010). Significant paternal-origin linkage was found to regions on chromosome 4, 15 and 20.

Parent-of-origin effects have been shown in a number of genetic disorders linked to ASD. Most of these conditions involve loci on chronmosome 15:

15q11-q13 duplication (Cook E.H. *et al.* 1997);

GABA(A) receptor differences in oculocutaneous albinism (including 15q11.2–12) (DeLong 2007);

Prader-Willi syndrome (15q12, 15q11-q13)(Nicholls, Saitoh and Horsthemke 1998);

Turner syndrome (Xp22.33) (Donnelly *et al.* 2000; Sagi *et al.* 2007).

In Angelman syndrome, a grandparent-of-origin effect has also been shown (Buiting *et al.* 1998)

Parent of origin effects are typically the result of differential methylation between the sexes (Biliya and Bulla 2010), but can also arise purely a a result of maternal effects (Hager, Cheverud and Wolf 2008).

3. *Recognizing the role of genetic modifiers –* the wide phenotypic variability often seen in conditions where a core genetic mechanism (a 'target gene') has been identified is also increasing interest in the role of 'genetic modifiers' (Nadeau 2001; Slavotinek and Biesecker 2003). These are genes that are neither necessary nor sufficient for the occurrence of a condition, but which, when present, affect the expressed phenotype.

We will go on to discuss conditions such as Biedl-Bardet syndrome [17] where such effects are known, and other possible modifier effects such as the role of GRIK2, which has been established as a factor in the expression of Huntington's disease (Rubinsztein *et al.* 1997). GRIK2 is involved in glutamate metabolism, and is a gene which has been linked to autism in screening studies (Jamain *et al.* 2002; Shuang *et al.* 2004).

4. *The importance of copy number variations (CNVs)* in understanding the variation in heritability across the human population in general (for discussion, see Feuk, Carson and Scherer 2006), and the variations seen across different ethnic populations (Redon *et al.* 2006) – CNVs (deletions, duplications and large copy number variants) are common, introduce a variety of mechanisms by which genetic differences arise, and were, until recently, relatively unknown. They are not readily detected by single nucleotide polymorphism (SNP) technology, and as a result many of the genetic screening studies that have been carried out using SNP-only methods are likely to have missed many cases where such genetic differences may have been important.

5. *Understanding the interplay between biologically determined factors and the effects of social environment –* for a simple introduction to many of these issues, see Jablonka and Lamb (2005). There is increasing data which suggests that gene expression *can* be affected by factors such as early parental care and

attention or early-life environmental stressors (Kaffman and Meaney 2007; Weaver, Meaney and Szyf 2006; Murgatroyd *et al.* 2009).

6. *The roles of translated non-coding RNA* – in contrast to the widely expressed view that much DNA is accumulated 'junk', it now appears that a high proportion of human DNA is expressed, despite the fact that only around 1.5 per cent of human DNA codes for proteins (Wong and Nielsen 2004); the rest is translated into non-coding RNA (^{nc}RNA) which is thought to be involved in processes such as epigenetic imprinting (Cavaille *et al.* 2000, 2002) and within-cell transactions (Mattick 2004). Epigenetic imprinting is involved in a range of mechanisms which are relevant to factors such as disease susceptibility (Jirtle, Sander and Barrett 2000), and the effects of toxic exposure (Murphy and Jirtle 2000).

7. *Understanding the biological products of genetic differences* expressed in ASD – proteomics, the study of differences in protein expression associated with a given condition, is beginning to demonstrate differences in the ASD population (Corbett *et al.* 2007).

8. *The potential role of toxic agents in disrupting epigenetic processes* – it is known that inhibition of histone deacetylation and DNA methylation disrupt imprinting (Hu, Oruganti, Vu and Hoffman; Hu, Vu and Hoffman 1996 and 1998; Svensson *et al.* 1998). A number of environmental toxins can be involved in this process, potentially leading to increased prevalence of a particular genetic cause as a result of genetic–environmental interaction (Edelson and Cantor 1998).

The above factors, in varying combinations, account for many of the variations typically seen across those with a given genetic predisposing factor, and also for the apparent absence of a genetic contribution in many of the cohort screening studies.

It is not rare for two ASD members of the same family (even for identical twins) with the same genetic condition to differ markedly in how severely they are affected, and to differ by the presence or absence of associated features such as epilepsy or cardiac problems.

As the sufficient independent causes of ASDs have become more apparent, there has been increasing interest in, and work on, many speciality areas related to differentiation within the ASDs and better understanding of the ASDs:

- **bacteriology** (Finegold *et al.* 2002)

- **gastroenterology** (Afzal *et al.* 2003; Galli-Carminati, Horvath and Perman 2002b; Chauvet and Deriaz 2006; Sullivan 2008a; White 2003)

- **genetics** (Autism entry – OMIM No. 209850 accessed at: www.ncbi.nlm.nih. gov/entrez/dispomim.cgi?id=209850; Autism Genome Project Consortium 2007; Folstein and Rosen-Sheidley 2001; Freitag 2007; Lauritsen and Ewald 2001; Muhle, Trentacoste and Rapin 2004; Schaefer and Lutz 2006; Sykes and Lamb 2007)

- **immunology** (Ashwood, Wills and Van de Water 2006; Burger and Warren 1998; Cabanlit *et al.* 2007; Stern *et al.* 2005; Zimmerman *et al.* 2007;)

- **metabolic differences** (James, Culver and Golabi 2006; MacFabe *et al.* 2007; Page 2000; Zimmerman *et al.* 2005;)

- **neurology** (Bauman 2005; Ito 2004; Tuchman and Rapin 2002b)

- **neurovirology** (Hornig and Lipkin 2001; Hornig, Chian and Lipkin 2004; Pletnikov 2002)

There is considerable debate over the 'diagnostic yield' from such lines of investigation and whether any or all of the above should constitute part of a standard biological assessment for those with ASD (Hahn and Neubauer 2005; Stern *et al.* 2005; Tomas Vila 2004).

Recent claims suggest that while conventional genetic analysis gives a diagnostic yield of some 10 per cent (Battaglia and Carey 2006; Herman *et al.* 2007), it produces a far higher diagnositc yield of between 40 and 65 per cent of cases when a more detailed protocol is adopted (Aitken 2008; Cass, Sekaran and Baird 2006; Schaefer and Lutz 2006; Schaefer and Mendelsohn 2008; for further discussion, see Martin and Ledbeter 2007).

Many of the investigations required to test for rarer genetic disorders are currently difficult to access in many areas, for a variety of practical reasons (Willems 2008), which means that significant improvement in routine genetic screening for many of the disorders discussed is unlikely to be widespread for some time to come. Moreover, because these other assessments are not currently included in the diagnostic process, for the time being, irrespective of their results, they will not affect diagnosis. (A particular constellation of behaviours fulfils criteria for an ASD diagnosis, irrespective of the results of lymphocyte profiling/serum glutamate levels/abnormalities of melatonin release/ EEG abnormalities… The relevance of such tests has been marginalized, based on the hypothesis that one common mechanism underpins all of the ASDs.) The same is true of more widely accepted components of assessment, such as neuropsychological profiling: identifying executive function, working memory and NVLD (non-verbal learning disability) difficulties can be important in informing appropriate interventions, but does not at present play any part in the diagnostic process.

In one study of 182 patients seen by the Mayo clinic over the period 1995–1998 (Challman, Barbaresi, Katusic and Weaver 2003), 'aetiologically relevant' conditions were identified in around four per cent of cases; however, only a proportion of cases underwent testing and a far higher percentage showed evidence of epilepsy, EEG and structural brain abnormalities, and abnormalities of uncertain significance.

New genetic links to ASD are continually being identified. In 2008, an association between reciprocal duplication of 1q21.1 and ASD were first described (Mefford *et al.* 2008). This duplication was seen in 9 out of 5,218 individuals screened. A number of screening studies have identified an ASD risk locus at 5p14.1 (Ma 2009; Wang *et al.* 2009). A recent large-scale study of CNVs in 996 ASD cases (from 1,275 screened) and 1,287 controls has identified a large number of rare CNVs that appear to be associated with ASD (Pinto *et al.* 2010).

In practice, the range of assessments which are available and used in routine clinical practice is expanding all the time, and changing as newer techniques replace older ones. (For example, the wide availability of functional magnetic resonance imaging (fMRI) and its relative safety, compared to older brain imaging techniques which relied on radioactivity, has made study of how the brain is working during many activities far easier, for far greater numbers of subjects.) Clinical developments in this area are both driven and constrained by their utility and cost-effectiveness, with the most rapid progress being made in the North American private healthcare systems. (For discussion, see Williams M.S. 2003).

3. 'Biological factors do not contribute to the genesis of autism, nor to its development'

The past 20 years have seen a gradual realization that the earlier view of autism (as psychiatric, psychogenic, non-genetic and untreatable) is incorrect. Today, the neurobiological understanding of ASDs is moving on at the same rapid pace as biological understanding in many other areas of neuroscience.

The MRC Research Review (Medical Research Council 2001) identified a number of biomedical areas of potential clinical importance from the published literature and submissions to the review panel. Prioritized investigation in several areas was recommended: the relevance of casein- and gluten-free diets (see Aitken 2009); sulphation problems (Alberti 1999; McFadden 1996); immune abnormalities; and gastrointestinal problems. Further investigation has yielded information in all of these areas, some of which will be discussed further below.

It is clear that many intrinsic and extrinsic biological factors contribute to the nature and severity of ASD and that understanding gene–environment interactions is likely to be one of the crucial areas of future work on ASD.

4. 'Autism is mainly a concern of child psychiatry, and of limited interest to adult services'

It is clear that at the time of writing there is little research on adult autism; there are few well-developed adult clinical services and few other adult resources.

The epidemiological work to date suggests that the prevalence of *diagnosed* ASD in adults is low, compared to children and adolescents. This is probably because Asperger and Rett syndromes did not officially exist until 1994, and re-diagnosis of people who already have an established clinical diagnosis is uncommon. The heavy reliance on early developmental history in establishing diagnosis is another factor that can make late diagnosis more complex.

Clinicians, researchers and politicians are now starting to appreciate the economic effect of ASD persisting into adult life (Jarbrink *et al.* 2007).

Current understanding suggests that the following should be reflected in our knowledge of ASD.

- A large number of conditions are sufficient to result in ASD behaviour.
- Appropriate assessment should involve a range of medical and non-medical specialities.
- Genetic, epigenetic and metabolic factors are important, and in many instances knowledge of these factors is critical to providing the most appropriate help to those with ASD.
- Problems such as sleep difficulties, epilepsy, digestive problems and poor immune function are common. Whether they are part of the ASD condition or epiphenomenal, they should not be ignored, and should in many cases be part of the routine assessment process.

Clinical practice in many areas, however, has failed to keep pace with the exponential increase in biological understanding. The massive injection of research funding in this area since 2006, particularly in the USA will see this avalanche of information accelerate.

EARLY PRESENTING FEATURES AND RISK FACTORS

One of the few factors over which there has been reasonable consensus in recent years in the area of ASD has been that, using appropriate methods, earlier intervention results in better outcome. Early identification of individuals with ASD has thus become the 'Holy Grail' of autism research – *identify early* > *intervene early* > *improve outcome.*

The past decade has seen steady improvement in age at first detection of concern over development, and a shortening of the period from referral to diagnosis, in many Western countries. There is increasing evidence for the benefits of early intervention in generally enhancing developmental progress (Dawson *et al.* 2010; Zwaigenbaum 2010).

There is conflicting evidence concerning a lower age limit to such early identification. Teitelbaum's work suggests that early movement analysis may be able to discriminate subsequently diagnosed children (Teitelbaum *et al.* 1998), while more recent prospective studies of high-risk groups focusing more on early interactional variables suggest that at six months, at least, it is not possible to discriminate ASD cases reliably from others (Ozonoff *et al.* 2010). It is possible that some of the larger prospective cohort studies such as MoBa (den norske **Mo**r and **Ba**rn-undersokelsen – see Magnus *et al.* 2006) will provide clearer data, allowing key predictive variables to be identified.

There is information to suggest that obstetric risk factors increase the likelihood of an ASD child. However, none of these factors, as yet, is sufficiently well established to be useful in screening (Kolevzon, Gross and Reichenberg 2007).

A range of standardized early screening tools is now available to the clinician to aid in early identification – such as the Checklist for Autism in Toddlers. (For a recent overview, see Scambler, Hepburn and Rogers 2006.)

The substantial and sustained rise in reported cases (see, for example, MMWR 2007a, 2007b, 2007c) is, however, putting a steadily increasing burden on clinicians involved in this process. Improvements in detection need to be backed up with clarification of the basis to the condition, and with optimized intervention to achieve the best quality of life for the individual.

There is still much confusion over the concept of regression in ASD. Many parents perceive their child's development to have been normal in the first year to 18 months – the point at which parents begin to develop concerns over the development of their ASD child (De Giacomo and Fombonne 1998). Various factors may be relevant to regressive phenomena in the ASD population:

> There is now some evidence to suggest that boys with autism and an MeCP2 gene defect, more typically reported in association with Rett syndrome [*63a, 63b*], may be more likely to show developmental regression. (Xi *et al.* 2007)

A subset of autistic children has been reported where developmental regression is linked to gene differences at 21q and 7q. (Molloy, Keddache and Martin 2005)

The effects of having co-morbid epilepsy are often complex, but it is common for children with epilepsy and ASD to show loss of language skills, autistic regression or both. [*See Tuchman 2006 for a review and discussion.*] The regressive factors specific to epilepsy such as the language loss in Landau-Kleffner syndrome are additional to the ASD-specific problems often seen in the same individuals.

Unrecognized metabolic factors can result in regression, as with B12 depletion due to vegan diet. (Casella, Valente, de Navarro and Kok *et al.* 2005)

What sort of things should give rise to early concern?
Parental age
A link between increasing parental age and risk of ASD has been found in a number of studies (for example, Hultman, Sparen and Cnattingius 2002; Mouridsen, Rich and Isager 1993; Reichenberg *et al.* 2006; Shelton, Tancredi and Hertz-Picciotto 2010). This finding has been corroborated in a study of families contributing to the Autism Genetic Resource Exchange (AGRE) (Cantor , Yoon, Furr and Lajonchere 2007). The most recent studies to address the issue of parental age (Croen, Najjar, Fireman and Grether 2007; Durkin *et al.* 2008) have both found that increasing maternal and paternal age seem to be independently associated with an increased risk of ASD.

It seems likely that parental age may be associated with a number of the genetic conditions discussed here in systematic ways.

Table A3: Conditions associated with regressive onset of ASD

• Adenylosuccinate lyase (ADSL) deficiency	[9]
• B12 depletion	(Casella, Valente, de Navarro and Kok 2005)
• Bannayan-Riley-Ruvalcaba syndrome	[15]
• Basal cell nevus syndrome	[16]
• Cortical Dysplasia–Focal Epilepsy (CDFE) syndrome	[19]
• Cowden syndrome	[26]
• Duchenne muscular dystrophy	[33]
• L-2-hydroxyglutaric aciduria	[40]
• Landau-Kleffner syndrome	(see Tuchman 2006)
• Proteus syndrome	[62]
• Rett syndrome	[63a]
• Rett syndrome (Hanefeld variant)	[63b]
• Schindler disease	[65]
• Male autistics with a MeCP2 defect	(Xi *et al.* 2007)
• Mitochondrial gene defects	(Poling, Frye, Shoffner and Zimmerman 2006)

- The likelihood of Down syndrome [31], for example, has long been known to increase with increasing maternal age (Penrose 1933).

- The increasing prevalence with ageing of defects in mitochondrial DNA would also provide a possible risk process linking autism to parental age. Many conditions linked with epilepsy have a mitochondrial component. Most mitochondrial inheritance is matrilineal (from the mother), suggesting that the likelihood of co-morbid epilepsy will become much greater as maternal reproductive age increases, than it will as paternal age increases.

- The prevalence of sperm containing both an X and a Y chromosome, instead of the more normal single X or single Y sex chromosome, makes it appear more likely that as paternal reproductive age increases, so does the risk of Klinefelter's (XYY) syndrome in boys (Lowe *et al.* 2001).

A recent overview of Californian birth cohort data from almost 5 million birth records from 1992 to 2000 has suggested that having an older mother represents a higher risk of autism than having an older father (King, Fountain, Dakhlallah and Bearman 2009).

Parental health

Mothers of autistic children are significantly more likely to have autoimmune problems such as type I diabetes, adult rheumatoid arthritis, hypothyroidism, systemic lupus erythematosus (Comi *et al.* 1999) and epilepsy (Leonard, de Klerk, Bourke and Bower 2006), compared to controls. Whether this is in some way causally related to the subsequent development of the affected child, or both are linked to some further factor, has not yet been established.

A long-term follow-up of Danish parents of children diagnosed with infantile autism has suggested associations with paternal type I diabetes and maternal ulcerative colitis (Mouridsen, Rich, Isager and Nedergaard 2007). As we shall see, the fragile-X tremor ataxia syndrome is being found to affect some mothers and maternal grandparents of boys with fragile-X.

The at-risk pregnancy

Studies of perinatal risk show little apparent association between specific birth and/ or perinatal difficulties and ASD. There is a slight increase in perinatal difficulties overall, but no specific difficulty appears to convey a significant increase in risk. (See, for example, Stein, Weizman, Ring and Barak 2006.)

Although the idea may seem biologically plausible, the evidence to date does not seem to support the notion that ASD arises as a consequence of factors such as increased head circumference (by making the baby more difficult to deliver, or increasing the chance of problems such as perinatal anoxia) or congenital malformation. (See Maimburg and Vaeth 2006.) One recent study has found that there is no evidence of accelerated brain growth *in utero* (Hobbs *et al.* 2007). A number of studies have demonstrated a higher rate of pre- and perinatal risk factors (for example, abnormal growth rate, both *in utero* and after birth; enlarged head at birth; bleeding in pregnancy; and low Apgar scores) in those who receive a subsequent diagnosis of autism (Dementieva *et al.* 2005; Glasson *et al.* 2004; Hultman, Sparen and Cnattingius 2002; Redcay and Courchesne 2005; Torrey, Dhavale, Lawlor and Yolken 2004).

Studies of umbilical cord blood samples have suggested that differences in levels of various neuropeptides and neurotrophins can, in some cases, differentiate between infants who go on to receive diagnoses of autism and other groups. The variations in findings across studies by the same research group suggest, however, that this evidence cannot be used at the present time to differentiate reliably (Nelson *et al.* 2001, 2006).

One study (Anderson G.M. *et al.* 2007) found significantly higher rates of trophoblast inclusions in a small group of archived placental samples from autistic births (6/27 or 22.2 per cent) compared to an anonymous control series (12/154 or 7.8 per cent). Inclusions were found in a proportion of both groups, so were not ASD-specific; however, as no attempt was made to look for other biological factors in the ASD group, and the positive controls could not be further investigated, the most that can be said at this point is that, if replicated, the finding could form part of an early high-risk screening process.

Approximately five per cent of the variance in head circumference can be explained on the basis of the HOXA1 A218G G allele (Conciatori *et al.* 2004) – so a genetic basis underpins a small proportion of the general group differences in cephalic growth.

The at-risk infant

Prematurity with very low birthweight is a factor that is associated with a subsequently increased ASD risk (Indredavik, Vik, Skranes and Brubakk 2008). One recent screening study using the Modified Checklist for Autism in Toddlers with 91 two-year-olds who had weighed less than 1.5kg at birth found 26 per cent of them to have ASD (Limperopoulos *et al.* 2008). Whether this is a consequence of increased learning, motor and behavioural and social difficulties experienced by this population, or is due to factors that also predispose to premature birth, is uncertain. Another recent study systematically reviewed all

healthcare records for three-year-old children in Atlanta born in 1981–1993 and found that a birthweight of less than 2.5kg doubled the likelihood of ASD diagnosis – but this was particularly for autism with associated learning problems and there was a major gender effect, with a much stronger risk in girls (Schendel and Bhasin 2008).

A large all-Denmark prospective birth cohort study of 698 autistic children born since 1962 with 25 controls per case found a range of perinatal factors were associated with autistic diagnosis. Breech presentation, low 5 minute Apgar scores, birth at <35 weeks GA and parental psychiatric history particularly of schizophrenia-like or affective conditions were all factors that were significantly associated with autistic diagnosis (Larsson *et al.* 2005).

There is a range of markers in infancy that can also indicate increased likelihood of developing ASD (Gray and Tonge 2001), particularly pre-verbal and non-verbal communication skills (which we have elsewhere called aspects of 'intersubjectivity' – see Trevarthen and Aitken 2001; Trevarthen *et al.* 2006) and pre-verbal play.

One recent study of a high-risk cohort followed from 14 to 36 months of age clearly differentiated an early-diagnosed group who exhibited differences in play, social functioning and communication by 14 months, and a second, later diagnosed group who, although not distinguishable from controls at 14 months, were clearly exhibiting similar difficulties by 24 months (Landa, Holman and Garrett-Mayer 2007).

There is an increased risk of ASD in the children of women with diabetes, who are almost three times as likely to have an ASD child, and of women with epilepsy whose risk is more than quadrupled (Leonard, de Klerk, Bourke and Bower 2006). These findings should help identify at-risk pregnancies and children who should receive more intensive early follow-up.

Sodium valproate is an antiepileptic medication that is a safe treatment for epilepsy but a teratogen to the developing foetus, and increases the risk of autism (Alsdorf and Wyszynski 2005). Risks from antenatal valproate exposure in epileptic women, who require treatment through pregnancy, can be minimized through various strategies (Genton, Semah and Trinka 2006).

Some markers should be high on the public health agenda, such as the significantly increased risk to infants who are given non-supplemented formula feeds (feeds not supplemented with docosahexaenoic and arachidonic acid) (Schultz et al. 2006), or who are on vegan breast or bottlemilk (Casella, Valente, de Navarro and Kok 2005), or are placed on early vegan diets (Cundiff and Harris 2006).

The beneficial effects of breastfeeding in organic acidaemias and the possible links between ASD and methylmalonic acidaemia also lend support to the benefits of breastfeeding in ASD in most cases (Gokcay, Baykal, Gokdemir and Demirkol 2006).

As long-chain polyunsaturated fatty acids are principally incorporated into the grey matter of the developing brain and their presence is highly dependent on dietary sources (Wainwright 2002), the above findings are unsurprising. Here, changes in public awareness and a change in policy concerning formula preparation could both have a marked impact on prevalence of ASD. This factor is most likely to have an effect in the USA, where formula supplementation is optional and parental decision-making is often based on relative cost.

Cord blood samples may help to predict subsequent ASD diagnosis from the levels of several biochemical compounds: substance P (SP), vasoactive intestinal peptide (VIP), pituitary adenylate cyclase-activating polypeptide (PACAP), calcitonin gene-related peptide (CGRP) and the neurotrophins nerve growth factor (NGF), brain-derived neurotrophic factor (BDNF), neurotrophin 3 (NT3) and neurotrophin 4/5 (NT4/5). BDNF differences look to be the most promising predictor (Nelson et al. 2001, 2006). However, one recent study has failed to corroborate its usefulness as an early biomarker (Croen et al. 2008). Material which makes such studies possible is available in some areas (in California, umbilical cord blood samples are stored from every birth) where the retrospective studies to date have been carried out, but collection of such samples is not yet a routine part of health surveillance in most places today.

Although not currently identifying large numbers of cases (Sempere et al. 2010), newborn metabolic and endocrine screening can be used to identify and intervene with a range of conditions (Braun et al. 2003).

As antenatal diagnosis through techniques such as serum sampling, amniocentesis and chorionic villous sampling of a range of genetic conditions becomes more widely used, coupled with the high potential demand for such screening as clear preventative treatment implications become apparent (Caughey, Washington, Gildengorin and Kuppermann 2004), early interventions should become more feasible.

A range of early behavioural features is seen in infants and preschoolers, particularly in respect of early reciprocal social interaction and pre-verbal play (Gray and Tonge 2001). The Checklist for Autism in Toddlers (CHAT) studies have shown that various early behaviours can predict a proportion of cases, based on three specific behaviours (Baron-Cohen *et al.* 2000b):

1. lack of *protodeclarative* pointing (pointing to draw joint attention to something – 'Look at this, Mummy!') as opposed to *protoimperative* pointing (pointing to obtain something – 'Get me that!')

2. lack of or poor eye contact

3. lack of fantasy and/or pretend play.

There have been various refinements to the CHAT, such as the M-CHAT (Robins, Fein, Barton and Green 2001) and most successfully the as yet unreplicated CHAT-23 (Wong *et al.* 2004). There are various other early screening tools available. The First Year Inventory (FYI) (Watson, L.R. *et al.* 2007) may prove useful, but has had limited validation and seems to have a significant false negative rate. The Early Screening for Autistic Traits (ESAT) Questionnaire (Dietz *et al.* 2006) appears to have comparable sensitivity and specificity. This would not require administration by a clinician and would therefore prove simpler to administer for early screening (Groen, Swinkels, van der Gaagand and Buitelaar 2007).

There is now a rich body of early family videotape material (see Palomo, Belinchon and Ozonoff 2006 for a recent overview). In summary, there is now evidence for early differences which can identify a subgroup of cases. However, a high proportion of currently diagnosed children where earlier videotape evidence is available show no obvious early evidence for differences – video evidence can, on current evidence, be used to 'rule-in' or confirm cases, but not to 'rule-out' or exclude them.

It seems almost a truism, but age at recognition of differences correlates with factors such as the severity of the disorder, the degree of associated learning difficulty and the extent of associated medical problems (Baghdadi *et al.* 2003). That said, a recent US study using the Autism Diagnostic Interview – Revised (ADI-R) (Chawarska *et al.* 2007) found that age at initial concern in autism was 14.7 months (N=51) while in PDD-NOS (a less severe diagnosis on the US DSM system) it was 14.9 months (N=24). There was, however, an association between severity of early social disability and subsequent diagnosis – greater early social disability increased the likelihood that a child would receive a later diagnosis of autism.

There is some work to suggest that discrete subgroups of infants can be identified, based on tools such as the Infant Behavioral Summarized Evaluation (IBSE), which predict distinct clinical subtypes of autistic disorder from early behaviour (Malvy *et al.* 2004).

There is also some evidence to suggest that early diagnosis may be possible on the basis of patterns of movement and facial expressions such as mouth shape (Teitelbaum *et al.* 1998). This is exciting and potentially related to some of the conditions discussed here – the 'Mobius mouth' reported as a common feature in this study of early videotapes is a typical feature of those with a cranial nerve VI and VII palsy and is seen classically in Mobius syndrome [48]. However, not all cases of Mobius syndrome have an ASD. Further validation of the technique on unselected cases, and ascertainment of false positive and false negative rates – the number of misdiagnosed and the number of missed cases – would need to be clarified before this could be used as a screening test in isolation.

Without specific interventions or therapies, there is clear evidence that some children diagnosed with ASD in infancy improve. One recent paper compares a group of 13 children who 'lost' their ASD diagnosis by age four with a group of 60 who maintained their diagnosis over time and a group of 17 normal controls. The only factor that appeared to discriminate the children who outgrew their ASD was that they had significantly better motor skills on the Vineland adaptive behaviour scales than those who did not (Sutera *et al.* 2007).

As awareness of ASD improved in the late twentieth and early twenty-first centuries, decreasing age at diagnosis was a phenomenon that produced a transient increase in apparent numbers. Recent research suggests that the impact of this phenomenon has now largely dissipated and that the continuing increase in reported numbers of newly diagnosed cases is not significantly affected by it (Hertz-Picciotto and Delwiche 2009).

Conclusion

At present, a significant proportion of those with ASD can be identified in the first two years of life if appropriate screening assessments are used by adequately trained clinicians. The limited number of trained clinicians in many areas is a barrier to such screening. A number of methods can be used to identify high-risk groups, based on risk factors such as maternal epilepsy and diabetes, and certain lifestyle factors such as vegan diet. Some screening tests may be able to pick up 'at-risk' cases with birth screening of blood biochemistry, but much further work is required before such techniques are likely to become reliable and sensitive enough to use in routine clinical practice.

PHYSICAL DIFFERENCES

A large number of clinical conditions are known to be associated with autism (Gillberg and Coleman 1996; Kielinen, Rantala, Timonen, Linna and Moilanen 2004; Zafeiriou, Ververi and Vargiami 2006; this volume), particularly when genetic effects or exposure are at a similar time post-conception. (For an early discussion of this idea, see Aitken 1991.)

A number of physical differences are seen more commonly in ASDs, and minor physical anomalies, particularly of the head, ears, mouth and hands, are prevalent in this group (Tripi *et al.* 2007).

This section briefly discusses some of the main physical anomalies that can give rise to concerns.

Abnormal glutamate metabolism

The amino-acid neurotransmitters glutamate and gamma-amino butyric acid (GABA) have received limited attention in the study of ASDs (Dhossche *et al.* 2002). Researchers have only recently begun to investigate the role of these factors in the pathogenesis and development of ASD and the potential implications for treatment.

GABA receptor subunit gene differences have been found to occur frequently in particular patterns in the ASD population (Ma *et al.* 2005).

The Affymetrix 'Genchip' study (also referred to as the NAAR Autism Genome Project) is an international collaborative project that has screened large numbers of multiplex ASD families, using a SNP high-density micro-array (a technology that enables rapid screening of large numbers of single nucleotide polymorphisms – see Carter N.P. 2007 for review) that can screen genotypes and copy number variations across large samples to develop a clinical database of ASD susceptibility genes. (For recent findings from this project, see Weiss *et al.* 2009.)

Glutamate is the principal excitatory amino-acid neurotransmitter found in all vertebrate nervous systems. An imbalance between excitatory and inhibitory transmitter systems provides a reasonable theoretical model for certain presentations of ASD (Rubenstein and Merzenich 2003).

The Affymetrix study of autism risk loci (Autism Genome Project Consortium 2007), although not identifying glutamate-specific genes within its own dataset, makes much in its discussion of the large number of reported ASD susceptibility genes affecting glutamatergic neurotransmission (such as 2q13; 4q28.3; 7q21.3; 9p24.2; 9q34.11; 11q13–12; and 15q25.2), which are implicated as promising candidate genes for ASD. They note that in both fragile-X [35, 36] and tuberous sclerosis [73] there is dysregulation of glutamate signalling.

The physiological effects of glutamate are ubiquitous (Carlson 2001; Kandel, Schwartz and Jessell 1995). GABA is converted from glutamate by the enzyme glutamic acid decarboxylase (GAD). Pyridoxal phosphate (vitamin B6) is an essential co-enzyme in this process. GAD is the rate-limiting step in the synthesis of GABA, and reduction in GAD activity leads to excess levels of glutamate. There are some preliminary results suggesting that ASD may be associated with abnormal GABA A receptor genes on chromosome 4 (Vincent, Zhong, Nabi and Mahbubal Huq 2004), and with a defect in the metabotropic glutamate receptor 8 at chromosome 7q13 (Seragee, Zhong, Nabi and Mahbubal Huq 2003).

Abnormalities in neuroligin 3 and neuroligin 4 have both been reported in association with ASD (Blasi et al. 2006; Chocholska, Rossier, Barbi and Kehrer-Sawatzki 2006; Jamain et al. 2003; Laumonnier et al. 2004). As with many such associations, the findings are not common in larger population samples (Vincent et al. 2004). Neuroligins are critical for synapse formation, and recent developments in research on the homologous *nlg*-1 gene in nematodes is providing a clearer understanding of the role played by neuroligins in central nervous system development, and the effect that neuroligin defects exert on their ability to cope with oxidative stress and mercury toxicity (Hunter et al. 2010). There is increasing evidence for oxidative stress in autism (Chahuan and Chahuan 2006; Laura et al. 2011) and in specific related ASD conditions such as Down Syndrome.

Examination of brain levels of GAD in five autistic and eight control subjects at postmortem found that this enzyme was reduced by 48–61 per cent in parietal and cerebellar areas of the brain in individuals with autism, compared to controls (Fatemi et al. 2002). As the 'excitotoxic' effects of glutamate interfere with neuronal development, and have their maximal effect during the second year of human life (Kornhuber et al. 1989), it seems plausible that such a difference in glutamate metabolism may be implicated in the brain differences reported in the ASDs. A further recent study of adult autistic serum levels of glutamate also provides support for

the involvement of abnormal glutamergic neurotransmission in autism (Shinohe et al. 2006).

As well as being the period of maximal effects of glutamate on neural maturation, the middle of the second year is the time when parents typically first note concerns over development in those children who go on to receive a diagnosis of autism (De Giacomo and Fombonne 1998).

A further postmortem study of 10 autistic and 23 group-matched control brains found a range of neurogenetic differences, particularly of interest here being that mRNA levels of excitatory amino acid transporter 1 and glutamate receptor AMPA 1 were elevated, specifically in cerebellum, while AMPA-type glutamate receptor density was significantly reduced, also selectively in cerebellum (Purcell et al. 2001).

The interactions between glutamate, GABA and the other neurotransmitter systems involved in brain development, such as serotonin and dopamine, are complex (Sodhi and Sanders-Bush 2004) and not yet fully understood. (See Attwell 2000 and Lam, Aman and Arnold 2005 for recent reviews of the neurochemistry.)

Various environmental factors, including chronic stress, increase circulating glutamate levels (Abraham, Juhasz, Kekesi and Kovacs 1998), activating N-methyl D-aspartate (NMDA) receptors and increasing the likelihood of cell death (Kandel, Schwartz and Jessell 1991).

There is also increasing interest in a possible link between glutamate receptor differences and a heightened risk of various conditions, including ADHD (Turic et al. 2004), epilepsy (Smith P.F. 2005) and hepatic encephalopathy (Platt 2007).

Anti-glutamergic agents are receiving increasing attention for their potential role in the management of ASDs (see, for review, King and Bostic 2006). Glutamatergic overactivity is also known to be associated with an increased risk of seizures (Hussman 2001). It is well recognized that seizure problems are more common in the autistic population (Tuchman and Rapin 2002a), with more severely impaired individuals having a greater likelihood of also having seizures (Gabis, Pomeroy and Andriola 2005). However, the potential link between these various aspects has yet to be systematically explored.

Researchers have found abnormalities of cellular development in the limbic system and cerebellum at postmortem (Lawrence, Kemper, Bauman and Blatt 2010; Raymond, Bauman and Kemper 1996; Schumann and Amaral 2006) consistent with abnormal antenatal development of these structures.

We now have evidence for differences in the GABA receptor pathways (as indicated by the abnormal GAD levels reported above), in the ionotrophic glutamate receptor system (as indicated by the AMPA 1 differences above), and in metabotropic glutamate receptors (as we will see in the sections on fragile-X [35, 36]).

IN SUMMARY: Glutamate abnormalities appear to occur in ASDs at a higher than expected rate. These may be primary and genetic in origin, driven by secondary factors such as anxiety, or a compound of such effects. As we will go on to discuss, in some conditions, such as fragile-X [35, 36], response to certain receptor-blocking agents in animal knockout models provides strong evidence for reversibility, and human clinical trials are underway. Whether the more extensive abnormalities of glutamate metabolism that have been reported in ASD may respond similarly to manipulation of glutamate pathways remains to be tested.

Abnormal sterol metabolism

Sterols, such as cholesterol, are complex hydrocarbons that are key elements in cell membranes. Abnormalities could have effects on the permeability of structures like the lining of the intestine and the integrity of the blood–brain barrier.

The complex role played by dietary sterols in conditions as disparate as heart attacks, obesity and Alzheimer's disease is fascinating, and the role of dietary sterols is becoming better appreciated. The history of the science in this area is intriguing and is well reviewed in a popular book by American science journalist Susan Allport (Allport 2006). The potential role of abnormal cholesterol metabolism in ASD is highlighted by a number of disparate findings in the clinical literature.

A variety of abnormalities in short chain fatty acid metabolism have been hypothesized as being involved in some forms of ASD (Brown and Austin 2009; Porter 2002). Abnormal long chain acyl-CoA dehydrogenase (LCAD), for example, has been found in an autistic patient, with consequent defects in the beta-oxidation of branched and unsaturated fatty acids, reduced synthesis of omega-3 DHA, and abnormal cholesterol metabolism (Clark-Taylor and Clark-Taylor 2004). A small French series showed marked plasma omega-3 deficiencies but no reduction in omega-6 in ASD cases (N=15) compared to learning-disabled controls (N=18) (Vancassel et al. 2001).

Reporting on a chance finding, Bell, Sargent, Tocher and Dick (2000) described abnormal erythrocyte cell membrane phospholipids – in particular, reduced levels of highly unsaturated fatty acids (HUFAs), which were most obvious after cold storage. This suggested the possibility that these compounds are more rapidly metabolized in those with ASDs. In a later paper by Bell *et al.* (2004), the initial findings were replicated. In addition, physical symptoms of fatty acid deficiency were found to be over-represented in the ASD population. These features were noted to occur more commonly in those whose presentation was regressive than in those with 'classical' autism. A study by Bell and colleagues (Bell *et al.* 2009) compared autistic children (N = 45) with matched typically developing controls and 38 non-autistic developmentally disabled children. Within the autistic group, those taking fish oil supplements were compared to those who were not. In most respects the results showed no differences between groups with the exception of a high alpha linolenic acid to eicosapentanoic acid ratio in the un-supplemented but not the supplemented autistics. This suggests that there may be a highly unsaturated fatty acid imbalance in ASD that is correctable by supplementation. Further controlled studies would be required to confirm this finding and look for demonstrable effects on symptomology or behaviour.

A small study from IBRD (the Institute for Basic Research in Developmental Disabilities; Chauhan V. *et al.* 2004) has shown an increased level of amino-glycerophospholipids in the plasma of 14 autistic children, compared to their non-autistic sibling controls. This supports the earlier finding of Bell and colleagues that there is abnormal erythrocyte membrane composition in those with autistic disorder, and, presumably, differences in the membranes of many or all body tissues. This raises the possibility of differences in membrane integrity both in the intestine – a possible basis for 'leaky gut syndrome' – and at the blood–brain barrier (currently a hotly debated topic in terms of both infiltration (Shusta 2005) and development of more effective pharmacotherapies

(Egelton and Davis 2005). BBB transport of glutamate, for example, is a biologically complex process that may be important in conditions such as Fragile-X (see: Smith 2000).

A study carried out by Tierney *et al.* (2006) at the Kennedy Krieger Institute at Johns Hopkins in Baltimore has found that a significantly larger than expected proportion of those with ASD had abnormally low lipid levels, with 19 of the 100 samples analysed showing cholesterol levels below the fifth centile, compared to the expected general population values.

A further study of 22 adults with Asperger's syndrome found significantly elevated whole cholesterol and LDL (low density lipoprotein) levels, compared to closely matched controls (Dziobek, Gold, Wolf and Convit 2007).

A considerable amount of research has now been carried out on the biology of Smith-Lemli-Opitz syndrome (SLOS) [66] (Tierney, Nwokoro and Kelley 2000). This is a condition caused by a defect in the final stage of cholesterol biosynthesis, due to an inborn error in the gene for 3 beta-hydroxysteroid Delta7-reductase (DHCR7) that commonly results in ASD if it is not treated by early cholesterol supplementation.

Recent epidemiological and clinical studies have suggested that DHCR7 may be the most prevalent genetic deficit that can be linked to ASD (Ciara *et al.* 2006) and that it can show a beneficial response to early dietary intervention.

Dietary deficiencies in essential fatty acid intake appear to be relatively common in children with neurological disabilities (Hals *et al.* 2000).

A study of lipid profiles in Smith-Magenis syndrome [67] found cholesterol levels to be elevated above the 95th centile for the general population in 57 per cent (Smith A.C.M. *et al.* 2002). This suggests a possible genetic basis to abnormal cholesterol metabolism linked to 17p11.2 deletion.

A small, double-blinded, group-matched, randomized and placebo-controlled pilot study of omega-3 fatty acid supplementation in autistic children provides evidence for a significant effect on hyperactivity and stereotypy in an unselected autistic population (Amminger *et al.* 2006; for comment, see Gilbert 2007). A further recent open trial of PUFA (polyunsaturated fatty acid) supplementation found significant improvements in ASD symptomology in 20/30 cases as rated on the Childhood Autism Rating Scale (CARS), and normalization of blood PUFA levels assessed by means of thumb-prick blood testing (Meguid, Atta, Gouda and Khalil 2008).

A final factor of possible relevance is that in the Avon Longitudinal Study of Parents and Children (ALSPAC) cohort there is a reported association between low omega-3 fatty acid intake from fish and postpartum maternal depressive symptomology (Golding *et al.* 2009). As postnatal depression is known to have a negative impact on early child development (Trevarthen and Aitken 2001), it seems likely that this would compound the effects of other factors predisposing to ASD.

IN SUMMARY: Abnormalities of sterol metabolism are common in the ASD population. Some of the biological bases have clear, well-understood mechanisms and effective intervention approaches.

Anxiety, overrarousal, self-injury, aggression, sleep and behaviour problems

A range of behavioural and emotional problems is common in autistic spectrum disorders. Anxiety, overarousal, self-injurious behaviours, aggressive behaviours, sleep problems and stereotypies are typically reported as being both amongst the most common and the most distressing.

In some clinical conditions, there is a predictable pattern of comorbidities. In fragile-X syndrome [35, 36], for example, the constellation of ASD, anxiety disorder, specific learning problems and global learning disability is commonly seen.

The effects of stress and anxiety on behaviour and development begin before birth. In animal models, antenatal psychological stress results in a significant reduction in cell proliferation, in particular in midbrain structures (such as the nucleus accumbens and hippocampus) (Kawamura *et al.* 2006).

Stress and anxiety are amongst the commonest problems seen in clinical practice, and are modulated by glutamate. There is now a considerable body of research on differences in glutamate receptor function (Chen, Tracy and Nam 2007), on glutamate metabolism linked to differences in levels of anxiety and stress, and on clinical response to modulation of metabotropic glutamate receptors (Bergink, van Megen and Westenberg 2004; Swanson *et al.* 2005). There is also recent work suggesting a role for secretin, both in the central nervous system and in the gastrointestinal system, as a stress-regulating neuropeptide (Welch M.G. *et al.* 2006).

In a study of normal healthy humans there was a correlation between the level of stress (rated on the Derogatis Stress

Profile) and the size of the anterior portion of the hippocampus (Szeszko *et al.* 2006). A recent study of children with ASD found an association between the size of the amygdala and assessed level of anxiety on a standardized scale, with the size of the right side of the amygdala varying in proportion to the level of anxiety (Juranek *et al.* 2006).

In one study carried out with rats, it was shown that a large number of gene effects (upwards of 500) are mediated by the pattern of maternal care, and effects on the development of hippocampal structure and of glutamate mGluR5 receptors were down-regulated where mothers showed lower levels of licking, grooming and arched-back nursing, compared to others (Weaver, Meaney and Szyf 2006). It also appears that such effects of early experience are potentially reversible. As we shall see, glutamate mGluR5 receptors are implicated in fragile-X syndrome [35, 36].

Self-injurious behaviour is a well-recognized problem that is over-represented in many forms of ASD, such as SLOS [66] (Tierney *et al.* 2001) and fragile-X syndrome [35, 36] (Symons *et al.* 2003).

In one interesting study with adults with ASD (McDougle *et al.* 1996) tryptophan depletion led to a significant increase in behaviours such as whirling, flapping, pacing, banging and hitting self, rocking, and toe walking. Abnormal tryptophan levels in ASD have been a well-recognized feature for many years (Jorgensen, Mellerup and Rafelsen 1970).

Toe walking is a poorly understood but common phenomenon in ASD, which is associated with language impairment (Accardo and Whitman 1989). It can

Table A4: Genetic conditions associated with ASD and sleep difficulties

• XXY	[3]
• Angelman syndrome	[11]
• Cortical Dysplasia–Focal Epilepsy (CDFE) syndrome	[19]
• Down syndrome	[31]
• Dravet's syndrome	[32]
• Hypothyroidism	[43]
• Joubert syndrome	[44]
• Neurofibromatosis type 1	[51]
• Potocki-Lupski syndrome	[60]
• Prader-Willi syndrome	[61]
• Rett syndrome	[63a]
• Rubinstein-Taybi syndrome	[64]
• Smith-Lemli-Opitz syndrome	[66]
• Smith-Magenis syndrome	[67]
• Succinic semialdehyde dehydrogenase (SSADH) deficiency	[69]
• Tourette syndrome	[71]

respond to behavioural treatment interventions (Marcus, Sinnott, Bradley and Grey 2010), but surgical intervention to improve flexion is not uncommon (Caselli, Rzonca and Lue 1988; McMulkin, Baird, Caskey and Ferguson 2006).

Aggression is another type of challenging behaviour that is frequently reported in ASD (Dunlap, Robbins and Darrow 1994).

There are also a number of mechanisms involved in anxiety that may contribute to difficulties in those with ASDs. Neuroendocrine factors such as oxytocin (a neuropeptide) reduce the responses of the hypothalamic–pituitary–adrenal (HPA) axis to stress (Heinrichs and Gaab 2007). The oxytocin receptor gene located at 3p24.1 has been identified as being associated with ASD (Ylisaukko-oja et al. 2004, 2006).

Anxiety, aggressive behaviour and psychosis can all be presenting features of epilepsy (Kanner 2004), and this should be considered as a possible basis where these features occur.

In adults with Asperger syndrome, a number of markers of abnormal phospholipid metabolism (with elevation of cholesterol and low-density lipoprotein levels) correlate with increased ratings of both anxiety and obsessive-compulsive symptoms (Dziobek, Gold Wolf and Convit 2007). This suggests that modifying what are normally thought of as cardiac risk markers may reduce both OCD and anxiety.

Consistently, despite the rising prevalence of reported cases of ASD, a strong excess of males seems to be a robust characteristic of the ASD population – significantly more boys than girls are diagnosed. Given the sex bias, an 'extreme male brain theory' of autism has been proposed (Baron-Cohen 2002). This theory provides support for the possible role of sexually dimorphic neuroendocrine

mechanisms in the pathogenesis of ASD. Despite only cursory acknowledgement in Baron-Cohen (2002), the idea seems strongly reminiscent of the earlier work of Geschwind and Galaburda on the effects of testosterone on brain development and developmental psychopathology (Geschwind and Galaburda 1985a, 1985b, 1985c).

Much emphasis has been given to the possible role of in utero testosterone exposure. Although much has been made of a link between 'male behaviour' and conditions such as congenital adrenal hyperplasia [25], the evidence to date is far from clear or convincing. Two other potentially relevant neuro-hormonal sex differences are in arginine vasopressin (an androgen-dependent neuropeptide which strongly influences male behaviour) and oxytocin (an analogous neuropeptide with many similar behavioural functions in females) (Carter C.S. 2007).

One interesting finding is that in a double-blind, placebo-controlled within-subjects study with healthy male volunteers, inhalation of 24 IU of oxytocin significantly improved their performance on a 'mind-reading' task (Domes et al. 2007), which suggests that such neuropeptide mechanisms may be important in social perception, and relevant to the deficits seen in ASD. For an overview of the effects of oxytocin and vasopressin, see Caldwell and Young (2006).

Sleep problems are commonly reported in those with ASD (Liu, Hubbard, Fabes and Adam 2006). There is evidence that both central factors, such as abnormalities of melatonin production (Tordjman et al. 2005), and associated problems, such as gastro-oesophageal reflux (Horvath et al. 1999), may be involved in individual cases.

A recent study shows that in some cases reduced levels of melatonin synthesis are associated with polymorphisms in the

ASMT gene that encodes the final enzyme ASMT (acetylserotonin methyltransferase, aka hydroxyindole-o-methyltransferase) which is involved in melatonin biosynthesis (Melke *et al.* 2007). In some cases of ASD the section of the X or Y chromosome involving the ASMT gene (Xpter–p22.32/ Ypter–p11.2 respectively) is deleted.

Certain of the conditions associated with ASD appear to result in elevated rates of sleep problems. Table A4 shows those that are the most likely to result in significant sleep difficulties.

The use of melatonin supplementation appears successful in a high percentage of published cases (Phillips and Appleton 2004; Wirojanan *et al.* 2009) and in the first, albeit small, randomized controlled trial (Garstang and Wallis 2006). Melatonin has also proved beneficial in certain specific conditions, such as Angelman syndrome (Braam, Didden, Smits and Curfs 2008).

An oddity of the US licensing system has made prescription licensing of melatonin difficult because it is already available as an over-the-counter supplement. As a consequence, synthetic analogue melatonin agonists such as Ramelteon (Rozerem [Takeda Pharmaceutical Company Ltd, Osaka, Japan], aka TAK-375) are being explored as patentable alternatives (Pandi-Perumal *et al.* 2007).

In the UK, after a period of over-the-counter sale as a food supplement, melatonin was reclassified as 'medicinal by use' and became a non-product-licensed, prescription-only substance. This means that current recommendation is that melatonin is only available on prescription by a hospital-based consultant.

A further factor that has been shown to be associated with sleep difficulties in some ASD cases is low serum ferritin, secondary to dietary iron insufficiency. In a study of 33 children, 77 per cent had restless sleep, all of whom responded with significant improvement to treatment with 6mg/kg of elemental iron per day (Dosman *et al.* 2007). Levels of serum transferrin, an antioxidant iron-binding protein, have been found to be significantly reduced in ASD, and to correlate (along with abnormally low levels of ceruloplasmin, a copper-binding protein) with loss of language skills (Chauhan A. *et al.* 2004).

Table A5: Genetic conditions associated with ASD and cancer risk

• XXY	[3]
• Bannayan-Riley-Ruvalcaba syndrome	[15]
• Basal cell nevus syndrome	[16]
• CATCH22	[18]
• Cowden syndrome	[26]
• Down syndrome	[31]
• Neurofibromatosis type 1	[51]
• Noonan syndrome	[52]
• Sotos syndrome	[68]
• Xeroderma pigmentosa	[79]
• X-linked ichthyosis	[80]

IN SUMMARY: Anxiety, overrarousal, self-injurious behaviour, aggression, sleep and behaviour problems are all more common in the ASD population. Some of these, such as anxiety and sleep difficulties, are particularly associated with certain specific conditions, and can have direct implications for management.

Cancer risk

A number of the genetic conditions linked to ASD have been reported in association with specific cancers. One survey has attempted to correlate rates of 46 specific cancers occurring in different geographical regions of the USA with rates of ASD diagnosis. A robust statistical association could be found only for *in situ* breast cancer (Kao *et al.* 2010). A number of conditions have been noted where such associations have been described (see Table A5).

IN SUMMARY: A range of physical features is found in association with certain presentations of ASD. A number of these associations are linked with specific clinical syndromes and conditions.

Cardiac abnormalities

A number of ASD conditions have associated cardiac abnormalities. Some are complex, such as tetralogy of Fallot, and, although uncommon, require early attention, while others may require careful monitoring.

Table A6: Genetic conditions associated with ASD and cardiac abnormalities

• CATCH22	[18]
• CHARGE syndrome	[20]
• Coffin-Lowry syndrome	[21]
• de Lange syndrome	[27]
• DiGeorge syndrome I	[29a]
• Down syndrome	[31]
• Noonan syndrome	[52]
• Timothy syndrome	[70]
• Velocardiofacial syndrome	[76]
• Williams syndrome	[77]

Table A7: Genetic conditions associated with ASD and connective tissue disorders

• Ehlers-Danlos syndrome	[34]
• Marfan's syndrome	
• Williams syndrome	[77]

Connective tissue disorders

Several conditions that result in defects of connective tissue have been linked to ASD.

'Cupid's bow' upper lip (aka 'Mobius mouth')

This feature is typically associated with a cranial nerve VI and VII palsy. It is seen in Mobius syndrome [48] and Smith-Magenis syndrome [67], 'Mobius mouth' has also been reported in non-Mobius ASD cases from ratings of a series of early autism videos by Teitelbaum *et al.* (1998). Mobius syndrome is also associated with abnormal ear rotation (see below).

Enlarged head circumference

Many people with ASDs have larger than average heads, and a range of 'overgrowth syndromes' such as Sotos syndrome [68] are reported. There are also reports that in some cases this can be related to a genetic differerence in a specific homeobox gene (the HOXA1 A218G polymorphism) (Conciatori *et al.* 2004); or else part of a general picture of increased somatic growth (Torrey, Dhavale, Lawlor and Yolken 2004). The pattern is typically one of accelerated head growth during the first year, followed by a marked deceleration during the second year, which coincides with behavioural worsening of autistic symptomology (Dawson *et al.* 2007). There is marked variation, however, with some studies reporting accelerated growth through the preschool period (see Redcay and Courchesne 2005 for review). There is also a suggestion that the accelerated brain growth is regionally specific, being more obvious in frontal association areas (Carper and Courchesne 2005) – something that would be consistent with the results seen on functional neuroimaging studies.

Some preliminary data (based on 45 autistic and 222 normal control subjects) suggests that overall foetal head growth in ASD is not outside of normal limits (Hobbs *et al.* 2007).

A recent, albeit small, study found that, within a fragile-X [35, 36] population, in the first year of life there was no difference in head growth between those who fulfilled criteria for autism and those who did not, but that by 30 and 60 months, those with autism showed evidence of increased head circumference, whereas those with fragile-X alone were no different from the general population norms (Chiu *et al.* 2007).

Macrocephaly can be benign, and can also be associated with immune problems in the absence of any features consistent with ASD (Cogulu *et al.* 2007). In one recent study of a large sample (N=241) of nonsyndromic autistic subjects, there was a significant association between larger head size and the prevalence of allergic/immune disorders (Sacco *et al.* 2007a). This finding fits with the early speculations of Norman Geschwind and Albert Galaburda (Geschwind and Galaburda 1985a, 1985b, 1985c) who related this general association between increased head circumference and immune problems to increased levels of *in utero* testosterone exposure. When this is artificially manipulated in other species, there is increased head growth, coupled with retarded development of immune structures such as the thymus gland (Geschwind and Galaburda 1985a, 1985b, 1985c).

Table A8: Genetic conditions associated with ASD and gastrointestinal disturbance

• Angelman syndrome	[11]
• Autism secondary to autoimmune lymphoproliferative syndrome (ALPS)	[14]
• Bannayan-Riley-Ruvalcaba syndrome	[15]
• Down syndrome	[31]
• Williams syndrome	[77]

Facial asymmetries (hemifacial microsomia)

Differences in the rate of growth of the two sides of the jaw and associated facial musculature, often with partial development of the lower ear, are seen in Goldenhar syndrome [38]. Hemi-overgrowth is also seen in neurofibromatosis [51] and Proteus syndrome [62].

Gastrointestinal disturbance

Gastrointestinal problems have been reported in ASD in a significant proportion of cases. Although the majority of the literature has looked at gastrointestinal problems in *all* ASD, some studies have also found such problems in several of the genetic conditions linked to ASD.

In addition, the MET receptor tyrosine kinase variant at 7q31 (Campbell D.B. *et al.* 2006, 2008), which is a pleiotropic gene involved in both brain development and gastrointestinal repair, has been shown from a screening of 918 individuals on the Autism Genetic Resource Exchange (AGRE) database to be associated with the co-morbid presentation of gastrointestinal problems and ASD (Campbell *et al.* 2009).

The issue of gastrointestinal involvement in ASD has been hotly debated, in large part due to the controversies surrounding the issue of a putative link between the measles–mumps–rubella (MMR) vaccine

and autism. The initial theory advanced for a possible link between MMR vaccine exposure and a novel form of bowel disorder called 'ileal-lymphoid-nodular hyperplasia' (ILNH) or 'autistic enterocolitis' suggested that there might be a causal link between MMR vaccine exposure and the subsequent development of ASD. This was based on research suggesting that persistent viral infection was detectable in intestinal biopsy samples (Uhlmann *et al.* 2002). Subsequent research using rigorous methods and involving the laboratories which had made the original claims has validated the methodology but failed to replicate the suggestion of persistent vaccine strain virus (Hornig *et al.* 2008).

ILNH is an unusual bowel pathology and has been reported recently in a case of Bannayan-Riley-Ruvalcaba syndrome [15] linked to ASD (Boccone *et al.* 2006).

Gastrointestinal disturbance has often been attributed to faddy eating, and it is true that extreme self-imposed food restriction does occur in some cases, and can have major developmental consequences (Uyanik *et al.* 2006).

A number of systematic reviews of the literature on gastrointestinal problems in ASD are now available (Erickson *et al.* 2005; Horvath and Perman 2002a, 2002b; White 2003). All of these reviews suggest that there is a significantly elevated prevalence of gastrointestinal symptomology in ASD.

Various reasons for possible gastrointestinal disturbance being linked to ASD have been advanced. Abnormal intestinal permeability (often called the 'leaky gut hypothesis') has been strongly advocated by several groups who claim to have found evidence of high levels of diet-derived peptides in the urine of a high percentage of those with ASDs. These peptides, often called casomorphins and gluteomorphins, are thought to derive from casein and gluten in the diet (Anderson *et al.* 2002; Reichelt and Knivsberg 2003). The early history of interest in casein- and gluten-derived neuropeptides has been reviewed comprehensively elsewhere (Klavdieva 1996).

Critics of this view have made highly contrasting claims. A group based in York in the UK has claimed that the presence of IAG (indolyl-3-acryloylglycine – one of the gluten-derived opioids said to be involved in ASD) in the urine of individuals with ASD was not important, since, although they could detect IAG at significant levels in their urine, they could also find similar levels of IAG in all of the other children tested, including non-autistic age-, sex- and school-matched controls (Wright *et al.* 2005).

A second group, from Edinburgh in Scotland, could not isolate opioid peptides either from the urine of 11 autistic children, or from their non-autistic sibling controls, or from adult controls (Hunter L.C. *et al.* 2003).

There are, of course, conditions which we will go on to discuss, such as Down syndrome [31] and Williams syndrome [77], where coeliac disease can often result in a clear clinical indication of gluten intolerance (Giannotti *et al.* 2001). In such cases, antibody testing and appropriate intervention should be a routine part of clinical assessment and management.

The potential clinical utility of casein and gluten restriction (CFGF) diets was identified as a research priority in the Medical Research Council Research Review (MRC 2001), but, at the time of writing, no such research has been funded.

In spite of controversy over the mechanism, the data, albeit limited, on effects of intervention with restriction diet are positive (Knivsberg, Reichelt, Hoien and Nodland 2002; Reichelt and Knivsberg 2003). Some further limited support comes from the finding of reduced autistic symptomology in response to long-term naltrexone treatment (Cazzullo *et al.* 1999). Naltrexone is a selective opioid-receptor blocking agent that would also attenuate the effects of exorphins.

It could, of course, prove to be the case that casein and gluten restriction are beneficial, but for reasons different to those which have been proposed, such as ketogenesis (Aitken 2009), or gastrointestinal problems caused by a PTEN defect such as Bannayan-Riley-Ruvalcaba syndrome [15] (Boccone *et al.* 2006).

The current situation, therefore, with respect to the usefulness of CFGF diets is that they appear to be helpful for a proportion of those with ASD, but no large-scale, systematic studies have been carried out, and there continues to be controversy over why such diets might be effective.

A systematic review published in 2002 (Horvath and Perman 2002a) documents the high prevalence of gastrointestinal symptomology in the ASD population.

This association is now generally widely accepted among clinicians so that, despite continuing debate over what causes such problems, their presence and the need to adequately investigate and treat them should be well accepted.

In a 2003 case series of 103 autistic and 29 normal controls who were suffering from abdominal pain (Afzal *et al.* 2003), a significantly higher proportion of the autistic group was reported as having megacolon (an enlarged lower intestine) on rectosigmoid loading. This was seen in 54 per cent of the autistic group, compared to 24 per cent of their controls. The ASD cases were also more likely to suffer with severe constipation (seen in 36 per cent, compared to 10 per cent of the controls).

A survey of 500 families with children with ASD (Lightdale, Siegel and Heyman 2001) found that approximately 50 per cent of those with ASD had loose stools or diarrhoea; one in three suffered from abdominal pain; and one in five had frequent bowel motions (three or more per day). There were no controls, however, and it is unclear how subjects were asked to participate in the study.

A further study (Melmed *et al.* 2000) reported on 385 children attending the local ASD centre in Phoenix, Arizona, plus 102 unrelated controls and 48 sibling controls. They found in their ASD group that 19 per cent had diarrhoea, 19 per cent had constipation, and 7 per cent alternated between the two. The combined rate for these problems was under 10 per cent in both of the control groups. How the problems were defined is not clear from the paper, but we can assume that it was the same for all three groups – indicating that such problems were four-and-a-half times more common in this ASD group than in the controls.

Karoly Horvath at Johns Hopkins University Medical School in Baltimore reported on a questionnaire survey of 412 children with ASD and 43 normal controls, and subsequently on interview validation with a subset (112 of their children with ASD and the 44 siblings then of age to take part) (Horvath, Medeiros and Rabszlyn 2000; Horvath and Perman 2002a, 2002b). Their data show clear differences in prevalence of gastrointestinal symptomology between their ASD cases and controls. In an earlier case series they had shown that in ASD cases with gastro-oesophageal reflux there was a high prevalence of sleep disorders which responded to appropriate management of the reflux (Horvath *et al.* 1999).

One study has found clear differences in the level of gastrointestinal symptomology in ASD compared both to those with other developmental problems and to those with no such difficulties (Valicenti-McDermott *et al.* 2006). In this study the group differences were also strongly associated with self-restricted diet and rejection of novel foods by the ASD group compared to the others. No link between gastrointestinal symptomology and a family history of autoimmune problems was found in this series.

A further paper by Valicenti-McDermott *et al.* (2008) has looked for possible overlap between ASD, language regression, gastrointestinal symptomology and a family history of autoimmune problems in a series of 100 families. Within this group, language regression and abnormal gastrointestinal function were associated with a family history of autoimmune problems (specifically with a history of coeliac or irritable bowel disease or rheumatoid arthritis).

In the ASD population there does not seem to be a relationship between the extent or severity of gastrointestinal symptomology and dietary intake of calories, carbohydrates, fats or protein (Levy S.E. *et al.* 2007). This absence of an association suggests that the problems seen are likely to be constitutional in origin rather than an effect of diet *per se*. One early study suggested that some cases of autism who manifest lactic acidosis have a defect in carbohydrate metabolism (Coleman and Blass 1985).

It is interesting, in one study of congenital anomalies, that defects are, on the whole, more common in a subsequently diagnosed ASD population than in an age-, sex- and hospital-of-birth-matched cohort. However, when broken into congenital anomaly by organ system, only gastrointestinal anomalies were significantly more common in the ASD group (Wier *et al.* 2006).

In a review of the evidence concerning gastrointestinal problems in ASD (Erickson *et al.* 2005), the general conclusion was that the data was difficult to interpret if looking for ASD-specific gastroenterological symptoms. It is clear, however, from the studies reviewed, that the rate of such symptoms in people with ASD was significantly higher than in the general population.

In one recent Swiss survey of a sample of 118 learning-disabled adults, 43 with and 75 without co-morbid PDD (PDD, or pervasive developmental disorder, can be taken as synonymous with ASD), clinical reports of gastrointestinal disorders were found for 48.8 per cent of the ASD group, and 8 per cent of those with learning disability alone. The authors conclude that 'gastrointestinal disorders may be considered as a feature of PDD' (Galli-Carminati, Chauvet and Deriaz 2006, p.711).

There is ongoing debate over the extent to which such problems are caused by some process or difference that can be said to be ASD-specific (Buie *et al.* 2010a, 2010b; MacDonald T.T. and Domizio 2007).

One study of 24 consecutive autistic children of unknown aetiology found no clear evidence of a link between autism and the presence of intestinal inflammatory markers (nitric oxide and calprotectin), except in two of the children – one who had recently had severe *clostridium difficile* gastrointestinal problems, and one with extreme constipation (Fernell, Fagerberg and Hellstrom 2007).

IN SUMMARY: Gastrointestinal problems are significantly more common in people with ASD than in others, but the nature and severity of such problems based on presenting clinical symptoms is not specific. They should be investigated on clinical merit in the individual case, and there is no reason to support the view that the comorbidity of ASD and gastrointestinal disturbance should lead to the latter not being investigated. If anything, the presence of an ASD should indicate to the clinician the need to collect a clear history of this aspect of the person's development and functioning, and to treat these aspects as indicated in line with current best practice guidelines.

General physical overgrowth

There is a general tendency for those with an ASD to have increased physical stature. Are there specific ASD conditions that might make someone larger than normal?

Yes. A number of overgrowth syndromes are associated with ASD. The classic, but fairly technical, overview of overgrowth syndromes, which deals with most of those we discuss here, is Cohen, Neri and Weksberg (2002).

Overgrowth syndromes associated with ASD

The conditions found in Table A9 are all associated with being significantly larger than would be predicted, based on family size (excluding other family members who also have the gene in question).

In general terms, larger parents will have larger children, with the stronger effect on

Table A9: Genetic conditions associated with ASD and overgrowth syndromes

• Bannayan-Riley-Ruvalcaba syndrome (macrocephaly/autism syndrome)	[15]
• Basal cell nevus syndrome	[16]
• Cortical Dysplasia–Focal Epilepsy (CDFE) syndrome	[19]
• Cole-Hughes macrocephaly syndrome	[24]
• Cowden syndrome	[26]
• Orstavik 1997 syndrome	[56]
• Proteus syndrome	[62]
• Sotos syndrome	[68]

the size of the child being maternal build and placental function. (A smaller mother and a larger father will tend to have a smaller child, while a larger mother with a smaller father will tend to have a larger child).

Although a number of overgrowth syndromes are more commonly seen in ASD, the association in these conditions is far from 100 per cent (not everyone with, say, Sotos syndrome has an ASD), and there are many other overgrowth syndromes that have not been found in association with ASD.

Table A10 below lists the more common overgrowth syndromes with no known link to ASD at the time of writing.

Immune dysfunction

The immune system consists of cells and antibodies throughout the body that are primarily involved in recognizing and combating infections, identifying foreign materials and recognizing foodstuffs likely to provoke reactions.

Autoimmune problems occur where, rather than warding off infection, the immune system reacts to factors within the individual. This can result from processes such as 'molecular mimicry', where antibodies that typically react to an infection react to structures within the individual instead. A good example of this is 'PANDAS' (paediatric autoimmune neurodevelopmental disorder secondary to group A streptococcal infection). This is a type of movement disorder seen in children. It often starts shortly after a throat infection, where the antibodies raised by the immune system to fight the throat infection go on to affect parts of the central nervous system motor system, reacting to them as if they were the same as the infection. (See Pavone, Parano, Rizzo and Trifiletti 2006 for a recent discussion.)

What is the evidence of immune dysfunction in ASDs?

One recent study compared serum antibodies to brain endothelial cells and to nuclei in two children with Landau-Kleffner syndrome, 11 children with Landau-Kleffner syndrome variant, 11 with ASD, 20 with other neurological conditions and 22 with non-neurological conditions (Connolly *et al.* 1999). IgG autoantibodies to brain tissue were found in 27 per cent of the ASD cases and in 45 per cent of the Landau-Kleffner syndrome variant cases, but in only 2 per cent of controls. IgM autoantibodies were found in 36 per cent of ASD and 9 per cent of

Landau-Kleffner syndrome variant cases, but were not present in controls. This suggests an autoimmune component to some cases of ASD. A further paper from the same group highlighted an interaction between immune differences and elevated brain-derived neurotrophic factor (BDNF) in both ASD and childhood disintegrative disorder (Connolly *et al.* 2006).

In recent reviews researchers from the MIND institute and UC Davis (Ashwood, Wills and Van de Water 2006; Goines and Van de Water 2010; Heuer *et al.* 2008) emphasize the discovery of defects in a number of genes in ASD that are known to be involved in immune function (human leukocyte antigen-DRB1 and complement C4 alleles), in a range of factors which indicate abnormal immune function:

• abnormal, or skewed, T-helper cell type 1 TH1/TH2 cytokine profiles

• decreased lymphocyte numbers

• decreased T-cell mitogen response

• imbalance of serum immunoglobulin levels.

These authors have suggested an association between reduced immune function and behavioural symptom severity.

In 2003 a single family pedigree with three children, the first normal, the second with ASD and third with severe specific language impairment, was reported, in which maternal neuronal antibodies were identified. The same antibodies were shown to have effects on coordination and cerebellar function in mice, and were speculated to be associated with the children's developmental problems (Dalton *et al.* 2003). A further small study of 11 mothers of children with ASD looked at antibodies from the mothers which reacted to foetal brain tissue, and found that the mothers did have specific serum antibodies which reacted to foetal but not to postnatal tissue, and which were not found in controls – suggesting that such autoantibodies could have crossed the placenta and affected foetal brain development (Zimmerman A.W. *et al.* 2007).

Pioglitazone is a medication that has been noted to reduce glial mediated inflammatory responses through its action on tyrosine kinsase in animal inflammatory models. It is marketed respectively as Actos® in the USA and Glustin® in Europe by the pharmaceutical companies Takeda and Eli Lilly. It is a thiazolidinedione

Table A10: Overgrowth syndromes which have not to date been linked to ASD

• Beckwith-Wiedemann syndrome	
• Hemihyperplasia	[84]
• Klippel-Trelaunay syndrome	
• Maffucci syndrome	
• PEHO syndrome	[86]
• Perlman syndrome	
• Parkes Weber syndrome	
• Simpson-Golabi-Behmel syndrome type 1	[87]
• Sturge-Weber syndrome	[88]
• Weaver syndrome	[89]

which acts as an agonist of the peroxisome proliferator activated receptor gamma (PPARγ), a nuclear hormone receptor that modulates insulin sensitivity and has been used in treating type 2 diabetes. It has recently been suggested as a novel treatment approach in ASD in cases where such inflammatory TH2-type immune differences are seen (Emanuele, Lossano, Politti and Barale 2007).

There has been only one clinical trial of pioglitazone to date (Boris *et al.* 2007). This was an open trial with 25 children, over 3–54 months of treatment. Significant beneficial effects were noted on irritability, lethargy, stereotypy and hyperactivity as rated on the Autism Behaviour Checklist, with no medical side effects. Proper double-blinded trials in individuals with ASD, matched for such inflammatory markers, would be required before pioglitazone treatment could be advocated in management of ASD cases with immune dysfunction.

Another immune modulating medication, spironolactone (marketed variously as Aldactone®, Novo-Spiroton®, Spiractin®, Spirotone®, or Berlactone®) is an aldosterone antagonist. It has potassium-sparing, diuretic, anti-inflammatory and immune modifying actions. It lowers androgen levels and has been used extensively in the management of acne, hirsutism and precocious puberty. It reduces the levels of inflammatory markers such as TNFα and MCP-1 incell culture. It has recently been proposed as a treatment for appropriately profiled ASD cases (Bradstreet *et al.* 2007). Bradstreet *et al.* also detail the positive response seen in a single ASD case. As with pioglitazone, proper double-blinded trials in individuals with ASD, matched for inflammatory markers, would be required before spironolactone treatment could be advocated in management of ASD cases with immune dysfunction.

Animal research now clearly demonstrates that antibody subsets to systemic *lupus erythematosus* (one of several autoimmune conditions overrepresented in the families of people with ASD) (Comi *et al.* 1999) can affect both cognitive functions (such as associative memory) and emotional behaviours (such as fear-conditioning). They can also cause damage to hippocampal neurons when given to mice whose blood–brain barrier function has been weakened by administration of lipopolysaccharide (Huerta *et al.* 2006).

IN SUMMARY: There is clear evidence of immune dysfunction in a significant proportion of ASD cases, and in close family members. However, in clinical practice it is not typical at the present time for immune status to be assessed. A family history of autoimmune conditions may be relevant to pathogenesis. The clinical interventions mentioned above are currently speculative, and could not be advocated on the basis of the level of current evidence without further supportive clinical research.

Methylmalonic acidaemia, vitamin B12 (methylcobalamin) and cobalt levels

The structure of vitamin B12 was first described in 1956 (Hodgkin *et al.* 1956). Methylmalonic acidaemia (MMA) was first described in children in 1967 (Oberholzer, Levin, Burgess and Young 1967; Stokke *et al.* 1967). MMA is one of the most common organic acidemias (Hori *et al.* 2005; Wajner *et al.* 2009) MMA presents early in infancy with encephalopathy. It is a progressive disorder with a number of sufficient genetic causes. It had previously been described in adults with pernicious anaemia. It results from a deficiency of either methylmalonyl-CoA mutase (the principal enzyme involved in converting methylmalonyl-CoA to succinyl-CoA) or adenosine cobalamin, an essential co-factor that is derived from vitamin B12 (cobalamin). MMA is a branched-chain organic aciduria like maple syrup urine disease (MSUD), isovaleric acidaemia (IVA) and propionic aciduria (PA) (Cox and White 1962).

Cobalamin deficiency is a well-recognized problem in infants (de Baulny and Saudubray 2002) and in the elderly (Andres *et al.* 2004), where it is often a problem of malabsorption rather than of dietary deficiency.

There are well-recognized neurological-psychiatric sequelae of an inborn error of metabolism that impairs the intracellular synthesis of adenosylcobalamin and methylcobalamin (cobalamin C disease) (Roze *et al.* 2003).

Vitamin B12 deficiency can arise for a variety of reasons, including the mother adhering to a vegan diet during pregnancy and while breastfeeding (Casella, Valente, de Navarro; Kok 2005 and Ciani *et al.* 2000), or strict adherence to a vegan diet taken by the subjects themselves (Cundiff and Harris 2006). Such restriction of B12 intake can result in developmental regression with hypotonia and cerebral atrophy (Casella 2005), and in West syndrome with hypotonia and developmental delay (Erol, Alehan and Gümüs 2007). The few cases reported to date suggest that improvements in response to intramuscular vitamin B12 injections can be rapid and dramatic.

A genetic basis to some forms of vitamin B12-dependent MMA has now been identified (Dobson *et al.* 2002). Imerslund-Gräsbeck disease is an autosomal recessive problem with B12 absorption, coupled with proteinurea (Gräsbeck 2006).

There are, therefore, as outlined above, a number of possible causes of tissue B12 deficiency, such as:

1. inadequate B12 intake (typically seen in vegans)

2. malabsorption of B12 (seen in pernicious anaemia)

3. defective cell delivery due to a defect in transcobalamin II

4. failure of cellular adenosylcobalamin synthesis

5. failure of cellular methylcobalamin synthesis

6. Imerslund-Gräsbeck disease (14q32, 10p12.1)

7. Biermer's disease (Zittoun 2001)

8. a primary cobalt deficiency.

The above are usually associated with megaloblastic anaemia and MMA.

Research indicates surprisingly little association between improved biochemical indicators of response to B12 and the lack of apparent clinical benefit as evidenced by measures of anaemia, and gastrointestinal or neurological changes in randomized controlled trials with a community sample of adults treated for elevated plasma MMA levels (Hvas, Ellegaard and Nexø 2001).

In general, the prognosis for MMA has been steadily improving over recent decades (de Baulny *et al.* 2005). Improved newborn screening techniques may make early detection and intervention a much more standardized aspect of early screening programmes (Dionisi-Vici *et al.* 2006).

The neuropathlogy of non-B12 responsive MMA, though scant, is consistent with that reported in general in the ASD literature (Kanaumi *et al.* 2006), with a reduction in granule cell density, hypomyelination and abnormalities of the cerebral cortex, limbic system and cerebellum.

There is some evidence for abnormalities in methylation in ASD and for amelioration of the identified biochemical defects by the use of a combination of folinic acid, betaine and methylcobalamin (James *et al.* 2004).

From the literature to date, there are clinical cases that appear to show beneficial effects of supplementation with vitamin B12. However, as the prevalence of such cases is uncertain, no clear general recommendations could be given at this time.

One paper (James *et al.* 2006) introduces the concept of metabolic endophenotypes in ASD associated with transmethylation and transsulphuration of methionine, demonstrating abnormal rates of allele frequency or gene–gene interactions in the following:

1. reduced folate carrier (RFC 80G > A)

2. transcobalamin II (TCN2 776G > C)

3. catechol-O-methyltransferase (COMT 472G > A)

4. methylenetetrahydrofolate reductase (MTHFR 677C > T and 1298A > C)

5. glutathione-S-transferase (GSTM1).

Another paper documented a slight increase in the prevalence of glutathione S-transferase M1 (GSTM1) differences in parents of children with autism (Buyske *et al.* 2006). GSTM1 is a condition where it is difficult to ascertain the prevalence of heterozygous carriers, making conventional heritability estimates problematic. A further paper from the same group (Williams T.A. *et al.* 2007) described the increased prevalence of a glutathione-S-transferase P1 haplotype in mothers of autistic children. They examined 137 family members from 49 ASD families. Where mothers carried a specific glutathione-S-transferase P1 haplotype (specifically had the *GSTP1–313* genotype) this increased the likelihood of ASD in their children, suggesting that the effect was due to differences in the foetal environment resulting from this gene difference.

A screening study looking for folate abnormalities in a group of 138 children with ASD found that MTHFR C677T is a significant risk factor, being found in 16.3 per cent of those with ASD compared to 6.5 per cent of non-ASD controls (Mohammad *et al.* 2009).

In one Chinese series of 77 cases of MMA, two cases were reported as showing autistic symptoms, but no further detail is given (Yang *et al.* 2006b).

Some autistic children who self-restrict their diet have very limited protein intake. This can cause them to develop optic atrophy and visual loss. When identified and corrected in time, this can be partially reversed through treatments to normalize B12 levels. A recent paper described clinical improvement in three such cases through intramuscular B12 injection (Pineles, Avery and Liu 2010).

Much has been made in the literature on comparative and alternative medicine of the benefits of cobalamin and the need to use alternative routes for administration due to the high level of vitamin breakdown when taken orally. B12 is absorbed in the ileum, so absorption is not affected by gut dysbiosis. Various preparations have been employed, including transdermal creams, transdermal patches, subcutaneous injections and nasal sprays. A synthetic form of B12, and compounded methylcobalamin sprays, are also available.

Although it is true that there is a high level of breakdown with oral administration, there is an extensive literature on the effective use of high dose oral B12 (Conley *et al.* 1951; Kuzminski *et al.* 1998; Unglaub and Goldsmith 1955).

Although one subcutaneous methylcobalamin study is nearing completion (see http://clinicaltrials.gov/ct), no comparative studies of B12 response are currently available. At the time of writing, only the James *et al.* small-N open dose study of combined folinic acid, betaine and subcutaneous methylcobalamin (James *et al.* 2004) is available in the peer-reviewed published literature.

The progressive visual condition Leber's hereditary optic neuropathy (LHON) is associated with B12 deficiency (Pott and Wong 2006). However, B12 supplementation, particularly with cyanocobalamin, has been reported to accelerate the condition, perhaps due to the reduced liver activity of thiosulphate sulphur transferase, which rids the body of cyanide seen in such cases (Cagianut, Schnebli, Rhymer and Furrer 1984). Cyanide is a compound that is part of the synthetic cyanocobalamin form of B12. It is important, therefore, that this approach be used with caution in ASD cases with optic neuropathy.

LHON is different from Leber's amaurosis, a condition that has been reported in association with autism (Rogers and Newhart-Larson 1989). As the diagnostic validity of Leber's amaurosis is currently uncertain (see Traboulsi, Koenekoop and Stone 2006), it has not been given specific treatment in this volume. It is interesting to note, however, that recent clinical research on intra-ocular gene therapy appears to be producing beneficial effects in cases diagnosed with Leber's amaurosis (Cideciyan *et al.* 2008).

IN SUMMARY: A range of factors affecting vitamin B12 metabolism have been described that impact on development. These seem to be more common in ASD than was previously appreciated, and the preliminary studies to date show promising responses to treatment interventions. Adequate trials in selected ASD groups are required before we can be clear about possible clinical benefits from this approach.

Evidence for the selective benefits from different methods of B12 administration is not available. Assessment for optic neuropathy may be advisable.

Muscular involvement

A range of conditions has been reported where ASD is linked to a neuromuscular problem. (For a review, see Hinton *et al.* 2009.) Whether one or other aspect is causal, or both are linked due to associations with other mechanisms, has yet to be ascertained. Management and treatment of several of these conditions have recently undergone major developments that will be discussed later – the treatment of Duchenne muscular dystrophy with tamoxifen and reversal of the Rett phenotype in animal models of the disease seem particularly promising.

Clinically, where there is a consistent developmental history of slower motor development (late walking, poor functional hand use, skill regression) or atypical development (such as 'Gower's sign' – using the hands to push up the body when first standing, which is the classic feature in Duchenne), evaluation is important.

The neuromuscular conditions in Table A11 have been reported in association with ASD and should be part of the differential diagnosis in cases where development of motor skills has been abnormal.

Obesity

Although not a universal feature, excess body fat is a common aspect of a number of the genetic syndromes associated with ASD. The conditions in which obesity tends to be reported are found in Table A12:

Table A11: Genetic conditions associated with ASD and muscular involvement

• Adenylosuccinate lyase (ADSL) deficiency	[9]
• Becker muscular dystrophy	[33]
• Duchenne muscular dystrophy	[33]
• GAMT deficiency	[37]
• Myotonic dystrophy type 1/Steinert's myotonic dystrophy	[50]
• Rett syndrome	[63a]
• Rett syndrome (Hanefeld variant)	[63b]
• Schindler disease	[65]
• Sotos syndrome	[68]

Table A12: Genetic conditions associated with ASD and obesity

• Biedl-Bardet syndrome	[17]
• Cohen syndrome	[23]
• Fragile-X syndrome	[35]
• Prader-Willi syndrome	[61]
• Rubinstein-Taybi syndrome	[64]

A useful review of genetic obesity syndromes can be found in Goldstone and Beales (2008).

Two recent studies have suggested a possible link between deletion of a gene (SH2B1 at 16p11.2) that has previously been linked to ASD in a small proportion (@0.6 per cent) of cases from the Autism Genetic Resource Exchange (AGRE) database (Weiss *et al.* 2008) and the development of severe obesity (Bochukova *et al.* 2010; Walters *et al.* 2010).

Palatal abnormalities

Several conditions are associated with abnormalities of the palate, a number of which may require surgical correction. Amongst the most common are those in Table A13.

Seizures, fits and epilepsy

There is continuing debate amongst epileptologists over the increasing clinical benefits of being able to apply genetic information to diagnosis and treatment for seizures. (See Delgado-Escueta and Bourgeois 2008.)

In general, seizure problems are significantly more common in people with ASD than in comparable non-ASD populations. ASD symptomology is also more common within the epileptic population (Clarke *et al.* 2005). Some case series, however, have reported lower rates of epilepsy in autistic subjects (Pavone *et al.* 2004). On balance the rate is higher, but variations may reflect factors such as the nature of the clinical populations reported on – tertiary neurological clinics will see a higher proportion of neurogenetic disorders, compared with what might be seen in general paediatric clinics, and are likely to have a higher proportion of epileptic cases referred to them.

A useful review of the literature on epilepsy and ASD can be found in Spence and Schneider (2009), and an overview of the management of epilepsy in people with autism can be found in Peake, Notghi and Philip (2006). Investigation of seizures should be on a clinical basis with each case.

In reviewing all Icelandic cases of epilepsy for the 18 years 1982–2000, Saemundsen, Ludvigsson, Hilmarsdottir and Rafnsson (2007) found a higher prevalence of autism in those who had presented with unprovoked seizures in the first year of life. All children whose parents had concerns over their development were studied (N=84), of whom six (7.1 per cent) (four girls and two boys – a similar sex ratio to the overall group) had an ASD. All six had an associated learning disability.

There is currently insufficient evidence to recommend either for or against the use of routine EEG screening in ASDs (Kagan-Kushnir, Roberts and Snead 2005). However, in one recent clinical series of 889 patients with ASDs collected by a Chicago clinic over a nine-year period (Chez et al. 2006), none of whom had epilepsy or a known genetic condition or clinical malformation, over 60 per cent showed evidence of epileptiform activity on ambulatory EEG recording. In the majority, the clinical activity was over the right temporal lobe. Of 176 who were treated prophylactically with sodium valproate (i.e. where it was prescribed on the basis of the EEG recording alone, and not, as would be more usual, on a clinical diagnosis of epilepsy), 80 showed normalization of the EEG, and of those, 30 showed clinical improvements.

One issue which warrants further study is 2-ketoglutaric aciduria in drug resistant infantile seizures in infants with early onset ASD, progressive lethargy, and sparse hair (Colamaria et al. 1989). This can result from partial biotinidase deficiency (Zaffanello et al. 2003). In the Colamaria et al case there was dramatic improvement on biotin supplementation and in the younger of the children treated prospectively by Zaffanello he had a partial biotinidase deficxiency but was clinically normal while his older brother showed no improvement when treatment was commenced at age 4 years. Inborn

Table A13: Genetic conditions associated with ASD and palatal abnormalities

• Apert syndrome	[12]
• Basal cell nevus syndrome	[16]
• Biedl-Bardet syndrome	[17]
• CATCH22	[18]
• CHARGE syndrome	[20]
• de Lange syndrome	[27]
• DiGeorge syndrome I	[29a]
• Hypomelanosis of Ito	[42]
• SLOS	[66]
• Smith-Magenis syndrome	[67]
• Velocardiofacial syndrome	[76]

errors of biotin metabolism are reviewed by Nyhan (1987).

One recent retrospective case series (Park 2003) found that of 59 autistic patients with previously poorly controlled seizures who had then been treated with an implanted vagal nerve stimulator, 58 per cent showed at least a 50 per cent reduction in seizure frequency and 76 per cent showed improvements in 'quality of life', particularly in alertness, by one year after the device was implanted. The study discriminated between types of seizure activity, but not between types/causes of ASD. In a single adult case of Asperger syndrome with temporal lobe epilepsy, both seizure severity and behavioural components of his Asperger symptomology (judged on the Yale-Brown Obsessions and Compulsions scale and a physician rating of quality of life) were significantly improved through use of an implanted vagal nerve stimulator (Warwick *et al.* 2007).

Within the ASD population epilepsy is more prevalent, with three factors being associated: prevalence increases with age; there is a second peak for seizure onset at adolescence, in addition to the more typical onset peak in the preschool years (Volkmar and Nelson 1990); and there is a lower level of cognitive functioning and poorer receptive language skills (Tuchman and Rapin 2002a). These factors may also

Table A14: Genetic conditions associated with ASD and epilepsy

• 15q11–q13 duplication	[1]
• 22q13 deletion syndrome	[7]
• Adenylosuccinate lyase (ADSL) deficiency	[9]
• Angelman syndrome	[11]
• ARX gene mutations	[13]
• CATCH22	[18]
• Juvenile dentatorubral-pallidoluysian atrophy	[28]
• Down syndrome	[31]
• Dravet's syndrome	[32]
• Fragile-X syndrome	[35]
• GAMT deficiency	[37]
• HEADD syndrome	[39]
• Neurofibromatosis	[51]
• NAPDD	[53]
• Orstavik 1997 syndrome	[56]
• Phenylketonuria	[57]
• Rett syndrome	[63a]
• Rett syndrome (Hanefeld variant)	[63b]
• Schindler disease	[65]
• Sotos syndrome	[68]
• Tuberous sclerosis	[73]

provide an index of the extent of organic involvement – in tuberous sclerosis [73] for example, the numbers of tubers seen on brain scanning increase with age, indicating the progressive nature of the condition (Wong and Khong 2006).

Cases have been reported where epilepsy has been linked to a neurometabolic disorder, as with creatine defects due to either GAMT deficiency [37], or arginine:glycine amidionotransferase deficiency. These disorders are reported to respond clinically to treatment with creatinine monohydrate (Leuzzi 2002).

It is possible that in some cases ASD behaviour is an iatrogenic effect of antiepileptic medication, and cases are recorded where paradoxical normalization has occurred in response to a change in medication (Amir and Gross-Tzur 1994).

It has also recently been argued that in some conditions, such as Landau-Kleffner syndrome, tuberous sclerosis [73] and CSWS (continuous spike and wave in slow wave sleep), the epilepsy is a causal factor in the pathogenesis of ASD (Deonna and Roulet 2006).

Often parents can get confused, as so many different words and sets of terms are used in describing epilepsy.

Types of structural difference seen in the epileptic brain

Differences in the brain structures involved and how these arise can be important. The overlapping neurological differences apparent in ASD are now becoming quite well documented (see, for review, Stanfield et al. 2007). A number of types of structural differences in the brain underpin the neuropathology of epilepsy:

- **Focal cortical dysplasia (FCD)** (Taylor, Falconer, Bruton and Corsellis 1971) covers a group of disorders (Palmini and Luders 2002), some of which are thought to be a mild variant of tuberous sclerosis. The associated epilepsy can be difficult to control. Surgical intervention is often considered as a treatment of last resort. At present, there is no agreed classification within this group of conditions.

- **Periventricular heterotopia (PVH)** means clustering of nerve cells around the ventricles. Seizure onset in such cases is not usually until late adolescence, with concomitant reading difficulties (Chang et al. 2005). PVH is a neural migration abnormality that has been reported in fragile-X syndrome [35] (Moro et al. 2006).

- **Polymicrogyria** is where there are an excessive number of smaller than normal gyri. A variety of polymicrogyric presentations have been described (Barkovich et al. 2001). The distribution can be on one or both sides of the brain, the most common form being bilateral perisylvian polymicrogyria (BSP – affecting both sides of the cortex and predominantly around the sylvian fissure; see Barkovich, Hevner and Guerrini 1999). BSP presents with epilepsy, pseudobulbar palsy, spastic quadriplegia and learning disability. Unilateral polymicrogyria can be associated with mutations to the PAX6 homeobox gene at 11p13 (Mitchell et al. 2003). 11p13 is a gene position which has been linked to ASD (Yonan et al. 2003).

- **Lissencephaly** is typically associated with the microtubule binding gene LIS1 (Reiner and Coquelle 2005), and in a proportion of the remaining cases with the expanding group of doublecortin (DCX) mutations at Xq22.3–q23 (doublecortin is a gene associated with the development of new nerve cells – neurogenesis; defects can result in lissencephaly) (Reiner *et al.* 2006). Developmental problems are normally of early onset, with hypotonia, profound learning disability and severe epilepsy. A mild form of lissencephaly, associated with cerebellar hypoplasia, has been reported in association with the Reelin mutation (Boycott *et al.* 2005; Hong *et al.* 2000). The Reelin gene, at 7q21–q36, is a susceptibility locus for ASD (Serajee, Zhong and Mahbubul Huq 2006; Dutta *et al.* 2008).

- **Subcortical band heterotopias** affect females with DCX mutations. (In males, DCX mutations result in lissencephaly.) A separate band of cells forms between the cortical mantle and the ventricular zone, clearly visible on MRI, and the extent of developmental problems and severity of epilepsy appear to correlate inversely with the thickness of the subcortical band (Lian and Sheen 2006).

- **Dysembryoplastic neuroepithelial tumours (DNETs)** are small areas of abnormal nerve cell proliferation within cortical tissue, which are associated with focal epilepsy. The tumours are not malignant and can respond well to stereotactic surgical removal (Daumas-Duport *et al.* 1988).

This clinical pathology underpinning seizure activity based on the above classifications has been systematically reviewed (Lian and Sheen 2006; Sisodiya 2004).

A further important point to note is that treatment with anti-epileptic medications increases excretion of D-glucaric acid (Park and Kitteringham 1988; Tutor-Crespo, Hermida and Tutor 2005). Urinary porphyrins are also elevated in treated epileptic patients. However, coproporphyrin levels do not correlate with either D-glucaric acid levels or enzymatic effects of medication, so may originate in a renal problem common to those with epilepsy, with or without an ASD. (For discussion, see Tutor-Crespo, Hermida and Tutor 2005.) As no study has so far been conducted looking at porphyrin levels in drug-naive epileptic subjects, it is also possible that porphyrin levels are elevated by the presence of epilepsy *per se*. Given the high rates of epileptic activity in those with ASD, this is an important factor to address in any systematic clinical overview of such issues (Chez *et al.* 2006).

There is current interest in elevated levels of porphyrins as a possible marker variable in ASD (Austin and Shandley 2008; Nataf *et al.* 2006). This is being used by some to identify individuals who are said to be candidates for chelation therapy. It is important to be aware that elevated porphyrin levels will occur with anti-epileptic medication, whether or not a person is autistic, so the results of testing taken in isolation have the potential to be misleading if the person is taking medication for epilepsy, and could result in the use of inappropriate and potentially dangerous treatment.

With some forms of epilepsy, the association with ASD seems to be related to the site and type of seizure activity. In West syndrome (often referred to as 'infantile spasms'), for example, the presence of hypsarrythmia, particularly when detected from the frontal lobes of the brain, is strongly associated with the later onset of ASD (Kayaalp *et al.* 2007). One recent early-onset West syndrome case was secondary to the infant breastfeeding from a mother with mild methylmalonic aciduria. The infant presented with seizures, hypotonia and developmental delay (Erol, Alehan and Gümüs 2007). In this case, intramuscular vitamin B12 injections resulted in rapid and dramatic normalization of development and the cessation of epilepsy.

A rare but well-recognized subgroup of epilepsies is caused by defects in the autosomal recessive gene responsible for production of glutamic acid decarboxylase. (See, for review, Rajesh and Girija 2003.) These cases are responsive to treatment with pyrodoxine (vitamin B6).

Recent findings suggest that there is an association between low selenium levels and both an increased likelihood of epilepsy and lowered levels of the selenium dependent antioxidant glutathione peroxidase (Ashrafi, Shams *et al.* 2007).

A further issue of interest is that abnormal glutamate metabolism is involved in some forms of epilepsy which are seen in ASD. In such cases, it seems likely from the research to date that anti-epileptic medications such as topiramate (which has a selective effect on glutamatergic systems) may prove beneficial. Here, the problem lies in the mGluR5 receptor pathway, especially in the kainate systems of the amygdala (Gryder and Rogawski 2003; Kaminski, Banerjee and Rogawski 2004; Rogawski *et al.* 2003), and medications that affect this pathway are likely to be selectively beneficial.

As fragile-X selectively affects the mGluR5 pathway and is associated with both ASD and epilepsy, this group in particular may benefit from topiramate.

Recent studies have found that there is a direct effect of leptin levels on seizures. Leptin is a peripheral hormone, the levels of which are directly proportional to body fat stores, and appears to be linked to seizure control. (For discussion, see Diano and Horvath 2008.)

There is increasing evidence for beneficial effects of ketogenic diets in the control of seizure activity (Neal *et al.* 2008) and in the management of ASD (Evangeliou *et al.* 2003). (This literature is summarized in Aitken 2009.) These findings strengthen the clinical importance of evaluating phospholipid function in individuals with ASD, particularly where this is associated with co-morbid epilepsy.

IN SUMMARY: Epilepsy is a common problem seen in the ASD population. Epilepsy treatments may complicate the interpretation of other biomedical parameters, and as 'subclinical' EEG abnormalities are common in the ASD population, screening for such difficulties should be a more routine component of baseline assessment.

In addition to medication and surgical interventions a number of factors may be relevant to seizure control, including dietary factors such as level of glutamate and cobalamin (vitamin B12) intake.

Skin pigmentation differences
Café-au-lait spots (skin hyperpigmentation)
These are 'coffee-coloured' patches of skin. The most common genetic cause is neurofibromatosis (NF1) [51].

There are case reports of unusual pigmentation abnormalities. One report, for example, documents a case with developmental delay and ASD which appears to combine the typical skin lesions seen in both tuberous sclerosis [73] and neurofibromatosis [51], while testing negative for both conditions (Buoni *et al.* 2006b).

A number of conditions can result in 'depigmentation', a loss or reduction of 'melanophores' from the skin. These are the cells that contain melanin and produce tanning in response to sunlight.

'Mongolian' spots
These are dense collections of 'melanophores'. The skin in these areas is a deep blueish-brown in colour. The lesions tend to be most pronounced at birth and to

fade with age. They are the most common birthmark, and are typically benign, but can be associated with inborn errors of metabolism such as lysosomal storage disease and the mucopolysaccharidoses (Ashrafi, Shabanian, Mohammadi and Kavusi 2006).

Conditions that show pigmentation differences in association with ASD are listed in Table A15.

'Chicken skin'
This term is used to describe areas of bumpy skin found usually on the upper arms and thighs in people with phospholipid deficiencies. This appearance typically indicates problems with lipid metabolism and may be an indication for phospholipid (Meguid, Atta, Gouda and Khalil 2008) or in some cases cholesterol (Aneja and Tierney 2008) supplementation.

The apparent benefits from cholesterol supplementation in conditions such as SLOS [66] contrast with the hypercholesterolaemia that has been reported in some ASD populations (Dziobek, Gold, Wolf and Convit 2007). As elevated cholesterol levels appear linked

Table A15: Genetic conditions associated with ASD and skin pigmentation differences

• Adrenomyeloneuropathy	[10]
• Bannayan-Riley-Ruvalcaba syndrome	[15]
• Hypomelanosis of Ito	[42]
• Neurofibromatosis type 1	[51]
• Oculocutaneous albinism	[55]
• Proteus syndrome	[62]
• Tuberous sclerosis	[73]
• Xeroderma pigmentosa (complementation group C)	[79]

Table A16: Genetic conditions associated with ASD and other skin differences

• Bannayan-Riley-Ruvalcaba syndrome	[15]
• Basal cell nevus syndrome	[16]
• Cowden syndrome	[26]
• DiGeorge syndrome I	[29a]
• Hyper IgE syndrome with autism	[41]
• Hypomelanosis of Ito	[42]
• Neurofibromatosis type 1	[51]
• Noonan syndrome	[52]
• Prader-Willi syndrome	[61]
• Proteus syndrome	[62]
• Tuberous sclerosis	[73]
• X-linked ichthyosis	[80]

to elevated levels of anxiety and OCD behaviour, normalization of short-chain fatty acid metabolism seems the best aim from current evidence.

Other skin differences

A number of the specific genetic ASD conditions we go on to discuss have been linked to skin problems of various sorts. Those where dermatological differences are commonly reported are principally the ones found in Table A16.

Several of these conditions are known as 'phacomatoses' (see Nowak 2007) that have combined differences in the skin and possible neurological involvement. The conditions typically classified as phacomatoses that are associated with ASD are Bannayan-Riley-Ruvalcaba syndrome [15]; neurofibromatosis type 1 [51]; Proteus syndrome [62]; and tuberous sclerosis [73].

Thumb adduction, external ear rotation, upper limb malformation and 6th and 7th cranial nerve abnormalities

The combination of thumb, ear, upper limb and cranial nerve anomalies seems to be associated with a group of autistic conditions that result from interference with embryonic development at the same stage during pregnancy. They are well documented in cases of ASD and result from various teratogens (thalidomide, valproic acid and misoprostal having been most carefully studied), while for certain other causes clear genetic origins have been identified (for example, fragile-X [35, 36] and Mobius syndrome [48]). For discussion, see Miller *et al.* (2005).

Vitamin B6 and magnesium

One of the earliest alternative biological treatments for autism was the use of high-dose vitamin B6 and magnesium supplementation. The finding came about through analysis of the first 1,000 E2 questionnaires completed and returned to the Autism Research Institute in San Diego (an E2 questionnaire provides a profile of sociodemographic, developmental and behavioural features in diagnosed ASD cases). After behavioural management advice, the next most likely thing to be reported as having produced a significant clinical benefit was a multivitamin supplement, and the sole factor common to the vitamin supplements used was vitamin B6. In initial studies with high-dose B6 supplements, many verbal children with ASD reported tingling in fingers and toes, a sign of peripheral neuropathology that is a well-recognized and reversible side-effect of excess vitamin B6 (Parry and Bredesen 1985; Schaumburg *et al.* 1983).

The problem was found to be due to magnesium depletion, and magnesium supplementation was found to be necessary to ensure there were no peripheral nerve problems.

There are a range of conditions and disorders that can result in a need for additional vitamin B6, typically given as pyrodoxal 5 phosphate (P5P), the most readily absorbed form. (See Clayton 2006 for a more detailed discussion than can be given here.)

A defect in the PNPO (pyridox(am)ine 5'-phosphate oxidase) gene that converts B6 from the diet into intracellular pyrodoxal 5 phosphate results in a severe condition called neonatal epileptic encephalopathy (Mills P.B. *et al.* 2005). The gene for PNPO is at 17q21.2, a site which has been found to be linked to ASD (with a

Maximum Lod) (Logarithm of Difference) Score (MLS) of 2.26), and is also the site of HOXB1, a homeobox gene involved in the development of the nervous system (McCauley *et al.* 2005). It has long been known that treatment with intravenous B6 can be highly effective in management of otherwise intractable neonatal or early infant seizures (Kroll 1985). However, worsening of seizures is also sometimes seen (Hammen, Wagner, Berkhoff and Donati 1998).

Levels of P5P have been found generally to be lower in unsupplemented autistic children than in controls (Adams and Holloway 2004). The enzyme pyridoxal phosphate, which converts B6 to P5P, has been reported as showing lower binding affinity in people with autism. A recent study has found high plasma levels of B6 in a series of 35 unsupplemented autistic children compared to controls (Adams *et al.* 2007). Taken together, these three, albeit small, studies suggest difficulties in the conversion of B6 to P5P in many of those with ASD, and provide support to a rational biological basis for P5P supplementation being beneficial in a proportion of ASD cases.

Two French publications provide some further information that bears on this issue. A first study (Mousain-Bosc *et al.* 2006a) looked at 40 children with ADHD and 36 non-intervention controls. This showed deficiencies in erythrocyte magnesium in the ADHD group pre-supplementation, which improved with B6–Mg supplementation, paralleled by improvements in ratings of hyperactivity, hypermotivity/aggressiveness and school attention. Deterioration occurred after cessation of supplementation.

In a second study by the same group (Mousain-Bosc *et al.* 2006b) an open trial of B6–Mg in 33 autistic children was reported and compared with 36 non-treatment normal controls. The study demonstrated significant group differences in pre-supplementation levels of erythrocyte magnesium, which improved with magnesium supplementation, and this improvement coincided with clinical improvement in PDD symptomology in 23/33. As in the ADHD study, deterioration occurred after cessation of supplementation, suggesting an ongoing need for the substrate.

As noted at many other points in this volume, there are a number of conditions in which both ADHD and ASD symptomology co-occur.

IN SUMMARY: Vitamin B6 supplementation has a long history of anecdotal support in the literature, but of equivocal results in controlled supplementation trials with unselected ASD cases. As the problem in some cases may lie with the PNPO gene involved in the conversion of B6 to P5P, which shows a significant link to ASD, and studies have not been set up to intervene specifically with this subgroup, the results are unsurprising. The literature to date suggests that a more systematic evaluation of this treatment approach should be undertaken, and that P5P has a higher likelihood of showing successful treatment response than vitamin B6.

GENETIC CONDITIONS SEEN IN THE ASDS

The remainder of this book provides a summary of many of the biological conditions that have been reported in people with ASDs: what the conditions look like, how they present, and factors which can be important in their assessment and treatment. The 'Physical Differences' section has presented some of this information in table form for ease of comparison across these conditions.

Some conditions, like fragile-X and SLOS, are common causes of ASD; many of the others are not frequently considered and may easily be missed.

As the science progresses, we are discovering that there is sometimes considerable overlap between identified genetic conditions with different genotypes, and equally (and giving rise to equal confusion) there is in some cases wide variation between individuals with the same genetic difference.

To give two brief examples:

1. Angelman syndrome

Angelman syndrome is a condition that typically results from deletions, paternal isodisomy (getting both copies of the affected 15q11–q13 gene from father), or imprinting defects in the 15q11–q13 gene (Baker, Piven, Scwartz and Patil 1994; Bolton et al. 2004; Shao et al. 2003; Thomas, Roberts and Browne 2003). The process of gene expression is turning out to be more complex than originally anticipated (Hogart, Leung et al. 2008).

Angelman syndrome has also been reported without 15q11–q13 defects but in association with the MeCP2 gene defect typically seen in Rett syndrome and found on the X chromosome at Xq28 (Kishino, Lalande and Wagstaff 1997). At a gross level at least, the same genotype gives rise to a different phenotype.

2. 22q11.2

22q11 is a chromosome region that is closely involved in programming the embryonic development of the forebrain, the heart and the limbs (Maynard et al. 2003).

Several phenotypes can be found with the same genetic difference. A number of clinical conditions that were first thought to be separable have turned out to have deletions on chromosome 22 at 22q11.2. (See Scambler 2000 and Table A17 below.) Most of these were described and grouped clinically on the physical and behavioural phenotype (on physical differences and differences in behaviour), well before genetic testing became available, and this was the basis for discriminating, for example, between DiGeorge syndrome and velocardiofacial syndrome. (See, for discussion, Hall J.G. 1993; Shprintzen 1994.) It now seems clear that both of these conditions as previously defined are extremely variable and overlapping. (For further discussion of 22q11DS, see Ousley *et al.* 2007.)

Takao velocardiofacial syndrome, described in Japanese groups, is reported as having a much more obvious cardiac component but the same genetic anomaly (Shimizu, Takao, Ando and Hirayama 1984); it seems similar in clinical description to another 22q11.2 syndrome called Cayler cardiofacial syndrome (Giannotti *et al.* 1994).

Sedlackova syndrome, described in 1955 in a series of 26 Czech children with hypernasal speech, shortening of the soft palate and facial dysmorphism, was also described (Sedlackova 1955). Subsequent cases were detailed with associated cleft palate and heart defects. Most recently it has been described as a variant of velocardiofacial syndrome (Fokstuen *et al.* 2001).

Now that we can screen relatives of people identified with such 22q11.2 deletions and pick up other family members who also have the deletion, it has come as a surprise to some that only around half of the children and a third of the adults who carry the deletion have any problems which would have brought them to clinical attention (McDonald-McGinn *et al.* 2001).

The clinical presentation in monozygotic twins can also vary, and it is relatively common, for example, for one twin to have a serious heart problem, while their brother or sister with the same genetic condition has none (Vincent M-C. *et al.* 1999).

So, a genetic screen showing up a deletion/problem at 22q11.2 may be benign or could be associated with any of a broad range of clinical conditions (see Table A17).

The variations seen both within and between the various 22q11.2 conditions may be due to differences in the epigenetic mechanisms highlighted earlier, to different subsets of 22q11.2 genes being involved, to environmental exposures at critical times

Table A17: 22q11.2 conditions associated with ASD

Condition	Gene locus	Key references
• CATCH 22	22q11.2	Niklasson, Rasmussen, Oskarsdottir and Gilberg 2002; Roubertie *et al.* 2001
• Cayler cardiofacial syndrome	22q11.2	Giannotti *et al.* 1994
• DiGeorge syndrome I	22q11.2	Lajiness-O'Neill *et al.* 2005
• Shprintzen's syndrome/ velocardiofacial syndrome	22q11.2	Shprintzen, Goldberg, Young and Wolford 1981
• Sedlackova syndrome	22q11.2	Fokstuen *et al.* 2001; Sedlackova 1955
• Takao velocardiofacial syndrome (conotruncal anomaly face syndrome)	22q11.2	Shimizu, Takao, Ando and Hirayama 1984; Matsuoka *et al.* 1994
• 22q11.2 deletion syndrome	22q11.2	Fernández *et al.* 2005
• Unselected relative findings (lack of clear genotype–phenotype correlation)	22q11.2	McDonald-McGinn *et al.* 2001
• Opitz G/BBB syndrome	22q11.2	Fryburg, Breg and Lindgren 1991; LaCassie and Arriaza 1996; McDonald-McGinn *et al.* 1995

in early development, to a combination of such factors or to other factors affecting variation in phenotypic expression.

A similar cluster of conditions is seen at 22p11.2, with ARX [13], Coffin-Lowry syndrome [21], oculocutaneous albinism [55], Rett syndrome [63a, 63b] and X-linked ichthyosis [80] all being linked to defects in the same small area of DNA.

IN SUMMARY: For many of the conditions discussed in this volume, at our current level of understanding the link between genotype and phenotype is, as yet, poorly understood, and in many cases involves mechanisms such as mitochondrial function and epigenetic factors which are not yet part of routine clinical investigation. One important consequence of this is that an atypical phenotype should not rule out a role for genetic investigation.

SECTION B

Genetic Conditions Seen in the Autistic Spectrum Disorders

But words are things, and a small drop of ink, falling, like dew, upon a thought produces that which makes thousands, perhaps millions think.

Lord Byron, Don Juan (canto III, st. 88)

They do certainly give very strange, and newfangled, names to diseases.

Plato, The Republic (427–347BC)

1.

15q11–q13 duplication

aka • idic(15)

GENE LOCUS: 15q11–q13

KEY ASD REFERENCES: Bolton *et al.* 2004; Christian *et al.* 2008; Hogart *et al.* 2008; Ouldim, Natiq, Jonveaux and Sefiani 2007; Thomas, Roberts and Browne 2003; Wu *et al.* 2009.

SUMMARY: This is a condition that results from duplication of the region of chromosome 15 that, when deleted, results in Angelman or Prader-Willi syndrome. Few 15q11–q13 duplication cases have been reported. Typically the duplication is inherited from the mother and results in learning disability, hypotonia, epilepsy and lactic acidosis in addition to ASD.

HOW COMMON IS 15Q11–Q13 DUPLICATION? Only a small number of (non-Angelman or Prader-Willi) cases have so far been described, so no clear idea of prevalence can be given at present. Angelman and Prader-Willi are both deletion syndromes. The other conditions reported are low copy repeat duplication syndromes. One estimate is that around one per cent of all ASD cases result from deletion or duplication abnormalities of 15q11–q13 (Depienne *et al.* 2009).

MAIN CLINICAL FEATURES: Epilepsy; learning problems; hypotonia; motor delay; lactic acidosis.

Clinically and genetically, there is an overlap with both Angelman [11] and Prader-Willi [61] syndromes (both of which are caused by a 15q11–q13 deletion abnormality).

IS THERE A LINK BETWEEN 15Q11–Q13 DUPLICATION AND ASD? 15q abnormalities are amongst the most common genetic disorders (Smalley 1997), and have been found in between 0.5 and three per cent of ASD cases so far reported (Browne *et al.* 1997; Cook E.H. *et al.* 1997; Schroer *et al.* 1998; Sebat *et al.* 2007; Weiss *et al.* 2008).

A link with autism was first suggested in a paper on two patients (Baker, Piven, Schwartz and Patil 1994). A subsequent paper (Flejter *et al.* 1996) reported on a further two cases where autism was seen in association with epilepsy, learning problems and mild hypotonia. In all four cases, the affected chromosome appeared to have been inherited from the mother. A further study to suggest a link between 15q11–q13 stressed the parent-of-origin effect: of three affected children, two inherited the duplication from their mothers, while the third had an apparently *de novo* mutation (Cook E.H. *et al.* 1997).

In a further study of a group of 100 ASD cases, four were shown to have proximal 15q abnormalities, all inherited from their mothers (Schroer *et al.* 1998).

One study (Wolpert *et al.* 2000) reported on three unrelated autistic patients with maternally inherited isodicentric chromosomes, in all of which the proximal region of 15q11.2 was affected. Their review of earlier case reports had suggested a number of possibly associated features – delayed milestones, learning disability, hypotonia and seizures.

In 2003 two autistic children were described with moderate motor delay, lactic acidosis and severe hypotonia, and with normal EEG and MRI, both of whom had a 15q11–q13 inverted duplication (Filipek *et al.* 2003). Both boys had muscle enzyme results on biopsy that showed evidence of excessive mitochondrial activity and a respiratory chain block, suggesting that

15q11–13 may be critical in affecting mitochondrial function.

In one recent series of three families with an interstitial duplication (15q11–q13) (Thomas, Roberts and Browne 2003), two families demonstrated multigenerational matrilineal inheritance. The affected cases had minor anomalies with learning disability, with four of the five children examined meeting criteria for an autistic diagnosis, or stated to be in the 'autistic range'.

In 1997, 15q11–q13 was identified as a candidate gene region for autism susceptibility (Pericak-Vance *et al.* 1997).

In one recent study of 221 autistic individuals, using autism as a covariate yielded evidence for linkage to 15q11–q13 with a Lod score of 4.71 (Shao *et al.* 2003).

In 2009, David Wu and colleagues (Wu *et al.* 2009) reported on a boy with autism and a 15q13.2 duplication arising from a paternally inherited translocation with 9q34.12. He exhibited the characteristic profile of learning disability, autism, hypotonia and mild abnormal facies (including epicanthic folds, prominent ears and a submucosal cleft palate). He had had multiple episodes of otitis media and had delayed puberty.

DIFFERENTIAL DIAGNOSIS: The principal conditions that can present with this phenotype are the Angelman and Prader-Willi syndromes, both of which more typically result from deletion of genetic material from 15q11–q13.

MANAGEMENT AND TREATMENT: No specific treatment approaches have so far been developed. The link to defective mitochondrial function may lead to specific treatments focused on correcting respiratory chain activity.

ANIMAL MODELS: No animal studies of this condition have yet been published.

2.

Chromosome 2q37 deletion

aka • Albright hereditary osteodystrophy-like syndrome;

• brachydactyly-mental retardation syndrome

GENE LOCUS: 2q37

KEY ASD REFERENCES: Burd, Martsolf, Kerbeshian and Jalal 1988; Felder *et al.* 2009; Galasso *et al.* 2008); Ghaziuddin and Burmeister 1999; Lukusa *et al.* 2004

SUMMARY: This is a rare condition with dysmorphic features (large forehead, broad nose, small hands and feet) and mild learning disability.

HOW COMMON IS CHROMOSOME 2Q37 DELETION? Prevalence is not known, but the condition is assumed to be rare.

MAIN CLINICAL FEATURES: Hypotonia (muscle weakness), large forehead, broad nose, small hands and feet, mild developmental delay, poor eye contact, overactivity and anxiety.

IS THERE A LINK BETWEEN CHROMOSOME 2Q37 DELETION AND ASD? An early genetic paper (Burd, Martsolf, Kerbeshian and Jalal 1988) described an ASD case with a partial trisomy 6p and a 2q37–qter. A number of the dysmorphic features described such as prominent forehead are also seen with 2q37 deletion alone.

The first paper to suggest a possible association between 2q37 deletion and ASD reported two cases of ASD associated with dysmorphic features and distal deletions of the long arm of chromosome 2 (Ghaziuddin and Burmeister 1999).

In 2004, Lukusa and colleagues reported the case of a 12-year-old girl with a terminal 2q37.3 cryptic deletion. She had presented with hypotonia and feeding difficulties during infancy. She had coarse facial features, with a notably prominent forehead and eyebrow ridges, broad flat nasal bridge and round cheeks. She had small hands and feet, with bilateral brachymetaphalangism, proximal implantation of the thumbs and short toenails. She had a mild degree of learning disability and presented with autistic behaviour. The specific behaviours which were reported as autistic included early lack of eye contact and limited social interaction, propensity to be stereotypically busy and to get easily and excessively anxious. She had two older siblings with a similar but less extensive 2q37 gene deletion who were not ASD.

A 2008 paper from the University of Rome (Galasso *et al.* 2008) described a further girl with learning difficulties, dysmorphic features, gastrointestinal anomalies and autistic traits.

A further case of 2q37 deletion in association with ASD and brachymetaphalangy was found to have downregulation of three genes involved in somatic differentiation – FARP2 (FERM, RhoGEF and pleckstrin domain protein 2), HDLBP (high-density lipoprotein binding protein) and PASK (proline-alanine-rich STE20-related kinase).

The association of 2q37 deletions with learning disability and dysmorphic features has been reported for some time (Wilson L.C. *et al.* 1995).

One study, of three cases of autism where a 2q37.3 terminal deletion was found, identified deletions that involved the centaurin gamma-2 gene (CENTG2) (Wassink *et al.* 2005). CENTG2 is involved in membrane trafficking and seems an attractive candidate gene for ASD.

Reports have also appeared suggesting an association of 2q37 deletion with partial callosal agenesis (failure of development of part of the major fibre tract that connects the two hemispheres of the brain (Sherr *et al.* 2005), and with osteodystrophy (Smith M. *et al.* 2001).

DIFFERENTIAL DIAGNOSIS: The main conditions that can be confused with 2q37 deletion syndrome are Albright hereditary osteodystrophy (Falk and Casas 2007) and Turner syndrome [74].

MANAGEMENT AND TREATMENT: No specific treatment approaches have so far been developed.

ANIMAL MODELS: No animal studies have yet been published.

3.

XXY syndrome

aka • Klinefelter's syndrome

GENE LOCUS: Those with Klinefelter's syndrome possess an additional copy of the X chromosome (a condition only affecting males). In addition, mitochondrial DNA (mtDNA) haplotypes in Klinefelter individuals seem to be unique and appear different from their mother (typically mtDNA is inherited from the mother), suggesting that in addition to the chromosome aneuploidy there is an unusual pattern of mitochondrial involvement and inheritance in this condition (Oikawa *et al.* 2002).

KEY ASD REFERENCES: Jha, Sheth and Ghaziuddin 2007; Merhar and Manning-Courtney 2007; Stuart, King and Pai 2007; van Rijn, Swaab, Aleman and Kahn 2006, 2008.

SUMMARY: Klinefelter's syndrome is an eponymous term, being named after Henry Klinefelter, who first described a group of symptoms found in some men with an additional X chromosome. Even though all men with Klinefelter's syndrome have an extra X chromosome, not every XXY male has all of the symptoms he first described; as a result, the term 'XXY male' is typically used to describe those with Klinefelter's syndrome.

Clinical presentation varies widely and many people with XXY have no clinically significant features. Typically, developmental milestones are achieved more slowly and IQ is one standard deviation below the population mean.

HOW COMMON IS XXY SYNDROME? XXY syndrome is the most common sex chromosome copy number difference, and one of the most common genetic anomalies seen in humans overall. It is seen in approximately one in 500 liveborn males (Nielsen and Wohlert 1991).

MAIN CLINICAL FEATURES: Many males with an additional X chromosome are asymptomatic and do not come to clinical attention. There is a wide variability in clinical presentation.

Early physical development tends to be slow, with later achievement of early motor milestones, and poor muscle tone and power. Individuals with XXY are often late in talking and have problems with processing both spoken and written language. For around 25 per cent of people with XXY, their language difficulties continue to have a significant effect into adult life. This is typically associated with an IQ that is 15–16 points lower than in the general population. (See, for review, Visootsak and Graham 2006.)

XXY syndrome is a genetically defined disorder characterized by the presence of an additional X chromosome. It can reveal insights into genotype–phenotype associations. Increased vulnerability to psychiatric disorders characterized by difficulties in social interactions, such as schizophrenia and autism, has been reported in people with XXY.

Klinefelter's syndrome is a relatively common sex chromosome aneuploidy, seen in approximately one in 700 men. Men with Klinefelter's have one or more additional X chromosomes and are, most typically, 47,XXY.

The normal increase in testicular volume that occurs at around 11–12 years of age in boys fails to occur in Klinefelter's, and testicular volume falls away from normal centile levels (having been normal pre-pubertally). This is typically coupled with lack of, or severe reduction in, spermatogenesis, and 95–99 per cent of individuals with Klinefelter's are sterile. However, XXY males can have normal sex lives.

Most boys with Klinefelter's are of broadly normal intelligence, but with a slight skewing down of the overall distribution. In addition, on neuropsychological assessment they show evidence of executive function problems relative to their overall ability level (Temple and Sanfilippo 2003). There is often a delay in speech development, typically involving auditory memory and receptive and expressive language skills (Bender et al. 1983), and this should be addressed by appropriate speech and language therapy.

A number of health concerns are more common in adulthood, including autoimmune conditions such as systemic lupus erythematosus and autoimmune hepatitis (Sasaki et al. 2006), breast cancer (Aguirre et al. 2006), veinous diseases, osteoporosis, and tooth decay.

Often those with XXY are shy, quiet and less active than others. They tend to be poorer at sport, as they tend to tire easily and have motor difficulties.

IS THERE A LINK BETWEEN XXY SYNDROME AND ASD? Three publications to date point to a possible association:

- Jha, Sheth and Ghaziuddin (2007) described two cases of autism in association with supernumary sex chromosomes – one with an XXY genotype and the other with an XXYY genotype.

- Merhar and Manning-Courtney (2007) presented two autistic boys both with severe communication disorders and abnormal EEGs. In addition, one of the boys also had clinical seizures.

- Stuart, King and Pai (2007) presented the case of a seven-year-old boy with autism and an XXY genotype, who also had a 3p21.31 duplication.

In addition to the reported cases of ASD, there is clear evidence of impaired social perception in individuals with Klinefelter's syndrome (van Rijn, Swaab, Aleman and Kahn 2006) and of higher self-ratings on autism screening tools (van Rijn, Swaab, Aleman and Kahn 2008).

In line with the more general evidence of differences in the structure and function of the amygdala in ASD (Schulkin 2007), there is now structural imaging data which demonstrates that the amygdala is significantly reduced in size in individuals with XXY (Patwardhan *et al.* 2002).

DIFFERENTIAL DIAGNOSIS: Although easily diagnosed on genetic testing, XXY can be confused phenotypically with Kallman syndrome. In Kallman syndrome, in addition to underdeveloped genitalia, affected individuals also lack a sense of smell (anosmia) (Rugarli 1999). The prevalence of Kallman syndrome, which is more common in males, is thought to be one in 10,000.

MANAGEMENT AND TREATMENT: Motor function, muscle development, vocal tone and the appearance of facial and body hair can be changed considerably by testosterone replacement therapy (TRT) at puberty (typically @ 11–12 years). This can be achieved using oral preparations that do not affect hepatic (liver) function such as testosterone undecanoate – an ester of testosterone which converts into testosterone in the body – or through injections of testosterone preparations. Excessive sleepiness is another common problem reported by people with XXY that often improves with TRT, which is also thought to reduce the later risk of osteoporosis, immune disorders and breast cancer (Nielsen, Pelsen and Sorensen 1988).

One recent paper (Swarts, Leisegang, Owen and Henderson 2007) describes an ornithine transcarbamylase deficiency in a 20-month-old boy with XXY syndrome who showed clinical improvement on a low-protein diet with accompanying treatment with benzoate and phenylbutyrate. Ornithine transcarbamylase deficiency is a separate genetic disorder that interferes with the body's ability to metabolize the amino acid alanine.

ANIMAL MODELS: No animal studies have yet been published.

4.

XYY syndrome

GENE LOCUS: Those affected have a supernumary Y chromosome.

KEY ASD REFERENCES: Geerts, Steyaert and Fryns 2003; Gillberg, Winnergard and

Wahlstrom 1984; Nicolson, Bhalerao and Sloman 1998

SUMMARY: 47,XYY is a sex chromosome aneuploidy caused by the presence of an additional Y chromosome that often goes undetected in early life. It is not associated with learning disability. It is associated with being taller, leaner, having proneness to speech delay, hyperactive behaviour and educational problems. To date, there is a paucity of information on any central nervous system sequelae. There have been a number of case reports of XYY in association with ASD. However, no systematic assessments of this association have been carried out.

HOW COMMON IS XYY SYNDROME? It is a relatively common genetic anomaly, being found in between one in 1,200 and one in 1,800 live births (Hansteen 1982; Jacobs et al. 1974; Nielsen and Wohlert 1991). Birthweight typically does not differ from controls (Ratcliffe, Butler and Jones 1990; Robinson, Bender. Linden and Salbenblatt 1990).

Mosaicism, where some cells are 47,XYY and some are 46,XY, is found in approximately 10–20 per cent of all cases (Jacobs et al. 1974; Nielsen and Wohlert 1991.) The cause is always nondisjunction of the Y chromosome at either the second meiotic division or after mitosis of the zygote.

MAIN CLINICAL FEATURES: Various screening methods could pick up an affected baby before birth. The methods include amniocentesis and chorionic villous sampling. (Other findings can be suggestive, such as increased 'nuchal translucency' – a fluid-filled space behind the base of the baby's neck, which can be seen on ultrasound. This feature is more commonly seen in association with Down syndrome [31].) These methods would not

form part of routine screening, and it is not typically the case that XYY is identified antenatally (Sebire et al. 1998; Spencer, Tul and Nicolaides 2000). The exception is where screening is carried out for other reasons, such as increased maternal age (Abramsky and Chapple 1997), or when screening for Down syndrome (Ryall et al. 2001). It is therefore likely that an age bias in clinical (but not in epidemiological) samples reflects the correlation between increased likelihood of screening and increased maternal age.

Obvious physical abnormalities are not seen in infancy (Buyse 1990; Jacobs et al. 1974), there is no increased risk of learning difficulties, and overt behaviour problems are not common. Early year postnatal diagnosis is therefore uncommon (Abramsky and Chapple 1997; Nielsen and Videbech 1984), and the condition is more likely to be found by chance than deliberate clinical intent.It does appear that there is a heightened incidence of speech delay, hyperactivity and educational difficulties, particularly in the postnatally diagnosed XYY population (Buyse 1990; Linden, Bender and Robinson 1996; Walzer, Bashir and Silbert 1990). The lower rates of developmental difficulties reported in the prenatally diagnosed population (Linden and Bender 2002) could, however, represent an ascertainment bias, as routine karyotyping would be considered more often in those presenting clinically with issues such as speech delay, hyperactivity and educational problems. In general, psychosocial problems are common but tend to be mild in the XYY population and are not typically severe enough to result in psychiatric diagnosis (Fryns, Kleczkowska, Kubien and Van den Berghe 1995). Physically those with XYY tend to be taller and leaner than average (Buyse 1990; Linden, Bender and Robinson 1996). Those with 47,XYY are typically fertile (Linden, Bender and Robinson 1996).

However, they are more likely to have a number of genital anomalies, including hypospadias and small or undercended testes (Buyse 1990).

One case of 47,XYY in an individual who was phenotypically female has been reported in the clinical literature (Benasayag *et al.* 2001). There is no increased risk of 47,XYY linked to later maternal age at conception (Ferguson-Smith and Yates 1984) – perhaps unsurprising, given that the origin of the additional chromosome will be paternal. Neither does there appear to be increased risk with increasing age of fathers producing aneuploid sperm (over the age range from 22 to 80 years of age) (Wyrobek *et al.* 2006). This suggests that there is something about spermatogenesis in the fathers of those with XYY that predisposes to this process. 47,XYY has been reported in infants conceived by intracytoplasmic sperm injection (ICSI) (Aboulghar *et al.* 2001), but not, to date, through any other means of assisted conception.

IS THERE A LINK BETWEEN XYY SYNDROME AND ASD? Three papers to date have pointed to a possible association:

- Gillberg, Winnergard and Wahlstrom (1984) note previous cases of childhood psychosis in association with XYY, and present a case of infantile autism with XYY.
- Nicolson, Bhalerao and Sloman (1998) described two boys, both with an XYY genotype. One fulfilled criteria for autistic disorder, the other for the DSM-III diagnosis of pervasive developmental disorder – not otherwise specified (PDD-NOS).
- Geerts, Steyaert and Fryns (2003) presented perhaps the most useful dataset to date, describing a series of 38

children with XYY, which indicated that, although many children with XYY are of normal ability, psychosocial problems are noted in around half of all cases, and the likelihood of ASD diagnosis seems to rise with age, perhaps suggesting that the presentation is more suggestive of Asperger's syndrome than autism.

DIFFERENTIAL DIAGNOSIS: While XYY is easily diagnosed on genetic testing, phenotypically it could be confused with other conditions resulting in taller, thinner stature, such as Marfan syndrome (De Paepe *et al.* 1996).

MANAGEMENT AND TREATMENT: XYY, although associated with ASD, appears remarkably benign. No major difficulties have been reported for which specific treatments appear warranted at the present time. The biological effects of having an additional Y chromosome are not well known.

ANIMAL MODELS: No animal studies have yet been published.

5.

10p terminal deletion

GENE LOCUS: 10p

KEY ASD REFERENCE: Verri *et al.* 2004

SUMMARY: 10p terminal deletion is a rare condition, and has only been reported to date in one ASD case. This 33-year-old man was reported in addition as having hypoparathyroidism, severe mental retardation, and calcification of the basal ganglia.

HOW COMMON IS 10P TERMINAL DELETION? There have been no

population studies of the prevalence of this condition, but it is thought to be very rare. As cases have been reported in conditions themselves linked to ASD, the association, though uncommon, may indicate a specific pathogenic mechanism that is involved in a subgroup of people with an ASD diagnosis.

MAIN CLINICAL FEATURES: Large forehead; small teeth; congenital heart defect; kidney problems; dilated cerebral ventricles; developmental delay.

IS THERE A LINK BETWEEN 10P TERMINAL DELETION AND ASD? The 10p region is not identified, from the various gene marker studies, as being associated with ASD.

There is one clinical report of an association (Verri *et al.* 2004). It may prove relevant, as 10p deletions have been reported in association with both the DiGeorge II [29b] (Yatsenko *et al.* 2004) and velocardiofacial [76] syndromes (Gottlieb *et al.* 1998). (See also Daw *et al.* 1996.) Both of these conditions are overrepresented in the ASD population, and typically the case reports of 10p terminal deletion to date have not looked in any detail for possible ASD behaviour.

In a review of 36 patients with a 10p deletion (van Esch *et al.* 1999), affected individuals showed a phenotype similar to a partial DiGeorge syndrome I [29a]. However, a consistent additional feature of those with 10p deletion was that they also had a sensorineural hearing loss.

In one paper (Sunada, Rash and Tam 1998) the association of partial 10p monosomy with seizures and cortical atrophy is well documented, as well as the previously reported phenotypic characteristics − bossing of the frontal bones of the skull; small teeth; congenital heart defect; kidney problems; dilated cerebral ventricles; and developmental delay.

MANAGEMENT AND TREATMENT: The biological basis to this association is not known at the present time, and no specific treatment approach has been developed to date.

ANIMAL MODELS: No animal studies of 10p terminal deletion have yet been published.

6.

45,X/46,XY mosaicism

GENE MARKER: 45X/46XY

KEY ASD REFERENCES: Fontenelle, Mendlowicz, Menezes and Martins 2004; Telvi *et al.* 1999

SUMMARY: 45,X/46,XY mosaicism (a Turner syndrome mosaic) is an extremely rare presentation. In Turner syndrome, all cells are 45,X. Here, the individual has a combination of normal male 46,XY cells and 45,X Turner syndrome cells, giving a range of possible phenotypes. Three cases of ASD so far reported and the broad clinical phenotype do not allow for generalizations to be drawn at this time.

HOW COMMON IS 45,X/46,XY MOSAICISM? This is seen in fewer than two per cent of Turner syndrome cases (Van Dyke and Wiktor 2006). Turner syndrome affects some 32/100,000 (Gravholt, Juul, Naeraa and Hansen 1996), so in every million people we would expect to find 324.6 people with the full 45X Turner syndrome, and 6.4 people with a Turner mosaic genotype.

MAIN CLINICAL FEATURES: In typical Turner syndrome cases [74], all cells are 45,XO, the individual is missing a sex chromosome, and the person is phenotypically female. A person who is genotypically 46,XY has a full chromosome complement and is phenotypically male. In 45,X/46,XY mosaicism, some cells are 45,X and some are 46,XY. The proportion of cells of each type is currently not possible to predict.

As a mosaic condition, 45,X/46,XY shows a wide range of phenotypic presentation, from normal male to Turner syndrome female. Some 90 per cent of antenatally diagnosed cases are male, while a broader range of postnatally diagnosed phenotypes is seen. This pattern may change with greater use of antenatal diagnostics. The most common features currently reported are 'Ullrich-Turner stigmata' (drooping of the upper eyelid, coupled with 'webbing' on the neck). Most individuals with this karyotype are phenotypically normal males with unexplained short stature, but tend not to be routinely screened for 45,X/46,XY mosaicism. This should be done, and where found, checks should be done for possible problems associated more typically with Turners syndrome:

• an echocardiogram to check for possible heart defects

• a renal ultrasound to check kidney function

• a cognitive assessment to check for a non-verbal learning disability profile.

Short stature in children with an apparently normal male phenotype can result from 45,X/46,XY mosaicism and can respond successfully to growth hormone treatment. In a study by Richter-Unruh et al. (2004), 5/6 cases responded favourably to growth hormone replacement, while one was unresponsive. The unresponsive case was not commenced on treatment until after he was 14 years old.

IS THERE A LINK BETWEEN 45,X/46,XY MOSAICISM AND ASD? Only two papers to date have examined this issue.

• Fontenelle, Mendlowicz, Menezes and Martins (2004) reported a single male Brazilian case of Asperger's syndrome with obsessive compulsive disorder, who also developed major depression.

• Telvi et al. (1999) reported on a series of 27 45,X/46,XY mosaic cases, four of whom were learning disabled and two of whom had a diagnosis of autism. If this rate were reflected in larger samples, it would seem to indicate a strong association between the two presentations.

DIFFERENTIAL DIAGNOSIS: The phenotype shows wide variations, from normal male to a classic Turner syndrome presentation. Differential diagnosis based on phenotype would be dependent on the presentation in the individual case.

MANAGEMENT AND TREATMENT: Ongoing care and management should be dependent on clinical findings, not on genotype.

ANIMAL MODELS: No animal studies have yet been published.

7.

22q13 deletion syndrome

aka • Phelan-McDermid syndrome

GENE LOCUS: 22q13.3

KEY ASD REFERENCES: Cusmano-Ozog, Manning and Hoyme 2007; Goizet et al. 2000; Manning et al. 2004; Moessner et al. 2007; Phelan 2008; Prasad et al. 2000

IN SUMMARY: Developmental delay, failure of speech development and hypotonia are typical features. Large hands and in-growing toenails are common, as are slower breathing, chewing on non-food objects (pica) and reduced sensitivity to pain. They are prone to minor ear infections which could, in part, account for delayed language development. Acquisition of bowel and bladder control tends to be slower, due in part to more global motor problems and communication difficulties. Speech is often acquired to a limited extent and then regresses, but with greater preservation of receptive language skills.

The neurobehavioural profile associated with 22q13.3 deletions is variable in severity but consistent in the domains affected (Philippe *et al.* 2008). Hypotonia, sleep problems, delayed speech, sensory processing and neuromotor problems are consistent findings. Social deficits are more varied and although early lack of interest is common, reciprocal interaction usually improves through the preschool years.

HOW COMMON IS 22Q13 DELETION SYNDROME? 22q13 deletion syndrome is relatively rare, with fewer than 150 cases reported in the world literature. To date there is no clear indication of the prevalence of this condition, as the phenotype is not well recognized and the deletion does not form a routine part of clinical chromosome studies. In one subtelomeric chromosome deletion survey, it was the second most common deletion seen after deletions of 1p36.3 (Heilstedt *et al.* 2003).

MAIN CLINICAL FEATURES: Dysfunction of a 100kb segment of DNA at 22q13 appears to be the critical factor in this condition (Anderlid *et al.* 2002). Clinically, the use of two gene probes – the arylsulphatase A probe and a specific subtelomere probe (D22S1726) – should identify 100 per cent of cases.

From a review of 56 cases, there does not seem to be any association between the size of the gene deletion and the resultant phenotype (Wilson H.L. *et al.* 2003), which can be anywhere between 100kb and 9mb.

The deletion can be inherited from either parent, but in 80–85 per cent of cases is a *de novo* deletion in the affected individual. Where a deletion has been inherited, in most cases it is from the paternal chromosome (Luciani *et al.* 2003; Wilson H.L. *et al.* 2003). The gene locus lies close to the gene defect at 22q13.1 that causes adenylosuccinate lyase deficiency [9]. No gene markers with Lod scores above 2.2 have been identified at any location on chromosome 22.

In around 75 per cent of cases, the defect is a simple deletion, while in the others it arises from an unbalanced translocation or other chromosomal rearrangement.

Typical features in 22q13 deletion are developmental delay, failure of speech development and hypotonia. Features seen in a significant minority of cases are epileptic seizures and a number of craniofacial features, including the presence of epicanthic folds, large prominent ears, long eyelashes, a prominent brow, pointed chin and irregular dentition. Many of those affected have large hands and in-growing toenails. Slower breathing, chewing on non-food objects (pica) and a reduced sensitivity to pain are also reported to be more common. Many cases show lack of perspiration, so have difficulty regulating their body temperature – extra care should be taken with exposure to sunlight and during periods of illness. Minor ear infections are common and could in part account for delayed language development. Lymphoedema is seen in around 10 per cent of cases (Phelan 2008). Gastro-esophageal reflux is not uncommon (seen in @ 30 per cent of cases), with cyclical vomiting reported in 25 per cent. Taking smaller, more frequent meals coupled with avoidance of spicy foods can prove helpful. Most reported cases have been born at term, appropriately sized for their gestational age. Most cases have grown normally but experienced global developmental delay, with slower acquisition of motor milestones and either slowed or absent development of communication skills. Acquisition of bowel and bladder control also tends to be slow, in part due to more global motor problems and in part due to communication difficulties. Speech is often acquired to a limited extent and then regresses, but with greater preservation of receptive language skills. Occasional neurological abnormalities have been reported, arachnoid cysts being the most common. Reduced size of the frontal lobes, agenesis of the corpus callosum and dilated ventricles have also been reported. There are no characteristic findings on EEG or structural neuroimaging.

In some cases, hyperactivity, anxiety and self-stimulatory behaviours are sufficiently extreme to warrant treatment. Sleep problems are quite common and may be linked to reduced production of melatonin.

No individuals with 22q13.3 have reproduced, but puberty and menstruation occur normally in girls and conception would appear possible.

IS THERE A LINK BETWEEN 22Q13 DELETION SYNDROME AND ASD? Individuals with 22q13 deletion typically have poor eye contact, motor stereotypies and severe communication difficulties in association with learning disability. These features are consistent with ASD in many cases, but can also reflect the overall level of learning disability.

Several papers have reported a possible association with ASD.

- Cusmano-Ozog, Manning and Hoyme (2007) review the evidence for a consistent phenotype associated with 22q13 deletion syndrome, suggesting that the constellation of developmental delay, hypotonia, delayed or absent speech, receptive language difficulties and autistic behaviour, with normal growth and head circumference, form a consistent phenotype as seen in 22q13 deletion.

- Goizet et al. (2000) described a case of autism, developmental delay and communication difficulties associated with a de novo cryptic 22q13 deletion detected by FISH (fluorescence in-situ hybridization).

- Manning et al. (2004) described 11 cases of ASD with severe speech and language delay and hypotonia in association with a microdeletion at 22q13.3.

- In one cohort of 400 screened ASD cases, three defects in SHANK 3 were found (Moessner et al. 2007), indicating, assuming this sample is representative, that possibly 0.75 per cent of ASD may present with such problems. Estimates of the prevalence of ASD within those with 22q13 deletion range from under five per cent to 54 per cent of cases. This variability reflects a range of factors, such as changing diagnostic criteria and diagnostic overshadowing.

- Phelan (2008) provides a detailed overview of 22q13 deletion.

- Prasad et al. (2000) documented three clinical cases with 22q13 deletions. One of the three cases met criteria on the Childhood Autism Rating Scale for an autism diagnosis with co-morbid learning disability. Her initial diagnosis had been thought to be 22q11 and she had been included in an earlier case series and reported as such (Chudley, Gutierrez, Jocelyn and Chodirker 1998).

WHAT CAUSES 22Q13 DELETION SYNDROME? The gene involvement in this condition is deletion of the gene known as SHANK 3 or PROSAP 2 (proline-rich synapse associated protein 2). This gene produces a scaffolding protein for the postsynaptic density complex where it binds with neuroligins (Meyer *et al.* 2004), which are important in combination with neurexins, particularly at glutamatergic synapses. Both neuroligin defects (Jamain *et al.* 2003) and abnormalities of glutamatergic transmission have been described in association with ASD, the latter particularly in fragile-X [35], so defective production of a protein involved in the function of these substances is not surprising. SHANK 3 also has a role in the development of the dendritic spines of nerve cells (Boeckers, Bockmann, Kreutz and Gundelfinger 2002).

A study of 56 individuals examined the size of the 22q13 deletion and the parental origin of the deletion (Wilson H.L. *et al.* 2003). They also studied the gene SHANK 3 (also called PROSAP 2). Approximately two-thirds of the deletions found were in the paternally inherited chromosome and one third in the maternally inherited one. Deletions varied in size between 130 kilobases and 9 megabases, with no association between the size of the deletion and the physical or behavioural phenotype. A degree of both developmental and speech delay occurred in all of these cases.

A number of other conditions can present with phenotypic and behavioural similarities to 22q13 deletion syndrome, amongst the more commonly suggested being the ones listed in Table A17 on page 98.

Ring chromosome 22 has been reported in association with autism (MacLean, Teshima, Szatmari and Nowaczyk 2000). It appears that where the association is seen, the expression of SHANK 3 has been affected (Jeffries *et al.* 2005), with a larger deletion from the distal portion of what would normally have been the long arm of the chromosome.

Ring chromosome 22 cases are more likely to show short stature (seen in a quarter of cases) and microcephaly (seen in one third), both of which are uncommon in 22q13.3 cases (Ishmael *et al.* 2003; Luciani *et al.* 2003).

DIFFERENTIAL DIAGNOSIS: As 22q13 deletion presents with hypotonia and developmental delay, the early presentation can be confused with a number of other syndromes that have also been linked to ASD: Angelman syndrome [11]; fragile-X syndrome [35]; Prader-Willi syndrome [61]; Smith-Magenis syndrome [67]; Sotos syndrome [68]; velocardiofacial syndrome [76]; Williams syndrome [77]; and ring chromosome 22. Ring chromosome 22 is more likely than 22q13 deletion to present with short stature and microcephaly.

Both cerebral palsy and trichorhinophalangeal syndrome can present with similar physical phenotypes.

MANAGEMENT AND TREATMENT: There is only one study to date that has investigated a specific treatment in Phelan-McDermid syndrome. This was an exploratory trial of intranasal insulin. The results of this small trial are encouraging, but clinical use of this approach is not yet warranted in improving intellectual functioning (Schmidt H. *et al.* 2008).

ANIMAL STUDIES: No specific animal models for Phelan-McDermid syndrome have so far been developed. The 22q13.3 area has been linked to MNGIE (mitochondrial neurogastrointestinal encephalomyopathy), and mouse models being investigated for this condition may also have application as models of Phelan-McDermid (Haraguchi *et al.* 2002).

8.

Aarskog syndrome

aka • Aarskog-Scott syndrome

GENE LOCUS: At present the gene locus has not been definitively located, but mutations in the FGD1 gene (Xp11.21) have been described in some cases (Orrico, Hayek and Burroni 1999).

KEY ASD REFERENCE: Assumpcao, Santos, Rosario and Mercadante 1999

SUMMARY: Aarskog syndrome is a rare condition with short stature, hypertelorism and 'shawl scrotum', learning difficulties and behavioural problems. Three of the approximately 200 cases so far reported have an ASD. Further research is required to confirm whether this represents a clinically significant association. A recent overview paper summarizes clinical presentation and genetic characterization to date (Orrico *et al.* 2004)

HOW COMMON IS AARSKOG SYNDROME? Aarskog syndrome, first described by Aarskog (1970), is a rare connective tissue condition that has been reported in less than 200 cases in total worldwide (Grier, Farrington, Kendig and Mamunes 1983; Teebi, Rucquoi and Meyn 1993; Welch 1974).

MAIN CLINICAL FEATURES: Aarskog syndrome is typically reported as being associated with short stature, hypertelorism and 'shawl scrotum' (see Grier 1983, Farrington, Kendig and Mamunes for review). In addition, learning difficulties, behavioural problems and hyperactivity have been reported (Fryns 1992). In one family, males in three successive generations were affected (Welch 1974).

IS THERE A LINK BETWEEN AARSKOG SYNDROME AND ASD? There is a brief report on an association between this condition and autism (Assumpcao, Santos, Rosario and Mercadante 1999), in which three case descriptions are given of boys, all of whom had significant learning difficulties, hyperactivity and the physical phenotype characteristic of Aarskog syndrome. All three fulfilled DSM criteria for autistic disorder.

DIFFERENTIAL DIAGNOSIS: The main differential diagnoses are Noonan syndrome [52] and Robinow syndrome (see Patton and Afzal 2002).

MANAGEMENT AND TREATMENT: Two specific areas of treatment have been studied. The use of growth hormone supplementation has been shown to be useful in correction of short stature (Darendeliler *et al.* 2003; Petryk, Richton, Sy and Blethen 1999), and restorative dental care is both feasible and potentially useful (Batra *et al.* 2003).

No treatments specific to the behavioural aspects of ASD in Aarskog syndrome have been reported.

ANIMAL MODELS: No animal studies have yet been published.

9.

Adenylosuccinate lyase (ADSL) deficiency

GENE LOCUS: 22q13.1

KEY ASD REFERENCES: Edery *et al.* 2003; Jaeken and van den Berghe 1984; Jaeken *et al.* 1988

SUMMARY: ADSL is an autosomal recessive clinical disorder of purine synthesis that has been reported in association with mental retardation and autism (Jaeken and van den Berghe 1984). It was the first known defect of human purine synthesis to be found. The purine synthesis pathway is complex, involving ten discrete steps in converting 5-phosphoribosylpyrophosphate (PRPP) to inosine monophosphate (IMP). The adenine and guanine nucleotides of DNA are formed from IMP.

ADSL is associated with the build-up of two enzyme substrates in body fluids – suc-cinylaminoimidazolecarboxamide (SAICA) riboside, and succinyladenosine (S-Ado) (Race, Marie, Vincent and van de Berghe 2000). The ratio of these two compounds predicts the severity of the condition (Kmoch et al. 2000) and is likely to be the key to effective treatment. From the available information to date, it is inferred that levels of SAICA are critical in predicting level of disability, and that higher relative levels of S-Ado are protective (Jaeken et al. 1992). An overview of 14 different gene defects interfering with ADSL has shown that variations in the ratio of SAICA to S-Ado are strongly predicted by the gene lesion involved (Zikanova et al. 2010).

S-Ado is reduced in ADSL and can be tested for reliably (Maddocks and Reed 1989).

There is a recent review by Spiegel, Colman and Patterson (2006) of many of the issues. At the present time there is a wide variability in the gene mutations, the biochemistry and the behaviour that are taken to characterize ADSL.

HOW COMMON IS ADSL? There are no screening studies as yet, so prevalence is unknown. Fewer than 100 cases have been reported to date in the clinical literature. Five cases were identified in 2,000 children screened with neurodevelopmental disorders in one Czech series, suggesting a very low prevalence in the learning-disabled population (Sebesta et al. 1997). Recent, and so far unique, single cases have recently been reported from Poland (Jurkiewicz, Mierzewska and Kusmierska 2007) and the UK (Marinaki et al. 2004).

In one Czech study (Sebesta et al. 1997) urine samples from more than 2,000 children with unexplained neurological disease were screened. Two boys and three girls in four kindreds were identified with ADSL. Two of the four kindreds were of Romany origin.

Most cases of ADSL are detected through metabolic testing of infants with severe psychomotor retardation. However, the initial presentation can be of infantile seizures (Maaswinkel-Mooij et al. 1997; Marinaki et al. 2004).

MAIN CLINICAL FEATURES: Psychomotor retardation; hypotonia-ataxia; seizures; poor eye contact; stereotypies. Approximately 50 per cent of reported cases fulfil criteria for a diagnosis of autism.

Two forms of the disorder are recognized (Jaeken et al. 1988): the first presents with early onset epilepsy and severe psychomotor retardation; the second with psychomotor retardation and autistic symptomology. A variety of additional features have been reported in some but not in all cases, such as microcephaly, brain atrophy, lissencephaly and delayed myelin formation. (See, for example, Edery et al. 2003; Holder-Espinasse et al. 2002; Nassogne et al. 2000.)

Some cases present with a clinical phenotype that is very similar to Angelman syndrome. Gitaux et al. (2009) present two sisters, aged 11 and 12, both with learning difficulties and seizures but with an Angelman-like clinical phenotype.

WHAT DO WE KNOW OF THE GENETICS? Despite its rarity, a wide variety of both missense and point mutations have been reported in ADSL (Kmoch *et al.* 2000; Marie *et al.* 1999; Stone *et al.* 1992).

IS THERE A LINK BETWEEN ADSL AND ASD?

- In 1984, Jaeken and van den Berghe described three children with severe psychomotor delay and autism. They identified two specific compounds – succinyladenosine (S-Ado) and succinylaminoimidazole carboxamide (SAICA) ribotide – in the cerebro-spinal fluid, plasma and urine at well above normal levels (normally at detectable levels only in urine). These authors concluded that ADSL is a clinically specific cause of autism.

- In a subsequent paper on eight children with ADSL (Jaeken *et al.* 1988), seven showed significant developmental delay, epilepsy was noted in five, autistic features in three, and growth retardation associated with muscular wasting in two siblings. One girl was only mildly delayed (and was strikingly less developmentally delayed than the others), and she showed lesser biochemical differences.

- Maddocks and Reed (1989) published results of a urinary test for succinyladenosine, which could discriminate between urine from ADSL autistic cases and urine from normal control samples in a blinded assay.

- One recent paper (Edery *et al.* 2003) described three siblings, all of whom had the same homozygous ADSL mutation. Two had presented with autism and the third with psychomotor regression coupled with atrophy of the cerebellar vermis.

- A screen carried out with 119 Canadian patients with autism found no subjects to have a point mutation on the ADSL gene, and on the subset tested there was no evidence of novel mutations on any of the four ADSL exons (Fon *et al.* 1995), suggesting that, although ADSL is a specific cause of autism, it is also a rare one.

DIFFERENTIAL DIAGNOSIS: ADSL deficiency is one of a number of inborn errors of purine and pyrimidine metabolism (Jurecka 2009), several of which have been associated with ASD: dihydropyrimidine dehydrogenase deficiency [30]; NAPDD [53]; and hereditary xanthinuria type I.

MANAGEMENT AND TREATMENT: Treatment approaches to date have met with limited success. Only one published study, using D-ribose supplementation, has shown positive effects on both purine synthesis and behaviour (Salerno *et al.* 1999). In this single case, improved purine metabolism was paralleled by decreased ataxia, stereotypies and seizure activity, and increased eye contact. A further series of four cases has failed to show similar treatment response (Jurecka *et al.* 2008).

One area that gives some promise for the development of genetic interventions is the identification of Exon skipping as at least one of the mechanisms that can result in ADSL (Hide *et al.* 2001). This type of mechanism has been found to be important in various other conditions discussed here, such as Duchenne muscular dystrophy [33] and velocardiofacial syndrome [76]. In Duchenne, in particular, results to date are extremely promising. (See, for review, Muntoni and Wells 2007.)

ANIMAL STUDIES: The importance of developing animal models has been emphasized (see, for example, Spiegel, Colman and Patterson 2006). No animal models have been published to date.

10.

Adrenomyeloneuropathy (AMN)

GENE LOCUS: Xq28

KEY ASD REFERENCE: Swillen, Hellmans, Steyaert and Fryns 1996

SUMMARY: Adrenomyeloneuropathy (AMN) is a mild form of adrenoleukodystrophy (ALD). ALD can take seven primary forms (Moser *et al.* 2000). In AMN, as in the other forms, the problem is an inability to metabolize very long chain fatty acids (VLCFAs), resulting in a build-up in both plasma and body tissues. The essential biochemistry appears the same in AMN and ALD (Lazo *et al.* 1988).

They are peroxisomal disorders, affecting the membranes of peroxisomes – small, subcellular organelles that have been known since the 1950s to be involved, alongside mitochondria, in α- and β-oxidation of fatty acids. (For an overview, see Tabak, Braakman and Distel 1999.) Peroxisomes differ in their role in fatty acid oxidation, as they lack a Krebs cycle and can only shorten the chain length of fatty acids where mitochondria can completely oxidize them (Hashimoto 1999).

The gene defect identified is in the gene for a peroxisome membrane transporter protein, not for the enzyme very long chain fatty acyl-CoA synthetase (VLCS). This structural defect, in turn, interferes with the function of VLCS (Smith K.D. *et al.* 1999).

HOW COMMON IS AMN? AMN is a rare condition. It affects approximately one in 50,000 liveborn boys. It was first reported almost a century ago (von Neusser and Wiesel 1910), but late and incomplete recognition has resulted in less research being carried out than on the more severe or rapidly progressing forms of ALD.

A large number of deletions and point mutations have been reported, with no apparent correlation between these and the nature of the resulting phenotype. Phenotypic variations between identical twins with the same Xq28 gene defect suggest that other factors also affect expression (Rzeski *et al.* 1999).

Most of those affected with AMN are the brothers or other close relatives of patients with classic adrenoleukodystrophy.

MAIN CLINICAL FEATURES: Impaired β-oxidation and build-up of VLCFAs. (See, for reviews, Wanders 1999; Wanders *et al.* 2001.) There is no apparent change in tissue levels of VLCFAs with age.

VLCFAs accumulate in the adrenal glands and the testes, interfering with the function of these glands (Spurek, Taylor-Gjevre, Van Uum and Khandwala 2004). Primary adrenocortical insufficiency is seen in around 70 per cent of cases, and testicular atrophy is common.

There is progressive muscle weakness and weight loss. Problems with bladder function are common, with urgency, frequency or incontinence. Many people with ALD are wheelchair bound by between five and 15 years old. Muscle weakness is greatest in the lower limbs. There is progressive pansensory loss and loss of proprioceptive abilities, affecting balance and coordination. The skin is typically hyperpigmented, so would tend, in fair-skinned families, to be darker than in other family members.

Physical and cognitive prognosis is better, without gross MRI evidence of neurological involvement (seen in around 50 per cent of those affected). As neuroimaging improves, it may be possible to discriminate more subtle central nervous system changes which help to classify cases and aid in monitoring change (Teriitehau *et al.* 2007).

Brain auditory evoked responses are abnormal in all affected males and around 50 per cent of females carrying the condition.

VLCFAs are elevated in around 85 per cent of female carriers, who typically have a late-onset myelopathy (between the ages of 20 and 55). This is a non-inflammatory myelopathy that mainly affects the glial cells that support axonal function (Powers *et al.* 2000).

Affective disorders are common in this condition (Walterfang, O'Donovan, Fahey and Velakoulis 2007), but the extent to which anxious and depressive symptomology is seen is not related to adrenal status.

IS THERE A LINK BETWEEN AMN AND ASD? To date there has only been a single paper that has suggested a possible link between AMN and ASD (Swillen, Hellemans, Steyaert and Fryns 1996). In this paper, a single autistic case in a Dutch residential home was also diagnosed with AMN.

DIFFERENTIAL DIAGNOSIS: Principal differential diagnoses are with amyotrophic lateral sclerosis, and with other peroxisomal disorders which result in VLCFA abnormalities, such as infantile Refsum's disease and Zellweger syndrome. AMN is not easily confused with other conditions that have been associated with an ASD diagnosis.

MANAGEMENT AND TREATMENT: A variety of strategies have been used or advocated for use with AMD:

- gene therapy (Unterrainer, Molzer, Forss-Petter and Berger 2000)

- bone marrow transplantation (Krivit *et al.* 1995; Moser *et al.* 1992)
- cholesterol-lowering medication (Singh, Khan, Key and Pai 1998)
- 'Lorenzo's oil' (Moser *et al.* 1992, 2005, 2007)
- antioxidants (Deon *et al.* 2007; Perlman 2002)

Although there are benefits from the use of medications to lower cholesterol (Singh, Khan, Key and Pai 1998), it is important to recognize that such medications can have a deleterious effect on liver function through lowering coenzyme Q10 levels (Folkers *et al.* 1990).

Steroid replacement has been used successfully to address the adrenal problems.

Large studies have now been carried out to evaluate, particularly, the efficacy of 'Lorenzo's oil'. At present the results suggest that, once the patient becomes symptomatic, outcome is not improved in the majority (van Geel *et al.* 1999), but that outcome is more likely to be improved where the treatment is started early, while the person is asymptomatic (Moser *et al.* 2005).

The use of allogeneic haemopoetic cell transplants from matched donor cells has been available for some time (Cartier and Aubourg 2008). A paper has described the use of gene therapy for whom matched donors could not be found (Cartier *et al.* 2009). This was achieved by modifying the subject's own CD34+ cells with a lentiviral vector coding for the unaffected gene. This arrested deterioration in two seven-year-old boys with ALD, with success equivalent to allogeneic haemopoetic cell transplants. Further research is needed to confirm the safety of this technique, especially as earlier apparent gene therapy successes have had initially unrecognized side effects (Nienhuis, Dunbar and Sorrentino 2006).

ANIMAL MODELS: So far, only a mouse model of AMN has been produced. In the knockout mouse model, the same β-oxidation abnormalities are seen that we see in human AMN, but there is no evidence of neurological defects, and there has, as yet, been no attempt to look at behavioural effects (Lu J.F. *et al.* 1997).

A further contrast is that while in the mouse model there is no evidence of oxidative stress (in adrenal cortex, brain, kidney or liver), in human ALD there is clear evidence of oxidative stress in both the adrenal cortex and the brain (Powers *et al.* 2005).

11.

Angelman syndrome (AS)

aka • 'happy puppet syndrome',

• 'marionette joyeuse',

• 'pantin hilaire'

GENE LOCI: Xq28, 15q11–q13

KEY ASD REFERENCES: Bonati *et al.* 2007; Bundey *et al.* 1994; O'Donnell *et al.* 2010; Pelc, Cheron and Dan 2008; Peters, Beaudet, Madduri and Bacino 2004; Trillingsgaard and Østergaard 2004

SUMMARY: Angelman syndrome is named after Harry Angelman, the British paediatrician from Warrington who first described the condition (Angelman 1965). Angelman claimed that his term 'puppet children' was not an attempt to capture their usually happy disposition, but derived from his associating the characteristic jerky movements with Giovanni Francesco Caroto's sixteenth-century painting *Boy with a Puppet*.

Clinical overviews of AS are provided in Cassidy and Schwartz (1998), Clayton-

Smith and Laan (2003) and Clayton-Smith and Pembrey (1992). The first detailed clinical description of the type of children that Angelman had originally identified appeared in 1967 (Bower and Jeavons 1967). Bower and Jeavons coined the term 'happy puppet syndrome', considered pejorative today, in an attempt to capture the happy disposition and frequent bouts of laughter that seemed to typify people with the condition. The term 'Angelman syndrome' was suggested by Williams and Frias (1982) as a more acceptable alternative.

AS is a complex disorder and can be caused by four main genetic factors that have different methods of action and give rise to different patterns of presentation. Most people with AS have delayed milestones, severe learning and communication difficulties, epilepsy, motor difficulties and gastrointestinal problems. They often have obsessions with foods and can be prone to becoming overweight.

Recent detailed reviews of Angelman syndrome can be found in Dan (2008) and Pelc, Cheron and Dan (2008).

O'Donnell *et al.* (2010), in a recent screening study of 105 individuals with 18q deletions, found that 45 (43 per cent) of the sample screened as positive for likely ASD on the Gilliam Autism Rating Scale. TCF4, one of the genes sufficient for AS, was found to be associated with an increased risk of ASD (as were two other 18q deletions: NETO1 and FBXO15).

HOW COMMON IS ANGELMAN SYNDROME? There is no indication of a skewed sex ratio, or any difference in ethnic distribution. No prevalence studies have been published to date, but the estimated prevalence is thought to be between approximately one in 10,000 and one in 40,000 (Buckley, Dinno and Weber 1998;

Kyllerman 1995; O'Brien and Yule 1996), with milder cases often going undetected.

MAIN CLINICAL FEATURES: Angelman syndrome is associated with severe learning disabilities. Most children are non-verbal but some develop a small vocabulary of up to 50 words. Around 80–96 per cent of people with AS develop epilepsy, most commonly with myoclonic, atonic, generalized tonic-clonic or atypical absence seizures (Buntinx et al. 1995; Galvan-Manso, Campistol, Conill and Sanmarti 2005; Smith A. et al. 1996; Valente, Koiffemann et al. 2006). Epilepsy is often seen before AS diagnosis is made, and there is a tendency for seizure control to improve with age. Severe myoclonic epilepsy seems to be specific to those who inherit a maternal deletion of 15q11–q13 (Minassian et al. 1998), the other genetic forms of AS being associated with milder types of epilepsy. The basis to the epilepsy seen in the 15q11–q13 forms of AS is likely to be the lack of the β3 subunit of the $GABA_A$ receptor which results from the AS 15q11–q13 deletion, which would also help to explain why the UBE3A cases, who do not have such a deletion, are less likely to be epileptic. As it provides a possible therapeutic target, modification of GABAergic activity is an active area of research (Meldrum and Rogawski 2007).

The EEG pattern seen appears to be characteristic of the condition (Berg and Pakula 1972; Viani et al. 1995), with 20 per cent showing febrile convulsions before the age of two, with 95 per cent going on to develop epilepsy, of whom approximately 50 per cent develop transient myoclonic status epilepticus. There are still a number of unanswered questions concerning the epilepsies seen in Angelman syndrome. However, valproic acid and clonazepam appear well tolerated and to be the most effective reported antiepileptic medications (Galvan-Manso, Campistol, Conill and Sanmarti 2005). An EEG is sometimes helpful in clarifying early diagnosis (Boyd, Harden and Patton 1988; Dorries, Spohr and Kunze 1988; Galvan-Manso, Campistol, Conill and Sanmarti 2005).

People with AS typically walk stiffly, with their legs wider apart than normal. They typically have fine peripheral muscle tremors, hand flapping and arm jerks. Their head circumference is below average, and they typically have a brachycephalic (broader than normal) head shape. The rear of the skull often appears 'flattened'. Fair hair and blue eyes are more common (being seen in approximately 60 per cent of Caucasian cases). The pale blue irises are a result of abnormal choroidal pigmentation, as noted in several case series (Berg and Pakula 1972; Dickinson, Fielder, Duckett and Young 1988; Fryburg, Breg and Lindgren 1991). Pale skin is reported in between 40 and 75 per cent of

Table B11.1: Genetic bases to AS and their reported prevalence

Genetic basis	Typically reported in:
• maternal de novo deletions at 15q11–q13	@70 per cent of cases
• paternal isodisomy of 15q11–q13	@2 per cent of cases
• imprinting defects at 15q11–q13	@3 per cent of cases
• mutations in the ubiquitin-protein ligase gene (UBE3A) at Xq28	@8 per cent of cases
• TCF4 at 18q21.1	@2 per cent of cases

cases (King, Wiesner, Townsend and White 1993), typically in combination with pale blue eyes (Clayton-Smith 1993; Smith A. *et al.* 1996). (A similar hypopigmentation pattern is also seen in Prader-Willi syndrome [61] and hypomelanosis of Ito [42].) Hypopigmentation is the only feature that appears to be restricted to non-deletion cases (Saitoh *et al.* 1994).

A number of minor facial features are also reported – large, protruding jaw (prognathism); widely spaced teeth; thin upper lip; wide mouth; tongue protrusion (the proportion of cases in which this is reported lessens markedly with age); deepset eyes – but limited data is available on how commonly these features are found. In one study, tongue protrusion was found in all cases (Buntinx *et al.* 1995). A squint is reported in 40 per cent of cases, and curvature of the spine (scoliosis) in 10 per cent.

Delayed early motor and communication milestones are typical. Feeding problems are also common, and in three–quarters of cases early problems are seen in sucking. Consequently there is often poor early weight gain.

Severe learning difficulty is typical, as are concentration difficulties and hyperactive behaviour.

Individuals with AS are sociable and laugh frequently during social exchanges.

As in many other ASD syndromes, a poor sleep–wake pattern or diminished sleep is common, as are fascination with running water and tactile materials such as crinkly paper or plastic, and increased heat sensitivity. Food-related and gastrointestinal problems are also commonly reported – obsessions with certain foodstuffs, diet-related obesity and constipation in particular.

A recent consensus on diagnostic criteria for AS has been produced (Williams *et al.* 2006).

The clinical features of AS persist into adulthood (Sandanam *et al.* 1997).

A positive response to the high-pitched sound of a tuning fork has been suggested to discriminate those with AS. However, this is based on a small sample of seven cases so far reported (Hall 2002; Hall and Cadle 2002).

WHAT DO WE KNOW ABOUT THE GENETIC MECHANISMS? Several genetic mechanisms can result in Angelman syndrome (see table on p.125).

The mechanisms underpinning AS are therefore complex and involve a number of discrete epigenetic mechanisms (Lalande and Calciano 2007).

The association with 15q11–q13 has been well described in a number of studies (Baker, Piven, Schwartz and Patil 1994; Bolton *et al.* 2004; Shao *et al.* 2003; Thomas, Roberts and Browne 2003). For the link with UBE3A, see Kishino, Lalande and Wagstaff (1997).

The majority of AS cases result from *de novo* deletions at 15q11–q13. These are expected to have a low risk of recurrence. In one series, 87 per cent of 93 AS cases were due to such deletions (Chan *et al.* 1993), in another, 75 per cent of cases (18/24) (Malcolm *et al.* 1990), and in a further study, 100 per cent of 25 cases (Smith, J.C. *et al.* 1992). A low recurrence risk is also seen in paternal isodisomy cases (Stalker and Williams 1998). Recurrence risks for AS arising from imprinting defects or mutations of UBE3A, which account for some 13 per cent of cases, can, in contrast, be as high as 50 per cent.

An interesting fact is that a gene deletion at 15q11–q13 that results in AS if inherited from the mother can cause Prader-Willi syndrome [61] if inherited from the father (Donlon 1988; Knoll *et al.* 1989). It seems that the specific genes sufficient for the two conditions are slightly different, but lie side by side, and both genes are often affected in either condition (Jiang, Tsai, Bressler and Braudet 1998).

A number of patients with a clinical diagnosis of AS on clinical and behavioural phenotype have been shown to have a MeCP2 deletion on subsequent genetic testing. This may be because the MeCP2 difference found in Rett syndrome interferes with UBE3A expansion, an imprinting defect seen in 25 per cent of AS cases (Makedonski et al. 2005).

In a series of 86 AS cases, two were found to have TCF4 mutations (Takano et al. 2010). If this is replicated in other samples, it suggests that perhaps two per cent of AS cases, negative for lesions at 15q11–q13 or Xq28, result from mutations at this site.

Approximately 70 per cent of cases are caused by absence of a maternal contribution to the imprinted region on chromosome 15q11–q13, two per cent from paternal uniparental isodisomy of the same region and some two–three per cent from imprinting defects of this region. The other 25 per cent of cases appear to result from mutations to the gene for ubiquitin-protein ligase at Xq28 (Kishino, Lalande and Wagstaff 1997). Prader-Willi syndrome [61] is a clinically distinct disorder resulting from paternal deletion of part of the same 15q11–q13 region.

IS THERE A LINK BETWEEN AS AND ASD?
Two recent overviews have suggested that there is a low prevalence of ASD in the AS population (Cohen D. et al. 2005; Veltman, Craig and Bolton 2005). However, a number of co-morbid cases have been described in the literature, and two recent studies outlined below do suggest a high prevalence of ASD in people with AS. A number of papers are suggestive of a link:

• The first publication to suggest that AS and ASD could co-occur was by Bundey et al. (1994). They described a single male case with a maternally inherited 15q11–q13 duplication, autism, epilepsy and ataxia.

• Williams, Lossie and Driscoll (2001) suggest that AS may have a phenotype that mimics other conditions such as ASD.

• Trillingsgaard and Østergaard (2004) assessed 16 children with AS on the ADOS-G (Autism Diagnostic Observation Scale – Generic). Ten fulfilled criteria for ASD and three for PDD-NOS. The authors felt that there was possible overdiagnosis of ASD due to the severity of co-morbid learning disability.

• Peters, Beaudet, Madduri and Bacino (2004) used the ADOS-G and ADI-R to characterize autistic symptomology in a sample of 19 children with AS. They found that dysregulation of the UBE3A was most likely to be seen in those who fulfilled criteria for ASD. Eight children (42 per cent) fulfilled ADOS-G criteria for ASD.

• Bonati et al. (2007) also found ASD diagnosis in AS cases to be associated with UBE3A mutation. They reviewed 23 AS cases and found 14 (61 per cent) to meet criteria for co-morbid ASD diagnosis on the ADOS algorithm. ASD diagnosis in this group tends to be associated with lower developmental level, and this is in turn linked to a higher rate of repetitive sensory and motor behaviour and poorer communication skills.

• Pelc, Cheron and Dan (2008) reviewed the studies on autistic behaviour in AS, and concluded that there was a risk of overdiagnosis due to the nature of the social and communication impairments seen in AS.

For a general discussion of the relationship between autism and 15q11–q13 disorders, see Dykes, Sutcliffe and Levitt (2004).

DIFFERENTIAL DIAGNOSIS: Several conditions can present with a similar phenotype to Angelman syndrome (Williams, Lossie and Driscoll 2001). Some have been linked to ASD: 22q13 deletion syndrome [7] and mitochondrial conditions such as HEADD syndrome [39]; in girls, Rett syndrome [63a] can sometimes be confused with Angelman syndrome. In addition, present with similar features cerebral palsy and Mowat-Wilson syndrome (Zweier *et al.* 2005).

A number of case reports have detailed multiple affected children in the same family and led to the initial conclusions concerning a genetic basis to AS. (See, for example, Baraitser *et al.* 1987; Robb *et al.* 1989.)

A recent review (Jedele 2007) has pointed to the clinical overlap between Angelman and Rett syndromes, and possible commonalities at the level of their biological bases.

MORE DETAILED GENETIC INFORMATION:
1. *Maternal 15q deletions and genomic imprinting:* These are the most common basis to AS, being found as newly occurring lesions in approximately 70 per cent of all cases.

- Magenis *et al.* (1988) proposed that patients with AS and Prader-Willi syndrome share an identical deletion on chromosome 15q11. They did suggest that the more severe learning and communication difficulties typically seen in AS were likely to be due to larger deletions. More recent work has shown that most of the genes responsible for AS and Prader-Willi syndrome are overlapping and are in the same region of 15q11–q13, but are different both in position and in mode of action (Jiang, Tsai, Bressler and Braudet 1998; Saitoh *et al.* 1998).

- A high-resolution cytogenetic study of ten children with AS, and their parents in nine cases, and seven children with Prader-Willi syndrome (Magenis *et al.* 1990) found that the same proximal band, 15q11.2, was deleted in both disorders. In AS, the deletion tended to be larger, though of variable size, including q12 and part of q13. AS was maternally inherited, while in Prader-Willi syndrome the deletion was typically inherited from the father.

- Two families provide evidence in support of genomic imprinting. The first

Table B11.2: Differential diagnoses similar to Angelman syndrome

• Rett syndrome (see Scheffer, Brett, Wilson and Baraitser 1990; Watson *et al.* 2001)	[63a]
• Alpha-thalassaemia retardation syndrome (ATR-X) (see Williams, Lossie and Driscoll 2001)	[81]
• Gurrieri syndrome (see Williams, Lossie and Driscoll 2001)	[83]
• MTHFR deficiency (see Williams, Lossie and Driscoll (2001))	[85]
• Cerebral palsy	
• Pervasive developmental delay	

(Greenstein 1990) came from a kindred in which both Prader-Willi and AS were presented, with maternal transmission of AS and paternal transmission of Prader-Willi syndrome. In the second family also (Hulten *et al.* 1991), with two cases of Prader-Willi syndrome and one of AS, females passed on the predisposition to AS, while males passed on the risk of Prader-Willi syndrome.

2. Defects in the imprinting centre

- A small (6kb) area of chromosome 15 has been established as sufficient to cause AS, while insufficient to cause Prader-Willi syndrome (Saitoh *et al.* 1998).

- Methylation abnormalities consistent with imprinting defects have been reported in several studies (Beuten *et al.* 1996; Reiss *et al.* 1994).

- In an interesting pair of papers (Wagstaff *et al.* 1992; Wagstaff, Shugart and Lalande 1993), AS was transmitted from a grandfather through his son to three sisters, who in turn had four children with AS, indicating that maternal transmission was necessary for expression. A sister of the grandfather had transmitted the same genotype to four children, all of whom were phenotypically normal. This finding is consistent with the view that the effects of the imprinting centre involved in AS and Prader-Willi syndrome depend for their expression on the sex of the grandparent transmitting the difference (Buiting *et al.* 1995). This suggestion was borne out by further work suggesting a grandparent-of-origin effect in a series of cases where an imprinting basis to AS was found (Buiting *et al.* 1998).

3. Possible imprinting defects associated with male infertility treatment

- A number of cases have been reported where AS has been linked to a particular form of treatment for infertility – intracytoplasmic sperm injection (ICSI) (Cox *et al.* 2002; Orstavik *et al.* 2003; Sanchez-Albisua *et al.* 2007).

- Some evidence counts against the mechanism, that had been thought to operate, specifically an increased risk of faulty imprinting. This is due to the way in which the sperm are taken from subfertile fathers (Hartmann *et al.* 2006).

- In a further series of 16 people with AS born to subfertile couples (Ludwig *et al.* 2005), it appeared that the link to fertility difficulties was a more general one, and that such problems might in some more general way increase the chance of an AS conception, rather than being specific to ICSI.

4. Paternal uniparental disomy:
In approximately two per cent of cases AS can be caused by inheritance of both copies of 15q11–q13 from the father (Malcolm *et al.* 1991). The ways in which such paternal uniparental isodisomy can arise are reviewed in Engel (1993).

5. Mutations in the UBE3A gene

- Mutations of UBE3A were first noted as a cause of AS in 1997 (Matsuura *et al.* 1997).

- In a study of 56 AS patients, 30 per cent had a number of disease-causing mutations of UBE3A (Fang *et al.* 1999).

- In a separate case series (Lossie *et al.* 2001), seven out of 104 AS cases had UBE3A mutations. Those with UBE3A changes tended to be less severely affected, were taller and heavier than others with AS and were less likely to require antiepileptic medication.

- Two first cousins have been reported with the same UBE3A frameshift mutations but with discordant phenotypes – one with AS, the other with severe asymmetric motor problems (Molfetta *et al.* 2004) – suggesting possible cell mosaicism.

- In 7/45 screened AS cases without obvious 15q11–13 abnormalities, UBE3A mutations were identified. In addition, all cases were screened for MeCP2 mutations but none were found (Hitchins *et al.* 2004).

6. *Genotype–phenotype associations:* 15q11–q13 deletion forms of AS appear to be more severely affected than non-deletion forms (due to parental isodisomy, imprinting defects and UBE3A mutations (Moncla *et al.* 1999).

- A series of seven patients has been reported (Gillessen-Kaesbach *et al.* 1999) with mild learning disability, obesity and hypotonia, but none of the other characteristics typical of AS. Methylation studies of two AS-specific sites – SNRPN and D15S63 – were consistent with AS, but chromosome analyses were routinely normal, suggesting a possible mosaicism or partial imprinting defect.

- In a small study comparing 21 deletion with four uniparental isodisomy cases, age at diagnosis was later for uniparental isodisomy cases, in whom walking tended to be earlier, language development was less impaired, and epilepsy developed later (Fridman *et al.* 2000).

- A further study compared presentation in 58 AS patients, of whom nine had a uniparental isodisomy (Varela, Kok, Otto and Koiffmann 2004). Again, uniparental isodisomy (UPD) was associated with lower severity of associated difficulties – swallowing problems were seen in 73.9 per cent of deletion cases, and only 22.2 per cent

of UPD cases. Hypotonia was seen in 73.3 per cent of deletion and 28.57 per cent of UPD cases. Those with UPD were less likely to take seizures (44.4 per cent vs 89.4 per cent) or be microcephalic (11.1 per cent vs 54.35 per cent). They were more likely to have speech (33.3 per cent vs 8.5 per cent), and were reported as more able. They were also more likely to be overweight (55.5 >75 percentile vs 17.5 >75 percentile). The authors suggest that AS secondary to UPD was more likely to go undetected as a consequence of the less severe phenotype. Average age at UPD case diagnosis was nine years.

- In addition, Varela, Kok, Otto and Koiffmann (2004) compared groups with the two most common 15q deletion forms of AS – Class 1, who have BP1 and BP3 breakpoints (N = 13), and Class 2, who have BP2 and BP3 breakpoints (N = 22). Low muscle tone was more common in the Class 1 cases (84.6 per cent vs 61.1 per cent), as was lack of speech (100 per cent vs 61.9 per cent). Swallowing difficulties, in contrast, were more common in Class 2 cases (75 per cent vs 42.85 per cent). Mean age at diagnosis was 5y4m for Class 1 and 6y1m for Class 2.

The above studies suggest that there is some merit in subclassifying AS dependent on the genetic basis. However, the numbers analysed to date are small and the findings need to be treated as preliminary.

MANAGEMENT AND TREATMENT: At the time of writing, there is no specific treatment for AS. The findings concerning specific GABA receptor abnormalities may lead to development of specific targeted medications for the seizure problems in AS (Meldrum and Rogawski 2007).

As there is a specific deletion in the GABA-A receptor region linked to the presence of seizure activity in AS (Saitoh *et al.* 1992), and as this has been implicated in the excitatory–inhibitory balance in epilepsy (Fritschy 2008), it seems possible that medications which have a specific effect on GABA-A function, such as stiripentol, could potentially be beneficial. Stiripentol has not been licensed in Europe or the USA for this purpose, but is used with a much wider range of seizure conditions in Asia. (See discussion of zonizamide in Shorvon 2005.)

Many people with AS have epilepsy that is poorly controlled on existing medications. In one series of 45 AS cases, Valente, Koiffmann *et al.* (2006) reported four who had been poorly controlled on drug therapies, but whose epilepsy responded well to ketogenic diet. (For further discussion of ketogenic diets, see Aitken 2009.) A survey of 150 UK families found only one that was using ketogenic diet, but in this case there was reported to be a good response, with improved seizure control (Ruggieri and McShane 1998). Currently Massachusetts General Hospital Pediatric Epilepsy Program is conducting a study of low GI diets in AS and their effect on seizure control.

There is some evidence of beneficial effects of melatonin for the sleep problems seen in AS (Braam, Didden, Smits and Curfs 2008). Melatonin supplementation can reduce time taken getting to sleep, lengthen time slept and reduce night wakening. (Currently, melatonin is available as an over-the-counter supplement in the USA but prescription-only in the UK.) To date there has been no work to investigate whether there is an abnormal pattern of melatonin production in AS, as has been reported in a number of other conditions linked to ASD (Kulman *et al.* 2000; Tordjman *et al.* 2005).

Early work to maximize communication skills is important, given the progressive nature of the communication difficulties in many cases. Simple forms of communication using alternative and augmentative systems should be emphasized, given that the likely level of adult communication will be limited.

Other aspects to care and management should be dealt with on a case-by-case basis, depending on clinical presentation – gastrointestinal problems should be investigated where present, and likewise obsessive and stereotyped behaviours.

ANIMAL MODELS: Several mouse models of AS have been developed (Sinkkonen, Homanics and Korpi 2003). In the earliest of these (Cattanach *et al.* 1997), it was shown that mice with paternal duplication of the area on mouse chromosome 7, analogous to 15q11–q13 in human DNA, exhibited characteristics analogous to AS. Although of small skeletal size, these mice showed progressive obesity, a feature noted in a subset of AS patients (Smith A. *et al.* 1996). In addition, they had smaller brains and abnormal patterns of brain electrical activity. From weaning they exhibited hyperactivity on open-field testing.

In a transgenic mouse model (Jiang, Tsai, Bressler and Braudet 1998), with UBE3A knocked out (the Xq28 gene defect seen in up to 25 per cent of human AS cases), abnormal hippocampal and Purkinje cell development together with an AS-like behavioural phenotype were seen.

A further group (DeLorey *et al.* 1998; Handforth, Delorey, Homanics and Olsen 2005) has studied the role of the GABRB3 gene in the development of epilepsy in a mouse model of Angelman syndrome. As this results in the lack of the β_3 subunit of the $GABA_A$ receptor, it is likely to be the biological basis to epilepsy in AS cases, other than in those caused by UBE3A defects. GABRB3 differences have been reported in autism (Buxbaum *et al.* 2002), and the genetic location of GABRB3 is adjacent to UBE3A on chromosome 15. UBE3A abnormalities were also found to be overrepresented in autistic family pedigrees (Nurmi *et al.* 2001).

A recent paper (Wu Y. *et al.* 2008) has described the development of several drosophila mutations that have defects in the genetic equivalent to UBE3A (dube3a). This may provide one of the most promising animal models for future research.

A useful review of research developments in AS that discussed the animal work on GABA$_A$ and NMDA receptor function can be found in Dan (2008).

FURTHER INFORMATION:

- A useful summary and resource listing can be found in Randi Hagerman's excellent, if slightly dated, little book, *Neurodevelopmental Disorders: Diagnosis and Treatment*, published by Oxford University Press (Hagerman 1999).

- Information on a study of ketogenic diet sponsored by the Angelman Syndrome Foundation can be found at www.angelman.org.

- For one family's account of their child with AS who responded to ketogenic diet, see www.ourangeltyler.com.

12.

Apert syndrome

GENE LOCUS: 10q26

KEY ASD REFERENCE: Morey-Canellas, Sivagamasundari and Barton 2003

SUMMARY: Apert syndrome is a genetic disorder caused by defects in the FGFR2 gene at 10q26. It results in abnormal skull growth and fusion of the fingers and toes.

It is one of a group of craniosynostosis syndromes. (For reviews, see Cohen 1973, 1977.)

Apert syndrome is a rare condition characterized by an unusual skull shape – brachysphenocephaly – and dental abnormalities that increase the complexity of dental management (Hohoff *et al.* 2007). In typical cases, a single fingernail joins across fingers two to four. The first clinical description, of the skull shape and syndactyly of the hands and feet, was published in France in 1906 (Apert 1906).

There is a clinical overlap, in terms of the skull abnormalities seen, with a number of other conditions: Carpenter, Crouzon and Pfeiffer syndromes; isolated cloverleaf skull, and thanatophoric dysplasia. Differentiation is on genetic criteria and on clinical phenotype – in Crouzon syndrome, for example, chronic herniation of the cerebellar tonsils is far more common, being seen in over 70 per cent of cases, as opposed to between two and 17 per cent of Apert cases (Cinalli *et al.* 1995; Quintero-Rivera *et al.* 2006). Fusion of the spinal vertebrae is common in Apert (affecting some 68 per cent, and usually vertebrae C5–C6), while in Crouzon syndrome it is seen in @25 per cent of cases (usually affecting vertebrae C2–C3 only) (Kreiborg, Barr and Cohen 1992). To date Apert syndrome is the only craniosynostosis condition in which ASD has been reported.

Based on a large series of cases (N = 136), cardiovascular (10 per cent) and genitourinary abnormalities (9.6 per cent) are common in this population, and should be screened for. Gastrointestinal anomalies are less common (1.5 per cent) (Cohen and Kreiborg 1993).

Cases are typically sporadic (there is no family association). However, familial inheritance has been reported, with two families having an affected mother and daughter (Roberts and Hall 1971; Weech 1927); one an affected mother and son (Van den Bosch cited in Blank 1960); one an affected father and daughter (Rollnick 1988); and one in which two sisters were affected (Allanson 1986).

HOW COMMON IS APERT SYNDROME? In the only large epidemiological survey, carried out in California by the California Birth Defects Monitoring Program, prevalence was found to be one in 80,645 live births, based on a population cohort of 53 cases in a total population of almost 2.5 million births (Tolarova, Harris, Ordway and Vargervik 1997). Apert syndrome did not show a sex bias, being as common in boys and girls, was most prevalent in Asiatic families, and was associated with advanced paternal age with almost 50 per cent of fathers being over 35 at the time of the affected child's birth (Tolarova, Harris, Ordway and Vargervik 1997). The prevalence figures agree reasonably well with an earlier Hungarian study which reported a birth prevalence of one per 101,010 live births (Czeizel, Elek and Susanszky 1993), and a multi-population survey which reported a slightly higher rate of one per 64,516 live births (Cohen et al. 1992).

The literature is varied on developmental level in Apert syndrome. In one early series of cases, 14/29 cases were of normal or borderline normal IQ, while the rest of the sample had IQs of 70 or below (Patton, Goodship, Hayward and Lansdown 1988). A survey of known cases with obvious central nervous system abnormalities (Cohen and Kreiborg 1990), which may therefore have been weighted towards more severe presentations, concluded that a high proportion of cases, many of whom had callosal and limbic abnormalities and nonprogressive hydrocephalus, had significant learning disabilities.

MAIN CLINICAL FEATURES: Apert syndrome is a congenital disorder characterized primarily by craniosynostosis, midface hypoplasia, and syndactyly of the hands and feet, with a tendency to fusion of bony structures. Cases are typically *de novo* and sporadic. However, autosomal dominant inheritance has also been reported (Mantilla-Capacho, Arnaud, Diaz-Rodriguez and Barros-Nunez 2005). Fusion of the fingers is varied in severity, from all digits being fused (so-called 'mitten hand') to fusion across the second to fourth digits, with similar variability in the extent of toe fusion. Occasionally, additional digits are also seen. In general the upper limbs are more severely affected (Cohen and Kreiborg 1995). A coding system for severity of syndactyly has been developed (Wilkie et al. 1995).

The skin is typically moist, and becomes oily at adolescence, with a tendency to acne (Cohen and Kreiborg 1993, 1995).

In a review of brain imaging results from 30 patients with Apert syndrome, Quintero-Rivera et al. (2006) reported on 30 patients. A variety of abnormalities were documented – three–quarters had dilated cerebral ventricles, while 1/6 showed absence of the septum pellucidum and 1/6 had low cerebellar tonsils (both also indicative of periods of increased CSF pressure); two-thirds had abnormal formation of the semi-circular canals in the inner ear, approximately a quarter had partial agenesis of the corpus callosum, while hydrocephalus was found in 13 per cent. Given these signs of raised CSF pressure, it is unsurprising that 28/30 cases had jugular foraminal stenosis, as is reported in cases where raised intracranial pressure is associated with craniosynostosis (Rich, Cox and Hayward 2003).

Progressive synostosis seems to be the typical feature, though the degree of fusion and pattern of progression is varied (Blank 1960; Schauerte and St-Aubin 1966).

In two series of cases with Aperts syndrome where intelligence was assessed, normal or borderline normal IQ was seen in approximately 50 per cent of cases (Patton, Goodship, Hayward and Lansdown 1988; Reiner *et al.* 1996). In the Reiner *et al.* series, early cranial surgery to decompress the skull seemed to be associated with better cognitive outcome, as was continuing to live with their biological family.

Additional fingers and toes have been reported to date in nine cases, but only in one where genetic confirmation of a FGFR2 mutation has been carried out (Mantilla-Capacho, Arnaud, Diaz-Rodriguez and Barros-Nunez 2005).

A range of ophthalmic problems is common, but many are amenable to craniofacial surgical correction (Khong *et al.* 2006).

One study has analysed proliferation and differentiation of calvaria cells (bone cells taken from the base of the skull) from infants and foetuses with FGFR2 mutations (Lomri *et al.* 1998). The findings suggest premature development and increased numbers of cells that go on to form skull bone in Apert syndrome, resulting in the abnormal rate and pattern of growth. If similar distal acceleration of osteoblast formation is seen (perhaps with greater severity in the P253R variant mutation, in which a higher severity of syndactyly is seen), this may be the primary mechanism which accounts for the physical phenotype.

A 1995 paper (Wilkie *et al.* 1995) presented 40 unrelated cases of Apert syndrome and found one of two mutations in exon 7 of the FGFR2 gene: S252W (176943.0010) or P253R (176943.0011).

Oldridge *et al.* (1999) studied a series of 260 cases of Apert syndrome. They found that two mutations in the fibroblast growth factor receptor (FGFR2) accounted for 257 of their cases. (172 showed the S252W mutation; 85 the P253R mutation.) Two further patients had an aluminium-element insertion in or near exon 9. A further case series found the two mutations accounted for 35 of 36 cases (Lajeunie *et al.* 1999), again with @ two-thirds of cases showing the S252W mutation. A different large FGFR2 (in exon IIIb) has been reported in Apert syndrome in association with craniosynostosis (Bochukova *et al.* 2009).

The likelihood of FGFR2 mutations in sperm increases with age (Glaser *et al.* 2003), and a paternal age effect has been noted. New mutations causing Apert syndrome seem to arise exclusively from the father (Moloney *et al.* 1996). The ageing effect is not sufficient to explain the birth pattern of Apert syndrome, and various other mechanisms have been considered.

In one study of 36 Apert cases, there was no clear differentiation between the clinical features seen with the two most common FGFR2 mutations (Park W-J. *et al.* 1995). Another series of 70 unrelated cases found the S252W mutation to be more commonly associated with cleft palate, while the P253R mutation was seen with more severe syndactyly (Slaney *et al.* 1996). These differences have some implications for the likely benefits of cosmetic surgery (von Gernet *et al.* 2000).

Considerable phenotypic variation is seen across individuals with the same genetic basis to their condition (Lajeunie *et al.* 1999). Some individuals with the gene markers do not show evidence of craniosynostosis, while others have forms of syndactyly atypical to those typically reported.

IS THERE A LINK BETWEEN APERT SYNDROME AND ASD? Morey-Canellas, Sivagamasundari and Barton (2003) have described a seven-year-old boy with Apert syndrome, developmental delay and ASD.

The reported link to autistic spectrum disorder is consistent with the evidence of increased head growth in ASD (Maimburg and Vaeth 2006). The structural brain studies report abnormalities of the cerebellum and limbic system, both areas implicated in ASD pathogenesis (Raymond, Bauman and Kemper 1996; Schumann and Amaral 2006).

DIFFERENTIAL DIAGNOSIS: Several other conditions characterized by craniosynostosis, midface hypoplasia and syndactyly need to be considered: Crouzon syndrome (Glaser *et al.* 2000); Jackson-Weiss syndrome (Jackson *et al.* 1976); and Pfeiffer syndrome (Cohen 1973, 1977).

MANAGEMENT AND TREATMENT: To date, no Apert-specific treatment strategies are known, but could, presumably, target processes such as calvaria cell differentiation and osteoblast formation. The high rate of ventricular enlargement could also provide a focus for earlier identification and treatment.

ANIMAL MODELS: To date, animal models of Apert syndrome are limited. One study (Hajihosseini, Wilson, De Moerlooze and Dickson 2001) found that abnormalities of a fibroblast growth factor receptor in mice affected embryogenesis, resulting in an Apert/Pfeiffer-like physical phenotype (FgfR2-IIIc), suggesting that the two FGFR2 mutations seen in over 90 per cent of the cases reported by Park *et al.* (Park W-J. 1995) are likely to be causal.

PARENTAL ACCOUNT: McDermott, J. (2000) *Babyface: A Story of Heart and Bones.* Bethesda: Woodbine House.

13.

ARX gene mutations

GENE LOCUS: Xp22.1.1–p22.3

KEY ASD REFERENCES: Kato *et al.* 2004; Sherr 2003; Strømme *et al.* 2002c; Turner *et al.* 2002

SUMMARY: ARX stands for the 'aristaless related homeobox gene', important in the development of the brain. This group of conditions has sometimes been called Partington syndrome after the principal author of the first paper to describe them (Partington *et al.* 1988). ARX gene mutations are a group of X-linked conditions that typically combine mild to moderate learning disability and dystonic hand movements with a variable physical phenotype. ARX mutations are seen in approximately one per cent of learning disabled populations, but the rate of co-morbid ASDs is currently unclear.

HOW COMMON IS ARX? ARX is a well documented but rare cause of autism in learning disabled populations. ARX screening is warranted, however, in autistic individuals with severe learning disability, on the basis of the range of disorders that have now been documented in such individuals with Xp22.1.1–p22.3 mutations.

A recent Danish study screened 682 males with learning difficulties and found only seven with ARX mutations (Grønskov, Hjalgrim, Nielsen and Brondum-Nielsen 2004), concluding that it was a rare cause of learning disability. A small number of autistic individuals were also examined; none were found to have ARX mutations. ARX mutation was also found in 1/188 normal male controls.

How ARX mutations affect development, through transcription repression, is just beginning to be understood (McKenzie *et al.* 2007). This is through the binding of the ARX protein to a molecule called TLE (Groucho/transducin-like enhancer of split cofactor proteins).

MAIN CLINICAL FEATURES: The clinical spectrum seen with ARX mutations is broad. This is not too surprising, given the large number of reported mutations. ARX mutations have been implicated in a range of disorders with severe mental retardation, including West syndrome, with a variable phenotype that can include lissencephaly, hand dystonia, epilepsy, autism, and abnormalities of the genitals.

Subsequent studies have indicated a wide variation in clinical presentation with the same mutation (Partington, Turner, Boyle and Gecz 2004). In one study of 18 individuals with the same ARX defect, all had learning disability but only two-thirds had hand dystonia, and one third epileptiform EEGs, so that the majority could be said to have Partington syndrome, while one third could not (Szczaluba *et al.* 2006).

The combined prevalence of ARX mutations warrants systematic screening in non-syndromic X-linked learning disability syndromes (Poirier *et al.* 2006). To date, some 59 ARX mutations have been reported in seven different X-linked clinical disorders associated with learning disability. (For an overview, see Gecz, Cloosterman and Partington 2006.)

ARX mutations have been reported in a subgroup of West syndrome (a condition with infantile spasms, an unusual EEG pattern (hypsarrythmia), and progressive learning disability) (Scheffer *et al.* 2002), in Ohtahara syndrome (another early onset seizure disorder with an unusual EEG pattern of 'burst-suppression') (Kato *et al.* 2007), and in a recently described syndrome of infantile spasms, subclinical seizures, and complex movements (Poirier *et al.* 2008).

As cases accumulate, clear associations between specific ARX defects and specific clinical and endophenotypes are being found (Kato *et al.* 2004). Clearly, interference with the ARX homeobox can have wide effects across a range of characteristics (usually called pleiotropy).

Generally, larger deletions, frameshifts, nonsense mutations (see p.360) and splice site mutations in exons 1–4 caused X-linked lissencephaly and anomalous genitalia (XLAG) (Kitamura *et al.* 2002; Uyanik *et al.* 2003) or hydranencephaly (a rare condition with normal development of the skull, but where the skull is largely filled with cerebrospinal fluid), also with abnormal genitalia (Kato *et al.* 2004). Nonconservative missense mutations within the homeobox caused less severe XLAG, whereas conservative substitution in the homeodomain caused agenesis of the corpus callosum with abnormal genitalia (Proud, Levine and Carpenter 1992).

Both syndromic and non-syndromic mental retardation can result from defects in the same ARX gene (Frints, Froyen, Marynen and Fryrs 2002).

One XLAG case has been reported with significant gastrointestinal involvement, with severe watery diarrhoea that responded to a medication, octreotide, that reduces intestinal secretion (Nanba, Oka and Ohno 2007). There is no evidence at present on the prevalence of such symptoms in ARX.

IS THERE A LINK BETWEEN ARX AND ASD?

- The first paper to suggest a link between ARX mutations and ASD was Strømme et al. (2002c). This paper presented data on ARX screening in 50 learning disabled cases. Four of those screened had co-morbid autism, all with the 428–451 duplication mutation.

- Kato et al. (2004) also note the association between ASD and a mild ARX mutation phenotype, but do not go into any detail in the paper on this association.

- Two studies have explicitly looked for, but failed to find ARX autistic cases:

  ○ Grønskov, Hjalgrim, Nielsen and Brondum-Nielsen (2004) established a general population rate of 1/188 for ARX mutations, but failed to find evidence of ARX defects in a small number of autistic cases examined.

  ○ Chaste et al. (2007) screened 226 males with ASD and failed to find evidence of ARX mutations in this group.

- Strømme et al. (2002b) identified the ARX gene, and its association with X-linked mental retardation and epilepsy. Using Northern blotting and expressed sequence tag (EST) analyses, their work indicates that ARX is expressed predominantly in foetal and adult brain and skeletal muscle. In animals, the same group identified ARX protein as important in various types of nerve cells in the cortex, and in axonal guidance (Strømme et al. 2002b).

ARX is transmitted as an X-linked recessive condition, so female carriers are clinically unaffected.

DIFFERENTIAL DIAGNOSIS: There is wide variation within the ARX mutation group, with a number of clinical disorders being defined. However, the genotype–phenotype variation is wide, and as screening studies are being conducted, unaffected ARX carrier males are being identified (Grønskov, Hjalgrim, Nielsen and Brondum-Nielsen 2004), The presence of lissencephaly, with ambiguous development of the genitalia, coupled with hand dystonia, is fairly unambiguously related to ARX mutation; however, the range of more mildly presenting phenotypes – typically with learning disability, but occasionally without, often with seizure activity or abnormalities on EEG – strongly suggests that this is a potential diagnosis in a wider range of ASD cases. The presence of dysarthria (in a quarter of cases) and long, triangular facial features has been remarked upon (Szczaluba et al. 2006).

MANAGEMENT AND TREATMENT: There are few specific treatments that have been investigated for the management of ARX. In some single case reports patients have proved responsive to symptomatic treatments (Kato et al. 2003) and treatment of gastrointestinal symptoms with octreotide (Nanba, Oka and Ohno 2007).

Treatment at present needs to be focused on the presenting clinical features – appropriate physiotherapy and occupational therapy for the motor control issues, where present; treatment for seizures, where present and depending on presentation; and assessment and treatment of gastrointestinal features, where present.

At the present time there is no specific approach to treatment and management. The characterization of the condition as affecting primarily GABAergic neuronal systems suggests that treatments targeting glutamate pathways may hold some promise, as has been the case in fragile-X, where the mGLUr5 receptor is affected.

ANIMAL MODELS: In animal models, the ARX protein genes are expressed primarily in the cerebral cortex and brain floorplate, suggesting a similar role in human brain development and maintenance (Miura, Yanazawa, Kato and Kitamura 1997).

A detailed study of ARX expression in developing and adult mouse neurons found that ARX is most strongly expressed in GABAergic neurons, throughout the central nervous system, in the developing mouse brain, and more specifically in the amygdala and olfactory bulb in the adult (Poirier *et al.* 2004). It is also strongly expressed in testes (Kitamura *et al.* 2002) and pancreas (Collombat *et al.* 2003).

The exception is that there is no expression of ARX in the cerebellum at any stage of the development of the mouse nervous system (Bienvenu *et al.* 2002).

The expression in GABAergic neurons, and selective interference with these systems resulting from ARX mutations, could account for the high prevalence of epilepsy in ARX mutation syndromes, and for interference with the sense of smell (Yoshihara *et al.* 2005).

Three of the ARX mutations reported in humans have been found to produce learning problems, epilepsy and lissencephaly when mutated in mouse models (Kitamura *et al.* 2009).

14.

Autism secondary to autoimmune lymphoproliferative syndrome (ALPS)

aka
- Canale-Smith syndrome
- Evans syndrome
- autoimmune haemolytic anaemia
- idiopathic thrombocytopenia
- Coombs-positive hemolytic anaemia
- immune thrombocytopenia

GENE LOCUS: 10q24.1

KEY ASD REFERENCE: Shenoy, Arnold and Chatila 2000

SUMMARY: ALPS is a rare condition that affects the production of a key protein involved in immune function. Often it goes unnoticed and is not diagnosed until well into adult life. A single case linked to ASD has so far been described, with regressive onset of ASD symptomology at around 18 months of age. At the present time, although it has been widely cited in the literature, it is uncertain whether the association is a chance finding or is of biological relevance.

Table B14: Conditions with presentations similar to ALPS

- common variable immunodeficiency disease (CVID) (Piqueras *et al.* 2003) – although features of both can be seen in the same individuals with caspase-8 mutations (Chun *et al.* 2002)
- hyper IgM (HIGM) syndrome
- X-linked lymphoproliferative syndrome (XLP)
- Wiskott-Aldrich syndrome (WAS)
- B-cell or T-cell lymphoma

HOW COMMON IS ALPS? The prevalence is currently not established. The condition is found in both sexes, and appears not to be more common in particular racial or ethnic populations.

The limited data available indicate that the condition can be compatible with survival well into adult life (Drappa *et al.* 1996).

ALPS is a fairly recently recognized condition. The earliest clinical description of ALPS (Canale and Smith 1967) suggested a common clinical presentation in childhood, with enlargement of the lymph glands and the spleen, autoimmune haemolytic anaemia and thrombocytopenia. Later series (for example, Straus, Lenardo and Puck 1997) suggest greater clinical variability.

Essentially, ALPS is a condition where cells produced by the immune system accumulate, with resulting enlargement of the lymph nodes and the spleen. These are secondary problems, with autoimmune damage to other organ systems, including anaemia due to the destruction of red blood cells.

Two recent reviews summarize the features and genetics of the condition (Bleesing, Johnson and Zhang 2007; Le Deist 2004). One paper has raised the possibility that any association between ALPS and ASD is coincidental (Accardo and Roseman 2000).

MAIN CLINICAL FEATURES: ALPS is a pleiotropic condition, whose clinical presentation can vary (Straus, Lenardo and Puck 1997). The most common presenting features are: an enlarged spleen and liver (often seen referred to as 'hepatospenomegaly'); enlarged lymph nodes, especially in the neck and under the arms; urticarial skin rashes; and frequent nosebleeds and bruising, with lengthened clotting time for cuts and abrasions. Slow wound healing and haemolytic anaemia are characteristic, with low platelet levels, an increase in certain types of white blood cells (including a rarer form with double-negative T-cells) (Holzelova *et al.* 2004), and gastrointestinal symptoms. ALPS interferes with the production of a specific lymphoid protein called Fas.

The clinical features are typically apparent by age five years. Lymphoma, seen in some cases, is not typically diagnosed until late in the third decade of life (Straus *et al.* 2001), and risk can be increased by certain immunosuppressant treatment.

Fas is involved in programmed cell death (also called apoptosis, the main process by which embryonic development takes place), and in ALPS leads specifically to a build-up of immune system T-cells.

IS THERE A LINK BETWEEN ALPS AND ASD? In the *Journal of Pediatrics* in 2000, Shenoy and colleagues reported on a child who had been developmentally normal but who regressed, losing speech, gestures and eye contact at around 18 months coincident with development of lymphoproliferative symptoms and haemolytic anaemia (Shenoy, Arnold and Chatila 2000). He had regular speech and occupational therapy over the following 15 months, but continued to deteriorate. At 33 months, oral treatment with prednisone dramatically improved physical symptoms: both chronic diarrhoea and a skin rash improved. The size of his spleen and lymph nodes also reduced. There was a gradual improvement in autistic symptomology, and he had built up a vocabulary of over 200 spoken words after one year of steroid therapy.

DIFFERENTIAL DIAGNOSIS: The differential diagnosis of ALPS from other ASDs is based on the presence of lymphatic, spleen and haematologic differences. As regressive onset ASD symptomology coupled with gastrointestinal problems is being reported more frequently, gastrointestinal function should be explored in ALPS cases (Werner and Dawson 2006). Currently there is uncertainty over the aetiology (Hornig *et al.* 2008).

Differential diagnosis of ALPS from other immunodeficiency disorders can be found in Table B14.

MANAGEMENT AND TREATMENT: At present there is no treatment that can cure ALPS. Current approaches focus on limiting the effects of lymphoproliferation in the spleen and lymph system, treatment of haematologic effects, and in later years, where required, management of lymphoma. Lymphoma, when it does arise, appears as responsive to conventional treatments as lymphomas in non-ALPS presentations. Blood transfusions may be required where anaemia is severe.

Increased problems from prolonged bleeding time and slow wound healing need to be addressed, and infection risk should be kept to a minimum. Urticarial rashes should be addressed as for other contact allergic reactions.

Immunosuppressive agents are used when the condition restricts breathing or to limit autoimmune effects, but side effects can be severe and symptoms return when treatment is stopped (Bleesing 2003). Mycophenolate mofetil seems effective where there is a chronic loss of blood cells (both red and white) (Rao *et al.* 2005), and can reduce the need for steroids in such cases. Unfortunately it increases the risk of later developing lymphomas, and can increase lymphoproliferative problems associated with Epstein-Barr virus (O'Neill, Vernino, Gogan and Giannini 2007).

There are some helpful reviews of treatment and prognosis (Bleesing 2003; Bleesing, Johnson and Zhang 2007).

PREVENTION OF PRIMARY MANIFESTA-TIONS: It would appear that ALPS can be successfully treated with bone-marrow transplantation (Benkerrou *et al.* 1997; Kahwash *et al.* 2007; Sleight *et al.* 1998).

Use of steroids: Steroids are widely used as the primary treatments in acute autoimmune episodes, presenting with haemolytic anaemia and immune-mediated very low platelet counts. One common steroid is prednisone. It is often given for a short time, but sometimes it is needed for longer periods (Shenoy, Arnold and Chatila 2000). Side effects are common with long-term use and/or at high doses, so should be avoided where possible.

There are a variety of possible long-term side effects of steroid use:

* osteoporosis
* poorer wound healing
* difficulty fighting infection
* type II diabetes
* cataracts
* mood swings
* excessive weight gain
* physiological dependence.

ANIMAL MODELS: The mouse model that appears to most closely approximate to that seen in ALPS is *lpr* (Watanabe-Fukunaga *et al.* 1992), which also results in a build-up of T-cells (Krammer 2000).

In a recent study, *Fas*-deficient lymphoproliferative mice were found to develop a Parkinson's disease-like phenotype when given a dopaminergic neurotoxin that did not affect mice with normal *Fas* expression (Landau *et al.* 2005).

15.

Bannayan-Riley-Ruvalcaba syndrome

aka • BRRS

- Bannayan-Zonana syndrome (BZS)
- macrocephaly, with multiple lipomas, and haemangiomata
- macrocephaly with pseudopapilloedema, and multiple haemangiomata
- Riley-Smith syndrome
- Ruvalcaba-Myhre-Smith syndrome (RMSS)

GENE LOCUS: 10q23.31

KEY ASD REFERENCES: Boccone *et al.* 2006; Butler *et al.* 2005; Lynch, Lynch, McMenamin and Webb 2009.

SUMMARY: The term 'Bannayan-Riley-Ruvalcaba syndrome' was suggested by Cohen (1990) to unify three previously recognized syndromes with apparently similar clinical characteristics. Various other nomenclatures have been suggested, including those listed above and also PTEN MATCHS (Phosphatase and Tensin Homologue – Macrocephaly, Autosomal dominant, Thyroid disease, Cancer, Hamartomata and Skin abnormalities) (DiLiberti 1998) and PHTS (PTEN hamartoma tumour syndrome) (Marsh *et al.* 1999). BRRS is a condition that presents with macrocephaly, vascular malformations, pigmented macules and lipomas. Macrocephaly is common in ASD and has so far been reported in eight of 24 BRRS cases evaluated. PTEN defects would appear to be a common cause of macrocephaly associated with ASD.

HOW COMMON IS BRRS? Over 50 cases have been described in the clinical literature, but no true prevalence studies have been carried out. Prevalence has been estimated at one in 200,000 (Nelen *et al.* 1999).

A number of other conditions have overlapping clinical features. These include Proteus syndrome, Klippel-Trelaunay syndrome (Jacob *et al.* 1998), Cowden syndrome (Celebi *et al.* 1999; Lachlan, Lucassen, Bunyan and Temple 2007) and macrocephaly/autism syndrome. Some of the research to date suggests that Cowden syndrome and BRRS may be essentially slightly different manifestations of the same geneotype (Marsh *et al.* 1999).

MAIN CLINICAL FEATURES: BRRS is an overgrowth syndrome with associated macrocephaly, lipomas and vascular malformations. The typical presentation is early in life with macrocephaly, developmental delay and hypotonia, resulting in slower early achievement of milestones. Growths such as intestinal polyps and subcutaneous and visceral lipomas are common, as are vascular malformations. The skin is often affected with pigmented macules, often referred to as café-au-lait spots, particularly on the penis.

The earliest clear descriptions of cases with the triad of impairments now classified as BRRS were made at autopsy in a single paediatric case by George Bannayan at Johns Hopkins Hospital in Baltimore in 1971. Shortly after, Zonana, Rimoin and Davis (1976) and Zonana, Rimoin and Fisher (1976) described the same triad of features in a father and two sons.

One group (Gorlin, Cohen, Condon and Burke 1992) has suggested that a high proportion of BRRS cases have Hashimoto's thyroiditis (7/12 cases tested). At the time of writing this finding has yet to be replicated.

More complex clinical presentations in association with PTEN mutations are reported in the clinical literature. For example, one of the cases reported by Zigman *et al.* (1997) had a complex heart defect, in addition to the characteristic BRRS phenotype and bilateral clubfoot.

Because it is a lipid storage problem affecting body tissues, there had been a suggestion that BRRS may result from a 3-hydroxyacyl-coenzyme A dehydrogenase (L-CHAD) deficiency (Fryburg, Pelegano, Bennett and Bebin 1994). An earlier study suggested that this was a lipid storage myopathy based on muscle biopsy findings (DiLiberti, D'Agostino, Ruvalcaba and Schimschock 1984). DiLiberti suggested, on the basis of abnormal lipid storage test results in 13/14 cases, that there was an overlap between benign familial macrocephaly (Day and Schutt 1979), Ruvalcaba-Myhre-Smith syndrome and Bannayan-Zonana syndrome, both of the latter now being accepted as synonymous with BRRS. Subsequent research (for example, Otto *et al.* 1999) has failed to find evidence that this is a common cause of BRRS. As cases are reported where there is no evidence of a PTEN defect (Carethers *et al.* 1998), it is possible that an L-CHAD defect can result in a phenocopy disorder in a small proportion of atypical cases.

Occasional cases without a PTEN defect but with other chromosomal anomalies are reported, such as 19q translocation (Israel, Lessick, Szego and Wong 1991).

IS THERE A LINK BETWEEN BRRS AND ASD? Butler and colleagues (2005) looked at a group of 18 autistic subjects aged 3–18 (15 males and 3 females), all with macrocephaly. Three of the male subjects were found to have the PTEN mutations seen in BRRS.

PTEN mutations are seen in a number of conditions that have been linked to ASD. In addition to BRRS these include BCNS [16], Cowden syndrome [26] and Proteus syndrome [62]. PTEN is known as a tumour-suppressor gene, and defects in this gene are associated with vascular malformations and an increased risk of tumour formation. Useful discussions of the functions of PTEN can be found in Eng (2003) and Waite and Eng (2002).

- A Sardinian case has been reported (Boccone *et al.* 2006), with the classic physical features of BRRS together with autism and reactive ileo-colonic nodular lymphoid hyperplasia.

- In a recent series of six BRRS cases (Lynch, Lynch, McMenamin and Webb 2009), two were reported to have autistic features and one a diagnosis of Asperger's syndrome. In all three cases, the mother also carried the PTEN mutation.

So, although further information is required, the limited studies to date suggest that BRRS is important to investigate in ASD cases with macrocephaly.

DIFFERENTIAL DIAGNOSIS: The constellation of features overlaps with a number of other disorders, and cases have been reported variously. Sotos syndrome was reported in two cases with macrocephaly, intestinal polyps, and pigmented macules on the penis (Ruvalcaba, Myhre and Smith 1980).

MANAGEMENT AND TREATMENT: A recent study (Tan *et al.* 2007) highlights the range of vascular abnormalities with PTEN mutations and the importance of monitoring for early detection and treatment of growths in thyroid, breast and endometrial tissues. In addition, it has been recommended that there should be annual screening from infancy for intestinal hamartomas (Hendriks *et al.* 2003).

Low muscle carnitine levels are common and appear to respond to supplementation in many cases. In one study of 27 cases from 17 families (Powell, Budden and Buist 1993) increased muscle lipid content and typical clinical features were seen in all of the clinical cases studied (11) and in affected relatives (4) tested. They also had significantly low muscle carnitine levels. An L-carnitine supplement was given to all 27 cases and clinical benefit was noted in 17 (63 per cent). For a general overview of effects of carnitine deficiency, see Points and de Vivo (1995).

ANIMAL MODELS: A number of mouse models of defective production of PTEN protein have been developed. The role of the PTEN gene as a tumour suppressor has been confirmed.

Mutation in the PTEN system causes abnormal cell growth in multiple organ systems in mice (Podsypanina *et al.* 1999). PTEN deficiency can specifically accelerate mammary tumours in certain transgenic mice (Li Y. *et al.* 2001).

To date, no animal models of behavioural differences with PTEN mutations have been reported.

16.

Basal cell naevus syndrome (BCNS)

aka • nevoid basal cell carcinoma syndrome
• Gorlin syndrome
• Gorlin-Goltz syndrome
• épithéliomatose multiple généralisée

• fifth phacomatosis
• hereditary cutaneomandibular polyoncosis
• multiple basalioma syndrome

GENE LOCUS: 9q22.3

KEY ASD REFERENCE: Swillen, Hellemans, Steyaert and Fryns 1996

SUMMARY: Basal cell naevus syndrome (BCNS) is an autosomal dominant condition. It is known as a phacomatosis (Nowak 2007). This term signifies that it involves the pairing of abnormal tissue growth, particularly in the nervous system, with the presence of (typically pigmented) birthmarks. In BCNS, multiple jaw keratocysts develop typically between age 10 and 20, and/or basal cell carcinomas between 20 and 30 years of age. In approximately two-thirds of cases there is a recognizable physical phenotype with macrocephaly, bossing of the forehead, facial milia and coarse facial features.

HOW COMMON IS BASAL CELL NAEVUS SYNDROME? Prevalence estimates vary. A screening study in the UK gave a figure of one in 57,000 (Evans, Birch and Orton 1991). However, the rate is likely to be higher still as milder cases are likely to have been missed.

MAIN CLINICAL FEATURES: Wideset eyes, a broad nasal bridge, a prominent forehead and a protruding chin are common features, together with the basal cell naevi that give the condition its name.

Diagnosis is currently based on having two major diagnostic factors, or one major and three minor criteria (Evans D.G. *et al.* 1993). Genetic screening is highlighting a broader phenotype than is identified on clinical features alone.

Major criteria:

1. calcification of the falx on skull X-ray (seen in 90+ per cent by age 20)

2. keratocyst of the jaw (mainly with adolescent onset)

3. small pits on the palms or soles of the feet, showing up as small white/pink areas

4. multiple basal cell carcinomas (small areas of pink, orange or brownish skin)

5. having an affected first-degree relative (70–80 per cent risk).

Minor criteria:

1. childhood primitive neuroectodermal tumour (PNET) in @5 per cent (aka medulloblastoma)

2. cysts of the lymphatic system, the mesentery or the pleura

3. large head (OFC above the 97th centile)

4. cleft lip or palate (5 per cent)

5. abnormal vertebrae

6. extra fingers

7. fibromas of the ovary (2 per cent) or heart (20 per cent) (Evans D.G., Riffaud, Brassier and Morandi 1993; Gorlin 1987)

8. various ocular abnormalities, including abnormal retinal pigmentation and cataract (Black *et al.* 2003).

Diagnosis is typically made at around two years of age.

Large head size is often noted first, and many babies with BCNS are born by caesarean section because of pelvic disparity.

PNETs are usually detected at around two years of age, and respond favourably to surgical excision (Amlashi, Riffaud, Brassier and Morandi 2003).

Jaw keratocysts usually present in adolescence as painless swelling, but can lead to abnormal dentition if left unattended.

Although basal cell naevi provide the label for this condition, one in ten BCNS cases do not have any such lesions. Their occurrence is partly dependent on skin type, and pale skin which burns easily in sunlight seems particularly susceptible.

Children who present with medulloblastoma (a type of malignant brain tumour which originates in the cerebellum or posterior fossa) need to be investigated for BCNS, as radiotherapy used in the management of the tumour can accelerate basal cell carcinomas. The mean age for presentation of medulloblastoma in the population is around seven years, but in BCNS it is around three years, suggesting that the intact PTCH gene acts as a tumour suppressor (Cowan *et al.* 1997).

The PTCH gene defect at 9q22.3 can be identified in @70 per cent of cases that conform to current clinical criteria. It is typically a truncated mutation of the gene (65 per cent), with missense (16 per cent) and splice (13 per cent) mutations making up the bulk of other cases.

Typically, a series of X-rays are key to diagnosis (due to the abnormalities often seen in the skull, jaw, vertebrae and ribs). Repeat X-rays are not advisable, as people with BCNS seem particularly susceptible to effects from radiation, with possible development of multiple basal cell carcinomas (Evans, Birch and Orton 1991).

There is normal life expectancy in most cases.

IS THERE A LINK BETWEEN BCNS AND ASD? To date few cases of BCNS in association with ASD have been reported. The overlap with other conditions which are more strongly linked to ASD, together with the specific problems associated with this condition, make it an important consideration in cases which have clinical features consistent with this disorder.

DIFFERENTIAL DIAGNOSIS: In a child presenting with autistic behaviour and a large head, the principal differential diagnoses will be Bannayan-Riley-Ruvalcaba syndrome [15], Cole-Hughes macrocephaly syndrome [24], Cowden syndrome [26], Proteus syndrome [62] and Sotos syndrome [68]. A rarer possibility would be Orstavik 1997 syndrome [56]. Arsenic toxicity is a separate factor that can result in basal cell carcinoma through exposure.

Where the differential diagnosis is based on the skin anomalies, BCNS needs to be discriminated from various dermal conditions, primarily from Bazex syndrome, in which there is also basal cell carcinoma, and where the backs of the hands tend to be particularly badly affected.

As this is a disorder with significant risk of complications, and only arises *de novo* in 20–30 per cent of cases, screening of at-risk relatives is important. Where a parent is also affected, there will be a 50 per cent risk that siblings and offspring of the affected individual will also be affected.

MANAGEMENT AND TREATMENT: This is a complex disorder affecting multiple organ systems and requires ongoing monitoring and care by specialists in several areas, such as orthopaedics, ophthalmology, cardiology, dentistry and plastic surgery, depending on the nature and extent of the clinical presentation. Head growth and heart function should be closely monitored in early life.

Both keratocysts and basal cell carcinomas should be treated promptly when present. Current best practice is that ovarian fibromas that require surgical excision should be treated, leaving as much ovarian tissue in situ as possible (Seracchioli *et al.* 2001).

Treatment of basal cell carcinoma can be carried out in various ways with high levels of success. Treatments range from surgical excision to topical treatment with methyl aminolevulinate (Rhodes *et al.* 2007). Photodynamic therapy appears to be safe and effective for treatment of basal cell carcinomas (Haylett, Ward and Moore 2003; Rhodes *et al.* 2007). Various topical treatments are under investigation (Stockfleth *et al.* 2002). Many of the important considerations are preventative, such as minimizing exposure to X-rays and protecting against excessive exposure to sunlight.

ANIMAL MODELS: The gene involved is homologous to the drosophila gene PATCHED (Hahn *et al.* 1996).

Several groups have now produced research on mouse knockout models of BCNS with a knockout of the gene for *Ptc1*, the protein that acts as a receptor for Sonic hedgehog (Shh; hedgehog genes are highly conserved genes involved in specifying the process of somatic development) (Corcoran and Scott 2001; Pazzaglia 2006). The Sonic-Patched-Gli pathway that articulates this process appears to be extremely sensitive to protein concentration (Villavicencio, Walterhouse and Iannaccone 2000).

Some novel approaches to treatment are being tested which may lead to human application, such as by up-regulation of Sonic hedgehog signalling (Vogt *et al.* 2004).

Basal cell tumours have also been induced in *Ptc1* inactivated mice by radiation and studied as a model for human basal cell carcinoma (Mancuso *et al.* 2004).

17.

Biedl-Bardet syndrome (BBS)

aka • Bardet-Biedl syndrome
 • Laurence-Moon-Bardet-Biedl syndrome

GENE LOCI: 20p12, 16q21, 15q22.3–q23, 14q32.1, 12q21.2, 11q13, 9q31–q34.1, 7p14, 4q27, 3p12–q13, 2q31

KEY ASD REFERENCES: Barnett *et al.* 2002; Gillberg and Wahlstrom 1985

SUMMARY: Biedl-Bardet syndrome (BBS) was first described in 1866 by Laurence and Moon in a London family. George Bardet described two affected French girls in his thesis submitted in 1920. Arthur Biedl described two Austrian children in a research report published in 1922.

It is an autosomal recessive condition, diagnosed on the basis of a number of clinical features. Diagnosis is currently on clinical features, not genetic findings, in over two-thirds of cases. Diagnosis is based on a combination of four primary or three primary and two secondary features (Beales 2005; Beales *et al.* 1999, 2001).

A useful recent review of BBS can be found in Ross and Beales (2007). Diagnosis is often only after some years as a result of the onset of obvious visual impairment, the other early features (unless the child has additional fingers or toes) being quite non-specific.

Currently a dozen genes have been identified as causes of BBS (see Table B17). Only the p.M390R gene that causes BBS1 is tested for clinically, and accounts for approximately 35 per cent of cases. C91fsX95 causes BBS10 and accounts for a further 10 per cent of cases with the

Table B17: The principal BBS genes

Gene	Gene locus	Percentage of BBS cases reported with this anomaly	Key reference
BBS1	11q13	~23.2%	Katsanis 2004
BBS2	16q21	~8.1%	Katsanis 2004
ARL6/BBS3	3p12–q13	~0.4%	Chiang *et al.* 2004; Katsanis 2004
BBS4	15q22.3–q23	~0.4%	Katsanis 2004
BBS5	2q31	Not yet known	Katsanis 2004
MKKS/BBS6	20p12	~5.8%	Katsanis 2004
BBS7	4q27	~1.5%	Katsanis 2004
TTC8/BBS8	14q32.1	~1.2%	Katsanis 2004
B1/BBS9	7p14	Not yet known	Nishimura *et al.* 2005
BBS10	12q21.2	~20%	Stoetzel *et al.* 2006
BBS11/TRIM32	9q31–q34.1	<0.4%	Chiang *et al.* 2006; Katsanis 2004
BBS12	4q27	~5%	Stoetzel *et al.* 2007

other known genes causing only small numbers of cases.

HOW COMMON IS BBS? The typically reported prevalence is one in 160,000 in European (Klein and Ammann 1969) and one in 100,000 in North American (Croft and Swift 1990) populations. Higher rates have been reported in Newfoundland, where the prevalence of one in 17,500 is thought to be due to a 'founder effect' (Green *et al.* 1989), and in the Bedouin population of Kuwait, where the reported prevalence of one in 13,500 is thought to be a result of higher rates of consanguineous marriages (Farag and Teebi 1988).

MAIN CLINICAL FEATURES: The main presenting features in a person with BBS are obesity (progressive, usually after being born of normal weight, with accumulation of fat particularly around the stomach), a progressive retinal dystrophy (the visual problems are slow to develop but progressive, with night blindness present typically by 7–8 years, and most children being diagnosed as functionally blind by their mid teens), polydactyly, small genitals in affected boys, moderate learning disability and kidney dysfunction. (Kidney problems are chronic and can be fatal.) A number of secondary problems are also seen.

Elevated cholesterol levels and diabetes are characteristics that require ongoing monitoring and management.

Speech acquisition is often delayed, with words being used typically from around four years of age (Moore *et al.* 2005).

Primary features:

1. cone–rod dystrophy – progressive with age, and not usually apparent before the age of five (Hamel 2007; Riise *et al.* 1996). By 17 there is rarely more than a small central visual field (Jacobson,

Borruat and Apathy 1990; Riise, Andreasson, Wright and Tornqvist 1996). Macular degeneration is clear by some time in the teenage years, but occasionally earlier (Fulton, Hansen and Glynn 1993)

2. truncal obesity (body mass index above the 97th centile)

3. postaxial polydactyly – additional fingers on the ulnar side of the hand, or toes on the fibular side of the foot, in 58–69 per cent of cases (Ammann 1970; Beales *et al.* 1999; Green *et al.* 1989; Ramirez, Marrero, Carlo and Cornier 2004)

4. learning disability (Barnett *et al.* 2002; Beales *et al.* 1999; Green *et al.* 1989; Moore S.J. *et al.* 2005)

5. males show hypogonadotrophic hypogonadism (small penis/reduced testicular volume), while affected females show various complex female genitourinary malformations (Stoler, Herrin and Holmes 1995)

6. renal dysfunction (a characteristic combination of calyceal clubbing, tubular cystic diverticula, and persistent foetal lobulation) is common, but reported rates vary widely, with chronic renal failure reported in 5–100 per cent of cases (Beales *et al.* 1999; Harnett *et al.* 1988; O'Dea *et al.* 1996.

Secondary features:

1. speech delay/disorder (Beales *et al.* 1999; Garstecki, Borton, Stark and Kennedy 1972)

2. strabismus/cataracts/astigmatism

3. brachydactyly of both hands and feet is common, and syndactyly between the second and third toes is common (Rudling, Riise, Tornqvist and Jonsson 1996)

4. developmental delay (delayed milestones are frequently reported in both motor and social development)

5. polyuria/polydipsia (nephrogenic diabetes insipidus) (often without any obvious renal involvement)

6. ataxia/poor coordination/imbalance

7. mild hypertonia (especially lower limbs)

8. diabetes mellitus (typically type II diabetes, often in association with obesity)

9. dental crowding, hypodontia, small dental roots, high-arched palate (Borgstrom, Riise, Tornqvist and Garanath 1996)

10. cardiovascular anomalies – seen in approximately 7 per cent of cases (Beales et al. 1999), valvular stenoses and atrial/ventricular septal defects being the most common (Elbedour et al. 1994)

11. hepatic problems (Nakamura, Sasaki, Kajihara and Yamanoue 1990)

12. hypertension – seen in 50–66 per cent of cases (Fralick, Leichter and Sheth 1990; Harnett et al. 1988; O'Dea et al. 1996; Riise 1996)

13. subclinical hearing loss – apparent on testing in almost half of all cases (Beales et al. 1999; Ross A.J. et al. 2005).

There is a characteristic facial appearance, with a narrow forehead, large ears and narrow eyelids, a long, shallow nasal philtrum, a thin upper lip and small, downturned mouth. Most affected males have a receding hairline (Beales et al. 1999; Lorda-Sanchez, Ayuso, Sanz and Ibanez 2001; Moore S.J. et al. 2005).

To date there is no clear indication of an association between the genotype and phenotype in BBS.

A further confusing aspect is that in some families it appears to require three of the BBS genes for the condition to manifest: triallelic inheritance (Katsanis et al. 2001), which may account for some 10 per cent of cases.

A recent development in our understanding of BBS proteins has come from discovering that the various BBS proteins are conserved ciliary proteins, which are important factors in intracellular transport (Avidor-Reiss et al. 2004; Li J.B. et al. 2004). Ansley et al. (2003) have found that these proteins are involved in formation of the basal bodies of ciliated cells. For a discussion of these developments, see Mykytyn and Sheffield (2004).

As ciliary functions are important in a range of human functions, from lung clearance and the sense of smell to sperm motility, it is not surprising that BBS cases have been reported with ciliary problems in lung function (Shah et al. 2008) and both partial and complete anosmia (Iannaccone et al. 2005; Kulaga et al. 2004).

IS THERE A LINK BETWEEN BBS AND ASD?
BBS was identified in one of 66 ASD cases screened for genetic conditions reported from a Swedish case series (Gillberg and Wahlstrom 1985). No further fully documented cases have been reported to date in the clinical literature.

In a more recent series of 21 BBS cases (Barnett et al. 2002), aged 3–18, 12 families consented to screening for ASD symptomology using the Childhood Autism Rating Scale (CARS) (Schopler et al. 1980). Two cases scored as severely autistic and two as mild–moderate on the CARS. However, no more detailed assessments were carried out. Parental interviews established that a number of behaviours were common to this BBS group as a whole, including social and emotional immaturity (90.5 per cent), obsessions (80.9 per cent), routines (57.1 per cent) and repetitive play (42.9 per cent).

Clearly, more detailed assessment of ASD in this population is warranted. No attempt has been made to date to link the specific gene differences that cause BBS to particular patterns of behaviour.

DIFFERENTIAL DIAGNOSIS:
1. McKusick-Kaufman syndrome (MKKS)

Gene: 20p (MKKS), which is also a BBS susceptibility gene.

Primary clinical features: abnormal genital development (hydrometrocolpos (HMC)) in girls additional digits (postaxial polydactyly (PAP)), and congenital heart disease (CHD).

MKKS and Bardet-Biedl syndrome have significant overlap in both their symptomology and their genetic basis (David A. *et al.* 1999; Sheffield, Nishimura and Stone 2001; Slavotinek and Biesecker 2000; Slavotinek *et al.* 2000), and may be best seen as part of the same phenotypic spectrum.

2. Alström syndrome

Gene: 2p13 (ALMS1)

Primary clinical features: this condition also causes a cone–rod dystrophy, obesity, a dilated cardiomyopathy, type II diabetes, and developmental delay. There is, in addition, a progressive sensorineural hearing impairment.

3. Biemond 2 syndrome

Gene: none has so far been identified.

Primary clinical features: learning disability; obesity; iris coloboma; additional digits (postaxial polydactyly); smaller genitalia (hypogonadism); hydrocephalus; and facial synostosis.

MANAGEMENT AND TREATMENT: A significant area of help where individuals with BBS require specialist care and advice is the use of visual aids and communication that takes account of their progressive loss of vision. At present there is no treatment that prevents or slows the visual deterioration.

Early educational interventions and speech and language input also need to make allowance for progressive visual loss and greater reliance on auditory and tactile processing with age. (Here the differential diagnosis of Alström syndrome is important, given the additional problems of progressive hearing loss.)

Dietary approaches can help with management of obesity, elevated cholesterol, elevated blood pressure, and type II diabetes. As these are later onset aspects of the condition, regular monitoring is important to identify difficulties at an early stage and institute secondary preventative measures.

Additional fingers and toes often require surgical removal to minimize problems with hand function and walking.

ANIMAL MODELS: Specific mouse knockouts have been produced for several of the BBS genes: BBS1 (Kulaga *et al.* 2004), BBS2 (Nishimura *et al.* 2004), BBS4 (Kulaga *et al.* 2004; Mykytyn *et al.* 2004) and BBS6 (Fath *et al.* 2005; Ross A.J. *et al.* 2005). These have provided support for ciliary dysfunction in BBS. Several ciliary dysfunctions have been noted in mouse models – in sperm motility, in retinal function, in lung function and in olfactory function.

A number of mouse models for the various forms of BBS are being developed. A knock-in mouse model of BBS1 has a range of consistent physical features including cilia defects, enlarged cerebral ventricles, retinopathy and obesity (Davis R.E. *et al.* 2007). Rahmouni *et al.* (2008) have recently published on the role of leptin in both obesity and hypertension in mouse models.

18.

CATCH22

aka • Cayler cardiofacial syndrome
 • DiGeorge syndrome
 • Takao velocardiofacial syndrome
 • conotruncal anomaly face syndrome
 • 22q11.2 deletion syndrome
 • Sedlackova syndrome
 • Shprintzen syndrome
 • velocardiofacial syndrome
 • Opitz G/BBB syndrome

GENE LOCUS: 22q11.2

KEY ASD REFERENCES: Fine *et al.* 2005; Kozma 1998; Niklasson *et al.* 2001, 2002; Roubertie *et al.* 2001

SUMMARY: The term CATCH22 is an acronym, coined by John Burn. The term stands for **C**ardiac anomaly, **A**nomalous face, **T**hymus hypoplasia/aplasia, **C**left palate and **H**ypocalcaemia (Burn 1999). It is caused in almost all cases by a gene deletion of genetic material at 22q11.2 (see, for example, Desmaze *et al.* 1993).

HOW COMMON IS CATCH22? It is estimated that 22q11.2 deletions are found in one in every 4,000 live births (Tézenas du Montcel *et al.* 1996). This is felt to be an underestimate, as it is based on cases identified by phenotype, and milder and somatic mosaic cases have also been reported. One recent study has found a mean IQ of 71 in a series of 100 22q11 cases, and a neuropsychological profile more strongly associated with 22q11 than with the presence of ASD within the population (Niklasson and Gillberg 2010). Estimates of prevalence vary from one in

3,800 in US Hispanic populations (Botto *et al.* 2003) to one in 6,395 (Devriendt *et al.* 1998). The mean annual incidence in one large Swedish study was one in every 7,090 live births (Oskarsdóttir, Vujic and Fasth 2004; Oskarsdóttir, Belfrage *et al.* 2005; Oskarsdóttir, Persson *et al.* 2005).

MAIN CLINICAL FEATURES: Most people with CATCH22 have a learning disability (Moss *et al.* 1995). Immune problems are also seen in a high proportion (around 70 per cent). Complex heart problems are found in around three–quarters of cases, tetralogy of Fallot being the most common and affecting more than one in five cases. Over 90 per cent of fatalities result from complications of such cardiac difficulties. Renal problems are seen in around one third of cases.

Overviews of the physical and behavioural phenotype can be found in Antshel *et al.* (2005) and Arriola-Pereda, Verdú-Pérez and de Castro-De Castro (2009).

A 22q11.2 deletion is the gene defect most commonly associated with having a cleft palate. The deletion is found in around seven per cent of cases, and over two-thirds of those with the deletion have palatal problems. Heart defects, often complex ones, affect almost three–quarters of cases. Around half of all cases have hypocalcaemia, but the effect lessens with age. Seizure problems, when seen, are usually associated with hypocalcaemia. One in three have significant problems with feeding, which can be severe and could require nasogastric tube feeding and/or gastrostomy. The gene typically occurs as a *de novo* mutation in the affected individual, but can be inherited (in approximately seven per cent of cases), and is transmitted as an autosomal dominant condition. Parents of an affected child should also be tested, as mildly affected parents, and parents with somatic mosaic status, have both been reported (McDonald-McGinn *et al.* 2001). Where a parent is also affected the risk to siblings will be 50 per cent, but in *de novo* cases the risk appears low. Children of an affected individual will have a 50 per cent risk of also being affected.

Typically there are delays in both motor and communication milestones (mean age at walking 18 months; first speech at two to three years). Around 80 per cent of cases show severe motor delay, with the same proportion showing some degree of learning difficulty.

A non-verbal learning disability profile on IQ is most commonly reported (i.e. a significant gap between verbal and non-verbal skills) (Wang *et al.* 1998). However, the results are variable, both within and across studies (for example, Sobin *et al.* 2005; Stiers *et al.* 2005). Problems with numeracy skills seem amongst the most common (Simon *et al.* 2002).

A range of behavioural features is seen in CATCH22 – both disinhibition and impulsiveness and shyness and withdrawal are more common (Swillen *et al.* 1999). Inattention, anxiety and executive deficits such as perseveration are seen, as are difficulties with social interaction (Niklasson *et al.* 2001; Swillen *et al.* 1999).

Abnormalities of immune function are also common. Juvenile rheumatoid arthritis is around 20 times as common as it is in the general population, and a variety of other immune conditions, including coeliac disease, is also seen (Keenan, Sullivan, McDonald-McGinn nad Zackai 1997; Sullivan *et al.* 1997). Immune problems such as haemolytic anaemia and juvenile arthritis are more common because of abnormal development of the thymus gland and a reduction in T-cell production (Sullivan 2004). However, this problem tends to lessen with age.

Kidney and genitourinary problems are reported in approximately one third of cases (Wu *et al.* 2002).

Hearing can be affected, and chronic ear and nasal infections are common, due to poorer ability to fight off infections. It is advised that, where immune abnormalities are present, live vaccinations are delayed in this group unless there is a high background rate of disease, as their immune status increases the risk of atypical reactions.

There are a number of reports of hepatoblastoma, a form of liver cancer that is rare in the general population, suggesting a possible association with 22q11.2 (Patrone, Chatten and Weinberg 1990; Scattone *et al.* 2003).

Characteristic facial features are seen in Caucasian populations. These include abnormalities of the ear and nose, 'hooded eyelids', ocular hypertelorism, cleft lip and palate, asymmetric crying facies (Cayler 1969; Sanklecha, Kher and Bharucha 1992), craniosynostosis (McDonald-McGinn, Gripp *et al.* 2005), and a long face and flat cheeks. These features do not seem to be characteristic of affected individuals from Africa-American populations (McDonald-McGinn, Minugh-Purvis *et al.* 2005).

Although adult stature is within normal limits, children are often growth retarded, and in some cases benefit from growth hormone treatment (Weinzimer *et al.* 1998).

Seizures are less common, being reported in seven per cent (27/383) in one case series (Kao *et al.* 2004). Ataxia and cerebellar atrophy have been reported, but to date only in single case (Lynch D.R. *et al.* 1995).

Skeletal abnormalities of the ribs and vertebrae are also fairly common (Ricchetti *et al.* 2004).

Enlargement of the sylvian fissures has been reported, detectable on brain scanning in infancy, but the findings have not been independently replicated (Bingham et al. 1997). Functional MRI scans indicate reduced volume of the dominant hemisphere in the occipito-parietal cortex compared to matched controls (Barnea-Goraly et al. 2003; Bearden, van Erp et al. 2004; Bish et al. 2004; Kates et al. 2004).

A detailed description of 250 22q11.2 deletion cases can be found in McDonald-McGinn et al. (1999). Despite the complex nature of the phenotype and the relatively large numbers who have been studied, there is no clear association between the extent of the lesion and the phenotype (McDonald-McGinn et al. 2001).

The typical neuropsychological profile seen in 22q11.3 as with many ASD conditions, shows particular difficulties with executive functioning and working memory.

Ninety-five per cent of cases with the clinical phenotype show a positive genetic test on fluorescence in situ hybridization (FISH).

A number of psychiatric disorders have been reported in association with 22q11.2. In particular, schizophrenia, seen in around 25 per cent of adult cases (Bassett et al. 2005, 2008; Chow, Bassett and Weksberg 1994; Murphy, Jones and Owen 1999), bipolar disorder, anxiety, ADHD and depression (Baker and Skuse 2005) are commonly reported.

IS THERE A LINK BETWEEN CATCH22 AND ASD? Several papers have commented on the level of ASD symptomology in people with CATCH22. Lena Niklasson and her colleagues from Goteborg in southern Sweden have published two papers describing the neuropsychological and neuropsychiatric phenotype in 22q11.2 and raised the idea of an association with ASD symptomology (Niklasson et al. 2001, 2002).

Agatha Roubertie and colleagues from Montpellier published detailed neurological descriptions of three cases, one of whom was autistic and the others affected by epilepsy (Roubertie et al. 2001).

A separate group from Philadelphia published neuropsychological data on 80 22q11.2 microdeletion cases and described a consistent profile of non-verbal learning disability, with additional language and social deficits (Woodin et al. 2001).

Fine and colleagues (Fine et al. 2005) systematically examined the prevalence of ASD symptomology in 98 children who had a confirmed 22q11.2 deletion. Twenty-two showed significant levels of autistic symptomology, 14 had an autistic spectrum diagnosis and, of these, 11 had autism. Significant autistic symptoms were thus seen in around 20 per cent of cases, and an ASD in around 15 per cent.

DIFFERENTIAL DIAGNOSIS: The conditions which present with the most similar physical symptomology in conjunction with ASD are Goldenhar syndrome [38], a 14q32 deletion which results in complex symptomology typically involving reduced growth of one side of the face, and Smith-Lemli-Opitz syndrome [66], an overgrowth condition which can be identified genetically and results in a defect in cholesterol metabolism.

The central nervous system and phenotypic characteristics also overlap with those reported in Opitz G/BBB syndrome (Guion-Almeida and Richieri-Costa 1992; MacDonald M.R. et al. 1993; Neri et al. 1987), a condition linked to Xp22. Although similarities are seen in the physical phenotype, there have been no reports of Opitz G/BBB in association with ASD. Xp22 is the area on the X chromosome which is affected in a number of other ASD conditions: CHARGE syndrome [20], DiGeorge syndrome I [29a] and velocardiofacial syndrome (VCFS) [76].

A large number of conditions have been named and described in association with a 22q11.2 gene deletion. Given the variability in presenting phenotype, there is ongoing debate concerning differentiation within this population. Much emphasis has been placed on a specific gene, TBX1, that is sufficient but not necessary for the presentation of the 22q11.2 phenotype. The recent discovery of a number of candidate genes that interfere with mitochondrial function on the same section of chromosome 22q11.2 (Maynard et al. 2008) suggests that these may be involved in the phenotypic variability observed.

Sedlackova syndrome (or velofacial hypoplasia) was thought to be a distinct entity, until a recent study (Fokstuen et al. 2001) indicated that 80 per cent of those tested with a DiGeorge/VCFS region-specific probe showed evidence of a 22q11.2 deletion in the same region.

A recent study has described elevated proline levels in a subset of cases (Raux et al. 2007).

MANAGEMENT AND TREATMENT: Most 22q11.2 cases require regular follow-up by a range of specialisms.

Screening for heart problems should be undertaken at an early stage, and this is often how the condition is first identified. Treatment is no different than it would be for others with the same cardiac problem.

Palatal abnormalities may require surgical correction and need to be evaluated by a craniofacial surgical team.

Feeding problems may require modified cutlery, antacids for gastro-oesophageal reflux, medication to improve gastric motility and modified seating to improve digestion.

Bleeding problems are more common in this group and should be treated as in others where they are found, so should be assessed and, where required, treated by a haematologist.

Growth retardation is also more common and growth hormone supplementation may be beneficial in some cases.

Hypocalcaemia is common, and low serum calcium concentration can be corrected with calcium supplementation. An increased risk of kidney stones from long-term use of calcium supplements needs to be borne in mind, keeping oxalate levels to a minimum (Aitken 2009).

Where there are immune problems, as seen in the majority of cases, assessment by a clinical immunologist is advisable, and in some cases prophylactic antibiotics, intravenous immunoglobulin or a thymus transplant may be required.

Early intensive intervention to improve interaction and communication skills are as for other ASD conditions, and should ideally involve an appropriate team of psychologists, speech and language therapists and early education specialists. Ideally, baseline speech and language assessments should be carried out as early as possible. These can also aid in recognition of more subtle palatal defects. Given the profile of learning problems which characterizes this group, strategies should be put in place to aid with non-verbal learning disabilities, where present.

Where psychiatric symptomology is seen – especially ADHD, anxiety, bipolar or psychotic features – these should be evaluated, and where necessary treated by appropriate mental health professionals.

ANIMAL MODELS: *Tbx1* knockout mouse models have been developed and their effect on embryonic growth has been evaluated (Jerome and Papaioannou 2001; Lindsay et al. 2001; Merscher et al. 2001). The mice that were heterozygous for the null mutation were viable and survived with defects similar to those seen in the human 22q11.2 deletion syndrome. Studies of the phenotype in *Tbx1*-null mice have shown the same pattern of physical anomalies as are seen in the 22q11 deletion syndrome (Liao *et al.* 2004).

19.

Cortical Dysplasia–Focal Epilepsy (CDFE) syndrome

GENE LOCUS: 7q36

KEY ASD REFERENCES: Alarcón *et al.* 2008; Arking *et al.* 2008; Bakkaloglu *et al.* 2008; Fisher and Scharff 2009; Jackman, Horn, Molleston and Sokol 2009; Poot *et al.* 2010; Rossi *et al.* 2008; Strauss *et al.* 2006

SUMMARY: CDFE is caused by an abnormality in the contactin associated protein-like 2 (CASPR2) which is encoded by the CNTNAP2 gene at 7q35–q36. The CNTNAP2 gene is involved in the regulation of axonal membrane proteins and controlling potassium channels at the nodes of Ranvier in axonal cells in the nervous system (Traka *et al.* 2003). It is thus important for salutatory conduction (the way in which electrical signals transmit more rapidly by jumping from node to node) (Poliak and Peles 2003).

It was first described in the Old Order Amish of Pennsylvania. Having previously been identified as a risk factor for early language delay, it has now been confirmed as a risk factor for ASD in four independent studies. Most individuals have larger than average heads and absent deep tendon reflexes.

HOW COMMON IS CDFE? This is a rare condition, first described in 2001. The multiple independent replications of a link between CNTNAP2 and ASD in different populations suggests that the co-morbid prevalence rate may be high. It has been identified as a cause of developmental disability in Old Order Amish, a population in which ASD has historically been reported to be infrequent. The lack of population prevalence data makes these findings difficult to evaluate until further epidemiology is carried out.

MAIN CLINICAL FEATURES: The key diagnostic features are, unsurprisingly, cortical dysplasia and focal epilepsy. The head is larger than predicted from familial head size, but growth is within normal parameters in other respects. Diminished deep-tendon reflexes are usually seen. Epileptic seizures are seen in most cases from early childhood and are often difficult to control. Seizures, typically simple, partial or complex partial types, usually begin between 14 and 20 months of age. The seizures tend to resolve spontaneously but only after a number of years. Slow early language development or language regression is typical of cases so far described. Hyperactivity, impulsive and aggressive behaviour and learning disability were reported in all of the Old Amish series originally described (Strauss *et al.* 2006).

IS THERE A LINK BETWEEN CDFE AND ASD?

- In a clinical series of nine CDFE cases (Strauss *et al.* 2006), 6/9 fulfilled criteria for ASD. All had learning disabilities and 7/9 fulfilled criteria for ADHD. Hyperactivity, inattention and aggression were the most common behavioural difficulties reported in this series between seizure episodes. All cases had complex partial seizures, and in addition, four had secondary generalized seizures, three status epilepticus and three simple partial seizures. All of the cases in this series came from Old Amish families of Lancaster, Pennsylvania, in the USA. This is a population in which autism has been infrequently reported.

• Alarcón et al. (2008) published a screening study of DNA material from the AGRE database of established autistic cases. A strong association was found between autistic diagnosis and CNTNAP2 variants; this was preferentially found in males. By screening 304 independent parent–child trios an association between CNTNAP2 and age at first word in ASD was demonstrated. This followed on from an earlier study which had linked 7q35 defects to language learning problems in ASD (Alarcón, Cantor et al. 2005).

• Arking et al. (2008) also used data from the AGRE database. Their analysis based on 78 sibling pairs and 145 parent–child trios also found CNTNAP2 to be an autism susceptibility gene, with a gender effect – more commonly associated with male gender – and a parent of origin effect which seems to be inherited through the female line.

• Bakkaloglu et al. (2008) sequenced the CNTNAP2 gene in 635 ASD and 942 control cases. In the ASD cases 13 nonsynonymous changes in CNTNAP2 were found, while in the controls there were 11. This is a small absolute difference, suggesting that there is an association, but that this is a relatively rare factor in the overall ASD population.

• Rossi et al. (2008) have recently reported a case of an adult female with a deletion spanning 7q33–q35. This has deleted two genes, CNTNAP2, the gene linked to ASD in the above studies, and

NOBOX, which has been associated with primary amenorrhoea. This lady's case is well described, and includes both ASD and amenhorroea. She had shown delayed early speech, with first words only by around age four years. She had had frequent nocturnal wakening in infancy and had two isolated seizures at age 16. Her IQ could not be formally assessed, but appears likely to have been in the moderately learning disabled range, based on her vocabulary and her scoring on other materials reported (Ravens coloured matrices and the Token test).

• A recent case study (Poot et al. 2010) presented a boy with mildly dysmorphic facial feartures, speech delay and ASD. This boy had a deletion of the CNTNAP2 region, including the FOX2. His presentation was genetically more complex, with a total of seven chromosome 7 breaks and a further three breaks on chromosome 1 with additional transpositions and insertions.

• Fisher and Scharff (2009) reviewed the genetic evidence for the FOX2 gene being linked to both specific language impairments and to ASD, and the evidence that FOX2 is a highly conserved gene through vertebrate evolution and also a strong candidate as a gene for linguistic communication.

• A further recent study (Roohi et al. 2008) has identified contactin-4 abnormalities that have a different genetic basis but some functional similarities in some individuals with ASD. This is a 3p deletion syndrome that has a distinct neurocognitive phenotype.

DIFFERENTIAL DIAGNOSIS: CNTNAP2 deletions have also been reported in association with Gilles de la Tourette syndrome [71] in two affected children who had a father with a diagnosis of OCD

(Verkerk *et al.* 2003). As Tourette syndrome is also associated with ASD and was not screened for in this pedigree, this could indicate an alternative clinical phenotype or a co-morbidity.

MANAGEMENT AND TREATMENT: To date there are no specific treatments which have been implemented or evaluated, as CDFE has only been characterized in the past two years. From the phenotype described to date, early identification of cases and provision of early intervention on communication may help to minimize language delays and improve cognitive outcome. Monitoring for early seizure activity and prophylactic treatment may also be of benefit. The extent to which other problems, such as sleep difficulties, are characteristic of, or overrepresented in, CDFE is yet to be established.

ANIMAL MODELS: From work on drosophila, CNTNAP2 has been shown to produce a neurexin that is important in blood–brain barrier function (Baumgartner *et al.* 1996).

The pattern of cortical expression in mouse and rat CNTNAP2 models is not similar to that seen in humans (Su *et al.* 2002). In humans, there is enriched expression of the gene in anterior regions, while in murine models there is no such differential expression. (For discussion, see Abrahams *et al.* 2007.) In human foetal tissue, it is consistently expressed in multiple brain areas – the prefrontal and anterior temporal cortex, as well as in the dorsal thalamus, caudate, putamen and amygdala.

To date, there have been no attempts to model behavioural or physical phenotype based on modification or deletion of CNTNAP2.

20.

CHARGE syndrome

aka • Hall-Hittner syndrome

GENE LOCI: 8q12.1; 7q21.1

KEY ASD REFERENCES: Davenport, Hefner and Mitchell 1986; Fernell *et al.* 1999; Graham, Rosner, Dykens and Visootsak 2005; Hartshorne, Grialou and Parker 2005; Hartshorne, Nicholas, Grialou and Russ 2007; Johansson *et al.* 2006; Johansson, Gillberg and Råstam 2009; Jure, Rapin and Tuchman 1991; Rapin and Ruben 1976; Sanlaville and Verloes 2007; Simon Harvey, Leaper and Bankier 1991; Smith, Nichols, Issekutz and Blake 2005; Vervloed *et al.* 2006; Wiznitzer, Rapin and Van de Water 1987

SUMMARY: The name CHARGE is an acronym which stands for **C**oloboma of the eye, **H**eart defects, **A**tresia of the choanae, **R**etardation of growth and/or development, **G**enital and/or urinary abnormalities, and **E**ar abnormalities and deafness. This set of physical and sensory features is used in making a clinical diagnosis.

The first descriptions of CHARGE were provided by Hall (1979) and Hittner, Hirsch, Kreh and Rudolph (1979).

HOW COMMON IS CHARGE SYNDROME?
The best current estimate is that CHARGE syndrome affects between one in 12,000 (Kallen *et al.* 1999) and one in 8,500 live births (Issekutz *et al.* 2005). Around one in 42,500 live births will have CHARGE syndrome and go on to receive a diagnosis of ASD.

MAIN CLINICAL FEATURES:

1. *choanal atresia* (an overgrowth condition where the nasal passages are blocked due to an overgrowth of bone or tissue), and/or cleft palate

2. *ocular coloboma* (a currently untreatable defect in the development of the eye that can result in retinal detachment or glaucoma and requires regular assessment)

3. *cranial nerve abnormalities* resulting in problems with olfaction, swallowing, facial palsy, deafness, or a combination of these

4. *ear malformation* (cup shape to the outer ear, often with inner ear abnormalities and deafness)

5. *heart anomalies* (various cardiac defects are reported, including tetralogy of Fallot, atrioventricular (AV) canal defects and aortic arch abnormalities)

6. *learning disability*, with delayed motor and cognitive milestones

7. *growth retardation*

8. *genital hypoplasia*

9. *cleft lip/palate.*

The number and severity of features is highly variable. From their review of 444 cases of choanal atresia, Harris, Robert and Kallen (1997) concluded that at least three of the above features, excluding growth retardation, would need to be present to conclude that an individual had the CHARGE association. This study did not attempt to match the phenotype against any genetic information on the cases.

- As more cases are reported, the clinical phenotype is broadening. One recent case, for example, presented (in addition to the recognized clinical characteristics) with preaxial polydactyly (Douglas and Lam 2010).

- Swallowing problems and gastro-oesophageal reflux are common features in this population, and when not monitored and treated effectively can prove problematic, or may even be fatal (Bergman, Blake *et al.* 2010).

- Sleep disturbance is seen in approximately 60 per cent of cases, and more commonly in those who are deaf–blind, with frequent middle-ear infections and with delayed walking (Hartshorne *et al.* 2009).

- Devriendt *et al.* (1998) described a girl with a 22q11 deletion and features of the CHARGE association: iris coloboma, a large ventricular septal heart defect, external ear abnormalities, severe growth retardation, and moderate learning disability. This child would now be said to have a velocardiofacial syndrome [76] or CATCH22 [18].

- Van Meter and Weaver (1996) described two cases who both showed features of the CHARGE association and Goldenhar syndrome [38].

- The symptomology overlaps significantly with Kallman syndrome, in which the combination of hypogonadotropic hypogonadism and a diminished or absent sense of smell are typical features, and a number of Kallman syndrome cases are also being found to have CHD7 mutations (Jongmans *et al.* 2009).

- Tetralogy of Fallot is the most frequent type of heart defect reported in the CHARGE association (Cyran *et al.* 1987), being seen in approximately one third of cases with cardiac lesions (Wyse, Al-Mahdawi, Burn and Blake 1993).

- Choanal atresia is strongly associated with central nervous system anomalies. Lin, Siebert and Graham (1990) noted malformations in some 55 per cent, predominantly of the frontal structures.

- In a report in 1996, Tellier *et al.* reviewed 41 CHARGE cases and noted a correlation with increased paternal, but not maternal, age.
- Genital hypoplasia is most obvious in boys, but affects both sexes (Wheeler, Quigley, Sadeghi-Nejad and Weaver 2000). Hormonal measurements in infancy can aid in diagnosis and enable treatment to minimize secondary difficulties.

GENETIC BASIS: Two specific genes appear linked to CHARGE association: CHD7, seen in the majority of cases, and SEMA3E, so far reported in only two cases (Lalani *et al.* 2004).

The CHD7 gene at 8q12 has been found to be mutated in a high percentage of cases. From two series, sequencing genes from 217 cases in all, some 62 per cent of cases have the defective gene, but genotype–phenotype associations are weak (Jongmans *et al.* 2006; Lalani *et al.* 2006).

Antenatal detection and follow-up of CHD7 cases has demonstrated an association between the extent of the CHD7 truncation and the clinical phenotype. Noteworthy is the fact that features that had not previously been reported – arhinencephaly and agenesis of the semicircular canals – were found to be consistent features across all ten cases in a series reported by Sanlaville *et al.* (2006). These physical features would be consistent with the anosmia and balance difficulties reported as consistent features of the behavioural phenotype.

The SEMA3E translocation, in a well-described CHARGE association case (Martin, Sheldon and Gorski 2001), resulted from a balanced *de novo* chromosome 2–7 translocation, and in one further case was identified through screening a group of other CHARGE cases.

IS THERE A LINK BETWEEN CHARGE AND ASD?

- Davenport, Hefner and Mitchell (1986) described 15 CHARGE cases, concluding that the constellation of features was a true disorder. The ear malformations and audiogram results were felt to be key diagnostic features, and facial paralysis was viewed as very common, as were feeding difficulties. They also commented on one child as seemingly autistic with a profound level of learning disability, that they have described in further publications (for example, Hartshorne, Hefner and Davenport 2005).
- Wiznitzer, Rapin and Van de Water (1987) reported on neurological findings in 100 children with ear malformations: 65 had central nervous system involvement, and of these, 45 had learning disabilities – seven with autism, and one with the CHARGE association.
- Jure, Rapin and Tuchman (1991) carried out a review of 46 children, including a number with the CHARGE association, who had both hearing problems and ASD. In 11 children autism was diagnosed only several years after the hearing loss, while in ten the opposite delay was seen. The importance of assessment of both areas in parallel was stressed for appropriate early education.
- In 1999, Elisabeth Fernell *et al.* from Sweden described three cases of CHARGE syndrome who were all reported to be autistic, and two of whom had significant learning difficulties.
- Graham, Rosner, Dykens and Visootsak (2005) compared a series of 14 boys with CHARGE to 20 with Down syndrome [31], 17 with Prader-Willi syndrome [61] and 16 with Williams syndrome [77]. The view of the authors

was that the autistic-like behaviours seen in the CHARGE cases, in contrast to the other groups, were secondary to sensory impairments – all 14 were deaf and 10 were classified as blind.

- In one survey of 160 ABC checklists (returned from 204 families asked to participate, with a 78 per cent return rate), 27.5 per cent would be classified as autistic (Hartshorne, Grialou and Parker 2005). This suggests that as a minimum around one in five people with CHARGE syndrome might be classified as autistic.

- Hartshorne, Nicholas, Grialou and Russ (2007) published a study on executive function (EF) in CHARGE syndrome and the association between EF and ASD symptomology. This is a large study of 98 children, using the Behavior Rating Inventory of Executive Function (BRIEF) and the Autism Behavior Checklist (ABC), and demonstrates higher ABC scores than in other deaf–blind groups, but lower than in typical ASD populations. There was a correlation between EF deficits and ABC scores.

- Johansson et al. (2006) presented data on 31 individuals aged from one month to 31 years with CHARGE. ASD ascertainment proved impossible in three infants and three deaf–blind cases. Of the remaining 25, five were classified as autistic, five as autistic-like and seven as having autistic traits, suggesting autistic symptomology in some two-thirds of cases. Visual problems were seen in all of the autistic children. Hearing problems appeared to be independently associated with severity of ASD. Learning difficulties (LD) did not appear to correlate with ASD symptomology, but all of those with ASD diagnosis had co-morbid LD diagnoses.

- Sanlaville and Verloes (2007), in a useful update review, conclude that there is still no consensus on whether the ASD symptomology reported is true ASD, or ASD behaviour secondary to sensory impairment.

- Smith, Nicholas, Issekutz and Blake (2005), in a preliminary paper from a Canadian epidemiological study that includes 78 CHARGE cases, described the completed data on the ten cases aged above four to five years on whom screening data was completed. From telephone interview data, six of the ten were judged to present moderate to strong evidence of ASD.

- In a study by Vervloed et al. (2006) attempting to correlate medical difficulties with presenting problems, deaf–blindness was associated with delayed communication, while cardiac problems were associated with a lower level of behavioural difficulties. No association between medical presentation and ASD was found.

- A survey of several genetic disorders that included a group of 31 CHARGE cases found that 68 per cent fitted criteria for an ASD diagnosis using the ADI-R, CARS and ABC scales and two independent clinical diagnoses. The authors caution about the use of diagnostic scales alone in assessing deaf–blind cases (Johansson, Gillberg and Råstam 2009).

Across individuals diagnosed with CHARGE syndrome and classified as having an ASD, there is wide variation in behavioural profile on screening instruments for autistic behaviour.

A recent study has evaluated the use of various ASD scales with this population, questioning the applicability of current diagnostic tools such as the Autism Diagnostic Interview – Revised

(ADI-R), the Childhood Autism Rating Scale (CARS) and the Autistic Behaviour Checklist (ABC) in this population if the subject is deaf–blind (Johansson, Gillberg and Råstam 2009).

DIFFERENTIAL DIAGNOSIS: In addition to ASD, a range of mental health conditions are diagnosed in CHARGE, the most common being ASD, obsessive-compulsive disorder, attention deficit disorder, and Tourette syndrome. The likelihood of tics is linked to presence and severity of cardiac problems (Sanlaville and Verloes 2007).

MANAGEMENT AND TREATMENT: This is a very complex disorder that is likely to require, at the least, close monitoring and follow-up of cardiac function, airway function, and swallowing. Correction of choanal atresia, cardiac problems and palatal abnormalities may be required. There are to date no studies to suggest that any aspects of ASD presentation are specifically related to the CHARGE association, other than the increased severity of communication difficulties that can arise from palatal abnormalities, and the increased likelihood of motor tics related to severity of cardiac problems.

A recent single-case study from Taiwan has reported beneficial effects of a casein- and gluten-free diet in a boy with CHARGE syndrome, reporting significant improvements in growth, eye contact and language use over an 11-month period after commencing the diet at age 3 years and 6 months (Hsu *et al.* 2009).

ANIMAL MODELS: As CHARGE has a strong phenotypic overlap with VACTERL (Shaw-Smith 2006), it seems likely that the mouse models of Sonic hedgehog that are relevant to VACTERL (Kim, Kim and Hui 2001) may also prove helpful in the study of the CHARGE association.

Recent work on a *Chd7* mouse model has investigated the prevalence of anosmia and hypogonadotrophic hypogonadism which are reported in the majority of human cases. These features could not be consistently demonstrated, and there was marked variation in these aspects of the phenotype despite genetic homogeneity (Bergman, Bosman *et al.* 2010).

A review of CHARGE syndrome can be found at: Blake, K.D. and Prasad, C. (2006) 'CHARGE syndrome.' *Orphanet Journal of Rare Diseases*, 1: 34, doi:10.1186/1750-1172-1-34, www.ojrd.com.

21.

Coffin-Lowry syndrome (CLS)

GENE LOCUS: Xp22.2

KEY ASD REFERENCE: Manouvrier-Hanu *et al.* 1999

SUMMARY: Coffin-Lowry syndrome (CLS) is a clinical disorder resulting from a defect in the RPS6KA3 gene at Xp22.2 (Jacquot, Zeniou, Touraine and Hanaver 2002). There is little apparent correlation between the genotype and the clinical phenotype. A large number of *de novo* defects are reported – 44/45 cases in one recent series (Delaunoy, Dubos, Marques Periera and Hanaver 2006). There have been reports of cases with the CLS phenotype but different gene defects thought to interfere with the same pathways (MAP Kinase) as RPS6KA3. For example, McCandless *et al.* (2000) report a case where a 10q25.1–25.3 deletion was found with no abnormality at Xp22.2.

CLS was first described by Coffin, Siris and Wegienka in 1966, and later by Lowry,

Miller and Fraser in 1971, and in 1972 by Procopis and Turner. Credit for recognizing that there was a common underlying condition to the presenting phenotype goes to Temtamy, Miller and Hussels-Maumenee, who recognized in 1975 that all of the reported cases had a similar pattern of facial features, abnormalities of the fingers and toes, and learning disability.

HOW COMMON IS COFFIN-LOWRY SYNDROME? There are no accurate data available. One author (Hanauer 2001) has given an estimate of between one in 50,000 and one in 100,000.

MAIN CLINICAL FEATURES: Affected males have severe to profound levels of learning disability. They are typically of short stature and commonly microcephalic. They have fleshy hands with short, tapering fingers. There are characteristic facial features, with large ears, large mouth with full lips, and broad, flattened nose. Scoliosis (progressive curvature of the spine) is a common feature that is progressive and seen in almost half of all males with CLS (Hunter 2002). Obesity is a common problem, but may be secondary to the fact that many individuals need to be in wheelchairs due to frequent stimulus-induced drop episodes (SIDEs). SIDEs are a form of attack brought on by being suddenly startled, which results in the person dropping down without loss of consciousness. These attacks are seen in approximately one in five cases (Stephenson et al. 2005), with epilepsy being seen in some five per cent, usually as a progression from these to myoclonic epilepsy and tonic spasms.

Cardiac problems are also common and can take a variety of forms (Hunter 2002).

Problems with intestinal function, teeth, vision and hearing have all been reported (Hartsfield et al. 1993; Sivagamasundari et al. 1994), but on current evidence are less characteristic of CLS.

In the only small systematic study of cognitive function to date, Simensen et al. (2002) reported on two African-American families with three normal male and three normal female family members, six affected males and seven carrier females. There was a clear association between genetic status and IQ, with the following average scores on standardized testing: unaffected – 90.8; carrier – 65; affected – 43.2.

In one small study, Harum, Alemi and Johnston (2001) found in a sample of five boys and two girls with CLS that there was a correlation between their level of cognitive functioning and levels of CREB (factor cAMP response element-binding protein). CREB production is affected by RPS6KA3. It was suggested that genes responsive to CREB could be implicated in other phenotypic characteristics, such as the facial and skeletal differences seen in CLS.

A recent brain-imaging report compared individuals from two families with CLS to matched controls. The study found the brains of those with CLS to be consistently smaller, particularly the cerebellum and hippocampus, with a suggestion that the extent of difference in hippocampal size is associated with cognitive level (Kesler et al. 2007).

Behavioural difficulties such as self-injury and destructive behaviour have been reported, but whether they are common is unknown (Hunter, Schwartz and Abidi 2007).

Clinical presentation can vary widely.

• Facher et al. (2004) described a boy with developmental and physical features of CLS who presented at 14 years of age with sudden onset of symptoms of congestive heart failure.

• Heterozygous females have developmental levels ranging from normal to profound learning disability. They also show the characteristic hand differences and are prone to develop scoliosis in around a third of cases.

- Depression has been reported in several papers (Haspeslagh *et al.* 1984; Partington *et al.* 1988; Sivagamasundari *et al.* 1994) but it is unclear whether this is a biologically driven or a reactive process, and no systematic research has been undertaken.

A useful recent summary of CLS can be found in Hunter, Schwartz and Abidi (2007).

IS THERE A LINK BETWEEN COFFIN-LOWRY SYNDROME AND ASD? In 1999 Manouvrier-Hanu *et al.* reported on two brothers with a mild Coffin-Lowry syndrome phenotype, and a previously unreported RSK2 missense mutation genotype. Both boys had transient but severe hypotonia, large heads and delayed closure of the fontanelles, and both had mild learning disability. In the first sibling, psychomotor regression and slow language acquisition, with progressive social isolation and development of motor stereotypies, led to a diagnosis of autism, intensive early psychotherapy and an improvement in social engagement. Continence was delayed, and motor and communication development remained slow.

No systematic screening of CLS cases for the presence of ASD symptomology has yet been carried out.

DIFFERENTIAL DIAGNOSIS: Several syndromes share some characteristics with Coffin-Lowry syndrome, including alpha-thalassaemia mental retardation syndrome and Borjeson-Forssman-Lehmann syndrome, but none have the characteristic hand features seen in CLS. Williams syndrome [77] is the most relevant to be considered in a person with an ASD.

MANAGEMENT AND TREATMENT:

- SIDEs can be distressing and can be managed using antiepileptic medication (O'Riordan, Patton and Schon 2006).
- Self-injurious and destructive behaviours can occur, and there is some evidence that medication can be helpful in reducing these (Valdovinos *et al.* 2002).
- The major clinical features which are important to monitor and to treat as necessary are the cardiac features, where present, and the scoliosis. Both of these would be managed as in anyone else with the same clinical presentation, but as both can have a major impact on both quality and length of life, they should be regularly monitored and managed as appropriate when found.

ANIMAL MODELS: To date, no specific animal models of CLS have been reported.

22.

Coffin-Siris syndrome

aka • fifth digit syndrome

GENE LOCUS: Not established. There is a suggestion from two cases (McGhee *et al.* 2000; McPherson *et al.* 1997) that the gene may be on 7q32–q34.

KEY ASD REFERENCES: Hersh, Bloom and Weisskopf 1982; Swillen, Glorieux, Peeters and Fryns 1995

SUMMARY: The condition was first described by Coffin and Siris in 1970. They gave details of three unrelated girls, all with learning disability and a missing nail and last section of the fifth finger. The equivalent portion of the little toe was also absent, or reduced in size, on both feet. These finger and toe abnormalities gave rise to the alternative term 'fifth digit syndrome'. There was no family history in any of Coffin and Siris' original cases. However, two cases have now been reported where there is partial expression in one parent (Haspeslagh, Fryns and van den Berghe 1984; Tunnessen, McMillan and Levin 1978).

HOW COMMON IS COFFIN-SIRIS SYNDROME? This is an uncommon disorder. To date only around 40 cases have been reported in the world literature. Estimation of the prevalence of ASD is not possible on current information.

MAIN CLINICAL FEATURES: Coffin-Siris syndrome is a syndrome with learning disability, abnormalities to the little fingers and toes, coarsening of facial features, and excessive hair growth, associated with multiple congenital anomalies. Feeding problems and frequent infections are also common features (Fleck *et al.* 2001).

Several pieces of information have been taken to suggest an autosomal recessive pattern of inheritance, in particular the occurrence of affected siblings (Carey and Hall 1978; Franceschini *et al.* 1986) and a child born to consanguineous parents (Richieri-Costa, Monteleone-Neto and Gonzales 1986). There is still some debate over the inheritance pattern.

CENTRAL NERVOUS SYSTEM FEATURES: Several cases have been reported with a 'Dandy–Walker malformation' (Coffin and Siris 1970; DeBassio, Kemper and Knoefel 1985; Imai *et al.* 2001; Tunnessen, McMillan and Levin 1978) – a condition with abnormal development of the outer layers of the cerebellar vermis and dilation of the fourth cerebral ventricle, but without enlargement of the other cerebral ventricles. This pattern is well described in the autism literature by Courchesne (1997) and others.

IS THERE A LINK BETWEEN COFFIN-SIRIS SYNDROME AND ASD? The case described by Hersh, Bloom and Weisskopf (1982) was as six-year-old girl with growth retardation, dysmorphic facial features and abnormal little fingers and toes consistent with the Coffin-Siris phenotype. She had learning disability, and a 'severe behavioural relating disorder was observed which was consistent with a diagnosis of childhood autism'.

In a series of 12 cases aged 2.5 to 19 years, documented by Swillen, Glorieux, Peeters and Fryns (1995), all exhibited learning difficulties (three mild and nine moderate). All showed significant expressive language delay, but those old enough to be systematically assessed showed language comprehension commensurate with their mental age, and gross motor skills were also developmentally appropriate. Five showed pervasive developmental disorder, a DSM-III-R diagnosis consistent with ASD. Obsessional routines and rituals and unusual fears characterized the older children, while difficult, aggressive and disruptive behaviour was more typical of the younger children.

DIFFERENTIAL DIAGNOSIS: The condition that can present with similar features to Coffin-Siris syndrome and is also reported in association with ASD is Cornelia de Lange syndrome [27] (Fryns 1986; Musio *et al.* 2006).

Choanal atresia, a typical feature of the CHARGE association [20], has been reported in Coffin-Siris and could result in confusion between the two conditions (DeJong and Nelson 1992).

MANAGEMENT AND TREATMENT: To date, there are no specific treatment or management approaches that have been shown to be helpful, based on the diagnosis of Coffin-Siris syndrome.

ANIMAL MODELS: There are no Coffin-Siris animal models at the present time.

23.

Cohen syndrome

aka • Pepper syndrome

GENE LOCUS: 8q22–q23

KEY ASD REFERENCES: Cohen *et al.* 1973; Howlin 2001; Howlin, Karpf and Turk 2005; Karpf, Turk and Howlin 2004

SUMMARY: Typically, Cohen syndrome presents with motor delay and hypotonia; coordination problems; microcephaly; joint hyperlaxity; myopia and progressive retinal problems; and intermittent neutropenia. Those affected usully have a happy disposition. It is an autosomal recessive condition that results from a defect in the COH1 gene.

HOW COMMON IS COHEN SYNDROME? Cohen syndrome is a rare condition. The prevalence has been estimated as one in 105,000. However, the numbers of cases reported suggest that many cases go undetected, so that currently the prevalence of Cohen syndrome has not been clearly established (Falk, Wang and Traboulski 2006). Over 100 cases have so far been reported, but in case series rather than from epidemiological studies.

MAIN CLINICAL FEATURES: Cohen syndrome is an autosomal recessive condition that is more common in families of Finnish descent (Norio 2003). In this population the phenotype is characteristic – mild to moderate motor delay; clumsiness; microcephaly; joint hyperlaxity; childhood hypotonia; a progressive retinochoroid dystrophy; myopia; intermittent neutropenia;

and a happy disposition (Kolehmainen *et al.* 2003). Progressive myopia seems to be a characteristic seen in the majority of cases (Seifert *et al.* 2006).

This phenotype has also been described in non-Finnish populations (Chandler *et al.* 2003).

In addition, there are characteristic facial features that seem more specific to Finnish Cohen syndrome individuals: high-arched or wave-shaped eyelids; short, broad nostrils; thick hair; and a low hairline. Retinal mottling appears to be another feature specific to Finnish cases (Kondo, Nagataki and Miyagi 1990). Facial measurements on Finnish cases show the upper face to be normally proportioned and the lower face to be narrower, making the face seem more pointed (Hurmerinta, Pirinen, Kovero and Kivitie-Kallio 2002).

The widely variable clinical features seem to result from the wide range of mutations that are sufficient for the condition to express. In one study of 20 cases from 12 family pedigrees from Brazil, Germany, Lebanon, Oman, Poland and Turkey, 17 separate novel mutations of COH1 were found (Hennies *et al.* 2004). Seifert *et al.* (2006) identified 25 different COH1 mutations in 24 patients from a variety of ethnic backgrounds.

An MRI study of 18 people with Cohen syndrome (Kivitie-Kallio, Larsen, Kajasto and Norio 1998) and 26 volunteer controls found that there was an enlarged corpus callosum in the context of an overall microcephaly. This is an unusual finding in learning disability. Grey and white matter intensities appeared normal, with an overall reduction in central nervous system volume. Further research may confirm this as a clear diagnostic marker of Cohen syndrome diagnosis.

The same research group published the first detailed clinical description of neuropsychological and behavioural features, documenting the same cohort of 18 cases used in their MRI study (Kivitie-Kallio, Larsen, Kajasto and Norio 1999). Psychomotor retardation and microcephaly were the first obvious clinical features. Behavioural stereotypies and mannerisms were common, but all had cheerful sociable personalities and none exhibited significant behavioural issues.

IS THERE A LINK BETWEEN COHEN SYNDROME AND ASD?

- The first paper to suggest a possible link between ASD and Cohen syndrome was published in 2001 (Howlin 2001). It presented information from a postal survey of families of 33 affected individuals (18 male, 15 female), between two and 45 years of age. From 19 of these, the results obtained were consistent with criteria for autism. If substantiated, this suggests that approximately 57 per cent of Cohen syndrome individuals may have autism.

- Karpf, Turk and Howlin (2004) reported results from cognitive, linguistic and adaptive assessments of a group of 45 individuals clinically diagnosed with Cohen syndrome. Twenty (10 male and 10 female) were classed as 'definite' cases, based on clinical features. In the 'definite' group there was wide variation in performance IQ: from 20 to 104 (average 48.1). Scores in all areas on the Vineland Adaptive Behavior Scales were low, in general in line with the performance/non-verbal intelligence quotient (PIQ), but the sociable temperament seen in Cohen syndrome perhaps helps to explain the slightly stronger scores on the socialization scale.

- Howlin, Karpf and Turk (2005) reported on behaviour and autistic features in the cohort already described by Karpf,

Turk and Howlin (2004). On the ADOS (Autism Diagnostic Observation Scale), 23/43 (53 per cent) fitted criteria for autism, and 34 (79 per cent) for ASD.

- The original paper describing this condition was published by Michael Cohen et al. in 1973. It described a brother and sister and a further unrelated patient with poor muscle tone, obesity, high nasal bridge, and prominent incisor teeth. All the cases had a learning disability.

DIFFERENTIAL DIAGNOSIS:

- Similarities have been noted between Cohen syndrome and Prader-Willi syndrome [61] (Fraccaro et al. 1983; Fuhrmann-Rieger, Kohler and Fuhrmann 1984).

- Kolehmainen et al. (2004) assessed a cohort of 76 individuals who were thought to have possible Cohen syndrome on the basis of clinical phenotype. The aim was to try to link genotype to clinical phenotype. Comparison was on the basis of the number of criteria met – the presence or absence of eight features:

1. developmental delay
2. microcephaly
3. typical Cohen syndrome facial gestalt
4. truncal obesity with slender extremities
5. overly sociable behaviour
6. joint hypermobility
7. high myopia and/or retinal dystrophy
8. neutropenia.

Of the individuals who met six or more criteria (N=37) 22 had COH1 mutations at 8q22–q23. None of the 39 who met five or fewer criteria had COH1 mutations.

- Eight individuals from two large Amish kindreds have been described (Falk *et al.* 2004) who had early-onset pigmentary retinopathy and myopia, global learning disability, microcephaly, short stature, low muscle tone, joint hyperlaxity, small hands and feet, and a friendly disposition, and the genetic basis was mapped to COH1 at 8q22–q23. This provides evidence of a second genetic condition which has been linked to ASD within the Amish (the other being Cortical Dysplasia–Focal Epilepsy [19]).

MANAGEMENT AND TREATMENT: To date no specific treatments have been developed for Cohen syndrome that differ from those for others with ASD. The fairly specific retinal problems require careful monitoring and treatment as required.

ANIMAL MODELS: At the present time there are no animal models of the Cohen syndrome phenotype.

24.

Cole-Hughes macrocephaly syndrome (CHMS)

aka • macrocephaly/autism syndrome

GENE LOCUS: Not clearly established. Some cases have mutations of the PTEN tumour suppressor gene (Butler *et al.* 2005). There may be an overlap with Bannayan-Riley-Ruvalcaba syndrome [15].

KEY ASD REFERENCES: Butler *et al.* 2005; Naqvi, Cole and Graham 2000

SUMMARY: Cole-Hughes macrocephaly syndrome has characteristic craniofacial features, with a pronounced but narrow forehead and a square jaw. There is progressive weight gain starting off from a normal birthweight, and poor language and social development.

HOW COMMON IS CHMS? There is no prevalence information available on CHMS. If it is genetically contiguous with Bannayan-Riley-Ruvalcaba syndrome [15], as the features of BRRS are broadly defined, the two conditions may be turn out to be phenotypically identical, despite the apparent lack of BRRS features in the subjects reported by Butler *et al.* (2005).

MAIN CLINICAL FEATURES: CHMS was first recognized in a larger cohort study looking for Sotos syndrome [68] (Cole and Hughes 1991). Six of the cases they described had a characteristic physical and behavioural phenotype. In these six (of the 79 individuals evaluated), the same craniofacial characteristics were seen – a square outline to the face, with a pronounced forehead, a narrow forehead, and long, narrow nostrils. Birthweight and body proportions were normal at birth, but there was rapid weight gain and the individuals were obese on follow-up. In addition, their language and social skills were significantly poorer developmentally than their motor function.

In a review of 100 ASD cases, Stevenson *et al.* (1997) had found progressive postnatal macrocephaly in 24, of whom 15 (62 per cent) had one or both parents also with macrocephaly.

IS THERE A LINK BETWEEN CHMS AND ASD? In 2000, Naqvi, Cole and Graham described two patients with the features reported in CHMS who also showed characteristics consistent with co-morbid diagnoses of ASD and ADHD.

Butler *et al.* (2005) studied a group of 18 subjects aged from three to 18 with ASD and a significant degree of macrocephaly. There were no features suggestive of Bannayan-Riley-Ruvalcaba syndrome [15], except for pigmented macules on the glans penis of one boy, nor of Cowden syndrome [26]. As a number of other conditions are now known to produce this phenotype (such as basal cell naevus syndrome [16]; Cortical Dysplasia–Focal Epilepsy syndrome [19]; Orstavik 1997 syndrome [56]; Proteus syndrome [62]; and Sotos syndrome [68]), Butler et al.'s conclusion of CHMS by exclusion is not adequate to characterize their group. In three of the 18 cases there was a PTEN mutation consistent with BRRS.

DIFFERENTIAL DIAGNOSIS: CHMS presents with a pronounced macrocephaly, and the other conditions listed in Table A9 should be considered along with benign familial megalencephaly/macrocephaly (Day and Schutt 1979).

MANAGEMENT AND TREATMENT: No specific treatment or management implications can be drawn from our current level of understanding of this putative condition.

ANIMAL MODELS: There are no animal models of this condition, as the genotype has not been clearly characterized.

25.

Congenital adrenal hyperplasia (CAH)

aka • 21-hydroxylase-deficient congenital adrenal hyperplasia
• adrenogenital syndrome (AG syndrome)
• C-21-hydroxylase deficiency
• congenital adrenocortical hyperplasia

GENE LOCUS: 6p21.3

KEY ASD REFERENCES: Falter, Plaisted and Davis 2008; Knickmeyer et al. 2006; Sieg 2009

SUMMARY: This is a group of autosomal recessive disorders that interfere with the body's ability to manufacture cortisol from cholesterol by the adrenal cortex. It most commonly results from a gene defect in CYP21A2, the gene responsible for the production of 21-hydroxylase (21-OHD).

HOW COMMON IS CAH? There are so-called 'classic' and 'non-classic' forms of CAH. (See 'Main Clinical Features' below.) Current estimates for the overall prevalence of CAH are that it affects approximately one in every 10,000 live births (Orphanet 2009).

For 'classic' CAH, the analysis of approximately 6.5 million newborns screened in different populations worldwide gave an overall incidence of one in every 15,000 live births (Pang and Shook 1997). The prevalence in specific populations varies widely, from one in 300 in the Yupik Eskimos of Alaska to one in 23,000 in the New Zealand population (Wilson et al. 2007). The classic form further divides into the virilizing (approximately 25 per cent) and salt-wasting (approximately 75 per cent) subgroups.

There is less information on the prevalence of 'non-classic' CAH. The prevalence in the general population of New York City was estimated to be one in 100, with the highest nonclassic disease prevalence (1/27) in the Ashkenazi Jewish population. High rates are also reported in several other New York ethnic groups, such as Hispanic (1/40) and Slav (1/50), while the rate in New York Italians is somewhat lower (1/300) (Speiser et al. 1985).

MAIN CLINICAL FEATURES:
1. Classic
In all classic cases, there is deficient cortisol production. The classic form of CAH, if not

treated neonatally, presents in both sexes with virilization, with genital enlargement in both sexes (but smaller testes in males). Over time there is accelerated appearance of pubic and underarm hair, rapid physical growth and accelerated bone age. Severe acne is common. Premature epiphyseal fusion results in short adult stature, compared to unaffected family members. Shorter adult stature does not seem to be corrected by cortisol treatment. Untreated girls have a high incidence of menstrual problems, hirsutism, male pattern baldness and reduced fertility.

2. Non-classic

The non-classic form does not typically result in lowered cortisol production, and is a later onset problem, but in many other respects presents similar issues. Premature bone fusion can cause short stature (as in the classic type), and hirsutism, acne and other virilizing aspects of excessive androgen exposure can be seen. Females with the non-classic form can have reduced fertility (seen in around half of reported cases) and severe menstrual problems (10 per cent). Polycystic ovaries are common.

Clinical diagnosis: The diagnosis is usually made or suspected in four situations:

- in children born to affected individuals
- in girls with precocious or accelerated virilization
- in boys who show virilization in childhood (i.e. pseudoprecocious puberty)
- in any infant with a salt-losing crisis in the first four weeks of life.

IS THERE A LINK BETWEEN CAH AND ASD?

In 2006, Knickmeyer and colleagues from the Autism Research Centre in Cambridge published a paper on scoring on the Autism Spectrum Quotient by individuals with congenital adrenal hyperplasia (34 females,

26 males) and their unaffected relatives (24 females, 25 males). Based on the extreme male brain theory of ASD, the prediction was that androgenized females with CAH would have elevated scores on this scale compared to their unaffected female relatives, while males with CAH would not demonstrate an effect. The results bore out this prediction. However, it is important to note that, although statistically significant, the size of the effect still placed the CAH female scores (mean score 18.44+/−5.51, compared to control scores of 16+/−4.25) well below the cut-off for clinical suspicion (26 or more).

A recent single-case report (Sieg 2009) presented a 12-year-old Caucasian boy with CAH who fulfilled criteria for autism, with an overall score of 126 on the Autism Behavior Checklist. (Scores of 67 or more are typically taken as indicative of ASD.)

The 'extreme male brain' theory of ASD (Baron-Cohen 2002) developed from a more general theory concerning neurodevelopmental disorders, proposed by Geschwind and Galaburda (1985a, 1985b, 1985c). The basic theory suggested that an increased prevalence of neurodevelopmental disorders *per se* could be related to increased *in utero* exposure to male sex hormones, which could result in megalencephaly, with greater cerebral symmetry, an increased rate of anomalous handedness, a greater prevalence of immune disorders and a higher likelihood of epilepsy, and which would be overrepresented in males. One test of this general model has been to evaluate the effects of conditions (such as 'classic' CAH in girls) which result in increased exposure to male sex hormones – and whether increased *in utero* exposure to testosterones results in more masculinized behaviour. The results to date appear to support this hypothesis. (See, for example, Pasterski *et al.* 2007.)

A further questionnaire survey, using the Testosterone-related Medical Questionnaire, based on the predictions of the 'extreme male brain' theory, investigated the presence of medical cases consistent with elevated testosterone in a sample of 54 women with ASD, 74 mothers of children with ASD, and 183 controls. The theory would predict that some of the women with ASD and possibly the mothers of children with ASD would have elevated levels of testosterone compared to the controls. Some conditions related to increased testosterone were more common in the ASD cases and mothers but CAH, contrary to prediction, was seen in none of the mothers or ASD cases, but in two affected controls (Ingudomnukul, Baron-Cohen, Wheelwright and Knickmeyer 2007).

In utero androgen exposure significantly affects somatic development in both the male and the female foetus (Okten, Kalyoncu and Yaris 2002), but Falter, Plaisted and Davis (2008) argue that increased androgen exposure alone cannot account for all of the findings in CAH. They review the evidence from growth studies – largely, to date, the relative length of the second and fourth fingers, coupled with the level of testosterone exposure – and discuss genetic conditions that alter *in utero* androgen exposure levels. They conclude that *in utero* androgen exposure is not sufficient to account for the cognitive aspects of CAH, and challenge the view that it is sufficient to result in ASD.

DIFFERENTIAL DIAGNOSIS: CAH has been reported in association with a sex chromosome aneuploidy (XYY) [4], which would of itself have accelerated *in utero* virilization by increasing circulating testosterone levels (Mallin and Walker 1972). This has only been reported in a single case and is unlikely to be a common

factor, but rather a reason for this particular boy to have come to clinical attention.

Phenotypic cases have also been reported in association with muscular dystrophy [33] with glycerol kinase deficiency (Francke *et al.* 1987), and with Ehlers-Danlos syndrome [34], hypermobility type. The association with Ehlers-Danlos is due to contiguity of the CYP21A2 involved in CAH, and the TNX gene involved in this variant of Ehlers-Danlos (Schalkwijk *et al.* 2001). The cases reported do not appear to have an ASD.

MANAGEMENT AND TREATMENT: In non-classic cases, treatment is not always required. However, in classic cases the disorder is lifelong and requires treatment and monitoring throughout life.

Treatment for classic 21-OHD CAH includes glucocorticoid replacement therapy, which needs to be increased during periods of stress. Individuals with the salt-wasting form of 21-OHD CAH require treatment with 9alpha-fludrohydrocortisone and often sodium chloride.

Bilateral adrenalectomy may be indicated for individuals with severe 21-OHD CAH who are homozygous and has been reported as helpful in some homozygous cases that have not responded to hormone replacement (Meyers and Grua; Van Wyk *et al.* 1996 2000).

Given that the link between CAH and ASD is theoretical rather than substantial at this point (despite screening of groups in whom one might have expected to find cases, had the link been substantive and significant), no further information will be given here. There are several excellent and fairly recent reviews of CAH and its clinical implications (Forest 2004; New 2004; Ogilvie *et al.* 2006; Speiser and White 2003) and the reader is referred to these for more specific information on CAH.

A downloadable guide for patients and families to CAH caused by 21-hydroxylase deficiency can be found at www.hopkinschildrens.org.

ANIMAL MODELS: Target disruption to StAR (steroidogenic acute regulatory protein) provides a knockout mouse model of CAH in steroidgenesis (Caron *et al.* 1997). However, there have been no further publications on this model.

There are no direct animal models of the phenotypic effects of defects at the CAH gene locus. The chromosomal area involved is interesting as it is highly conserved (Tripodis *et al.* 2000) and is adjacent to the centromeric end of the major histocompatability complex involved in peptide generation (Kasahara *et al.* 1996).

26.

Cowden syndrome (CS)

aka • PTEN hamartoma tumour syndrome (PHTS)

• Bannayan-Ruvalcaba-Riley syndrome

• Bannayan-Riley-Ruvalcaba syndrome

• Bannayan-Zonana syndrome

• Riley-Smith syndrome

• Ruvalcaba-Myhre-Smith syndrome

• Proteus syndrome

GENE LOCI: 10q23.31, 10q22.3

KEY ASD REFERENCES: Butler *et al.* 2005; Goffin *et al.* 2001

SUMMARY: Cowden syndrome is one of a number of overlapping hamartoma disorders. It presents with macrocephaly and mild learning disability, and with slowly developing trichilemmomas and papilloma which develop over the early decades of life.

The difficulty in presenting separate sections in this volume dealing with the various hamartoma disorders that have been reported in association with ASD concerns the current uncertainty over the extent to which these are discrete conditions, and the extent to which they overlap with one another, or are actually synonymous. Butler *et al.* (2005), for example, talk about 'Cowden syndrome (a cancer syndrome) *and other **related** hamartoma disorders* such as Bannayan-Riley-Ruvalcaba syndrome, Proteus syndrome, and Proteus-like conditions' (my emphases), i.e. they assume that the conditions are discrete. Marsh *et al.* (1998) in contrast, drawing on PTEN mutation genotype–phenotype data from 43 BRRS [15] and 37 Cowden syndrome cases, conclude that they may be overlapping phenotypic presentations of the same genetic condition. Others (see, for example, Gustafson, Zbuk, Scacheri and Eng 2007) subsume these various conditions under the umbrella term of PTEN hamartoma tumour syndrome (PHTS).

PTEN mutations are seen in approximately 80 per cent of CS cases. Nuclear PTEN appears to mediate cell cycle arrest, while cytoplasmic PTEN is required for apoptosis (Chung and Eng 2005). Abnormalities of apoptosis can result in brain overgrowth, as the major factor that produces normal brain differentiation is selective cell death. PTEN appears to remove phosphate groups from three amino acids – tyrosine, serine and threonine. It plays an important role in the inhibition of cell migration, a factor that is important in keeping cancer growth in check.

HOW COMMON IS COWDEN SYNDROME?
Due to the diagnostic uncertainties mentioned above, 10q22–q23 defects tend to be estimated on joint prevalence. The true prevalence is unknown, but has been estimated at one in 200,000 (Nelen *et al.* 1999); if we assume CS to be a discrete condition, this figure is likely to be an underestimate. The variable and sometimes mild or absent phenotypic features (Haibach *et al.* 1992; Schrager *et al.* 1998) mean that many individuals go undiagnosed, and may in effect have the genotype without phenotypic manifestations (McDonald-McGinn *et al.* 2001). This factor may also lead to a misleading indication of likely severity.

MAIN CLINICAL FEATURES: CS is a multiple hamartoma syndrome with a high risk of both benign and malignant thyroid, breast and endometrial cancers. Affected individuals usually have macrocephaly, trichilemmomas (a tumour which forms around the hair follicles) and papilloma (small benign skin tumours), and all are typically present by the time the person is in their late twenties. The lifetime risk of developing breast cancer is 25–50 per cent, with an average age of diagnosis between 38 and 46 years (Starink *et al.* 1986). Breast cancer has been noted in male as well as female cases (Fackenthal *et al.* 2001), and is strongly associated with the presence of PTEN mutations (Marsh *et al.* 1998). Thyroid nodules, adenoma and goitre occur in up to 75 per cent of CS cases (Harach *et al.* 1999) while the lifetime risk for thyroid cancer (usually follicular, rarely papillary, but never medullary thyroid) is around 10 per cent. The risk of endometrial cancer is not well documented but may be around 5–10 per cent.

Most cases have clear clinical features indicative of the disorder by their third decade of life.

Cowden syndrome has consensus diagnostic criteria that are regularly updated (see Eng 2000). IQ is typically in the mild learning disability range.

PTEN mutations are found in a high proportion of PHTS cases:

- in 85 per cent of individuals who meet the diagnostic criteria for CS (Marsh *et al.* 1998; Zhou *et al.* 2003)

- in 65 per cent of individuals with a clinical diagnosis of BRRS (Marsh *et al.* 1998; Zhou *et al.* 2003); but

- the proportion of Proteus syndrome cases with PTEN mutations is at present not known.

IS THERE A LINK BETWEEN CS AND ASD?

- Goffin *et al.* (2001) reported a mother and son with a diagnosis of Cowden syndrome and a PTEN mutation. The boy presented with autistic behaviour and learning disability. His mother had normal intelligence and social skills. The authors stressed the association of progressive macrocephaly and pervasive developmental disorder, and its association with PTEN mutations.

- Butler *et al.* (2005) presented information on a series of 18 cases of ASD who had associated extreme macrocephaly (head circumference 2.5 to 8.0 SD above the population mean).

DIFFERENTIAL DIAGNOSIS: The main differential diagnoses, assuming that the conditions are separable, are BRRS and Proteus syndrome, as well as certain other hamartoma syndromes – juvenile polyposis syndrome (JPS), where the primary clinical presentation is with intestinal polyps of the lamina propria, and Peutz-Jeghers syndrome (PJS), which also gives rise to intestinal polyps and abnormal mucocutaneous pigmentation.

Other possible but less likely differential diagnoses associated with ASD are neurofibromatosis type 1 [51] and basal cell naevus syndrome [16].

The clinical presentation in BRRS is argued to be somewhat different. The cancer risks are equivalent, which may be related to the PTEN gene defect in both conditions (Marsh *et al.* 1999). There is clear symptom overlap between the two diagnoses (Marsh *et al.* 1999), as well as a demonstrated genetic overlap with Proteus syndrome, cases of which have been described with mutations that have been identified as causing CS and BRRS (Zhou *et al.* 2000, *et al.* 2001).

Proteus syndrome (PS) [62], like BRRS, is an overgrowth condition affecting multiple tissues and associated with a PTEN defect. As currently defined, Proteus syndrome is selectively associated with a number of rarer types of tumour (of the central nervous system and genitourinary system) that have not been reported in either BRRS or CS. As a significant number of cases of Proteus syndrome without PTEN deletions have been found, there may be different genetic mechanisms operating in this overgrowth disorder (Thiffault, Schwartz, Der Kaloustian and Foulkes 2004).

Relatives can be tested, and if they do not have the PTEN mutation they are not at increased cancer risk. If parents carry the mutation, then siblings have a 50 per cent risk of having the mutation. Where parents do not, the risk to siblings is low.

All children of someone carrying a PTEN mutation have a 50 per cent risk of being affected. Where one parent carries the mutation, their blood relatives are also at increased risk of being affected.

MANAGEMENT AND TREATMENT: The most serious consequences of CS relate to the increased risk of breast, thryoid, endometrial and renal cancers, and so the most important aspect of management, as for other PTEN defects, is increased cancer surveillance and appropriate management of identified cancers. Information on an appropriate surveillance regime can be found in Zbuk, Stein and Eng (2006).

There is no evidence to date for beneficial effects of prophylactic treatment of cases to reduce cancer risk.

mTOR inhibitors are showing promise in the treatment of malignancies in individuals who have a germline PTEN mutation. These are not yet available for clinical use. No clinical trials have yet been carried out specifically with individuals with any PTEN hamartoma tumour syndrome.

ANIMAL MODELS: mTOR inhibitory effects have been extensively studied from the point of view of interfering with PTEN effects in tumourigenesis (Neshat *et al.* 2001).

In a tissue-specific PTEN model of prostate cancer in the mouse, upregulation of PTEN activity, with reduction in tumour growth and an increase in lifespan, was achieved through dietary omega-3 enrichment (Berquin *et al.* 2007).

A model that results in PTEN loss in all tissues has yet to be achieved (Lu T.L. *et al.* 2007).

27.

de Lange syndrome (CdLS)

aka • Cornelia de Lange syndrome

- Brachmann-de Lange syndrome (BDLS)

Includes:

- NIPBL-Related Cornelia de Lange syndrome
- SMC1L1-Related Cornelia de Lange syndrome

GENE LOCI: 5p13.1 (NIPBL), Xp11.22–p11.21 (SMC1L1), 10q25 (SMC3 and SMC1A)

KEY ASD REFERENCES: Basile, Villa, Selicorni and Molteni 2007; Bhuiyan *et al.* 2006; Moss *et al.* 2008

SUMMARY: A probable case of CdLS was first described by Willem Vrolik in 1849 (Vrolik 1849; also see Oostra, Baljet and Hennekam 1994).

The condition is named after the Dutch paediatrician Cornelia de Lange, who first described cases in 1933, originally using the term 'degeneration' ('*typus Amstelodamensis*)'. It first became known in English as 'Amsterdam dwarfism' ('*typus degenerativus Amstelodamensis*') (de Knecht-van Eekelen and Hennekam 1994; de Lange 1933; MacDonald 1973). The earlier term 'Brachmann-de Lange syndrome' honours an earlier descriptive monograph by the German physician Winfried Brachmann (1916), who described in detail the physical characteristics of a child who had similar features but had died of pneumonia at 19 days old.

CdLS is inherited either as an X-linked or as an autosomal dominant condition. To date, four genes have been identified as causing the de Lange phenotype. The first, NIPBL, accounts for around 50 per cent of cases tested, while SMC1L1 has been reported in one family and one sporadic case (Musio *et al.* 2006), and SMC3–SMC1A in a single case (Deardorff *et al.* 2007). The severity of the phenotype is linked to the genotype, and the extent to which the cohesin system is impaired. Cohesinopathies (amongst those so far identified being de Lange, Roberts and Warsaw breakage syndromes) are multisystem developmental disorders that result from defects in the system that maintains chromosome cohesion between replicating sister chromatids.

Typically CdLS arises as a *de novo* mutation, with fewer than one per cent of people affected having the gene difference identified in either of their parents. Therefore, on this basis and in view of the lowered likelihood of someone who is affected wanting children, it is unlikely that others in the family will be affected. If a parent carries the mutation, then the likelihood of a sister being affected will be 50 per cent, but 50 per cent for a brother only when the mother carries the mutation. Affected men could only pass on a CdLS gene to their daughters and not to their sons.

One genetic basis to CdLS, a gene defect in NIPBL, was identified in 2004 (Krantz *et al.* 2004). Three other genes have also been identified as linked (SMC1L1, SMC1A and SMC3). An early suggestion of a link to 3q has not been borne out (Krantz *et al.* 2004) and mutations in this area are now a differential diagnosis. To date a genetic basis is identifiable in around 70 per cent of cases diagnosed by phenotype, suggesting that other sites or sub-threshold defects may be involved (Borck *et al.* 2004).

CdLS is one of a group of disorders known as cohesinopathies where the primary defect is in one of the mechanisms involved in chromosome segregation (McNairn and Gerton 2008a, 2008b).

HOW COMMON IS DE LANGE SYNDROME?
De Lange syndrome is equally common in males and females. It is thought to have a prevalence of 1.24 in 100,000 births

(Barisic *et al.* 2008). As milder phenotypes are often not recognized, this may be an underestimate, and figures as high as one in 10,000 have been suggested by some (Opitz 1985).

MAIN CLINICAL FEATURES: In the European Surveillance of Congenital Anomalies (Barisic *et al.* 2008; also see www.eurocat-network.eu), the most common associated physical features are as follows:

- limb defects (73.1 per cent)
- heart defects (45.6 per cent)
- central nervous system malformations (40.2 per cent)
- cleft palate (21.7 per cent)

Low birthweight is seen in around two-thirds of cases, and lower birthweight is associated with more severe complications. Boys are significantly more likely to have limb malformations.

The main diagnostic features of CdLS include:

- dysmorphic facial features (a low frontal hairline, a small, upturned nose with a triangular tip, a crescent-shaped mouth, arched eyebrows, often with synophrys – a single eyebrow across both eyes – and small, widely spaced teeth) (Jackson L. *et al.* 1993)
- hirsutism in general
- slow antenatal and postnatal growth
- microcephaly
- reduced upper limb growth – the most common feature, with relative preservation of the lower limbs
- cardiac defects – seen in around a quarter of all cases (Mehta and Ambalavanan 1997; Tsukahara *et al.* 1998), and may be complex, but ventricular septal and atrial-septal defects are the most common

- cleft palate, seen in 20 per cent of cases (Sataloff *et al.* 1990).

Other problems which are reported include gastrointestinal dysfunctions; seizures, which are seen in around 25 per cent of cases; hearing loss (in 80 per cent) (Sataloff *et al.* 1990); and visual problems (Levin A.V. *et al.* 1990).

An unusual low-pitched cry is described in three–quarters of cases in infancy (Jackson L. *et al.* 1993), but to date this has not been specifically studied or recorded.

Milder physical phenotypes with the same gene mutation are reported more commonly than the classic presentation described above. (See, for example, Allanson, Hennekam and Ireland 1997.)

Self-injurious behaviour is seen in around 55 per cent of cases (Oliver *et al.* 2003).

Slower growth is typical of those with CdLS, most having noticeable intrauterine growth retardation (Boog *et al.* 1999), being born at lower birthweight (Barisic *et al.* 2008) and remaining below the fifth centile throughout their lives (Kline, Barr and Jackson 1993; Kousseff, Thomson-Meares, Newkirk and Rook1993).

Intellectual functioning varies widely. Most individuals are of limited ability, with the mean reported IQ being 53 (Kline *et al.* 1993). A number of cases have been reported of normal IQ, typically seen in those of higher birthweight (>2.5 kilos) and without associated limb malformations (Saal *et al.* 1993). (See also discussion in Basile Villa, Selicorni and Molteria 2007.)

A wide range of NIPBL gene mutations has been reported in CdLS (truncating, splice-site, missense, in-frame deletion and regulatory) (Selicorni *et al.* 2007). Gene deletions have been reported, but do not appear to be viable (Hulinsky, Byrne, Lowichik and Viskochil 2005).

One unusual feature which has been reported is that the chromatids separate earlier than normal during cell division, something called precocious sister chromatid separation (PSCS) (Kaur *et al.* 2005).

A number of abnormalities overlap phenotypically with those seen in CdLS, including certain 3p deletion and 12q duplication abnormalities (DeScipio *et al.* 2005).

Mottling of the skin ('*cutis marmorata*') is seen in around 60 per cent of cases. Single palmar creases and abnormal finger whorls are also commonly reported (Smith G.F. 1966).

Incomplete development of the nipples and the umbilicus is seen in around 50 per cent of cases.

Gastro-oesophageal reflux is seen in almost all classic cases (Bull, Fitzgerald, Heifetz and Brei 1993), and can require surgical correction (Jackson L. *et al.* 1993). A variety of other gastrointestinal problems are reported, including pyloric stenosis (which causes persistent vomiting in around 25 per cent), diaphragmatic hernia and intestinal malrotation.

Undescended testes (73 per cent) and small genitalia (57 per cent) are seen in a high percentage of males, and kidney problems are seen in around 12 per cent (Jackson L. *et al.* 1993).

A range of orthopaedic problems has been reported, but none are characteristic and few require surgical intervention. Of 34 patients referred for orthopaedic evaluation in Toronto, only two required surgery, both for bilateral equinovarus (clubfoot) (Roposch *et al.* 2004).

A low platelet count has been reported in some cases (Froster and Gortner 1993; Fryns and Vinken 1994), but no further papers have appeared in recent years and the diagnostic and clinical significance is not known.

Increased nuchal translucency (a collection of fluid behind the nape of the foetal neck, which can be seen on ultrasound) (Huang and Porto 2002) has been described in the first trimester. This is a finding more typically reported in association with Down syndrome.

The facial features consistent with CdLS can be recognized from ultrasound scanning *in utero* (Boog *et al.* 1999; Urban and Hartung 2001).

There is a suggestion of genotype–phenotype association, with truncating mutations resulting in more severely affected cases and missense mutations in a milder phenotype (Gillis *et al.* 2004). However, as over 50 genetic NIPBL variants have so far been reported (Borck *et al.* 2004; Gillis *et al.* 2004; Krantz *et al.* 2004; Tonkin *et al.* 2004) and numbers of clinical cases remain small, the strength of this association is unclear.

IS THERE A LINK BETWEEN CDLS AND ASD? A number of early clinical and review papers described autistic-like behaviours in de Lange syndrome (Bay, Mauk, Radcliffe and Kaplan 1993; Bryson, Sakati, Nyhan and Fish 1971; Johnson H.G. *et al.* 1976; Opitz 1985; Shear, Nyhan, Kirman and Stern 1971; Sarimski 1997).

- The first paper to suggest that there might be an association between ASD and de Lange syndrome was a fairly recent one (Bhuiyan *et al.* 2006). This study, of 39 cases, used two standardized assessment scales: the Developmental Behaviour Checklist and the Diagnostic Interview for Social and Communication Disorders (DISCO). Both scales identified seven cases as fulfilling criteria for autism, albeit slightly different but overlapping subsets of this population. Bhuiyan *et al.* speculate that the autistic behaviours might have been a reflection of the level of global learning disability – the more severely disabled cases were more likely to be autistic – but that more research would be needed to clarify the issue.

- Basile, Villa, Selicorni and Molteni (2007) carried out a questionnaire survey of 56 Italian children with de Lange syndrome. They also employed standardized rating scales of autistic symptomology – the Childhood Autism Rating Scale (CARS) and Autism Behaviour Checklist (ABC). Fifteen of the children presented behaviour consistent with an autistic pattern. As in the study by Bhuiyan et al., ASD symptomology was correlated with learning disability.

- The most recent study (Moss et al. 2008), again used standardized screening measures – the ADOS (Lord et al. 2000), which uses direct observation, and the SCQ (Social Communication Questionnaire, formerly known as the Autism Screening Questionnaire (ASQ) (Rutter, Bailey and Lord 2003) – to screen 34 de Lange cases, of which 21 (62 per cent) were found to be above the autism cut-off. In a comparison group of children with cri du chat syndrome, a condition not to date linked to ASD, 39.2 per cent were also above the clinical cut-off.

DIFFERENTIAL DIAGNOSIS: Four conditions have clinical presentation similar to CdLS:

1. partial 3q trisomy, with both translocation and duplication being reported (Falek, Schmidt and Jervis 1966; Fear and Briggs 1979; Ireland et al. 1991, 1995; Tranebjaerg, Baekmark, Dyhr-Nielsen and Kreiborg 1987). This can present with similar facial features and cardiac and palatal abnormalities

2. 2q31 deletion (Del Campo et al. 1999), which presents with the upper limb abnormalities but not the facial characteristics

3. Fryns syndrome (Fryns et al. 1979), which has many similar characteristics: poor development of the forearms and lower leg is seen in 75 per cent; cleft palate in 30 per cent; cardiac, kidney and genital abnormalities are also common

4. foetal alcohol syndrome (Miles, Takahashi, Haber and Hadden 2003; Nash, Sheard, Rovet and Koren 2008), which can result in intrauterine growth problems and early failure to thrive, sinophrys, a small nose and cardiac defects.

MANAGEMENT AND TREATMENT: This is a complex disorder with a variable phenotype, so initial assessment must be multidisciplinary. The extent of follow-up assessments would depend on the findings at the initial stage.

- Gastrointestinal, cardiac and renal function should be evaluated and a neurological screening, including an EEG, carried out.

- Audiology and ophthalmology assessments should be undertaken, once these are feasible.

- Regular assessment of growth against CdLS centiles would be sensible.

- Platelet and white blood cell levels should be measured, although the significance has not yet been established.

- Orthopaedic assessment is sensible, as scoliosis can occur, and equinovarus (clubfoot) can impair motor development.

- Speech and language, physiotherapy, occupational therapy and cognitive/developmental assessments should be carried out to guide self-help and communicative development.

- An assessment of ASD symptomology using a standardized scale, such as the Autism Diagnostic Observation Schedule, should also be carried out as a baseline.

A number of possible complications of CdLS may require surgical intervention:

- gastro-oesophageal reflux
- intestinal malrotation
- severe failure to thrive (possibly requiring gastrostomy tube placement)
- cardiac defects
- poor manipulation of hands, and/or correct clubfoot
- undescended testes.

Medication may be required for seizure control, and antibiotics may be required in the management of kidney problems.

Problems with the regulation of body temperature can be seen, and this can be an important factor during any type of surgical procedure (Papadimos and Marco 2003).

ANIMAL MODELS: There are no recent animal models, and none that relate the genotype to the phenotypic presentation. One paper (Seller and Wallace 1993) suggested a possible model for conditions that present with transverse limb defects, such as the de Lange and Mobius syndromes, but to date no animal models for the behavioural aspects of CdLS have been published or proposed.

A USEFUL BOOK ON SELF-INJURY IN CDLS: Oliver, C., Moss, J., Petty, J., Arron, K., Sloneem, J. and Hall, S. (2003) *Self-injurious Behaviour in Cornelia de Lange Syndrome: A Guide for Parents and Carers.* Coventry: Trident Communications Ltd. This can be downloaded from www.cdlsusa.org.

28.

Juvenile dentatorubral-pallidoluysian atrophy (JDPLA)

aka • Naito-Oyanagi disease

GENE LOCUS: 12p13.31

KEY ASD REFERENCES: Licht and Lynch 2002; Wada *et al.* 1998

SUMMARY: JDPLA is inherited as an autosomal dominant condition. It was first described in 1958 by Smith J.K., Conda and Malamud (1958), and the term 'dentatorubral-pallidoluysian atrophy' first appears in Smith's chapter in the classic *Handbook of Clinical Neurology* by Vinken and Bruyn (1975). A useful review can be found in Kanazawa (1998).

'Haw River syndrome' in the USA is caused by the same triplet repeat poly-alanine expansion, but it presents with a different clinical phenotype, without the myoclonic seizures seen in JDPLA and with calcification to the basal ganglia and subcortical demyelinization that are not reported in JDPLA. To date only a small number of Haw River syndrome cases have been reported, and all have been from African-American families (Burke *et al.* 1996). Both Haw River syndrome and JDPLA result from the same CAG triplet expansion.

The defining features of the condition, seen at autopsy, that give the condition its rather cumbersome name, are the combined degeneration of the *dentatorubral system*, a nerve fibre system beginning in the dentate nucleus in the cerebellum and projecting to the red nucleus in the midbrain, and the *pallidoluysian system*, which projects from the globus pallidus (part of the lentiform nucleus in the midbrain) to subthalamic nuclei.

One model which has been proposed is that the polyalanine expansions seen with CAG repeats, and which are found in at least five separate triplet expansion conditions (including JDPLA and Huntington's chorea), interfere with protein–protein interactions in different but very specific fashions, resulting in the specific physical phenotypes. Burke *et al.* (1996) showed that unaffected protein from the Huntington's chorea expansion – 'huntingtin' – and from the DRPLA site – 'atrophin-1' – bind to the enzyme GAPD (glyceraldehyde-3-phosphate dehydrogenase). GAPD is a strongly conserved gene, and has also been shown to bind to amyloid precursor protein, and to be linked to late onset Alzheimer's disease (Li Y. *et al.* 2004; Myers *et al.* 2002). Roses (1996) has reviewed the findings on polyalanine expansions.

HOW COMMON IS JDPLA? JDPLA is a disorder that appears rare in European Caucasian populations (prevalence estimated at <1,000,000). It is significantly more common in Japan. The prevalence estimate from one combined review of Japanese and Caucasian cases estimates overall prevalence at 0.2–0.7 per 100,000 (Takano *et al.* 1998).

It appears that JDPLA is significantly more common in Japanese populations, in whom it was first clearly described (Naito and Oyanagi 1982). Several other Japanese series have been reported (for example, Iizuka, Hirayama and Maehara 1984). It may also be more common in other Asiatic groups. However, so far such cases have only been reported from Hong Kong (Yam *et al.* 2004). There are reports of Portuguese families of Asiatic origin who have a high prevalence of DPLA (Martins *et al.* 2003), and there is a higher than expected prevalence in South

Wales (Wardle *et al.* 2007). Otherwise only sporadic cases have been reported from Spain (Muñoz *et al.* 1999), the UK (Warner, Williams and Harding 1994), Denmark (Norremolle, Nielsen, Sorensen and Hasholt 1995) and the USA (Licht and Lynch 2002). A survey of a large group of 117 patients with spinocerebellar atrophy in France failed to find any DPLA cases (Dubourg *et al.* 1995).

MAIN CLINICAL FEATURES: The juvenile or early onset form of dentatorubral-pallidoluysian atrophy typically presents with progressive myoclonic epilepsy and dementia. The clinical features and progression of JDPLA are highly variable, even within the same family (Saitoh *et al.* 1998). However, most of those affected are completely dependent by between five and 20 years of age.

It is a CAG triplet expansion condition, where a small section of DNA found at 12p13.31 has been copied significantly more often than normal, resulting in abnormal production of mRNA and hence interfering with normal protein production. Triplet repeats are seen in a number of ASD-related conditions, the best-known and best-studied being fragile-X syndrome [35]. There is mounting consensus that triplet repeat disorders are underpinned by the same general mechanism (see Kaplan, Itzkovitz and Shapiro 2007) despite their differences in clinical presentation.

As with a number of the other triplet repeat expansion conditions, there seems to be a link between the size of the expansion and the pattern of progression, with larger expansions resulting in an earlier onset and more severe presentation (Ikeuchi *et al.*; Koide *et al.* 19941995) – although care needs to be taken in interpreting this information, as so few cases have been reported (Potter 1996). From the work of Koide *et al.* it appears that maternal transmission leads to a shortening of the repeated DNA sequence, while paternal transmission leads to a lengthening. As longer triplet sequences are associated with greater severity and earlier onset, the parent of origin is an important aspect of assessment where the condition is inherited rather than a *de novo* mutation.

Hirayama, Iizuka, Maehara and Watanabe (1981) tried to characterize three distinct forms of dentatorubro-pallidoluysian atrophy (DRPLA):

1. an ataxic-choreoathetoid form
2. a pseudo-Huntington form
3. a myoclonic epilepsy form.

It seems likely at the time of writing that, as described above, there is a link between the expansion size, age of onset and phenotype, with the largest expansion being seen in type 3, intermediate in type 2, and smallest in type 1. Childhood onset presentation normally includes myoclonic epilepsy, while later onset cases are seldom epileptic (Tomoda *et al.* 1991). For example, Shimojo *et al.* (2001) report two unrelated cases with very early onset, cortical atrophy, severe motor and seizure difficulties and particularly large CAG expansions. It may also prove to be the case that the pseudo-Huntington form results from the effects of a secondary gene such as GRIK2 (Rubinsztein *et al.* 1997). This gene is involved in glutamate metabolism, and has been linked to autism in screening studies (Jamain *et al.* 2002; Shuang *et al.* 2004). DRPLA has been reported in cases diagnosed with Huntington's chorea (Connarty *et al.* 1996), and this issue should be explored further.

Anticipation has been shown in some families – progressive severity in successive generations suggesting increasing expansion. For example, in a family reported by Aoki *et al.* (1994), documented over three generations, the first showed late onset (aged 52–60 years) with mild cerebellar ataxic symptoms; the mother in the second generation showed severe cerebellar ataxia with onset in her thirties; and the child in the third generation had learning difficulties and myoclonic epilepsy, beginning at age 8. In 71 affected individuals from 12 Japanese families, Komure *et al.* (1995) found between 7 and 23 CAG repeats in unaffected family members, and between 53 and 88 in those affected, with longer repeat length being associated with earlier age of onset. Vinton *et al.* (2005) describe similar differences in presentation, dependent on age at presentation and expansion size, in a three-generation Caucasian family of Balkan origin.

From studies of sperm in affected men, and in men with several other expansion disorders, CAG expansion in DRPLA produces the strongest anticipation effect seen to date in a triplet expansion disorder (Takiyama *et al.* 1999).

In contrast, however, cases are reported where the same level of expansion results in very different phenotypes (Saitoh *et al.* 1998), suggesting that factors other than expansion are involved.

IS THERE A LINK BETWEEN JDPLA AND ASD? The first suggestion of a link with ASD appears in a paper by Wada *et al.* (1998). They reported on an 11-year-old boy with ASD who had had psychomotor difficulties from infancy, with cerebellar ataxia. At six years he began having myoclonic seizures. Genetic testing identified that he had a 12p13.31 expansion.

Licht and Lynch (2002) report on six North American cases, two of whom, cousins and the youngest in the family pedigree, had JDPLA and autism. These were the youngest affected family members. The basis for autistic diagnosis is unclear.

DIFFERENTIAL DIAGNOSIS: There is a complex differential diagnosis within the ataxias (Manto 2005; Poretti, Wolf and Boltshauser 2008), but JDPLA is the only such condition so far reported in association with ASD.

JDPLA has a highly variable early presentation. The differential diagnosis in ASD would most probably be with other conditions resulting in certain early motor problems and/or seizure involvement. The principal conditions that would need to be considered are: adenylosuccinate lyase deficiency [9]; Angelman syndrome [11]; ARX mutations [13]; Becker muscular dystrophy [33]; CATCH22 [18]; Down syndrome [31]; Dravet's syndrome [32]; Duchenne muscular dystrophy [33]; fragile-X syndrome [35]; GAMT deficiency [37]; Schindler disease [65]; Steinert's myotonic dystrophy/myotonic dystrophy type 1 [50]; and (in girls) Rett syndrome [63a] and Rett syndrome (Hanefeld variant) [63b].

A further consideration in the early stages, particularly in Nordic populations, would be infantile neural ceroid lipofuscinosis. However, the lack of reported cases in this population would appear to make diagnostic confusion unlikely.

Some cases present with the appearance of Huntington's chorea (Hirayama, Iizuka, Maehara and Watanabe 1981; Norremolle, Nielsen, Sorensen and Hasholt 1995). However, these cases tend to be of later onset.

MANAGEMENT AND TREATMENT: At the present time there is no specific treatment for JDPLA. Clinical management is focused on physiotherapy for the motor problems, together with medical management of the epilepsy that is typically seen in the juvenile form. A recent paper describes a 16-year-old girl whose seizure control had shown a positive response to ketogenic diet (Matsuura *et al.* 2009).

If there is a common basis to triplet expansion, as has been suggested (Kaplan, Itzkovitz and Shapiro 2007), successful therapeutic strategies, such as appear likely in fragile-X syndrome [35], hold out some promise for the possibility of targeted clinical intervention in JDPLA.

ANIMAL MODELS: There is a transgenic mouse model of DRPLA (Schilling *et al.* 1999). Yamada, Sata, Tsuji and Takahashi (2002) have used the transgenic model to investigate the white matter degeneration seen in DRPLA and its association with the degeneration of oligodendrocytes.

In the transgenic mouse model, atrophin-1 fragments accumulate in neurons in a similar fashion to the accumulations seen in fragile-X neurons (Wood *et al.* 2000), suggesting similarities in the pathogenesis.

Recent research has highlighted the role of atrophin-1, the gene product of DRPLA, and its gene interactions in the drosophila, particularly its role in transcription repression (Haecker *et al.* 2007).

A simple description of the neurology of DRPLA can be found on the HOPES (Huntington's Outreach Project for Education at Stanford) website, accessible at http://images.google.co.uk.

29a.

DiGeorge syndrome I (DGS I)

GENE LOCUS: 22q11.2

KEY ASD REFERENCES: Antshel *et al.* 2007; Evers, Vermaak, Engelen and Curfs

2006; Fine *et al.* 2005; Lajiness-O'Neill *et al.* 2005; Mukaddes and Herguner 2007; Niklasson, Rasmussen, Oskarsd and Gillberg 2001; Paylor *et al.* 2006

See also CATCH22 [18]; velocardiofacial syndrome [76].

SUMMARY: DiGeorge syndrome I is a condition which affects the migration of nerve cells and has effects on a number of organ systems, including the development of the thymus gland and cardiovascular system. It was first described in 1965 by Angelo DiGeorge, a paediatrician from Temple University School of Medicine in Philadelphia, who described the constellation of hypoplasia of the thymus gland, T-lymphocyte deficiency, congenital hypoparathyroidism, hypocalcaemia and moderate facial dysmorphism (DiGeorge 1965). In a more formal paper that appeared in 1968, DiGeorge drew a comparison between the various immune and metabolic effects he was observing in his clinical cases and the effects of absence of the thymus gland in the chicken in describing three cases that his team was investigating.

The first paper to link this phenotype to a genetic condition was by de la Chapelle, Herva, Koivisto and Aula (1981). These French authors reported on 20/22 translocation and suggested that DiGeorge syndrome might be due to a deletion within chromosome 22 or partial duplication of 20p. They suggested that DiGeorge syndrome might result from 22q11 monosomy. This speculation was confirmed the following year by Kelley *et al.* (1982), when three DiGeorge patients with 22q11 translocation were reported.

Most cases of DiGeorge syndrome occur as spontaneous mutations and are not inherited, but in around seven per cent the condition is inherited as an autosomal dominant condition. It is more common, in the inherited cases, for the gene anomaly to be inherited from the mother (Demczuk *et al.* 1995).

The typical person with a DiGeorge syndrome diagnosis has a large deletion at 22q11.2 that involves some 30 genes. Few of these have been well characterized and the variation across these various genes is likely to account for much of the wide phenotypic variation observed.

HOW COMMON IS DIGEORGE SYNDROME?
The combined prevalence of DiGeorge syndrome I + II has been estimated as between 13.2 and 23.3 in 100,000 (Burn *et al.* 1995; Oskarsdóttir, Vujec and Fasth 2004). Overall, 22q11 defects are reported as being present in around one in 4,000 live births (Burn *et al.* 1995).

In a large study by Goodship, Cross, Scambler and Burn (1998) of 207 infants with congenital heart disease, drawn from a birth cohort of 69,129, five had 22q11 deletions consistent with DiGeorge syndrome. This gives a birth prevalence of approximately 13 per 100,000. As the rate of cardiac problems in DiGeorge syndrome is reported as being around 75 per cent, this suggests that either there may be under-ascertainment, or that the prevalence of DiGeorge syndrome in those with cardiac anomalies is the same as in those without. In any event, the data demonstrate that 22q11 deletions are the second most likely genetic factor associated with congenital cardiac problems after Down syndrome [31].

MAIN CLINICAL FEATURES: DiGeorge syndrome is one of a number of conditions affecting T-box genes (Packham and Brook 2003). The genetic basis to DiGeorge syndrome was first identitfied in 1997 (Chieffo *et al.* 1997). Individuals with a 22q11.2 deletion are typically of short stature and have mild to moderate learning disability. The typical facial features are low-set ears, a bulbous nose, small mouth and jaw, and cleft palate, with resultant hypernasal speech and occasionally cleft lip.

The early presenting features are typically cardiac problems, immune abnormalities (low T-cells resulting in increased susceptibility to infections due to poor development of the thymus gland), and/or hypocalcaemia due to hypoparathyroidism (often presenting as neonatal seizures, due to poor development of the parathyroid gland).

Stewart, Irons, Cowan and Bianchi (1999) found that 5/13 22q11.2 microdeletion cases had kidney problems. Kujat, Schulz, Strenge and Froster (2006) found that 5/6 cases studied had kidney problems. This has not been investigated in larger screening studies to date.

In 39 22q11.2 deletion children (mean age 11y) Campbell L.E. et al. (2006) found an IQ of 67+/−10, while in 26 sibling controls (mean age 11y) they found an IQ of 102+/−12. Individuals with a 22q11.2 deletion typically exhibit deficits in executive functions (normally viewed as problems with anticipating consequences, mental flexibility and interpreting the actions of others) (Bearden, Reus and Freimer 2004).

Structural studies of the brain have shown that the amygdala is enlarged (Kates et al. 2006), the cerebellum is smaller than normal (van Amelsvoort et al. 2004), and that there are differences in the development of the prefrontal cortex (Kates et al. 2005). All are differences that have been reported in the autism literature. According to the study by Antshel et al. (2007), the amygdala is significantly larger in those who have both 22q11.2 deletions and ASD than in those with 22q11.2 alone, and in most this is also in the context of further psychiatric co-morbidity. On brain

imaging, polymicrogyria is commonly reported (Robin et al. 2006), particularly on the right hemisphere.

In adult cases, psychiatric presentations, particularly schizophrenia and depressive disorder, are more common than would be expected. In one series of 78 adult cases (Bassett et al. 2005), over 22 per cent were found to be schizophrenic, while over 92 per cent had learning difficulties. Some adult cases also present with late-onset hypocalcaemia (Kar, Ogoe, Poole and Meeking 2005).

A proportion of people with 22q11.2 deletions have virtually no symptomology. This may be true of 10–25 per cent of cases (Levy, Michel, Lemerrer and Philip 1997). As 'benign' cases are unlikely to be screened in the general population, prevalence estimates based on clinical presentation may be low.

Discordant clinical phenotypes in MZ twins suggest that factors other than the 22q11.2 deletion are required to produce the clinical phenotype. (See, for example, Goodship, Cross, Scambler and Burn 1995; Vincent et al. 1999; Wilson D.I. et al. 1991.)

In a study of 13 DiGeorge phenotype cases with no apparent 22q11 deletion, Yagi et al. (2003) identified several TBX1 mutations as sufficient to cause the five major phenotypic features (described above): typical facial features; conotruncal cardiac defects; cleft palate; hypoplasia of the thymus gland; and parathyroid dysfunction with hypocalcaemia. Unlike deletion cases, mutations did not appear to result in any associated learning difficulties.

Several reports have now documented hyperthyroidism (Graves disease) in DiGeorge syndrome. Kawame et al. (2001) described five patients with chromosome 22q11.2 deletion (four girls and one boy) who manifested Graves disease between the ages of 27 months and 16 years, in one case with seizure disorder, and suggested that Graves disease may be part of the clinical spectrum of this disorder. Gosselin *et al.* (2004) documented three further cases of Graves disease in association with 22q11.2.

In one series of 35 DiGeorge cases, 33 were shown to have either deletion or microdeletion, using high-resolution banding, FISH and molecular dosage analyses (Carey *et al.* 1992; Wilson D.I. *et al.* 1992). In a further series, Driscoll, Budarf and Emanuel (1992) identified molecular deletions in all of 14 cases.

One study (Bearden, Jawad *et al.* 2004) looked at 44 children 11.1y+/−3.2 with 22q11.2 deletions. Sixteen were Met-hemizygous and 28 were Val-hemizygous. The val-form is associated with high and the Met-form with low catechol-O-methyl-transferase (COMT) enzyme activity. Their results suggested that the type of genotype influences the likelihood of executive functioning problems with Met-hemizygous people performing better than those who were Val-hemizygous. Shashi *et al.* (2006) studied 21 22q11.2 children aged 7–16 and found the Met-hemizygous children had greater frontal dopaminergic activity, better prefrontal functioning and higher overall cognitive ability than those who were Val-hemizygous. In contrast, Glaser B. *et al.* (2006) tested 34 children and young adults but found no significant differences between those who were Val- or Met-hemizygous, suggesting that COMT polymorphisms are either marginal in their effects, or of no relevance to IQ, verbal memory or EF difficulties.

IMMUNE DIFFERENCES: Poor or absent function of the thymus gland results in reduced or absent T-cells, which can be measured by assessing levels of CD4 cells (Wilson D.I. *et al.* 1993). Parathyroid abnormality can be assessed by measuring any reduction of thyrocalcitonin immunoreactive cells (C cells) (Burke *et al.* 1987; Palacios, Gamallo, Garcia and Rodriguez 1993). Jawad, McDonald-McGinn, Zackai and Sullivan (2001) studied 195 patients with chromosome 22q11 deletion syndrome and found that diminished T-cell counts in the peripheral blood are common. Four presented with juvenile rheumatoid arthritis, and idiopathic thrombocytopenic purpura was seen in eight cases. A variety of autoimmune conditions were seen in individual cases.

A general overview of immunological aspects of DiGeorge syndrome can be found in McLean-Tooke, Barge, Spickett and Gennery (2008), who also reported on T-cell abnormalities in a further series of 27 child cases with findings similar to Jawad, McDonald-McGinn, Zackai and Sullivan (2001).

IS THERE A LINK BETWEEN DIGEORGE SYNDROME I AND ASD?

- A neuropsychiatric review of 39 cases of 22q11.2 deletion was carried out in southern Sweden (Niklasson, Rasmussen, Oskarsdóttir and Gillberg 2001). ADHD was seen in 44 per cent and an ASD in 31 per cent, while only 6 per cent were of normal overall IQ.

- In 2005, as part of a special issue of the journal *Child Neuropsychology* on 22q11.2, Lajiness-O'Neill *et al.* compared the memory function of a group of children with 22q11.2 deletion syndrome, and their siblings, with a group of children dignosed with autism, and their siblings. Although slight differences were found between the groups, on most measures both showed similar deficits in verbal memory and memory for faces, compared to siblings, suggesting that both groups show differences in the functioning of the dorsolateral prefrontal cortex.

- In the first systematic study, Fine *et al.* (2005) reported on a series of 98 people with a 22q11.2 deletion screened for ASD. Fourteen qualified for a diagnosis of ASD based on the Autism Diagnostic Interview – Revised (ADI-R) (Lord, Rutter and Le Couteur 1994), and 22 displayed significant levels of ASD symptomology.

- Evers, Vermaak, Engelen and Curfs (2006) documented a 52-year-old adult case with a 22q11.2 deletion, a diagnosis of velocardiofacial syndrome with dementia and 'autistic features'. He had shown progressive cognitive decline since the age of 36. He was reported as having an autistic sister who also carried the deletion.

- In a paper describing Tbx1 haploinsufficiency, Paylor *et al.* (2006) describe one family with an affected mother and two sons, where the mother had a major depressive illness and one of the sons had a diagnosis of Asperger's syndrome.

- Antshel *et al.* (2007), again using the ADI-R, found that 17/41 (41 per cent) of a series of 22q11.2 children aged 6.5–15.8 years fulfilled diagnostic criteria for an ASD. This was a significantly higher proportion of individuals than reported in the general population, and in the Fine *et al.* (2005) study. The discrepancy between the Antshel *et al.* (2007) findings and the earlier result could be because of the change in the ADI-R scoring algorithm used in the two studies.

- Mukaddes and Herguner (2007) reported on a nine-year-old girl with a 22q11.2 duplication, who was diagnosed with autistic disorder, language delay and behavioural problems.

DIFFERENTIAL DIAGNOSIS: A variety of other clinical diagnoses are given to individuals with 22q11.2 deletion anomalies. Amongst the most common are: CATCH22 [18]; CATCH phenotype; Cayler cardiofacial syndrome; Shprintzen's syndrome/velocardiofacial syndrome [76]; Takao velocardiofacial syndrome (conotruncal anomaly face syndrome); 22q11.2 deletion syndrome; and Opitz G/BBB syndrome; or, more rarely, Kousseff syndrome (Forrester *et al.* 2002; Kousseff 1984; Maclean *et al.* 2004; Toriello, Sharda and Beaumont 1985). As several of these conditions have been reported specifically in association with ASD and there is still debate over their differentiation, separate discussion is given to a number of these elsewhere in the current volume. Shprintzen (1994), for example, believed velocardiofacial syndrome to be a specific condition, while he viewed DiGeorge syndrome as heterogeneous. Burn (1999) suggests that the primary presentation in the individual case should dictate the diagnostic label used – Takao syndrome, where the major problem was cardiac defect; DiGeorge syndrome, where there is neonatal presentation with hypocalcaemia and hypoplasia of the thymus gland; velocardiofacial syndrome, where there is abnormality of the palate with speech problems; replacing CATCH22 with CATCH phenotype for people with the combination of a cardiac abnormality, T-cell deficit, cleft palate and hypocalcaemia. He also thought the term '22q11 deletion syndrome' was an acceptable diagnostic term. De Decker and Lawrenson (2001) suggest a common gene defect with a diverse phenotype.

A recently described distal deletion of 22q11.2 shows some phenotypic overlap but the presentation seems sufficiently different to be treated as a separate condition (Ben-Shachar *et al.* 2008). Mosaic microdeletion cases are also now being reported with cardiac anomalies, learning disability and dysmorphic facial features (Halder, Jain, Kabra and Gupta 2008).

Several other genetic differences have been reported in association with the DiGeorge phenotype. Greenberg *et al.* (1988) reported one case in association with del10p13 (now known as DiGeorge II [29b]) and a further case with a 18q21.33 deletion, while Fukushima *et al.* (1992) reported on a female infant with a deletion at 4q21.3–q25. It is possible that these early cases would also be found to have 22q11.2 microdeletions on present-day testing.

A DiGeorge-like phenotype can also be produced by the teratogenic effects of foetal exposure to alcohol or to low levels of retinoic acid (from vitamin A) during pregnancy. (See Vermot *et al.* 2003 for discussion.)

MANAGEMENT AND TREATMENT:

- Calcium supplementation can be helpful, as most cases have marked hypocalcaemia.

- The poor immune status of many can present complications for surgical intervention such as may be required for thymus transplant or corrective heart surgery.

- In the small proportion of patients who do not have a thymus gland (approximately one per cent), thymus transplantation is generally well tolerated and can in some cases restore normal immune function (Markert *et al.* 1999, 2007). There have been steady improvements in the techniques involved (Hudson *et al.* 2007). Markert *et al.* (1999) suggest that early transplantation may hold out the greatest hope for correction of immune problems.

- There is a range of conotruncal cardiac defects seen in association with 22q11.2, including tetralogy of Fallot, pulmonary

atresia with ventricular septal defect, truncus arteriosus, interrupted aortic arch, isolated anomalies of the aortic arch, and ventricular septal defects (Carotti *et al.* 2008; Marino *et al.* 2001).

- Treatment for cardiac abnormalities should be as for any other people with similar defects, bearing in mind the complications secondary to compromised immune status.

- Speech and language therapy may be required, particularly where articulatory problems are present.

- Therapies aimed at improving executive functioning and working memory may be helpful once assessment to establish a baseline level of functioning has been carried out.

ANIMAL MODELS: A variety of animal models of DiGeorge syndrome have been reported. Some are phenocopy conditions without genetic synteny (for example, Chisaka and Capecchi 1991), while others are models based on defects in the syntenous gene regions to human 22q11.2.

A region on the mouse chromosome 16 has been identified as syntenic with the 22q11 region implicated in DiGeorge syndrome (Schinke and Izumo 2001). Seven key genes in this area have been identified in this region (Galili *et al.* 1997).

The *Tbx1* gene in mice has been shown to provide a molecular basis to the cardiac defects seen in DiGeorge syndrome (Lindsay *et al.* 1999; reviewed by Baldini 2002), but does not model the immune abnormalities.

The picture is not a simple one, however. Puech *et al.* (2000) have generated a mouse deletion that does not result in such cardiac anomalies. Varying cardiac malformations can be produced in the mouse model by varying *Tbx1* dosage (Liao *et al.* 2004).

In the mouse, Chisaka and Capecchi (1991) described a knockout of Hox A3 (1.5) that produced a recessive phenocopy very similar to DiGeorge syndrome I. This gene maps to human chromosome 7, an area not yet implicated in the cause of the human syndrome.

Based on data from various animal models (mouse and zebrafish), and of the human literature, Stalmans *et al.* (2003) found that absence of the Vegf (vascular endothelial growth factor) isoform that binds the enzyme neuropilin-1 exacerbates the cardiovascular defects seen in 22q11.2.

Lindsay *et al.* (2001) have identified the chromosomal region (*Tbx1*) responsible for the cardiac defects seen in the mouse model of DiGeorge syndrome.

Jerome and Papaioannou (2001) produced a mouse with a null mutation of *Tbx1*. This has most of the physical phenotypic features seen in DiGeorge syndrome, with hypoplasia of the thymus and parathyroid glands, conotruncal cardiac defects, cleft palate and facial dysmorphism.

29b.

DiGeorge syndrome II (DGS II)

aka • velocardiofacial syndrome II
 • 10p13–p14 deletion syndrome
 • HDR syndrome

GENE LOCUS: 10p13–14

KEY ASD REFERENCE: No specific papers to date (see discussion below).

SUMMARY: Cases with an apparent DiGeorge phenotype who have a deletion at 10p, but no 22q11.2 deletion, were first reported in 1988 by Greenberg *et al.* in a series of DiGeorge phenotype cases who were screened for genetic anomalies. A subsequent paper (Daw *et al.* 1996) described considerable phenotypic variability across affected individuals with 10p deletions who presented with a DiGeorge or velocardiofacial syndrome phenotype.

The critical gene region for DGS II has been identified by mapping the deletion in 12 patients with 10p deletions, nine of whom showed a DiGeorge phenotype (Schuffenhauer *et al.* 1998).

HOW COMMON IS DGS II? Investigation of DGS II is typically considered when there is a DiGeorge phenotype with a negative finding on deletion testing of 22q11.2, the gene implicated in DGS I. The prevalence of DGS II is uncertain at this time. Bartsch *et al.* (2003) studied a series of 295 patients with a DiGeorge phenotype and did not identify any with a 10p14 defect – they recommend that screening for 10p anomalies is not warranted on the basis of clinical phenotype. That said, no studies in other groups have been carried out and prevalence could be lower in central European groups.

MAIN CLINICAL FEATURES: The main clinical features reported are as for DiGeorge syndrome I ([29a] above), including hypoparathyroidism, conotruncal cardiac defects, immune deficiency, deafness and kidney abnormalities. For example, Yatsenko *et al.* (2004) described a boy with an interstitial 10p deletion, craniofacial dysmorphology, developmental delay and an atrial-septal heart defect.

These findings suggest that the key genetic features in both DiGeorge syndromes impact on the same neurodevelopmental and somatic processes as are affected in DGS I.

IS THERE A LINK BETWEEN DGS II AND ASD? DGS II is included here for discussion as the phenotype is highly similar to that described in DiGeorge syndrome I. Many people given a DiGeorge syndrome diagnosis are 22q11.2 deletion negative and no systematic screening has yet been carried out. It seems likely that there will be ASD cases with DGS II. However, as the prevalence is small compared to 22q11.2, the likelihood of identifying cases is smaller.

10p13–14 has not shown up as having significant linkage to ASD.

DIFFERENTIAL DIAGNOSIS: A study by Villanueva *et al.* (2002) found that in cell lines from two female patients with DGS II the nebulette gene (NEBL) was deleted. NEBL deletion has been associated with both craniofacial and cardiac abnormalities. Both patients had several key DiGeorge phenotypic features. Cell lines raised from two further cases with HDR syndrome (**h**ypoparathyroidism with sensorineural **d**eafness and **r**enal dysplasia) had a more distal deletion of 10p13–14 and did not show NEBL deletion.

DGS II and HDR (see Hasegawa *et al.* 1997; Lichtner *et al.* 2000) are non-overlapping defects at 10p13–14. HDR has been shown to result from haploinsufficiency of GATA3 (Van Esch *et al.* 2000), which may provide a reliable way in which to discriminate the two conditions.

One recent case in which there is a translocation of 10p13-pter with 22q11-pter (Dasouki *et al.* 1997) shows only marginal overlap with the previous smallest area of deletion sufficient to cause DGS II, suggesting either that a fairly precise locus had been defined or that more than one specific locus was sufficient. Using flourescence in-situ hybridization (FISH) and polymerase chain reaction (PCR), the DGS II critical region has now been mapped to a small region mapped within a 1 centimorgan interval (Schuffenhauer *et al.* 1998).

MANAGEMENT AND TREATMENT: Although uncommon, severe hypocalcaemia in such cases (as recently reported in a paternally inherited balanced translocation of 10p13 and 3q29) can lead to cardiac failure unless the hypocalcaemia is aggressively managed (Chao, Chao, Hwang and Chung 2009).

ANIMAL MODELS: As for DiGeorge syndrome I ([29a] above). A number of animal models have been developed based on phenotype rather than genetic synteny, that apply to both DiGeorge syndromes.

30.

Dihydropyrimidine dehydrogenase (DPYS) deficiency

---

aka • uraciluria thyminuria

GENE LOCUS: 1p22

KEY ASD REFERENCES: Berger *et al.* 1984; Marshall *et al.* 2008; van Gennip, Abeling, Vreken and van Kuilenburg 1997; van Kuilenburg *et al.* 1999

SUMMARY: DPYS deficiency is an inborn error of metabolism. It is an autosomal recessive disorder of pyrimidine catabolism. Lack of the enzyme dihydropyrimidine dehydrogenase (DPYD) interrupts the first stage in the catabolism of uracil and thymine by the liver, with consequent excess of uracil, thymine and 5-hydroxymethyluracil, which can all be detected at high levels in the urine of those affected. A Dutch group first described it in 1984 (Berger *et al.* 1984).

DPYS deficiency has two major metabolic consequences: it alters the metabolism of the amino acids thymine and valine, and this in turn results in a build-up of beta-aminoisobutyric acid. These two metabolic consequencesmay provide a direct focus for treatment, as they have effects on the levels of alanine-containing peptides (van Kuilenburg et al. 2004, 2006).

The principal interest to date has been in the effect of DPSY deficiency in causing severe adverse reactions to 5-fluoracil-based cancer chemotherapy (Morrison et al. 1997). 5-fluoracil is used extensively in the treatment of various cancers, including HIV-associated malignancies. As DYPD breaks down 5-fluoracil in normal circumstances, an unrecognized lack of the enzyme can lead to severe toxicity or fatality due to toxic build-up (Ezzeldin and Diasio 2004; van Kuilenburg et al. 2001). This is potentially a problem for up to one in 20 people receiving cancer chemotherapy, but screening for DPYS deficiency is not routine, even in individuals requiring 5-fluoracil cancer chemotherapy (van Kuilenburg 2006). Effects on the action of a range of medications used in cancer therapy, muscle problems and viral and fungal infections are now known. (See Schmidt et al. 2005.)

HOW COMMON IS DPYS DEFICIENCY? There is no general epidemiological data on prevalence of DPYS deficiency. Wide variations in DPYD activity in the general population have been reported (Ridge et al. 1998). From studies in cancer, rates in Caucasian populations are around 3–5 per cent (Lu, Zhang and Diasio 1993; Lu et al. 1998; Relling, Lin, Ayers and Evans 1992). There is limited information on other ethnic groups, with reported Indian (Saif et al. 2006), Pakistani (Yau, Shek, Chan and Chan 2004) and Japanese

(Ogura 2006) cases. However, the only systematic data is on African-American populations, which have higher rates, particularly in females, in whom over 12 per cent are affected (Mattison et al. 2006). Limited screening to date has shown G>A splice site mutations to be fairly common in Finnish and Taiwanese populations (Wei et al. 1996).

MAIN CLINICAL FEATURES: As the general population prevalence figures reported are high, it would appear that for most situations the effects of DPYS deficiency are benign and that there is no obvious physical or behavioural phenotype. In children presenting with problems, the presentation can be varied, with a range of features reported, including craniofacial abnormalities, ocular problems, seizures, microcephaly, developmental delay, hypotonia, brisk reflexes and autistic features (van Gennip, van Gennip, Abeling, Vreken and van Kuilenburg 1997; van Kuilenburg et al. 1999; Yau, Shek, Chan and Chan 2004).

The catabolism of pyrimidine is the only source of alanine in humans (Gonzalez and Fernandez-Salguero 1995; Wasternack 1980). As dihydropyrimidines do not accumulate in DPYS deficiency, urine needs to be tested for metabolites (van Gennip et al. 1994). Clinical findings that suggest screening for disorders of purine and pyrimidine metabolism have been discussed by Duran et al. (1997).

IS THERE A LINK BETWEEN DPYS DEFICIENCY AND ASD?

- In the initial paper (Berger et al. 1984), three cases were described: two boys and one girl. The first boy (8y) had slow speech development and solitary behaviour with autistic features, but was described as of normal intelligence; the second boy (3y) had severe growth retardation, microcephaly and learning difficulties; the girl (13y) had absence seizures, dry skin and learning difficulties.

- Van Gennip, Abeling, Vreken and van Kuilenburg 1997) first systematically reported autistic features in a series of DPYS cases, and in a systematic review, van Kuilenburg *et al.* (1999) reported autism as affecting five of their 22 cases (23 per cent).

The various linkage studies to date have not reported a significant association between 1p22 and ASD. A recent, genome-wide copy-number variation study (Marshall *et al.* 2008) did identify this as a novel, previously unreported ASD susceptibility locus.

At the present time this appears to be a rare but important association of a condition with a high population prevalence.

DIFFERENTIAL DIAGNOSIS: The constellation of features reported in DPYS deficiency could be confused phenotypically with other conditions such as INCL (infantile neural ceroid lipofuscinosis) (Wisniewski, Kida, Connell and Zhong 2000), Rett syndrome [63a] and Rett syndrome (Hanefeld variant) [63b], in which there are also hypotonia, microcephaly, and autistic symptomology. As all have a specific genotype and DPYS deficiency has a clear metabolic profile, clinical differentiation should not be problematic.

A number of ASD conditions are also linked to increased cancer risk, and it is important to differentiate between these and DPYS deficiency because of the specific risks from 5-fluoracil chemotherapy in DPYS. ASD conditions reported in association with cancer are: XXY [3]; Bannayan-Riley-Ruvalcaba syndrome [15]; basal cell naevus syndrome [16]; CATCH22 [18]; Cowden syndrome [26]; Down syndrome [31]; neurofibromatosis type 1 [51];

Noonan syndrome [52]; Sotos syndrome [68]; xeroderma pigmentosa [79]; and X-linked ichthyosis [80], where treatment using chemotherapies metabolized by dihydropyrimidine dehydrogenase may be important as failure to recognize this could be dangerous.

MANAGEMENT AND TREATMENT: Assessment for DPYS deficiency may be advisable where there are neurological symptoms such as epileptic seizures, with or without learning disability (Schmidt *et al.* 2005).

In addition to a build-up of uracil, thymine and 5-hydroxymethyluracil, a direct consequence of DPYS deficiency is lack of alanine. Alanine is usually a non-essential amino acid as it is derived through this pathway. Deficits are therefore likely only in DPYS deficiency in combination with a diet low in alanine-containing foods – principally meat, seafood and dairy, but lower levels are also derived from cereals, nuts, some legumes and yeast. Alanine is produced alongside lactate during anaerobic exercise – the alanine is converted to glucose in the liver, with urea as a byproduct. Alanine is required for the metabolism of tryptophan, and is important in maintaining glucose levels.

Although no trials have yet been carried out, it seems possible that alanine supplementation may be beneficial in DPYS deficiency.

ANIMAL MODELS: No murine or primate models of DPYS deficiency have been produced to date. There are several drosophila mutations, which are syntenic (Rawls 2006), but these have not been explored with respect to their effects on behaviour.

31.

Down syndrome (DS)

aka • mongolism (historical)
• trisomy 21

GENE LOCUS: trisomy of chromosome 21

KEY ASD REFERENCES: Bregman and Volkmar 1988; Buckley 2005; Carter *et al.* 2007; Cohen *et al.* 2005; Ghaziuddin 1997, 2000; Tsai and Ghaziuddin 1992; Howlin, Wing and Gould 1995; Kent, Perry and Evans 1998; Prasher and Clarke 1996; Rasmussen, Borjesson, Wentz and Gillberg 2001; Reilly (2009) (Review); Starr *et al.* 2005; Wakabayashi 1979

SUMMARY: Down syndrome (DS) is the most frequent genetic cause of learning disability and is caused by trisomy of normally all, but at least part of, the DS critical portion of chromosome 21. In 95 per cent of cases there are three copies of chromosome 21, which are clearly visible on karyotyping. In the other five per cent of cases, one copy is translocated to another chromosome, typically 14 or 21.

The prevalence of co-morbid DS and ASD remains unclear. However, the studies to date suggest that the association is not uncommon and that there is a characteristic behavioural phenotype in DS–ASD that differs from that seen in DS without ASD.

From the studies which have been published, there does not appear to be a difference between individuals who are co-morbid and others with DS, in terms of the likelihood of their showing other DS-specific features, such as cardiac anomalies, helicobacter pylori infection, coeliac disease, and thyroid, gallbladder, sensory or EEG abnormalities. However, for many of these features there is a lack of systematic research.

Problems such as coeliac disease, leukaemia, melatonin production and oxidative stress, coupled with the unusual physiology of people with DS, are important to explore in all such cases, and may have implications for more individualized management approaches.

HOW COMMON IS DOWN SYNDROME? The prevalence of Down syndrome is currently estimated at 50 in 100,000 live births (Orphanet 2009). Prevalence figures vary with a number of factors, such as sociodemographic and ethnic differences (Khoshnood *et al.* 2004), differences in antenatal screening (Khoshnood *et al.* 2004), and increase in maternal age at conception (Morris and Alberman 2009). Prevalence at birth does not seem to vary markedly across ethnic groups. However, research on this issue is sparse. (See Carothers, Hecht and Hook 1999; Sherman, Allen, Bean and Freeman 2007.)

MAIN CLINICAL FEATURES: First described in an essay that was printed in 1866, published in 1867 and elaborated in a book that appeared two decades later (Down 1867, 1887), DS is the first clearly described and differentiated form of learning disability. Down syndrome was first documented, based on the clinical phenotype of characteristic facial and physical features in combination with learning disability. Down syndrome remains one of the most common chromosome anomalies seen in clinical practice in learning disability, and there is now a huge clinical literature, with over 23,000 clinical and research papers published.

In contrast to the sex chromosome aneuploidies (see [3, 4]), the risk of having a child with trisomy 21 increases with maternal age. The risk of having a child with Down syndrome at age 30 is one in 1,000, and at age 40 it is one in 110

(Hook, Cross and Schreinemachers 1983; Lamson and Hook 1980). (There is also a significant independent effect of age of maternal grandmother on likelihood of Down syndrome (Malini and Ramachandra 2006).) The effect of maternal age is confounded with sociodemographic/ethnic factors (Khoshnood *et al.* 2000), suggesting that findings need to be replicated across different cultural groups. No equivalent paternal age effect has so far been reported – Roecker and Huethner (1983) found no such effect in a US Caucasian population) – however, no recent large studies or studies in different ethnic groups are available.

To date, no study has attempted to link maternal age either to the likelihood of co-morbid autism, or to the possibility of an interaction between the paternal age effect in autism and maternal age effect in DS.

Median age at death has steadily improved, but shows major disparities, in the USA at least (MMWR 2001). For the most recent year on which data has been published (1997), the median age at death for white individuals with DS was 50, for black individuals with DS 25, and for other ethnic groups with DS @11 years of age.

A range of somatic characteristics is common in those with DS, including:

- 'epicanthic folds' – small folds of skin at the side of the nose that obscure the inner edge of the eye, giving the appearance of more widely spaced eyes. These are seen in most infants but typically disappear as the nasal bridge develops
- a flattened nasal bridge
- slightly protruding (sometimes called 'cockleshell') ears
- 'hypoglossia' – an enlarged tongue
- a hypotonic lower lip

- a receding chin
- small hands
- short stature.

The facial and oral differences seen in DS may contribute to a variety of difficulties – poorer articulation; lower self-esteem; poorer peer relationships. There is some evidence that the use of palatal plates (Bäckman *et al.* 2007), started early in life, can lead to improved oromotor function, facial expression and speech. Whether there are benefits in cosmetic facial surgery is hotly debated (see Roizen 2005 for discussion), and currently purely cosmetic operations are not actively encouraged. That said, there is an extensive literature in this area, and it may be that some surgery has functional benefits – for example, the shape of the ear can be corrected successfully (O'Malley *et al.* 2007), and the effect of this may be both cosmetic and beneficial to hearing.

A number of malformations and disorders are significantly more common in individuals with DS:

1. *cardiac problems* are seen in up to 40 per cent of cases. The majority of these are the same as are seen in the general population. However, two types of heart defect – atrioventricular septal defect and tetralogy of Fallot – are both more common in DS and carry greater operative risks (Stos *et al.* 2004)

2. *gastrointestinal malformations* are more common – duodenal stenosis or atresia, imperforate anus and Hirschsprung disease all being more common than would be expected (Cleves *et al.* 2007). Coeliac disease is also significantly more common (Wallace 2007)

3. *gallbladder problems* are seen in @25 per cent of cases – five times more likely than in matched general population

adult controls (Tyler, Zyzanski and Runser 2004)

4. *leukaemia* is some 10–20 times more common in DS than in the general population, with an increased risk of acute lymphoblastic leukaemia (ALL), but principally because of a marked increase in acute megakaryoblastic leukaemia (AML) within the DS population (Puumala *et al.* 2007)

5. *differences in neurochemistry* are apparent from the early stages of antenatal brain development (Engidawork and Lubec 2003). Accelerated onset and increased prevalence of dementia, and particularly of Alzheimer's disease, are not inevitable but are commonly seen in DS (Margallo-Lana *et al.* 2007)

6. *seizure problems* are not commonly cited as a feature of DS. However, in two large series, epilepsy was reported in some eight per cent of cases (Goldberg-Stern *et al.* 2001; Prasher 1994)

7. *thyroid problems* are common in DS, with a wide variation in reported rates, some series reporting as many as 35 per cent of DS cases with thyroid dysfunction. (See Prasher 1999 for extensive review.)

8. *early cataract formation* is a further sensory difficulty experienced by some 1.4 per cent of children with DS (Haargaard and Fledelius 2006)

The following list of medical conditions aims is to provide a reasonably thorough but brief overview of factors which are important to rule in/rule out in someone with DS. Many of these conditions have direct implications for help – coeliac individuals require good dietary advice and help and may benefit from calcium and iron supplementation, for example.

• High-altitude pulmonary oedema is common in DS (Durmowicz 2001),

typically related to a preexisting cardiac condition. This suggests that DS children, particularly those with a history of cardiac problems, should exercise caution when considering air travel or high-altitude activities such as mountaineering.

• A recent review of gastrointestinal (GI) concerns in adults attending a general clinic for DS (Wallace 2007) found 36/37 had GI problems. Of these, 6/51 tested positive for (likely) coeliac disease; 29/43 who were tested had helicobacter pylori; 13/53 tested had hepatitis B; and 17/47 tested had hepatitis A. Only 12 had a history of institutional care, the factor to which such infections have typically been attributed.

Coeliac disease is a common concomitant of DS which is now well recognized in the literature (Gale, Wimalaratna, Brotodiharjo and Duggan 1997; Shamaly *et al.* 2007; Swigonski *et al.* 2006; Zachor, Mroczek-Musulman and Brown 2000), and there appears to be a strong link between coeliac and the presence of more generalized autoimmune disorders (over 30 per cent compared to 15 per cent in the DS population in general). One large study screened 1,202 DS cases and found 55 with coeliac disease (4.6 per cent) (Bonamico *et al.* 2001). This is an important factor to screen for in all DS cases. In addition to their antibody profiles, those with coeliac had low serum calcium and iron.

• Both acute lymphoblastic and acute myeloblastic leukaemia (ALL and AML) are 10 to 20 times as common in those with DS compared to the general population (Robinson 1992), while megakaryocytic leukaemia is 200 to 400 times as common (Zipursky, Peeters and Poon 1987). There is some evidence that periconceptional vitamin supplementation by mothers of those with DS significantly lowers subsequent likelihood of ALL but not of AML (Ross J.A. *et al.* 2005). AML in DS appears to respond well to treatment with ultra low-dose cytarabine (Al-Ahmari *et al.* 2006).

- A range of neurological differences has been shown in those with DS, including cerebellar hypoplasia with reduced granule cell density (Aylward *et al.* 1997; Moldrich, Dauphinot, Laffaire, Rossier and Potier 2007). The volume of the hippocampus is significantly reduced in DS from early in life (Pinter *et al.* 2001).

- Individuals with DS develop features of Alzheimer's disease more commonly and much earlier than those without a trisomy 21 (Wisniewski, Wisniewski and Wen 1985). From the neuropathology to date, the typical plaques and tangles of Alzheimer's neuropathology are seen earlier than is usual (Wisniewski, Wisniewski and Wen 1985), possibly accelerated by triplication of the gene on Ch21 for amyloid precursor protein. It appears that genetic risk factors such as APOE 4 increase Alzheimer's risk in DS (Deb *et al.* 2000). An APOE 4 carrier individual has a 2.7-fold increased risk of developing Alzheimer's disease (Rubinsztein *et al.* 1999). A range of medications have been used in the management of Alzheimer's disease in individuals with DS (Prasher 2004).

The premature onset of Alzheimer's may be related to higher amyloid precursor protein and/or elevated levels of the inflammatory marker neopterin in children and adolescents with DS, both of which are now being reported in some cases (Coppus *et al.* 2007; Mehta, Capone, Jewell and Freedland 2007). No follow-up studies have yet

been carried out which indicate the extent and clinical significance of this association. It is interesting to note that in adults with DS and Alzheimer's type neuropathology, the neurochemistry is different from other cases of Alzheimer's and does not show the same degree of cortical and cerebellar GABA depletion (Seidl *et al.* 2001).

- Ninety percent of all Down syndrome patients have a significant hearing loss, usually of the conductive type (Mazzoni, Ackley and Nash 1994).

Oxidative Stress and DS: Oxidative stress is linked to the pathogenesis of ASD (James S.J. *et al.* 2004), Alzheimer's disease and DS (Zana, Janka and Kalman 2007). As the therapeutic implications are of potential significance, further research on this issue is important to pursue.

Much of the theoretical interest in the possible role of oxidative stress in DS comes from the fact that a key enzyme in the oxidation of free radicals to hydrogen peroxide (superoxide dismutase/SOD1) is encoded on chromosome 21 (at 21q22.1). There is evidence from multiple studies for increased SOD1 activity in trisomy 21 DS, but of normal SOD1 activity in translocation and mosaic DS. (See, for example, De-la-Torre *et al.* 1996.)

There is evidence of increased oxidative stress in individuals with DS (Jovanovic, Clements and MacLeod 1998), and of the presence of biological factors that may account for this, such as elevation of thiobarbituric acid reactive substances (TBARS), uric acid, and seric superoxide dismutase and catalase (Garces, Perez and Salvador 2005).

At the present time, there is no reason to suppose that an individual with DS and ASD is any less likely to benefit from treatment approaches that have established benefit in others with ASD.

GENETIC FACTORS IN DS: Three principal genetic mechanisms can result in Down syndrome:

1. most affected individuals (@95 per cent) with trisomy 21 have three separate copies of chromosome 21 (Lejeune, Gautier and Turpin 1959)

2. in about five per cent of patients, one copy of the critical region is translocated to another acrocentric chromosome, most often to either chromosome 14 or an additional section of chromosome 21 incorporated through expansion (Petersen *et al.* 1991)

3. in around two to four per cent of cases there is a mosaicism, combining a trisomic and a normal cell line, and here only a proportion of cells have an extra copy of chromosome 21. Depending on the stem lines involved, these cases tend to be less severely affected (Mikkelsen 1977; Niikawa and Kajii 1984).

Some of the more usual clinical features have been incorporated into the phenotypic maps of chromosome 21. (See Delabar *et al.* 1993; Epstein *et al.* 1991; Korenberg, Bradley and Disteche 1992.)

Down syndrome is also occasionally associated with a ring chromosome 21 (McGinniss *et al.* 1992).

Genetic models alone are not sufficient to account for the phenotypic variations seen across DS which result from a range of influences (see: Reeves, Baxter and Richtsmeier 2001).

The origins of free trisomy 21: Where there is an additional copy of chromosome 21, this is typically of maternal origin. About 70 per cent of cases result from an error in meiosis I, with some 20 per cent resulting from an error in meiosis II. In these cases there is a correlation with maternal age. In the further five per cent that arise from errors in mitosis, and five per cent where the error is in spermatogenesis, there is no link to maternal age.

The origins of the translocation forms of trisomy 21: All of the *de novo* t(14;21) trisomies studied to date are of maternal origin (Shaffer *et al.* 1992). In *de novo* t(21;21) Down syndrome the situation is different (Antonarakis *et al.* 1990; Grasso *et al.* 1989; Shaffer *et al.* 1992). In most cases (14 out of 17) the t(21;21) is an isochromosome (dup21q), formed by transverse as opposed to the normal longitudinal division of the chromosome. Maternal and paternal inheritance of isochromosome (dup21q) appears equally likely. In a small number of cases, the *de novo* t(21;21) is a maternal Robertsonian translocation – here both long arms of chromosome 21 are inherited from one parent rather than one long and one short arm from each.

The region of chromosome 21 critical for the development of DS: MX1, a locus found in band 21q22.3, has been associated with many of the physical characteristics and developmental problems associated with DS (Delabar *et al.* 1993), including learning difficulties, epicanthic folds, flat nasal bridge, short stature and unusual fingerprints. Using a panel of cell lines from individuals with DS and matching the genetic profiles to the physical phenotypes, a number of other regions also appear to contribute to many of these phenotypic features (Korenberg, Bradley and Disteche 1994).

Separable regions within the Down syndrome critical region: Four separate sufficient Down syndrome critical regions have been identified within the section of chromosome 21 that results, when triplicated, in the DS phenotype:

1. DSCR1 (Fuentes *et al.* 1995) – highly expressed in CNS and cardiac tissues (21q22.1–q22.2)

2. DSCR2 (Vidal-Taboada *et al.* 1998) (21q22.3)

3. DSCR3 (Nakamura, Hattori and Sakaki 1997a) (21q22.2)

4. DSCR4 (Nakamura, Hattori and Sakaki 1997b) – predominantly expressed in the placenta (21q22.2).

A transcription factor, REST, which is important for neurite formation, neuron plasticity and brain development, is significantly down-regulated in DS neuronal precursor cells compared to controls (Bahn *et al.* 2002).

Genetic risk factors for leukaemia in DS: One study (Wechsler *et al.* 2002) indicates that the increased risk is associated with mutations in the GATA1 gene, a transcription factor which affects myeloid lineage commitment (Look 2002). The link with GATA1 is strengthened by the results of other studies which link GATA1 to transient myeloproliferative disorder in DS, a condition which precedes acute megakaryoblastic leukaemia (AMKL) in some 30 per cent of cases (Hitzler *et al.* 2003; Mundschau *et al.* 2003).

Genetic risk for atrioventricular septal defects in DS: A specific gene mutation in the CRELD1 gene found at 3p25.3 has been linked to atrioventricular septal heart defects and found to be present in 2/39 of a DS series (Maslen *et al.* 2006).

MTHFR polymorphisms and DS: Methionine tetrahydrofolate reductase (MTHFR) polymorphisms have been linked to ASD. (See Boris, Goldblatt, Galanko and James 2004 and [85] in this book.) It is interesting, therefore, that the presence of the same MTHFR polymorphisms in mothers significantly increases their risk of having a child with DS (Acácio *et al.* 2005; Boduroglu, Alana, Koldan and Tuncbilek 2004; Hobbs *et al.* 2000; Rai *et al.* 2006). In those with DS, the presence of the MTHFR

677T allele has been linked to lower IQ, as has a specific transcobalamin 776G allele (Gueant *et al.* 2005). This suggests the possibility that altered methylation and abnormal B12 metabolism may be implicated in the severity of certain aspects of the DS phenotype.

There are wide ethnic variations in the prevalence of the 677T allele in the general population (Botto and Yang 2000). However, there has been no research to date attempting to link the prevalence of this allele to the prevalence of DS.

IS THERE A LINK BETWEEN DS AND ASD?

Historically, the typical description of the child with DS has been the antithesis of the ASD stereotype – sociable, affectionate and outgoing (see, for example, Gibbs and Thorpe 1983) – and ASD has been said to be uncommon in DS (Rutter and Schopler 1988). Although occasional single cases were described (for example, Bregman and Volkmar 1988; Prasher and Clarke 1996; Wakabayashi 1979), these were thought of as uncommon exceptions.

The first paper to suggest that there might be an association between DS and ASD (Howlin, Wing and Gould 1995) described four boys with DS and co-morbid autism, and noted the difficulties in getting clinical recognition of ASD in this group.

A series of case reports from Michigan reported by Ghaziuddin (Ghaziuddin 1997, 2000; Ghaziuddin, Tsai and Ghaziuddin 1992) provided further case material and illustrated autistic features in the parents of co-morbid cases.

A paper by Rasmussen, Borjesson, Wentz and Gillberg (2001) documented a case series of 25 co-morbid DS–ASD cases that had presented to the Queen Sylvia Hospital in Goteborg over a 15-year period. This series illustrated a number of factors – the relatively late age at ASD diagnosis (mean: 14.4y); prevalence of severe infections, principally recurrent otitis media (72 per cent); prevalence of ASD in first or second degree relatives (20 per cent); and prevalence of epilepsy (20 per cent). This is a clinical, not a population, series, with no indication of the overall numbers of DS cases seen over this period, but does suggest that DS–ASD comorbidity is a significant clinical issue.

In a small study of a self-selected group of 13 DS families (Starr et al. 2005), the ADI-R and Adapted Pre-Linguistic Autism Diagnostic Observation Schedule (A-PL-ADOS) were used to screen for possible ASD. Of the 13, five could be considered to have an ASD. This study again provides evidence for the possibility of comorbidity, but does not allow any conclusions concerning the prevalence of such a link to be drawn.

A recent study by Carter et al. (2007), again of a selected sample, provides evidence concerning the behavioural profile of 127 subjects with DS, approximately 70 per cent male, with a mean age of 8.4 years. Sixty-four were found to have co-morbid ASD, 19 stereotypic movement disorder, 18 disruptive behaviours, and 26 had no behavioural comorbidities, when assessed on two standardized scales: the Aberrant Behavior Checklist and Autism Behavior Checklist. The principal conclusion in the current context is that those with ASD showed a distinctive pattern of behaviour that was characteristic and different from that in the other groups. In particular, they were characterized by anxiety, social withdrawal and odd stereotyped behaviours.

No studies to date have attempted to differentiate DS–ASD cases from non-ASD cases on the basis of factors such as genetic differences or neurobiology. A recent genetic review (Cohen et al. 2005) comes to no clear conclusions over the extent of the association.

The limited epidemiological research that has looked for a possible link antedates the currently reported high prevalence rates which may reduce the prevalence of DS within the broader ASD population, but studies using cases diagnosed primarily on pre-ICD-10 and DSM-IV-TR criteria are quoted as between 1.7 per cent and 2.5 per cent (Fombonne, Du Mazaubrun, Cans and Grandjean 1997; Ritvo et al. 1990).

It may prove to be the case that there is no biological association between DS and ASD, but a link is more commonly perceived between the two because of their shared association with learning disability. Whatever transpires to be the case, there are significant numbers of people who have both DS and ASD. The complexity of their presentation requires knowledge of the biological factors that operate in both conditions.

DIFFERENTIAL DIAGNOSIS: Genetic diagnosis is definitive; however, in early life several other diagnoses may give a similar phenotype: trisomy 18, aka Edward syndrome (Kitanovski, Ovcak and Jazbec 2009); multiple X chromosomes; Zellweger syndrome; and other peroxisomal problems (Yik et al. 2009).

There are now several cases of Down syndrome (trisomy 21) who also have fragile-X syndrome (Arinami et al. 1987; Collacott et al. 1990; Stevens, Tartaglia, Hagerman and Riley 2010). The last of these cases, a 14-year-old boy, is the first in which assessment for autism has also been carried out, and he presents with a mixed physical phenotype with joint hyperlaxity, a DSM-IV diagnosis of autistic disorder, a DQ in the 30–50 range and facial features consistent with DS, together with the macro-orchidism, prominent forehead and jaw consistent with fragile-X.

MANAGEMENT AND TREATMENT:

The possible role of complementary therapies in DS: Treatments for the cardiac, haematologic, seizure and other biological comorbidities seen in DS have been remarkably successful in improving mortality in DS, and have resulted in marked improvements in life expectancy, from a median age of survival of one year in 1968 to 49 in 1997 for individuals with DS in the USA (MMWR 2001).

At present, despite the best efforts over the past 140 years, there is no medical approach to the treatment of the developmental and psychosocial aspects of DS that has shown any robust and appreciable benefits for the condition. As a consequence, many families have turned to complementary and alternative therapies, but many of the claims of benefit have proved difficult to justify.

Systematic reviews of prenatal multivitamin supplementation does not suggest that this conveys a reduced risk of DS (Goh, Bollano, Einarson and Koren 2006), although, as mentioned above, it does appear that periconceptional use by women who go on to have a DS child does reduce leukaemia in those children.

Dietary factors in DS: There has been long-standing and extensive debate and argument over the role of dietary factors in the care of those with DS (Ani, Grantham-McGregor and Muller 2000; Ciaccio *et al.* 2003; Golden 1984; Roizen 2005; Sacks and Buckley 1998; Salman 2002).

A wide range of supplements have been used, individually and in combination, including:

• **5HTP and tryptophan:** There was only one early controlled clinical trial of tryptophan use with infants with DS (Airaksinen 1974). Tryptophan was banned from use by the Federal Drug Administration (FDA) due to the appearance of a condition – eosinophilia myalgia syndrome – which killed 37 and permanently disabled 1,500 US Americans and was linked to a tryptophan supplement produced by Showa Denko. (As far as I am aware, this was the first vitamin supplement to be produced by genetically engineered bacteria.) The problem was due to a toxin from the GM production process and not due to tryptophan itself. (For a detailed discussion of the case, see Smith 2003.) Tryptophan has since has been re-approved for use as a supplement.

5HTP is the intermediate between tryptophan, a dietary amino acid, and the neurotransmitter serotonin. Serotonin in turn is metabolized to produce melatonin, the chronobiotic compound which controls the sleep–wake cycle. There is little evidence that 5HTP affects the sleep pattern in DS (Petre–quadens and de Lee 1975).

Three studies have looked at behavioural effects of 5HTP supplementation in DS (Partington and MacDonald 1971; Pueschel, Reed, Cronk and Goldstein 1980; Weise, Koch, Shaw and Rosenfeld 1974). Although there were some differences in favour of the supplemented children, results are difficult to interpret.

• **Calcium:** Serum calcium levels are lower in those with DS and coeliac disease (Bonamico *et al.* 2001). No studies of specific calcium supplementation (except in older cases, to prevent bone demineralization) have been undertaken to date.

• **Carnitine:** There is some evidence for lower carnitine levels in younger children with DS, normalizing compared to control values, from around five years of age (Seven, Cengiz, Tüzgen and Iscan 2001). As carnitine has been found to be helpful in some cases of dementia, it was proposed that supplementation might be beneficial in DS. The only controlled study to date, with 40 adult DS patients aged 18–30, found no beneficial effects of supplementation using a battery of tests of IQ, attention and behaviour (Pueschel 2006). No baseline assessment of carnitine levels was made in this study, and it may be that positive effects would result from supplementation at an earlier stage.

- *Folate:* Folate levels are reduced in epileptics on active medication (Botez, Botez, Ross-Chouinard and Lalonde 1993). As folate levels are also low in those with DS (David O. *et al.* 1996), they have an eight per cent likelihood of having co-morbid epilepsy (Goldberg-Stern *et al.* 2001; Prasher 1994), and with some 60 per cent of those with ASD showing EEG evidence of epileptiform activity (Chez *et al.* 2006), folate supplementation in DS may prove to be clinically useful. In epilepsy, folate supplementation can reduce the levels of anticonvulsant required to achieve seizure control (Mattson, Gallagher, Reynolds and Glass 1973).

  A recent randomized placebo-controlled trial of folinic acid and antioxidants, alone or in combination, in 156 infants with DS, begun at @4 months and continued through 22 months, failed to demonstrate any significant effects on development (Ellis *et al.* 2008).

  Low folate levels are also associated with leukaemia (Zittoun 1995), DNA damage and increased cancer risk (Blount and Ames 1995).

  A more general discussion of dietary factors in Down Syndrome and epilepsy can be found in Thief and Fowkes (2004).

- *Iron:* No supplementation studies have been carried out. Again, those individuals with DS and coeliac appear to have lowered serum iron levels (Bonamico *et al.* 2001).

- *Melatonin:* There is some, albeit limited, evidence of a wide variation in melatonin production by individuals with Down syndrome (Reiter *et al.* 1996). Some with DS have normal circadian release, whilst others show no fluctuation through the day – the normal pattern is high levels at night and low levels through the day.

  Recent evidence in learning disabled children in general suggests that melatonin supplementation is well tolerated and largely effective in the long-term treatment of otherwise treatment-resistant circadian rhythm sleep disorders. In a long-term randomized placebo-controlled follow-up study of 50 individuals with such problems, including a subgroup with DS, results in terms of clinical benefit, side effects and acceptability were highly positive (Carr *et al.* 2007; Wasdell *et al.* 2008).

  There is also evidence of effects of melatonin on SOD1 levels and antioxidant function in general, which may be important in DS (Rodriguez *et al.* 2004).

- *Phenylalanine:* A small, unreplicated Russian study of four DS patients subjected to phenylalanine loading compared to ten normal controls (Shaposh-nikov, Khal'chitskii and Shvarts 1979) found biochemical changes in the DS cases consistent with impaired liver phenylalanine hydroxylase activity. This finding suggested that the DS subjects they studied would have had problems in metabolizing normal dietary levels of phenylalanine.

A single case study has reported marked improvements in an individual with DS treated through adherence to a low phenylalanine diet (Marsh and Cabaret 1972).

- **Selenium:** Serum selenium levels appear to be low in DS (Kadrabová, Madáric, Sustrová and Ginter 1996).

  A reasonable case has been made for the biological rationale supporting selenium supplementation in DS (Antila and Westermarck 1989). These authors argue for the importance of selenium as an antioxidant in limiting the effects of overexpression of SOD1.

  In the only reasonably well-controlled study of selenium supplementation in DS (Antila, Nordberg, Syväoja and Westermarck 1990), there was, as predicted, improvement in immune function.

- **Vitamin A:** A large number of early studies suggested that individuals with DS had abnormally low levels of vitamin A, but there is wide variation in reported levels. There is only one paper that has attempted to address the effects of vitamin A supplementation systematically (Palmer 1978), in randomly assigned DS–sibling pairs, both of whom took a vitamin A supplement (1,000 IU/kg/day) or placebo for six months. The study showed a steady reduction in infection rates in the DS cases treated with vitamin A over time, compared to their siblings; however, the results are not simple to interpret.

  There has been some speculation that ASD may in some cases have a basis in abnormal vitamin A processing (Megson 2000). However, caution has been urged in the therapeutic use of vitamin A and close monitoring should be undertaken during use, as supplementation can lead to liver damage with both chronic low dose (Geubel et al. 1991) and acute high dose use (Castaño, Etchart and Sookoian 2006).

- **Vitamin B6:** Two randomized controlled trials of vitamin B6 in DS have been published (Coleman et al. 1985; Pueschel, Reed, Cronk and Goldstein 1980). In the first study there were ten subjects and nine controls, monitored on the Stanford-Binet/Bayley scales of infant development. In the second, 23 patients treated with B6, 24 with B6 and 5-HTP, and 26 non-treatment controls were monitored on the Bayley scales and the Vineland Social Maturity Scales. In the second study, B6 was given alone or in combination with 5-HTP, the precursor of serotonin. Both groups followed up their subjects for three years. Outcome in both studies was that there was no effect of B6 supplementation on developmental outcome.

  It appears that in general plasma B6 levels are elevated in unsupplemented children with autism when compared to controls (James, George and Audhya 2006).

- **Vitamin B12:** In one early paper a three-year-old girl with DS was found to have a problem with B12 metabolism without proteinurea (Cartlidge and Curnock 1986).

  In contrast, in 1990, a large series of 83 children with DS was assessed on various biochemical parameters including B12 (Ibarra et al. 1990), and all were shown to have normal B12 levels.

  As B12 supplementation can cause problems in some metabolic liver conditions (Linnell and Matthews 1984) and there is evidence of liver dysfunction in at least some cases of DS (Shaposhnikov, Khal'chitskii and Shvarts 1979), with no information on the prevalence of such differences, use of B12 supplementation in DS should be considered carefully before use.

- **Vitamin E:** Beneficial effects of vitamin E have been reported in Alzheimer's disease (Sano *et al.* 1997). No studies on DS have been published.

- **Zinc:** The findings of low serum, plasma and whole blood zinc are amongst the more robust in the DS literature. (For review, see Sacks and Buckley 1998.) Supplementation has been shown to normalize the pattern and strengthen immune function (Björkstén *et al.* 1980).

  Zinc sulphate as been shown to be beneficial in reducing thyroid-stimulating hormone levels in hypothyroid DS cases (Bucci *et al.* 1999). However, there are some reservations (Bucci *et al.* 2001).

Combined supplement effects: A recent study of adults with DS (Fillon-Emery *et al.* 2004) has shown that plasma homocysteine levels could be significantly lowered through the use of folic acid, B6 and B12 supplementation.

Summary of individual nutrient approaches: In summary, the wide range of studies to date, with the exception of selenium and zinc, have shown limited evidence of efficacy. In many cases, this may be because limited research has been done, rather than evidence that they are ineffective.

Earlier approaches to multiple supplementation in DS: A history of the use of vitamin and mineral supplements by private organizations, but without systematic research evidence, extends back at least to 1940, when a supplement approach was introduced in the USA by Dr Henry Turkel. Turkel used a mixture of vitamins, minerals, fatty acids, digestive enzymes, lipotropic nutrients, glutamic acid, thyroid hormone, antihistamines, nasal decongestants and a diuretic. The treatment was called his 'U

series', and was said to adhere to a method known as orthomolecular therapy (Turkel 1975; Turkel and Nusbaum 1985). A variety of similar products have been used ('HAP CAPS', 'Nutrivene-D', 'MSB'), but with little peer-reviewed, empirical research evidence (Bumbalo, Morelewicz, Berens and Buffalo 1964).

In the 1980s Dr Ruth Harrell and colleagues proposed a similar multimineral (N=11), multivitamin I (N=8) and (variable) thyroid hormone supplement as improving IQ in a learning disabled group (including DS), based on their own earlier work (Harrell *et al.* 1981). Again the outcome of this study is difficult to interpret, as various tests and various assessors were used.

Historically, there has been considerable clinical scepticism over claims made for the benefits from supplementation.

As with many other conditions, interventions in DS to date have relied on the view that there will be no differences within the population that would be likely to affect response to treatment. Biologically distinct subgroups can be identified – at the genetic level, ring 21, mosaic and translocation cases can all differ in severity, comorbidity, outcome and response to intervention, from supernumary 21 cases. At the behavioural level it is currently unclear whether specific behavioural phenotypes such as DS–ASD have differences in their response to treatment. At the biomedical level, hearing loss, cardiac difficulties, coeliac disease, gallbladder disease, leukaemia, epilepsy, differences in phenylalanine hydroxylase activity and/or differences in oxidative stress may all have critical effects on development and outcome.

Our increased knowledge of the underpinning biology of DS gives a situation where, for the first time, treatment interventions can be based on knowledge of many of the biological factors involved.

The increasing evidence of specific problems with oxidative stress, and the role of factors such as selenium, zinc and SOD1 in these processes, are leading to more biologically grounded and testable treatment hypotheses (Garcez, Perez and Salvador 2005).

ANIMAL MODELS: One mouse model (Shinohara *et al.* 2001) created chimeric mice using a technique called microcell-mediated chromosome transfer. This produced mice with DNA containing human chromosome 21. The resulting chromosome was essentially intact with a small deletion. Some cell lines lost the chromosome insertion, resulting in mice with varying degrees of mosaicism. Central nervous system retention of chromosome 21 impaired learning and emotional behaviour in various standardized tests. A high proportion of the chimeric foetuses examined showed evidence of retarded development of the immune system and cardiac defects – primarily atriventricular (A-V) canal malformations.

A further transgenic mouse model which shows overexpression of *Dyrk1A* (Altafaj *et al.* 2001) demonstrates impairments in spatial learning and cognitive flexibility, with hyperactivity and poor motor skill learning but unimpaired working memory.

The Ts65Dn mouse is a partial trisomy model of DS that changes the structure of the cerebellum (Saran *et al.* 2003). It does not markedly alter behaviour, but does produce marked effects on gene function.

A recent study suggests that, in the Ts65Dn mouse model, the use of a specific GABA A antagonist, pentylenetetrazole, results in a significant improvement in cognition (Fernandez *et al.* 2007). The GABA A gene, located at 15q11–13, is involved in formation of the palate and central nervous system development, and has been implicated in ASD and in several specific associated genetic conditions, such as Angelman syndrome [11] (Saitoh *et al.* 1992). GABRB3 mouse models of autism has been produced (Buxbaum *et al.* 2002; Delorey *et al.* 2008). The precise role of the B3 subunit is under active investigation (Ferguson *et al.* 2007).

A mouse trisomy model for the chromosomes equivalent to human chromosome 21 (Olson, Richtsmeier, Leszl and Reeves 2004) examined craniofacial dysmorphogenesis, concluding that the DS critical region was neither necessary nor specific for the generation of the typical skeletal differences seen in DS.

A close analogue to human DS has been engineered in a mouse line which has a free, almost complete copy of human chromosome 21 and shows many of the phenotypic characteristics of DS in humans, including abnormalities of cerebellar structure and heart development (O'Doherty *et al.* 2005).

In the mouse model of DS, the transcriptome for cerebellar development is completely disrupted (Saran, Pletcher, Natale, Cheng and Reeves 2003). Roper *et al.* (2006) identified abnormal cerebellar granule cell development in their mouse model of DS. This was reversible through administering an agonist to the Hedgehog protein signalling pathway.

USEFUL BOOKS:

Pueschel, S.M. (2001) *A Parent's Guide to Down Syndrome: Towards a Brighter Future.* (Revised and updated.) Baltimore: Paul Brookes.

Sears, M. and Soper, K.L. (eds.) (2007) *Gifts: Mothers Reflect on How Children with Down Syndrome Enrich Their Lives.* Bethesda: Woodbine House.

32.

Dravet's syndrome

aka • Severe myoclonic epilepsy in infancy (SMEI)
• SCN1A-related seizure disorders

Includes:

• intractable childhood epilepsy with generalized tonic-clonic seizures
• SCN1A-related generalized epilepsy with febrile seizures
• severe myoclonic epilepsy in infancy
• simple febrile seizures

GENE LOCI: 5q31.1–q33.1, 2q24

KEY ASD REFERENCES: Caraballo and Fejerman 2006; Weiss *et al.* 2003; Wolff, Casse-Perrot and Dravet 2006

SUMMARY: Dravet's syndrome is a form of epilepsy resulting from a mutation in the SCN1A gene on chromosome 2 at 2q24. It is named after Charlotte Dravet, a French psychiatrist and epileptologist who worked at the Centre St Paul in Marseille from 1965 to 2000. Also known as severe myoclonic epilepsy in infancy (SMEI), it was first described by Dravet (1978). Upwards of 500 clinical cases have been reported in the literature to date.

Formal international recognition came in 1989 when the revised classification of the International League Against Epilepsy placed this syndrome under 'epilepsies and syndromes undetermined as to whether they are focal or generalized', since the syndrome shows both generalized and localized features (Commission on Classification and Terminology of the International League Against Epilepsy 1989).

A number of general books on epilepsy and epilepsy management have useful sections on Dravet's syndrome (Arzimanoglou, Guerrini and Aicardi 2003; Roger *et al.* 2005; Shorvon 2005; Wallace and Farrell 2004).

HOW COMMON IS DRAVET'S SYNDROME? A precise estimate is currently not known (Hurst 1990; Yakoub *et al.* 1992). Prevalence is thought to be between one in 20,000 and one in 40,000.

MAIN CLINICAL FEATURES: Before seizures start, development is recorded as normal. Severe myoclonic epilepsy always begins in the first year. Over time, seizure activity usually starts with unilateral clonic or generalized seizures, often alternating from one side of the body to the other without any warning signs, and as these progress, myoclonic jerks and partial seizures normally appear. Progressive developmental delay from time of seizure onset is typical, becoming more apparent through the second year, with ataxia and corticospinal signs appearing later.

The initial seizures can vary in duration. In most cases, the first seizure appears in association with a raised body temperature, typically from fever, but sometimes even triggered by a hot bath (Awaya *et al.* 1990).

The same types of seizures often recur, sometimes without increase in temperature, and can be difficult to classify. A variety of other types of seizure also occur in this condition, with the pattern changing as the condition evolves: myoclonic seizures, absence seizures, complex partial seizures and status epilepticus are all seen (Dravet *et al.* 1992).

The initial EEGs after febrile episodes may not show any epileptiform activity. Later, the EEG between seizure events shows varied features, with a strong response to photic stimulation being seen in a large proportion of cases. EEGs carried out between seizures show a complex picture characterized by generalized, focal and multifocal anomalies (Dravet *et al.* 2005). There is a light-strength-dependent photosensitive response in many cases (Takahashi, Fujiwara, Yagi and Seino 1999), and often a sleep EEG will show more evidence of abnormality than an awake EEG (Dravet *et al.* 2005).

In one autopsied case, neuropathology demonstrated cerebellar and cerebrocortical microdysgenesis (Renier and Renkawek 1990), suggesting a problem with apoptosis. However, for most, no significant pathology has been reported. Structural neuroimaging may show mild diffuse atrophy, but is not usually helpful (Dravet *et al.* 2005).

In the majority of cases (around 80 per cent), there is no family history of Dravet's or of other types of epilepsy. The finding of a number of concordant identical (Fujiwara *et al.* 1990; Ohki *et al.* 1997) and one concordant non-identical twin pair (Ohtsuka *et al.* 1991), and of families with more than one affected sibling (Dravet *et al.* 2005; Ogino *et al.* 1989), strongly suggested a genetic aetiology. Long-term follow-up of one identical twin pair shows a strong similarity in clinical progression (Fujiwara 2006).

A genetic basis to Dravet's syndrome was first reported in 2001, when Claes *et al.* reported a defect in the SCN1A gene in all of a series of seven cases. SCN1A is involved in sodium channel function in the central nervous system. Lower rates of SCN1A gene defects in association with the Dravet phenotype have been reported in a number of other studies (for example, Wallace *et al.* 2003 (33.3 per cent); Fukuma *et al.* 2004 (44.8 per cent)). However, the range of SC1A mutations is huge

(Ceulemans, Claes and Lagae 2004), with 338 separate mutations being reported at the last count, 309 of which are associated with Dravet's syndrome and three which have been reported in association with autism (Weiss *et al.* 2003).

Defects in SCN1A are examples of one class of ion channelopathies, now known to be involved in a range of epilepsy syndromes. (For review, see Hirose 2006.)

IS THERE A LINK BETWEEN DRAVET'S SYNDROME AND ASD? To date, three studies have appeared which have suggested a possible link between Dravet's syndrome and ASD.

- The first paper was a screening study looking for SCN1A, SCN2A and SCN3A channelopathies in 117 multiplex ASD families involved with the AGRE project (Weiss *et al.* 2003). The screening identified six families with variants that could have an effect on sodium channel function (five on SCN1A and one on SCN2A).

- Caraballo and Fejerman (2006) reviewed casenotes on 55 cases that fitted the International League Against Epilepsy's criteria for Dravet's syndrome. The cases had been seen at their clinic in Argentina over a 14-year period (1990–2004). The authors found two cases (3.5 per cent) that fitted criteria for autism. Eighty-five per cent of cases fitted criteria for hyperactivity. It is not possible from the report to draw any conclusions concerning comorbidity.

- Wolff, Casse-Perrot and Dravet (2006) discuss the natural history of Dravet's syndrome, drawing on their analysis of a series of 20 cases. 'Autistic traits' and hyperactivity are both described as 'frequent', but no further information is given, except that this description applies to behaviour over the period from two to four years of age, during which there is typically developmental deterioration, followed by a severe level of learning difficulty, after previously normal development.

Various studies have commented on individuals with the same clinical course and outcome, but without the polyclonias and characteristic EEG described by Dravet. (See, for example, Doose, Lunau, Castiglione and Waltz 1998.) It transpires that these cases have genetic profiles somewhat different to Dravet's syndrome.

DIFFERENTIAL DIAGNOSIS: As Dravet's syndrome often begins with febrile convulsions, differentiation from more benign febrile fits is important in the early stages. In Dravet's syndrome onset is usually earlier and the convulsions are often clonic and one-sided rather than bilateral and tonic-clonic.

A further, much milder epileptic condition – generalized epilepsy with febrile seizures plus (GEFS+) – which also has onset with febrile convulsions, is also linked to defects in SCN1A (Escayg et al. 20001).

At the current level of understanding, a diagnosis can neither be ruled in nor ruled out by testing for an SCN1A defect. Diagnosis is currently based on the pattern of evolution of clinical symptoms.

MANAGEMENT AND TREATMENT: Although the research evidence to date is unreplicated and on small numbers, it appears that ketogenic diet can reduce seizure frequency in a significant proportion of the cases where it has been tried (Caraballo et al. 1998, 2005). Two medications – stiripentol (Chiron et al. 2000; Kassaï et al. 2008; Landmark and Johannessen 2008) and topiramate (Coppola et al. 2002; Kröll-Seger, Portilla, Dulac and Chiron 2006) – have been shown to be effective, both individually and in combination, in controlling seizure activity, though again in fairly small numbers of cases and centres.

There is one randomized controlled trial of stiripentol that in 15/21 patients produced a 50 per cent drop in clonic and tonic-clonic seizures (Kanazawa and Shirane 1999). Stiripentol appears to work through a direct influence on the GABA A receptor (Fisher 2008). Stiripentol (zonizamide) interacts with a number of other antiepileptic medications and has a number of possible side effects, such as renal stones and rash. (See discussion in Shorvon 2005.)

Other medications have also shown efficacy, sodium valproate, clonazepam and lorazepam being found the most useful, while other medications have been helpful in certain types of seizures – phenobarbital and potassium bromide in convulsive seizures, and ethosuximide in myoclonic and absence seizures. Carbamazepine and lamotrigine have been reported to exacerbate seizure activity (Guerrini et al. 1998; Wallace S.J. 1998).

As raised temperature and infection appear to be strong triggers for seizure activity in Dravet's syndrome, avoidance and prompt treatment of these are important for achieving the best level of fit control.

The outcome in Dravet's syndrome has historically been of significantly reduced life expectancy and deteriorating seizure control, coupled with significant learning disability, but recent developments in medical management of cases, particularly the positive results with use of stiripentol, topiramate and ketogenic diet, coupled with the possibilities of earlier identification through genetic screening, may lead to significantly improved outcomes.

ANIMAL MODELS: In the mouse, Malo et al. (1991) showed that SCN1A and SCN2A are tightly linked, and separated by a distance of only 0.7 centimorgans. The latter gene had previously been mapped to human chromosome 2; SCN1A was predicted, correctly, also to be located on human chromosome 2. Shortly after, using flourescence in-situ hybridization (FISH), Malo *et al.* (1994a, 1994b) were able to map the SCN1A gene to chromosome 2q24.

The progress in our understanding of the specific types of SCN1A defects that result in Dravet's syndrome and in ASD should now enable animal modelling of these conditions to be usefully developed (Yamakawa 2006).

33.

Duchenne (DMD) and Becker (BMD) muscular dystrophy

aka • Duchenne disease

• muscular dystrophy – Duchenne type

• [Duchenne] benign pseudohypertrophic muscular dystrophy

GENE LOCI: Xp21.2, 12q21

KEY ASD REFERENCES: Hendriksen and Vles 2008; Hinton *et al.* 2009; Komoto, Usui, Otsuki and Terao 1984; Kumagai *et al.* 2001; Wu J.Y. *et al.* 2005; Zwaigenbaum and Tarnopolsky 2003

SUMMARY: Duchenne muscular dystrophy was first described in 1836 (Conte and Gioia 1836). Duchenne muscular dystrophy is named after Guillaume-Benjamin Duchenne (1806–1875), the French neurologist. Becker muscular dystrophy is

named after the German neurologist Peter Emil Becker (1908–2000).

Duchenne and Becker muscular dystrophies are X-linked dominant genetic conditions that result in production of defective dystrophin protein, a key constituent of skeletal muscle. Dystrophin is a cytoplasmic protein that is over 3,500 amino acids in length and coded for by the longest human gene so far detected. Dystrophun isoforms are involved in a variety of tissue functions (see Muntoni, Torelli and Ferlini 2003). The immediate consequences of this defect is inability to form normal muscle, with muscle wasting and loss of functional mobility.

In DMD virtually no functional dystrophin is produced, while in BMD a truncated (shortened) form of the dystrophin protein is produced, with some functionality. There is variability depending on the specific gene defect, and the clinical phenotype is largely dependent on the amount of functional dystrophin produced (Monaco *et al.* 1988).

There are two genetic 'hotspots' – one at exons 2–20 (seen in 30 per cent of cases with identified gene deletions), and one at exons 44–53 (seen in 70 per cent) – which are implicated in both DMD and BMD (Den Dunnen *et al.* 1989).

HOW COMMON IS DMD? Estimates vary between one in 5,618 live male births (Bushby, Thambyayah and Gardner-Medwin 1991) and one in 50,000 live male births (Orphanet 2009).

Ethnic variations in the prevalence of different types of DMD mutation have been reported, with high rates of *de novo* mutation in northern Indian (Sinha *et al.* 1996) and Mexican (Alcántara *et al.* 1999) populations, and a high frequency of duplications in the Japanese population (Hiriashi, Kato, Ishihara and Takano 1992).

HOW COMMON IS BMD? For BMD the prevalence is estimated at one in 18,450 live male births (Bushby, Thambyayah and Gardner-Medwin 1991).

MAIN CLINICAL FEATURES: DMD typically presents in early childhood with slow achievement of early motor milestones. Proximal weakness causes a waddling gait and difficulty with climbing, and the classic 'Gower's sign' (with the child pulling him/herself to standing using the arms). DMD is associated with a progressive reduction in mobility. As a result, boys with DMD have decreasing bone density due to postural decalcification and an increased risk of bone fractures (Soderpalm et al. 2007). The motor problems progress rapidly, with most children being in a wheelchair by @12 years. Almost all individuals with DMD will be nonambulant by age 13. DMD and BMD are typically distinguished by the age at which those affected become wheelchair dependent: those with DMD before age 13 years and those with DMD after age 16 years. In practice, there is an overlap between the groups. Parents are typically first concerned over generally slow motor development in over 40 per cent of cases. Gait problems, including persistent toe-walking and flat-footedness, are cause for concern in almost a third, and delayed walking in one fifth of cases. Parents typically do not identify 'Gower's sign' as abnormal (Marshall and Galasko 1995). Clinical diagnosis is typically given at about four years ten months (range: 16 months–8 years) (Bushby 1999).

In BMD weakness develops more slowly and affected individuals are often independently mobile into their twenties. In addition, other aspects of development are delayed, such as acquisition of language milestones (Cyrulnik et al. 2007).

Overall, studies of intellectual function in DMD have shown a lower IQ (approximately one third of DMD cases have associated learning difficulties, i.e. IQ <70) (Mochizuki et al. 2008), predominantly with a lower verbal than performance IQ (Bresolin et al. 1994; Leibowitz and Dubowitz 1981; Moizard et al. 1998). This profile has been linked to a short-term memory impairment as this has greater impact on verbal than non-verbal IQ test results (Hinton et al. 2000, 2001; Wicksell, Kihlgren, Melin and Eeg-Olofsson 2004).

A particular isoform of dystrophin (Dp140) appears to be specifically associated with learning difficulties in DMD (Felisari et al. 2000). It may also prove to be the case that the Dp140 isoform is important for intellectual development in others.

Most DMD and BMD cases (around 90 per cent) have some degree of cardiac involvement. It is the cause of death in one in five DMD and one in two BMD cases. Heart problems secondary to DCM are the most common cause of death (Cox and Kunkel 1997). Heart muscle weakness is typical by age 18 years. Few of those affected with DMD survive through their thirties, with complications of respiratory infection or cardiac problems being the main causes of death, typically a few years after onset of congestive heart failure in males with slower progression in females (Beggs 1997). The typical presentation of cardiomyopathy is of left ventricular dilation and congestive heart failure between 20 and 40 years of age in men, and somewhat later in women. Life expectancy in BMD is typically into the mid-forties (Bushby and Gardner-Medwin 1993).

DCM is seen in both BMD and DMD (Palmucci et al. 2000). In DCM the ventricles of the heart are typically enlarged but do not function normally. Boys with DCM will present in their twenties and thirties; they will typically survive for up to two years after the diagnosis has been made (Finsterer and Stollberger 2003). Female carriers of DMD mutations are more likely to develop dilated cardiomyopathy with later onset, typically in the forties to fifties, and with a slower rate of progression. DCM is increasingly frequent with age – in boys, 95 per cent being affected by their early twenties, and 80 per cent by their mid-fifties (Nigro, Comi, Politano and Bain 1990).

In DMD-related DCM the mutations in the DMD gene affect two gene areas that specifically transcribe dystrophin used in cardiac muscle.

ECG abnormalities, due to dystrophin deficiency, are found in over 90 per cent of DMD cases (Takami et al. 2008).

Isolated DCM is also seen, with a failure to produce dystrophin specifically in cardiac muscle (Ferlini et al. 1999), and elevated CPK (Towbin et al. 1993).

Two dystrophin-producing genes prevent effects in skeletal muscles (Beggs 1997). Only 30 per cent of normal dystrophin levels are required to prevent muscular dystrophy (Neri et al. 2007).

With clear delineation of the genotype, mildly affected BMD cases are now being identified in adulthood, including some with very late onset of symptoms (see, for example, Quinlivan et al. 1995; Yazaki et al. 1999).

Parents of children with DMD perceive themselves as under high levels of stress, primarily as a consequence of their child's problem behaviours, particularly in social interaction, as opposed to the physical difficulties of their disease (Nereo, Fee and Hinton 2003).

Ethnic variations in the prevalence of different types of DMD mutation have been reported, with high rates of de novo mutation in northern Indian (Sinha et al. 1996) and Mexican (Alcántara et al. 1999) populations, and a high frequency of duplications in the Japanese (Hiriashi, Kato, Ishihara and Takano 1992).

Female presentation: Female DMD carriers can show features of DMD and BMD where X chromosome rearrangements involve the DMD locus, a single X chromosome, or non-random X-inactivation (Bodrug et al. 1987; Richards et al. 1990). It is not uncommon for DMD and BMD carriers to show symptoms of mild muscular weakness and cardiac involvement that are seen in around one in five (Hoogerwaard et al. 1999). As onset of cardiac problems is delayed in females compared to males, monitoring can usually begin in the teenage years (Nolan, Jones, Pedersen and Johnston 2003).

Girls who are affected can have DMD through four major mechanisms:

- an X chromosome rearrangement involving Xp21.2
- an X chromosome deletion involving Xp21.2
- complete absence of one X chromosome (as seen in Turner syndrome)
- a maternal uniparental X chromosome isodisomy.

Co-morbidity: In some boys with DMD additional X-linked disorders have been reported such as retinitis pigmentosa (seen in Biedl-Bardet syndrome [17]), chronic granulomatous disease, McLeod red cell phenotype, glycerol kinase deficiency and adrenal hyperplasia [25] (Darras and Francke 1988; Francke et al. 1985, 1987). The conditions that have been reported are due to contiguous gene deletion syndromes.

Clinical diagnosis: A diagnosis is arrived at if there is a positive family history suggesting X-linked recessive inheritance that is supportive. In addition the following clinical findings are present. There is progressive bilateral muscular weakness, greater for the upper arms and legs, sometimes with enlargement of the calf and the muscles of the tongue; the enlarged muscle is gradually replaced by fat and connective tissue, hence the use of the term 'pseudohypertrophic'. Symptoms are typically obvious before the child is five years old.

Serum creatine phosphokinase levels are elevated (in DMD typically to more than tenfold normal levels, and in BMD to over five times normal levels) in all cases. In female carriers, elevated levels are seen in around 50 per cent.

As DMD and BMD people get older, there is a gradual drop in serum creatine kinase, with the loss of dystrophic muscle fibres (Zatz et al. 1991). Normal concentrations of serum CPK have been reported in some cases of DMD-related dilated cardiomyopathy (Mestroni et al. 1999).

GENETIC TESTING: Clinical testing should first establish that there is an elevated level of CPK, and, in the context of associated clinical findings, this should lead on to genetic testing, which, if negative, as it would be in one third of cases, would lead on to muscle biopsy.

A number of genetic techniques can detect the deletions that account for the majority of mutations in both DMD and BMD. Southern blotting and quantitative PCR can also detect duplications that account for the mutations in some six to ten per cent of DMD and BMD mutations (Den Dunnen et al. 1989; Galvagni et al. 1994). For the remainder of the mutations so far found, mutation scanning and sequence analysis detect the small deletions or insertions, single-base changes and splicing mutations seen (Bennett et al. 2001; Dolinsky, de Moura-Neto and Falcao-Conceicao 2002).

Quantitative real-time PCR can now successfully identify mutations caused by deletion or duplication in most cases (Joncourt et al. 2004).

A variety of testing methods like SCAIP (single condition amplification internal primer sequencing) (Flanigan et al. 2003), DGGE (denaturing gradient gel electrophoresis-based whole-gene mutation scanning) (Hofstra et al. 2004) and MLPA (multiplex ligation-dependent probe amplification) (Hwa et al. 2007) are being developed to attempt to identify the one third or so of cases where the genetic basis cannot currently be identified using conventional techniques.

GENETIC INHERITANCE: Males with DMD do not survive long enough to have children. As BMD is an X-linked condition, affected fathers do not pass it on to their sons (who will inherit their X chromosome from their mother), but all of their daughters will be carriers, as they will inherit an affected X-chromosome. Mothers who carry a defective BMD or DMD gene will pass this on to their sons, and have a 50 per cent chance of passing the gene on to their daughters.

Genetic risk factors: The gene is inherited from the mother; fathers will not carry the disease mutation (although this could be possible with improvements in survival; recently a family has been described with five affected family members over two generations and apparent patrilineal inheritance (Purushottam et al. 2008)).

If the mother of an affected boy has another affected relative, she is an 'obligate heterozygote' and will be a carrier of a DMD gene defect.

Where a mother has more than one affected son and there is no other family history, there are various genetic possibilities (van Essen et al. 1992; van Essen et al. 1997; van Essen et al. 2003).

Genetic investigation will be required to clarify whether there is somatic or germline mosaic inheritance, or a maternal *de novo* mutation.

Risk to siblings of an affected person: Risks to a sibling depend on the mother's carrier status. Where the mother is a carrier, then 50 per cent of brothers will be affected and 50 per cent of sisters will be carriers.

If the mother has a germ-line mosaic, there is a 15–20 per cent risk of siblings being affected (van Essen *et al.* 2003). If the affected person has a *de novo* gene mutation, there is no increased risk to siblings.

Risk to children of an affected person: Males with DMD currently die before coming of age to father children, or are physically too severely affected to reproduce. The consequence of improvements in management may result in some males with DMD fathering offspring. If this were to happen, they would have affected daughters (all of whom would inherit their father's DMD X-chromosome), while sons would be unaffected.

Males with BMD or with DMD-related dilated cardiomyopathy (DCM) can usually father children. When this happens, they will have affected daughters (all of whom will inherit their father's DMD X-chromosome), while sons will be unaffected.

Mothers of DMD and BMD cases have an increased risk of DCM, and should be monitored.

IS THERE A LINK BETWEEN DMD AND ASD?

- The initial report of DMD in association with what at the time was known as infantile autism was a single case study of an 11-year-old boy (Komoto, Usui, Otsuki and Terao 1984).

- Kumagai and colleagues subsequently reported on a series of DMD (N=94)

and BMD (N=43) cases (Kumagai *et al.* 2001). Eight patients in their DMD series and two of those with BMD were diagnosed as autistic. The reported prevalence of ASD in this clinic series was well above what would be predicted from population prevalence. However, there is a possibility of ascertainment bias. The variation in ASD phenotype in 3/8 sibling pairs with the same genetic dystrophin defect in this series suggests that the association may be due to other mechanisms, or to other genetic factors.

- Two further reported cases of autism associated with muscular dystrophy from North America (Zwaigenbaum and Tarnopolsky 2003) transpired in one instance to be BMD type, and in the other, congenital autosomal recessive muscular dystrophy.

- In a series reported by Wu J.Y. *et al.* (2005), eight boys with both autism and DMD were identified, from a total population of 158 boys with DMD in the state of Massachusetts. Within the population with DMD in the state of Massachusetts, this gives a rate of one in 26 – that is significantly above the rate of concordance that would be predicted by chance. Again, however, there is a problem of ascertainment bias – virtually all muscular dystrophy cases will be identified, and they will be closely monitored for any developmental concerns, thereby inflating recognized co-morbidity levels.

- In 2008, Hendriksen and Vles reported on a questionnaire survey of parents of 351 DMD cases. The specific topics of interest were ADHD, obsessive-compulsive disorder and ASD. Based on the questionnaire data, 11.7 per cent were co-morbid for ADHD, 4.8 per cent for OCD and 3.1 per cent for ASD, the general conclusion being that DMD affects brain function as well as the peripheral nervous system, increasing the likelihood of 'neuropsychiatric' conditions.

- A 2009 study reviewed 85 boys with either DMD or BMD (Hinton *et al.* 2009). Using the Social Communication Questionnaire as a screening measure, 21 boys (approximately 25 per cent) but none of their siblings (23 brothers and 28 sisters) scored as possible ASD cases. All mothers of possible cases were interviewed using the ADI-R – 16 (around 19 per cent) met ASD criteria.

- Reports on ASD behavioural phenotypes can also be found in various other sources (Hinton, Fee, De Vivo and Goldstein 2006; Poysky 2007).

DMD and BMD are two of the nine primary muscular dystrophies, the other seven being:

- congenital
- distal
- Emery-Dreifuss
- facioscapulohumeral
- limb-girdle
- myotonic
- oculopharyngeal.

To date the only reported associations with ASD (other than the single case of congenital muscular dystrophy reported by Zwaigenbaum and Tarnopolsky) are cases of DMD and BMD. As no screening across the other seven types has yet been carried out, it is not possible to say at this point whether the association is specific to the DMD and BMD types, or is a more general association with the muscular dystrophies. There is an overrepresentation of neuromuscular disorders in ASD (see Table A9).

DIFFERENTIAL DIAGNOSIS: Duchenne and Becker muscular dystrophies need to

be distinguished from one another, based on the level of dystrophin expression.

Differentiation needs to be made from other dystrophic conditions linked to ASD:

- myotonic dystrophy (DM1)/Steinert's myotonic dystrophy [50]

- congenital autosomal recessive muscular dystrophies (CARMD) (Muntoni and Voit 2004). This term covers a number of genetic dystrophies caused by genes, including laminin-alpha 2 chain, fukutin-related protein, LARGE and fukutin. A single case of CARMD with ASD has also been reported (Zwaigenbaum and Tarnopolsky 2003).

Differentiation also needs to be made from other muscular dystrophies not to date reported in association with ASD:

- Emery-Dreifuss muscular dystrophy (EDMD) (Bonne, Leturcq, Récan-Budiartha and Yaou 2007). It is caused by a gene defect in the production of emerin at Xp28

- facioscapulohumeral muscular dystrophy (FSHMD), which is the most common type of muscular dystrophy. It is an autosomal dominant condition resulting in upper body muscle wasting and is typically due to abnormality in a region of 4q35 (Lemmers *et al.* 2007)

- limb-girdle muscular dystrophy (Bushby 1999). This diagnosis also needs to be considered, and has recently been shown to result from absence of the protein c-FLIP (Benayoun *et al.* 2008)

- oculopharyngeal dystrophy (OPD), which is a late onset dystrophic condition (usually in the sixties) caused by a 14q11.2–q13 gene defect in the PABPN1 gene coding for polyadenylate-binding protein 2 (Brais *et al.* 1995)

- spinal muscular atrophy (SMA), which has recently been associated with mutations to the UBE1 gene (Ramser *et al.* 2008)

- distal muscular dystrophy is the term for a group of muscular disorders affecting the hands or feet typically involving a gene at 2p13 that codes for dysferlin, a protein involved in repair of skeletal muscle (von Tell *et al.* 2003)

- dilated cardiomyopathy as a discrete presentation (Mestroni *et al.* 1999).

MANAGEMENT AND TREATMENT: At the time of writing, there are no treatments to prevent the primary features of either DMD or BMD.

SURVEILLANCE AND MONITORING: There should be routine monitoring of cardiac and lung function, particularly from the stage at which a person becomes wheelchair dependent. Treatment of DCM with ACE-inhibitors and beta-blockers as needed can, in most cases, result in normalization of the size of the left ventricle and normal systolic function early on (Towbin, J.A. 2003). A heart transplant may be required in the most severe and intractable cases. Care should be taken to minimize risk of respiratory infection.

Regular monitoring of possible orthopaedic complications, from osteoporosis and scoliosis in particular, need to be monitored and treated as appropriate. Supplementation with vitamin D and calcium should be used, particularly once the person is non-ambulant, to reduce the risks of osteoporosis and bone fracture.

Physical and occupational therapy should be used to maintain functional mobility and prevent flexion contractures of the ligaments.

As activity level reduces, care should be taken to ensure there is no excess weight gain.

Medications: A number of medications are used with good effect in controlling some of the symptoms of both DMD and BMD. In particular, *prednisolone* has been shown to improve muscular strength and physical abilities (Backman and Henriksson 1995; Fenichel *et al.* 1991; Mendell *et al.* 1989) and to prolong walking (DeSilva, Drachman, Mellits and Kuncl 1987). Prednisolone is a steroid that is converted in the liver from prednisone, a corticosteroid medication. Prednisolone has been shown to slow the muscular deterioration in DMD without marked negative effects on quality of life (Beenakker *et al.* 2005; Manzur, Kuntzer, Pike and Swan 2008), but various side effects are reported, including significant weight gain (40 per cent) with a 'cushingoid' appearance, elevated blood pressure, behavioural deterioration, slowing of physical growth, and the development of cataracts (Griggs *et al.* 1993; Mendell *et al.* 1989).

The optimal age for prednisolone treatment, and the appropriate duration of treatment, have not been established, but current recommendations suggest beginning as soon as a diagnosis has been made (Merlini *et al.* 2003). No long-term or large group controlled trials have been so far been conducted.

Deflazacort, which is an artificial prednisolone derivative, is available in Europe but not currently in the USA. It appears to produce less weight gain (Mesa *et al.* 1991), but has a significantly increased risk of causing asymptomatic cataracts (30 per cent) (Biggar *et al.* 2004). A systematic review and meta-analysis of 15 studies found improved muscle strength and motor function compared to placebo (Campbell and Jacob 2003). To date there are no direct trials of deflazacort against prednisolone.

Oxandrolone is an anabolic steroid that has been shown in a pilot study to have effects similar to prednisolone, but has fewer reported side effects (Fenichel *et al.*

1997). In one randomized controlled trial oxandrolone was shown to produce minor improvements in muscle strength (Fenichel et al. 2001).

Therapies under investigation for the prevention of secondary complications: A number of experimental gene therapies are currently under investigation (Gregorevic and Chamberlain 2003; Nowak and Davies 2004; Tidball and Spencer 2003; van Deutekom and van Ommen 2003).

• *Gentamycin* is an aminoglycoside that can override premature stop codon defects in DMD. One preliminary open study gave two weeks of gentamicin (7.5 mg/kg/day) to four people with DMD. No full-length dystrophin was produced by their muscles (Wagner et al. 2001).

  In some 13 per cent of cases, DMD is due to a nonsense mutation that results in premature insertion of a stop codon. This means that a functional version of the essential muscle protein, dystrophin, is not produced. Administering gentamycin enables the gene to 'skip' over the stop codon and produce the dystrophin protein by ignoring the stop codon and reading the full genetic sequence. The side effects of gentamycin with long-term use – deafness and kidney damage – make this problematic as a treatment approach. Other aminoglycoside antibiotics have similar effects and similar, though less severe, side effect profiles. *Negamycin* has shown some promise in animal models (Arakawa et al. 2003). For a useful recent discussion of this topic, and of the phase III trials of genetic approaches underway at the time of writing, see Muntoni and Wells (2007).

• *Stem cell therapy* is under investigation but at this time remains an experimental rather than a clinical treatment (Blau

2008; Gussoni et al. 1997, 1999, 2002; Skuk et al. 2004).

• *Creatine monohydrate* has been studied as potential treatment in muscular dystrophies and neuromuscular disorders (Louis et al. 2003) with slightly improved bone density. In a recent randomized, controlled, crossover treatment study, 30 boys with DMD were given creatine (aproximately 0.1 g/kg/day) over an eight-month period (Tarnopolsky et al. 2004). Modest benefits were found in muscle mass and grip strength, but with no improvement in function. For a recent overview of creatine supplementation, see Athanasios, Konstantina, Paraskevi and Nikolaidis (2009).

• Another novel treatment showing promise is *PTC124*, an experimental 1,2,4-oxadiazole nonaminoglycoside medication (Hamed 2006). It has effects similar to gentamycin on the production of dystrophin in nonsense cases, but without the side effects (Hirawat et al. 2007; Welch et al. 2007). PTC124 is showing promise in phase II clinical trials that began in May 2007. (For further information see www.ptcbio.com.) This type of approach may prove helpful where the DNA sequence for dystrophin is present but disrupted, but it would not work in DMD cases where the gene is deleted or rearranged.

• Some recently published work on the long-term use of *perindopril*, an 'ACE-inhibitor' (angiotensin-converting enzyme inhibitor), reports a significant reduction in mortality over a ten-year period as a result of its protective effects on cardiac and respiratory muscle function (Duboc et al. 2007). This study randomly assigned patients (aged 9 to 13.5 years at the start of the trial) blindly to two groups: 28 receiving perindopril, 29 placebo. Over a ten-year follow-up period, 26 of the 28 receiving active medication survived, compared to only 19 of 29 in the control group.

Dietary approaches to managing problems secondary to treatments such as steroids are important, but as yet poorly researched. (See, for review, Davidson and Truby 2009).

There is some RCT evidence for beneficial effects of coenzyme Q10 supplementation on physical performance and cardiac function (Folkes and Simonsen 1995).

Gene therapies: The most exciting developments in potential treatment for DMD involve gene therapies (Cossu and Sampaolesi 2007). There are a number of limitations to gene therapies as currently developed, particularly in their ability to improve cardiac function. A number of novel approaches to gene delivery that hope to circumvent current limitations are in active development. (See, for example, Goncalves *et al.* 2008; Nelson, Crosbie, Miceli and Spencer 2009).

Mechanical devices to prolong mobility: Orthotic devices to maintain physical movement in muscular dystrophy as physical power diminishes are being developed. Dr Tariq Rahman at the University of Delaware has one of the more advanced programmes, involving a device called WREX (the Wilmington Robotic Exoskeleton). (See Rahman *et al.* 2001, and the Nemours website: www.udel.edu/bio/nemours.)

ANIMAL MODELS: The *mdx* (a mouse model for Duchenne muscular dystrophy) mouse provides a useful knockout model for DMD. One important suggestion from this model is that the effects of lack of dystrophin are developmentally dependent, producing a DMD-like phenotype when affected between three and eight weeks after birth in the mouse, but not earlier

or later (Gharamani Seno *et al.* 2008). As dystrophin has a long half-life in muscle tissue, this suggests that gene therapy to restore dystrophin before this critical phase may be able to arrest the disorder.

Gregorevic *et al.* (2004) reported systemic administration of rAAV6 vectors, resulting in successful delivery of the DMD gene to affected muscles of dystrophin-deficient *mdx* mice.

Gentamycin (see above) is showing positive results in the *mdx* mouse model (Barton-Davis *et al.* 1999; Barton *et al.* 2005).

In a recent study Wu, B. *et al.* (2008) used the *mdx* mouse model to demonstrate that a phosphorodiamidate morpholino oligomer with a designed cell-penetrating peptide (PPMO) could improve cardiac muscle strength. This was achieved with negligible toxicity or immune response, suggesting it may be helpful in DMD patients.

Adult mouse dystrophin knockdown does not result in muscular dystrophic pathology (Ghahramani Senov *et al.* 2008), suggesting that if early dystrophin production can be maintained, the benefits may last for a considerable time.

A helpful paper for parents, 'Research Approaches for a Therapy of Duchenne Muscular Dystrophy', by Dr Guenter Scheuerbrandt (2008), can be downloaded from www.endduchenne.org.

34.

Ehlers-Danlos syndrome (EDS)

aka • Chernogubov's syndrome
• Danlos' syndrome

- Meekeren-Ehlers-Danlos syndrome
- Sack's syndrome
- Sack-Barabas syndrome
- Van Meekeren's syndrome I

GENE LOCI:

- Type I (17q21.31–q22; 9q34.2–q34.3; 2q31)
- Type II (9q34.2–q34.3)
- Type III (6p21.3; 2q31)
- Type IV (2q31)
- Type V (not known)
- Type VI (1p36.3–p36.2; 16q2)
- Type VII (17q21.31–q22)
- Type VII (5q23)
- Type VIII (12p13)
- Cardiac valvular form (7q22.1)
- Progeroid form (5q35.2–q35.3)
- Type X (2q34–q36)
- Periventricular heterotopia variant (Xq28)

KEY ASD REFERENCES: Fehlow, Bernstein, Tennstedt and Walther 1993; Lumley *et al.* 1994; Sieg 1992

SUMMARY: The first clinical description of EDS was by a Dutch surgeon, Job Janszoon Van Meekeren, who presented the case of George Albes, a Spanish sailor, to senior physicians at the Academy of Leiden in 1657. Albes was well known for being able to stretch the skin on his chest out to arm's length. This early account was published two years after Van Mekeren's death in 1668. Edvard Ehlers, a Danish dermatologist, described clinical cases in 1901, and Henri-Alexandre Danlos, a Parisian physician, published further descriptions in 1908.

EDS is the term now used to describe a group of disorders of collagen, the main protein found in connective tissues in the body. All of the EDS gene defects produce abnormalities of collagen, with a variety of physical features: most result in hyperextensible joints, some in skin fragility, some in easy bruising, and some in scoliosis. To date, there are 14 distinct genetic sites that have been linked to EDS, and over ten recognized distinct subtypes. (For an overview, see Mao and Bristow 2001.)

The Villefranche classification, which is commonly used, classifies six distinct subtypes (Beighton *et al.* 1998), as can be seen in Table B34.

Improving clinical assessment may lead to clear differentiation among all of the genetic variants.

Most forms of EDS are inherited in an autosomal dominant fashion. However, two – kyphoscoliosis (EDS type VI), which results from a defect in lysyl-hydroxylase, and dermatosparaxis (EDS type VIIc), which results from a defect in procollagen

Table B34: The Villefranche classification of Ehlers-Danlos syndrome

- classical (type I/II)
- hypermobility (type III)
- vascular (type IV)
- kyphoscoliosis (type VI)
- arthrochalasia (type VIIa,b)
- dermatosparaxia (type VIIc)

N-peptidase – are autosomal recessive conditions. Exon skipping appears to be the mechanism which results in a number of the specific forms of EDS identified in type I, type II, type IV, type VIIa, and type VIIb (Nicholls *et al.* 1996).

HOW COMMON IS EHLERS-DANLOS SYNDROME? The best current estimate for the Ehlers-Danlos group of conditions is 3.5 per 100,000 (Orphanet 2009). However, some estimates are as high as one in 5,000 (Steinmann, Royce and Superti-Furga 1993).

MAIN CLINICAL FEATURES: All of the EDS gene defects produce abnormalities of collagen, with a variety of physical features: most result in hyperextensible joints, some in skin fragility, some in easy bruising, and some (particularly type VI) in scoliosis. Gastrointestinal involvement is seen and can sometimes present with severe complications (Saucy, Eidus and Keeley 1980; Shaikh and Turner 1988).

Cardiac problems are reported in a small proportion of cases but appear to be a rare concomitant of EDS (Beighton 1969; D'Aloia *et al.* 2008).

Overviews of the vascular form of EDS (type IV) can be found in Germain (2007) and Germain and Herrera-Guzman (2004).

Central nervous system involvement is reported, with an association between one variant of EDS and periventricular heterotopia (Cupo *et al.* 1981; Sheen *et al.* 2005; Thomas P. *et al.* 1996). This association has been linked to a common defect in the filamin (Thomas P. *et al.* 1996), a gene that has not been reported in other forms of EDS. Filamin A is at Xq28 (Fox *et al.* 1998; Sheen *et al.* 2005; Sheen and Walsh 2006). In the vascular (type IV) form, intracerebral aneurysms have been reported (Kato *et al.* 2001).

IS THERE A LINK BETWEEN EDS AND ASD? Several reports of cases in which individuals with Ehlers-Danlos syndrome also have ASD have been published. However, to date no systematic studies of this issue have appeared. It is unclear, therefore, whether this is a chance association or there is some causal linkage involved, and as the association has not been with a specific type of EDS, the genetic basis, if any, is still unclear.

- Sieg (1992) published the first case report as a letter in the *American Journal of Child and Adolescent Psychiatry.*

- Fehlow, Bernstein, Tennstedt and Walther (1993) described a 19-year-old patient with EDS, early infantile autism and learning disability, who died after extreme distension of the stomach induced by aerophagy (air-swallowing).

- Lumley and colleagues, from Wayne State University in Detroit, interviewed and tested 48 people with EDS – 41 adults and 7 children (Lumley *et al.* 1994). More than two-thirds of those examined had a history of mental health problems. The authors suggest that these problems are linked to chronic pain and dissatisfaction with the medical system. Many of the difficulties they report – interpersonal concerns and avoidance of relationships and social activities – could easily reflect an ASD. In much of the literature EDS has been linked with 'alexithymia' (a term which is not in the DSM or ICD systems, but which is used to describe a personality disorder in which there are problems in understanding, processing and describing emotions).

- In a separate paper Lumley and colleagues (1996) included a sample of 40 subjects with EDS along with normal controls in a study of alexithymia, health problems and perceived social support. Using a number of scales of alexithymia and the PILL (Pennebaker Inventory of Limbic Languidness (Pennebaker 1982)), they were able to demonstrate an association between physical symptomology, poor social support and poor perceived social skills (suggesting that a difficulty in understanding, processing and describing emotions characterizes the EDS behavioural phenotype).

DIFFERENTIAL DIAGNOSIS: The features of EDS are not typically confused with other conditions. However, Williams syndrome [77], which results in a defect in connective tissue due to defective production of elastin, and Marfan's syndrome, which presents with similar features due to defects in the production of both elastin and fibrillin-1 (a further protein important in connective tissue formation – see discussion in Dietz 2007), have both been linked wth ASD. (See Tantam, Evered and Hersov 1990 on the co-occurrence of Marfan's syndrome and ASD.) Supravalvular aortic stenosis (SVAS), a feature of both William syndromes and Marfan's syndrome, is specific to defects in elastin but is not seen in any type of EDS.

MANAGEMENT AND TREATMENT: As the features of EDS are highly variable, the treatment approach cannot be prescriptive. At the present time, there is insufficient information to give separable behavioural phenotypes for the different forms of EDS. However, there are emerging suggestions of different behavioural phenotypes associated with the different types of EDS (Lumley et al. 1994).

ANIMAL MODELS: There are no specific animal models of EDS. However, there is a veterinary literature on the same types of connective tissue problems in various other animals, including dogs and mink (Hegreberg 1975).

A number of the genes that have been identified in forms of EDS have direct homologues in the mouse (Searle, Edwards and Hall 1994).

35.

Fragile-X syndrome

aka • Martin-Bell syndrome
 • Marker-X syndrome

GENE LOCUS: Xq27.3 (FMR1: fragile-X mental retardation 1)

KEY ASD REFERENCES: August and Lockhart 1984; Blomquist et al. 1985; Brown et al. 1982a, 1982b; Cohen I.L. et al. 1991 (review); Gillberg 1983; Hatton et al. 2006; Hernandez et al. 2009; Kaufmann et al. 2004; Loesch et al. 2007; Meryash, Szymanski and Gerald 1982 (But see Klauck et al. 1997 – they conclude there is no association between FMR1 and ASD.)

SUMMARY: There are a large number of genes (over 130 currently known) which can result in X-linked mental retardation (XLMR), and a significant proportion of which result in clinically indistinguishable non-syndromic forms (NS-XLMR) where the genetics is inferred from the familial inheritance pattern (Ropers 2006). The most common X-linked condition that causes neurodevelopmental problems is known as fragile-X syndrome. It is the genetic condition most commonly linked to autism in the clinical literature. Fragile-X syndrome is thought to be the second most common genetic cause of learning disability after Down syndrome (Rousseau et al. 1995).

Fragile-X syndrome results from a triplet repeat expansion of the FMR1 locus. It is inherited as an X-linked dominant condition. A normal FMR1 gene is some 38 kilobases of DNA, with 17 exons (Eichler, Richards, Gibbs and Nelson 1993). This mechanism was first described in fragile-X syndrome by a group from Rotterdam (Verkerk *et al.* 1991; De Boulle *et al.* 1993). Although originally thought to be unusual, over 40 neuromuscular, neurodegenerative and neurological disorders have now been described which result from triplet repeat expansions (Pearson, Edamura and Cleary 2005). Structurally, fragile-X results in morphologically distinct spinal neurons (Bagni and Greenough 2005).

The FMR1 gene ceases to function in 99 per cent of cases due to a triplet expansion with direct effects on methylation. The FMR1 region codes for the RNA-binding protein known as fragile-X mental retardation protein (FMRP) (Kooy, Willemsen and Oostra 2000). FMRP is primarily expressed in neurons (Devys *et al.* 1993), with a role in the maturation and apoptosis of synapses (Weiler and Greenough 1999).

In the other @1 per cent of cases, the condition arises from deletions (Hammond, Macias, Tarleton and Shashidhar Pai 1997) or point mutations (Wang Y.C. *et al.* 1997) within the same FMR1 locus. Fragile-X syndrome is thus caused by inactivation of the gene and the reduction or absence of FMRP. The transcription process is partly controlled by two other genes, Nrf-1 and Sp1, and is not regulated by DNA methylation alone (Smith, Coffee and Reines 2004; Garber, Smith, Reines and Warren 2006).

Although most fragile-X cases result from a triplet repeat expansion of the FMR1 region, small deletions within the FMR1 region can also result in the phenotype (Lugenbeel, Peier, Carson, Chudley and Nelson 1995).

The cytosine-guanine-guanine (CGG) nucleic acid sequence involved in the production of FMRP repeats some 6–55 times in the general population. In mothers of affected individuals the same CGG sequence repeats some 55–230 times (which used to be called a 'pre-mutational' expansion; but see FXTAS below), while in diagnosed individuals some 230 to 1,000 copies are typically seen (Fryns *et al.* 2000). The condition usually affects the X chromosome in boys, who will have inherited their Y chromosome from their father and their X chromosome from their mother. Although *de novo* mutation and uniparental isodisomy with patrilineal inheritance are theoretically possible, neither has been reported to date.

FMR1 expansions are not invariably associated with developmental problems. One paper documents a woman with a full mutation who is of above average IQ, but has an anxiety disorder and specific learning disabilities (Angkustsiri *et al.* 2008). Unmethylated FMR1 expansions with normal development have been reported (Hagerman, Ono and Hagerman 2005), as have cases of normal development with partial methylation (Rousseau *et al.* 1994b).

The first clinical account of the fragile-X syndrome phenotype is commonly accepted as a 1943 paper written by two clinicians working at Queen Square in London (Martin and Bell 1943), and the condition was subsequently referred to as Martin-Bell syndrome. (See, for example, Opitz, Westphal and Daniel 1984.) Many of the cases in the initial report by Martin and Bell were children of the daughters of two unaffected brothers.

The first identification of a chromosomal defect on the X chromosome in such cases was reported in 1969, when an X chromosome defect was identified in chromosomes cultured in a folate-reduced medium (Lubs 1969). It was in 1977 that Sutherland demonstrated the importance of folate reduction for FMR1 expansion to be visible.

For overviews of the importance of Julia Bell in the development of clinical genetics, see Bundey (1996) and Harper (2005).

HOW COMMON IS FRAGILE-X SYNDROME?

The full mutation form of the fragile-X expansion is found in some one in 3,717 to one in 8,918 of the male Caucasian population (Crawford, Acuna and Sherman 2001). The phenotype associated with fragile-X syndrome is significantly more common in boys.

There appear to be ethnic differences in prevalence – the Afro-American male population is reported as having a higher prevalence rate of some one in 1,289 to one in 2,545 (Crawford *et al.* 2002). A higher prevalence of certain alleles that are rare in Caucasian populations has also been reported in the African-Brazilian population (Mingroni-Netto *et al.* 2002).

A Taiwanese study found only one query positive case on bloodspot screening of 10,046 neonates, with six premutational cases, suggesting that there is a substantively lower prevalence in the Taiwan Chinese population (Tzeng *et al.* 2005).

The prevalence of pre-mutational and mutational expansion in women is far higher than might be expected. A French-Canadian screening study of 10,624 women found one in 259 were pre-mutational carriers of an FMR1 expansion (Rousseau *et al.* 1995). A more recent Israeli study of 14,334 women found 127 carriers, three with full mutations, giving a prevalence of one in 113, with one in 69 having more than 50 repeats (Toledano-Alhadef *et al.* 2001).

MAIN CLINICAL FEATURES: The early physical phenotype is not obvious, and without genetic testing diagnostic confusion is common (Stoll 2001). Stoll emphasized the importance of fragile-X DNA testing in all children presenting with developmental concerns. Ideally DNA testing should be routine for children presenting with delayed milestones, autistic behaviour or obvious learning disability without obvious cause, or where there is a positive family history.

The clinical diagnosis relies on the identification of an FMR1 expansion on genetic testing (or, more rarely, point mutation; deletion; or missense mutation interfering with FMR1 function), coupled with abnormal methylation.

Fragile-X can be diagnosed antenatally by chorionic villus sampling (Sutherland *et al.* 1991).

The most obvious early signs of the condition are marked gaze avoidance and hand flapping. An enlarged forehead (occipitofrontal head circumference of > 50 per cent) is common. The physical features that are typically quoted – long face, protruding ears and large testes – become markedly more prominent after puberty and are often unremarkable earlier.

In fragile-X there is a well-recognized behavioural and physical phenotype (Hagerman and Cronister 1996). Seizure problems affect some 10–20 per cent of cases, with complex partial seizures being most common (Sutherland, Gecz and Mulley 2002).

In affected males with an FMR1 expansion, a range of behavioural features are commonly seen and after puberty a number of physical features become more characteristic.

Key behavioural features:

• learning disability (IQ typically 30–50), often in the context of a family history of learning disability

• hyperactivity

• short attention span

Table B35.1: Physical and behavioural features of boys with fragile-X syndrome

Feature	Boys with feature (%)
• perseveration	95
• hyperactivity	89
• poor eye contact	88
• hand flapping	85
• flat feet	82
• hyperextensible metacarpophalangeal joints	81
• prominent ears	78
• tactile defensiveness	76
• long face	64
• hand biting	64
• double-jointed thumbs	58
• high-arched palate	51
• hand calluses	18

(Adapted from Hagerman and Hagerman 2002a)

Table B35.2: Common physical problems in males with fragile-X

Common problem in males with FMR1	Males with feature (%)
• recurrent otitis media	85
• strabismus	36
• recurrent emesis	31
• sinusitis	23
• seizures	22
• motor tics	19
• failure to thrive	15
• hernia	15
• apnoea	10
• joint dislocation	3

(Adapted from Hagerman and Hagerman 2002a)

- tactile defensiveness
- hand flapping
- hand biting
- poor eye contact
- perseverative speech.

Poor fine-motor control appears to differentiate fragile-X with ASD from fragile-X without ASD (Zingerevich *et al.* 2009).

Key physical features (usually more obvious after puberty): With a full mutation, boys typically show delayed milestones for both motor development and communication, walking and talking with clear words at @20 months.

Other key physical features are:

- hyperextensible metacarpophalangeal joints
- large or prominent ears
- large testes (macroorchidism)
- Simian crease or single palmar crease. (A single palmar crease is seen in a range

of ASD conditions including Aarskog syndrome [8]; de Lange syndrome [27]; Down syndrome [31]; and Smith-Lemli-Opitz syndrome [66].)

Macroorchidism is commonly reported in males with FMR1. The evidence to date suggests that there is an association, with some 44 per cent of those with FMR1 and learning disability having macroorchidism. This can be of greater degree than in the general learning-disability male population, and may be associated more with degree of learning disability than with FMR1 per se (Vatta *et al.* 1998).

The physical phenotype reported in women with a full FMR1 expansion (poor eye contact and increased rate of stereotyped behaviours) is similar to the features reported in full mutation FMR1 males.

It is clear from the prevalence and range of features, in both affected males and females, that, although they clearly identify

Table B35.3: Physical and behavioural features in women with the full fragile-X mutation

Feature	Women with feature (%)
• poor eye contact	73
• long face	66
• high-arched palate	59
• double-jointed thumbs	42
• prominent ears	42
• hyperextensible metacarpophalangeal joints	24
• flat feet	24
• scoliosis	22
• strabismus	20
• hand flapping	17
• hand biting	7

(Adapted from Hagerman and Hagerman 2002a)

differences from the normal population, none are either necessary or specific.

Certain other features, such as sleep difficulties, appear to be common in fragile-X syndrome (Tirosh and Borochowitz 1992; Weiskop, Richdale and Matthews 2005) and may be related to biological differences. From the work to date, aspects such as melatonin secretion seem extremely variable (Gould *et al.* 2000).

There have been reports of cardiac abnormalities, such as mitral valve prolapse (Hagerman and Synhorst 1984; Pyeritz *et al.* 1982) and mild dilatation of the aorta (Hagerman and Synhorst 1984). No recent studies of cardiac function have been published.

Ligamentous laxity has also been reported in two earlier studies (Hagerman, Van Housen, Smith and McGavran 1984; Opitz, Westphal and Daniel 1984). However, again no recent studies have been conducted on this issue.

A small-scale study of early videotapes of development in children with fragile-X (N=11) compared this group to other children with autism (N=11), children with other developmental disorders (N=10), and normal controls (N=11) (Baranek *et al.* 2005). The results suggested that those with fragile-X showed early differences in their sensorimotor development compared to those with autism without fragile-X. The findings in the fragile-X group were most similar to those seen in the other developmental disorders (not including ASD). This suggests a possible difference between fragile-X autism and other autistics. One limitation is that the study did not discriminate within the fragile-X group between those who would have qualified for an ASD diagnosis (normally around 20–30 per cent in reported samples to date) (Feinstein and Reiss 1998; Rogers,

Wehner and Hagerman 2001), and those who would not.

A further study, comparing a group of 24 21–48-month-old fragile-X cases to 27 with autism and 23 with developmental delay on various instruments (Rogers, Wehner and Hagerman 2001), found that one third of the fragile-X cases clearly met criteria for an ASD while the rest did not, suggesting additional genetic influences on the behavioural phenotype in fragile-X syndrome.

When we look at the proportion of those with an ASD diagnosis who have a fragile-X expansion on genetic testing, the results vary widely, with somewhere between none and 16 per cent of cases typically being reported. (See Dykens and Volkmar 1997 for review.) The proportion of fragile-X positive cases is likely to have fallen with the broadening of diagnostic criteria in the ICD-10 and DSM-IV criteria introduced in 1994. One systematic study in particular, which reviewed a large ASD sample (Klauck *et al.* 1997), concludes that, although cases where fragile-X and ASD co-occur can be found, the level of the association is minimal. In this study, the authors concluded that a link between autism and fragile-X at Xq27.3 was non-existent. A screening study found that the rate of FMR1 in the ASD population was similar to that in the learning disabled population in general (Hagerman, Wilson *et al.* 1994).

Within the fragile-X population, receptive language skills appear to be an area of relative strength, except in those who also fulfil criteria for autism. Those with fragile-X autism, in common with most other autistics, show relative deficits in receptive language (Philofsky *et al.* 2004). Where early population screening is available, this may prove to be a way of distinguishing within the fragile-X population those who are at risk of ASD, and targeting early interventions.

In a German study, Backes et al. (2000) assessed 49 boys with fragile-X syndrome and 16 controls in a group comparison study. The fragile-X group had mild to moderate learning disability assessed on the Kaufman Assessment Battery for Children. ADHD, oppositional defiant disorder, enuresis and encopresis were the most common mental health difficulties. There was no clear association between the phenotype and genotype.

An early study established that FMR1 expression in the foetal brain is most pronounced in the nucleus basalis magnocellularis and the hippocampus (Abitbol et al. 1993). FMRP is localized in dendrites and reduced in synapses by activation of the specific metabotropic glutamate receptor mGluR5 (Antar et al. 2004). In rats, at least, mGluR5 can be detected during embryonic development (Lopez-Bendito, Shigemoto, Fairen and Lujan 2002), and is most prominent in zones of active neurogenesis (Gerevini et al. 2004). Its expression rises through the first two postnatal weeks, then falls to adult levels (Romano, Smout, Miller and O'Malley 2002).

Neuroanatomically, fragile-X results in an excess of long, thin dendritic spines seen in both human central nervous system autopsy tissue from affected individuals (Irwin, Galvez and Greenough 2000) and in brain tissue from genetically engineered knockout mice (Comery et al. 1997). Dendritic anomalies are common to a number of disorders associated with learning problems. However, the nature, location and extent of these defects seem to be disorder-specific (Kaufmann and Moser 2000; Ramackers 2002). In fragile-X, the effect of the FMRP defect is to produce a syndrome-specific abnormality of dendritic spine morphology (Vanderklish and Edelman 2005).

Studies of the brain in fragile-X have shown both structural differences, with enlargement of the hippocampus and reduction in the size of the cerebellum and the superior temporal gyrus (Reiss et al. 1991; Reiss, Lee and Freund 1994), functional differences (Rivera et al. 2002), and differences in neuroendocrine function, particularly affecting the hypothalamo-gonadal-pituitary axis (Hessl, Rivera and Reiss 2004). The presence of periventricular heterotopias in unrelated cases (Moro et al. 2006) suggests that one aspect of fragile-X is a neural migration defect.

In certain brain areas, expression of FMRP mRNA is regulated by brain-derived neurotrophic factor (Castre et al. 2002). A complex range of mRNAs binds to fragile-X gene products, partly accounting for the wide variation in phenotype (Gantois and Kooy 2002; Jin et al. 2004). Studies are beginning to elucidate the metabolic chain that culminates in fragile-X syndrome (Pietrobono et al. 2005).

A systematic review (Cornish et al. 2004) has suggested that a neuroconstructivist systems view of development in fragile-X best captures the subtle and complex interplay of genetic, brain and environmental factors.

The considerable recent interest in the neurobiology of fragile-X syndrome (Belmonte and Bourgeron 2006; Hagerman 2006; Miller 2006) has been stimulated by several major developments, outlined here in the following.

First, the recognition that the grandfathers of those affected by fragile-X syndrome often presented in later life with a condition now known as fragile-X-associated tremor/ataxia syndrome (FXTAS) (Amiri, Hagerman and Hagerman 2008; Berry-Kravis et al. 2007; Hagerman and Hagerman 2004; Hagerman et al. 2001, 2004, 2005; Jacquemont et al. 2003, 2004; Leehey et al. 2003). FXTAS has also been reported in carrier sisters who have preferential activation of the premutational X allele (Berry-Kravis *et al.* 2005). It appears that FXTAS does not convey the same increased risk of dementia in carrier women as it does in males, although it does present with tremor and ataxia (Hagerman *et al.* 2004).

Approximately one in 25 adult onset cerebellar ataxias in men is thought to result from a pre-mutational FMR1 expansion (Brussino *et al.* 2005).

There is also a possible link between pre-mutational expansion and risk of autism, with several cases and one systematic study having being reported (Farzin *et al.* 2006; Goodlin-Jones, Tassone, Gane and Hagerman 2004). This suggests that pre-mutational expansions may not be benign, but may convey risk in pre-mutational males.

Recent studies have shown that it is the inclusion of untranslated FMR1 messenger RNA that results in the inclusion bodies seen in the glial cells and neurons in the hippocampus and cerebral cortex of pre-mutational males (Chiurazzi, Tabolacci and Neri 2004; Welt, Smith and Taylor 2004).

Second, there is strong evidence of premature ovarian failure in approximately 20 per cent of female carriers of a pre-mutational expansion (typically classified as ceasing menstruation before age 40) (Bretherick, Fluker and Robinson 2005; Sherman 2000) – but not of other potentially associated difficulties (Hundscheid *et al.* 2003). A large international collaborative study of some 790 women from fragile-X families clearly established the link between female FMR1 carrier status and premature ovarian failure (Allingham-Hawkins *et al.* 1999).

There is a particular neuropsychological profile in some female carriers with problems of selective attention (Steyaert, Legius, Borghgraef and Fyrns 2003). There

is, in addition, a small effect of carrier status and of the size of pre-mutational expansion on verbal IQ in female carriers that explains some four per cent of the variance (Allen *et al.* 2005).

The main effect of the fragile-X expansion is to interfere with metabotropic glutamate receptor-coupled pathways (specifically of those involving mGluR5) (Bear 2005). This theory was first proposed in 2004 (Bear, Huber and Warren 2004) and has quickly established empirical support from both animal and human studies. An interesting recent finding is that mGluR5 receptors respond to glutamate preferentially, but also to cysteine, aspartate and asparagines (Frauli *et al.* 2006).

The introduction of mGluR5 antagonists such as 2-methyl-6 (phenylethynyl) pyridine (MPEP) can, *in vitro* at least, block many of the effects resulting from absence of FMRP (Aschrafi, Cunningham, Edelman and Vanderklish 2005). Studies are beginning to appear on clinical trials of glutamate-blocking agents such as fenobam (Hagerman *et al.* 2008).

Various brain areas, including the cerebellum and limbic system, have high numbers of glutamate receptors. Researchers have theorized that overactivity of glutamate could result in 'excitotoxicity', which could cause aberrant neuronal development (Bittigau and Ikonomidou 1997). In mice, FMR1 deletion affects the development of a wide range of neural structures with abnormal mGluR1-dependent long-term depression in the hippocampus and in cerebellum (Huber, Gallagher, Warren and Bear 2002). If the glutamergic system is hyperfunctional, it is likely that neuronal growth and connectivity would be damaged during critical periods of early development.

The potential role of glutamate in a number of conditions as disparate as post-traumatic stress disorder,

Alzheimer's disease, anxiety disorders and schizophrenia has been well recognized (Bergink, van Megen and Westenberg 2004; Javitt 2004).

The role of mGluR5 in learning and memory has been extensively studied (Simonyi, Schactman and Christoffersen 2005). From the animal research to date, there are two splice variants – mGluR5a and mGluR5b, with the b variant predominating in the adult brain, and mGluR5 mRNA being found predominantly in the hippocampus, amygdala, caudate-putamen and cortex.

There has been a steadily growing interest in metabotropic glutamate receptors as a potential target for pharmacotherapy (Nicoletti et al. 1996). A number of specific pre- and post-synaptic mGluR5 antagonists have now become available (Gasparini et al. 1999; O'Leary, Morsesyan, Vicini and Faden 2000; Schoepp, Jane and Monn 1999; and see Berry-Kravis and Potanos 2004 for a more broad-ranging review of pharmacotherapy in fragile-X).

There is some evidence of NMDA receptor abnormality in Fragile-X (O'Leary, Morsesyan, Vicini and Faden 2000). The NMDA receptor antagonist memantine has shown clinical benefit in around 2/3 of patients in an open-label trial (Erickson, Mullett and McDougle 2009).

From the variety of phenotypes associated with differences in FMR1, and the increasing evidence of benefits from therapeutic intervention, there is increasing interest in population screening (Hagerman and Hagerman 2008; Tassone et al. 2008).

Testing FMRP levels: Levels of fragile-X mental retardation protein (FMRP) have been shown to correlate inversely with level of ASD symptomology (Hatton et al. 2006; Loesch et al. 2007). Testing levels is not routine, but can be performed (Willemsen et al. 1997) and may be helpful in population screening and in profiling individuals for biological markers of severity (Tassone et al. 1999).

PCR: Results of PCR can vary, particularly in cellular mosaics (Orrico et al. 1998; Schmucker and Seidel 1999), sometimes giving false negative PCR results. This can usually be clarified by using other methods, such as Southern blot analysis. The recent development of a rapid PCR bloodspot test suitable for population screening may result in wider population screening for clinical use (Tassone et al. 2008).

Etablishing methylation status: The methylation status of the expansion may be important, and several methods are available that allow this to be established (Das et al. 1997–1998; Weinhausel and Haas 2001). There have been FMR1 cases reported with methylation mosaicism or with completely unmethylated full mutations that have been of normal intelligence (Hagerman, Hull et al. 1994; Rousseau, et al. 1994b; Smeets et al. 1995).

GENOTYPE–PHENOTYPE CORRELATIONS: Most research has been carried out on the triplet repeat forms of FMR1, as it is the most prevalent presentation. This does not necessarily match what is typical in other types of FMR1 condition, like deletion or point mutation cases.

Pre-mutational expansions: There is an extensive literature on the effects of fragile-X premutational expansion. (See Bourgeois et al. 2009.)

Pre-mutational expansions (59–200 CGG repeats): These can result in symptoms consistent with a full mutation (Hagerman, Wilson et al. 1994, 1996; Hagerman, and Hagerman 2002b; Riddle et al. 1998). Some 'transmitting' males who have pre-mutational expansions are of normal ability and are fertile. There is some evidence of neuropsychological difficulties in pre-mutational males with deficits in executive functions and working memory (Moore et *al.* 2004). Some studies have also shown there to be an association between pre-mutational expansions and autism (Farzin *et al.* 2006; Goodlin-Jones, Tassone, Gane and Hagerman 2004).

Transmitting males and carrier females are at risk of developing tremor-ataxia syndrome in later life. With maternal pre-mutational expansions to over 90 repeats, the majority of offspring are likely to be born with full mutations; with less than 70 repeats, fewer than six per cent of children will have full mutations (Nolin *et al.* 2003).

Full mutation (200 repeats or more): Individuals with a full FMR1 mutation are said to have fragile-X syndrome. Males typically have moderate to severe learning disability. Gaze avoidance, distractibility and hand-flapping are typical in childhood; both may improve with age. The physical features, although common, are not always found, and overlap considerably with a number of other conditions. Around 50 per cent of females with a full FMR1 expansion are similarly affected, but typically they are slightly more able than males. The extent of developmental problems in women appears to be inversely associated with the level of FMRP that they produce.

Mosaic presentations: FMR1 mosaics account for 15–20 per cent of cases. Mosaics can present with either a combination of pre-mutational and full mutational expansions, or with methylation mosaicism where only a proportion of the expansions are methylated (Hagerman, Wilson *et al.* 1994; Rousseau *et al.* 1994b; Smeets *et al.* 1995). As the effect of mosaicism on levels of FMRP is less than in the full mutation (Tassone *et al.* 1999), the phenotype is less severe, with higher cognitive functioning (Coffee *et al.* 2008; McConkie-Rosell *et al.* 1993). However, the more severe fragile-X phenotype has also been reported (MacKenzie, Sumargo and Taylor 2006).

De novo FMR1 expansion has never been reported. The most likely way in which a fragile-X mutation is inherited is from a mother with either a pre-mutational or a full expansion. Pre-mutational expansions will typically result in larger expansions in offspring who inherit the mutation. However, reduction in CGG repeats have been reported, both mother-to-daughter transmission (Vits *et al.* 1994) and mother-to-son (Tabolacci *et al.* 2008).

In very rare cases, both parents have FMR1 expansions (Linden *et al.* 1999; Mila *et al.* 1996; Russo *et al.* 1998).

Founder effects have been demonstrated in populations in the USA and Australia (Hirst *et al.* 1993; Richards R.I. *et al.* 1992), Finland (Haataja *et al.* 1994), and Israel (Dar *et al.* 1995). Different founder genotypes have been identified in different circumpolar clinical populations (Norwegian, Kola Saami and Siberian Nenet) (Larsen *et al.* 2001). The length of CGG repeats seen in fragile-X within given populations appears to correlate with the time that fragile-X has been found within that population, suggesting increasing expansion over historical time (Kunst *et al.* 1996). Some populations, such as Nova Scotia, appear not to have fragile-X expansions or mutations at the present time (Beresford *et al.* 2000).

IS THERE A LINK BETWEEN FRAGILE-X AND ASD? That the association of fragile-X with autism is at well above chance levels is now well accepted (Goodlin-Jones, Tassone, Gane and Hagerman 2004). The recent reporting of cases where autism has been found in children with pre-mutational expansions (Miller 2006) strengthens the idea of a common underlying pathophysiology to both the fragile-X-specific physical and behavioural phenotype and the behavioural phenotype of autism. This may lead on to a clearer understanding of sufficient neurobiological mechanisms in the pathogenesis and maintenance of autistic symptomology.

- The first papers to suggest an association between ASD and fragile-X were a brace of publications by Brown *et al.* (1982a, 1982b) describing four male cases of autism in association with an FMR1 expansion.

- Another paper published in the same year also suggested an association (Meryash, Szymanski and Gerald 1982).

- In 1983, Gillberg reported triplets who were moderately learning disabled, and who all showed physical characteristics consistent with fragile-X syndrome. The triplets were all diagnosed with infantile autism on Rutter's criteria. Each showed 8–12 per cent fragile-X positive cells. Their mother and singleton sister also had high numbers of fragile-X positive cells.

- In 1983 August suggested that fragile-X was a gene marker associated with autism, and the following year, August and Lockhart (1984) presented two brothers with autism, learning disability and fragile-X mutations, who had had twin brothers with autism and learning disability. The twins had died in a fire before any genetic assessment was carried out.

- In 1985 a Swedish multicentre study (Blomquist *et al.* 1985) studied 212 children with diagnoses of infantile autism. Fragile-X was found in 13 of 83 boys, but in none of the 129 girls tested.

- Demonstration of a fragile-X mutation in 18 out of a series of 144 male autistic cases provided strong evidence of an association between the two conditions, as distinct from cases where the two co-occur by chance (Fisch *et al.* 1986).

- In 1991, Ira Cohen and colleagues reviewed the literature, noting inconsistent findings to that time, but concluding overall that autism and fragile-X are associated and that a clearer understanding of X-chromosome abnormalities may be important in understanding the aetiology of autism.

- Kaufmann *et al.* (2004) at the Kennedy Krieger Institute in Baltimore examined the profiles of 56 boys with fragile-X on a battery of measures of cognition, autistic behaviour, behaviour problems, adaptive behaviours and language. This was an attempt to look for fragile-X-specific ASD profiles and found a strong association between impaired social interaction and ASD diagnosis. It clearly indicated that there is a subgroup of fragile-X individuals who fulfil criteria for ASD diagnosis.

- A further paper from the same group (Kau *et al.* 2004) compared and contrasted various groups, including fragile-X, with autism, developmental language delay with autism, and idiopathic autism (without either language delay or fragile-X). This study reported that there was a specific profile seen in those with fragile-X autism who were less impaired both on the Aschenbach Child Behavior Checklist withdrawn subscale and on the ADI-R assessment of reciprocal social interaction, but scored more highly on measures of behavioural stereotypy and communication difficulty.

- Hatton *et al.* (2006), from the University of North Carolina at Chapel Hill, documented autistic behaviour in a large sample of children with fragile-X syndrome. Twenty-seven out of 129 cases (21 per cent) were above the clinical cutoff for diagnosis on the CARS. They also reported on a longitudinal subset of 116 children. CARS scores increased over time, and there was an inverse correlation between levels of fragile-X mental retardation protein (FMRP) and severity of autistic behaviour. This was also a finding in earlier research (Tassone *et al.* 1999).

- An Australian–US collaborative study (Loesch *et al.* 2007) found that both in full mutation (N=147) and in pre-mutational cases (N=59) scores on the ADOS-G were significantly elevated compared with non-fragile-X relatives (N=59). Full-scale IQ and executive functioning skills were the major predictors of ASD diagnosis, with social interaction and communication difficulties correlating strongly and inversely with levels of fragile-X mental retardation protein (FMRP) but contributing to a lesser extent to ASD diagnosis.

- A recent longitudinal follow-up of 56 fragile-X cases from the Kennedy Krieger group (Hernandez *et al.* 2009) established that the fragile-X with autism group is a remarkably stable and distinctive subphenotype of fragile-X.

- A German group (Klauck *et al.* 1997) presented data on 141 autistic patients from 105 simplex and 18 multiplex families. Blood samples were collected from all cases and tested for FMR1 expansion. Only in two males, both from the same multiplex family, was there an FMR-1 expansion. Both had a mosaic expansion with a partly functional gene. One met ASD criteria; the other had a mild learning disability. The authors concluded that there was no association between FMR1 and ASD. In the context of the other research reviewed above, this suggests that there may, in addition to the ethnic differences in prevalence noted above, be marked differences in geographic/population prevalence.

DIFFERENTIAL DIAGNOSIS: As the physical phenotype only becomes obvious postpubertally, and prepubertal physical and cognitive features are variable, a range of alternative diagnoses need to be explored in someone presenting with a fragile-X phenotype. Testing for FMR1 is now a routine part of screening in many centres, so alternative possible diagnosis are most likely to be relevant where the person has screened as FMR1 negative.

Developmental delay and/or mental retardation is seen in most cases, but, since only one in 20 learning disabled cases will have an FMR1 expansion, other causes should be investigated (Curry *et al.* 1997; Shevell *et al.* 2003).

A number of other overgrowth conditions should be considered, such as Bannayan-Riley-Ruvalcaba syndrome (BRRS) [15]; basal cell naevus syndrome [16]; Cortical Dysplasia–Focal Epilepsy (CDFE) syndrome [19]; Cole-Hughes macrocephaly syndrome (macrocephaly/autism syndrome) [24]; Cowden syndrome [26]; fragile-XE syndrome (Hamel *et al.* 1994; Mulley *et al.* 1995); Orstavik 1997 syndrome [56]; Prader-Willi syndrome [61]; Proteus syndrome [62]; and Sotos syndrome [68].

There is some evidence for a phenotype similar to that of Prader-Willi syndrome (de Vries *et al.* 1993, 1995; Schrander-Stumpel *et al.* 1994).

Fragile-X expansion can co-occur with Down syndrome (Arinami *et al.* 1987; Collacott *et al.* 1990) and a case has been reported with fragile-X, Down syndrome and autism diagnosed in the same individual (see further discussion on p.190 above).

MANAGEMENT AND TREATMENT: A range of ameliorative strategies is available to address patterns of presentation as appropriate to the specific individual.

Seizures, cardiac problems and ophthalmic and cosmetic issues should be treated as in other cases (Hagerman 1997, 1999; Hagerman and Cronister 1996).

Until very recently, there were no treatment approaches that were thought to substantively improve function in fragile-X syndrome. Based on the exciting findings in animal models discussed below, several approaches are being actively pursued, and promising intervention studies have recently appeared.

A number of treatment approaches are being actively explored in attempts to correct the biological differences found. Simple summaries of this work can be found in Berry-Kravis (2008), Hagerman et al. (2009), Reiss and Hall (2007) and Rueda, Ballesteros and Tejade (2009).

Folic acid: Folic acid has been shown to be of some benefit (see, for example, Hagerman et al. 1986). However, not all studies have yielded positive results (Rosenblatt et al. 1985) and it is thought that it might exacerbate seizure activity in some cases. Folic acid deficiency is implicated in a range of conditions including epilepsy, vascular disease and neurodevelopmental defects (Moore 2005).

Certain antibiotics containing trimethoprim, or other antagonists to folate production, have been suggested as potentially hazardous to children with fragile-X (Lejeune et al. 1982), and it has been suggested that they should be avoided during pregnancies where there is a risk of fragile-X (Hecht and Glover 1983).

MGluR5 antagonists: The biology of glutamatergic differences in fragile-X syndrome is now becoming well understood (Dölen and Bear 2008). The results of treatment studies in animal models are highly encouraging.

Lithium has been shown to reverse the memory problems seen in fragile-X

drosophila (McBride et al. 2005). Audiogenic seizures are seen in fragile-X mice (Chen and Toth 2001), and there are reports that these are also reduced in response to lithium (Berry-Kravis 2008; Berry-Kravis et al. 2008).

Various medications that block the mGluR5 pathway have been undergoing evaluation, including fenobam (Hagerman et al. 2008) and MPEP.

Human trials of an mGluR5 antagonist (STX107) are underway in the USA at the time of writing. (See www.seasidetherapeutics.com.)

Ampakine and mifepristone: Two other treatment approaches are being evaluated at present. *Ampakine* (CX516), an AMPA receptor activator, is being evaluated, based on findings in knockout mice in which memory is impaired and cortical AMPA receptors are reduced in number. Preliminary results of a randomized placebo-controlled trial (N=49) suggest that, while well tolerated for the most part, there were no effects on memory, language, executive functions or behaviour overall. Benefits were observed, however, only in those subjects who were already receiving antipsychotic medication, and it is possible that the dosage of ampakine used was sub-therapeutic.

Mifepristone, which is being researched by Dr Alan Reiss's group at Stanford University, blocks the effects of cortisol. In one preliminary study, cortisol has been shown to be elevated at rest in children with fragile-X, and to increase in response to social stress (Wisbeck et al. 2000). No results of this work are available at the current time.

GABA agonists: Drugs that increase GABA (gamma-aminobutyric acid) pathway activity are known to reduce glutamatergic receptor activity by competition. On this basis, a number of GABA agonists are being investigated for their potential use in the treatment of fragile-X. In particular, baclofen, which is known to reduce aggressive and self-injurious behaviour, and ganaloxone (Kerrigan *et al.* 2000), which is showing some success in seizure control, are being investigated.

P21 activated kinase (PAK) inhibitors: PAK is involved in the activation of protein synthesis by mGluRs. There has been promising animal research (Hayashi *et al.* 2007), and some of the medications in development for the treatment of neurofibromatosis type 1 [51] are PAK inhibitors which could also prove beneficial in the treatment of fragile-X.

Ampakines: AMPA receptor activity is reduced with FMRP deficiency (Nakamoto *et al.* 2007); AMPA increases the activation of brain derived neurotrophic factor (BDNF), and BDNF activity is reduced in fragile-X. This suggests that increased AMPA activation could be beneficial. One medication, piracetam, which upregulates AMPA activity, has been shown to have positive effects in autism in combination with risperidone (Akhondzadeh *et al.* 2008). The ampakine 'CX515' has been the subject of a randomized, double-blind, placebo-controlled trial in adults with fragile-X, and was well tolerated. However, effects on cognition and behaviour were minimal except when used in conjunction with risperidone (Reiss and Hall 2007).

Minocyclidine: Minocyclidine is a medication that has been used in the treatment of acne. Its mode of action is reduction of one of the proteins regulated by FMRP. A recently approved NIH-funded study will provide evidence on possible efficacy (July 2008, NIH Trial Number: NCT00409747, web ref: www.clinicaltrials.gov/ct).

ANIMAL MODELS:

- In an early study, Kooy *et al.* (1999) showed that there were no appreciable volumetric changes in the fragile-X mouse brain that paralleled those reported in human studies. Despite a lack of structural similarities, Qin, Kang and Smith (2002) found that there was widespread hypermetabolism, compared to controls.

- Zhang *et al.* (2001) showed that, in a drosophila FMR1 model, peripheral synapses were significantly altered, with structural defects and defective neurotransmission. The same group (Pan, Zhang, Woodruff and Broadie 2004) have shown in their drosophila model that in the central brain the fragile-X model results in abnormal development of structures involved in learning and memory. Zhang and Broadie (2005) detail several of the mechanisms they have identified concerning regulation of RNA, development of the microtubule cytoskeleton, and complexity of brain architecture.

- Morales *et al.* (2002) have developed a drosophila model of fragile-X, in which they have shown that the drosophila analogue to FMR1 is critical to neurite extension, branching and guidance, suggesting that there is a likely role in the drosophila equivalent to that played by neural cell adhesion molecules in human axonal guidance.

- Gruss and Braun (2001) were the first to show that there are regionally specific alterations in neural amino acid metabolism which parallel lack of FMRP in the FMR1 knockout juvenile mouse.

- Entezam *et al.* (2007) have demonstrated that a knock-in mouse FMR1 model is capable of showing similarly rapid repeat expansion, an inverse relationship between repeat expansion and FMRP levels, and reduction in purkinje cell density. Entezam and Usdin (2008) have shown that in their mouse model there is an interaction between expansion and mutations in ATR (ataxia telangiectasia and rad3-related kinase). This is critical in their model to the rapid expansion in ATR seen with maternal inheritance that also characterizes human fragile-X (Entezam and Usdin 2008).

There is currently much interest in the development of pharmacological treatments targeted at addressing both the abnormal dendritic formation seen at postmortem in the fragile-X brain (Koekkoek et al. 2005) and also in the knockout mouse model of human FMR1 (Greenough et al. 2001). There is exaggerated long-term depression of responses caused by the absence of feedback inhibition of mGluR5-induced dendritic translation by FMRP. Long-term depression eliminates AMPA (alpha-amino-3-hydroxy-5-methyl-4-isoxazole propionic acid) receptors from the synapse (Malinow and Malenka 2002). The interactions in this system are complex, involving a range of other factors including DARPP-32 phosphorylation that is regulated by glutamate (Nishi et al. 2003, 2005).

There appear to be multiple roles for FMRP. For example, FMRP granules are expressed in response to oxidative stress and there is variability of co-localization of FMRP and T-cell internal antigen (TIA-1). TIA-1 is a stress granule marker protein (Dolzhanskay, Merz and Denman 2006).

In the drosophila *dfmr1* knockout model (Gao 2002), many behavioural abnormalities that result from the gene knockout mirror those seen in human fragile-X patients. Of potential importance is that many of these differences can be corrected through the use of glutamate antagonists (Dölen and Bear 2005; McBride et al. 2005).

Several studies are showing reversal of fragile-X characteristics in FMR1 knockout mouse models. In one study (Hayashi et al. 2007) it was demonstrated that inhibition of PAK (p21-activated kinase) can ameliorate many of the synaptic and behavioural differences seen in fragile-X knockout mice. A further study, by Dölen et al. (2007), engineered an mGluR5 deficient mouse (lacking one of the key cell membrane glutamate receptors), demonstrating a clear link between deficient glutamate pathway function and the resultant behavioural phenotype.

Certain antagonists such as MPEP (2-methyl-6-(phenylethynyl)-pyridine) are showing particular promise in reversing the fragile-X physical and behavioural phenotype in animal knockout models, and may hold promise in human treatment (Yan, Rammal, Tranfaglia and Bauchwirtz 2005). MPEP is a potent mGluR5 receptor antagonist that has been used to selectively block this glutamate pathway in animal models (Gasparini et al. 1999; Yan, Rammal, Tranfaglia and Bauchwirtz 2005). MPEP can correct memory problems in the fragile-X drosophila (Bolduc et al. 2008).

Currently, there are significant advances being made in identification of biochemical factors that can normalize glutamatergic function in drosophila fragile-X phenotypes (Chang et al. 2008).

GSK-3 (glycogen synthase kinase-3) is another enzyme involved in activation of protein synthesis by mGluRs that has been shown to be critically involved in murine fragile-X models (Min et al. 2008). Research has shown that the GSK-3 specific inhibitors SB-216763 (Bain et al. 2007; Coghlan et al. 2000) and AR-A014418 (Bain et al. 2007; Bhat et al. 2003) can normalize the mutant fragile-x phenotype.

36.

Fragile-X permutation (partial methylation defects)

GENE LOCUS: Xq27.3

KEY ASD REFERENCES: Nolin *et al.* 1994; Reddy 2005

Premutation defects have been covered to some extent under fragile-X syndrome [35] above.

SUMMARY: Premutations are partial methylation defects due to mosaicism, resulting in a partial form of the normal, full fragile-X expansion condition.

MAIN CLINICAL FEATURES: The effects on function are largely as for [35], the more typical fragile-X presentation. See clinical description under section 35 above.

HOW COMMON IS FRAGILE-X PREMUTA-TION? The overall literature on fragile-X premutation suggests that some 15–20 per cent of cases show some degree of mosaicism (Petek *et al.* 1999; Pieretti *et al.* 1991; Rousseau *et al.* 1991, 1994a; van den Ouweland *et al.* 1994).

IS THERE A LINK BETWEEN FRAGILE-X PREMUTATION AND ASD? Fragile-X pre-mutation appears to be more common in ASD than might be expected, with Reddy (2005) reporting 43 per cent of the fragile-X ASD males in her study to be mosaics, and Nolin *et al.* (1994) reporting a rate of 41 per cent in affected males.

As no studies of the tissue distribution of mosaicism have yet been undertaken, the significance of this finding is currently uncertain, and it could reflect differences in technique or sampling.

Matching premutation against levels of FMRP activity may provide some insight into the apparent level of association and how this may be linked to central nervous system factors.

DIFFERENTIAL DIAGNOSIS: As for fragile-X syndrome.

MANAGEMENT AND TREATMENT: Largely as for fragile-X [35].

ANIMAL MODELS: As for fragile-X [35].

37.

GAMT deficiency (guanidinoacetate methyltransferase deficiency)

GENE LOCUS: 19p13.3

KEY ASD REFERENCES: Mercimek-Mahmutoglu *et al.* 2006; Sykut-Cegielska, Gradowska, Mercimek-Mahmutoglu and Stöckler-Ipsiroglu 2004; see also Lion-François *et al.* 2006

SUMMARY: GAMT deficiency is a recently described autosomal recessive condition. It is an inborn error of creatine metabolism that interferes with the body's ability to produce guanidinoacetate, the metabolic precursor of creatine. Creatine is a compound derived from animal protein in the diet and also through metabolic processes in the body (see Figure B37 below). It is likely, therefore, that the condition would have a more pronounced effect on those adhering to a vegan or vegetarian diet who do not have alternative dietary sources of creatine. There are a number of inborn errors of creatine metabolism which have been systematically reviewed (Nasrallah,

Feki and Kaabachi 2010; Stromberger, Bodamer and Stöckler-Ipsiroglu 2003).

Most of the small numbers of cases described to date are Portuguese or of Portuguese origin (Almeida *et al.* 2007), suggesting a possible founder effect. However, a number of Turkish cases have also been reported. Systematic screening of other populations does not yet appear to have been carried out. A recent US series of eight GAMT cases is from a wide variety of ethnic backgrounds (Dhar *et al.* 2009).

The first paper to describe the condition was published by Stöckler *et al.* (1994).

The GAMT gene was mapped to chromosome 19p13.3 by somatic cell hybridization and radiation hybrid analysis in 1998 (Chae *et al.* 1998). It is one of three genetic factors which have an effect on creatine metabolism, the other

two being defects in the X-linked creatine transporter gene SLC6A8 (Salomons *et al.* 2001; DeGraw *et al.* 2003) and AGAT (arginine: glycine amidinotransferase deficiency) (Item *et al.* 2001).

Defects in creatine metabolism are a newly recognized group of inborn errors of metabolism. The key clinical features are mental retardation, communication difficulties and epilepsy, which are present in all of the defects of creatine metabolism (GAMT, AGAT and CT1 defects) so far described. Autistic behaviour and hyperactivity are commonly reported in more mildly affected GAMT cases. They may be present in AGAT and CT1 cases. However, this has yet to be investigated. As these other conditions appear equally responsive to treatment intervention (for AGAT, see Battini *et al.* 2006; for CT1

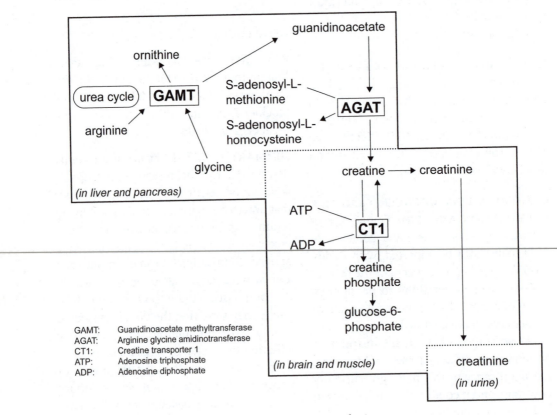

GAMT: Guanidinoacetate methyltransferase
AGAT: Arginine glycine amidinotransferase
CT1:   Creatine transporter 1
ATP: Adenosine triphosphate
ADP: Adenosine diphosphate

Figure B37: The metabolic pathway for creatine and creatinine production

see Chilosi *et al.* 2008), it is possible that a significant subgroup of ASD cases may have treatment-responsive abnormalities of creative metabolism.

Metabolic screening for creatinine transporter abnormalities can result in high numbers of false positive results depending on diet. In one screening study 29/33 cases from a screened population of 1600 proved to be dietary false positives with only four true deficiency cases identified (Ariani *et al.* 2008).

HOW COMMON IS GAMT DEFICIENCY?

At present, there is no epidemiological data on the prevalence or incidence of GAMT. Given the positive response to treatment and the potential benefits from antenatal identification, neonatal screening and early intervention, it is important that this is established. Cerebral creatine deficiency syndromes overall appear to be fairly common in males with unexplained learning difficulties. In a survey of 188 children (114 boys, 74 girls) referred to a paediatric neurology department for investigation of unexplained learning problems with a normal karyotype and no fragile-X expansion (Lion-François *et al.* 2006), GAMT deficiency was established in one and a creatine transporter defect in four. All of those affected were boys. The boy with GAMT deficiency and two of those with transporter defects were reported as showing autistic behaviour. All were reported to have language impairments. The boy with GAMT deficiency and one of those with a transporter defect had seizure problems.

As I have previously discussed (Aitken 2008), urinary creatinine levels are lower in the ASD population (Whiteley *et al.* 2006), and this correlates with reduced creatine levels (Sykut-Cegielska, Gradowska, Mercimek-Mahmutoglu and

Stöckler-Ipsiroglu 2004). It therefore seems probable that GAMT/AGAT/CT1 abnormalities may account for a significant subgroup of those with ASD.

MAIN CLINICAL FEATURES: The disease usually presents with concerns over delayed development in the first months after birth. Various neurological symptoms may be reported, including muscle weakness, poor head control, movement problems and seizures. Seizures, hyperactive and autistic behaviour and self-injury have all been reported in a significant proportion of the older cases that have been described in the literature. Learning difficulties, seizures and speech delay characterize the presentation of all of the genetic disorders of creatine metabolism.

As might be expected, given that more extreme cases are typically the first to be characterized, the earlier cases reported fall into the 'severe' category (Sykut-Cegielska, Gradowska, Mercimek-Mahmutoglu and Stöckler-Ipsiroglu 2004). Stöckler *et al.* (1994), for example, reported a 22-month-old boy with hypotonia and a progressive extrapyramidal movement problem. He showed extremely low urinary excretion of creatinine, and low creatine and creatine phosphate, with accumulation of guanidinoacetate in the central nervous system detected by magnetic resonance spectroscopy (MRS). Stöckler, Hanefeld and Frahm (1996) described their original case and a further four-year-old female patient with severe learning difficulties, hypotonia, ataxia, uncontrolled epilepsy and a similar biochemical profile.

Schulze *et al.* (1997) described a Kurdish girl who presented at two years six months and was clearly regressing at age three. She had had *grand mal* seizures from 14 months. She was the child of a consanguineous marriage. MRS established creatine depletion and guanidinoacetate build-up in the central nervous system. Urinary creatinine was reduced, but there was no clinical response to creatine supplementation.

Cases have been reported of central nervous system-specific creatine deficiency with associated mental retardation and language delay, with normalization on creatine monohydrate supplementation, and concomitant developmental improvement (Bianchi *et al.* 2000).

IS THERE A LINK BETWEEN GAMT DEFICIENCY AND ASD? Two recent papers are of particular note concerning a GAMT link with ASD.

Sykut-Cegielska, Gradowska, Mercimek-Mahmutoglu and Stöckler-Ipsiroglu (2004), based on a systematic review of creatine deficiency syndromes, suggest that there are three 'types' of GAMT phenotypic presentation graded by severity:

1. Severe

- intractable epilepsy
- early global developmental delay
- extrapyramidal movement disorder
- abnormalities of the basal ganglia.

2. Intermediate

- moderate/severe learning disability
- speech delay
- autistic and hyperkinetic behaviour
- epilepsy.

3. Mild

- learning disability
- autistic behaviour
- speech delay.

The second paper, by Mercimek-Mahmutoglu *et al.* (2006), looked at a large international series of individuals, all of whom had a GAMT defect. Twenty-one of the 27 patients (78 per cent) reported on were 'hyperactive, autistic and self-injurious'.

Two cases where autistic behaviour has been noted in association with a creatine transporter defect have also been recorded by Lion-François *et al.* (2006).

DIFFERENTIAL DIAGNOSIS: As diagnosis is typically based on biochemical features coupled with the behaviours that are seen in all of the creatine disorders, differentiation is based on biochemistry coupled with brain MRS. At the present time, no reports on the behavioural phenotype associated with either AGAT or CT1 abnormalities have been published, and a possible link to ASD based on a common pathophysiology cannot be excluded.

A screening study of 180 residential patients with severe learning disabilities identified four with GAMT deficiency, of whom three were related, and all of whom had absent or limited language development (Caldeira Araujo *et al.* 2005).

From the screening study by Lion-François *et al.* (2006) detailed above, it may be that CT1 abnormalities are more common and possibly also linked to ASD.

MANAGEMENT AND TREATMENT: From the clinical reports to date, GAMT deficiency can respond successfully to creatine supplementation (Ganesan *et al.* 1997; Schulze *et al.* 1997; Stöckler *et al.* 1996). It has also been shown that creatine supplementation can have more general effects, not least the ability to improve performance in endurance sports (Engelhardt, Neumann, Berbalk and Reuter 1998). In a double-blind, placebo-controlled, crossover trial it has been shown that oral creatine monohydrate supplementation can significantly improve the memory (backward digit span) and cognitive performance (on Ravens advanced progressive matrices) of vegan and vegetarian subjects aged 18–40 (Rae, Digney, McEwan and Bates 2003).

In an early study, Stöckler et al. (1994) were able to show that oral supplementation with creatine monohydrate and arginine, but not arginine alone, improved cerebral creatine and normalized urinary and serum creatinine, as well as improving neurological symptoms and motor development, in a 22-month-old boy.

A separate factor which appears to link to the often intractable seizures seen in GAMT is the accumulation of central nervous system guanidinoacetate. This appears to be the result of a creatine-dependent negative-feedback mechanism, and to respond to the combination of arginine restriction and ornithine supplementation with improved seizure control and developmental outcome (Schulze, Ebinger, Rating and Mayatepek 2001; Schulze, Mayatepek and Rating 2000).

The combined use of creatine monohydrate, arginine restriction and ornithine supplementation, when used from an early stage, appears able to reverse the neurochemical, structural, epileptic and behavioural abnormalities seen in the GAMT and AGAT creatine deficiency syndromes (Schulze 2003). To date, there has been no successful treatment strategy that has ameliorated the creatine deficiency cases that are caused by creatine transporter abnormalities (Stöckler, Schutz and Salomons 2007).

With population screening, pre-symptomatic identification and treatment is likely to provide the best clinical outcome (Schulze and Battini 2007).

ANIMAL MODELS: The region of mouse DNA corresponding to the GMT locus in humans is on chromosome 10 (Chae et al. 1998).

Schmidt et al. (2004) produced a knockout mouse model for GAMT deficiency with equivalent patterns of reduced creatine and creatinine in brain, serum and urine. The brain and skeletal muscle were both affected, with lifelong reduction in body fat mass, muscle hypotonia, reduced lifespan and a reduction in male fertility.

A recent GAMT knockout mouse study (Schneider et al. 2008) has demonstrated, consistent with the findings to date in humans (see discussion in Sykut-Cegielska, Gradowska, Mercimek-Mahmutoglu and Stöckler-Ipsiroglu 2004), no differences in cardiac structure or function in males or females with age, despite the prediction that the lower levels of available creatine would progressively affect the heart.

In the rat, Braissant et al. (2005) have studied in detail the expression of the GAMT, AGAT and creatine transporter gene CT1 throughout the body. Their work suggests that the effects on development are well established from the early stages of in utero development, particularly in the central nervous system.

A summary of GAMT deficiency by Sylvia Stöckler-Ipsiroglu can be found at www.orpha.net.

A further recent review (in Spanish) can be found in Arias-Dimas et al. (2006).

38.

Goldenhar syndrome

aka • Goldenhar-Gorlin syndrome
• Franceschetti-Goldenhar syndrome
• hemifacial microsomia (HFM)

- oculoauriculovertebral dysplasia (OAV dysplasia)
- facioauriculovertebral sequence (FAV sequence)
- oculoauriculovertebral spectrum (OAVS)

GENE LOCUS: 14q32

KEY ASD REFERENCES: Johansson *et al.* 2007; Landgren, Gillberg and Stromland 1992; Miller *et al.* 2004, 2005; Stromland *et al.* 2007

SUMMARY: Goldenhar syndrome is named after the Belgian-American ophthalmologist and general practitioner, Maurice Goldenhar, who published a review of cases in 1952. The first clinical description consistent with the condition was in a work on eye conditions by the German physician, Carl Ferdinand von Arlt, in 1881.

HOW COMMON IS GOLDENHAR SYNDROME? Goldenhar syndrome is thought to affect approximately one in 20,000 live births (Araneta *et al.* 2002). Lower rates have been reported – one Northern Irish study estimated a minimum prevalence of one in 45,000 (Morrison, Mulholland, Craig and Nevin 1992). There are reports of higher prevalence. Gorlin (1990) reported a general population rate of one in 5,800. A study of the offspring of US Gulf War veterans (Araneta *et al.* 2002) reported a rate of one in 6,800.

Rollnick *et al.* (1987) found male cases to be almost twice as common as female cases (191 to 103).

MAIN CLINICAL FEATURES:
Physical features:
- unilateral or bilateral underdevelopment of the lower jaw (mandible)
- unilateral or bilateral microtia (reduced size/absence of the outer ear)
- unilateral or bilateral reduction in size and flattening of the maxilla (upper jaw)
- narrowing of the opening of the eye
- coloboma of the upper eyelid
- epibulbar dermoids – small benign tumours that typically form over the lateral aspect of one eye and can impair vision.

Goldenhar syndrome is typically described as being characterized by the triad of *hemifacial microsomia* (a common birth defect involving the first and second branchial arch derivatives), *epibulbar dermoid cysts* and *abnormal development of the vertebrae and ribs*. Ocular anomalies are seen in over half of all cases, lipodermoid being the most common. Lipodermoids are usually localized in the inferotemporal epibulbar area and can often be missed. Abnormal ear development is found in over 70 per cent of cases. Various abnormalities of the vertebrae and ribs are found; anomalies include absent vertebrae, hemivertebrae, fused ribs, kyphosis and scoliosis. Cleft lip and palate are reported in approximately two per cent of cases.

The main classifications in use for hemifacial microsomia are the OMENS (Vento, LaBrie and Mulliken 1991) and subsequently OMENS Plus (Horgan, Padwa, LaBrie and Mulliken 1995) systems. The acronym stands for **O**rbital asymmetry; **M**andibular hypoplasia; **E**ar deformity; **N**erve involvement; and **S**oft tissue deficiency. The system seems both simple and clinically useful (Poon, Meara and Heggie 2003).

There are reports of abnormal caruncles at the medial angle of the eye. Nijhawan, Morad, Seigel-Bartelt and Levin (2002) reported seven such cases.

Tracheoesophageal fistulas have been reported in five per cent of cases in one clinical series (Sutphen *et al.* 1995).

A recent review of a series of 87 cases has identified cardiac abnormalities in 28 (32 per cent) (Digilio *et al.* 2008), with conotruncal, atrial and ventriculoseptal defects accounting for the greatest proportion (71 per cent of cardiac anomalies).

Frank neurological defects are seen, typically in association with more severe physical features such as anopthalmia or cleft lip and palate (Schrander-Stumpel *et al.* 1992).

Rollnick and Kaye (1983) found that, in the 433 first-degree relatives of 97 Goldenhar cases, eight per cent had the same or a similar anomaly, while six per cent of 176 siblings were similarly affected.

Possible anticipation has been reported in one affected mother with two affected pregnancies (Stoll, Viville, Tressier and Gasser 1998).

CAUSAL MECHANISMS: A recent study (Wieczorek *et al.* 2007) found an excess of monozygotic twins in a cohort of normally conceived individuals with Goldenhar syndrome, and an excess of Goldenhar cases in a series of assisted conceptions. The study was conducted by comparing a sample of 72 Goldenhar cases and a series of 3,372 assisted conceptions (by intracytoplasmic sperm injection) to normal population data. The excess of twin cases may go some way in explaining the research reports of higher rates of twinning in autism in some series (Betancur, Leboyer and Gillberg 2002; Ho, Todd and Constantino 2005).

Over 20 discordant identical twins, where one has hemifacial microsomia and one does not, have now been reported (Balci, Engiz, Yilmaz and Baltaci 2006; Boles, Bodurtha and Nance 1987; Burck 1983; Connor and Fernandez 1984;

Ebbesen and Petersen 1982; Setzer *et al.* 1981; Wieczorek *et al.* 2007). Three separate cases in sets of triplets where only one was affected (Jongbloet 1987; Roesch *et al.* 2001; Yovich *et al.* 1985) have now also been reported.

Most cases of Goldenhar syndrome arise sporadically. However, some familial cases have been reported that show autosomal dominant inheritance.

There are anecdotal reports of links to exposure to toxins such as dioxin, ingestion of some known teratogenic agents (cocaine, thalidomide, retinoic acid, tamoxifen), various environmental exposures (insecticides, herbicides) and effects of maternal diabetes.

Wang, Martinez-Frias and Graham (2002) reported on a series of 30 Spanish cases and found a significantly increased risk of Goldenhar syndrome associated with maternal diabetes, suggesting that this can interfere with neural crest migration. Maternal diabetes has not been found to be a risk factor for the development of autism (Hultman, Sparen and Cnattingius 2002).

PRENATAL DIAGNOSIS: One paper reviewed ultrasound analyses of 21 foetal cases with multiple congenital anomalies scanned between 14 and 35 weeks post-conception (Castori *et al.* 2006). A wide range of physical anomalies was evident and demonstrable in around half of all cases.

IS THERE A LINK BETWEEN GOLDENHAR SYNDROME AND ASD? The initial report on co-ocurrence of Goldenhar syndrome and autism was a report on two girls (Landgren, Gillberg and Stromland 1992). In the first of these cases, Goldenhar syndrome was diagnosed in the early weeks of life and autism was diagnosed at age five years. In the second case, both diagnoses were made at age seven, when the child was referred for ASD assessment.

Between 1998 and 2007 a series of 20 cases of Goldenhar syndrome was studied and reported in three papers (Johansson *et al.* 2007; Miller *et al.* 2004, 2005).

Johansson's group reported various multisystem malformations and functional problems. Three individuals were diagnosed with an ASD. All three had associated gastrointestinal problems. Johansson *et al.* (2007) presented data on the ADI-R assessments of this group and also evidence from structural neuroimaging (Johansson *et al.* 2007).

A more recent review of 18 patients produced by the same group (Stromland *et al.* 2007) also reported high rates of functional impairment, but provided less detail on milder ASD symptomology (see Table B38.2):

High rates of hyperactivity are also reported in this population.

There are few reports of other mental health problems associated with Goldenhar syndrome, apart from one case reported as 'schizophreniform disorder' in a 27-year-old male (Brieger, Bartel-Friedrich, Haring and Marneros 1998).

Research into Goldenhar syndrome, along with Mobius syndrome [48] and thalidomide embryopathy, has helped to produce a model according to which it is thought that the ASD behavioural phenotype can arise if neural development is disrupted within a critical 'temporal window' in embryogenesis. This suggests that, for one group of ASD disorders at least, genetic and/or environmental factors can result in ASD, provided they act on neural development at certain crucial times in embryogenesis. (See Aitken 1991, Miller *et al.* 2005 and Rodier *et al.* 1996 for further discussion.) More detailed knowledge of the associated timing in

Goldenhar cases may help to specify this association, as the patterns of microtia and associated abnormalities appear to cluster into distinct groupings, and this may indicate a time at which development is affected. (For discussion, see Kaye *et al.* 1989; Miller *et al.* 2005.)

DIFFERENTIAL DIAGNOSIS: In classical Goldenhar cases where there is hemi-microsomia, differential diagnosis is not usually problematic. Where there is a bilateral growth defect, the issue is more complex. Unilateral cases are roughly twice as common as bilateral ones (193 to 98 in the series reported by Rollnick *et al.* 1987).

Several factors point to a link between Goldenhar and CHARGE syndrome [20]. An early paper (Van Meter and Weaver 1996) described two infants (a male and a female) with significant symptoms found in both conditions. More recently, Kallen *et al.* (2004) studied the relationships between different malformations, identifying individuals with Goldenhar, CHARGE, VATER (vertebral anomalies/ dysgenesis, vascular anomalies; anal atresia; tracheoesophageal fistula; esophageal atresia; and renal anomalies) and OEIS (omphalocele; exstrophy; imperforate anus; and spinal defects) from data held on 5,260 infants on four large congenital malformation registers. Goldenhar symptomology thus seems to overlap with other conditions with known gene loci at 8q12.1 and 7q21.1. An overlap between the clinical features of Goldenhar syndrome, VATER and sirenomelia has also been noted (Duncan and Shapiro 1993).

There has also been a case report of a male infant who presents with the clinical features of both the Goldenhar and *cri du chat* syndromes (Choong, Watts, Little and Beck 2003). This suggests that the genetic bases to the two conditions in this case may be contiguous, and a possible gene locus for Goldenhar syndrome near to the 5p14 locus for *cri du chat* syndrome identified in this case. The genetics of *cri du chat* are not fully clarified at the time of writing; the 5p region produces a variety of clinical presentations of *cri du chat* (Mainardi 2006).

A case with a Goldenhar-like phenotype has been reported in a boy with a 22q11 deletion and a conotruncal heart defect (Derbent *et al.* 2003). 22q11 deletions are strongly associated with ASD.

In series of eight cases with a Goldenhar phenotype and anal anomalies consistent with Townes-Brocks syndrome, one proved

Table B38.1: Common problems in Goldenhar syndrome

Problem	No. (%)
Systemic/ocular malformations	
• microsomia	15/20 (75)
• ear tags	14/20 (70)
• ocular dermoids	13/20 (65)
• lipodermoid	13/20 (65)
• gastrointestinal	11/20 (55)
• epibulbar dermoids	10/20 (50)
• microtia	10/20 (50)
• vertebral anomaly	10/20 (50)
• genitourinary	7/20 (35)
• cardiovascular	6/20 (30)
• fistula	4/20 (20)
Cranial nerve involvement	
• facial nerve palsy	8/20 (40)
• neurosensory deafness	3/20 (15)
Functional problems	
• hearing	14/20 (70)
• all-developmental delay	7/20 (35)
• severe developmental delay	4/19 (21)
All ASD	11/20 (55)
• autistic traits	5/20 (25)
• possible autistic spectrum disorder	3/20 (15)
• autistic disorder	2/20 (10)
• autistic-like condition	1/20 (5)

(Table based on Johansson *et al.* 2007; Miller *et al.* 2004, 2005.)

to have a nonsense mutation of the SALL1 gene at 16q12.1 (Keegan, Mulliken, Wu and Korf 2001).

Most reported cases are sporadic, and routine genetic analysis has been unrewarding. Autosomal dominant transmission has been shown in three families with multiple affected members and male-to-male transmission (Godel, Regenbogen, Goya and Goodman 1982; Regenbogen, Godel, Goya and Goodman 1982; Summitt 1969).

A study by Kaye et al. (1992) looked at physical malformations in the families of 74 individuals with Goldenhar. Their analysis demonstrated patterns consistent with an autosomal dominant pattern of inheritance.

The genotype is currently speculative. Linkage to a site at 14q32 has been reported based on one family pedigree (Kelberman et al. 2001), but could not be found either in a further family pedigree, or from analysis of a large series of 120 sporadic cases.

A separate site on chromosome 14 (14q11.2–q12) has been found to be associated with an autosomal dominant ear defect (accessory auricular anomaly) (Yang et al. 2006a).

A number of cases are described where Goldenhar syndrome is associated with chromosome 22 defects – terminal 22q deletion (Herman, Greenberg and Ledbetter 1988): complete (Kobrynski et al. 1993), partial (Balci, Engiz, Yilmaz and Baltaci 2006), or mosaic (Pridjian, Gill and Shapira 1995) trisomy 22.

In one Goldenhar case with a t(4;8) translocation, the chromosome 4 breakpoint was found to be close to the BAPX1 gene (Fischer et al. 2006), a homeobox gene involved in craniofacial development and inner ear formation (Tucker et al. 2004).

A further case report describes a case of Goldenhar syndrome in a girl with a pericentric (p11:q13) inversion of chromosome 9 (Stanojevic, Stipoljev, Koprcina and Kurjak 2000).

MANAGEMENT AND TREATMENT: Various aspects of Goldenhar syndrome may need to be addressed (Cousley and Calvert 1997).

Surgical treatment may be indicated to correct the size and shape of the mandible and maxilla on the affected side (Lima et al. 2007), to rebuild the structure of the outer ear (Romo, Fozo and Sclafani 2000; Romo, Presti and Yalamanchili 2006), and to build up the structure of the cheeks. Where present, surgery may be required to correct cleft lip and palate. Orthodontic supervision is essential, and dental management can be complex (Moulin-

Table B38.2: Problems in Goldenhar syndrome (Table based on Stromland et al. 2007.)

• hearing impairment	15 (83%)
• visual impairment	5 (28%)
• combined visual and hearing impairment	5 (28%)
• feeding difficulties	9 (50%)
• articulation problems	10 (56%)
• mental retardation	7 (39%)
• severe autistic symptoms	2 (11%)

Romsee, Verdonck, Schoenaers and Carels 2004). Surgical correction of scoliosis may be required for those cases where vertebral problems are significant (Anderson and David 2005).

ANIMAL MODELS: Naora *et al.* (1994) described a transgenic mouse line developed by producing a heterozygous cross of wild type and 643 transgenic mice (Otani *et al.* 1991). Homozygous 643 foetal mice did not survive past gestational day 13, and homozygosity was presumed to be lethal. The gene was mapped to mouse chromosome 10. Cousley *et al.* (2002) confirmed the validity of this transgenic mouse model for Goldenhar syndrome.

39.

HEADD syndrome (Hypotonia, Epilepsy, Autism and Developmental Delay)

GENE LOCUS: mitochondrial DNA defects (found in only 5/12 of the reported cases)

KEY ASD REFERENCES: Fillano, Goldenthal, Rhodes and Marin-Garcia 2002; Oliveira *et al.* 2005

SUMMARY: HEADD syndrome is a clinical phenotype associated with a defect in mitochondrial function. The term is an acronym that stands for **H**ypotonia, **E**pilepsy, **A**utism and **D**evelopmental **D**elay.

There are few reports of ASD series in which an assessment of mitochondrial function has been performed. Consequently it is difficult to estimate the likely prevalence of mitochondrial dysfunction in this population.

A useful overview is provided in Smith, Spence and Flodman (2009).

HOW COMMON IS HEADD? The recent increase in interest in mitochondrial dysfunction has found mitochondriopathies to be far more common than had previously been appreciated.

The only publication that reports HEADD is a case series and does not provide information that allows prevalence or incidence to be calculated (Fillano, Goldenthal, Rhodes and Marin-Garcia 2002).

MAIN CLINICAL FEATURES: The clinical features of HEADD syndrome, namely hypotonia, intractable seizures, autism and developmental delay have so far only been reported in one case series of 12 children who underwent investigation for possible mitochondrial abnormalities. In most, metabolic, structural and/or genetic evidence of a mitochondrial defect was identified. 7/8 had muscle biopsy evidence of mitochondrial enzyme activity; 5 had large mitochondrial DNA deletions; and 3/4 had structural abnormalities of their mitochondria.

IS THERE A LINK BETWEEN HEADD AND ASD? This is a circular question – because autism is a key feature required to arrive at the diagnosis, the two 'conditions' must be linked, assuming that HEADD is a valid diagnostic entity.

Fillano *et al.* (2002) described a group of 12 children who presented with hypotonia, epilepsy, autism and developmental delay. The results obtained indicated that defects in mitochondrial DNA, enzyme activity and/or ultrastructure could be identified in most of the cases. The variation in results suggests that the common factor is interferences with mitochondrial energy metabolism, rather than a precise gene defect.

A number of other series have been reported in which mitochondrial function has been assessed, but in none of these has HEADD been specifically reported.

In one Portuguese series of 120 ASD cases (Oliveira *et al.* 2005), 69 had plasma lactate levels checked to screen for possible mitochondrial dysfunction, with 14 being found to be abnormally elevated, and five of these due to a mitochondrial disorder. All of the five mitochondrial cases had severe autism (rated on the CARS), were positive on the ADI-R and had moderate to severe learning disability. None, however, was epileptic. (Mitochondrial defects are well recognized as being associated with childhood epilepsy (Kang *et al.* 2007).)

A systematic review of 25 patients with ASD and a mitochondrial disorder (Weissman *et al.* 2008) found that, compared to others with ASD, the group was characterized by excessive fatiguability (76 per cent), unusual patterns of developmental regression (40 per cent), and marked delay in early milestones (32 per cent).

Defects in beta-oxidation indicate mitochondriopathy and are commonly reported in ASD, often due to specific mitochondrial defects such as LCAD (Clark-Taylor and Clark-Taylor 2004).

DIFFERENTIAL DIAGNOSIS: The primary differential diagnosis is from other mitochondriopathies affecting energy metabolism (Finsterer 2004).

MANAGEMENT AND TREATMENT: A recent Cochrane review (Chinnery, Majamaa, Turnball and Thoburn 2006) found six randomized controlled trials of treatments for mitochondrial disorders, with varying results. From this review there is some evidence for supplementation with coenzyme Q10, some for the use of creatine, and some for the use of dichloroacetate. The heterogeneous nature of the population is likely to be the key factor in outcome variability.

ANIMAL MODELS: No relevant animal models for mitochondriopathy have been developed.

40.

L-2-hydroxyglutaric aciduria (L-2 HGAA)

GENE LOCUS: 14q22.1

KEY ASD REFERENCE: Zafeiriou *et al.* 2007

SUMMARY: L-2 HGAA is a rare autosomal recessive condition. It results in a disorder of glycosylation – the process that adds sugars to proteins and fats on cell surfaces of the endoplasmic reticulum of the cell. It is a progressive metabolic condition resulting in intellectual, communicative and motoric regression together with macrocephaly and seizures.

This inborn error of metabolism results from a difficulty in metabolizing certain sugars including galactose, a sugar uniquely derived from lactose (found only in milk in the Western diet). An overview of the biochemistry of L-2 HGAA can be found in Van Schaftingen, Rzem and Veiga-da-Cunha (2009).

HOW COMMON IS L-2-HYDROXYGLUTARIC ACIDURIA? The prevalence is currently not known, but reports are more common in areas with higher rates of consanguineous marriage (Shafeghati, Vakili and Entezari 2006). It has been described worldwide in around 75 cases to date.

MAIN CLINICAL FEATURES: The condition is progressive in nature, with gradual intellectual decline; deterioration in motor skills with cerebellar ataxic gait, intention tremor, macrocephaly and seizures are the most characteristic physical features. (See, for example, Barbot *et al.* 1997; Topçu *et al.* 2005.) These changes are accompanied by metabolic differences – elevated L-2-hydroxyglutaric acid and elevated levels of lysine in plasma, urine and CSF (Barth *et al.* 1992).

L-2-hydroxyglutaric aciduria has been linked to a number of developmental problems including infantile spasms and psychomotor regression, with subcortical abnormalities (Mahfoud *et al.* 2004; Seijo-Martínez *et al.* 2005).

There is as yet no robust evidence on the mechanisms involved. There is preliminary evidence for the presence of a central nervous system-toxic, FAD-dependent L-2-hydroxyglutarate dehydrogenase mutation, initially in rat tissue and subsequently in two affected families with L-2-hydroxyglutaric aciduria (Rzem *et al.* 2004).

IS THERE A LINK BETWEEN L-2-HYDROXYGLUTARIC ACIDURIA AND ASD? A recent study detailing the development of a single three-year-old boy with L-2 HGAA has suggested an association between L-2-hydroxyglutaric aciduria and ASD (Zafeiriou *et al.* 2007). He presented with mild motor delay, profound difficulties with communication and a score on the CARS (44/60) consistent with severe autism.

DIFFERENTIAL DIAGNOSIS: As for a number of the other conditions we discuss in this book, diagnosis is clear after genetic and metabolic testing, but in the initial stages, differential diagnosis should consider other conditions that are associated with macrocephaly (Shafeghati, Vakili and Entezari 2006). (Refer to Table A9 on page 86).

MANAGEMENT AND TREATMENT: Knowledge of the biochemistry involved has led to reports of beneficial treatment. Samuraki *et al.* (2008) report on an adult female case who had developed normally through elementary school and graduated from high school, but who showed a gradual deterioration in gait and increase in hand tremor, coupled with a decline in intellectual function to an assessed IQ of 47 at age 43. She was treated with flavin adenine dinucleotide sodium (a metabolic derivative of riboflavin) and levocarnitine chloride (involved in fatty acid transport across mitochondrial cell membranes). This combined treatment reversed the problems in her gait and tremor, and further cognitive decline was arrested.

A further recent report of treatment of an adolescent boy with L-2 HGAA reports beneficial effects from treatment with riboflavin (vitamin B2) (Yilmaz 2009).

Many families claim to see clinical benefit from casein- and gluten-free diets or casein-, gluten-, soy- and egg-free diets, and from the 'specific carbohydrate diet'. Such approaches are time-consuming and require considerable commitment to undertake and persevere with. There is a clinical literature that is supportive of such dietary interventions in some cases (Anderson *et al.* 2002; Klavdieva 1996; Knivsberg, Reichelt, Hoien and Nodland 2002; Reichelt and Knivsberg 2003). However, the mechanisms that underlie such apparent improvement are far from clear. As one of the genes involved in lactose digestion corresponds to the highest Lod score locus for ASD so far reported – 3q26.1–q26.3 – it seems likely that, for some cases at least, where removal of milk products has proved beneficial, the difference may result from removal of lactose rather than from removal of casein.

The prevailing theory for why this type of approach may be of benefit concerns deficiency of gut enzymes involved in casein digestion, coupled with increased intestinal permeability, resulting in the entry of opioid-like compounds into the bloodstream and ultimately into the brain. (For discussion of this model see information on the ESPA Research website: www.espa-research.gov.uk). There are various possible reasons for such factors, one being the presence of heterozygous sequence variants of the secretin gene at 11p15.5 (Yamagata *et al.* 2002). Such a difference could increase intestinal permeability by increasing intestinal acidity and altering gut flora.

Another possible reason for beneficial effects from this nutritional approach may be the removal of galactose from the diet. Galactose is one of the two sugars produced by the degradation of lactose (milk sugar) – the other being glucose. One of the key genes involved in galactose metabolism is found at 3q26.1–q26.3. To date, from the gene marker studies, this site on chromosome 3 has the highest reported Lod score for ASD of any gene association so far reported – 4.81 (Auranen *et al.* 2002).

ANIMAL MODELS: No genetically engineered animal models for L-2 HGAA have been made. There are, however, natural equivalents in the dog. Two separate studies have identified homologous natural gene defects in a specific breed of dog (the Staffordshire bull terrier) which have similar phenotypic characteristics to the human condition (Abramson *et al.* 2003; Penderis *et al.* 2007).

41.

Hyper IgE syndrome with autism (HiES)

aka • Buckley syndrome
• Job syndrome

GENE LOCI: 4q21 (precise location not yet known), 17q21

KEY ASD REFERENCE: Grimbacher *et al.* 1999a

SUMMARY: Hyperimmunoglobulin E syndrome (HiES) was first described in 1966 in two red-haired girls (Davis, Schaller and Wedgwood 1966). It was originally called 'Job's syndrome', as a feature of the condition was recurrent staphylococcal abscesses. (In the Bible, Job's body was covered in boils by Satan, and those affected by HiES show a weakened, inflammatory response to infection.) The patients reported on by Davis *et al.* presented with boils, eczema, hyperextensible joints, and distinctive, coarse facial features.

In addition to the immune component, Hyper-IgE is known to be a multisystem disorder, affecting all organ systems in the body (Grimbacher *et al.* 1999b). A genetic basis to the condition has been linked to chromosome 4 (Grimbacher *et al.* 1999c). Recently a second genetic factor – defects in the interleukin-6 mediator STAT3 (17q21) – has been reported in a series of HiES cases (Holland *et al.* 2007) and appears to provide a second sufficient genetic mechanism.

HOW COMMON IS HIES? There are no studies to date which indicate the incidence or prevalence of HiES. It is a rare disorder that appears to affect both sexes equally and all racial groups so far examined.

MAIN CLINICAL FEATURES: Elevated serum IgE levels were first reported by Buckley, Wray and Belmaker (1972), and are associated with recurrent lung and skin infections, principally staphylococcus aureus and candida. A number of immune problems are reported – TH1/TH2 lymphocyte skewing, elevated IL-4 (Borges, Augustine and Hill 2000) with reductions in chemokine (Chehimi *et al.* 2001), and 1-selectin production (Vargas *et al.* 1999).

The early features are typically severe eczema, with infection, and recurrent otitis media and sinusitis which persist into adult life.

A recent paper documents the MRI findings in a series of 50 patients with HiES (Freeman A.F. *et al.* 2007). Central nervous system abnormalities, particularly hyperintensities apparent on T2 imaging, were common, being seen in 70 per cent of cases.

There appear to be both autosomal dominant (Grimbacher *et al.* 1999b) and autosomal recessive (Renner *et al.* 2004) forms of HiES. Neurological complications appear more common in the recessive form. Sporadic cases typically resemble the dominant form (Grimbacher, Holland and Puck 2005). It seems likely that the co-morbid case reported by Grimbacher *et al.* (1999a) had the dominant phenotype.

The autosomal dominant form (but not the recessive form) has a distinctive facial appearance (Borges *et al.* 1998) that is seen by mid-childhood: typically, those affected have a prominent forehead, a broad bridge to the nose, and a bulbous nose. A cleft lip and palatal abnormalities have been reported. A few cases have been documented with craniosynostosis.

A variety of joint and skeletal abnormalities are also seen – some 70 per cent are reported to have hyperextensible joints; those affected are prone to fractures, have osteoporosis, and typically develop scoliosis over time. They are typically late in losing their milk teeth.

Neither the facial nor the skeletal characteristics can be explained on the basis of the immune differences so far described.

IS THERE A LINK BETWEEN HIES AND ASD? Only one paper to date has documented ASD in an individual with HiES (Grimbacher *et al.* 1999a). This describes a 17-year-old boy with has mild learning disability, autism and a sporadic HiES. He had an analphoid ring marker chromosome derived from an interstitial deletion of 4q21 on the maternally inherited chromosome.

DIFFERENTIAL DIAGNOSIS: Atopic dermatitis is the most likely alternative (but does not have the typical facial and skeletal appearance found in HiES).

Other primary immunodeficiencies with eczematous dermatitis include Wiskott-Aldrich syndrome (WAS) and chronic granulomatous disease (CGD). These also lack the typical facial and skeletal appearance found in HiES.

Omenn syndrome (an 11p13 condition) is a severe combined immunity disease (SCID) variant that has elevated IgE, as part of a more complex symptomology that is fatal if untreated. It can be successfully treated by bone marrow transplantation (Gomez *et al.* 1995) in contrast to HiES (Gennery, Flood, Abinun and Cant 2000).

Common variable immunodeficiency disease (CVID) has similar immunological features, but without the skeletal or facial differences seen in HiES.

IPEX (immune dysregulation, poly-endocrinopathy, enteropathy, X-linked inheritance syndrome) has early onset diabetes as part of the clinical presentation (Bennett *et al.* 2001).

Raised level of IgE is a rare manifestation of HIV infection (Seroogy *et al.* 1999).

MANAGEMENT AND TREATMENT: HiES is treated prophylactically with chronic antibiotics to help protect against staphylococcal infection and candidiasis (DeWitt, Bishop, Buescher and Stone 2006). Medium and high-dose intravenous gamma-globulin have been used successfully in cases with severe eczema (Bilora, Petrobelli, Boccioleti and Pomerri 2000; Kimata 1995). Skeletal abnormalities should be treated as required, with monitoring for possible scoliosis and ensuring adequate calcium intake to protect against osteoporosis.

ANIMAL MODELS: No HiES animal models have so far been developed. A murine model for Omenn syndrome is the closest parallel (Wong and Roth 2007), but the genetic basis to these two conditions is different.

42.

Hypomelanosis of Ito (HI)

aka • incontinentia pigmenti achromians

GENE LOCI: various genes have been reported – 9q33–qter, 15q11–q13, and Xp11

KEY ASD REFERENCES: Akefeldt and Gillberg 1991; Davalos, Merikangas and Bender 2001; Gomez-Lado *et al.* 2004; Hermida-Prieto *et al.* 1997; Pascual-Castroviejo *et al.* 1988, 1998; von Aster *et al.* 1997; Zappella 1993

SUMMARY: HI was first described, purely as a cutaneous phenomenon, by Ito (1952), who described a 22-year-old Japanese woman with a curious pattern of depigmentation but who was otherwise normal. She had depigmented areas on her trunk and spine, and linear depigmentation on her arms.

The clinical presentation of HI is very varied but around three–quarters of cases have abnormalities of other organ systems, particularly of the central nervous system.

HI is thought to be the third most common neurocutaneous condition after neurofibromatosis type 1 [51] and tuberous sclerosis [73].

HOW COMMON IS HI? The incidence in live births and the population prevalence are reported as being one in 7,540 and one in 82,000 respectively (Ruggieri and Pavone 2000). HI appears to be around twice as common in girls as in boys.

MAIN CLINICAL FEATURES: HI was previously called *incontinentia pigmenti achromians*. It results in hypopigmented skin, particularly the formation of asymmetric, but typically bilateral, depigmented macules across the chest along the 'Blaschko lines' (Nehal, PeBenito and Orlow 1996), in zigzag patterns on the spine, and in vertical lines on the arms (Donnai, Read, McKeown and Andrews 1988). A range of other congenital organ system defects are also reported, with multiple congenital defects, particularly of the central nervous system, but with additional skeletal, hair and dental findings. The cutaneous features are visible from birth.

HI also presents with ocular abnormalities (Amon, Menapace and Kirnbauer 1990; Weaver, Martin and Zanolli 1991).

The most commonly associated problems are congenital anomalies, learning disability and epileptic seizures, all of which should be kept under review.

Pascual-Castroviejo *et al.* (1998) reviewed 76 cases of HI. They reported that 57 per cent of patients had an IQ score of less than 70, of whom 40 per cent had an IQ below 50. A high proportion of cases have mild to moderate learning disabilities.

Most cases appear to arise *de novo* with no previous family history.

IS THERE A LINK BETWEEN HI AND ASD?
A number of papers have suggested a link between hypomelanosis of Ito and ASD.

- In a review of neurological complications in 34 cases of HI, Pascual-Castroviejo *et al.* (1988) noted that four had a diagnosis of autism.

- Akefeldt and Gillberg (1991) described three cases – two girls and one boy, all with typical features of HI and all with ASD. One was autistic, one had Asperger's, and one was atypical autistic. The authors recommended that skin examination should be part of the clinical workup for those with an ASD.

- Davalos, Merikangas and Bender (2001) described a 35-year-old female case of HI whose clinical presentation was consistent with an autistic disorder.

- Zappella (1993) presented two twin pairs – one MZ and one DZ pair. Both pairs were concordant for HI and autism.

- Hermida-Prieto *et al.* (1997) described two further female HI cases, one with learning disability in addition to autism.

- Von Aster *et al.* (1997) described a 13-year-old boy who had presented neonatally with failure to thrive, and on follow-up had a diagnosis of atypical autism.

- Pascual-Castroviejo *et al.* (1998) presented the first large case series of HI. They described the presentation of 76 cases seen over a 30-year period. Fifty-six per cent had significant learning disability and ten per cent of those were co-morbidly autistic. Twenty-two per cent were of normal overall IQ (>85). Forty-nine per cent were epileptic. Twelve were macrocephalic and six were microcephalic. Fourteen were significantly hypotonic. (It is not clear whether this series extends the series reported earlier by this group in 1988, but this seems likely to be the case.)

- In 2004, Gomez-Lado and colleagues retrospectively reviewed 14 cases of HI. Learning disability was noted in 11, with co-morbid autism in two. Abnormal dentition was noted in six, hyperacusis in five, and seizures in two.

Table B42: Problems in hypomelanosis of Ito

• seizures	(Pascual-Castroviejo *et al.* 1988)
• palatal abnormalities	(Fryns *et al.* 1993)
• dental malformations	(Fryns *et al.* 1993; Happle and Vakilzadeh 1982)
• hearing loss	(Griebel, Krageloh-Mann and Michaelis 1989)
• visual problems	(Scott, Micallef, Hale and Watts 2008)
• renal problems	(Coward *et al.* 2001; Vergine *et al.* 2008)
• orthopaedic problems	(Pascual-Castroviejo *et al.* 1988)

As HI is a rare condition, the number of reported cases with ASD, typically associated with central nervous system involvement and learning disability, suggests that there is an association that has a common biological basis.

DIFFERENTIAL DIAGNOSIS: The range of genes which appear to interfere with melanin metabolism and the reports of mosaicism (Donnai, Read, McKeown and Andrews 1988; Fritz *et al.* 1998) are thought to account for the high degree of phenotypic variability (Glover, Brett and Atherton 1989). There have been cases reported with 15q11–13 (Pellegrino *et al.* 1995), an area of chromosome 15 implicated in oculocutaneous albinism [55] and Angelman [11] and Prader-Willi [61] syndromes.

Type 2 oculocutaneous albinism and Angelman and Prader-Willi syndromes can all present with hypopigmentation. All, like HI, can result from a 15q11 defect, and all can be found with ASD.

Several rare cutaneous conditions can present with similar features to HI: fourth stage of *incontinentia pigmenti*; linear and whorled nevoid hypermelanosis; and *nevus depigmentus*.

MANAGEMENT AND TREATMENT: The cutaneous aspects of HI do not require any specific management approach. However, there are a number of approaches to treating hypopigmentation, which may be used where the cosmetic aspects cause distress (Brenner and Hearing 2008; Schaffer and Bolognia 2003). In other respects, the biology is not yet understood to a level where there are any specific treatment implications.

A number of specific problems have been reported in association with HI that may require additional treatment on a case-by-case basis (see Table B42).

ANIMAL MODELS: No specific animal models of HI have been developed. There are a number of animal models of albinism and other cutaneous pigmentary deficits. The mouse pink-eyed dilution locus on chromosome 7 is syntenic with 15q11 and has been proposed as a model for Angelman, Prader-Willi and HI (Brilliant 1992).

43.

Hypothyroidism

GENE LOCI: 8q23–q24, 2q33

KEY ASD REFERENCES: Comi *et al.* 1999; Gillberg, Gillberg and Kopp 1992; Molloy *et al.* 2006; Raja and Azzoni 2008; Sweden *et al.* 2006

SUMMARY: Hypothyroidism typically results from abnormal structural development of the thyroid gland (seen in 75 per cent of cases) but can also result from abnormal development of the compounds which metabolize iodine, or other enzymes involved in the production of thyroxine (10 per cent), abnormal pituitary function (5 per cent), or secondary to maternal hypothyroidism/transplacental exposure to maternal antibodies (10 per cent).

Hypothyroidism is one of the most common metabolic disorders. It is estimated that around ten per cent of women of childbearing age have some degree of thyroid dysfunction.

Hypothyroidism can arise due to chronic iodine deficiency. Today iodine is added to table salt and deficiency is virtually unknown; it is extremely unlikely, except in some isolated, land-locked, mountainous regions such as parts of the Himalayas. However, other maternal dietary factors such as flavonoid ingestion could cause transient foetal hypothyroidism and affect brain development (Román 2007).

HOW COMMON IS HYPOTHYROIDISM?

On US figures, congenital hypothyroidism is reported to affect one in 3,500 of the general population. Rates vary markedly, however, depending on the population studied and criteria used, with one epidemiological study giving a rate of 46/1,000 or more than one in 21 (Hollowell *et al.* 2002).

There are differences in racial prevalence, with Hispanics being most likely to be affected, followed by Caucasians, while Afro-Caribbeans are the least likely to suffer from hypothyroidism. Thyroid problems are more common in girls, who are twice as likely to be affected.

MAIN CLINICAL FEATURES: A number of early features are characteristic: babies tend to be born past their due date and are heavy for their gestational age. They tend to be slow in developing a bowel pattern, have prolonged jaundice, are hypoactive and feed poorly, are prone to hypothermia and have laboured breathing and a hoarse cry. If left untreated, there is markedly delayed physical growth and progressive cognitive decline (a rare condition known as cretinism, possibly due to a form of iodine deficiency historically common in parts of Crete).

Neonatal screening detects the vast majority of cases, and early treatment (typically by giving thyroxine replacement) prevents emergence of the later features of the condition.

IS THERE A LINK BETWEEN HYPOTHY-ROIDISM AND ASD? Several studies point to a possible link between thyroiditis and ASD:

- Gillberg, Gillberg and Kopp (1992) described three boys and two girls, two with mothers who were likely to have been hypothyroid during their pregnancies, and three who had hypothyroidism themselves. They suggest that there is a possible link between the conditions, due either to effects of low thyroid hormone exposure on early central nervous system development, or to autoimmune factors involved in both conditions. These cases are therefore associated with abnormal foetal thyroid exposure or congenital hypothyroidism. Discussion below will deal with these effects of early thyroid abnormalities and will not discuss later acquired forms of hypothyroidism.

- Comi *et al.* (1999) surveyed families to look for links between family autoimmune problems and ASD, comparing questionnaire responses from families of 61 autistic patients to families of 46 healthy controls. Mothers were eight times as likely to report autoimmune disorders compared to mothers of controls (16 per cent vs 2 per cent), with type 1 diabetes, adult rheumatoid arthritis, hypothyroidism and systemic lupus erythematosus being the most commonly reported conditions.

- Sweeten *et al.* (2003) carried out a large questionnaire study of 101 families with a child with ASD, 101 families with a child presenting with an autoimmune disorder and families of 101 healthy controls. The frequency of autoimmune problems was significantly higher in the families of children with ASD than in the other two groups, particularly the prevalence of Hashimoto's thyroiditis and rheumatic fever. Hashimoto's thyroiditis is a later-onset autoimmune condition where the thyroid becomes damaged.

- Molloy *et al.* (2006) carried out telephone interviews about family history of autoimmune problems with the families of 308 children with ASD who were part of the Collaborative Programs of Excellence in Autism (CPEA) network. They specifically compared those who had a history of regression (N = 155) to those with no regressive history (N = 153). The only significant difference between the groups was that families whose children had regressed were significantly more likely to report a family history of autoimmune thyroid disease (64 vs 38).

- In a recent paper by Raja and Azzoni (2008) on comorbidity of Asperger's syndrome and bipolar disorder, one of the cases presented was a 30-year-old man with adrenal insufficiency and hypothyroidism as part of his clinical presentation.

Clearly there is a need for further systematic research on this issue. However, the published literature to date suggests that lower than normal levels of thyroid hormone exposure may be a risk factor for the development of ASD, and particularly for ASD with a regressive onset. Since in many of the cases to date the reported link is with maternal hypothyroidism during pregnancy, in families with a history of autoimmune problems, thyroid levels should be closely monitored antenatally.

The lack of any systematic screening of thyroid function in ASD to date makes it impossible to speculate on the strength on any possible link.

DIFFERENTIAL DIAGNOSIS: One other deficiency syndrome that results in autistic behaviour and has a similar clinical presentation as part of a complex and severe neurodevelopmental disorder is 5-oxoprolinase deficiency (Cohen L.H. *et al.* 1997).

MANAGEMENT AND TREATMENT: In most cases, underactivity of the thyroid gland can be corrected by supplementation with thyroxine/levothyroxine. Response to treatment is monitored by checking levels of thyroid stimulating hormone (TSH). This is a compound produced by the pituitary gland which normally controls thyroid function, and levels of which are controlled by negative feedback of circulating thyroxine levels.

ANIMAL MODELS: One animal model has been proposed to date as relevant to a connection between hypothyroidism and ASD. Sadamatsu and colleagues from Shiga University in Japan have proposed a rat model, induced by giving propylthiouracil (PTU) to lactating rats. This impairs brain development in their offspring, which exhibit mild transient hypothyroidism (Sadamatsu *et al.* 2006). This model results in abnormal cerebellar development similar to that reported in autistic humans (Sadamatsu and Watanabe 2005) and increases susceptibility to audiogenic seizures (Yasuda *et al.* 2000).

44.

Joubert syndrome

GENE LOCI: 2q13, 3q11.2, 6q23.3, 8q, 9q34.3, 9q34.3, 11p12–13.3, 12q21.32, 16q11.2

KEY ASD REFERENCES: Alvarez Retuerto *et al.* 2008; Holroyd, Reiss and Bryan 1991; Ozonoff, Williams, Gale and Miller 1999; but see also Takahashi, Farmer *et al.* 2005

SUMMARY: Joubert syndrome was first described by Joubert, Eisenring, Robb and Andermann (1969) in a paper which

Table B44.1: The eight Joubert syndrome gene loci

Gene locus	Gene product	Key reference/s
• 2q13	NPHP1	Castori *et al.* 2005; Parisi *et al.* 2004
• 3q11.2	ARL13B	Cantagrel *et al.* 2008
• 6q23.3	AHI1	Dixon-Salazar *et al.* 2004; Ferland *et al.* 2004; Parisi *et al.* 2006, Utsch *et al.* 2006
• 12q21.32	CEP290 (NPHP6)	Sayer *et al.* 2006; Valente *et al.* 2006b
• 8q21.1–q22.1	MKS3 (TMEM67)	Baala *et al.* 2007
• 9q34.3	JBTS1/CORS1	Saar *et al.* 1999; Valente *et al.* 2005
• 11p12–q13.3	JBTS2/CORS2	Keeler *et al.* 2003; Valente *et al.* 2003
• 16q11.2	RPGRIP1L	Arts *et al.* 2007; Brancati *et al.* 2008; Delous *et al.* 2007

Table B44.2: Diagnoses reported to show the 'molar tooth sign'

• COACH syndrome	Gentile *et al.* 1996
• Cogan oculomotor apraxia syndrome	Betz *et al.* 2000
• Dekaban-Arima syndrome	Dekaban 1969
• Leber congenital amaurosis-like	Steinlin, Scmid, Landau and Boltshauser 1997
• nephronophthisis	Otto *et al.* 2003, 2005
• oculomotor apraxia	Steinlin, Schmid, Landau and Boltshauser 1997
• Senior-Løken syndrome	Løken, Hanssen, Halvorsen and Jolster 1961; Senior, Friedmann and Braudo 1961
• Varadi-Papp syndrome	Munke *et al.* 1990

presented cases with an inherited pattern in which there was poor development of the cerebellar vermis in association with periodic rapid breathing, motor ataxia, abnormal eye movements and learning difficulties. The clinical picture is complex, with variable clinical features, and has a range of severity and possible complications.

It is a cerebello-oculo-renal syndrome, affecting motor control, vision and kidney function. It has an autosomal recessive pattern of inheritance.

A number of helpful summaries of Joubert syndrome are now available. (See Parisi, Doherty, Chance and Glass 2007; Parisi and Glass 2007.)

HOW COMMON IS JOUBERT SYNDROME? No good epidemiological studies have been carried out. The best estimate that is currently available is 0.85 per 100,000 (Orphanet 2009).

HERITABILITY: Joubert syndrome is an autosomal recessive condition.

As each parent must be a recessive carrier and is asymptomatic, each child has a 50 per cent chance of inheriting an affected gene from each parent, so one in four will inherit two affected genes and have Joubert syndrome, two in four will be carriers, and one in four will inherit two unaffected genes. The aunts and uncles of an affected person will have a 50 per cent risk of carrying the recessive gene involved.

It is possible that someone with Joubert syndrome could reproduce, although to date no such cases have been reported. Affected males are likely to have lowered fertility due to their ciliary defect.

Tracing the ancestry of the French-Canadian family first described with the condition, Joubert, Eisenring, Robb and Andermann (1969) revealed a 'founder effect' identifying that the condition began with an individual who emigrated from France to Quebec in the 1600s (Badhwar, Andermann, Valerio and Andermann 2000).

MAIN CLINICAL FEATURES: The key behavioural features are infantile hypotonia with subsequent development of truncal ataxia, a variable developmental delay or learning disability, together with either abnormal respiration (alternating tachypnoea and/or apnoea which can improve with age) (Maria *et al.* 1999b) or abnormal eye movements (typically oculomotor apraxia or difficulty in smooth visual pursuit and jerkiness in gaze and tracking) (Bennett, Meuleman, Glass and Chance 2003; Maria *et al.* 1999a; Saraiva and Baraitser 1992; Steinlin, Schmid, Landau and Boltshauser 1997; Zaki *et al.* 2008). In some cases rhythmic tongue movements result in enlargement of the tongue and difficulties with vocalization. Truncal ataxia is typical of what would be expected with central vermal hypoplasia. There is a broad range of cognitive ability, from severe learning disability to normal IQ.

The typical facial features are a long, narrow face with low-set ears; high, arched eyebrows; a protruding jaw; prominent bridge to the nose; and small triangular mouth. To date, however, these features have not been characterized well or consistently enough in the literature or linked to the specific genotypic markers to tell how consistently they are present.

A range of other physical and metabolic features has been reported in some cases. Epilepsy has been reported in individual cases, but the prevalence is not known (Saraiva and Baraitser 1992).

It is now clear that there are a number of Joubert-like syndromes with separate genetic aetiologies (Valente *et al.* 2005, 2006a). These are sometimes referred to as the cerebello-oculo-renal syndromes, and eight distinct genetic forms have so far been described (see Table B44.1). One of these forms involves mutations to the AHI1 gene (Ferland *et al.* 2004), and has both cerebellar hypoplasia and cortical polymicrogyria (Dixon-Salazar *et al.* 2004). As defects in AHI1 have recently been reported in cases diagnosed as having Joubert syndrome (Alvarez Retuerto *et al.* 2008), the diagnostic picture is currently somewhat confused.

The 'molar tooth sign': In Joubert syndrome the cerebellum and brainstem are malformed. The classic physical feature is the 'molar tooth sign' seen on MRI, indicating vermal hypoplasia (lack of development of the vermis of the cerebellum), with impaired axonal decussation (with a deep interpeduncular notch), and thick abnormally oriented superior cerebellar peduncles. (See Limperopoulos and du Plessis 2006 for discussion of conditions involving cerebellar development.) Essentially this produces a pattern on an axial brain scan of the base of the brain that looks like a drawing of a molar tooth.

Diagnosis is currently on the basis of the phenotype combined with the 'classic' molar tooth appearance (see above) on axial brain imaging of the area where the pons and midbrain join (Maria *et al.* 1997, 1999b; Quisling, Barkovich and Maria 1999). The molar tooth sign is seen as a necessary feature for a diagnosis of Joubert syndrome to be given.

A number of the genes involved in Joubert syndrome – NPHP1, AHI1, CEP290, RPGRIP1L, TMEM67 and ARL13B – are involved in ciliary function.

The molar tooth sign has also been described in other clinical syndromes (Gleeson *et al.* 2004; Satran, Pierpont and Dobyns 1999), so is not truly diagnostic of Joubert syndrome. A number of other diagnosed conditions are reported in association with the 'molar tooth sign': cerebellar abnormalities, learning disability, and varying combinations of the other features also reported in Joubert syndrome (see Table B44.2).

There is ongoing debate over whether these are varying presentations of the same condition, or separable conditions with discrete aetiologies. To date, the lack of a consistent protocol for investigation has not allowed this issue to be successfully addressed. The finding of the molar tooth sign in all of the above (Chance *et al.* 1999; Gleeson *et al.* 2004; Pellegrino, Lensch, Muenke and Chance 1997; Satran, Pierpont and Dobyns 1999) has been used to argue for a common aetiology.

A recent study of Egyptian cases has been used to propose a classification system for molar tooth cases based on clinical criteria (Zaki *et al.* 2008). As the sample used was small and 9/13 cases reviewed were not linked to known loci, a larger validation study is needed to test this system.

In those people with CEP290 mutations where neuroimaging has been carried out, the molar tooth sign and/or cerebellar vermal hypoplasia have been shown, usually in combination with retinal dystrophy or congenital blindness (Sayer *et al.* 2006; Valente *et al.* 2006a).

Other abnormalities of the central nervous system: In addition to the molar tooth sign, a number of other central nervous system abnormalities have been reported. These have not been screened across the various associated genotypes and could be genotype-specific. At the time of writing, Joubert syndrome can be found in association with enlargement of the fourth ventricle (the fluid-filled space between the pons and the cerebellum) which is reported in around ten per cent of cases (Maria *et al.* 2001). Hydrocephalus is also reported without fourth ventricle dilatation (Genel, Atlihan, Ozdemir and Targan 2004). In some, the corpus callosum has failed to develop (Valente *et al.* 2005). Some show evidence of occipital encephalocele (a small, fluid-filled sac at the rear of the skull) or meningocele, a similar sac connecting to the membranes covering the brain (Genel, Atlihan, Ozdemir and Targan 2004). Heterotopias, or small areas of 'misplaced' neural tissue (Saraiva and Baraitser 1992), and neuroepithelial cysts (Marsh *et al.* 2004) have been reported. Polymicrogyria is also reported (Gleeson *et al.* 2004). This finding of excessive convolutions on the surface of the cortex indicated that selective cell death (apoptosis) has not occurred normally, so that there are excessive numbers of neurons. This may be a finding that is specific to those with AHI1 mutations (Dixon-Salazar *et al.* 2004).

Variability in presentation: The presentation of Joubert syndrome is highly variable.

Serial prenatal ultrasound can be successful in identifying phenotypically obvious at-risk cases (Doherty *et al.* 2005). However, the variability in phenotype means that this can be used to rule in, but not to exclude, possible diagnosis.

In the original cases reported (Joubert, Eisenring, Robb and Andermann 1969), one case had an occipital meningoencephalocele and agenesis of the cerebellar vermis, and one only agenesis of the cerebellar vermis, while two had agenesis only of the posterior occipital cerebellar vermis.

Behaviourally and phenotypically discordant identical girl twins have been reported (Raynes *et al.* 1999). Both showed the molar tooth sign on MRI. At the time of the report, the girls were 7.5 years of age and had a 21-month-old affected sister with ocular abnormalities, motor delay, the molar tooth sign and cerebellar vermal hypoplasia. The twins had very different physical and behavioural phenotypes, one being ambulant, verbal and not reported as autistic, the other wheelchair-bound, non-verbal and reportedly autistic. The genotype in these three cases is not known.

Intellectual function is variable, from normal ability to severe learning disability. In one follow-up study, 11/15 had intelligible speech and six were in mainstream education at five years of age (Hodgkins *et al.* 2004). A further study (Braddock, Henley and Maria 2007) found that there was an equivalent level of language comprehension in children with Joubert syndrome, irrespective of motor communicative skills. Some can go on to attend college independently.

A variety of behavioural difficulties are reported in some, but not in all, cases. Behavioural problems, including impulsivity, inattention, overactivity and temper tantrums, are present in perhaps 20 per cent of those with Joubert syndrome (Deonna and Ziegler 1993; Hodgkins *et al.* 2004). These problem behaviours are associated with high levels of parental stress (Farmer *et al.* 2006).

Physical characteristics of Joubert syndrome: A range of physical features may be seen, including the following.

- *Ophthalmologic findings.* The retinal problems reported in Joubert syndrome resemble those seen in Leber's congenital amaurosis. Leber's amaurosis has recently been reported in association with a number of the genetic ciliary defects implicated in Joubert syndrome, such as CEP290 and RPGRIP1 (den Hollander, Roepman, Koenekoop and Cremers 2008).

  A variety of visual apractic defects are reported, and incomplete retinal development is not uncommon (Saraiva and Baraitser 1992).

- *A variety of renal problems* can occur, normally progressively with age (Saraiva and Baraitser 1992; Steinlin, Schmid, Landau and Boltshauser 1997). Several of these reported features are characteristic of other 'molar tooth disorders' and strengthen the idea of diagnostic overlap:

  o Cystic dysplasia (which is seen as a feature of Dekaban-Arima syndrome (Dekaban 1969)). Juvenile nephronophthisis typically presents in adolescence with thirst, excess urine production, growth retardation and low iron levels (Saunier, Salomon and Antignac 2005).

  o The kidneys often become small and scarred, and kidney transplantation is sometimes required.

It has been proposed that these two kidney problems are on a continuum representing the same renal problem presenting at different ages or stages (Kumada *et al.* 2004).

- *Polydactyly* of the fingers and/or toes are frequently documented (Saraiva and Baraitser 1992).

- *Abnormalities of the tongue* are common and can often lead to problems with chewing, swallowing and breathing.

In those cases who have a NPHP1 defect, renal impairment seems typical and retinal abnormalities have also been reported (Castori *et al.* 2005; Parisi *et al.* 2004).

In contrast, with AHI1 defects, most cases show retinal dystrophy, while renal problems are uncommon (Parisi *et al.* 2006; Utsch *et al.* 2006) and can be late-onset.

IS THERE A LINK BETWEEN JOUBERT SYNDROME AND ASD? Several studies have noted a possible link between Joubert syndrome and ASD.

- Holroyd, Reiss and Bryan (1991) described two cases of Joubert syndrome, one of whom met DSM-III-R criteria for autism, while the other showed autistic features. The genetic basis to the cases was not described.

- Ozonoff, Williams, Gale and Miller (1999) assessed 11 children with Joubert syndrome using the ADI-R and the ADOS-G. Three met criteria for autistic disorder and one for pervasive developmental disorder not otherwise specified, while all of the other seven exhibited some features of autistic spectrum disorders. The genetic basis to these cases was not described.

- Alvarez Retuerto *et al.* (2008) have looked at a possible association between variants in the AHI1 gene at chromosome 6q23.3, which is seen in a significant proportion of Joubert syndrome cases, and autism, using the Autism Genetic Resource Exchange (AGRE) database. A significant association between AHI1 variants and autistic diagnosis was found.

- Takahashi, Farmer *et al.* (2005), however, compared 31 Joubert syndrome families to families with autism and to Down syndrome controls. None of the Joubert syndrome children met ASD criteria on the Autism Behavior Checklist (ABC), and family histories were not similar to the other groups, suggesting that Joubert syndrome was aetiologically distinct. The ABC is a less robust tool for ASD diagnosis than the ADI-R. However, the finding is on a large sample and the contrasting prevalence result is surprising.

To date, no attempt has been made to examine the prevalence of ASD symptomology in specific genetic forms of Joubert syndrome, and it could transpire that the link is with particular genetic types of Joubert syndrome and not with the diagnosis *per se*.

DIFFERENTIAL DIAGNOSIS:

- *Biedl-Bardet syndrome* (BBS [17]). BBS is another autosomal recessive condition in which ciliary defects have been implicated and ASD behaviour has been reported. Kidney problems, visual impairment and ataxia are common features of BBS. However, structural impairment of the cerebellum is rare (Baskin *et al.* 2002).

- *Cogan syndrome* is an autosomal, recessive, congenital oculomotor apraxia that impairs horizontal voluntary eye movements and results in jerky lateral eye movements. In some cases, the cerebellar vermis is incompletely formed and the molar tooth sign is present on MRI (Sargent, Poskitt and Jan 1997; Whitsel, Castillo and D'Cruz 1995), and some cases present with kidney problems. The NPHP1 homozygous deletion, also found in Joubert syndrome, Senior-Løken syndrome and juvenile nephronophthisis type I, has been found in cases diagnosed as Cogan syndrome (Betz *et al.* 2000).

- **C**olobomas, **O**ligophrenia (learning disability), **A**taxia, **C**erebellar vermis hypoplasia, and **H**epatic fibrosis (*COACH syndrome*) (Gentile *et al.* 1996) also presents with the molar tooth sign.

- *The Dandy-Walker malformation* is a condition characterized by abnormal development of the hindbrain, cerebellar vermal hypoplasia, and an enlarged collection of cerebrospinal fluid contiguous with the fourth ventricle. In addition, some cases have callosal agenesis and hydrocephalus affecting the other parts of the ventricular system (Patel and Barkovich 2002). Structural neuroimaging shows different patterns of brainstem development in Dandy-Walker malformation that does not present the molar tooth sign (Maria *et al.* 2001).

- *X-linked cerebellar hypoplasia* is a condition that has been linked to defects in the OPHN1 gene (Bergmann C. *et al.* 2003). It typically presents in males, with hypotonia from birth and moderate learning difficulties (Philip *et al.* 2003).

- *Ataxia and oculomotor apraxia types 1 and 2* are autosomal recessive disorders (Le Ber, Brice and Durr 2005). They are caused by mutations in the genes encoding ataxin (APTX) (9p13.3) and senataxin (SETX) (9q34), respectively. Both are characterized by progressive cerebellar ataxia with onset in later childhood, and oculomotor apraxia. Cerebellar atrophy is present on neuroimaging.

- *Congenital disorders of glycosylation* (CDG) show developmental delay, hypotonia, ataxia and oculomotor abnormalities. In CDG, renal problems, breathing problems, polydactyly and the molar tooth sign have not been reported, and a number of abnormal features, including subcutaneous fat distribution

in infancy and inverted nipples (Jaeken and Hagberg 1991), are not reported in Joubert syndrome. Abnormalities of glycoprotein glycosylation are typical of CDG. Serum transferrin isoelectric focusing is normal in Joubert syndrome but abnormal in most forms of glycosylation defect, so is helpful in differential diagnosis (Morava *et al.* 2004).

- *3-C syndrome (cranio-cerebello-cardiac syndrome or Ritscher-Schinzel syndrome)* is thought to be an autosomal recessive condition. It presents with cerebellar vermal hypoplasia, and often with fourth ventricle enlargement, similar to the Dandy-Walker malformation. Heart defects, cleft palate and ocular colobomas are also reported (Kosaki, Curry, Roeder and Jones 1997; Leonardi, Pai, Wilkes and Lebel 2001). Learning disability is a common part of the presentation but not obligatory. The genetic basis to 3-C is unknown at the present time.

- *The pontocerebellar hypoplasias/atrophies* are a group of rare conditions with vermal hypoplasia and limited development of the pons, but without the molar tooth sign (Barth 1993). They can be genetic and pre- or perinatal in origin. Most show severe learning difficulties and progressive muscular impairment.

- *Oral-facial-digital (OFD) syndrome type II* (Mohr syndrome) (Reardon *et al.* 1989) presents with facial clefting, tongue abnormalities, polydactyly and cerebellar vermal agenesis, and *type III* (Sugarman, Katakia and Menkes 1971) presents with learning disability and polydactyly.

- *Meckel-Gruber syndrome* presents with polycystic kidneys, polydactyly and an occipital encephalocele. Cerebellar vermal hypoplasia has been noted in some cases, and hepatic fibrosis has also been documented. A number of gene loci have been mapped and two genes have been identified: MKS1 (Kyttala *et al.* 2006), and MKS3 (Morgan *et al.* 2002; Smith U.M. *et al.* 2006). One study has found that the MKS3 gene mutated in Meckel-Gruber syndrome is also mutated in some cases of Joubert syndrome (Baala *et al.* 2007). The pattern of inheritance is autosomal recessive.

• Nephronophthisis is also a common feature (Sayer *et al.* 2006). The combination of nephronopythesis, retinal dystrophy and molar tooth sign are the key features of *Senior-Løken syndrome*.

MANAGEMENT AND TREATMENT: At the present time there are no treatment approaches that are specific to Joubert syndrome. As the presentation is complex and variable, assessment, therapy and follow-up need to be on a case-by-case basis.

A number of separate genes are involved and independently sufficient to cause Joubert syndrome. At present it is not clear that all cases have a genetic basis, and there is considerable overlap with several other presentations. It seems likely that there will be no single approach to management, but a number of approaches focused on the specific genes and gene products involved. Animal models are beginning to show some potential for early treatment of renal impairment resulting from the lack of a specific compound 'nephrocystin-6', caused by CEP290 knockdown (Tobin and Beales 2008).

Assessment and follow-up should be focused on detailed evaluation of the various systems that may be involved:

• genetic investigation of individuals with a Joubert syndrome phenotype to screen for the known genes

• detailed neuroimaging, particularly of the cerebellum, ventricular system and axially through the midbrain (to image the 'molar tooth sign' where present)

• neurological assessment and management as appropriate – for example, of encephalocele, hypotonia, oculomotor and oromotor function (mastication, swallowing and articulation); gastrostomy feeding can be required in severely dysphagic cases; and management of seizures and ventricular dilatation where these are present

• assessment of respiratory function with treatment as required

• assessment and correction as appropriate of physical abnormalities such as palatal clefting, polydactyly and tongue restrictions; physical growth can be restricted and should be monitored

• ophthalmological assessment, particularly of retinal function, with treatment as required

• assessment of renal and hepatic function and endocrine screening are important. Dialysis or transplantation may be required for renal problems.

Once age-appropriate, assessment of cognitive and language development, and of activities of daily living skills, should be carried out, and difficulties and delays addressed when identified.

Parenting stress should be assessed and support provided as appropriate, including management help in those cases where stress is related to behavioural difficulties such as poor impulse control or anger control issues.

ANIMAL MODELS: CEP290 is a gene involved in ciliary function. In experimental knockdown models of CEP290, which prevent production of nephrocystin-6 in zebrafish, there is abnormal development of the cerebellum, kidneys and retina

(Sayer *et al.* 2006). A recent study in zebrafish (Tobin and Beales 2008) has shown that a number of renal ciliopathies can be modelled by gene knockdown, and that the cystic lesions and functional kidney defects can be reversed through pharmacological treatment.

There is also evidence that nephrocystin-6 is expressed in the cerebellum during embryonic development in the mouse (Valente *et al.* 2006b).

45.

Kleine-Levin syndrome

aka • Kleine-Levin hibernation
syndrome

GENE LOCUS: 6p21.3 in some but not all reported cases

KEY ASD REFERENCES: Berthier, Santamaria, Encabo and Tolosa 1992; Mukaddes, Fateh and Kilincasian 2008

SUMMARY: First reported in 1862 by Brierre de Boismont, the condition is named after two early twentieth-century clinicians: Willi Kleine, who described various cases of episodic hypersomnia (Kleine 1925), and Max Levin, who noted the association between hypersomnia and hyperphagia (Levin 1929, 1936).

An infectious aetiology was first proposed by Critchley and Hoffman (1942), and subsequently a number of cases have been reported with onset shortly after infection (Dauvilliers *et al.* 2002; Katz and Ropper 2002). A useful overview can be found in Lisk (2009).

There is increasing evidence that Kleine-Levin syndrome results from factors that interfere with the functioning of the major histocompatibility complex at DQB1 on chromosome 6p (see, for example, BaHammam *et al.* 2007; Dauvilliers *et al.* 2002) and possibly provide a mechanism for increased susceptibility to infection.

HOW COMMON IS KLEINE-LEVIN SYNDROME? At the present time, the prevalence of Kleine-Levin syndrome is not known. Around 300 cases are reported in the clinical literature to date (Arnulf *et al.* 2005, 2008; Schenck, Arnulf and Mahowald 2007).

MAIN CLINICAL FEATURES: The behavioural aspects reported appear to be episodic, with normal behaviour in these respects between attacks. (See, for example, Popper, Hsia, Rogers and Yuen 1980).

Table B45: Clinical features of Kleine-Levin syndrome

• hypersomnia	100%
• cognitive changes (including a specific feeling of derealization)	96%
• eating disturbances	80%
• depressed mood	48%
• hypersexuality	43%
• compulsions	29%

(Adapted from Arnulf *et al.* 2005)

IS THERE A LINK BETWEEN KLEINE-LEVIN SYNDROME AND ASD? Two papers have reported co-morbid cases.

- Berthier, Santamaria, Encabo and Tolosa (1992) described two adolescent males with Asperger's syndrome who also had recurrent bouts of hypersomnia. The report preceded the adoption of ICD or DSM criteria for Asperger's syndrome, but has been quoted in the literature as an association between ASD and Kleine-Levin syndrome (for example, Zafeiriou, Ververi and Vargiami 2006).

- Mukaddes, Fateh and Kilincasian (2008) have presented a further two cases of Kleine-Levin syndrome with associated autistic disorder.

A number of papers have highlighted neuropsychiatric symptomology in Kleine-Levin syndrome (Masi, Favilla and Millepiedi 2000; Mukaddes, Alyanak, Kora and Polvan 1999). A systematic review has detailed 186 cases reported between 1962 and 2004 (Arnulf *et al.* 2005). This review indicated a mean age of onset in the mid-teens and, as with many neuropsychiatric disorders, a higher prevalence in males but greater severity in presenting females.

DIFFERENTIAL DIAGNOSIS: The presentation is unusual, episodic and distinctive. It is unlikely that Kleine-Levin syndrome would be confused with other types of presentation.

MANAGEMENT AND TREATMENT: There is a lack of evidence concerning pharmacological treatments for Kleine-Levin syndrome (Oliveira, Conti, Saconato and Fernandes do Prado 2009).

The most successful reported treatment to date for the recurrent hypersomnia is lithium (Arnulf *et al.* 2005). In some cases at least, there appears to be a close association between lithium level achieved and clinical improvement (Muratori, Bertini and Masi 2002).

A recent case has been described who went into complete remission on carbamazepine (El Hajj *et al.* 2009).

ANIMAL MODELS: No animal models for Kleine-Levin syndrome have been reported to date.

46.

Lujan-Fryns syndrome

aka • mental retardation, X-linked, with Marfanoid habitus

GENE LOCUS: Xq13, and a reported additional link to terminal 5p deletion

KEY ASD REFERENCES: Guerrieri and Neri 1991; Lerma-Carrillo *et al.* 2006; Purandare and Markar 2005; Spaepen, Hellemans and Fryns 1994; Stathopulu, Ogilvie and Flinter 2003; Swillen, Hellemans, Steyaert and Fryns 1996

SUMMARY: The syndrome was first described in 1984 by J. Enrique Lujan (Lujan, Carlin and Lubs 1984).

Those affected are tall and slim with long, slender fingers and toes, and narrow faces with small jaws and prominent foreheads.

A useful review of Lujan-Fryns syndrome can be found in Van Buggenhout and Fryns (2006).

HOW COMMON IS LUJAN-FRYNS SYNDROME? There have been no prevalence studies to date. As the genes implicated in this condition have only recently been identified, the possibility of screening studies has only just become available.

MAIN CLINICAL FEATURES: The majority of reported cases are male. Mild to moderate learning disability is seen in most cases, but normal levels of cognitive function are reported. (See, for example, Williams 2006.) In the case described by Williams, despite normal IQ there were major problems with learning and memory and a complex behavioural presentation that included elements of ODD, ADHD and conduct disorder, together with extreme shyness. The phenotype is described as 'Marfanoid', and both hyperextensible joints and cardiac defects are reported (Wittine, Josephson and Williams 1999), such as are seen in Marfan's syndrome (Le Parc 2005).

A tall, slender physique with limited subcutaneous fat, long fingers and toes, an aqualine nose, thin upper lip, prominent forehead, maxillary hypoplasia and small jaw are typical, as is macroorchidism.

Behaviourally, in addition to the ASD features, shyness (Lacombe *et al.* 1993) and hyperactivity (De Hert *et al.* 1996; Wittine, Josephson and Williams 1999) are frequently reported.

Epilepsy is reported in some cases, but how common and how consistent a feature is uncertain.

There is progressive scoliosis in many cases, which may require surgical correction in some.

Recent research with some of the originally reported families has identified a missense mutation in the MED12 gene at Xq13 (Schwartz *et al.* 2007), while terminal 5p deletion has also been reported in association with the condition (Stathopulu, Ogilvie and Flinter 2003).

IS THERE A LINK BETWEEN LUJAN-FRYNS AND ASD? Despite the limited literature on Lujan-Fryns, a number of papers have suggested an association with ASD.

- Guerrieri and Neri (1991) reported on a brother and sister with Lujan-Fryns and co-morbid ASD.

- Spaepen, Hellemans and Fryns (1994) reported on a series of 14 Lujan-Fryns cases and found that 12 of the 14 exhibited autistic or autistic-like behaviour.

- Swillen, Hellemans, Steyaert and Fryns (1996) reported that four of the 21 residential learning-disabled ASD cases they reported had the Lujan-Fryns phenotype.

- Stathopulu, Ogilvie and Flinter (2003) describe a 16-year-old male with a Lujan-Fryns phenotype and a small terminal 5p deletion. This may prove to be a phenocopy disorder with a separate aetiology.

- Purandare and Markar (2005) provided a systematic review of the psychiatric symptomology reported in association with Lujan-Fryns.

- Lerma-Carrillo *et al.* (2006) documented a 23-year-old male with borderline IQ, who had been admitted to psychiatric hospital because of behavioural disturbance and firesetting. He had the classic Lujan-Fryns phenotype and a history of ADHD and disturbed behaviour. His presenting behaviour was consistent with an ASD. On MRI he was found to have callosal agenesis. A maternal uncle had a similar presentation, abnormal dentition and a heart defect. They suggest from their review of the literature and their own cases that around 90 per cent of cases have ASD symptomology.

- Lalatta *et al.* (1991) were the first to suggest that psychotic presentations may be common in this condition. A number of cases have been described with visual and auditory hallucinations, and schizophrenia has been diagnosed in some cases (De Hert *et al.* 1996; Purandare and Markar 2005).

DIFFERENTIAL DIAGNOSIS: The differential diagnosis should include assessment to exclude XXY [3] and XYY [4] aneuploidies; 22q11 deletion syndromes [18, 29, 76]; fragile-X syndrome [35, 36]; Marfan syndrome; and homocystinuria – all of which can present with a similar phenotype.

MANAGEMENT AND TREATMENT: At the present time there is no specific treatment for Lujan-Fryns syndrome. The likelihood of scoliosis and joint problems, cardiac abnormalities and the risk of seizures should all be monitored.

The ASD, ADHD and social shyness that are characteristics of the condition should respond to approaches used with others. The increased likelihood of hallucinations should be monitored and treated where present.

ANIMAL MODELS: Most animal models to date are in zebrafish. It has been shown that *med12* deficient fish have defects in brain, neural crest and kidney development (Hong *et al.* 2005), and that *med12* is involved in the regulation of various other signalling pathways and the *Sox9* gene (Rau, Fischer and Neumann 2006; Wang *et al.* 2006).

47.

2-methylbutyryl-CoA dehydrogenase deficiency

aka • short/branched-chain acyl-CoA dehydrogenase deficiency (SBCADD/2-MBADD)

GENE LOCUS: 10q25–q26

KEY ASD REFERENCE: Kanavin *et al.* 2007.

SUMMARY: This is an inborn error of metabolism. It was first reported by Gibson *et al.* (1999). It results in a problem in metabolizing isoleucine and valine and, when not appropriately managed, results in developmental delay, seizures, limited social responsiveness and motor difficulties.

HOW COMMON IS 2-METHYLBUTYRYL-COA DEHYDROGENASE DEFICIENCY?
2-methylbutyryl-CoA dehydrogenase deficiency is thought to be rare, but no population prevalence or incidence figures have been reported, except in the Hmong population of southeastern Asia (the Hmong are originally thought to be from Laos, Cambodia and southern China) and in Hmong American families, where between one in 250 and one in 500 people are affected (van Calcar *et al.* 2007). Several cases have been reported in the clinical literature from Eritrea and Somalia, suggesting that the condition may also have a significant prevalence in these populations.

MAIN CLINICAL FEATURES: Typically, SBCADD cases present with severe developmental delay, seizures, poor social responsiveness and motor problems diagnosed variously as hypotonia, muscle wastage and cerebral palsy (Akaboshi *et al.* 2001; Andresen *et al.* 2000; Gibson *et al.* 2000; Madsen *et al.* 2006).

This is an autosomal recessive inborn error of metabolism, specifically concerned with the metabolism of the amino acids isoleucine and valine (Andresen *et al.* 2000). It is typically detected by the presence of the compounds 2-methylbutyryl glycine and 2-methylbutyryl-carnitine in urine.

A number of gene differences are sufficient to result in SBCADD. These produce a range of levels of deficiency and some, particularly missense variants, are common in the general population (Pedersen *et al.* 2008). As a number of the reported cases appear to have one parent with 2-methylbutyryl glycinuria but without any clinical symptomology, SBCADD may be a condition that requires an additional factor to manifest. The possibility of changes in diet coinciding with a critical phase in foetal development may be one possibility, given the reported cases in Eritrean, Somali and Hmong now domiciled in Europe or North America.

IS THERE A LINK BETWEEN SBCADD AND ASD? To date, only a single ASD case with SBCADD and autism has been reported (Kanavin *et al.* 2007). The case is a four-year-old Somali boy born to healthy parents. The child had presented in Somalia with seizures, but the details were lost to follow-up when the family moved to Norway when he was 18 months old.

A recent paper from Sweden (Barnevik-Olsson, Gillberg and Fernell 2008) suggests that the rate of autism in the Somali population of Stockholm is three to four times higher than the indigenous rate amongst Swedes.

SBCADD is an inborn error of metabolism that is common in the Somali population and would be markedly less problematic on the indigenous Somali diet. This is low in protein with Tef as the grain staple – Tef is high in lysine and methionine from which l-carnitine is synthesized. Thus SBCADD Somali children on their natural diet would be less likely to demonstrate developmental problems than they would on a Western diet.

DIFFERENTIAL DIAGNOSIS: 2-methyl-butyryl-CoA dehydrogenase deficiency should be differentiated from other inborn errors of isoleucine metabolism. (See Korman 2006.)

MANAGEMENT AND TREATMENT: Current clinical management typically involves the use of protein restriction together with l-carnitine supplementation. In one girl whose mother had started this routine antenatally after a first affected child, her development to age 4 years 8 months was reported as asymptomatic with normal development (Madsen *et al.* 2006). Postnatal dietary management has not been found to be beneficial.

ANIMAL MODELS: There are no animal models of this condition to date.

48.

Mobius syndrome

aka • Moebius syndrome
 • Möbius syndrome

GENE LOCUS: 13q12.2–q13

KEY ASD REFERENCES: Bandim *et al.* 2003; Briegel 2006; Gillberg 1992; Gillberg and Steffenburg 1989; Gillberg and Winnergard 1984; Johansson *et al.* 2001; Verzijl, van der Zwaag, Cruysberg and Padberg 2003

SUMMARY: A probable case of Mobius syndrome was first described by Alfred von Graefe in 1880. However, the description by the German neurologist Paul Julius Möbius in 1888 is usually taken as the first clinical account. (For a brief biography of Möbius, see Steinberg 2005.) It is a facial nerve palsy that results in flattening of facial affect and a characteristic cupid's-bow shape to the mouth.

HOW COMMON IS MOBIUS SYNDROME? There is only one epidemiological study to date on Mobius syndrome (Verzijl, van der Zwaag, Cruysberg and Padberg 2003). Based on a Dutch population survey, this paper estimated the incidence of Mobius syndrome in the Dutch population in 1996 to be 0.002 per cent. (Four cases were found in 189,000 births.) There is no indication of a higher prevalence in either sex or in particular racial groups.

MAIN CLINICAL FEATURES: The condition typically involves abnormal function of cranial nerves VI and VII, resulting in flattened facial affect. A number of other cranial nerves can also be affected. In addition to cranial nerve function, a variety of other features can be present, and there are several diagnostic systems that are not in full agreement concerning necessary and sufficient factors for diagnosis.

The hypoglossal nerve is affected in around 25 per cent of cases, resulting in difficulties with tongue protrusion and articulation.

The condition is typically noted in infancy due to poor sucking, drooling, lack of eyelid closure during sleep and flattened facial affect. The persistence of flattened facial affect makes it difficult for the person to convey emotion through facial expression, compounding difficulties with social interaction. Because of the lack of facial innervation there is an absence of skin wrinkling and the appearance of the face is exceptionally smooth. External ocular nerve palsies are seen in around 80 per cent of cases.

Intelligence is typically within the normal range. (See, for example, Verzijl, van der Zwaag, Cruysberg and Padberg 2003.) However, a subgroup has mild learning disabilities.

One small (N=13) recent study has reported behavioural difficulties, particularly aggressive behaviour, oppositional defiance and anxiety in boys, to be reasonably common in a sample of preschool children with Mobius syndrome (Briegel, Hofmann and Schwab 2007). Caregivers also reported a high level of perceived stress in themselves.

Sucking and swallowing problems can be severe in infancy and can contribute, along with respiratory problems, to increased early mortality. It is common for those affected to have small mouths with large lips and to be unable to fully close their mouth, which adds to their swallowing difficulties. It also makes it difficult to produce certain sounds, and speech is often indistinct as a result.

Inability to fully close the eyelids during sleep leads to an increased risk of recurrent conjunctivitis. No systematic study of sleep problems in Mobius syndrome has been carried out.

There is a high incidence of other congenital abnormalities. *Talipes equinovarus* (or clubfoot) is a commonly associated abnormality seen in around one third of cases. Abnormalities of the hand (syndactyly, brachydactyly and finger webbing) and hypoplastic thumb and jaw are also common, as is abnormal formation of the microtia/inner ear.

Four separate cases of cataplexy (a rare condition where the person collapses without warning while laughing) have been reported: one single case report (Tyagi and Harrington 2003) and three from a series of 19 attending a sleep clinic in south London (Parkes 1999).

In a study of 37 Dutch Mobius patients aged from six months to 53 years (Verzijl, van der Zwaag, Cruysberg and Padberg 2003), 86 per cent were noted as having had feeding difficulties from birth due to abnormalities of the palate and pharynx; 90 per cent had craniofacial abnormalities; 86 per cent had abnormalities of the hands and/or feet; and 88 per cent were noted to have motor clumsiness.

Genetic and epigenetic factors: The pattern of inheritance is still unclear. Family pedigrees have been reported which are consistent with X-linked recessive inheritance (Journel, Roussey and Le Maree 1989), and with both autosomal dominant and autosomal recessive inheritance (Legum, Godel and Nemet 1981).

Two early papers suggested a link to genetic defects at 13q12.2–q13 (Slee, Smart and Viljoen 1991; Ziter, Wiser and Robinson 1977). Various patterns of inheritance have been reported consistent with autosomal dominant and recessive and with X-linked recessive patterns of inheritance, or with several sufficient genetic mechanisms. Overall the risk of inheritance from someone affected by the condition is said to be approximately two per cent (Baraitser 1977, 1982). However, there have been no recent studies of this issue.

One family presented with a Mobius phenotype across three generations, where all of those affected had reciprocal translocations between 1p34 and 13q13 but unaffected family members did not (Ziter, Wiser and Robinson 1977). In the second case, Mobius syndrome was associated with a 13q12.2 deletion in a two-and-a-half-year-old girl (Slee, Smart and Viljoen 1991).

A number of environmental factors have also been reported to be independently sufficient causes. In particular, thalidomide, which was used for a number of years in the management of morning sickness in early pregnancy, has been shown to have teratogenic effects which can cause both Mobius syndrome and ASD (Miller *et al.* 2005). Misoprostol (Bandim *et al.* 2003), an abortifacient, has also been found capable of producing the combination of Mobius syndrome and ASD. Cases have also been reported in association with ergotamine exposure (Smets, Zecic and Willems 2004) and cocaine use during pregnancy (Puvabanditsin, Garrow and Augustin 2005). It is important, therefore, in exploring the pathogenesis, to identify any possible exposures to relevant teratogenic agents.

The common factors appear to be the stage at which neural development has been affected, and that the factor – whether toxic, traumatic or genetic – affects critical aspects of vascular development in the central nervous system. A useful discussion of the embryology underpinning Mobius syndrome and the link between constellation of features and timing of disruption to early growth can be found in Miller *et al.* (2005).

IS THERE A LINK BETWEEN MOBIUS SYNDROME AND ASD?

- Gillberg and Winnergard (1984) described a five-year-old boy with Mobius syndrome, a mild to moderate level of learning difficulty and a childhood psychosis described as 'possibly infantile autism'. This was the first such case described in the clinical literature.

- Gillberg and Steffenburg (1989) presented data from a screening study of 17 children and young adults with Mobius syndrome. Using the Checklist for Autism developed by Mildred Creak (Creak 1963), five were said to fulfil criteria for a DSM-III-R diagnosis of autism.

- Gillberg (1992) reviewed 59 autism cases with a variety of co-morbid medical conditions including Mobius syndrome. He concluded that there were clear differences in the behavioural phenotype that depended on the associated medical condition.

- Johansson *et al.* (2001) published a detailed assessment of 22 Mobius syndrome cases using the Autism Diagnostic

Interview – Revised (ADI-R), the Childhood Autism Rating Scale (CARS) and the Autism Behavior Checklist (ABC) for ASD assessment. Six cases fulfilled diagnostic criteria for autism, all of whom had co-morbid learning disability.

- A study in northeastern Brazil (Bandim *et al.* 2003) screened 23 Mobius syndrome cases for possible autism, using DSM-IV criteria and the CARS. Of those aged under two years, 2/5 showed autistic features, while of those over two years of age, 5/18 met diagnostic criteria for autism. All had co-morbid learning disability. One of the cases under two and three of the older cases had been exposed to misoprostol during the first trimester. Misoprostol is used in the treatment of stomach ulcers, and is also an abortifacient that can produce teratogenic effects consistent with those seen in the genetic form of Mobius syndrome (Miller *et al.* 2005).

- Verzijl, van der Zwaag, Cruysberg and Padberg (2003) carried out a screening study of 37 Dutch Mobius syndrome cases. No specific assessment of ASD was used, but it is noted incidentally that two of the school-age cases have a diagnosis of autism, and the paper implies that both may have co-morbid learning disability, as it comments that the other school-age cases have IQs of over 80.

A review of the neuropsychiatric sequelae of Mobius syndrome can be found in Briegel (2006).

Overall (with the exception of the lower rate found by Verzijl, van der Zwaag, Cruysberg and Padberg 2003), this suggests that perhaps 28 per cent of those with Mobius syndrome fulfil criteria for ASD, so co-morbid cases may occur in perhaps one in 140,000 of the population,

if the limited epidemiology is broadly correct.

A recent study has evaluated the use of various ASD scales with this population, questioning the applicability of current diagnostic tools such as the ABC, CARS and ADI-R in this population, if the subject is deaf–blind (Johansson, Gillberg and Råstam 2009).

DIFFERENTIAL DIAGNOSIS: The principal differential diagnoses are the neuromuscular conditions, and initial differentiation can be difficult (Imamura *et al.* 2007). Alternative possible diagnoses include:

- hereditary congenital facial paresis (Verzijl *et al.* 2003, 2005), which only affects the facial nerves and has no central or brainstem component

- facioscapulohumeral muscular dystrophy (Tawil 2008)

- infantile myotonic dystrophy (Yoshimura, Sasaki, Akimoto and Yoshimura 1989)

- Charcot-Marie-Tooth disease (Herrmann 2008).

A recent paper has detailed a Mobius-like syndrome that presents with similar muscular impairment but very distinct neuroimaging (Dumars *et al.* 2008).

There have been rare cases of Mobius syndrome in combination with other anomalies such as Goldenhar syndrome [38] and hypoglossia-hypodactyly (Preis *et al.* 1996).

MANAGEMENT AND TREATMENT: This is a static and not a progressive condition. Treatment is dependent on the clinical profile in the individual case.

Surgical treatment can be required to correct deformities of the hand, foot or jaw. Surgery may also be considered to correct strabismus (crossed eyes) and to address flattened facial affect through transfer of innervation and musculature to animate the corners of the mouth.

A tracheotomy may sometimes be required to help those with severe breathing difficulties.

Some will require some form of assisted alimentation, such as nasogastric tube feeding.

ANIMAL MODELS: To date, no genetic models that are similar to Mobius syndrome have been developed. A targeted mouse model with disruption to *Hoxb-1* fails to develop the VIIth nerve motor nucleus, and so has morphological similarity to Mobius syndrome. However, the syntenic human gene to HOXB-1-1 is 17q21–q22, and not the 13q12.2–q13 region implicated in Mobius syndrome (Goddard, Rossel, Manley and Capecchi 1996).

49.

Myhre syndrome

aka • growth-mental deficiency syndrome of Myhre

GENE LOCUS: not yet identified

KEY ASD REFERENCES: Burglen *et al.* 2003; Titomanlio *et al.* 2001

SUMMARY: In 1981, Myhre and colleagues described two unrelated learning-disabled young men with similar physical phenotypes (Myhre, Ruvalcaba and Graham 1981). Both were short and heavily built, with small mouths, jaws and noses, limited joint movement, undescended testes and hearing loss. Older paternal age was noted in both cases. A number of similar case reports followed this initial description. (See, for example, Garcia-Cruz *et al.* 1993; Soljak, Aftimos and Gluckman 1983.)

Recent reviews of Myhre syndrome can be found in Becarra-Solano *et al.* (2008) and Burglen *et al.* (2003).

HOW COMMON IS MYHRE SYNDROME? The prevalence and incidence are not currently known. Only 20 cases have so far been reported.

MAIN CLINICAL FEATURES: The most widely reported features are short stature; heavy, muscular build; hearing loss; decreased joint mobility; thickened, hard skin; underdeveloped upper jaw and prominent lower jaw; and narrow eyelids. Typically, these features are associated with learning disability. However, there is a report of the Myhre syndrome phenotype in association with normal intelligence (Rulli *et al.* 2005).

A paper from Scotland (Whiteford *et al.* 2001) described a single case – a 13-year-old male with short stature, learning disability, hearing difficulty, heavy muscular build and limited joint mobility.

IS THERE A LINK BETWEEN MYHRE SYNDROME AND ASD? One paper (Titomanlio *et al.* 2001) describes a 14-year-old boy with the clinical features of Myhre syndrome (including impaired growth) and a co-morbid ASD diagnosis.

Burglen *et al.* (2003) reported on four cases of Myhre, one of whom was reported to have an 'autistic-like' condition.

A further case of an 11-year-old boy with autism and similar neurocutaneous findings, but with physical overgrowth, has been reported (Buoni *et al.* 2006b).

Whether two cases from a world literature of around 20 in total constitutes a meaningful association between these conditions will await the reporting of a larger clinical population.

There is no genetic marker for Myhre syndrome and the extent of phenotypic variability in this condition is unknown. Variation can be marked in many of the conditions we have considered. The above may be presentations of the same underlying mechanism, but could conceivably represent similar phenotypes with differing underlying bases.

DIFFERENTIAL DIAGNOSIS: A number of other conditions should be considered in the differential diagnosis, which also present with the combination of short stature, small hands and feet and limited joint mobility. These include Moore-Federman syndrome (Moore and Federman 1965), geleophysic dysplasia (Wraith *et al.* 1990) and acromicric dysplasia (Maroteaux, Stanescu, Stanescu and Rappaport 1986).

MANAGEMENT AND TREATMENT: No specific treatment approaches have been developed to date.

ANIMAL MODELS: As the aetiology is currently uncertain and no specific genetic abnormalities have been reported, no animal models have yet been reported.

50.

Myotonic dystrophy type 1 (MD1)

aka • dystrophia myotonica 1
• Steinert's muscular dystrophy

GENE LOCUS: 19q13.2–q13.3

KEY ASD REFERENCES: Blondis, Cook, Koza-Taylor and Finn 1996; Ekström *et al.* 2008; Paul and Allington-Smith 1997; Yoshimura, Sasaki, Akimoto and Yoshimura 1989

SUMMARY: Myotonic dystrophy type 1 is the second most common type of muscular dystrophy after Duchenne [33]. It is an autosomal dominant CTG triplet repeat expansion disorder affecting the production of dystrophia myotonica-protein kinase (DMPK). In the general population,

CTG repeats of up to 37 copies are seen. Anticipation is seen in MD1, so one or other parent typically has a pre-mutational expansion of 37 to 50 copies. Larger mutations are usually associated with maternal transmission. Affected individuals have between 50 and 4,000 copies. With shorter expansions (50–400 copies), there is a correlation between repeat length and age of onset; above 400 copies, earlier onset is consistently seen.

MD1 was originally called Steinert's muscular dystrophy after the German nineteenth-century neurologist Hans Gustav Wilhelm Steinert, who described the condition in a paper published in 1910.

There are a number of useful reviews of MD1, such as Schara, Benedikt and Schoser (2006) and Bird T.D. (2007).

HOW COMMON IS MYOTONIC DYSTROPHY TYPE 1? Estimates of prevalence vary for myotonic dystrophy type 1. The current best overall estimate is a rate of between one in 20,000 and one in 100,000 (Bird T.D. 2007). Reported rates vary from one in 100,000 in Japan to one in 10,000 in Iceland.

MAIN CLINICAL FEATURES: MD1 is a multisystem disorder that affects all major body systems except the skeleton. It is an autosomal dominant condition caused by a mutation at 19q13.2–q13.3. This is a region transcribed into RNA but not into protein. The principal effects appear to be on the chloride channel CIC-1, resulting in myotonia, and the insulin receptor INSR, resulting in insulin resistance (Cho and Tapscott 2007).

There are effects on both skeletal and smooth muscle, as well as the eye, heart, endocrine system, and central nervous system.

MD1 is typically divided into three groups:

1. mild, in which the typical presentation is of a sustained but slight myotonia combined with cartaract and normal life expectancy

2. classic, in which gradual-onset hypotonia, myotonia and muscle wasting, combined with cataract, are typical, cardiac problems are common, and life expectancy is shortened

3. congenital, characterized by congenital hypotonia and severe weakness, breathing difficulties, learning disability in most cases, and short life expectancy.

A recent study of cognitive and adaptive abilities in a sample of 31 male and 24 female DM1 cases (mean age 12 years 1 month; range from 2 years 7 months to 21 years 5 months) found a negative association between severity of dystrophy and both IQ and adaptive level on the Vineland Adaptive Behavior Scales (Ekström, Hakenäs-Plate, Tulinius and Wentz 2009).

IS THERE A LINK BETWEEN MD1 AND ASD?

- In the earliest case report, Yoshimura, Sasaki, Akimoto and Yoshimura (1989) described an 11-year-old girl with congenital myotonic dystrophy and infantile autism.

- Blondis, Cook, Koza-Taylor and Finn (1996) described one 10-year-old girl with MD1 and co-morbid Asperger syndrome.

- Paul and Allington-Smith (1997) described two boys with MD1 and diagnoses of Asperger syndrome, one aged 16, one 14.

Despite its being a well recognized and physically quite obvious condition, the first paper to systematically investigate an association between myotonic dystrophy and ASD did not appear until 2008 (Ekström *et al.* 2008). This paper examined 57 children and adolescents with MD1 (26 girls and 31 boys). Based on the ADI-R, typically accepted as the 'gold-standard' diagnostic tool, 46 per cent of the MD1 cases they examined fulfilled criteria for an ASD diagnosis, suggesting a strong but previously largely unrecognized association between the two conditions.

DIFFERENTIAL DIAGNOSIS: There are no other causes of multi-system myotonic dystrophy which have been identified. Diagnosis is based on identifying the presence of a CTG expansion of the DMPK gene at 19q13.2–q13.3. As in most triplet repeat expansion conditions, there is anticipation – the carrier parent will have a shorter expansion than the affected person, and there is an association between the severity of the condition and the size of the expansion. In the normal population, the number of CTG copy repeats is between five and 30. A typical person with MD1 will have 50–80 copies, but expansions of up to 2,000 repeats have been reported.

MANAGEMENT AND TREATMENT: The wide range of presentation leads to a range of appropriate treatment interventions depending on the main areas of difficulty.

A recent review of medication for the management of myotonia has appeared in the Cochrane Library (Trip, Drost, van Engelen and Faber 2009). The review identified ten small randomized trials. However, the quality of the published studies was poor. One small study demonstrated a significant beneficial effect of taurine (Durelli, Mutani and Fassio 1983), but despite its finding of significant benefits and lack of apparent side effects, it remains unreplicated 25 years later.

There is some RCT evidence for beneficial effects of coenzyme Q10 supplementation on physical performance and cardiac function (Folkes and Simonsen 1995).

As gradual muscle wastage is a common feature, systematic approaches to exercise are being evaluated. One study (Omgreen, Olsen and Vissing 2005) has shown improvements in oxygen uptake and muscle function through the use of a graded aerobic exercise regime on static exercise bikes. As respiratory problems are one of the most important predictors of life expectancy, such graded exercise programmes may prove particularly beneficial.

As the basis for the association between ASD and MD1 is unclear, and interest in the association is very recent, the implications (if any) for treatment or management of ASD are unclear.

As a consequence of the wide range of presentation of MD1, a number of specialist services may be involved in assessment and ongoing management – the muscular abnormalities can lead to problems with motor control, respiration, cardiac function and digestion. There are associated problems with vision – cataract is a common finding that may require surgical correction.

In the congenital form, significant breathing problems can be present from birth and result in a need for ventilator support (Keller, Reynolds, Lee and Garcia-Prats 1998).

Males with MD1 often have low testosterone levels (Griggs et al. 1985), but are typically not infertile. Obstetric difficulties are common. However, only women with multi-system involvement appear at significantly increased risk of having affected offspring (Koch, Grimm, Harley and Harper 1991).

ANIMAL MODELS: A large number of animal models of MD1 have been published, some of which will be briefly discussed here.

One of the important findings is that different adjacent genes account for different aspects of the clinical phenotype – DMPK appears to have effects primarily on cardiac development; CIC-1 defects cause chloride channel problems that result in myopathy, and SIX5 defects result in ocular problems such as cataract and abnormal development of sperm.

In 1996, Jansen et al. demonstrated marginal effects of over-expression of the human DMPK transgene in mice. There was a minimal effect except for a copy number dependent cardiomyopathy, suggesting that other factors than the presence or size of the expansion were likely to be important for the MD1 phenotype. A similarly cardiac-specific DMPK mouse model has more recently been reported by Wang G.S. et al. (2007).

Reddy et al. (1996) have developed a mouse with a disrupted *Dmpk* gene resulting in reduced levels of DMPK and skeletal myopathy.

Two separate research groups developed *Six5* disrupted mouse models (Klesert et al. 2000; Sarkar et al. 2000). Both models developed cataracts. Sarkar, Paul, Han and Reddy (2004) also reported that *Six5* disrupted mice had abnormal spermatogenesis.

Mankodi et al. (2000) were able to demonstrate that the build-up of toxic RNA from CUG repeats is sufficient to impair muscle fibre function. In a subsequent paper they demonstrated that the CUG expansion triggers abnormal CIC-1 function and chloride channel dysfunction (Mankodi et al. 2002).

Mahadevan et al. (2006) have demonstrated that CUG-BP1 (a binding protein to the CUG triplet) is over-expressed and builds up to toxic levels in both cardiac and skeletal muscle in MD1 mouse models. The build-up of CUG-BP1 was reversible by transgene silencing.

Muscle chloride channel dysfunction appears to be a central factor in MD1 and has been effectively modelled in the mouse (Lueck *et al.* 2007).

A recent study (Wheeler *et al.* 2007) has demonstrated that in a mouse model of MD1, by introducing a morpholino antisense oligonucleotide (AON), it was possible to produce exon skipping, correct the CIC-1 gene defect responsible for the chloride channel abnormalities and correct the myotonia. The effects were localized and required multiple injections, but this study demonstrates the potential benefit of such approaches.

The results of recent mouse models have demonstrated that the phenotype can be decomposed into a number of specific factors that result in different aspects of the condition, and have also shown that interventions that significantly alter the phenotype through mechanisms such as exon skipping are likely to prove clinically useful, as they have proved to be in other neuromuscular disorders such as Duchenne muscular dystrophy.

51.

Neurofibromatosis type 1 (NF1)

aka • von Recklinghausen disease

GENE LOCI: 17q11.2, 2p22–p21

KEY ASD REFERENCES: Folstein and Rutter 1988; Gillberg 1992; Havlovicova *et al.* 2007; Marui *et al.* 2004a; Mbarek *et al.* 2000; Mouridsen *et al.* 1992; Williams and Hersh 1998

SUMMARY: Genetically, NF1 is complex, with over 240 separate constitutional mutations having so far been recorded. It is inherited in an autosomal dominant fashion, once established. Over half of cases appear to arise as *de novo* mutations, making it one of the most common forms of spontaneous mutation so far reported. The condition results in loss or production of truncated forms of neurofibromin. At the present time the normal function of neurofibromin is not fully understood – it appears to be a negative regulator of the RAS signal transduction pathway (Ormerovic *et al.* 2007), and is the basis for the frequent occurrence of plexiform neurofibromas (Packer *et al.* 2002).

Recent systematic reviews of clinical and genetic issues in NF1 can be found in Ferner (2007), Lee and Stephenson (2007) and Friedman (2007).

Physically, NF1 is characterized by the growth of non-cancerous tumours called neurofibromas. It is classified as a phacomatosis (Nowak 2007) – a condition that is dysplastic (results in abnormal tissue growth), tending to form tumours in the skin, nervous system and viscera. Other phacomatoses are Bannayan-Riley-Ruvalcaba syndrome [15]; hypomelanosis of Ito [42]; Proteus syndrome [62]; and tuberous sclerosis [73]. The process of tumour growth in NF1 is complex and determined by multiple genetic loci (Upadhyaya *et al.* 2004).

The best-known individual case, and one that has appeared in many textbooks dealing with neurofibromatosis, is Joseph Carey Merrick (1862–1890), better known as 'the Elephant Man'. The diagnosis of NF1 in this case was first suggested in a paper by Parkes Weber in 1909. Merrick's clinical features do not, however, correspond clearly to NF1 (Tibbles and Cohen 1986), and he is now thought most probably to have had Cowden syndrome [26].

NF1 was described in 1768 by Mark Akenside, a London medical practitioner.

It was for many years known as von Recklinghausen's syndrome, after the German pathologist Friedrich Daniel von Recklinghausen, who published detailed autopsy reports on two cases in 1882.

HOW COMMON IS NEUROFIBROMATOSIS TYPE 1? Most prevalence estimates for NF1 mutations vary between one in 2,000 and one in 5,000 of the general population (Friedman 1999; Lammert, Friedman, Kluwe and Mautner 2005; Rasmussen and Friedman 2000). Prevalence of the condition is typically quoted as being one in 4,000 and one in 5,000 (Ferner 2007; Huson, Compton, Clark and Harper 1989), but reports vary from one in 960 (Garty, Laor and Danon 1994) to one in 7,800 (Sergeyev 1975). The wide differences in reported rates in different populations may reflect differences in their genetic makeup.

MAIN CLINICAL FEATURES: The clinical features of NF1 vary in presentation and severity (Friedman and Birch 1997).

In those with a positive family history, recognition tends to be earlier, most cases through the presence of café-au-lait spots (DeBella, Szudek and Friedman 2000). Children without a positive family history are often not recognized as having the condition in their early years.

Through childhood, the features of NF1 tend to become more noticeable with age, and most *de novo* cases meet diagnostic criteria by around age eight (DeBella, Poskitt, Szudek and Friedman 2000). Many features of NF1 increase in frequency with age (DeBella, Szudek and Friedman 2000; Friedman and Birch 1997; Wolkenstein, Freche, Zeller and Revuz 1996). In contrast, features such as UBOs (see below) appear to become less common through adolescence and into adulthood (Gill, Hyman, Steinberg and North 2006; Hyman *et al.* 2003).

The typical picture in neurofibromatosis is of multiple café-au-lait (coffee coloured) spots, under the arm and most commonly across the abdomen.

Multiple discrete dermal neurofibromas and iris Lisch nodules (small benign tumours on the iris) are seen in most, except for certain mosaic cases.

Affected individuals tend to be below average height, with above average head circumference (Bale, Amos, Parry and Bale 1991; Clementi *et al.* 1999; Szudek, Birch and Friedman 2000; Virdis *et al.* 2003). Puberty is often delayed (Virdis *et al.* 2003).

The brain is typically larger than normal, but there is no correlation between grey matter volume and cognitive function (Greenwood *et al.* 2005).

Hyperintense 'unidentified bright objects' (UBOs) are seen on structural scans in some two-thirds of children (Goh *et al.* 2004, 2006), and appear to indicate patchy areas of abnormal myelination (Alkan *et al.* 2005; Tognini *et al.* 2005), which on neuropathology are areas of spongiform encephalopathy (DiPaolo *et al.* 1995). UBOs can appear throughout the nervous system and to be less common with age (Gill, Hyman, Steinberg and North 2006; Hyman *et al.* 2003). Their presence, size, location and number appear to have no bearing on the extent of any co-morbid learning problems (Feldmann *et al.* 2003; Goh *et al.* 2004; Hyman *et al.* 2003; North 1999; North *et al.* 1997).

Some degree of learning difficulty is noted in around half of all cases (North 1999; North *et al.* 1997). However, the effect is a small one and not found in all studies. (See review in Levine *et al.* 2006.)

Headaches are frequently reported. Seizures (Vivarelli *et al.* 2003) and hydrocephalus (Creange *et al.* 1999; North 1998) have been reported, but only rarely.

Hypertension is seen, but age of onset varies (Friedman 1999; Lama *et al.* 2004). In one series of 75 cases under 16 (McKeever, Shepherd, Crawford and Morrison 2008) only one case of hypertension was reported. It can be essential hypertension, but can also arise from specific NF1-related lesions, and a specific abnormality affecting both cardiovascular and renal function is often found (Fossali *et al.* 2000; Han and Criado 2005).

Vascular lesions to the heart or brain are uncommon, but have potentially serious or fatal consequences when present (Friedman 1999; Kanter, Graham, Fairbrother and Smith 2006).

A diffuse pattern of polyneuropathy, which is probably due to multiple nerve root tumours and a high risk of malignant peripheral nerve sheath tumours, has been reported (Ferner *et al.* 2004).

There have been various estimates of the proportion of individuals with NF1 who have specific learning difficulties (Hyman, Shores and North 2005, 2006; Kayl and Moore 2000; Levine *et al.* 2006; McKeever, Shepherd, Crawford and Morrison 2008; North 1999; North *et al.* 1997; Riccardi and Eichner 1986; Rosser and Packer 2003), ranging from 3.4 per cent (Riccardi and Eichner 1986) to 11 per cent (Wadsby, Lindenhamer and Eeg-Olofsson 1989). A range of difficulties are reported, the most common being visual–spatial deficits on performance tasks and problems with sustained attention and concentration (Hyman, Shores and North 2006; Koth, Cutting and Denckla 2000; Levine *et al.* 2006; Mautner, Kluwe, Thakker and Leark 2002; Schrimsher, Billingsley, Slopis and Moore 2003). Learning difficulties continue to be reported through adulthood (Pavol *et al.* 2006; Zoller, Rembeck and Backman 1997).

Children with NF1 often show difficulties in their social skills (Barton and North 2004). Quality of life has been reported to be poor in children and adolescents (Graf, Landolt, Mori and Boltshauser 2006; Wolkenstein *et al.* 2008) and in adults (Page *et al.* 2006). Sleep problems are reported as being more common (Johnson H. *et al.* 2005).

Skeletal problems are common, abnormal skeletal growth and pseudoarthrosis being the most common and problematic (Alwan, Tredwell and Friedman 2005), and have significant impact on quality of life (Wolkenstein *et al.* 2008). Scoliosis is seen in some 10 per cent of cases (Akbarnia, Gabriel, Beckman and Chalk 1992), developing usually between six and ten years of age, and often requires complex surgical correction (Shen *et al.* 2005).

Various abnormalities of the nervous system are seen, including plexiform neurofibromas (with proliferation of Schwann cells within the nerve sheath), which are apparent in some 30 per cent of cases (Darrigo, Geller, Filho and Azulay 2007; Ferner 2007; Kreusel 2005); gliomas of the optic nerve, which can lead to blindness in some cases; central nervous system gliomas, thought to affect some 15 per cent of cases (Thiagalingam, Flaherty, Billson and North 2004); and malignant peripheral nerve sheath tumours, seen in one to two per cent of cases (Evans *et al.* 2002). Lisch nodules (benign tumours of the iris) are seen in 63 per cent of prepubertal and 92 per cent of adult cases (Nichols, Amato and Chung 2003).

The number with plexiform neurofibromas is likely to be significantly greater than recorded. However, the majority are internal, symptom-free and cannot be found on routine physical examination (Tonsgard, Kwak, Short and Dachman 1998).

Cardiovascular problems are more common in individuals with NF1 than in the general population (Lin *et al.* 2000) and specific recommendations have been made concerning their management (Friedman *et al.* 2002).

The average life expectancy of individuals with NF1 appears to be shorter than normal. One US study suggests that it is reduced by about 15 years (Rasmussen, Yang and Friedman 2001) – a mean life expectancy of 54.4 years compared to 70.1 years for the same geographic population, with malignant tumours being the most likely specific cause of death identified.

The most frequent cancerous growths seen in NF1 are malignant peripheral nerve sheath tumours that are seen in around ten per cent of cases (Evans *et al.* 2002; Walker *et al.* 2006) and which tend to occur in adulthood, but at a much younger age in NF1 than in the general population, and with poorer prognosis (Evans *et al.* 2002; Hagel *et al.* 2006).

NF1 has been linked with lower-than-expected serum 25-hydroxyvitamin D concentrations (Lammert *et al.* 2006), with mean levels less than half of those in controls, and with an inverse correlation between levels and numbers of dermal neurofibromas.

There is a positive family history in around half of all cases. Where a parent is positive for an NF1 defect, the risk to siblings is 50 per cent, but where neither parent is affected, the risk is low. Half of the children of someone with NF1 are also likely to be affected.

More than one independent spontaneous NF1 mutation has been reported in two separate family pedigrees (Klose *et al.* 1999; Upadhyaya *et al.* 2003).

Ultrasound examination in pregnancy is not usually informative, but can identify severe malformation in high-risk cases (McEwing *et al.* 2006).

NF1 is an unusually large gene that has introns coding for several other genes within it. Its protein product, neurofibromin, was identified in 1990 (Cawthon *et al.* 1990; Wallace *et al.* 1990), and the coding sequence detailed some three years later (Viskochil, White and Cawthon 1993).

A large number of genetic variants and types of defect have been described that interfere with the production of neurofibromin, but none in more than a small percentage of families studied (Ars *et al.* 2003). The majority interfere with mRNA splicing (Ars *et al.* 2000, 2003; Messiaen *et al.* 2000, 2001).

Neurofibromin activates ras GTPase, limiting cell proliferation and thereby suppressing tumour development (Cichowski and Jacks 2001; Gottfried, Amos, Parry and Bale 2006; Trovo-Marqui and Tajara 2006; Viskochil 1999; Zhu and Parada 2001). Recent work suggests that this is in tandem with c-kit activation in mast cells. (See Yang *et al.* 2008 under 'Animal models' below.) Preliminary evidence suggests that interfering with this process (using imatinib mesylate (Gleevec)) can effectively limit the development of neurofibromas.

Neurofibromin is involved in a range of other metabolic processes (see, for example, Gottfried, Viskochil, Fults and Couldwell 2006; Ismat, Xu, Lu and Epstein 2006 2006; Trovo-Marqui and Tajara 2006; Yohay 2006).

DIAGNOSTIC CRITERIA: The clinical criteria for NF1 were broadly agreed upon in an NIH conference statement (NIH Consensus Development Conference 1988).

Two or more of the following need to be met for clinical diagnosis:

- six or more café-au-lait patches > 15mm in adults and > 5mm in children

- two or more neurofibromas or one plexiform neurofibroma

- axillary or groin freckling

- Lisch nodules (iris hamartomas)
- optic pathway glioma
- a distinctive osseous lesion such as sphenoid wing dysplasia or thinning of the long bone cortex, with or without pseudoarthrosis
- a first-degree relative with NF1.

(From Gutmann *et al.* 1997)

GENETIC INFORMATION:

Genetic testing: The steps involved in detection of mutations in those who meet the clinical criteria for NF1 are well described (Messiaen *et al.* 2000, 2001):

1. identifying a truncated version of the neurofibromin protein
2. FISH testing for complete NF1 deletion
3. RT-PCR and Southern blot analysis to detect intragenic deletions
4. sequencing to identify large-scale rearrangements.

Large or complete NF1 gene deletions are seen in one to four cases (Kluwe *et al.* 2004) and can be assessed using various techniques (Wimmer *et al.* 2006). These are tested for when suspected clinically in light of maternal transmission, early appearance of numbers of cutaneous neurofibromas and associated learning disability (Mensink *et al.* 2006; Spiegel *et al.* 2005; Tonsgard *et al.* 1997; Upadhyaya *et al.* 1998; Venturin *et al.* 2004).

IS THERE A LINK BETWEEN NF1 AND ASD?

- A link between neurofibromatosis type 1 and ASD has been suggested since 1988 when, in a prescient paper, Susan Folstein and Michael Rutter suggested that it was likely that more than one genetic factor might be implicated in the pathogenesis of autism, and that neurofibromatosis type 1 and fragile-X were amongst such factors.

- Mouridsen *et al.* (1992) reviewed 341 children seen in two Danish clinics over a 25-year period but could only identify a single case of NF1 in their series. Their conclusion was that, at 0.3 per cent, although the two conditions could co-occur, they did not do so in a way suggesting any aetiological relationship.

- Christopher Gillberg (1992) reviewed 59 cases of infantile autism and noted the occurrence of a number of known genetic conditions including NF1 in this group.

- Williams and Hersh (1998) provide a brief report on three cases co-morbid for NF1 and autism.

- Mbarek *et al.* (2000) suggest that, although NF1 is a rare factor in ASD, it is still some 150 times more common than in the general population. This estimate needs to be revised down considerably on current ASD prevalence figures, but perhaps a ten-fold increased likelihood of co-occurrence seems realistic. From screening a French series of 85 ASD cases and 213 controls, this group identify one specific allele (allele 5 of the GXAlu marker) which appears to be specific to ASD/NF1 cases, and which is associated with a severe clinical picture with poorer motor development and muscle tone in 4.3 per cent of their ASD cases. An attempt to replicate this finding in a South Carolina series of 204 cases (Plank *et al.* 2001) failed to find any GXAlu cases in a group of 204 ASD patients or in 200 controls. Similarly, Marui *et al.* (2004a) failed to find evidence of this six-allele repeat polymorphism in a Japanese ASD cohort.

- Lauritsen, Mors, Morstensen and Ewald (2002), in their review of medical co-morbidities, suggest that the literature states anywhere between 0.2 per cent and 14 per cent of ASD cases are found to have NF1, and note that Mouridsen *et al.* (1992) had suggested a weighted probability of 1.8 per cent.

Some concerns have been voiced concerning the current tendency to consider cases such as individuals with NF1 and other neurogenetic conditions (fragile-X, tuberous sclerosis) and cases of 'idiopathic autism' as a single specific syndrome. (See, for example, Benaron 2003.)

Marui *et al.* (2004b), although failing to confirm the link found by Mbarek *et al.* (2000), did identify differences in NF1 allele distribution in 74 autistic subjects compared to 122 controls, suggesting a pattern that could be consistent with increased susceptibility.

A paper from the Czech Republic (Havlovicova *et al.* 2007) describes a young girl with atypical autism (assessed on the ADI-R), hyperactivity, distractibility, learning disability (IQ 45), mild dysmorphic features, growth retardation and epilepsy. Genetic testing showed her to have a mosaic ring chromosome 17.

DIFFERENTIAL DIAGNOSIS:
In someone presenting with a physical phenotype consistent with NF1 and a behavioural phenotype consistent with ASD, several alternative possibilities should be investigated if an NF1 defect is excluded. The conditions most likely to present in this way are:

- other ASD-linked phacomatoses – Bannayan-Riley-Ruvalcaba syndrome [15]; hypomelanosis of Ito [42]; Proteus syndrome [62]; and tuberous sclerosis [73] – Noonan syndrome [52]; LEOPARD syndrome (a condition genetically related to Noonan syndrome but with skin pigment changes); and Klippel-Trenaunay-Weber syndrome (an overgrowth condition genetically related to Proteus syndrome)

- piebaldism (typically presenting with areas of cutaneous pigmentation and depigmentation, hyperpigmented borders of the unpigmented areas, a white forelock and white hair down the midline of the body, sleep difficulties and gastrointestinal problems). This condition, which results from a defect in the gene for endothelin-3 and has a fairly clear physical and behavioural phenotype, should also be considered. Piebaldism has not yet been reported in the literature on ASD, but to date several such cases have been seen by the present author.

A number of conditions not linked to date to ASD symptomology can also present with an NF1 physical phenotype, in particular:

- phacomatoses with no known link to ASD – Sturge-Weber syndrome (Rodríguez-Bujaldón, Vázquez-Bayo, Jiménez-Puya and Moreno-Giménez 2008); neurofibromatosis type 2 (Nowak 2007)

- homozygosity for one of the genes for hereditary non-polyposis colon cancer (HNPCC/Lynch syndrome) caused by a defect in MSH2 (Østergaard, Sunde and Okkels 2005; Raevaara *et al.* 2004)

- Schwannomatosis (MacCollin *et al.* 2003)

- multiple café-au-lait spots (Hoo and Shrimpton 2005; Riccardi 1980)

- McCune-Albright syndrome (Chanson, Salenave and Orcel 2007; Zacharin 2007)

- multiple endocrine neoplasia type 2B

- multiple lipomatosis

- juvenile hyaline fibromatosis

- congenital generalized fibromatosis
- Weaver syndrome [89]
- multiple intradermal naevi.

A number of cases have been reported with an NF1 genotype but without an NF1 or NF1-like phenotype.

- A two-year-old boy presented with encephalocraniocutaneous lipomatosis (ECCL/Fishman syndrome) (Legius *et al.* 1995).

- There have been reports of three families with multiple spinal neurofibromas but without the café-au-lait spots characteristic of NF1 (Kaufmann *et al.* 2001; Kluwe, Tatagibam Funsterer and Mautner 2003).

- Finally, there has been a report of a man with an isolated optic glioma, but no other diagnostic features (Buske *et al.* 1999).

Around one in 19 cases present with a phenotype which is similar to Noonan syndrome [52] (Colley, Donnai and Evans 1996) but with an NF1 genotype (De Luca *et al.* 2005; Huffmeier *et al.* 2006). The genetic bases for this association are not fully understood, and more than one mechanism has been identified (Bertola *et al.* 2005; Carey 1998).

A small 3-bp in-frame deletion of exon 17 results in the typical café-au-lait skin lesions seen in NF1, but without the other phenotypic features (Upadhyaya *et al.* 2007).

MANAGEMENT AND TREATMENT: Because of the wide variation in presenting phenotype and clinical progression seen in NF1, there is no simple approach to assessment and monitoring, which are largely dictated by individual clinical presentation.

Routine initial evaluation should include a standard medical history, paying particular attention to family history and clinical features of NF1; a detailed physical examination with particular attention to the skin; and assessment of vision and optic nerve function, central nervous system, skeleton and cardiovascular system. A neurodevelopmental assessment is also recommended. Some authorities also recommend EEG, brain MRI, body X-rays, brainstem auditory evoked potentials (BAEPs) and audiography (Riccardi 1999). Aspects that show abnormality should be the subjects of regular review.

The cosmetic aspects and physical inconvenience of NF1 are often the most distressing factors for those affected (Wolkenstein *et al.* 2000).

Response to surgical removal of plexiform neurofibromas can be poor, and these have a tendency to recur (Gottfried, Viskochil, Fults and Couldwell, 2006; Kim *et al.* 2005; Packer and Rosser 2002; Packer *et al.* 2002).

The development of several of the associated lesions seen in NF1 is often slower than would otherwise be expected. This is true of optic gliomas and of brainstem and cerebellar gliomas, and complicates the approach to management. A static picture or slower progression of optic gliomas is well documented in several series (Czyzyk, Jozwiak, Roszkowski and Schwartz 2003; Rosser and Packer 2002; Singhal *et al.* 2002), and spontaneous regression has been noted in a number of papers (Parsa *et al.* 2001; Perilongo *et al.* 1999; Rosser and Packer 2002; Zizka, Elias and Jakubec 2001). This complicates decisions concerning best management (Sylvester, Drohan and Sergott 2006). Similarly, brain stem and cerebellar astrocytomas develop less rapidly than normal (Korf 2000; Pollack, Shultz and Mulvihill 1996; Rosser and Packer 2002; Vinchon, Soto-Ares, Ruchoux and Dhellemmes 2000). There are also reports of spontaneous regression (Leisti, Pyhtinen and Poyhonen 1996; Rosser and Packer 2002; Schmandt, Packer, Vezina and Jane 2000).

The number and size of neurofibromas may increase during pregnancy (Dugoff and Sujansky 1996). This is thought to be due to increased production of lysophosphatidic acid through the pregnancy, a factor that increases the migration and survival of Schwann cells (Nebesio *et al.* 2007). Hypertension may begin during or be exacerbated by pregnancy.

The use of radiation therapy has been found to accelerate the development of malignant peripheral nerve sheath tumours (Evans D.G. *et al.* 2002; Sharif *et al.* 2006).

Therapies under investigation: A number of medical treatments for plexiform and spinal neurofibromas are under investigation (Liebermann and Korf 1999; Packer *et al.* 2002; Packer and Rosser 2002). These include *pirfenidone*, which inhibits collagen synthesis and blocks fibroblast proliferation (Babovic-Vuksanovic *et al.* 2006), *tifiparnib*, which interferes with RAS protein function (Widemann *et al.* 2006), and *surgical intervention* (Gottfried, Viskochil, Fults and Couldwell 2006).

The diffuse plexiform neurofibromas that can be found on the face have in some cases been shown to respond to treatment with radiofrequency therapy (Baujat *et al.* 2006).

There has been considerable interest in the possible use of statins in treating the cognitive difficulties seen in NF1. Preliminary published results show no benefit (Krab *et al.* 2008).

A useful listing of ongoing clinical therapeutic trials can be found on the Children's Tumour Foundation website at www.ctf.org

ANIMAL MODELS: One early mouse model showed that the learning deficits and alterations in GABA-ergic function seen

in *Nf1* (+/−) mice can be reversed by a farnesyl-transferase inhibitor that decreases Ras function (Costa *et al.* 2002).

A recent paper (Yang *et al.* 2008) has considerably advanced understanding of the mechanism of formation and growth of plexiform neurofibromas through the interaction of NF1 deficient Schwann cells and NF1+/− mast cells, and a method for containing their growth. Formation could be induced by transplantation with NF1+/− bone marrow, while the growth could be reduced by treatment with Gleevec, which inhibits production of c-kit (a mast cell factor that is known to accelerate tumour growth). In a single human clinical case, Gleevec was shown to reduce the size of a tumour which was obstructing the airway of a patient and not suitable for surgical excision.

Neurofibromin has been found to regulate the ERK signalling pathways, which have an effect on GABA release. GABA release has an important role in hippocampal long-term potentiation and learning. NF1 deletions interfere with this process in a manner that could explain the learning problems that sometimes accompany neurofibromatosis 1 (Cui *et al.* 2008).

A further recent mouse model found reduced body weight related to reduced size of the anterior pituitary gland and reduced levels of neurofibrin in the hypothalamus (Hegedus *et al.* 2008).

'Understanding NF1', a resource about neurofibromatosis 1 for parents, patients and carers, can be accessed at www.understandingnf1.org.

52.

Noonan syndrome

GENE LOCI: SOS1 at 2p22–p21; PTPN11 at 12q24.1; KRAS at 12p12.1

KEY ASD REFERENCES: Ghaziuddin, Bolyard and Alessi 1994; Paul, Cohen and Volkmar 1983

SUMMARY: The first case description of Noonan syndrome may have been that of a 20-year-old German male described in the late nineteenth century (Kobylinski 1883). The condition is named after Jacqueline Anne Noonan, an American paediatric cardiologist, who together with Dorothy Ehmke first described the condition in six boys and three girls in a conference abstract in 1963. All cases were of short stature, with pulmonary stenosis, hypertelorism and abnormal skeletal development. In 1968 Noonan described 19 cases with this clinical phenotype. They were reported as resembling Turner's syndrome, but without the obvious karyotype. The term 'Noonan syndrome' was first used in a conference abstract published in 1965 (Opitz, Summitt, Smith and Sarto 1965).

For a historical overview of our understanding of the condition, see Noonan (2002).

HOW COMMON IS NOONAN SYNDROME?

The best current estimates of prevalence are one in 1,000–2,500 (Sharland, Burch, McKenna and Paton 1992; Tartaglia and Gelb 2005).

Noonan syndrome appears equally common in males and females.

MAIN CLINICAL FEATURES: Feeding difficulties are common in early life (Sharland *et al.* 1992). Low–normal short stature is typically reported (Noonan, Raaijmakers and Hall 2003), but growth is slower than normal. Ocular abnormalities (Lee, Kelly and Sharland 1992), congenital heart defects (typically pulmonary stenosis, but more complex problems are reported – see Ishizawa *et al.* 1996), and ECG abnormalities are common, even without apparent structural defects (Sharland *et al.* 1992).

Physical characteristics include:

- broad or webbed neck (*pterygium colli*)
- unusual chest shape with protrusion of the upper part and intrusion of the lower portion – sometimes called a 'shield-shaped' chest
- apparently low-set nipples
- cryptorchidism in males
- characteristic facies which become less obvious with age (Allanson *et al.* 1985), including low hairline, epicanthic folds, low-set, backward-turned ears, wide-spaced blue or blue-green eyes and small lower jaw
- café-au-lait spots noted in some cases.

Blood clotting problems, easy bruising and lymphatic dysplasias are common features (Sharland, Patton *et al.* 1992). Renal problems are seen in around ten per cent of cases (George *et al.* 1993). Speech difficulties are seen in around two-thirds of cases, but respond well to speech therapy (Allanson 1987).

Effects on male sexual development are varied. In girls, onset of menstruation tends to be late, but fertility appears to be normal (Sharland *et al.* 1992).

A study of 48 children with Noonan syndrome found a mean IQ of 84, with 25 per cent having learning difficulties (Lee *et al.* 2005). Approximately 50 per cent showed evidence of motor clumsiness on the Stott-Moyes-Henderson Test of Motor Impairment – Revised (TOMI-R) (Henderson 1987). Ten to fifteen per cent were placed in special education (Sharland *et al.* 1992; van der Burgt *et al.* 1999).

Lee *et al.* (2005), using several well-validated scales, were unable to identify any consistent behavioural phenotype associated with Noonan syndrome.

GENETIC TESTING AND HERITABILITY: Standard karyotyping gives normal results. On molecular genetic testing, 50 per cent of cases test positive for PTPN11 abnormalities at 12q24.1, ten per cent for abnormalities of SOS1 at 2p22–p21, and five per cent for abnormalities of KRAS at 12p12.1 (Schubbert *et al.* 2006). Tests for all three sites are available on a clinical basis and would be screened for, based on clinical phenotype.

Inheritance is autosomal dominant. An affected parent is identified in 35–40 per cent of cases and the rest arise from *de novo* mutations, with no family history. A child of someone with Noonan syndrome has a 50 per cent risk of being similarly affected.

Where the condition has been inherited, in all cases reported to date, inheritance has been from the father (Tartaglia *et al.* 2004), predominantly to male offspring, and correlated with older paternal age than in other Noonan cases.

Where a mutation has been found in the presenting case, parents should be screened, and if a parent tests positive, siblings should also be screened, as they will be at 50 per cent risk. The children of the individual will also be at 50 per cent risk of being similarly affected.

IS THERE A LINK BETWEEN NOONAN SYNDROME AND ASD? Paul, Cohen and Volkmar (1983) reported on a boy with Noonan syndrome who had a severe learning disability, communication disorder, limited social interest and motor stereotypies and was described as having autistic features.

Ghaziuddin, Bolyard and Alessi (1994) describe Noonan syndrome comorbidity with mild learning disability and ASD.

As few cases have been described with both the Noonan syndrome phenotype and ASD, but as these predate genetic screening, it is unclear whether there is an association with any of the three Noonan syndrome susceptibility sites. At the present time there are no clear phenotypic features to distinguish the three genotypes found in Noonan syndrome.

Although Noonan syndrome appears in many review papers on genetic syndromes associated with ASD, it is difficult to tell from the cases reported to date whether the association is greater than chance.

DIFFERENTIAL DIAGNOSIS: The principal differential diagnoses are Aarskog syndrome [8]; neurofibromatosis type 1 [51]; Turner syndrome [74]; and Williams syndrome [77].

LEOPARD syndrome (**L**entigines, **E**CG abnormalities, **O**cular hypertelorism, **P**ulmonary stenosis, **A**bnormal genitalia, **R**etardation of growth, **D**eafness) overlaps clinically with Noonan syndrome and has been shown to result from a PTPN11 mutation (Digilio *et al.* 2002; Legius *et al.* 2002).

Three other rare conditions show phenotypic overlap:

- cardiofaciocutaneous (CFC) syndrome (Rodriguez-Viciana *et al.* 2006), which has been linked to defects in the MAPKinase pathway

- Watson syndrome (Allanson *et al.* 1991)

- Costello syndrome (Troger *et al.* 2003), which has been linked to the HRAS proto-oncogene (Aoki *et al.* 2005).

For reviews of the common pathways involved in these conditions, see Gelb and Tartaglia (2006) and Tidyman and Rauen (2008).

MANAGEMENT AND TREATMENT: In view of the multiple organ systems that can be involved, after initial diagnosis baseline assessments of growth, cardiac and renal function, vision, hearing and central nervous system are required.

The cardiovascular abnormalities in Noonan syndrome can be managed as for other people with the same heart problems. Summaries of the surgical cardiac issues in Noonan syndrome are reviewed in Formigari *et al.* (2008).

Results of growth hormone supplementation studies show that this is an effective approach to increasing adult height in Noonan syndrome (Noordam *et al.* 2008; Ogawa *et al.* 2004).

In view of the blood and liver problems that are often seen, medications that affect blood clotting should only be used under medical advice.

ANIMAL MODELS: No behavioural models of Noonan syndrome have yet been published.

To date, models have been developed to study the embryological development of knockdown *Shp2* zebrafish models of the region syntenic to the human PTPN11 gene (Jopling, van Geemen and den Hertog 2007). Mouse models have also been developed to look at the effects of *Ptpn11* defects on the development of the heart (Nakamura *et al.* 2007).

53.

NAPDD

GENE LOCUS: not known

KEY ASD REFERENCES: Page 2000; Page, Yu, Fontanesi and Nyhan 1997

SUMMARY: The term NAPDD stands for 'nucleotidase-associated pervasive developmental disorder'. The first use of the term appears in a paper by Page, Yu, Fontanesi and Nyhan (1997).

A nucleotidase is an enzyme that catalyses the hydrolysis of a nucleotide into a nucleoside and a phosphate. In this case, the affected nucleotidase catalyses purines and pyrimidines.

NAPDD may constitute the basis for a hypouricosuric form of 'purine autism'. Hyperuricosuric forms (with elevated rather than lowered uric acid and urate levels) have also been documented (Page and Coleman 2000).

HOW COMMON IS NAPDD? At the time of writing, the frequency of this condition is unknown. To date it has only been reported by one clinical group working in Southern California.

MAIN CLINICAL FEATURES: A variety of behavioural and physical features have been reported to characterize those with NAPDD: extreme hyperactivity, impulsiveness, absent or greatly delayed speech, abnormal social interaction, seizures, ataxia and frequent infections.

IS THERE A LINK BETWEEN NAPDD AND ASD? By definition, all NAPDD cases fulfil criteria for ASD. However, the prevalence of NAPDD within the ASD population is not established.

The first paper (Page, Yu, Fontanesi and Nyhan 1997) described four cases, and the review of metabolic factors in autism (Page 2000) documents a number of further cases, but without detailed case information. No independent reports of cases have so far been published in the literature.

Metabolic differences in cytosolic 5' nucleotidase activity have been reported in this group (Trifilio and Page 2000). It is possible that this metabolic difference is a causally sufficient factor in ASD.

DIFFERENTIAL DIAGNOSIS: The principal differential diagnoses are other ASD conditions with overlapping symptomology such as Angelman syndrome [11]; CATCH22 [18]; JDPLA [28]; and fragile-X [35].

MANAGEMENT AND TREATMENT: NAPDD is potentially important in view of the apparent response to intervention.

In a small double-blinded, placebo-controlled trial of uridine in four cases, remarkable improvement in speech and behaviour were reported together with a decrease in both seizure activity and frequency of infection. There was rapid regression on all parameters when on placebo (Page, Yu, Fontanesi and Nyhan 1997). In a review of treatment approaches Page (2000) notes a further eight clinical cases with varying degrees of benefit from uridine. The way in which uridine operates is currently unclear. It could be through its effects on dopamine receptor function.

A more recent single case report of treatment over a two-year period with reversals resulting in behavioural deterioration has also been published (Page and Mosely 2002).

In his review, Page (2000) notes other treatments to have been of some benefit, including intravenous immunoglobulin and a combined treatment with ribose, UMP (uridine-5 monophosphate) and CMO (cetyl myristoleate). These are commented on *passim* with no referencing.

As the 5°-nucleotidases act to regulate nucleotide and drug metabolism, the implications for various aspects of management may be fairly broad-ranging (Hunsucker, Mitchell and Spychala 2005).

ANIMAL MODELS: There are no specific animal models of NAPDD.

54.

Ornithine carbamyltransferase deficiency (OCTD)

aka • ornithine transcarbamylase deficiency (OTD)

GENE LOCUS: Xp21.1

KEY ASD REFERENCE: Gorker and Tuzun 2005

SUMMARY: Ornithine carbamyltransferase is a nuclear-encoded mitochondrial matrix enzyme on the short arm of the X chromosome that codes for the second enzyme of the urea cycle. It is the most common X-linked disorder of the urea cycle. The principal consequence of this condition is an inability to metabolize the amino acid alanine from protein in the diet.

The molecular basis to the clinical variation observed in the presentation of ornithine carbamyltransferase deficiency (OCTD) is beginning to be unravelled, and shows the likely operation of multifactorial causes, rather than the operation of a single gene abnormality. (See Tuchman, McCullough and Yudkoff 2000.)

HOW COMMON IS OCTD? The best current estimate of prevalence is that OCTD occurs in one in 40,000 of the general population (Wraith 2001).

MAIN CLINICAL FEATURES: The clinical presentation of OCTD is varied. Boys with a full mutation can present with anything from neonatal failure to thrive, encephalopathy and severe hyperammonaemia, to chance asymptomatic cases detected in adulthood (Matsuda *et al.* 1996). Boys with later presentation typically present with disturbed behaviour, vomiting and drowsiness (Drogari and Leonard 1988).

In female carriers, the severity of the phenotype is dependent on the extent of inactivation of the affected X chromosome in liver cells, but appears to be independent of peripheral X chromosome status (Yorifuji *et al.* 1998). The extent of hyperammonaemia is correlated with the level of X inactivation of the affected chromosome, in liver but not in peripheral cells.

Well over 300 mutations to the OCTD gene have now been reported (Yamaguchi *et al.* 2006), and OCTD mosaicism in males has been reported (Maddalena, Sosnoski, Berry and Nussbaum 1988). It has been known for a number of years that this can present with 'psychotic' behaviour in response to elevated protein intake (DiMagno, Lowe, Snodgrass and Jones 1986). However, the prevalence of this is at present not known.

IS THERE A LINK BETWEEN OCTD AND ASD? A single case report to date details the case of a girl with PDD-NOS (pervasive developmental disorder – not otherwise specified) together with aggression and hyperactivity (Gorker and Tuzun 2005). The girl was found to have an ornithine carbamyltransferase deficiency together with an arginase deficiency.

DIFFERENTIAL DIAGNOSIS: A number of other inborn errors affect urea cycle metabolism, but to date only one, argininosuccinic acid synthetase, has been reported in association with psychiatric sequelae, in which postpartum psychotic features have been reported (Enns *et al.* 2005).

Other possible factors that can have similar presentation are vascular liver damage and viral liver infection (Summar and Tuchman 2003).

MANAGEMENT AND TREATMENT: Useful reviews of treatment can be found in Grompe, Jones and Caskey (1990) and Wraith (2001). Treatment response in males presenting neonatally (typically to protein restriction and citrulline supplementation) are uniformly poor to date. In girls and in later presenting boys, results are more optimistic. Accurate diagnosis and rapid treatment can lead to good recovery from acute encephalopathy (Mak *et al.* 2007).

One recent paper (Swarts, Leisegang, Owen and Henderson 2007) describes an ornithine transcarbamylase deficiency in a 20-month-old boy with XXY syndrome [3]. He showed clinical improvement on a low-protein diet together with benzoate and phenylbutyrate.

In the ASD case reported by Gorker and Tuzun (2005), the girl was treated with a combination of protein restriction, coupled with sodium benzoate and arginine supplementation. After one year of treatment, her hyperactivity and autistic symptoms had resolved.

ANIMAL MODELS: The closest parallel to the human disorder is seen in the OTCD 'sparse fur' mouse (DeMars, LeVan, Trend and Russell 1976). No studies have been published of the behavioural phenotype (if there is any distinguishing behavioural profile) associated with the gene mutation.

55.

Oculocutaneous albinism (OCA)

GENE LOCI:

- type 1 (TYR): 11q14.3
- type 2 (OCA2): 15q11.2–12, 16q24.3

- type 3 (TYRP1): 9p23
- type 4 (MAT P): 5p13.3

KEY ASD REFERENCES: Bakare and Ikegwuonu 2008; Ornitz, Guthrie and Farley 1977; Rogawski, Funderburk and Cederbaum 1978

SUMMARY: OCA is one of a number of 'inborn errors of metabolism' first described in 1908 by Sir Archibald Garrod (Garrod 1909). It is an error in the production and/ or distribution of melanin, primarily in the skin, hair and visual system of the affected individual. Melanin is produced from the essential amino acid tyrosine.

A recent review of OCA can be found in Grønskov, Ek and Brondum-Nielsen (2007), and a review more specifically of OCA2 in King and Oetting (2007).

HOW COMMON IS OCA? There are four main forms of OCA. In total, the best estimate is that the various forms of OCA have a cumulative population prevalence of 7.15 per 100,000 (Orphanet 2009). OCA2 specifically is reported to occur in between one in 38,000 and one in 40,000 of the population worldwide. There is a markedly higher prevalence in African and African-American populations, being found in between one in 1,500 and one in 8,000 (Lund *et al.* 1997; Spritz, Fukai, Holmes and Luande 1995; Stevens, Ramsay and Jenkins 1997; Stevens, van Beukering, Jenkins and Ramsay 1995).

MAIN CLINICAL FEATURES: OCA is characterized by reduced skin, iris and hair pigmentation, and a number of specific ocular changes. The iris is light coloured – typically blue or grey, but may be brown. Nystagmus and increased translucency of the iris are seen. The fovea is hypoplastic, resulting in reduced visual acuity (Creel, O'Donnell and Witkop 1978). A number of features are due to the misrouting of the optic nerves through the optic chiasma, with alternating strabismus, a consequent reduction in stereoscopic vision, and altered visual evoked potentials (Bouzas, Caruso, Drews-Bankiewicz and Kaiser-Kupfer 1994).

In OCA2, there is some degree of pigmentation that develops with age, while in the type 1 (TYR) form there is complete lack of pigmentation.

Those with OCA have normal levels of intelligence, normal life expectancy and normal fertility.

IS THERE A LINK BETWEEN OCA AND ASD? The first mention of OCA in ASD is in a paper by Ornitz, Guthrie and Farley (1977). They noted OCA in one four-year-old boy in a retrospective analysis of early development in a series of 74 young autistic children.

Rogawski, Funderburk and Cederbaum (1978) published a paper detailing the association in two further autistic boys.

In 2007, Robert DeLong reported a link between GABA(A) receptor differences, parent-of-origin effects and OCA in some cases of ASD.

Bakare and Ikegwuonu (2008) reported on a 13-year-old Nigerian boy with ASD who clearly presents with the OCA2 form.

It seems likely that the cases of OCA reported in association with ASD are type 2. This form results from a lack of a tyrosine transporter referred to as polypeptide P, and not of tyrosinase, the enzyme that converts tyrosine to melanin (and which is missing in the type 1 form).

This suggests a possible common mechanism for the development of ASD in OCA, Angelman and Prader-Willi syndromes and hypomelanosis of Ito, due to a common genetic mechanism in the 15q11 region. It is possible that the common mechanism involves dysfunction of the GABA A receptor alpha-5 polypeptide that has been mapped to 15q11.2–q12 and implicated in Angelman and Prader-Willi syndromes (Wagstaff *et al.* 1991) and in OCA2 (DeLong 2007). We will not provide any detail here on types 1, 3 and 4 of OCA, which are reviewed in Grønskov, Ek and Brondum-Nielsen (2007).

DIFFERENTIAL   DIAGNOSIS: Hypomelanosis of Ito [42] and Angelman [11] and Prader-Willi [61] syndromes can all present with hypopigmentation. Each, like OCA2, can result from a 15q11 defect, and all can be found with ASD.

Other conditions which present with hypopigmentation (Hermansky-Pudlak syndrome, Chediak-Higashi syndrome, Griscelli syndrome and Waardenburg syndrome type II) have not been reported in ASD.

MANAGEMENT AND TREATMENT: The principal issues in treatment and ongoing management of OCA2 are twofold. (See Grønskov, Ek and Brondum-Nielsen 2007.)

1. *the skin:* low levels of pigmentation make those affected more prone to sunburn, and could increase the risk of skin cancers without adequate precautions (hats, adequate sunscreen and clothing) to block ultraviolet light.

2. *eye problems:*

   • *lack of iris pigmentation* results in difficulties in coping with bright light. This can be helped with the use of dark glasses or tinted contact lenses

   • *poor visual acuity* because of the poor development of the fovea, visual acuity is typically poor, and corrective glasses are usually required

   • *nystagmus* (oscillating rhythmic eye movements) may improve with contact lenses, or may require surgery to the eye muscles

   • *strabismus* (where the eyes are not focused on the same point) can respond to eye patching to encourage better use of the non-dominant eye.

It is possible that specific GABA receptor-based treatment strategies will be developed that target the biological defect resulting in autism. Such a treatment would be likely to be of benefit in Angelman syndrome, Prader-Willi syndrome and hypomelanosis of Ito, as well as in OCA2 cases.

ANIMAL MODELS: A number of mouse models have been developed for Angelman syndrome and Prader-Willi syndrome that are also possible models for OCA. (See, for example, Gabriel *et al.* 1999; Pagiliardini, Ren, Wevrick and Greer 2005; Stefan *et al.* 2005.)

56.

Orstavik 1997 syndrome

GENE LOCUS: not known at time of writing

KEY ASD REFERENCES: Orstavik *et al.* 1997; Steiner, Guerreiro and Marquis-de-Faria 2003

SUMMARY: The constellation of features reported makes this presentation a candidate for a genetic condition. However, the lack of more detailed biological information and genetic testing makes it impossible to draw any more specific conclusions.

HOW COMMON IS ORSTAVIK 1997 SYNDROME? As to date only one family pedigree has been reported, and a second with a similar presentation has been

Table B56: Features reported in Orstavik 1997 syndrome

	Sister 1	Sister 2
• OFC at birth (cm)	36	34
• birthweight (g)	3,600	2,600
• macrocephaly	from birth and progressive	small at birth but progressive
• psychomotor delay	Yes	Yes
• epilepsy	Yes	Yes
• autistic features	Yes	Yes
• large forehead	Yes	Yes
• short philtrum	Yes	Yes
• bush eyebrows	Yes	Yes
• additional feature		coeliac disease

suggested; coupled with the lack of a known gene marker, prevalence is currently unknown.

This condition has been reported to date in a single family pedigree from Norway, with two affected sisters. There was no associated genotype, but the constellation of features was felt to constitute a previously unrecognized clinical syndrome. Sister 2 died at the age of five years, probably from an epileptic seizure.

Phenotypically similar cases – a pair of eight-year-old female twins and their four-year-old brother – have been noted in one Brazilian clinic series (Steiner, Guerreiro and Marques-de-Faria 2003): both girls fulfilled criteria for autism, and all were noted to be learning disabled. None was noted to have a seizure problem. There remains no gold-standard method of identifying the syndrome.

DIFFERENTIAL DIAGNOSIS: Given the paucity of information, differential diagnosis is difficult. The reported phenotype with macrocephaly and epilepsy suggests that Sotos syndrome [68] should be considered as a potential differential diagnosis.

MANAGEMENT AND TREATMENT: No specific treatment approaches have been developed.

ANIMAL MODELS: As no mechanism is currently known, no animal models have been developed.

57.

Phenylketonuria (PKU)

aka • Folling disease
  • *imbecillitas phenylpyruvica* (historical)
  • *oligophrenica phenylpyruvica* (historical)

GENE LOCUS: 12q24.1

KEY ASD REFERENCES: Baieli *et al.* 2003; Chen and Hsiao 1989; Lowe *et al.* 1980; Miladi *et al.* 1992

SUMMARY: Phenylketonuria is an inborn error of metabolism. The condition was first identified in two affected children in 1934 in Norway by the Scandinavian paediatrician Asbjörn Folling (Folling 1934; see Centerwall and Centerwall 2000). He used a ferric chloride urine test, which normally turns reddish-brown in response to the presence of ketones; the test unexpectedly, and repeatedly on testing, turned green – a previously unrecorded reaction. Subsequent analysis of 20 litres of urine, collected faithfully over several months by the mother of the children, led to identification of the compound causing the effect – phenylpyruvic acid. Folling used the terms *imbecillitas phenylpyruvica* and *oligophrenica phenylpyruvica* to identify the condition. Penrose and Questel suggested the term 'phenylketonuria' in 1937. In 1947 Jervis identified the metabolic problem as an inability to oxidize phenylalanine in order to convert it to tyrosine.

The classic form of PKU is an autosomal recessive condition, with most variation being due to the individual being heterozygous for a mutant allele.

PKU is typically caused by a defect in the gene at 12q24.1, involved in the production of the liver-specific enzyme phenylalanine hydroxylase (PAH). (See, for example, Chao, Hsiao and Su 2001.) Failure to produce phenylalanine hydroxylase results in a problem in metabolizing the amino acid phenylalanine, with a build-up of circulating levels and a condition known as *hyperphenylalaninaemia* (if below a clinical cut-off level for PKU) or *phenylketonuria* (if above this level). Phenylalanine hydroxylase requires a further compound, 6(R)-erythro-5,6,7,8-tetrahydrobiopterin (BH4), to function. PAH mRNA can be detected in some PKU liver biopsy specimens (Guttler and Woo 1986), but is absent in others (Ledley *et al.* 1988).

No phenylalanine hydroxylase activity or immunoreactive protein was detected in the liver of one foetal case of PKU (Ledley *et al.* 1988). Both compounds could be measured in control specimens of similar gestational age.

An early paper speculated that the reason for developmental problems in PKU, rather than hepatic damage, is that phenylpyruvic acid inhibits the action of pyruvate decarboxylase in the brain, thus interfering with myelin formation and nerve cell development (Bowden and McArthur 1972). This model would be consistent with the beneficial effects of LCPUFA supplementation.

In addition to a 12q24.1 gene defect a number of other factors can cause a build-up of phenylalanine (Scriver, Eisensmith, Woo and Kaufman 1994) – for example, GTP cyclohydrolase deficiency; 6-pyruvoyl-tetrahydropterin synthase deficiency; dihydropteridine reductase deficiency; and pterin-4α carbinolamine dehydratase deficiency all typically result in PKU levels of serum phenylalanine, but are unresponsive to a phenylalanine-restricted diet.

The PAH locus was identified as 12q22–q24.1 by in situ hybridization (Woo *et al.* 1984), allowing for reliable prenatal diagnosis.

PKU was the first example of a treatable inborn error of metabolism. 'Classic' PKU is now a rare cause of ASD, but should be considered where neonatal screening may have been missed. ASD is virtually unknown in early detected and early treated PKU. PKU autism provides a clear demonstration of a genetic factor leading to a correctable imbalance which, if not addressed, can lead to ASD. Dietary intervention can produce improvement even after late diagnosis.

Note. Hyperphenylalaninaemia, a milder problem than classical PKU, breeds true in families, with phenylalanine hydroxylase levels around five per cent of normal being found on liver biopsy (Kaufman, Max and

Kang 1975). As many as one in ten infants who have a positive Guthrie test result are hyperphenylalaninaemic, as opposed to having classic PKU, and are not currently considered to require dietary treatment. In the Northern Irish population this is typically (in 70 per cent of cases) associated with one particular mutation, T380M (Zschocke *et al.* 1994).

Guthrie (1996) discusses the introduction of newborn screening for PKU. The first recorded case of a phenylalanine-restricted diet being used to improve the condition of a child with PKU and learning disability is well described in three papers by Bickel and colleagues: Bickel, Gerrard and Hickmans (1953); Bickel, Gerrard and Hickmans (1954); and Bickel (1996), where the results of a phenylalanine-restricted casein hydrolysate feed resulted in dramatic improvement in the status of a girl patient at the University Children's Hospital in Zurich (detected using a ferric chloride test in 1949). Low phenylalanine diets have proved highly successful, but are also unpalatable.

A huge range of over 400 PAH mutation variants have now been reported. Most of these can be reviewed on the PAH Mutation Analysis Consortium Database. (See, for discussion, Hoang, Byck, Prevost and Scriver 1996; Nowacki, Byck, Prevost and Scriver 1997.) A wide range of allelic variants of PKU have been reported. For specific detail on these, the reader should consult the relevant entry in OMIM at www.ncbi.nlm.nih.gov.

The first PKU mutation identified was a single base change in the PAH gene (DiLella *et al.* 1986a, 1986b). Marvit *et al.* (1987) found that the GT-to-AT substitution at the 5-prime splice donor site of intron 12 resulted in the skipping of the preceding exon during RNA splicing. More recently, Chao, Hsiao and Su (2001) identified an intron 11 change which also results in exon

skipping. As techniques are now being developed which partially correct exon skipping in some other conditions such as Duchenne muscular dystrophy [33], identification of this mechanism may prove to have important clinical implications, and could result in strategies that can correct such defects.

A major European collaborative study (Guldberg *et al.* 1998) examined 686 PAH patients from seven centres and looked in more detail at the phenotypic characteristics of 297 functionally hemizygous patients. They were able to demonstrate a close association between the genetic deficit identified and the severity of the resulting clinical phenotype.

HOW COMMON IS PKU? Peculiarities in the ethnic and geographical distribution of PKU have been noted. The condition is rare in Ashkenazi Jewish populations (Centerwall and Neff 1961; Cohen B.E., Bodonyi and Szeinberg 1961). It occurs in one in 100,000 of the Finnish population (Guldberg *et al.* 1995). In Ireland, the rate is quoted as one in 4,500; in Scotland, one in 5,550; and in Turkey, the highest reported rate, one in 2,600 (Smith M. 2006). In western Poland the prevalence is one in 5,000 (Jaruzelska *et al.* 1991). In the USA incidence is around one in 8,000, and in Switzerland one in 16,000 (DiLella *et al.* 1986b). From ten years of newborn-screening data collected in Maryland, Hofman, Steel, Kazazian and Valle (1991) concluded that PKU affects some one in 50,000 US Black nationals. This is one-third of the rate seen in Caucasians.

The gene abnormalities which manifest PKU also vary – 80 per cent of Chinese and Japanese cases would appear to be caused by the same haplotype 4 PKU defects (Daiger *et al.* 1989b), while in European PKU a wider variety of mechanisms are prevalent (Daiger *et al.* 1989a). The range of PAH mutant alleles also varies markedly in Turkish families, compared to those from northern European countries (Stuhrmann, Riess, Monch and Kurdoglu 1989).

The wide variation in mutations responsible for PAH suggests strongly that the evolution of these mutations arose after divergence of the different racial groups (Eisensmith *et al.* 1992). One detailed study established that the major haplotypes associated with severe PKU in Caucasian populations are not seen in the Polynesian population (Hertzberg *et al.* 1989).

Historically in the UK, a large proportion of those with PKU are from families who derive from Ireland and the West of Scotland (Carter and Woolf 1961), areas that are thought to have the highest prevalence of PKU. There is a great diversity of PAH causing mutations in the UK populations (Tyfield *et al.* 1997). Some of the mutations seen in the Celtic population of Ireland and Western Scotland are consistent with those found in Norwegian families (Zschocke, Mallory, Eiken and Nevin 1997). Whether this indicates an influence of Celtic mutations on the Norwegian population or of Viking mutations on the Celtic population has been the subject of much debate (Saugstad 1975a, 1975b; Zschocke, Mallory, Eiken and Nevin 1997). A similarly elevated prevalence is reported in the Lithuanian population, arising from a different origin (Eisensmith *et al.* 1992).

In a Kuwaiti series (Teebi *et al.* 1987), seven cases of PKU were identified in a residential population of 451 learning disabled people (1.9 per cent of that population).

MAIN CLINICAL FEATURES: It is well known that the cognitive profiles of those with PKU reflect their level of dietary control, with control at age two years being

a reasonable predictor of later IQ. (See, for example, Griffiths *et al.* 2000.)

In a study comparing ten boys and ten girls who were off-diet but early treated PKU patients at age 11, then later at 14, compared to 20 age-, sex- and IQ-matched controls (Weglage *et al.* 1999), initial results showed a correlation between neuropsychological performance and blood phenylalanine levels. Follow-up testing, although showing continued elevated levels, found that the initial deficits recorded in the PKU cases had decreased, indicating that central nervous system vulnerability to elevated PKU seems to diminish over time.

There is evidence that later diagnosis and poorer dietary control are associated with significant reductions in the volume of motor and premotor cortex and thalamus (Pérez-Dueñas *et al.* 2006).

Cases of PKU who are unresponsive to low phenylalanine diet and who develop neurological sequelae have been reported for several decades (Danks 1978). The mechanisms, typically involving BH4 deficiency, have slowly been unravelled (Dhond, Ardouin, Hayte and Farriaux 1981). BH4 (tetradrobiopterin) is one of a group of compounds known as pterins that are cofactors in the catalysis of enzymes.

BH4 supplementation: BH4 deficiency both causes severe developmental problems *and* responds to supplementation. It should be screened for in all neonates who show persistent levels of phenylalanine elevation unresponsive to diet (Smith M. 2006).

A study of BH4 in the treatment of PKU (Matalon *et al.* 2004) produced positive responses to oral supplementation in 21 of 36 (58.3 per cent) cases. A single daily dose of 10 mg/kg resulted in a reduction of over 30 per cent in blood phenylalanine levels. Treatment response was greatest in those patients who had PAH mutations involving the BH4 binding domains. (BH4 is able to prevent the rapid breakdown of the PAH variants produced by a number of the milder PKU and phenylalaninaemic variants (Pey *et al.* 2004).)

It is interesting that pterin levels are also reported as elevated in the ASD population (Harrison and Pheasant 1995; Messahel *et al.* 1998), and there is a literature on the use of BH4 in the treatment of individuals with ASD.

An open clinical study found marked-to-moderate clinical improvement in 52/97 ASD cases on dosages of 1–3mg/kg/day, with significantly improved social, language and cognitive functioning, with follow-up over a period of up to two years (Takesada *et al.* 1992).

A further study has reported improvements in social functioning and eye contact in a (N=6) group of three- to five-year-olds treated with BH4 over a three-month period and monitored with standardized measures (the Griffiths Developmental Scales and the Parental Satisfaction Survey) (Fernell *et al.* 1997).

There is some preliminary evidence from one small double-blind, randomized, controlled trial (N=12) for significant benefits in social interaction from BH4 supplementation in children who had lowered pre-treatment levels of BH4

cerebrospinal fluid (CSF) (Danfors *et al.* 2005).

Tyrosine: H4 acts as a co-factor in the conversion of phenylalanine into tyrosine. It is also essential in the regulation of tyrosine and tryptophan hydroxylase, and involved in the rate-limiting steps in the production of the neurotransmitters dopamine, norepinephrine, epinephrine and serotonin (Pearl, Capp, Novotny and Gibson 2005).

There is a clear association between tyrosine levels and phenylalanine metabolism, and low tyrosine levels in PKU may impact on neurotransmitter levels. This is well illustrated in one recent study of PKU plasma tyrosine levels (Hanley *et al.* 2000) – see Table B57.1.

Disturbances to tyrosine levels are reported in ASD. However, both elevated (Aldred, Moore, Fitzgerald and Waring 2003) and lowered (Arnold, Hyman, Mooney and Kirby 2003) plasma levels have been reported, and to date no attempt has been made to link these findings either to genetic factors, or to the severity of ASD. It would be interesting to know if the BH4 responsive cases had abnormal tyrosine levels.

BH4 responsiveness seems to characterize a high proportion of those patients @50 per cent with mild hyperphenylalaninaemia

Table B57.1: Plasma tyrosine levels in PKU

	Non-fasting plasma tyrosine level	No.
• classical PKU	41.1 micromol/litre	99
• mild PKU	53.3 micromol/litre	26
• mild hyperphenylalaninaemia	66.6 micromol/litre	35
• non-PKU controls (hospital data)	64.0 micromol/litre	102
• private practice volunteers	69.1 micromol/litre	58
• literature values for infants, children and adolescents	64–78.8 micromol/litre	

(elevated levels of phenylalanine but below the clinical cut-off for PKU), or with mild phenylketonuria (above the clinical cut-off level but at the low end of the clinical distribution). Some 87 per cent of cases in one series (N=31) showed lowered blood phenylalanine levels; while none of the seven classical PKU cases reported derived benefit from BH4 (Muntau *et al.* 2002). Erlandsen and Stevens (2001) suggested that BH4-responsive patients might have missense mutations of the phenylalanine hydroxylase gene. Two cases, both with PAH missense mutations, have been reported who would have been likely treatment responders on this basis: neither showed a plasma phenylalanine-lowering response to clinical treatment with BH4 neonatally, but both show positive responses at an older age (Lassker, Zschocke, Blau and Santer 2002).

More detail on specific conditions and BH4 deficiencies can be obtained from the commercially sponsored site www.bh4. org.

The effect of maternal phenylketonuria: Poor dietary control during the pregnancy of women with PKU can result in developmental problems in their offspring. As more women with PKU and lesser variant PAH defects are now developing normally and having children, this has become a significant clinical issue. (For an early discussion, see Komrower, Sardharwalla, Coutts and Ingham 1979.) A recent study has shown a clear association between poorer dietary control during pregnancy and poorer developmental outcome in the children of mothers with PKU (Maillot *et al.* 2008), an effect which was found even when maternal phenylalanine levels were within the target range for good control.

Huntley and Stevenson (1969) described two sisters with PKU who had a total of 28 pregnancies, of which 16 ended in spontaneous foetal loss within the first trimester. All of the babies they carried to term were growth retarded with microcephaly, and 75 per cent had associated cardiac malformations.

In one study of five children born to mothers who had PKU which was poorly controlled through pregnancy, compared to two siblings of a mother with well-controlled PKU (Levy H.L. *et al.* 1996), there was evidence of underdevelopment of the corpus callosum in the poorly controlled cases, but there was also evidence, in all cases, of behavioural effects such as hyperactivity, irrespective of pregnancy control.

The Maternal Phenylketonuria Collaborative Study (MPKUCS) reported in 1997 on a collaborative study of children born to mothers with PKU (Rouse *et al.* 1997). The frequency of malformations such as congenital heart defects, small head size and facial anomalies rose with maternal phenylalanine levels in the earlier stages, and neurological involvement rose with higher levels through the pregnancy.

A further report from the MPKUCS (Guttler *et al.* 1999) reported findings concerning genetic make-up, biochemical phenotype and IQ in females with phenylalanine hydroxylase deficiency. In a series of 222 hyperphenylalaninaemic mothers, a total of 84 different PAH mutations were identified, with an association between the mutation type and the severity of their clinical presentation.

Phenylalanine control through pregnancy, genotype and developmental outcome (Rouse *et al.* 2000) was studied in a large group of 354 pregnant women with PKU. Thirty-one of the resulting infants had congenital heart disease and 17 had microcephaly. Both problems were strongly associated with poor control of phenylalanine levels through pregnancy, and all of those infants affected were the result of poor control over the first eight weeks of the pregnancy.

A large study of 149 children with PKU and 33 with hyperphenylalaninaemia (Waisbren *et al.* 2000), using the McCarthy Scales of Children's Abilities (a standardized IQ scale) at age four years, compared children on the basis of stage of pregnancy when metabolic control was gained. Later control correlated with poorer performance on the ability scale. Where maternal control was achieved before conception, IQ was normal for age (99); where control had not been achieved by five months post-conception, IQ averaged 70 or below, with 30 per cent showing social and behavioural problems. The link here may be due to poorer dietary control being exercised by more stressed families (Olsson, Montgomery and Alm 2007; Walter *et al.* 2002), underlining the need for good medical and family supports in such circumstances.

A further report from the MPKUCS (Levy H.L. *et al.* 2001) reported on 416 babies born of PKU pregnancies. In 14 per cent of the 235 cases with poor metabolic control through the first two months there was congenital heart disease, compared to one of 100 non-PKU controls, and one of 50 hyperphenylalaninaemic cases.

Cerebral abnormalities: Alterations in brain white matter were seen in ten individuals with PKU (age 15–30 years) not adhering to a phenylalanine-free diet, and clinical phenotype was found to correlate with brain concentration of phenylalanine measured by *in vivo* proton magnetic resonance spectroscopy (Leuzzi *et al.* 2000).

In a study of 15 adolescent patients with good dietary control, abnormalities on structural MRI brain scanning were either absent (10) or slight (5) (Ullrich *et al.* 1994). There was no association between blood phenylalanine levels, age or sex and MRI findings.

In another study of MRI scans of PKU patients (34 cases, aged 8–33), severity of MRI changes was related both to concurrent plasma phenylalanine levels and (in those not currently on a diet) to time since diet cessation (Thompson *et al.* 1993). Adults who have received effective dietary treatment through childhood continue to show evidence of impaired cerebral metabolism in response to phenylalanine loading (Pietz *et al.* 2003). A recent study of 27 cases (mean age 27 ± 7y) and matched controls found an association between grey matter volume and dietary control, with reduced volume correlating with lower IQ and later age at diagnosis. All of these findings are consistent with the fact that in animal studies increased levels of phenylalanine have been shown to reduce myelinization (Reynolds, Burri and Herschkowitz 1993).

Even in those cases with good early dietary control, a variety of brain structures have been found to be demonstrably smaller in PKU cases than in controls, in particular the cerebral cortex, corpus callosum, hippocampus and pons (Pfaendner *et al.* 2005) – presumably as a result of *in utero* exposure to phenylalanine.

Cognitive impairments: The principal focus of work characterizing the cognitive impairments in PKU has highlighted executive functioning (EF) deficits as being characteristic even of those who have received early dietary treatment. (See Christ, Moffitt and Peck 2010 for review.) It is becoming clear, however, that the range of cognitive effects is significantly broader, with impairments in non-EF cognitive abilities such as information processing, fine motor skills and visuospatial abilities (Janzen and Nguyen 2010).

IS THERE A LINK BETWEEN PKU AND ASD? PKU no longer causes autism or learning disability where universal neonatal screening and appropriate dietary management supports are in place. The Guthrie heelstick blood test (Guthrie and Susi 1963) is administered to all neonates in most of Western Europe and North America, usually within the first three days, and allows the prevention of problems by the early introduction of a special 'phenylalanine-free' diet.

With current screening methods, few cases are missed and those who are typically show evidence of learning disability. In one large 'post Guthrie test introduction' screening study of 280,919 adults (Levy, Karolkewicz, Houghton and MacCready 1970), only three previously unknown cases with PKU were identified, of whom all had a learning disability.

There are, however, many countries where such neonatal screening is not as comprehensive. (For a recent series illustrating that autism can still be caused by later treated PKU, see Vanli, Yilmaz, Tokatli and Anlar 2006.)

An early paper which suggested a link between PKU and autism (Lowe *et al.* 1980) screened 65 children with ASDs and found three with untreated PKU. The three children with PKU showed symptomatic and developmental improvement when placed on phenylalanine-free diets.

Since the widespread introduction of the Guthrie test, such cases have become far less common, but occasional single case reports have been published. In 1989,

Table B57.2: Recent developments in PKU treatment

Mode of action	Therapeutic approach
More palatable phenylalanine-free formulae	New phenylalanine-free formulae (Macdonald *et al.* 2004)
Reduced intestinal uptake of phenylalanine	Purified phenylalanine ammonia-lyase (for original basis, see Hoskins *et al.* 1980; Kim *et al.* 2004)
Alternative degradation pathways	Recombinant phenylalanine ammonia-lyase (mouse model – Sarkissian *et al.* 1999) Pegylated phenylalanine ammonia-lyase (under development see Gámez *et al.* 2005; Ikeda *et al.* 2005; Sarkissian and Gámez 2005)
Increasing PAH enzymatic activity	Tetrahydrobiopterin (BH4) supplementation (Matalon *et al.* 2004)
Competition for blood–brain barrier carriers	Large neutral amino acids supplementation (mouse model – Koch *et al.* 2003; Matalon *et al.* 2003)
Gene therapy	Low immunogenic vectors PAH expression in tissues other than liver (see, for reviews, Ding, Harding and Thöny 2004; dos Santos *et al.* 2006)
Improved cell membrane integrity	Long-chain polyunsaturated fatty acid supplementation (adjunctive) (Agostoni *et al.* 2000)

(Expanded and adapted from dos Santos *et al.* 2006)

a case report of a 12-year-old Chinese boy with autism who was discovered to have PKU on clinical investigation was published (Chen and Hsiao 1989). In 1992, a three-and-a-half-year-old Tunisian girl with autism was also found to have PKU on clinical investigation (Miladi *et al.* 1992).

Two recent studies have suggested that the ASD link is with poor dietary control, and not an obligatory link with a gene defect in phenylalanine hydroxylase:

- A paper published in 2003 (Baieli *et al.* 2003) reviewed 243 patients with various levels of PKU and milder forms of hyperphenylalaninaemia. They were investigated for possible ASD, using the ADI-R and the CARS. Only two cases (5.71 per cent) who met criteria for ASD were identified, both of whom were male and were late diagnosed.

- A more recent study from Turkey (Vanli, Yilmaz, Tokatli and Anlar 2006) described a case series of 146 PKU cases. Fifteen (10.27 per cent) were found to be autistic and all of these were late-diagnosed and late-treated. Only 47 of the children in this series received treatment before two months of age. Seventy per cent of the children who received early treatment were of normal cognitive ability while only three (three per cent) of the 99 who were commenced on treatment after two months were. As the authors point out, their series appears to have more severe problems than some other reported groups, and this may reflect a severity bias in their population that led to paediatric neurology referral.

It is interesting to note that in a study comparing well and poorly controlled PKU cases to a group with high functioning ASD and a group with closed head injuries (Dennis *et al.* 1999), the closest similarity is between the group with poorly controlled PKU and the group with ASD. Both groups showed relatively good performance on block design (a visuo-spatial constructional task) compared to comprehension. This profile has been well documented in the ASD population (Shah and Frith 1993). No attempt has so far been made to match this finding to phenylalanine hydroxylase levels.

Although 12q24.1 has been established as the locus for phenylketonuria and for Noonan syndrome [52], it has not shown up as a linkage site for ASD from the various gene marker studies.

In addition to possible ASD, a number of other features characterize untreated or later treated PKU cases (Paine 1957; Vanli, Yilmaz, Tokatli and Anlar 2006): learning disability; the presence of a 'mousey' odour (caused by the excretion of phenylacetic acid); hypopigmentation; unusual gait, stance and sitting posture; eczema; and epilepsy.

DIFFERENTIAL DIAGNOSIS: The wide use of screening means that most cases are identified in the early neonatal period. The metabolism of phenylalanine is well documented (Williams, Mamotte and Burnett 2008). Differential diagnosis is from other genetic anomalies that interfere with the metabolism of tetrahydrobiopterin (Thöny, Auerbach and Blau 2000; Frye 2010).

MANAGEMENT AND TREATMENT: Current evidence suggests that only when phenylalanine intake is limited prior to conception can foetal damage be prevented (Drogari, Smith, Beasley and Lloyd 1987). However, dietary restriction through pregnancy does limit the extent of damage and developmental problems (Hanley *et al.* 1996). In one UK series, 3/6 babies born to mothers with PKU who exercised dietary control only post-conception had congenital heart disease, and two infants died from this, while none of 34 babies born to mothers with PKU after good pre-conceptional dietary control had evidence of heart disease (Brenton and Lilburn 1996).

Dietary factors: A range of dietary factors can affect plasma phenylalanine levels.

1. *Aspartame:* Aspartame, an artificial sweetener, is 50 per cent phenylalanine, 30 per cent aspartic acid and 20 per cent ethanol. Digestion of aspartame frees a significant amount of phenylalanine into the bloodstream. One study (Stegink et al. 1989) examined whether aspartame intake from artificially sweetened drinks would affect levels in persons heterozygous for PKU. Moderate and clinically insignificant elevations were seen when measured 30–45 minutes after drinking. A further study (Trefz et al. 1994) has shown no effects on cognitive function, but significantly increased plasma levels, in a double-blinded, placebo-controlled crossover trial. These results suggest that, despite the minimal effects on the individual, aspartame intake should be minimized through pregnancy to limit the potential effects on the foetus.

   In individuals homozygous for PKU the effects of aspartame will be markedly more pronounced (Janssen and van der Heijden 1988).

   In a study of 125 Northern Irish children with classical PKU and hyperphenylalaninaemia, there was an association between likely reduction of IQ after dietary relaxation and level of residual enzyme activity: the lower the residual enzyme activity, the higher the likelihood of cognitive decline on dietary relaxation between ages 8, 14 and 18 (Greeves et al. 2000).

2. *Long-chain polyunsaturated fatty acids:* A low phenylalanine diet is typically low in the long-chain polyunsaturated fatty acids (LCPUFA). LCPUFAs are essential for the formation of cell membranes and myelination of the brain and peripheral nervous system. A study of 12-month supplementation with LCPUFAs found enhanced levels of docosahexaenoic acid (DHA), an increase in lipid levels in blood cell membranes, and enhanced visual function on electrophysiological assessment (Agostoni et al. 2000). A further study by the same group (Agostoni et al. 2003) found that group differences seen in the first study had disappeared three years after ceasing supplementation.

3. *Carnitine:* Another factor that is deficient unless supplemented in those on a PKU diet is carnitine. Carnitine production requires precursors derived from phenylalanine. This seems to be correctable by appropriate oral supplementation (Vilaseca et al. 1993). Mild carnitine deficiency has been noted as a general feature in ASD and is thought to indicate mitochondrial dysfunction (Filipek et al. 2004). Carnitine supplementation has also proved beneficial in small-scale trials with Rett syndrome [63a] (Ellaway et al. 2001). For a general overview of effects of carnitine deficiency, see Points and de Vivo (1995).

4. *Amino acid supplementation:* Giving large neutral amino acid supplements (supplementing with tyrosine, tryptophan, threonine, isoleucine, leucine, valine, methionine and histidine) could work, and does in the mouse model, by means of these other amino acids competing for the same transporter mechanism as phenylalanine to cross the blood–brain barrier (Oldendorf and Szabo 1976).

Some supplement regimes can prove problematic in those with phenylalanine processing difficulties. A 16-year-old with mild hyperphenylalalinaemia developed a range of problems (headache, deteriorating school performance and mild depression) while taking a high-protein body-building supplement. The problems reversed when the supplement was stopped, and clinical improvement was found with BH4 supplementation (Koch *et al.* 2003b).

It seems likely that high-protein diets in general will be problematic for many with clinical and subclinical phenylalanine difficulties. This could be important for foetal development, even in mild hyperphenylalalinaemia, as many circulating factors are concentrated in foetal blood.

There is some evidence that in certain, typically milder, cases of PAH deficient PKU and hyperphenylalaninaemia tetrahydrobiopterin supplementation can be of benefit (Gramer, Burgard, Garbade and Lindner 2007).

Note: To date, there have been few studies of the effects of dietary factors on foetal development in *hyperphenylalaninaemia*. The results to date suggest that, with similar preconceptional and antenatal care, the effects are less than with PKU; however, they can still be significant. One survey of 86 affected mothers (all of normal IQ, 47 per cent college graduates) identified PKU in 22 children (13 per cent of the sample), congenital heart disease in four, and other severe anomalies in a further five. For mothers who had phenylalanine levels above 400 micromole/litre, there was a negative association between level and the child's IQ (based on 81 tested children), but all were functioning within the normal IQ range (Levy *et al.* 1995).

Recent developments in treatment of PKU: A recent study (Koch *et al.* 2000) suggests that blood and brain phenylalanine levels can diverge, with low brain and high blood levels being seen in some individuals with normal IQ (the implication being that magnetic resonance spectroscopy may be of use in recommending sensible dietary levels of phenylalanine). In general, however, small fluctuations in phenylalanine level have marked effects on cognitive function, particular effects being seen on tasks requiring sustained attention and working memory (Huijbregts *et al.* 2002).

Based on a 32-year follow-up study of 70 from an original cohort of 125 children, the long-term maintenance of dietary restriction into adulthood is associated with a lower prevalence of mental problems (Koch *et al.* 2002). At follow-up, 61 were off-diet and 9 were continuing to exercise dietary restriction, so numbers are small, but nevertheless, approximately twice the proportion of those off-diet experienced mental health difficulties, such as depression and phobias, compared to the continuers (22/59 vs 2/9).

In the UK, the NSPKU provides excellent dietary information that can be used by members in conjunction with a dietician, and information on what is available on prescription. These can be downloaded from their website at www.nspku.org.

One extreme treatment for PKU is liver transplant. This would not normally be considered, given the good response to other treatments and the lack of concomitant liver problems. In one ten-year-old boy with PKU and unrelated cirrhosis, his PKU was cured when he underwent a liver transplant to address the cirrhosis (Vajro *et al.* 1993).

ANIMAL MODELS: In 1987, one group established by *in situ* hybridization that the *Pah* gene in the mouse was localized to chromosome 10 (Ledbetter, Ledbetter, Ledley and Woo 1987). Three years later, two groups mapped location of the *Pah* gene on mouse chromosome 10. One group (McDonald, Bode, Dove and Shedlovsky 1990) created a mutated germ line mouse which showed hyperphenylalaninaemia with damage on mouse chromosome 10 at or near the *Pah* locus. The other (Justice *et al.* 1990) also mapped the *Pah* locus as part of a more detailed molecular study, using interspecific backcross analysis to create a genetic linkage map of the whole of mouse chromosome 10.

Two further chemically induced genetic models of PKU have been induced in mice, with differing severities; the mouse mutations demonstrate close genotype–phenotype associations that resemble those seen in human PKU (McDonald and Charlton 1997). Recent studies have used this mouse model to study abnormalities of brain protein production (Smith and Kang 2000), and it may prove a useful model for testing novel treatment approaches.

58.

Pituitary deficiency

GENE LOCI: 3p11, 3p21.2–p21.1, 5q, 9q34.3

KEY ASD REFERENCES: Gingell, Parmar and Sungum-Paliwal 1996; Hoshino *et al.* 1984; Polizzi *et al.* 2006; Ritvo *et al.* 1990

SUMMARY: ASD cases of pituitary deficiency are typically associated with HESX1 mutations (at 3p21.2–p21.1). These result in a specific physical phenotype with hypopituitarism and septo-optic dysplasia (SOD). Most, but not

all, cases (Gingell, Parmar and Sungum-Paliwal 1996) are therefore blind. Various midline central nervous system structures are also hypoplastic.

HOW COMMON IS PITUITARY DEFICIENCY? Overall growth hormone deficiencies related to pituitary dysfunction are fairly common, affecting one in 4,000 to one in 10,000 live births (Procter, Phillips and Cooper 1998). The type of combined pituitary hormone deficiency linked to SOD and ASD that has been reported with defects in HESX1 is far rarer, accounting for a small percentage of such cases (Viera, Boldarine and Abucham 2007).

MAIN CLINICAL FEATURES: Homozygous inactivating mutations of HESX1 mutations result in a specific physical phenotype with hypopituitarism, SOD and structural agenesis of various midline structures in the nervous system.

To date, some 13 separate mutations have been identified that are associated with SOD and hypopituitarism. (See discussion in Sajedi *et al.* 2008.) In addition, a number of heterozygous missense HESX1 mutations have now been identified in individuals with a range of mild pituitary abnormalities (Thomas P.Q. *et al.* 2001).

IS THERE A LINK BETWEEN PITUITARY DEFICIENCY AND ASD? Only four papers have so far appeared which bear on this issue.

- Hoshino *et al.* (1984) were the first to suggest that there were abnormalities of pituitary function associated with some cases of ASD, after demonstrating abnormal plasma growth hormone levels in response to L-5HTP loading.

- Ritvo *et al.* (1990) documented 12 rare diseases in their epidemiological survey of 233 cases of ASD in Utah. One of these was a boy with pituitary deficiency diagnosed shortly after birth. He also had a SOD, so was blind from birth. As blindness is an independent factor associated with ASD, interpretation of the role of pituitary dysfunction in contributing to his ASD was problematic.

- Gingell, Parmar and Sungum-Paliwal (1996) described a nine-year-old boy with ASD who also had multiple pituitary deficiency. This is the only case reported to date without additional complications.

- Polizzi *et al.* (2006) described a series of eight cases of ASD associated with SOD, similar to the original case described by Ritvo *et al.* (1990). They point out that midline hypothalamic–pituitary structural malformations are commonly seen in addition to the optic nerve dysplasia, and that autistic behaviour is a frequent concomitant.

The association of septo-optic dysplasia and pituitary dysfunction has been found to be linked to a mutation/deletion of the HESX1 gene at 3p21.2–p21.1. The phenotype associated with HESX1 is broad and usually, but not always, includes SOD. Of the ASD cases associated with pituitary dysfunction, 9/10 also presented with SOD. Based on this, discussion will be confined to multiple pituitary deficiency resulting from HESX1.

DIFFERENTIAL DIAGNOSIS: Mutations in a number of separate genes can result in pituitary deficiency.

MANAGEMENT AND TREATMENT: Optimal management of pituitary deficiencies depends on the basis to the disorder, the range of hormone imbalances, and the age and sex of the affected individual. As there is a wide range of phenotypic presentation in HESX1 cases, good baseline assessment and monitoring

of response to appropriate treatment as required are important.

ANIMAL MODELS: There is only one animal paper (Nicot, Otto, Brabet and Dicicco-Bloom 2004) to date that has examined a possible link between pituitary factors and ASD. This paper studied mice that were deficient in the pituitary adenylate cyclase-activating polypeptide (PACAP) type I receptor. *Pac1*-deficient mice are socially impaired, particularly for olfactory social exploration. However, this does not appear to be a particularly useful analogue to the pituitary effects of human HESX1 gene defects. The human HESX1 gene is found at 3p21.2–p21.1, while the mouse *Pac1* gene is syntenic to PACAP38 at 18p11.

A number of mouse models have been developed to investigate the link between HESX1 SOD and hypopituitarism (Sajedi *et al.* 2008). However, no attempts have been made to date to investigate the associated behavioural phenotype as a possible model for ASD. Structurally, *Hesx1* deletion in the mouse results in disruption to the development of the posterior forebrain structures, mirroring some of the structural differences reported in the brains of humans with ASD (Andoniadou *et al.* 2007).

59.

Port-wine facial staining and autism

GENETIC BASIS: The gene RASA1 at 5q13.3 has been implicated in some cases of Sturge-Weber syndrome [88] (Eerola *et al.* 2003), but has not been tested for in the cases reported by Chugani *et al.* (2007).

KEY ASD REFERENCE: Chugani *et al.* 2007

SUMMARY: This is a previously unreported condition that appears phenotypically to resemble Sturge-Weber syndrome, but a key feature of Sturge-Weber syndrome that is *not* seen in these cases is leptomeningeal angioma – dilated blood vessels on the surface of the affected areas of the brain, thought to result in seizures and brain injury. Leptomeningeal angiomas can be subtle and can sometimes be overlooked or too small to be detected at the resolution of the imaging system being used (Fischbein, Barkovich, Wu and Berg 1998; Juhasz and Chugani 2007; Mentzel *et al.* 2005).

HOW COMMON IS PORT-WINE FACIAL STAINING IN ASSOCIATION WITH AUTISM? As the aetiology is uncertain at the present time, the prevalence of this condition is not known. It may turn out that this is a variant of one of the neurocutaneous conditions such as Sturge-Weber syndrome that have not previously been reported in association with ASD. In this case, overall prevalence should be ascertainable from the clinical literature on Sturge-Webber syndrome.

MAIN CLINICAL FEATURES: This condition is characterized by deep purple-red-coloured patches on the skin of the face or scalp, caused by the growth of a net of abnormal blood vessels in the affected areas.

Of the four cases reported by Chugani *et al.* (2007), three had a history of seizures; two were ongoing and maintained on medication at the time of the report. Two had eye problems that would be consistent with Sturge-Weber syndrome. All were established as autistic based on the ADI-R, and three had typical ASD scores on the Gilliam Autism Rating Scale. (The fourth case did not have this assessment carried out.)

IS THERE A LINK BETWEEN PORT-WINE FACIAL STAINING AND ASD? As the aetiology is currently uncertain, it is difficult to say whether these cases are from a known clinical group such as Sturge-Weber, in which ASD has not previously been reported, or whether they represent a novel aetiology that is more strongly associated with ASD.

DIFFERENTIAL DIAGNOSIS: Whether there is a clear differentiation between these cases and more phenotypically normal Sturge-Weber syndrome remains to be established.

MANAGEMENT AND TREATMENT: As only four cases have so far been reported, no specific treatments are known. It seems likely that there will be a high likelihood of seizures in this group, and monitoring and treatment of seizure activity would seem sensible. Assuming that Sturge-Weber syndrome is the underlying aetiology, there have been recent developments in best practice that may also be relevant here. (See Comi 2006, 2007.)

ANIMAL MODELS: As the basis to these cases is currently unclear, no animal models can be said to be consistent with the condition.

60.

Potocki-Lupski syndrome (PTLS)

aka • ((dup)17(11.2p.11.2))

GENE LOCUS: 17p11.2

KEY ASD REFERENCES: Moog *et al.* 2004; Potocki *et al.* 2000, 2007

SUMMARY: Potocki-Lupski syndrome is a recently described reciprocal microduplication syndrome which is the homologous recombination reciprocal of Smith-Magenis syndrome [67] (Potocki *et al.* 2000a). It was the first such reciprocal microduplication syndrome to be predicted. The first paper to describe 17p11.2 duplication was one describing two unrelated males with developmental delay and mild dysmorphic features (Brown *et al.* 1996).

HOW COMMON IS PTLS? There is no data on the prevalence of PTLS at the time of writing.

MAIN CLINICAL FEATURES: The first description of the clinical presentation of ((dup)17(11.2p.11.2)) was by Brown *et al.* (1996), of two unrelated male cases with learning disability and slightly dysmorphic facial features. The consistent clinical features are:

- delayed early development
- language impairment
- learning disability
- hypotonia
- failure to thrive.

Additional common features are:

- poor feeding in infancy
- oral–pharyngeal dysphasia
- autism
- obstructive and central sleep apnoea
- structural cardiovascular abnormalities
- epileptiform electroencephalogram (EEG) abnormalities
- scoliosis
- hypermetropia.

As only a small number of cases have been reported to date, and it is likely that few milder cases have been screened, caution should be exercised in interpreting the genotype–phenotype results to date as providing a strong indication of the likely or typical phenotype in PTLS.

IS THERE A LINK BETWEEN PTLS AND ASD? The first paper to suggest a link between PTLS and ASD (Potocki *et al.* 2000) described seven unrelated learning disabled cases with *de novo* 17(11.2p.11.2) duplications. The clinical features described included mild facial dysmorphic features, dental malformations, short stature, mild learning disabilities, and behavioural features including ADHD and autism.

A further case, a six-year-old boy, was reported in 2004 (Moog *et al.* 2004). He had moderate learning disability, a gait disturbance, an 'autism-related disorder' and mild facial dysmorphic features, with a broad forehead, thin upper lip and ear anomalies. Genetic testing had identified duplication consistent with hereditary motor and sensory neuropathy type 1A (Charcot-Marie-Tooth disease). It is now known that the abnormalities in the gene region identified can result in four disorders: Charcot-Marie-Tooth disease type 1A; hereditary neuropathies with liabilities to pressure palsies; Smith-Magenis syndrome; and what is now known as Potocki-Lupski syndrome.

In their most recent case series Potocki *et al.* (2007) reported on ten subjects. Delayed early development (10/10), language impairment (10/10), learning disability (10/10) and hypotonia (10/10) were the most characteristic clinical features. In addition, poor feeding (8/10) and failure to thrive (10/10) in infancy, oral-pharyngeal dysphasia (8/9), autism (9/10), obstructive and central sleep apnoea (8/9), structural cardiovascular abnormalities (5/9), epileptiform electroencephalogram (EEG) abnormalities (5/9) and hypermetropia (8/10) were common features. The majority of cases (9/10) were reported as exhibiting autism.

A recent paper (Greco *et al.* 2008) used well standardized tools (CARS in one and ADI-R and ADOS-G in the other two) to characterize the behavioural phenotype in three PTLS cases. This study failed to find evidence of ASD, but replicated the other reported findings – all three showed hypotonia, failure to thrive and language delay; two showed early developmental delay; and all exhibited learning disability (Greco *et al.* 2008).

The most recent case described, using ADI-R and ADOS-G, was autistic with a co-morbid severe expressive language delay (Nakamine *et al.* 2008).

From the cases reported to date, there is clearly a significant group that exhibits autistic behaviour, typically in the context of learning disability, communication disorder, early feeding difficulties and sleep problems.

DIFFERENTIAL DIAGNOSIS: There is a clinical overlap between PTLS and Smith-Magenis syndrome [67] (which also results from a deletion at 17p11.2), and with two of the hereditary neuropathies (Charcot-Marie-Tooth disease type 1A; hereditary neuropathies with liabilities to pressure palsies).

MANAGEMENT AND TREATMENT: At the time of writing there is insufficient understanding of this condition to provide any specific guidance on treatment. As for a number of the other conditions discussed, management needs to be on a case-by-case basis. No cases are reported with epilepsy, but a number have been reported with generalized and focal epileptiform EEG abnormalities, and non-epileptic abnormalities were fairly consistently (7/8 cases) associated with obstructive sleep apnoea (Potocki *et al.* 2007).

ANIMAL MODELS: Walz *et al.* (2003) engineered both deletion and duplication mouse models of the syntenic region to human 17p11.2. This would be expected to result in models of Smith-Magenis syndrome [67] and Potocki-Lupski syndrome respectively. The deletion mice had craniofacial abnormalities, seizures, marked obesity, and male-specific reduced fertility, while those with the duplication were underweight, did not have seizures or craniofacial abnormalities, and were fertile.

Walz *et al.* (2004) have further advanced their study of their mouse models by showing that a range of behavioural characteristics are seen in their 17p11.2 duplication mice, particularly hyperactivity and impaired contextual fear conditioning. Combining this work with their 17p11.2 deletion phenotype, they have shown that some behaviours are deletion or duplication specific, while others are sensitive to the number of active copies of this region of chromosome 17.

Walz *et al.* (2006) developed a mouse model with different numbers of copies of the retinoic acid inducible 1 (Rai1) gene. Absence of Rai1 is sufficient to result in Smith-Magenis syndrome [67]. Disomic activation of the Rai1 gene is sufficient to prevent the PTLS mouse behavioural genotype.

61.

Prader-Willi syndrome (PWS)

aka • Prader-Labhart-Willi syndrome

GENE LOCI: 15q12, 15q11–q13

KEY ASD REFERENCES: Bolton *et al.* 2001; Descheemaeker, Govers, Vermeulen and Fryns 2006; Dimitropoulos and Schultz

2007; Milner *et al.* 2005; Veltman, Craig and Bolton 2005

SUMMARY: The English physician John Langdon Haydon Down described the first patient who would today be given a diagnosis of PWS in 1887. His description was of a 25-year-old woman with learning disability, short stature, small hands and feet, hypogonadism and marked obesity. She was reported to have a voracious appetite.

The Swiss clinicians Andrea Prader, Alexis Labhart and Heinrich Willi reported a series of patients with similar phenotypes in 1956, and this led to the characterization of the condition we now know as Prader-Willi syndrome (PWS).

In 1981, Ledbetter *et al.* identified chromosome 15 deletions, specifically of 15q11–13 as the cause of PWS. PWS results, in the majority of cases, from inheriting paternal mutation of 15q11–13, while maternal inheritance of the same mutation typically results in Angelman syndrome [11].

PWS was the first clinical disorder to be attributed to genomic imprinting.

PWS is a disorder caused by defects in the functioning of genes on the short arm of chromosome 15, caused by loss of the paternal allele, *either* as a result of deletion of this section of the paternal allele (70 per cent), *or* inheritance of both copies of the chromosome from the mother (uniparental idodisomy) (28 per cent), *or*, more rarely, translocation, other structural alteration or deletion of the imprinting centre (two per cent).

HOW COMMON IS PWS? A variety of prevalence rates have been reported in the literature, from one in 8,000 to one in 52,000. (See Akefeldt, Gillberg and Larsson 1991; Burd, Vesely, Martsolf and Kerbeshian 1990; Whittington *et al.* 2001.) It is equally common in both sexes and no racial differences in prevalence are reported. There do, however, appear to be racial differences in the phenotype (Hudgins, Geer and Cassidy 1998).

MAIN CLINICAL FEATURES: Consensus criteria for PWS were published in 1993 by Holm *et al.*, as follows, with separate cut-off levels for children under three years of age (five points, with at least three from major criteria), and those over three years (eight points, with at least five from major criteria):

Major criteria (one point for each):

- infantile central hypotonia
- infantile feeding problems and/or failure to thrive
- nutrition: rapid weight gain from 1 to 6 years
- characteristic facial features, such as narrow bifrontal diameter, almond-shaped palpebral fissures, narrow nasal bridge, and down-turned mouth
- hypogonadism
- learning disability.

Minor criteria (one half-point for each):

- decreased foetal movement/infantile lethargy
- sleep disturbance and/or sleep apnoea
- short stature for predicted height by mid-adolescence (if not on growth hormone treatment)
- hypopigmentation
- small hands and feet
- narrow hands with straight ulnar border
- Esotropia/myopia
- thick viscous saliva
- speech articulation defects
- skin picking/rectal poking.

In cases of PWS it is often reported that the baby had diminished foetal movement.

The typical clinical presentation is of clinical obesity, hypotonia, with a weak cry and poor sucking, learning disability, short stature, hypogonadotropic hypogonadism, strabismus, a 'shield-shaped' chest and small hands and feet. From early in the first year, hyperphagia is common, with progressive weight gain compared to the centile charts.

The development of pubic and body hair may be precocious but other primary and secondary sexual characteristics tend to be delayed. Descent of the testes in boys and start of ovulation in girls can be extremely delayed.

Most PWS cases have growth hormone deficiency. However, there is variation, and there does not appear to be a link between growth hormone levels and likelihood of obesity (Thacker et al. 1998).

Mild learning disability is seen in most cases. In addition, behavioural problems, such as temper outbursts, obsession and compulsions, often impair access to learning.

Hyperphagia is typical where access to food is not tightly controlled, and secondary problems such as impaired exercise tolerance, heart problems, type II diabetes and sleep apnoea are common.

Various factors may be directly related to the morbid obesity that typically accompanies PWS. Abnormalities of anterior pituitary hormone secretion such as insulin-like growth factor (IGF1) are reported in almost all people with PWS, and structural abnormalities of the pituitary gland are seen in most cases (74 per cent vs 8 per cent in controls). Similar profiles are seen in early-onset morbid obesity without PWS, and may be the basis to the obesity component of the condition (Miller J.L. et al. 2008).

Elevated levels of ghrelin, both when fasted and under normal conditions, are reported in PWS. Ghrelin acts both as a gastrointestinal hormone, modifying appetite, and as a neuropeptide, affecting brain levels of serotonin (Nonogaki, Ohashi-Nozue and Oka 2006). Ghrelin abnormalities may be involved in the satiety problems that characterize people with PWS.

IS THERE A LINK BETWEEN PWS AND ASD?

- Bolton et al. (2001) studied 21 people from six families who had duplications of the 15q11–13 region affected in PWS and Angelman syndrome. Four of the people they studied had a pervasive developmental disorder, and one was diagnosed as autistic. Most of the mutations giving rise to pervasive developmental disorders were maternal in origin, as would be seen in Angelman syndrome but not PWS. The authors concluded that developmental delay, but not specifically ASD, was associated with maternal inheritance of 15q11–13 defects.

- Milner et al. (2005) studied a large sample of 96 PWS cases, using a variety of measures including the ASQ, ADI and ADOS. They compared cases where there was a maternally inherited uniparental disomy (where there had been no inheritance of a parternal chromosome 15 but both copies came from the mother), with cases where there was an inherited 15q11–13 deletion on the paternally inherited chromosome. Their results indicated a strong association between paternally inherited 15q11–13 deletions and ASD. Larger deletions were associated with lower intellectual level, but not with an increased likelihood of ASD diagnosis.

- Descheemaeker, Govers, Vermeulen and Fryns (2006) used a standardized scale – the Pervasive Developmental Disorder

Mental Retardation Scale (PDD-MR Scale) – to evaluate comorbidity in 59 PWS individuals and 59 matched controls with non-specific forms of learning disability, matched on gender, age and IQ. Most of those with PWS presented with a higher rate of autistic-like behaviour. However, using strict criteria (on DSM-III-R), 19 per cent of those with PWS were classified as having ASD, and 15 per cent of those as having non-specific learning disabilities.

- Veltman, Craig and Bolton (2005), acknowledging the role of 15q11–13 in ASD, reviewed the various studies of maternally and paternally inherited deletions and uniparental disomies in both PWS and Angelman syndrome. Based on the studies available up to that time, all types of 15q11–13 deletion, and uniparental disomy in Angelman syndrome, confer an increased risk, but the risk conveyed by maternally inherited uniparental disomy in Prader-Willi syndrome conveys a significantly elevated risk compared to the other 15q11–13 mechanisms.

- Dimitropoulos and Schultz (2007) provide a further review of the evidence for genetic risk of ASD in those with PWS from loss or damage to 15q11–13. They conclude, as did Veltman, Craig and Bolton (2005), that ASD appears to be most strongly linked to loss of the paternally inherited chromosome, particularly through inheritance of two copies of the maternal chromosome and none from the father (maternally inherited uniparental disomy). For a general discussion of the relationship between autism and 15q11–q13 disorders, see Dykes, Sutcliffe and Levitt (2004).

DIFFERENTIAL DIAGNOSIS: Genetic conditions affecting 15q11–13 include Angelman syndrome [11] and oculocutaneous albinism [55], which should be considered. Neither condition is easily confused with PWS, as they result in markedly different phenotypes. However, genetic studies could suggest these conditions.

Biedl-Bardet syndrome [17], Cohen syndrome [23] and fragile-X syndrome [35] present with overlapping clinical phenotypes and should be included in the differential diagnosis.

MANAGEMENT AND TREATMENT: As PWS is a multi-system disorder with both structural and hormonal differences in the pituitary and other endocrine structures, good metabolic and imaging assessments are important as part of a comprehensive initial assessment. As a number of genetic factors can result in the clinical phenotype and may prove to be amenable to different approaches, ascertaining the genetic basis is also important. Treatment should be based on the outcome of such assessment.

A major practical problem for many with PWS is obesity due to overeating. This compounds the skeletal problems, in particular exacerbating difficulties due to scoliosis, and increasing rates of sleep apnoea.

Early dietary intervention can be effective in controlling weight gain, but can result in short stature (Schmidt et al. 2008). It has been suggested therefore that diet should be coupled with growth hormone treatment. Unfortunately, the evidence to date is varied concerning clinical benefit (Mogul et al. 2008) and is coupled with a significant increase in obstructive sleep apnoea (Fillion, Deal and Van Vliet 2008). It may be that the differences in ghrelin production and metabolism are critical to control of hunger.

As obesity is one of the major factors in morbidity and mortality for individuals with PWS, this is a critical aspect of ongoing care and management.

For an overview of management issues, see Butler, Lee and Whitman (2006).

As with Angelman syndrome [11] and oculocutaneous albinism [55], PWS shows evidence of dysfunction of the GABA system (Verhoeven and Tuinier 2006). Further elucidation of the nature of this abnormality and possible links to motor dysfunction and sleep problems may be important for future approaches to management.

ANIMAL MODELS: See discussions of models under Angelman syndrome [11] and oculocutaneous albinism [55]. The same models have relevance here.

62.

Proteus syndrome

GENE LOCUS: Not yet identified. Suggestions of a link to PTEN defects have been reported in a number of cases (Smith J.M. et al. 2002; Zhou et al. 2000, 2001).

KEY ASD REFERENCE: Butler et al. 2005

SUMMARY: This syndrome is named after the Greek God Proteus, 'the old man of the sea', who was said to be able to change his shape to avoid being caught (Wiedemann et al. 1983). It is best known by one of those who was severely affected – the nineteenth-century 'Elephant Man', Joseph Merrick (Cohen 1988).

It occurs as a sporadic mutation, and the clinical picture is progressive throughout life.

HOW COMMON IS PROTEUS SYNDROME? Proteus syndrome is a rare condition, with only around 200 cases reported so far

worldwide (Orphanet 2009). There is no apparent difference in prevalence across racial groups. It is reported to be almost twice as common in males as in females (Turner et al. 2004).

MAIN CLINICAL FEATURES: The main clinical features are macrocephaly, hamartomas and lipomas. Physical overgrowth is typically asymmetric. Overgrowth of the long bones in the arms and legs is typical (Nguyen et al. 2004) and scoliosis is common (del Rosario Barona-Mazuera et al. 1997). Tumours can occur in a range of body tissues (Jamis-Dow, Turner, Biesecker and Choyke 2004).

This is a hamartomatous overgrowth condition that overlaps clinically with BRRS [15], BCNS [16] and Cowden syndrome [26]. Detailed discussion of such PTEN defects and their effects is provided in these other sections, and will not be repeated here.

Based on current consensus, these conditions are perhaps best grouped under a common heading of PHTSs (PTEN hamartoma–tumour syndromes) (see Marsh et al. 1999; Waite and Eng 2002). There is marked variation in what is reported as being Proteus syndrome in the published literature – Turner, Cohen and Biesecker (2004) reviewed 205 cases in the literature, of which only 47.3 per cent would appear to meet current criteria.

IS THERE A LINK BETWEEN PROTEUS SYNDROME AND ASD? Butler et al. (2005) reviewed a series of 18 ASD cases with macrocephaly and identified three cases with previously unreported PTEN mutations. Proteus syndrome is included here as one of the group of PTEN conditions with genotypic and phenotypic overlap that have been reported in association with ASD.

DIFFERENTIAL DIAGNOSIS: Differential diagnoses are as for the other PHTSs discussed, as indicated above, and for the other differential diagnoses discussed there.

MANAGEMENT AND TREATMENT: As for the other PHTSs, at the present time treatment is largely symptomatic.

ANIMAL MODELS: Again, these are as for the other PHTSs. See BRRS [15], BCNS [16] and Cowden syndrome [26].

63a.

Rett syndrome (RTT)

GENE LOCUS: Xq28

KEY ASD REFERENCES: Carney *et al.* 2003; Hagberg, Aicardi, Dias and Ramos 1983; Lam *et al.* 2000; Rett 1986

SUMMARY: Rett syndrome (RTT) is named after the Viennese paediatric neurologist Andreas Rett. He first described a group of girls who all presented with very similar difficulties in a paper published in 1966, and later reviewed the development of the evidence for a distinct clinical ohenotype in a paper published in 1986. His initial findings were the result of chance observation of the similarities in two unrelated girls sitting in a clinic waiting area. One characteristic documented in these early cases but not replicated in later work was his finding of raised blood ammonia levels (hyperammonaemia) (Rett 1977).

The biological basis to RTT has proved far more difficult to unravel than its clinical description. Clinical criteria for RTT were published in 1985 (Hagberg *et al.* 1985). A 2001 consensus panel of the European Paediatric Neurology Society has produced what are probably the clearest criteria in current use (see Hagberg, Hanefeld, Percy and Skjeldal 2002). They suggest eight necessary criteria (normal pre- and perinatal history; normal psychomotor development over the first six months; normal birth OFC; postnatal deceleration in head growth compared to normative range (in most but not all cases); achievement of functional hand use and subsequent loss by between 6 and 30 months; stereotyped hand movements; regression in social learning and communicative functions; static or regressing motor function); eight supportive criteria (breathing disturbance; bruxism; impaired sleep pattern; abnormal muscle tone; peripheral vasomotor problems; progressive scoliosis/kyphosis; growth retardation; small hands and feet); and five exclusion criteria (evidence of storage disease; visual problems such as retinopathy, optic atrophy or cataract; evidence of peri- or postnatal brain damage; evidence for a progressive neurological disease; evidence of traumatic or infective CNS damage). Delineation of the condition was based on a collaborative European series of cases (Hagberg, Aicardi, Dias and Ramos 1983).

The initial view of RTT as a condition found exclusively in females that may result in non-viable male conceptions has had to be changed, as a significant number of male cases have now been reported.

A number of pairs of concordant identical twins have been reported (Partington 1988; Tariverdian, Kanter and Vogel 1987; Zoghbi *et al.* 1990), suggesting a probable genetic aetiology. However, although typically concordant for RTT diagnosis, clinical presentation and progression can vary across twins (Bruck, Philippart, Giraldi and Antoniuk 1991), making it likely that environmental factors affect the expression of the genotype.

In a now classic genetics paper, Hudah Zoghbi's group from Baylor College in Houston showed that in some cases of RTT the defective gene was the X-linked methyl-CpG-binding protein 2 (MeCP2) (Amir *et al.* 1999).

RTT is one of a group of human chromatin structure or modification disorders, many of which, such as ARX [13], Coffin-Lowry syndrome [21] and Rubinstein-Taybi syndrome [64] (reviewed in Hendrich and Bickmore 2001), are linked to ASD.

Hagberg (1995) reviewed 170 Swedish female cases, diagnosed on clinical phenotype, and aged between two and 52 years. Seventy-five per cent presented with the 'classic' Rett phenotype, while 25 per cent were 'atypical'. Today, a number of clinical variants are recognized, including the preserved speech variant (Renieri *et al.* 2009) – see below – and the clinical variation within the RTT group is also proving to be broader than had initially been thought, with some individuals showing development of skills such as writing and drawing, and preservation of verbal ability into teenage years, in contrast to the normal regressive picture more typically described in the literature (Kerr *et al.* 2006). As the more obvious clinical phenotypes are those most likely to be identified, until such time as a genetic test becomes clinically available, this leads to greater apparent consistency in the current clinical literature than may actually be the case. As the genotype comes into use as the gold standard for diagnosis, clinical variability in the phenotype is becoming greater. For example, a recent case with a novel frameshift deletion was described with macrocephaly (Oexle, Thamm-Mucke, Mayer and Tinschert 2005).

Although much of the genetics has superseded it, one of the most useful overviews of RTT remains Kerr and Witt Engerstrom's overview (2001).

There is no association between RTT and increased maternal age (Martinho *et al.* 1990).

HOW COMMON IS RETT SYNDROME? Several studies have provided prevalence estimates that are broadly similar.

Suzuki, Hirayama and Arima (1989) report a rate of one in 20,000 girls affected in Tokyo. Hagberg (1995) estimated the overall prevalence in southern Sweden at around one in 15,000. Burd, Vesely, Martsolf and Kerbeshian (1991) estimated the prevalence in girls aged up to 18 years in South Dakota as one in 19,786. In Texas, the prevalence has been estimated as one in 22,800 (Kozinetz *et al.* 1993).

The lack of good epidemiological studies is offset by the obvious clinical phenotype in many cases. However, the existence of mild RTT variants (Huppke *et al.* 2003, 2006) and of male cases (Maiwald *et al.* 2002; Philippart 1990; Schanen and Francke 1998) – see below – makes accurate estimation difficult.

MAIN CLINICAL FEATURES: Those affected with RTT typically have a frail build, rapid, energetic movements (including hand-wringing/washing and hand-biting), and bursts of rapid breathing. They typically have normal caloric intake and are hypometabolic, compared to controls (Motil *et al.* 1994), which suggests that their growth failure is due to their level of involuntary activity.

Reduced bone density seems common, being seen in 12/16 cases reported by Leonard *et al.* (1995).

Heart function is abnormal in many individuals with Rett syndrome. Sekul *et al.* (1994), Ellaway *et al.* (1999) and Guideri *et al.* (1999) have all reported prolonged QT intervals and reduced heart rate variability in patients with Rett syndrome, suggesting impairment of the autonomic nervous system (Glaze 2002).

An early multi-centre European paper (Hagberg, Aicardi, Dias and Ramos 1983) provided clinical details on 35 girls from France, Portugal and Sweden. This paper essentially detailed the criteria used in describing the RTT phenotype. There is some variation across the cases described. However, all the girls showed a progressive encephalopathy. Development was reported as normal until the age of 7–18 months, at which point speech stopped (often after a small vocabulary had developed) and functional hand use was lost. Where head circumference data was available, there was evidence of progressive microcephaly – the rate of head growth slowed relative to normal growth charts. Rate of head growth is associated with developmental progression in RTT: larger head size and better early head growth is associated with greater likelihood of walking (Leonard and Bower 1998).

A large study looking for more pervasive genotype–phenotype associations was unable to identify any consistent pattern (Weaving et al. 2003). Two more recent studies, on the other hand, have found consistent patterns. Schanen et al. (2004) studied a cohort of 85 RTT cases, 65 of whom had one of the eight main reported mutations. Missense mutations had the least effect – better language and lower overall symptom severity – with one particular mutation (R306C) being associated with the least impairment. A further large study of 524 RTT females found marked differences in survival across the different reported mutations (Jian et al. 2005).

A study using the Australian Rett syndrome database (Robertson L. et al. 2006) found associations between particular behavioural characteristics and several of the specific RTT mutations. Hand washing

and hand flapping were more commonly seen with R270X or R255X mutations, excessive fear or anxiety in those with mutations to R133C and R306C, while body rocking, facial grimacing and low mood with less frequent hand movements were seen in those with an R294X mutation. Jerky, ataxic movements were typical, with gradual loss of lower limb function, most cases confined to wheelchairs by their mid-teens, and onset of epilepsy during the second decade. There is evidence for progressive changes in a variety of neurotransmitter pathwatys in RTT, particularly in AMPA and NMDA receptor density in putamen and kainate receptor density in the causdate (Blue, Naidu and Johnston 1999).

A number of immune differences, such as abnormal CD4+/CD8+ ratios and low levels of natural killer cells, have been found in a study of 20 RTT patients (Fiumara et al. 1999). Elevated levels of auto-antibodies that selectively targeted nerve growth factor were found on repeated testing of five girls with RTT (Klushnik, Gratchev and Belichenko 2001).

The clearest evidence of consistent neuropathology in Rett syndrome is a reduction in dendritic branching, found on detailed ultrastructural examination of a series of 16 RTT brains (Armstrong, Dunn, Antalffy and Trivedi 1995). Differences were primarily seen in neurons projecting from primary areas into association cortices and the limbic system of those with RTT.

Rett syndrome, congenital variant is a rare variant of the Rett phenotype associated with a mutation in the FOXG1 gene at 14q13. To date only ten cases have been reported, 8 girls (Ariani et al. 2008; Mencarelli et al. 2010; Philippe et al. 2010) and two boys (Mencarelli et al. 2009; Le Guen et al. 2010). The phenotype has very early onset with concerns raised usually by 3 months, but in other respects the cases reported to date resemble classic Rett syndrome.

The preserved speech variant of RTT: A number of reports describe the preserved speech variant (PSV) of RTT (De Bona *et al.* 2000; Zappella 1997; Zappella, Gillberg and Ehlers 1998). The PSV appears to have a broadly similar but slowed progression, little evidence of seizure activity, muscle wastage or scoliosis, with preservation of communicative skills, and often with recovery of functional hand use. A recent paper has outlined criteria and provided detailed clinical description of this preserved speech or 'Zapella' variant (Renieri *et al.* 2009).

All cases of PSV so far reported appear to be due to late truncating missense mutations (Zappella *et al.* 2001).

Male Rett syndrome:

- Coleman (1990) reported one possible case of male RTT, and Philippart (1990) two cases – these were reported as possible male Rett on the basis of the physical and behavioural phenotype, as the MeCP2 gene mutation was not identified until 1999.

- In 1998, Schanen *et al.* described two boys with neonatal encephalopathy born into families with RTT girls, suggesting a possible common genetic aetiology.

- Mildly presenting male RTT with MeCP2 somatic mosaicism and slow motor development has been reported (Clayton-Smith, Watson, Ramsden and Black 2000).

- Villard *et al.* (2000) presented two boys who died in infancy of severe neonatal encephalopathy and had a sister with classic RTT. The authors identified a missense mutation in the MeCP2 gene in the sister, tissue from one of the brothers and on the inactive X chromosome in the mother.

- Topçu *et al.* (2005) reported a boy with a MeCP2 deletion and a 'classic' RTT phenotype.

- Zeev *et al.* (2002) described a brother and sister, both with MeCP2 mutations, where the sister had a classic RTT presentation and the brother had a severe neonatal encephalopathy.

- Maiwald *et al.* (2002) described a phenotypic male with a 46,XX (female) karyotype and a MeCP2 deletion and phenotype.

- Leuzzi *et al.* (2004) reported on a 28-month-old boy with a MeCP2 mutation and neurophysiological findings consistent with reduced dendritic branching.

- Budden, Dorsey, Robert and Steiner (2005) and Dayer *et al.* (2007) present further single male RTT cases with mothers carrying mutated MeCP2 genes on their inactivated X chromosomes.

IS THERE A LINK BETWEEN RTT AND ASD? Rett syndrome is a specific clinical subgroup within the autistic spectrum disorders that is recognized on both the DSM-IV and ICD-10 classification systems. It does not really make sense to evaluate whether individuals with RTT have symptomology consistent with ASD, as it is a particular type of ASD with a known genetic basis. Prior to the introduction of the Rett criteria to both systems in 1994, individuals with Rett syndrome would typically receive a diagnosis of autism.

DIFFERENTIAL DIAGNOSIS: As a regressive onset ASD with apparently normal early development and progressive microcephaly that typically affects females, most cases of RTT are easily identified and MeCP2 screening is now widely available to confirm clinical suspicion. CDKL5 Rett syndrome [63b] and Angelman syndrome

[11] are the two most likely alternative diagnoses.

A number of conditions show similar patterns of early developmental regression. Those which could be confused with RTT on behavioural grounds are the various PTEN defects such as BRRS [15] (but these are typically seen in association with macrocephaly); certain inborn errors of metabolism [9, 40]; certain of the epilepsies [19]; and Landau-Kleffner syndrome. Infantile Neural Ceroid Lipofuscinos (INCL)/Batten's disease can also show a similar early pattern; however, the progression is more rapid.

A male Rett case with a supernumerary, paternally inherited X chromosome (Rett + Klinefelter's syndrome) has been reported (Schwartzman et al. 1999).

Recently, it has become clear that MeCP2 defects are also found in Angelman syndrome, neonatal onset encephalopathy, other ASDs, and non-specific X-linked mental retardation in males (Hammer et al. 2002). A recent study also suggests that boys with autism and a MeCP2 gene defect may be more likely to show evidence of developmental regression (Xi et al. 2007).

Lam et al. (2000) reported MeCP2 mutations in both RTT phenotypic female patients and in one four-year-old girl with a clinical diagnosis of infantile autism, out of a screened group of 21 ASD cases.

Carney et al. (2003) screened a population of 69 diagnosed ASD cases and found that two had de novo MeCP2 mutations.

MANAGEMENT AND TREATMENT: As RTT is a progressive disorder with apparently normal early development through the first year, the availability of MeCP2 screening, both antenatally and in early infancy, provides a window of opportunity for clinical intervention before the more obvious manifestations appear.

Boys with a RTT-like phenotype are often not tested for MeCP2. However, the rising numbers of male positive cases reported suggest that this should be a more regular part of diagnostic screening.

A number of treatment approaches have been found to have some efficacy in providing symptomatic improvements: magnesium supplementation has been found beneficial in the treatment of hyperventilation (Egger, Hofacker, Schiel and Holthausen 1992); melatonin for sleep difficulties (McArthur and Budden 1998); and l-carnitine is reported to produce general improvements in well-being (Ellaway et al. 2001).

Prolonged QT intervals are noted in cardiac monitoring of individuals with RTT in general and suggest that a range of medications that affect heart function should be avoided. (See Weaving, Ellaway, Gecz and Christodoulou 2005 for discussion.)

Treatment of seizure activity is as for any other cases (Huppke et al. 2006). Seizure onset is often in adolescence, unlike the Hanefeld variant, in which there is neonatal seizure onset in most cases. One study on seizure control in 8 drug-resistant RTT girls found levetiracetam (Keppra) reduced seizure frequency with consequently improved quality of life in all cases. Seizures reduced in frequency from an average of 21.3 to 1.5 seizures per month after 6 months (Specchio et al. 2009).

Scoliosis often requires corrective surgery and should be closely monitored in classic RTT cases, as secondary effects on breathing and organ restriction are common (Harrison and Webb 1990; Kerr, Webb, Prescott and Milne 2003).

There is ongoing research on the possible role of histone deacetylase inhibitors (HDACIs) in the treatment of RTT, but no published studies on this approach have yet appeared. (See, for discussion, Abel and Zukin 2008; Kalin, Butler and Kozikowski 2009.)

ANIMAL MODELS: In the first reported model, Shahbazian *et al.* (2002) generated mice that expressed a truncated MeCP2 protein similar to those found in RTT patients. After several weeks of apparently normal early development, they developed a progressive neurologic disease with many features seen in RTT: tremors, motor problems, decreased activity levels, seizures and stereotyped movements.

A paper from a group at Harvard Medical School (Ogier *et al.* 2007) has shown in a mouse model that the severe respiratory problems that characterize RTT are linked to reduced levels of brain derived neurotrophic factor (BDNF), which can be reversed by means of an ampakine medication that upregulates glutamatergic AMPA receptors. This treatment results in normal breathing frequency and volume, and holds promise for possible human application.

Adrian Bird and colleagues from the Wellcome Trust Centre for Cell Biology in Edinburgh have contributed a number of important studies on MeCP2. They have shown that a mouse model of RTT, with physiological and behavioural features similar to those seen in affected people, can be reversed through a procedure that makes the MeCP2 gene function normally (Guy *et al.* 2007). In this study a 'loc-cassette' was introduced into the MeCP2 gene sequence to disable, producing a knockout RTT mouse model. Tamoxifen was then given by intraperitoneal injection, displacing the cassette and correcting the gene defect. The consequence in the mice that survived the procedure was a reversal of the behavioural phenotype (the odd motor and breathing patterns seen), and a normalization of brain structure. This happened even when the treatment was administered to adult mice.

The same group has recently begun to elucidate the hydrophilic mechanism by which MeCP2 functions to repress DNA transcription (Ho *et al.* 2008), and the factors that lead to high level of MeCP2 expression. It appears that high levels mirror elevated histones. As both excessive and reduced levels have deleterious effects on cell functioning (Skene *et al.* 2010), this goes some way towards clarifying the neurobiology.

A group at the Massachusetts Institute of Technology in Cambridge, Massachusetts (Giacometti, Luikenhuis, Beard and Jaenisch 2007), has also engineered a transgenic mouse model that can be reversed at different developmental stages, showing that lifespan can be extended and neurologic symptomology delayed by this approach.

A recent paper by Tropea *et al.* (2009) showed that many Rett-like features of the MeCP2-deficient mouse – abnormal heart rate and breathing pattern, low brain weight, reduced life expectancy and abnormal locomotion, and a number of aspects of central nervous system structure such as reduced spinal density and cortical plasticity – were partially corrected by the administration of insulin-like growth factor 1 (IGF1).

A number of animal studies are showing the ability to reverse the effects of MeCP2 defects typically produced by the introduction of a 'STOP cassette' that can be displaced. A recent study has shown that administration of insulin-like growth factor 1 (IGF1) can partially reverse much RTT symptomology. However, IGF1 levels have not been shown to be reduced in RTT (Riikonen 2003), and this approach has *not* been trialled in human RTT.

63b.

Rett syndrome (Hanefeld variant) (RSHV)

GENE LOCUS: Xp22

KEY ASD REFERENCES: Goutieres and Aicardi 1986; Grosso *et al.* 2007a; Hagberg and Skjeldal 1994; Hanefeld 1985; Nectoux *et al.* 2006; Scala *et al.* 2005; Tao *et al.* 2004; Weaving *et al.* 2004

SUMMARY: The Hanefeld variant was first described in a 1985 paper by Folker Hanefeld, and has been termed Rett syndrome (Hanefeld variant). The gene defect involves Cyclin-dependent kinase-like 5 (CDKL5), aka serine-threonine protein kinase 9 (STK9).

The literature, somewhat confusingly, at times differentiates between 'serine/ threonine kinase 9 (STK9) defects', an 'early seizure variant of Rett syndrome' and 'Rett syndrome (Hanefeld variant)'. (See, for example, the discussion in Bahi-Buisson *et al.* 2008a on STK9 cases discussed in Kalscheuer *et al.* 2003.)

All three diagnoses are reported with essentially the same early seizure onset and Rett symptomology, in association with the same CDKL5 gene mutations at Xp22 (in contrast to the 'classic' Rett syndrome MeCP2 mutation at Xq28). It seems reasonable, given the synonymous gene defect and clinical presentation, to suggest that these three diagnoses are different terms for the same condition.

RSHV is a variant of the phenotype found in typical Rett syndrome due to a different gene defect at a different position on the X chromosome. It is similar in clinical presentation – however, typically, in addition to the Rett features (progressive microcephaly; loss of functional hand use; stereotyped hand movements), there is an early onset of seizure activity that is not seen in the MeCP2 form, with a fairly consistent pattern of seizure evolution (Bahi-Buisson *et al.* 2008b). The pattern of seizure activity has been called myoclonic encephalopathy (Buoni *et al* 2006a). One paper that reviewed the literature and presented three new cases found that 13 of 14 CDKL5 patients presented with seizures before three months of age (Evans *et al.* 2005).

CDKL5, like MeCP2, is a kinase, and appears to affect the same physiological pathway (Mari *et al.* 2005), which may explain the overlapping clinical phenotype.

A recent review of clinical cases of early infantile spasms, however, indicates that CDKL5 abnormalities are overrepresented in this broader clinical group, irrespective of Rett phenotype (Archer *et al.* 2006). As is also the case with MeCP2 Rett syndrome, the genotype–phenotype association is not as strong as was initially suspected.

HOW COMMON IS RETT SYNDROME (HANEFELD VARIANT)? The clinical phenotype is largely as for MeCP2 Rett syndrome, and this is classified on both ICD-10 and DSM-IV-Tr as an autistic spectrum disorder. No large-scale screening has so far been conducted; however, Bahi-Buisson *et al.* (2008b) screened 183 girls with encephalopathy and early seizures and identified CDKL5 abnormalities in 20 of them. The most common presentation, seen in five of the eight girls with a RTT-like presentation, was the combination of early onset epilepsy, severe hypotonia and a normal inter-ictal EEG.

MAIN CLINICAL FEATURES: Early onset seizures, usually within the first six weeks after birth; severe early onset hypotonia with delayed motor milestones; normal inter-ictal EEG. Other features as for Rett syndrome [63a].

IS THERE A LINK BETWEEN RETT SYNDROME (HANEFELD VARIANT) AND ASD?

As the RTT phenotype with or without early onset seizures constitutes an ASD diagnosis, this section is circular. The following studies can be taken as clarifying the nature of the condition.

- In 1985 Folker Hanefeld described one child with infantile spasms who went on to develop the clinical phenotype of Rett syndrome. The girl's two sisters had already received a diagnosis of Rett syndrome. This suggested a different mechanism to MeCP2 in these cases.

- Goutieres and Aicardi (1986) described a series of seven girls who partially fulfilled criteria for Rett syndrome but where the presentation was unusual. Five of the girls did not show normal early development, and two had early and intense seizure activity. At least two are likely to be CDKL5 rather than MeCP2 cases.

- Hagberg and Skjeldal (1994) proposed a classification for atypical Rett syndrome variants and applied their criteria to 16 learning disabled girls with 'partial' Rett syndrome. Two of the cases detailed as congenital variants had a history of early seizure as the principal feature of their initial presentation.

- Scala et al. (2005) report frameshift mutations in CDKL5 in two girls with a Rett phenotype but with onset of epilepsy in both cases in the early weeks of life. MeCP2 and ARX mutations were screened for and excluded. (The authors note that CDKL5 mutations have also been reported in West syndrome, another epileptic condition with early onset that has been linked to ASD, but usually with later onset of ASD symptomology (Erol, Alehan and Gümüs 2007; Kayaalp et al. 2007).)

- Tao et al. (2004) were the first to identify CDLK5 defects in two unrelated female cases with a behavioural phenotype consistent with atypical Rett syndrome and no defect in MeCP2. They also presented information on a pair of 41-year-old identical female twins with a Rett phenotype including episodic hyperventilation, marked hypotonia, scoliosis and a CDKL5 transversion. They point out in their review that while in 'classic' Rett cases the majority show evidence of MeCP2 mutation/deletion, this is true only of 20–40 per cent of atypical cases.

- Weaving et al. (2004) reported on two families. In the first family there were three children with single nucleotide CDKL5 deletions: a pair of 19-year-old identical twin girls, one with an atypical Rett phenotype, severe learning disability and a history of complex epilepsy, the other with autism and mild–moderate learning disability (IQ @70) but with good verbal ability and no history of seizures, while a brother with the same deletion had had complex early-onset epilepsy and severe learning difficulties and had died at age 16 from aspiration pneumonia. The second family had two half-sisters, one with a CDKL5 deletion and a Rett-like phenotype, and the second with a 'classic' Rett phenotype and no seizures nor evidence of either a CDKL5 or a MeCP2 deletion.

- Nectoux et al. (2006) documented a girl with a RTT phenotype and generalized convulsions that started at ten days who had an insertion, nonsense and missense mutations of CDKL5 and matrilineal inheritance.

- Grosso et al. (2007a) review the 27 cases reported up to that time and present a case with sleep-related hyperkinetic seizures, suggesting that the range of seizure problems seen with CDKL5 mutation may be broader than had originally been thought.

- Bahi-Buisson *et al.* (2008b) screened a large population of 183 females with learning disability and early onset seizures for CDKL5 mutations, and identified 18 mutations in 20 unrelated cases. Eight had encephalopathy with Rett-like features, five had infantile spasms, and seven had encephalopathy with refractory epileptic seizures. The consistent pattern was of early onset epilepsy and severe hypotonia, together with normal inter-ictal EEG.

DIFFERENTIAL DIAGNOSIS: MeCP2 Rett syndrome [63a] and Angelman syndrome [11] are the two most likely alternative diagnoses.

Netrin G1 translocation on chromosome 1 has been reported in a single case of early seizure variant Rett syndrome without a CDKL5 or MeCP2 mutation (Borg *et al.* 2005). Four non-pathogenic sequence variants but no further cases were found in a large case series screening of 115 Rett phenotype cases with neither CDKL5 or MeCP2 mutations, 52 of whom had early onset seizures (Archer *et al.* 2008).

MANAGEMENT AND TREATMENT: As most studies to date on treatment have not looked specifically at the Hanefeld variant as a separate group, treatment should be as for classical Rett syndrome, in which a number of treatments have been found to have some efficacy: magnesium in the treatment of hyperventilation (Egger, Hofacker, Schiel and Holthausen 1999); melatonin for sleep difficulties (McArthur and Budden 1998); and l-carnitine, which is reported to produce general improvements in well-being (Ellaway *et al.* 1999, 2001).

Specific approaches to the management of seizures should be as for other conditions resulting in infantile spasms. The treatment of choice, despite earlier concerns over visual field restriction, would still seem to be vigabatrin. (See review and update in Willmore *et al.* 2009.) Longer-term outcome studies of vigabatrin use in infancy show fewer lesser effects on visual fields than had been predicted (Gaily, Jonsson and Lappi 2009).

Prolonged QT intervals are noted in cardiac monitoring of individuals with Rett syndrome in general, and suggest that a range of medications that can affect heart function should be avoided. (See Weaving, Ellaway, Gecz and Christodoulou 2005 for discussion.)

ANIMAL MODELS: No specific CDKL5 animal models have been reported at this time.

64.

Rubinstein-Taybi syndrome

aka • broad thumb hallux syndrome

GENE LOCI: 22q13, 16p13.3

KEY ASD REFERENCE: Hellings, Hossain, Martin and Baratang 2002

SUMMARY: First described by Jack Herbert Rubinstein and Hooshang Taybi (1963) this is a malformation syndrome characterized by distinctive facial features and learning disability, together with broad thumbs, and broad big toes. (This combination is the first to alert clinicians to the possible diagnosis.) Children with this condition are typically small for age, have feeding difficulties, fail to thrive, have frequent chest infections, exhibit congenital heart disease and show evidence of developmental delay.

HOW COMMON IS RUBINSTEIN-TAYBI SYNDROME? The best estimate at present is one in 100,000 to one in 125,000 (Hennekam, Van Den Boogaard, Sibbles and Von Spijker 1990). It appears to affect males and females in equal numbers. No differences in prevalence in different racial groups have been reported.

MAIN CLINICAL FEATURES: Initial presentation is often of failure to thrive, as feeding difficulties are common and compounded by a slower rate of skeletal growth. A third of cases present with cardiac problems which often compound respiratory infections.

Motor and other developmental milestones are typically delayed, with an average IQ of 51 being reported. Speech development is often poor.

Broad thumbs and great toes are always seen. Other digits are also commonly enlarged, and in some there is syndactyly or polydactyly.

Reduced development of the upper jaw (hypoplastic maxilla) with a narrow palate is typical. Most of those affected also have a prominent 'beaked' nose, down-slanted eyelids and low-set ears. A third of cases have significantly smaller heads than normal for their overall body size.

Some 80 per cent of boys have undescended testes. Three–quarters of girls have excess body hair. Hypotonia is noted in around two-thirds of cases. Around two-thirds of cases have some degree of strabismus. Around one third of cases show EEG abnormalities, but no significant association with seizure activity has been reported. Tumours of various types are seen in some one in 20 cases.

Sleep problems such as sleep apnoea are reported to be common, but there is no systematic research on this issue (Zucconi et al. 1993).

Milder versions of the condition have been reported, typically described as 'incomplete Rubinstein-Taybi syndrome'. (See, for example, Zimmerman et al. 2007.)

IS THERE A LINK BETWEEN RUBINSTEIN-TAYBI SYNDROME AND ASD? One paper suggests a possible link between Rubinstein-Taybi syndrome and ASD. Hellings, Hossain, Martin and Baratang (2002) describe an adult female with a complex clinical presentation. She had a severe learning disability, overactivity, inattention and recurrent manic episodes with aggression, and had received a dual psychiatric diagnosis of bipolar mood disorder and autism.

Note: The authors suggest a possible link with GABA receptor or transmitter function, as abnormalities in GABAergic function have been linked to 16p13.3 deletion, a site implicated in Rubinstein-Taybi syndrome. This would be consistent with other GABA mechanisms (such as the defect seen in OCA2 [55] at 15q11.2) that have recently been suggested in ASD (DeLong 2007). It may also account for the high level of side-effects with neuroleptic medication reported in this condition (Levitas and Reid 1998).

DIFFERENTIAL DIAGNOSIS: Several other conditions that have been reported in association with ASD, or which overlap with ASD-associated conditions, can present with similar clinical features:

- Aarskog syndrome [8]
- Simpson-Golabi-Behmel syndrome [87]
- Weaver syndrome [89].

In addition, a number of other rare overgrowth conditions have a similar phenotype:

- Greig syndrome
- Larsen syndrome
- Pfeiffer syndrome (Cohen 1973, 1977)

- Saethre-Chotzen syndrome.

(See Cohen, Neri and Weksberg 2002.)

MANAGEMENT AND TREATMENT: The high level of side effects with conventional neuroleptic medication was noted above (Levitas and Reid 1998).

There can be problems with anaesthesia due to difficulties with intubation (Twigg and Cook 2002). There is a particular susceptibility to adverse reactions to certain anaesthetics such as succinylcholine (Stirt 1981). Wiley *et al.* (2003) have provided medical guidelines for clinical management and surveillance of patients with Rubinstein-Taybi syndrome.

The specific nature of the physiological defects underlying Rubinstein-Taybi suggests that pharmacological approaches which modify the cyclic AMP response element binding protein (CREB) mapped to 16p13.3 may have direct effects on the cognitive and long-term memory problems seen in Rubinstein-Taybi (Hallam and Bourtchouladze 2006). This provides a specific focus for a novel therapeutic approach to this condition that addresses some of its core features.

A second gene site at 22q13 (EP300) has been identified as sufficient to cause the Rubinstein-Taybi phenotype (Roelfsema *et al.* 2005). This gene encodes a histone acetyltransferase that is important in cell proliferation and differentiation. This may respond differently to clinical treatment.

There is ongoing research on the possible role of histone deacetylase inhibitors (HDACIs) in the treatment of Rubinstein-Taybi, but no published studies on this approach have yet appeared. (See, for discussion, Abel and Zukin 2008; Kalin, Butler and Kozikowski 2009.)

ANIMAL MODELS: A fairly accurate mouse model of Rubinstein-Taybi syndrome has been produced through insertion mutation of the CPB gene. This results in the production of a truncated CPB protein (Oike *et al.* 1999). The resulting mice show many of the key clinical features of Rubinstein-Taybi syndrome, such as retarded bone maturation, growth retardation and hypoplastic maxilla with a narrow palate.

Behaviourally, the mouse Rubinstein-Taybi syndrome model has problems with long-term memory, and it has been shown that these can be ameliorated with phosphodiesterase 4 inhibitors (Bourtchouladze *et al.* 2003).

65.

Schindler disease

aka
- neuroaxonal dystrophy, Schindler type
- alpha-N-acetylgalactosaminidase deficiency, type I
- NAGA deficiency, type I

GENE LOCUS: 22q11

KEY ASD REFERENCE: Blanchon, Gay, Gibert and Lauras 2002

SUMMARY: Schindler disease is a lysosomal disease caused by lack of the enzyme alpha-N-acetylgalactosaminidase. It was first described by Schindler and colleagues from Rotterdam (Schindler *et al.* 1989; van Diggelen *et al.* 1988). There has recently been debate about a possible role for mutations in the phospholipase-2 greoul 6 gene (PLA2G6) at 22q13.1 as a second independent genetic factor in Schindler's disease that could account for the phenotypic heterogeneity (see: Westaway, Gregory and Hayflick 2006). PLA2G6 is a calcium dependent enzyme that catalyses glycerophospholipid hydrolysis. Mutation leads to a neurodegenerative picture with iron accumulation in the basal ganglia (Kurian *et al.* 2008).

HOW COMMON IS SCHINDLER DISEASE? No epidemiological studies have been carried out, so prevalence is currently unknown. However, given its obvious and progressive course, it is an extremely rare presentation, with only a dozen reported cases in the world literature. On current understanding it seems unlikely that any benign or *forme fruste* variants of the condition will be identified.

MAIN CLINICAL FEATURES: Schindler disease is a type of lysosomal storage disorder that is caused by a lesion to the alpha-N-acetylgalactosaminidase gene. It is a neuroaxonal dystrophy with similar neuropathology to other forms (Wolfe, Schindler and Desnick 1995).

There is considerable phenotypic variability, and two types are recognized: type 1, which is infantile onset, and type 2, also known as Kanzaki disease, with onset in adulthood. The co-morbid case reported by Blanchon *et al.* is clearly type 1.

In affected infants (type 1) development appears normal in the early months of life, after which there is rapid deterioration with frequent myoclonic seizures, severe motor delay and cortical blindness.

IS THERE A LINK BETWEEN SCHINDLER DISEASE AND ASD? To date, there is only a single case of Schindler disease that has been reported in association with ASD. This was a 12-year-old boy with an IQ of 48 who met ADI-R criteria for autistic disorder, reported in 2002 by a group from the Kanner Centre in Saint Etienne in France (Blanchon, Gay, Gibert and Lauras 2002). As the prevalence of Schindler disease is not known, it is unclear whether there is a true association, and a biological basis to any link can only be speculated about. As so many overlapping conditions associated with ASD are located at 22q11, the link could be due to contiguous affected regions. It is clear that Schindler disease and ASD can co-occur; whether there is an increased ASD that results from Schindler disease is a question that awaits further research.

DIFFERENTIAL DIAGNOSIS: Predominantly other neuroaxonal dystrophies, such as Seitelberger disease (Wang A.M. *et al.* 1988).

MANAGEMENT AND TREATMENT: At present no specific treatments for Schindler disease have been found.

ANIMAL MODELS: There are currently no animal models.

66.

Smith-Lemli-Opitz syndrome (SLOS)

aka • RHS syndrome

GENE LOCUS: 11q12–q13

KEY ASD REFERENCES: Aneja and Tierney 2008; Sikora *et al.* 2006; Tierney, Nwokoro and Kelley 2000; Tierney *et al.* 2001, 2006

SUMMARY: Smith-Lemli-Opitz syndrome was first reported in a paper by David Weyhe Smith, John Marius Opitz and Luc Lemli (Smith, Lemli and Opitz 1964). It is the first reported metabolic syndrome to be reported that results in multiple congenital malformations and a distinct behavioural phenotype. It shows an autosomal recessive pattern of inheritance.

A more severe form, 'Smith-Lemli-Opitz type II' (Curry *et al.* 1987), will not be discussed here.

SLOS results from a gene defect that affects the production of the enzyme 7-dehydrocholesterol reductase (Mobius *et al.* 1998; Tint *et al.* 1994). The gene has been mapped to 11q12–q13 (Wassif *et al.* 1998). A number of useful overviews are available which deal with cholesterol biosynthesis and the problems seen in SLOS and other related conditions (Opitz and de la Cruz 1994; Herman 2003; Salen *et al.* 1996). Recent general reviews on SLOS can be found in Irons (2007) and Porter (2008).

The two major northern european SLOS alleles, c.964–IG>C and p.Trp151X, would appear to have first appeared approximately 3000 years ago (Witsch-Baumgartner *et al.* 2008).

HOW COMMON IS SLOS? This is currently not firmly established. A review of all diagnosed cases in the UK from 1984 to 1998 suggested a rate of one in 60,000 (Ryan *et al.* 1998). The availability of reliable screening techniques (for example, Scalco *et al.* 2003) has considerably widened the reported clinical phenotype.

One US study (Battaile *et al.* 2001) screening 1,503 anonymous blood samples for one specific SLOS mutation (IVS8-1G-C) has estimated the carrier frequency for all SLOS mutations to be as high as one in 30, with a predicted prevalence of SLOS of between one in 1,590 and one in 13,500. This is the most prevalent mutation in populations of Western European ancestry. However, in other populations, such as those of Czech and Slovak descent, it is uncommon (Kozak *et al.* 2000), and carrier frequency may be significantly lower in such groups.

Rates of SLOS in the Czech Republic have been estimated at one in 10,000 (Opitz 1999) and in Slovakia at one in 15,000 to one in 20,000 (Bzduch, Beluchova and Skodova 2000).

Based on population prevalence of carriers for the gene in a recent Polish screening study of the most common mutations (Ciara *et al.* 2006), the prevalence of SLOS in this population is likely to be in the region of one in 2,300 to one in 3,900. On this basis SLOS could be a common cause of ASD, and would be the most common known genetic cause if similar rates were seen in other populations. SLOS is thought to be more common in Central Europe. However, this finding may not generalize to other populations, as the different mutations have been reported to occur at very different rates. One study comparing 59 British, Polish, German and Austrian cases found different patterns of mutation in the different populations (Witsch-Baumgartner *et al.* 2001).

GENETICS: A large number of genetic factors have been identified as sufficient to result in SLOS, with more than 120 separate mutations so far having been described, the majority being missense mutations (well over 85 per cent are of this type), with smaller numbers of nonsense mutations (see p.395–396), small deletions and insertions and mutations that affect splicing or translation initiation (Correa-Cerro and Porter 2005; Nowaczyk and Waye 2001; Yu and Patel 2005).

It seems likely that variations in the gene mutations involved relate to the biochemical differences in cholesterol synthesis and to the clinical phenotype (Neklason, Andrews, Kelley and Metherall 1999). One suggested mechanism by which the gene defects found in SLOS may result in developmental pathology is through interference with hedgehog signalling proteins that are normally modified by cholesterol (Kelley *et al.* 1996; Porter, Young and Beachy 1996).

ANTENATAL DETECTION: Antenatal diagnosis of SLOS by biochemical profiling has been possible for some years (Johnson J.A. *et al.* 1994; McGaughran, Donnai, Clayton and Mills 1994). Reliable diagnosis is possible (Irons and Tint 1998) from testing of amniotic fluid (Dallaire *et al.* 1995; Kratz and Kelley 1999), chorionic villus sampling (Kratz and Kelley 1999) or maternal urinary steroid levels (Jezela-Stanek *et al.* 2006).

Antenatal screening demonstrates low maternal urinary oestriol (Jezela-Stanek *et al.* 2006) and elevated plasma oestriol levels (Shackleton, Roitman, Kratz and Kelley 1999) and can be useful in early detection of SLOS. Shackleton's group also demonstrated the presence of equine-type oestriols that are not normally found but made up over half of the oestrogens detected in the mother carrying a foetus affected by SLOS. It has been speculated that the effects on oestriol levels may be due to abnormal development of the foetal adrenal glands (McKeever and Young 1990), and adrenal insufficiency has been found to be a complicating factor in some cases (Andersson *et al.* 1999).

Note: Several other conditions show similar differences in urinary and blood marker oestriol levels, in particular Down syndrome [31] (Craig *et al.* 2006) and X-linked ichthyosis [80], but abnormalities can be found in a range of other presentations (Duric *et al.* 2003; Kim *et al.* 2000).

A number of abnormalities are detectable on ultrasound. Intrauterine growth retardation is most common, being seen in two-thirds of cases (Goldenberg *et al.* 2004).

MAIN CLINICAL FEATURES: Smith-Lemli-Opitz syndrome is a condition that affects a gene critical to the body's production of cholesterol. The gene is called 3 beta-hydroxysteroid Delta7-reductase, or DHCR7. There is now an extensive body of research on DHCR7 and on how it affects development. (See Yu and Patel 2005 for a review.) Defects in the gene can result in a range of physical abnormalities (Kelley 2000).

There is a wide range of severity reported in SLOS, and this is thought primarily to reflect dietary levels of cholesterol intake (Curry *et al.* 1987; Kelley 1998; Kelley and Hennekam 2000; Nowaczyk *et al.* 2001b; Opitz and de la Cruz 1994; Opitz, Gilbert-Barness, Ackerman and Lowichik 2002; Porter 2000; Ryan *et al.* 1998; Smith, Lemli and Opitz 1964; Waye *et al.* 2002).

In the 25 cases reported by Ryan *et al.* (1998), 98 per cent had learning disability, 80 per cent had second/third toe syndactyly, and 72 per cent had congenital cardiac problems. In this series, serum 7-dehydrocholesterol levels did not appear linked to clinical severity of the disorder.

Typical physical features include microcephaly with bitemporal narrowing, ptosis, epicanthic folds, a short nose with anteverted nostrils, capillary haemangioma of the forehead, postaxial polydactyly, and second/third toe syndactyly. Growth retardation is a common feature. A high, arched, narrow palate is common and cleft palate is not uncommon, and hypospadias is common in males (Cowell 1978; Kelley and Hennekam 2000; Nowaczyk and Waye 2001; Nowaczyk *et al.* 2001b; Opitz and de la Cruz 1994; Opitz, Gilbert-Barness, Ackerman and Lowichik 2002; Porter 2000; Smith, Lemli and Opitz 1964; Waye *et al.* 2002).

Ambiguous genital development has been reported in a number of genetically male cases (Bialer *et al.* 1987; Fukazawa *et al.* 1992; Lachman *et al.* 1991; Scarbrough, Huddleston and Finley 1986).

In infancy, poor sucking, irritability and failure to thrive are commonly noted (Pinsky and DiGeorge 1965).

The typical behavioural presentation includes learning disability; some are in the low normal range of intelligence (Anderson A.J. *et al.* 1998; Langius *et al.* 2003; Mueller *et al.* 2003; Nowaczyk, Whelan and Hill (1998), and have behavioural abnormalities (Tierney *et al.* 2000, 2001).

Tactile, visual and auditory sensitivity are reported to be common problems (Anstey and Taylor 1999; Tierney, Nwokoro and Kelley 2000). Sleep problems are reported to be a common feature, but lessen with age and are usually not significant after puberty. Self-injury and aggression are significant issues for many and may require specific approaches to management.

Structural brain anomalies are seen in around a third of those with SLOS. The main anomalies reported include central cerebellar vermal hypoplasia, partial or complete callosal dysgenesis (failure of formation of) and hypoplasia of the frontal lobes (Gorlin, Cohen and Levin 1990). The brain is smaller than normal in some 84 per cent. (See Kelley and Hennekam 2000 and Hennekam 2005 for reviews.) Complete callosal agenesis, together with partial development of the frontal lobes, has also been reported (Kelley *et al.* 1996). Holoprosencephaly has been reported in a number of cases (Kelley 1998; McKeever and Young 1990; Nowaczyk *et al.* 2001a).

The clinical features of SLOS are partly modified by the maternal genotype, and in particular the effects of the ApoE genotype on transmission of cholesterol from the maternal blood supply to the developing embryo (Witsch-Baumgartner *et al.* 2004).

IS THERE A LINK BETWEEN SMITH-LEMLI-OPITZ SYNDROME AND ASD?
The first published paper to suggest a link between SLOS and ASD appeared in 2000 (Tierney, Nwokoro and Kelley 2000). Tierney and colleagues reviewed their own and others' work, and noted that six out of 13 cases they had presented at an American Academy of Child and Adolescent Psychiatry (AACAP) meeting in 1999 had scored as autistic on both the ADI-R and on DSM-IV criteria.

- Tierney *et al.* (2001) used multiple age-dependent postal questionnaires and telephone interviews to evaluate the behavioural phenotype of 56 subjects with SLOS. Forty-seven were later followed up with direct observation and interview. The authors concluded that individuals with SLOS manifest a characteristic behavioural profile of cognitive delay, sensory hyperreactivity, irritability, language impairment, sleep-cycle disturbance, self-injurious behaviour, syndrome-specific motor movements, upper body opisthotonus and autism spectrum behaviours. Nine of the 17 subjects (53 per cent) who were assessed on the ADI-R met criteria for autistic disorder.

- In 2006 Sikora *et al.* published a study of 14 children with SLOS, aged between three and 16, using questionnaire, interview and direct observational measures. Depending on the measures used, 71–86 per cent fulfilled criteria for an ASD, with some 50 per cent fulfilling criteria for autistic disorder.

In a study of cholesterol in an unselected series of 100 ASD cases obtained from the Autism Genetic Resource Exchange (AGRE) specimen bank, Tierney *et al.* (2006) found low cholesterol levels (below the normal population fifth centile levels) in 19 cases. No cases had levels consistent with SLOS, but this report suggests that a significant proportion of ASD cases have abnormal sterol metabolism.

The most recent paper on ASD and SLOS (Aneja and Tierney 2008) is a review of the role of cholesterol in autism, using SLOS as a paradigm case. It provides information on the various mechanisms

by which sterol deficiencies can result in developmental abnormalities, namely:

- the role of cholesterol in embryonic and foetal development (Tabin and McMahon 1997)
- cholesterol as a precursor in the formation of neuroactive steroids (Marcos et al. 2004)
- cholesterol's role in the formation of myelin (Saher et al. 2005)
- cholesterol as a modulator of oxytocin receptors (Gimpl, Wiegand, Burger and Fahrenholz 2002)
- cholesterol as a modulator of serotonin 1A receptor (Chattopadhyay et al. 2005).

A recent study compared excretion levels of two compounds: 8-hydroxy-2-deoxyguanosine (8-OHdG) and 8-isoprostane-F2alpha (8-iso-PGF2alpha). The study compared 33 autistic children with 29 healthy, group-matched controls, and a slight overall group difference was found. The autistic group's distribution was bimodal and a small subgroup of the autistic children showed a far more marked elevation than controls, suggesting that a subgroup had a specific defect in sterol metabolism (Ming et al. 2005).

DIFFERENTIAL DIAGNOSIS: A marker found almost exclusively in SLOS is the particular pattern of second/third toe (Y-shaped) syndactyly (Gofflot et al. 2003). It is reported in a high proportion of cases (in 79/80 in the series reported by Cunniff et al. 1997, and in 40/55 of those reported by Johnson V.P. 1975).

Various SLOS features are seen in other conditions, and the phenotypic variability within SLOS is wide. However, the biochemical profile (Seller et al. 1997) and genetics are specific.

A number of other conditions present with similar abnormalities of sterol metabolism, including:

- beta-sitosterolaemia (Parsons et al. 1995)
- CHILD syndrome (Porter 2003)
- desmosterolosis (Porter 2003)
- mevalonic aciduria (Bretón Martínez et al. 2007)
- X-linked dominant chondrodysplasia punctata (Martanová et al. 2007).

A number of conditions present with varying combinations of features that overlap with those seen in SLOS, and some are reported as co-occurring in the same individuals:

- Dubowitz syndrome (Tsukahara and Opitz 1996)
- Meckel-Gruber syndrome (Alexiev, Lin, Sun and Brenner 2006)
- Noonan syndrome [52]
- Nguyen syndrome (Nakane, Hayashibe and Nakazawa 2005)
- Russell-Silver syndrome (Plotts and Livermore 2007)
- Simpson-Golabi-Behmel syndrome [87]
- trisomy 13 syndrome (both conditions can co-exist) (Alkuraya, Picker, Irons and Kimonis 2005)
- trisomy 18 (Edwards) syndrome (Edwards et al. 1960)
- pseudo-trisomy 13 syndrome (Cohen and Gorlin 1991)
- Pallister-Hall syndrome (Azzam et al. 2005).

MANAGEMENT AND TREATMENT:

Cholesterol supplementation: Antenatal cholesterol supplementation is feasible and produces *in utero* improvement in foetal plasma cholesterol and red cell volume (Irons et al. 1999). To date no reports have been published on the effects of this approach on subsequent development.

The age at which cholesterol supplementation and correction of

7-dehydrocholesterol build-up is addressed may be critical, as effects on myelin development and blood–brain barrier function in the nervous system may be difficult to reverse (Morell and Jurevics 1996).

Irons *et al.* (1994) provided an early report on improvements in cholesterol levels in a severely affected girl with SLOS treated with bile salts and cholesterol. Post-treatment cholesterol levels were, however, still well below normal values.

In an early review Kelley (1998) noted reports of marked improvements in physical growth and development, communication, self-injurious behaviour and agitation. Elias *et al.* (1997) reported similar results in six children they had treated, with, in addition, reduced skin sensitivity, better infection tolerance, reduced gastrointestinal symptomology and improved developmental progress, with no reported adverse reactions. Nwokoro and Mulvihill (1997) reported on bile acid/cholesterol replacement in six cases with reported behavioural improvements and improvements in quality of life, but variable effects on plasma cholesterol levels. Irons *et al.* (1997) reported biochemical and clinical improvement (in growth and neurodevelopmental status) in 14 SLOS patients in parallel with increase in plasma cholesterol and per cent sterol as cholesterol after treatment with cholesterol alone (3) or cholesterol in combination with bile acids (11).

Linck *et al.* (2000) were able to show reductions in 7-dehydrocholesterol and increases in cholesterol in serum through dietary cholesterol supplementation.

Sikora *et al.* (2004) reported no improvement in development in 14 SLOS cases who were followed up over a six-year period of cholesterol supplementation. This study did, however, find wide variation in the results obtained, with two cases showing substantial improvement (but

full data was obtained on only two cases). Initial cholesterol levels, not response to supplementation, seemed the best predictor of outcome.

Improvements in skin sensitivity to ultraviolet light have been documented in response to cholesterol supplementation (Azurdia, Anstey and Rhodes 2001; Starck, Lovgren-Sandblom and Bjorkhem 2002a).

Simvastatin: As part of the metabolic problem may result from the build-up of 7-dehydrocholesterol in body tissues, studies are being conducted on the use of simvastatin to reduce 7-dehydrocholesterol in parallel with cholesterol supplementation. Results on development are mixed (Haas *et al.* 2007; Jira *et al.* 2000; Starck, Lovgren-Sandblom and Bjorkhem 2002b), but the combined treatment appears well tolerated and has the predicted metabolic effects (Chan *et al.* 2009).

Other aspects of care: A variety of management issues are discussed in Kelley and Hennekam (2000) and in Irons (2007).

There are minor issues in anaesthetic care where diagnostic imaging or surgical management is required (Choi and Nowaczyk 2000), and other issues in surgical management have been discussed (Craigie, Ba'ath, Fryer and Baillie 2005). Minor issues in dental treatment have also been reported (Muzzin and Harper 2003).

Haloperidol can exacerbate symptomology as it can bind to the DHCR7 binding site leading to an excessive build-up of 7-dehydrocholesterol.

ANIMAL MODELS: Fitzky *et al.* (1998) identified the syntenic regions for the human and mouse delta-7-sterol reductase genes on 11q13 and 7F5.

SLOS-like phenotype in offspring resulted from use of a 7-dehydrocholesterol inhibitor with pregnant, cholesterol-deficient mice (Dehart, Lanone, Tint and

Sulik 1997; Roux, Horvath and Dupuis 1979; Suzuki and De Paul 1971).

In one mouse model of SLOS, where the same gene defect was produced, similarly lowered levels of both serum and tissue cholesterol were found, and an impaired response to glutamate in frontal neurons in the cerebral cortex was seen (Wassif *et al.* 2001). The mice exhibited intrauterine growth retardation and craniofacial abnormalities, including palatal clefting. Behaviourally, they were hypotonic with decreased activity and poor sucking.

A more recent mouse model of SLOS (Waage-Baudet *et al.* 2003) produced mice with the following structural central nervous system differences: commissural deficiencies, hippocampal abnormalities, with enlargement of serotonergic neurons.

In a subsequent study (Waage-Baudet *et al.* 2005), the same group studied differences in hindbrain development, highlighting abnormalities in axonal guidance and commissural development.

Allergies are a common feature in SLOS. A study of abnormalities of lipid rafts and mast cell activation in *Dhcr7* −/− mice provides evidence on one possible mechanism (Kovarova *et al.* 2006).

67.

Smith-Magenis syndrome (SMS)

GENE LOCUS: 17p11.2, typically with interstitial deletion, but also with specific mutation of RAI1

KEY ASD REFERENCES: Cohen *et al.* 2005; de Almeida, Reis and Martins 1989; Dykens, Finucane and Gayley 1997; Hicks, Ferguson, Bernier and Lemay 2008; Lockwood *et al.* 1988; Mariner *et al.* 1986;

Vostanis, Harrington, Prendergast and Farndon 1994

SUMMARY: The first paper to describe a clinical series detailed nine SMS cases with 17p11.2 deletions (Smith *et al.* 1986); a paper describing a further small series of six cases appeared later the same year (Stratton *et al.* 1986). All 15 cases were described as conforming to the same clinical phenotype – physically they were described as brachycephalic, having midface hypoplasia and prognathism, and as being growth retarded. They had hoarse voices, speech delay, delayed milestones and behavioural problems.

Martin, Wolters and Smith (2006) highlight the high degree of maladaptive behaviour seen in individuals with SMS. Global cognitive functioning in SMS is delayed and is generally consistent with the person's communication and daily living skills, whereas socialization is often better than would be expected from IQ scores.

The current view of SMS is that it is a microdeletion syndrome that results from a mutation/deletion that includes the retinoic-acid induced 1 (RAI1) gene. RAI1 seems sufficient to produce the SMS phenotype (Slager *et al.* 2003), while in most cases (90 per cent) this is part of a 3.7-Mb interstitial deletion in chromosome 17p11.2 (Potocki *et al.* 2000a). RAI1 is within the larger Smith-Magenis chromosome region (Girirajan, Elsas, Devriendt and Elsea 2005) that results in the variable cardiac and renal problems seen in most cases.

For a recent review of SMS, see Gropman, Elsea, Duncan and Smith (2007).

HOW COMMON IS SMS? The best recent estimate is that the population prevalence of SMS is between one in 15,000 and one in 25,000 (Juyal *et al.* 1996; Smith A.C.M.

et al 2006). Prevalence of one in 600 has been found in a population with learning disability of unknown cause (Struthers, Carson, McGill and Khalifa 2002).

Similar numbers of male and female cases are reported. There have been no reports of any association with racial group.

MAIN CLINICAL FEATURES: The first clinical report of a child with Smith-Magenis syndrome (Patil and Bartley 1984) gave details of a four-year-old girl with a slight build (50th percentile for height and head circumference but fifth centile for weight). She had a significant learning disability, delayed speech and language, generalized hypotonia, small ears, and a conductive hearing loss. She was found to have an interstitial deletion of chromosome 17p11.2.

Commonly reported early features are infantile hypotonia and failure to thrive. Infant development does not seem to show autistic features, which become more apparent with age, typically between two and three years of age (Wolters *et al.* 2009).

A number of physical features are consistently seen:

- brachycephaly
- flattened midface
- broad bridge to the nose
- Mobius/Cupid's bow mouth shape
- short stature.

(See Lockwood *et al.* 1988)

Other commonly reported problems include:

- otolaryngolic abnormalities
- ocular abnormalities
- cleft lip/palate
- peripheral nerve problems
- scoliosis
- heart defects
- abnormal genitalia

- epilepsy

(Greenberg *et al.* 1991).

Learning disability is typically present, but of variable level, typically with an IQ of between 40 and 60, although the reported range is wider (Greenberg *et al.* 1996). Communication is typically impaired.

A number of behavioural features are thought to be characteristic, particularly self-mutilation and inserting objects into body orifices such as the ears. (See, for example, Greenberg *et al.* 1991.)

Sleep disturbance is seen in a high proportion of those with SMS: in 62 per cent of those reported by Greenberg *et al.* in 1991 and in 75 per cent of those they reported on in 1996; in 60 per cent of those studied by Dykens, Finucane and Gayley (1997); in a series of 19 cases reported by Potocki *et al.* (2000b), all of whom had abnormal excretion of a melatonin metabolite; and in a further series of 20 cases (De Leersnyder *et al.* 2001), 40 per cent of whom showed evidence of an abnormal pattern of melatonin release. Some (2/32 cases studied by Greenberg *et al.* 1991) have absent REM (rapid eye movement) sleep.

Smith A.C.M. *et al.* (2002) carried out lipid profiling on 49 SMS cases and noted that cholesterol levels were elevated above the 95th centile in 57 per cent.

Parental age does not appear to be an additional risk factor.

Genetic aspects of SMS: It is possible that various aspects of the SMS phenotype, particularly hypotonia, seizure activity, learning disability and the behavioural phenotype, result from mitochondrial abnormalities due to mutation or deletion of the 5-Prime-@ Nucleotidase, Mitochondrial (NT5M) gene which is in the SMS critical region of 17p11.2 (Lucas *et al.* 2001; Rampazzo *et al.* 2000). NT5M is a deoxyribonucleoside, which is imported into mitochondria where it is converted to a deoxyribonucleoside kinase and limits the accumulation of thymidine triphosphate.

Specific deletion of the RI1 gene can result in a phenotype without short stature or gastrointestinal involvement, but with the craniofacial differences – brachiocephaly and midface hypoplasia – and the behavioural components of SMS – self-injury, temper, and sleep disturbance (Girirajan, Elsas, Devriendt and Elsea 2005). This is similar to the restricted SMS phenotype shown in animal models with selective *Rai1* deletion (Walz *et al.* 2006). The genetic mechanisms that in part account for the heterogeneity of the phenotype aare complex and only just becoming better understood (see, for example: Bi *et al.* 2003)

IS THERE A LINK BETWEEN SMS AND ASD? A number of papers have so far been published reporting cases with Smith-Magenis syndrome and ASD:

- Mariner *et al.* (1986) published an early paper on autosomal gene defects associated with ASD and learning difficulties. One of the cases they describe is the first *de novo* 17p deletion reported in association with ASD.

- Lockwood *et al.* (1988) discussed three cases with 17p11.2 deletions, one of whom, a 17-year-old Caucasian girl with an IQ of 40, was described as having some autistic behaviour but good eye contact.

- De Almeida, Reis and Martins (1989) presented a further single SMS case: a three-year-old boy with delayed development, a broad face with hypoplastic midface, prognathism, and behavioural anomalies consistent with an ASD.

- Vostanis, Harrington, Prendergast and Farndon (1994) described two autosomal genetic conditions in association with ASD. One of these cases, a 17-year-old boy, had an interstitial chromosome 17 deletion.

- Dykens, Finucane and Gayley (1997) published a study on the behavioural and cognitive profile of a small series of ten individuals (two male; eight female) with SMS, aged 14–51. A battery of cognitive and attainment tests were reported: the Vineland Adaptive Behavior Scales and the Reiss Maladaptive Behavior screen. The paper does not present data on the autism scores from the Reiss screen. All that can be concluded is that fewer than five of these people were scored above the risk cut-off for autism on this measure.

- Hicks, Ferguson, Bernier and Lemay (2008) recently reported on a pair of three-and-a-half-year-old identical male twins concordant for SMS, learning disability, communication delay, motor stereotypies, self-injurious behaviour and ASD. This is the first description of SMS in twins. The twins were divergent on a number of features – particularly the presence of cardiac and renal abnormalities and the extent of their language problems and behavioural issues. Despite their zygosity, the twins had marked differences in presentation, including divergence for cardiac anomalies (twin A had atrio- and ventriculo-septal defects and pulmonary stenosis while twin B was normal) and renal anomalies (twin A had bilateral reflux while twin B was normal), delayed expressive language development (more severe in twin A), and behavioural phenotype (destructive behavioural outbursts were markedly worse in twin B).

DIFFERENTIAL DIAGNOSIS: All of the differential diagnoses are other genetic conditions that have been linked to ASD.

The principal differential diagnosis to be considered is fragile-X [35]; other conditions that can sometimes present with a similar phenotype are 22q11.2 deletion syndromes [18, 29a, 76]; Prader-Willi syndrome [61]; and Williams syndrome [77]. Down syndrome [31] can occasionally be confused with SMS in the neonatal period.

MANAGEMENT AND TREATMENT: In one study with nine children (De Leersnyder et al. 2001) acebutolol, a selective beta-1-adrenergic antagonist, was given early in the morning. A significant decrease in inappropriate behaviour and improvement in concentration were noted. In addition, delayed sleep onset, lengthened sleep and delayed waking were also seen.

There is clear evidence that hypercholesterolaemia is linked to SMS, as is an increased risk of cardiac malformation. Treatment strategies to lower particularly LDL cholesterol would seem advisable, and maintenance management with cholesterol-lowering agents may be useful to consider.

Sleep problems are common in SMS, and appear linked to a defect in the production of serotonin and abnormal circadian release of melatonin. This suggests that serotonin supplementation, or supplementation with precursors, may also be helpful.

There is a particular constellation of challenging behaviour difficulties that appear to result in an SMS-specific behavioural phenotype. The general literature on treatment of such behaviours in ASD suggests that consideration of medications such as risperidone may be warranted where behavioural strategies have proved ineffective. However, this needs to be carefully monitored, as side effects can be significant (Yang and Tsai 2004).

ANIMAL MODELS: A number of animal models have been developed to approximate the 17p11.2 deletions seen in human SMS cases.

• Bi et al. (2002) were the first to identify a SMS critical region on the chromosome mouse 11 region syntenic to human 17p11.2.

• Walz et al. (2003) developed syntenic mouse chromosome 11 models. Deletions in the equivalent region resulted in craniofacial anomalies, seizures, obesity, abnormal circadian rhythm and reduced male fertility.

• In a subsequent study Walz et al. (2006) selectively preserved the *Rai1* gene by generating compound heterozygous mice with a Dp(11)17 allele and a null *Rai1* allele, resulting in normal disomic gene dosage of *Rai1*. This demonstrated that *Rai1* was a critical region both for weight control and for the behavioural phenotype of their earlier syntenic knockout models, as the 18 other 17p11.2 genes could be removed without producing the same physical or behavioural effects which appeared to be sensitive to *Rai1* dosage.

• Yan, Bi and Lupski (2007) produced a mouse strain with a size of deletion intermediate between the large v17q11.2 deletions that were originally produced to simulate SMS and the microdeletions which showed the critical effect of *Rai1*. The phenotypes produced were intermediate between the two earlier models, suggesting that a range of background genetic factors influence the expression of the *Rai1* gene deletion.

68.

Sotos syndrome

aka • cerebral gigantism

GENE LOCUS: 5q35

KEY ASD REFERENCES: Cohen 2003; Finegan *et al.* 1994; Morrow, Whitman and Accardo 1990; Mouridsen and Hansen 2002; Rutter and Cole 1991; Zapella 1990

SUMMARY: Sotos syndrome is an overgrowth condition – people who have it are significantly larger than would be expected for their families.

The syndrome was first described in 1964 (Sotos *et al.* 1964) in a paper on five children with a disorder characterized by excessively rapid growth, acromegalic features, and a nonprogressive cerebral disorder with learning disability. A high-arched palate and a prominent jaw were noted in several of these cases. The children were large at birth, their length being between the 90th and 97th centiles, with advanced bone age in most.

An earlier report (Schlesinger 1931) appears to document a remarkably similar phenotype and may be the earliest account identified to date.

The key features are accelerated bone ageing (a wrist X-ray to identify accelerated bone age was the diagnostic tool before the 5q35 abnormality was identified) over the first four years, acromegaly, and non-progressive neurological deficits.

The NSD1 gene (nuclear receptor-binding Su-var, enhancer of Zeste, and trithorax domain protein 1) has been implicated in a high proportion of cases, with varying specific NSD1 defects in different populations (microdeletions appear particularly prevalent in the Japanese)

(Douglas *et al.* 2003; Kamimura *et al.* 2003; Kurotaki *et al.* 2002; Rio *et al.* 2003). The localization of Sotos syndrome to NSD1 at 5q35 is a fairly recent finding (Kurotaki *et al.* 2002). NSD1 defects do not appear to be common in other overgrowth conditions (Türkmen *et al.* 2003).

There are two recent Orphanet reviews of Sotos syndrome (Baujat and Cormier-Daire 2007; Tatton-Brown and Rahman 2007), and a further useful review can be found in Gosalakkal (2004).

HOW COMMON IS SOTOS SYNDROME? Sotos syndrome is assumed in the literature to be common, as a large number of clinical cases have been reported. However, no epidemiological studies have been carried out to date.

MAIN CLINICAL FEATURES: The main clinical characteristics of Sotos syndrome are detailed in Tatton-Brown and Rahman (2004). There are three key features:

- a typical facial gestalt which becomes more pronounced with age (with lengthening of the face and the jaw-line becoming more prominent – Allanson and Cole 1996)

- significant macrocephaly

- learning difficulties. All three features are seen in over 90 per cent of cases (Tatton-Brown and Rahman 2004).

Other fairly common features are:

- childhood physical overgrowth

- advanced bone age

- cardiac and genitourinary anomalies

- neonatal jaundice

- neonatal hypotonia

- febrile convulsions

- tumours

- scoliosis.

Cole and Hughes (1990) note that the physical features tend to become less obvious with age. Cardiac problems are reported in some 50 per cent of cases (Kaneko *et al.* 1987).

Clinical diagnosis based on phenotype (macrocephaly, facial features and size) is successful in identifying NSD1 Sotos syndrome in 99 per cent of cases, suggesting that the NSD1 phenotype can be reliably diagnosed in the majority of cases (Tatton-Brown *et al.* 2005).

Sotos can be found with normal intelligence (Cole and Hughes 1994; De Boer *et al.* 2004; van Haelst *et al.* 2005). The two series where IQ/DQ has been reported identify a wide range of functioning, with mean scores in the high 70s:

- Cole and Hughes 1994: mean 78, range 40–129 (78 cases)
- De Boer *et al.* 2004: mean 76, range 47–105 (21 cases).

Most cases arise as sporadic mutations with no family history. Both concordant (Hook and Reynolds 1967) and discordant (Brown W.T. *et al.* 1998) identical twin pairs have been reported. Where a family history is reported, the pattern of inheritance is typically consistent with autosomal dominant inheritance (Hansen and Friis 1976; Van Haelst *et al.* 2005; Winship 1985; Zonana, Romoin and Fisher 1976, 1977).

IS THERE A LINK BETWEEN SOTOS SYNDROME AND ASD? Many of the early accounts of cerebral gigantism would be consistent with an ASD diagnosis. Kjellman (1965), for example, described a girl with aggressive, wilful and avoidant behaviour who had apparently normal motor skills but was nonverbal; and as early as 1984, Varley and Crnic documented social deficits in Sotos syndrome. However, none of the cases they described were thought to have an ASD.

- The first publication to suggest a link between Sotos syndrome and autism was a single case study published in 1990 by Morrow and colleagues from St Louis. The paper described a boy aged 4 years, 11 months, of normal intelligence (assessed on the Stanford-Binet), but with delayed early milestones, immediate and delayed echolalia, abnormal eye contact and self-injury (head-banging and hair-pulling). He fulfilled criteria for autistic disorder. Also in 1990, Michele Zapella, a paediatric neurologist from Sienna in Northern Italy, published a similar case report.

- The following year, Rutter and Cole (1991) published a case series of 16 children with Sotos syndrome, aged 5–15. Two-thirds of these children had IQs in the normal range. A number of behaviours were seen as characteristic: tantrums, destructiveness, social withdrawal, eating and sleeping difficulties. Several of the children were said to display autistic tendencies, but no standardized assessments of ASD were carried out.

- Finegan *et al.* (1994) studied 27 cases of Sotos syndrome and compared their profiles to 20 other non-specific overgrowth cases. In the Sotos group, 21 had IQ scores in the average range – a greater proportion than in the comparison group. Expressive and receptive language levels were commensurate with IQ. The children with Sotos syndrome were more likely to be irritable, had higher rates of stereotyped behaviour, had a high rate of ADHD (seen in 38 per cent), and were more socially withdrawn. Several were thought to be autistic.

- Mouridsen and Hansen (2002) described two Sotos cases, one of whom had low normal IQ, ADHD and autistic features; the other had a moderate learning disability and met ICD-10 criteria for autistic disorder.

- Cohen (2003) reviewed the evidence on behavioural and cognitive phenotypes in the various overgrowth syndromes, including Sotos syndrome.

- A recent paper presents a 20-year-old male case of Sotos syndrome who presented with apparent delusions and hallucinations and a long-standing history of learning disability, seizures, asthma, difficulties with peer relationships and temper outbursts (Compton, Celentana, Price and Furman 2004).

DIFFERENTIAL DIAGNOSIS: Differential diagnosis is between Sotos syndrome and a number of other overgrowth syndromes, some of which have been linked to ASD, such as BRRS [15]; BCNS [16]; CDFE syndrome [19]; Cole-Hughes macrocephaly syndrome [24]; Cowden syndrome [26]; Orstavik 1997 syndrome [56]; and Proteus syndrome [62], and some which have not, such as Weaver syndrome [89].

Weaver syndrome presents with the greatest degree of phenotypic similarity, but can usually be discriminated by the absence of an NSD1 defect (the genetic finding that is typically seen in Sotos syndrome). There are, however, cases reported as Weaver syndrome that also have NSD1 mutations (Baujat *et al.* 2005; Douglas *et al.* 2003; Rio *et al.* 2003).

Sotos syndrome has also been reported in association with fragile-X syndrome [35] (Beemer, Veenema and de Pater 1986; Verloes, Sacré and Geubelle 1987). However, no such cases have been reported

to date with co-morbid ASD, and an NSD1 mutation was not tested for in these cases.

At the time of writing, studies are appearing in which Sotos phenotype cases are being reported with other gene abnormalities, such as 11p15 (Baujat *et al.* 2004); and other clinical conditions (besides Weaver syndrome, which is phenotypically similar) are being reported with 5q35 defects (Baujat and Cormier-Daire 2007).

MANAGEMENT AND TREATMENT: As a multi-system disorder, Sotos requires multidisciplinary review to identify difficulties in the individual case and to put in place appropriate monitoring and treatment as required. As cardiac problems, genitourinary problems and scoliosis are potential areas that will require management, it is important that these are reviewed and treatment provided as required. See the discussion of general management issues in Baujat and Cormier-Daire (2007).

ANIMAL MODELS: No specific models for Sotos syndrome have yet been developed. An NSD1 mouse model has been used to examine bone maturation, and demonstrated that NSD1 defects are associated with advanced bone age (Rayasam *et al.* 2003), but no attempts have been made to assess the behavioural phenotype in this mouse model.

69.

Succinic semialdehyde dehydrogenase (SSADH) deficiency

GENE LOCUS: 6p22

KEY ASD REFERENCES: Knerr, Gibson, Jakobs and Pearl 2008; Pearl *et al.* 2003

SUMMARY: SSADH deficiency is an inborn error of metabolism that is a rare autosomal recessive disorder of gamma aminobutyric acid (GABA) metabolism.

The first case identified was reported in 1981 by Jakobs *et al.* – a Turkish child of consanguineous parents with neurologic abnormalities and elevated urinary excretion of gamma-hydroxybutyrate (GHB). He had a mild learning difficulty but was markedly ataxic and hypotonic. The same child, when followed up at age five, had elevated levels of GABA in both urine and cerebrospinal fluid (Gibson *et al.* 1984). Various other reports of affected children from consanguineous relationships have been reported, suggesting autosomal recessive inheritance (Gibson *et al.* 1997b; Haan, Brown, Mitchell and Danks 1985).

HOW COMMON IS SSADH DEFICIENCY? SSADH deficiency has been described to date in over 400 cases in the literature, but at present there is no accurate estimate of the likely population prevalence (Pearl *et al.* 2003).

MAIN CLINICAL FEATURES: The first large clinical series to be described (N=23) (Gibson *et al.* 1997a) reported delayed motor, cognitive and language development, hypotonia, ataxia, seizures, diminished reflexes, behavioural problems and EEG abnormalities to be the most commonly reported features. These can be seen reflected in the more recent series reported by Pearl *et al.* (2003) and Knerr, Gibson, Jakobs and Pearl (2008) – see Table B69.

Although limited, long-term follow-up suggests that the behavioural phenotype is fairly static and does not worsen over time (Crutchfield, Haas, Nyhan and Gibson 2008).

THE NEUROCHEMISTRY OF SSADH: The missing mitochondrial enzyme, found in astrocytes, catalyses the transformation of succinic semialdehyde into succinic acid, which would normally then provide gamma-hydroxybutyrate as a key factor in the tricarboxylic/Krebs cycle. For a brief synopsis of Pyruvate metabolism, see Pitukpakorn (2005).

IS THERE A LINK BETWEEN SSADH AND ASD? Pearl *et al.* (2003) reviewed 53 cases, all with early developmental delay, and over 80 per cent with learning disability at the time of review. Sleep disturbances were common, being seen in 68 per cent, and one case was described as having autistic behaviour – the age and sex are not specified in the paper.

Knerr, Gibson, Jakobs and Pearl (2008) reviewed 33 adolescent and adult cases, four of whom had a diagnosis of PDD or autism.

Pearl *et al.* presented a collation of 14 newly reported cases, together with a review of previously published cases (age range 1–21 years), and Knerr *et al.* a series of adolescent and adult cases from the database maintained at the Children's National Medical Center in Washington.

Between them, these two papers describe five cases of ASD within a total of 86 cases of SSADH, giving a combined likelihood of @8 per cent. There may be a slight overlap in the cases in the two reports.

The main autistic features that have been noted are withdrawn affect, poor eye contact, poor pretend play, stereotypies, inability to transition and a strong preference for routine (Pearl *et al.* 2009).

MANAGEMENT AND TREATMENT: The principal metabolic abnormalities seen in SSADH deficiency are elevations in gamma aminobutyric acid (GABA) and gamma-hydroxybutyrate (GHB).

Table B69: Main clinical features of SSADH deficiency

	Pearl et al. 2003		Knerr, Gibson, Jakobs and Pearl 2008	
	N	%	N	%
Clinical findings	(N = 53)		(N = 33)	
Developmental delay	53	100	33	100
Mental retardation	43	81		
Hypotonia	35	66	15	45
Behaviour problems	37	70	27	82
Seizures	24	45	19	58
Ataxia	28	53	20	61
Language delay	18	34		
Neuropsychiatric problems	(N = 37)	70	(N = 27)	82
Aggression	6	16	6	18
Anxiety	11	30	12	36
Hallucinations	4	11	5	15
Hyperactivity	15	41	13	39
Inattention	19	51	18	55
OCD	13	35	11	33
Sleep disturbance	25	68	15	45
PDD/autism	1	3	4	12
Ataxia			(N = 20)	60
Decreased balance			8	24
Uncoordinated movements			8	24
Wide-based gait			7	21
Uncoordinated walking			7	21
Hand tremors			6	18
Excessive movements			4	12
Tripping			2	6
Seizures	(N = 25)	47	(N = 19)	57
Generalized tonic-clonic	14	56	14	42
Absence	10	40	12	36
Myoclonic	5	20	3	9
Unspecified	3	12	9	27
Other (ALTE, atonic, partial, febrile)	7	28		
EEG studies	(N = 28)	53		

Background abnormal/slowing	7	25
Spike discharges	8	29
ESES	1	4
Photosensitivity	2	7
Normal	10	36
Neuroimaging	**N = 30**	**57**
Increased T2 signal		
Globus pallidi	13	43
White matter	2	7
Dentate nucleus	5	17
Brainstem	2	7
Cerebral atrophy	3	10
Cerebellar atrophy	2	7
Delayed myelination	2	7
Normal MRI	13	43

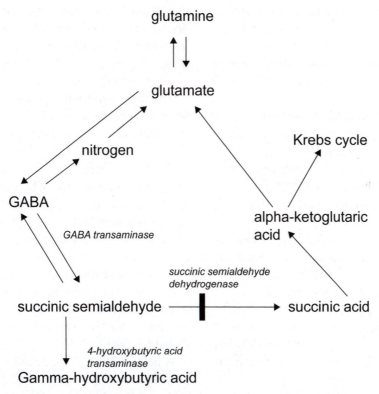

Figure B69: A succinic semialdehyde dehydrogenase deficiency affects the metabolism of glutamate.

Treatments to date have largely involved the use of GABA inhibitors such as vigabatrin (Gropman 2003), other medications which are known to modulate the GABA system (Knerr *et al.* 2007) and amino acids such as taurine, which has the same receptor binding (Pearl and Gibson 2004; Pearl *et al.* 2009).

In an interesting recent report (Leuzzi *et al.* 2007) two brothers with SSADH deficiency developed dystonic movements that were brought on by exercise. In both cases the problem improved with the use of vigabatrin, and in one there was a parallel improvement in walking and a reduction in seizure activity.

ANIMAL MODELS: There is a large body of animal research on syntenic knockout models for human SSADH.

Gupta *et al.* (2004) demonstrated a range of amino acid and neurotransmitter imbalances in the SSADH-deficient mouse, including abnormalities in the neurotransmitter GABA that seemed important for the evolution of seizure activity.

Drasbek *et al.* (2008) have shown clear evidence of abnormal GABAergic function in the SSADH-deficient mouse cortex, concluding that SSADH deficiency leads to elevated extracellular GABA levels and increased GABAergic neurotransmission in the mouse cerebral cortex.

Donarum *et al.* (2006) have found that there is an unexpected and significant downregulation of myelin development and compaction, predominantly in the cortex and hippocampus of the SSADH-deficient mouse. This suggests that in addition to its role in GABA modulation, SSADH is likely to have a significant impact on brain development.

A more recent paper has provided further evidence of abnormal lipids associated with SSADH deficiency in the mouse (Barcelo-Coblijn *et al.* 2007).

A recent study has demonstrated that ATP levels and hippocampal mitochondrial function can be normalized in SSADH-deficient mice by ketogenic diet (Nylen *et al.* 2009).

70.

Timothy syndrome

GENE LOCUS: 12p13.3

KEY ASD REFERENCES: Splawski *et al.* 2004, 2006

SUMMARY: Timothy syndrome is a specific calcium channelopathy, (Cav1.2) n. It is named after the American cardiologist Dr Katherine W. Timothy, who was instrumental in much of the early research on long QT syndromes. Timothy syndrome is one of ten such conditions.

Timothy syndrome results from a defect on chromosome 12 that results in an abnormality of calcium metabolism. This is a single nucleotide substitution that results in an amino acid substitution of an arginine for a glycine. The gene defect affects calcium flow, with a build-up of excess calcium in cells.

Around half of the cases so far reported have dysmorphic facial features, typically with the constellation of a flat nasal bridge, small upper jaw, low-set ears and small teeth. Syndactyly (webbing) of the fingers and several toes is seen in all cases, and all are bald at birth.

A helpful review of calcium signalling abnormalities seen in seizure disorders, migraine and ASD can be found in Gargus (2009) and for a more specific discussion of calcium channel mutations in Tompathy syndrome, see Splawski *et al.* (2005).

HOW COMMON IS TIMOTHY SYNDROME?

Not currently established – only 20 cases have been reported to date worldwide, so the prevalence would appear likely to be low, given the clinical presentation.

MAIN CLINICAL FEATURES: All individuals with this defect have cardiac involvement, with QT prolongation (the period of activation and recovery of the ventricular heart muscle calculated from an ECG reading) seen in all cases, and arrythmia in well over 90 per cent. One in three has an enlarged heart. More complex cardiac defects such as ventriculo-septal defects and tetralogy of Fallot are seen in approximately one in four cases.

Only 25 per cent of those with Timothy syndrome have a learning disability and one in five will have a seizure disorder.

Breathing difficulties are common, with pneumonia or bronchitis being seen in just under half of the reported cases. One in three has a brisk gag reflex that complicates feeding.

Low blood sugar levels are regularly recorded in one third of cases, as are low calcium levels.

Recurrent infections are common, being seen in over 40 per cent of cases.

IS THERE A LINK BETWEEN TIMOTHY SYNDROME AND ASD?

In 2004 Splawski and co-workers reviewed the literature and presented data on 17 clinical cases. This paper established that Timothy syndrome results in a multi-system disorder with a characteristic phenotype, including cardiac arrythmia in all cases, ASD in 80 per cent, and learning disability in 25 per cent. In each case, ASD was as a consequence of a *de novo* missense mutation at 12p13.3.

From the cases reported to date, some 80 per cent have an ASD and 60 per cent meet full criteria for autism.

Splawski *et al.* (2006) screened 461 individuals with ASD for evidence of the gene mutation CACNA1H at 12p13.3 that causes Timothy syndrome. Missense mutations were identified in six cases, and in none of 480 'ethnically matched' controls.

DIFFERENTIAL DIAGNOSIS: The principal differential diagnoses are the other long QT syndromes (see Splawski *et al.* 2000), and other ASD syndromes which also present with syndactyly. BBS [17] and SLOS [66] are the two most likely. Having conjoined second and third toes is an unusual presentation that can be seen in Timothy syndrome and is often assumed to be a phenotypic marker of SLOS.

MANAGEMENT AND TREATMENT: Studies to date on the use of calcium channel blocking agents that successfully treat angina in adults are showing some promising results (Jacobs A. *et al.* 2006; Napolitano, Bloise and Priori 2006).

An experimental model of the effects of Timothy syndrome on cardiac function at the cellular level is showing positive effects of a drug, ranolazine, but no clinical trials of its use have so far taken place (Sicouri *et al.* 2007).

ANIMAL MODELS: Animal models have been developed that are syntenic to most of the other long QT syndromes. However, no mode for Timothy syndrome has so far been developed. (See Salama and London 2007.)

71.

Tourette syndrome

aka • Gilles de la Tourette syndrome (GTS)

GENE LOCI: 7q31, 8q, 11q23, 13q31.1, 16p, 17q25

KEY ASD REFERENCES: Barabas and Matthews 1983; Baron-Cohen *et al.* 1999a, 1999b; Burd *et al.* 1987, 2009; Canitano and Vivanti 2007; Comings and Comings 1991; Healy 1965; Hebebrand *et al.* 1994; Kadesjo and Gillberg 2000; Kano, Ohta and Nagai 1987; Kano *et al.* 1988; Kerbeshian and Burd 1986, 1996; Nelson and Pribor 1993; Realmuto and Main 1982; Ringman and Jankovic 2000; Ritvo *et al.* 1990; Stern and Robertson 1997; Sverd 1991; Sverd, Montero and Gurevich 1993

SUMMARY: The condition is known as Gilles de la Tourette syndrome after the French clinician, a student of Charcot at the Salpêtrière in Paris, who wrote an early description of the condition. (See discussion in Kushner 1995; Lees 1986.) Tourette published his best known paper on the condition, '*Étude sur une affection nerveuse caractérisée par de l'incoordination motrice, acompagnée de l'écholalie et de coprolalie*', in 1885.

The first case to arouse interest was the Marquise de Dampierre, a Parisian aristocrat who was first described by Itard in 1825. The Marquise was the subject of Tourette's 1885 paper, but it is unlikely that Tourette ever met or examined her – if still alive, she would have been 86 at the time of his first publication – and from the historical records it also seems unlikely that Charcot would have met or treated her

(Kurlan 2004; Teive, Chien, Munhoz and Barbosa 2008).

Tourette syndrome (GTS) is diagnosed on the basis of chronic vocal and motor tics. In its extreme form, GTS can be socially disabling, as it may also include involuntary obscene vocalizations (coprolalia) and involuntary obscene gestures (copropraxia).

It can be caused by mutations in the SLITRK1 gene at 13q31. However, this is a rare cause, being seen in around one in 60 cases (Abelson *et al.* 2005). Linkage of the GTS phenotype to several other chromosomal sites has also been proposed.

A number of useful overviews of GTS have been produced: Comings (1990), Kurlan (2004), Leckman and Cohen (1999), Robertson (2000) and Singer (2005), and remain amongst the most detailed and helpful. An excellent historical overview of the development of our understanding of Tourette syndrome can be found in Kushner (1999).

HOW COMMON IS TOURETTE SYNDROME? A number of epidemiological studies are published, with varying prevalence rates, those reported ranging from 0.05 per cent of boys and 0.03 per cent of girls aged 16–17 years (Apter *et al.* 1992), through 1.05 per cent of boys and 0.1 per cent of girls aged 6–15 years (Comings, Himes and Comings 1990) to 3.3 per cent of children aged 13–14 years (Mason *et al.* 1998).

Kadesjo and Gillberg (2000) studied 409 11-year-old children in a total population cohort. GTS was four times as prevalent in boys as in girls (N=5, 4:1), and two-thirds had significant comorbidity. A second component to the paper was a study of 435 children aged 5–15 referred to a national GTS clinic over a three-year period. All attended mainstream school, and three were of borderline ability. ADHD was the most common co-morbid feature, affecting 64 per cent. Asperger disorder was diagnosed in three (5 per cent) and PDD-NOS in ten (17 per cent).

Khalifa and von Knorring (2003) carried out a questionnaire survey of 4,479 7–15-year-olds. In total, some 6.6 per cent had experienced some type of tic disorder in the preceding year, with 0.6 per cent fulfilling criteria for GTS.

GTS is overrepresented in certain ethnic groups (such as the Ashkenazi Jewish population) and appears to be rare in others – for example, few Afro-Caribbean cases have been reported.

MAIN CLINICAL FEATURES: GTS syndrome is a neurological disorder in which the diagnostic features are major chronic motor and vocal tics with associated behavioural abnormalities. As with most neuro-developmental disorders, there is a preponderance of males, with a 4:1 male to female ratio. (See, for example, Comings and Comings 1985.) This could indicate that GTS is more prevalent in males, that the presentation is more severe in males, or that the presentation is different between the sexes. The majority of those diagnosed are children or adolescents. In around one in ten cases, there is a positive family history – an older first-degree relative has received the diagnosis.

Diagnosis of Tourette syndrome is based on the clinical presentation of chronic major motor and vocal tics. (It is important to recognize that tics themselves have a high prevalence in the child and adolescent population (with an estimated lifetime prevalence of around ten per cent), and that the majority of tics spontaneously remit with age.) Typically, the first symptoms are motor tics around the head or neck, and there is a gradual 'cephalocaudal' progression – the motor tics affect more and more of the body, moving from head to foot. With progression of the disease other motor features may appear, such as echopraxia, and vocal tics such as echolalia, sniffing, coughing, grunting and coprolalia may develop. Coprolalia and copropraxia are not necessary features for diagnosis – the latter is seldom reported in the clinical literature, while coprolalia is seen in around eight per cent of current cases (Goldenberg, Brown and Weiner 1994). Prior to 1987, both coprolalia and copropraxia were necessary for diagnosis, and consequently GTS was far less commonly diagnosed. It is not uncommon for the affected person to be unaware of their own tics (Kurlan et al. 1987).

From some of the studies carried out (for example, Nee et al. 1980; Pauls and Leckman 1986; Pauls et al. 1988), there seems to be an association between GTS and a positive family history of tics, GTS and obsessive-compulsive disorder.

A family history where both parents have certain GTS features – tics, OCD or anxiety – is common. Walkup et al. (1996) found a positive family history for this broader phenotype in a high percentage of cases – 19 per cent where both parents were or had been affected. Kurlan et al. (1994) found that in families with a significant history of GTS, the broader phenotype was seen in both parents in 41 per cent of cases.

Suggestions that a difference in dopamine systems is important have come from studies which show benefits from the use of treatments such as haloperidol that block the dopamine D2 receptor, and exacerbation of symptoms through medications that increase dopaminergic activity.

GENETIC FACTORS: One study of a family with a paternal history of OCD and a boy and girl, both with OCD and GTS together with learning disability, identified an insertion/translocation involving chromosomes 2 and 7 which interrupted the CNTNAP2 gene (Verkerk *et al.* 2003). This is potentially important, as it is the first gene region to be identified as an ASD risk factor in several independent studies (Alarcón *et al.* 2008; Arking *et al.* 2008; Bakkaloglu *et al.* 2008; Rossi *et al.* 2008). It has also been shown to be a risk factor for CDFE syndrome [19] as a specific ASD condition associated with seizure problems and abnormal cortical development; and for communication problems (Alarcón *et al.* 2005a).

Comings (1990) has suggested that there may be a link between GTS and mutations in the tryptophan 2.3 dioxygenase gene. This enzyme is the first rate-limiting factor in the breakdown pathway from tryptophan to kynurenine and is involved in development of the central nervous system. It is interesting that an association has also been noted between mutations of this gene and ASD (Nabi *et al.* 2004). This mutation, where present, would be likely to result in elevated levels of serotonin.

IS THERE A LINK BETWEEN TOURETTE SYNDROME AND ASD? A large number of co-morbid cases are reported in the clinical literature.

- The first paper to suggest a link between GTS and ASD was an early Irish report of an adolescent boy (Healy 1965).

- Realmuto and Main (1982) also described a single co-morbid clinical case – a 15-year-old boy.

- Barabas and Matthews (1983) described a further boy diagnosed at age two with autism, and additionally at 15 with GTS.

- Kerbeshian and Burd (1986) described six cases of atypical pervasive developmental disorder (also identified as fulfilling criteria for Asperger syndrome), three of whom also presented with co-morbid GTS.

- Burd *et al.* (1987) presented data on 59 patients with autism or PDD-NOS. Twelve of their series had co-morbid GTS which developed after their ASD symptomology. The authors noted that those who developed GTS had higher IQs and better expressive and receptive language than the rest of their group.

- Kano, Ohta and Nagai (1987) presented two cases of GTS with infantile autism, and took issue with the conclusion of Burd *et al.* that the development of GTS appears to parallel improvement in autistic symptomology.

- The paper by Kano *et al.* (1988) appears to be a re-presentation of data on the two boys described in Kano, Ohta and Nagai (1987).

- The study by Ritvo *et al.* (1990) of 233 people with autism in Utah looked specifically for medical comorbidities and reported a number of cases with co-morbid GTS.

- Comings and Comings (1991) reviewed the literature on pervasive developmental disorder up to that time and identified 41 cases who would today be diagnosed as having ASD, and who were subsequently diagnosed with GTS. They reported a further 16 cases with co-morbid presentations, and three further families where both conditions were found. They also reported a high incidence of other disorders in extended family members of their cases, and suggested a possible link to abnormalities of serotonin metabolism.

- Sverd (1991) presented a further ten cases of comorbidity, suggesting that individuals with GTS alone may have a single copy of the critical gene involved, while homozygous inheritance (where the affected person carries two affected copies) could result in the reported co-morbid cases.

- Sverd, Montero and Gurevich (1993) reported two children and two adults with autistic disorder, an additional schizophrenia-like psychosis, and tics or GTS. The authors suggested that co-morbid GTS may be a factor that increases the liklihood of ASD developing into a more schizophrenic type of psychotic presentation.

- Nelson and Pribor (1993) described the case of a calendrical calculator (someone who can, apparently without effort, link days of the week to dates) with ASD and GTS. The possibility that obsessive-compulsive features provide a critical link between the two conditions is raised by these authors.

- In the first paper to provide evidence of a link between ASD, GTS and a specific genetic defect, Hebebrand et al. (1994) reported a partial trisomy 16p in a 14-year-old boy with an ASD and GTS. He had complex motor and vocal phenomena, including simple tics that had been present since childhood.

- Kerbeshian and Burd (1996) noted that both bipolar disorder and ASD had been reported in association with GTS. They identified four patients in North Dakota for whom these three diagnoses had been given, and the chronology. ASD diagnosis preceded GTS diagnosis, which preceded bipolar disorder diagnosis in all cases. The authors suggest that there may be common factors which underlie the aetiology of this observed association.

- Stern and Robertson (1997) reviewed the 90 or so cases of ASD co-morbid with GTS reported to that date, and the arguments for and against a biological association between the conditions.

- Two studies by the Cambridge Autism Research Centre group have looked at the prevalence of GTS in ASD populations:
  - Baron-Cohen et al. (1999a) reviewed 37 children attending an ASD school and found that three (8.1 per cent) met criteria for a co-morbid diagnosis of GTS.
  - Baron-Cohen et al. (1999b) extended the initial study with a review of 497 pupils from nine further schools for children with ASD. Overall, 4.3 per cent had definite and 2.2 per cent probable GTS; 7.1 per cent of those with an autism diagnosis were co-morbid, as were 7.7 per cent of those with Asperger syndrome and 5 per cent of those with another ASD diagnosis.

- Kadesjo and Gillberg (2000) reported an epidemiological screening of 407 children (50 per cent of all 11-year-olds in a small town in central Sweden). This first study identified five children with GTS: four boys and one girl. The girl and one of the boys had no co-morbid diagnoses. The other boys had diagnoses of Asperger syndrome, Disorders of Attention, Motor Control and Perception (DAMP), and ADHD. A second study screened all children diagnosed with GTS from the same area, aged 5–15 (N = 58). A high rate of comorbidity was found, particularly for ADHD (64 per cent), with ASD being seen in 22 per cent of cases (Asperger syndrome 5 per cent and PDD-NOS 17 per cent). As the majority of the cases identified in the 11-year-old screening had not been clinically identified, the second study is likely to suffer from ascertainment bias and may have exaggerated the incidence of comorbidity, as such cases are more likely to come to clinical attention.

- Ringman and Jankovic (2000) described a series of 12 ASD cases that had been referred to a movement disorders clinic in Texas. The authors discriminated Asperger syndrome cases on the basis of normal language development, and on this basis all of the GTS cases reported were classified as having Asperger syndrome. Three of the GTS cases had severe sensory deficits. The cases classified as being autistic had complex motor stereotypies in addition to simple tics.

- Canitano and Vivanti (2007) described a survey of the prevalence of tic disorders in a sample of 105 people with ASD. Twenty-four showed evidence of significant tic disorders. Overall, tic disorders were seen in 22 per cent of the sample, with 11 per cent having chronic motor tics and 11 per cent having additional vocal tics sufficiently chronic to qualify for a diagnosis of GTS. In this sample, all of those examined had some degree of learning disability. There was an association between the severity of tics and the severity of learning disability.

- Burd et al. (2009) used an international database of 7,288 people with GTS to identify cases with co-morbid ASD (called in the paper 'pervasive developmental disorders'). Three hundred and thirty-four co-morbid cases were identified, giving a rate of 4.6 per cent. As a group, these cases were more complex in their presentation: 98.8 per cent had additional comorbidity, while this was only true of 13.2 per cent of those with GTS but without ASD.

In summary, there is a large body of both case report and clinical series evidence to suggest that GTS and ASD co-occur at a significantly higher rate than would be expected unless there were some common underlying process to the two conditions.

DIFFERENTIAL DIAGNOSIS: A number of conditions can present with similar features, but typically with later onset (as in Huntington's chorea) or with other obvious features (as in Wilson's disease and Hallevorden-Spatz syndrome). The only other condition that also significantly overlaps with ASD and may be confused with GTS is tuberous sclerosis [73].

MANAGEMENT AND TREATMENT: A wide range of pharmacological, behavioural, neurosurgical and 'alternative' treatment approaches have been tried. The literature on this topic is voluminous and cannot be covered in any detail here. The interested reader is referred to some helpful reviews (Lavenstein 2003; Silay and Jankovic 2005). Suffice it to say that there is a wide range of treatments that appear to have significantly benefited subgroups. Much of this literature predates the identification of the large number of apparently sufficient genes for the development of GTS, and the possibility that particular genetic causes are selectively benefited by particular therapies has not yet been fully explored.

The most commonly used medications are haloperidol, clonidine and sulpiride.

Risperidone, a medication which inhibits the re-uptake of serotonin, has proved beneficial in controlling tics in some cases (Dion, Annable, Sandor and Chouinard 2002; Scahill et al. 2003).

Nicotine has been claimed to produce significant clinical benefits, improving attention and reducing compulsions and complex tics on self-report, though failing to reduce observed symptom severity. There has been only a small amount of well-controlled research to date and this has shown limited effects (Howson et al. 2004).

Transcranial magnetic resonance stimulation has been advocated as a possible treatment, but the results to date in well-controlled studies are also disappointing. (See, for example, Orth *et al.* 2005.)

Deep brain stimulation with surgically implanted electrodes aimed at correcting the abnormal patterns of electrical activity, particularly around the parahippocampal gyrus, is an extreme treatment strategy that has proved beneficial in some cases, but this could only be undertaken in neurosurgical centres with appropriate expertise (Skidmore *et al.* 2006).

At the present time there is nothing to suggest that any particular aetiology of GTS is more likely to be linked to ASD than any other. The implications, if any, of GTS comorbidity for which approach is likely to be the most beneficial in management of ASD are currently unclear.

ANIMAL MODELS: DAT1 is a dopamine transporter gene, mutation of which has been linked to ADHD in humans; the defect results in excessive levels of circulating dopamine. Berridge, Aldridge, Houchard and Zhuang (2005) have presented data on a DAT knockdown mouse model which, they suggest, provides a model for OCD and GTS. This is a potentially useful model, assuming that the neurochemical differences in GTS result from a defect in dopaminergic function. There is support for this view from various sources: positive response to neuroleptic medication (Robertson and Cavanna 2008) in a significant proportion of cases, levels of metabolites in cerebrospinal fluid (Singer *et al.* 1982), and functional neuroimaging (Serra-Mestres *et al.* 2004; Wong *et al.* 1997).

At the present time this mouse model is only relevant to the dopaminergic forms of GTS. As these appear to account only for a proportion of cases, the overall relevance

of such a model is not certain. Abnormal serotonergic metabolism seems equally important. (See, for example, discussion in Singer 2005.)

Two useful books for families are:

Chowdhury, U. (2004) *Tics and Tourette Syndrome: A Handbook for Parents and Professionals.* London: Jessica Kingsley Publishers.

Robertson, M. and Cavanna, A. (2008) *Tourette Syndrome (The Facts).* (2nd edn.) Oxford: Oxford University Press.

There is also a DVD which gives a useful vignette of someone affected with GTS – the subject, John, does not have a co-morbid ASD:

John's Not Mad (1989) (BBC Q.E.D. Documentary). Available from Amazon.co.uk.

72.

Trichothiodystrophy (TTD)

aka
- brittle hair–intellectual impairment–decreased fertility–short stature (BIDS) syndrome
- onychotrichodysplasia
- chronic neutropenia and mild mental retardation syndrome (ONMRS)
- Amish brittle hair syndrome
- hair–brain syndrome
- Polit syndrome
- Tay syndrome
- Sabinas syndrome

GENE LOCI: 19q13.2–q13.3, 6p25.3, 2q21

KEY ASD REFERENCE: Schepis, Elia, Siragusa and Barbareschi 1997

SUMMARY: Trichothiodystrophy (TTD) is the term used for a rare group of genetic disorders, all of which affect organ systems including the skin, that arise from the neuroectoderm (Bergmann and Egly 2001). This is one of a range of defects involving DNA damage response that result in neurodevelopmental disorders. (See Barzilai, Biton and Shiloh 2008.)

HOW COMMON IS TRICHOTHIODYSTRO-PHY? The prevalence of TTD is thought to be low, with some 20 cases reported in the clinical literature to date (Rossi and Cantisani 2004). As most cases have not been genotyped, the relative prevalence of the different forms is not known at this time. The TTD-A form has been characterized (Giglia-Mari *et al.* 2004), but is thought to be rare (Stefanini *et al.* 1993).

MAIN CLINICAL FEATURES: The term 'trichothiodystrophy' was introduced as a descriptive label for the combination of brittle hair, brittle nails and ichthyotic skin. Brittle hair and nails are due to sulphur deficiency (Price, Odom, Ward and Jones 1980). Limited subcutaneous fat is also characteristic (Happle, Traupe, Grobe and Bonsmann 1984). One review suggested that low birthweight, small head circumference, small genitalia, cataracts and recurrent infection are also characteristic (Blomquist *et al.* 1991). Most cases, in addition, demonstrate delayed motor development and some degree of learning disability. Sensitivity to sunlight is also common, being reported in approximately half of reported cases (Broughton *et al.* 2001).

Key features (adapted and extended from Bergmann and Egly 2001, page 280):
Skin abnormalities:

• brittle hair and nails
• ichthyosis (dried and crackled skin covered with thin adherent scales, with low sulphur content
• collodion baby (transparent shiny skin at birth)

• erythroderma, eczema
• photosensitivity (in some 50 per cent of cases, but without apparent increased skin cancer risk).

Morphologic changes and dysmorphia:
• growth retardation
• microcephaly
• skeletal deformations: receding chin, protruding ears, thin, beaked nose

	SVAS reference	ASD reference
Marfan syndrome	Grimm and Wesselhoeft 1980	Tantam, Evered and Hersov 1990
rubella embryopathy	Varghese, Izukawa and Rowe 1969	Chess 1971
Thalidomide embryopathy	Jorgensen 1972	Miller *et al.* 2005

• impaired development of primary sexual characteristics
• decreased subcutaneous fat, with failure to form breast tissue in females
• dental abnormalities, increased carie formation.

Neurological dysfunctions:
• learning disability
• spasticity/paralysis, ataxia, intention tremor
• impaired motor control
• progeric facial features
• dysmyelination.

Ocular abnormalities:
• cataracts
• conjunctivitis.

Immune system:
• recurrent infections.

Although it is common to see a mild level of learning disability in individuals who show this constellation of features, presentation is variable, and normal intelligence has been reported (Verhage *et al.* 1987).

The first cases reported were a brother and a sister, of Asian first-cousin parents (Tay 1971). Both showed ichthyosiform erythroderma, were growth retarded and learning disabled, and one died neonatally from an intestinal obstruction.

In one case, who has been followed for over a decade (Jorizzo, Atherton, Crounse and Wells 1982; Stefanini *et al.* 1993), there was no indication of any progressive problems, except for hand joint contractures secondary to ichthyosiform involvement of the palms of the hands.

One form of TTD has been shown to result from reduced production of transcription factor IIH (TFIIH) (Vermeulen *et al.* 2000). This is also due to a small gene mutation that contributes to TFIIH stability and concentration (Cleaver 2005).

A particular form of TDD that seems to be exacerbated by temperature has been reported (Kleijer, Beemer and Boom 1994), and has been shown to be characterized by a specific TFIIH transcription factor mutation (Vermeulen *et al.* 2001).

IS THERE A LINK BETWEEN TTD AND ASD? To date, only one case has been reported in the literature in association with ASD: a 14-year-old Italian boy with autism associated with TTD, absence seizures with diffuse spike-and-wave discharges apparent on EEG, short stature, and learning disability (Schepis, Elia, Siragusa and Barbareschi 1997). The genotype in this case was not reported.

Given the low overall reported prevalence of TTD, it is impossible to comment on the extent to which the conditions are linked, or whether this is a chance co-occurrence of unrelated factors.

The biological basis to TTD appears to be similar to that causing xeroderma pigmentosa [79], which, although not common, is significantly more prevalent. The condition results from abnormalities of the TFIIH DNA transcription/repair system. As this system involves ten separate proteins, a number of separate genetic defects may prove to be involved, three of which have so far been reported, with two gene loci identified.

It is possible that defects in the TFIIH system, which is involved in repair of oxidative DNA damage, may prove to be a more general genetic factor in several forms of ASD.

DIFFERENTIAL DIAGNOSIS: The skin involvement is usually apparent within the first two months after birth, and is not easily confused with other ASD conditions, the most common alternative causes being immunodeficiency, papulosquamous dermatitis and Netherton syndrome (Pruszkowski *et al.* 2000). There are a number of other genetic ichthyoses (see, for example, Nakabayashi *et al.* 2005), all of which appear to operate through effects on DNA nucleotide excision repair (Kraemer *et al.* 2007).

There are a number of nucleotide excision repair syndromes. None is common, but all have been reported in association with ASDs, and there appears to be significant phenotypic overlap. Using complementation testing by cell fusion, two specific defects were identified in one study of TDD (Hoeijmakers 1994). A third complementation group has been identified in one child of a consanguineous marriage (Weeda *et al.* 1997).

MANAGEMENT AND TREATMENT: No specific treatment strategies have been reported to date. The characterization in the clinical description provided does not allow for any conclusions to be drawn concerning best management. It is possible that advances in our understanding of nucleotide excision repair mechanisms will lead to targeted treatment approaches.

ANIMAL MODELS: A progeric mouse model caused by an ERCC2 defect (de Boer *et al.* 2002) causes accelerated ageing. Combining this with an XPA defect (a subunit of the TFIIH system) produces greatly accelerated ageing compared to ERCC2 alone. This demonstrates that blocking the TFIIH system amplifies oxidative DNA damage and prevents adequate repair.

Both xeroderma pigmentosa [79] and TTD are caused by changes to the function of a 10-protein DNA repair/transcription system called TFIIH. A recent paper (Aguilar-Fuentes *et al.* 2008) describes a drosophila model in which p8/TTDA, a subunit of this complex, has been modified, giving rise to phenotypic similarities to human TTD.

A useful review of mouse models of nucleotide excision repair defects and their effects on neurological development has recently appeared (Niedernhofer 2008).

73.

Tuberous sclerosis complex (TSC)

aka • Bourneville syndrome

• epiloia

GENE LOCI: 16p13.3 (TSC2), 12q14, 9q34 (TSC1)

KEY ASD REFERENCES: Asano *et al.* 2001; Askalan *et al.* 2003; Baker, Piven and Sato 1998; Bolton and Griffiths 1997; Bolton *et al.* 2002; Critchley and Earl 1932; Curatolo, Porfirio, Manzi and Seri 2004; Datta, Mandal and Bhattacharya 2009; de Vries, Hunt and Bolton 2007; Gillberg,

Gillberg and Ahlsen 1994; Humphrey, Higgins, Yates and Bolton 2004; Hunt and Dennis 1987; Hunt and Shepherd 1993; Khare *et al.* 2001; Kothur, Ray and Malhi 2008; Lewis J.C. *et al.* 2004; Riikonen and Simell 1990; Seri, Cerquiglini, Pisani and Curatolo 1999; Smalley 1998; Smalley, Tanguay, Smith and Gutierrez 1992

SUMMARY: The original term for this condition was 'Bourneville syndrome', after the French neurologist Désiré-Magloire Bourneville, who first described cases in 1880. The term 'tuberous sclerosis' was used to describe the appearance of the brain on autopsy – there was the clear appearance of swollen structures that resemble the tubers of a potato.

The term 'epiloia' was introduced as an acronym standing for 'epilepsy, low intelligence, and adenoma sebaceum'. However, this term has not superseded TSC in clinical use, partly because the term 'adenoma sebaceum' is not an accurate description of the cutaneous features.

The association of TSC with two principal genes – TSC1 and TSC2 – was clarified by two studies (Kandt *et al.* 1992; Povey *et al.* 1994). Taken together, these studies indicate that just over half of cases are caused by TSC2 mutations, and the rest by TSC1.

For more detail on TSC than could easily be given here, the reader is referred to three sources – a recent clinical overview (Curatolo 2003), a detailed review of the biology (Crino, Nathanson and Henske 2006), and an overview of recent advances in our understanding of the neurobiology (Napolioni, Moavero and Curatolo 2009).

The mechanisms by which synapse development and the control of axonal guidance are affected in TSC are becoming much more clearly understood (Knox *et al.* 2007). There are two principal abnormal gene products – *hamartin* (a TSC1 product) and *tuberin* (a TSC2 product). The pathways involved result in abnormal protein synthesis and involve a group of kinases that were called TORs (targets of rapamycin). These had been identified as being affected by a compound, rapamycin, an FDA approved agent, which had been used as an antifungal agent but had fallen out of favour clinically due to its immunosuppressive effects. Rapamycin can correct the abnormalities of behaviour and brain structure shown in animal TSC models.

Individuals with TSC commonly present with four key features: epilepsy; learning difficulties; behaviour problems; and lesions to the skin ('depigmented macules'). Various kidney problems are also common (typically angiomyolipomas and renal cysts).

HOW COMMON IS TUBEROUS SCLEROSIS?
The most recent prevalence estimate for TSC is one in 24,956 (Devlin, Shepherd, Crawford and Morrison 2006). This is in broad agreement with earlier estimates. The rate in childhood is higher, at some one in 12,000 (Sampson *et al.* 1989). TSC is the second most common neurocutaneous disorder after neurofibromatosis type 1.

MAIN CLINICAL FEATURES: TSC seems equally common in all races and both sexes. There is no association with increased age of either parent.

The condition first came to light because of the characteristic skin lesions that can occur without other major problems. As with many of the conditions noted here, the phenotype is broad, with varying levels of intelligence and varying severity of physical phenotype.

The skin lesions usually referred to as 'depigmented macules' were first clearly documented in the late 1960s (Fitzpatrick *et al.* 1968). They are typically present

at birth in most cases, allowing early diagnosis, but may only be evident under a Wood's light examination (ultraviolet light examination in a dark room).

Infantile spasms progressing to seizure activity are seen in a significant proportion of TSC cases, and some 70 per cent of such cases are diagnosed with ASD.

Renal problems are common, with 60–80 per cent of cases having angiomyolipomas (benign growths in the fatty tissue of the kidney), but often go unrecognized. In one review (Cook, Oliver, Mueller and Sampson 1996) of 139 cases, 61 per cent had evidence of renal damage on ultrasound. Some problems can be more severe, and kidney failure is amongst the leading causes of death in TSC.

There is a reported association between the extent of renal involvement and the level of learning disabilities (O'Callaghan, Noakes and Osborne 2000). This is probably an indication of the general severity of the condition, with more severe cases being more likely to have problems with kidney and with central nervous system function, rather than evidence of any direct causal link between renal problems and intellectual function.

Pitting in the enamel of the teeth is a further common characteristic, seen in over 70 per cent of cases (Flanagan *et al.* 1997).

IS THERE A LINK BETWEEN TUBEROUS SCLEROSIS AND ASD?

- In 1932 (well before autism was characterized by Kanner), Critchley and Earl described 'a combination of intellectual defect and a primitive form of psychosis' in TSC.

- Hunt and Dennis (1987) described the psychiatric status of a sample of 90 children with tuberous sclerosis. Hyperkinetic behaviour was described in 59 per cent. Half of the sample had 'psychotic' behaviour, and 13 per cent were severely aggressive. Of those with infantile spasms, 57 per cent were diagnosed as autistic.

- Riikonen and Amnell (1981) surveyed 192 Finnish children with infantile spasms. Twenty-four had ASD diagnoses, of which 14 were transient. They noted an association between infantile spasms and the co-occurrence of autism and tuberous sclerosis. Riikonen and Simell (1990) reviewed the association between TSC and infantile spasms in 24 cases, indicating that, without appropriate therapy, the prognosis was worse than for infantile spasms that are idiopathic, and that the relapse rate was higher after stopping ACTH therapy.

- Smalley, Tanguay, Smith and Gutierrez (1992) reviewed the literature up to that time, noting that between 17 per cent and 58 per cent of TSC cases were noted to have ASD, where the association had been looked for. In a series of seven co-morbid cases, the only clear discrimination from others with TSC appeared to be a higher proportion of males in the co-morbid group (with an even sex ratio in the rest of their TSC cases).

- Hunt and Shepherd (1993) interviewed the parents of 21 children with TSC and categorized five as ASD, and four (all girls) as having behaviour consistent with PDD-NOS.

- Gillberg, Gillberg and Ahlsen (1994) describe a series of 28 TSC cases, 24 of whom had 'autistic features', and 17 of those fulfilled (DSM-III-R) criteria for autistic disorder.

- Patrick Bolton and Paul Griffiths (1997) were the first to report on an association between the numbers of temporal lobe tubers and the likelihood of ASD diagnosis in TSC cases. They reported a strong association between increasing numbers of temporal tubers, decreased IQ and likelihood of ASD diagnosis, from a series of 18 referred TSC cases whose brain scans were reviewed.

- Smalley (1998) suggested a possible association between maternal depression and genetic factors predisposing to ASD and TS in offspring, with the finding that mothers who had co-morbid children were more likely to have experienced depression that antedated the conception of the affected child.

- Baker, Piven and Sato (1998) screened a clinic sample of 20 TSC cases on the Autism Behavior Checklist, and then carried out ADI and observational recording on the children who scored as likely cases. They 'conservatively' estimated ASD to be present in 20 per cent of their cases.

- In one of the few neurophysiological studies of TS, Seri, Cerquiglini, Pisani and Curatolo (1999) compared brainstem auditory evoked responses between 14 children with TSC, seven with autistic disorder and seven without. The results indicated that those with autistic disorder had a central auditory processing disorder, coupled with automatic memory problems, and associated with unilateral or bilateral temporal lobe lesions.

- Asano et al. (2001) assessed nine autistic, nine learning-disabled non-autistic, and eight non-learning-disabled children with TSC, using MRI and PET scanning. Bilateral temporal hypometabolism was associated with ASD and with communication difficulties, as was hypermetabolism in deep cerebellar nuclei.

- Khare et al. (2001) examined a family with a missense mutation of the TSC2 gene affecting 19 out of 34 family members, 17 of whom had a TSC diagnosis. Two of those affected had a co-morbid ASD diagnosis – one of autism and one of PDD.

- The earlier findings of Bolton and Griffiths (1997) concerning temporal lobe tubers were confirmed in a more detailed but overlapping retrospective analysis (Bolton *et al.* 2002). This paper presented data from 53 TSC cases, 19 of whom had an ASD diagnosis.

- Askalan *et al.* (2003) published a small cross-over pilot study of the treatment of infantile spasms in nine infants aged 3–16 months. The study used two medications – corticotrophin (ACTH) and vigabatrin. The study sample was too small to draw conclusions concerning treatment efficacy, but the authors did find that those with symptomatic spasms were more likely to develop epilepsy and to be autistic at follow-up. (All were assessed on the ADOS-G at two years of age.) All three of those with ASD had developed epilepsy and all showed a positive response to medication. (Two improved on vigabatrin, and one on vigabatrin and ACTH in combination.)

- In a study of 94 TSC patients (Lewis J.C *et al.* 2004), an association was found between TSC2 mutations, diagnosis of autism, presence of infantile spasms and lower IQ. No such association was found for TSC1. This suggests that the TSC2 locus at 16p13.3 may be a specific susceptibility locus for ASD.

- In 2004, Humphrey, Higgins, Yates and Bolton published on a male monozygotic twin pair with TSC. The twins were discordant for autism, and the affected twin had a lower IQ, earlier onset seizures and larger central nervous system tubers.

- De Vries, Hunt and Bolton (2007) carried out a postal survey of 265 families with members who had TSC. The overall rate

of ASD was 48 per cent (119 of 246 returns). A high proportion (66 per cent) had co-morbid learning disability (96/146) while 17 per cent (13/78) were of normal intelligence. This indicated a strong association between learning disability and likelihood of ASD diagnosis in people with TSC.

- Kothur, Ray and Malhi (2008) describe two Indian cases of ASD in TSC, in association with temporal lobe tubers.

- Datta, Mandal and Bhattacharya (2009) described a six-year-old boy with a history of convulsions from the age of four months, who had both a learning disability and autism in combination with TSC. In this case it is not entirely clear how the diagnosis of autism was made, as the Conners Rating Scale mentioned in the paper is an ADHD, not an ASD, rating measure.

There have been a number of useful recent reviews of the association between TSC and ASD. (See, for example, Curatolo, Portirio, Manzi and Seri 2004; Wiznitzer 2004.)

DIFFERENTIAL DIAGNOSIS: The principal differential diagnoses would be neurofibromatosis (NF1) [51] and the various PTEN hamartoma tumour syndromes, such as Cowden syndrome [26].

MANAGEMENT AND TREATMENT: TSC in association with ASD appears more likely to be associated with the TSC2 susceptibility gene at 16p13.3. It is likely to occur after infantile spasms and in association with learning disability, both of which are also more likely to be seen with the TSC2 mutation. From the animal work discussed briefly below, it appears that seizure activity, learning and memory problems, and structural abnormalities of brain development can be minimized or prevented by early or prophylactic treatment.

The neurobiology of TSC predicts problems with GABAergic function. The beneficial effects reported from the limited trial data so far suggest that the treatment of infantile spasms with vigabatrin, or with vigabatrin and ACTH, can improve outcome. (See, for example, Askalan *et al.* 2003; Riikonen and Simell 1990.) As vigabatrin has been largely discontinued due to concerns over possible visual field defects, such an approach would require regular monitoring for possible side effects.

Two clinical studies to date provide evidence for some positive effects of rapamycin in patients. An initial study (Franz *et al.* 2006) found in a small series that treatment resulted in reduction in the size of astrocytomas, but that when treatment was stopped, there was regrowth. A recent study demonstrated that renal and cardiac problems could also be improved, but that there was a high rate of side effects (Bissler *et al.* 2008).

Long-term treatment with rapamycin in humans can be difficult to maintain, due to the high rate of side effects, including elevated blood lipid levels, mouth ulcers and increased susceptibility to infection. In adults this has led to a high proportion of patients discontinuing long-term treatment.

As prophylactic treatment would be possible, longer-term treatment has not been evaluated. The possible side effects are both predictable and treatable. The results to date look promising, and this is an urgent area for further systematic research.

ANIMAL MODELS: Knockout drosophila models of *dTsc1* and *dTsc2* have been developed (Potter, Huang and Xu 2001). Results show that the rapamycin pathway, critically involved in several aspects of cell growth and differentiation (Gao and Pan 2001), is affected by knockouts equivalent to those seen in TSC.

A number of mouse models of TSC have been developed which have enabled the testing of various approaches to clinical treatment. These have been used to test predictions (made from the drosophila work) that correction of the mTOR rapamycin pathway by treatment with rapamycin will affect development of the TSC-like phenotype.

Zeng, Xu, Gutmann and Wong (2008) examined the effects of rapamycin on *Tsc1* knockout mice. The results indicate that the structural pathology can be avoided and epilepsy, which normally appears in unmedicated mice by four weeks, does not emerge.

A further study of a slightly different *Tsc1* knockout model (Meikle *et al.* 2007) examined effects on both behavioural phenotype and central nervous system structure, and found improvements in both aspects as a result of administering rapamycin and a related compound (Meikle *et al.* 2008).

Ehninger *et al.* (2008a) have developed a *Tsc2* knockout mouse model with deficits in spatial learning and contextual discrimination that are reversed by rapamycin.

There is reduced expression and function of glutamate transporters in mouse astrocytes in one *Tsc1* KO mouse model. This was associated with increased neuronal death and epileptogenesis. Early treatment with a cephalosporin antibiotic was effective in increasing astrocyte glutamatergic transport and in preventing the development of seizures (Zeng *et al.* 2010).

74.

Turner syndrome

aka • Morgagni-Turner syndrome
• Morgagni-Turner-Albright syndrome
• Shereshevskii-Turner syndrome
• Turner-Albright syndrome
• Turner-Vary syndrome
• Morgagni-Shereshevskii-Turner-Albright syndrome
• Ullrich-Turner syndrome
• Bonnevie-Ullrich syndrome
• gonadal dysgenesis
• monosomy X

GENE LOCUS: Xp22.33

KEY ASD REFERENCES: Creswell and Skuse 2000; Donnelly *et al.* 2000; Lewis, Lubetsky, Wenger and Steele 1995; Skuse 2000; Skuse *et al.* 1997

SUMMARY: Turner syndrome is named after the American endocrinologist Henry Hubert Turner, who described a series of seven cases in a paper published in 1938.

Turner syndrome was identified at an early stage in clinical genetics, as it results from the absence of one copy of the X chromosome. It is a sex chromosome aneuploidy – a condition resulting from an atypical number of sex chromosomes. It was easy to identify on karyotyping due to the gross nature of the difference. It affects only females. Diagnosis is by routine karyotyping and can be made at any point after conception.

Girls with Turner syndrome had previously been described by several clinicians, including the Italian anatomist Giovanni Morgagni in 1768; in a Russian clinical paper by Nikolai Shereshevskii in 1925; and in a paper by Otto Ullrich in the German clinical literature in 1930.

HOW COMMON IS TURNER SYNDROME? Turner syndrome occurs in approximately one in 2,000 female live births (Gravholt 2005a; Gravholt, Juul, Naeraa and Hansen 1996). It is a sex chromosome aneuploidy that results from the total or partial absence of the second sex chromosome, resulting in a 46,XO rather than 46,XX phenotype. There is a clear parent-of-origin effect – where the X chromosome is of paternal origin, girls with Turner syndrome have a higher likelihood of ocular abnormalities and a tendency to be of higher cognitive ability. Some 20 per cent of Turner syndrome cases inherit their X chromosome from their fathers (Sagi *et al.* 2007).

MAIN CLINICAL FEATURES: The most common physical abnormalities affecting girls with TS include short stature (unless growth hormone supplemented), infertility, oestrogen deficiency, hypertension, elevated hepatic enzymes, middle ear infection, micrognathia, bone age retardation, decreased bone mineral content, *cubitus valgus*, and poor growth in the first postnatal year with swollen hands and feet. Females with TS also have significantly higher risks for certain diseases compared to the general population, including hypothyroidism, diabetes, heart disease, osteoporosis, congenital malformations (heart, urinary system, face, neck, ears) such as webbed necks, drooping eyelids and a broad, flat shield-shaped chest, neurovascular disease and cirrhosis of the liver, as well as colon and rectal cancers (Gravholt 2005b).

IS THERE A LINK BETWEEN TURNER SYNDROME AND ASD? There have been four papers to date that suggest a link between Turner syndrome and ASD.

- Lewis, Lubetsky, Wenger and Steele (1995) detailed a number of genetic disorders in a US psychiatric population. Included in their series were the first individuals to be reported with a co-morbid diagnosis of Turner syndrome and ASD.

- Skuse *et al.* (1997) reported on a series of 80 Turner syndrome cases, with 55 X chromosomes being of maternal origin and 25 of paternal origin. Comparison of the two groups showed that those who had inherited a paternal X chromosome were better socially adjusted, had higher verbal IQs and better executive function skills than those who had inherited a maternal X chromosome. Three of those with maternally inherited X chromosomes fulfilled criteria for autism.

Note: This suggested that the X chromosome contains a gene or genes that are imprinted and are not expressed by the maternal X chromosome. As males inherit their X chromosome almost exclusively from their mothers, this could help to explain the increased rates of developmental disorders of social cognition in boys. Skuse (2000) provides an overview of the evidence for imprinted X-linked genes in autism, based on his research group's work on Turner syndrome. A more general overview of X-chromosome factors in ASD including updated information on Turner syndrome can be found in Marco and Skuse (2006).

- Creswell and Skuse (2000) presented five cases of autism in girls with Turner syndrome from a clinical population of 150 Turner cases. This would indicate a rate at least five times higher than in the general population, if the sample were representative of Turner syndrome. (The authors claim a 300 times increased likelihood of autism; however, they base this on a one in 10,000 rate for the general population.) All five cases had inherited a maternal X chromosome. It is unclear whether or not these cases were from an expanded cohort, drawing on an earlier series reported by this group in 1997, or from a newly ascertained series.

- Donnelly *et al.* (2000) presented a further case of autism in a Turner syndrome girl with a maternally inherited X chromosome, strengthening the hypothesis of a parent-of-origin effect on social cognition.

A general discussion of the factors that would seem to link increased autism susceptibility to differences in the X chromosome can be found in Marco and Skuse (2006).

OTHER ASPECTS: A recent review of social cognition in Turner syndrome relates the differences in functional neuroanatomy, particularly of the amygdala and other limbic structures, to the specific deficits in gaze perception and emotion recognition, and emphasizes the parallels to the structural and functional differences seen in ASD and the over-representation of ASD in the Turner syndrome population (Burnett, Reutens and Wood 2010).

Parent-of-origin effects are not confined to the behavioural phenotype. A recent study on an Israeli series of 83 Turner syndrome cases (Sagi *et al.* 2007) has found parent-of-origin effects with kidney problems, higher body mass index, but lower LDL and total cholesterol, being found with inheritance of a maternal X chromosome, and increased ocular problems and higher academic achievement being more common with inheritance of a paternal X.

DIFFERENTIAL DIAGNOSIS: The clinical presentation in Turner syndrome is usually quite distinctive and apparent, but there are a small number of rare alternative diagnoses:

- autoimmune thyroiditis
- gonadal dysgenesis
- lymphoedema
- XY gonadal agenesis syndrome.

However, diagnosis should be simple on karyotyping (except in mosaic cases).

MANAGEMENT AND TREATMENT: For most aspects of Turner syndrome with ASD, management is the same as for other ASD conditions. As it is a multi-system condition, those with Turner syndrome need to be helped and treated by a multidisciplinary team. A useful overview of the issues involved in ongoing treatment and management can be found in Hjerrild, Mortensen and Gravholt (2008).

Short stature is a matter of concern for many with Turner syndrome (Sutton *et al.* 2005), but infertility and lack of development of sexual characteristics are viewed by many as the most difficult aspects of the condition. Improved glucose tolerance and reduced risk of developing type II diabetes appear to be direct health consequences of growth hormone replacement (Wooten, Bakalov, Hill and Bondy 2008).

Both physical growth and development of sexual characteristics can be promoted by growth hormone treatment (Bakalov, Shawker, Ceniceros and Bondy 2007). Concerns over possible negative effects on heart development appear to be unsubstantiated (Matura *et al.* 2007).

ANIMAL MODELS:

- Davies *et al.* (2006) studied the effects of a knockout XO mouse model on attention in an attentional task in comparison to XX and X*Y mice. The absence of a second sex chromosome

resulted in impaired function, and no parent-of-origin effect was seen.

- Lynn and Davies (2007) suggest that the 39,XO mouse may be a good biological model for studying aspects of the behavioural phenotype of sex-biased neuropsychiatric disorders such as autism and ADHD.
- Probst, Cooper, Cheung and Justice (2008) discuss the utility of the 39,XO mouse as a model for the investigation of Turner syndrome at the genetic, phenotypic or karyotypic levels.

75.

Unilateral cerebellar hypoplasia syndrome

GENE LOCUS: no specific gene linked to this presentation

KEY ASD REFERENCE: Ramaekers *et al.* 1997

SUMMARY: Unilateral cerebellar hypoplasia syndrome is a neurodevelopmental presentation. It is one of the more common presentations of cerebellar structural abnormalities, but does not have a clear genetic or metabolic pathogenesis (Ramaekers *et al.* 1997). It is typically associated with developmental delay (Patel and Barkovich 2002).

HOW COMMON IS UNILATERAL CEREBELLAR HYPOPLASIA SYNDROME? Unilateral cerebellar malformations are rare, with various causes of hypoplasia gradually becoming clarified (Poretti, Wolf and Boltshauser 2008). A clear idea of prevalence awaits clarification of the extent of co-morbidity with Mobius [48] and Joubert [44] syndromes, and clarification of the extent of, and the genetic basis/ bases to, the remainder of such cases.

MAIN CLINICAL FEATURES: At present, there is no clear aetiology to this presentation. However, it seems most likely to have a genetic aetiology. As no clear genetic basis to this neuropathology has so far been identified, this pattern is not recognized in current classifications of cerebellar malformation (Patel and Barkovich 2002).

IS THERE A LINK BETWEEN UNILATERAL CEREBELLAR HYPOLASIA SYDROME AND ASD? There is one report of two unrelated male cases of ASD in association with unilateral cerebellar hypoplasia (Remaekers *et al.* 1997). Both cases were microcephalic, and in both there was an associated ipsilateral choreido-retinal coloboma.

Cases of cerebellar hypoplasia are well documented in the ASD literature (see, for example, Courchesne *et al.* 1994), and cases of unilateral cerebellar hypoplasia have been reported in association with a number of genetic conditions linked to ASD, including Mobius [48] (Harbord *et al.* 1989) and Joubert [44] (Pellegrino, Lensch, Muenke and Chance 1997) syndromes.

DIFFERENTIAL DIAGNOSIS: Some ASD cases are reported in association with Mobius [48] and Joubert [44] syndromes. However, the pathogenesis in the cases reported by Raemaekers *et al.* (1997) is unclear at this time, and no genetic basis has been reported.

MANAGEMENT AND TREATMENT: No specific treatment or management approaches are known at this time.

ANIMAL MODELS: There are no specific animal models. Some of the more general models for lateralized growth conditions such as Goldenhar syndrome (hemifacial microsomia) [38] may prove to be informative (Naora *et al.* 1994; Otani *et al.* 1991).

76.

Velocardiofacial syndrome (VCFS)

See also

- CATCH22 [18]
- CHARGE syndrome [20]
- DiGeorge syndrome I [29a]

GENE LOCUS: 22q11.2

KEY ASD REFERENCES: Chudley, Gutierrez, Jocelyn and Chodirker 1998; Kates *et al.* 2007a, 2007b; Kozma 1998; Niklasson , Rasmussen, Oskarsdóttir and Gillberg 2001

SUMMARY: VCFS has been included here for completeness, because the term is still in common use and there are support groups in the USA and Australia that use it. The core material has been covered in several other sections dealing with cases which have been identified as CATCH22 [18], CHARGE syndrome [20] and DiGeorge syndrome I [29a], and will not be duplicated here. Turn to these other sections for further information which is relevant to people who have a diagnosis of VCFS.

A recent review of the history of work on VCFS can be found in Shprintzen (2008), which links to these other literatures.

HOW COMMON IS VCFS? See sections covering CATCH22 [18], CHARGE syndrome [20] and DiGeorge syndrome I [29a].

IS THERE A LINK BETWEEN VCFS AND ASD?

- Chudley, Gutierrez, Jocelyn and Chodirker (1998) documented a series of cases with 22q11 deletions and ASD. One of their original series has been reclassified as having a 22q13 defect, not a 22q11 deletion as originally thought.

- Kozma (1998) presented a case of a girl with diagnoses of VCFS and ASD, a cardiac defect and profound learning disability.

- Niklasson, Rasmussen, Oskarsdóttir and Gillberg (2001) reviewed 32 children with '22q11 deletion syndrome'. Ninety-four per cent had associated learning disability, 28 per cent had ADHD alone, 15 per cent had ASD alone, and 16 per cent fulfilled criteria for both ADHD and ASD.

- In a meticulous study using the ADI-R to compare five groups (ASD + VCFS children to VCFS alone; siblings of VCFS children; a group with idiopathic autism; and community controls), Kates et al. (2007a, 2007b) were able to show that there was a range of VCFS-specific behaviours which were seen irrespective of ASD comorbidity, and also a number of behaviours seen in idiopathic cases but not typically seen in those with 'VCFS autism'. In particular, difficulties in sharing attention, limited gestural communication, difficulty in initiating conversation and the presence of circumscribed interests were seen in VCFS, with or without ASD. Limited fantasy play, increased ritualistic behaviour, presence of motor stereotypies and repetitive use of objects were seen in idiopathic ASD, but not in VCFS with no associated ASD. This study provides a helpful template to aid

in evaluating the effects of treatment interventions.

DIFFERENTIAL DIAGNOSIS: A variety of overlapping clinical disorders, all associated with 22q11.2 defects, are reported. The overlap in both phenotype and genotype suggests that a variety of conditions should be considered. (Refer to Table A17 on page 102.)

ANIMAL MODELS: See sections covering CATCH22 [18], CHARGE syndrome [20] and DiGeorge syndrome I [29a].

77.

Williams syndrome (WS)

aka • Williams-Beuren syndrome (WBS)
     • infantile hypercalcaemia -

GENE LOCUS: 7q11.23

KEY ASD REFERENCES: Berg *et al.* 2007; Edelmann *et al.* 2007; Gillberg and Rasmussen 1994; Herguner and Mukaddes 2006; Klein-Tasman *et al.* 2007, 2009; Laws and Bishop 2004; Reiss *et al.* 1985

SUMMARY: A paper from New Zealand is usually taken as the first clear description of WS: Williams, Barratt-Boyes and Lowe (1961) described four older children with supravalvular aortic stenosis (SVAS), learning difficulty and a particular constellation of facial features.

Williams syndrome (WS) has been argued by many to be a mirror opposite of ASD, those with the condition being typically described as sociable, sometimes even overfriendly, with good eye contact, and often as hyperverbal. The issue of comorbidity has aroused much controversy and debate. However, there is now a substantial literature detailing individuals with both the clinical and genetic characteristics of Williams syndrome who also have an ASD.

HOW COMMON IS WS? The population prevalence has been estimated as approximately one in 10,000 live births (Grimm and Wesselhoeft 1980). One recent Norwegian survey has arrived at a figure of one in 7,500 (Strømme *et al.* 2002a).

MAIN CLINICAL FEATURES: In WS, a number of classic features are seen:

- a specific congenital heart defect, supravalvular aortic stenosis (SVAS), with multiple peripheral pulmonary arterial stenoses
- an elfin face (shortened eyelid fissures, a depressed nasal bridge, heavy eyebrows, a slightly upturned nose and full lips)
- short stature
- a characteristic pattern of dental malformation (with small crowns and failure of formation of one or more permanent teeth)
- infantile hypercalcaemia
- learning difficulty.

There is often a 'stellate' or 'lacy' pattern to the iris (Holmstrom *et al.* 1990), and individuals are predominantly blue-eyed (77 per cent) (Winter *et al.* 1996).

As regards behaviour, hyperacusis is a common feature, affecting 41/49 cases (84 per cent) in one series (Gothelf *et al.* 2006), and 54/54 (100 per cent) in another (Mari *et al.* 1995). It is thought that both the hyperacusis and high-frequency sensorineural hearing loss commonly seen in the same individuals could result from an abnormality of the auditory nerve. Hyperacusis is commonly associated with fears and phobias in people with WS. (It was seen in 58 per cent of a sample of 38 Swedish individuals with WS, compared to

2.5 per cent of a control sample (Blomberg, Rosander and Andersson 2006).)

A useful review of the early development of our understanding of WS (Jones 1990) focuses on the early hypocalcaemic component, contrasting this with the milder form of hypocalcaemia induced by excessive vitamin D supplementation (as occurred in the UK and parts of mainland Europe in the period immediately after World War II).

WS is a multi-system disorder (Cherniske *et al.* 2004). A systematic assessment of a group of 20–30-year-old individuals with WS showed a high prevalence of the following:

- high-frequency sensorineural hearing loss
- cardiovascular disease
- hypertension
- gastrointestinal symptoms
- diabetes and abnormal glucose tolerance
- subclinical hypothyroidism
- decreased bone mineral density
- anxiety problems.

Hypertension is a common problem in WS that is seen in approximately 50 per cent of cases (Broder *et al.* 1999; Del Campo *et al.* 2006).

From examining a series of 96 WS cases, it was found that those people who lacked the NCF1 gene as part of their deletion were significantly less likely to be hypertensive. This was probably because they had reduced levels of oxidative stress. Based on these findings, Del Campo *et al.* suggest that antioxidant therapies focused on reducing nicotinamide adenine dinucleotide phosphate (NADPH) oxidase activity may be beneficial, particularly for those WS cases who are hypertensive.

Premature greying of the hair and development of cataracts were also common in this group, suggesting accelerated ageing.

Several genes are known to be involved in Williams syndrome, including the elastin gene and the LIM kinase-1 gene, RFC2 (aka activator 1) and CYLN2 (aka cytoplasmic linker protein 115/CLIP 115), all of which have been mapped to 7q11.23 (Hoogenraad *et al.* 2002). Tassabehji *et al.* (2005) demonstrated that both GTF2IRD1 (7q11.23) and GTF2I (7q11.23), known to be involved in craniofacial and cognitive development, are also responsible for the principal features seen in Williams syndrome.

There is an association between the extent of the gene microdeletion and the physical and cognitive phenotype seen in WS (Tassabehji 2003).

A rare parental inversion variant has been described in two children in the same pedigree who have the 7q11.23 deletion in the context of a WBS Inv-1 parental anomaly (Scherer *et al.* 2005).

Many of the clinical features of WS are associated with defects in the elastin gene. Elastin is an essential component in the construction of the vascular system, with defects resulting in supravalvular aortic stenosis (SVAS) (Li, Brooke *et al.* 1998). Elastin disorders are seen in a range of clinical conditions in addition to WS, including:

- SVAS
- *cutis laxa*
- Marfan syndrome
- isolated skeletal features of Marfan syndrome
- *ectopia lentis*
- familial thoracic aortic aneurysms and dissections
- MASS syndrome
- Shprintzen Goldberg syndrome
- congenital contractural arachnodactyly.
  (Milewicz, Urbán and Boyd 2000)

It is interesting to note that several of the other possible causes of SVAS have also been associated with ASD:

	SVAS reference	ASD reference
Marfan syndrome	Grimm and Wesslhoeft 1980	Tantam, Evered and Hersov 1990
rubella embryopathy	Varghese, Izukawa and Rowe 1969	Chess 1971
thalidomide embryopathy	Jorgensen 1972	Miller *et al.* 2005

Connective tissue abnormalities and both facial and general myopathy are common, and well described in WS (Voit *et al.* 1991), typically with delayed motor milestones, muscle pains and hypotonia. In extreme cases, there may be joint contractures and scoliosis. Abnormalities of elastin are typically seen on skin biopsy and may prove to be a useful assessment of the extent of the elastin defect (Dridi *et al.* 1999).

These features are not always seen, however, and a number of pairs of MZ twins have been described where only one twin shows obvious features (see, for example, Castorina *et al.* 1997; Pankau, Gosch, Simeon and Wessel 1993), while similar variability in connective tissue problems is seen in other members of the affected person's family (Pankau *et al.* 2001).

Cardiac features: Cardiac problems are not always present, and in one recent review of a series of 75 patients (Eronen *et al.* 2002), 47 per cent had cardiovascular symptoms identified at birth, SVAS was present in 73 per cent over time, and 55 per cent exhibited hypertension in adulthood.

The condition presents with considerable variability, and early reports did not make the link between the cardiac component (SVAS) and infantile hypercalcaemia. This association was first proposed by Beuren (1972).

Cardiac problems may be significant but undetected: in an early study of a group of 19 patients with Williams syndrome (Jones and Smith 1975), 13 were found to have significant cardiac problems. These appear to be significantly more likely in boys than girls. In girls, however, they tend to be detected earlier, and are of greater severity (Sadler et al. 2001).

Stenosis of the supravalvular aorta is one of the most consistent findings in WS. It was seen in 57/59 cases examined in one series, with surgical intervention being required in 17 (Wessel et al. 1994).

In one large series of 75 cases, SVAS was the most common cardiac diagnosis, being seen in 32/44 (73 per cent). Pulmonary arterial stenosis (PAS) was seen in 18/44 (41 per cent); an aortic or mitral valve defect in 5/44 (11 per cent); and tetralogy of Fallot was seen in one case (2 per cent) (Eronen et al. 2002).

Cerebral arteries: Narrowing of the cerebral arteries in WS, when unrecognized and untreated, can result in strokes and brain damage (Kaplan, Levinson and Kaplan 1995).

Kidney function: Kidney abnormalities, including calcium deposition, and narrowing of the renal arteries due to elastin defects, are seen in approximately 18 per cent of cases (Biesecker, Laxova and Friedman 1987; Pober et al. 1993).

Thyroid function: Thyroid hypoplasia is common in WS, being seen in up to 75 per cent of cases, and 25 per cent having elevated levels of thyroid stimulating hormone (Cherniske et al. 2004; Selicorni et al. 2006; Stagi et al. 2005). Regular thyroid function testing is a recommended part of routine monitoring of WS cases (Cambiaso et al. 2007; Selicorni et al. 2006).

Stature: Both boys and girls with WS tend to be smaller than average, mean height tracking the third centile. They have normal pubertal growth spurts, achieving adult heights again around the third centile. *In utero* growth is more typically within the normal range (Pankau et al. 1992).

Limited supination at the elbow due to radioulnar synostosis is a common feature, being seen in @7.5 per cent of a series of 119 cases (Pankau, Gosch, Simeon and Wessel 1993).

Vocal pattern: A hoarse or brassy tone of voice has typically been described (Gosch, Stading and Pankau 1994). It has been speculated that this may be a direct function of the abnormalities of elastin in the vocal cords themselves in WS (Vaux, Wojtozak, Benirschke and Lyons Jones 2003).

Unrecognized cases of WS: It is possible for the presentation of WS to be benign and unnoticed until another family member is identified. One paper describes three families in which an affected parent was only identified as having WS once the child had been diagnosed (Morris, Thomas and Greenberg 1993).

Puberty: Puberty is often advanced in WS, while emotional-social development is typically slowed. It has been argued that this may give grounds, in some cases, for the use of medication or hormonal interventions to delay sexual maturation. One case of extreme precocity has been documented (Scothorn and Butler 1997), in a girl with onset of puberty at 7.5 years and of menarche at 8.5 years. However, a large series of 86 girls with WS found a mean age at menarche of 11.5 years +/− 1.7 years compared to 12.9 +/− 1.1 years in a population sample of 759 girls (Partsch et al. 2002).

Coeliac disease: In an interesting study six (9.5 per cent) out of a series of 63 WS patients (Giannotti et al. 2001), as compared to only one (0.54 per cent) of 184 controls, tested positive for the presence of antiendomesial and antigliadin antibodies, the presence of which is indicative of coeliac disease.

Screening for coeliac should, on this basis, form part of the assessment of those with Williams syndrome, with appropriate dietary intervention where it is identified (Hill *et al.* 2005).

Intelligence: From the literature to date, the range of overall ability documented in WS is wide, ranging from severe learning disability to good average ability, with a mean IQ in the mild learning disability range (Ewart *et al.* 1993; Plissart *et al.* 1994).

Epilepsy: Epilepsy is not a recognized concomitant of WS. Three papers have documented infantile spasms in a total of four cases (Mizugushi, Yamanaka, Kuwajima and Kondo 1998; Morimoto *et al.* 2003; Tsao and Westman 1997).

Learning disability: A consistent finding in the literature is one of non-verbal learning disability, with significantly better verbal than performance abilities and the differences in spatial ability reported (Mervis, Robinson and Pani 1999). Concentration problems, motor restlessness and attention-seeking behaviour have been found to be common in WS.

As with many of the features discussed, there is no clear association, within the WS population with the full deletion, between the genotype and the severity of the clinical phenotype. This may be because of the uniformity of the deletion in the majority of cases, with 95 per cent of cases showing the same 1.55-Mb deletion (Bayes *et al.* 2003).

Neurological features: Two of the earliest imaging studies of WS were carried out by Jernigan and colleagues. In the first of these (Wang P.P. *et al.* 1992) the researchers demonstrated that, whereas in

Down syndrome the neocerebellar tonsils are smaller when compared to controls matched for age, IQ and cerebral volume, in WS these structures are larger than either Down syndrome or non-specific age, IQ and cerebral volume matched controls. The authors suggest that this may be linked to the preserved verbal abilities and affect seen in WS. In the second study (Jernigan *et al.* 1993) the analysis was extended to cerebral structures and indicated that, in comparison to Down syndrome, some prefrontal and temporal-limbic structures are relatively preserved in WS, while a number of abnormalities were apparent in basal ganglia and diencephalic structures across both groups.

There is a gradual change from hypotonia to hypertonia with age in WS (Chapman, du Plessis and Pober 1996). A neurological study of 47 WS cases (Gagliardi, Martelli, Burt and Borgatti 2007) documented problems with gross and fine motor control, mild cerebellar signs, and a progressive pattern of soft extrapyramidal signs through late childhood into early adolescence.

An fMRI study of auditory processing in a small group of five people with WS and matched controls found highly atypical patterns of brain activation in response to background noise and music. In contrast to the general population, who showed increased temporal lobe cortical activation, the WS subjects showed reduced activation in these areas, coupled with increased activation in the right amygdala, an area more typically activated in emotional processing. This difference may account for the common finding of hyperacusis in this population (Levitin *et al.* 2003).

In a study of 14 patients with Williams syndrome, compared to 48 group-matched controls, Rae *et al.* (1998) found a correlation between the performance of their WS group on a range of psychometric tests, and decreases in the amount of neocerebellar N-acetylaspartate when this was normalized to levels of choline or creatine.

The behavioural phenotype in Williams syndrome suggests a dorsal and/or ventral developmental dissociation, with defects in dorsal but not the ventral hemispheric visual stream. A shortened extent of the dorsal central sulcus has been observed in autopsy specimens. A study of the gross dorsal and ventral anatomy of the visual system in 21 WS cases compared with age and sex matched controls (Galaburda et al. 2001) found differences in the dorsal aspects of the visual pathways within the hemispheres, but not the ventral pathways. The study is consistent with subsequent work by the same group (for example, Thompson P.M. et al. 2005) and with the visuospatial difficulties reported in this population.

There is some evidence of differences in the development of the corpus callosum (the large fibre tract which connects the two hemispheres of the brain) from one study of 12 WS cases and 12 controls (Tomaiuolo et al. 2002) and from a subsequent study of 24 cases and controls demonstrating a shorter, thinner callosal section in WS (Luders et al. 2007).

One MRI study of 20 WS cases found an increased degree of cerebral symmetry (Schmitt, Eliez, Bellugi and Reiss 2001), suggesting, in line with later research from the same group (Gaser et al. 2006), that there may be accelerated in utero brain growth that is specific to the dorsal aspects of the frontal areas of the brain.

From a study of 11 WS cases and matched controls engaged in a facial recognition task, the WS cases showed a different pattern of cortical activation, with increased frontal and temporal flow compared to the controls, who activated primary and secondary visual cortex (Mobbs et al. 2004).

In one multimodal neuroimaging study of visual processing of 13 WS cases and 11 controls, there was clear evidence of hypoactivation of the dorsal visual pathways, which closely paralleled reduced volume of areas of grey matter during tasks which involved visualizing an object as a set of components, or construction of a replica (Meyer-Lindenberg et al. 2004).

A further study (Meyer-Lindenberg et al. 2005) examined the structure and activity of the hippocampus in WS. The study used multimodal neuroimaging to characterize the hippocampi in 12 WS cases with normal IQ and 12 age-, sex- and IQ-matched healthy controls. Using PET and fMRI they found evidence of marked reduction in the resting anterior flow, but normal posterior hippocampal blood flow, in the WS group. There were also lower levels of N-acetylaspartate, suggesting lower synaptic activity.

In a recent study of 43 adult WS cases and 40 controls (Reiss et al. 2004), the former had smaller volume and reduced density of the thalamic and occipital lobes (areas involved in visuo-spatial processing). A recent French study of nine children with WS and 11 age-matched controls (Boddaert et al. 2006) reported similar differences in parieto-occipital grey matter.

A further study of cortical thickness in WS, comparing 42 WS to 40 control cases, identified an area of the right hemisphere perisylvian and inferior temporal zone that is significantly increased in depth in the WS cases (Thompson P.M. et al. 2005).

In a study comparing gyri in the occipital cortex and precuneus in 42 WS cases and 40 controls (Gaser et al. 2006), there were consistently significantly more gyri in the WS cases. This finding suggests that there is a defect in selective cell apoptosis, the principal mechanism involved in early postnatal development of the central nervous system.

A recent detailed analysis of cortical folding patterns in 16 WS and 13 control brains found differences in a broad range of cortical areas bilaterally, and in both anterior and posterior cortex (Van Essen *et al.* 2006).

GENETIC FACTORS:

Deletion at the ELN (elastin) gene locus: Several studies suggest that the variability of presentation in WS may result from deletions that are broader than the core mechanism sufficient to produce the WS phenotype (see, for example, Ewart *et al.* 1993); and as many deletions extend to regions outside the core WS area of chromosome 7, the severity of the phenotype may often be an indication of the involvement of genes that are not part of the WS genotype (Dutly and Schinzel 1996; Ewart *et al.* 1993; Urban *et al.* 1996).

From two studies looking in total at 104 WS cases, deletion of the elastin gene was found in over 90 per cent of cases (Mari *et al.* 1995; Nickerson *et al.* 1995).

Deletions of other genes: There is evidence for the deletion of a number of genes other than ELN in WS cases. In one study, the RFC2 gene, also found at 7q11.23, was deleted in 100 per cent of 18 cases assessed (Osborne *et al.* 1996; Peoples *et al.* 1996). The authors speculated that this might be the gene that is involved in the observed pattern of growth retardation in WS.

Several research groups have also reported deletions of the LIM-kinase gene (Frangiskakis *et al.* 1996; Osborne *et al.* 1996; Tassabehji *et al.* 1996).

One group (Frangiskakis *et al.* 1996) studied Williams syndrome patients who showed particularly poor visuo-spatial constructive skills. In two of the families studied, who had both the LIM-kinase and ELN gene deletion, they hypothesized that the LIM-kinase defect was the basis to their visuo-spatial difficulties. They also found that an ELN deletion alone was insufficient to produce such problems.

Papers are starting to appear concerning the contributions of genes adjacent to the WS region that are commonly deleted in combination with ELN and LIM-kinase. A recent report suggests that CYLN2 and GTF2IRD1 contribute significantly to the learning difficulties and to the specific WS cognitive profile (van Hagen *et al.* 2007).

Delineation of the WBS critical region: Typically the gene deletion found in WS is large (some 1.5–2.5 megabytes), and deletes 17 or more genes. A physical gene map of a 500 kb region of chromosome 7 was created to determine the deleted region in a series of 30 WS cases (Osborne *et al.* 1996). The study determined that the typical deleted region included the genes for ELN, LIMK1, RFC2 and WSCR1.

The minimal region required for the expression of a WS phenotype was determined in a study using a series of ten micro-satellite markers and five fluorescence in-situ hybridization (FISH) probes (Wu *et al.* 1998). Analysing data from 51 patients, in those with WS both a LIM-kinase and an ELN deletion were always found. In one case who had SVAS but did not present with WS, there was an ELN deletion but LIM-kinase was intact.

As hemizygous LIM-kinase is specifically implicated in WS visuo-spatial difficulties and ELN in SVAS, one group (Meng *et al.* 1998) carried out a mapping exercise of commonly deleted genes to look for further associations. Three further genes were identified in the area typically deleted in WS: TBL2, BCL7B and WBSCR14. However, no clear phenotypic correspondence was found.

Genotype/phenotype correlations: In one large case series of 85 (Wang *et al.* 1999), there was little in the way of association between genotype and phenotype – infantile hypercalcaemia was associated with the lacy/stellate iris pattern, and maternally inherited deletions were associated with increased head circumference, but otherwise there was no statistically significant association between factors such as deletion size, gender and parental transmission, and the resulting clinical phenotype.

In contrast, in a further series of 65 cases (Perez Jurado *et al.* 1996), where deletion size and parent of origin were ascertained, maternally derived deletions were associated with more severe microcephaly and growth retardation.

If, instead of a microdeletion of the WS locus, a duplication occurs, then in contrast to the normal language fluency and hyperverbal pattern seen in WS, there is a severe delay in expressive language, and a relative strength in visuo-spatial abilities (Berg *et al.* 2007; Depienne *et al.* 2007; Somerville *et al.* 2005).

Genetic comorbidities: A single case report of WS in association with Klinefelter syndrome has been reported in a four-year-old Chinese boy co-morbid for the two conditions – an additional X chromosome together with a 7q11.23 deletion. He was growth-retarded despite adequate nutrition, and presented with a ventriculo-septal heart defect (Lee *et al.* 2006).

IS THERE A LINK BETWEEN WS AND ASD? In 1985, Alan Reiss and colleagues described two six-year-old cases of WS who fulfilled criteria for autism (Reiss *et al.* 1985).

A Swedish paper in 1994 described four further cases of WS with autistic behaviour (Gillberg and Rasmussen 1994). All were preschool, two girls and two boys.

In a study of language use in 19 children and young adults with WS, compared to similar groups with Down syndrome [31] and specific language impairment (Laws and Bishop 2004), the broad conclusions were as follows:

> ...this study suggests that individuals with Williams syndrome have pragmatic language impairments, poor social relationships and restricted interests. Far from representing the polar opposite of autism, as suggested by some researchers, Williams syndrome would seem to share many of the characteristics of autistic disorder. (Laws and Bishop 2004)

A recent case report of a 12-year-old boy with WS and ASD, and an accompanying literature review (Herguner and Mukaddes 2006), suggests that a defect in the elastin gene at 7q11.23 results in the core features seen in WS, and that co-morbid autistic symptomology may result from disruption to genes which flank the elastin locus. This notion is lent support by a recent molecular genetics study, based on study of an atypical WS deletion in a six-and-a-half-year-old girl with ASD, which arrives at a similar conclusion (Edelmann *et al.* 2007).

An ADOS study of 29 children with WS aged from two to five years classified approximately half the group as being on the autistic spectrum, and three as having autism (Klein-Tasman *et al.* 2007). The same group has suggested that many young children with WS show social and communicative difficulties, and that there may be issues of diagnostic overshadowing (failing to pick up on the social difficulties) as a result of identifying WS as the primary issue (Klein-Tasman *et al.* 2009).

Microduplication of the 7q11.23 region that results in WS when deleted results in delayed speech and ASD (Berg *et al.* 2007). A case involving triplication of the WS-critical region has been reported with similar phenotypic characteristics to the duplication cases (Beunders *et al.* 2009).

One suggestion for the neurobiology underpinning the behavioural phenotype in WS duplication is a regionally selective defect in neural migration. The authors discuss an illustrative 13-year-old female case (Torniero *et al.* 2007).

From the above, it is clear that the co-occurrence of ASD and WS is now a well-established phenomenon, and that the communication pattern seen in WS is similar to that typically described in ASD. It seems likely that the genetic basis to the co-occurrence is due to genetic factors which overlap with 7q11.23 – a deletion in this region may be necessary, but seems on its own not to be sufficient to result in an ASD. Williams syndrome is associated with ASD in approximately 50 per cent of cases. Given the population prevalence of WS, this suggests that WS co-occurs with ASD in approximately one in every 15,000 live births.

MANAGEMENT AND TREATMENT: There are useful general overviews of treatment and management for WS aimed at both the primary care physician (Lashkari, Smith and Graham 1999), and at those managing adult WS cases (Pober and Morris 2007).

The various associated problems with growth, hypercalcaemia, cardiac, thyroid and kidney function and coeliac disease are all important to keep under review and to manage and treat as appropriate.

The relatively low prevalence has meant that to date there have been no systematic studies of the effects of approaches which have demonstrable efficacy in some of the other conditions discussed in this volume.

There is now growing evidence for the efficacy of growth hormone therapy in addressing the short stature seen in those

with WS (Kuijpers, De Vroede, Knol and Jansen 1999; Xekouki *et al.* 2005).

Infantile hypercalcaemia, a factor that is thought to be associated with the extent of cardiac problems, can be successfully treated through the use of biphosphonate (Cagle *et al.* 2004; Oliveri *et al.* 2004).

Although there is no systematic research on the issues, from the literature to date it seems likely that both vitamin D and calcium supplementation are contraindicated in those with WS.

Treatments to address oxidative stress in those who present with hypertension may be of benefit (Del Campo *et al.* 2006). However, there is no intervention research to date that has addressed this issue.

ANIMAL MODELS: One group has been able to demonstrate, by engineering a heterozygous mouse model for the human elastin gene deletion seen in WS (Li, Brooke *et al.* 1998), that mice with this defect show a reduction in the RNA for elastin and a 50 per cent drop in the protein itself, compared to genetically normal mice. As in humans, this resulted in an increase in both smooth muscle and elastic lamellae in the arterial walls.

Excessive vitamin D intake can result in reduced elastin expression in addition to hypercalcaemia (Hinek, Botney and Mecham 1991; Vijayakumar and Kurup 1974). In animal models, increased vitamin D intake can result in SVAS (Chan *et al.* 1979; Friedman and Roberts 1966).

Mice with a homozygous loss of *Gtf2ird1* have craniofacial abnormalities that are similar to those seen in WBS; in addition, they demonstrate growth retardation and neurologic abnormalities (Durkin, Keck-Waggoner, Popescu and Thorgeirsson 2001).

One study has identified a mouse gene, *Cyln2*, that codes for cytoplasmic linker protein 115 (Hoogenraad *et al.* 2002). This gene is commonly expressed in the brain, is involved in intracellular communication, and is commonly deleted in WS.

Mice with an elastin defect appear in most cases to develop a stable hypertensive pattern (Faury *et al.* 2003). On this basis, mouse models do not provide a useful model of human WS; humans appear to be particularly sensitive to elastin disorders (Milewicz, Urbán and Boyd 2000).

Homozygous loss of the *Gtf2ird1* gene in the mouse produces craniofacial abnormalities reminiscent of those seen in WS. The mice also show evidence of growth retardation and neurological differences (Durkin, Keck-Waggoner, Popescu and Thorgeirsson 2001).

A best-practice genetic guideline has been published:

Committee on Genetics, American Academy of Pediatrics (2001) 'Health care supervision for children with Williams syndrome.' *Pediatrics*, 107: 1192–1204.

A useful overview can be found in the following short book:

Bellugi, U. and St George, M. (eds.) (2001) *Journey from Cognition to Brain to Gene: Perspectives from Williams syndrome.* Massachusetts: MIT Press.

78.

Hereditary xanthinuria type II

GENE LOCUS: At the time of writing the genetic locus is not certain (hereditary xanthinuria type I which affects the production of xanthine dehydrogenase alone has been localized to 2p23–p22).

KEY ASD REFERENCE: Zannolli *et al.* 2003

SUMMARY: This is a rare autosomal recessive disorder which results in defects

in two specific enzymes – xanthine dehydrogenase and aldehyde oxidase. The genes for these enzymes are both on chromosome 2 (at 2p22 and 2q33 respectively), but their separation makes mutation of both an unlikely cause. Individuals with this mutation are unable to metabolize allopurinol.

A defect in the gene for human molybdenum cofactor sulphatase (HMCS) has been identified in independent cases. This results in defects in the production of xanthine dehydrogenase and aldehyde oxidase, with the additional inactivation of sulphite oxidase (Ichida *et al.* 2001).

HOW COMMON IS HEREDITARY XANTHINURIA TYPE II? It is a rare disorder with few reported cases (Simmonds 2003).

MAIN CLINICAL FEATURES: The clinical presentation is varied, from around 20 per cent of cases who are asymptomatic, to a small percentage at the opposite extreme who present with acute renal failure. Most cases have xanthine calculi and crystalluria. Some ten per cent of cases present with duodenal ulcers, myopathy or arthropathy.

IS THERE A LINK BETWEEN HEREDITARY XANTHINURIA TYPE II AND ASD? To date a single case has been reported in which the combination of features has been reported. This was an 11-year-old boy with learning disability, autistic features, vocal and motor tics, cortical and renal cysts, osteopenia, hair and teeth defects, and a range of behavioural symptoms, including aggressiveness with temper tantrums, and ADHD.

At the present time, there is no understanding of a biological basis that could underpin the co-occurrence of ASD and xanthinuria type II.

DIFFERENTIAL DIAGNOSIS: Hereditary xanthinuria type I presents with similar physical problems to type II, but with a less complex metabolic profile with a mutation in the gene for xanthine dehydrogenase and without an affect on aldehyde oxidase. There are no other conditions that present with the same clinical pattern.

MANAGEMENT AND TREATMENT: High fluid intake and purine restriction are the current recommended treatments specific to this form of xanthinuria (Simmonds 2003).

ANIMAL MODELS: The problems with allopurinol metabolism that this condition presents may make it a candidate for trials of xanthine oxidase inhibitors, which are showing evidence of effects in animal models (Nishino *et al.* 2005; Pacher, Nivorozhkin and Szabo 2006).

79.

Xeroderma pigmentosa (complementation group C)

GENE LOCUS: 3p25

KEY ASD REFERENCE: Khan *et al.* 1998

SUMMARY: Xeroderma pigmentosa is a condition in which the skin cannot repair damage to DNA caused by ultraviolet light (Slor *et al.* 2000). It results in thinning of the skin, odd patterns of skin pigmentation, and telangectasia (spidery, fine blood vessels). Basal cell carcinoma (cancer of the basal skin cells) is also common.

A summary of the genetic mechanisms involved in xeroderma pigmentosa can be found in Cleaver, Thompson, Richardson and States (1999).

HOW COMMON IS XERODERMA PIGMENTOSA? The best current estimate of prevalence is one in 250,000 (Hedera and Fink 2007).

MAIN CLINICAL FEATURES: Skin, eye and central nervous system effects should be monitored. The nature and extent of any such involvement is largely dependent on the extent of sun exposure. Lack of vitamin D can also result in brittle bones if not addressed.

IS THERE A LINK BETWEEN XERODERMA PIGMENTOSA AND ASD? To date, a single case – a four-year-old Korean boy with xeroderma pigmentosa complementation group C – has been reported with ASD. The complementation group C form appears to have the least neurological sequelae (Anttinen *et al.* 2008).

DIFFERENTIAL DIAGNOSIS: A number of other genetic conditions can result in photosensitivity and increased risk of UV skin damage:

- XP with neurologic abnormalities
- Cockayne syndrome (CS) (including cerebrooculofacioskeletal syndrome (COFS))
- the XP/CS complex
- trichothiodystrophy (TTD) [72]
- the XP/TTD complex
- UV-sensitive syndrome.

MANAGEMENT AND TREATMENT: Protection from ultraviolet in sunlight is the primary treatment. UVC from some house lighting can also cause damage and levels should be checked. Where the condition is identified early in life there is a possibility of low vitamin D levels, and supplementation should be considered.

ANIMAL MODELS: There are currently no direct animal models of the complementation group C form of xeroderma pigmentosa.

80.

X-linked ichthyosis (XLI)

aka • steroid sulphatase deficiency

GENE LOCUS: Xp22.32

KEY ASD REFERENCE: Kent *et al.* 2008

SUMMARY: XLI was first described in 1965 in a clinical study of 81 affected males (Wells and Kerr 1965). It is a dermatological condition arising from abnormalities of steroid sulphatase that result from deletions or mutations at Xp22.32.

XLI results from a defect, typically a deletion, seen in @ 85 per cent of cases (Hernandez-Martin, Gonzalez-Sarmiento and De Unamuno 1999), or point mutation, seen in the remaining 15 per cent. (Six separate point mutations of the steroid sulphatase (STS) gene at Xp22.32 have been reported (Alperin and Shapiro 1997).) (First reported by Jöbsis *et al.* 1980.)

Antenatal detection is possible by screening, and, since around one in five cases is co-morbid for ASD, screening would detect the one in 25,000 live births who are likely to have both XLI and an ASD.

In the cases where an ASD has been reported in XLI, there is a deletion of the contiguous NLGN4 gene, which has also been linked to ASD in non-XLI cases.

Treatment should be as for other cases with NLGN4 deletion, coupled with management of the dermatological problems.

XLI expresses differently in males and females with girls typically producing higher levels of steroid sulphatase and being more mildly affected. Most reported clinical cases are male. Transmission is typically from heterozygous carrier mothers to their sons.

Consistent with maternal transmission of STS deletion, in the majority of reported cases there is absent STS activity, and mothers show reduced STS activity levels consistent with carrier status (Cuevas-Covarrubias, Kofman-Alfaro, Orozco Orozco and Diaz-Zagoya 1995; Valdes-Flores, Kofman-Alfaro, Jimenez-Vaca and Cuevas-Covarrubias 2001).

Shapiro *et al.* (1978) showed that arylsulphatase deficiency is X-linked and that it is expressed in postnatal life as X-linked ichthyosis.

HOW COMMON IS XLI? The best current estimate of prevalence is one in 5,043 males (Ingordo *et al.* 2003).

MAIN CLINICAL FEATURES: XLI is typically noticed shortly after birth through peeling of large scales of skin. Scales are primarily on the neck, trunk and backs of the hands and feet. The typical scaling on the neck gave rise to the term 'dirty neck disease'. The face, palms and soles are typically spared. XLI improves during the summer, while *ichthyosis vulgaris* does not. There is no apparent improvement with age.

Some patients may present with additional features, such as undescended testes and testicular cancer. Corneal opacities are seen in between 50 and 100 per cent of cases, and in the majority of female carriers (Sever, Frost and Weinstein 1968).

Although epilepsy has been reported with ichthyosis (Quattrini *et al.* 1986), it is not clear whether any of the reported cases had XLI, and prevalence is uncertain.

In a large early series of 50 affected families reported by Lykkesfeldt *et al.* (1985), 42 families had more than one affected member, which strongly suggests a genetic aetiology.

Both undescended testes (Lykkesfeldt *et al.* 1985) and hypogonadism (Pike *et al.* 1989) appear to be more common in XLI than would be expected in the general population.

IS THERE A LINK BETWEEN XLI AND ASD? Only one study to date has examined a possible link between XLI and ASD (Kent *et al.* 2008). This study screened 25 children with XLI (who had been detected through antenatal screening of maternal urinary oestriol to identify steroid sulphatase deficiencies). The children were aged five years and above. Five children were found, from screening on the Childhood Asperger Screening Test (CAST) and Autism Screening Questionnaire (ASQ) now known as the Social Communication Questionnaire (SCQ), followed by more detailed assessment of ASD symptomology and communication, to have an autistic spectrum disorder or language/communication disorder. All of the children identified, in contrast to the other children screened, had large deletions that included deletion of the NLGN4 gene.

GENETIC FACTORS: The gene responsible for XLI is contiguous to the NLGN4 gene, which has been linked to ASD (Blasi *et al.* 2006; Chocholska, Rossier, Barbi and Kehrer-Sawatzki 2006; Jamain *et al.* 2003; Laumonnier *et al.* 2004; Lawson-Yuen, Saldivar, Sommer and Picker 2008; Yan *et al.* 2008). Often the NLGN4 gene is deleted in individuals with XLI.

A number of models for the possible role of NLGN4 in the genesis of ASD have been proposed. (See, for example, Bourgeron 2007; De Jaco, Comoletti, King and Taylor 2008; Talebizadeh *et al.* 2006.)

There are, however, cases with features of XLI and NLGN4 deletion, but without ASD symptomology (Macarov *et al.* 2007), and several studies have failed to replicate

evidence of NLGN4 defects in ASD (Gauthier *et al.* 2005; Vincent *et al.* 2004; Ylisaukko-Oja *et al.* 2005), suggesting that there may be variations in the prevalence of NLGN4 defects in different populations.

DIFFERENTIAL DIAGNOSIS: XLI differs in various ways, both clinically and histologically, from autosomal dominant ichthyosis (Wells and Jennings 1967). The distribution of scaling can also be helpful in differentiating XLI from *ichthyosis vulgaris* (Okano *et al.* 1988).

The differential diagnosis of XLI is from other ichthyoses, such as autosomal dominant ichthyosis, hereditary and acquired *ichthyosis vulgaris*, and lamellar ichthyosis. (It also needs to be differentiated from asteatotic eczema and atopic dermatitis.) The various forms of ichthyosis can be discriminated using skin biopsy staining (Lake *et al.* 1991).

None of these other ichthyotic conditions has been reported to date in association with ASD.

One case of ichthyosis has been described in a girl with Turner syndrome (Solomon and Schoen 1971), with a positive paternal family history. Recently a specific Turner syndrome neurocognitive phenotype has been mapped to Xp22.3 by examining women with partial X-chromosome deletions (Zinn *et al.* 2007). In one such case a son with the same partial deletion had XLI.

A clinical overlap between XLI and Kallmann syndrome (also an Xp22.3 condition) has been noted in a number of papers (for example, Ballabio *et al.* 1986, 1987; Krishnamurthy, Kapoor and Yadav 2007; Weissortel *et al.* 1998).

Wieacker, Davies, Mevorah and Ropers (1983) looked for linkage between the RC8 sequence at Xp21.2 implicated in Duchenne muscular dystrophy [33] and the steroid sulphatase (STS) locus in XLI.

No cases of XLI together with Duchenne have so far been reported.

Monozygotic twins have been reported with a concordant phenotype (XLI, learning disability, and *grand mal* epilepsy in both cases) (Gohlke *et al.* 2000).

MANAGEMENT AND TREATMENT: Management and treatment of XLI is primarily directed at keeping the skin hydrated and supple, to prevent scaling (Janniger and Schwartz 2008).

Good results have been reported, in various studies, from the topical application of cholesterol-based creams (Lykkesfeldt and Hoyer 1983; Zettersten *et al.* 1998), and retinoid creams (Shwayder 2004). It is thought that the formation of scales is a result of accumulation of undegraded cholesterol sulphate, increasing corneodesmosome retention and reducing cholesterol synthesis (Elias *et al.* 1984, 2008).

Freiberg *et al.* (1997) were able to demonstrate correction of STS expression and histology in skin cells from XLI patients grafted onto immunodeficient mice, where a retroviral expression vector was used to correct gene function.

Spirito, Meneguzzi, Danas and Mezzina (2001) have reviewed the evidence of such gene therapy approaches to the treatment of cutaneous diseases.

ANIMAL MODELS: Attempts to produce animal models for XLI have been problematic for several reasons.

- It would appear that during primate evolution there has been a pericentric inversion of the portion of the X chromosome involved, making it difficult to produce non-simian equivalents to the chromosome region that is implicated (Laval and Boyd 1993; Yen *et al.* 1988).

- The size of the STS gene is far larger in humans than in rodents (the human gene is over 146 kilobytes in length, while the equivalent rat gene is 8.2 kilobytes) (Li X.M. *et al.* 1996); however, several regions appear highly conserved.

- Cloning of the mouse *Sts* gene using human reagents has been unsuccessful (Salido *et al.* 1996), suggesting that mouse and human genes differ substantially. The mouse gene is also pseudoautosomal (Kipling, Salido, Shapiro and Cooke 1996), suggesting divergence both from the rat and from human genes, which are not (Kawano *et al.* 1989; Li X.M. *et al.* 1996).

SECTION C

Some Conditions with Similarities to ASD

The following conditions have many features that are similar to those in some of the recognized ASD conditions. Some are becoming considered as synonymous with disorders covered in Section B, but the literature continues to make sufficient distinction that these are presented here is separable disorders.

81.

Alpha-thalassaemia/ mental retardation syndrome, nondeletion type, X-linked (ATRX)

aka • mental retardation–hypotonic facies syndrome
• Smith-Fineman-Myers syndrome
• Carpenter-Waziri syndrome
• Chudley-Lowry syndrome
• Juberg-Marsidi syndrome
• Holmes-Gang syndrome

GENE LOCUS: Xq13

KEY REFERENCE: Gibbons *et al.* 1995; Gong *et al.* 2008

SUMMARY: ATRX is a complex neurodevelopmental disorder with variable degrees of learning disability, sensorineural deafness, undescended testes with ambiguous genital development or hypospadias in 4/5 and progressive slowing of head growth in 3/4. Various other features such as epilepsy and cardiac malformations are more common but not characteristic. For an overview of ATRX see Gibbons (2006).

It is an X-linked recessive condition, shown in boys when passed on from the mother or arising from de novo mutation. Those affected are extremely unlikely to reproduce and no case of paternal transmission has been reported. It is caused by mutation of a SWI2/SNF2 DNA helicase/ATPase gene (Picketts *et al.* 1996). The ATRX gene is known to interact with MeCP2 (defects which cause Rett syndrome [63a]) (Nan *et al.* 2007).

HOW COMMON IS ATRX? As only around 150 affected individuals have been described to date, no clear idea of population prevalence can currently be given. There is nothing in the published literature to suggest a higher or lower prevalence in any particular racial or ethnic group, although most reported cases have been of Mediterranean descent. The prevalence of ATRX is thus uncertain at the time of writing. It has been estimated at <1–9 per 1,000,000 (Gibbons 2006).

Those with ATRX are often described as appearing to be in a world of their own and avoiding eye contact (Gibbons, Picketts, Villard and Higgs 1995). They can present with obsessional repetitive behaviours. An association with ASD has been brought to light through analysis of ASD families with skewed maternal X-chromosome inactivation (Gong *et al.* 2008).

MAIN CLINICAL FEATURES:
• moderate to profound learning difficulties (in 95 per cent of cases)
• sensorineural deafness, with secondary expressive language problems
• cryptorchidism; ambiguous genitalia or hypospadias (in 80 per cent)
• progressive microcephaly (in 75 per cent)
• gastrointestinal problems – gastrooesophageal reflux, regurgitation, vomiting and urinary tract infections
• epilepsy (in 30 per cent)
• spasticity, often progressive

- severe behaviour problems (repetitive behaviours similar to Angelman syndrome [11])
- cardiac malformations (in 20 per cent).

The facial features are characteristic: affected individuals have a small head circumference, telecanthus or ocular hypertelorism, a small triangular nose with retracted columella, a cupid's-bow-shaped upper lip, a large lower lip, and an open mouth. Abnormal ear structure is not uncommon, as are widely spaced teeth and a larger protruding tongue. There is progressive coarsening of the facial features over time.

The typical features are a severe level of cognitive delay with slow achievement of early milestones usually being the first signs that give rise for concern. Various physical and haematological differences are also characteristic (Stevenson, Schwartz and Schroer 2000). Hypotonia is typical, and contributes to both the facial manifestations and the learning difficulties. There are also pedigrees described in which some individuals with the gene difference do not show either the same degree of cognitive deficit or physical phenotype (Guerrini *et al.* 2000; Yntema *et al.* 2002).

Alpha-thalassaemia (an inherited form of anaemia which limits levels of the alpha chains of haemoglobin) is present in 90 per cent of cases and in 25 per cent of carriers. Between 1 in 30 and 1 in 1,000 erythrocytes show beta-globin tetramers on staining with cresyl blue (Gibbons *et al.* 1992, 1995).

Poor food intake, food refusal and excessive drooling are also common; the latter, if excessive, may require medication or surgical intervention. Food refusal should result in gastrointestinal investigation to exclude, for example, peptic ulcers. High-calorie feeds and gavage feeding may be necessary if food intake is poor. GI factors such as gastric ulcers and helicobacter pylori should be investigated and weight should be monitored closely. A variety of possible treatments can be used to reduce drooling where this is problematic – excessive salivation often causes skin irritation.

There are typically minor abnormalities of the external genitalia that can include first-degree hypospadias, undescended testes, and underdevelopment of the scrotum. Occasionally, more severe genital defects are present such as second- and third-degree hypospadias, micropenis, and ambiguous genitalia. Gonadal dysgenesis can be a result of limited in utero testosterone exposure and result in inadequate subsequent testosterone production, leading to somatic feminization and normal-appearing female external genitalia despite a male genotype. Typically, such individuals are brought up as girls (see, for example, Reardon, Gibbons, Winter and Baraitser 1995). Although a wide range of genital anomalies can be seen, the type of anomaly present appears to be consistent within families.

Antenatal detection of affected offspring can be achieved by chorionic villous sampling at 10–12 weeks or by amniocentesis at 15–18 weeks of pregnancy in heterozygous women in most cases. Germline mosaicism has been reported and is a possibility (Bachoo and Gibbons 1999). Despite negative leukocyte testing, women with an ATRX mosaic who have had an affected child may pass on the mutation in subsequent pregnancies. Prenatal diagnosis should be offered in all cases where there is a previous affected child and an XY foetus. Where the mother is a carrier there is a 50 per cent risk of her having a child who is either a female carrier or an affected male child.

GENETICS: All individuals reported to date with ATRX have shown a normal 46,XY karyotype. ATRX at Xq13 is the only gene associated with the syndrome. It can be tested for clinically and abnormalities are detected in about 90 per cent of phenotypic cases.

Individuals who have ATRX do not have children themselves. Most women who are carriers have skewed X-chromosome inactivation (Gibbons *et al.* 1992) and have a 50 per cent chance of having an affected child – girls have a 50 per cent chance of being unaffected carriers and boys of being affected.

Penetrance is presumed to be 100 per cent in males as Xq13 mutations have not been reported in unaffected males.

Most allelic variants of ATRX are found in the zinc finger domain transcription factor (exons 7–9) (Borgione *et al.* 2003; Gibbons, Picketts, Villard and Higgs 1995; Villard and Fontes 2002; Villard *et al.* 1996, 1999). Missense mutations are the most common finding, with frameshift and nonsense mutations being seen less often, while various other deletions, insertions and missense, nonsense and splice mutations have also been identified.

Germline and gonadosomal mosaicism have been described (Bachoo and Gibbons 1999).

ATRX appears to play a role in chromatin remodelling (Ausio *et al.* 2003; Tang, Park, Marshall Graves and Harley 2004). This effect is the likely cause of the thalassaemia, CNS and physical malformations, learning disabilities and ASD.

Skewed X-chromosome inactivation is seen in most unaffected female carriers, but is not sufficient itself to confirm or exclude carrier status (Gibbons *et al.* 1992).

Xq13 mutations are not unique to ATRX and have been reported both in cases of nonsyndromic X-linked mental retardation and X-linked mental retardation with spastic paraplegia (Lossi *et al.* 1999; Yntema *et al.* 2002).

DIFFERENTIAL DIAGNOSIS: ATRX and Coffin-Lowry syndrome (CLS) [21] are similar in clinical presentation and can sometimes be confused on presenting phenotype. CLS is due to a defect at Xp22.2, so can be differentiated genetically.

MANAGEMENT AND TREATMENT: Councelling needs to be on the basis of genetic testing in the individual case.

ANIMAL MODELS: There are no specific models of ATRX and how it affects development. However, mouse models are being used to explore the process influencing ATRX expression.

Like many other X-linked syndromes resulting in learning disability, ATRX shows highly skewed X-chromosome inactivation in maternal carriers. In the mouse model this has been shown not to be present close to conception, when the proportions of inactive cells appear evenly balanced, but to be restricted to specific stages of development (Muers *et al.* 2007).

In a mouse model ATRX was found to interact with MeCP2 (Nan *et al.* 2007). MeCP2 is the methyl-CpG-binding protein implicated in Rett syndrome [63a] and in some forms of XLMR. The pericentromeric heterochromatin domain of ATRX is disturbed in the neurons of MeCP2-null mice, suggesting that this may be one of the pathogenic mechanisms involved in the learning disability associated with MeCP2.

82.

Carbohydrate-deficient glycoconjugate syndrome, Type 1a (CDG1A)

aka • olivopontocerebellar atrophy
• Jaeken syndrome
• Norman-Jaeken ataxia
• phosphomannomutase 2 deficiency

GENE LOCUS: 16p13.3–p13.2

KEY REFERENCE: Barone *et al.* 2008; Grunewald 2009

The gene locus was identified as significantly associated with ASD in the International Molecular Genetic Study of Autism Consortium (2001) study. 16p13 has been shown to be the gene site for phosphomannomutase (PMM), and PMM deficiency is the cause of carbohydrate-deficient glycoconjugate syndrome type 1a (CDG1A).

The condition is the same as Norman ataxia and the authors of one paper have suggested that the term Norman-Jaeken ataxia might be adopted (Pascual-Castroviejo, Pascual-Pascual, Quijano-Roy and Gutiérrez-Molina 2006). However, additional features such as abnormalities of carbohydrate metabolism, and retinopathy, suggest that this nomenclature would not capture the essence of the condition.

A clear description of the condition is given in Jaeken, Matthijs, Barone and Carchon (1997).

CDG1A is a complex multi-system disease, which includes cerebellar atrophy, ataxia, pigmentary retinopathy and strabismus, peripheral neuropathy, stroke-like episodes and, in some cases, epilepsy. Affected individuals seldom progress to walking independently, but there is no regression in motor skills.

In a single case to date, the static nature of the motor impairments reported is in contrast to the neurophysiological findings, with a slow and progressive deterioration in nerve conduction velocity, and progressive impairment in visual evoked responses and electroretinography (Veneselli, Biancheri, di Rocco and Tortorelli 1998).

One study to date has documented the early development and neuropsychological profile of four young adults with CDG1A (Barone *et al.* 1999).

No treatments are presently available for CDG1A. However, recent developments in the genetic characterization of the condition are leading to possible mutation-specific approaches (Vega *et al.* 2009).

DIFFERENTIAL DIAGNOSIS: Hypotonia, developmental delay and failure to thrive are seen in CDG1A, but are also consistent with a number of other conditions – in particular, Prader-Willi syndrome [61], muscular dystrophies such as Duchenne and Becker [33], myopathies (as seen in Williams syndrome [77]), mitochondrial disorders (see Section D1), peroxisomal disorders such as adrenomyeloneuropathy [10] and abnormalities of the urea cycle.

ANIMAL MODELS: No animal models of CDG1A have been investigated.

83.

Gurrieri syndrome

aka • Gurrieri-Sammito-Bellussi syndrome

GENE LOCUS: none yet identified, but some cases linked to proximal 15q deletion

KEY REFERENCES: Battaglia and Gurrieri 1999; Battaglia, Orsitto and Gibilisco 1996; Gurrieri, Sammito, Bellussi and Neri 1992; Orrico, Hayek and Burroni 1999

Gurrieri syndrome (Gurrieri, Sammito, Bellussi and Neri 1992) typically presents with moderate to severe mental retardation, epilepsy, short stature and skeletal dysplasia. The short stature is associated with various spinal differences and with slower bone age. In addition there are abnormalities of the retina, short fingers (brachydactyly), a large jaw (prognathism) and misalignment of the upper and lower teeth (dental malocclusion, often caused by being large-jawed).

Some, but not all, of the reported cases have shown absence of the maternal proximal 15q allele typically seen in Angelman syndrome. In 1996, Battaglia, Orsitto and Gibilisco published a case study on a male with severe mental retardation, epilepsy, short stature and skeletal dysplasia. In a subsequent paper (Battaglia and Gurrieri 1999) they showed that the 1996 case was missing the maternal proximal 15q allele. They also found that this was true of two of the four cases in the originally reported 1992 pedigree.

The most recent family described (Orrico, Hayek and Burroni 1999) consisted of two affected siblings (a brother and sister) with features consistent with Gurrieri syndrome (short stature, severe mental retardation and epilepsy), but with some additional features: retinal abnormalities, abnormal bone development (osteodysplasia), a larger skull (brachydactyly), a protruding jaw (prognathism) and poorly aligned teeth (dental malocclusion).

DIFFERENTIAL DIAGNOSIS: The pathogenesis is currently unclear. The phenotype is quite specific, but as there is no gold standard diagnostic measure or gene marker, diagnosis is by exclusion of other conditions such as Rett syndrome [63a, 63b] and infantile neural ceroid lipofuscinosis (Vanhanen, Raininko, Autti and Santavuori 1995).

ANIMAL MODELS: No animal models have been developed as the pathogenesis is unclear.

84.

Hemihyperplasia

GENE LOCUS: 11p15

KEY REFERENCE: Hoyme et al. 1998

SUMMARY: The hemihyperplastic syndromes result from excessive cell proliferation, with body overgrowth on one side of the body.

HOW COMMON IS HEMIHYPERPLASIA? Hemihyperplasia is estimated to affect one in 86,000 of the population.

MAIN CLINICAL FEATURES: Hemihyperplasia is associated with an increased risk of embryonal cancers in childhood, particularly Wilms tumour (Shuman et al. 2006). It appears to be most common when 11p15 is inherited as a uniparental disomy (where both copies of the chromosome are inherited from one parent), as was reported in 16 per cent of the cases in this study.

A detailed review of the various hemihyperplastic syndromes can be found in Hoyme et al. (1998). A more specific review of craniofacial hemihypertrophic conditions can be found in Cohen (1995).

DIFFERENTIAL DIAGNOSIS: Hemi-overgrowth can be seen in a number of other ASD-related conditions, such as Goldenhar syndrome [38] (where there is a specific hemifacial overgrowth), neurofibromatosis

[51], Proteus syndrome and unilateral cerebellar hypoplasia syndrome [75].

Proteus syndrome is frequently confused with hemihyperplasia (Biesecker *et al.* 1998), and there would appear to be a subgroup of patients who show hemihyperplasia with multiple typically static or mildly progressive lipomata.

One pair of discordant MZ female twins in which hemihyperplasia was present in one twin has been reported (West, Love, Stapleton and Winship 2003). Genetic testing identified a mosaic pattern of paternally inherited uniparental isodisomy for 11p15 in the affected twin.

A recent study (Martin, Grange, Zehnbauer and DeBaun 2005) has found that a high proportion of those with isolated hemihyperplasia show an epigenetic defect in the methylation of two genes – LIT1 and H19.

ANIMAL MODELS: No animal models for hemihyperplasia have been developed.

85.

Methylenetetrahydrofolate reductase (MTHFR) deficiency (+/− homocystinuria)

GENE LOCUS: 1p36.3

KEY REFERENCES: Boris, Goldblatt, Galanko and James 2004; James *et al.* 2004, 2006

SUMMARY: MTHFR deficiency is caused by a mutation in the 5,10-alpha-methylenetetrahydrofolate reductase gene. It is an inborn metabolic error, and the primary problem produced is a defect in folate metabolism with a wide range of phenotypic expression.

HOW COMMON IS MTHFR DEFICIENCY? Different MTHFR alleles have markedly different prevalence in different ethnic groups with consequent effects on folate status (Guéant-Rodriguez *et al.* 2006). The TT allele, for example, is found in some 35 per cent of Mexican women (Mutchinick *et al.* 1999). In the UK, the prevalence of this allele is some 8 per cent, while in Asia the prevalence appears to be approximately 4 per cent. In indigenous African populations the prevalence appears to be 0 per cent, and in the Middle East it is approximately 1.5 per cent (Schneider, Rees, Liu and Clegg 1988).

There is a suggested link between prevalence of the certain MTHFR polymorphisms and the prevalence of neural tube defects (Christensen *et al.* 1999) In particular, the TT allele creates a higher risk due to a higher requirement for folate than is seen in those who have either the CC or CT forms of MTHFR. There is still debate over the extent to which this should affect recommendations concerning folate supplementation (Bailey and Gregory 1999).

One study to date (of 138 autistic and 138 age and sex matched controls) has suggested a link between ASD susceptibility risk and the presence of the MTHFR 677T allele (Mohammad *et al.* 2009).

Strong sunlight results in folate depletion and there is a latitude effect on the prevalence of the 677TT MTHFR genotype suggesting that there has been an evolutionary selection pressure with selection for the 677TT genotype in less equatorial latitudes where the beneficial effects (reduced rates of colon cancer and ALL) are advantages when a folate rich diet can be obtained (Cordain and Hickey 2006).

IS THERE A LINK BETWEEN MTHFR DEFICIENCY AND ASD? There is now a body of literature that suggests ASD can be associated with metabolic abnormalities of folate metabolism (James *et al.* 2004, 2006, 2009).

There is also data suggesting that an association with abnormal folate metabolism can result from a significantly higher prevalence of the 677CT and 677TT MTHFR alleles in ASD than in the general population (Boris, Goldblatt, Galanko and James 2004; Mohammad *et al.* 2009).

It has been suggested that the association between the 677CT and TT MTHFR alleles and ASD may result from increased oxidative stress and a decreased methylation capacity in these groups (Deth *et al.* 2008; James *et al.* 2006; Zecavati and Spence 2009).

MAIN CLINICAL FEATURES: The most typical features reported in association with an MTHFR deficiency are developmental delay with subsequent diagnosis of learning disability, motor abnormalities with abnormal gait, seizures, psychotic or ASD symptomology and homocysteinaemia.

MTHFR polymorphisms have been reported as overrepresented in a number of clinical disorders including coronary artery disease, cleft lip and palate, leukaemia and neural tube defects.

Coronary artery disease: MTHFR has been reported at higher rates in some populations with coronary artery disease.

This association has been reported in the Japanese (Morita *et al.* 1997) but not replicated in Western Australian (van Bockxmeer, Mamotte, Vasikaran and Taylor 1997) or North American non-Hispanic female (Schwartz *et al.* 1997) populations.

Being homozygous for the MTHFR 677CT polymorphism increases cardiovascular risk, particularly in association with having low red blood cell folate levels (Klerk *et al.* 2002).

Cleft lip/palate: There seems to be a slightly raised risk of cleft lip/palate associated with maternal MTHFR mutation frequency rather than with either paternal or embryonic genotype of the affected child (Martinelli *et al.* 2001).

Studies on the hypothesized link between cleft lip/palate and MTHFR deficiency have produced varied results. An Irish study found that homozygosity for the (TT) thermolabile form of MTHFR was three times higher in a cleft palate group and was elevated but less so in those with cleft lip (Mills *et al.* 1999). A Polish study has found no link between the 677CT polymorphism and increased risk (Mostowska, Hozyasz and Jagodzinski 2006).

Leukaemia: A recent UK study (Wiemels *et al.* 2001) reported associations of MTHFR polymorphisms with three paediatric leukaemic subgroups. Comparing a large group of 253 paediatric leukaemia patients to 200 healthy newborn controls for the MTHFR polymorphisms 677CT and 1298AC, a significant association for carriers of 677CT was demonstrated for leukemias with MLL translocations when compared with controls. This is the same 677CT polymorphism that has been found by one group (Boris, Goldblatt, Galanko and James 2004) to be overrepresented in the autistic population when compared to normal controls.

Leukaemia and folate abnormalities are both overrepresented in XXY [3] and in Down syndrome [31] (Roman and Beral 1991).

Folate abnormalities can be an increased risk factor for Down syndrome in offspring (Hobbs *et al.* 2000); although the risk may be different in different populations and could not be substantiated in a Turkish cohort (Boduroglu, Alana, Koldan and Tuncbilek 2004).

Abnormal folate metabolism has also been found to result in an increased risk of developing a variety of other forms of cancer (Paz *et al.* 2002).

Neural tube defects: MTHFR defects may increase the risk of neural tube defects (Ou *et al.* 1996; Papapetrou, Lynch, Burn and Edwards 1996; van der Put, Eskes and Blom 1997); however, there are some findings that would argue against such a link (Mornet *et al.* 1997).

A link with neural tube defects seems to be synergistic with folic acid status during pregnancy, with a significantly elevated risk being associated with the combination of low red blood cell folate and being homozygous for the MTHFR 677CT polymorphism.

Other vascular problems: Ischaemic stroke has been found to be more common in adults with the 677CT substitution form of MTHFR deficiency (Casas, Hingorani, Bautista and Sharma 2004); however, the presence of this substitution did not appear to increase risk in a Chinese population (Lu *et al.* 2002).

Retinal artery occlusion is reported and seems to be associated with the presence of hyperhomocysteinaemia (Weger *et al.* 2002).

Hypertension: Both the 677CT and 677TT polymorphisms appear to be risk factors for essential hypertension (Ilhan *et al.* 2008).

The presence of the 677TT polymorphism in hypertensive adolescents also appears to be predictive of the subsequent development of early onset coronary artery disease (Koo, Lee and Hong 2007).

A significantly elevated risk of preeclampsia has been reported in one Japanese study (Sohda *et al.* 1997); however, a second Japanese study found no association (Kobashi *et al.* 2000). Further

work is required to establish whether there is a real association.

A study of a Cretan population found a higher rate of spontaneous abortion to foetuses that carried an MTHFR mutation (Zetterberg *et al.* 2002). This suggests a potential role for preconceptional and early foetal folic acid supplementation in at-risk families. There is some evidence to suggest a link between abnormal folic acid and homocysteine metabolism, and increased risk of preeclampsia and spontaneous abortion (see, for example, Ray and Laskin 1999).

DIFFERENTIAL DIAGNOSIS: A number of other metabolic conditions can show similar patterns of presentation. Cystathionine beta-synthetase deficiency causes classical homocystinuria and has a similar pattern of presentation (Bishop *et al.* 2008). A number of cobalamin pathway abnormalities such as methylmalonyl-CoA mutase deficiency or a defect in adenosine cobalamin can also present with similar features. Differentiation can be clinically important, given the differences in aetiology, biochemistry and treatment across the various conditions that affect homocysteine metabolism (Kuhara, Ohsea, Ohdoi and Ishida 2000). Glutamate formiminotransferase deficiency shows metabolic similarities. It is the second most common inborn error of folate metabolism and results in elevated levels of formiminoglutamic acid in urine (Hilton *et al.* 2003).

MANAGEMENT AND TREATMENT: In an early paper (Freeman, Finkelstein, Mudd and Uhlendorf 1972), a 15-year-old black girl with mild learning disability was described. She presented with progressive withdrawal, delusions and hallucinations and with catatonic rigidity. Her presentation was unresponsive to psychotherapy. Blood biochemistry found homocystinuria without elevation of plasma methionine (Freeman, Finkelstein and Mudd 1975). Her psychotic symptoms gradually disappeared with administration of pyridoxine (vitamin B6) and folic acid. A sister had the same chemical findings but was asymptomatic. A decrease was shown in methylenetetrahydrofolate reductase. Preliminary enzyme and biochemistry results were reported (Mudd et al. 1972). A number of subsequent studies showed clinical responses to supplements such as betaine – shown to produce biochemical and clinical improvement in a three-year-old developmentally delayed girl (Wendel and Bremer 1984) – and combination treatments such as methionine, folinic acid, pyrodoxine and vitamin B12 – which produced clinical improvement in an infant (Harpey et al. 1981).

Similarities to the original Freeman et al. report can be seen in a more recent sibling pair (Haworth et al. 1993). The two brothers both had a folate deficiency and MTHFR defect. The elder brother had shown no symptoms when seen at 37 years of age. His younger brother had developed muscle weakness, poor coordination, paresthesiae, and was having memory lapses by 15 years; he was wheelchair dependent by his early twenties. On testing, both brothers showed elevated homocysteine and low plasma methionine. Their parents had intermediate enzyme activities, and the father had paraparesis and homocysteinaemia. The biochemistry in both brothers improved but did not fully normalize on treatment with folate and betaine therapy.

A small study of 20 autistic children were compared to 33 group-matched controls. The autistic group showed increased oxidative stress as indicated by decreased plasma levels of methionine, S-adenosylmethionine, homocysteine, cystathionine, cysteine and total glutathione with elevated levels of S-adenosylhomocysteine, adenosine and oxidized glutathione (James et al. 2004). In a small subset of the autistic group (N=8), methylcobalamin (75 µg), folinic acid (800 µg) and betaine (1,000 mg) were administered with significant normalization of their metabolic profiles.

In a further study (James et al. 2006) plasma levels of metabolites in methionine transmethylation and transsulphuration pathways were measured in 80 autistic and 73 control children, and in a separate study of 360 autistic and 205 age-matched controls common polymorphic variants that are known to modulate these metabolic pathways were evaluated. The results indicated that plasma methionine and the ratio of S-adenosylmethionine to S-adenosylhomocysteine were significantly decreased in the autistic children. Differences in a number of genes involved in folate metabolism were established between the groups.

One open-label trial treated 40 autistic children (age 0.8–4.8 years) with metabolic evidence of reduced methylation capacity (a reduced ratio of plasma S-adenosylmethionine to S-adenosylhomocysteine) or a reduced GSH redox ratio (a reduced level of glutathione (GSH) to its oxidized disulphide form (GSSG)) with 75 µg/kg methylcobalamin (two times/week) and 400 µg folinic acid (two times/day) for three months. These were out of a sample of 68 autistic children, 17 of whom did not meet metabolic criteria; four dropped out and four were lost to follow-up. The sample was matched to age and sex controls and showed significant but incomplete normalization of methylation capacity over the course of the intervention.

ANIMAL MODELS: An MTHFR knockout mouse has been developed (Chen et al. 2001). Whether heterozygous or homozygous, knockout mice were significantly hyperhomocysteinaemic. In addition, the homozygous knockout mice also showed cerebellar pathology and developmental delays. There was gradual lipid deposition in the aorta in both groups. (For a more general overview of aniimal models of hyperhomocysteinaemic conditions, see Troen 2005.)

86.

PEHO syndrome (progressive encephalopathy with oedema, hypsarrythmia and optic atrophy

aka • infantile cerebellooptic atrophy

GENE LOCUS: none yet identified

KEY REFERENCES: Rikonen, R. 2001; Field *et al.* 2003

SUMMARY: PEHO syndrome presents with progressive microcephaly that develops over the first year, after normal head size at birth. Nerve conduction and evoked responses are abnormal. Infantile spasms are common, usually beginning in the first six months. Poor visual fixation is common, as is peripheral oedema.

HOW COMMON IS PEHO SYNDROME? The prevalence of PEHO syndrome is uncertain. A large number of Finnish cases have been reported, suggesting a possible founder effect, but cases have now been reported from a number of diverse ethnic backgrounds: a small series of PEHO and PEHO-like cases has been reported from Australia (Field *et al.* 2003). A further two siblings of Japanese descent (Fujimoto, Yokochi, Nakano and Wada 1995) have

been reported, but without peripheral oedema, and cases have been reported from Canada (Shervell *et al.* 1996), Holland, Turkey, Spain, Hungary (Vanthatalo, Somer and Barth 2002) and Switzerland (Klein, Schmitt and Boltschauser 2004).

MAIN CLINICAL FEATURES: The initial clinical description was of a series of 14 patients (Salonen *et al.* 1991). The clinical features in these initial cases were severe hypotonia, convulsions with hypsarrhythmia, a profound level of learning disability, hyperreflexia, transient or persistent oedema, and optic atrophy. In addition, microcephaly and cerebellar and brainstem atrophy were described.

One detailed neuropathological study has described eight cases (Haltia and Somer 1993), including three of the patients originally described by Salonen *et al.* (1991). Two of the cases were siblings. In two further cases, the first had one, and the second two, affected siblings, strongly suggesting a heritable basis to the condition. All the cases had both cortical atrophy and pronounced cerebellar atrophy. In all cases, the neuropathology showed abnormalities of the cerebellum and the optic nerve. The inner granular layer of the cerebellum was abnormal, with severe depletion of neurons and small deformed Purkinje cells. These sites of neuronal abnormality appear similar to that described in the work of Bauman and Kemper on autism (Bauman 2005), but the reduction in Purkinje cell density which they described in autism was not seen in the PEHO cases.

Characteristic facial features include a 'pear shape' to the face, protruding lower parts of the earlobes, a short nose, an open mouth with curved upper lip, and peripheral oedema. The oedema of the hands and tapering to the fingers described is similar to that seen in cases of Coffin-Lowry syndrome [21].

PEHO syndrome now has recognized clinical characteristics, diagnostic criteria and genetics. Somer (1993) reviewed 21 possible cases of PEHO syndrome and found that ten fitted criteria. They showed progressive microcephaly over the first year, after normal head size at birth (as seen in Rett syndrome [63a]). Nerve conduction velocities slowed with age, and brainstem somatosensory and auditory evoked responses were abnormal. Infantile spasms typically started within the first six months. Visual fixation was absent or lost early in life. Peripheral oedema was reported in nine cases. In total, 19 of the 21 cases were felt to be consistent with a PEHO diagnosis, and these cases came from 14 families. The inheritance pattern was felt to be consistent with an autosomal recessive condition.

PEHO syndrome is associated with cerebellar abnormalities, typically with a pontocerebellar hypoplasia (Ramaekers *et al.* 1997). Some cases have been described with the clinical phenotype but without the cerebellar hypoplasia apparent on neuroimaging, which has been taken as necessary for clinical diagnosis (Chitty *et al.* 1996; Longman, Tolmie, McWilliam and MacLennan 2003).

DIFFERENTIAL DIAGNOSIS: In PEHO syndrome hypotonia, convulsions, mental retardation, oedema and optic atrophy are found, in association with cerebellar and brainstem atrophy on neuroimaging. A condition similar to PEHO has been reported in which hypotonia, convulsions, mental disability, oedema and optic atrophy are found, but without concomitant abnormalities on brain imaging (Chitty *et al.* 1996).

A large number of conditions with some degree of phenotypic overlap present with cerebellar atrophy on neuroimaging.

(See Poretti, Wolf and Boltshauser 2008 for a systematic review.)

ANIMAL MODELS: No animal models of PEHO syndrome have so far been developed.

87.

Simpson-Golabi-behmel syndrome type 1 (SGBS1)

aka
- bulldog syndrome
- dysplasia gigantism syndrome, X-linked (DGSX)
- Golabi-Rosen syndrome
- Simpson dysmorphia syndrome (SDYS)

GENE LOCUS: Xq26

KEY REFERENCES: Garganta and Bodurtha 1992; Neri, Gurrieri, Zanni and Lin 1998

SUMMARY: Simpson-Golabi-Behmel syndrome type 1 (SGBS1) is an X-linked condition with both pre- and postnatal overgrowth, coarsening of facial features, congenital heart defects and other congenital abnormalities (Xuan, Hughes-Benzie and MacKenzie 1999). The term 'Simpson-Golabi-Behmel syndrome' was first proposed by Neri *et al.* (1988).

The condition was described by Simpson, Landey, New and German (1975) in two male first cousins born to two sisters. Both were of normal intelligence. They had similar physical phenotypes: both had large protruding jaws, a retroussé nose, with a wide bridge to the nose, and an enlarged tongue. They were both of picnic build, with short hands and fingers. One had a cleft in his lower lip. The family description of the boys was 'bulldog-like'.

Their condition was not linked to hypo-thyroidism.

SGBS1 is an overgrowth disorder caused by a defect in the gene GPC3 at Xq26. This gene codes for a particular membrane constituent, called a glypican. It was first discovered in 1996 (Pilia *et al.* 1996). This group also reported a case where the genes for both GPC3 and GPC4 were affected. A simple discussion of GPC3 and the role of glypicans (i.e. the class of membrane-bound heparan sulphate proteoglycans, to which it belongs) can be found in Filmus and Selleck (2001). The unusual factor about GPC3 is that, unlike other glypicans, it has a role in controlling body size.

Two studies have localized the gene defect in SGBS1 to Xq26 (Orth *et al.* 1994; Xuan *et al.* 1994).

HOW COMMON IS SGBS1? The condition would appear to be rare, but prevalence is not known. For a clinical overview of SGBS1, see James, Culver and Golabi (2006).

MAIN CLINICAL FEATURES: In early development of clinical criteria SGBS1 has been confused with both Weaver syndrome [89] (Tsukahara, Tanaka and Kajii 1984) and Beckwith-Wiedemann syndrome. (For discussion, see Verloes *et al.* 1995.) A GPC3 defect, which appears common in SGBS1, is not reported in Beckwith-Wiedemann syndrome, but is seen in some cases diagnosed with Sotos syndrome [68] and Perlman syndrome (Li *et al.* 2001). As more individuals with the gene defect have been identified, the clinical picture in SGBS1 is broadening, with learning disability, hydrocephalus and epilepsy being reported in some cases (Young, Wishnow and Nigro 2006). Approximately half of reported cases have cardiac defects with a third having obvious structural malformations

of the heart (Lin, Neri, Hughes-Benzie and Weksberg 1999).

The earlier cases described were consistent in being large from birth, with a large head and short neck, broad, short hands and feet, and early motor clumsiness which resolved with age. Additional nipples are also a commonly reported feature. The cases reported by Simpson and Behmel were of normal intelligence (Behmel, Plochl and Rosenkranz 1984; Simpson, Landey, New and German 1975). Golabi reported the same physical features, but in the context of mental retardation (Golabi and Rosen 1984).

Several groups have commented on the high apparent incidence of sudden infant death in those with the condition. There is some suggestion of a subtype with early lethality, but currently there is no means of distinguishing this from others with a GPC3 defect (Terespolsky, Farrell, Siegel-Bartelt and Weksberg 1995).

Recent findings suggest that the clinical phenotype is broader than was originally proposed, with a mild phenotype in female carriers, and a number of previously un-described features, such as an additional lumbar vertebra (Rodriguez-Criado *et al.* 2005).

DIFFERENTIAL DIAGNOSIS: SGBS1 has phenotypic similarities with Beckwith-Wiedemann syndrome (BWS), another overgrowth syndrome that has been linked to deregulation of imprinted genes in the 11p15 region. In both conditions physical overgrowth with a large tongue, cleft palate and cardiac complications are common. BWS has also been linked (rarely) to the 5q35 region implicated in Sotos syndrome [68].

There is also Simpson-Golabi-Behmel syndrome type 2 (SGBS2), which has been associated with a mutation at Xp22 in the CXORF5 gene. Gene differences at Xp22 are implicated in a number of ASD conditions (ARX gene mutations [13]; Coffin-Lowry syndrome [21]; oculocutaneous albinism [55]; Rett syndrome [63a]; and Rett syndrome (Hanefeld variant) [63b].

ANIMAL MODELS: No specific animal models of SGBS1 have so far been published.

88.

Sturge-Weber syndrome

aka • 'the fourth phacomatosis'

GENE LOCUS: none as yet established, but there are some suggestions of a link to the gene RASA1 (Eerola *et al.* 2003) at 5q13.3

KEY REFERENCES: Juhasz *et al.* 2007; Madaan, Dewan, Ramaswamy and Sharma 2006

SUMMARY: Sturge-Weber syndrome is a neurocutaneous condition (it affects both the skin and the central nervous system). It is characterized by port-wine stains (deep purple-coloured areas of skin pigmentation), typically only on one side of the body; blood vessel abnormalities of the eye (glaucoma is a common feature); and abnormal brain blood vessels (leptomeningeal angioma) (Baselga 2004; Comi 2006). It is a phacomatosis (a condition characterized by the development of hamartomas in various body tissues). Other phacomatoses include tuberous sclerosis [73] and neurofibromatosis [51].

Usually Sturge-Weber cases arise *de novo*. Debicka and Adamczak (1979) described a father and son, both of whom were affected, and both with central nervous system involvement.

One study correlating PET findings with clinical course and severity of cognitive difficulties found that the more extreme the asymmetry of cortical metabolism, the less severely affected were cognitive functions (Lee *et al.* 2001)., This suggested to the study authors that functional reorganization was more effective with more severe lateralized cortical involvement.

A review of 52 adult cases by Sujansky and Conradi (1995) reviewed outcome, and ascertained the prevalence of different presenting features:

- port-wine stains
  - cranial (98 per cent)
  - extracranial (52 per cent)
- glaucoma (60 per cent)
- seizures (83 per cent)
- neurological deficit (65 per cent).

Useful recent reviews can be found in Baselga (2004) and Comi (2006).

There is now prospective evidence to suggest that the major negative metabolic effects of Sturge-Weber occur before three years of age, and that with good seizure control there can be a degree of recovery over time after this point (Juhasz *et al.* 2007). Hypermetabolism and hyperfusion can often be detected at an early stage in the cortical areas before any obvious clinical symptomology (Reid *et al.* 1997), with progressive hypometabolism and hypometabolism being seen with advancing stages of the condition (Juhasz *et al.* 2007).

As central nervous system involvement is variable and associated with the extent of cutaneous involvement, it may be (as is the case with the extent and nature of seizure activity) that any ASD behaviours are consistent with the site of the central nervous system lesions, rather than associated with presence of the condition *per se*. Should this prove to be the case, prediction of any such association will await the ability to predict the pattern of phenotypic expression.

DIFFERENTIAL DIAGNOSIS: Port-wine facial staining and autism [59] presents with overlapping clinical features and is the only condition likely to be considered in the differential diagnosis.

It is possible that the pathogenesis of the two conditions is the same genetically, with epigenetic factors influencing severity of phenotypic expression.

ANIMAL MODELS: There are no animal models of SWS at the present time.

89.

Weaver syndrome

(may be synonymous with Sotos syndrome [68], also now localized to 5q35)

aka • Weaver-Smith syndrome

GENE LOCUS: 5q35

KEY REFERENCES: See Sotos syndrome [68].

SUMMARY: More than 75 per cent of those with Sotos syndrome [68] show evidence of mutation of the NSD1 gene at 5q35. A gene defect in this region is reported in three of seven cases diagnosed as having Weaver syndrome (Douglas et al. 2003). The genetic co-localization of these phenotypes discriminates them from other overgrowth syndromes, and suggests that they may either result from similar defects, or be clinically synonymous.

HOW COMMON IS WEAVER SYNDROME? As there is probable diagnostic overlap with Sotos syndrome, prevalence is uncertain. Sotos syndrome itself does not have a robust epidemiology but is assumed to be relatively common on the basis of the significant numbers of reported cases.

MAIN CLINICAL FEATURES: In 1974, Weaver and colleagues described a syndrome with accelerated growth rate and bone maturation, craniofacial abnormalities, camptodactyly, hypertonia and an unusual hoarse, low-pitched cry (Weaver, Graham, Thomas and Smith 1974). Relatively few cases are reported in the world literature, but other features reported are psychomotor delay, lax skin, and hernias.

Occasional cases have been reported with apparently associated conditions – for example, Freeman B.M et al. (1999) reported a phenotypic case of Weaver syndrome with pachygyria.

Weaver cases are being reported with other gene abnormalities, such as 11p15 (Baujat et al. 2004).

There has been much debate in the literature over whether Weaver syndrome and Sotos syndrome can be differentiated (Cole 1998; Opitz, Weaver and Reynolds 1998). Opitz, Weaver and Reynolds (1998) discuss Sotos and Weaver syndromes and their differentiation. Possible phenotypic differences they highlighted were as follows.

• Sotos syndrome may be a cancer syndrome, whereas Weaver syndrome is not (although a case with neuroblastoma had been reported in the latter disorder).

• Sotos syndrome is associated with advanced dental maturation, but this feature has rarely been commented on in Weaver syndrome.

• In Weaver syndrome, there are more conspicuous contractures and a facial appearance that has been argued to differentiate from that in Sotos syndrome.

DIFFERENTIAL DIAGNOSIS: Differential diagnosis is between Weaver syndrome and a number of other overgrowth syndromes, some of which have been linked to ASD, such as Bannayan-Riley-Ruvalcaba syndrome (BRRS) [15]; basal cell naevus syndrome [16]; Cortical Dysplasia–Focal Epilepsy (CDFE) syndrome [19]; Cole-Hughes macrocephaly syndrome [24]; Cowden syndrome [26]; Orstavik 1997 syndrome [56]; Proteus syndrome [62]; and Simpson-Golabi-Behmel syndrome type 1 (SGBS1) [87].

Some cases of Weaver syndrome have also been reported with NSD1 mutations (Baujat *et al.* 2005; Douglas *et al.* 2003; Rio *et al.* 2003).

ANIMAL MODELS: There are no specific animal models for either Weaver or Sotos syndrome. An NSD1 mouse model has been used to examine bone maturation and demonstrated that NSD1 defects are associated with advanced bone age (Rayasam *et al.* 2003). No behavioural studies have been carried out.

SECTION D

Some Promising Recent Developments in ASD Research

1. Mitochondrial defects

Mitochondria are the energy-producing subcellular organelles found in cells throughout the body. The only exception is nerve cells. These, because they have no mitochondria, are dependent on a continuous supply of energy and exquisitely sensitive to the effects of energy deprivation. This occurs when key compounds are missing from the diet or metabolic pathway, or when circulation is arrested.

To date, HEADD syndrome [39] is the only mitochondriopathy to have been reported specifically in association with ASD. Most studies have not tested subjects with ASD for possible mitochondrial dysfunction. Where such testing has been done, it is concluded that mitochondrial energy defects may be amongst the most commonly associated biological factors (Oliveira *et al.* 2005). An additional complication is that, as mitochondria are heteroplasmic, testing for mitochondrial mutations may often prove negative in one tissue, while positive in another. A recent study of a late onset mitochondrial encephalomyopathy gave negative results on blood testing, but positive results when affected skeletal muscle fibres were tested (Sanaker, Nakkestad, Downham and Bindoff 2010).

A large number of genes are involved in interaction with mitochondria, and a recent study on 22q11 candidate genes has identified six genes which encode mitochondrial proteins (Maynard *et al.* 2008). These genes may account for the phenotypic variability seen in 22q11 conditions and the difficulties that have been experienced in classifying them. (See, for example, Burn 1999.)

Recently it has been established that mitochondrial DNA (mtDNA) mutations, previously thought to be rare, are common in the general population, with pathogenic mtDNA mutations being present in approximately one in 200 people (Elliott *et al.* 2008). It is unsurprising, therefore, that mitochondrial disorders appear to be similarly common in those with autistic spectrum disorders (Weissman *et al.* 2008), and here mitochondria are fascinating, and potentially relevant, for many reasons:

1. they possess their own separate ring chromosome, and so have a different inheritance system from the other chromosomes in the body

2. they are almost always inherited exclusively from the mother, because the mitochondria in sperm are coiled around the tail, and the tail is shed as the sperm enters the egg

3. the numbers of mitochondria per cell vary, and at cell division which mitochondria go into in each divided cell, and how they themselves multiply, is not yet fully understood

4. as mitochondria are critical to energy production, mitochondrial defects are commonly seen in conditions where energy production within the organism is abnormal, such as epilepsy

5. mitochondrial defects are 'heteroplasmic': where a mitochondrial DNA defect arises, it is often found to differing extents in different cell lines within the body, depending on the proportion of abnormal mitochondria present

6. as discussed earlier, systematic mitochondrial DNA defects are found in some other ASD conditions which were previously thought to be due to nuclear DNA differences – for example, as in Klinefelter's syndrome (Oikawa *et al.* 2002)

7. mitochondrial dysfunctions are associated with oxidative stress (Sas, Robotka, Toldi and Vécseia 2007), a factor which has been recognized as common in people with ASD (James *et al.* 2004, 2006).

A simple introduction to the role and importance of the mitochondria can be found in Nick Lane's excellent little tome *Power, Sex, Suicide: Mitrochondria and the Meaning of Life* (Lane 2005), and a general introduction to the issue of mitochondrial disorders and dysfunction can be found in Naviaux (2000).

The possibility that autism could be caused by a mitochondrial defect was first raised in 1998 (Lombard 1998), and a range of studies indicate problems with mitochondrial function in some people with ASD – which in some cases seems most likely to be an indication of a mitochondrial gene defect (Chugani *et al.* 1999; Correia *et al.* 2006; Graf *et al.* 2000; Oliveira *et al.* 2005; Pons *et al.* 2004), while in others, it may indicate a defect in nuclear DNA mechanisms which interact with mitochondrial function (as with the inverse duplication of chromosome 15q11–q13 (Filipek *et al.* 2003)).

There have been a number of discussions of mitochondrial defects in ASD in the clinical literature (for example, Lerman-Sagie, Leshinsky-Silver, Watemberg and Lev 2004; Pons *et al.* 2004; Tsao and Mendell 2007), most of which present small case series, but with several different defects in mitochondrial DNA.

One recent case has received considerable attention, as it is a child with a regressive autistic presentation, growth failure and clear evidence of a metabolic disturbance of mitochondrial function (Poling, Frye, Shoffner and Zimmerman 2006). This child has reduced levels of all of the biochemical markers of oxidative phosphorylation. The authors also present data from a retrospective casenote review of clinic cases, which suggests that approximately 40 per cent of ASD cases had test results (for aspartate aminotransferase and/or serum creatine kinase) that would be consistent with such defects.

A number of factors can affect oxidative phosphorylation in addition to mitochondrial genetics. It has been found, for example, that valproic acid actively inhibits dihydrolipoyl dehydrogenase, thus down regulating oxidative phosphorylation (Luis *et al.* 2007).

A number of avenues for the treatment of mitochondrial gene defects currently show promise. (See, for review, Swerdlow 2007; Wallace 2005.)

2. Gene markers

Gene markers are DNA markers that are associated with specific phenotypic traits – in this case with ASD diagnosis. Typically, the role or function of the genes in the marker region itself are not known.

The following table details genes with significant linkage to ASD. The chromosome position and the markers for each are given, together with the scan group reporting the association, and, where detailed, the candidate gene loci.

Table D2.1: Gene positions with linkage to ASD diagnoses

Chr	Position	Marker (at or near)	Scan group*	MLS (multipoint Lod score)	Candidate gene locus
1	1p13.2	D1S1675	1	2.63+?	
	1q21–22	D1S1653	1	2.63	
	1q22	D1S2721	2	2.88	
	1q23.3	D1S484	2	3.58	
	1q42.2	D1S1656	3	3.06	
2	2q31.1	D2S2188	4 (but see 15)	4.80	DLX1/2
	2q31.1	D2S355	3 (but see 15)	3.32	DLX1/2
3	3p24.1	D3S2432	2	3.32	
	3p25.3	D3S3691	5	2.22	
	3q22.1	D3S3045–D3S1736	6	3.10	
	3q26.32	D3S3715/D3S3037	1	4.81	
4	4q23	D4S1647	3	2.87	
	4q27	D4S3250	3	2.73	
	4q32.3	D4S2368	2	2.82	
5	5p13.1	D5S2494	7	2.54	
	5p13.1	D5S2494	8	2.55	
6	6q14.3	D6S1270	3	2.61	
	6q16.3	D6S283	9	2.23	
7	7q21.2	D7S1813	10	2.20	PON1
	7q22.1	D7S477	4 (but see 16)	3.55	RELN
	7q32.1–34	D7S530–D7S684	11	3.55	WNT2
	7q34–36.2	D7S1824–D7S3058	6	2.98	EN2
	7q36.1	D7S483	12	2.37	
9	9p22.2	D9S157	4	3.11	
	9q34.3	D9S1826	4	3.59	
11	11p11.2–13	D11S1392/D11S1993	7	2.24	BDNF
13	13q12.3	D13S217/12229	10	2.30	
	13q22	D13S800	10	2.30	
	13q32.1–32.3	D13S793–D13S1271	2	2.86	
15	15q21.2	CYP19	4	2.21	
16	16p13	D16S3102	4	2.93	
	16p13.2	D16S407	4	2.22	
17	17p11.2	D17S1298–D17S1299	6	2.22	SLC6A4

Chr	Position	Marker (at or near)	Scan group*	MLS (multipoint Lod score)	Candidate gene locus
	17q11.2	D17S1294–D17S798	13	4.30	SLC6A4
	17q11.2	D17S1294	5	2.85	SLC6A4
	17q11.2	D17S1800	7	2.83	SLC6A4
	17q11.2	HTTINT2	4	2.34	SLC6A4
	17q21.2	D17S1299	5	2.26	HOXB1
	17q21.32	D17S2180	14	4.41	HOXB1
	17q24.3	D17S1290–D17S1301	6	2.84	
19	19p	D19S433	8	[3.36]	
	19p13.11	D19S930	5	2.77	
	19p13.12	D19S714	8	2.53	
	19p13.12	D19S714	3	2.31	
21	21q21.1	D21S1437	12	3.40	
X	Xq21.33	DXS6789	1	2.54	
	Xq25	DXS1047	8	2.67	
	Xq	DXS1047	8	[2.27]	

Note: For ease of presentation and simplicity, I have adopted the standard convention of reporting only linkage Lod scores of 2.2 or greater. (See Lander and Kruglyak 1995.)

* *Scan groups*

1. Auranen *et al.* 2002
2. Ylisaukko-oja *et al.* 2004
3. Buxbaum *et al.* 2004
4. International Molecular Genetic Study of Autism Consortium 2001
5. McCauley *et al.* 2005
6. Alarcón *et al.* 2005b
7. Yonan *et al.* 2003
8. Liu *et al.* 2001
9. Philippe *et al.* 1999
9. Barrett *et al.* 1999
10. International Molecular Genetic Study of Autism Consortium 1998
11. Mills *et al.* 2005

12. Stone *et al.* 2004
13. Cantor *et al.* 2005
14. Shao *et al.* 2002
15. Rabionet *et al.* 2004
16. Devlin *et al.* 2004

Table D2.2 matches the marker genes that have shown up on linkage analyses (with Lod scores of 2.2 or above) against the reported clinical phenotypes discussed earlier in the book.

Table D2.2: Syndromes, gene loci and genes

- A gene locus in plain type and with no linked syndrome is one that has been reported in association with ASD, but with no known association to a specific clinical phenotype.
- Regular text is used for associated clinical phenotypes so far reported.
- *Italic* indicates a close match of an associated clinical phenotype to a gene marker.
- **Bold italic** indicates loci for associated behavioural phenotypes genetically contiguous with high Lod score linkage sites.

Linked syndrome, if any	Gene locus	Gene
	1p13.2	
dihydropyrimidine dehydrogenase (DPYS) deficiency [30]	1p22	
Down syndrome [31]	1p35.2–p33	
Ehlers-Danlos syndrome [34]	1p36.3–p36.2	
	1q21–22	
	1q22	
	1q23.3	
	1q42.2	
Down syndrome [31]	1q43	
neurofibromatosis type 1 [51]	2p22–p21	
hypothyroidism [43]	2q12–q14	
Joubert syndrome [44]	2q13	
Biedl-Bardet syndrome [17]	***2q31***	
Ehlers-Danlos syndrome [34]	***2q31***	
Ehlers-Danlos syndrome [34]	***2q31***	
	2q31.1	*DLX 1/2*
Ehlers-Danlos syndrome [34]	2q34	
Biedl-Bardet syndrome [17]	3p12–q13	
pituitary deficiency [58]	3p21.2–p21.1	HESX1
	3p24.1	
xeroderma pigmentosa [79]	***3p25***	
	3p25.3	
	3q22.3	
fragile-X syndrome [35, 36]	3q28	
phenylketonuria [57]	4p15.31	
hyper IgE syndrome [41]	4q21	
	4q23	

Linked syndrome, if any	Gene locus	Gene
	4q27	
	4q32.3	
pituitary deficiency [58]	5p13–p12	
de Lange syndrome [27]	*5p13.1*	
	5p13.1	
Ehlers-Danlos syndrome [34]	5q23	
Ehlers-Danlos syndrome [34]	5q35.2–q35.3	
Weaver syndrome [89]	5q35	
Sotos syndrome [68]	5q35	
Lujan-Fryns syndrome [46]	5q terminal	
congenital adrenal hyperplasia [25]	6p21.3	
Ehlers-Danlos syndrome [34]	6p21.3	
succinic semialdehyde dehydrogenase deficiency [69]	6p22	
trichothiodystrophy [72]	6p25.3	
	6q14.3	
	6q16.3	
Joubert syndrome [44]	6q23.3	
Biedl-Bardet syndrome [17]	7p14, 4q27	
trichothiodystrophy [72]	7p14	
congenital adrenal hyperplasia [25]	7q11.2	
Williams syndrome [77]	7q11.23	
CHARGE [20]	7q21.1	
Ehlers-Danlos syndrome [34]	7q22.1	
	7q21.2	PON1
	7q22.1	RELN
	7q32.1–34	WNT2
	7q34–36.2	EN2
	7q36	
	7q36.1	EN2
congenital adrenal hyperplasia [25]	8p11.2	
CHARGE [20]	8q12.1	
congenital adrenal hyperplasia [25]	8q21	
Cohen syndrome [23]	8q22–q23	
	9p22.2	
basal cell nevus syndrome [16]	9q22.3	

Linked syndrome, if any	Gene locus	Gene
Biedl-Bardet syndrome [17]	9q31–q34.1	
tuberous sclerosis [73]	9q34	
	9q34.3	
pituitary deficiency [58]	*9q34.3*	
Joubert syndrome [44]	*9q34.3*	
Ehlers-Danlos syndrome [34]	*9q34.2–q34.3*	
Di George syndrome I [29a]	10p14–10p13	
Cowden syndrome [26]	10q22.3	
Cowden syndrome [26]	10q23.31	
Bannayan-Riley-Ruvalcaba syndrome [15]	10q23.31	
ALPS [14]	10q24.1	
congenital adrenal hyperplasia [25]	10q24.3	
Apert syndrome [12]	10q26	
	11p11.2–13	BDNF
Joubert syndrome [44]	11p12–13.3	
Smith-Lemli-Opitz syndrome [66]	11q12–q13	
Biedl-Bardet syndrome [17]	11q13	
Tourette syndrome [71]	11q23	
phenylketonuria [57]	11q22.3–q23.3	
Noonan syndrome [52]	12p12.1	
Timothy syndrome [70]	12p13.3	
tuberous sclerosis [73]	12q14	
Duchenne's disease [33]	12q21	
Biedl-Bardet syndrome [17]	12q21.2	
Joubert syndrome [44]	12q21.3	
phenylketonuria [57]	12q24.1	
Noonan syndrome [52]	12q24.1	
	13q12.3	
Mobius syndrome [48]	13q12.2–q13	
Fragile-X syndrome [35, 36]	13q14	
	13q22	
Tourette syndrome [71]	13q31	
	13q32.1–32.3	
L-2-hydroxyglutaric aciduria [40]	14q22.1	
phenylketonuria [57]	14q22.1–q22.2	

Linked syndrome, if any	Gene locus	Gene
hypothyroidism [43]	14q31	
Goldenhar syndrome [38]	14q32	
Biedl-Bardet syndrome [17]	14q32.1	
Angelman syndrome [11]	15q11–q13	
Prader-Willi syndrome [61]	15q11–q13	
Prader-Willi syndrome [61]	15q12	
oculocutaneous albinism [55]	15q11.2–q12	
	15q21.2	
Biedl-Bardet syndrome [17]	15q22.3–q23	
congenital adrenal hyperplasia [25]	15q23–q24	
	16p13	
	16p13.2	
tuberous sclerosis [73]	16p13.3	
Biedl-Bardet syndrome [17]	16q21	
Smith-Magenis syndrome [67]	*17p11.2*	
Potocki-Lupski syndrome [60]	*17p11.2*	
fragile-X syndrome [35, 36]	17p13.1	
	17q11.2	*SLC6A4*
neurofibromatosis type 1 [51]	*17q11.2*	
	17q21.2	*HOXB1*
	17q21.32	HOXB1
Ehlers-Danlos syndrome [34]	17q21.31–q22	
	17q24.3	
pituitary deficiency [58]	17q22–q24	
	19p	
	19p13.11	
	19p13.12	
myotonic dystrophy (MD1) [50]	19q13.2–q13.3	
GAMT deficiency [37]	19p13.3	
trichothiodystrophy [72]	19q13.2–13.3	
Biedl-Bardet syndrome [17]	20p12	
	21q21.1	
Down syndrome [31]	21q22.1–q22.2	
Down syndrome [31]	21q22.3	
CATCH22 [18]	*22q11.2*	

Linked syndrome, if any	Gene locus	Gene
CHARGE [20]	*22q11.2*	
Di George syndrome I [29a]	*22q11.2*	
Velocardiofacial syndrome [76]	*22q11.2*	
adenylosuccinate lyase deficiency [9]	22q13.1	
Down syndrome [31]	22q22.2	
de Lange syndrome [27]	Xp11.21	
Down syndrome [31]	Xp11.23	
hypomelanosis of Ito [42]	Xp11.30	
ornithine carbamyltransferase deficiency [54]	Xp21.1	
Duchenne's disease [33]	Xp21.2	
Rett syndrome (Hanefeld variant) [63b]	*Xp22*	*CDKL5*
Rett syndrome [63a]	*Xp22*	*MeCP2*
Coffin-Lowry syndrome [21]	Xp22.2–p22.1	
ARX gene mutations [13]	Xp22.13	
oculocutaneous albinism [55]	Xp22.3	
X-linked ichthyosis [80]	Xp22.32	
	Xq	
Lujan-Fryns syndrome [46]	Xq13	
	Xq21.33	
	Xq25	
Simpson-Golabi-Behmel syndrome type 1 [87]	Xq26	
Angelman syndrome [11]	Xq28	
Ehlers-Danlos syndrome [34]	Xq28	
fagile-X syndrome [35, 36]	*Xq27.3*	*FMR1*
Angelman syndrome [11]	*Xq28*	*UBE3A*
Rett syndrome [63a]	*Xq28*	*MeCP2*
Rett syndrome (Hanefeld variant) [63b]	*Xq28*	*CDKL5*
fragile-X syndrome [35, 36]	*Xq28*	*FMR1*

Definitions of gene acronyms

BDNF	brain derived neurotrophic factor
CDKL5	cyclin-dependent kinase-like 5
DLX 1/2	distal-less homeobox 1/2
EN2	engrailed 2
FMR1	fragile-X mental retardation protein 1
HESX1	homeobox gene expressed in ES cells
HOXB1	homeobox B1
MeCP2	methyl-CpG binding protein 2
PON1	paroxonase 1
RELN	reelin
SLC6A4	solute carrier family 6 (Neurotransmitter transporter, serotonin) member 4
UBE3A	ubiquitin-protein ligase E3A
WNT2	wingless-type MMTV integration site family, member 2

The studies reported to date have not reported on Y chromosome abnormalities, except for the association with a supernumary Y chromosome in XYY syndrome [4]. Given the high male to female ratio for ASD, Y chromosome abnormalities could be an important factor in some forms of ASD. There is a high degree of homology between the functional areas of the Y chromosome and the X chromosome. There are Y-specific genes such as the SRY gene (Quintana-Murci and Fellous 2001), which could be important. Research on such factors is ongoing (Smith M., Spence and Flodman 2009).

Some of the gene markers identified appear to have specific associated behavioural phenotypes. The serotonin transporter SLC6A4, for example seems to be associated with an increased likelihood of rigid compulsive behaviour in association with ASD diagnosis (Sutcliffe *et al.* 2005), while SHANK3 is associated with more severe learning disability (Sykes *et al.* 2009).

One gene marker (3q26.32) which we go on to discuss below is important in the metabolism of galactose. It is, to date, the candidate region with the strongest association with likelihood of ASD diagnosis. This association may help to provide an explanatory mechanism alternative to the 'opioid hypothesis' regarding the beneficial effects reported in many cases through the removal of milk and milk products from the diet.

The opioid hypothesis, which states that autistic behaviour can result from exogenous opioid compounds resulting from the incomplete digestion of casein and gluten, had had some theoretical and empirical support (Anderson *et al.* 2002; Reichelt and Knivsberg 2003), but several failures to substantiate the empirical basis to the hypothesis have appeared (see, for example, Hunter *et al.* 2003; Wright *et al.* 2005).

In addition to those identified in such screening studies, there are many other gene differences which have been reported in a proportion of individuals with ASDs – such as the recently described MET receptor tyrosine kinase variant at 7q31 (Campbell, Sutcliffe *et al.* 2006). This pathway is under the control of a number of genetic factors (Campbell D.B. *et al.* 2008). A polymorphism in the GLO1 gene at 6p21.3–p21.2 has also been reported (Junaid *et al.* 2004), although the latter has recently been questioned, by reason of the low GLO1 allele frequencies in the control group of the Junaid group study (Sacco *et al.* 2007).

A further recent study has highlighted the variable clinical phenotypes, including an ASD-specific one, associated with recurrent rearrangements of 1q21.1 (Mefford *et al.* 2008).

A recent review highlights many of the genotype–phenotype associations seen in ASD (Lintas and Persico 2008).

A further recent study has shown the importance of matching on behavioural phenotype, with high Lod scores being obtained using factors such as delayed onset of phrase speech and low IQ, which were not seen in overall ASD populations (Liu X–Q. *et al.* 2008).

This is an area of active ongoing research. Several large cohort analyses have appeared mapping risk loci and rare copy number variants (Anney *et al.* 2010; Autism Genome Project Consortium *et al.* 2007; Pinto *et al.* 2010).

Autism spectrum disorders (ASDs) are common, heritable neurodevelopmental conditions. The genetic architecture of ASDs is complex, requiring large samples to overcome heterogeneity. Here we broaden coverage and sample size relative to other studies of ASDs by using Affymetrix 10K SNP arrays and 1,181 [corrected] families with at least two affected individuals, performing the largest linkage scan to date while also analyzing copy number variation in these families. Linkage and copy number variation analyses implicate chromosome 11p12–p13 and neurexins, respectively, among other candidate loci. Neurexins team with previously implicated neuroligins for glutamatergic synaptogenesis, highlighting glutamate-related genes as promising candidates for contributing to ASDs.

Table D3: Nonsense mutations associated with ASD

• ARX	[13]
• Biedl-Bardet syndrome	[17]
• Coffin-Lowry syndrome	[21]
• Cohen syndrome	[23]
• Cowden syndrome	[26]
• Rett syndrome	[63a]
• neuroligin 3 and neuroligin 4 defects	Jamain *et al.* 2003
• FOXP2	Gong *et al.* 2004
• creatine transporter defect	Poo-Arguelles *et al.* 2006

3. Potential correction of 'nonsense' mutations

Nonsense mutations are mutations in a chromosome which prevent a ribosome from fully reading a given portion of DNA, and thereby block the production of the appropriate RNA to manufacture a given protein.

Nonsense mutations have been reported in a number of ASD-relevant conditions and dysfunctions, shown in Table D3.

A recent study (Welch et al. 2007) has provided evidence for the possibility of identifying and correcting nonsense mutation defects which, when left untreated, result in metabolic abnormalities.

4. Differences in the gastrin-releasing peptide receptor (GRPR) gene

GENE LOCUS: Xp22.3–p21.2

In female carriers of many X-linked mental retardation conditions, such as Williams syndrome [77] and Aarskog syndrome [8], there is skewed inactivation of the affected chromosome. (See Plenge et al. 2002 for discussion.) As a result, the mutation is present on the preferentially inactive chromosome (Gong et al. 2008). There is some evidence to suggest that this pattern can be seen in GRPR (Talebizadeh et al. 2005), and also that deletions in this area of Xp can be associated with autism in girls (Thomas et al. 1999).

Non-random X chromosome inactivation is seen in females in many conditions related to ASD – for example:

- in an unselected series of female cases diagnosed with autism (Talebizadeh et al. 2005)
- in four Rett syndrome cases without MeCP2 mutation [63a, 63b] (Villard et al. 2001)
- in carriers of X-linked adrenoleukodystrophy [10] (Maier et al. 2002).

Given the abnormal sex ratio, with approximately four times more boys affected than girls, and the presence of X chromosome differences in many of the female cases reported, it is thought that X chromosome genes may be of particular importance in the development of autism.

GRPR, a gene which is widely expressed in various organ systems, including the central nervous system and the gastrointestinal tract, is found on the short arm of the X chromosome fairly close to the gene involved in ARX [13] and the gene for neuroligin 4 (Blasi et al. 2006; Chocholska, Rossier, Barbi and Kehrer-Sawatzki 2006; Laumonnier et al. 2004). It is expressed early in embryonic development (Battey, Wada and Wray 1994).

The first paper to suggest a link between autism and a break point in the X chromosome at the site of the GRPR gene was a single case study published by Rao et al. in 1994. A second case was reported shortly after (Bolton et al. 1995), where a GRPR abnormality was subsequently characterized (Ishikawa-Brush et al. 1997). These two papers both describe the phenotype and genetic profile of a 27-year-old female patient who had, in addition to autism, multiple extoses – bony lumps – on the long bones (of the legs, arms, fingers, toes), on the pelvis and on the shoulder blades, learning disability (IQ of 35), grand mal epilepsy, brachycephaly and short stature.

Why might GRPR be relevant? A number of studies have shown abnormalities in such 'bombesin-like' peptides and their receptors in other biological conditions affecting mental functioning, such as schizophrenia and Alzheimer's disease. (See Roesler et al. 2006a for review.) (They are called 'bombesin-like' because they belong to a structurally similar class of peptides, the first of which to be characterized was isolated from the skin of the frog '*bombina bombina*'.) In an interesting experiment, Presti-Torres et al. (2007) showed that neonatal rats whose GRPR pathway was blockaded with bombesin showed impairment in both social interaction and novel object memory. The study authors hypothesize that impairment in the action of gastrin-releasing peptide may be a useful model for neurodevelopmental disorders such as autism. Shumyatsky et al. (2002) have shown that, in mice, gastrin-releasing peptide is strongly expressed both in the lateral nucleus of the amygdala and in the regions that convey fearful auditory information to the lateral nucleus, and in the GABAergic interneurons of the lateral nucleus. Gastrin-releasing peptide excited these interneurons and increased their inhibition of principal neurons. In GRPR-deficient mice inhibition of principal neurons was decreased by the interneurons with more pronounced and persistent long-term fear memory. Defects in GRPR, then, are involved in structural differences in the amygdala and in the development of heightened fear responses, both of which are common features in ASD.

As abnormalities of interneuron function have been proposed as a basis for neurodevelopmental disorders (Levitt, Eagleson and Powell 2004), and structural defects in the amygdala have been proposed as core neuroanatomical abnormalities (Amaral, Bauman and Schumann 2003; Baron-Cohen et al. 2000a), the presence of GRPR defects in some ASD cases, and the direct effect that they have on interneuron development within the amygdala, is potentially of great importance and warrants further systematic study.

It is important to note that there may be large ethnic variation in the prevalence of GRPR differences. The polymorphic sites which appear to be significantly associated in North American studies appear far less prevalent in Japanese populations (Marui et al. 2004a, 2004b).

Some animal work is beginning to emerge demonstrating effects of GRPR antagonists on memory consolidation, which could have clinical implications for improving memory consolidation (Santos Dantas, Luft, Henriques and Schwartsmann 2006). Studies in rodent models have shown that GRPRs in the hippocampus are important regulators of memory consolidation (Roesler et al. 2006b).

5. Differences in glutamate mechanisms and metabolism

The evidence concerning possible glutamate abnormalities in autism come from several sources.

1. There are a number of genes implicated in glutamate metabolism which have been highlighted from various genome studies in autistic populations:

   - the glutamate G6 receptor gene GRIK2 at 6p21 (Jamain et al. 2002; Shuang et al. 2004)

   - the glutamate G5 receptor gene mGluR5, affected by the FMR1 site at Xq27.3 (Westmark and Malter 2007)

- the glutamate G8 receptor gene GRM8 at 7q31 (Seragee, Zhong, Nabi and Mahbubal Huq 2003).

2. In animal models, at least, induction of central hypoglutamatergia through the use of antipsychotics can induce autistic-like behaviour (Nilsson *et al.* 2001).

3. Elevated glutamate levels are seen as a consequence of anxiety, a common clinical feature in ASD (Gillott, Furniss and Walter 2001).

4. With specific conditions such as fragile-X [35, 36] and tuberous sclerosis [73] it is clear that there is a problem due to the absence of specific components of the glutamate pathway (in fragile-X, through the absence of one specific glutamate receptor – mGluR5).

Preliminary findings to date show some promise; however, early reports are of cases selected on ASD diagnosis, not concurrent anxiety (Niederhofer 2007).

6. Differences in oxytocin

Oxytocin is a sexually dimorphic neuropeptide expressed most in the female. There has been considerable discussion of its possible role in ASD (Carter 2007; Hammock and Young 2006). Oxytocin is important as a modulator of the functioning of the hypothalamic–pituitary–adrenal axis in situations of social stress and social interaction. (See Heinrichs and Gaab 2007 for a recent overview.) It is noteworthy that intranasal administration of oxytocin significantly increases trust in social situations and willingness to take social risks, based on personal judgement (Kosfeld *et al.* 2005).

The oxytocin receptor gene is located at a linkage site for ASD (3p25–p26),

identified by McCauley *et al.* (2005), and several pieces of published evidence point to a role for oxytocin in the ASDs:

- the HOXA1 and EN2 genes which are implicated in autism are involved in the oxytocin-vasopressin system (for discussion, see Badcock and Crespi 2006)

- plasma levels of oxytocin are lower in an unselected ASD population when compared to age-matched controls (Modahl *et al.* 1998)

- in one study, oxytocin infusion significantly reduced repetitive behaviours in a group of adults with diagnoses of autism and Asperger's syndrome, compared to the effects of sham infusion (Hollander *et al.* 2003)

- in a randomized, placebo-controlled study of 30 normal, non-ASD adults performance on a task where subjects inferred the mental state of others from facial expression (the 'Reading the Mind in the Eyes' Test), a single 24 IU intranasal spray of oxytocin significantly improved performance on difficult-to-discriminate items. (Domes *et al.* 2007)

- oxytocin receptor gene abnormalities have been found to be overrepresented in both Caucasian (Jacob *et al.* 2007) and Chinese Beijing HapMap and Han ASD samples (Wu S. *et al.* 2005).

7. Ghrelin differences

GENE LOCUS: 3p26–p25

Ghrelin is a gastrointestinal hormone and neuropeptide which has been arousing much recent interest. (See Anderson *et al.* 2005 for a general review.) It is involved in central nervous system, immune and gastrointestinal function, and seems, in animal studies at least, to be protective against stress-induced gastrointestinal dysfunction (Brzozowski *et al.* 2004).

In mice and rats, ghrelin affects both synapse formation and dopaminergic activity of the *nucleus accumbens* in the midbrain (Abizaid *et al.* 2006).

Abnormalities of ghrelin production have been implicated in a range of conditions which range from epilepsy (Berilgen, Mungen, Ustundag and Demira 2006) and irritable bowel disease (Peracchi *et al.* 2006) to immune dysfunction (Dixit and Taub 2005).

In animal models an association has been found between plasma ghrelin levels and brain levels of serotonin (Nonogaki, Ohashi-Nozue and Oka 2006). Given the extensive data on serotonergic defects in ASD, together with the immune and gastrointestinal components discussed earlier, ghrelin may prove to be of clinical importance in some of the cases that show this constellation of features.

8. Ciliopathies

Cilia can be viewed as sensory cellular antennae that coordinate signalling pathways, either to produce particular patterns of motility or to coordinate processes involved in cell division and differentiation. Cilia perform a wide variety of functions in mammals – from clearing our lungs of debris, helping our intestines to process food and affording information to our senses, to providing the 'outboard motor' for sperm motility and for the movement of the egg out of the ovary. First described as early as 1835 (Purkinje and Valentin 1835), the various functions of cilia, their presence in a range of body systems and their high degree of phylogenic preservation have only recently come to be appreciated.

We now know that defects in the genetics of cilia are involved in a number of human neurodevelopmental disorders, including Alstrom syndrome (Collin *et al.* 2002); Biedl-Bardet syndrome (BBS) [17] (Ansley *et al.* 2003; Avidor-Reiss *et al.* 2004; Li J.B. *et al.* 2004; Mykytyn and Sheffield 2004); Joubert syndrome [44] (Arts *et al.* 2007; Brancati *et al.* 2008; Cantagrel *et al.* 2008; Delous *et al.* 2007; Gorden *et al.* 2008); Meckel-Gruber syndrome (Kyttala *et al.* 2006); Loken-Senior syndrome (Otto *et al.* 2005); and oral-facial-digital syndrome and polycystic kidney disease (Afzelius 2004; Badano, Mitsuma, Beales and Katsanis 2006; Bisgrove and Yost 2006; Fliegauf, Benzig and Omran 2007; Gorden *et al.* 2008; Marshall 2008; Satir and Christensen 2008). Abnormalities of the cilia are also now recognized to be involved in cancer, and particularly in the growth of tumours (Mans, Voest and Giles 2008). Ciliary dysfunction has also been found to be associated with the development of obesity (Mok, Héon and Zhen 2010).

As both BBS [17] and Joubert syndrome [44] have been reported in association with ASD, while other ciliopathies such as oral-facial-digital syndrome have many features in common, it seems likely that for some ASD conditions this may provide a link between the diagnosis and associated gastrointestinal, sensory, respiratory and reproductive problems.

A recent development in our understanding of the abnormal proteins implicated in the development of BBS has come from discovering that these are variants of highly conserved ciliary proteins. These proteins are important in intracellular transport and are involved in formation of the basal bodies of ciliated cells. For a discussion of these developments, see Section B17. BBS cases have been reported with ciliary problems in lung function

(Shah *et al.* 2008), and with both partial and complete anosmia (Iannaccone *et al.* 2005; Kulaga *et al.* 2004).

Specific mouse knockouts have been produced for several of the BBS genes: BBS1 (Kulaga *et al.* 2004), BBS2 (Nishimura *et al.* 2004), BBS4 (Kulaga *et al.* 2004; Mykytyn *et al.* 2004) and BBS6 (Fath *et al.* 2005; Ross A.J. *et al.* 2005). Several ciliary dysfunctions have been noted in BBS mouse models – in sperm motility, retinal function and lung and olfactory function – and these have provided support for the role of ciliary dysfunction in BBS.

9. Aquaporins

There is increasing interest in the role of aquaporins in bodily function. These are a family of genetic factors that regulate water-selective cell membrane channels, controlling fluid homeostasis and glycerol transport (Krane and Goldstein 2007). They are critically involved in fluid balance in a range of body systems such as the eye, lungs, salivary and sweat glands, the gastrointestinal tract and the kidneys.

Aquaporins are a class of compounds that form water channels in cell membranes. A range of factors are likely to alter aquaporin function. In animal models, aquaporin expression in the gastrointestinal system can be altered by the induction of food allergy (Yamamoto, Kuramoto and Kadowaki 2007), which affects water absorption through the gut wall.

There is some system specificity to the various aquaporins so far discovered. Aquaporin-1, for example, appears to be erythrocyte (red blood cell) specific, while aquaporin-4 is central nervous system specific.

There is increasing interest in the role of certain of the aquaporin channels, and their controlling genes. Aquaporins 0, 1, 2, 4, 5, 6 and 8 are specific channels involved in water transport, while aquaporins 3, 7, 9 and 10 are involved in glycerol release and transport. Aquaporins 7 and 9 allow glycerol to move through cell membranes (Hara-Chikuma and Verkman 2006) and are implicated in various conditions, including type 2 diabetes, obesity, and various other metabolic disorders (Hibuse *et al.* 2005; Wintour and Henry 2006).

Genetic defects in aquaporin-4 (Zhou J. *et al.* 2008) can affect blood–brain barrier development and function, and could increase the impact of peripheral glutamate levels on central nervous system glutamatergic function.

Viral exposure at certain critical points in early brain development can affect the functioning of aquaporin-4 (Fatemi *et al.* 2008a, 2008b). As aquaporin-4 is involved in the migration of glial cells, neural signal transduction and in brain oedema (Verkman *et al.* 2006), it may have a major effect in neural development. To date this has not been linked to abnormalities of glutamatergic function. Our understanding of aquaporins and their functions is very recent. Peter Agre of Johns Hopkins University in Baltimore shared the Nobel Prize for Chemistry in 2003 for the discovery and investigation of aquaporin channels (Agre 2006).

Defects in aquaporin-4 are known to occur in some of the neuromuscular conditions that have been associated with ASD, such as Duchenne muscular dystrophy [33], and in epilepsy (Benga 2006; Obeid and Herrmann 2006).

SECTION E

Appendices

APPENDIX A: INFORMATION AND SUPPORT

The following lists of contacts and information resources are not comprehensive – new resources and new information become available all the time. The charities working in this area have changed considerably during the period when this book was being compiled. Treat these as a starting point rather than a definitive listing.

1. Genetic information and support

The Autism Genetic Database

http://wren.bcf.ku.edu/
This site, established in 2009 by the Bioinformatics Department of the University of Kansas, provides a reasonably comprehensive searchable database of autism susceptibility genes.
Information on the site and how to use it can be found in:
Matuszek, G. and Talabizadeh, Z. (2009) 'Autism Genetic Database: A comprehensive database for autism susceptibility gene-CNVs integrated with known noncoding RNAs and fragile sites.' *BMC Medical Genetics*, 10: 102. doi:10.1186/1471-2350-10-102

Chromosome Help-Station

www.chromosomehelpstation.com
A general link site for support for people and families with rare chromosome disorders.

Chromosome Deletion Outreach, Inc.

P.O. Box 724
Boca Raton
FL 33429-0724
USA
Family helpline: (561) 395-4252
E-mail: info@chromodisorder.org
Website: www.chromodisorder.org
Another useful site for families with members who have been found to have rarer genetic differences, such as deletions, duplications, trisomies, inversions, translocations or ring chromosomes.

CLIMB (Children Living with Inherited Metabolic Diseases)

Climb Building
176 Nantwich Road
Crewe
CW2 6BG
UK *Tel.* 0800 652 3181 or 0845 241 2172
Mon–Fri 10.00am–4.00pm GMT
E-mail: info.svcs@climb.org.uk
Website: www.climb.org.uk/contact.php
CLIMB provides an excellent information resource covering a wide range of inherited metabolic disorders. Also provides disease-specific information and family support.

The Genetic and Rare Diseases Information Center

P.O. Box 8126
Gaithersburg
Maryland
MD 20898-8126
USA
Tel: (888) 205-2311 (phone)
(888) 205-3223 (TTY)
(301) 519-3194 (International Telephone Access Number)
Fax: (240) 632-9164
E-mail: GARDinfo@nih.gov
Website: http://rarediseases.info.nih.gov

This service, established by the National Human Genome Research Institute (NHGRI) and the Office of Rare Diseases (ORD), provides information to the public, and to clinical and research professionals, on genetic and rare diseases.

GeneTests: Medical Genetics Information Resource (online database)
Copyright, University of Washington, Seattle. 1993–2007. www.ncbi.nlm.nih.gov/sites/GeneTests
Another excellent website for clinical and genetic information.

The Council for Responsible Genetics
5 Upland Road, Suite 3
Cambridge
MA 02140
USA
Tel: (617) 868-0870
Fax: (617) 491-5344
E-mail: crg@gene-watch.org
Website: www.gene-watch.org
This site is dedicated to monitoring the development of genetic and biotechnology advances and their ethical implications. An interesting section on autism can currently be found here.

geneimprint
www.geneimprint.com
or
www.geneimprint.org
This site was established in 1997 and is run by the Jirtle Laboratory at Duke University. It provides access to a wide range of material on genomic imprinting.

Genetics of Learning Disability (GOLD)
http://goldstudy.cimr.cam.ac.uk
The GOLD study is a project based at the Cambridge Institute for Medical Research in England. It is investigating genetic causes of learning disabilities in families with more than one affected family member, using a range of techniques.

NCBI GenBank
Human/Mouse Homology Relationships
Michael F. Seldin
Rowe Program in Genetics

Departments of Biological Chemistry and Medicine
University of California Davis
Website: www.ncbi.nlm.nih.gov/Omim/Homology
This is a more technical site that allows people to search for genetic information on human and mouse gene homologies.

The Jackson Laboratory
www.jax.org
This is the world's largest mammalian genetics research institute. The website gives access to information on a wide range of research, and to bibliography on ongoing work in areas such as neurodevelopment.

2. Sites providing information on particular aspects of ASD

The Autism Research Institute
4182 Adams Avenue
San Diego
CA 92116
USA
Fax: 619-563-6840
E-mail: media@autismresearchinstitute.com
Website: www.autism.com

ESPA Research
The Robert Luff Laboratory
Unit 133I
North East Business & Innovation Centre (BIC)
Sunderland Enterprise Park
Wearfield
Sunderland
SR5 2TA
Tel: 0191 549 9300
E-mail: info@espa-research.org.uk
Website: www.espa-research.org.uk

UC Davis MIND Institute
(Medical Investigation of Neurodevelopmental Disorders)
2825 50th Street
Sacramento
CA 95817

California
USA
Tel: (916) 703-0280
Website: www.ucdmc.ucdavis.edu
An excellent resource is the series of recorded talks in the MIND Institute lecture series on neurodevelopmental disorders, which can be viewed through University of California Television at www.uctv.tv.

Autism Research Centre (ARC)
Section of Developmental Psychiatry
University of Cambridge
Douglas House
18b Trumpington Road
Cambridge
CB2 8AH
UK
Tel: 01223-746057
Fax: 01223-746033
E-mail: raj33@medschl.cam.ac.uk (ARC administrator)
Website: www.autismresearchcentre.com

3. Autism research charities

In the USA:
Autism Speaks
2 Park Avenue
11th Floor
New York
NY 10016
USA
Tel: (212) 252-8584
Fax: (212) 252-8676
E-mail: contactus@autismspeaks.org
Website: www.autismspeaks.org

The Simons Foundation
101 Fifth Avenue
5th Floor
New York
NY 10003
USA
E-mail: admin@simonsfoundation.org
Website: http://home/simonsfoundation.org

In the UK:
Autism Speaks UK
North Lea House
66 Northfield End
Henley-on-Thames
Oxfordshire
RG9 2BE
UK
Tel: 01491 412311
Fax: 01491 571921
E-mail: info@autismspeaks.org.uk
Website: www.autismspeaks.org.uk

In Canada:
Autism Speaks Canada
8 King Street East
Ste 1104
Toronto
Ontario
M5C 1B5
Canada
Tel: (888) 362-6227
E-mail: slanthier@autismspeaks.org
Website: www.autismspeaks.ca

4. Some relevant organizations and charities dealing with and funding research on related conditions

PACE (People Against Childhood Epilepsy)
7 East 85th Street
Suite A3
New York
NY 10028
USA
Tel: (212) 665-(PACE) 7223
Fax: (212) 327-3075
E-mail: pacenyemail@aol.com
Website: www.paceusa.org

Tourettes Action
Southbank House
Black Prince Road
London
SE1 7SJ
UK
TS helpline: 0845 458 1252
E-mail: help@tourettes-action.org.uk
Administration: 020 7793 2356
E-mail: admin@tourettes-action.org.uk
Website: www.tourettes-action.org.uk

Bill and Melinda Gates Foundation
PO Box 23350
Seattle
WA 98102
USA Tel: (206) 709-3100 (reception)
(206) 709-3140 (grant inquiries)
E-mail: info@gatesfoundation.org
Website: www.gatesfoundation.org

Medical Research Council
20 Park Crescent
London
W1B 1AL
UK
Tel: 020 7636 5422
Fax: 020 7436 6179
E-mail: corporate@headoffice.mrc.ac.uk
Website: www.mrc.ac.uk

The Wellcome Trust
Gibbs Building
215 Euston Road
London
NW1 2BE
UK
Tel: 020 7611 8888
Fax: 020 7611 8545
E-mail: contact@wellcome.ac.uk
Website: www.wellcome.ac.uk

5. Some relevant professional organizations

The International Molecular Genetic Study of Autism Consortium (IMGSAC)
Contact links for most of those involved in this group are available on their website: www.well.ox.ac.uk

The International Society for Autism Research (INSAR)
INSAR is a professionals-only organization for those working in the area of autism research. The principal function of the society at present is setting up and running the annual International Meeting for Autism Research. Specific requests for information on INSAR should be directed to
Dr Nurit Yirmiya: NuritYirmiya@huji.ac.il
INSAR Conference Homepage: www.cevs.ucdavis.edu

Society for the Study of Behavioural Phenotypes (SSBP)
This is an international organization that started in 1987 with a specific interest in investigating behavioural and emotional aspects of biologically determined clinical syndromes associated with intellectual disability.
SSBP
Robbie Fountain, Administrative Secretary
2nd Floor
Douglas House
18b Trumpington Road
Cambridge
CB2 8AH
UK
Tel: 01223 746100
Fax: 01223 746122
E-mail: ssbpRobbie@aol.com
Website: www.ssbp.co.uk

6. General information on rare biomedical conditions

A range of self-help groups and organizations provide information and support for families with many of the conditions described in this volume. Many are specific groups dedicated to a specific identified condition, and have been included in the preceding lists, as far as possible.

In addition to those condition-specific groups, several 'umbrella' groups exist to support and work with a range of conditions, while others, such as NORD and Unique, provide information on rare disorders for which no specific support groups have been established.

In the USA:

The MAGIC Foundation
Corporate Office
6645 W. North Avenue
Oak Park
Illinois 60302
USA
Tel: (708) 383-0808
Toll-free parent helpline: (800) 3MAGIC3
or (800) 362-4423
Fax: (708) 383-0899
Website: www.magicfoundation.org

National Organization for Rare Disorders (NORD)
55 Kenosia Avenue
P.O. Box 1968
Danbury
CT 06813-1968
USA
Tel: (203) 744-0100
Toll-free: (800) 999-6673 (voicemail only)
TDD number: (203) 797-9590
Fax: (203) 798-2291
E-mail: orphan@rarediseases.org
Website: www.rarediseases.org

Genetic Alliance
4301 Connecticut Ave, NW
Suite 404
Washington, DC 20008–2304
USA
Tel: (800) 336-GENE (4363) or
(202) 966-5557
Fax: (202) 966-8553
E-mail: info@geneticalliance.org
Website: www.geneticalliance.org

The Children's Craniofacial Association
13140 Coit Road
Suite 307
Dallas
Texas
TX 75240
USA
Toll-free: (800) 535-3643
Tel: (214) 570-9099
Fax: (214) 570-8811
E-mail: contactCCA@ccakids.com
Website: www.ccakids.com

In Europe:

The European Organisation for Rare Diseases (EURODIS)
Plateforme Maladies Rares
102, rue Didot
75014 Paris
France
Tel: +33 (1) 56.53.52.10
Fax: +33 (1) 56.53.52.15
E-mail: eurordis@eurordis.org
Website: www.eurordis.org
EURODIS is a parent-driven alliance of patient organizations and individuals living with rare diseases.

In the UK:

Unique
P.O. Box 2189
Surrey
CR3 5GN
UK
Telephone helpline: 01883 330766
E-mail: info@rarechromo.org
Website: www.rarechromo.org
Rare chromosome disorder support group.

Genetic Interest Group
Unit 4D
Leroy House
436 Essex Road
London
N1 3QP
UK
Tel: 020 7704 3141
Fax: 020 7359 1447
E-mail: mail@gig.org.uk
Website: www.gig.org.uk

Contact a Family
209–211 City Road
London
EC1V 1JN
UK
Tel: 020 7608 8700
Freephone for parents and families (10am–4pm,
Mon–Fri): 0808 808 3555
Textphone: 0808 808 3556
Fax: 020 7608 8701
E-mail: info@cafamily.org.uk
Website: www.cafamily.org.uk
Linking site for families with the same
condition: www.makingcontact.org

In Canada:
The London Health Sciences Centre
800 Commissioners Road East
P.O. Box 5010
London
Ontario
N6A 5W9
Canada
Tel: (519) 685-8500
Website: www.lhsc.on.ca

Maintains **The Canadian Directory of
Genetic Support Groups**

In Sweden:
The Swedish Association of Rare Disorders
Sällsynta diagnoser
Box 1386
172 27 Sundbyberg
Sweden
Tel: 08-764 49 99
Fax: 08-546 40 494
Website: www.sallsyntadiagnoser.nu

In Australasia:
AGSA (The Association of Genetic Support of
Australasia Inc.)
66 Albion Street
Surry Hills
NSW 2010
Australia
E-mail: info@agsa-geneticsupport.org.au
Website: www.agsa-geneticsupport.org.au

7. Searching for further information

To search for further information on specific conditions, a variety of other resources are helpful:

The National Center for Biotechnology Information (NCBI), provided as a free resource by the National Institutes for Health in the USA, gives a rapid means of searching the medical literature on a number of databases. The most relevant is **PubMed**, which can search a huge proportion of the peer-reviewed medical literature (over 16 million papers at the time of writing).
www.ncbi.nlm.nih.gov
Searching on all databases through the NCBI search window accesses a large number of clinical and research papers that can be downloaded as open-access PDF files.

Online Mendelian Inheritance in Man (OMIM) is a catalogue of known human genetic disorders.
www.ncbi.nlm.nih.gov

The Birth Disorder Information Directory provides a detailed list of clinical disorders with brief definitions.
www.bdid.com

genetests currently provides technical information on 373 genetic conditions, and international directories of genetic testing laboratories and diagnostic clinics.
www.ncbi.nlm.nih.gov/sites/GeneTests

8. Some clinical and academic journals relevant to neurobiological issues in ASD

Autism
http://aut.sagepub.com

Autism Research
www3.interscience.wiley.com

Biological Psychiatry
www.journals.elsevierhealth.com

Brain and Development
www.elsevier.com

Development and Psychopathology
http://journals.cambridge.org

Developmental Medicine and Child Neurology (DMCN)
www.wiley.com

Journal of the American Academy of Child and Adolescent Psychiatry (JAACAP)
www.jaacap.com

Journal of Autism and Developmental Disorders (JADD)
www.springer.com

Journal of Child Neurology
http://jcn.sagepub.com

Journal of Child Psychology and Psychiatry (JCPP)
http://ev.wiley.com

Journal of Inherited Metabolic Disease
www.springer.com

Mental Retardation and Developmental Disabilities Research Reviews (MRDDRR)
http://eu.wiley.com

Molecular Psychiatry
www.nature.com

Proceedings of the National Academy of Science (PNAS)
www.pnas.org

Trends in Neurosciences
www.elsevier.com

APPENDIX B: FURTHER READING

For those who require an easy introduction to genetics, biology and their relevance to everyday human life, I would recommend these simple but well-written books:

Chiu, L.S. (2006) *When a Gene Makes You Smell Like a Fish…and Other Tales about the Genes in Your Body.* New York: Oxford University Press.

Collins, F. (2010) *The Language of Life: DNA and the Revolution in Personalised Medicine.* New York: HarperCollins.

Moalem, S. (2007) *Survival of the Sickest: A Medical Maverick Discovers Why We Need Disease.* London: HarperCollins.

There are many excellent books which provide far greater coverage of elements of this extensive field than has been possible here. The following are particularly commended to those who wish to read further in areas relevant to the neurobiology of ASD:

Allis, C.D., Jenuwein, T., Reinberg, D. and Caparros, M-L. (eds.) (2006) *Epigenetics.* Cold Spring Harbour: Cold Spring Harbor Press.

Arbib, M.A. (2006) *Action to Language via the Mirror Neuron System.* Cambridge: Cambridge University Press.

Baxter, P. (ed.) (2001) *Vitamin Responsive Conditions in Paediatric Neurology.* Cambridge: MacKeith Press.

Berthoz, A., Andres, C., Barthelemy, C., Massion, J. and Roge, B. (eds.) (2005) *L'Autisme: de la recherche a la pratique.* Paris: Odile Jacob.

Butler, M.G. and Meaney, F.J. (eds.) (2005) *Genetics of Developmental Disabilities.* Boca Raton: Taylor and Francis.

Cassidy, S.B. and Allanson, J.E. (eds.) (2005) *Management of Genetic Syndromes* (2nd edn.). Hoboken, New Jersey: John Wiley and Sons.

Charman, T. and Stone, W. (eds.) (2006) *Social and Communication Development in Autism Spectrum Disorders: Early Identification, Diagnosis, and Intervention.* New York: Guilford Press.

Cicchetti, D. and Cohen, D.J. (eds.) (2006) *Developmental Psychopathology* (2nd edn.). (Three vols.) Hoboken, New Jersey: John Wiley and Sons.

Cohen, M. Jr., Neri, G. and Weksberg, R. (2002) *Overgrowth Syndromes.* New York: Oxford University Press.

Coleman, M. (ed.) (2005) *The Neurology of Autism.* Oxford: Oxford University Press.

Dhossche, D.M. (ed.) (2005) *GABA in Autism and Related Disorders.* New York: Academic Press.

Doerfler, W. and Bohm, P. (eds.) (2006) *DNA Methylation: Development, Genetic Disease and Cancer.* Berlin: Springer.

Fisch, G.S. and Flint, J.M.D. (eds.) (2006) *Transgenic and Knockout Models of Neuropsychiatric Disorders.* Tolowa, New Jersey: Humana Press.

Gibson, G. and Muse, S.V. (2004) *A Primer of Genome Science* (2nd edn.). Massachusetts: Sinauer Associates Ltd.

Gillberg, C. and Coleman, M. (2000) *The Biology of the Autistic Syndromes* (3rd edn.). London: MacKeith Press, (Clinics in Developmental Medicine No. 15 3/4).

Gluckman, P. and Hanson, M. (2005) *The Foetal Matrix: Evolution, Development and Disease.* Cambridge: Cambridge University Press.

Hagerman, R. (1999) *Neurodevelopmental Disorders: Diagnosis and Treatment.* Oxford: Oxford University Press.

Harris, J.C. (1995) *Developmental Neuropsychiatry.* (Two vols.) New York: Oxford University Press.

Harris, J.C. (2006) *Intellectual Disability: Understanding its Development, Causes, Classification, Evaluation, and Treatment.* New York: Oxford University Press.

Hurst, J.A., Firth, H.V. and Hall, J.G. (eds.) (2005) *Oxford Desk Reference Clinical Genetics.* Oxford: Oxford University Press.

Jones, K. (2005) *Smith's Recognizable Patterns of Human Malformation* (6th edn.). Amsterdam: Saunders (Elsevier).

McKinlay Gardner, R.J. and Sutherland, G.R. (2003) *Chromosome Abnormalities and Genetic Counseling.* Oxford: Oxford University Press.

Moldin, S.O. and Rubenstein, J.L.R. (eds.) (2006) *Understanding Autism: From Basic Neuroscience to Treatment.* Boca Raton: Taylor and Francis.

Nyhan, W.L., Barshop, B.A. and Ozand, P.T. (2006) *Atlas of Metabolic Diseases* (2nd edn.). London: Chapman and Hall.

Oldstone, M.B.A. (ed.) (2005) *Molecular Mimicry: Infection Inducing Autoimmune Disease.* New York: Springer.

Ozonoff, S., Rogers, S.J. and Hendren, R.L. (eds.) (2003) *Autism Spectrum Disorders: A Research Review for Practitioners.* Washington: American Psychiatric Publishing.

Peres, J.M., Gonzalez, P.M., Comi, M.L. and Nieto, C. (eds.) (2007) *New Developments in Autism: The Future is Today.* London: Jessica Kingsley Publishers.

Rogers, S.J. and Williams, J.H.G. (eds.) (2006) *Imitation and the Social Mind: Autism and Typical Development.* New York: Guilford Press.

Romer, D. and Walker, E.F. (2007) *Adolescent Psychopathology and the Developing Brain.* New York: Oxford University Press.

Runge, M.S. and Patterson, C. (eds.) (2006) *Principles of Molecular Medicine* (2nd edn.). Tolowa, New Jersey: Humana Press.

Shore, S.M. and Rastelli, L.G. (2006) *Understanding Autism for Dummies.* Wiley: Hoboken. Shorvon, S. (2005) *Handbook of Epilepsy Treatment* (2nd edn.). Oxford: Blackwell Publishing.

Sicile-Kira, C. (2003) *Autism Spectrum Disorders: The Complete Guide*. London: Vermillion.

Smith, M. (2006) *Mental Retardation and Developmental Delay: Genetic and Epigenetic Factors*. Oxford: Oxford University Press.

Smith, R. (2006) *The Trouble with Medical Journals*. London: The Royal Society of Medicine Press.

Stamenov, M.I. and Gallese, V. (eds.) (2002) *Mirror Neurons and the Evolution of Brain and Language*. Amsterdam: John Benjamins.

Tager-Flusberg, H. (ed.) (1999) *Neurodevelopmental Disorders*. Cambridge, Massachusetts: MIT Press.

Tuchman, R. and Rapin, I. (eds.) (2006) *Autism: A Neurological Disorder of Early Brain Development*. Cambridge: Cambridge University Press.

Volkmar, F.R., Paul, R., Klin, A. and Cohen, D. (eds.) (2005) *Handbook of Autism and Developmental Disorders* (3rd edn.). (Two vols.) Hoboken, New Jersey: John Wiley and Sons.

REFERENCES

Aarskog, D. (1970) 'A familial syndrome of short stature associated with facial dysplasia and genital anomalies.' *Journal of Pediatrics*, 77: 856–861.

Abel, T. and Zukin, R.S. (2008) 'Epigenetic targets of HDAC inhibition in neurodegenerative and psychiatric disorders.', *Current Opinion in Pharmacology*, 8: 57–64.

Abelson, J.F., Kwan, K.Y., O'Roak, B.J., Baek, D.Y. *et al.* (2005) 'Sequence variants in SLITRK1 are associated with Tourette's syndrome.', *Science*, 310: 317–320.

Abitbol, M., Menini, C., Delezoide, A-L., Rhyner, T. *et al.* (1993) 'Nucleus basalis magnocellularis and hippocampus are the major sites of FMR-1 expression in the human foetal brain.', *Nature Genetics*, 4: 147–153.

Abizaid, A., Liu, Z-W., Andrews, Z.B., Shanabrough, M. *et al.* (2006) 'Ghrelin modulates the activity and synaptic input organization of midbrain dopamine neurons while promoting appetite.', *Journal of Clinical Investigation*, 116(12): 3229–3239.

Aboulghar, H., Aboulghar, M., Mansour, R., Serour, G. *et al.* (2001) 'A prospective controlled study of karyotyping for 430 consecutive babies conceived through intracytoplasmic sperm injection.', *Fertility and Sterility*, 76: 249–253.

Abraham, I., Juhasz, G., Kekesi, K.A. and Kovacs, K.J. (1998) 'Corticosterone peak is responsible for stress-induced elevation of glutamate in the hippocampus.' *Stress*, 2: 171–181.

Abrahams, B.S., Tentler, D., Perederiy, J.V., Oldham, M.C. *et al.* (2007) 'Genome-wide analyses of human perisylvian cerebral cortical patterning.', *Proceedings of the National Academy of Science USA*, 104(45): 17849–17854.

Abramsky, L. and Chapple, J. (1997) '47,XXY (Klinefelter syndrome) and 47,XYY: estimated rates of and indication for postnatal diagnosis with implications for prenatal counselling.', *Prenatal Diagnosis*, 17: 363–368.

Abramson, C.J., Platt, S.R., Jakobs, C., Verhoeven, N.M. *et al.* (2003) 'L-2-hydroxyglutaric aciduria in Staffordshire Bull Terriers.', *Journal of Veterinary Internal Medicine*, 17(4): 551–556.

Acácio, G.L., Barini, R., Bertuzzo, C.S., Couto, E.C. *et al.* (2005) 'Methylenetetrahydrofolate reductase gene polymorphisms and their association with trisomy 21.', *Prenatal Diagnosis*, 25(13): 1196–1199.

Accardo, P.J. and Roseman, B. (2000) 'By any other name.', *The Journal of Pediatrics*, 136(5): 576–577.

Accardo, P. J. and Whitman, B. (1989) 'Toe walking: a marker for language disorders in the developmentally disabled.', *Clinical Pediatrics*, 28(8): 347–350.

Adams, J.B. and Holloway, C. (2004) 'Pilot study of a moderate dose multivitamin/mineral supplement for children with autistic spectrum disorder.', *Journal of Alternative and Complementary Medicine*, 10(6): 1033–1039.

Adams, M., Lucock, M., Stuart, J., Fardell, S. *et al.* (2007) 'Preliminary evidence for involvement of the folate gene polymorphism 19 bp deletion-DHFR in occurrence of autism.', *Neuroscience Letters*, 422: 24–29.

Afzal, N., Murch, S., Thirrupathy, K., Berger, L. *et al.* (2003) 'Constipation with acquired megarectum in children with autism.' *Pediatrics*, 112: 939–942.

Afzelius, B.A. (2004) 'Cilia-related diseases.', *Journal of Pathology*, 204: 470–477.

Agre, P. (2006) 'Aquaporin water channels: from atomic structure to clinical medicine.' *Nanomedicine: Nanotechnology, Biology, and Medicine*, 2: 266–267.

Aguilar-Fuentes, J., Fregoso, M., Herrera, M., Reynaud, E. *et al.* (2008) 'P8/TTDA overexpression enhances UV-irradiation resistance and suppresses TFIIH mutations in a Drosophila trichothiodystrophy model.', *PLoS Genetics*, 4(11): e1000253.

Aguirre, D., Nieto, K., Lazos, M., Pena, Y.R. *et al.* (2006) 'Extragonadal germ cell tumors are often associated with Klinefelter syndrome.', *Human Pathology*, 37: 477–480.

Agostoni, C., Massetto, N., Biasucci, G., Rottoli, A. *et al.* (2000) 'Effects of long-chain polyunsaturated fatty acid supplementation on fatty acid status and visual function in treated children with hyperphenylalaninemia.', *Journal of Pediatrics*, 137: 504–509.

Agostoni, C., Verduci, E., Massetto, N., Fiori, L. *et al.* (2003) 'Long term effects of long chain polyunsaturated fats in hyperphenylalaninemic children.', *Archives of Disease in Childhood*, 88: 582–583.

Agrelo, R. and Wutz, A. (2010) 'X inactivation and disease.', *Seminars in Cell and Developmental Biology*, 21: 194–200.

Airaksinen, E.M. (1974) 'Tryptophan treatment of infants with Down's syndrome.', *Annals of Clinical Research*, 6(1): 33–39.

Aitken, K.J. (1991) 'Examining the evidence for a common structural basis to autism.' *Developmental Medicine and Child Neurology*, 33: 930–934.

Aitken, K.J. (1998) 'Behavioural phenotypes.', *Association for Child Psychology and Psychiatry Occasional Papers Series*, 15: 5–20.

Aitken, K.J. (2008) 'Intersubjectivity, affective neuroscience, and the neurobiology of autistic spectrum disorders: a systematic review.' *The Keio Medical Journal*, 57(1): 15–36.

Aitken, K.J. (2009) *Dietary Interventions in the ASDs – Why They Work When They Do, Why They Don't When They Don't.* London: Jessica Kingsley Publishers.

Akaboshi, S., Ruiters, J., Wanders, R.J.A., Andresen, B.S. et al. (2001) 'Divergent phenotypes in siblings with confirmed 2-methylbutyryl-CoA dehydrogenase (2-MBAD) deficiency.', *Journal of Inherited Metabolic Disease*, 24(Supp.1): 58.

Akbarnia, B.A., Gabriel, K.R., Beckman, E. and Chalk, D. (1992) 'Prevalence of scoliosis in neurofibromatosis.', *Spine*, 17(8 Suppl): S244–248.

Akefeldt, A. and Gillberg, C. (1991) 'Hypomelanosis of Ito in three cases with autism and autistic-like conditions.' *Developmental Medicine and Child Neurology*, 33: 737–743.

Akefeldt, A., Gillberg, C. and Larsson, C. (1991) 'Prader-Willi syndrome in a Swedish rural county: epidemiological aspects.', *Developmental Medicine and Child Neurology*, 33(8): 715–721.

Akenside, M. (1768) 'Observations on cancers.', *Medical Transactions of the Royal College of Physicians of London*, 1: 64–92.

Akhondzadeh, S., Tajdar, H., Mohammadi, M.R., Mohammadi, M. et al. (2008) 'A double-blind placebo controlled trial of piracetam added to risperidone in patients with autistic disorder.', *Child Psychiatry and Human Development*, 39(3): 237–245.

Al-Ahmari, A., Shah, N., Sung, L., Zipursky, A. and Hitzler, J. (2006) 'Long-term results of an ultra low-dose cytarabine-based regimen for the treatment of acute megakaryoblastic leukaemia in children with Down syndrome.' *British Journal of Haematology*, 133(6): 646–648.

Alarcón, M., Abrahams, B.S., Stone, J.L., Duvall, J.A. et al. (2008) 'Linkage, association, and gene-expression analyses identify CNTNAP2 as an autism-susceptibility gene.', *American Journal of Human Genetics*, 82(1): 150–159.

Alarcón, M., Cantor, R.M., Liu, J., Gilliam, T.C., Geschwind, D.H., and the AGRE Consortium (2005a) 'Evidence for a language quantitative trait locus on chromosome 7q in multiplex autism families.' *American Journal of Human Genetics*, 70: 60–71.

Alarcón, M., Yonan, A.L., Gilliam, T.C., Cantor, R.M. and Geschwind, D.H. (2005b) 'Quantitative genome scan and ordered-subsets analysis of autism endophenotypes support language QTLs.' *Molecular Psychiatry*, 10: 747–757.

Alberti, A., Pirrone, P., Elia, M., Waring, R.H. and Romano, C. (1999) 'Sulphation deficit in "low-functioning" autistic children: a pilot study.' *Biological Psychiatry*, 46(3): 420–424.

Alcántara, M.A., Villarreal, M.T., Del Castillo, V., Gutiérrez, G. et al. (1999) 'High frequency of de novo deletions in Mexican Duchenne and Becker muscular dystrophy patients: implications for genetic counselling.', *Clinical Genetics*, 55(5): 376–380.

Aldred, S., Moore, K.M., Fitzgerald, M. and Waring, R.H. (2003) 'Plasma amino acid levels in children with autism and their families.', *Journal of Autism and Developmental Disorders*, 33(1): 93–97.

Alexiev, B.A., Lin, X., Sun, C.C. and Brenner, D.S. (2006) 'Meckel-Gruber syndrome: pathologic manifestations, minimal diagnostic criteria, and differential diagnosis.', *Archives of Pathology and Laboratory Medicine*, 130(8): 1236–1238.

Alkan, A., Sigirci, A., Kutlu, R., Ozcan, H. et al. (2005) 'Neurofibromatosis type 1: diffusion weighted imaging findings of brain.', *European Journal of Radiology*, 56: 229–234.

Alkuraya, F.S., Picker, J., Irons, M.B. and Kimonis, V.E. (2005) 'Smith-Lemli-Opitz syndrome in trisomy 13: how does the mix work?' *Birth Defects Research A: Clinical and Molecular Teratology*, 73(8): 569–571.

Allanson, J.E. (1986) 'Germinal mosaicism in Apert syndrome.', *Clinical Genetics*, 29: 429–433.

Allanson, J.E. (1987) 'Noonan syndrome.', *Journal of Medical Genetics*, 24: 9–13.

Allanson, J.E. and Cole, T.R.P. (1996) 'Sotos syndrome: evolution of facial phenotype subjective and objective assessment.' *American Journal of Medical Genetics*, 65: 13–20.

Allanson, J.E., Hall, J.G., Hughes, H.E., Preus, M. and Witt, R.D. (1985) 'Noonan syndrome: the changing phenotype.', *American Journal of Medical Genetics*, 21: 507–514.

Allanson, J.E., Hennekam, R.C. and Ireland, M. (1997) 'De Lange syndrome: subjective and objective comparison of the classical and mild phenotypes.', *Journal of Medical Genetics*, 34: 645–650.

Allanson, J.E., Upadhyaya, M., Watson, G.H., Partington, M. et al. (1991) 'Watson syndrome: is it a subtype of type 1 neurofibromatosis?' *Journal of Medical Genetics*, 28: 752–756.

Allen, E.G., Sherman, S., Abramowitz, A., Leslie, M. et al. (2005) 'Examination of the effect of the polymorphic CGG repeat in the FMR1 gene on cognitive performance.' *Behavioural Genetics*, 35: 435–445.

Allingham-Hawkins, D.J., Babul-Hirji, R., Chitayat, D., Holden, J.J.A. et al. (1999) 'Fragile-X premutation is a significant risk factor for premature ovarian failure: the international collaborative POF in fragile-X study – preliminary data.' *American Journal of Medical Genetics*, 83: 322–325.

Allport, S. (2006) *The Queen of Fats: Why Omega-3s Were Removed from the Western Diet and What We Can Do to Replace Them*. Berkeley, University of California Press.

Almeida, L.S., Vilarinho, L., Darmin, P.S., Rosenberg, E.H. et al. (2007) 'A prevalent pathogenic GAMT mutation (c.59G>C) in Portugal.', *Molecular Genetics and Metabolism*, 91: 1–6.

Alperin, E.S. and Shapiro, L.J. (1997) 'Characterization of point mutations with X-linked ichthyosis: effects on the structure and function of the steroid sulfatase protein.', *Journal of Biological Chemistry*, 272: 20756–20763.

Alsdorf, R. and Wyszynski, D.F. (2005) 'Teratogenicity of sodium valproate.', *Expert Opinion on Drug Safety*, 4(2): 345–353.

Altafaj, X., Dierssen, M., Baamonde, C., Marti, E. et al. (2001) 'Neurodevelopmental delay, motor abnormalities and cognitive deficits in transgenic mice overexpressing Dyrk1A (minibrain), a murine model of Down's syndrome.', *Human Molecular Genetics*, 10: 1915–1923.

Alvarez Retuerto, A.I., Cantor, R.M., Gleeson, J.G., Ustaszewska, A. et al. (2008) 'Association of common variants in the Joubert syndrome gene (AHI1) with autism.', *Human Molecular Genetics*, 17(24): 3887–3896.

Alwan, S., Tredwell, S.J. and Friedman, J.M. (2005) 'Is osseous dysplasia a primary feature of neurofibromatosis 1 (NF1)?' *Clinical Genetics, 67*(5): 378–390.

Amaral, D.G., Bauman, M.D. and Schumann, C.M. (2003) 'The amygdala and autism: implications from non-human primate studies.' *Genes, Brain and Behaviour, 2*: 295–302.

Amir, N. and Gross-Tzur, V. (1994) 'Paradoxical normalization in childhood epilepsy.' *Epilepsia, 35*(5): 1060–1064.

Amir, R.E., Van den Veyver, I.B., Wan, M., Tran, C.Q. *et al.* (1999) 'Rett syndrome is caused by mutations in X-linked MeCP2, encoding methyl-CpG-binding protein 2.' *Nature Genetics, 2*(3): 185–188.

Amiri, K., Hagerman, R.J. and Hagerman, P.J. (2008) 'Fragile-X associated tremor/ataxia syndrome an aging face of the fragile-X gene.', *Archives of Neurology, 65*(1): 19–23.

Amlashi, S.F., Riffaud, L., Brassier, G. and Morandi, X. (2003) 'Nevoid basal cell carcinoma syndrome: relation with desmoplastic medulloblastoma in infancy. A population-based study and review of the literature.', *Cancer, 98*: 618–624.

Ammann, F. (1970) 'Investigations clinique et genetique sur le syndrome de Bardet-Biedl en Suisse.' *Journal of Human Genetics, 18*, 1–310.

Amminger, G.P., Berger, G.E., Schafer, M.R., Klier, C. *et al.* (2006) 'Omega-3 fatty acids supplementation in children with autism: a double-blind randomized, placebo-controlled pilot tudy.' *Biological Psychiatry, 61*(4): 551–553.

Amon, M., Menapace, R. and Kirnbauer, R. (1990) 'Ocular symptomatology in familial hypomelanosis of Ito. incontinentia pigmenti achromians.', *Ophthalmologica, 200*(1): 1–6.

Anderlid, B.M., Schoumans, J., Anneren, G., Tapia-Paez, I. *et al.* (2002) 'FISH-mapping of a 100-kb terminal 22q13 deletion.', *Human Genetics, 110*: 439–443.

Anderson, A.J., Stephan, M.J., Walker, W.O. and Kelley, R.I. (1998) 'Variant RSH/Smith-Lemli-Opitz syndrome with atypical sterol metabolism.' *American Journal of Medical Genetics, 78*: 413–418.

Anderson, G.M., Jacobs-Stannard, A., Chawarska, K., Volkmar, F.R. and Kliman H.J. (2007) 'Placental trophoblast inclusions in autism spectrum disorder.', *Biological Psychiatry, 61*: 487–491.

Anderson, L.L., Jeftinija, S., Scanes, C.G., Stromer, M.H. *et al.* (2005) 'Physiology of ghrelin and related peptides.' *Domestic Animal Endocrinology, 29*: 111–144.

Anderson, P.J. and David, D.J. (2005) 'Spinal anomalies in Goldenhar syndrome.', *The Cleft Palate-Craniofacial Journal, 42*(5): 477–480.

Anderson, R.J., Bendell, D.J., Garnett, I., Groundwater, P.W. *et al.* (2002) 'Identification of indolyl-3-acryloylglycine in the urine of people with autism.' *Journal of Pharmacy and Pharmacology, 54*: 295–298.

Anderson, S.R. and Romanczyck, R.G. (1999) 'Early intervention for young children with autism: Continuum-based behavioural models.' *Journal of the Association for Persons with Severe Handicaps, 24*: 162–173.

Andersson, H.C., Frentz, J., Martinez, J.E., Tuck-Muller, C.M. and Bellizaire, J. (1999) 'Adrenal insufficiency in Smith-Lemli-Opitz syndrome.', *American Journal of Medical Genetics, 82*: 382–384.

Andoniadou, C.L., Signore, M., Sajedi, E., Gaston-Massuet, C. *et al.* (2007) 'Lack of the murine homeobox gene Hesx1 leads to a posterior transformation of the anterior forebrain.', *Development, 134*(8): 1499–1508.

Andres, E., Loukili, N.H., Noel, E., Kaltenbach, G. *et al.* (2004) 'Vitamin B12 (cobalamin) deficiency in elderly patients.' *Canadian Medical Association Journal, 171*: 251–259.

Andresen, B.S., Christensen, E., Corydon, T.J., Bross, P. *et al.* (2000) 'Isolated 2-methylbutyrylglycinuria caused by short/branched-chain acyl-CoA dehydrogenase deficiency: identification of a new enzyme defect, resolution of its molecular basis, and evidence for distinct acyl-CoA dehydrogenases in isoleucine and valine metabolism.', *American Journal of Human Genetics, 67*: 1095–1103.

Aneja, A. and Tierney, E. (2008) 'Autism: the role of cholesterol in treatment.', *International Review of Psychiatry, 20*(2): 165–170.

Angell, M. (2004) *The Truth About the Drug Companies: How They Deceive Us and What to Do About It.* New York: Random House.

Angelman, H. (1965) '"Puppet children": a report of three cases.', *Developmental Medicine and Child Neurology, 7*: 681–688.

Angkustsiri, K., Wirojanan, J., Deprey, L.J., Gane, L.W. and Hagerman, R.J. (2008) 'Fragile-X syndrome with anxiety disorder and exceptional verbal intelligence.', *American Journal of Medical Genetics, 146A*: 376–379.

Ani, C., Grantham-McGregor, S. and Muller, D. (2000) 'Nutritional supplementation in Down syndrome: theoretical considerations and current status.', *Developmental Medicine and Child Neurology, 42*: 207–213.

Anney, R., Klei, L., Pinto, D., Regan, R., Conroy, J. *et al.* (2010) 'A genome-wide scan for common alleles affecting risk for autism.' *Human Molecular Genetics, 19(20)*: 4072–4082.

Ansley, S.J., Badano, J.L., Blacque, O.E., Hill, J. *et al.* (2003) 'Basal body dysfunction is a likely cause of pleiotropic Bardet-Biedl syndrome.', *Nature, 425*: 628–633.

Anstey, A.V. and Taylor, C.R. (1999) 'Photosensitivity in the Smith-Lemli-Opitz syndrome: the US experience of a new congenital photosensitivity syndrome.', *Journal of the American Academy of Dermatology, 41*: 121–123.

Antar, L.N., Afroz, R., Dictenberg, J.B., Carroll, R.C. and Bassell, G.J. (2004) 'Metabotropic glutamate receptor activation regulates fragile-X mental retardation protein and *Fmr1* mRNA localization differentially in dendrites and synapses.' *The Journal of Neuroscience, 24*: 2648–2655.

Antila, E., Nordberg, U.R., Syväoja, E.L. and Westermarck, T. (1990) 'Selenium therapy in Down syndrome (DS): a theory and a clinical trial.', *Advances in Experimental Medicine and Biology, 264*: 183–186.

Antila, E. and Westermarck, T. (1989) 'On the etiopathogenesis and therapy of Down syndrome.', *International Journal of Developmental Biology, 33*: 183–188.

Antonarakis, S.E., Adelsberger, P.A., Petersen, M.B., Binkert, F. and Schinzel, A.A. (1990) 'Analysis of DNA polymorphism suggests that most *de novo* dup(21q) chromosomes in patients with Down syndrome are isochromosomes and not translocations.', *American Journal of Human Genetics, 47*: 968–972.

Antshel, K.M., Aneja, A., Strunge, L., Peebles, J. *et al.* (2007) 'Autistic spectrum disorders in velocardiofacial syndrome (22q11.2 deletion).', *Journal of Autism and Developmental Disorders, 37*: 1776–1786.

Antshel, K.M., Kates, W.R., Roizen, N., Fremont, W. and Shprintzen, RJ. (2005) '22q11.2 deletion syndrome: genetics, neuroanatomy and cognitive/behavioural features.', *Child Neuropsychology, 11*(1): 5–19.

Anttinen, A., Koulu, L., Nikoskelainen, E., Portin, R. *et al.* (2008) 'Neurological symptoms and natural course of xeroderma pigmentosum.', *Brain, 131*(8): 1979–1989.

Aoki, M., Abe, K., Kameya, T., Watanabe, M. and Itoyama, Y. (1994) 'Maternal anticipation of DRPLA.', *Human Molecular Genetics, 3*: 1197–1198.

Aoki, Y., Niihori, T., Kawame, H., Kurosawa, K. *et al.* (2005) 'Germline mutations in HRAS proto-oncogene cause Costello syndrome.', *Nature Genetics, 37*: 1038–1040.

Apert, M.E. (1906) 'De l'acrocephalosyndactylie.', *Bulletins et mémoires de la Société médicale des hôpitaux de Paris, 23*: 1310–1330.

Apter, A., Pauls, D.L., Bleich, A., Zohar, A.H. *et al.* (1992) 'A population-based epidemiological study of Tourette syndrome among adolescents in Israel.', *Advances in Neurology, 58*: 61–65.

Arakawa, M., Shiozuka, M., Nakayama, Y., Hara, T. *et al.* (2003) 'Negamycin restores dystrophin expression in skeletal and cardiac muscles of mdx mice.', *Journal of Biochemistry (Tokyo), 134*(5): 751–758.

Araneta, M.R.G., Moore, C., Olney, R.S., Edmonds, L.D. *et al.* (2002) 'Goldenhar syndrome among infants born in military hospitals to Gulf War veterans.', *Teratology, 56*(4): 244–251.

Archer, H.L., Evans, J.C., Edwards, S., Colley, J. *et al.* (2006) 'CDKL5 mutations cause infantile spasms, early onset seizures and severe mental retardation in female patients.' *Journal of Medical Genetics, 12*: 729–734.

Archer, H.L., Evans, J.C., Millar, D.S., Thompson, P.W. *et al.* (2008) '*NTNG1* Mutations are a rare cause of Rett syndrome.', *American Journal of Medical Genetics A, 140*(7): 691–694.

Ariani, F., Hayek, G., Rondinella, D., Artuso, R. *et al.* (2008) 'FOXG1 is responsible for the congenital variant of Rett syndrome.', *American Journal of Human Genetics, 83*: 89–93.

Arias, A., Corbella, M., Fons, C., Sempere, A. *et al.* (2007) 'Creatine transporter deficiency: prevalence among patients with mental retardation and pitfalls in metabolite screening.', *Clinical Biochemistry*, doi:10.1016/j.clinbiochem.2007.07.010.

Arias-Dimas, A., Vilaseca, M.A., Artuch, R., Ribes, A. and Campistol, J. (2006) ['Diagnosis and treatment of brain creatine deficiency syndromes.'] [Article in Spanish.] *Revista de Neurologia, 43*(5): 302–308.

Arinami, T., Kondo, I., Hamaguchi, H., Tamura, K. and Hirano, T. (1987) 'A fragile X female with Down syndrome.' *Human Genetics, 77*: 92–94.

Arking, D.E., Cutler, D.J., Brune, C.W., Teslovich, T.M. *et al.* (2008) 'A common genetic variant in the neurexin superfamily member CNTNAP2 increases familial risk of autism.', *American Journal of Human Genetics, 82*(1): 160–164.

Arlt, C.F. von (1881) *Klinische Darstellung der Krankheiten des Auges zunächst der Binde-, Horn- und Lederhaut, dann der Iris und des Ciliarkörpers.* Wien: Braumüller.

Armstrong, D., Dunn, J.K., Antalffy, B. and Trivedi, R. (1995) 'Selective dendritic alterations in the cortex of Rett syndrome.', *Journal of Neuropathology and Experimental Neurology, 54*: 195–201.

Arnold, G.L., Hyman, S.L., Mooney, R.A. and Kirby, R.S. (2003) 'Plasma amino acids profiles in children with autism: potential risk of nutritional deficiencies.', *Journal of Autism and Developmental Disorders, 33*(4): 449–454.

Arnulf, I., Zeitzer, J.M., File, J., Farber, N. and Mignot, E. (2005) 'Kleine-Levin syndrome: a systematic review of 186 cases in the literature.' Brain, 128(12): 2763–2776.

Arnulf, I., Zeitzer, J.M., File, J., Farber, N. and Mignot, E. (2008) 'Kleine–Levin syndrome: a systematic review of 186 cases in the literature.', *Brain, 128*: 2763–2776.

Arriola-Pereda, G., Verdú-Pérez, A. and de Castro-De Castro, P. (2009) ['Cerebral polymicrogyria and 22q11 deletion syndrome'] [Article in Spanish.] *Revista de Neurologia, 48*(4): 188–190.

Ars, E., Kruyer, H., Morell, M., Pros, E. *et al.* (2003) 'Recurrent mutations in the NF1 gene are common among neurofibromatosis type 1 patients.', *Journal of Medical Genetics, 40*: e82.

Ars, E., Serra, E., Garcia, J., Kruyer, H. *et al.* (2000) 'Mutations affecting mRNA splicing are the most common molecular defects in patients with neurofibromatosis type 1.', *Human Molecular Genetics, 9*: 237–247.

Arts, H.H., Doherty, D., van Beersum, S.E.C., Parisi, M.A. *et al.* (2007) 'Mutations in the gene encoding the basal body protein RPGRIP1L, a nephrocystin-4 interactor, cause Joubert syndrome.', *Nature Genetics, 39*: 882–888.

Arzimanoglou, A., Guerrini, R. and Aicardi, J. (2003) *Aicardi's Epilepsy in Children* (3rd edn.). Philadelphia: Lippincott, Williams and Wilkins.

Asano, E., Chugani, D.C., Muzik, O., Behen, M. *et al.* (2001) 'Autism in tuberous sclerosis complex is related to both cortical and subcortical dysfunction.', *Neurology, 57*(7): 1269–1277.

Aschrafi, A., Cunningham, B.A., Edelman, G.M. and Vanderklish, P.W. (2005) 'The fragile-X mental retardation protein and group 1 metabotropic glutamate receptors regulate levels of mRNA granules in brain.' *Proceedings of the National Academy of Science USA, 102*: 2180–2185.

Ashrafi, M.R., Shabanian, R., Abbaskhanian, A., Nasirian, A. *et al.* (2007) 'Selenium and intractable epilepsy: is there any correlation?' *Pediatric Neurology, 36*: 25–29.

Ashrafi, M.R., Shabanian, R., Mohammadi, M. and Kavusi, S. (2006) 'Extensive Mongolian spots: a clinical sign merits special attention.' *Pediatric Neurology, 34*(2): 143–145.

Ashrafi, M.R., Shams, S., Nouri, M., Mohseni, M. *et al.* (2007) 'A probable causative factor for an old problem: selenium and glutathione peroxidase appear to play important roles in epilepsy pathogenesis.', *Epilepsia*, *48*(9): 1750–1755.

Ashwood, P., Wills, S. and Van de Water, J. (2006) 'The immune response in autism: a new frontier for autism research.' *Journal of Leukocyte Biology*, *80*(1): 1–15.

Askalan, R., Mackay, M., Brian, J., Otsubo, H. *et al.* (2003) 'Prospective preliminary analysis of the development of autism and epilepsy in children with infantile spasms.', *Journal of Child Neurology*, *18*: 165–170.

Assaf, M., Jagannathan, K., Calhoun, V.D., Miller, L. *et al.* (2010) 'Abnormal functional connectivity of default mode sub-networks in autism spectrum disorder patients.', *Neuroimage*, *53*(1): 247–256.

Assumpcao, F., Santos, R.C., Rosario, M. and Mercadante, M. (1999) 'Brief report: autism and Aarskog syndrome.' *Journal of Autism and Developmental Disorders*, *29*: 179–181.

Athanasios, E. Konstantina, V., Paraskevi, K. and Nikolaos, N. (2009) 'Clinical applications of creatine supplementation on paediatrics.', *Current Pharmaceutical Biotechnology*, *10*: Sep 13. [Epub ahead of print]

Attwell, D. (2000) 'Brain uptake of glutamate: food for thought.' *Journal of Nutrition*, *130*: 1023S–1025S.

August, G.J. (1983) 'A genetic marker associated with infantile autism.', *American Journal of Psychiatry*, *140*(6): 813.

August, G.J. and Lockhart, L.H. (1984) 'Familial autism and the fragile-X chromosome.', *Journal of Autism and Developmental Disorders*, *14*(2): 197–204.

Auranen, M., Vanhala, R., Varilo, T., Ayers, K. *et al.* (2002) 'A genomewide screen for autism-spectrum disorders: evidence for a major susceptibility locus on chromosome 3q25–27.' *American Journal of Human Genetics*, *71*: 777–790.

Ausio, J., Levin, D.B., De Amorim, G.V., Bakker, S. and Macleod, P.M. (2003) 'Syndromes of disordered chromatin remodeling.' *Clinical Genetics*, *64*: 83–95.

Austin, D.W. and Shandley, K. (2008) 'An investigation of porphyrinuria in Australian children with autism.', *Journal of Toxicology and Environmental Health, Part A*, *71*: 1349–1351.

Autism Genome Project Consortium (2007) 'Mapping autism risk loci using genetic linkage and chromosomal rearrangements.', *Nature Genetics*: online, 18th Feb 2007: doi:10.1038/ng1985.

Avidor-Reiss, T., Maer, A.M., Koundakjian, E., Polyanovsky, A. *et al.* (2004) 'Decoding cilia function: defining specialized genes required for compartmentalized cilia biogenesis.', *Cell*, *117*: 527–539.

Awaya, Y., Satoh, F., Oguni, H., Miyamoto, M. *et al.* (1990) 'Study of the mechanism of seizures induced by hot bathing – ictal EEG of hot bathing induced seizures in severe myoclonic epilepsy in infancy (SMEI).', (In Japanese.) M Seino and S. Ohtahara, (Eds.) *Annual Report of the Japanese Epilepsy Research Foundation* (Osaka), *2*: 103–110.

Aylward, E.H., Habbak, R., Warren, A.C., Pulsifer, M.B. *et al.* (1997) 'Cerebellar volume in adults with Down syndrome.', *Archives of Neurology*, *54*: 209–212.

Aymé, S. (2000) 'Bridging the gap between molecular genetics and metabolic medicine: access to genetic information.', *European Journal of Pediatrics*, *159* (Supp.3): S183–S185.

Azurdia, R.M., Anstey, A.V. and Rhodes, L.E. (2001) 'Cholesterol supplementation objectively reduces photosensitivity in the Smith-Lemli-Opitz syndrome.', *British Journal of Dermatology*, *144*: 143–145.

Azzam, A., Lerner, D.M., Peters, K.F., Wiggs, E. *et al.* (2005) 'Psychiatric and neuropsychological characterization of Pallister-Hall syndrome.', *Clinical Genetics*, *67*(1): 87–92.

Baala, L., Romano, S., Khaddour, R., Saunier, S. *et al.* (2007) 'The Meckel–Gruber syndrome gene, MKS3, is mutated in Joubert syndrome.', *American Journal of Human Genetics*, *80*: 186–194.

Babovic-Vuksanovic, D., Ballman, K., Michels, V., McGrann, P. *et al.* (2006) 'Phase II trial of pirfenidone in adults with neurofibromatosis type 1.', *Neurology*, *67*: 1860–1862.

Bachner-Melman, R., Dina, C., Zohar, A.H., Constantini, N. *et al.* (2005) 'AVPR1a and SLC6A4 gene polymorphisms are associated with creative dance performance.' *PLoS Genetics*, *1*: e42.

Bachoo, S. and Gibbons, RJ. (1999) 'Germline and gonosomal mosaicism in the ATR-X syndrome.', *European Journal of Human Genetics*, *7*: 933–936.

Backes, M., Genc, B., Schreck, J., Doerfler, W. *et al.* (2000) 'Cognitive and behavioural profile of fragile-X boys: correlations to molecular data.' *American Journal of Medical Genetics*, *95*: 150–156.

Bäckman, B., Grevér-Sjölander, A.C., Bengtsson, K., Persson, J. and Johansson, I. (2007) 'Children with Down syndrome: oral development and morphology after use of palatal plates between 6 and 48 months of age.', *International Journal of Paediatric Dentistry*, *17*(1): 19–28.

Backman, E. and Henriksson, K.G. (1995) 'Low-dose prednisolone treatment in Duchenne and Becker muscular dystrophy.', *Neuromuscular Disorders*, *5*: 233–241.

Badano, J.L., Mitsuma, N., Beales, P.L. and Katsanis, N. (2006) 'The ciliopathies: an emerging class of human genetic disorders.', *Annual Reviews of Genomics and Human Genetics*, *7*: 125–148.

Badcock, C. and Crespi, B. (2006) 'Imbalanced genomic imprinting in brain development: an evolutionary basis for the aetiology of autism.' *Journal of Evolutionary Biology*, *19*(4): 1007–1032.

Badhwar, A., Andermann, F., Valerio, R.M. and Andermann, E. (2000) 'Founder effect in Joubert syndrome.', *Annals of Neurology*, *48*: 435–436.

Baer, D., Wolf, M., and Risley, R. (1968) 'Some current dimensions of applied behavior analysis.' *Journal of Applied Behavior Analysis*, *1*(1): 91–97.

Baghdadi, A., Picot, M.C., Pascal, C., Pry, R. and Aussilloux, C. (2003) 'Relationship between age of recognition of first disturbances and severity in young children with autism.' *European Journal of Child and Adolescent Psychiatry*, *12*: 122–127.

Bagni, C. and Greenough, W.T. (2005) 'From mRNP trafficking to spine dysmorphogenesis: the roots of fragile-X syndrome.', *Nature Reviews Neuroscience*, *6*(5): 376–387.

BaHammam, A.S., GadEl Rab, M., Owais, S.M., Alswat, K. and Hamam, K.D. (2007) 'Clinical characteristics and HLA typing of a family with Kleine-Levin syndrome.', *Sleep Medicine, 9*(5): 575–578.

Bahi-Buisson, N., Kaminska, A., Boddaert, N., Rio, M. *et al.* (2008a) 'The three stages of epilepsy in patients with *CDKL5* mutations.', *Epilepsia, 49*(6): 1027–1037.

Bahi-Buisson, N., Nectoux, J., Rosas-Vargas, H.E., Milh, M. *et al.* (2008b) 'Key clinical features to identify girls with CDKL5 mutations.', *Brain, 131*: 2647–2661.

Bahn, S., Mimmack, M., Ryan, M., Caldwell, M.A. *et al.* (2002) 'Neuronal target genes of the neuron-restrictive silencer factor in neurospheres derived from fetuses with Down's syndrome: a gene expression study.', *Lancet, 359*: 310–315.

Baieli, S., Pavone, L., Meli, C., Fiumara, A. and Coleman, M. (2003) 'Autism and phenylketonuria.' *Journal of Autism and Developmental Disorders, 33*: 201–204.

Bailey, L.B. and Gregory, J.F. 3rd (1999) 'Polymorphisms of methylenetetrahydrofolate reductase and other enzymes: metabolic significance, risks and impact on folate requirement.', *Journal of Nutrition, 129*: 919–922.

Bain, J., Plater, L., Elliott, M., Shpiro, N. *et al.* (2007) 'The selectivity of protein kinase inhibitors: a further update.', The *Biochemical Journal, 408*(3): 297–315.

Bakalov, V.K., Shawker, T., Ceniceros, I. and Bondy, C.A. (2007) 'Uterine development in Turner syndrome.', *Journal of Pediatrics, 151*(5): 528–531.

Bakare, M.O. and Ikegwuonu, N.N. (2008) 'Childhood autism in a 13 year old boy with oculocutaneous albinism: a case report.', *Journal of Medical Case Reports, 2*: 56, doi:10.1186/1752-1947-2-56.

Baker, K.D. and Skuse, D.H. (2005) 'Adolescents and young adults with 22q11 deletion syndrome: psychopathology in an at-risk group.', *British Journal of Psychiatry, 186*: 115–120.

Baker, P., Piven, J. and Sato, Y. (1998) 'Autism and tuberous sclerosis complex: prevalence and clinical features.', *Journal of Autism and Developmental Disorders, 28*(4): 279–285.

Baker, P., Piven, J., Schwartz, S. and Patil, S. (1994) 'Duplication of chromosome 15q11–13 in two individuals with autistic disorder.' *Journal of Autism and Developmental Disorders, 24*: 529–535.

Bakkaloglu, B., O'Roak, B.J., Louvi, A., Gupta, A.R. *et al.* (2008) 'Molecular cytogenetic analysis and resequencing of contactin associated protein-like 2 in autism spectrum disorders.', *American Journal of Human Genetics, 82*: 165–173.

Balci, S., Engiz, O., Yilmaz, Z. and Baltaci, V. (2006) 'Partial trisomy (11;22) syndrome with manifestations of Goldenhar sequence due to maternal balanced t(11;22).', *Genetic Counselling, 17*(3): 281–289.

Baldini, A. (2002) 'DiGeorge syndrome: the use of model organisms to dissect complex genetics.', *Human Molecular Genetics, 11*(20): 2363–2369.

Bale, S.J., Amos, C.I., Parry, D.M. and Bale, A.E. (1991) 'Relationship between head circumference and height in normal adults and in the nevoid basal cell carcinoma syndrome and neurofibromatosis type I.', *American Journal of Medical Genetics, 40*(2): 206–210.

Ballabio, A., Parenti, G., Tippett, P., Mondello, C. *et al.* (1986) 'X-linked ichthyosis, due to steroid sulphatase deficiency, associated with Kallmann syndrome (hypogonadotropic hypogonadism and anosmia): linkage relationships with Xg and cloned DNA sequences from the distal short arm of the X chromosome.', *Human Genetics, 72*: 237–240.

Ballabio, A., Sebastio, G., Carrozzo, R., Parenti, G. *et al.* (1987) 'Deletions of the steroid sulphatase gene in "classical" X-linked ichthyosis and in X-linked ichthyosis associated with Kallmann syndrome.', *Human Genetics, 77*: 338–341.

Bamshad, M. and Guthery, S.L. (2007) 'Race, genetics and medicine: does the color of a leopard's spots matter?' *Current Opinion in Pediatrics, 19*: 613–618.

Bandim, J.M., Ventura, L.O., Miller, M.T., Almeida, H.C. and Costa, A.E.S. (2003) 'Autism and Mobius sequence: an exploratory study of children in northeastern Brazil.', *Arquivos de Neuro-psiquiatria, 61*(2–A): 181–185.

Barabas, G. and Matthews, W.S. (1983) 'Coincident infantile autism and Tourette syndrome: a case study.', *Journal of Developmental and Behavioural Pediatrics, 4*: 280–282.

Baraitser, M. (1977) 'Genetics of Möbius syndrome.', *Journal of Medical Genetics, 14*(6): 415–417.

Baraitser, M. (1982) 'Heterogeneity and pleiotropism in the Moebius syndrome.', (Letter), *Clinical Genetics, 21*: 290.

Baraitser, M., Patton, M., Lam, S.T.S., Brett, E.M. and Wilson, J. (1987) 'The Angelman (happy puppet) syndrome: is it autosomal recessive?' *Clinical Genetics, 31*: 323–330.

Baranek, G.T., Danko, C.D., Skinner, M.L., Bailey, D.B. Jr. *et al.* (2005) 'Video analysis of sensory-motor features in infants with fragile-X syndrome at 9–12 months of age.', *Journal of Autism and Developmental Disorders, 35*(5): 645–656.

Barbosa-Gonçalves, A., Vendrame-Goloni, C.B., Martins, A.L. and Fett-Conte, A.C. (2008) 'Subtelomeric region of chromosome 2 in patients with autism spectrum disorders.', *Genetics and Molecular Research, 7*(2): 527–533.

Barbot, C., Fineza, I., Diogo, L., Maia, M. *et al.* (1997) 'L-2-hydroxyglutaric aciduria: clinical, biochemical and magnetic resonance imaging in six Portuguese pediatric patients.', *Brain and Development, 19*: 268–273.

Barcelo-Coblijn, G., Murphy, E.J., Mills, K., Winchester, B. *et al.* (2007) 'Lipid abnormalities in succinate semialdehyde dehydrogenase (Aldh5a1 −/−) deficient mouse brain provide additional evidence for myelin alterations.', *Biochimica et Biophysica Acta, 1772*(5): 556–562.

Bardet, G. (1920) 'Sur un Syndrome d'Obedite Congenitale avec Polydactylie at Retinite Pigmentaire (Contribution a l'etude des lormes clinique de l'Obesite typophysaire).', (Thesis – Paris.)

Barisic, I., Tokic, V., Loane, M., Bianchi, F. *et al.* (2008) 'Descriptive epidemiology of Cornelia de Lange syndrome in Europe.', *American Journal of Medical Genetics A, 146A*(1): 51–59.

Barkovich, A.J., Hevner, R. and Guerrini, R. (1999) 'Syndromes of bilateral symmetrical polymicrogyria.' *American Journal of Neuroradiology, 20*: 1814–1821.

Barkovich, A.J., Kuzniecky, R.I., Jackson, G.D., Guerrini, R. and Dobyns, W.B. (2001) 'Classification system for malformations of cortical development: update.', *Neurology, 57*: 2168–2178.

Barnea-Goraly, N., Menon, V., Krasnow, B., Ko, A. *et al.* (2003) 'Investigation of white matter structure in velocardiofacial syndrome: a diffusion tensor imaging study.', *American Journal of Psychiatry, 160*(10): 1863–1869.

Barnett, S., Reilly, S., Carr, L., Ojo, I. *et al.* (2002) 'Behavioural phenotype of Bardet-Biedl syndrome.', *Journal of Medical Genetics, 39*: e76, www.jmedgenet. com/cgi/content/full/39/12/e76.

Barnevik-Olsson, M., Gillberg, C. and Fernell, E. (2008) 'Prevalence of autism in children born to Somali parents living in Sweden: a brief report.', *Developmental Medicine and Child Neurology, 50*(8): 598–601.

Baron-Cohen, S. (2002) 'The extreme male brain theory of autism.', *Trends in Cognitive Science, 6*: 248–254.

Baron-Cohen, S., Mortimore, C., Moriarty, J., Izaguirre, J. and Robertson, M. (1999a) 'The prevalence of Gilles de la Tourette's syndrome in children and adolescents with autism.', *Journal of Child Psychology and Psychiatry, 40*: 213–218.

Baron-Cohen, S., Ring, H.A., Bullmore, E.T., Wheelwright, S. *et al.* (2000a) 'The amygdala theory of autism.', *Neuroscience and Biobehavioural Reviews, 24*: 355–364.

Baron-Cohen, S., Scahill, V.L., Izaguirre, J., Hornsey, H. and Robertson, M.M. (1999b) 'The prevalence of Gilles de la Tourette syndrome in children and adolescents with autism: a large scale study.', *Psychological Medicine, 29*(5): 1151–1159.

Baron-Cohen, S., Wheelwright, S., Cox, A., Baird, G. *et al.* (2000b) 'Early identification of autism by the Checklist for Autism in Toddlers (CHAT).' *Journal of the Royal Society of Medicine, 93*(10): 521–525.

Barone, R., Pavone, L., Fiumara, A., Bianchini, R. and Jaeken, J. (1999) 'Developmental patterns and neuropsychological assessment in patients with carbohydrate-deficient glycoconjugate syndrome type 1A (phosphomannomutase deficiency).', *Brain and Development, 21*: 260–263.

Barone, R., Sturiale, L., Sofia, V., Ignoto, A. *et al.* (2008) 'Clinical phenotype correlates to glycoprotein phenotype in a sib pair with CDG-Ia.' *American Journal of Medical Genetics A, 146A*(16): 2103–2108.

Barrett, S., Beck, J.C., Bernier, R., Bisson, E. *et al.* (1999) 'An autosomal genomic screen for autism: collaborative linkage study of autism.' *American Journal of Medical Genetics, 88*: 609–615.

Barth, P.G. (1993) 'Pontocerebellar hypoplasias: an overview of a group of inherited neurodegenerative disorders with foetal onset.', *Brain and Development, 15*: 411–422.

Barth, P.G., Hoffmann, G.F., Jaeken, J., Lehnert, W. *et al.* (1992) 'L-2-hydroxyglutaric acidemia: a novel inherited neurometabolic disease.', *Annals of Neurology, 32*(1): 66–71.

Barton, B. and North, K. (2004) 'Social skills of children with neurofibromatosis type 1.', *Developmental Medicine and Child Neurology, 46*: 553–563.

Barton, E., Zadel, M., Welch, E., Rotta, C. *et al.* (2005) 'PTC124 nonsense mutation suppression therapy of Duchenne muscular dystrophy (DMD).', *Neurology, 54*(Suppl 1): A176.

Barton-Davis, E.R., Cordier, L., Shoturma, D.I., Leland, S.E. *et al.* (1999) 'Aminoglycoside antibiotics restore dystrophin function to skeletal muscles of mdx mice.', *Journal of Clinical Investigation, 104*(4): 375–381.

Bartsch, O., Nemecková, M., Kocárek, E., Wagner, A. *et al.* (2003) 'DiGeorge/velocardiofacial syndrome: FISH studies of chromosomes 22q11 and 10p14, and clinical reports on the proximal 22q11 deletion.', *American Journal of Medical Genetics A, 117A*(1): 1–5.

Barzilai, A., Biton, S. and Shiloh, Y. (2008) 'The role of the DNA damage response in neuronal development, organization and maintenance.', *DNA Repair, 7*: 1010–1027.

Baselga, E. (2004) 'Sturge-Weber syndrome.' *Seminars in Cutaneous Medicine and Surgery, 23*(2): 87–98.

Basile, E., Villa, L., Selicorni, A. and Molteni, M. (2007) 'The behavioural phenotype of Cornelia de Lange syndrome: a study of 56 individuals.', *Journal of Intellectual Disability Research, 51*(9): 671–681.

Baskin, E., Kayiran, S.M., Oto, S., Alehan, F. *et al.* (2002) 'Cerebellar vermis hypoplasia in a patient with Bardet-Biedl syndrome.', *Journal of Child Neurology, 17*: 385–387.

Bassett, A.S., Chow, E.W., Husted, J., Weksberg, R. *et al.* (2005) 'Clinical features of 78 adults with 22q11 deletion syndrome.', *American Journal of Medical Genetics A, 138*: 307–313.

Bassett, A.S., Marshall, C.R., Lionel, A.C., Chow, E.W. *et al.* (2008) 'Copy number variations and risk for schizophrenia in 22q11.2 deletion syndrome.', *Human Molecular Genetics, 17*(24): 4045–4053.

Batra, P., Kharbanda, O.P., Duggal, R., Reddy, P. and Parkash, H. (2003) 'Orthodontic treatment of a case of Aarskog syndrome.' *Journal of Clinical Pediatric Dentistry, 27*(3): 229–233.

Battaglia, A. and Carey, J.C. (2006) 'Etiologic yield of autistic spectrum disorders: a prospective study.', *American Journal of Medical Genetics Part C – Seminars in Medical Genetics, 142C*(1): 3–7.

Battaglia, A. and Gurrieri, F. (1999) 'Case of apparent Gurrieri syndrome showing molecular findings of Angelman syndrome.', (Letter) *American Journal of Medical Genetics, 82*: 100.

Battaglia, A., Orsitto, E. and Gibilisco, G. (1996) 'Mental retardation, epilepsy, short stature, and skeletal dysplasia: confirmation of the Gurrieri syndrome.' *American Journal of Medical Genetics, 62*: 230–232.

Battaile, K.P., Battaile, B.C., Merkens, L.S., Maslen, C.L. and Steiner, R.D. (2001) 'Carrier frequency of the common mutation IVS8–1G>C in DHCR7 and estimate of the expected incidence of Smith-Lemli-Opitz syndrome.', *Molecular Genetics and Metabolism, 72*(1): 67–71.

Battey, J., Wada, E. and Wray, S. (1994) 'Bombesin receptor gene expression during mammalian development.' *Annals of the New York Academy of Science, 739*: 244–252.

Battini, R., Alessandrì, M.G., Leuzzi, V., Moro, F. et al. (2006) 'Arginine:glycine amidinotransferase (AGAT) deficiency in a newborn: early treatment can prevent phenotypic expression of the disease.', Journal of Pediatrics, 148(6): 828–830.

Baujat, B., Krastinova-Lolov, D., Blumen, M., Baglin, A.C. et al. (2006) 'Radiofrequency in the treatment of craniofacial plexiform neurofibromatosis: a pilot study.', Plastic and Reconstructive Surgery, 117: 1261–1268.

Baujat, G. and Cormier-Daire, V. (2007) 'Sotos syndrome.', Orphanet Journal of Rare Diseases, 2: 36 doi:10.1186/1750-1172-2-36.

Baujat, G., Rio, M., Rossignol, S., Sanlaville, D. et al. (2004) 'Paradoxical NSD1 mutations in Beckwith-Wiedemann syndrome and 11p15 anomalies in Sotos syndrome.' American Journal of Human Genetics, 74: 715–720.

Baujat, G., Rio, M., Rossignol, S., Sanlaville, D. et al. (2005) 'Clinical and molecular overlap in overgrowth syndromes.', American Journal of Medical Genetics C, 137C(1): 4–11.

Bauman, M. (Ed.) (2005) The Neurology of Autism. Oxford: Oxford University Press

Baumgartner, S., Littleton, J.T., Broadie, K., Bhat, M.A. et al. (1996) 'A drosophila neurexin is required for septate junction and blood-nerve barrier formation and function.', Cell, 87(6): 1059–1068.

Bay, C., Mauk, J., Radcliffe, J. and Kaplan, P. (1993) 'Mild Brachmann-de Lange syndrome: delineation of the clinical phenotype, and characteristic behaviours in a six-year-old boy.', American Journal of Medical Genetics, 47: 965–968.

Bayes, M., Magano, L.F., Rivera, N., Flores, R. and Perez Jurado, L.A. (2003) 'Mutational mechanisms of Williams-Beuren syndrome deletions.', American Journal of Human Genetics, 73: 131–151.

Beales, P.L. (2005) 'Lifting the lid on Pandora's box: the Bardet-Biedl syndrome.' Current Opinion in Genetics and Development, 15: 315–323.

Beales, P.L., Elcioglu, N., Woolf, A.S., Parker, D. and Flinter, F.A. (1999) 'New criteria for improved diagnosis of Bardet-Biedl syndrome: results of a population survey.' Journal of Medical Genetics, 36: 437–446.

Beales, P.L., Katsanis, N., Lewis, R.A., Ansley, S.J. et al. (2001) 'Genetic and mutational analyses of a large multiethnic Bardet-Biedl cohort reveal a minor involvement of BBS6 and delineate the critical intervals of other loci.' American Journal of Human Genetics, 68: 606–616.

Bear, M.F. (2005) 'Therapeutic implications of the mGluR theory of fragile-X mental retardation.' Genes, Brain and Behaviour, 4(6): 393–398.

Bear, M.F., Huber, K.M. and Warren, S.T. (2004) 'The mGluR theory of fragile-X mental retardation.' Trends in the Neurosciences, 27: 370–377.

Bearden, C.E. and Freimer, N.B. (2006) 'Endophenotypes for psychiatric disorders: Ready for primetime?' Trends in Genetics, 22(6): 306–313.

Bearden, C.E., Jawad, A.F., Lynch, D.R., Sokol, S. et al. (2004) 'Effects of a functional COMT polymorphism on prefrontal cognitive function in patients with 22q11.2 deletion syndrome.', American Journal of Psychiatry, 161(9) 1700–1702.

Bearden, C.E., Reus, V.I. and Freimer, N.B. (2004) 'Why genetic investigation of psychiatric disorders is so difficult.', Current Opinion in Genetics and Development, 14(3): 280–286.

Bearden, C.E., van Erp, T.G., Monterosso, J.R., Simon, T.J. et al. (2004) 'Regional brain abnormalities in 22q11.2 deletion syndrome: association with cognitive abilities and behavioural symptoms.', Neurocase, 10: 198–206.

Becerra-Solano, L.E., Díaz-Rodriguez, M., Nastasi-Catanese, J.A., Toscano-Flores, J.J. et al. (2008) 'The fifth female patient with Myhre syndrome: further delineation.', Clinical Dysmorphology, 17: 113–117.

Beemer, F.A., Veenema, H. and de Pater, J.M. (1986) 'Cerebral gigantism (Sotos syndrome) in two patients with FRA(X) chromosomes.', American Journal of Medical Genetics, 23(1–2): 221–226.

Beenakker, E.A., Fock, J.M., Van Tol, M.J., Maurits, N.M. et al. (2005) 'Intermittent prednisone therapy in Duchenne muscular dystrophy: a randomized controlled trial.', Archives of Neurology, 62: 128–132.

Beggs, A.H. (1997) 'Dystrophinopathy, the expanding phenotype: dystrophin abnormalities in X-linked dilated cardiomyopathy.', [Editorial; comment.] Circulation, 95: 2344–2347.

Behmel, A., Plochl, E. and Rosenkranz, W. (1984) 'A new X-linked dysplasia gigantism syndrome: identical with the Simpson dysplasia syndrome?' Human Genetics, 67: 409–413.

Beighton, P. (1969) 'Cardiac abnormalities in the Ehlers-Danlos syndrome.', British Heart Journal, 31(2): 227–232.

Beighton, P., De Paepe, A., Steinmann, B., Tsipouras, P. and Wenstrup, R.J. (1998) 'Ehlers-Danlos syndromes: revised nosology, Villefranche, 1997. Ehlers-Danlos National Foundation (USA) and Ehlers-Danlos Support Group (UK).', American Journal of Medical Genetics, 77: 31–37.

Bell, J.G., MacKinlay, E.E., Dick, J.R., MacDonald, D.J. et al. (2004) 'Essential fatty acids and phospholipase A2 in autistic spectrum disorders. Prostaglandins Leukotrienes and Essential Fatty Acids, 71: 201–204.

Bell, J.G., Miller, D., Macdonald, D.J., MacKinlay, E.E. et al. (2009) 'The fatty acid compositions of erythrocyte and plasma polar lipids in children with autism, developmental delay or typically developing controls and the effect of fish oil intake.', British Journal of Nutrition, 9: 1–8.

Bell, J.G., Sargent, J.R., Tocher, D.R. and Dick, J.R. (2000) 'Red blood cell fatty acid compositions in a patient with autistic spectrum disorder: a characteristic abnormality in neurodevelopmental disorders?' Prostaglandins Leukotrienes and Essential Fatty Acids, 63: 21–25.

Belmonte, M.K. and Bourgeron, T. (2006) 'Fragile-X syndrome and autism at the intersection of genetic and neural networks.' Nature Neuroscience, 9(10): 1221–1225.

Benaron, L.D. (2003) 'Inclusion to the point of dilution.' (Commentary) Journal of Autism and Developmental Disorders, 33(3): 355–359.

Benasayag, S., Rittler, M., Nieto, F., Torres de Aguirre, N. et al. (2001) '47,XYY karyotype and normal SRY in a patient with a female phenotype.', Journal of Pediatric Endocrinology and Metabolism, 14: 797–801.

Benayoun, B., Baghdiguian, S., Lajmanovich, A., Bartoli, M. *et al.* (2008) 'NF-κB-dependent expression of the antiapoptotic factor c-FLIP is regulated by calpain 3, the protein involved in limb-girdle muscular dystrophy type 2A.', *The FASEB Journal, 22*: 1521–1529.

Bender, B., Fry, E., Pennington, B., Puck, M. *et al.* (1983) 'Speech and language development in 41 children with sex chromosome anomalies.', *Pediatrics, 71*(2): 262–267.

Benga, I. (2006) 'Priorities in the discovery of the implications of water channels in epilepsy and Duchenne muscular dystrophy.' *Cellular and Molecular Biology (Noisy-le-grand), 52*(7): 46–50.

Benkerrou, M., Le Deist, F., de Villartay, J.P., Caillat-Zucman, S. *et al.* (1997) 'Correction of Fas (CD95) deficiency by haploidentical bone marrow transplantation.', *European Journal of Immunology, 27*: 2043–2047.

Bennett, C.L., Meuleman, J., Glass, I.A. and Chance, P.F. (2003) 'Clinical and genetic aspects of the Joubert syndrome: a disorder characterized by cerebellar vermian hypoplasia and accompanying brainstem malformations.', *Current Genomics, 4*: 123–129.

Bennett, R.R., den Dunnen, J., O'Brien, K.F., Darras, B.T. and Kunkel, L.M. (2001) 'Detection of mutations in the dystrophin gene via automated DHPLC screening and direct sequencing.', *BMC Genetics, 2*: 17.

Ben-Shachar, S., Ou, Z., Shaw, C.A., Belmont, J.W. *et al.* (2008) '22q11.2 distal deletion: a recurrent genomic disorder distinct from DiGeorge syndrome and velocardiofacial syndrome.', *American Journal of Human Genetics, 82*: 214–221.

Beresford, R.G., Tatlidil, C., Riddell, D.C., Welch, J.P., *et al.* (2000) 'Absence of fragile-X syndrome in Nova Scotia.' *Journal of Medical Genetics, 37*, 77–79.

Berg, J.M. and Pakula, Z. (1972) 'Angelman's ("happy puppet") syndrome.' *American Journal of Diseases of Childhood, 123*: 72–77.

Berg, J.S., Brunetti-Pierri, N., Peters, S.U., Kang, S.H. *et al.* (2007) 'Speech delay and autism spectrum behaviours are frequently associated with duplication of the 7q11.23 Williams-Beuren syndrome region.', *Genetics in Medicine, 9*(7): 427–441.

Berger, R., Stoker-de Vries, S.A., Wadman, S.K., Duran, M. *et al.* (1984) 'Dihydropyrimidine dehydrogenase deficiency leading to thymine-uraciluria: an inborn error of pyrimidine metabolism.', *Clinica Chimica Acta, 141*(2–3): 227–234.

Bergink, V., van Megen, H.J.G.M. and Westenberg, H.G.M. (2004) 'Glutamate and anxiety.', *European Neuropsychopharmacology, 14*: 175–183.

Bergman, J.E.H., Blake, K.D., Bakker, M.K., du Marchie Sarvaas, G.J., Freed, R.H., and van Ravenswaaij-Arts, C.M.A. (2010) 'Death in CHARGE syndrome after the neonatal period.', *Clinical Genetics, 77*: 232–240.

Bergman, J.E., Bosman, E.A., van Ravenswaaij-Arts, C.M. and Steel, K.P. (2010) 'Study of smell and reproductive organs in a mouse model for CHARGE syndrome.', *European Journal of Human Genetics, 18*(2): 171–177.

Bergmann, C., Zerres, K., Senderek, J., Rudnik-Schoneborn, S. *et al.* (2003) 'Oligophrenin 1 (OPHN1) gene mutation causes syndromic X-linked mental retardation with epilepsy, rostral ventricular enlargement and cerebellar hypoplasia.', *Brain, 126*: 1537–1544.

Bergmann, E. and Egly, J-M. (2001) 'Trichothiodystrophy, a transcription syndrome.', *Trends in Genetics, 17*(5): 279–286.

Berilgen, M.S., Mungen, B., Ustundag, B. and Demira, C. (2006) 'Serum ghrelin levels are enhanced in patients with epilepsy.' *Seizure, 15*: 106–111.

Berquin, I.M., Min, Y., Wu, R., Wu, J. *et al.* (2007) 'Modulation of prostate cancer genetic risk by omega-3 and omega-6 fatty acids.', *Journal of Clinical Investigation, 117*(7): 1866–1875.

Berridge, K.C., Aldridge, J.W., Houchard, K.R. and Zhuang, X. (2005) 'Sequential super-stereotypy of an instinctive fixed action pattern in hyper-dopaminergic mutant mice: a model of obsessive compulsive disorder and Tourette's.', *BMC Biology, 3*: 4, doi:10.1186/1741-7007-3-4

Berry-Kravis, E. (2008) 'Fragile-X research: a status report.', *The National Fragile-X Foundation Quarterly, 31*: 12–16.

Berry-Kravis, E., Abrams, L., Coffey, S.M., Hall, D.A. *et al.* (2007) 'Fragile-X-associated tremor/ataxia syndrome: clinical features, genetics, and testing guidelines.', *Movement Disorders, 22*(14): 2018–2030.

Berry-Kravis, E. and Potanos, K. (2004) 'Psychopharmacology in fragile-X syndrome – present and future.' *Mental Retardation and Developmental Disabilities Research Reviews, 10*: 42–48.

Berry-Kravis, E., Potanos, K., Weinberg, D., Zhou, L. and Goetz, C.G. (2005) 'Fragile-X-associated tremor/ataxia syndrome in sisters related to X-inactivation.' *Annals of Neurology, 57*: 144–147.

Berry-Kravis, E., Sumis, A., Hervey, C., Nelson, M. *et al.* (2008) 'Open-label treatment trial of lithium to target the underlying defect in fragile-X syndrome.', *Journal of Developmental and Behavioural Pediatrics, 29*: 293–302.

Berthier, M.L., Santamaria, J., Encabo, H. and Tolosa, E.S. (1992) 'Recurrent hypersomnia in two adolescent males with Asperger's syndrome.' *Journal of the American Academy of Child and Adolescent Psychiatry, 31*: 735–738.

Bertola, D.R., Pereira, A.C., Passetti, F., de Oliveira, P.S. *et al.* (2005) 'Neurofibromatosis–Noonan syndrome: molecular evidence of the concurrence of both disorders in a patient.', *American Journal of Medical Genetics A, 136*: 242–245.

Bertrand, J., Mars, A., Boyle, C., Bove, F. *et al.* (2001) 'Prevalence of autism in a United States population: the Brick Township, New Jersey, investigation.', *Pediatrics, 108*(5): 1155–1161.

Betancur, C., Leboyer, M. and Gillberg, C. (2002) 'Increased rate of twins among affected sibling pairs with autism.', *American Journal of Human Genetics, 70*: 1381–1383.

Bettelheim, B. (1955) *Truants From Life: The Rehabilitation of Emotionally Disturbed Children.* Glencoe: IL Free Press.

Bettelheim, B. (1967) *The Empty Fortress: Infantile Autism and the Birth of the Self.* New York: Free Press

Betz, R., Rensing, C., Otto, E., Mincheva, A. *et al.* (2000) 'Children with ocular motor apraxia type Cogan carry deletions in the gene (NPHP1) for juvenile nephronophthisis.', *Journal of Pediatrics, 136*: 828–831.

Beunders, G., van de Kamp, J.M., Veenhoven, R.H., van Hagen, J.M. *et al.* (2009) 'A triplication of the Williams-Beuren syndrome region in a patient with mental retardation, a severe expressive language delay, behavioural problems and dysmorphisms.', *Journal of Medical Genetics, JMG Online,* doi:10.1136/ jmg.2009.070490.

Beuren, A.J. (1972) 'Supravalvular aortic stenosis: a complex syndrome with and without mental retardation.' *Birth Defects Original Articles Series,* VIII, *5*: 45–56.

Beuten, J., Hennekam, R.C.M., Van Roy, B., Mangelschots, K. *et al.* (1996) 'Angelman syndrome in an inbred family.' *Human Genetics, 97*: 294–298.

Bhat, R., Xue, Y., Berg, S., Hellberg, S. *et al.* (2003) 'Structural insights and biological effects of glycogen synthase kinase 3-specific inhibitor AR-A014418.', *Journal of Biological Chemistry, 278*(46): 45937–45945.

Bhuiyan, Z., Klein, M., Hammond, P., Mannens, M.M., Van Haeringen, A. *et al.* (2006) 'Genotype-phenotype correlations of 39 patients with Cornelia de Lange syndrome: the Dutch experience.' *Journal of Medical Genetics, 43*: 237–250.

Bi, W., Park, S-S., Shaw, C.J., Withers, M.A. *et al.* (2003) 'Reciprocal crossovers and a positional preference for strand exchange in recombination events resulting in deletion or duplication of chromosome 17p11.2.' *American Journal of Human Genetics, 73*: 1302–1315.

Bi, W., Yan, J., Stankiewicz, P., Park, S-S. *et al.* (2002) 'Genes in a refined Smith-Magenis syndrome critical deletion interval on chromosome 17p11.2 and the syntenic region of the mouse.', *Genome Research, 12*: 713–728.

Bialer, M.G., Penchaszadeh, V.B., Kahn, E., Libes, R. *et al.* (1987) 'Female external genitalia and mullerian duct derivatives in a 46,XY infant with the Smith-Lemli-Opitz syndrome.', *American Journal of Medical Genetics, 28*: 723–731.

Bianchi, M.C., Tosetti, M., Fornai, F., Alessandri, M.G. *et al.* (2000) 'Reversible brain creatine deficiency in two sisters with normal blood creatine level.', *Annals of Neurology, 47*(4): 511–513.

Bickel, H. (1996) 'The first treatment of phenylketonuria.' *European Journal of Pediatrics, 155* (suppl. 1): 2–3.

Bickel, H., Gerrard, J. and Hickmans, E.M. (1953) 'Influence of phenylalanine intake on phenylketonuria.', *Lancet 262*(6790): 812–813.

Bickel, H., Gerrard, J. and Hickmans, E. M. (1954) 'The influence of phenylalanine intake on the chemistry and behaviour of a phenylketonuric child.', *Acta Paediatrica, 43*: 64–77.

Biedl, A. (1922) 'Ein Geschwisterpaar mit adipose-genitaler dystrophie.', *Deutsch Medizin Wochenschrift, 48*: 1630.

Bienvenu, T., Poirier, K., Friocourt, G., Bahi, N. *et al.* (2002) 'ARX, a novel Prd-class-homeobox gene highly expressed in the telencephalon, is mutated in X-linked mental retardation.', *Human Molecular Genetics, 11*(8): 981–991.

Biesecker, L.G., Laxova, R. and Friedman, A. (1987) 'Renal insufficiency in Williams syndrome.', *American Journal of Medical Genetics, 28*: 131–135.

Biesecker, L.G., Peters, K.F., Darling, T.N., Choyke, P. *et al.* (1998) 'Clinical differentiation between Proteus syndrome and hemihyperplasia: description of a distinct form of hemihyperplasia.' *American Journal of Medical Genetics, 79*: 311–318.

Biggar, W.D., Politano, L., Harris, V.A., Passamano, L. *et al.* (2004) 'Deflazacort in Duchenne muscular dystrophy: a comparison of two different protocols.', *Neuromuscular Disorders, 14*: 476–482.

Biliya, S. and Bulla, L.A. Jr. (2010) 'Genomic imprinting: the influence of differential methylation in the two sexes.' *Experimental Biology and Medicine, 235*: 139–147.

Bilora, F., Petrobelli, F., Boccioletti, V. and Pomerri, F. (2000) 'Moderate-dose intravenous immunoglobulin treatment of Job's syndrome: case report.', *Minerva Medica, 91*: 113–116.

Bingham, P.M., Zimmerman, R.A., McDonald-McGinn, D., Driscoll, D. *et al.* (1997) 'Enlarged sylvian fissures in infants with interstitial deletion of chromosome 22q11.', *American Journal of Medical Genetics, 74*: 538–543.

Bird A. (2007) 'Perceptions of epigenetics.', *Nature Insight, 447*(7143): 396–398.

Bird, T.D. (2007) (update) 'Myotonic dystrophy type 1 (Steinert's Disease).', *GENEReviews*:

Bisgrove, B.W. and Yost, H.J. (2006) 'The roles of cilia in developmental disorders and disease.', *Development, 133*(21): 4131–4143.

Bish, J.P., Nguyen, V., Ding, L., Ferrante, S. and Simon, T.J. (2004) 'Thalamic reductions in children with chromosome 22q11.2 deletion syndrome.', *Neuroreport, 15*: 1413–1415.

Bishop, L., Kanoff, R., Charnas, L., Krenzel, C., Berry, S.A. and Schimmenti, L.A. (2008) 'Severe methylenetetrahydrofolate reductase (MTHFR) deficiency: a case report of nonclassical homocystinuria.', *Journal of Child Neurology, 23*: 823–828.

Bissler, J.J., McCormack, F.X., Young, L.R., Elwing, J.M. *et al.* (2008) 'Sirolimus for angiomyolipoma in tuberous sclerosis complex or lymphangioleiomyomatosis.', *New England Journal of Medicine, 358*(2): 140–151.

Bittigau, P. and Ikonomidou, C. (1997) 'Glutamate in neurologic diseases.' *Journal of Child Neurology, 12*: 471–485.

Björkstén, B., Bäck, O., Gustavson, K.H., Hallmans, G. *et al.* (1980) 'Zinc and immune function in Down's syndrome.', *Acta Paediatrica Scandinavica, 69*(2): 183–187.

Black, G.C., Mazerolle, C.J., Wang, Y., Campsall, K.D. *et al.* (2003) 'Abnormalities of the vitreoretinal interface caused by dysregulated Hedgehog signaling during retinal development.', *Human Molecular Genetics, 12*: 3269–3276.

Blake, K.D. and Prasad, C. (2006) 'CHARGE syndrome.', *Orphanet Journal of Rare Diseases, 1*: 34, doi:10.1186/1750-1172-1-34, www.ojrd.com/ content/1/1/34.

Blanchon, Y.C., Gay, C., Gibert, G. and Lauras, B. (2002) 'A case of N-acetyl galactosaminidase deficiency (Schindler disease) associated with autism.' *Journal of Autism and Developmental Disorders, 32*: 145–146.

Blank, C.E. (1960) 'Apert's syndrome (a type of acrocephalosyndactyly): observations on a British series of thirty-nine cases.', *Annals of Human Genetics*, *24*: 151–164.

Blasco, M.A. (2007) 'The epigenetic regulation of mammalian telomeres.', *Nature Reviews: Genetics*, 8: 299–309.

Blasi, F., Bacchelli, E., Pesaresi, G., Carone, S. *et al.* (2006) 'Absence of coding mutations in the X-linked genes neuroligin 3 and neuroligin 4 in individuals with autism from the IMGSAC collection.' *American Journal of Medical Genetics B: Neuropsychiatric Genetics*, *141*(3): 220–221.

Blau, H.M. (2008) 'Cell therapies for muscular dystrophy.', *New England Journal of Medicine*, *359*(13): 1403–1405.

Blaxill, M.X. (2004) 'What's going on? The question of time trends in autism.', *Public Health Reports*, *119*(6): 536–551.

Bleesing, J.J. (2003) 'Autoimmune lymphoproliferative syndrome (ALPS).', *Current Pharmaceutical Design*, 9: 265–278.

Bleesing, J.J.H., Johnson, J., and Zhang, K. (2007) 'Autoimmune lymphoproliferative syndrome.', *GENEReviews*, web-based resource.

Blomberg, S., Rosander, M. and Andersson, G. (2006) 'Fears, hyperacusis and musicality in Williams syndrome.', *Research in Developmental Disabilities*, 27: 668–680.

Blomquist, H.K., Back, O., Fagerlund, M., Holmgren, G. and Stecksen-Blicks, C. (1991) 'Tay or IBIDS syndrome: a case with growth and mental retardation, congenital ichthyosis and brittle hair.', *Acta Paediatrical Scandinavica*, 80: 1241–1245.

Blomquist, H.K., Bohman, M., Edvinsson, S.O., Gillberg, C. *et al.* (1985) 'Frequency of the fragile-X syndrome in infantile autism: a Swedish multicenter study.', *Clinical Genetics*, 27: 113–117.

Blondis, T.A., Cook, E. Jr., Koza-Taylor, P. and Finn, T. (1996) 'Asperger syndrome associated with Steinert's myotonic dystrophy.', *Developmental Medicine and Child Neurology*, 38: 840–847.

Blount, B.C. and Ames, B.N. (1995) 'DNA damage in folate deficiency.', *Bailliere's Clinical Haematology*, *8*(3): 461–478.

Blue, M.E., Naidu, S. and Johnston, M.V. (1999) 'Altered development of glutamate and GABA receptors in the basal ganglia of girls with Rett syndrome.', *Experimental Neurology*, *156*(2): 345–352.

Boccone, L., Dessi, V., Zappu, A., Piga, S. *et al.* (2006) 'Bannayan-Riley-Ruvalcaba syndrome with reactive nodular lymphoid hyperplasia and autism and a PTEN mutation.', (Letter) *American Journal of Medical Genetics*, *140A*: 1965–1969.

Bochukova, E.G., Huang, N., Keogh, J., Henning, E. *et al.* (2010) 'Large, rare chromosomal deletions associated with severe early-onset obesity.', *Nature*, *463*(7281): 666–670.

Bochukova, E.G., Roscioli, T., Hedges, D.J., Taylor, I.B. *et al.* (2009) 'Rare mutations of FGFR2 causing Apert syndrome: identification of the first partial gene deletion, and an Alu element insertion from a new subfamily.', *Human Mutation*, *30*(2): 204–211.

Boddaert, N., Belin, P., Chabane, N., Poline, J-B. *et al.* (2003) 'Perception of complex sounds: abnormal pattern of cortical activation in autism.', *American Journal of Psychiatry*, *160*: 2057–2060.

Boddaert, N., Chabane, N., Belin, P., Bourgeois, M. *et al.* (2004) 'Perception of complex sounds in autism: abnormal auditory cortical processing in children.' *American Journal of Psychiatry*, *161*: 2117–2120.

Boddaert, N., Mochel, F., Meresse, I., Seidenwurm, D. *et al.* (2006) 'Parieto-occipital grey matter abnormalities in children with Williams syndrome.', *NeuroImage*, *30*: 721–725.

Bodfish, J.W. (2004) 'Treating the core features of autism: are we there yet?' *Mental Retardation and Developmental Disabilities Research Reviews*, *10*(4): 318–326.

Bodrug, S.E., Ray, P.N., Gonzalez, I.L., Schmickel, R.D. *et al.* (1987) 'Molecular analysis of a constitutional X-autosome translocation in a female with muscular dystrophy.' *Science*, *237*(4822): 1620–1624.

Boduroglu, K., Alana, Y., Koldan, B. and Tuncbilek, E. (2004) 'Methylenetetrahydrofolate reductase enzyme polymorphisms as maternal risk for Down syndrome among Turkish women.', *American Journal of Medical Genetics A*, *127A*(1): 5–10.

Boeckers, T.M., Bockmann, J., Kreutz, M.R. and Gundelfinger, E.D. (2002) 'ProSAP/Shank prot.', *Journal of Neurochemistry*, *81*: 903–910.

Bolduc, F.V., Bell, K., Cox, H., Broadie, K.S. *et al.* (2008) 'Excess protein synthesis in drosophila fragile-X mutants impairs long-term memory.', *Nature Neuroscience*, *11*(10): 1143–1145.

Boles, D.J., Bodurtha, J. and Nance, W.E. (1987) 'Goldenhar complex in discordant monozygotic twins: a case report and review of the literature.' *American Journal of Medical Genetics*, *28*: 103–109.

Bolton, P.F., Dennis, N.R., Browne, C.E., Thomas, N.S. *et al.* (2001) 'The phenotypic manifestations of interstitial duplications of proximal 15q with special reference to the autistic spectrum disorders.', *American Journal of Medical Genetics*, *105*(8): 675–685.

Bolton, P.F. and Griffiths, P.D. (1997) 'Association of tuberous sclerosis of temporal lobes with autism and atypical autism.', *Lancet*, *349*: 392–395.

Bolton, P.F., Park, R.J., Higgins, J.N., Griffiths, P.D. and Pickles, A. (2002) 'Neuro-epileptic determinants of autism spectrum disorders in tuberous sclerosis complex.', *Brain*, *125*(6): 1247–1255.

Bolton, P.F, Powell, J., Rutter, M., Buckle, V. *et al.* (1995) 'Autism, mental retardation, multiple exostoses and short stature in a female with 46,X,t(X;8) (p22.13;q22.1).' *Psychiatric Genetics*, *5*(2): 51–55.

Bolton, P.F., Veltman, M.W., Weisblatt, E., Holmes, J.R. *et al.* (2004) 'Chromosome 15q11–13 abnormalities and other medical conditions in individuals with autism spectrum disorders.' *Psychiatric Genetics*, *14*: 131–137.

Bonamico, M., Mariani, P., Danesi, H.M., Crisogianni, M. *et al.* (2001) 'Prevalence and clinical picture of coeliac disease in Italian Down syndrome patients: a multicenter study.', *Journal of Pediatric Gastroenterology and Nutrition*, *33*(2): 139–143.

Bonati, M.T., Russo, S., Finelli, P., Valsecchi, M.R. *et al.* (2007) 'Evaluation of autism traits in Angelman syndrome: a resource to unfold autism genes.', *Neurogenetics*, *8*(3): 169–178.

Bonne, G., Leturcq, F., Récan-Budiartha, D. and Yaou, R.B. (2007) 'Emery-Dreifuss muscular dystrophy.', *GeneReviews*, web-based resource.

Boog, G., Sagot, F., Winer, N., David, A. and Nomballais, M.F. (1999) 'Brachmann-de Lange syndrome: a cause of early symmetric foetal growth delay.', *European Journal of Obstetrics, Gynecology and Reproductive Biology*, 85: 173–177.

Borgione, E., Sturnio, M., Spalletta, A., Angela, L. *et al.* (2003) 'Mutational analysis of the ATRX gene by DGGE: a powerful diagnostic approach for the ATRX syndrome.', *Human Mutation*, 21: 529–534.

Borgstrom, M.K., Riise, R., Tornqvist, K. and Granath, L. (1996) 'Anomalies in the permanent dentition and other oral findings in 29 individuals with Laurence-Moon-Bardet-Biedl syndrome.', *Journal of Oral Pathology Medicine*, 25: 86–89.

Borck, G., Redon, R., Sanlaville, D., Rio, M. *et al.* (2004) 'NIPBL mutations and genetic heterogeneity in Cornelia de Lange syndrome.', *Journal of Medical Genetics*, 41: e128.

Borg, I., Freude, K., Kubart, S., Hoffmann, K. *et al.* (2005) 'Disruption of Netrin G1 by a balanced chromosome translocation in a girl with Rett syndrome.', *European Journal of Human Genetics*, 13: 921–927.

Borges, W.G., Augustine, N.H. and Hill, H.R. (2000) 'Defective IL-12/interferon-gamma pathway in patients with hyperimmunoglobulinemia E syndrome.', *Journal of Pediatrics*, 136(2): 176–180.

Borges, W.G., Hensley, T., Carey, J.C., Petrak, B.A. and Hill, H.R. (1998) 'The face of Job.', *Journal of Pediatrics*, 133(2): 303–305.

Boris, M., Goldblatt, A., Galanko, J. and James, S.J. (2004) 'Association of MTHFR gene variants with autism.' *Journal of American Physicians and Surgeons*, 9(4): 106–108.

Boris, M., Kaiser, C.C., Goldblatt, A., Elice, M.W. *et al.* (2007) 'Effect of pioglitazone treatment on behavioural symptoms in autistic children.', *Journal of Neuroinflammation*, 4: 3, doi:10.1186/1742-2094-4-3.

Botez, M.I., Botez, T., Ross-Chouinard, A. and Lalonde, R. (1993) 'Thiamine and folate treatment of chronic epileptic patients: a controlled study with the Wechsler IQ scale.' *Epilepsy*, 16(2): 157–163.

Botto, L.D., May, K., Fernhoff, P.M., Correa, A. *et al.* (2003) 'A population-based study of the 22q11.2 deletion: phenotype, incidence, and contribution to major birth defects in the population.', *Pediatrics*, 112: 101–107.

Botto, L.D. and Yang, Q. (2000) '5,10-methylenetetrahydrofolate reductase gene variants and congenital anomalies: a HuGE review.', *American Journal of Epidemiology*, 151: 862–877.

Bourgeois, J., Coffey, S., Rivera, S.M., Hessl, D. *et al.* (2009) 'Fragile-X premutation disorders – expanding the psychiatric perspective.', *Journal of Clinical Psychiatry*, 70(6): 852–862.

Bourgeron, T. (2007) 'The possible interplay of synaptic and clock genes in autism spectrum disorders.', *Cold Spring Harbor Symposia in Quantative Biology*, 72: 645–654.

Bourtchouladze, R., Lidge, R., Catapano, R., Stanley, J. *et al.* (2003) 'A mouse model of Rubinstein-Taybi syndrome: defective long-term memory is ameliorated by inhibitors of phosphodiesterase 4.', *Proceedings of the National Academy of Science USA*, 100(18): 10518–10522.

Bouzas, E.A., Caruso, R.C., Drews-Bankiewicz, M.A. and Kaiser-Kupfer, M.I. (1994) 'Evoked potential analysis of visual pathways in human albinism.' *Ophthalmology*, 101: 309–314.

Bowden, J.A. and McArthur, C.L. III (1972) 'Possible biochemical model for phenylketonuria.', *Nature*, 235: 230.

Bower, B.D. and Jeavons, P.M. (1967) 'The "happy puppet" syndrome.' *Archives of Diseases in Childhood*, 42: 298–301.

Boycott, K.M., Flavelle, S., Bureau, A., Glass, H.C. *et al.* (2005) 'Homozygous deletion of the very low density lipoprotein receptor gene causes autosomal recessive cerebellar hypoplasia with cerebral gyral simplification.', *American Journal of Human Genetics*, 77: 477–483.

Boyd, S.G., Harden, A. and Patton, M.A. (1988) 'The EEG in early diagnosis of the Angelman (happy puppet) syndrome.' *European Journal of Pediatrics*, 147: 508–513.

Braam, W., Didden, R., Smits, M.G. and Curfs, L.M. (2008) 'Melatonin for chronic insomnia in Angelman syndrome: a randomized placebo-controlled trial.', *Journal of Child Neurology*, 23(6): 649–654.

Brachmann, W. (1916) 'Ein Fall von symmetrischer Monodaktylie durch Ulnadefekt, mit symmetrischer Flughautbildung in den Ellenbogen, sowie anderen Abnormalitaten (Zwerghaftigkeit, Halsrippen, Behaarung).', *Jahrbuch Kinderheilkd*, 84: 225–235.

Braddock, S.R., Henley, K.M. and Maria, B.L. (2007) 'The face of Joubert syndrome: a study of dysmorphology and anthropometry.', *American Journal of Medical Genetics A*, 143A(24): 3235–3242.

Bradford, Y., Haines, J., Hutcheson, H., Gardiner, M. *et al.* (2001) 'Incorporating language phenotypes strengthens evidence of linkage to autism.', *American Journal of Medical Genetics*, 105: 539–547.

Bradstreet, J., Geier, D.A., Kartzinel, J.J., Adams, J.B. and Geier, M.R. (2003) 'A case-control study of mercury burden in children with autistic spectrum disorders.', *Journal of American Physicians and Surgeons*, 8(3): 76–79.

Bradstreet, J.J., Smith, S., Granpeesheh, D., El-Dahr, J.M. and Rossignol, D. (2007) 'Spironolactone might be a desirable immunologic and hormonal intervention in autism spectrum disorders.' *Medical Hypotheses*, 68: 979–987.

Brais, B., Xie, Y.G., Sanson, M., Morgan, K. *et al.* (1995) 'The oculopharyngeal muscular dystrophy locus maps to the region of the cardiac alpha and beta myosin heavy chain genes on chromosome 14q11.2–q13.' *Human Molecular Genetics*, 4(3): 429–434.

Braissant, O., Henry, H., Villard, A.M., Speer, O. *et al.* (2005) 'Creatine synthesis and transport during rat embryogenesis: spatiotemporal expression of AGAT, GAMT and CT1.', *BMC Developmental Biology*, 5: 9.

Brancati, F., Travaglini, L., Zablocka, D., Boltshauser, E. *et al.* (2008) 'RPGRIP1L mutations are mainly associated with the cerebello-renal phenotype of Joubert syndrome-related disorders.', *Clinical Genetics, 74*: 164–170.

Braun, K., Van, N., Yeargin-Allsopp, M., Schendel, D. and Fernhoff, P. (2003) 'Long-term developmental outcomes of children identified through a newborn screening program with a metabolic or endocrine disorder: a population-based approach.', *Journal of Pediatrics, 143*: 236–242.

Bregman, J.D. and Volkmar, F.R. (1988) 'Autistic social dysfunction and Down syndrome.', *Journal of the American Academy of Child and Adolescent Psychiatry, 27*: 440–441.

Brenner, M. and Hearing, V.J. (2008) 'Modifying skin pigmentation – approaches through intrinsic biochemistry and exogenous agents.', *Drug Discovery Today: Disease Mechanisms, 5*(2): e189–e199.

Brenton, D.P. and Lilburn, M. (1996) 'Maternal phenylketonuria: a study from the United Kingdom.', *European Journal of Pediatrics, 155* (suppl. 1): 177–180.

Bresolin, N., Castelli, E., Comi, G.P., Felisari, G. *et al.* (1994) 'Cognitive impairment in Duchenne muscular dystrophy.', *Neuromuscular Disorders, 4*: 359–369.

Bretherick, K.L., Fluker, M.R. and Robinson, W.P. (2005) 'FMR1 repeat sizes in the gray zone and high end of the normal range are associated with premature ovarian failure.', *Human Genetics, 117*, 376–382.

Bretón Martínez, J.R., Cánovas Martínez, A., Casaña Pérez, S., Escribá Alepuz, J. and Giménez Vázquez, F. (2007) 'Mevalonic aciduria: report of two cases.', *Journal of Inherited Metabolic Disease, 30*(5): 829.

Briegel, W. (2006) 'Neuropsychiatric findings of Moebius sequence – a review.', *Clinical Genetics, 70*: 91–97.

Briegel, W., Hofmann, C. and Schwab, K.O. (2007) 'Moebius sequence: behaviour problems of preschool children and parental stress.', *Genetic Counselling, 18*: 267–275.

Brieger, P., Bartel-Friedrich, S., Haring, A. and Marneros, A. (1998) 'Oculo-auriculo-vertebral spectrum disorder (Goldenhar "syndrome") coexisting with schizophreniform disorder.' (Letter) *Journal of Neurology, Neurosurgery and Psychiatry, 65*(1): 135–136.

Brierre de Boismont, A. (1862) *Des hallucinations*, (3rd edn.). Paris: Germer Bailliere.

Brilliant, M.H. (1992) 'The mouse pink-eyed dilution locus: a model for aspects of Prader-Willi syndrome, Angelman syndrome, and a form of hypomelanosis of Ito.', *Mammalian Genome, 3*(4): 187–191.

Broder, K., Reinhardt, E., Ahern, J., Lifton, R. *et al.* (1999) 'Elevated ambulatory blood pressure in 20 subjects with Williams syndrome.', *American Journal of Medical Genetics, 83*: 356–360.

Broughton, B.C., Berneburg, M., Fawcett, H., Taylor, E.M. *et al.* (2001) 'Two individuals with features of both xeroderma pigmentosum and trichothiodystrophy highlight the complexity of the clinical outcomes of mutations in the XPD gene.', *Human Molecular Genetics, 10*: 2539–2547.

Brown, A., Phelan, M.C., Patil, S., Crawford, E. *et al.* (1996) 'Two patients with duplication of 17p11.2: the reciprocal of the Smith-Magenis syndrome deletion?' *American Journal of Medical Genetics, 63*: 373–377.

Brown, C.M. and Austin, D.W. (2009) 'Commentary: fatty acids, breastfeeding and autism spectrum disorder.', *Electronic Journal of Applied Psychology: Innovations in Autism, 5*(1): 49–52.

Brown, J. (2010) *Writers on the Spectrum: How Autism and Asperger Syndrome Have Influenced Literary Writing.* London: Jessica Kingsley Publishers.

Brown, W.T., Friedman, E., Jenkins, E.C., Brooks, J. *et al.* (1982a) 'Association of fragile-X syndrome with autism.', *Lancet, 319*(8263): 100.

Brown, W.T., Jenkins, E.C., Friedman, E., Brooks, J. *et al.* (1982b) 'Autism is associated with the fragile-X syndrome.', *Journal of Autism and Developmental Disorders, 12*: 303–308.

Brown, W.T., Wisniewski, K.E., Sudhalter, V., Keogh, M. *et al.* (1998) 'Identical twins discordant for Sotos syndrome.' *American Journal of Medical Genetics, 79*: 329–333.

Browne, C.E., Dennis, N.R., Maher, E., Long, F.L. *et al.* (1997) 'Inherited interstitial duplications of proximal 15q: genotype–phenotype correlations.', *American Journal of Human Genetics, 61*: 1342–1352.

Bruck, I., Philippart, M., Giraldi, D. and Antoniuk, S. (1991) 'Difference in early development of presumed monozygotic twins with Rett syndrome.', *American Journal of Medical Genetics, 39*: 415–417.

Brussino, A., Gellera, C., Saluto, A., Mariotti, C. *et al.* (2005) 'FMR1 gene premutation is a frequent genetic cause of late-onset sporadic cerebellar ataxia.', *Neurology, 64*: 145–147.

Bryson, Y., Sakati, N., Nyhan, W.L. and Fish, C.H. (1971) 'Self mutilative behaviour in the Cornelia de Lange syndrome.', *American Journal of Mental Deficiency, 76*: 319–324.

Brzozowski, T., Konturek, P.C., Konturek, S.J., Kwiecien, S. *et al.* (2004) 'Exogenous and endogenous ghrelin in gastroprotection against stress-induced gastric damage.' *Regulatory Peptides, 120*: 39–51.

Bucci, I., Napolitano, G., Giuliani, C., Lio, S. *et al.* (1999) 'Zinc sulphate supplementation improves thyroid hypofunction in hypozincemic Down children.', *Biological Trace Element Research, 67*: 257–268.

Bucci, I., Napolitano, G., Giuliani, C., Lio, S. *et al.* (2001) 'Concerns about using Zn supplementation in Down's syndrome (DS) children.', *Biological Trace Element Research, 82*(1–3): 273–275.

Buckley, R.H., Dinno, N. and Weber, P. (1998) 'Angelman syndrome: are the estimates too low?' *American Journal of Medical Genetics, 80*: 385–390.

Buckley, R.H., Wray, B.B. and Belmaker, E.Z. (1972) 'Extreme hyperimmunoglobulinemia E and undue susceptibility to infection.', *Pediatrics, 49*(1): 59–70.

Buckley, S.J. (2005) 'Autism and Down syndrome.', *Down Syndrome News and Update, 4*(4): 114–120.

Budden, S.S., Dorsey, H.C., Robert D., and Steiner, R.D. (2005) 'Clinical profile of a male with Rett syndrome.', *Brain and Development, 27*: S69–S71.

Buie, T., Campbell, D.B., Fuchs, G.J. III, Furuta, G.T. *et al.* (2010a) 'Evaluation, diagnosis, and treatment of gastrointestinal disorders in individuals with ASDs: a consensus report.', *Pediatrics, 125*: S1–S18 doi:10.1542/peds.2009-1878C.

Buie, T., Fuchs, G.J. III, Furuta, G.T., Kooros, K. *et al.* (2010b) 'Recommendations for evaluation and treatment of common gastrointestinal problems in children with ASDs.', *Pediatrics, 125*: S19–S29 doi:10.1542/peds.2009-1878D.

Buiting, K., Dittrich, B., Gross, S., Lich, C. *et al.* (1998) 'Sporadic imprinting defects in Prader-Willi syndrome and Angelman syndrome: implications for imprint-switch models, genetic counseling, and prenatal diagnosis.' *American Journal of Human Genetics, 63*: 170–180.

Buiting, K., Saitoh, S., Gross, S., Dittrich, B. *et al.* (1995) 'Inherited microdeletions in the Angelman and Prader-Willi syndromes define an imprinting centre on human chromosome 15.', *Nature Genetics, 9*: 395–400.

Bull, M.J., Fitzgerald, J.F., Heifetz, S.A. and Brei, T.J. (1993) 'Gastrointestinal abnormalities: a significant cause of feeding difficulties and failure to thrive in Brachmann-de Lange syndrome.', *American Journal of Medical Genetics, 47*: 1029–1034.

Bumbalo, T.S., Morelewicz, H.V., Berens, D.L. and Buffalo, M.D. (1964) 'Treatment of Down's syndrome with the "U" series of drugs.', *Journal of the American Medical Association, 187*: 361.

Bundey, S. (1996) 'Julia Bell, MRCS LRCP FRCP (1879–1979): steamboat lady, statistician and geneticist.', *Journal of Medical Biography, 4*: 8–13.

Bundey, S., Hardy, C., Vickers, S., Kilpatrick, M.W. and Corbett, J.A. (1994) 'Duplication of the 15q11–13 region in a patient with autism, epilepsy and ataxia.' *Developmental Medicine and Child Neurology, 36*: 736–742.

Buntinx, I.M., Hennekam, R.C.M., Brouwer, O.F., Stroink, H. *et al.* (1995) 'Clinical profile of Angelman syndrome at different ages.' *American Journal of Medical Genetics, 56*: 176–183.

Buoni, S., Zannolli, R., Colamaria, V., Macucci, F. *et al.* (2006a) 'Myoclonic encephalopathy in the CDKL5 gene mutation.', *Clinical Neurophysiology, 117*: 223–227.

Buoni, S., Zannolli, R., de Santi, M., Macucci, F. *et al.* (2006b) 'Neurocutaneous syndrome with mental delay, autism, blockage in intracellular vescicular trafficking and melanosome defects.' *European Journal of Neurology, 13*(8): 842–851.

Burck, U. (1983) 'Genetic aspects of hemifacial microsomia.', *Human Genetics, 64*: 291–296.

Burd, L., Fisher, W.W., Kerbeshian, J. and Arnold, M.E. (1987) 'Is development of Tourette disorder a marker for improvement in patients with autism and other pervasive developmental disorders?' *Journal of the American Academy of Child and Adolescent Psychiatry, 26*(2): 162–165.

Burd, L., Li, Q., Kerbeshian, J., Klug, M.G. and Freeman, R.D. (2009) 'Tourette syndrome and co-morbid pervasive developmental disorders.', *Journal of Child Neurology, 24*(2): 170–175.

Burd, L., Martsolf, J.T., Kerbeshian, J. and Jalal, S.M. (1988) 'Partial 6p trisomy associated with infantile autism.', *Clinical Genetics, 33*(5): 356–359.

Burd, L., Vesely, B., Martsolf, J. and Kerbeshian, J. (1990) 'Prevalence study of Prader-Willi syndrome in North Dakota.' *American Journal of Medical Genetics, 37*: 97–99.

Burd, L., Vesely, B., Martsolf, J.T. and Kerbeshian, J. (1991) 'Prevalence study of Rett syndrome in North Dakota children.' *American Journal of Medical Genetics, 38*(4): 565–568.

Burgdorf, J. and Panksepp, J. (2006) 'The neurobiology of positive emotions.', *Neuroscience and Biobehavioural Reviews, 30*: 173–187.

Burger, R.A. and Warren, R.P. (1998) 'Possible immunogenetic basis for autism.', *Mental Retardation and Developmental Disabilities Research Reviews, 4*: 137–141.

Burglen, L., Heron, D., Moerman, A., Dieux-Coeslier, A. *et al.* (2003) 'Myhre syndrome: new reports, review, and differential diagnosis.' *Journal of Medical Genetics, 40*: 546–551.

Burke, B.A., Johnson, D., Gilbert, E.F., Drut, R.M. *et al.* (1987) 'Thyrocalcitonin-containing cells in the Di George anomaly.', *Human Pathology, 18*(4): 355–360.

Burke, J.R., Enghild, J.J., Martin, M.E., Jou, Y.S. *et al.* (1996) 'Huntingtin and DRPLA proteins selectively interact with the enzyme GAPDH.', *Nature Medicine, 2*: 347–350.

Burn, J. (1999) 'Closing time for CATCH22.', *Journal of Medical Genetics, 36*: 737–738.

Burn, J., Wilson, D.I., Cross, I., Atif, U. *et al.* (1995) 'The clinical significance of 22q11 deletion.', In E.B Clark, R.R Markwald and A Takao (eds.): *Developmental Mechanisms of Heart Disease.* New York: Futura Publishers, pp.559–567.

Burnett, A.C., Reutens, D.C. and Wood, A.G. (2010) 'Social cognition in Turner's syndrome.', *Journal of Clinical Neuroscience, 17*: 283–286.

Bushby, K.M. (1999) 'The limb-girdle muscular dystrophies – multiple genes, multiple mechanisms.', *Human Molecular Genetics, 8*: 1875–1882.

Bushby, K.M. and Gardner-Medwin, D. (1993) 'The clinical, genetic and dystrophin characteristics of Becker muscular dystrophy. I. Natural history.', *Journal of Neurology, 240*: 98–104.

Bushby, K.M., Thambyayah, M. and Gardner-Medwin, D. (1991) 'Prevalence and incidence of Becker muscular dystrophy.', *Lancet, 337*: 1022–1024.

Buske, A., Gewies, A., Lehmann, R., Ruther, K. *et al.* (1999) 'Recurrent NF1 gene mutation in a patient with oligosymptomatic neurofibromatosis type 1 (NF1).', *American Journal of Medical Genetics, 86*: 328–330.

Butler, M.G. (2010) 'Genomic imprinting disorders in humans: a mini-review.' *Journal of Assisted Reproduction and Genetics, 26*: 477–486.

Butler, M.G., Dasouki, M.J., Zhou, X.P., Talebizadeh, Z. *et al.* (2005) 'Subset of individuals with autism spectrum disorders and extreme macrocephaly associated with germline PTEN tumour suppressor gene mutations.' *Journal of Medical Genetics, 42*: 318–321.

Butler, M.G., Lee, P.D.K. and Whitman, B.Y. (eds.) (2006) *Management of Prader-Willi Syndrome* (3rd edn.). New York: Springer.

Buxbaum, J.D., Silverman, J., Keddache, M., Smith, C.J. et al. (2004) 'Linkage analysis for autism in a subset families with obsessive-compulsive behaviours: evidence for an autism susceptibility gene on chromosome 1 and further support for susceptibility genes on chromosome 6 and 19.' *Molecular Psychiatry*, 9: 144–150.

Buxbaum, J.D., Silverman, J.M., Smith, C.J., Greenberg, D.A. et al. (2002) 'Association between a GABRB3 polymorphism and autism.', *Molecular Psychiatry*, 7: 311–316.

Buyse, M.E. (ed.) (1990) 'Chromosome X, chromosome XYY.', In: *Birth Defects Encyclopedia*. Cambridge, Massachusetts: Blackwell Scientific Publications, 400–401.

Buyske, S., Williams, T.A., Mars, A.E., Stenroos, E.S. et al. (2006) 'Analysis of case-parent trios at a locus with a deletion allele: association of GSTM1 with autism.', *BMC Genetics*, 7: 8, doi:10.1186/1471-2156-7-8

Bzduch, V., Beluchova, D. and Skodova, J. (2000) 'Incidence of Smith–Lemli–Opitz syndrome in Slovakia.', *American Journal of Medical Genetics*, 90: 260.

Cabanlit, M., Wills, S., Goines, P., Ashwood, P. and Van de Water, J. (2007) 'Brain-specific autoantibodies in the plasma of subjects with autistic spectrum disorder.', *Annals of the New York Academy of Science*, 1107: 92–103.

Cagianut, B., Schnebli, H.P., Rhyner, K. and Furrer, J. (1984) 'Decreased thiosulfate sulfur transferase (rhodanese) in Leber's hereditary optic atrophy.', *Journal of Molecular Medicine*, 62(18): 850–854.

Caglayan, A.O. (2010) 'Genetic causes of syndromic and non-syndromic autism.' *Developmental Medicine and Child Neurology*, 52(2): 130–138.

Cagle, A.P., Waguespack, S.G., Buckingham, B.A., Shankar, R.R. and Dimeglio, L.A. (2004) 'Severe infantile hypercalcemia associated with Williams syndrome successfully treated with intravenously administered pamidronate.', *Pediatrics*, 114(4): 1091–1095.

Caldeira Araujo, H., Smit, W., Verhoeven, N.M., Salomons, G.S. et al. (2005) 'Guanidinoacetate methyltransferase deficiency identified in adults and a child with mental retardation.', *American Journal of Medical Genetics*, 133A: 122–127.

Caldwell, H.K. and Young, W.S. 3rd (2006) 'Oxytocin and vasopressin: genetics and behavioural implications.' Ch.25, pp.573–607. In R. Lim (ed.) *Handbook of Neurochemistry and Molecular Neurobiology: Neuroactive Proteins and Peptides* (3rd edn.) New York: Springer Verlag.

Cambiaso, P., Orazi, C., Digilio, M.C., Loche, S. et al. (2007) 'Thyroid morphology and subclinical hypothyroidism in children and adolescents with Williams syndrome.', *Journal of Pediatrics*, 150(1): 62–65.

Campbell, C. and Jacob, P. (2003) 'Deflazacort for the treatment of Duchenne dystrophy: a systematic review.', *BMC Neurology*, 3: 7.

Campbell, D.B., Buie, T.M., Winter, H., Bauman, M. et al. (2009) 'Distinct genetic risk based on association of MET in families with co-occurring autism and gastrointestinal conditions.', *Pediatrics*. 123(3): 1018–1024.

Campbell, D.B., Li, C., Sutcliffe, J.S., Persico, A.M. and Levitt, P. (2008) 'Genetic evidence implicating multiple genes in the MET receptor tyrosine kinase pathway in autism spectrum disorder.', *Autism Research*, 1(3): 159–168.

Campbell, D.B., Sutcliffe, J.S., Ebert, P.J., Militerni, R. et al. (2006) 'A genetic variant that disrupts MET transcription is associated with autism.', *Proceedings of the National Academy of Science USA*, 103(45): 16834–16839.

Campbell, L.E., Daly, E., Toal, F., Stevens, A. et al. (2006) 'Brain and behaviour in children with 22q11.2 deletion syndrome: a volumetric and voxel-based morphometry MRI study.', *Brain*, 129: 1218–1228.

Canale, V.C. and Smith, C.H. (1967) 'Chronic lymphadenopathy simulating malignant lymphoma.', *Journal of Pediatrics*, 70: 891–899.

Canitano, R. and Vivanti, G. (2007) 'Tics and Tourette syndrome in autism spectrum disorders.', *Autism*, 11(1): 19–28.

Cannon, T.D. and Keller, M.C. (2006) 'Endophenotypes in the genetic analyses of mental disorders.', *Annual Review of Clinical Psychology*, 2: 7.1–7.24.

Cantagrel, V., Silhavy, J.L., Bielas, S.L., Swistun, D. et al. (2008) 'Mutations in the cilia gene ARL13B lead to the classical form of Joubert syndrome.', *American Journal of Human Genetics*, 83(2): 170–179.

Cantor, R.M., Kono, N., Duvall, J.A., Alvarez-Retuerto, A. et al. (2005) 'Replication of autism linkage: fine-mapping peak at 17q21.' *American Journal of Human Genetics*, 76: 1050–1056.

Cantor, R.M., Yoon, J.L., Furr, J. and Lajonchere, C.M. (2007) 'Paternal age and autism are associated in a family-based sample.', (Letter) *Molecular Psychiatry*, 12: 419–423.

Caraballo, R.H., Cersosimo, R.O., Sakr, D., Cresta, A. et al. (2005) 'Ketogenic diet in patients with Dravet syndrome.', *Epilepsia*, 46(9): 1539–1544.

Caraballo, R.H. and Fejerman, N. (2006) 'Dravet syndrome: study of 53 patients.', *Epilepsy Research*, 70(Supp 1): S231–S238.

Caraballo, R.H, Tripoli, J., Escobal, L., Cersosimo, R. et al. (1998) 'Ketogenic diet: efficacy and tolerability in childhood intractable epilepsy.', *Revista de Neurologia*, 26: 61–64.

Carethers, J.M., Furnari, F.B., Zigman, A.F., Lavine, J.E. et al. (1998) 'Absence of PTEN/MMAC1 germ-line mutations in sporadic Bannayan-Riley-Ruvalcaba syndrome.', *Cancer Research*, 58: 2724–2726.

Carey, A.H., Kelly, D., Halford, S., Wadey, R. et al. (1992) 'Molecular genetic study of the frequency of monosomy 22q11 in DiGeorge syndrome.', *American Journal of Human Genetics*, 51: 964–970.

Carey, J.C. (1998) 'Neurofibromatosis–Noonan syndrome.', *American Journal of Medical Genetics*, 75: 263–264.

Carey, J.C. and Hall, B.D. (1978) 'The Coffin-Siris syndrome: five cases including two siblings.', *American Journal of Diseases of Childhood*, 132: 667–671.

Carlson, N.R. (2001) *Physiology of Behaviour* (7th edn, pp.96–129). Boston: Allyn and Bacon.

Carney, R.M., Wolpert, C.M., Ravan, S.A., Shahbazian, M. et al. (2003) 'Identification of MeCP2 mutations in a series of females with autistic disorder.' *Pediatric Neurology*, 28: 205–211.

Caron, K.M., Soo, S.C., Wetsel, W.C., Stocco, D.M. *et al.* (1997) 'Targeted disruption of the mouse gene encoding steroidogenic acute regulatory protein provides insights into congenital lipoid adrenal hyperplasia.', *Proceedings of the National Academy of Science USA*, 94(21): 11540–11545.

Carothers, A.D., Hecht, C.A. and Hook, E.B. (1999) 'International variation in reported livebirth prevalence rates of Down syndrome, adjusted for maternal age.', *Journal of Medical Genetics*, 36: 386–393.

Carotti, A., Digilio, M.C., Piacentini, G., Saffirio, C. *et al.* (2008) 'Cardiac defects and results of cardiac surgery in 22q11.2 deletion syndrome.', *Developmental Disabilities Research Reviews*, 14(1): 35–42.

Carper, R.A. and Courchesne, E. (2005) 'Localized enlargement of the frontal cortex in early autism.', *Biological Psychiatry*, 57: 126–133.

Carr, R., Wasdell, M.B., Hamilton, D., Weiss, M.D. *et al.* (2007) 'Long-term effectiveness outcome of melatonin therapy in children with treatment-resistant circadian rhythm sleep disorders.', *Journal of Pineal Research*, 43: 351–359.

Carter, C.O. and Woolf, L.I. (1961) 'The birthplaces of parents and grandparents of a series of patients with phenylketonuria in southeast England.' *Annals of Human Genetics*, 25: 57–64.

Carter, C.S. (2007) 'Sex differences in oxytocin and vasopressin: implications for autism spectrum disorders?' *Behavioural Brain Research*, 176: 170–186.

Carter, J.A., Lees, J.A., Goma, J.K., Murira, G. *et al.* (2006) 'Severe falciparum malaria and acquired childhood language disorder.', *Developmental Medicine and Child Neurology*, 48: 51–57.

Carter, J.C., Capone, G.T., Gray, R.M., Cox, C.S. and Kaufmann, W.E. (2007) 'Autistic-spectrum disorders in Down syndrome: further delineation and distinction from other behavioural abnormalities.', *American Journal of Medical Genetics, B Neuropsychiatric Genetics*, 144(1): 87–94.

Carter, N.P. (2007) 'Methods and strategies for analyzing copy number variation using DNA microarrays.' *Nature Genetics*, 39(Suppl 7): S16–S21.

Cartier, N. and Aubourg, P. (2008) 'Hematopoietic stem cell gene therapy in Hurler syndrome, globoid cell leukodystrophy, metachromatic leukodystrophy and X-adrenoleukodystrophy.', *Current Opinion in Molecular Therapeutics*, 10(5): 471–478.

Cartier, N., Hacein-Bey-Abina, S., Bartholomae, C.C., Veres, G. *et al.* (2009) 'Hematopoietic stem cell gene therapy with a lentiviral vector in X-linked adrenoleukodystrophy.', *Science*, 326(5954): 818–823.

Cartlidge, P.H. and Curnock, D.A. (1986) 'Specific malabsorption of vitamin B12 in Down's syndrome.', *Archives of Disease in Childhood*, 61(5): 514–515.

Casas, J.P., Hingorani, A.D., Bautista, L.E. and Sharma, P. (2004) 'Meta-analysis of genetic studies in ischemic stroke: thirty-two genes involving approximately 18000 cases and 58000 controls.' *Archives of Neurology*, 61: 1652–1662.

Casella, E.B., Valente, M., de Navarro, J.M. and Kok, F. (2005) 'Vitamin B12 deficiency in infancy as a cause of developmental regression.' *Brain and Development*, 27(8): 1–3.

Caselli, M.A., Rzonca, E.C. and Lue, B.Y. (1988) 'Habitual toe-walking: evaluation and approach to treatment.', *Clinics in Podiatric Medicine and Surgery*, 5(3): 547–559.

Cass, H., Sekaran, D. and Baird, G. (2006) 'Medical investigation of children with autistic spectrum disorders.' *Child: Care, Health and Development*, 32(5): 521–533.

Cassidy, S.B. and Schwartz, S. (1998) 'Prader-Willi and Angelman syndromes: disorders of genomic imprinting.' *Medicine*, 77: 140–151.

Castaño, G., Etchart, C. and Sookoian, S. (2006) 'Vitamin A toxicity in a physical culturist patient: a case report and review of the literature.', *Annals of Hepatology*, 5(4): 293–295.

Castellanos, F.X. and Tannock, R. (2002) 'Neuroscience of attention deficit/hyperactivity disorder: the search for endophenotypes.', *Nature Reviews: Neuroscience*, 3: 617–628.

Castori, M., Brancati, F., Rinaldi, R., Adami, L. *et al.* (2006) 'Antenatal presentation of the oculo-auriculo-vertebral spectrum (OAVS).', *American Journal of Medical Genetics*, 140A: 1573–1579.

Castori, M., Valente, E.M., Donati, M.A., Salvi, S. *et al.* (2005) 'NPHP1 gene deletion is a rare cause of Joubert syndrome related disorders.', *Journal of Medical Genetics*, 42: e9.

Castorina, P., Selicorni, A., Bedeschi, F., Dalpra, L. and Larizza, L. (1997) 'Genotype-phenotype correlation in two sets of monozygotic twins with Williams syndrome.', *American Journal of Medical Genetics*, 69: 107–111.

Castre, M., Lampinen, K.E., Miettinen, R., Koponen, E. *et al.* (2002) 'BDNF regulates the expression of fragile-X mental retardation protein mRNA in the hippocampus.' *Neurobiology of Disease*, 11: 221–229.

Cattanach, B.M., Barr, J.A., Beechey, C.V., Martin, J. *et al.* (1997) 'A candidate model for Angelman syndrome in the mouse.', *Mammalian Genome*, 8: 472–478.

Caughey, A.B., Washington, A.E., Gildengorin, V. and Kuppermann, M. (2004) 'Assessment of demand for prenatal diagnostic testing using willingness to pay.', *Obstetrics and Gynecology*, 103(3): 539–545.

Cavaille, J., Buiting, K., Kiefmann, M., Lalande, M. *et al.* (2000) 'Identification of brain-specific and imprinted small nucleolar RNA genes exhibiting an unusual genomic organization.', *Proceedings of the National Academy of Science USA*, 97: 14311–14316.

Cavaille, J., Seitz, H., Paulsen, M., Ferguson-Smith, A.C. and Bachellerie, J.P. (2002) 'Identification of tandemly-repeated C/D snoRNA genes at the imprinted human 14q32 domain reminiscent of those at the Prader-Willi/Angelman syndrome region.' *Human Molecular Genetics*, 11: 1527–1538.

Cawthon, R.M., Weiss, R., Xu, G.F., Viskochil, D. *et al.* (1990) 'A major segment of the neurofibromatosis type 1 gene: cDNA sequence, genomic structure, and point mutations.', *Cell*, 62: 193–201.

Cayler, G.G. (1969) 'Cardiofacial syndrome: congenital heart disease and facial weakness, a hitherto unrecognized association.', *Archives of Disease in Childhood*, 44: 69–75.

Cazzullo, A.G., Musetti, M.C., Musetti, L., Bajo, S. et al. (1999) 'B-endorphin levels in peripheral blood mononuclear cells and long-term naltrexone treatment in autistic children.', European Neuropsychopharmacology, 9(4): 361–366.

Celebi, J.T., Tsou, H.C., Chen, F.F., Zhang, H. et al. (1999) 'Phenotypic findings of Cowden syndrome and Bannayan-Zonana syndrome in a family associated with a single germline mutation in PTEN.', Journal of Medical Genetics, 36: 360–364.

Centerwall, S.A. and Centerwall, W.R. (2000) 'The discovery of phenylketonuria: the story of a young couple, two retarded children, and a scientist.', Pediatrics, 105(1): 89–103.

Centerwall, W.R. and Neff, C.A. (1961) 'Phenylketonuria: a case report of children of Jewish ancestry.', Archives of Pediatrics, 78: 379–384.

Ceponiene, R., Lepisto, T., Shestakova, A., Vanhala, R. et al. (2003) 'Speech–sound-selective auditory impairment in children with autism: they can perceive but do not attend.' Proceedings of the National Academy of Science USA, 100(9): 5567–5572.

Ceulemans, B.P.G.M., Claes, L.R.F. and Lagae, L.G. (2004) 'Clinical correlations of mutations in the SCN1A gene: from febrile seizures to severe myoclonic epilepsy in infancy.', Pediatric Neurology, 30(4): 236–243.

Chae, Y-J., Chung, C-E., Kim, B-J., Lee, M-H. and Lee, H. (1998) 'The gene encoding guanidinoacetate methyltransferase (GAMT) maps to human chromosome 19 at band p13.3 and to mouse chromosome 10.' Genomics, 49: 162–164.

Chahuan, A. and Chahuan, V. (2006) 'Oxidative stress in autism.', Pathophysiology, 13(3): 171–181.

Challman, T.D., Barbaresi, W.J., Katusic, S.K. and Weaver, A. (2003) 'The yield of the medical evaluation of children with pervasive developmental disorders.', Journal of Autism and Developmental Disorders, 33(2): 187–192.

Chan, C-T.J., Clayton-Smith, J., Cheng, X-J., Buxton, J. et al. (1993) 'Molecular mechanisms in Angelman syndrome: a survey of 93 patients.', Journal of Medical Genetics, 30: 895–902.

Chan, G.M., Buchino, J.J., Mehlhorn, D., Bove, K.E. et al. (1979) 'Effect of vitamin D on pregnant rabbits and their offspring.', Pediatric Research, 13: 121–126.

Chan, Y.M., Merkens, L.S., Connor, W.E., Roullet, J.B. et al. (2009) 'Effects of dietary cholesterol and simvastatin on cholesterol synthesis in Smith-Lemli-Opitz syndrome.', Pediatric Research, 65(6): 681–685.

Chance, P.F., Cavalier, L., Satran, D., Pellegrino, J.E. et al. (1999) 'Clinical nosologic and genetic aspects of Joubert and related syndromes.', Journal of Child Neurology, 14: 660–666.

Chandana, S.R., Behen, M.E., Juhasz, C., Muzik, O. et al. (2005) 'Significance of abnormalities in developmental trajectory and asymmetry of cortical serotonin synthesis in autism.', International Journal of Developmental Neuroscience, 23: 171–182.

Chandler, K.E., Kidd, A., Al-Gazali, L., Kolehmainen, J. et al. (2003) 'Diagnostic criteria, clinical characteristics, and natural history of Cohen syndrome.' Journal of Medical Genetics, 40: 233–241.

Chang, B.S., Ly, J., Appignani, B., Bodell, A. et al. (2005) 'Reading impairment in the neuronal migration disorder of periventricular nodular heterotopia.', Neurology, 64: 799–803.

Chang, S., Bray, S.M., Li, Z., Zarnescu, D.C. et al. (2008) 'Identification of small molecules rescuing fragile-X syndrome phenotypes in drosophila.', Nature Chemical Biology, 4(4): 256–263.

Chanson, P., Salenave, S. and Orcel, P. (2007) 'McCune-Albright syndrome in adulthood.', Pediatric Endocrinology Reviews, 4(Supplement 4): 453–462.

Chao, H-K., Hsiao, K-J. and Su, T-S. (2001) 'A silent mutation induces exon skipping in the phenylalanine hydroxylase gene in phenylketonuria.', Human Genetics, 108: 14–19.

Chao, P.H., Chao, M.C., Hwang, K.P. and Chung, M.Y. (2009) 'Hypocalcemia impacts heart failure control in DiGeorge 2 syndrome.', Acta Paediatrica, 98(1): 195–198.

Chapman, C.A., du Plessis, A. and Pober, B.R. (1996) 'Neurologic findings in children and adults with Williams syndrome.' Journal of Child Neurology, 11(1): 63–65.

Charlton, N. and Wallace, K.L. (2009) 'Post-chelator challenge urinary metal testing.', American College of Medical Toxicology Position Statement on Post-Chelator Challenge Urinary Metal Testing, www.acmt.net/cgi/page.cgi?aid=2999and_id=52&zine=show.

Charman, T. and Clare, P. (2004) Mapping Autism Research: Identifying Autism Priorities for the Future. London: National Autistic Society.

Chartrand, J-P., Filon-Bilodeau, S. and Belin, P. (2007) 'Brain response to birdsongs in bird experts.' NeuroReport, 18(4): 335–340.

Chaste, P., Nygren, G., Anckarsäter, H., Råstam, M. et al. (2007) 'Mutation screening of the ARX gene in patients with autism.', American Journal of Medical Genetics B Neuropsychiatric Genetics, 144B(2): 228–230.

Chattopadhyay, A., Jafurulla, M., Kalipatnapu, S., Pucadyil, T.J. and Harikumar, K.G. (2005) 'Role of cholesterol in ligand binding and G-protein coupling of serotonin1A receptors solubilized from bovine hippocampus.', Biochemical and Biophysical Research Communications, 327: 1036–1041.

Chauhan, A., Chauhan, V., Brown, W.T. and Cohen, I. (2004) 'Oxidative stress in autism: increased lipid peroxidation and reduced serum levels of ceruloplasmin and transferrin – the antioxidant proteins.', Life Sciences, 75: 2539–2549.

Chauhan, V., Chauhan, A., Cohen, I.L., Brown, W.T. and Sheikh, A. (2004) 'Alteration in amino-glycerophospholipids levels in the plasma of children with autism: a potential biochemical diagnostic marker.' Life Sciences, 74: 1635–1643.

Chawarska, K., Paul, R., Klin, I., Hannigen, S. et al. (2007) 'Parental recognition of developmental problems in toddlers with autism spectrum disorders.', Journal of Autism and Developmental Disorders, 37: 62–72.

Chehimi, J., Elder, M., Greene, J., Noroski, L. et al. (2001) 'Cytokine and chemokine dysregulation in hyper-IgE syndrome.', Clinical Immunology, 100: 49–56.

Chen, C.H. and Hsiao, K.J. (1989) 'A Chinese classic phenylketonuria manifested as autism.' *British Journal of Psychiatry*, 155: 251–253.

Chen, L. and Toth, M. (2001) 'Fragile-X mice develop sensory hyperreactivity to auditory stimuli.', *Neuroscience*, 103(4): 1043–1050.

Chen, L., Tracy, T. and Nam, C.I. (2007) 'Dynamics of postsynaptic glutamate receptor targeting.', *Current Opinion in Neurobiology*, 17: 53–58.

Chen, Z., Karaplis, A.C., Ackerman, S.L., Pogribny, I.P. *et al.* (2001) 'Mice deficient in methylenetetrahydrofolate reductase exhibit hyperhomocysteinemia and decreased methylation capacity, with neuropathology and aortic lipid deposition.' *Human Molecular Genetics*, 10: 433–443.

Cherniske, E.M., Carpenter, T.O., Klaiman, C., Young, E. *et al.* (2004) 'Multisystem study of 20 older adults with Williams syndrome.', *American Journal of Medical Genetics*, 131A: 255–264.

Chess, S. (1971) 'Autism in children with congenital rubella.', *Journal of Autism and Childhood Schizophrenia*, 1(1): 33–47.

Chez, M.B., Memon, S. and Hung, P.C. (2004) 'Neurologic treatment strategies in autism: an overview of medical intervention strategies.', *Seminars in Pediatric Neurology*, 11: 229–235.

Chez, M.G., Shoaib Memon, S. and Hung, P.C. (2004) 'Neurologic Treatment Strategies in Autism: An Overview of Medical Intervention Strategies.' *Seminars in Pediatric Neurology*, 11: 229–235.

Chez, M.G., Chang, M., Krasne, V., Coughlan, C. *et al.* (2006) 'Frequency of epileptiform EEG abnormalities in a sequential screening of autistic patients with no known clinical epilepsy from 1996 to 2005.' *Epilepsy and Behaviour*, 8: 267–271.

Chiang, A.P., Beck, J.S., Yen, H.J., Tayeh, M.K. *et al.* (2006) 'Homozygosilty mapping with SNP arrays identitfies TRIM32, an E3 ubiquitain ligase, as a Bardet-Biedl syndrome gene (BBS11).' *Proceedings of the National Academy of Science*, 103 (16): 6287–6292.

Chiang, A.P., Nishimura, D., Searby, C., Elbedour, K. *et al.* (2004) 'Comparative genomic analysis identifies an ADP-ribosylation factor-like gene as the cause of Bardet-Biedl syndrome (BBS3).', *American Journal of Human Genetics*, 75(3): 475–484.

Chieffo, C., Garvey, N., Gong, W., Roe, B. *et al.* (1997) 'Isolation and characterization of a gene from the DiGeorge chromosomal region homologous to the mouse Tbx1 gene.', *Genomics*, 43: 267–277.

Chilosi, A., Leuzzi, V., Battini, R., Tosetti, M. *et al.* (2008) 'Treatment with l-arginine improves neuropsychological disorders in a child with creatine transporter defect.', *Neurocase*, 14(2): 151–161.

Chinnery, P., Majamaa, K., Turnbull, D. and Thorburn, D. (2006) 'Treatment for mitochondrial disorders.', *Cochrane Database of Systematic Reviews*, Issue 1. Art. No.: CD004426, doi: 10.1002/14651858. CD004426.pub2.

Chiron, C., Marchand, M.C., Tran, A., Rey, E. *et al.* (2000) 'Stiripentol in severe myoclonic epilepsy in infancy: a randomized placebo-controlled syndrome-dedicated trial. STICLO study group.', *Lancet*, 356(9242): 1638–1642.

Chisaka, O. and Capecchi, M.R. (1991) 'Regionally restricted developmental defects resulting from targeted disruption of the mouse homeobox gene hox-1.5.', *Nature*, 350(6318): 473–479.

Chisolm, J.J. Jr. (2001) 'The road to primary prevention of lead toxicity in children.' *Pediatrics*, 107(3): 581–583.

Chitty, L.S., Robb, S., Berry, C., Silver, D. and Baraitser, M. (1996) 'PEHO or PEHO-like syndrome?' *Clinical Dysmorphology*, 5: 143–152.

Chiu, S., Wegelin, J.A., Blank, J., Jenkins, M. *et al.* (2007) 'Early acceleration of head circumference in children with fragile-X syndrome and autism.' *Journal of Developmental and Behavioural Pediatrics*, 28(1): 31–35.

Chiurazzi, P., Tabolacci, E. and Neri, G. (2004) 'X-linked mental retardation (XLMR): from clinical condition to cloned gene.' *Critical Reviews in Clinical and Laboratory Science*, 41: 117–158.

Cho, H. and Tapscott, S.J. (2007) 'Myotonic dystrophy: emerging mechanisms for DM1 and DM2.', *Biochimica et Biophysica Acta*, 1772: 195–204.

Chocholska, S., Rossier, E., Barbi, G. and Kehrer-Sawatzki, H. (2006) 'Molecular cytogenetic analysis of a familial interstitial deletion Xp22.2–22.3 with a highly variable phenotype in female carriers.' *American Journal of Medical Genetics A*, 140(6): 604–610.

Choi, P.T. and Nowaczyk, M.J. (2000) 'Anesthetic considerations in Smith-Lemli-Opitz syndrome.', *Canadian Journal of Anaesthesiology*, 47: 556–561.

Choong, Y.F., Watts, P., Little, E. and Beck, L. (2003) 'Goldenhar and cri-du-chat syndromes: a contiguous gene deletion syndrome?' *Journal of the American Academy for Pediatric Ophthalmology and Strabismus*, 7: 226–227.

Chow, E.W., Bassett, A.S. and Weksberg, R. (1994) 'Velocardiofacial syndrome and psychotic disorders: implications for psychiatric genetics.', *American Journal of Medical Genetics*, 54: 107–112.

Chowdhury, U. (2004) *Tics and Tourette Syndrome: A Handbook for Parents and Professionals.* London: Jessica Kingsley Publishers.

Christ, S.E., Moffitt, A.J. and Peck, D. (2010) 'Disruption of prefrontal function and connectivity in individuals with phenylketonuria.', *Molecular Genetics and Metabolism*, 99: S33–S40.

Christensen, B., Arbour, L., Tran, P., Leclerc, D. *et al.* (1999) 'Genetic polymorphisms in methylenetetrahydrofolate reductase and methionine synthase, folate levels in red blood cells, and risk of neural tube defects.' *American Journal of Medical Genetics*, 84: 151–157.

Christian, S.L., Brune, C.W., Sudi, J., Kumar, R.A. *et al.* (2008) 'Novel submicroscopic chromosomal abnormalities detected in autism spectrum disorder.', *Biological Psychiatry*, 15: 1111–1117.

Critchley, M. and Hoffman, H.L. (1942) 'The Syndrome of Periodic Somnolence and Morbid Hunger (Kleine-Levin Syndrome).', *British Medical Journal*, 1 (4230): 137–139.

Chudley, A.E., Gutierrez, E., Jocelyn, L.J. and Chodirker, B.N. (1998) 'Outcomes of genetic evaluation in children with developmental disorder.' *Journal of Developmental and Behavioural Pediatrics*, 19: 321–325.

Chugani, D.C., Sundram, B.S., Behen, M., Lee, M. and Moore, G.J. (1999) 'Evidence of altered energy metabolism in autistic children.' *Progress in Neuro-Psychopharmacology and Biological Psychiatry, 23*: 635–641.

Chugani, H.T., Juhász, C., Behen, M.E., Ondersma, R. and Muzik, O. (2007) 'Autism with facial port-wine stain: a new syndrome?' *Pediatric Neurology, 37*: 192–199.

Chun, H.J., Zheng, L., Ahmad, M., Wang, J. *et al.* (2002) 'Pleiotropic defects in lymphocyte activation caused by caspase-8 mutations lead to human immunodeficiency.', *Nature, 419*(6905): 395–399.

Chung, J.H. and Eng, C. (2005) 'Nuclear-cytoplasmic partitioning of phosphatase and tensin homologue deleted on chromosome 10 (PTEN) differentially regulates the cell cycle and apoptosis.', *Cancer Research, 65*: 8096–8100.

Ciaccio, M., Piccione, M., Giuffrè, M., Macaione, V. *et al.* (2003) 'Aminoacid profile and oxidative status in children affected by Down syndrome before and after supplementary nutritional treatment.', *Italian Journal of Biochemistry, 52*(2): 72–79.

Ciani, F., Poggi, G.M., Pasquini, E., Donati, M.A. and Zammarchi, E. (2000) 'Prolonged exclusive breast-feeding from vegan mother causing an acute onset of isolated methylmalonicaciduria due to a mild mutase deficiency.', *Clinical Nutrition, 19*(2): 137–139.

Ciara, E., Popowska, E., Piekutowska-Abramczuk, D., Jurkiewicz, D. *et al.* (2006) 'SLOS carrier frequency in Poland as determined by screening for Trp151X and Val326Leu DHCR7 mutations.' *European Journal of Medical Genetics, 49*(6): 499–504.

Cichowski, K. and Jacks, T. (2001) 'NF1 tumor suppressor gene function: narrowing the GAP.', *Cell, 104*: 593–604.

Cideciyan, A.V., Aleman, T.S., Boye, S.L., Schwartz, S.B. *et al.* (2008) 'Human gene therapy for RPE65 isomerase deficiency activates the retinoid cycle of vision but with slow rod kinetics.', *Proceedings of the National Academy of Science USA, 105*(39): 15112–15117.

Cinalli, G., Renier, D., Sebag, G., Sainte-Rose, C. *et al.* (1995) 'Chronic tonsillar herniation in Crouzon's and Apert's syndromes: the role of premature synostosis of the lambdoid suture.', *Journal of Neurosurgery, 83*: 575–582.

Claes, L., Del-Favero, J., Ceulemans, B., Lagae, L. *et al.* (2001) 'De novo mutations in the sodium-channel gene SCN1A cause severe myoclonic epilepsy of infancy.', *American Journal of Human Genetics, 68*(6): 1327–1332.

Clarke, D.F., Roberts, W., Daraksan, M., Dupuis, A. *et al.* (2005) 'The prevalence of autistic spectrum disorder in children surveyed in a tertiary care epilepsy clinic.' *Epilepsia, 46*: 1970–1977.

Clark-Taylor, T. and Clark-Taylor, B.E. (2004) 'Is autism a disorder of fatty acid metabolism? Possible dysfunction of mitochondrial beta-oxidation by long chain acyl-CoA dehydrogenase.' *Medical Hypotheses, 62*: 970–975.

Clayton, P.T. (2006) 'B6-responsive disorders: a model of vitamin dependency.' *Journal of Inherited Metabolic Disease, 29*(2–3): 317–326.

Clayton-Smith, J. (1993) 'Clinical research on Angelman syndrome in the United Kingdom: observations on 82 affected individuals.' *American Journal of Medical Genetics, 46*: 12–15.

Clayton-Smith, J. and Laan, L. (2003) 'Angelman syndrome: a review of the clinical and genetic aspects.', *Journal of Medical Genetics, 40*: 87–95.

Clayton-Smith, J. and Pembrey, M.E. (1992) 'Angelman syndrome.' *Journal of Medical Genetics, 29*: 412–415.

Clayton-Smith, J., Watson, P., Ramsden, S. and Black, G.C.M. (2000) 'Somatic mutation in MeCP2 as a non-fatal neurodevelopmental disorder in males.', *Lancet, 356*: 830–832.

Cleaver, J.E. (2005) 'Splitting hairs – discovery of a new DNA repair and transcription factor for the human disease trichothiodystrophy.', *DNA Repair, 4*: 285–287.

Cleaver, J.E., Thompson, L.H., Richardson, A.S. and States, J.C. (1999) 'A summary of mutations in the UV-sensitive disorders: xeroderma pigmentosum, Cockayne syndrome, and trichothiodystrophy.' *Human Mutation, 14*: 9–22.

Clementi, M., Milani, S., Mammi, I., Boni, S. *et al.* (1999) 'Neurofibromatosis type 1 growth charts.', *American Journal of Medical Genetics, 87*: 317–323.

Cleves, M.A., Hobbs, C.A., Cleves, P.A., Tilford, J.M. *et al.* (2007) 'Congenital defects among liveborn infants with Down syndrome.', *Birth Defects Research A Clinical and Molecular Teratology, 79*(9): 657–663.

Coffee, B., Ikeda, M., Budimirovic, D.B., Hjelm, L.N. *et al.* (2008) 'Mosaic FMR1 deletion causes fragile-X syndrome and can lead to molecular misdiagnosis: a case report and review of the literature.', *American Journal of Medical Genetics A, 146A*(10): 1358–1367.

Coffin, G.S. and Siris, E. (1970) 'Mental retardation with absent fifth fingernail and terminal phalanx.', *American Journal of Diseases in Childhood, 119*: 433–439.

Coffin, G.S., Siris, E. and Wegienka, L.C. (1966) 'Mental retardation with osteocartilaginous anomalies.', *American Journal of Diseases of Childhood, 112*: 205–213.

Coghlan, M.P., Culbert, A.A., Cross, D.A., Corcoran, S.L. *et al.* (2000) 'Selective small molecule inhibitors of glycogen synthase kinase-3 modulate glycogen metabolism and gene transcription.', *Chemistry and Biology, 7*(10): 793–803.

Cogulu, O., Aykut, A., Kutukculer, N., Ozkinay, C. and Ozkinay, F. (2007) 'Two cases of macrocephaly and immune deficiency.' *Clinical Dysmorphology, 16*: 81–84.

Cohen, B.E., Bodonyi, E. and Szeinberg, A. (1961) 'Phenylketonuria in Jews.', *Lancet, I*: 344–345.

Cohen, D., Pichard, N., Tordjman, S., Baumann, C. *et al.* (2005) 'Specific genetic disorders and autism: clinical contribution towards their identification.' *Journal of Autism and Developmental Disorders, 35*: 103–116.

Cohen, I.L., Sudhalter, V., Pfadt, A., Jenkins, E.C. *et al.* (1991) 'Why are autism and the fragile-X syndrome associated? Conceptual and methodological issues.', *American Journal of Human Genetics, 48*: 195–202.

Cohen, L.H., Vamos, E., Heinrichs, C., Toppet, M. *et al.* (1997) 'Growth failure, encephalopathy, and endocrine dysfunctions in two siblings, one with 5-oxoprolinase deficiency.', *European Journal of Pediatrics, 156*(12): 935–938.

Cohen, M.M. Jr. (1973) 'An etiologic and nosologic overview of craniosynostosis syndromes.' *Birth Defects Original Articles Series, XI*(2): 137–189.

Cohen, M.M. Jr. (1977) 'Genetic perspectives on craniosynostosis and syndromes with craniosynostosis.' *Journal of Neurosurgery, 47*: 886–898.

Cohen, M.M. Jr. (1988) 'Further diagnostic thoughts about the Elephant Man.', *American Journal of Medical Genetics, 29*: 777–782.

Cohen, M.M. Jr. (1990) 'Bannayan-Riley-Ruvalcaba syndrome: renaming three formerly recognized syndromes as one etiologic entity.', (Letter) *American Journal of Medical Genetics, 35*: 291 only.

Cohen, M.M. Jr. (1995) 'Perspectives on craniofacial asymmetry. IV. Hemi-asymmetries.' *International Journal of Oral and Maxillofascial Surgery, 24*: 134–141.

Cohen, M.M. Jr. (2003) 'Mental deficiency, alterations in performance, and central nervous system abnormalities in overgrowth syndromes.' *American Journal of Medical Genetics C Seminars in Medical Genetics, 117*: 49–56.

Cohen, M.M. Jr. and Gorlin, R.J. (1991) 'Pseudo-trisomy 13 syndrome.', *American Journal of Medical Genetics, 39*(3): 332–335.

Cohen, M.M. Jr., Hall, B.D., Smith, D.W., Graham, C.B. and Lampert, K.J. (1973) 'A new syndrome with hypotonia, obesity, mental deficiency, and facial, oral, ocular and limb anomalies.', *Journal of Pediatrics, 83*: 280–284.

Cohen, M.M. Jr. and Kreiborg, S. (1990) 'The central nervous system in the Apert syndrome.', *American Journal of Medical Genetics, 35*: 36–45.

Cohen, M.M. Jr. and Kreiborg, S. (1993) 'Visceral anomalies in the Apert syndrome.', *American Journal of Medical Genetics, 45*: 758–760.

Cohen, M.M. Jr. and Kreiborg, S. (1995) 'Hands and feet in the Apert syndrome.', *American Journal of Medical Genetics, 57*: 82–96.

Cohen, M.M. Jr., Kreiborg, S., Lammer, E.J., Cordero, J.F. *et al.* (1992) 'Birth prevalence study of the Apert syndrome.', *American Journal of Medical Genetics, 42*: 655–659.

Cohen, M.M. Jr., Neri, G. and Weksberg, R. (2002) *Overgrowth syndromes.* Oxford Monographs in Medical Genetics, 43. Oxford: Oxford University Press.

Colamaria, V., Burlina, A.B., Gaburro, D., Pajno-Ferrara, F. *et al.* (1989) 'Biotin-responsive infantile encephalopathy: EEG-polygraphic study of a case.', *Epilepsia, 30*(5): 573–578.

Cole, T. (1998) 'Growing interest in overgrowth.' *Archives of Diseases in Childhood, 78*: 200–204.

Cole, T.R.P. and Hughes, H.E. (1990) 'Sotos syndrome.' *Journal of Medical Genetics, 27*: 571–576.

Cole, T.R.P. and Hughes, H.E. (1991) 'Autosomal dominant macrocephaly: benign familial macrocephaly or a new syndrome?' *American Journal of Medical Genetics, 41*: 115–124.

Cole, T.R.P. and Hughes, H.E. (1994) 'Sotos syndrome: a study of the diagnostic criteria and natural history.' *Journal of Medical Genetics: 31*, 20–32.

Coleman, M. (1990) 'Is classical Rett syndrome ever present in males?' *Brain and Development, 12*: 31–32.

Coleman, M. (ed.) (2005) *The Neurology of Autism.* Oxford: Oxford University Press.

Coleman, M. and Blass, J.P. (1985) 'Autism and lactic acidosis.', *Journal of Autism and Developmental Disorders, 15*(1): 1–8.

Coleman, M. and Gillberg, C. (1985) *The Biology of the Autistic Syndromes.* New York: Praeger Publishing.

Coleman, M., Sobel, S., Bhagavan, H.N., Coursin, D. *et al.* (1985) 'A double blind study of vitamin B6 in Down's syndrome infants. Part 1 – clinical and biochemical results.', *Journal of Mental Deficiency Research, 29*: 233–240.

Collacott, R., Duckett, D.P., Mathews, D., Warrington, J.S. and Young, I.D. (1990) 'Down's syndrome and fragile-X syndrome in a single patient.' *Journal of Mental Deficiency Research, 34*: 81–86.

Colley, A., Donnai, D. and Evans, D.G. (1996) 'Neurofibromatosis/Noonan phenotype: a variable feature of type 1 neurofibromatosis.', *Clinical Genetics, 49*: 59–64.

Collier, D.A. (2008) 'Schizophrenia: the polygene princess and the pea.', *Psychological Medicine, 38*: 1687–1691.

Collin, G.B., Marshall, J.D., Ikeda, A., So, W.V. *et al.* (2002) 'Mutations in ALMS1 cause obesity, type 2 diabetes and neurosensory degeneration in Alstrom syndrome.', *Nature Genetics, 31*: 74–78.

Collis, M.S. (1951) *The Discovery of LS Lowry.* London: Alex Reid and Lefevre.

Collombat, P., Mansouri, A., Hecksher-Sorensen, J., Serup, P. *et al.* (2003) 'Opposing actions of Arx and Pax4 in endocrine pancreas development.', *Genes and Development, 17*(20): 2591–2603.

Comery, T.A., Harris, J.B., Willems, P.J., Oostra, B.A. *et al.* (1997) 'Abnormal dendritic spines in fragile-X knockout mice: maturation and pruning deficits.' *Proceedings of the National Academy of Science USA, 94*: 5401–5404.

Comi, A.M. (2006) 'Advances in Sturge-Weber syndrome.' *Current Opinion in Neurology, 19*: 124–128.

Comi, A.M. (2007) 'Update on Sturge-Weber syndrome: diagnosis, treatment, quantitative measures, and controversies.', *Lymphatic Research and Biology, 5*(4): 257–264.

Comi, A.M., Zimmerman, A.W., Frye, V.H., Law, P.A. and Peeden, J.N. (1999) 'Familial clustering of autoimmune disorders and evaluation of medical risk factors in autism.', *Journal of Child Neurology, 14*(6): 388–394.

Comings, D.E. (1990) *Tourette Syndrome and Human Behaviour.* Duarte: Hope Press.

Comings, D.E. and Comings, B.G. (1985) 'Tourette syndrome: clinical and psychological aspects of 250 cases.', *American Journal of Human Genetics, 37*: 435–450.

Comings, D.E. and Comings, B.G. (1991) 'Clinical and genetic relationships between autism-pervasive developmental disorder and Tourette syndrome: a study of 19 cases.', *American Journal of Medical Genetics, 39*: 180–191.

Comings, D.E., Himes, J.A. and Comings, B.G. (1990) 'An epidemiologic study of Tourette's syndrome in a single school district.', *Journal of Clinical Psychiatry, 51*(11): 463–469.

Commission on Classification and Terminology of the International League Against Epilepsy (1989) 'Proposal for revised classification of epilepsies and epileptic syndromes.' *Epilepsia, 30*: 289–299.

Committee on Genetics, American Academy of Pediatrics. (2001) 'Health care supervision for children with Williams syndrome.' *Pediatrics, 107*: 1192–1204.

Compton, M.T., Celentana, M., Price, B. and Furman, A.C. (2004) 'A case of Sotos syndrome (cerebral gigantism) and psychosis.', *Psychopathology, 37*: 190–194.

Conciatori, M., Stodgell, C.J., Hyman, S.L., O'Bara, M. *et al.* (2004) 'Association between the HOXA1 A218G polymorphism and increased head circumference in patients with autism.' *Biological Psychiatry, 55*: 413–441.

Condon, W.S. and Sander, L.W. (1974) 'Synchrony demonstrated between movements of the neonate and adult speech.', *Child Development, 45*: 456–462.

Conley, C.L., Krevans, J.R., Chow, B.F., Barrows, C. and Lang, C.A. (1951) 'Observations on the absorption, utilization and excretion of vitamin B12.', *Journal of Laboratory and Clinical Medicine, 38*: 84–94.

Connarty, M., Dennis, N.R., Patch, C., Macpherson, J.N. and Harvey, J.F. (1996) 'Molecular re-investigation of patients with Huntington's disease in Wessex reveals a family with dentatorubral and pallidoluysian atrophy.', *Human Genetics, 97*: 76–78.

Connolly, A.M., Chez, M.G., Pestronk, A., Arnold, S.T. *et al.* (1999) 'Serum autoantibodies to brain in Landau-Kleffner variant, autism, and other neurologic disorders.', *The Journal of Pediatrics, 134*(5): 607–613.

Connolly, A.M., Chez, M., Streif, E.M., Keeling, R.M. *et al.* (2006) 'Brain-derived neurotrophic factor and autoantibodies to neural antigens in sera of children with autistic spectrum disorders, Landau-Kleffner syndrome, and epilepsy.', *Biological Psychiatry, 59*(4): 354–363.

Connor, J.M. and Fernandez, C. (1984) 'Genetic aspects of hemifacial microsomia.', (Letter) *Human Genetics, 68*: 349.

Conte, G. and Gioia, L. (1836) 'Scrofola del sistema muscolare.', *Annali Clinici dell'ospedale degli Incurabili, Napoli, 2*: 66–79.

Conway, B.R. (2007) 'Colour vision: mice see hue too.', *Science, 17*(12): R457–R560.

Cook, E.H. Jr., Lindgren, V., Leventhal, B.L., Courchesne, R. *et al.* (1997) 'Autism or atypical autism in maternally but not paternally derived proximal 15q duplication.', *American Journal of Human Genetics, 60*(4): 928–934.

Cook, J.A., Oliver, K., Mueller, R.F. and Sampson, J. (1996) 'A cross sectional study of renal involvement in tuberous sclerosis.' *Journal of Medical Genetics, 33*: 480–484.

Coppola, G., Capovilla, G., Montagnini, A., Romeo, A. *et al.* (2002) 'Topiramate as add-on drug in severe myoclonic epilepsy in infancy: an Italian multicenter open trial.', *Epilepsy Research, 49*(1): 45–48.

Coppus, A.W., Fekkes, D., Verhoeven, W.M.A., Tuinier, S. *et al.* (2007) 'Plasma amino acids and neopterin in healthy persons with Down's syndrome.', *Journal of Neural Transmission, 114*(8): 1041–1045.

Corbett, B.A., Kantor, A.B., Schulman, H., Walker, W.L. *et al.* (2007) 'A proteomic study of serum from children with autism showing differential expression of apolipoproteins and complement proteins.', *Molecular Psychiatry, 12*: 292–306.

Corcoran, R.B. and Scott, M.P. (2001) 'A mouse model for medulloblastoma and basal cell naevus syndrome.', *Journal of Neurooncology, 53*(3): 307–318.

Cordain, L. and Hickey, M.S. (2006) 'Ultraviolet radiation represents an evolutionary selective pressure for the south-to-north gradient of the MTHFR 677TT genotype.', *American Journal of Clinical Nutrition, 84*(5): 1243.

Cornish, K.M., Turk, J., Wilding, J., Sudhalter, V. *et al.* (2004) 'Annotation. Deconstructing the attention deficit in fragile-X syndrome: a developmental neuropsychological approach.', *Journal of Child Psychology and Psychiatry, 45*(6): 1042–1053.

Correa-Cerro, L.S. and Porter, F.D. (2005) '3beta-hydroxysterol Delta7-reductase and the Smith-Lemli-Opitz syndrome.', *Molecular Genetics and Metabolism, 84*(2): 112–126.

Correia, C., Coutinho, A.M., Diogo, L., Grazina, M. *et al.* (2006) 'Brief report. High frequency of biochemical markers for mitochondrial dysfunction in autism: no association with the mitochondrial aspartate/glutamate carrier SLC25A12 gene.', *Journal of Autism and Developmental Disorders, 36*: 1137–1140.

Cossu, G. and Sampaolesi, M. (2007) 'New therapies for Duchenne muscular dystrophy: challenges, prospects and clinical trials.', *TRENDS in Molecular Medicine, 13*(12): 520–526.

Costa, R.M., Federov, N.B., Kogan, J.H., Murphy, G.G. *et al.* (2002) 'Mechanism for the learning deficits in a mouse model of neurofibromatosis type 1.', *Nature, 415*(6871): 526–530.

Courchesne, E. (1997) 'Brainstem, cerebellar and limbic neuroanatomical abnormalities in autism.', *Current Opinion in Neurobiology, 7*(2): 269–278.

Courchesne, E., Saitoh, O., Townsend, J.P., Yeung-Courchesne, R. *et al.* (1994) 'Cerebellar hypoplasia and hyperplasia in infantile autism.', *Lancet, 343*(8888): 63–64.

Cousley, R., Naora, H., Yokoyama, M., Kimura, M. *et al.* (2002) 'Validity of the Hfm transgenic mouse as a model for hemifacial microsomia.', *Cleft Palate-Craniofacial Journal, 39*(1): 81–92.

Cousley, R.R. and Calvert, M.L. (1997) 'Current concepts in the understanding and management of hemifacial microsomia.', *British Journal of Plastic Surgery, 50*(7): 536–551.

Cowan, R., Hoban, P., Kelsey, A., Birch, J.M. *et al.* (1997) 'The gene for the naevoid basal cell carcinoma syndrome acts as a tumour-suppressor gene in medulloblastoma.', *British Journal of Cancer, 76*: 141–145.

Cowell, H.R. (1978) 'The genetics of foot disorders.', *Orthopaedic Review, 7*: 55–58.

Coward, R.J.M., Risdon, R.A., Bingham, C., Hattersley, A.T. and Woolf, A.S. (2001) 'Kidney disease in hypomelanosis of Ito.' *Nephrology, Dialysis, Transplantation, 16*: 1267–1269.

Cox, E.V. and White, A.M. (1962) 'Methylmalonic acid excretion: index of vitamin Bq12 deficiency.', *Lancet, 280*(7261): 853–856.

Cox, G.F., Burger, J., Lip, V., Mau, U.A. *et al.* (2002) 'Intracytoplasmic sperm injection may increase the risk of imprinting defects.', *American Journal of Human Genetics*, 71: 162–164.

Cox, G.F. and Kunkel, L.M. (1997) 'Dystrophies and heart disease.', *Current Opinion in Cardiology*, 12: 329–343.

Craig, W.Y., Haddow, J.E., Palomaki, G.E., Kelley, R.I. *et al.* (2006) 'Identifying Smith-Lemli-Opitz syndrome in conjunction with prenatal screening for Down syndrome.', *Prenatal Diagnosis*, 26(9): 842–849.

Craigie, R.J., Ba'ath, M., Fryer, A. and Baillie, C. (2005) 'Surgical implications of the Smith-Lemli-Opitz syndrome.', *Pediatric Surgery International*, 21(6): 482–484.

Crawford, D.C., Acuna, J.M. and Sherman, S.L. (2001) 'FMR1 and the fragile-X syndrome: human genome epidemiology review.', *Genetics in Medicine*, 3: 359–371.

Crawford, D.C., Meadows, K.L., Newman, J.L., Taft, L.F. *et al.* (2002) 'Prevalence of the fragile-X syndrome in African-Americans.', *American Journal of Medical Genetics*, 110: 226–233.

Creak, E.M. (1963) 'Childhood psychosis: a review of 100 cases.', *British Journal of Psychiatry*, 109: 84–89.

Creange, A., Zeller, J., Rostaing-Rigattieri, S., Brugieres, P. *et al.* (1999) 'Neurological complications of neurofibromatosis type 1 in adulthood.', *Brain*, 122(3): 473–481.

Creel, D., O'Donnell, F.E. Jr. and Witkop, C.J. Jr. (1978) 'Visual system anomalies in human ocular albinos.' *Science*, 201: 931–933.

Cremin, J.D. Jr., Luck, M.L., Laughlin, N.K. and Smith, D.R. (1999) 'Efficacy of succimer chelation for reducing brain lead in a primate model of human lead exposure.', *Toxicology and Applied Pharmacology*, 161(3): 283–293.

Creswell, C. and Skuse, D. (2000) 'Autism in association with Turner syndrome: implications for male vulnerability.', *Neurocase*, 5: 511–518.

Crino, P.B., Nathanson, K.L. and Henske, E.P. (2006) 'The tuberous sclerosis complex.' *New England Journal of Medicine*, 355: 1345–1356.

Critchley, M. and Earl, C.J.C. (1932) 'Tuberose sclerosis and allied conditions.', *Brain*, 55: 311–346.

Croen, L.A., Goines, P., Braunschweig, D., Yolken, R. *et al.* (2008) 'Brain-derived neurotrophic factor and autism: maternal and infant peripheral blood levels in the Early Markers for Autism (EMA) Study.', *Autism Research*, 1(2): 130–137.

Croen, L.A., Najjar, D.V., Fireman, B. and Grether, J.K. (2007) 'Maternal and paternal age and risk of autism spectrum disorders.' *Archives of Pediatric and Adolescent Medicine*, 161: 334–340.

Croft, J.B. and Swift, M. (1990) 'Obesity, hypertension, and renal disease in relatives of Bardet-Biedl syndrome sibs.', *American Journal of Medical Genetics*, 36: 37–42.

Crow, T.J. (2008) 'The emperors of the schizophrenia polygene have no clothes.', *Psychological Medicine*, 38: 1681–1685.

Crutchfield, S.R., Haas, R.H., Nyhan, W.L. and Gibson, K.M. (2008) 'Succinic semialdehyde dehydrogenase deficiency: phenotype evolution in an adolescent patient at 20-year follow-up.', *Developmental Medicine and Child Neurology*, 50(11): 880–881.

Cuevas-Covarrubias, S.A., Kofman-Alfaro, S., Orozco Orozco, E. and Diaz-Zagoya, J.C. (1995) 'The biochemical identification of carrier state in mothers of sporadic cases of X-linked recessive ichthyosis.', *Genetic Counselling*, 6: 103–107.

Cui, Y., Costa, R.M., Murphy, G.G., Elgersma, Y. *et al.* (2008) 'Neurofibromin regulation of ERK signaling modulates GABA release and learning.', *Cell*, 135(3): 549–560.

Cunniff, C., Kratz, L.E., Moser, A., Natowicz, M.R. and Kelley, R.I. (1997) 'Clinical and biochemical spectrum of patients with RSH/Smith-Lemli-Opitz syndrome and abnormal cholesterol metabolism.', *American Journal of Medical Genetics*, 68: 263–269.

Cundiff, D.K. and Harris, W. (2006) 'Case report of 5 siblings: malnutrition? Rickets? DiGeorge syndrome? Developmental delay?' *Nutrition Journal*, 5: 1, doi:10.1186/1475-2891-5-1

Cupo, L.N., Pyeritz, R.E., Olson, J.L., McPhee, S.J. *et al.* (1981) 'Ehlers-Danlos syndrome with abnormal collagen fibrils, sinus of Valsalva aneurysms, myocardial infarction, panacinar emphysema and cerebral heterotopias.', *American Journal of Medicine*, 71: 1051–1058.

Curatolo, P. (ed.) (2003) *Tuberous Sclerosis Complex: From Basic Science to Clinical Phenotypes*. Cambridge: MacKeith Press.

Curatolo, P., Porfirio, M.C., Manzi, B. and Seri, S. (2004) 'Autism in tuberous sclerosis.' *European Journal of Paediatric Neurology*, 8: 327–332.

Curry, C.J.R., Carey, J.C., Holland, J.S., Chopra, D. *et al.* (1987) 'Smith-Lemli-Opitz syndrome-type II: multiple congenital anomalies with male pseudohermaphroditism and frequent early lethality.' *American Journal of Medical Genetics*, 26: 45–57.

Curry, C.J.R, Stevenson, R.E., Aughton, D., Byrne, J. *et al.* (1997) 'Evaluation of mental retardation: recommendations of a consensus conference. American College of Medical Genetics.', *American Journal of Medical Genetics*, 72: 468–477.

Cusmano-Ozog, K., Manning, M.A. and Hoyme, H.E. (2007) '22q13.3 deletion syndrome: a recognizable malformation syndrome associated with marked speech and language delay.', *American Journal of Medical Genetics C: Seminars in Medical Genetics*, 145C(4): 393–398.

Cyran, S.E., Martinez, R., Daniels, S., Dignan, P.S.J. and Kaplan, S. (1987) 'Spectrum of congenital heart disease in CHARGE association.', *Journal of Pediatrics*, 110: 576–580.

Cyrulnik, S.E., Fee, R.J., De Vivo, D.C., Goldstein, E. and Hinton, V.J. (2007) 'Delayed developmental language milestones in children with Duchenne's muscular dystrophy.', *Journal of Pediatrics*, 150(5): 474–478.

Czeizel, A.E., Elek, C. and Susanszky, E. (1993) 'Birth prevalence study of Apert syndrome.', (Letter) *American Journal of Medical Genetics*, 45: 392.

Czyzyk, E., Jozwiak, S., Roszkowski, M. and Schwartz, R.A. (2003) 'Optic pathway gliomas in children with and without neurofibromatosis 1.', *Journal of Child Neurology*, 18: 471–478.

Daiger, S.P., Chakraborty, R., Reed, L., Fekete, G. *et al.* (1989a) 'Polymorphic DNA haplotypes at the phenylalanine hydroxylase (PAH) locus in European families with phenylketonuria (PKU).', *American Journal of Human Genetics*, 45: 310–318.

Daiger, S.P., Reed, L., Huang, S-S., Zeng, Y-T. *et al.* (1989b) 'Polymorphic DNA haplotypes at the phenylalanine hydroxylase (PAH) locus in Asian families with phenylketonuria (PKU).', *American Journal of Human Genetics*, 45: 319–324.

Dallaire, L., Mitchell, G., Giguere, R., Lefebvre, F. *et al.* (1995) 'Prenatal diagnosis of Smith-Lemli-Opitz syndrome is possible by measurement of 7-dehydrocholesterol in amniotic fluid.', *Prenatal Diagnosis*, 15: 855–858.

D'Aloia, A., Vizzardi, E., Zanini, G., Antonioli, E. *et al.* (2008) 'Young woman affected by a rare form of familial connective tissue disorder associated with multiple arterial pulmonary stenosis and severe pulmonary hypertension.', *Circulation Journal*, 72: 164–167.

Dalton, P., Deacon, R., Blamire, A., Pike, M. *et al.* (2003) 'Maternal neuronal antibodies associated with autism and a language disorder.', *Annals of Neurology*, 53(4): 533–537.

D'Amelio, M., Ricci, I., Sacco, R., Liu, X. *et al.* (2005) 'Paraoxonase gene variants are associated with autism in North America, but not in Italy: possible regional specificity in gene–environment interactions.', *Molecular Psychiatry*, 10: 1006–1016.

Dan, B. (2008) *Angelman Syndrome*, Clinics in Developmental Medicine. London: MacKeith Press, Wiley-Blackwell.

Danks, D.M. (1978) 'Pteridines and phenylketonuria: report of a workshop. Introductory comments.', *Journal of Inherited Metabolic Disease*, 1(2): 47–48.

Danfors, T., von Knorring, A.L., Hartvig, P., Langstrom, B. *et al.* (2005) 'Tetrahydrobiopterin in the treatment of children with autistic disorder: a double-blind placebo-controlled crossover study.', *Journal of Clinical Psychopharmacology*, 25(5): 485–489.

Danlos, H-A. (1908) 'Un cas de cutis laxa avec tumeurs par contusion chronique des coudes et des genoux (xanthome juvénile pseudo-diabetique de MM Hallopeau et Macé de Lépinay).', *Bulletin de la Société française de dermatologie et de syphiligraphie*, Paris, 19: 70–72.

Dar, H., Schaap, T., Bait-Or, H., Borochowitz, Z. *et al.* (1995) 'Ethnic distribution of the fragile-X syndrome in Israel: evidence of founder chromosomes(?).', *Israeli Journal of Medical Science*, 31: 323–325.

Darendeliler, F., Larsson, P., Neyzi, O., Price, A.D. *et al.* (2003) 'Growth hormone treatment in Aarskog syndrome: analysis of the KIGS (Pharmacia International Growth Database) data.', *Journal of Pediatric Endocrinology and Metabolism*, 16(8): 1137–1142.

Darras, B.T. and Francke, U. (1988) 'Myopathy in complex glycerol kinase deficiency patients is due to 3' deletions of the dystrophin gene.', *American Journal of Human Genetics*, 43: 126–130.

Darrigo Jr., L.G., Geller, M., Filho, A.B. and Azulay, D.R. (2007) 'Prevalence of plexiform neurofibroma in children and adolescents with type I neurofibromatosis.', *Jornal de Pediatria (Rio J)*, 83(6): 571–573.

Das, S., Kubota, T., Song, M., Daniel, R. *et al.* (1997–1998) 'Methylation analysis of the fragile-X syndrome by PCR.', *Genetic Testing*, 1: 151–155.

Dasouki, M., Jurecic, V., Phillips, J.A. 3rd, Whitlock, J.A. and Baldini, A. (1997) 'DiGeorge anomaly and chromosome 10p deletions: one or two loci?' *American Journal of Medical Genetics*, 73(1): 72–75.

Danfors, T., von Knorring, A.L., Hartvig, P., Langstrom, B. *et al.* (2005) 'Tetrahydrobiopterin in the treatment of children with autistic disorder: a double-blind placebo-controlled crossover study.', *Journal of Clinical Psychopharmacology*, 25(5): 485–489.

Danks, D.M. (1978) 'Pteridines and phenylketonuria: report of a workshop: Introductory comments.', *Journal of Inherited Metabolic Disease*, 1(2): 47–48.

Datta, A.K., Mandal, S. and Bhattacharya, S. (2009) 'Autism and mental retardation with convulsion in tuberous sclerosis: a case report.', *Cases Journal*, 2: 7061, doi:10.4076/1757-1626-2-7061.

Daumas-Duport, C., Scheithauer, B.W., Chodkiewicz, J.P., Laws, E.R. Jr. and Vedrenne, C. (1988) 'Dysembryoplastic neuroepithelial tumor: a surgically curable tumor of young patients with intractable partial seizures. Report of thirty-nine cases.', *Neurosurgery*, 23: 545–556.

Dauvilliers, Y., Mayer, G., Lecendreux, M., Neidhart, E. *et al.* (2002) 'Kleine-Levin syndrome: an autoimmune hypothesis based on clinical and genetic analyses.', *Neurology*, 59: 1739–1745.

Davalos, D.B., Merikangas, J. and Bender, S. (2001) 'Psychosis in hypomelanosis of Ito.', *Journal of the Royal Society of Medicine*, 94(3): 140–141.

Davenport, S.L.H., Hefner, M.A. and Mitchell, J.A. (1986) 'The spectrum of clinical features in CHARGE syndrome.', *Clinical Genetics*, 29: 298–310.

David, A., Bitoun, P., Lacombe, D., Lambert, J.C. *et al.* (1999) 'Hydrometrocolpos and polydactyly: a common neonatal presentation of Bardet-Biedl and McKusick-Kaufman syndromes.', *Journal of Medical Genetics*, 36: 599–603.

David, O., Fiorucci, G.C., Tosi, M.T., Altare, F. *et al.* (1996) 'Hematological studies in children with Down syndrome.', *Pediatric Hematology and Oncology*, 13(3): 271–275.

Davidson, Z.E. and Truby, H. (2009) 'A review of nutrition in Duchenne muscular dystrophy.', *Journal of Human Nutrition and Dietetics*, 22(5): 383–393.

Davies, W., Humby, T., Isles, A.R., Burgoyne, P.S. and Wilkinson, L.S. (2006) 'X-monosomy effects on visuospatial attention in mice: a candidate gene and implications for Turner syndrome and attention deficit hyperactivity disorder.', *Biological Psychiatry*, 61(12): 1351–1360.

Davis, R.E., Swiderski, R.E., Rahmouni, K., Nishimura, D.Y. *et al.* (2007) 'A knockin mouse model of the Bardet–Biedl syndrome 1 M390R mutation has cilia defects, ventriculomegaly, retinopathy, and obesity.', *Proceedings of the National Academy of Science USA*, 104(49): 19422–19427.

Davis, S.D., Schaller, J. and Wedgwood, R.J. (1966) 'Job's syndrome: recurrent, "cold", staphylococcal abscesses.' *Lancet*, 287(7445): 1013–1015.

Daw, S.C.M., Taylor, C., Kraman, M., Call, K. *et al.* (1996) 'A common region of 10p deleted in DiGeorge and velocardiofacial syndromes.' *Nature Genetics*, 13: 458–461.

Dawson, G., Munson, J., Webb, S.J., Nalty, T. *et al.* (2007) 'Rate of head growth decelerates and symptoms worsen in the second year of life in autism.', *Biological Psychiatry*, 61: 458–464.

Dawson, G., Rogers, S., Munson, J., Smith, M. *et al.* (2010) 'Randomized, controlled trial of an intervention for toddlers with autism: the Early Start Denver Model.', *Pediatrics*, 125(1): e17–23.

Day, R.E. and Schutt, W.H. (1979) 'Normal children with large heads – benign familial megalencephaly.', *Archives of Disease in Childhood*, 54: 512–517.

Dayer, A.G., Bottani, A., Bouchardy, I., Fluss, J. *et al.* (2007) 'MeCP2 mutant allele in a boy with Rett syndrome and his unaffected heterozygous mother.', *Brain and Development*, 29: 47–50.

de Almeida, J.C., Reis, D.F. and Martins, R.R. (1989) 'Interstitial deletion of (17) (p11.2): a microdeletion syndrome. Another example.', *Annals of Genetics*, 32: 184–186.

Deardorff, M.A., Kaur, M., Yaeger, D., Rampuria, A. *et al.* (2007) 'Mutations in cohesin complex members SMC3 and SMC1A cause a mild variant of Cornelia de Lange syndrome with predominant mental retardation.', *American Journal of Human Genetics*, 80(3): 485–494.

Deb, S., Braganza, J., Norton, N., Williams, H. *et al.* (2000) 'APOE epsilon 4 influences the manifestation of Alzheimer's disease in adults with Down's syndrome.', *British Journal of Psychiatry*, 176: 468–472.

DeBassio, W.A., Kemper, T.L. and Knoefel, J.E. (1985) 'Coffin-Siris syndrome: neuropathologic findings.', *Archives of Neurology*, 42: 350–353.

de Baulny, H.O., Benoist, J.F., Rigal, O., Touati, G. *et al.* (2005) 'Methylmalonic and propionic acidaemias: management and outcome.' *Journal of Inherited Metabolic Disorders*, 28: 415–423.

de Baulny, H.O. and Saudubray, J.M. (2002) 'Branched-chain organic aciduria.' *Seminars in Neonatology*, 7: 65–74.

DeBella, K., Poskitt, K., Szudek, J. and Friedman, J.M. (2000) 'Use of "unidentified bright objects" on MRI for diagnosis of neurofibromatosis 1 in children.', *Neurology*, 54: 1646–1651.

DeBella, K., Szudek, J. and Friedman, J.M. (2000) 'Use of the national institutes of health criteria for diagnosis of neurofibromatosis 1 in children.', *Pediatrics*, 105: 608–614.

Debicka, A. and Adamczak, P. (1979) 'A case of hereditary Sturge-Weber syndrome.' [In Polish]. *Klinicka Oczna*, 81(9): 541–542.

de Boer, J., Andressoo, J.O., de Wit, J., Huijmans, J. *et al.* (2002) 'Premature aging in mice deficient in DNA repair and transcription.', *Science*, 296: 1276–1279.

De Boer, L., Kant, S.G., Karperien, M., Van Beers, L. *et al.* (2004) 'Psychosocial, cognitive, and motor dysfunctioning in patients with suspected Sotos syndrome: a comparison genotype-phenotype correlation in patients suspected of having Sotos syndrome.', *Hormone Research*, 62: 197–207.

De Bona, C., Zappella, M., Hayek, G., Meloni, I. *et al.* (2000) 'Preserved speech variant is allelic of classic Rett syndrome.', *European Journal of Human Genetics*, 8: 325–330.

De Boulle, K., Verkerk, A.J.M.H., Reyniers, E., Vits, L. *et al.* (1993) 'A point mutation in the FMR-1 gene associated with fragile-X mental retardation.' *Nature Genetics*, 3: 31–35.

De Decker, H.P. and Lawrenson, J.B. (2001) 'The 22q11.2 deletion: from diversity to a single gene theory.', *Genetics in Medicine*, 3(1): 2–5.

De Giacomo, A. and Fombonne, E. (1998) 'Parental recognition of developmental abnormalities in autism.', *European Child and Adolescent Psychiatry*, 7(3): 131–136.

DeGrauw, T.J., Cecil, K.M., Byars, A.W., Salomons, G.S. *et al.* (2003) 'The clinical syndrome of creatine transporter deficiency.', *Molecular and Cellular Biochemistry*, 244: 45–48.

Dehart, D.B., Lanoue, L., Tint, G.S. and Sulik, K.K. (1997) 'Pathogenesis of malformations in a rodent model for Smith-Lemli-Opitz syndrome.', *American Journal of Medical Genetics*, 68: 328–337.

De Hert, M., Steemans, D., Theys, P., Fryns, J.P. and Peuskens, J. (1996) 'Lujan-Fryns syndrome in the differential diagnosis of schizophrenia.' *American Journal of Medical Genetics*, 67: 212–214.

De Jaco, A., Comoletti, D., King, C.C. and Taylor, P. (2008) 'Trafficking of cholinesterases and neuroligins mutant proteins: an association with autism.', *Chemico-Biological Interactions*, 175: 349–351.

DeJong, G. and Nelson, M.M. (1992) 'Choanal atresia in two unrelated patients with the Coffin-Siris syndrome.', *Clinical Genetics*, 42: 320–322.

Dekaban, A.S. (1969) 'Hereditary syndrome of congenital retinal blindness (Leber), polycystic kidneys and maldevelopment of the brain.', *American Journal of Ophthalmology*, 68: 1029–1037.

de Knecht-van Eekelen, A. and Hennekam, R.C. (1994) 'Historical study: Cornelia C. de Lange (1871–1950) – a pioneer in clinical genetics.', *American Journal of Medical Genetics*, 52: 257–266.

Delabar, J.M., Theophile, D., Rahmani, Z., Chettouh, Z. *et al.* (1993) 'Molecular mapping of twenty-four features of Down syndrome on chromosome 21.', *European Journal of Human Genetics*, 1: 114–124.

de la Chapelle, A., Herva, R., Koivisto, M. and Aula, P. (1981) 'A deletion in chromosome 22 can cause DiGeorge syndrome.', *Human Genetics*, 57: 253–256.

de Lange, C. (1933) 'Sur un type nouveau de degeneration (typus Amstelodamensis) [On a new type of degeneration (type Amsterdam)], *Archives de Medecine des Enfants* 36: 713–719

De-la-Torre, R., Casado, A., Lopez-Fernandez, E., Carrascosa, D. *et al.* (1996) 'Overexpression of copper–zinc superoxide dismutase in trisomy 21.', *Experientia*, 52: 871–873.

Delaunoy, J.P., Dubos, A., Marques Pereira, P. and Hanauer, A. (2006) 'Identification of novel mutations in the RSK2 gene (RPS6KA3) in patients with Coffin-Lowry syndrome.' *Clinical Genetics*, 70: 161–166.

Del Campo, M., Antonell, A., Magano, L.F., Munoz, F.J. *et al.* (2006) 'Hemizygosity at the NCF1 gene in patients with Williams-Beuren syndrome decreases their risk of hypertension.', *American Journal of Human Genetics*, 78: 533–542.

Del Campo, M., Jones, M.C., Veraksa, A.N., Curry, C.J. et al. (1999) 'Monodactylous limbs and abnormal genitalia are associated with hemizygosity for the human 2q31 region that includes the HOXD cluster.', American Journal of Human Genetics, 65: 104–110.

De Leersnyder, H., de Blois, M-C., Vekemans, M., Sidi, D. et al. (2001) 'Beta-1-adrenergic antagonists improve sleep and behavioural disturbances in a circadian disorder, Smith-Magenis syndrome.', Journal of Medical Genetics, 38: 586–590.

Delgado-Escueta, A.V. and Bourgeois, B.F. (2008) 'Debate: Does genetic information in humans help us treat patients? PRO–genetic information in humans helps us treat patients. CON–genetic information does not help at all.', Epilepsia, 49 (Suppl 9): 13–24.

DeLong, R. (2007) 'GABA (A) receptor alpha 5 subunit as a candidate gene for autism and bipolar disorder: a proposed endophenotype with parent-of-origin and gain-of-function features, with or without oculocutaneous albinism.', Autism, 11(2): 135–147.

DeLorey, T.M., Handforth, A., Anagnostaras, S.G., Homanics, G.E. et al. (1998) 'Mice lacking the B3 subunit of the GABAA receptor have the epilepsy phenotype and many of the behavioural characteristics of Angelman syndrome.' Journal of Neuroscience, 18: 8505–8514.

DeLorey, T.M., Sahbaie, P., Hashemi, E., Homanics, G.E. et al. (2008) 'Gabrb3 gene deficient mice exhibit impaired social and exploratory behaviours, deficits in non-selective attention and hypoplasia of cerebellar vermal lobules: a potential model of autism spectrum disorder.', Behavioural Brain Research, 187(2): 207–220.

Delous, M., Baala, L., Salomon, R., Laclef, C. et al. (2007) 'The ciliary gene RPGRIP1L is mutated in cerebello-oculo-renal syndrome (Joubert syndrome type B) and Meckel syndrome.', Nature Genetics, 39: 875–881.

del Rosario Barona-Mazuera, M., Hidalgo-Galvan, L.R., de la Luz Orozco-Covarrubias, M., Duran-McKinster, C. et al. (1997) 'Proteus syndrome: new findings in seven patients.', Pediatric Dermatology, 14(1): 1–5.

De Luca, A., Bottillo, I., Sarkozy, A., Carta, C. et al. (2005) 'NF1 gene mutations represent the major molecular event underlying neurofibromatosis-Noonan syndrome.', American Journal of Human Genetics, 77: 1092–1101.

DeMars, R., LeVan, S.L., Trend, B.L. and Russell, L.B. (1976) 'Abnormal ornithine carbamyltransferase in mice having the sparse-fur mutation.', Proceeings of the National Academy of Science USA, 73(5): 1693–1697.

Demczuk, S., Levy, A., Aubry, M., Croquette, M-F. et al. (1995) 'Excess of deletions of maternal origin in the DiGeorge/velocardiofacial syndromes: a study of 22 new patients and review of the literature.', Human Genetics, 96: 9–13.

Dementieva, Y.A., Vance, D.D., Donnelly, S.L., Elston, L.A. et al. (2005) 'Accelerated head growth in early development of individuals with autism.' Pediatric Neurology, 32: 102–108.

Den Dunnen, J.T., Grootscholten, P.M., Bakker, E., Blonden, L.A. et al. (1989) 'Topography of the Duchenne muscular dystrophy (DMD) gene: FIGE and cDNA analysis of 194 cases reveals 115 deletions and 13 duplications.', American Journal of Human Genetics, 45: 835–847.

den Hollander, A.I., Roepman, R., Koenekoop, R.K. and Cremers, F.P.M. (2008) 'Leber congenital amaurosis: genes, proteins and disease mechanisms.', Progress in Retinal and Eye Research, 27: 391–419.

Dennis, M., Lockyer, L., Lazenby, A.L., Donnelly, R.E. et al. (1999) 'Intelligence patterns among children with high-functioning autism, phenylketonuria, and childhood head injury.', Journal of Autism and Developmental Disorders, 29(1): 5–17.

Deon, M., Sitta, A., Barschak, A.G., Coelho, D.M. et al. (2007) 'Induction of lipid peroxidation and decrease of antioxidant defenses in symptomatic and asymptomatic patients with X-linked adrenoleukodystrophy.', International Journal of Developmental Neuroscience, 25: 441–444.

Deonna, T. and Roulet, E. (2006) 'Autistic spectrum disorder: evaluating a possible contributing or causal role of epilepsy.', Epilepsia, 47(Supp 2): 79–82.

Deonna, T. and Ziegler, A.L. (1993) 'Cognitive development and behaviour in Joubert syndrome.', Biological Psychiatry, 33: 854–855.

De Paepe, A., Devereux, R.B., Dietz, H.C., Hennekam, R.C.M. and Pyeritz, R.E. (1996) 'Revised diagnostic criteria for the Marfan syndrome.', American Journal of Medical Genetics, 62: 417–426.

Depienne, C., Héron, D., Betancur, C., Benyahia, B. et al. (2007) 'Autism, language delay and mental retardation in a patient with 7q11 duplication.', Journal of Medical Genetics, 44(7): 452–458.

Depienne, C., Moreno-De-Luca, D., Heron, D., Bouteiller, D. et al. (2009) 'Screening for genomic rearrangements and methylation abnormalities of the 15q11–q13 region in autism spectrum disorders.', Biological Psychiatry, 66: 349–359.

Derbent, M., Yilmaz, Z., Baltaci, V., Saygili, A. et al. (2003) 'Chromosome 22q11.2 deletion and phenotypic features in 30 patients with conotruncal heart defects.', American Journal of Medical Genetics, 116A: 129–135.

Descheemaeker, M.J., Govers, V., Vermeulen, P. and Fryns, J.P. (2006) 'Pervasive developmental disorders in Prader-Willi syndrome: the Leuven experience in 59 subjects and controls.', American Journal of Medical Genetics, 140(11): 1136–1142.

DeScipio, C., Kaur, M., Yaeger, D., Innis, J.W. et al. (2005) 'Chromosome rearrangements in Cornelia de Lange syndrome (CdLS): report of a der(3) t(3;12)(p25.3;p13.3) in two half sibs with features of CdLS and review of reported CdLS cases with chromosome rearrangements.', American Journal of Medical Genetics A, 137: A276–282.

DeSilva, S., Drachman, D.B., Mellits, D. and Kuncl, R.W. (1987) 'Prednisone treatment in Duchenne muscular dystrophy: long-term benefit.', Archives of Neurology, 44: 818–822.

Desmaze, C., Scambler, P., Prieur, M., Halford, S. et al. (1993) 'Routine diagnosis of DiGeorge syndrome by fluorescent in situ hybridization.', Human Genetics, 90: 663–665.

Deth, R., Muratore, C., Benzecry, J., Power-Charnitsky, V-A. et al. (2008) 'How environmental and genetic factors combine to cause autism: a redox/methylation hypothesis.' Neurotoxicology, 29: 190–201.

Devlin, B., Bennett, P., Dawson, G., Figlewicz, D.A. *et al.* (2004) 'The CPEA Genetics Network and Schellenberg G.D. alleles of a reelin CGG repeat do not convey liability to autism in a sample from the CPEA network.' *American Journal of Medical Genetics B Neuropsychiatric Genetics, 126B*: 46–50.

Devlin, L.A., Shepherd, C.H., Crawford, H. and Morrison, P.J. (2006) 'Tuberous sclerosis complex: clinical features, diagnosis, and prevalence within Northern Ireland.', *Developmental Medicine and Child Neurology, 48*: 495–499.

Devriendt, K., Fryns, J.P., Mortier, G., van Thienen, M.N. and Keymolen, K. (1998) 'The annual incidence of DiGeorge/velocardiofacial syndrome.', (Letter) *Journal of Medical Genetics, 35*: 789–790.

Devriendt, K., Swillen, A. and Fryns, J.P. (1998) 'Deletion in chromosome region 22q11 in a child with CHARGE association.', *Clinical Genetics, 53*: 408–410.

de Vries, B.B.A., Fryns, J-P., Butler, M.G., Canziani, F. *et al.* (1993) 'Clinical and molecular studies in fragile-X patients with a Prader-Willi-like phenotype.', *Journal of Medical Genetics, 30*: 761–766.

de Vries, B.B.A., Robinson, H., Stolte-Dijkstra, I., Tjon Pian Gi, C.V. *et al.* (1995) 'General overgrowth in the fragile-X syndrome: variability in the phenotypic expression of the FMR1 gene mutation.', *Journal of Medical Genetics, 32*: 764–769.

de Vries, P.J., Hunt, A. and Bolton, P.F. (2007) 'The psychopathologies of children and adolescents with tuberous sclerosis complex (TSC): a postal survey of UK families.', *European Child and Adolescent Psychiatry, 16*(1): 16–24.

Devys, D., Lutz, Y., Rouyer, N., Bellocq, J-P. and Mandel, J-L. (1993) 'The FMR-1 protein is cytoplasmic, most abundant in neurons and appears normal in carriers of a fragile-X premutation.', *Nature Genetics, 4*: 335–340.

DeWitt, C.A., Bishop, A.B., Buescher, L.S. and Stone, S.P. (2006) 'Hyperimmunoglobulin E syndrome: two cases and a review of the literature.', *Journal of the American Academy of Dermatology, 54*: 855–865.

Dhar, S.U., Scaglia, F., Li, F-Y., Smith, L. *et al.* (2009) 'Expanded clinical and molecular spectrum of guanidinoacetate methyltransferase (GAMT) deficiency.', *Molecular Genetics and Metabolism, 96*: 38–43.

Dhond, J-L., Ardouin, P., Hayte, J-M. and Farriaux, J-P. (1981) 'Developmental aspects of pteridine metabolism and relationships with phenylalanine metabolism.', *Clinica Chimica Acta, 116*: 143–152.

Dhossche, D., Applegate, H., Abraham, A., Maertens, P. *et al.* (2002) 'Elevated plasma gamma-aminobutyric acid (GABA) levels in autistic youngsters: stimulus for a GABA hypothesis of autism.', *Medical Science Monitor, 8*(8): PR1–6.

Diano, S. and Horvath, T.L. (2008) 'Anticonvulsant effects of leptin in epilepsy.', *Journal of Clinical Investigation, 118*(1): 26–28.

Dickinson, A.J., Fielder, A.R., Duckett, D.P. and Young, I.D. (1988) 'Ocular and genetic findings in Angelman's syndrome.', (Abstract) *Journal of Medical Genetics, 25*: 642.

Dietz, C., Swinkels, S., Van Daalen, E., Van Engeland, H. and Buitelaar, J. (2006) 'Screening for autistic spectrum disorder in children aged 14–15 months: II, population screening with the Early Screening of Autistic Traits Questionnaire (ESAT), design and general findings.' *Journal of Autism and Developmental Disorders, 36*: 713–722.

Dietz, H.C. (2007) 'Marfan syndrome: from molecules to medicines.', *American Journal of Human Genetics, 81*: 662–667.

DiGeorge, A.M. (1965) 'Discussions on a new concept of the cellular basis of immunology.', *Journal of Pediatrics, 67*: 907.

DiGeorge, A.M. (1968) 'Congenital absence of the thymus and its immunologic consequences: concurrence with congenital hypoparathyroidism.', *Birth Defects Original Articles, Series IV*(1): 116–121.

Diggle, T.T.J. and McConachie, H.H.R. (2009) 'Parent-mediated early intervention for young children with autism spectrum disorder.' *Cochrane Database of Systematic Reviews*, 2009, Issue 2. Art. No.: CD003496, doi:10.1002/14651858.CD003496.

Digilio, M.C., Calzolari, F., Capolino, R., Toscano, A. *et al.* (2008) 'Congenital heart defects in patients with oculo-auriculo-vertebral spectrum (Goldenhar syndrome).', *American Journal of Medical Genetics A, 146A*(14): 1815–1819.

Digilio, M.C., Conti, E., Sarkozy, A., Mingarelli, R. *et al.* (2002) 'Grouping of multiple-lentigines/LEOPARD and Noonan syndromes on the PTPN11 gene.', *American Journal of Human Genetics, 71*: 389–394.

DiLella, A.G., Kwok, S.C.M., Ledley, F.D., Marvit, J. and Woo, S.L.C. (1986a) 'Molecular structure and polymorphic map of the human phenylalanine hydroxylase gene.', *Biochemistry, 25*: 743–749.

DiLella, A.G., Marvit, J., Guttler, F. and Woo, S.L.C. (1986b) 'Molecular genetics of phenylketonuria.', (Abstract) 7th International Congress on Human Genetics, Berlin, 665–666.

DiLiberti, J.H. (1998) 'Inherited macrocephaly-hamartoma syndromes.', *American Journal of Medical Genetics, 79*: 284–290.

DiLiberti, J.H., D'Agostino, A.N., Ruvalcaba, R.H.A. and Schimschock, J.R. (1984) 'A new lipid storage myopathy observed in individuals with the Ruvalcaba-Myhre-Smith syndrome.', *American Journal of Medical Genetics, 18*: 163–167.

DiMagno, E.P., Lowe, J.E., Snodgrass, P.J. and Jones, J.D. (1986) 'Ornithine transcarbamylase deficiency – a cause of bizarre behaviour in a man.', *New England Journal of Medicine, 315*: 744–747.

Dimitropoulos, A. and Schultz, R.T. (2007) 'Autistic-like symptomatology in Prader-Willi syndrome: a review of recent findings.' *Current Psychiatry Reports, 9*(2): 159–164.

Ding, Z., Harding, C.O. and Thöny, B. (2004) 'State-of-the-art 2003 on PKU gene therapy.', *Molecular Genetics and Metabolism, 81*(1): 3–8.

Dion, Y., Annable, L., Sandor, P. and Chouinard, G. (2002) 'Risperidone in the treatment of Tourette syndrome: a double-blind, placebo-controlled trial.', *Journal of Clinical Psychopharmacology, 22*: 31–39.

Dionisi-Vici, C., Deodato, F., Roschinger, W., Rhead, W. and Wilcken, B. (2006) '"Classical" organic acidurias, propionic aciduria, methylmalonic aciduria and isovaleric aciduria: long-term outcome and effects of expanded newborn screening using tandem mass spectrometry.' *Journal of Inherited Metabolic Disease, 29*: 383–389.

DiPaolo, D.P., Zimmerman, R.A., Rorke, L.B., Zackai, E.H. *et al.* (1995) 'Neurofibromatosis type 1: pathologic substrate of high-signal-intensity foci in the brain.', *Radiology, 195*: 721–724.

Dixit, V.D. and Taub, D.D. (2005) 'Mini review. Ghrelin and immunity: a young player in an old field.' *Experimental Gerontology, 40*: 900–910.

Dixon-Salazar, T., Silhavy, J.L., Marsh, S.E., Louie, C.M. *et al.* (2004) 'Mutations in the AHI1 gene, encoding jouberin, cause Joubert syndrome with cortical polymicrogyria.', *American Journal of Human Genetics, 75*: 979–987.

Dobson, C.M., Wai, T., Leclerc, D., Kadir, H. *et al.* (2002) 'Identification of the gene responsible for the cblB complementation group of vitamin B12-dependent methylmalonic aciduria.' *Human Molecular Genetics, 11*: 3361–3369.

Doherty, D., Glass, I.A., Siebert, J.R., Strouse, P.J. *et al.* (2005) 'Prenatal diagnosis in pregnancies at risk for Joubert syndrome by ultrasound and MRI.', *Prenatal Diagnosis, 25*: 442–447.

Dölen, G. and Bear, M.F. (2005) 'Courting a cure for fragile-X.' *Neuron, 45*: 642–644.

Dölen, G. and Bear, M.F. (2008) 'Role for metabotropic glutamate receptor 5 (mGluR5) in the pathogenesis of fragile X syndrome.' *Journal of Physiology, 586*(6): 1503–1508.

Dölen, G., Osterweil, E., Shankaranarayana Rao, B.S., Smith, G.B. *et al.* (2007) 'Correction of fragile-X syndrome in mice.', *Neuron, 56*(6): 955–962.

Dolinoy, D.C., Weidman, J.R. and Jirtle, R.L. (2007) 'Epigenetic gene regulation: linking early developmental environment to adult disease.', *Reproductive Toxicology, 23*: 297–307.

Dolinsky, L.C., de Moura-Neto, R.S. and Falcao-Conceicao, D.N. (2002) 'DGGE analysis as a tool to identify point mutations, de novo mutations and carriers of the dystrophin gene.', *Neuromuscular Disorders, 12*: 845–848.

Dolzhanskay, N., Merz, G. and Denman, R.B. (2006) 'Oxidative stress reveals heterogeneity of FMRP granules in PC12 cell neurites.' *Brain Research, 1112*: 56–64.

Domes, G., Heinrichs, M., Michel, A., Berger, C. and Herpertz, S.C. (2007) 'Oxytocin improves "mind-reading" in humans.' *Biological Psychiatry, 61*(6): 731–733.

Donarum, E.A., Stephan, D.A., Larkin, K., Murphy, E.J. *et al.* (2006) 'Expression profiling reveals multiple myelin alterations in murine succinate semialdehyde dehydrogenase deficiency.', *Journal of Inherited Metabolic Disease, 29*: 143–156.

Donlon, T.A. (1988) 'Similar molecular deletions on chromosome 15q11.2 are encountered in both the Prader-Willi and Angelman syndromes.', *Human Genetics, 80*: 322–328.

Donnai, D., Read, A.P., McKeown, C. and Andrews, T. (1988) 'Hypomelanosis of Ito: a manifestation of mosaicism or chimerism.' *Journal of Medical Genetics, 25*(12): 809–818.

Donnelly, S.L., Wolpert, C.M., Menold, M.M., Bass, M.P. *et al.* (2000) 'Female with autistic disorder and monosomy X (Turner syndrome): parent-of-origin effect of the X chromosome.', *American Journal of Medical Genetics, 96*(3): 312–316.

Doose, H., Lunau, H., Castiglione, E. and Waltz, S. (1998) 'Severe idiopathic generalized epilepsy of infancy with generalized tonic-clonic seizures.' *Neuropediatrics, 2*: 229–238.

Dorries, A., Spohr, H-L. and Kunze, J. (1988) 'Angelman ("happy puppet") syndrome – seven new cases documented by cerebral computed tomography: review of the literature.', *European Journal of Pediatrics, 148*: 270–273.

Dosman, C.F., Brian, J.A., Drmic, I.E., Senthilselvan, A. *et al.* (2007) 'Children with autism: effect of iron supplementation on sleep and ferritin.', *Pediatric Neurology, 36*: 152–158.

dos Santos, L.L., Magalhães, M. de C., Januário, J.N., Burle de Aguiar, M.J. and Carvalho, M.R.S. (2006) 'The time has come: a new scene for PKU treatment.', *Genetics and Molecular Research, 5*(1): 33–44.

Douglas, A.G.L. and Lam, W. (2010) 'Extending the phenotypic spectrum of CHARGE syndrome: a case with preaxial polydactyly.', *Clinical Dysmorphology, 19*: 33–34.

Douglas, J., Hanks, S., Temple, I.K., Davies, S. *et al.* (2003) 'NSD1 mutations are the major cause of Sotos syndrome and occur in some cases of Weaver syndrome but are rare in other overgrowth phenotypes.' *American Journal of Human Genetics, 72*: 132–143.

Down, J.L.H. (1867) 'Observations on an ethnic classification of idiots.' [*London Hospital Clinical Lecture Reports* (1866), *3*: 259. First printed in the *Journal of Mental Science*, 1867.] Reproduced in: *Mental Retardation* (1995), *33*(1): 54–56.

Down, J.L.H. (1887) *On Some of the Mental Affections of Childhood and Youth.* London: Churchill.

Drappa, J., Vaishnaw, A.K., Sullivan, K.E., Chu, J-L. and Elkon, K.B. (1996) 'Fas gene mutations in the Canale-Smith syndrome, an inherited lymphoproliferative disorder associated with autoimmunity.', *New England Journal of Medicine, 335*: 1643–1649.

Drasbek, K.R., Vardya, I., Delenclos, M., Gibson, K.M. and Jensen, K. (2008) 'SSADH deficiency leads to elevated extracellular GABA levels and increased GABAergic neurotransmission in the mouse cerebral cortex.', *Journal of Inherited Metabolic Disease, 31*(6): 662–668.

Dravet, C. (1978) 'Les epilepsies graves de l'enfant.', *Vie Medicale au Canada Francais, 8*: 543–548.

Dravet, C., Bureau, M., Guerrini, R., Giraud, N. and Roger, J. (1992) 'Severe myoclonic epilepsy in infants.', in: J. Roger, C. Dravet, M. Bureau, F.E. Dreifuss, A. Perret and P. Wolf (eds.). *Epileptic Syndromes in Infancy, Childhood and Adolescence.* (2nd edn.). London: John Libbey.

Dravet, C., Bureau, M., Oguni, H., Fukuyama, Y. and Cokar, O. (2005) 'Severe myoclonic epilepsy in infancy (Dravet syndrome).', in: J. Roger, M. Bureau, C. Dravet, P. Genton, C.A Tassinari, and P. Wolf (eds.) *Epileptic Syndromes in Infancy, Childhood and Adolescence*, (4th edn.). London: John Libbey.

Dridi, S.M., Ghomrasseni, S., Bonnet, D., Aggoun, Y. *et al.* (1999) 'Skin elastic fibers in Williams syndrome.', *American Journal of Medical Genetics, 87*: 134–138.

Driscoll, D.A., Budarf, M.L. and Emanuel, B.S. (1992) 'A genetic etiology for DiGeorge syndrome: consistent deletions and microdeletions of 22q11.' *American Journal of Human Genetics, 50*: 924–933.

Drogari, E. and Leonard, J.V. (1988) 'Late onset ornithine carbamoyl transferase deficiency in males.', *Archives of Disease in Childhood, 63*: 1363–1367.

Drogari, E., Smith, I., Beasley, M. and Lloyd, J.K. (1987) 'Timing of strict diet in relation to foetal damage in maternal phenylketonuria: an international collaborative study by the MRC/DHSS phenylketonuria register.', *Lancet, 330*(8565): 927–930.

Duboc, D., Meune, C., Pierre, B., Wahbi, K. *et al.* (2007) 'Perindopril preventive treatment on mortality in Duchenne muscular dystrophy: 10 years' follow-up.', *American Heart Journal, 154*(3): 596–602.

Dubourg, O., Durr, A., Chneiweiss, H., Stevanin, G. *et al.* (1995) 'La forme ataxo-choreique de DRPLA existe-t-elle en Europe? Recherche de la mutation dans 120 familles.', *Revue Neurologique* (Paris), *151*: 657–660.

Dugoff, L. and Sujansky, E. (1996) 'Neurofibromatosis type 1 and pregnancy.', *American Journal of Medical Genetics, 66*: 7–10.

Dumars, S., Andrews, C., Chan, W.M., Engle, E.C. and Demer, J.L. (2008) 'Magnetic resonance imaging of the endophenotype of a novel familial Möbius-like syndrome.', *Journal of the American Academy of Pediatric Ophthalmology and Strabismus, 12*(4): 381–389.

Duncan, P.A. and Shapiro, L.R. (1993) 'Interrelationships of the hemifacial microsomia-VATER, VATER, and sirenomelia phenotypes.', *American Journal of Medical Genetics, 47*(1): 75–84.

Dunlap, G., Robbins, F.R. and Darrow, M.A. (1994) 'Parents' reports of their children's challenging behaviours: results of a statewide survey.', *Mental Retardation, 32*(3): 206–212.

Duran, M., Dorland, L., Meuleman, E.E., Allers, P. and Berger, R. (1997) 'Inherited defects of purine and pyrimidine metabolism: laboratory methods for diagnosis.', *Journal of Inherited Metabolic Disease, 20*: 227–236.

Durelli, L., Mutani, R. and Fassio, F. (1983) 'The treatment of myotonia: evaluation of chronic oral taurine therapy.' *Neurology, 33*(5): 599–603.

Duric, K., Skrablin, S., Lesin, J., Kalafatic, D. *et al.* (2003) 'Second trimester total human chorionic gonadotropin, alpha-fetoprotein and unconjugated estriol in predicting pregnancy complications other than foetal aneuploidy.', *European Journal of Obstetrics, Gynecology and Reproductive Biology, 110*(1): 12–15.

Durkin, M.E., Keck-Waggoner, C.L., Popescu, N.C. and Thorgeirsson, S.S. (2001) 'Integration of a c-myc transgene results in disruption of the mouse Gtf2ird1 gene, the homologue of the human GTF2IRD1 gene hemizygously deleted in Williams–Beuren syndrome.', *Genomics, 73*: 20–27.

Durkin, M.S., Maenner, M.J., Newschaffer, C.J., Lee, L-C. *et al.* (2008) 'Advanced parental age and the risk of autism spectrum disorder.', *American Journal of Epidemiology, 168*(11): 1268–1276.

Durmowicz, A.G. (2001) 'Pulmonary oedema in 6 children with Down syndrome during travel to moderate altitudes.', *Pediatrics, 108*: 443–447.

Dutly, F. and Schinzel, A. (1996) 'Unequal interchromosomal rearrangements may result in elastin gene deletions causing the Williams-Beuren syndrome.', *Human Molecular Genetics, 5*(12): 1893–1898.

Dutta, S., Sinha, S., Ghosh, S., Chatterjee, A., Ahmed, S. and Usha, R. (2008) 'Genetic analysis of reelin gene (RELN) SNPs: no association with autism spectrum disorder in the Indian population.', *Neuroscience Letters, 441*(1): 56–60.

Dykens, E.M. Finucane, B.M. and Gayley, C. (1997) 'Brief report: cognitive and behavioural profiles in persons with Smith-Magenis syndrome.' *Journal of Autism and Developmental Disorders, 27*: 203–210.

Dykens, E.M.,, Sutcliffe, J.S. and Levitt, P. (2004) 'Autism and 15q11–q13 disorders: behavioural, genetic, and pathophysiological issues.', *Mental Retardation and Developmental Disabilities Research Reviews, 10*: 284–291.

Dykens, E.M. and Volkmar, F.R. (1997) 'Medical conditions associated with autism.', in: D. J. Cohen and F. R. Volkmar (eds.) *Handbook of Autism and Pervasive Developmental Disorders*. New York: John Wiley and Sons.

Dziobek, I., Gold, S.M., Wolf, O.T. and Convit, A. (2007) 'Hypercholesterolemia in Asperger syndrome: independence from lifestyle, obsessive–compulsive behaviour, and social anxiety.' *Psychiatry Research, 149*: 321–324.

Ebbesen, F. and Petersen, W. (1982) 'Goldenhar's syndrome: discordance in monozygotic twins and unusual anomalies.', *Acta Paediatrica Scandinavica, 71*: 685–687.

Edelmann, L., Prosnitz, A., Pardo, S., Bhatt, J. *et al.* (2007) 'An atypical deletion of the Williams–Beuren syndrome interval implicates genes associated with defective visuospatial processing and autism.' *Journal of Medical Genetics, 44*: 136–143.

Edelson, S.B. and Cantor, D.S. (1998) 'Autism: xenobiotic influences.' *Toxicology and Industrial Health, 14*: 553–563.

Edery, P., Chabrier, S., Ceballos-Picot, I., Marie, S. *et al.* (2003) 'Intrafamilial variability in the phenotypic expression of adenylosuccinate lyase deficiency: a report on three patients.', *American Journal of Medical Genetics, 120A*: 185–190.

Edwards, J.H., Harnden, D.G., Cameron, A.H., Crosse, V.M. and Wolff, O.H. (1960) 'A new trisomic syndrome.', *Lancet, 274*(7128): 787–790.

Eerola, I., Boon, L.M., Mulliken, J.B., Burrows, P.E. *et al.* (2003) 'Capillary malformation–arteriovenous malformation, a new clinical and genetic disorder caused by RASA1 mutations.' *American Journal of Human Genetics, 73*(6): 1240–1249.

Egelton, R.D. and Davis, T.P. (2005) 'Development of neuropeptide drugs that cross the blood-brain barrier.', *NeuroRx, 2*(1): 44–53.

Egger, J., Hofacker, N., Schiel, W. and Holthausen, H. (1992) 'Magnesium for hyperventilation in Rett's syndrome.', *Lancet, 340*: 621–622.

Ehlers, E.L. (1901) 'Cutis laxa. Neigung zu Haemorrhagien in der Haut, Lockering mehrerer Artikulationen.', *Dermatologische Zeitschrift*, Berlin, *8*: 173–174.

Ehninger, D., Han, S., Shilyansky, C., Zhou, Y. *et al.* (2008a) 'Reversal of learning deficits in a Tsc2+/− mouse model of tuberous sclerosis.', *Nature Medicine, 14*(8): 843–848.

Ehninger, D., Li, W., Fox, K., Stryker, M.P. and Silva, A.J. (2008b) 'Reversing neurodevelopmental disorders in adults.', *Neuron, 60*(6): 950–960.

Eichler, E.E., Richards, S., Gibbs, R.A. and Nelson, D.L. (1993) 'Fine structure of the human FMR1 gene.', [Published erratum: *Human Molecular Genetics*, 1994, *3*(4): 684–685] *Human Molecular Genetics, 2*: 1147–1153.

Eidinow, J. and Edmonds, D. (2002) *Wittgenstein's Poker*. London: Faber and Faber.

Eisensmith, R.C., Okano, Y., Dasovich, M., Wang, T. *et al.* (1992) 'Multiple origins for phenylketonuria in Europe.', *American Journal of Human Genetics, 51*: 1355–1365.

Ekström, A-B., Hakenäs-Plate, L., Samuelsson, L., Tulinius, M. and Wentz, E. (2008) 'Autism spectrum conditons in myotonic dystrophy type 1: a study on 57 individuals with congenital and childhood forms.', *American Journal of Medical Genetics Part B, 147B*(6):918–926.

Ekström, A-B., Hakenäs-Plate, L., Tulinius, M. and Wentz, E. (2009) 'Cognition and adaptive skills in myotonic dystrophy type 1: a study of 55 individuals with congenital and childhood forms.', *Developmental Medicine and Child Neurology, 51*(12): 982–990.

Elbedour, K., Zucker, N., Zalzstein, E., Barki, Y. and Carmi, R. (1994) 'Cardiac abnormalities in the Bardet-Biedl syndrome: echocardiographic studies of 22 patients.' *American Journal of Medical Genetics, 52*: 164–169.

El Hajj, T., Nasreddine, W., Korri, H., Atweh, S. and Beydoun, A. (2009) 'A case of Kleine-Levin syndrome with a complete and sustained response to carbamazepine.', *Epilepsy and Behaviour, 15*(3): 391–392.

Elias, E.R., Irons, M.B., Hurley, A.D., Tint, G.S. and Salen, G. (1997) 'Clinical effects of cholesterol supplementation in six patients with the Smith-Lemli-Opitz syndrome (SLOS).', *American Journal of Medical Genetics, 68*: 305–310.

Elias, P.M., Williams, M.L., Holleran, W.M., Jiang, Y.J. and Schmuth, M. (2008) 'Pathogenesis of permeability barrier abnormalities in the ichthyoses: inherited disorders of lipid metabolism.', *Journal of Lipid Research, 49*: 697–714.

Elias, P.M., Williams, M.L., Maloney, M.E., Bonifas, J.A. *et al.* (1984) 'Stratum corneum lipids in disorders of cornification: steroid sulfatase and cholesterol sulfate in normal desquamation and the pathogenesis of recessive X-linked ichthyosis.', *Journal of Clinical Investigation, 74*: 1414–1421.

Ellaway, C.J., Peat, J., Williams, K., Leonard, H. and Christodoulou, J. (2001) 'Medium-term open label trial of L-carnitine in Rett syndrome.', *Brain and Development, 23*(Suppl 1): S85–89.

Ellaway, C.J., Williams, K., Leonard, H., Higgins, G. *et al.* (1999) 'Rett syndrome: randomized controlled trial of L-carnitine.', *Journal of Child Neurology, 14*: 162–167.

Elliott, H.R., Samuels, D.C., Eden, J.A., Relton, C.L. and Chinnery, P.F. (2008) 'Pathogenic mitochondrial DNA mutations are common in the general population.', *American Journal of Human Genetics*, doi:10.1016/j.ajhg.2008.07.004.

Ellis, J.M., Tan, H.K., Gilbert, R.E., Muller, D.P.R. *et al.* (2008) 'Supplementation with antioxidants and folinic acid for children with Down's syndrome: randomised controlled trial.', *British Medical Journal, 336*: 594–597.

Emanuele, E., Lossano, C., Politi, P. and Barale, F. (2007) 'Pioglitazone as a therapeutic agent in autistic spectrum disorder.' *Medical Hypotheses, 69*(3): 699.

Eng, C. (2000) 'Will the real Cowden syndrome please stand up: revised diagnostic criteria.', *Journal of Medical Genetics, 37*: 828–830.

Eng, C. (2003) 'PTEN: one gene, many syndromes.', *Human Mutation, 22*: 183–198.

Engel, E. (1993) 'Uniparental disomy revisited: the first twelve years.', *American Journal of Medical Genetics, 46*: 670–674.

Engelhardt, M., Neumann, G., Berbalk, A. and Reuter, I. (1998) 'Creatine supplementation in endurance sports.', *Medicine and Science in Sport and Exercise, 30*(7): 1123–1129.

Engidawork, E. and Lubec, G. (2003) 'Molecular changes in foetal Down syndrome brain.', *Journal of Neurochemistry, 84*: 895–904.

Enns, G.M., O'Brien, W.E., Kobayashi, K., Shinzawa, H. and Pellegrino, J.E. (2005) 'Postpartum psychosis in mild argininosuccinate synthetase deficiency.', *Obstetrics and Gynecology, 105*: 1244–1246.

Entezam, A., Biacsi, R., Orrison, B., Saha, T. *et al.* (2007) 'Regional FMRP deficits and large repeat expansions into the full mutation range in a new fragile-X premutation mouse model.', *Gene, 395*(1–2): 125–134.

Entezam, A. and Usdin, K. (2008) 'ATR protects the genome against CGG-CCG-repeat expansion in fragile-X premutation mice.', *Nucleic Acids Research, 36*(3): 1050–1056.

Epstein, C.J., Korenberg, J.R., Anneren, G., Antonarakis, S.E. *et al.* (1991) 'Protocols to establish genotype-phenotype correlations in Down syndrome.', *American Journal of Human Genetics, 49*: 207–235.

Epstein, R.A. (2006) *Overdose: How Excessive Government Regulation Stifles Pharmaceutical Innovation*. New Haven and London: Yale University Press.

Erickson, C.A., Mullett, J.E. and McDougle, C.J. (2009) 'Open-label memantine in fragile-X syndrome.', *Journal of Autism and Developmental Disorders, 39*: 1629–1635.

Erickson, C.A., Stigler, K.A., Corkins, M.R., Posey, D.J. *et al.* (2005) 'Gastrointestinal factors in autistic disorder: a critical review.' *Journal of Autism and Developmental Disorders, 35*: 713–727.

Erlandsen, H. and Stevens, R.C. (2001) 'A structural hypothesis for BH(4) responsiveness in patients with mild forms of hyperphenylalaninaemia and phenylketonuria.', *Journal of Inherited Metabolic Disease, 24*: 213–230.

Erol, I., Alehan, F. and Gümüs, A. (2007) 'West syndrome in an infant with vitamin B12 deficiency in the absence of macrocytic anaemia.', *Developmental Medicine and Child Neurology, 49*: 774–776.

Eronen, M., Peippo, M., Hiippala, A., Raatikka, M. *et al.* (2002) 'Cardiovascular manifestations in 75 patients with Williams syndrome.' *Journal of Medical Genetics, 39*: 554–558.

Escayg, A., Heils, A., MacDonald, B.T., Haug, K. *et al.* (2001) 'A novel SCN1A mutation associated with generalized epilepsy with febrile seizures plus – and prevalence of variants in patients with epilepsy.', *American Journal of Human Genetics, 68*: 866–873.

Esch, B.E. and Carr, J.E. (2004) 'Secretin as a treatment for autism: a review of the evidence.', *Journal of Autism and Developmental Disorders, 34*(5): 543–556.

Evangeliou, A., Vlachonikolis, I., Mihailidou, H., Spilioti, M. *et al.* (2003) 'Application of a ketogenic diet in children with autistic behaviour: pilot study.', *Journal of Child Neurology, 18*(2): 113–118.

Evans, D. (2003) *Placebo: The Belief Effect.* London: HarperCollins Publishers.

Evans, D.G., Baser, M.E., McGaughran, J., Sharif, S. *et al.* (2002) 'Malignant peripheral nerve sheath tumours in neurofibromatosis 1.', *Journal of Medical Genetics, 39*: 311–314.

Evans, D.G., Birch, J.M. and Orton, C.I. (1991) 'Brain tumours and the occurrence of severe invasive basal cell carcinoma in first degree relatives with Gorlin syndrome.', *British Journal of Neurosurgery, 5*: 643–646.

Evans, D.G., Ladusans, E.J., Rimmer, S., Burnell, L.D. *et al.* (1993) 'Complications of the naevoid basal cell carcinoma syndrome: results of a population based study.', *Journal of Medical Genetics, 30*(6): 460–464.

Evans, J.C., Archer, H.L., Colley, J.P., Ravn, K. *et al.* (2005) 'Early onset seizures and Rett-like features associated with mutations in CDKL5.', *European Journal of Human Genetics, 13*(10): 1113–1120.

Evers, L.J.M., Vermaak, M.P., Engelen, J.J.M. and Curfs, L.M.G. (2006) 'The velocardiofacial syndrome in older age: dementia and autistic features.', *Genetic Counselling, 17*: 333–340.

Ewart, A.K., Morris, C.A., Atkinson, D., Jin, W. *et al.* (1993) 'Hemizygosity at the elastin locus in a developmental disorder, Williams syndrome.', *Nature Genetics, 5*: 11–16.

Exkorn, K.S. (2005) *The Autism Sourcebook: Everything You Need to Know About Diagnosis, Treatment, Coping and Healing.* New York: Harper and Collins.

Ezzeldin, H. and Diasio, R. (2004) 'Dihydropyrimidine dehydrogenase deficiency, a pharmacogenetic syndrome associated with potentially life-threatening toxicity following 5-fluorouracil administration.' *Clinical Colorectal Cancer, 4*(3): 181–189.

Facher, J.J., Regier, E.J., Jacobs, G.H., Siwik, E. *et al.* (2004) 'Cardiomyopathy in Coffin-Lowry syndrome.', *American Journal of Medical Genetics, 128A*: 176–178.

Fackenthal, J.D., Marsh, D.J., Richardson, A.L., Cummings, S.A. *et al.* (2001) 'Male breast cancer in Cowden syndrome patients with germline PTEN mutations.', *Journal of Medical Genetics, 38*: 159–164.

Falek, A., Schmidt, R. and Jervis, G.A. (1966) 'Familial de Lange syndrome with chromosome abnormalities.', *Pediatrics, 37*: 92–101.

Falk, M.J., Feiler, H.S., Neilson, D.E., Maxwell, K. *et al.* (2004) 'Cohen syndrome in the Ohio Amish.', *American Journal of Medical Genetics, 128A*: 23–28.

Falk, M.J., Wang, H. and Traboulski, E.I. (2006) 'Cohen Syndrome.', In: GeneReviews at GeneTests: Medical Genetics Information Resource [database online]. Copyright, University of Washington, Seattle, 1997–2006. Available at www.ncbi.nlm.nih.gov/sites/GeneTests.

Falk, R.E. and Casas, K.A. (2007) 'Chromosome 2q37 deletion: clinical and molecular aspects.', *American Journal of Medical Genetics, 145C*(4): 357–371.

Falls, J.G., Pulford, F.J., Wylie, A.A. and Jirtle, R.L. (1999) 'Review: genomic imprinting: implications for human disease.', *American Journal of Pathology, 154*: 635–647.

Falter, C.M., Plaisted, K.C. and Davis, G. (2008) 'Male brains, androgen, and the cognitive profile in autism: convergent evidence from 2D:4D and congenital adrenal hyperplasia.', *Journal of Autism and Developmental Disorders, 38*(5): 997–998.

Fang, P., Lev-Lehman, E., Tsai, T.F., Matsuura, T. *et al.* (1999) 'The spectrum of mutations in UBE3A causing Angelman syndrome.', *Human Molecular Genetics, 8*: 129–135.

Farag, T.I. and Teebi, A.S. (1988) 'Bardet-Biedl and Laurence-Moon syndromes in a mixed Arab population.', *Clinical Genetics, 33*: 78–82.

Farmer, J.E., Deidrick, K.M., Gitten, J.C., Fennell, E.B. and Maria, B.L. (2006) 'Parenting stress and its relationship to the behaviour of children with Joubert syndrome.', *Journal of Child Neurology, 21*: 163–167.

Farzin, F., Perry, H., Hessl, D., Loesch, D. *et al.* (2006) 'Autism spectrum disorders and attention-deficit/hyperactivity disorder in boys with the fragile-X premutation.', *Developmental and Behavioural Pediatrics, 27*(2): S137–S144.

Fatemi, S.H., Halt, A.R., Stary, J.M., Kanodia, R. *et al.* (2002) 'Glutamic acid decarboxylase 65 and 67 kDa proteins are reduced in autistic parietal and cerebellar cortices.' *Biological Psychiatry, 52*: 805–810.

Fatemi, S.H., Folsom, T.D., Reutiman, T.J. and Lee, S. (2008a) 'Expression of astrocytic markers aquaporin 4 and connexin 43 is altered in brains of subjects with autism.' *Synapse, 62*(7): 501–507.

Fatemi, S.H., Folsom, T.D., Reutiman, T.J. and Sidwell, R.W. (2008b) 'Viral regulation of aquaporin 4, connexin 43, microcephalin and nucleolin.' *Schizophrenia Research, 98*(1–3): 163–177.

Fath, M.A., Mullins, R.F., Searby, C., Nishimura, D.Y. *et al.* (2005) 'Mkks-null mice have a phenotype resembling Bardet-Biedl syndrome.', *Human Molecular Genetics, 14*(9): 1109–1118.

Faury, G., Pezet, M., Knutsen, R.H., Boyle, W.A. *et al.* (2003) 'Developmental adaptation of the mouse cardiovascular system to elastin haploinsufficiency.', *Journal of Clinical Investigation, 112*: 1419–1428.

Fear, C. and Briggs, A. (1979) 'Familial partial trisomy of the long arm of chromosome 3 (3q).', *Archives of Disease in Childhood, 54*: 135–138.

Fehlow, P., Bernstein, K., Tennstedt, A. and Walther, F. (1993) ['Early infantile autism and excessive aerophagy with symptomatic megacolon and ileus in a case of Ehlers-Danlos syndrome.'] [Article in German.] P*adiatrie und Grenzgebiete, 31*(4): 259–267.

Feinstein, C. and Reiss, A.L. (1998) 'Autism: the point of view from fragile-X syndrome.' *Journal of Autism and Developmental Disorders, 28*: 393–405.

Felder, B., Radlwimmer, B., Benner, A., Mincheva, A. *et al.* (2009) 'FARP2, HDLBP and PASK are downregulated in a patient with autism and 2q37.3 deletion syndrome.', *American Journal of Medical Genetics A, 149A*(5): 952–959.

Feldman, R. (2007) 'Parent–infant synchrony and the construction of shared timing: physiological precursors, developmental outcomes, and risk conditions.', *Journal of Child Psychology and Psychiatry, 48*(3/4): 329–354.

Feldmann, R., Denecke, J., Grenzebach, M., Schuierer, G. and Weglage, J. (2003) 'Neurofibromatosis type 1: motor and cognitive function and T2-weighted MRI hyperintensities.', *Neurology, 61*: 1725–1728.

Felisari, G., Martinelli Boneschi, F., Bardoni, A., Sironi, M. *et al.* (2000) 'Loss of Dp140 dystrophin isoform and intellectual impairment in Duchenne dystrophy.', *Neurology, 55*: 559–564.

Fenichel, G., Pestronk, A., Florence, J., Robison, V. and Hemelt, V. (1997) 'A beneficial effect of oxandrolone in the treatment of Duchenne muscular dystrophy: a pilot study.', *Neurology, 48*: 1225–1226.

Fenichel, G.M., Florence, J.M., Pestronk, A., Mendell, J.R. *et al.* (1991) 'Long-term benefit from prednisone therapy in Duchenne muscular dystrophy.', *Neurology, 41*: 1874–1877.

Fenichel, G.M., Griggs, R.C., Kissel, J., Kramer, T.I. *et al.* (2001) 'A randomized efficacy and safety trial of oxandrolone in the treatment of Duchenne dystrophy.', *Neurology, 56*: 1075–1079.

Ferguson, C., Hardy, S.L., Werner, D.F., Hileman, S.M., DeLorey, T.M. and Homanics, G.E. (2007) 'New insight into the role of the β3β3β3β3 subunit of the GABAA-R in development, behaviour, body weight regulation, and anesthesia revealed by conditional gene knockout.', *BMC Neuroscience, 8*: 85 doi:10.1186/1471-2202-8-85.

Ferguson-Smith, M.A. and Yates, J.R. (1984) 'Maternal age specific rates for chromosome aberrations and factors influencing them: report of a collaborative European study on 52,965 amniocenteses.', *Prenatal Diagnosis, 4*: 5–44.

Ferland, R.J., Eyaid, W., Collura, R.V., Tully, L.D. *et al.* (2004) 'Abnormal cerebellar development and axonal decussation due to mutations in AHI1 in Joubert syndrome.', *Nature Genetics, 36*: 1008–1013.

Ferlini, A., Sewry, C., Melis, M.A., Mateddu, A. and Muntoni, F. (1999) 'X-linked dilated cardiomyopathy and the dystrophin gene.', *Neuromuscular Disorders, 9*: 339–346.

Fernandez, F., Morishita, W., Zuniga, E., Nguyen, J. *et al.* (2007) 'Pharmacotherapy for cognitive impairment in a mouse model of Down syndrome.', *Nature Neuroscience, 10*(4): 411–413.

Fernández, L., Lapunzina, P., Pajares, I.L., Criado, G.R. *et al.* (2005) 'Higher frequency of uncommon 1.5–2 Mb deletions found in familial cases of 22q11.2 deletion syndrome.', *American Journal of Medical Genetics A, 136*(1): 71–75.

Fernell, E., Fagerberg, U.L. and Hellstrom, P.M. (2007) 'No evidence for a clear link between active intestinal inflammation and autism based on analyses of faecal calprotectin and rectal nitric oxide.', *Acta Paediatrica, 96*(7): 1076–1079.

Fernell, E., Olsson, V.A., Karlgren-Leitner, C., Norlin, B. *et al.* (1999) 'Autistic disorders in children with CHARGE association.', *Developmental Medicine and Child Neurology, 41*: 270–272.

Fernell, E., Watanabe, Y., Adolfsson, I., Tani, Y. *et al.* (1997) 'Possible effects of tetrahydrobiopterin treatment in six children with autism – clinical and positron emission tomography data: a pilot study.', *Developmental Medicine and Child Neurology, 39*(5): 313–318.

Ferner, R.E. (2007) 'Neurofibromatosis 1.', *European Journal of Human Genetics, 15*: 131–138.

Ferner, R.E., Hughes, R.A., Hall, S.M., Upadhyaya, M. and Johnson, M.R. (2004) 'Neurofibromatous neuropathy in neurofibromatosis 1 (NF1).', *Journal of Medical Genetics, 41*: 837–841.

Feuk, L., Carson, A.R. and Scherer, S.W. (2006) 'Structural variation in the human genome.' *Nature Reviews: Genetics, 7*: 85–97.

Field, M.J., Grattan-Smith, P., Piper, S.M., Thompson, E.M. *et al.* (2003) 'PEHO and PEHO-like syndromes: report of 5 Australian cases.' *American Journal of Medical Genetics, 122A*: 6–12.

Filipek, P.A., Juranek, J., Nguyen, M.T., Cummings, C. and Gargus, J.J. (2004) 'Relative carnitine deficiency in autism.', *Journal of Autism and Developmental Disorders, 34*(6): 615–623.

Filipek, P.A., Juranek, J., Smith, M., Mays, L.Z. *et al.* (2003) 'Mitochondrial dysfunction in autistic patients with 15q inverted duplication.' *Annals of Neurology, 53*: 801–804.

Fillano, J.J., Goldenthal, M.J., Rhodes, C.H. and Marin-Garcia, J. (2002) 'Mitochondrial dysfunction in patients with hypotonia, epilepsy, autism, and developmental delay: HEADD syndrome.' *Journal of Child Neurology, 17*: 435–439.

Fillion, M., Deal, C. and Van Vliet, G. (2008) 'Retrospective study of the potential benefits and adverse events during growth hormone treatment in children with Prader-Willi syndrome.', *Journal of Pediatrics, 154*(2): 230–233.

Fillon-Emery, N., Chango, A., Mircher, C., Barbe, F. *et al.* (2004) 'Homocysteine concentrations in adults with trisomy 21: effect of B vitamins and genetic polymorphisms 1–4.', *American Journal of Clinical Nutrition, 80*: 1551–1557.

Filmus, J. and Selleck, S.B. (2001) 'Glypicans: proteoglycans with a surprise.', *Journal of Clinical Investigation, 108*(4): 497–501.

Fine, S.E., Weissman, A., Gerdes, M., Pinto-Martin, J. *et al.* (2005) 'Autism spectrum disorders and symptoms in children with molecularly confirmed 22q11.2 deletion syndrome.', *Journal of Autism and Developmental Disorders, 35*(4): 461–470.

Finegan, J.K., Cole, T.R.P., Kingwell, E., Smith, M.L. *et al.* (1994) 'Language and behaviour in children with Sotos syndrome.', *Journal of the American Academy of Child and Adolescent Psychiatry, 33*: 1307–1315.

Finegold, S.M., Molitoris, D., Song, Y., Liu, C. *et al.* (2002) 'Gastrointestinal microflora studies in late-onset autism.' *Clinical Infectious Diseases, 35*(Suppl 1): S6–16.

Finsterer, J. (2004) 'Mitochondriopathies.', *European Journal of Neurology, 11*(3): 163–186.

Finsterer, J. and Stollberger, C. (2003) 'The heart in human dystrophinopathies.', *Cardiology, 99*: 1–19.

Fisch, G.S., Cohen, I.L., Wolf, E.G., Brown, W.T. *et al.* (1986) 'Autism and the fragile-X syndrome.', *American Journal of Psychiatry, 143*(1): 71–73.

Fischbein, N.J., Barkovich, A.J., Wu, Y. and Berg, B.O. (1998) 'Sturge-Weber syndrome with no leptomeningeal enhancement on MRI.', *Neuroradiology, 40*: 177–180.

Fischer, S., Ludecke, H-J., Wieczorek, D., Bohringer, S. *et al.* (2006) 'Histone acetylation dependent allelic expression imbalance of BAPX1 in patients with the oculo-auriculo-vertebral spectrum.', *Human Molecular Genetics, 15*(4): 581–587.

Fisher, J.L. (2008) 'The anti-convulsant stiripentol acts directly on the GABAA receptor as a positive allosteric modulator.', *Neuropharmacology, 56*(1): 190–197.

Fisher, S.E. and Scharff, C. (2009) 'FOXP2 as a molecular window into speech and language.', *Trends in Genetics, 25*(4): 166–177.

Fitzgerald, M. (2004) *Artistic Creativity: Is There a Link Between Autism in Men and Exceptional Ability?* Hove: Brunner-Routledge.

Fitzgerald, M. (2005) *The Genesis of Artistic Creativity.* London, Jessica Kingsley Publishers.

Fitzky, B.U., Witsch-Baumgartner, M., Erdel, M., Lee, J.N. *et al.* (1998) 'Mutations in the delta-7-sterol reductase gene in patients with the Smith-Lemli-Opitz syndrome.', *Proceedings of the National Academy of Science USA, 95*: 8181–8186.

Fitzpatrick, M. (2008) *Defeating Autism: A Damaging Delusion.* Abingdon: Routledge.

Fitzpatrick, T.B., Szabo, G., Hori, Y., Simone, A.A. *et al.* (1968) 'White leaf-shaped macules.' *Archives of Dermatology, 98*: 1–6.

Fiumara, A., Sciotto, A., Barone, R., D'Asero, G. *et al.* (1999) 'Peripheral lymphocyte subsets and other immune aspects in Rett syndrome.', *Pediatric Neurology, 21*(3): 619–621.

Flanagan, N., O'Connor, W.J., McCartan, B., Miller, S. *et al.* (1997) 'Developmental enamel defects in tuberous sclerosis: a clinical genetic marker?' *Journal of Medical Genetics, 34*: 637–639.

Flanigan, K.M., von Niederhausern, A., Dunn, D.M., Alder, J. *et al.* (2003) 'Rapid direct sequence analysis of the dystrophin gene.', *American Journal of Human Genetics, 72*: 931–939.

Fleck, B.J., Pandya, A., Vanner, L., Kerkering, K. and Bodurtha, J. (2001) 'Coffin-Siris syndrome: review and presentation of new cases from a questionnaire study.', *American Journal of Medical Genetics, 99*: 1–7.

Flejter, W.L., Bennett-Baker, P.E., Ghaziuddin, M., McDonald, M. *et al.* (1996) 'Cytogenetic and molecular analysis of inv dup(15) chromosomes observed in two patients with autistic disorder and mental retardation.' *American Journal of Medical Genetics, 61*: 182–187.

Fliegauf, M., Benzig, T. and Omran, H. (2007) 'When cilia go bad: cilia defects and ciliopathies.', *Nature Review Molecular and Cell Biology, 8*: 880–893.

Fokstuen, S., Vrticka, K., Riegel, M., Da Silva, V. *et al.* (2001) 'Velofacial hypoplasia (Sedlackova syndrome): a variant of velocardiofacial (Shprintzen) syndrome and part of the phenotypical spectrum of del 22q11.2.', *European Journal of Pediatrics, 160*: 54–57.

Folkers, K., Langsjoen, P., Willis, R., Richardson, P. *et al.* (1990) 'Lovastatin decreases coenzyme Q levels in humans.', *Proceedings of the National Academy of Science USA, 87*(22): 8931–8934.

Folkers, K. and Simonsen, R. (1995) 'Two successful double-blind trials with coenzyme Q10 (vitamin Q10) on muscular dystrophies and neurogenic atrophies.', *Biochimica and Biophysica Acta, 1271*(1): 281–286.

Folling, A. (1934) 'Ueber Ausscheidung von Phenylbrenztraubensaeure in den Harn als Stoffwechselanomalie in Verbindung mit Imbezillitaet.', *Zeitschrift fur Physiologische Chemie, 227*: 169–176.

Folstein, S. and Rutter, M. (1988) 'Autism: familial aggregation and genetic implications.', *Journal of Autism and Developmental Disorders, 18*(1): 3–30.

Folstein, S.E. and Rosen-Sheidley, B. (2001) 'Genetics of autism: complex aetiology for a heterogeneous disorder.' *Nature Reviews/Genetics, 2*: 943–955.

Fombonne, E. (2005) 'Epidemiology of autistic disorder and other pervasive developmental disorders.', *Journal of Clinical Psychiatry, 66* (Supp 10): 3–8.

Fombonne, E. (2009) 'Epidemiology of pervasive developmental disorders.', *Pediatric Research, 65*(6): 591–598.

Fombonne, E., Du Mazaubrun, C., Cans, C. and Grandjean, H. (1997) 'Autism and associated medical disorders in a French epidemiological survey.', *Journal of the American Academy of Child and Adolescent Psychiatry, 36*: 1561–1569.

Fombonne, E., Zakarian, R., Bennett, A., Meng, L. and McLean-Heywood, D. (2006) 'Pervasive developmental disorders in Montreal, Quebec, Canada: prevalence and links with immunizations.', *Pediatrics, 118*(1): e139–150. (Includes disclosure of conflict of interest declaration not in original paper.)

Fon, E.A., Sarrazin, J., Meunier, C., Alarcia, J. *et al.* (1995) 'Adenylosuccinate lyase (ADSL) and infantile autism: absence of previously reported point mutation.', *American Journal of Medical Genetics, 60*: 554–557.

Fontenelle, L.F., Mendlowicz, M.V., Menezes, G.B. and Martins, R. dos S. (2004) 'Asperger syndrome, obsessive-compulsive disorder, and major depression in a patient with 45,X/46,XY mosaicism.', *Psychopathology*, May/June *37*(3): 105–109.

Forest, M.G. (2004) 'Recent advances in the diagnosis and management of congenital adrenal hyperplasia due to 21-hydroxylase deficiency.', *Human Reproduction Update, 10*: 469–485.

Forrester, S., Kovach, M.J., Smith, R.E., Rimer, L. and Wesson, M. (2002) 'Kousseff syndrome caused by deletion of chromosome 22q11–13.', *American Journal of Medical Genetics, 112*: 338–342.

Formigari, R., Michielon, G., Digilio, M.C., Piacentini, G. *et al.* (2008) 'Genetic syndromes and congenital heart defects: how is surgical management affected?' *European Journal of Cardio-thoracic Surgery,* 35(4): 606–614.

Fossali, E., Signorini, E., Intermite, R.C., Casalini, E. *et al.* (2000) 'Renovascular disease and hypertension in children with neurofibromatosis.', *Pediatric Nephrology,* 14: 806–810.

Fox, J.W., Lamperti, E.D., Eksioglu, Y.Z., Hong, S.E. *et al.* (1998) 'Mutations in filamin 1 prevent migration of cerebral cortical neurons in human periventricular heterotopia.', *Neuron,* 21: 1315–1325.

Fraccaro, M., Zuffardi, O., Buhler, E., Schinzel, A. *et al.* (1983) 'Deficiency, transposition, and duplication of one 15q region may be alternatively associated with Prader-Willi (or a similar) syndrome: analysis of seven cases after varying ascertainment.', *Human Genetics,* 64: 388–394.

Fradin, D., Cheslack-Postava, K., Ladd-Acosta, C., Newschaffer, C. *et al.* (2010) 'Parent-Of-Origin Effects in Autism Identified through Genome-Wide Linkage Analysis of 16,000 SNPs.', *PLoS ONE,* 5(9): e12513. doi:10.1371/journal.pone.0012513

Fralick, R.A., Leichter, H.E. and Sheth, K.J. (1990) 'Early diagnosis of Bardet-Biedl syndrome.', *Pediatric Nephrology,* 4: 264–265.

Franceschini, P., Silengo, M.C., Bianco, R., Biagioli, M. *et al.* (1986) 'The Coffin-Siris syndrome in two siblings.', *Pediatric Radiology,* 16: 330–333.

Francke, U., Harper, J.F., Darras, B.T., Cowan, J.M. *et al.* (1987) 'Congenital adrenal hypoplasia, myopathy, and glycerol kinase deficiency: molecular genetic evidence for deletions.', *American Journal of Human Genetics,* 40: 212–227.

Francke, U., Ochs, H.D., de Martinville, B., Giacalone, J. *et al.* (1985) 'Minor Xp21 chromosome deletion in a male associated with expression of Duchenne muscular dystrophy, chronic granulomatous disease, retinitis pigmentosa, and McLeod syndrome.', *American Journal of Human Genetics,* 37: 250–267.

Frangiskakis, J.M., Ewart, A.K., Morris, C.A., Mervis, C.B. *et al.* (1996) 'LIM-kinase1 hemizygosity implicated in impaired visuospatial constructive cognition.', *Cell,* 86: 59–69.

Franz, D.N., Leonard, J., Tudor, C., Chuck, G. *et al.* (2006) 'Rapamycin causes regression of astrocytomas in tuberous sclerosis complex.', *Annals of Neurology,* 59: 490–498.

Frauli, M., Neuville, P., Vol, C., Pin, J-P. and Prezeau, L. (2006) 'Among the twenty classical l-amino acids, only glutamate directly activates metabotropic glutamate receptors.' *Neuropharmacology,* 50: 245–253.

Freeman, A.F., Collura-Burke, C.J., Patronas, N.J., Ilcus, L.S. *et al.* (2007) 'Brain abnormalities in patients with hyperimmunoglobulin E syndrome.', *Pediatrics,* 119(5):e112–11250.

Freeman, B.M., Breiter, S.N., Hoon, A.H. Jr. and Hamosh, A. (1999) 'Pachygyria in Weaver syndrome.', (Letter) *American Journal of Medical Genetics,* 86: 395–397.

Freeman, J.M., Finkelstein, J.D. and Mudd, S.H. (1975) 'Folate responsive homocystinuria and "schizophrenia": a defect in methylation due to deficient 5,10-methylenetetrahydrofolate reductase activity.' *New England Journal of Medicine,* 292: 491–496.

Freeman, J.M., Finkelstein, J.D., Mudd, S.H. and Uhlendorf, B.W. (1972) 'Homocystinuria presenting as reversible 'schizophrenia': a new defect in methionine metabolism with reduced methylene-tetrahydrofolate-reductase activity.' (Abstract), *Pediatric Research,* 6: 423.

Freiberg, R.A., Choate, K.A., Deng, H., Alperin, E.S. *et al.* (1997) 'A model of corrective gene transfer in X-linked ichthyosis.', *Human Molecular Genetics,* 6: 927–933.

Freitag, C.M. (2007) 'The genetics of autistic disorders and its clinical relevance: a review of the literature.' *Molecular Psychiatry,* 12: 2–22.

Fridman, C., Varela, M.C., Kok, F., Diament, A. and Koiffmann, C.P. (2000) 'Paternal UPD15: further genetic and clinical studies in four Angelman syndrome patients.' *American Journal of Medical Genetics,* 92: 322–327.

Friedman, J.M. (1999) 'Vascular and endocrine abnormalities.', In: J.M. Friedman, D.H. Gutmann, M. MacCollin and V.M. Riccardi (eds.) *Neurofibromatosis: Phenotype, Natural History, and Pathogenesis.* Baltimore: Johns Hopkins University Press.

Friedman, J.M. (2007) 'Neurofibromatosis 1.', Online review, GeneReviews, web-based resource.

Friedman, J.M., Arbiser, J., Epstein, J.A., Gutmann, D.H. *et al.* (2002) 'Cardiovascular disease in neurofibromatosis 1: report of the NF1 Cardiovascular Task Force.', *Genetics in Medicine,* 4(3): 105–111.

Friedman, J.M. and Birch, P.H. (1997) 'Type 1 neurofibromatosis: a descriptive analysis of the disorder in 1,728 patients.', *American Journal of Medical Genetics,* 70: 138–143.

Friedman, W.F. and Roberts, W.C. (1966) 'Vitamin D and the supravalvular aortic stenosis syndrome: the transplacental effects of vitamin D on the aorta of the rabbit.', *Circulation,* 34: 77–86.

Frints, S.G.M., Froyen, G., Marynen, P. and Fryns, J.P. (2002) 'X-linked mental retardation: vanishing boundaries between non-specific (MRX) and syndromic (MRXS) forms.', *Clinical Genetics,* 62: 423–432.

Fritschy, J.M. (2008) 'Epilepsy, E/I balance and GABA(A) receptor plasticity.', *Frontiers in Molecular Neuroscience,* 1: 5.

Fritz, B., Kuster, W., Orstavik, K.H., Naumova, A., Spranger, J. and Rehder, H. (1998) 'Pigmentary mosaicism in hypomelanosis of Ito: further evidence for functional disomy of Xp.', *Human Genetics,* 103(4): 441–449.

Froster, U.G. and Gortner, L. (1993) 'Thrombocytopenia in the Brachmann-de Lange syndrome.', *American Journal of Medical Genetics,* 46: 730–731.

Fryburg, J.S., Breg, W.R. and Lindgren, V. (1991) 'Diagnosis of Angelman syndrome in infants.' *American Journal of Medical Genetics,* 38: 58–64.

Fryburg, J.S., Pelegano, J.P. ,Bennett, M.J. and Bebin, E.M. (1994) 'Long-chain 3-hydroxyacyl-coenzyme A dehydrogenase (L-CHAD) deficiency in a patient with the Bannayan-Riley-Ruvalcaba syndrome.', *American Journal of Medical Genetics,* 52: 97–102.

Frye, R.E. (2010) 'Central tetrahydrobiopterin concentration in neurodevelopmental disorders.' *Frontiers in Neuroscience,* 4: Article 52, 1–8.

Fryns, J.P. (1986) 'On the nosology of the Cornelia de Lange and Coffin-Siris syndromes.', (Letter) *Clinical Genetics*, 29: 263–264.

Fryns, J.P. (1992) 'Aarskog syndrome: The changing phenotype with age.' *American Journal of Genetics*, 43: 420–427.

Fryns, J.P., Borghgraef, M., Brown, T.W., Chelly, J. *et al.* (2000) '9th International Workshop on fragile-X syndrome and X-linked mental retardation.' *American Journal of Medical Genetics*, 94: 345–360.

Fryns, J.P., Kleczkowska, A., Kubien, E. and Van den Berghe, H. (1995) 'XYY syndrome and other Y chromosome polysomies: mental status and psychosocial functioning.', *Genetic Counselling*, 6: 197–206.

Fryns, J.P., Lemaire, J., Timmermans, J., Soekarman, D. and Van den Berghe, H. (1993) 'The association of hemifacial microsomia, homolateral micro/anophthalmos, hemihypotrophy, dental anomalies, submucous cleft palate, central nervous system malformations and hypopigmented skin lesions following Blaschko's lines in two unrelated female patients: further evidence for a lethal mutation surviving in mosaic form in "hypomelanosis of Ito".', *Genetic Counselling*, 4(1): 63–67.

Fryns, J.P., Moerman, F., Goddeeris, P., Bossuyt, C. and Van den Berghe, H. (1979) 'A new lethal syndrome with cloudy corneae, diaphragmatic defects and distal limb deformities.', *Human Genetics*, 50: 65–70.

Fryns, J.P. and Vinken, L. (1994) 'Thrombocytopenia in the Brachmann-de Lange syndrome.', *American Journal of Medical Genetics*, 49: 360.

Fuentes, J.J., Pritchard, M.A., Planas, A.M., Bosch, A. *et al.* (1995) 'A new human gene from the Down syndrome critical region encodes a proline-rich protein highly expressed in foetal brain and heart.', *Human Molecular Genetics*, 4: 1935–1944.

Fuhrmann-Rieger, A., Kohler, A. and Fuhrmann, W. (1984) 'Duplication or insertion in 15q11–13 associated with mental retardation–short stature and obesity–Prader-Willi or Cohen syndrome?' *Clinical Genetics*, 25: 347–352.

Fujimoto, S., Yokochi, F., Nakano, M. and Wada, Y. (1995) 'Progressive encephalopathy with oedema, hypsarrhythmia, and optic atrophy (PEHO syndrome) in two Japanese siblings.' *Neuropediatrics*, 26: 270–272.

Fujiwara, T. (2006) 'Clinical spectrum of mutations in SCN1A gene: severe myoclonic epilepsy in infancy and related epilepsies.' *Epilepsy Research*, 70S: S223–S230.

Fujiwara, T., Nakamura, H., Watanabe, M., Yagi, K. *et al.* (1990) 'Clinicoelectrographic concordance between monozygotic twins with severe myoclonic epilepsy in infancy.', *Epilepsia*, 31: 281–286.

Fukazawa, R., Nakahori, Y., Kogo, T., Kawakami, T. *et al.* (1992) 'Normal Y sequences in Smith-Lemli-Opitz syndrome with total failure of masculinization.', *Acta Paediatrica*, 81: 570–572.

Fukuma, G., Oguni, H., Shirasaka, Y., Watanabe, K. *et al.* (2004) 'Mutations of neuronal voltage-gated Na+ channel 1 subunit gene SCN1A in core severe myoclonic epilepsy in infancy (SMEI) and in borderline SMEI(SMEB).', *Epilepsia*, 45: 140–148.

Fukushima, Y., Ohashi, H., Wakui, K., Nishida, T. *et al.* (1992) 'DiGeorge syndrome with del(4)(q21.3q25): possibility of the fourth chromosome region responsible for DiGeorge syndrome.', (Abstract) *American Journal of Human Genetics*, 51 (suppl.): A80.

Fulton, A.B., Hansen, R.M. and Glynn, R.J. (1993) 'Natural course of visual functions in the Bardet-Biedl syndrome.', *Archives of Ophthalmology*, 111: 1500–1506.

Gabis, L., Pomeroy, J. and Andriola, M.R. (2005) 'Autism and epilepsy: cause, consequence, comorbidity, or coincidence?' *Epilepsy and Behaviour*, 7: 652–656.

Gabriel, J.M., Merchant, M., Ohta, T., Ji, Y., Caldwell, R.G. *et al.* (1999) 'A transgene insertion creating a heritable chromosome deletion mouse model of Prader-Willi and Angelman syndromes.', *Proceedings of the National Academy of Science USA*, 96: 9258–9263.

Gage, N.M., Siegel, B., Callen, M., Timothy P.L. and Roberts, T.P.L. (2003) 'Cortical sound processing in children with autism disorder: an MEG investigation.', *NeuroReport*, 14: 2047–2051.

Gagliardi, C., Martelli, S., Burt, M.D. and Borgatti, R. (2007) 'Evolution of neurologic features in Williams syndrome.', *Pediatric Neurology*, 36: 301–306.

Gaily, E., Jonsson, H. and Lappi, M. (2009) 'Visual fields at school-age in children treated with vigabatrin in infancy.', *Epilepsia*, 50(2): 206–216.

Galaburda, A.M., Schmitt, J.E., Atlas, S.W., Eliez, S. *et al.* (2001) 'Dorsal forebrain anomaly in Williams syndrome.', *Archives of Neurology*, 58: 1865–1869.

Galasso, C., Lo-Castro, A., Lalli, C., Nardone, A.M. *et al.* (2008) 'Deletion 2q37: an identifiable clinical syndrome with mental retardation and autism.', *Journal of Child Neurology*, 23(7): 802–806.

Gale, L., Wimalaratna, H., Brotodiharjo, A. and Duggan, J.M. (1997) 'Down's syndrome is strongly associated with coeliac disease.', *Gut*, 40: 492–496.

Galili, N., Baldwin, H.S., Lund, J., Reeves, R. *et al.* (1997) 'A region of mouse chromosome 16 is syntenic to the DiGeorge, velocardiofacial syndrome minimal critical region.', *Genome Research*, 7: 17–26.

Galli-Carminati, G., Chauvet, I. and Deriaz, N. (2006) 'Prevalence of gastrointestinal disorders in adult clients with pervasive developmental disorders.' *Journal of Intellectual Disability Research*, 50(10): 711–718.

Galvagni, F., Saad, F.A., Danieli, G.A., Miorin, M. *et al.* (1994) 'A study on duplications of the dystrophin gene: evidence of a geographical difference in the distribution of breakpoints by intron.', *Human Genetics*, 94: 83–87.

Galvan-Manso, M., Campistol, J., Conill, J. and Sanmarti, F.X. (2005) 'Analysis of the characteristics of epilepsy in 37 patients with the molecular diagnosis of Angelman syndrome.' *Epileptic Disorders*, 7(1): 19–25.

Gámez, A., Sarkissian, C.N., Wang, L., Kim, W. *et al.* (2005) 'Development of pegylated forms of recombinant *Rhodosporidium toruloides* phenylalanine ammonia-lyase for the treatment of classical phenylketonuria.', *Molecular Therapy*, 11: 986–989.

Ganesan, V., Johnson, A., Connelly, A., Eckhardt, S. and Surtees, R.A. (1997) 'Guanidinoacetate methyltransferase deficiency: new clinical features.' *Pediatric Neurology*, 17: 155–157.

Gantois, I. and Kooy, R.F. (2002) 'Targeting fragile-X.', *Genome Biology, 3*(5): 1–5.

Ganz, M.L. (2007) 'The Lifetime Distribution of the Incremental Societal Costs of Autism'. *Archives of Pediatric and Adolescent Medicine, 161:* 343–349.

Gao, F-B. (2002) 'Understanding fragile-X syndrome: insights from retarded flies.' *Neuron, 34:* 859–862.

Gao, X. and Pan, D. (2001) 'TSC1 and TSC2 tumor suppressors antagonize insulin signaling in cell growth.', *Genes and Development, 15:* 1383–1392.

Garber, K., Smith, K.T., Reines, D. and Warren, S.T. (2006) 'Transcription, translation and fragile-X syndrome.' *Current Opinion in Genetics and Development, 16:* 270–275.

Garces, M.E., Perez, W. and Salvador, M. (2005) 'Oxidative stress and hematologic and biochemical parameters in individuals with Down syndrome.', *Mayo Clinic Proceedings, 80*(12): 1607–1611.

Garcia-Cruz, D., Figuera, L.E., Feria-Velazco, A., Sanchez-Corona, J. *et al.* (1993) 'The Myhre syndrome: report of two cases.', *Clinical Genetics, 44:* 203–207.

Garganta, C.L. and Bodurtha, J.N. (1992) 'Report of another family with Simpson-Golabi-Behmel syndrome and a review of the literature.', *American Journal of Medical Genetics, 44:* 129–135.

Gargus, J.J. (2009) 'Genetic calcium signaling abnormalities in the central nervous system: seizures, migraine and autism.', *Annals of the New York Academy of Science, 1151:* 133–156.

Garrod, A. (1909) *Inborn Errors of Metabolism:* The Croonian Lectures Delivered Before the Royal College of Physicians of London in June 1908. London: *Oxford University Press.*

Garrod, A.E. (1902) 'The incidence of alkaptonuria, a study in chemical individuality.', *Lancet, 160*(4137): 1616–1620.

Garrod, A.E. (1931) *Inborn Factors in Disease.* Oxford: Oxford University Press.

Garstang, J. and Wallis M. (2006) 'Randomized controlled trial of melatonin for children with autistic spectrum disorders and sleep problems.', *Child: Care, Health and Development, 32*(5): 585–589.

Garstecki, D.C., Borton, T.E., Stark, E.W. and Kennedy, B.T. (1972) 'Speech, language, and hearing problems in the Laurence-Moon-Biedl syndrome.' *Journal of Speech and Hearing Disorders, 37:* 407–413.

Garty, B.Z., Laor, A. and Danon, Y.L. (1994) 'Neurofibromatosis type 1 in Israel: survey of young adults.', *Journal of Medical Genetics, 31*(11): 853–857.

Gaser, C., Luders, E., Thompson, P.M., Lee, A.D. *et al.* (2006) 'Increased local gyrification mapped in Williams syndrome.', *NeuroImage 33,* 46–54.

Gasparini, F., Lingenhohl, K., Stoehr, N., Flor, P.J. *et al.* (1999) '2-methyl-6-(phenylethynyl)-pyridine (MPEP), a potent, selective and systemically active mGlu5 receptor antagonist.' *Neuropharmacology, 38:* 1493–1503.

Gauthier, J., Bonnel, A., St-Onge, J., Karemera, L. *et al.* (2005) 'NLGN3/NLGN4 gene mutations are not responsible for autism in the Quebec population.', *American Journal of Medical Genetics B: Neuropsychiatric Genetics, 132B*(1): 74–75.

Gecz, J., Cloosterman, D. and Partington, M. (2006) 'ARX: a gene for all seasons.', *Current Opinion in Genetics and Development, 16:* 308–316.

Gedeon, A.K., Baker, E., Robinson, H., Partington, M.W. *et al.* (1992) 'Fragile-X syndrome without CCG amplification has an FMR1 deletion.', *Nature Genetics, 1:* 341–344.

Geerts, M., Steyaert, J. and Fryns, J.P. (2003) 'The XYY syndrome: a follow-up study on 38 boys.' *Genetic Counselling, 14:* 267–279.

Gelb, B.D. and Tartaglia, M. (2006) 'Noonan syndrome and related disorders: dysregulated RAS-mitogen activated protein kinase signal transduction.', *Human Molecular Genetics, 15*(Spec No 2):R220–226.

Genel, F., Atlihan, F., Ozdemir, D. and Targan, S. (2004) 'Development of hydrocephalus in a patient with Joubert syndrome.' *Journal of Postgraduate Medicine, 50*(2): 153.

Gennery, A.R., Flood, T.J., Abinun, M. and Cant, A.J. (2000) 'Bone marrow transplantation does not correct the hyper IgE syndrome.', *Bone Marrow Transplant, 25*(12): 1303–1305.

Gentile, M., Di Carlo, A., Susca, F., Gambotto, A. *et al.* (1996) 'COACH syndrome: report of two brothers with congenital hepatic fibrosis, cerebellar vermis hypoplasia, oligophrenia, ataxia, and mental retardation.', *American Journal of Medical Genetics, 64:* 514–520.

Genton, P., Semah, F. and Trinka, E. (2006) 'Valproic acid in epilepsy: pregnancy-related issues.' *Drug Safety, 29*(1): 1–21.

George, C.D., Patton, M.A., el Sawi, M., Sharland, M. and Adam, E.J. (1993) 'Abdominal ultrasound in Noonan syndrome: a study of 44 patients.', *Pediatric Radiology, 23:* 316–318.

Gerevini, V.D., Di Caruso, A., Cappuccio, I., Vitiani, L.R. *et al.* (2004) 'The mGlu5 metabotropic glutamate receptor is expressed in zones of active neurogenesis of the embryonic and postnatal brain.' *Developmental Brain Research, 150:* 17–22.

Gerlai, J. and Gerlai, R. (2003) 'Autism: a large unmet medical need and a complex research problem.' *Physiology and Behaviour, 79:* 461–470.

Germain, D.P. (2007) 'Ehlers-Danlos syndrome type IV.', *Orphanet Journal of Rare Diseases, 2:* 32 doi:10.1186/1750-1172-2-32

Germain, D.P. and Herrera-Guzman, Y. (2004) 'Vascular Ehlers-Danlos syndrome.', *Annales de génétique, 47:* 1–9.

Geschwind, D.H. and Levitt, P. (2007) 'Autism spectrum disorders: developmental disconnection syndromes.' *Current Opinion in Neurobiology, 17:* 103–111.

Geschwind, N. and Galaburda, A.M. (1985a) 'Cerebral lateralisation: biological mechanisms, associations and pathology. I. A hypothesis and program for research.' *Archives of Neurology, 42*(5): 428–459.

Geschwind, N. and Galaburda, A.M. (1985b) 'Cerebral lateralisation: biological mechanisms, associations and pathology. II. A hypothesis and program for research.' *Archives of Neurology, 42*(6): 521–552.

Geschwind, N. and Galaburda, A.M. (1985c) 'Cerebral lateralisation: biological mechanisms, associations and pathology. III. A hypothesis and a program for research.' *Archives of Neurology, 42:* 634–654.

Geubel, A.P., De Galocsy, C., Alves, N., Rahier, J. and Dive, C. (1991) 'Liver damage caused by therapeutic vitamin A administration: estimate of dose-related toxicity in 41 cases.', *Gastroenterology*, *100*(6): 1701–1709.

Ghahramani Seno, M.M., Graham, I.R., Athanasopoulos, T., Trollet, C. *et al.* (2008) 'RNAi-mediated knockdown of dystrophin expression in adult mice does not lead to overt muscular dystrophy pathology.', *Human Molecular Genetics*, *17*(17): 2622–2632.

Ghaziuddin, M. (1997) 'Autism in Down's syndrome: family history correlates.', *Journal of Intellectual Disability Research*, *41*(1): 87–91.

Ghaziuddin, M. (2000) 'Autism in Down's syndrome: a family history study.', *Journal of Intellectual Disability Research*, *44*(5): 562–566.

Ghaziuddin, M., Bolyard, B. and Alessi, N. (1994) 'Autistic disorder in Noonan syndrome.' *Journal of Intellectual Disability Research*, *38*: 67–72.

Ghaziuddin, M. and Burmeister, M. (1999) 'Deletion of chromosome 2q37 and autism: a distinct subtype?' *Journal of Autism and Developmental Disorders*, *29*(3): 259–263.

Ghaziuddin, M., Tsai, L.Y. and Ghaziuddin, N. (1992) 'Autism in Down's syndrome: presentation and diagnosis.', *Journal of Intellectual Disability Research*, *36*(5): 449–456.

Giacometti, E., Luikenhuis, S., Beard, C. and Jaenisch, R. (2007) 'Partial rescue of MeCP2 deficiency by postnatal activation of MeCP2.', *Proceedings of the National Academy of Science USA*, *104*(6): 1931–1936.

Giannotti, A., Digilio, M.C., Marino, B., Mingarelli, R. and Dallapiccola, B. (1994) 'Cayler cardiofacial syndrome and del 22q11: part of the CATCH22 phenotype.' *American Journal of Medical Genetics*, *53*: 303–304.

Giannotti, A., Tiberio, G., Castro, M., Virgilii, F., Colistro, F. *et al.* (2001) 'Coeliac disease in Williams syndrome.' *Journal of Medical Genetics*, *38*: 767–768.

Gibbons, R. (2006) 'Alpha thalassaemia-mental retardation, X linked.' *ORPHANET Journal of Rare Diseases*, *1*: 15 doi:10.1186/1750-1172-1-15.

Gibbons, R.J., Brueton, L., Buckle, V.J., Burn, J. *et al.* (1995) 'Clinical and hematologic aspects of the X-linked alpha-thalassaemia/mental retardation syndrome (ATR-X).' *American Journal of Medical Genetics*, *55*: 288–299.

Gibbons, R.J., Suthers, G.K., Wilkie, A.O., Buckle, V.J. and Higgs, D.R. (1992) 'X-linked alpha-thalassaemia/mental retardation (ATR-X) syndrome: localization to Xq12–q21.31 by X inactivation and linkage analysis.' *American Journal of Human Genetics*, *51*: 1136–1149.

Gibbons, R.J., Picketts., D.J., Villard, L. and Higgs, D.R. (1995) 'Mutations in a putative global transcriptional regulator cause X-linked mental retardation with alpha-thalassaemia (ATR-X syndrome).', *Cell*, *80*: 837–845.

Gibbs, M.V. and Thorpe, J.G. (1983) 'Personality stereotype of noninstitutionalized Down syndrome children.', *American Journal of Mental Deficiency*, *87*(6): 601–605.

Gibson, G. and Muse, S.V. (2004) *A Primer of Genome Science* (2nd edn.). Massachusetts: Sinauer Associates Ltd.

Gibson, K.M., Burlingame, T.G., Hogema, B., Jakobs, C. *et al.* (2000) '2-methylbutyryl-coenzyme A dehydrogenase deficiency: a new inborn error of L-isoleucine metabolism.', *Pediatric Research*, *47*(6): 830–833.

Gibson, K.M., Christensen, E., Jakobs, C., Fowler, B. *et al.* (1997a) 'The clinical phenotype of succinic semialdehyde dehydrogenase deficiency (4-hydroxybutyric aciduria): case reports of 23 new patients.', *Pediatrics*, *99*: 567–574.

Gibson, K.M., Doskey, A.E., Rabier, D., Jakobs, C. and Morlat, C. (1997b) 'Differing clinical presentation of succinic semialdehyde dehydrogenase deficiency in adolescent siblings from Lifu Island, New Caledonia.', *Journal of Inherited Metabolic Disease*, *20*: 370–374.

Gibson, K.M., Jansen, I., Sweetman, L., Nyhan, W.L. *et al.* (1984) '4-hydroxybutyric aciduria: a new inborn error of metabolism. III. Enzymology and inheritance.', *Journal of Inherited Metabolic Disorders*, *7*(Supp.1): 95–96.

Gibson, K.M., Sacks, M., Kiss, D., Pohowalla, P. *et al.* (1999) '2-methylbutyrylglycinuria in a neonate with central nervous system dysfunction: evidence for isolated 2-methylbutyryl-CoA dehydrogenase deficiency, and inborn error of L-isoleucine metabolism.', *Journal of Inherited Metabolic Disease*, *22*(Supp.1): 16.

Giglia-Mari, G., Coin, F., Ranish, J.A., Hoogstraten, D. *et al.* (2004) 'A new, tenth subunit of TFIIH is responsible for the DNA repair syndrome trichothiodystrophy group A.', *Nature Genetics*, *36*: 714–719.

Gilbert, D.L. (2007) 'Regarding Omega-3 fatty acids supplementation in children with autism: a double-blind randomized, placebo-controlled pilot study'., *Biological Psychiatry*, e-print, doi:10.1016/j.biopsych.2007.03.028.

Gill, D.S., Hyman, S.L., Steinberg, A. and North, K.N. (2006) 'Age-related findings on MRI in neurofibromatosis type 1.', *Pediatric Radiology*, *36*: 1048–1056.

Gillberg C. (1983) 'Identical triplets with infantile autism and the fragile-X syndrome.', *British Journal of Psychiatry*, *143*: 256–260.

Gillberg, C. (1992) 'Subgroups in autism: are there behavioural phenotypes typical of underlying medical conditions?' *Journal of Intellectual Disability Research*, *36*(3): 201–214.

Gillberg, C. and Billstedt, E. (2000) 'Autism and Asperger syndrome: coexistence with other clinical disorders.' *Acta Psychiatrica Scandinavica*, *102*: 321–330.

Gillberg, C. and Coleman, M. (1996) 'Autism and medical disorders: a review of the literature.', *Developmental Medicine and Child Neurology*, *38*: 191–202.

Gillberg, C. and Coleman, M. (2000) *The Biology of the Autistic Syndromes* (3rd edn.). London: MacKeith Press, (*Clinics in Developmental Medicine* No. 15 3/4).

Gillberg, C. and Rasmussen, P. (1994) 'Brief report: four case histories and a literature review of Williams syndrome and autistic behaviour.', *Journal of Autism and Developmental Disorders*, *24*(3): 381–393.

Gillberg, C. and Steffenburg, S. (1989) 'Autistic behaviour in Moebius syndrome.' *Acta Paediatrica Scandinavica*, *78*: 314–316.

Gillberg, C. and Wahlstrom, J. (1985) 'Chromosome abnormalities in infantile autism and other childhood psychoses: a population study of 66 cases.' *Developmental Medicine and Child Neurology, 27*: 293–304.

Gillberg, C. and Winnergard, I. (1984) 'Childhood psychosis in a case of Moebius syndrome.', *Neuropediatrics, 15*(3): 147–149.

Gillberg, I.C., Gillberg, C. and Ahlsen, G. (1994) 'Autistic behaviour and attention deficits in tuberous sclerosis: a population-based study.', *Developmental Medicine and Child Neurology, 36*(1): 50–56.

Gillberg, I.C., Gillberg, C. and Kopp, S. (1992) 'Hypothyroidism and autism spectrum disorders.' *Journal of Child Psychology and Psychiatry, 33*: 531–542.

Gillberg, C., Winnergard, I. and Wahlstrom, J. (1984) 'The sex chromosomes—one key to autism? An XYY case of infantile autism.', *Applied Research in Mental Retardation, 5*: 353–360.

Gillessen-Kaesbach, G., Demuth, S., Thiele, H., Theile, U., Lich, C. and Horsthemke, B. (1999) 'A previously unrecognized phenotype characterized by obesity, muscular hypotonia, and ability to speak in patients with Angelman syndrome caused by an imprinting defect.', *European Journal of Human Genetics, 7*: 638–644.

Gillis, L.A., McCallum, J., Kaur, M., DeScipio, C. *et al.* (2004) 'NIPBL mutational analysis in 120 individuals with Cornelia de Lange syndrome and evaluation of genotype-phenotype correlations.', *American Journal of Human Genetics, 75*: 610–623.

Gillott, A., Furniss, F. and Walter, A. (2001) 'Anxiety in high-functioning children with autism.', *Autism, 5*(3): 277–286.

Gimpl, G., Wiegand, V., Burger, K. and Fahrenholz, F. (2002) 'Cholesterol and steroid hormones: modulators of oxytocin receptor function.', *Progress in Brain Research, 139*: 43–55.

Gingell, K., Parmar, R. and Sungum-Paliwal, S. (1996) 'Autism and multiple pituitary deficiency.' *Developmental Medicine and Child Neurology, 38*: 545–549.

Girirajan, S., Elsas, L.J.II, Devriendt, K. and Elsea, S.H. (2005) 'RAI1 variations in Smith-Magenis syndrome patients without 17p11.2 deletions.', *Journal of Medical Genetics, 42*: 820–828.

Gitiaux, C., Ceballos-Picot, I., Marie, S., Valayannopoulos, V. *et al.* (2009) 'Misleading behavioural phenotype with adenylosuccinate lyase deficiency.', *European Journal of Human Genetics, 17*(1): 133–136.

Giunco, C.T., Moretti-Ferreira, D., Silva, A.E., Rocha, S.S. and Fett-Conte, A.C. (2008) 'MOMO syndrome associated with autism: a case report.', *Genetic and Molecular Research, 7*(4): 1223–1225.

Glaser, B., Debbane, M., Hinard, C., Morris, M.A. *et al.* (2006) 'No evidence for an effect of COMT val158-to-met genotype on executive function in patients with 22q11 deletion syndrome.', *American Journal of Psychiatry, 163*: 537–539.

Glaser, R.L., Broman, K.W., Schulman, R.L., Eskenazi, B., Wyrobek, A.J. and Jabs, E.W. (2003) 'The paternal-age effect in Apert syndrome is due, in part, to the increased frequency of mutations in sperm.', *American Journal of Human Genetics, 73*: 939–947.

Glaser, R.L., Jiang, W., Boyadjiev, S.A., Tran, A.K. *et al.* (2000) 'Paternal origin of FGFR2 mutations in sporadic cases of Crouzon syndrome and Pfeiffer syndrome.', *American Journal of Human Genetics, 66*: 768–777.

Glasson, E.J., Bower, C., Petterson, B., de Klerk, N. *et al.* (2004) 'Perinatal factors and the development of autism: a population study.', *Archives of General Psychiatry, 61*: 618–627.

Glaze, D.G. (2002) 'Neurophysiology of Rett syndrome.', *Mental Retardation and Developmental Disability Research Reviews, 8*(2): 66–71.

Gleeson, J.G., Keeler, L.C., Parisi, M.A., Marsh, S.E. *et al.* (2004) 'Molar tooth sign of the midbrain-hindbrain junction: occurrence in multiple distinct syndromes.', *American Journal of Medical Genetics A, 125*: 125–134.

Glover, M.T., Brett, E.M. and Atherton, D.J. (1989) 'Hypomelanosis of Ito: spectrum of the disease.', *Journal of Pediatrics, 115*(1): 75–80.

Goddard, J.M., Rossel, M., Manley, N.R. and Capecchi, M.R. (1996) 'Mice with targeted disruption of Hoxb-1 fail to form the motor nucleus of the VIIth nerve.', *Development, 122*: 3217–3228.

Godel, V., Regenbogen, L., Goya, V. and Goodman, R.M. (1982) 'Autosomal dominant Goldenhar syndrome.', *Birth Defects Original Articles Series, 18*(6): 621–628.

Goffin, A., Hoefsloot, L.H., Bosgoed, E., Swillen, A. and Fryns, J.P. (2001) 'PTEN mutation in a family with Cowden syndrome and autism.', *American Journal of Medical Genetics, 105*: 521–524.

Gofflot, F., Hars, C., Illien, F., Chevy, F. *et al.* (2003) 'Molecular mechanisms underlying limb anomalies associated with cholesterol deficiency during gestation: implications of Hedgehog signaling.', *Human Molecular Genetics, 12*(10): 1187–1198.

Goh, W.H., Khong, P.L., Leung, C.S. and Wong, V.C. (2004) 'T2-weighted hyperintensities (unidentified bright objects) in children with neurofibromatosis 1: their impact on cognitive function.', *Journal of Child Neurology, 19*: 853–858.

Goh, Y.I., Bollano, E., Einarson, T.R. and Koren, G. (2006) 'Prenatal multivitamin supplementation and rates of congenital anomalies: a meta-analysis.', *Journal of Obstetrics and Gynaecology Canada, 28*(8): 680–689.

Gohlke, B.C., Haug, K., Fukami, M., Friedl, W. *et al.* (2000) 'Interstitial deletion in Xp22.3 is associated with X linked ichthyosis, mental retardation, and epilepsy.', *Journal of Medical Genetics, 37*: 600–602.

Goines, P. and Van de Water, J. (2010) 'The immune system's role in the biology of autism.' *Current Opinion in Neurology, 23*: 111–117.

Goin-Kochel, R.P., Myers, B.J. and Mackintosh, V.H. (2007) 'Parental reports on the use of treatments and therapies for children with autism spectrum disorders.' *Research in Autism Spectrum Disorders, 11*(1): 195–209.

Goizet, C., Excoffier, E., Taine, L., Taupiac, E. *et al.* (2000) 'Case with autistic syndrome and chromosome 22q13.3 deletion detected by FISH.', *American Journal of Medical Genetics, 96*: 839–844.

Gokcay, G., Baykal, T., Gokdemir, Y. and Demirkol, M. (2006) 'Breast feeding in organic acidaemias.' *Journal of Inherited Metabolic Disease, 29*: 304–310.

Goldacre, B. (2009) *Bad Science.* London: Fourth Estate.

Goldberg-Stern, H., Strawsburg, R.H., Patterson, B., Hickey, F. *et al.* (2001) 'Seizure frequency and characteristics in children with Down syndrome.', *Brain and Development, 23*: 375–378.

Golabi, M. and Rosen, L. (1984) 'A new X-linked mental retardation-overgrowth syndrome.', *American Journal of Medical Genetics, 17*(1): 345–358.

Golden, G.S. (1984) 'Controversies in therapies for children with Down syndrome.', *Pediatrics in Review, 6*: 116–120.

Goldenberg, A., Wolf, C., Chevy, F., Benachi, A. *et al.* (2004) 'Antenatal manifestations of Smith-Lemli-Opitz (RSH) syndrome: a retrospective survey of 30 cases.', *American Journal of Medical Genetics, 124A*: 423–426.

Goldenberg, J.N., Brown, S.B. and Weiner, W.J. (1994) 'Coprolalia in younger patients with Gilles de la Tourette syndrome.' *Movement Disorders, 9*(6): 622–625.

Goldenhar, M. (1952) 'Associations malformatives de l'oeil et de l'oreille: en particulier, le syndrome: dermoide epibulbaire-appendices auriculaires–fistula auris congenita et ses relations avec la dysostose mandibulo-faciale.', *Journal de Genetique Humaine, 1*: 243–282.

Golding, J., Steer, C., Emmett, P., Davis, J.M. and Hibbeln, J.R. (2009) 'High levels of depressive symptoms in pregnancy with low omega-3 fatty acid intake from fish.', *Epidemiology, 20*: 598–603.

Goldstone, A.P. and Beales, P.L. (2008) 'Genetic obesity syndromes.', *Frontiers in Hormone Research, 36*: 37–60.

Gomez, L., Le Deist, F., Blanche, S., Cavazzana-Calvo, M. *et al.* (1995) 'Treatment of Omenn syndrome by bone marrow transplantation.', *Journal of Pediatrics, 127*: 76–81.

Gomez-Lado, C., Eiris-Punal, J., Blanco-Barca, O., del Rio-Latorre, E. *et al.* (2004) 'Hipomelanosis de Ito. Un sindrome neurocutaneo heterogeneo y posiblemente infradiagnosticado.' [Hypomelanosis of Ito. A possibly under-diagnosed heterogeneous neurocutaneous syndrome], *Revista de Neurologia, 38*(3): 223–228.

Goncalves, M.A.F.V., Holkers, M., van Nierop, G.P., Wieringa, R. *et al.* (2008) 'Human genome by a fiber-modified high-capacity adenovirus-based vector system.', *PLoS ONE, 3*(8): e3084. doi:10.1371/journal.pone.0003084.

Gong, X., Bacchelli, E., Blasi, F., Toma, C. *et al.* (2008) 'Analysis of X chromosome inactivation in autism spectrum disorders.' *American Journal of Medical Genetics B: Neuropsychiatric Genetics, 147B*(6): 830–835.

Gong, X., Jia, M., Ruan, Y., Shuang, M. *et al.* (2004) 'Association between the FOXP2 gene and autistic disorder in Chinese population.', *American Journal of Medical Genetics B: Neuropsychiatric Genetics, 127*(1): 113–116.

Gonzalez, F.J. and Fernandez-Salguero, P. (1995) 'Diagnostic analysis, clinical importance and molecular basis of dihydropyrimidine dehydrogenase deficiency.', *Trends in Pharmacological Science, 16*: 325–327.

Goodey, C.F. (2006) 'Behavioural phenotypes in disability research: historical perspectives.', *Journal of Intellectual Disability Research, 50*(6): 397–403.

Goodlin-Jones, B.L., Tassone, F., Gane, L.W. and Hagerman, R.J. (2004) 'Autistic spectrum disorder and the fragile-X premutation.' *Journal of Developmental and Behavioural Pediatrics, 25*: 392–398.

Goodship, J., Cross, I., LiLing, J. and Wren, C. (1998) 'A population study of chromosome 22q11 deletions in infancy.', *Archives of Disease in Childhood, 79*: 348–351.

Goodship, J., Cross, I., Scambler, P. and Burn, J. (1995) 'Monozygotic twins with chromosome 22q11 deletion and discordant phenotype.', *Journal of Medical Genetics, 32*: 746–748.

Gorden, N.T., Arts, H.H., Parisi, M.A., Coene, K.L.M. *et al.* (2008) 'CC2D2A is mutated in Joubert syndrome and interacts with the ciliopathy-associated basal body protein CEP290.', *American Journal of Human Genetics, 83*(5): 559–571.

Gorker, I. and Tuzun, U. (2005) 'Autistic-like findings associated with a urea cycle disorder in a 4-year-old girl.' *Journal of Psychiatry and Neuroscience, 30*: 133–135.

Gorlin, R.J. (1987) 'Nevoid basal-cell carcinoma syndrome.', *Medicine (Baltimore), 66*: 98–113.

Gorlin, R.J. (1990) 'Branchial arch and oro-acral disorders.' In: J.J. Gorlin, M.M. Jr. Cohen and L.S. Levin (Eds.). *Syndromes of the Head and Neck* (3rd edn.). Oxford: Oxford University Press.

Gorlin, R.J., Cohen, M.M. Jr., Condon, L.M. and Burke, B.A. (1992) 'Bannayan-Riley-Ruvalcaba syndrome.', *American Journal of Medical Genetics, 44*: 307–314.

Gorlin, R.J., Cohen, M.M. and Levin, L.S. (1990) *Syndromes of the Head and Neck* (3rd edn.). Oxford: Oxford University Press.

Gosalakkal, J.A. (2004) 'Sotos syndrome (cerebral gigantism): a review of neurobehavioural, developmental and neurological manifestations.', *International Pediatrics, 19*(3): 147–151.

Gosch, A., Stading, G. and Pankau, R. (1994) 'Linguistic abilities in children with Williams-Beuren syndrome.', *American Journal of Medical Genetics, 52*: 291–296.

Gosden, R.G. and Feinberg, A.P. (2007) 'Genetics and epigenetics – nature's pen-and-pencil set.' *New England Journal of Medicine, 356*(7): 731–733.

Gosselin, J., Lebon-Labich, B., Lucron, H., Marçon, F. and Leheup, B. (2004) 'Syndrome de délétion 22 q 11 et maladie de basedow. À propos de trois observations pédiatriques.' [Grave's disease in children with 22q11 deletion. Report of three cases], *Archives de Pediatrie, 11*(12): 1468–1471.

Gotham, K., Pickles, A. and Lord, C. (2008) 'Standardizing ADOS scores for a measure of severity in autism spectrum disorders.', *Journal of Autism and Developmental Disorders, 39*(5): 693–705.

Gothelf, D., Farber, N., Raveh, E., Apter, A. and Attias, J. (2006) 'Hyperacusis in Williams syndrome: characteristics and associated neuroaudiologic abnormalities.', *Neurology, 66*: 390–395.

Gottfried, O.N., Viskochil, D.H., Fults, D.W. and Couldwell, W.T. (2006) 'Molecular, genetic, and cellular pathogenesis of neurofibromas and surgical implications.', *Neurosurgery, 58*: 1–16.

Gottlieb, S., Driscoll, D.A., Punnett, H.H., Sellinger, B. *et al.* (1998) 'Characterization of 10p deletions suggests two nonoverlapping regions contribute to the DiGeorge syndrome phenotype.' *American Journal of Human Genetics, 62*(2): 495–498.

Gould, E.L., Loesch, D.Z., Martin, M.J., Hagerman, R.J. *et al.* (2000) 'Melatonin profiles and sleep characteristics in boys with fragile-X syndrome: a preliminary study.', *American Journal of Medical Genetics, 95*: 307–315.

Goutieres, F. and Aicardi, J. (1986) 'Atypical forms of Rett syndrome.', *American Journal of Medical Genetics*, (Supp. 1) *25*: 183–194.

Graefe, A. von (1880) *Handbuch dergesammten Augenheilkunde*, (eds.) A. von Graefe and T. Saemisch. Leipzig: W. Englemann.

Graf, A., Landolt, M.A., Mori, A.C. and Boltshauser, E. (2006) 'Quality of life and psychological adjustment in children and adolescents with neurofibromatosis type 1.', *Journal of Pediatrics, 149*: 348–353.

Graf, W.D., Marin-Garcia, J., Gao, H.G., Pizzo, S. *et al.* (2000) 'Autism associated with mitochondrial DNA G8363A transfer RNA (Lys) mutation.' *Journal of Child Neurology, 15*: 357–361.

Graham, J.M. Jr., Rosner, B., Dykens, E. and Visootsak, J. (2005) 'Behavioural features of CHARGE syndrome (Hall-Hittner syndrome) comparison with Down syndrome, Prader-Willi syndrome, and Williams syndrome.' *American Journal of Medical Genetics A, 133*: 240–247.

Gramer, G., Burgard, P., Garbade, S.F. and Lindner, M. (2007) 'Effects and clinical significance of tetrahydrobiopterin supplementation in phenylalanine hydroxylase-deficient hyperphenylalaninaemia.', *Journal of Inherited Metabolic Disease, 30*(4): 556–564.

Granpeesheh, D., Tarbox, J. and Dixon, D.R. (2009) 'Applied behaviour analytic interventions for children with autism: a description and review of treatment research.', *Annals of Clinical Psychiatry, 21*(3): 162–173.

Gräsbeck, R. (2006) 'Imerslund-Gräsbeck syndrome (selective vitamin B12 malabsorption with proteinuria). *ORPHANET Journal of Rare Diseases, 1*: 17, doi:10.1186/1750-1172-1-17.

Grasso, M., Giovannucci, M.L., Pierluigi, M., Tavellini, F. *et al.* (1989) 'Isochromosome, not translocation in trisomy 21q21q.', *Human Genetics, 84*: 63–65.

Gravholt, C.H. (2005a) 'Epidemiological, endocrine and metabolic features in Turner syndrome.', *Arquivos Brasilleries Endocrinologin e metabologia, 49*: 145–156.

Gravholt, C.H. (2005b) 'Clinical practice in Turner syndrome.', *Nature Clinical Practice in Endocrinology and Metabolism, 1*(1): 41–52.

Gravholt, C.H., Juul, S., Naeraa, R.W. and Hansen, J. (1996) 'Prenatal and postnatal prevalence of Turner's syndrome: a registry study.', *British Medical Journal, 312*: 16–21.

Gray, K.M. and Tonge, B.J. (2001) 'Are there early features of autism in infants and preschool children?' *Journal of Paediatrics and Child Health, 37*: 221–226.

Greco, D., Romano, C., Reitano, S., Barone, C. *et al.* (2008) 'Three new patients with dup(17) (p11.2p11.2) without autism.', (Letter) *Clinical Genetics, 73*: 294–296.

Green, J., Charman, T., McConachie, H., Aldred, C. *et al.* (2010) 'Parent-medicated communication-focused treatment in children with autism (PACT): a randomised controlled trial.' *British Medical Journal*, doi:10.1016/S0140-6736(10)60587-9.

Green, J.S., Parfrey, P.S., Harnett, J.D., Farid, N.R. *et al.* (1989) 'The cardinal manifestations of Bardet-Biedl syndrome, a form of Laurence-Moon-Biedl syndrome.', *New England Journal of Medicine, 321*: 1002–1009.

Greenberg, F., Elder, F.F.B., Haffner, P., Northrup, H. and Ledbetter, D.H. (1988) 'Cytogenetic findings in a prospective series of patients with DiGeorge anomaly.', *American Journal of Human Genetics, 43*: 605–611.

Greenberg, F., Guzzetta, V., Montes de Oca-Luna, R., Magenis, R.E. *et al.* (1991) 'Molecular analysis of the Smith-Magenis syndrome: a possible contiguous-gene syndrome associated with del(17)(p11.2).', *American Journal of Human Genetics, 49*: 1207–1218.

Greenberg, F., Lewis, R.A., Potocki, L., Glaze, D. *et al.* (1996) 'Multi-disciplinary clinical study of Smith-Magenis syndrome (deletion 17p11.2).', *American Journal of Medical Genetics, 62*: 247–254.

Greenough, W.T., Klintsova, A.Y., Irwin, S.A., Galvez, R. *et al.* (2001) 'Synaptic regulation of protein synthesis and the fragile-X protein.' *Proceedings of the National Academy of Science USA, 98*: 7101–7106.

Greenstein, M.A. (1990) 'Prader-Willi and Angelman syndromes in one kindred with expression consistent with genetic imprinting.', (Abstract) *American Journal of Human Genetics, 47* (suppl.): A59.

Greenwood, R.S., Tupler, L.A., Whitt, J.K., Buu, A. *et al.* (2005) 'Brain morphometry, T2-weighted hyperintensities, and IQ in children with neurofibromatosis type 1.', *Archives of Neurology, 62*: 1904–1908.

Greeves, L.G., Patterson, C.C., Carson, D.J., Thom, R. *et al.* (2000) 'Effect of genotype on changes in intelligence quotient after dietary relaxation in phenylketonuria and hyperphenylalaninaemia.', *Archives of Disease in Childhood, 82*: 216–221.

Gregorevic, P., Blankinship, M.J., Allen, J.M., Crawford, R.W. *et al.* (2004) 'Systemic delivery of genes to striated muscles using adeno-associated viral vectors.', *Nature Medicine, 10*: 828–834.

Gregorevic, P. and Chamberlain, J.S. (2003) 'Gene therapy for muscular dystrophy.', *Expert Opinion on Biological Therapy, 3*: 803–814.

Griebel, V., Krageloh-Mann, I. and Michaelis, R. (1989) 'Hypomelanosis of Ito – report of four cases and survey of the literature.', *Neuropediatrics, 20*(4): 234–237.

Grier, R.E., Farrington, F.H., Kendig, R. and Mamunes, P. (1983) 'Autosomal dominant inheritance of the Aarskog syndrome.' *American Journal of Medical Genetics, 15*: 39–46.

Griffiths, P.V., Demellweek, C., Fay, N., Robinson, P.H. and Davidson, D.C. (2000) 'Wechsler subscale IQ and subtest profile in early treated phenylketonuria.', *Archives of Disease in Childhood, 82*: 209–215.

Griggs, R.C., Kingston, W., Herr, B.E., Forbes, G. and Moxley, R.T. 3rd (1985) 'Lack of relationship of hypogonadism to muscle wasting in myotonic dystrophy.', *Archives of Neurology, 42*(9): 881–885.

Griggs, R.C., Moxley, R.T. 3rd, Mendell, J.R., Fenichel, G.M. *et al.* (1993) 'Duchenne dystrophy: randomized, controlled trial of prednisone (18 months) and azathioprine (12 months).', *Neurology*, *43*: 520–527.

Grimbacher, B., Dutra, A.S., Holland, S.M., Fischer, R.E. *et al.* (1999a) 'Analphoid marker chromosome in a patient with hyper-IgE syndrome, autism, and mild mental retardation.' *Genetics in Medicine*, *1*: 213–218.

Grimbacher, B., Holland, S.M., Gallin, J.I., Malech, H.L. *et al.* (1999b) 'Hyper-IgE syndrome with recurrent infections – an autosomal dominant multisystem disorder.', *New England Journal of Medicine*, *340*(9): 692–702.

Grimbacher, B., Holland, S.M. and Puck, J.M. (2005) 'Hyper-IgE syndromes.', *Immunological Reviews*, *203*: 244–250.

Grimbacher, B., Schaffer, A.A., Holland, S.M., Davis, J. *et al.* (1999c) 'Genetic linkage of hyper-IgE syndrome to chromosome 4.', *American Journal of Human Genetics*, *65*(3): 735–744.

Grimm, T. and Wesselhoeft, H. (1980) 'Zur Genetik des Williams-Beuren-Syndroms und der isolierten Form der supravalvulaeren Aortenstenose (Untersuchungen von 128 Familien).', *Zeitschrift fur Kardiologie*, *69*: 168–172.

Grinker, R.R. (2007) *Unstrange Minds: A Father, A Daughter and a Search for New Answers – Remapping the World of Autism.* New York: Basic Books.

Groen, W.B., Swinkels, S.H., van der Gaag, R.J. and Buitelaar, J.K. (2007) 'Finding effective screening instruments for autism using Bayes theorem.' *Archives of Pediatric and Adolescent Medicine*, *161*: 415–416.

Groen, W.B., van Orsouw, L., ter Huurne, N., Swinkels, S. *et al.* (2009) 'Intact spectral but abnormal temporal processing of auditory stimuli in autism.', *Journal of Autism and Developmental Disorders*, *39*: 742–750.

Grompe, M., Jones, S.N. and Caskey, C.T. (1990) 'Molecular detection and correction of ornithine transcarbamylase deficiency.', *Trends in Genetics*, *6*(10): 335–339.

Grønskov, K., Ek, J. and Brondum-Nielsen, K. (2007) 'Oculocutaneous albinism.', *Orphanet Journal of Rare Diseases*, *2*: 43 doi:10.1186/1750-1172-2-43.

Grønskov, K., Hjalgrim, H., Nielsen, I-M. and Brondum-Nielsen, K. (2004) 'Screening of the ARX gene in 682 retarded males.', *European Journal of Human Genetics*, *12*: 701–705.

Gropman, A. (2003) 'Vigabatrin and newer interventions in succinic semialdehyde dehydrogenase deficiency.', *Annals of Neurology*, *54*(Supp.6): S66–S72.

Gropman, A.L., Elsea, S., Duncan, W.C. Jr and Smith, A.C.M. (2007) 'New developments in Smith-Magenis syndrome (del 17p11.2).' *Current Opinion in Neurology*, *20*: 125–134.

Grosso, S., Brogna, A., Bazzotti, S., Renieri, A. *et al.* (2007a) 'Seizures and electroencephalographic findings in CDKL5 mutations: case report and review', *Brain and Development*, *29*: 239–242.

Grosso, S., Lasorella, G., Russo, A., Galluzzi, P. *et al.* (2007b) 'Aicardi syndrome with favourable outcome: case report and review.', *Brain and Development*, *29*(7): 443–446.

Grunewald, S. (2009) 'The clinical spectrum of phosphomannomutase 2 deficiency (CDG-Ia).' *Biochimica et Biophysica Acta*, *1792*: 827–834.

Gruss, M. and Braun, K. (2001) 'Alterations of amino acids and monoamine metabolism in male Fmrl knockout mice: a putative animal model of the human fragile-X mental retardation syndrome.', *Neural Plasticity*, *8*(4): 285–298.

Gryder, D.S. and Rogawski, M.A. (2003) 'Selective antagonism of GluR5 kainate receptor-mediated synaptic currents by topiramate in rat basolateral amygdala neurons.', *Journal of Neuroscience*, *23*: 7069–7074.

Gueant, J-L., Anello, G., Bosco, P., Gueant-Rodriguez, R-M. *et al.* (2005) 'Homocysteine and related genetic polymorphisms in Down's syndrome IQ.', *Journal of Neurology, Neurosurgery and Psychiatry*, *76*: 706–709.

Guéant-Rodriguez, R.M., Guéant, J.L., Debard, R., Thirion, S. *et al.* (2006) 'Prevalence of methylenetetrahydrofolate reductase 677T and 1298C alleles and folate status: a comparative study in Mexican, West African, and European populations.', *American Journal of Clinical Nutrition*, *83*(3): 701–707.

Guerrini, R., Dravet, C., Genton, P., Belmonte, A. *et al.* (1998) 'Lamotrigine and seizure aggravation in severe myoclonic epilepsy.', *Epilepsia*, *39*: 508–512.

Guerrini, R., Shanahan, J.L., Carrozzo, R., Bonanni, P., Higgs, D.R. and Gibbons, R.J. (2000) 'A nonsense mutation of the ATRX gene causing mild mental retardation and epilepsy.' *Annals of Neurology*, *47*: 117–121.

Guideri, F., Acampa, M., Hayek, G., Zappella, M. and Di Perri, T. (1999) 'Reduced heart rate variability in patients affected with Rett syndrome: a possible explanation for sudden death.', *Neuropediatrics*, *30*: 146–148.

Guion-Almeida, M.L. and Richieri-Costa, A. (1992) 'CNS midline anomalies in the Opitz G/BBB syndrome: report on 12 Brazilian patients.', *American Journal of Medical Genetics*, *43*: 918–928.

Guldager, B., Jørgensen, P.J. and Grandjean, P. (1996) 'Metal excretion and magnesium retention in patients with intermittent claudication treated with intravenous disodium EDTA.' *Clinical Chemistry*, *42*(12): 1938–1942.

Guldberg, P., Henriksen, K.F., Sipila, I., Guttler, F. and de la Chapelle, A. (1995) 'Phenylketonuria in a low incidence population: molecular characterization of mutations in Finland.', *Journal of Medical Genetics*, *32*: 976–978.

Guldberg, P., Rey, F., Zschocke, J., Romano, V. *et al.* (1998) 'A European multicenter study of phenylalanine hydroxylase deficiency: classification of 105 mutations and a general system for genotype-based prediction of metabolic phenotype.', *American Journal of Human Genetics*, *63*: 71–79.

Gupta, M., Polinsky, M., Senephansiri, H., Snead, O.C. *et al.* (2004) 'Seizure evolution and amino acid imbalances in murine succinate semialdehyde dehydrogenase (SSADH) deficiency.', *Neurobiology of Disease*, *16*: 556–562.

Gurrieri, F. and Neri, G. (1991) 'A girl with the Lujan-Fryns syndrome.', (Letter) *American Journal of Medical Genetics*, *38*: 290–291.

Gurrieri, F., Sammito, V., Bellussi, A. and Neri, G. (1992) 'New autosomal recessive syndrome of mental retardation, epilepsy, short stature, and skeletal dysplasia.' *American Journal of Medical Genetics*, *44*: 315–320.

Gussoni, E., Bennett, R.R., Muskiewicz, K.R., Meyerrose, T. *et al.* (2002) 'Long-term persistence of donor nuclei in a Duchenne muscular dystrophy patient receiving bone marrow transplantation.', *Journal of Clinical Investigation, 110*: 807–814.

Gussoni, E., Blau, H.M. and Kunkel, L.M. (1997) 'The fate of individual myoblasts after transplantation into muscles of DMD patients.', *Nature Medicine, 3*: 970–977.

Gussoni, E., Soneoka, Y., Strickland, C.D., Buzney, E.A. *et al.* (1999) 'Dystrophin expression in the mdx mouse restored by stem cell transplantation.', *Nature, 401*: 390–394.

Gustafson, S., Zbuk, K.M., Scacheri, C. and Eng, C. (2007) 'Cowden syndrome.', *Seminars in Oncology, 34*(5): 428–434.

Guthrie, R. (1996) 'The introduction of newborn screening for phenylketonuria: a personal history.', *European Journal of Pediatrics, 155* (Suppl. 1): 4–5.

Guthrie, R. and Susi, A. (1963) 'A simple phenylalanine method for detecting phenylketonuria in large populations of newborn infants.', *Pediatrics, 32*: 338–343.

Gutmann, D.H., Aylsworth, A., Carey, J.C., Korf, B. *et al.* (1997) 'The diagnostic evaluation and multidisciplinary management of neurofibromatosis 1 and neurofibromatosis 2.', *Journal of the American Medical Association, 278*: 51–57.

Guttler, F., Azen, C., Guldberg, P., Romstad, A. *et al.* (1999) 'Relationship among genotype, biochemical phenotype, and cognitive performance in females with phenylalanine hydroxylase deficiency: report from the maternal phenylketonuria collaborative study.', *Pediatrics, 104*: 258–262.

Guttler, F. and Woo, S.L.C. (1986) 'Molecular genetics of PKU.', *Journal of Inherited Metabolic Disease, 9* (Suppl.1): 58–68.

Guy, J., Jian, J., Selfridge, J., Cobb, S. and Bird, A. (2007) 'Reversal of neurological defects in a mouse model of Rett syndrome.' *Science, 315*(5815): 1143–1147.

Haan, E.A., Brown, G.K., Mitchell, D. and Danks, D.M. (1985) 'Succinic semialdehyde dehydrogenase deficiency – a further case.', *Journal of Inherited Metabolic Disease, 8*(3): 99.

Haargaard, B. and Fledelius, H.C. (2006) 'Down syndrome and early cataract.', *British Journal of Ophthalmology, 90*: 1024–1027.

Haas, D., Garbade, S.F., Vohwinkel, C., Muschol, N. *et al.* (2007) 'Effects of cholesterol and simvastatin treatment in patients with Smith-Lemli-Opitz syndrome (SLOS).', *Journal of Inherited Metabolic Disease, 30*(3): 375–387.

Haataja, R., Vaisanen, M-L., Li, M., Ryynanen, M. and Leisti, J. (1994) 'The fragile-X syndrome in Finland: demonstration of a founder effect by analysis of microsatellite haplotypes.', *Human Genetics, 94*: 479–483.

Haecker, A., Qi, D., Lilja, T., Moussian, B. *et al.* (2007) 'Drosophila brakeless interacts with atrophin and is required for tailless-mediated transcriptional repression in early embryos.', *PLoS Biology, 5*(6): e145, doi:10.1371/journal.pbio.0050145.

Hagberg, B. (1995) 'Rett syndrome: clinical peculiarities and biological mysteries.', *Acta Paediatrica, 84*(9): 971–976.

Hagberg, B., Aicardi, J., Dias, K. and Ramos, O. (1983) 'A progressive syndrome of autism, dementia, ataxia, and loss of purposeful hand use in girls. Rett syndrome: report of 35 cases.', *Annals of Neurology, 14*: 471–479.

Hagberg, B., Goutieres, F., Hanefeld, F., Rett, A. and Wilson, J. (1985) 'Rett syndrome: criteria for inclusion and exclusion.' *Brain and Development, 7*: 372–373.

Hagberg, B.A. and Skjeldal, O.H. (1994) 'Rett variants: a suggested model for inclusion criteria.', *Pediatric Neurology, 11*(1): 5–11.

Hagberg, B., Hanefeld, F., Percy, A. and Skjeldal, O. (2002) 'An update on clinically applicable diagnostic criteria in Rett syndrome.' *European Journal of Paediatric Neurology, 6*: 1–5

Hagel, C., Zils, U., Peiper, M., Kluwe, L. *et al.* (2006) 'Histopathology and clinical outcome of NF1-associated vs. sporadic malignant peripheral nerve sheath tumors.', *Journal of Neurooncology, 82*(2): 187–192.

Hager, R., Cheverud, J.M. and Wolf, J.B. (2008) 'Maternal Effects as the Cause of Parent-of-Origin Effects That Mimic Genomic Imprinting.', *Genetics, 178*: 1755–1762.

Hagerman, R. (1999) *Neurodevelopmental Disorders: Diagnosis and Treatment.* Oxford: Oxford University Press.

Hagerman, R.J. (1997) 'Fragile-X syndrome: molecular and clinical insights and treatment issues.', *Western Medical Journal, 166*: 129–137.

Hagerman, R.J. (2006) 'Lessons from fragile-X regarding neurobiology, autism, and neurodegeneration.', *Journal of Developmental and Behavioural Pediatrics, 27*(1): 63–74.

Hagerman, R.J., Berry-Kravis, E., Hessl, D., Coffey, S. *et al.* (2008) 'Trial of fenobam, an mGluR5 antagonist, in adults with fragile-X syndrome.', *Journal of Intellectual Disability Research, 52*(10): 814.

Hagerman, R.J., Berry-Kravis, E., Kaufmann, W.E., Ono, M.Y. *et al.* (2009) 'Advances in the treatment of fragile-X syndrome.', *Pediatrics, 123*(1): 378–390.

Hagerman, R.J. and Cronister, A. (1996) *Fragile-X Syndrome: Diagnosis, Treatment and Research* (2nd edn.). Baltimore: Johns Hopkins University Press.

Hagerman, R.J. and Hagerman, P.J. (2002a) *Fragile-X Syndrome: Diagnosis, Treatment, and Research.* (3rd edn.). Baltimore: Johns Hopkins University Press

Hagerman, R.J. and Hagerman, P.J. (2002b) 'The fragile-X premutation: into the phenotypic fold.', *Current Opinion in Genetics and Development, 12*: 278–283.

Hagerman, R.J. and Hagerman, P.J. (2004) 'The fragile-X premutation: a maturing perspective.', *American Journal of Human Genetics, 74*: 805–816.

Hagerman, R.J. and Hagerman, P.J. (2008) 'Testing for fragile-X gene mutations throughout the life span.', *Journal of the American Medical Association, 300*(20): 2419–2421.

Hagerman, R.J., Hull, C.E., Safanda, J.F., Carpenter, I. *et al.* (1994) High functioning fragile-X males: demonstration of an unmethylated fully expanded FMR-1 mutation associated with protein expression.' *American Journal of Medical Genetics, 51*: 298–308.

Hagerman, R.J., Jackson, A.W., Levitas, A., Braden, M. et al. (1986) 'Oral folic acid versus placebo in the treatment of males with the fragile-X syndrome.', American Journal of Medical Genetics, 23(1–2): 241–262.

Hagerman, R.J., Leavitt, B.R., Farzin, F., Jacquemont, S. et al. (2004) 'Fragile-X-associated tremor/ataxia syndrome (FXTAS) in females with the FMR1 premutation.', American Journal of Human Genetics, 74: 1051–1056.

Hagerman, R.J., Leehey, M., Heinrichs, W., Tassone, F. et al. (2001) 'Intention tremor, parkinsonism, and generalized brain atrophy in male carriers of fragile-X.', Neurology, 57: 127–130.

Hagerman, R.J., Ono, M.Y. and Hagerman, P.J. (2005) 'Recent advances in fragile-X: a model of autism and neurodegeneration.' Current Opinion in Psychiatry, 18: 490–496.

Hagerman, R.J., Staley, L.W., O'Conner, R., Lugenbeel, K. et al. (1996) 'Learning-disabled males with a fragile-X CGG expansion in the upper premutation size range.', Pediatrics, 97: 122–126.

Hagerman, R.J. and Synhorst, D.P. (1984) 'Mitral valve prolapse and aortic dilatation in the fragile-X syndrome.', American Journal of Medical Genetics 17: 123–131.

Hagerman, R.J., Van Housen, K., Smith, A.C.M. and McGavran, L. (1984) 'Consideration of connective tissue dysfunction in the fragile-X syndrome.', American Journal of Medical Genetics, 17: 111–121.

Hagerman, R.J., Wilson, P., Staley, L.W., Lang, K.A. et al. (1994) 'Evaluation of school children at high risk for fragile-X syndrome utilizing buccal cell FMR-1 testing.', American Journal of Medical Genetics, 51: 474–481.

Hahn, A. and Neubauer, B.A. (2005) 'Autismus und Stoffwechselerkrankungen – was ist gesichert? [Autism and metabolic disorders-a rational approach] Zeitschrift fur Kinder und Jugendpsychiatrie und Psychotherapie, 33: 259–271.

Hahn, H., Wicking, C., Zaphiropoulous, P.G., Gailani, M.R. et al. (1996) 'Mutations of the human homolog of drosophila patched in the nevoid basal cell carcinoma syndrome.', Cell, 85: 841–851.

Haibach, H., Burns, T.W., Carlson, H.E., Burman, K.D. and Deftos, L.J. (1992) 'Multiple hamartoma syndrome (Cowden's disease) associated with renal cell carcinoma and primary neuroendocrine carcinoma of the skin (Merkel cell carcinoma).', American Journal of Clinical Pathology, 97: 705–712.

Hajihosseini, M.K., Wilson, S., De Moerlooze, L. and Dickson, C. (2001) 'A splicing switch and gain-of-function mutation in FgfR2-IIIc hemizygotes causes Apert/Pfeiffer syndrome-like phenotypes.', Proceedings of the National Academy of Science, 98(7): 3855–3860.

Halder, A., Jain, M., Kabra, M. and Gupta, N. (2008) 'Mosaic 22q11.2 microdeletion syndrome: diagnosis and clinical manifestations of two cases.', Molecular Cytogenetics, 1: 18 doi:10.1186/1755-8166-1-18

Hall, B.D. (1979) 'Choanal atresia and associated multiple anomalies.', Journal of Pediatrics, 95: 395–398.

Hall, B.D. (2002) 'Adjunct diagnostic test for Angelman syndrome: the tuning fork response.' (Letter) American Journal of Medical Genetics, 109: 238–240.

Hall, B.D. and Cadle, R.G. (2002) 'Adjunct diagnostic test for Angelman syndrome: the tuning fork response.', (Letter) American Journal of Medical Genetics, 112: 249.

Hall, J.G. (1993) 'CATCH 22.' Journal of Medical Genetics, 30: 801–802.

Hallam, T.M. and Bourtchouladze, R. (2006) 'Rubinstein-Taybi syndrome: molecular findings and therapeutic approaches to improve cognitive dysfunction.', Cellular and Molecular Life Sciences, 63(15): 1725–1735.

Hallmayer, J., Glasson, E.J., Bower, C., Petterson, B. et al. (2002) 'On the twin risk in autism.' American Journal of Human Genetics, 71(4): 941–946.

Hals, J., Bjerve, K.S., Nilsen, H., Svalastog, A.G. and Ek, J. (2000) 'Essential fatty acids in the nutrition of severely neurologically disabled children.' British Journal of Nutrition, 83: 219–225.

Haltia, M. and Somer, M. (1993) 'Infantile cerebello-optic atrophy: neuropathology of the progressive encephalopathy syndrome with oedema, hypsarrhythmia and optic atrophy (the PEHO syndrome).' Acta Neuropathologica (Berl), 85: 241–247.

Hamed, S.A. (2006) 'Drug evaluation: PTC-124 – ~>a potential treatment of cystic fibrosis and Duchenne muscular dystrophy.', IDrugs, 9(11): 783–789.

Hamel, B.C., Smits, A.P., de Graaff, E., Smeets, D.F. et al. (1994) 'Segregation of FRAXE in a large family: clinical, psychometric, cytogenetic, and molecular data.', American Journal of Human Genetics, 55: 923–931.

Hamel, C.P. (2007) 'Cone rod dystrophies.', Orphanet Journal of Rare Diseases, 2: 7, doi:10.1186/1750-1172-2-7.

Hammen, A., Wagner, B., Berkhoff, M. and Donati, F. (1998) 'A paradoxical rise of neonatal seizures after treatment with vitamin B6.', European Journal of Paediatric Neurology, 2: 319–322.

Hammer, S., Dorrani, N., Dragich, J., Kudo, S. and Schanen, C. (2002) 'The phenotypic consequences of MeCP2 mutations extend beyond Rett syndrome.', Mental Retardation and Developmental Disabilities Research Reviews, 8(2): 94–98.

Hammock, E.A. and Young, L.J. (2006) 'Oxytocin, vasopressin and pair bonding: implications for autism.', Philosophical Transactions of the Royal Society of London B Biological Sciences, 361(1476): 2186–2198.

Hammond, L.S., Macias, M.M., Tarleton, J.C. and Shashidhar Pai, G. (1997) 'Fragile-X syndrome and deletions in FMR1: new case and review of the literature.', American Journal of Medical Genetics, 72: 430–434.

Han, M. and Criado, E. (2005) 'Renal artery stenosis and aneurysms associated with neurofibromatosis.', Journal of Vascular Surgery, 41: 539–543.

Hanauer, A. (2001) 'Coffin-Lowry syndrome (CLS).' Orphanet Encyclopaedia, www.orpha.net/data/patho/GB/uk-coffin.pdf.

Handforth, A., Delorey, T.M., Homanics, G.E. and Olsen, R.W. (2005) 'Pharmacologic evidence for abnormal thalamocortical functioning in GABA receptor beta3 subunit-deficient mice, a model of Angelman syndrome.' Epilepsia, 46(12): 1860–1870.

Hanefeld, F.(1985) 'The clinical pattern of the Rett syndrome.', *Brain and Development, 7*(3): 320–325.

Hanley, W.B., Koch, R., Levy, H.L., Matalon, R. *et al.* (1996) 'The North American Maternal Phenylketonuria Collaborative Study, developmental assessment of the offspring: preliminary report.', *European Journal of Pediatrics, 155* (suppl. 1): 169–172.

Hanley, W.B., Lee, A.W., Hanley, A.J.G., Lehotay, D.C. *et al.* (2000) 'Hypotyrosinemia' in phenylketonuria.' *Molecular Genetics and Metabolism, 69*: 286–294.

Hansen, F.J. and Friis, B. (1976) 'Familial occurrence of cerebral gigantism, Sotos syndrome.', *Acta Paediatrica Scandinavica, 65*: 387–389.

Happé, F., Ronald, A. and Plomin, R. (2006) 'Time to give up on a single explanation for autism.' *Nature Neuroscience, 9*: 1218–1220.

Happle, R., Traupe, H., Grobe, H. and Bonsmann, G. (1984) 'The Tay syndrome (congenital ichthyosis with trichothiodystrophy).', *European Journal of Pediatrics, 141*: 147–152.

Happle, R. and Vakilzadeh, F. (1982) 'Hamartomatous dental cusps in hypomelanosis of Ito.', *Clinical Genetics, 21*(1): 65–68.

Harach, H.R., Soubeyran, I., Brown, A., Bonneau, D. and Longy, M. (1999) 'Thyroid pathologic findings in patients with Cowden disease.', *Annals of Diagnostic Pathology, 3*: 331–340.

Hara-Chikuma, M. and Verkman, A.S. (2006) 'Physiological roles of glycerol-transporting aquaporins: the aquaglyceroporins.', *Cellular and Molecular Life Sciences, 63*: 1386–1392.

Haraguchi, M., Tsujimoto, H., Fukushima, M., Higuchi, I. *et al.* (2002) 'Targeted deletion of both thymidine phosphorylase and uridine phosphorylase and consequent disorders in mice.', *Molecular and Cellular Biology, 22*(14): 5212–5221.

Harbord, M.G., Finn, J.P., Hall-Craggs, M.A., Brett, E.M. and Baraitser, M. (1989) 'Mobius' syndrome with unilateral cerebellar hypoplasia.', *Journal of Medical Genetics, 26*: 579–582.

Harnett, J.D., Green, J.S., Cramer, B.C., Johnson, G. *et al.* (1988) 'The spectrum of renal disease in Laurence-Moon-Biedl syndrome.', *New England Journal of Medicine, 319*: 615–618.

Harper, P.S. (2005) 'Julia Bell and the treasury of human inheritance.', *Human Genetics, 116*: 422–432

Harpey, J-P., Rosenblatt, D.S., Cooper, B.A., Le Moel, G. *et al.* (1981) 'Homocystinuria caused by 5,10-methylenetetrahydrofolate reductase deficiency: a case in an infant responding to methionine, folinic acid, pyridoxine, and vitamin B12 therapy.' *Journal of Pediatrics, 98*: 275–278.

Harrell, R.F., Capp, R.H., Davis, D.R., Peerless, J. and Ravitz, L.R. (1981) 'Can nutritional supplements help mentally retarded children? An exploratory study.', *Proceedings of the National Academy of Science USA, 78*(1): 574–578.

Harris, J., Robert, E. and Kallen, B. (1997) 'Epidemiology of choanal atresia with special reference to the CHARGE association.', *Pediatrics, 99*: 363–367.

Harris, J.C. (2006) *Intellectual Disability: Understanding its Development, Causes, Classification, Evaluation and Treatment.* Oxford: Oxford University Press.

Harrison, D.J. and Webb, P.J. (1990) 'Scoliosis in the Rett syndrome: natural history and treatment.', *Brain and Development, 12*(1): 154–156.

Harrison, K.L. and Pheasant, A.E. (1995) 'Analysis of urinary pterins in autism.', *Biochemical Society Transactions, 23*(4): 603S.

Hartmann, S., Bergmann, M., Bohle, R.M., Weidner, W. and Steger, K. (2006) 'Genetic imprinting during impaired spermatogenesis.', *Molecular Human Reproduction, 12*(6): 407–411.

Hartsfield, J.K. Jr., Hall, B.D., Grix, A.W., Kousseff, B.G. *et al.* (1993) 'Pleiotropy in Coffin-Lowry syndrome: sensorineural hearing deficit and premature tooth loss as early manifestations.', *American Journal of Medical Genetics, 45*: 552–557.

Hartshorne, T.S., Grialou, T.L. and Parker, K.R. (2005) 'Autistic-like behaviour in CHARGE syndrome.' *American Journal of Medical Genetics A, 133*: 257–261.

Hartshorne, T.S., Hefner, M.A. and Davenport, S.L. (2005) 'Behaviour in CHARGE syndrome: introduction to the special topic.', *American Journal of Medical Genetics, 133A*(3): 228–231.

Hartshorne, T.S., Heussler, H.S., Dailor, A.N., Williams, G.L. *et al.* (2009) 'Sleep disturbances in CHARGE syndrome: types and relationships with behaviour and caregiver well-being.', *Developmental Medicine and Child Neurology, 51*(2): 143–150.

Hartshorne, T.S., Nicholas, J., Grialou, T.L. and Russ, J.M. (2007) 'Executive function in CHARGE syndrome.', *Child Neuropsychology, 13*(4): 333–344.

Harum, K.H., Alemi, L. and Johnston, M.V. (2001) 'Cognitive impairment in Coffin-Lowry syndrome correlates with reduced RSK2 activation.', *Neurology, 56*: 207–214.

Hasegawa, T., Hasegawa, Y., Aso, T., Koto, S. *et al.* (1997) 'HDR syndrome (hypoparathyroidism, sensorineural deafness, renal dysplasia) associated with del(10) (p13).', *American Journal of Medical Genetics, 73*: 416–418.

Hashimoto, T. (1999) 'Peroxisomal β-oxidation enzymes.', *Neurochemical Research, 24*(4): 551–563.

Haspeslagh, M., Fryns, J.P., Beusen, L., Van Dessel, F. *et al.* (1984) 'The Coffin-Lowry syndrome: a study of two new index patients and their families.', *European Journal of Pediatrics, 143*: 82–86.

Haspeslagh, M., Fryns, J.P. and van den Berghe, H. (1984) 'The Coffin-Siris syndrome: report of a family and further delineation.', *Clinical Genetics, 26*: 374–378.

Hatton, D.D., Sideris, J., Skinner, M., Mankowski, J. *et al.* (2006) 'Autistic behaviour in children with fragile-X syndrome: prevalence, stability, and the impact of FMRP.' *American Journal of Medical Genetics A, 140*: 1804–1813.

Havlovicova, M., Novotna, D., Kocarek, E., Novotna, K. *et al.* (2007) 'Clinical Report: a girl with neurofibromatosis type 1, atypical autism and mosaic ring chromosome 17.', *American Journal of Medical Genetics Part A, 143A*: 76–81.

Haworth, J.C., Dilling, L.A., Surtees, R.A.H., Seargeant, L.E. *et al.* (1993) 'Symptomatic and asymptomatic methylenetetrahydrofolate reductase deficiency in two adult brothers.', *American Journal of Medical Genetics, 45*(5): 572–576.

Hayashi, M.L., Shankaranarayana Rao, B.S., Seo, J-S., Choi, H-S. *et al.* (2007) 'Inhibition of p21-activated kinase rescues symptoms of fragile-X syndrome in mice.', *Proceedings of the National Academy of Science*, 104(27): 11489–11494.

Hayden, D. (2003) *Pox: Genius, Madness and the Mysteries of Syphilis*. New York: Basic Books.

Haylett, A.K., Ward, T.H. and Moore, J.V. (2003) 'DNA damage and repair in Gorlin syndrome and normal fibroblasts after aminolevulinic acid photodynamic therapy: a comet assay study.', *Photochemistry and Photobiology*, 78: 337–341.

Healy, N.M. (1965) 'Gilles de la Tourette syndrome in an autistic child.', *Journal of the Irish Medical Association*, 57: 93–94.

Hebebrand, J., Martin, M., Korner, J., Roitzheim, B. *et al.* (1994) 'Partial trisomy 16p in an adolescent with autistic disorder and Tourette syndrome.', *American Journal of Medical Genetics*, 54(3): 268–270.

Hecht, F. and Glover, T.W. (1983) 'Antibiotics containing trimethoprim and the fragile-X chromosome.', (Letter) *New England Journal of Medicine*, 308: 285–286.

Hedera, P. and Fink, J.K. (2007) 'Xeroderma pigmentosum.', *eMedicine*, www.emedicine.com/neuro/topic399.htm.

Hegedus, B., Yeh, T.H., Lee, D.Y., Emnett, R.J. *et al.* (2008) 'Neurofibromin regulates somatic growth through the hypothalamic-pituitary axis.', *Human Molecular Genetics*, 17(19): 2956–2966.

Hegreberg, G.A. (1975) 'Animal model of human disease: Ehlers-Danlos syndrome.', *American Journal of Pathology*, 79(2): 383–386.

Heilstedt, H.A., Ballif, B.C., Howard, L.A., Kashork, C.D. and Shaffer, L.G. (2003) 'Population data suggest that deletions of 1p36 are a relatively common chromosome abnormality.', *Clinical Genetics*, 64: 310–316.

Heinrichs, M. and Gaab, J. (2007) 'Neuroendocrine mechanisms of stress and social interaction: implications for mental disorders.' *Current Opinion in Psychiatry*, 20: 158–162.

Hellings, J.A., Hossain, S., Martin, J.K. and Baratang, R.R. (2002) 'Psychopathology, GABA, and the Rubinstein-Taybi syndrome: a review and case study.' *American Journal of Medical Genetics*, 114: 190–195.

Henderson, S. (1987) *The Test of Motor Impairment – Revised*. London: Department of Educational Psychology, Institute of Education.

Hendrich, B. and Bickmore, W. (2001) 'Human diseases with underlying defects in chromatin structure and modification.', *Human Molecular Genetics*, 10: 2233–2242.

Hendriks, Y.M., Verhallen, J.T., van der Smagt, J.J., Kant, S.G. *et al.* (2003) 'Bannayan-Riley-Ruvalcaba syndrome: further delineation of the phenotype and management of PTEN mutation-positive cases.', *Familial Cancer*, 2(2): 79–85.

Hendriksen, J.G. and Vles, J.S. (2008) 'Neuropsychiatric disorders in males with Duchenne muscular dystrophy: frequency rate of attention-deficit hyperactivity disorder (ADHD), autism spectrum disorder, and obsessive-compulsive disorder.' *Journal of Child Neurology*, 23: 477–481.

Hennekam, R.C., Van Den Boogaard, M.J., Sibbles, B.J. and Van Spijker, H.G. (1990) 'Rubinstein-Taybi syndrome in The Netherlands.', *American Journal of Medical Genetics*, Supplement, 6: 17–29.

Hennekam, R.C.M. (2005) 'Congenital brain anomalies in distal cholesterol biosynthesis defects.' *Journal of Inherited Metabolic Disorders*, 28: 385–392.

Hennies, H.C., Rauch, A., Seifert, W., Schumi, C. *et al.* (2004) 'Allelic heterogeneity in the coh1 gene explains clinical variability in Cohen syndrome.', *American Journal of Human Genetics*, 75: 138–145.

Herbert, J.D., Sharp, I.R. and Gaudiano, B.A. (2002) 'Separating Fact from fiction in the etiology and treatment of autism: a scientific review of the evidence.', *The Scientific Review of Mental Health Practice*, 1(1): 23–43.

Herguner, S. and Mukaddes, N.M. (2006) 'Autism and Williams syndrome: a case report.', *World Journal of Biological Psychiatry*, 7(3): 186–188.

Herman, G.E. (2003) 'Disorders of cholesterol biosynthesis: prototypic metabolic malformation syndromes.', *Human Molecular Genetics*, 12(Spec No 1): R75–88.

Herman, G.E., Greenberg, F. and Ledbetter, D.H. (1988) 'Multiple congenital anomaly/mental retardation (MCA/MR) syndrome with Goldenhar complex due to a terminal del(22q).', *American Journal of Medical Genetics*, 29(4): 909–915.

Herman, G.E., Henninger, N., Ratliff-Schaub, K., Pastore, M. *et al.* (2007) 'Genetic testing in autism: how much is enough?' *Genetics in Medicine*, 9(5): 268–274.

Hermida-Prieto, A., Eirís-Puñal, J., Álvárez-Moreno, A., Alonso-Martín, A., Barreiro Conde, J. and Castro-Gago, M. (1997) 'Hipomelanosis de Ito: autismo, dilatación segmentaria del colon y hallazgo inusual en neuroimagen.', *Revista de Neurologia*, 25: 71–74.

Hernandez, R.N., Feinberg, R.L., Vaurio, R., Passanante, N.M. *et al.* (2009) 'Autism spectrum disorder in fragile-X syndrome: a longitudinal evaluation.', *American Journal of Medical Genetics A*, 149A(6): 1125–1137.

Hernandez-Martin, A., Gonzalez-Sarmiento, R. and De Unamuno, P. (1999) 'X-linked ichthyosis: an update.', *British Journal of Dermatology*, 141: 617–627.

Herrmann, D.N. (2008) 'Experimental therapeutics in hereditary neuropathies: the past, the present, and the future.', *Neurotherapeutics*, 5: 507–515.

Hersh, J.H., Bloom, A.S. and Weisskopf, B. (1982) 'Childhood autism in a female with Coffin-Siris syndrome.' *Journal of Developmental and Behavioural Pediatrics*, 3: 249–251.

Hertz-Picciotto, I. and Delwiche, L. (2009) 'The rise in autism and the role of age at diagnosis.', *Epidemiology*, 20(1): 84–90.

Hertzberg, M., Jahromi, K., Ferguson, V., Dahl, H.H.M. *et al.* (1989) 'Phenylalanine hydroxylase gene haplotypes in Polynesians: evolutionary origins and absence of alleles associated with severe phenylketonuria.', *American Journal of Human Genetics*, 44: 382–387.

Hessl, D., Rivera, S.M. and Reiss, A.L. (2004) 'The neuroanatomy and neuroendocrinology of fragile-x syndrome.', *Mental Retardation and Developmental Disabilities Research Reviews*, 10(1): 17–24.

Heuer, L., Ashwood, P., Schauer, J., Goines, P. *et al.* (2008) 'Reduced levels of immunoglobulin in children with autism correlates with behavioural symptoms.', *Autism Research*, 1(5): 275–283.

Hibuse, T., Maeda, N., Funahashi, T., Yamamoto, K. *et al.* (2005) 'Aquaporin 7 deficiency is associated with development of obesity through activation of adipose glycerol kinase.' *Proceedings of the National Academy of Science USA*, 102(31): 10993–10998.

Hicks, M., Ferguson, S., Bernier, F. and Lemay, J-F. (2008) 'A case report of monozygotic twins with Smith-Magenis syndrome.', *Journal of Developmental and Behavioural Pediatrics*, 29: 42–46.

Hide, W.A., Babenko, V.N., van Heusden, P.A., Seoighe C. and Kelso, J.F. (2001) 'The contribution of exon-skipping events on chromosome 22 to protein coding diversity.', *Genome Research*, 11: 1848–1853.

Hill, I.D., Dirks, M.H., Liptak, G.S., Colletti, R.B. *et al.* (2005) 'Guideline for the diagnosis and treatment of coeliac disease in children: recommendations of the North American Society for Pediatric Gastroenterology, Hepatology and Nutrition.', *Journal of Pediatric Gastroenterology and Nutrition*, 40(1): 1–19.

Hilton, J.F., Christensen, K.E., Watkins, D., Raby, B.A. *et al.* (2003) 'The molecular basis of glutamate formiminotransferase deficiency.', *Human Mutation*, 22(1): 67–73.

Hinek, A., Botney, M.D. and Mecham, R.P. (1991) 'Inhibition of tropoelastin expression by 1,2 dihydroxyvitamin D3.', *Connective Tissue Research*, 26: 155–166.

Hinton, V.J., Cyrulnik, S.E., Fee, R.J., Batchelder, A. *et al.* (2009) 'Association of autistic spectrum disorders with dystrophinopathies.', *Pediatric Neurology*, 41: 339–346.

Hinton, V.J., De Vivo, D.C., Nereo, N.E., Goldstein, E. and Stern, Y. (2000) 'Poor verbal working memory across intellectual level in boys with Duchenne dystrophy.', *Neurology*, 54: 2127–2132.

Hinton, V.J., De Vivo, D.C., Nereo, N.E., Goldstein, E. and Stern, Y. (2001) 'Selective deficits in verbal working memory associated with a known genetic etiology: the neuropsychological profile of duchenne muscular dystrophy.', *Journal of the International Neuropsychological Society*, 7: 45–54.

Hinton, V.J., Fee, R.J., De Vivo, D.C. and Goldstein, E. (2006) 'Poor facial affect recognition among boys with Duchenne muscular dystrophy.', *Journal of Autism and Developmental Disorders*, 37(10): 1925–1933.

Hirawat, S., Welch, E.M., Elfring, G.L., Northcutt, V.J. *et al.* (2007) 'Safety, tolerability, and pharmacokinetics of PTC124, a nonaminoglycoside nonsense mutation suppressor, following single- and multiple-dose administration to healthy male and female adult volunteers.' *Journal of Clinical Pharmacology*, 47: 430–444.

Hirayama, K., Iizuka, R., Maehara, K. and Watanabe, T. (1981) 'Clinicopathological study of dentatorubro-pallidoluysian atrophy. Part 1. Its clinical form and analysis of symptomatology.', *Shinkei Kenkyu no Shinpo*, 25: 725–736.

Hiriashi, Y., Kato, S., Ishihara, T. and Takano, T. (1992) 'Quantitative Southern blot analysis in the dystrophin gene of Japanese patients with Duchenne or Becker muscular dystrophy: a high frequency of duplications.', *Journal of Medical Genetics*, 29: 897–901.

Hirose, S. (2006) 'A new paradigm of channelopathy in epilepsy syndromes: intracellular trafficking abnormality of channel molecules.', *Epilepsy Research*, 70(Supp.): S206–S217.

Hirst, M.C., Knight, S.J.L., Christodoulou, Z., Grewal, P.K. *et al.* (1993) 'Origins of the fragile-X syndrome mutation.', *Journal of Medical Genetics*, 30: 647–650.

Hitchins, M.P., Rickard, S., Dhalla, F., de Vries, B.B.A. *et al.* (2004) 'Investigation of UBE3A and MECP2 in Angelman syndrome (AS) and patients with features of AS.', *American Journal of Medical Genetics*, 125A: 167–172.

Hittner, H.M., Hirsch, N.J., Kreh, G.M. and Rudolph, A.J. (1979) 'Colobomatous microphthalmia, heart disease, hearing loss, and mental retardation – a syndrome.', *Journal of Pediatric Ophthalmology and Strabismus*, 16: 122–128.

Hitzler, J.K., Cheung, J., Li, Y., Scherer, S.W. and Zipursky, A. (2003) 'GATA1 mutations in transient leukemia and acute megakaryoblastic leukemia of Down syndrome.', *Blood*, 101: 4301–4304.

Hjerrild, B.E., Mortensen, K.H. and Gravholt, C.H. (2008) 'Turner syndrome and clinical treatment.', *British Medical Bulletin*, 86: 77–93.

Ho, A., Todd, R.D. and Constantino, J.N. (2005) 'Brief report: autistic traits in twins vs. non-twins – a preliminary study.', *Journal of Autism and Developmental Disorders*, 35: 129–133.

Ho, K.L., McNae, I.W., Schmiedeberg, L., Robert, J., Klose, R.J., Bird, A.P. and Walkinshaw, M.D. (2008) 'MeCP2 binding to DNA depends upon hydration at Methyl-CpG.', *Molecular Cell*, 29: 525–531.

Hoang, L., Byck, S., Prevost, L. and Scriver, C.R. (1996) 'PAH Mutation Analysis Consortium Database: a database for disease-producing and other allelic variation at the human PAH locus.', *Nucleic Acids Research*, 24: 127–131.

Hobbs, C.A., Sherman, S.L., Yi, P., Hopkins, S.E. *et al.* (2000) 'Polymorphisms in genes involved in folate metabolism as maternal risk factors for Down syndrome.' *American Journal of Human Genetics*, 67: 623–630.

Hobbs, K., Kennedy, A., DuBray, M., Bigler, E.D. *et al.* (2007) 'A retrospective foetal ultrasound study of brain size in autism.', *Biological Psychiatry*, 62: 1048–1055. doi:10.1016/j.biopsych.2007.03.020.

Hodgkin, D.C., Kamper, J., MacKay, M., Pickworth, J. *et al.* (1956) 'Structure of vitamin B12.' *Nature*, 178(4524): 64–66.

Hodgkins, P.R., Harris, C.M., Shawkat, F.S., Thompson, D.A. *et al.* (2004) 'Joubert syndrome: long-term follow-up.', *Developmental Medicine and Child Neurology*, 46: 694–699.

Hoeijmakers, J.H.J. (1994) 'Human nucleotide excision repair syndromes: molecular clues to unexpected intricacies.' *European Journal of Cancer*, 30A: 1912–1921.

Hofstra, R.M., Mulder, I.M., Vossen, R., de Koning-Gans, P.A. *et al.* (2004) 'DGGE-based whole-gene mutation scanning of the dystrophin gene in Duchenne and Becker muscular dystrophy patients.', *Human Mutation, 23*: 57–66.

Hofman, K.J., Steel, G., Kazazian, H.H. and Valle, D. (1991) 'Phenylketonuria in U.S. blacks: molecular analysis of the phenylalanine hydroxylase gene.', *American Journal of Human Genetics, 48*: 791–798.

Hogart, A., Leung, K.N., Wang, N.J., Wu, D.J. *et al.* (2008) 'Chromosome 15q11–13 duplication syndrome brain reveals epigenetic alterations in gene expression not predicted from copy number.', *Journal of Medical Genetics*, doi:10.1136/jmg.2008.061580.

Hogart, A., Wu, D., LaSalle, J.M. and Schanen, N.C. (2008) 'The comorbidity of autism with the genomic disorders of chromosome 15q11.2–q13.', *Neurobiology of Disease*, doi:10.1016/j.nbd.2008.08.011.

Hohoff, A., Joos, U., Meyer, U., Ehmer, U. and Stamm, T. (2007) 'The spectrum of Apert syndrome: phenotype, particularities in orthodontic treatment, and characteristics of orthognathic surgery.' *Head and Face Medicine, 3*(10): 1–24.

Hoksbergen, R., ter Laak, J., Rijk, K., van Dijkum, C. and Stoutjesdijk, F. (2005) 'Post-institutional autistic syndrome in Romanian adoptees.' *Journal of Autism and Developmental Disorders, 35*(5): 615–623.

Holder-Espinasse, M., Marie, S., Bourrouillou, G., Ceballos-Picot, I. *et al.* (2002) 'Towards a suggestive facial dysmorphism in adenylosuccinate lyase deficiency?' (Letter) *Journal of Medical Genetics, 39*: 440–442.

Holland, S.M., DeLeo, F.R., Elloumi, H.Z., Hsu, A.P. *et al.* (2007) 'STAT3 mutations in the hyper-IgE syndrome.', *New England Journal of Medicine, 357*(16): 1608–1619.

Hollander, E., Novotny, S., Hanratty, M., Yaffe, R. *et al.* (2003) 'Oxytocin infusion reduces repetitive behaviours in adults with autistic and Asperger disorders.' *Neuropsychopharmacology, 28*: 193–198.

Holliday, R. (2006) 'Epigenetics: a historical overview.', *Epigenetics, 1*(2): 76–80.

Hollowell, J.G., Staehling, N.W., Flanders, W.D., Hannon, W.H. *et al.* (2002) 'Serum TSH, T(4), and thyroid antibodies in the United States population (1988 to 1994): National Health and Nutrition Examination Survey (NHANES III).', *Journal of Clinical Endocrinology and Metabolism, 87*(2): 489–499.

Holm, V.A., Cassidy, S.B., Butler, M.G., Hanchett, J.M. *et al.* (1993) 'Prader-Willi syndrome: consensus diagnostic criteria.', *Pediatrics, 91*(2): 398–402.

Holmes, A.S., Blaxill, M.F. and Hayley, B.E. (2003) 'Reduced levels of mercury in first baby haircuts of autistic children.', *International Journal of Toxicology, 22*: 277–285.

Holmstrom, G., Almond, G., Temple, K., Taylor, D. and Baraitser, M. (1990) 'The iris in Williams syndrome.' *Archives of Diseases in Childhood, 65*: 987–989.

Holroyd, S., Reiss, A.L. and Bryan, R.N. (1991) 'Autistic features in Joubert syndrome: a genetic disorder with agenesis of the cerebellar vermis.' *Biological Psychiatry, 29*: 287–294.

Holzelova, E., Vonarbourg, C., Stolzenberg, M-C., Arkwright, P.D. *et al.* (2004) 'Autoimmune lymphoproliferative syndrome with somatic Fas mutations.', *New England Journal of Medicine, 351*: 1409–1418.

Honda, H., Shimizu, Y. and Rutter, M. (2005) 'No effect of MMR withdrawal on the incidence of autism: a total population study.' *Journal of Child Psychology and Psychiatry, 46*(6): 572–579.

Hong, S.E., Shugart, Y.Y., Huang, D.T., Shahwan, S.A. *et al.* (2000) 'Autosomal recessive lissencephaly with cerebellar hypoplasia is associated with human RELN mutations.', *Nature Genetics, 26*: 93–96.

Hong, S.K., Haldin, C.E., Lawson, N.D., Weinstein, B.M. *et al.* (2005) 'The zebrafish kohtalo/trap230 gene is required for the development of the brain, neural crest, and pronephric kidney.', *Proceedings of the National Academy of Science USA, 102*(51): 18473–18478.

Hoo, J. and Shrimpton, A.E. (2005) 'Familial hyper- and hypopigmentation with age-related pattern change.'. (Letter) *American Journal of Medical Genetics, 132A*: 215–218.

Hoogenraad, C.C., Koekkoek, B., Akhmanova, A., Krugers, H. *et al.* (2002) 'Targeted mutation of Cyln2 in the Williams syndrome critical region links CLIP-115 haploinsufficiency to neurodevelopmental abnormalities in mice.', *Nature Genetics, 32*: 116–127.

Hoogerwaard, E.M., Bakker, E., Ippel, P.F., Oosterwijk, J.C. *et al.* (1999) 'Signs and symptoms of Duchenne muscular dystrophy and Becker muscular dystrophy among carriers in The Netherlands: a cohort study.', *Lancet, 353*: 2116–2119.

Hook, E.B., Cross, P.K. and Schreinemachers, D.M. (1983) 'Chromosomal abnormality rates at amniocentesis and in live-born infants.', *Journal of the American Medical Association, 249*: 2034–2038.

Hook, E.B. and Reynolds, J.W. (1967) 'Cerebral gigantism: endocrinological and clinical observations of six patients including a congenital giant, concordant monozygotic twins, and a child who achieved adult gigantic size.', *Journal of Pediatrics, 70*: 900–914.

Horgan, J.E., Padwa, B.L., LaBrie, R.A. and Mulliken, J.B. (1995) 'OMENS-plus: analysis of craniofacial and extracraniofacial anomalies in hemifacial microsomia.', *The Cleft Palate-Craniofacial Journal, 32*(5): 405–412.

Hori, D., Hasegawa, Y., Kimura, M., Yang, Y. *et al.* (2005) 'Clinical onset and prognosis of Asian children with organic acidemias, as detected by analysis of urinary organic acids using GC/MS, instead of mass screening.', *Brain and Development, 27*(1): 39–45.

Hornig, M., Briese, T., Buie, T., Bauman, M.L. *et al.* (2008) 'Lack of association between measles virus vaccine and autism with enteropathy: a case-control study.', *PLoS ONE, 3*(9): e3140, doi:10.1371/journal.pone.0003140.

Hornig, M., Chian, D. and Lipkin, W.I. (2004) 'Neurotoxic effects of postnatal thimerosal are mouse strain dependent.' *Molecular Psychiatry, 9*: 833–845.

Hornig, M. and Lipkin, W.I. (2001) 'Infectious and immune factors in the pathogenesis of neurodevelopmental disorders: epidemiology, hypotheses, and animal models.' *Mental Retardation and Developmental Disabilities Research Reviews, 7*: 200–210.

Horrobin, D. (2001) *The Madness of Adam and Eve: How Schizophrenia Shaped Humanity.* London: Bantam Press.

Horrobin, D.F. (2003) 'Are large clinical trials in rapidly lethal diseases usually unethical?'(Personal Paper), *Lancet, 361*: 695–697.

Horvath, K., Medeiros, L. and Rabszlyn, A. (2000) 'High prevalence of gastrointestinal symptoms in autistic children with autistic spectrum disorder.' *Journal of Pediatric Gastroenterology and Nutrition, 31*: S174.

Horvath, K., Papadimitriou, J.C., Rabsztyn, A., Drachenberg, C. and Tildon, J.T. (1999) 'Gastrointestinal abnormalities in children with autistic disorder.' *Journal of Pediatrics, 135*: 559–563.

Horvath, K. and Perman, J. A. (2002a) 'Autism and gastrointestinal symptoms.' *Current Gastroenterology Reports, 4*: 251–258.

Horvath, K. and Perman, J.A. (2002b) 'Autistic disorder and gastrointestinal disease.' *Current Opinion in Pediatrics, 14*: 583–587.

Horvath, K., Stefanatos, G., Sokolski, K.N., Wachtel, R., Nabors, L. and Tildon, J.T. (1998) 'Improved social and language skills after secretin administration in patients with autistic spectrum disorders.', *Journal of the Association of the Academy of Minority Physicians, 9*(1): 9–15.

Hoshino, Y., Watanabe, M., Tachibana, R., Kaneko, M. and Kumashiro, H. (1984) 'The hypothalamo-pituitary function in autistic children.', *Neurosciences, 10*: 285–291.

Hoskins, J.A., Jack, G., Wade, H.E., Peiris, R.J.D. *et al.* (1980) 'Enzymatic control of phenylalanine intake in phenylketonuria.', *Lancet, 315*(8156): 392–394.

Howlin, P. (1997) 'Prognosis in autism: do specialist treatments affect long-term outcome?' *European Child and Adolescent Psychiatry, 6*(2): 55–72.

Howlin, P. (1998) 'Practitioner review: psychological and educational treatments for autism.', *Journal of Child Psychology and Psychiatry, 39*(3): 307–322.

Howlin, P. (2001) 'Autistic features in Cohen Syndrome: a preliminary report.', *Developmental Medicine and Child Neurology, 43*(10): 692–696.

Howlin, P. (2003) 'Can early interventions alter the course of autism?' *Novartis Foundation Symposium, 251*: 250–259.

Howlin, P., Karpf, J. and Turk, J. (2005) 'Behavioural characteristics and autistic features in individuals with Cohen syndrome.' *European Journal of Child and Adolescent Psychiatry, 14*: 57–64.

Howlin, P., Wing, L. and Gould, J. (1995) 'The recognition of autism in children with Down syndrome – implications for intervention and some speculations about pathology.' *Developmental Medicine and Child Neurology, 37*: 406–414.

Howson, A.L., Batth, S., Ilivitsky, V., Boisjoli, A., Jaworski, M., Mahoney, C. and Knott, V.J. (2004) 'Clinical and attentional effects of acute nicotine treatment in Tourette syndrome.', *European Psychiatry, 19*(2): 102–112.

Hoyme, H.E., Seaver, L.H., Jones, K.L., Procopio, F. *et al.* (1998) 'Isolated hemihyperplasia (hemihypertrophy): report of a prospective multicenter study of the incidence of neoplasia and review.' *American Journal of Medical Genetics, 79*: 274–278.

Hsu, C.-L., Lin, D.C.Y., Chen, C.-L., Wang, C-M. and Wong, A.M.K. (2009) 'The effects of a gluten and casein-free diet in children with autism: a case report.', *Chang Gung Medical Journal, 32*: 459–465.

Hu, J.F., Oruganti, H., Vu, T.H. and Hoffman, A.R. (1998) 'The role of histone acetylation in the allelic expression of the imprinted human insulin-like growth factor II gene.' *Biochemical and Biophysical Research Communications, 251*: 403–408.

Hu, J.F., Vu, T.H. and Hoffman, A.R. (1996) 'Promoter-specific modulation of insulin-like growth factor II genomic imprinting by inhibitors of DNA methylation.' *Journal of Biological Chemistry, 271*: 18253–18262.

Huang, W.H. and Porto, M. (2002) 'Abnormal first-trimester foetal nuchal translucency and Cornelia de Lange syndrome.', *Obstetrics and Gynecology, 99*: 956–958.

Huber, K.M., Gallagher, S.M., Warren, S.T. and Bear, M.F. (2002) 'Altered synaptic plasticity in a mouse model of fragile-X mental retardation.' *Proceedings of the National Academy of Science USA, 99*: 7746–7750.

Hudgins, L., Geer, J.S. and Cassidy, S.B. (1998) 'Phenotypic differerences in African Americans with Prader-Willi syndrome.', *Genetics in Medicine, 1*(1): 49–51.

Hudson, L.L., Markert, M.L., Devlin, B.H., Haynes, B.F. and Sempowski, G.D. (2007) 'Human T cell reconstitution in DiGeorge syndrome and HIV-1 infection.', *Seminars in Immunology, 19*(5): 297–309.

Huerta, P.T., Kowal, C., DeGiorgio, L.A., Volpe, B.T. and Diamond, B. (2006) 'Immunity and behaviour: antibodies alter emotion.', *Proceedings of the National Academy of Science USA, 103*(3): 678–683.

Huffmeier, U., Zenker, M., Hoyer, J., Fahsold, R. and Rauch, A. (2006) 'A variable combination of features of Noonan syndrome and neurofibromatosis type I are caused by mutations in the NF1 gene.', *American Journal of Medical Genetics A, 140*: 2749–2756.

Huijbregts, S.C.J., De Sonneville, L.M.J., Licht, R., van Spronsen, F.J. and Sergeant, J.A. (2002) 'Short-term dietary interventions in children and adolescents with treated phenylketonuria: effects on neuropsychological outcome of a well-controlled population.', *Journal of Inherited Metabolic Disease, 25*: 419–430.

Hulinsky, R., Byrne, J.L., Lowichik, A. and Viskochil, D.H. (2005) 'Fetus with interstitial del(5)(p13.1p14.2) diagnosed postnatally with Cornelia de Lange syndrome.', *American Journal of Medical Genetics A, 137*: 336–338.

Hulten, M., Armstrong, S., Challinor, P., Gould, C. *et al.* (1991) 'Genomic imprinting in an Angelman and Prader-Willi translocation family.', (Letter) *Lancet, 338*: 638–639.

Hultman, C.M., Sparen, P. and Cnattingius, S. (2002) 'Prenatal risk factors for infantile autism.', *Epidemiology, 13*: 417–423.

Humphrey, A., Higgins, J.N.P., Yates, J.R.W. and Bolton, P.F. (2004) 'Monozygotic twins with tuberous sclerosis discordant for the severity of developmental deficits.', *Neurology, 62*: 795–798.

Hundscheid, R.D., Smits, A.P., Thomas, C.M., Kiemeney, L.A. and Braat, D.D. (2003) 'Female carriers of fragile-X premutations have no increased risk for additional diseases other than premature ovarian failure.', *American Journal of Medical Genetics, 117*: 6–9.

Hunsucker, S.A., Mitchell, B.S. and Spychala, J. (2005) 'The 5'-nucleotidases as regulators of nucleotide and drug metabolism.' *Pharmacology and Therapeutics, 107*: 1–30.

Hunt, A. and Dennis, J. (1987) 'Psychiatric disorder among children with tuberous sclerosis.', *Developmental Medicine and Child Neurology, 29*(2): 190–198.

Hunt, A. and Shepherd, C. (1993) 'A prevalence study of autism in tuberous sclerosis.', *Journal of Autism and Developmental Disorders, 23*(2): 323–339.

Hunter, A.G.W. (2002) 'Coffin-Lowry syndrome: a 20-year follow-up and review of long-term outcomes.', *American Journal of Medical Genetics, 111*: 345–355.

Hunter, A.G.W., Schwartz, C.E. and Abidi, F.E. (2007) 'Coffin-Lowry syndrome.', *GeneREVIEWS*, http://clsf.info/Literature/GeneReviews.pdf.

Hunter, J.W., Mullen, G.P., McManus, J.R., Heatherly, J.M. *et al.* (2010) 'Neuroligin-deficient mutants of *C. elegans* have sensory processing deficits and are hypersensitive to oxidative stress and mercury toxicity.', *Disease Models and Mechanisms, 3*: doi:10.1242/dmm.003442.

Hunter, L.C., O'Hare, A., Herron, W.J., Fisher, L.A. and Jones, G.E. (2003) 'Opioid peptides and dipeptidyl peptidase in autism.' *Developmental Medicine and Child Neurology, 45*: 121–128.

Huntley, C.C. and Stevenson, R.E. (1969) 'Maternal phenylketonuria: course of two pregnancies.', *Obstetrics and Gynecology, 34*: 694–700.

Huppke, P., Held, M., Laccone, F. and Hanefeld, F. (2003) 'The spectrum of phenotypes in females with Rett syndrome.', *Brain and Development, 25*(5): 346–351.

Huppke, P., Maier, E.M., Warnke, A., Brendel, C., Laccone, F. and Gartner, J. (2006) 'Very mild cases of Rett syndrome with skewed X inactivation.', *Journal of Medical Genetics, 43*: 814–816.

Hurmerinta, K., Pirinen, S., Kovero, O. and Kivitie-Kallio, S. (2002) 'Craniofacial features in Cohen syndrome: an anthropometric and cephalometric analysis of 14 patients.', *Clinical Genetics, 62*: 157–164.

Hurst, D.L. (1990) 'Epidemiology of severe myoclonic epilepsy of infancy.', *Epilepsia, 31*(4): 397–400.

Hus, V., Pickles, A., Cook, E.H. Jr., Risi, S. and Lord, C. (2007) 'Using the autism diagnostic interview-revised to increase phenotypic homogeneity in genetic studies of autism.' *Biological Psychiatry, 61*: 438–448.

Huson, S.M., Compston, D.A.S., Clark, P. and Harper, P.S. (1989) 'A genetic study of von Recklinghausen neurofibromatosis in south east Wales. 1. Prevalence, fitness, mutation rate, and effect of parental transmission on severity.', *Journal of Medical Genetics, 26*: 704–711.

Hussman, J.P. (2001) 'Suppressed GABAergic inhibition as a common factor in suspected etiologies of autism.' *Journal of Autism and Developmental Disorders, 31*: 247–248.

Hvas, A-M., Ellegaard, J. and Nexø, E. (2001) 'Vitamin B12 treatment normalizes metabolic markers but has limited clinical effect: a randomized placebo-controlled study. *Clinical Chemistry, 47*(8): 1396–1404.

Hwa, H.L., Chang, Y.Y., Chen, C.H., Kao, Y.S. *et al.* (2007) 'Multiplex ligation-dependent probe amplification identification of deletions and duplications of the Duchenne muscular dystrophy gene in Taiwanese subjects.', *Journal of the Formosan Medical Association, 106*(5): 339–346.

Hyman, S.L., Gill, D.S., Shores, E.A., Steinberg, A. *et al.* (2003) 'Natural history of cognitive deficits and their relationship to MRI T2-hyperintensities in NF1.', *Neurology, 60*: 1139–1145.

Hyman, S.L., Shores, A. and North, K.N. (2005) 'The nature and frequency of cognitive deficits in children with neurofibromatosis type 1.', *Neurology, 65*(7): 1037–1044.

Hyman, S.L., Shores, E.A. and North, K.N. (2006) 'Learning disabilities in children with neurofibromatosis type 1: subtypes, cognitive profile, and attention-deficit-hyperactivity disorder.', *Developmental Medicine and Child Neurology, 48*: 973–977.

Iannaccone, A., Mykytyn, K., Persico, A.M., Searby, C.C. *et al.* (2005) 'Clinical evidence of decreased olfaction in Bardet-Biedl syndrome caused by a deletion in the BBS4 gene.', *American Journal of Medical Genetics A, 132*: 343–346.

Ibarra, B., Rivas, F., Medina, C., Franco, M.E. *et al.* (1990) 'Hematological and biochemical studies in children with Down syndrome.', *Annals of Genetics, 33*(2): 84–87.

Ichida, K., Matsumura, T., Sakuma, R., Hosoya, T. and Nishino, T. (2001) 'Mutation of human molybdenum cofactor sulfurase gene is responsible for classical xanthinuria type II.', *Biochemical and Biophysical Research Communications, 282*: 1194–1200.

Iizuka, R., Hirayama, K. and Maehara, K. (1984) 'Dentatorubro-pallidoluysian atrophy: a clinico-pathological study.' *Journal of Neurology, Neurosurgery and Psychiatry, 47*: 1288–1298.

Ikeda, K., Schiltz, E., Fujii, T., Takahashi, M. *et al.* (2005) 'Phenylalanine ammonia-lyase modified with polyethylene glycol: potential therapeutic agent for phenylketonuria.', *Amino Acids, 29*(3): 283–287.

Ikeuchi, T., Onodera, O., Oyake, M., Koide, R. *et al.* (1995) 'Dentatorubral-pallidoluysian atrophy (DRPLA): close correlation of CAG repeat expansions with the wide spectrum of clinical presentations and prominent anticipation.', *Seminars in Cell Biology, 6*(1): 37–44.

Ilhan, N., Kucuksu, M., Kaman, D., Ilhan, N. *et al.* (2008) 'The 677 C/T MTHFR polymorphism is associated with essential hypertension, coronary artery disease, and higher homocysteine levels.' *Archives of Medical Research, 39*(1): 125–130.

Imai, T., Hattori, H., Miyazaki, M., Higuchi, Y. *et al.* (2001) 'Dandy-Walker variant in Coffin-Siris syndrome.', *American Journal of Medical Genetics, 100*: 152–155.

Imamura, Y., Fujikawa, Y., Komaki, H., Nakagawa, E. *et al.* (2007) '[A case of Möbius syndrome presenting with symptoms of severe infantile form of congenital muscular disorder].', *No To Hattatsu, 39*(1): 59–62.

Indredavik, M.S., Vik, T., Skranes, J. and Brubakk, A-M. (2008) 'Positive screening results for autism in ex-preterm infants.', *Pediatrics, 122*: 222.

Ingordo, V., D'Andria, G., Gentile, C., Decuzzi, M. *et al.* (2003) 'Frequency of X-linked ichthyosis in coastal southern Italy: a study on a representative sample of a young male population.', *Dermatology, 207*(2): 148–150.

Ingudomnukul, E., Baron-Cohen, S., Wheelwright, S. and Knickmeyer, R. (2007) 'Elevated rates of testosterone-related disorders in women with autism spectrum conditions.', *Hormones and Behaviour, 51*(5): 597–604.

Inlow, J.K. and Restifo, L.L. (2004) 'Molecular and comparative genetics of mental retardation.', *Genetics, 166*: 835–881.

Insel, T.R. and Fenton, W.S. (2005) 'Psychiatric epidemiology: it's not just about counting anymore.' *Archives of General Psychiatry, 62*(6): 590–592.

International Molecular Genetic Study of Autism Consortium (1998) 'A full genome screen for autism with evidence for linkage to a region on chromosome 7q.' *Human Molecular Genetics, 7*: 571–578.

International Molecular Genetic Study of Autism Consortium (2001) 'A genomewide screen for autism: strong evidence for linkage to chromosomes 2q, 7q, and 16p.', *American Journal of Human Genetics, 69*: 570–581.

Ireland, M., English, C., Cross, I., Houlsby, W.T. and Burn, J. (1991) 'A *de novo* translocation t(3;17) (q26.3;q23.1) in a child with Cornelia de Lange syndrome.', *Journal of Medical Genetics, 28*: 639–640.

Ireland, M., English, C., Cross, I., Lindsay, S. and Strachan, T. (1995) 'Partial trisomy 3q and the mild Cornelia de Lange syndrome phenotype.', *Journal of Medical Genetics, 32*: 837–838.

Irons, M. (2007) 'Smith-Lemli-Opitz syndrome.', *GeneReviews*, web-based resource.

Irons, M., Elias, E.R., Abuelo, D., Bull, M.J. *et al.* (1997) 'Treatment of Smith-Lemli-Opitz syndrome: results of a multicenter trial.', *American Journal of Medical Genetics, 68*: 311–314.

Irons, M., Elias, E.R., Tint, G.S., Salen, G. *et al.* (1994) 'Abnormal cholesterol metabolism in the Smith-Lemli-Opitz syndrome: report of clinical and biochemical findings in four patients and treatment in one patient.', *American Journal of Medical Genetics, 50*: 347–352.

Irons, M.B., Nores, J., Stewart, T.L., Craigo, S.D. *et al.* (1999) 'Antenatal therapy of Smith-Lemli-Opitz syndrome.', *Foetal Diagnosis and Therapy, 14*(3): 133–137.

Irons, M.B. and Tint, G.S. (1998) 'Prenatal diagnosis of Smith-Lemli-Opitz syndrome.', *Prenatal Diagnosis, 18*: 369–372.

Irwin, S.A., Galvez, R. and Greenough, W.T. (2000) 'Dendritic spine structural anomalies in fragile-X mental retardation syndrome.', *Cerebral Cortex, 10*: 1038–1044.

Ishikawa-Brush, Y., Powell, J.F., Bolton, P., Miller, A.P. *et al.* (1997) 'Autism and multiple exostoses associated with an X;8 translocation occurring within the GRPR gene and 3' to the SDC2 gene.' *Human Molecular Genetics, 6*(8): 1241–1250.

Ishizawa, A., Oho, S., Dodo, H., Katori, T. and Homma, S.I. (1996) 'Cardiovascular abnormalities in Noonan syndrome: the clinical findings and treatments.', *Acta Paediatrica Japonica, 38*: 84–90.

Ishmael, H.A., Cataldi, D., Begleiter, M.L., Pasztor, L.M. *et al.* (2003) 'Five new subjects with ring chromosome 22.' *Clinical Genetics, 63*: 410–414.

Ismat, F.A., Xu, J., Lu, M.M. and Epstein, J.A. (2006) 'The neurofibromin GAP-related domain rescues endothelial but not neural crest development in Nf1 mice.', *Journal of Clinical Investigation, 116*: 2378–2384.

Israel, J., Lessick, M., Szego, K. and Wong, P. (1991) 'Translocation 19;Y in a child with Bannayan-Zonana phenotype.', *Journal of Medical Genetics, 28*: 427–428.

Issekutz, K.A., Graham, J.M. Jr., Prasad, C., Smith, I.M. and Blake, K.D. (2005) 'An epidemiological analysis of CHARGE syndrome: preliminary results from a Canadian study.', *American Journal of Medical Genetics, 133A*(3): 309–317.

Item, C.B., Stöckler-Ipsiroglu, S., Stromberger, C., Muhl, A. *et al.* (2001) 'Arginine: glycine amidinotransferase deficiency: the third inborn error of creatine metabolism in humans.', *American Journal of Human Genetics, 69*: 1127–1133.

Ito, M. (1952) 'Studies on melanin.' *Tohoku Journal of Experimental Medicine, 55*: 1–104.

Ito, M. (2004) '"Nurturing the brain" as an emerging research field involving child neurology.' *Brain and Development, 26*: 429–433.

Jablonka, E. and Lamb, M.J. (2005) *Evolution in Four Dimensions: Genetic, Epigenetic, Behavioural and Symbolic Variation in the History of Life.* Cambridge, Massachusetts: MIT Press.

Jablonski, N.G. and Chaplin, G. (2000) 'The evolution of human skin coloration.', *Journal of Human Evolution, 39*(1): 57–106.

Jackman, C., Horn, N.D., Molleston, J.P. and Sokol, D.K. (2009) 'Gene associated with seizures, autism, and hepatomegaly in an Amish girl.', *Pediatric Neurology, 40*: 310–313.

Jackson, C.E., Weiss, L., Reynolds, W.A., Forman, T.F. and Peterson, J.A. (1976) 'Craniosynostosis midface hypoplasia, and foot abnormalities: an autosomal dominant phenotype in a large Amish kindred.', *Journal of Pediatrics, 88*: 963–968.

Jackson, L., Kline, A.D., Barr, M.A. and Koch, S. (1993) 'De Lange syndrome: a clinical review of 310 individuals.', *American Journal of Medical Genetics, 47*: 940–946.

Jacob, A.G., Driscoll, D.J., Shaughnessy, W.J. Stanson, A.W. *et al.* (1998) 'Klippel-Trénaunay syndrome: spectrum and management.', *Mayo Clinic Proceedings, 73*(1): 28–36.

Jacob, S., Brune, C.W., Carter, C.S., Leventhal, B.L. *et al.* (2007) 'Association of the oxytocin receptor gene (OXTR) in Caucasian children and adolescents with autism.', *Neuroscience Letters*, doi:10.1016/j.neulet.2007.02.001.

Jacobs, A., Knight, B.P., McDonald, K.T. and Burke, M.C. (2006) 'Verapamil decreases ventricular tachyarrhythmias in a patient with Timothy syndrome (LQT8).', *Heart Rhythm, 3*(8): 967–970.

Jacobs, P.A., Brunton, M., Melville, M.M., Brittain, R.P. and McClemont, W.F. (1965) 'Aggressive behaviour, mental sub-normality and the XYY male.', *Nature*, 208: 1351–1352.

Jacobs, P.A., Melville, M., Ratcliffe, S., Keay, A.J. and Syme, J. (1974) 'A cytogenetic survey of 11,680 newborn infants.', *Annals of Human Genetics*, 37: 359–376.

Jacobson, S.G., Borruat, F.X. and Apathy, P.P. (1990) 'Patterns of rod and cone dysfunction in Bardet-Biedl syndrome.', *American Journal of Ophthalmology*, 109: 676–688.

Jacquemont, S., Hagerman, R.J., Hagerman, P.J. and Leehey, M.A. (2007) 'Fragile-X syndrome and fragile-X-associated tremor/ataxia syndrome: two faces of FMR1.', *Lancet, Neurology* 6(1): 45–55.

Jacquemont, S., Hagerman, R.J., Leehey, M., Grigsby, J. *et al.* (2003) 'Fragile-X premutation tremor/ataxia syndrome: molecular, clinical, and neuroimaging correlates.', *American Journal of Human Genetics*, 72: 869–878.

Jacquemont, S., Hagerman, R.J., Leehey, M.A., Hall, D.A. *et al.* (2004) 'Penetrance of the fragile-X-associated tremor/ataxia syndrome in a premutation carrier population.', *Journal of the American Medical Association*, 291: 460–469.

Jacquot, S., Zeniou, M., Touraine, R. and Hanauer, A. (2002) 'X-linked Coffin-Lowry syndrome (CLS, MIM 303600, RPS6KA3 gene, protein product known under various names: pp90rsk2, RSK2, ISPK, MAPKAP1).', *European Journal of Human Genetics*, 10: 2–5.

Jaeken, J. and Hagberg, B. (1991) 'Clinical presentation and natural course of the carbohydrate-deficient glycoprotein syndrome.', *Acta Paediatrica Scandinavica*, 375 (Suppl): 6–13.

Jaeken, J., Matthijs, G., Barone, R. and Carchon, H. (1997) 'Carbohydrate-deficient glycoprotein syndrome type 1.', *Journal of Medical Genetics*, 34: 73–76.

Jaeken, J. and van den Berghe, G. (1984) 'An infantile autistic syndrome characterized by the presence of succinylpurines in body fluids.' *Lancet*, 324(8411): 1058–1061.

Jaeken, J., van den Bergh, F., Vincent, M.F., Casaer, P. and Van den Berghe, G. (1992) 'Adenylosuccinase deficiency: a newly recognized variant.' *Journal of Inherited Metabolic Disease*, 15: 416–418.

Jaeken, J., Wadman, S.K., Duran, M., van Sprang, F.J. *et al.* (1988) 'Adenylosuccinase deficiency: an inborn error of purine nucleotide synthesis.', *European Journal of Pediatrics*, 148: 126–131.

Jaenisch, R. and Bird, A. (2003) 'Epigenetic regulation of gene expression: how the genome integrates intrinsic and environmental signals.' *Nature Genetics Supplement*, 33: 243–254.

Jakobs, C., Bojasch, M., Monch, E., Rating, D. *et al.* (1981) 'Urinary excretion of gamma-hydroxybutyric acid in a patient with neurological abnormalities: the probability of a new inborn error of metabolism.', *Clinica et Chimica Acta*, 111: 169–178.

Jamain, S., Betancur, C., Quach, H., Philippe, A. *et al.* (2002) 'Paris Autism Research International Sibpair (PARIS) Study, 2002: linkage and association of the glutamate receptor 6 gene with autism.' *Molecular Psychiatry*, 7: 302–310.

Jamain, S., Quach, H., Betancur, C., Rastam, M. *et al.* (2003) 'Mutations of the X-linked genes encoding neuroligins NLGN3 and NLGN4 are associated with autism.', *Nature Genetics*, 34(1): 27–29.

James, A., Culver, C. and Golabi, M. (2006) 'Simpson-Golabi-Behmel syndrome.', *GeneREVIEWS*, www.genetests.org.

James, J.B., George, F. and Audhya, T. (2006) 'Abnormally high plasma levels of vitamin B6 in children with autism not taking supplements compared to controls not taking supplements.', *Journal of Alternative and Comparative Medicine*, 12(1): 59–63.

James, S.J., Cutler, P., Melnyk, S., Jernigan, S. *et al.* (2004) 'Metabolic biomarkers of increased oxidative stress and impaired methylation capacity in children with autism.', *American Journal of Clinical Nutrition*, 80: 1611–1617.

James, S.J., Melnyk, S., Fuchs, G., Reid, T. *et al.* (2009) 'Efficacy of methylcobalamin and folinic acid treatment on glutathione redox status in children with autism.' *American Journal of Clinical Nutrition*, 89: 425–430.

James, S.J., Melnyk, S., Jernigan, S., Cleves, M.A. *et al.* (2006) 'Metabolic endophenotype and related genotypes are associated with oxidative stress in children with autism.', *American Journal of Medical Genetics B Neuropsychiatric Genetics*, doi:10.1002/amjg.b.30366.

Jamis-Dow, C.A., Turner, J., Biesecker, L.G. and Choyke, P.L. (2004) 'Radiologic manifestations of Proteus syndrome.', *Radiographics*, 24(4): 1051–1068.

Jamison, K.R. (1993) *Touched with Fire: Manic-Depressive Illness and the Artistic Temperament.* New York: Simon and Schuster.

Janniger, C.K. and Schwartz, R.A. (2008) 'Ichthyosis, X-linked.' *EMedicine*, downloadable from http://emedicine.medscape.com/article/1111398-overview.

Jansen, G., Groenen, P.J., Bächner, D., Jap, P.H. *et al.* (1996) 'Abnormal myotonic dystrophy protein kinase levels produce only mild myopathy in mice.', *Nature Genetics*, 13(3): 316–324.

Janssen, P.J. and van der Heijden, C.A. (1988) 'Aspartame: review of recent experimental and observational data.' *Toxicology*, 50(1): 1–26.

Janzen, D. and Nguyen, M. (2010) 'Beyond executive function: non-executive cognitive abilities in individuals with PKU.', *Molecular Genetics and Metabolism*, 99: S47–S51.

Jarbrink, K. and Knapp, M. (2001) 'The economic impact of autism.', *Autism*, 5(1): 7–22.

Jarbrink, K., McCrone, P., Fombonne, E., Zanden, H. and Knapp, M. (2007) 'Cost-impact of young adults with high-functioning autistic spectrum disorder.', *Research in Developmental Disabilities*, 28: 94–104.

Jaruzelska, J., Henriksen, K.F., Guttler, F., Riess, O. *et al.* (1991) 'The codon 408 mutation associated with haplotype 2 is predominant in Polish families with phenylketonuria.', *Human Genetics*, 86: 247–250.

Javitt, D.C. (2004) 'Glutamate as a therapeutic target in psychiatric disorders.' *Molecular Psychiatry*, 9: 984–997.

Jawad, A.F., McDonald-McGinn, D.M., Zackai, E. and Sullivan, K.E. (2001) 'Immunologic features of chromosome 22q11.2 deletion syndrome (DiGeorge syndrome/velocardiofacial syndrome).', *Journal of Pediatrics, 139*: 715–723.

Jedele, K.B. (2007) 'The overlapping spectrum of rett and Angelman syndromes: a clinical review.', *Seminars in Pediatric Neurology, 14*: 108–117.

Jeffries, A.R., Curran, S., Elmslie, F., Sharma, A. *et al.* (2005) 'Molecular and phenotypic characterization of ring chromosome 22.', *American Journal of Medical Genetics A, 137*: 139–147.

Jepson, B. and Johnson, J. (2007) *Changing the Course of Autism: A Scientific Approach for Parents and Physicians,* Boulder. Colorado: Sentient Publications.

Jernigan, T.L., Bellugi, U., Sowell, E., Doherty, S. and Hesselink, J.R. (1993) 'Cerebral morphologic distinctions between Williams and Down syndromes.', *Archives of Neurology, 50*(2): 186–191.

Jerome, L.A. and Papaioannou, V.E. (2001) 'DiGeorge syndrome phenotype in mice mutant for the T-box gene, Tbx1.', *Nature Genetics, 27*: 286–291.

Jervis, G.A. (1947) 'Studies on phenylpyruvic oligophrenia: the position of the metabolic error.', *Journal of Biological Chemistry, 169*: 651–656.

Jezela-Stanek, A., Malunowicz, E.M., Ciara, E., Popowska, E. *et al.* (2006) 'Maternal urinary steroid profiles in prenatal diagnosis of Smith-Lemli-Opitz syndrome: first patient series comparing biochemical and molecular studies.', *Clinical Genetics, 69*: 77–85.

Jha, P., Sheth, D. and Ghaziuddin, M. (2007) 'Autism spectrum disorder and Klinefelter syndrome.', *European Journal of Child and Adolescent Psychiatry,* Mar 30 [e-print], doi:10.1007/s00787-007-0601-8.

Jian, L., Archer, H.L., Ravine, D., Kerr, A. *et al.* (2005) 'p.R270X MeCP2 mutation and mortality in Rett syndrome.' *European Journal of Human Genetics, 13*(11): 1235–1238.

Jiang, Y., Armstrong, D., Albrecht, U., Atkins, C.M. *et al.* (1998) 'Mutation of the Angelman ubiquitin ligase in mice causes increased cytoplasmic p53 and deficits of contextual learning and long-term potentiation.', *Neuron, 21*: 799–811.

Jiang, Y., Tsai, T-F., Bressler, J. and Beaudet, A.L. (1998) 'Imprinting in Angelman and Prader-Willi syndromes.', *Current Opinion in Genetics and Development, 8*: 334–342

Jiang, Y-H., Bressler, J. and Beaudet, A.L. (2004) 'Epigenetics and human disease.', *Annual Review of Genomics and Human Genetics, 5*: 479–510.

Jin, P., Zarnescu, D.C., Ceman, S., Nakamoto, M. *et al.* (2004) 'Biochemical and genetic interaction between the fragile-X mental retardation protein and the microRNA pathway.', *Nature Neuroscience, 7*(2): 113–117.

Jira, P.E., Wevers, R.A., de Jong, J., Rubio-Gozalbo, E. *et al.* (2000) 'Simvastatin: a new therapeutic approach for Smith-Lemli-Opitz syndrome.', *Journal of Lipid Research, 41*(8): 1339–1346.

Jirtle, R.L., Sander, M. and Barrett, J.C. (2000) 'Genomic imprinting and environmental disease susceptibility.', *Environmental Health Perspectives, 108*(3): 271–278.

Jirtle, R.L. and Skinner, M.K. (2007) 'Environmental epigenomics and disease susceptibility.', *Nature Review: Genetics, 8*: 253–262.

Jöbsis, A.C., De Groot, W.P., Tigges, A.J., De Bruijn, H.W. *et al.* (1980) 'X-linked ichthyosis and X-linked placental sulfatase deficiency: a disease entity. Histochemical observations.' *American Journal of Pathology, 99*(2): 279–289.

Johansson, M., Billstedt, E., Danielsson, S., Strömland, K. *et al.* (2007) 'Autism spectrum disorder and underlying brain mechanism in the oculoauriculovertebral spectrum.', *Developmental Medicine and Child Neurology, 49*(4): 280–288.

Johansson, M., Gillberg, C. and Råstam, M. (2009) 'Autism spectrum conditions in individuals with Möbius sequence, CHARGE syndrome and oculo-auriculo-vertebral spectrum: Diagnostic aspects.', *Research in Developmental Disabilities,* Aug 24. [Epub ahead of print]

Johansson, M., Råstam, M., Billstedt, E., Danielsson, S. *et al.* (2006) 'Autism spectrum disorders and underlying brain pathology in CHARGE association.', *Developmental Medicine and Child Neurology, 48*: 40–50.

Johansson, M., Wentz, E., Fernell, E., Stromland, K. *et al.* (2001) 'Autistic spectrum disorders in Möbius sequence: a comprehensive study of 25 individuals.', *Developmental Medicine and Child Neurology, 43*(5): 338–345.

Johnson, H., Wiggs, L., Stores, G. and Huson, S.M. (2005) 'Psychological disturbance and sleep disorders in children with neurofibromatosis type 1.', *Developmental Medicine and Child Neurology, 47*: 237–242.

Johnson, H.G., Ekman, P., Friesen, W., Nyhan, W.L. and Fish, C.H. (1976) 'Behavioural phenotype in the Cornelia de Lange syndrome.', *Pediatric Research, 10*: 843–850.

Johnson, J.A., Aughton, D.J., Comstock, C.H., von Oeyen, P.T. *et al.* (1994) 'Prenatal diagnosis of Smith-Lemli-Opitz syndrome, type II.', *American Journal of Medical Genetics, 49*: 240–243.

Johnson, V.P. (1975) 'Smith-Lemli-Opitz syndrome: review and report of two affected siblings.', *Zeitschrift fur Kinderheilkundte, 119*: 221–234.

Joncourt, F., Neuhaus, B., Jostarndt-Foegen, K., Kleinle, S. *et al.* (2004) 'Rapid identification of female carriers of DMD/BMD by quantitative real-time PCR.', *Human Mutation, 23*: 385–391.

Jones, K.L. (1990) 'Williams syndrome: an historical perspective of its evolution, natural history, and etiology.', *American Journal of Medical Genetics,* (suppl.), *6*: 89–96.

Jones, K.L. and Smith, D.W. (1975) 'The Williams elfin facies syndrome: a new perspective.' *Journal of Pediatrics, 186*: 718–723.

Jongbloet, P.H. (1987) 'Goldenhar syndrome and overlapping dysplasias, in vitro fertilisation and ovopathy.', *Journal of Medical Genetics, 24*: 616–620.

Jongmans, M.C.J., Admiraal, R.J., van der Donk, K.P., Vissers, L.E.L.M. *et al.* (2006) 'CHARGE syndrome: the phenotypic spectrum of mutations in the CHD7 gene.', *Journal of Medical Genetics, 43*: 306–314.

Jongmans, M.C.J., van Ravenswaaij-Arts, C.M.A., Pitteloud, N., Ogata, T. *et al.* (2009) 'CHD7 mutations in patients initially diagnosed with Kallmann syndrome – the clinical overlap with CHARGE syndrome.', *Clinical Genetics, 75*: 65–71.

Jopling, C., van Geemen, D. and den Hertog, J. (2007) 'Shp2 knockdown and Noonan/LEOPARD Mutant Shp2-induced gastrulation defects.', *PLoS Genetics*, 3(12): e225, doi:10.1371/journal.pgen.0030225.

Jorgensen, G. (1972) 'Befunde bei speziellen angeborenen Angiokardiopathien (II).' In: P.E Becker (ed.), *Humangenetik: Ein kurzes Handbuch in fuenf Baenden*. Stuttgart: Thieme (pub.) III(II), p.345 only.

Jorgensen, O.S., Mellerup, E.T. and Rafelsen, O.J. (1970) 'Amino acid excretion in urine of children with various psychiatric diseases – a thin layer chromatographic study.', *Danish Medical Bulletin*, 17: 166–170.

Jorizzo, J.L., Atherton, D.J., Crounse, R.G. and Wells, R.S. (1982) 'Ichthyosis, brittle hair, impaired intelligence, decreased fertility and short stature (IBIDS syndrome).', *British Journal of Dermatology*, 106: 705–710.

Joubert, M., Eisenring, J.J., Robb, J.P. and Andermann, F. (1969) 'Familial agenesis of the cerebellar vermis: a syndrome of episodic hyperpnea, abnormal eye movements, ataxia, and retardation.', *Neurology*, 19: 813–825.

Journel, H., Roussey, M. and Le Marec, B. (1989) 'MCA/MR syndrome with oligodactyly and Moebius anomaly in first cousins: new syndrome or familial facial-limb disruption sequence?' *American Journal of Medical Genetics*, 34: 506–510.

Jovanovic, S.V., Clements, D. and MacLeod, K. (1998) 'Biomarkers of oxidative stress are significantly elevated in Down syndrome.', *Free Radical Biology and Medicine*, 25: 1044–1048.

Juhasz, C., Batista, C.E.A., Chugani, D.C., Muzik, O. and Chugani, H.T. (2007) 'Evolution of cortical metabolic abnormalities and their clinical correlates in Sturge-Weber syndrome.', *European Journal of Paediatric Neurology*, doi:10.1016/j.ejpn.2007.02.001.

Juhasz, C. and Chugani, H.T. (2007) 'An almost missed leptomeningeal angioma in Sturge-Weber syndrome.', *Neurology*, 68(3): 243.

Junaid, M.A., Kowal, D., Barua, M., Pullarkat, P.S. *et al.* (2004) 'Proteomic studies identified a single nucleotide polymorphism in glyoxalase I as autism susceptibility factor.', *American Journal of Medical Genetics*, 131A: 11–17.

Junien, C. (2006) 'Impact of diets and nutrients/drugs on early epigenetic programming.', *Journal of Inherited Metabolic Disease*, 29: 359–365.

Juranek, J., Filipek, P.A., Berenji, G.R., Modahl, C. *et al.* (2006) 'Association between amygdala volume and anxiety level: magnetic resonance imaging (MRI) study in autistic children.', *Journal of Child Neurology*, 21: 1051–1058.

Jure, R., Rapin, I. and Tuchman, R.F. (1991) 'Hearing-impaired autistic children.', *Developmental Medicine and Child Neurology*, 33: 1062–1072.

Jurecka, A. (2009) 'Inborn errors of purine and pyrimidine metabolism.', *Journal of Inherited Metabolic Disease*, 32: 247–263.

Jurecka, A., Tylki-Szymanska, A., Zikanova, M., Krijt, J. and Kmoch, S. (2008) 'D: -Ribose therapy in four Polish patients with adenylosuccinate lyase deficiency: absence of positive effect.', *Journal of Inherited Metabolic Disease*, July 12, doi:10.1007/s10545-008-0904-z.

Jurkiewicz, E., Mierzewska, H. and Kusmierska, K. (2007) 'Adenylosuccinate lyase deficiency: the first identified Polish patient.', *Brain and Development*, 29: 600–602.

Justice, M.J., Siracusa, L.D., Gilbert, D.J., Heisterkamp, N. *et al* (1990) 'A genetic linkage map of mouse chromosome 10: localization of eighteen molecular markers using a single interspecific backcross.', *Genetics*, 125: 855–866.

Juyal, R.C., Figuera, L.E., Hauge, X., Elsea, S.H. *et al.* (1996) 'Molecular analyses of 17p11.2 deletions in 62 Smith-Magenis syndrome patients.', *American Journal of Human Genetics*, 58(5): 998–1007.

Kadesjo, B. and Gillberg, C. (2000) 'Tourette disorder: epidemiology and comorbidity in primary school children.', *Journal of the American Academy of Child and Adolescent Psychiatry*, 39(5): 548–555.

Kadrabová, J., Madáric, A., Sustrová, M. and Ginter, E. (1996) 'Changed serum trace element profile in Down syndrome.', *Biological Trace Element Research*, 54(3): 201–206.

Kaffman, A. and Meaney, M.J. (2007) 'Neurodevelopmental sequelae of postnatal maternal care in rodents: clinical and research implications of molecular insights.' *Journal of Child Psychology and Psychiatry*, 48(3/4): 224–244.

Kagan-Kushnir, T., Roberts, S.W. and Snead, O.C. 3rd (2005) 'Screening electroencephalograms in autism spectrum disorders: evidence-based guideline.', *Journal of Child Neurology*, 20: 197–206.

Kahwash, S.B., Fung, B., Savelli, S., Bleesing, J.J. and Qualman, S.J. (2007) 'Autoimmune lymphoproliferative syndrome (ALPS): a case with congenital onset.', *Pediatric and Developmental Pathology*, 10(4): 315–319.

Kalin, J.H., Butler, K.V. and Kozikowski, A.P. (2009) 'Creating zinc monkey wrenches in the treatment of epigenetic disorders.', *Current Opinion in Chemical Biology*, 13(3): 263–271.

Kallen, K., Robert, E., Castilla, E.E., Mastroiacovo, P. and Kallen, B. (2004) 'Relation between oculo-auriculo-vertebral (OAV) dysplasia and three other non-random associations of malformations (VATER, CHARGE, and OEIS).', *American Journal of Medical Genetics*, 127A: 26–34.

Kallen, K., Robert, E., Mastroiacovo, P., Castilla, E.E. and Kallen, B. (1999) 'CHARGE association in newborns: a registry-based study.', *Teratology*, 60: 334–343.

Kalscheuer, V.M., Tao, J., Donnelly, A., Hollway, G. *et al.* (2003) 'Disruption of the serine/threonine kinase 9 gene causes severe X-linked infantile spasms and mental retardation.', *American Journal of Human Genetics*, 72: 1401–1411.

Kamimura, J., Endo, Y., Kurotaki, N., Kinoshita, A. *et al.* (2003) 'Identification of eight novel NSD1 mutations in Sotos syndrome.', *Journal of Medical Genetics*, 40(11): e126.

Kaminski, R.M., Banerjee, M. and Rogawski, M.A. (2004) 'Topiramate selectively protects against seizures induced by ATPA, a GluR5 kainate receptor agonist.', *Neuropharmacology*, 46: 1097–1104.

Kanaumi, T., Takashima, S., Hirose, S., Kodama, T. and Iwasaki, H. (2006) 'Neuropathology of methylmalonic acidemia in a child.', *Pediatric Neurology*, 34: 156–159.

Kanavin, O.J., Woldseth, B., Jellum, E., Tvedt, B. *et al.* (2007) '2-methylbutyryl-CoA dehydrogenase deficiency associated with autism and mental retardation: a case report.', *Journal of Medical Case Reports, 1*: 98, doi:10.1186/1752-1947-1-98.

Kanazawa, I. (1998) 'Dentatorubral-pallidoluysian atrophy or Naito-Oyanagi disease.', *Neurogenetics, 2*: 1–17.

Kanazawa, O. and Shirane, S. (1999) 'Can early zonizamide medication improve the prognosis in the core and peripheral types of severe myoclonic epilepsy in infants?' *Brain and Development, 21*: 503.

Kandel, E. (1979) 'Psychotherapy and the single synapse: the impact of psychiatric thought on neurobiological research.', *New England Journal of Medicine, 301*: 1028–1037.

Kandel, E.R. (2006) *In Search of Memory: The Emergence of a New Science of Mind.* New York: Norton.

Kandel, E.R., Schwartz, J.H. and Jessell, T.M. (Eds.) (1991) *Principles of Neuroscience.* New York: Elsevier.

Kandel, E.R., Schwartz, J.H. and Jessell, T.M. (1995) *Essentials of Neural Science and Behaviour.* (pp.296–297). Norwalk, Connecticut: Appleton and Lange.

Kandt, R.S., Haines, J.L., Smith, M., Northrup, H. *et al.* (1992) 'Linkage of a major gene locus for tuberous sclerosis to a chromosome 16 marker for polycystic kidney disease.', (Abstract) *American Journal of Human Genetics, 51*(supp): A4.

Kaneko, H., Tsukahara, M., Tachibana, H., Kurashige, H. *et al.* (1987) 'Congenital heart defects in Sotos sequence.', *American Journal of Medical Genetics, 26*: 569–576.

Kang, H.C., Kwon, J.W., Lee, Y.M., Kim, H.D. *et al.* (2007) 'Nonspecific mitochondrial disease with epilepsy in children: diagnostic approaches and epileptic phenotypes.', *Child's Nervous System, 23*(11): 1301–1307.

Kanner, A.M. (2004) 'Recognition of the various expressions of anxiety, psychosis, and aggression in epilepsy.', *Epilepsia, 45*(supp 2): 22–27.

Kanner, L. (1943) 'Autistic disturbances of affective contact.' *Nervous Child, 2*: 217–250.

Kano, Y., Ohta, M. and Nagai, Y. (1987) 'Two case reports of autistic boys developing Tourette disorder: indications of improvement?' *Journal of the American Academy of Child and Adolescent Psychiatry, 26*(6): 937–938.

Kano, Y., Ohta, M., Nagai, Y., Yokota, K. and Shimizu, Y. (1988) 'Tourette's disorder coupled with infantile autism: a prospective study of two boys.', *Japanese Journal of Psychiatry and Neurology, 42*(1): 49–57.

Kanter, R.J., Graham, M., Fairbrother, D. and Smith, S.V. (2006) 'Sudden cardiac death in young children with neurofibromatosis type 1.', *Journal of Pediatrics, 149*(5): 718–720.

Kao, A., Mariani, J., McDonald-McGinn, D.M., Maisenbacher, M.K. *et al.* (2004) 'Increased prevalence of unprovoked seizures in patients with a 22q11.2 deletion.', *American Journal of Medical Genetics A, 129*: 29–34.

Kao, H-T., Buka, S.L., Kelsey, K.T., Gruber, D.F. and Porton, B. (2010) 'The correlation between rates of cancer and autism: an exploratory ecological investigation.', *PLoS One, 5*(2): e9372, doi:10.1371/journal.pone.0009372.

Kaplan, P., Levinson, M. and Kaplan, B.S. (1995) 'Cerebral artery stenoses in Williams syndrome cause strokes in childhood.', *Journal of Pediatrics, 126*: 943–945.

Kaplan, S., Itzkovitz, S. and Shapiro, E. (2007) 'A universal mechanism ties genotype to phenotype in trinucleotide diseases.' *PLoS Computational Biology, 3*(11): e235, doi:10.1371/journal.pcbi.0030235

Kar, P.S., Ogoe, B., Poole, R. and Meeking, D. (2005) 'Di-George syndrome presenting with hypocalcaemia in adulthood: two case reports and a review.', *Journal of Clinical Pathology, 58*(6): 655–657.

Karpf, J., Turk, J. and Howlin, P. (2004) 'Cognitive, language, and adaptive behaviour profiles in individuals with a diagnosis of Cohen syndrome.', *Clinical Genetics, 65*: 327–332.

Kasahara, M., Hayashi, M., Tanaka, K., Inoko, H. *et al.* (1996) 'Chromosomal localization of the proteasome Z subunit gene reveals an ancient chromosomal duplication involving the major histocompatibility complex.' Proceedings of the National Academy of Science USA, 93(17): 9096–9101.

Kasari, C. and Lawton, K. (2010) 'New directions in behavioral treatment of autism spectrum disorders.' Current Opinion in Neurology, 23: 137–143.

Kassaï, B., Chiron, C., Augier, S., Cucherat, M. *et al.* (2008) 'Severe myoclonic epilepsy in infancy: a systematic review and a meta-analysis of individual patient data.', *Epilepsia, 49*(2): 343–348.

Kates, W.R., Antshel, K.M., Fremont, W.P., Shprintzen, R.J. *et al.* (2007a) 'Comparing phenotypes in patients with idiopathic autism to patients with velocardiofacial syndrome (22q11 DS) with and without autism.', *American Journal of Medical Genetics A, 143*(22): 2642–2650.

Kates, W.R., Antshel, K., Willhite, R., Bessette, B.A. *et al.* (2005) 'Gender-moderated dorsolateral prefrontal reductions in 22q11.2 deletion syndrome: implications for risk for schizophrenia.', *Child Neuropsychology, 11*(1): 73–85.

Kates, W.R., Burnette, C.P., Bessette, B.A., Folley, B.S. *et al.* (2004) 'Frontal and caudate alterations in velocardiofacial syndrome (deletion at chromosome 22q11.2).', *Journal of Child Neurology, 19*: 337–342.

Kates, W.R., Krauss, B.R., Abdulsabur, N., Colgan, D. *et al.* (2007b) 'The neural correlates of non-spatial working memory in velocardiofacial syndrome (22q11.2 deletion syndrome).', *Neuropsychologia, 45*: 2863–2873.

Kates, W.R., Miller, A.M., Abdulsabur, N., Antshel, K.M. *et al.* (2006) 'Temporal lobe anatomy and psychiatric symptoms in velocardiofacial syndrome (22q11.2 deletion syndrome).', *Journal of the American Academy of Child and Adolescent Psychiatry, 45*(5): 587–595.

Kato, M., Das, S., Petras, K., Sawaishi, Y. *et al.* (2003) 'Polyalanine expansion of ARX associated with cryptogenic West syndrome.', *Neurology, 61*: 267–276.

Kato, M., Das, S., Petras, K., Kitamura, K. *et al.* (2004) 'Mutations of ARX are associated with striking pleiotropy and consistent genotype-phenotype correlation.', *Human Mutation, 23*(2): 147–159.

Kato, M., Saitoh, S., Kamei, A., Shiraishi, H. *et al.* (2004) 'A longer polyalanine expansion mutation in the arx gene causes early infantile epileptic encephalopathy with suppression-burst pattern (Ohtahara syndrome).' *American Journal of Human Genetics, 81*: 361–366.

Kato, T., Hattori, H., Yorifuji, T., Tashiro, Y. and Nakahata, T. (2001) 'Intracranial aneurysms in Ehlers-Danlos syndrome type IV in early childhood.', *Pediatric Neurology*, 25: 336–339.

Katsanis, N. (2004) 'The oligogenic properties of Bardet-Biedl syndrome.', *Human Molecular Genetics*, 13 (Special No 1): R65–71.

Katsanis, N., Ansley, S.J., Badano, J.L., Eichers, E.R. *et al.* (2001) 'Triallelic inheritance in Bardet-Biedl syndrome, a Mendelian recessive disorder.', *Science*, 293: 2256–2259.

Katz, J.D. and Ropper, A.H. (2002) 'Familial Kleine-Levin syndrome: two siblings with unusually long hypersomnic spells.', *Archives of Neurology*, 59: 1959–1961.

Kau, A.S.M., Tierney, E., Bukelis, I., Stump, M.H. *et al.* (2004) 'Social behaviour profile in young males with fragile-X syndrome: characteristics and specificity.', *American Journal of Medical Genetics*, 126A: 9–17.

Kaufman, S., Max, E.E. and Kang, E.S. (1975) 'Phenylalanine hydroxylase activity in liver biopsies from hyperphenylalaninemia heterozygotes: deviation from proportionality with gene dosage.', *Pediatric Research*, 9: 632–634.

Kaufmann, D., Muller, R., Bartelt, B., Wolf, M. *et al.* (2001) 'Spinal neurofibromatosis without cafe-au-lait macules in two families with null mutations of the NF1 gene.', *American Journal of Human Genetics*, 69: 1395–1400.

Kaufmann, W.E., Cortell, R., Kau, A.S.I., Tierney, E. *et al.* (2004) 'Autism spectrum disorder in fragile-X syndrome: communication, social interaction, and specific behaviours.', *American Journal of Medical Genetics A*, 129: 225–234.

Kaufmann, W.E. and Moser, H.W. (2000) 'Dendritic anomalies in disorders associated with mental retardation.', *Cerebral Cortex*, 10: 981–991.

Kaur, M., Descipio, C., McCallum, J., Yaeger, D. *et al.* (2005) 'Precocious sister chromatid separation (PSCS) in Cornelia de Lange syndrome.', *American Journal of Medical Genetics A*, 138: A27–31.

Kawame, H., Adachi, M., Tachibana, K., Kurosawa, K. *et al.* (2001) 'Graves' disease in patients with 22q11.2 deletion.', *Journal of Pediatrics*, 139: 892–895.

Kawamura, T., Chen, J., Takahashi, T., Ichitani, Y. and Nakahara, D. (2006) 'Prenatal stress suppresses cell proliferation in the early developing brain.' *NeuroReport*, 17(14): 1515–1518.

Kawano, J., Kotani, T., Ohtaki, S., Mimamino, N. *et al.* (1989) 'Characterization of rat and human steroid sulfatases.', *Biochimica et Biophysica Acta*, 997: 199–205.

Kayaalp, L., Dervent, A., Saltik, S., Uluduz, D. *et al.* (2007) 'EEG abnormalities in West syndrome: correlation with the emergence of autistic features.', *Brain and Development*, 29: 336–345.

Kaye, C.I., Martin, A.O., Rollnick, B.R., Nagatoshi, K. *et al.* (1992) 'Oculoauriculovertebral anomaly: segregation analysis.' *American Journal of Medical Genetics*, 43: 913–917.

Kaye, C.I., Rollnick, B.R., Hauck, W.W., Martin, A.O. *et al.* (1989) 'Microtia and associated anomalies: statistical analysis.' *American Journal of Medical Genetics*, 34(4): 574–578.

Kayl, A.E. and Moore, B.D. 3rd (2000) 'Behavioural phenotype of neurofibromatosis, type 1.', *Mental Retardation and Developmental Disabilities Research Reviews*, 6: 117–124.

Keegan, C.E., Mulliken, J.B., Wu, B-L. and Korf, B.R. (2001) 'Townes-Brocks syndrome versus expanded spectrum hemifacial microsomia: review of eight patients and further evidence of a "hot spot" for mutation in the SALL1 gene.', *Genetics and Medicine*, 3: 310–313.

Keeler, L.C., Marsh, S.E., Leeflang, E.P., Woods, C.G. *et al.* (2003) 'Linkage analysis in families with Joubert syndrome plus oculo-renal involvement identifies the CORS2 locus on chromosome 11p12–q13.3.', *American Journal of Human Genetics*, 73: 656–662.

Keenan, G.F., Sullivan, K.E., McDonald-McGinn, D.M. and Zackai, E.H. (1997) 'Arthritis associated with deletion of 22q11.2: more common than previously suspected.' (Letter comment.) *American Journal of Medical Genetics*, 71: 488.

Keenan, M. and Dillenburger, K. (2011) 'When all you have is a hammer …: RCTs and the hegemony of science.' *Research in Autistic Spectrum Disorders, 5*(1): 1–13.

Kelberman, D., Tyson, J., Chandler, D.C., McInerney, A.M. *et al.* (2001) 'Hemifacial microsomia: progress in understanding the genetic basis of a complex malformation syndrome.', *Human Genetics*, 109: 638–645.

Keller, C., Reynolds, A., Lee, B. and Garcia-Prats, J. (1998) 'Congenital myotonic dystrophy requiring prolonged endotracheal and noninvasive assisted ventilation: not a uniformly fatal condition.', *Pediatrics*, 101: 704–706.

Kelley, R.I. (1998) 'RSH/Smith-Lemli-Opitz syndrome: mutations and metabolic morphogenesis.', (Editorial) *American Journal of Human Genetics*, 63: 322–326.

Kelley, R.I. (2000) 'Inborn errors of cholesterol biosynthesis.' *Advances in Pediatrics*, 47: 1–53.

Kelley, R.I. and Hennekam, R.C.M. (2000) 'The Smith-Lemli-Opitz syndrome.' *Journal of Medical Genetics*, 37: 321–335.

Kelley, R.I., Roessler, E., Hennekam, R.C., Feldman, G.L. *et al.* (1996) 'Holoprosencephaly in RSH/Smith-Lemli-Opitz syndrome: does abnormal cholesterol metabolism affect the function of Sonic Hedgehog?' *American Journal of Medical Genetics*, 66: 478–484.

Kelley, R.I., Zackai, E.H., Emanuel, B.S., Kistenmacher, M. *et al.* (1982) 'The association of the DiGeorge anomaly with partial monosomy of chromosome 22.', *Journal of Pediatrics*, 101: 197–200.

Kent, L., Emerton, J., Bhadravathi, V., Weisblatt, E. *et al.* (2008) 'X-linked ichthyosis (steroid sulfatase deficiency) is associated with increased risk of attention deficit hyperactivity disorder, autism and social communication deficits.', *Journal of Medical Genetics*, 45(8): 519–524.

Kent, L., Perry, D. and Evans, J. (1998) 'Autism in Down syndrome: three case reports.', *Autism*, 2: 259–361.

Kerbeshian, J. and Burd, L. (1986) 'Asperger's syndrome and Tourette syndrome: the case of the pinball wizard.', *British Journal of Psychiatry*, 148: 731–736.

Kerbeshian, J. and Burd, L. (1996) 'Case study: comorbidity among Tourette syndrome, autistic disorder, and bipolar disorder.', *Journal of the American Academy of Child and Adolescent Psychiatry, 35*(5): 681–685.

Kerr, A.M., Archer, H.L., Evans, J.C., Prescott, R.J. and Gibbon, F. (2006) 'People with MeCP2 mutation-positive Rett disorder who converse.', *Journal of Intellectual Disability Research, 50*(5): 386–394.

Kerr, A.M., Webb, P., Prescott, R.J. and Milne, Y. (2003) 'Results of surgery for scoliosis in Rett syndrome.', *Journal of Child Neurology, 18*(10): 703–708.

Kerr, A.M. and Witt Engerstrom, I. (eds.) (2001) *Rett Disorder and the Developing Brain.* Oxford: Oxford University Press.

Kerrigan, J.F., Shields, W.D., Nelson, T.Y., Bluestone, D.L. *et al.* (2000) 'Ganaxolone for treating intractable infantile spasms: a multicenter, open-label, add-on trial.', *Epilepsy Research, 42*(2–3): 133–139.

Kesler, S.R., Simensen, R.J., Voeller, K., Abidi, F. *et al.* (2007) 'Altered neurodevelopment associated with mutations of RSK2: a morphometric MRI study of Coffin-Lowry syndrome.', *Neurogenetics, 8*(2): 143–148.

Khalifa, N. and von Knorring, A-L. (2003) 'Prevalence of tic disorders and Tourette syndrome in a Swedish school population.', *Developmental Medicine and Child Neurology, 45*(5): 315–319.

Khan, S.G., Levy, H.L., Legerski, R., Quackenbush, E. *et al.* (1998) 'Xeroderma pigmentosum group C splice mutation associated with autism and hypoglycinemia.', *Journal of Investigative Dermatology, 111*: 791–796.

Khare, L., Strizheva, G.D., Bailey, J.N., Au, K-S. *et al.* (2001) 'A novel missense mutation in the GTPase activating protein homology region of TSC2 in two large families with tuberous sclerosis complex.', *Journal of Medical Genetics, 38*: 347–349.

Khong, J.J., Anderson, P., Gray, T.L., Hammerton, M. *et al.* (2006) 'Ophthalmic findings in Apert syndrome prior to craniofacial surgery.', *American Journal of Ophthalmology, 142*: 328–330.

Khoshnood, B., De Vigan, C., Vodovar, V., Goujard, J. and Goffinet, F. (2004) 'A population-based evaluation of the impact of antenatal screening for Down syndrome in France, 1981–2000.', *British Journal of Obstetrics and Gynaecology, 111*(5): 485–490.

Khoshnood, B., Pryde, P., Wall, S., Singh, J. *et al.* (2000) 'Ethnic Differences in the Impact of Advanced Maternal Age on Birth Prevalence of Down Syndrome.', *American Journal of Public Health, 90*: 1778–1781.

Kielinen, M., Rantala, H., Timonen, E., Linna, S.L. and Moilanen, I. (2004) 'Associated medical disorders and disabilities in children with autistic disorder: a population-based study.', *Autism, 8*(1): 49–60.

Kim, D.H., Murovic, J.A., Tiel, R.L., Moes, G. and Kline, D.G. (2005) 'A series of 397 peripheral neural sheath tumors: 30-year experience at Louisiana State University Health Sciences Center.' *Journal of Neurosurgery, 102*: 246–255.

Kim, J., Kim, P. and Hui, C.C. (2001) 'The VACTERL association: lessons from the Sonic hedgehog pathway.', *Clinical Genetics, 59*: 306–315.

Kim, S.Y., Kim, S.K., Lee, J.S., Kim, I.K. and Lee, K. (2000) 'The prediction of adverse pregnancy outcome using low unconjugated estriol in the second trimester of pregnancy without risk of Down syndrome.', *Yonsei Medical Journal, 41*(2): 226–229.

Kim, W., Erlandsen, H., Surendran, S., Stevens, R.C. *et al.* (2004) 'Trends in enzyme therapy for phenylketonuria.', *Molecular Therapy, 10*: 220–224.

Kimata, H. (1995) 'High-dose intravenous gamma-globulin treatment for hyperimmunoglobulinemia E syndrome.', *Journal of Allergy and Clinical Immunology, 95*(3): 771–774.

King, B.H. and Bostic, J.Q. (2006) 'An update on pharmacologic treatments for autism spectrum disorders.', *Child and Adolescent Psychiatric Clinics of North America, 15*: 161–175.

King, M. and Bearman, P.S. (2009) 'Diagnostic change and the increased prevalence of autism.' *International Journal of Epidemiology, 38*: 1224–1234.

King, M.D., Fountain, C., Dakhlallah, D. and Bearman, P.S. (2009) 'Estimated autism risk and older reproductive age.', *American Journal of Public Health, 99*: 1673–1679.

King, R.A. and Oetting, W.S. (2007) 'Oculocutaneous albinism type 2.' Downloadable from *GeneReviews*, web-based resource.

King, R.A., Wiesner, G.L., Townsend, D. and White, J.G. (1993) 'Hypopigmentation in Angelman syndrome.', *American Journal of Medical Genetics, 46*: 40–44.

Kipling, D., Salido, E.C., Shapiro, L.J. and Cooke, H.J. (1996) 'High frequency *de novo* alterations in the long-range genomic structure of the mouse pseudoautosomal region.', *Nature Genetics, 13*: 78–82.

Kishino, T., Lalande, M. and Wagstaff, J. (1997) 'UBE3A/E6-AP mutations cause Angelman syndrome.', *Nature Genetics, 15*: 70–73.

Kitamura, K., Itou, Y., Yanazawa, M., Ohsawa, M. *et al.* (2009) 'Three human ARX mutations cause the lissencephaly-like and mental retardation with epilepsy-like pleiotropic phenotypes in mice.', *Human Molecular Genetics, 18*(19): 3708–3724.

Kitamura, K., Yanazawa, M., Sugiyama, N., Miura, H. *et al.* (2002) 'Mutation of ARX causes abnormal development of forebrain and testes in mice and X-linked lissencephaly with abnormal genitalia in humans.', *Nature Genetics, 32*: 359–369.

Kitanovski, L., Ovcak, Z. and Jazbec, J. (2009) 'Multifocal hepatoblastoma in a 6-month-old girl with trisomy 18: a case report.', *Journal of Medical Case Reports, 3*: 8319.,doi:10.4076/1752-1947-3-8319.

Kivitie-Kallio, S., Autti, T., Salonen, O. and Norio, R. (1998) 'MRI of the brain in the Cohen syndrome: a relatively large corpus callosum in patients with mental retardation and microcephaly.', *Neuropediatrics. 29*(6): 298–301.

Kivitie-Kallio, S., Larsen, A., Kajasto, K. and Norio, R. (1999) 'Neurological and psychological findings in patients with Cohen syndrome: a study of 18 patients aged 11 months to 57 years.', *Neuropediatrics, 30*: 181–189.

Kjellman, B. (1965) 'Cerebral gigantism.', *Acta Paediatrica Scandinavica, 54*: 603–609.

Klauck, S.M., Munstermann, E., Bieber-Martig, B., Ruhl, D. *et al.* (1997) 'Molecular genetic analysis of the FMR-1 gene in a large collection of autistic patients.' *Human Genetics, 100*: 224–229.

Klavdieva, M.M. (1996) 'The history of neuropeptides IV.', *Frontiers in Neuroendocrinology, 17*: 247–280.

Kleijer, W.J., Beemer, F.A. and Boom, B.W. (1994) 'Intermittent hair loss in a child with PIBI(D)S syndrome and trichothiodystrophy with defective DNA repair-xeroderma pigmentosum group D.', *American Journal of Medical Genetics, 52*: 227–230.

Klein, A., Schmitt, B. and Boltchauser, E. (2004) 'Progressive encephalopathy with oedema, hypsarrythmia and optic atrophy (PEHO) syndrome in a Swiss child.', *European Journal of Paediatric Neurology, 8*: 317–321.

Klein, D. and Ammann, F. (1969) 'The syndrome of Laurence-Moon-Bardet-Biedl and allied diseases in Switzerland: clinical, genetic and epidemiological studies.', *Journal of Neurological Sciences, 9*: 479–513.

Kleine, W. (1925) 'Periodische Schlafsucht.', *Monatsschrift für Psychiatrie und Neurologie, 57*: 285.

Klein-Tasman, B.P., Mervis, C.B., Lord, C. and Phillips, K.D. (2007) 'Socio-communicative deficits in young children with Williams syndrome: performance on the autism diagnostic observation schedule.', *Child Neuropsychology, 13*(5): 444–467.

Klein-Tasman, B.P., Phillips, K.D., Lord, C., Mervis, C.B. and Gallo, F.J. (2009) 'Overlap with the autism spectrum in young children with Williams syndrome.', *Journal of Developmental and Behavioural Pediatrics, 30*: 289–299.

Klerk, M., Verhoef, P., Clarke, R., Blom, H.J. *et al.* (2002) 'MTHFR 677C-T polymorphism and risk of coronary heart disease: a meta-analysis.' *Journal of the American Medical Association, 288*: 2023–2031.

Klesert, T.R., Cho, D.H., Clark, J.I., Maylie, J. *et al.* (2000) 'Mice deficient in Six5 develop cataracts: implications for myotonic dystrophy.', *Nature Genetics, 25*: 105–109.

Kline, A.D., Barr, M. and Jackson, L.G. (1993) 'Growth manifestations in the Brachmann-de Lange syndrome.', *American Journal of Medical Genetics, 47*: 1042–1049.

Kline, A.D., Stanley, C., Belevich, J., Brodsky, K. *et al.* (1993) 'Developmental data on individuals with the Brachmann-de Lange syndrome.', *American Journal of Medical Genetics, 47*: 1053–1058.

Klose, A., Peters, H., Hoffmeyer, S., Buske, A. *et al.* (1999) 'Two independent mutations in a family with neurofibromatosis type 1 (NF1).', *American Journal of Medical Genetics, 83*: 6–12.

Klushnik, T.P., Gratchev, V.V. and Belichenko, P.V. (2001) 'Brain-directed autoantibodies levels in the serum of Rett syndrome patients.', *Brain and Development, 23*(Supp.1): 113–117.

Kluwe, L., Siebert, R., Gesk, S., Friedrich, R.E. *et al.* (2004) 'Screening 500 unselected neurofibromatosis 1 patients for deletions of the NF1 gene.', *Human Mutation, 23*: 111–116.

Kluwe, L., Tatagiba, M., Funsterer, C. and Mautner, V.F. (2003) 'NF1 mutations and clinical spectrum in patients with spinal neurofibromas.', *Journal of Medical Genetics, 40*: 368–371.

Kmoch, S., Hartmannova, H., Stiburkova, B., Krijt, J. *et al.* (2000) 'Human adenylosuccinate lyase (ADSL), cloning and characterization of full-length cDNA and its isoform, gene structure and molecular basis for ADSL deficiency in six patients.', *Human Molecular Genetics, 9*: 1501–1513.

Knapp, M., Romeo, R. and Beecham, J. (2009) 'Economic cost of autism in the UK.', *Autism, 13*(3): 317–336.

Knerr, I., Gibson, K.M., Jakobs, C. and Pearl, P.L. (2008) 'Neuropsychiatric morbidity in adolescent and adult succinic semialdehyde dehydrogenase deficiency patients.' *CNS Spectrums, 13*(7): 598–605.

Knerr, I., Pearl, P.L., Bottiglieri, T., Carter Snead, O. *et al.* (2007) 'Therapeutic concepts in succinate semialdehyde dehydrogenase (SSADH; ALDH5a1) deficiency (g-hydroxybutyric aciduria): hypotheses evolved from 25 years of patient evaluation, studies in Aldh5a1j/j mice and characterization of g-hydroxybutyric acid pharmacology.', *Journal of Inherited Metabolic Disease, 30*: 279–294.

Knickmeyer, R.C. and Baron-Cohen, S. (2006) 'Foetal testosterone and sex differences in typical social development and in autism.', *Journal of Child Neurology, 21*(10): 825–845.

Knickmeyer, R.C., Baron-Cohen, S., Fane, B.A., Wheelwright, S. *et al.* (2006) 'Androgens and autistic traits: a study of individuals with congenital adrenal hyperplasia.' *Hormones and Behaviour, 50*: 148–153.

Knivsberg, A.M., Reichelt, K.L., Hoien, T. and Nodland, M. (2002) 'A randomised controlled study of dietary intervention in autistic syndromes.', *Nutritional Neuroscience, 5*(4): 251–261.

Knoll, J.H.M., Nicholls, R.D., Magenis, R.E., Graham, J.M. Jr. *et al.* (1989) 'Angelman and Prader-Willi syndromes share a common chromosome 15 deletion but differ in parental origin of the deletion.' *American Journal of Medical Genetics, 32*: 285–290.

Knox, S., Ge, H., Dimitroff, B.D., Ren, Y. *et al.* (2007) 'Mechanisms of TSC-mediated control of synapse assembly and axonal guidance.', *PLoS ONE, 2*(4): e375, 1–13, doi:10.1371/journal.pone.0000375.

Kobashi, G., Yamada, H., Asano, T., Nagan, S. *et al.* (2000) 'Absence of association between a common mutation in the methylenetetrahydrofolate reductase gene and preeclampsia in Japanese women.', *American Journal of Medical Genetics, 93*: 122–125.

Kobrynski, L., Chitayat, D., Zahed, L., McGregor, D. *et al.* (1993) 'Trisomy 22 and facioauriculovertebral (Goldenhar) sequence.', *American Journal of Medical Genetics, 46*: 68–71.

Kobylinski, O. (1883) 'Uber eine flughautahnliche ausbreitung am haise.', *Archives of Anthropology, 14*: 342–348.

Koch, M.C., Grimm, T., Harley, H.G. and Harper, P.S. (1991) 'Genetic risks for children of women with myotonic dystrophy.', *American Journal of Human Genetics, 48*: 1084–1091.

Koch, R., Burton, B., Hoganson, G., Peterson, R. *et al.* (2002) 'Phenylketonuria in adulthood: a collaborative study.', *Journal of Inherited Metabolic Disorders, 25*: 333–346.

Koch, R., Moats, R., Guttler, F., Guldberg, P. and Nelson, M.Jr. (2000) 'Blood-brain phenylalanine relationships in persons with phenylketonuria.', *Pediatrics, 106*: 1093–1096.

Koch, R., Moseley, K.D., Yano, S., Nelson, M. Jr., and Moats, R.A. (2003a) 'Large neutral amino acid therapy and phenylketonuria: a promising approach to treatment.', *Molecular Genetics and Metabolism*, 79: 110–113.

Koch, R., Moseley, K.D., Moats, R., Yano, S. *et al.* (2003b) 'Danger of high-protein dietary supplements to persons with hyperphenylalaninaemia.' *Journal of Inherited Metabolic Disease*, 26(4): 339–342.

Koekkoek, S.K.E., Yamaguchi, K., Milojkovic, B.A., Dortland, B.R. *et al.* (2005) 'Deletion of FMR1 in purkinje cells enhances parallel fiber LTD, enlarges spines, and attenuates cerebellar eyelid conditioning in fragile-X syndrome.', *Neuron*, 47: 339–352.

Koide, R., Ikeuchi, T., Onodera, O., Tanaka, H. *et al.* (1994) 'Unstable expansion of CAG repeat in hereditary dentatorubral-pallidoluysian atrophy (DRPLA).', *Nature Genetics*, 6: 9–13.

Kolehmainen, J., Black, G.C.M., Saarinen, A., Chandler, K. *et al.* (2003) 'Cohen syndrome is caused by mutations in a novel gene, COH1, encoding a transmembrane protein with a presumed role in vesicle-mediated sorting and intracellular protein transport.', *American Journal of Human Genetics*, 72: 1359–1369.

Kolehmainen, J., Wilkinson, R., Lehesjoki, A-E., Chandler, K. *et al.* (2004) 'Delineation of Cohen syndrome following a large-scale genotype-phenotype screen.', *American Journal of Human Genetics*, 75: 122–127.

Kolevzon, A., Smith, C.J., Schmeidler, J., Buxbaum, J.D. and Silverman, J.M. (2004) 'Familial symptom domains in monozygotic siblings with autism.', *American Journal of Medical Genetics (Neuropsychiatric Genetics)*, 129B: 76–81.

Kolevzon, A., Gross R. and Reichenberg, A. (2007) 'Prenatal and Perinatal risk factors for autism: a review and intgegration of findings.', *Archives of Pediatric and Adolescent Medicine*, 161: 326–333.

Komoto, J., Usui, S., Otsuki, S. and Terao, A. (1984) 'Infantile autism and Duchenne muscular dystrophy.', *Journal of Autism and Developmental Disorders*, 14(2): 91–95.

Komrower, G.M., Sardharwalla, I.B., Coutts, J.M.J. and Ingham, D. (1979) 'Management of maternal phenylketonuria: an emerging clinical problem.', *British Medical Journal*, I: 1383–1387.

Komure, O., Sano, A., Nishino, N., Yamauchi, N. *et al.* (1995) 'DNA analysis in hereditary dentatorubral-pallidoluysian atrophy: correlation between CAG repeat length and phenotypic variation and the molecular basis of anticipation.', *Neurology*, 45: 143–149.

Kondo, I., Nagataki, S. and Miyagi, N. (1990) 'The Cohen syndrome: does mottled retina separate a Finnish and a Jewish type?' *American Journal of Medical Genetics*, 37: 109–113.

Koo, H.S., Lee, H.S. and Hong, Y.M. (2007) 'Methylenetetrahydrofolate reductase TT genotype as a predictor of cardiovascular risk in hypertensive adolescents.' *Pediatric Cardiology*, 29(1): 136–141.

Kooy, R.F., Reyniers, E., Verhoye, M., Sijbers, J. *et al.* (1999) 'Neuroanatomy of the fragile-X knockout mouse brain studied using in vivo high resolution magnetic resonance imaging.', *European Journal of Human Genetics*, 7: 526–532.

Kooy, R.F., Willemsen, R. and Oostra, B.A. (2000) 'Fragile-X syndrome at the turn of the century.' *Molecular Medicine Today*, 6: 193–198.

Korenberg, J., Bradley, C. and Disteche, C. (1992) 'Down syndrome: molecular mapping of congenital heart disease and duodenal stenosis.', *American Journal of Human Genetics*, 50: 294–302.

Korf, B.R. (2000) 'Malignancy in neurofibromatosis type 1.', *Oncologist*, 5: 477–485.

Korman, S.H. (2006) 'Inborn errors of isoleucine degradation: a review.', *Molecular Genetics and Metabolism*, 89: 289–299.

Kornhuber, J., Mack-Burhardt, F., Konradi, C., Fritze, J. *et al.* (1989) 'Effect of antemortem and postmortem factors on [3H]MK-801 binding in the human brain: transient elevation during early childhood.', *Life Science*, 45: 745–749.

Kosaki, K., Curry, C.J., Roeder, E. and Jones, K.L. (1997) 'Ritscher-Schinzel (3C) syndrome: documentation of the phenotype.', *American Journal of Medical Genetics*, 68: 421–427.

Kosfeld, M., Heinrichs, M., Zak, P.J., Fishbacher, U. and Fehr, E. (2005) 'Oxytocin increases trust in humans.' (Letter) *Nature*, 435: 673–676.

Koth, C.W., Cutting, L.E. and Denckla, M.B. (2000) 'The association of neurofibromatosis type 1 and attention deficit hyperactivity disorder.', *Child Neuropsychology*, 6: 185–194.

Kothur, K., Ray, M. and Malhi, P. (2008) 'Correlation of autism with temporal tubers in tuberous sclerosis complex.', *Neurology India*, 56(1): 74–76.

Kousseff, B.G. (1984) 'Sacral meningocele with conotruncal heart defects: a possible autosomal recessive trait.', *Pediatrics*, 74: 395–398.

Kousseff, B.G., Thomson-Meares, J., Newkirk, P. and Root, A.W. (1993) 'Physical growth in Brachmann-de Lange syndrome.', *American Journal of Medical Genetics*, 47: 1050–1052.

Kovarova, M., Wassif, C.A., Odom, S., Liao, K. *et al.* (2006) 'Cholesterol deficiency in a mouse model of Smith-Lemli-Opitz syndrome reveals increased mast cell responsiveness.', *Journal of Experimental Medicine*, 203: 1161–1171.

Kozak, L., Francova, H., Hrabnicova, E., Prochazkova, D. *et al.* (2000) 'Smith-Lemli-Opitz syndrome: molecular-genetic analysis of ten families.', *Journal of Inherited Metabolic Disease*, 23: 409–412.

Kozinetz, C.A., Skender, M.L., MacNaughton, N., Almes, M.J. *et al.* (1993) 'Epidemiology of Rett syndrome: a population-based registry.', *Pediatrics*, 91(2): 445–450.

Kozma, C. (1998) 'On cognitive variability in velocardiofacial syndrome: profound mental retardation and autism.', *American Journal of Medical Genetics*, 81: 269–270.

Kozul, C.D., Nomikos, A.P., Hampton, T.H., Warnke, L.A. *et al.* (2008) 'Laboratory diet profoundly alters gene expression and confounds genomic analysis in mouse liver and lung.', *Chemico-Biological Interactions*, 173: 129–140.

Krab, L.C., de Goede-Bolder, A., Aarsen, F.K., Pluijm, S.M. *et al.* (2008) 'Effect of simvastatin on cognitive functioning in children with neurofibromatosis type 1: a randomized controlled trial.', *Journal of the American Medical Association*, 300(3): 287–294.

Kraemer, K.H., Patronas, N.J., Schiffman, R., Brooks, B.P. *et al.* (2007) 'Xeroderma pigmentosum, trichothiodystrophy and Cockayne syndrome: a complex genotype-phenotype relationship.', *Neuroscience, 145*: 1388–1396.

Krammer, P.H. (2000) 'CD95's deadly mission in the immune system.', *Nature, 407*: 789–795.

Krane, C.M. and Goldstein, D.L. (2007) 'Comparative functional analysis of aquaporins/glyceroporins in mammals and anurans.', *Mammalian Genome, 18*: 452–462.

Krantz, I.D., McCallum, J., DeScipio, C., Kaur, M. *et al.* (2004) 'Cornelia de Lange syndrome is caused by mutations in NIPBL, the human homolog of drosophila melanogaster Nipped-B.', *Nature Genetics, 36*: 631–635.

Kratz, L.E. and Kelley, R.I. (1999) 'Prenatal diagnosis of the RSH/Smith-Lemli-Opitz syndrome.' *American Journal of Medical Genetics, 82*: 376–381.

Kreiborg, A., Barr, M. Jr. and Cohen, M.M. Jr. (1992) 'Cervical spine in the Apert syndrome.', *American Journal of Medical Genetics, 43*: 704–708.

Kreusel, K.M. (2005) 'Ophthalmological manifestations in VHL and NF 1: pathological and diagnostic implications.', *Familial Cancer, 4*: 43–47.

Krishnamurthy, S., Kapoor, S. and Yadav, S. (2007) 'Nephrotic syndrome with X-linked ichthyosis, Kallmann syndrome and unilateral renal agenesis.', *Indian Pediatrics, 44*(4): 301–303.

Krivit, K., Lockman, L.A., Watkins, P.A., Hirsch, J. and Shapiro, E.G. (1995) 'The future for treatment by bone marrow transplantation for adrenoleukodystrophy, metachromatic leukodystrophy, globoid cell leukodystrophy and Hurler syndrome.', *Journal of Inherited Metabolic Disease, 18*: 398–412.

Kroll, J.S. (1985) 'Pyridoxine for neonatal seizures: an unexpected danger.', *Developmental Medicine and Child Neurology, 985*(27): 377–379.

Kröll-Seger, J., Portilla, P., Dulac, O. and Chiron, C. (2006) 'Topiramate in the treatment of highly refractory patients with Dravet syndrome.', *Neuropediatrics, 37*(6): 325–329.

Kuczynski, E., Bertola, D.R., de Castro, C.I.E., Koiffmann, C.P. and Kim, C.A. (2009) 'Infantile autism and 47,XYY karyotype.', *Arquivos de Neuropsiquiatria, 67*(3-A): 717–718.

Kuhara, T., Ohsea, M., Ohdoi, C. and Ishida, S. (2000) 'Differential diagnosis of homocystinuria by urease treatment, isotope dilution and gas chromatography–mass spectrometry.', *Journal of Chromatography B, 746*: 103–114.

Kuhl, P.K. (2000) 'A new view of language acquisition.', *Proceedings of the National Academy of Science, 97*(22): 11850–11857.

Kuhl, P.K., Coffey-Corina, S., Padden, D. and Dawson, G. (2005) 'Links between social and linguistic processing of speech in preschool children with autism: behavioural and electrophysiological measures.', *Developmental Science, 8*(1): F1–F12.

Kuijpers, G.M., De Vroede, M., Knol, H.E. and Jansen, M. (1999) 'Growth hormone treatment in a child with Williams-Beuren syndrome: a case report.', *European Journal of Pediatrics, 158*(6): 451–454.

Kujat, A., Schulz, M.D., Strenge, S. and Froster, U.G. (2006) 'Renal malformations in deletion 22q11.2 patients.', (Letter) *American Journal of Medical Genetics, 140A*: 1601–1602.

Kulaga, H.M., Leitch, C.C., Eichers, E.R., Badano, J.L. *et al.* (2004) 'Loss of BBS proteins causes anosmia in humans and defects in olfactory cilia structure and function in the mouse.', *Nature Genetics, 36*: 994–998.

Kulman, G., Lissoni, P., Rovelli, F., Roselli, M.G. *et al.* (2000) 'Evidence of pineal endocrine hypofunction in autistic children.', *Neuro Endocrinology Letters, 21*(1): 31–34.

Kumada, S., Hayashi, M., Arima, K., Nakayama, H. *et al.* (2004) 'Renal disease in Arima syndrome is nephronophthisis as in other Joubert-related cerebello-oculo-renal syndromes.', *American Journal of Medical Genetics A, 131*: 71–76.

Kumagai, T., Miura, K., Ohki, T., Matsumoto, A. *et al.* (2001) '[Central nervous system involvements in Duchenne/Becker muscular dystrophy].' *No To Hattatsu, 33*(6): 480–486.

Kunst, C.B., Zerylnick, C., Karickhoff, L., Eichler, E. *et al.* (1996) 'FMR1 in global populations.', *American Journal of Human Genetics, 58*: 513–522.

Kurian, M.A., Morgan, N.V., MacPherson, L., Foster, K. *et al.* (2008) 'Phenotypic spectrum of neurodegeneration associated with mutations in the PLA2G6 gene (PLAN).', *Neurology, 70*(18): 1623–1629.

Kurlan, R. (2004) *Handbook of Tourette's Syndrome and Related Tic and Behavioural Disorder.* New York: Marcel Dekker.

Kurlan, R., Behr, J., Medved, L., Shoulson, I., Pauls, D. and Kidd, K.K. (1987) 'Severity of Tourette syndrome in one large kindred: implication for determination of disease prevalence rate.', *Archives of Neurology, 44*: 268–269.

Kurlan, R., Eapen, V., Stern, J., McDermott, M.P. and Robertson, M.M. (1994) 'Bilineal transmission in Tourette's syndrome families.', *Neurology, 44*: 2336–2342.

Kurotaki, N., Imaizumi, K., Harada, N., Masuno, M. *et al.* (2002) 'Haploinsufficiency of NSD1 causes Sotos syndrome.', *Nature Genetics, 30*: 365–366.

Kushner, H.I. (1995) 'Medical fictions: the case of the cursing Marquise and the (re)construction of Gilles de la Tourette's syndrome.', *Bulletin of the History of Medicine, 69*: 225–254.

Kushner, H.I. (1999) *A Cursing Brain? The Histories of Tourette Syndrome.* Cambridge, Massachusetts: Cambridge University Press.

Kuzminski, A.M., Del Giacco, E.J., Allen, R.H., Stabler, S.P. and Lindenbaum, J. (1998) 'Effective treatment of cobalamin deficiency with oral cobalamin.', *Blood, 92*(4): 1191–1198.

Kyllerman, M. (1995) 'On the prevalence of Angelman syndrome.', *American Journal of Medical Genetics, 59*(3): 405.

Kyttala, M., Tallila, J., Salonen, R., Kopra, O. *et al.* (2006) 'MKS1, encoding a component of the flagellar apparatus basal body proteome, is mutated in Meckel syndrome.', *Nature Genetics, 38*: 155–157.

LaCassie, Y. and Arriaza, M.I. (1996) 'Opitz GBBB syndrome and the 22q11.2 deletion.', *American Journal of Medical Genetics, 62*(3): 318.

Lachlan, K.L., Lucassen, A.M., Bunyan, D. and Temple, I.K. (2007) 'Cowden syndrome and BannayanRileyRuvalcaba syndrome represent one condition with variable expression and age-related penetrance: results of a clinical study of PTEN mutation carriers.', *Journal of Medical Genetics*, 44: 579–585.

Lachman, M.F., Wright, Y., Whiteman, D.A.H., Herson, V. and Greenstein, R.M. (1991) 'Brief clinical report: a 46,XY phenotypic female with Smith-Lemli-Opitz syndrome.', *Clinical Genetics*, 39: 136–141.

Lacombe, D., Bonneau, D., Verloes, A., Couet, D. *et al.* (1993) 'Lujan-Fryns syndrome (X-linked mental retardation with marfanoid habitus): report of three cases and review.', *Genetic Counseling*, 4: 193–198.

Lajeunie, E., Cameron, R., El Ghouzzi, V., de Parseval, N. *et al.* (1999) 'Clinical variability in patients with Apert's syndrome.', *Journal of Neurosurgery*, 90: 443–447.

Lajiness-O'Neill, R.R., Beaulieu, I., Titus, J.B., Asamoah, A. *et al.* (2005) 'Memory and learning in children with 22q11.2 deletion syndrome: evidence for ventral and dorsal stream disruption?' *Neuropsychological Development and Cognition C Child Neuropsychology*, 11: 55–71.

Lake, B.D., Smith, V.V., Judge, M.R., Harper, J.I. and Besley, G.T.N. (1991) 'Hexanol dehydrogenase activity shown by enzyme histochemistry on skin biopsies allows differentiation of Sjogren-Larsson syndrome from other ichthyoses.', *Journal of Inherited Metabolic Disease*, 14: 338–340.

Lalande, M. and Calciano, M.A. (2007) 'Molecular epigenetics of Angelman syndrome.', *Cellular and Molecular Life Sciences*, 64(7–8): 947–960.

Lalani, S.R., Safiullah, A.M., Fernbach, S.D., Harutyunyan, K.G. *et al.* (2006) 'Spectrum of CHD7 mutations in 110 individuals with CHARGE syndrome and genotype-phenotype correlation.', *American Journal of Human Genetics*, 78: 303–314.

Lalani, S.R., Safiullah, A.M., Molinari, L.M., Fernbach, S.D. *et al.* (2004) 'SEMA3E mutation in a patient with CHARGE syndrome.', *Journal of Medical Genetics*, 41: e94.

Lalatta, F., Livini, E., Selicorni, A., Briscioli, V. *et al.* (1991) 'X-linked mental retardation with marfanoid habitus: first report of four Italian patients.', *American Journal of Medical Genetics*, 38: 228–232.

Lam, C.W., Yeung, W.L., Ko, C.H., Poon, P.M. *et al.* (2000) 'Spectrum of mutations in the MeCP2 gene in patients with infantile autism and Rett syndrome.', *Journal of Medical Genetics*, 3: E41.

Lam, K.S.L., Aman, M.G. and Arnold, E. (2005) 'Neurochemical correlates of autistic disorder: a review of the literature.' *Research in Developmental Disabilities*, 27: 254–289.

Lama, G., Graziano, L., Calabrese, E., Grassia, C. *et al.* (2004) 'Blood pressure and cardiovascular involvement in children with neurofibromatosis type 1.', *Pediatric Nephrology*, 19: 413–418.

Lammert, M., Friedman, J.M., Kluwe, L. and Mautner, V.F. (2005) 'Prevalence of neurofibromatosis 1 in German children at elementary school enrollment.', *Archives of Dermatology*, 141: 71–74.

Lammert, M., Friedman, J.M., Roth, H.J., Friedrich, R.E. *et al.* (2006) 'Vitamin D deficiency associated with number of neurofibromas in neurofibromatosis 1.', *Journal of Medical Genetics*, 43: 810–813.

Lamson, S.H. and Hook, E.B. (1980) 'A simple function for maternal-age-specific rates of Down syndrome in the 20-to-49-year age range and its biological implications.', *American Journal of Human Genetics*, 32: 743–753.

Landa, R.J., Holman, K.C. and Garrett-Mayer, E. (2007) 'Social and communication development in toddlers with early and later diagnosis of autism spectrum disorders.', *Archives of General Psychiatry*, 64(7): 853–864.

Landau, A.M., Luk, K.C., Jones, M-L., Siegrist-Johnstone, R. *et al.* (2005) 'Defective Fas expression exacerbates neurotoxicity in a model of Parkinson's disease.', *Journal of Experimental Medicine*, 202: 575–581.

Lander, E. and Kruglyak, L. (1995) 'Genetic dissection of complex traits: guidelines for interpreting and reporting linkage results.', *Nature Genetics*, 11: 241–247.

Landgren, M., Gillberg, C. and Stromland, K. (1992)'Goldenhar syndrome and autistic behaviour.', *Developmental Medicine and Child Neurology*, 34: 999–1005.

Landmark, C.J. and Johannessen, S.I. (2008) 'Pharmacological management of epilepsy: recent advances and future prospects.', *Drugs*, 68(14): 1925–1937.

Lane, N. (2005) *Power, Sex, Suicide: Mitochondria and the Meaning of Life.* Oxford: Oxford University Press.

Langius, F.A., Waterham, H.R., Romeijn, G.J., Oostheim, W. *et al.* (2003) 'Identification of three patients with a very mild form of Smith-Lemli-Opitz syndrome.', *American Journal of Medical Genetics*, 122A(1): 24–29.

Larsen, L.A., Vuust, J., Nystad, M., Evseeva, I. *et al.* (2001) 'Analysis of FMR1 (CGG)n alleles and DXS548-FRAXAC1 haplotypes in three European circumpolar populations: traces of genetic relationship with Asia.', *European Journal of Human Genetics*, 9: 724–727.

Larsson, H.J., Eaton, W.W., Madsen, K.M., Vestergaard, M. *et al.* (2005) 'Risk factors for autism: perinatal factors, parental psychiatric history, and socioeconomic status.', *American Journal of Epidemiology*, 161(10): 916–925, discussion: 926–928.

Lashkari, A., Smith, A.K. and Graham, J.M. Jr. (1999) 'Williams-Beuren syndrome: an update and review for the primary physician.', *Clinical Pediatrics (Philadelphia)*, 38(4): 189–208.

Lassker, U., Zschocke, J., Blau, N. and Santer, R. (2002) 'Tetrahydrobiopterin responsiveness in phenylketonuria: two new cases and a review of molecular genetic findings.', *Journal of Inherited Metabolic Disease*, 25: 65–70.

Laumonnier, F., Bonnet-Brilhault, F., Gomot, M., Blanc, R. *et al.* (2004) 'X-linked mental retardation and autism are associated with a mutation in the NLGN4 gene, a member of the neuroligin family.', *American Journal of Human Genetics*, 74(3): 552–557.

Laura, V., Cristina, L., Paola, R., Luisa, A.M. *et al.* (2011) 'Metals, metallothioneins and oxidative stress in blood of autistic children.' *Research in Autism Spectrum Disorders*, 5: 286–293.

Laurence, J.Z. and Moon, R.C. (1866) 'Four cases of retinitis pigmentosa occurring in the same family and accompanied by general imperfection of development.', *Ophthalmological Review*, 2: 32–41.

Lauritsen, M.B. and Ewald, H. (2001) 'The genetics of autism.', *Acta Psychiatrica Scandinavica*, *103*: 411–427.

Lauritsen, M.B., Mors, O., Mortensen, P.B. and Ewald, H. (2002) 'Medical disorders among inpatients with autism in Denmark according to *ICD-8*: a nationwide register-based study.', *Journal of Autism and Developmental Disorders*, *32*(2): 115–119.

Laval, S.H. and Boyd, Y. (1993) 'Partial inversion of gene order within a homologous segment on the X chromosome.', *Mammalian Genome*, *4*: 119–123.

Lavenstein, B.L. (2003) 'Treatment approaches for children with Tourette's syndrome.', *Current Neurology and Neuroscience Reports*, *3*(2): 143–148.

Lawrence, Y.A., Kemper, T.L., Bauman, M.L. and Blatt, G.J. (2010) 'Parvalbumin-calbindin- and calretinin-immunoreactive hippocampal interneuron density in autism.', *Acta Neurologica Scandinavica*, *121*: 99–108.

Laws, G. and Bishop, D. (2004) 'Pragmatic language impairment and social deficits in Williams syndrome: a comparison with Down's syndrome and specific language impairment.', *International Journal of Language and Communication Disorders*, *39*: 45–64.

Lawson-Yuen, A., Saldivar, J.S., Sommer, S. and Picker, J. (2008) 'Familial deletion within NLGN4 associated with autism and Tourette syndrome.', *European Journal of Human Genetics*, *16*(5): 614–618.

Lazo, O., Contreras, M., Hashmi, M., Stanley, W. *et al.* (1988) 'Peroxisomal lignoceroyl-CoA ligase deficiency in childhood adrenoleukodystrophy and adrenomyeloneuropathy.', *Proceedings of the National Academy of Science USA*, *85*: 7647–7651.

Le Ber, I., Brice, A. and Durr, A. (2005) 'New autosomal recessive cerebellar ataxias with oculomotor apraxia.', *Current Neurology and Neuroscience Reports*, *5*: 411–417.

Leckman, J.F. and Cohen, D.J. (eds.) (1999) *Tourette's syndrome: Tics, Obsessions and Compulsions*. New York: John Wiley.

Ledbetter, D.H. (2008) 'Cytogenetic technology – genotype and phenotype.', *New England Journal of Medicine*, *359*(16): 1728–1730.

Ledbetter, D.H., Riccardi, V.M., Airhart, S.D., Strobel, R.J. *et al.* (1981) 'Deletions of chromosome 15 as a cause of the Prader-Willi syndrome.', *New England Journal of Medicine*, *304*(6): 325–329.

Ledbetter, S.A., Ledbetter, D.H., Ledley, F.D. and Woo, S. (1987) 'Localization of phenylalanine hydroxylase (PAH) and alpha-1 antitrypsin (AAT) loci in mouse genome by synteny and in situ hybridization.', (Abstract) *American Journal of Human Genetics*, *41*: A173 only.

Le Deist, F. (2004) 'Autoimmune lymphoproliferative syndrome.', *Orphanet Encyclopaedia*, www.orpha.net/data/patho/GB/uk-ALPS.pdf.

Le Guen T, Bahi-Buisson N, Nectoux J, Boddaert N, *et al.* (2010) 'A FOXG1 mutation in a boy with congenital variant of Rett syndrome.', *Neurogenetics*, doi: 10.1007/s10048-010-0255-4

Ledley, F.D., Koch, R., Jew, K., Beaudet, A. *et al.* (1988) 'Phenylalanine hydroxylase expression in liver of a fetus with phenylketonuria.', *Journal of Pediatrics*, *113*: 463–468.

Lee, D.A., Portnoy, S., Hill, P., Gillberg, C. and Patton, M.A. (2005) 'Psychological profile of children with Noonan syndrome.', *Developmental Medicine and Child Neurology*, *47*: 35–38.

Lee, J.S., Asano, E., Muzik, O., Chugani, D.C., Juhasz, C. *et al.* (2001) 'Sturge-Weber syndrome: correlation between clinical course and FDG PET findings.', *Neurology*, *57*: 189–195.

Lee, M.J. and Stephenson, D.A. (2007) 'Recent developments in neurofibromatosis type 1.', *Current Opinion in Neurology*, *20*(2): 135–141.

Lee, N.B., Kelly, L. and Sharland, M. (1992) 'Ocular manifestations of Noonan syndrome.', *Eye*, *6*(3): 328–334.

Lee, S-J. (2007) 'Sprinting without myostatin: a genetic determinant of athletic prowess.', *Trends in Genetics*, *23*(10): 475–477.

Lee, W.T., Weng, W.C., Peng, S.F. and Tzen, K.Y. (2009) 'Neuroimaging findings in children with paediatric neurotransmitter diseases.', *Journal of Inherited Metabolic Disease*, *32*(3): 361–370.

Lee, Y., Quek, S.C., Chong, S.S., Tan, A.S. *et al.* (2006) 'Clinical report: a case of Williams syndrome and Klinefelter syndrome.', *Annals of the Academy of Medicine of Singapore*, *35*(12): 901–904.

Leehey, M.A., Munhoz, R.P., Lang, A.E., Brunberg, J.A. *et al.* (2003) 'The fragile-X premutation presenting as essential tremor.', *Archives of Neurology*, *60*: 117–121.

Lees, A.J. (1986) 'Georges Gilles de la Tourette: the man and his times.', *Revue Neurologique* (Paris), *142*: 808–816.

Legius, E., Schrander-Stumpel, C., Schollen, E., Pulles-Heintzberger, C. *et al.* (2002) 'PTPN11 mutations in LEOPARD syndrome.', *Journal of Medical Genetics*, *39*: 571–574.

Legius, E., Wu, R., Eyssen, M., Marynen, P. *et al.* (1995) 'Encephalocraniocutaneous lipomatosis with a mutation in the NF1 gene.', *Journal of Medical Genetics*, *32*: 316–319.

Legum, C., Godel, V. and Nemet, P. (1981) 'Heterogeneity and pleiotropism in the Moebius syndrome.', *Clinical Genetics*, *20*: 254–259.

Leibowitz, D. and Dubowitz, V. (1981) 'Intellect and behaviour in Duchenne muscular dystrophy.', *Developmental Medicine and Child Neurology*, *23*: 577–590.

Leisti, E.L., Pyhtinen, J. and Poyhonen, M. (1996) 'Spontaneous decrease of a pilocytic astrocytoma in neurofibromatosis type 1.', *AJNR American Journal of Neuroradiology*, *17*: 1691–1694.

Lejeune, J., Gautier, M. and Turpin, R. (1959) 'Etude des chromosomes somatiques de neuf enfants mongoliens.' *Comptes Rendus de l'Academie des Sciences*, *248*: 1721–1722.

Lejeune, J., Legrand, N., Lafourcade, J., Rethore, M.-O. *et al.* (1982) 'Fragilite du chromosome X et effets de la trimethoprime.' *Annales de Genetique*, *25*: 149–151.

Lemmers, R.J.L.F., Wohlgemuth, M., van der Gaag, K.J., van der Vliet, P.J. *et al.* (2007) 'Specific sequence variations within the 4q35 region are associated with facioscapulohumeral muscular dystrophy.' *American Journal of Human Genetics*, *81*(5): 884–894.

Leonard, H. and Bower, C. (1998) 'Is the girl with Rett syndrome normal at birth?' *Developmental Medicine and Child Neurology*, *40*: 115–121.

Leonard, H., de Klerk, N., Bourke, J. and Bower, C. (2006) 'Maternal health in pregnancy and intellectual disability in the offspring: a population-based study.', *Annals of Epidemiology*, *16*(6): 448–454.

Leonard, H., Thomson, M., Bower, C., Fyfe, S. and Constantinou, J. (1995) 'Skeletal abnormalities in Rett syndrome: increasing evidence for dysmorphogenetic defects.', *American Journal of Medical Genetics, 58*: 282–285.

Leonardi, M.L., Pai, G.S., Wilkes, B. and Lebel, R.R. (2001) 'Ritscher-Schinzel cranio-cerebello-cardiac (3C) syndrome: report of four new cases and review.', *American Journal of Medical Genetics, 102*: 237–242.

Lerma-Carrillo, I., Molina, J.D., Cuevas-Duran, T., Julve-Correcher, C. *et al.* (2006) 'Psychopathology in the Lujan-Fryns syndrome: report of two patients and review.', *American Journal of Medical Genetics, 140A*: 2807–2811.

Lerman-Sagie, T., Leshinsky-Silver, E., Watemberg, N. and Lev, D. (2004) 'Should autistic children be evaluated for mitochondrial disorders?' *Journal of Child Neurology, 19*(5): 379–381.

Le Parc, J-M. (2005) 'Marfan syndrome.', *Orphanet Encyclopaedia*, Downloadable from www.orpha.net/data/pathol/GB/uk-marfan.pdf.

Leuzzi, V. (2002) 'Inborn errors of creatine metabolism and epilepsy: clinical features, diagnosis, and treatment.' *Journal of Child Neurology, 17*, Supplement 3: S89–S97.

Leuzzi, V., Bianchi, M.C., Tosetti, M., Carducci, C. *et al.* (2000) 'Clinical significance of brain phenylalanine concentration assessed by in vivo proton magnetic resonance spectroscopy in phenylketonuria.', *Journal of Inherited Metabolic Disease, 23*: 563–570.

Leuzzi, V., Di Sabato, M.L., Deodato, F., Rizzo, C. *et al.* (2007) 'Vigabatrin improves paroxysmal dystonia in succinic semialdehyde dehydrogenase deficiency.', *Neurology, 68*: 1320–1321.

Leuzzi, V., Di Sabato, M.L., Zollino, M., Montanaro, M.L. and Seri, S. (2004) 'Early-onset encephalopathy and cortical myoclonus in a boy with MeCP2 gene mutation.', *Neurology, 63*: 1968–1970.

Levin, A.V., Seidman, D.J., Nelson, L.B. and Jackson, L.G. (1990) 'Ophthalmologic findings in the Cornelia de Lange syndrome.', *Journal of Pediatric Ophthalmology and Strabismus, 27*: 94–102.

Levin, M. (1929) 'Narcolepsy (Gelineau's syndrome) and other varieties of morbid somnolence.', *Archives of Neurology and Psychiatry, 22*: 1172–1200.

Levin, M. (1936) 'Periodic somnolence and morbid hunger: a new syndrome.', *Brain, 59*: 494–504.

Levine, T.M., Materek, A., Abel, J., O'Donnell, M. and Cutting, L.E. (2006) 'Cognitive profile of neurofibromatosis type 1.', *Seminars in Pediatric Neurology, 13*: 8–20.

Levitas, A.S. and Reid, C.S. (1998) 'Rubinstein-Taybi syndrome and psychiatric disorders.', *Journal of Intellectual Disability Research, 42*(4): 284–292.

Levitin, D.J., Menon, V., Schmitt, J.E., Eliez, S. *et al.* (2003) 'Neural correlates of auditory perception in Williams syndrome: an fMRI study.', *Neuroimage, 18*(1): 74–82.

Levitt, P., Eagleson, K.L. and Powell, E.M. (2004) 'Regulation of neocortical interneuron development and the implications for neurodevelopmental disorders.', *Trends in the Neurosciences, 27*(7): 400–406.

Levy, A., Michel, G., Lemerrer, M. and Philip, N. (1997) 'Idiopathic thrombocytopenic purpura in two mothers of children with DiGeorge sequence: a new component manifestation of deletion 22q11?' *American Journal of Medical Genetics, 69*: 356–359.

Levy, H.L., Guldberg, P., Guttler, F., Hanley, W.B. *et al.* (2001) 'Congenital heart disease in maternal phenylketonuria: report from the Maternal PKU Collaborative Study.', *Pediatric Research, 49*: 636–642.

Levy, H.L., Karolkewicz, V., Houghton, S.A. and MacCready, R.A. (1970) 'Screening the "normal" population in Massachusetts for phenylketonuria.', *New England Journal of Medicine, 282*: 1455–1458.

Levy, H.L., Lobbregt, D., Barnes, P.D. and Poussaint, T.Y. (1996) 'Maternal phenylketonuria: magnetic resonance imaging of the brain in offspring.', *Journal of Pediatrics, 128*: 770–775.

Levy, H.L., Waisbren, S.E., Lobbregt, D., Allred, E. *et al.* (1995) 'Maternal mild hyperphenylalaninaemia: an international survey of offspring outcome.', *Obstetrical and Gynecological Survey, 50*(6): 430–431.

Levy, S.E. and Hyman, S.L. (2005) 'Novel treatments for autistic spectrum disorders.' *Mental Retardation and Developmental Disabilities Research Reviews, 11*: 131–142.

Levy, S.E., Mandell, D.S., Merhar, S., Ittenbach, R.F. and Pinto-Martin, J.A. (2003) 'Use of complementary and alternative medicine among children recently diagnosed with autistic spectrum disorder.' *Journal of Developmental and Behavioural Pediatrics, 24*(6): 418–423.

Levy, S.E., Souders, M.C., Ittenbach, R.F., Giarelli, E. *et al.* (2007) 'Relationship of dietary intake to gastrointestinal symptoms in children with autistic spectrum disorders.', *Biological Psychiatry, 61*: 492–497.

Lewis, J.C., Thomas, H.V., Murphy, K.C. and Sampson, J.R. (2004) 'Genotype and psychological phenotype in tuberous sclerosis.', (Letter) *Journal of Medical Genetics, 41*: 203–207.

Lewis, K.E., Lubetsky, M.J., Wenger, S.L. and Steele, M.W. (1995) 'Chromosomal abnormalities in a psychiatric population.', *American Journal of Medical Genetics, 60*(1): 53–54.

Li, D.Y., Brooke, B., Davis, E.C., Mecham, R.P. *et al.* (1998) 'Elastin is an essential determinant of arterial morphogenesis.', *Nature, 393*(6682): 276–280.

Li, D.Y., Faury, G., Taylor, D.G., Davis, E.C. *et al.* (1998) 'Novel arterial pathology in mice and humans hemizygous for elastin.', *Journal of Clinical Investigation, 102*: 1783–1787.

Li, J.B., Gerdes, J.M., Haycraft, C.J., Fan, Y. *et al.* (2004) 'Comparative genomics identifies a flagellar and basal body proteome that includes the BBS5 human disease gene.', *Cell, 117*: 541–552.

Liu, K-Y., King, M. and Bearman, P.S. (2010) 'Social Influence and the Autism Epidemic.' *American Journal of Sociology, 115*(5): 1387–1434.

Liu, K-Y., Zerubavel, N. and Bearman, P.S. (2010) 'Social Demographic Change and Autism.' *Demography, 47*(2): 327–343.

Li, M., Shuman, C., Fei, Y.L., Cutiongco, E. *et al.* (2001) 'GPC3 mutation analysis in a spectrum of patients with overgrowth expands the phenotype of Simpson-Golabi-Behmel syndrome.', *American Journal of Medical Genetics, 102*: 161–168.

Li, X.M., Salido, E.C., Gong, Y., Kitada, K. *et al.* (1996) 'Cloning of the rat steroid sulfatase gene (Sts), a non-pseudoautosomal X-linked gene that undergoes X inactivation.', *Mammalian Genome, 7*: 420–424.

Li, Y., Nowotny, P., Holmans, P., Smemo, S. *et al.* (2004) 'Association of late-onset Alzheimer's disease with genetic variation in multiple members of the GAPD gene family.' *Proceedings of the National Academy of Science USA, 101*: 15688–15693.

Li, Y., Podsypanina, K., Liu, X., Crane, A. *et al.* (2001) 'Deficiency of Pten accelerates mammary oncogenesis in MMTV-Wnt-1 transgenic mice.', *BMC Molecular Biology, 2*: 2, www.biomedcentral.com/1471-2199/2/2

Lian, G. and Sheen, V. (2006) 'Cerebral developmental disorders.', *Current Opinion in Pediatrics, 18*: 614–620.

Liao, J., Kochilas, L., Nowotschin, S., Arnold, J.S. *et al.* (2004) 'Full spectrum of malformations in velocardiofacial syndrome/DiGeorge syndrome mouse models by altering Tbx1 dosage.', *Human Molecular Genetics, 13*: 1577–1585.

Licht, D.J. and Lynch, D.R. (2002) 'Juvenile dentatorubral-pallidoluysian atrophy: new clinical features.', *Pediatric Neurology, 26*(1): 51–54.

Lichtner, P., König, R., Hasegawa, T., Van Esch, H. *et al.* (2000) 'An HDR (hypoparathyroidism, deafness, renal dysplasia) syndrome locus maps distal to the DiGeorge syndrome region on 10p13/14.', *Journal of Medical Genetics, 37*: 33–37.

Liebermann, F. and Korf, B.R. (1999) 'Emerging approaches toward the treatment of neurofibromatoses.', *Genetics and Medicine, 1*: 158–164.

Lightdale, J.R., Siegel, B. and Heyman, M.B. (2001) 'Gastrointestinal symptoms in autistic children.' *Clinical Perspectives on Gastroenterology, 1*: 56–58.

Lilienfeld, S.O. (2005) 'Scientifically unsupported and supported interventions for childhood psychopathology: a summary.', *Pediatrics, 115*: 761–764.

Lima, M.D.M., Marques, Y.M.F.S., Alves-Júnior, S.M., Ortega, K.L. *et al.* (2007) 'Distraction osteogenesis in Goldenhar syndrome: case report and 8-year follow-up.', *Medicina Oral, Patologia Oral Y Cirugia Bucal, 12*(7): E528–531.

Limperopoulos, C., Bassan, H., Sullivan, N.R., Soul, J.S. *et al.* (2008) 'Positive screening for autism in ex-preterm infants: prevalence and risk factors.', *Pediatrics, 121*(4): 758–765.

Limperopoulos, C. and du Plessis, A.J. (2006) 'Disorders of cerebellar growth and development.', *Current Opinion in Pediatrics, 18*: 621–627.

Lin, A.E., Birch, P.H., Korf, B.R., Tenconi, R. *et al.* (2000) 'Cardiovascular malformations and other cardiovascular abnormalities in neurofibromatosis 1.', *American Journal of Medical Genetics, 95*(2): 108–117.

Lin, A.E., Neri, G., Hughes-Benzie, R. and Weksberg, R. (1999) 'Cardiac anomalies in the Simpson-Golabi-Behmel syndrome.' *American Journal of Medical Genetics, 83*: 378–381.

Lin, A.E., Siebert, J.R. and Graham, J.M. Jr. (1990) 'Central nervous system malformations in the CHARGE association.', *American Journal of Medical Genetics, 37*: 304–310.

Linck, L.M., Lin, D.S., Flavell, D., Connor, W.E. and Steiner, R.D. (2000) 'Cholesterol supplementation with egg yolk increases plasma cholesterol and decreases plasma 7-dehydrocholesterol in Smith-Lemli-Opitz syndrome.', *American Journal of Medical Genetics, 93*: 360–365.

Linden, M.G. and Bender, B.G. (2002) 'Fifty-one prenatally diagnosed children and adolescents with sex chromosome abnormalities.', *American Journal of Medical Genetics, 110*: 118.

Linden, M.G., Bender, B.G. and Robinson, A. (1996) 'Intrauterine diagnosis of sex chromosome aneuploidy.', *Obstetric and Gynecology, 87*: 468–475.

Linden, M.G., Tassone, F., Gane, L.W., Hills, J.L. *et al.* (1999) 'Compound heterozygous female with fragile-X syndrome.', *American Journal of Medical Genetics, 83*: 318–321.

Lindor, N.M., Kasperbauer, J.L., Hoffman, A.D., Parisi, J.E. *et al.* (2002) 'Confirmation of existence of a new syndrome: LAPS syndrome.', *American Journal of Medical Genetics, 109*(2): 93–99.

Lindsay, E.A., Botta, A., Jurecic, V., Carattini-Rivera, S. *et al.* (1999) 'Congenital heart disease in mice deficient for the DiGeorge syndrome region.', *Nature, 401*: 379–383.

Lindsay, E.A., Vitelli, F., Su, H., Morishima, M. *et al.* (2001) 'Tbx1 haploinsufficiency in the DiGeorge syndrome region causes aortic arch defects in mice.', *Nature, 410*: 97–101.

Linnell, J.C. and Matthews, D.M. (1984) 'Cobalamin metabolism and its clinical aspects.', *Clinical Science, 66*(2): 113–121.

Lintas, C. and Persico, A.M. (2008) 'Autistic phenotypes and genetic testing: state-of-the-art for the clinical geneticist.', *Journal of Medical Genetics*, doi:10.1136/jmg.2008.060871.

Lion-François, L., Cheillan, D., Pitelet, G., Acquaviva-Bourdain, C. *et al.* (2006) 'High frequency of creatine deficiency syndromes in patients with unexplained mental retardation.', *Neurology, 67*(9): 1713–1714.

Lisk, D.R. (2009) 'Kleine-Levin syndrome.', *Practical Neurology, 9*(1): 42–45.

Liu, J., Nyholt, D.R., Magnussen, P., Parano, E. *et al.* (2001) 'A genomewide screen for autism susceptibility loci.', *American Journal of Human Genetics, 69*: 327–340.

Liu, X., Dietrich, K.N., Radcliffe, J., Ragan, N.B. *et al.* (2002) 'Do children with falling blood lead levels have improved cognition?' *Pediatrics, 110*(4): 787–791.

Liu, X., Hubbard, J.A., Fabes, R.A. and Adam, J.B. (2006) 'Sleep disturbances and correlates of children with autism spectrum disorders.' *Child Psychiatry and Human Development, 37*(2): 179–191.

Liu, X.-q., Paterson, A.D., Szatmari, P. and the Autism Genome Project Consortium (2008) 'Genome wide linkage analyses of quantitative and categorical autism subphenotypes.', *Biological Psychiatry, 64*: 561–570.

Lockwood, D., Hecht, F., Dowman, C., Hecht, B.K. *et al.* (1988) 'Chromosome subband 17p11.2 deletion: a minute deletion syndrome.', *Journal of Medical Genetics, 25*: 732–737.

Loesch, D.Z., Bui, Q.M., Dissanayake, C., Clifford, S. *et al.* (2007) 'Molecular and cognitive predictors of the continuum of autistic behaviours in fragile-X.', *Neuroscience and Biobehavioural Reviews, 31*: 315–326.

Løken, A.A., Hanssen, O., Halvorsen, S. and Jolster, N.J. (1961) 'Hereditary renal dysplasia and blindness.', *Acta Paediatrica, 50*: 177–184.

Lombard, J. (1998) 'Autism: a mitochondrial disorder?' *Medical Hypotheses, 50*: 497–500.

Lomri, A., Lemonnier, J., Hott, M., de Parseval, N. *et al.* (1998) 'Increased calvaria cell differentiation and bone matrix formation induced by fibroblast growth factor receptor 2 mutations in Apert syndrome.', *Journal of Clinical Investigation, 101*: 1310–1317.

Longman, C., Tolmie, J., McWilliam, R. and MacLennan, A. (2003) 'Cranial magnetic resonance imaging mistakenly suggests prenatal ischaemia in PEHO-like syndrome.', *Clinical Dysmorphology, 12*: 133–136.

Look, A.T. (2002) 'A leukemogenic twist for GATA1.', *Nature Genetics, 32*: 83–84.

Lopez-Bendito, G., Shigemoto, R., Fairen, A. and Lujan, R. (2002) 'Differential distribution of group 1 metabotropic glutamate receptors during rat cortical development.', *Cerebral Cortex, 12*: 625–638.

Lord, C., Risi, S., Lambrecht, L., Cook, E.H. Jr. *et al.* (2000) 'The autism diagnostic observation schedule-generic: a standard measure of social and communication deficits associated with the spectrum of autism.', *Journal of Autism and Developmental Disorders. 30*(3): 205–223.

Lord, C., Rutter, M. and Le Couteur, A. (1994) 'Autism Diagnostic Interview–Revised: a revised version of a diagnostic interview for caregivers of individuals with possible pervasive developmental disorders.', *Journal of Autism and Developmental Disorders, 24*(5): 659–685.

Lorda-Sanchez, I., Ayuso, C., Sanz, R. and Ibanez, A. (2001) 'Does Bardet-Biedl syndrome have a characteristic face?' *Journal of Medical Genetics, 38*: E14.

Lossi, A.M., Millan, J.M., Villard, L., Orellana, C. *et al.* (1999) 'Mutation of the XNP/ATR-X gene in a family with severe mental retardation, spastic paraplegia and skewed pattern of X inactivation: demonstration that the mutation is involved in the inactivation bias.', *American Journal of Human Genetics, 65*: 558–562.

Lossie, A.C., Whitney, M.M., Amidon, D., Dong, H.J. *et al.* (2001) 'Distinct phenotypes distinguish the molecular classes of Angelman syndrome.', *Journal of Medical Genetics, 38*: 834–845.

Louis, M., Lebacq, J., Poortmans, J.R., Belpaire-Dethiou, M.C. *et al.* (2003) 'Beneficial effects of creatine supplementation in dystrophic patients.', *Muscle and Nerve, 27*: 604–610.

Lowe, T.L., Tanaka, K., Seashore, M.R., Young, J.G. and Cohen, D.J. (1980) 'Detection of phenylketonuria in autistic and psychotic children.', *Journal of the American Medical Association, 243*: 126–128.

Lowe, X., Eskenazi, B., Nelson, D.O., Kidd, S. *et al.* (2001) 'Frequency of XY sperm increases with age in fathers of boys with Klinefelter syndrome.', *American Journal of Human Genetics, 69*: 1046–1054.

Lowry, R.B., Miller, J.R. and Fraser, F.C. (1971) 'A new dominant gene mental retardation syndrome: associated with small stature, tapering fingers, characteristic facies, and possible hydrocephalus.', *American Journal of Diseases of Childhood, 121*: 496–500.

Lu, J.F., Lawler, A.M., Watkins, P.A., Powers, J.M. *et al.* (1997) 'A mouse model for X-linked adrenoleukodystrophy.', *Proceedings of the National Academy of Science USA, 94*(17): 9366–9371.

Lu, T.L., Chang, J.L., Liang, C.C., You, L.R. *et al.* (2007) 'Tumor spectrum, tumor latency and tumor incidence of the Pten-deficient mice.', *PLoS One, 2*(11): e1237.

Lu, Y., Zhao, Y., Liu, G., Wang, X. *et al.* (2002) 'Factor V gene G1691A mutation, prothrombin gene G20210A mutation, and MTHFR gene C677T mutation are not risk factors for pulmonary thromboembolism in Chinese population.', *Thrombosis Research, 106*: 7–12.

Lu, Z., Zhang, R., Carpenter, J.T. and Diasio, R.B. (1998) 'Decreased dihydropyrimidine dehydrogenase activity in a population of patients with breast cancer: implication for 5-fluorouracil-based chemotherapy.', *Clinical Cancer Research, 4*(2): 325–329.

Lu, Z., Zhang, R. and Diasio, R.B. (1993) 'Dihydropyrimidine dehydrogenase activity in human peripheral blood mononuclear cells and liver: population characteristics, newly identified deficient patients, and clinical implication in 5-fluorouracil chemotherapy.', *Cancer Research, 53*: 5433–5438.

Lubs, H.A. Jr. (1969) 'A marker X chromosome.', *American Journal of Human Genetics, 21*: 231–244.

Lucas, R.E., Vlangos, C.N., Das, P., Patel, P.I. and Elsea, S.H. (2001) 'Genomic organisation of the ~1.5 Mb Smith-Magenis syndrome critical interval: transcription map, genomic contig, and candidate gene analysis.', *European Journal of Human Genetics, 9*: 892–902.

Luciani, J.J., de Mas, P., Depetris, D., Mignon-Ravix, C. *et al.* (2003) 'Telomeric 22q13 deletions resulting from rings, simple deletions, and translocations: cytogenetic, molecular, and clinical analyses of 32 new observations.', *Journal of Medical Genetics, 40*: 690–696.

Luders, E., Di Paola, M., Tomaiuolo, F., Thompson, P.M. *et al.* (2007) 'Callosal morphology in Williams syndrome: a new evaluation of shape and thickness.', *Neuroreport, 18*(3): 203–207.

Ludwig, M., Katalinic, A., Gross, S., Sutcliffe, A. *et al.* (2005) 'Increased prevalence of imprinting defects in patients with Angelman syndrome born to subfertile couples.', *Journal of Medical Genetics, 42*: 289–291.

Lueck, J.D., Mankodi, A., Swanson, M.S., Thornton, C.A. and Dirksen, R.T. (2007) 'Muscle chloride channel dysfunction in two mouse models of myotonic dystrophy.', *Journal of General Physiology, 129*(1): 79–94.

Lugenbeel, K.A., Peier, A.M., Carson, N.L., Chudley, A.E. and Nelson, D.L. (1995) 'Intragenic loss of function mutations demonstrate the primary role of FMR1 in fragile-X syndrome.', *Nature Genetics, 10*: 483–485.

Luís, P.B.M., Ruiter, J.P.N., Aires, C.C.P., Soveral, G. et al. (2007) 'Valproic acid metabolites inhibit dihydrolipoyl dehydrogenase activity leading to impaired 2-oxoglutarate-driven oxidative phosphorylation.', *Biochimica et Biophysica Acta (BBA) – Bioenergetics*, 1767(9): 1126–1133.

Lujan, J.E., Carlin, M.E. and Lubs, H.A. (1984) 'A form of X-linked mental retardation with marfanoid habitus.', *American Journal of Medical Genetics*, 17: 311–322.

Lukusa, T., Vermeesch, J.R., Holvoet, M., Fryns, J.P. and Devriendt, K. (2004) 'Deletion 2q37.3 and autism: molecular cytogenetic mapping of the candidate region for autistic disorder.', *Genetic Counselling*, 15(3): 293–301.

Lumley, M.A., Jordan, M., Rubenstein, R., Tsipouras, P. and Evans, M.I. (1994) 'Psychosocial functioning in the Ehlers-Danlos syndrome.', *American Journal of Medical Genetics*, 53(2): 149–152.

Lumley, M.A., Ovies, T., Stettner, L., Wehmer, F. and Lakey, B. (1996) 'Alexithymia, social support and health problems.', *Journal of Psychosomatic Research*, 41(6): 519–530.

Lund, P.M., Puri, N., Durham-Pierre, D., King, R.A. and Brilliant, M.H. (1997) 'Oculocutaneous albinism in an isolated Tonga community in Zimbabwe.', *Journal of Medical Genetics*, 34: 733–735.

Lykkesfeldt, G., Bennett, P., Lykkesfeldt, A.E., Micic, S. et al. (1985) 'Abnormal androgen and oestrogen metabolism in men with steroid sulphatase deficiency and recessive X-linked ichthyosis.', *Clinical Endocrinology*, 23: 385–393.

Lykkesfeldt, G. and Hoyer, H. (1983) 'Topical cholesterol treatment of recessive X-linked ichthyosis.', *Lancet*, 322(8363): 1337–1338.

Lynch, D.R., McDonald-McGinn, D.M., Zackai, E.H., Emanuel, B.S. et al. (1995) 'Cerebellar atrophy in a patient with velocardiofacial syndrome.', [See comments.] *Journal of Medical Genetics*, 32: 561–563.

Lynch, N.E., Lynch, S.A., McMenamin, J. and Webb, D. (2009) 'Bannayan-Riley-Ruvalcaba syndrome: a cause of extreme macrocephaly and neurodevelopmental delay.', *Archives of Disease in Childhood*, 94(7): 553–554.

Lynn, P.M. and Davies, W. (2007) 'The 39,XO mouse as a model for the neurobiology of Turner syndrome and sex-biased neuropsychiatric disorders.', *Behavioural Brain Research*, 179(2): 173–182.

Ma, D., Salyakina, D., Jaworski, J.M., Konidari, I. et al. (2009) 'A genome-wide association study of autism reveals a common novel risk locus at 5p14.1.' *Annals of Human Genetics*, 73(3): 263–273.

Ma, D.Q., Whitehead, P.L., Menold, M.M., Martin, E.R. et al. (2005) 'Identification of significant association and gene-gene interaction of GABA receptor subunit genes in autism.', *American Journal of Human Genetics*, 77: 377–388.

Maaswinkel-Mooij, P.D., Laan, L.A.E.M., Onkenhout, W., Brouwer, O.F. et al. (1997) 'Adenylosuccinase deficiency presenting with epilepsy in early infancy.', *Journal of Inherited Metabolic Disease*, 20: 606–607.

Macarov, M., Zeigler, M., Newman, J.P., Strich, D. et al. (2007) 'Deletions of VCX-A and NLGN4: a variable phenotype including normal intellect.', *Journal of Intellectual Disability Research*, 51(5): 329–333.

McArthur, A.J. and Budden, S.S. (1998) 'Sleep dysfunction in Rett syndrome: a trial of exogenous melatonin treatment.', *Developmental Medicine and Child Neurology*, 40: 186–192.

McBride, S.M.J., Choi, C.H., Wang, Y., Leibelt, D. et al. (2005) 'Pharmacological rescue of synaptic plasticity, courtship behaviour, and mushroom body defects in a drosophila model of fragile-X syndrome.', *Neuron*, 45: 753–764.

McCandless, J. (2007) *Children with Starving Brains: A Medical Treatment Guide for Autism Spectrum Disorder* (3rd ed.). North Bergen, NJ: Bramble Books.

McCandless, S.E., Schwartz, S., Morrison, S., Garlapati, K. and Robin, N.H. (2000) 'Adult with an interstitial deletion of chromosome 10 [del(10)(q25.1q25.3)]: overlap with Coffin-Lowry syndrome.' *American Journal of Medical Genetics*, 95: 93–98.

McCauley, J.L., Li, C., Jiang, L., Olson, L.M. et al. (2005) 'Genome-wide and ordered-subset linkage analyses provide support for autism loci on 17q and 19p with evidence of phenotypic and interlocus genetic correlates.', *BMC Medical Genetics*, 6: 1–11, doi:10.1186/1471-2350-6-1

McClung, C.A. and Nestler, E.J. (2007) 'Neuroplasticity mediated by altered gene expression.', *Neuropsychopharmacology REVIEWS*, 1–15, doi:10.1038/sj.npp.1301544.

MacCollin, M., Willett, C., Heinrich, B., Jacoby, L.B. et al. (2003) 'Familial schwannomatosis: exclusion of the NF2 locus as the germline event.', *Neurology*, 60: 1968–1974.

McConachie, H., Barry, R., Spencer, A., Parker, L. et al. (2009) 'Daslne: the challenge of developing a regional database for autism spectrum disorder.', *Archives of Disease in Childhood*, 94: 38–41.

McConkie-Rosell, A., Lachiewicz, A.M., Spiridigliozzi, G.A., Tarleton, J. et al. (1993) 'Evidence that methylation of the FMR-I locus is responsible for variable phenotypic expression of the fragile-X syndrome.', *American Journal of Human Genetics*, 53: 800–809.

MacDermott, S., Williams, K., Ridley, G., Glasson, E. and Wray, J. (2007) 'The prevalence of autism in Australia: can it be established from existing data?' Overview and Report. Australian Advisory Board on Autism Spectrum Disorders, www.autismaus.com.au/

Macdonald, A., Daly, A., Davies, P., Asplin, D. et al. (2004) 'Protein substitutes for PKU: what's new?' *Journal of Inherited Metabolic Disease*, 27: 363–371.

MacDonald, D.M. (1973) 'De Lange syndrome (Amsterdam dwarfism).', *Proceedings of the Royal Society of Medicine*, 66(12): 1171–1173.

McDonald, J.D., Bode, V.C., Dove, W.F. and Shedlovsky, A. (1990) 'Pah(hph-5): a mouse mutant deficient in phenylalanine hydroxylase.', *Proceedings of the National Academy of Science, USA*, 87: 1965–1967.

McDonald, J.D. and Charlton, C.K. (1997) 'Characterization of mutations at the mouse phenylalanine hydroxylase locus.', *Genomics*, 39: 402–405.

MacDonald, J.L. and Roskams, A.J. (2009) 'Epigenetic regulation of nervous system development by DNA methylation and histone deacetylation.', *Progress in Neurobiology*, 88: 170–183.

MacDonald, M.R., Schaefer, G.B., Olney, A.H., Tamayo, M. and Frias, J.L. (1993) 'Brain magnetic resonance imaging findings in the Opitz G/BBB syndrome: extension of the spectrum of midline brain anomalies.', *American Journal of Medical Genetics, 46*: 706–711.

MacDonald, T.T. and Domizio, P. (2007) 'Autistic enterocolitis: is it a histopathological entity?' *Histopathology, 50*: 371–379, doi:10.1111/j.1365-2559.2007.02606.x

McDonald-McGinn, D.M., Driscoll, D.A., Bason, L., Christensen, K. *et al.* (1995) 'Autosomal dominant "Opitz" GBBB syndrome due to a 22q11.2 deletion.', *American Journal of Medical Genetics, 59*(1): 103–113.

McDonald-McGinn, D.M., Gripp, K.W., Kirschner, R.E., Maisenbacher, M.K. *et al.* (2005) 'Craniosynostosis: another feature of the 22q11.2 deletion syndrome.', *American Journal of Medical Genetics A, 136*: 358–362.

McDonald-McGinn, D.M., Kirschner, R., Goldmuntz, E., Sullivan, K. *et al.* (1999) 'The Philadelphia story: the 22q11.2 deletion: report on 250 patients.', *Genetic Counselling, 10*: 11–24.

McDonald-McGinn, D.M., Minugh-Purvis, N., Kirschner, R.E., Jawad, A. *et al.* (2005) 'The 22q11.2 deletion in African-American patients: an underdiagnosed population?' *American Journal of Medical Genetics A, 134*: 242–246.

McDonald-McGinn, D.M., Tonnesen, M.K., Laufer-Cahana, A., Finucane, B. *et al.* (2001) 'Phenotype of the 22q11.2 deletion in individuals identified through an affected relative: cast a wide FISHing net!' *Genetics in Medicine, 3*: 23–29.

McDowell, T.L., Gibbons, R.J., Sutherland, H., O'Rourke, D.M. *et al.* (1999) 'Localization of a putative transcriptional regulator (ATRX) at pericentromeric heterochromatin and the short arms of acrocentric chromosomes.' *Proceedings of the National Academy of Science USA, 96*: 13983–13988.

McDougle, C.J., Naylor, S.T., Cohen, D.J., Aghajanian, G.K. *et al.* (1996) 'Effects of tryptophan depletion in drug-free adults with autistic disorder.', *Archives of General Psychiatry, 53*(11): 993–1000.

McEwing, R.L., Joelle, R., Mohlo, M., Bernard, J.P. *et al.* (2006) 'Prenatal diagnosis of neurofibromatosis type 1: sonographic and MRI findings.', *Prenatal Diagnosis, 26*: 1110–1114.

MacFabe, D.F., Cain, D.P., Rodriguez-Capote, K., Franklin, A.E. *et al.* (2007) 'Neurobiological effects of intraventricular propionic acid in rats: possible role of short chain fatty acids on the pathogenesis and characteristics of autism spectrum disorders.' *Behavioural Brain Research, 176*: 149–169.

McFadden, S.A. (1996) 'Phenotypic variation in xenobiotic metabolism and adverse environmental response: focus on sulfur-dependent detoxification pathways.' *Toxicology, 111*(1–3): 43–65.

McFee, R.B. and Caraccio, T.R. (2001) 'Intravenous mercury injection and ingestion: clinical manifestations and management.' *Journal of Toxicology and Clinical Toxicology, 39*(7): 733–738.

McGaughran, J., Donnai, D., Clayton, P. and Mills, K. (1994) 'Diagnosis of Smith-Lemli-Opitz syndrome.', (Letter) *New England Journal of Medicine, 330*: 1685–1686.

McGhee, E.M., Klump, C.J., Bitts, S.M., Cotter, P.D. and Lammer, E.J. (2000) 'Candidate region for Coffin-Siris syndrome at 7q32–34.', *American Journal of Medical Genetics, 93*: 241–243.

McGinniss, M.J., Kazazian, H.H. Jr., Stetten, G., Petersen, T.M.B. *et al.* (1992) 'Mechanisms of ring chromosome formation in 11 cases of human ring chromosome 21.', *American Journal of Human Genetics, 50*: 15–28.

McGue, M. and Bouchard, T.J. Jr. (1998) 'Genetic and environmental influences on human behavioural differences.' *Annual Review of Neuroscience, 21*: 1–24.

McKeever, K., Shepherd, C.W., Crawford, H. and Morrison, P.J. (2008) 'An epidemiological, clinical and genetic survey of neurofibromatosis type 1 in children under sixteen years of age.', *Ulster Medical Journal, 77*(3): 160–163.

McKeever, P.A. and Young, I.D. (1990) 'Smith-Lemli-Opitz syndrome II: a disorder of the foetal adrenals?' *Journal of Medical Genetics, 27*: 465–466.

MacKenzie, J.J., Sumargo, I. and Taylor, S.A.M. (2006) 'A cryptic full mutation in a male with a classical fragile-X phenotype.', *Clinical Genetics, 70*: 39–42.

McKenzie, O., Ponte, M., Mangelsdorf, M., Finnis, G. *et al.* (2007) 'Aristaless-related homeobox gene, the gene responsible for West syndrome and related disorders, is a Groucho/transducin-like enhancer of split dependent transcriptional repressor.', *Neuroscience*, doi:10.1016/j.neuroscience.2007.01.038.

McKusick, V.A. (1969) 'On Lumpers and Splitters, or the Nosology of Genetic Disease.' *Birth Defects: Original Article Series, 5*(1): 23–32.

MacLean, J.E., Teshima, I.E., Szatmari, P. and Nowaczyk, M.J. (2000) 'Ring chromosome 22 and autism: report and review.', *American Journal of Medical Genetics, 90*(5): 382–385.

Maclean, K., Field, M.J., Colley, A.S., Mowat, D.R. *et al.* (2004) 'Kousseff syndrome: a causally heterogeneous disorder.', *American Journal of Medical Genetics, 124A*: 307–312.

McLean-Tooke, A., Barge, D., Spickett, G.P. and Gennery, A.R. (2008) 'Immunologic defects in 22q11.2 deletion syndrome.', *Journal of Allergy and Clinical Immunology, 122*: 362–367.

McMulkin, M.L., Baird, G.O., Caskey, P.M. and Ferguson, R.L. (2006) 'Comprehensive outcomes of surgically treated idiopathic toe walkers.', *Journal of Pediatric Orthopedics, 26*(5): 606–611.

McNairn, A.J. and Gerton, J.L. (2008a) 'The chromosome glue gets a little stickier.', *Trends in Genetics, 24*(8): 382–389.

McNairn, A.J. and Gerton, J.L. (2008b) 'Cohesinopathies: one ring, many obligations.', *Mutation Research, 647*(1–2): 103–111.

McPherson, E.W., Laneri, G., Clemens, M.M., Kochmar, S.J. and Surti, U. (1997) 'Apparently balanced t(1;7)(q21.3;q34) in an infant with Coffin-Siris syndrome.', *American Journal of Medical Genetics, 71*: 430–433.

Madaan, V., Dewan, V., Ramaswamy, S. and Sharma, A. (2006) 'Behavioural manifestations of Sturge-Weber syndrome: a case report.', *Primary Care Companion to the Journal of Clinical Psychiatry.' 8*(4): 198–200.

Maddalena, A., Sosnoski, D.M., Berry, G.T. and Nussbaum, R.L. (1988) 'Mosaicism for an intragenic deletion in a boy with mild ornithine transcarbamylase deficiency.', *New England Journal of Medicine, 319*: 999–1003.

Maddocks, J. and Reed, T. (1989) 'Urine test for adenylosuccinase deficiency in autistic children.' (Letter) *Lancet, 338*(8630): 158–159.

Madsen, P.P., Kibaek, M., Roca, X., Sachidanandam, R. *et al.* (2006) 'Short/branched-chain acyl-CoA dehydrogenase deficiency due to an IVS3+3A-G mutation that causes exon skipping.', *Human Genetics, 118*: 680–690.

Magenis, R.E., Toth-Fejel, S., Allen, L.J., Black, M. *et al.* (1990) 'Comparison of the 15q deletions in Prader-Willi and Angelman syndromes: specific regions, extent of deletions, parental origin, and clinical consequences.', *American Journal of Medical Genetics, 35*: 333–349.

Magenis, R.E., Toth-Fejel, S., Allen, L.J., Cohen, R. *et al.* (1988) 'Angelman happy puppet and Prader Willi syndromes: do they share an identical deletion?' (Abstract) *American Journal of Human Genetics, 43*: A113.

Magnus, P., Irgens, L.M., Haug, K., Nystad, W. *et al.* (2006) 'Cohort profile: the Norwegian Mother and Child Cohort Study (MoBa).', *International Journal of Epidemiology, 35*(5): 1146–1150.

Mahadevan, M.S., Yadava, R.S., Yu, Q., Balijepalli, S. *et al.* (2006) 'Reversible model of RNA toxicity and cardiac conduction defects in myotonic dystrophy.', *Nature Genetics, 38*: 1066–1070.

Mahfoud, A., Domínguez, C.L., Pérez, A., Rodríguez, T. *et al.* (2004) ['L-2-hydroxyglutaric aciduria: clinical, biochemical and neuroradiological findings in two Venezuelan patients.'][Article in Spanish.] *Revista de Neurologia, 39*(4): 343–346.

Mahmood, A., Bibat, G., Zhan, A-L., Izbudak, I. *et al.* (2009) 'White matter impairment in Rett Syndrome: diffusion tensor imaging study with clinical correlations.', *American Journal of Neuroradiology,* 10.3174/ajnr.A1792 [Epub ahead of print].

Maier, E.M., Kammerer, S., Muntau, A.C., Wichers, M. *et al.* (2002) 'Symptoms in carriers of adrenoleukodystrophy relate to skewed X inactivation.', *Annals of Neurology, 52*: 683–688.

Maillot, F., Lilburn, M., Baudin, J., Morley, D.W. and Lee, P.J. (2008) 'Factors influencing outcomes in the offspring of mothers with phenylketonuria during pregnancy: the importance of variation in maternal blood phenylalanine.', *American Journal of Clinical Nutrition, 88*(3): 700–705.

Maimburg, R.D. and Vaeth, M. (2006) 'Perinatal risk factors and infantile autism.' *Acta Psychiatrica Scandinavica, 114*(4): 257–264.

Makedonski, K., Abuhatzira, L., Kaufman, Y., Razin, A. and Shemer, R. (2005) 'MeCP2 deficiency in Rett syndrome causes epigenetic aberrations at the PWS/AS imprinting center that affects UBE3A expression.', *Human Molecular Genetics, 14*(8): 1049–1058.

Mainardi, P.C. (2006) 'Cri du chat syndrome.', *Orphanet Journal of Rare Diseases, 1*: 33, doi:10.1186/1750-1172-1-33.

Maiwald, R., Bonte, A., Jung, H., Bitter, P. *et al.* (2002) '*De novo* MeCP2 mutation in a 46,XX male patient with Rett syndrome.', (Letter) *Neurogenetics, 4*: 107–108.

Mak, C.M., Siu, T.S., Lam, C.W., Chan, G.C. *et al.* (2007) 'Complete recovery from acute encephalopathy of late-onset ornithine transcarbamylase deficiency in a 3-year-old boy.', *Journal of Inherited Metabolic Disease, 30*(6): 981.

Malcolm, S., Clayton-Smith, J., Nichols, M., Robb, S. *et al.* (1991) 'Uniparental paternal disomy in Angelman's syndrome.', *Lancet, 337*: 694–697.

Malcolm, S., Webb, T., Rutland, P., Middleton-Price, H.R. and Pembrey, M.E. (1990) 'Molecular genetic studies of Angelman's syndrome.', (Abstract) *Journal of Medical Genetics, 27*: 205.

Malini, S.S. and Ramachandra, N.B. (2006) 'Influence of advanced age of maternal grandmothers on Down syndrome.', *BMC Medical Genetics, 7*: 4, doi:10.1186/1471-2350-7-4.

Malinow, R. and Malenka, R.C. (2002) 'AMPA receptor trafficking and synaptic plasticity.', *Annual Review of Neuroscience, 25*: 103–126.

Mallin, S.R. and Walker, F.A. (1972) 'Effects of the XYY karyotype in one of two brothers with congenital adrenal hyperplasia.', *Clinical Genetics, 3*(6): 490–494.

Malo, D., Schurr, E., Dorfman, J., Canfield, V. *et al.* (1991) 'Three brain sodium channel alpha-subunit genes are clustered on the proximal segment of mouse chromosome 2.', *Genomics, 10*: 666–672.

Malo, M.S., Blanchard, B.J., Andresen, J.M., Srivastava, K. *et al.* (1994a) 'Localization of a putative human brain sodium channel gene (SCN1A) to chromosome band 2q24.', *Cytogenetics and Cell Genetics, 67*: 178–186.

Malo, M.S., Srivastava, K., Andresen, J.M., Chen, X-N. *et al.* (1994b) 'Targeted gene walking by low stringency polymerase chain reaction: assignment of a putative human brain sodium channel gene (SCN3A) to chromosome 2q24–31.', *Proceedings of the National Academy of Science USA, 91*: 2975–2979.

Malvy, J., Barthélémy, C., Damie, D., Lenoir, P. *et al.* (2004) 'Behaviour profiles in a population of infants later diagnosed as having autistic disorder.', *European Journal of Child and Adolescent Psychiatry, 13*: 115–122.

Mancuso, M., Pazzaglia, S., Tanori, M., Hahn, H. *et al.* (2004) 'Basal cell carcinoma and its development: insights from radiation-induced tumors in *Ptch1*-deficient mice.', *Cancer Research, 64*: 934–941.

Mankodi, A., Logigian, E., Callahan, L., McClain, C. *et al.* (2000) 'Myotonic dystrophy in transgenic mice expressing an expanded CUG repeat.', *Science, 289*: 1769–1772.

Mankodi, A., Takahashi, M.P., Jiang, H., Beck, C.L. *et al.* (2002) 'Expanded CUG repeats trigger aberrant splicing of ClC-1 chloride channel pre-mRNA and hyperexcitability of skeletal muscle in myotonic dystrophy.', *Molecular Cell, 10*: 35–44.

Mankoski, R.E., Collins, M., Ndosi, N.K., Mgalla, E.H. *et al.* (2006) 'Etiologies of autism in a case-series from Tanzania.' *Journal of Autism and Developmental Disorders, 36*: 1039–1051.

Manning, M.A., Cassidy, S.B., Clericuzio, C., Cherry, A.M. *et al.* (2004) 'Terminal 22q deletion syndrome: a newly recognized cause of speech and language disability in the autism spectrum.' *Pediatrics, 114*: 451–457.

Manouvrier-Hanu, S., Amiel, J., Jacquot, S., Merienne, K. *et al.* (1999) 'Unreported RSK2 missense mutation in two male sibs with an unusually mild form of Coffin-Lowry syndrome.', *Journal of Medical Genetics, 36*: 775–778.

Mans, D.A., Voest, E.E. and Giles, R.H. (2008) 'All along the watchtower: is the cilium a tumor suppressor organelle?' *Biochimica et Biophysica Acta, 1786*: 114–125.

Mantilla-Capacho, J.M., Arnaud, L., Diaz-Rodriguez, M. and Barros-Nunez, P. (2005) 'Apert syndrome with preaxial polydactyly showing the typical mutation Ser252Trp in the FGFR2 gene.', *Genetic Counselling, 16*: 403–406.

Manto, M.U. (2005) 'The wide spectrum of spinocerebellar ataxias (SCAs).', *Cerebellum, 4*: 2–6.

Manzur, A.Y., Kuntzer, T., Pike, M. and Swan, A. (2008) 'Glucocorticoid corticosteroids for Duchenne muscular dystrophy.', (Update) *Cochrane Database Systematic Reviews*, (1): CD003725.

Mao, J-R. and Bristow, J. (2001) 'The Ehlers-Danlos syndrome: on beyond collagens.', *The Journal of Clinical Investigation, 107*(9): 1063–1069.

Marco, E.J. and Skuse, D.H. (2006) 'Autism-lessons from the X chromosome.', *SCAN (Social Cognitive and Affective Neuroscience), 1*: 183–193.

Marcos, J., Guo, L.W., Wilson, W.K., Porter, F.D. and Shackleton, C. (2004) 'The implications of 7-dehydrosterol-7-reductase deficiency (Smith-Lemli-Opitz syndrome) to neurosteroid production.', *Steroids, 69*: 51–60.

Marcus, A., Sinnott, B., Bradley, S. and Grey, I. (2010) 'Treatment of idiopathic toe-walking in children with autism using GaitSpot Auditory Speakers and simplified habit reversal.', *Research in Autism Spectrum Disorders, 4*: 260–267.

Margallo-Lana, M.L., Moore, P.B., Kay, D.W., Perry, R.H. *et al.* (2007) 'Fifteen-year follow-up of 92 hospitalized adults with Down's syndrome: incidence of cognitive decline, its relationship to age and neuropathology.', *Journal of Intellectual Disability Research, 51*(6): 463–477.

Mari, A., Amati, F., Mingarelli, R., Giannotti, A. *et al.* (1995) 'Analysis of the elastin gene in 60 patients with clinical diagnosis of Williams syndrome.', *Human Genetics, 96*: 444–448.

Mari, F., Azimonti, S., Bertani, I., Bolognese, F. *et al.* (2005) 'CDKL5 belongs to the same molecular pathway of MeCP2 and it is responsible for the early-onset seizure variant of Rett syndrome.', *Human Molecular Genetics, 14*: 1935–1946.

Maria, B.L., Boltshauser, E., Palmer, S.C. and Tran, T.X. (1999a) 'Clinical features and revised diagnostic criteria in Joubert syndrome.', *Journal of Child Neurology, 14*: 583–590.

Maria, B.L., Hoang, K.B., Tusa, R.J., Mancuso, A.A. *et al.* (1997) '"Joubert syndrome" revisited: key ocular motor signs with magnetic resonance imaging correlation.', *Journal of Child Neurology, 12*: 423–430.

Maria, B.L., Bozorgmanesh, A., Kimmel, K.N., Theriaque, D. and Quisling, R.G. (2001) 'Quantitative assessment of brainstem development in Joubert syndrome and Dandy-Walker syndrome.', *Journal of Child Neurology, 16*: 751–758.

Maria, B.L., Quisling, R.G., Rosainz, L.C., Yachnis, A.T. *et al.* (1999b) 'Molar tooth sign in Joubert syndrome: clinical, radiologic, and pathologic significance.', *Journal of Child Neurology, 14*: 368–376.

Marie, S., Cuppens, H., Heutersprete, M., Jaspers, M. *et al.* (1999) 'Mutation analysis in adenylosuccinate lyase deficiency: eight novel mutations in the re-evaluated full ADSL coding sequence.', *Human Mutation, 13*: 197–202.

Marinaki, A.M., Champion, M., Kurian, M.A., Simmonds, H.A. *et al.* (2004) 'Adenylosuccinate lyase deficiency – first British case.', *Nucleosides, Nucleotides and Nucleic Acids, 23*: 1231–1233.

Mariner, R., Jackson, A., Levitas, A., Hagerman, R. *et al.* (1986) 'Autism, mental retardation and chromosomal abnormalities.', *Journal of Autism and Developmental Disorders, 16*: 425–440.

Marino, B., Digilio, M.C., Toscano, A., Anaclerio, S. *et al.* (2001) 'Anatomic patterns of conotruncal defects associated with deletion 22q11.', *Genetics in Medicine, 3*(1): 45–48.

Markert, M.L., Boeck, A., Hale, L.P., Kloster, A.L. *et al.* (1999) 'Transplantation of thymus tissue in complete DiGeorge syndrome.', *New England Journal of Medicine, 341*: 1180–1189.

Markert, M.L., Devlin, B.H., Alexieff, M.J., Li, J. *et al.* (2007) 'Review of 54 patients with complete DiGeorge anomaly enrolled in protocols for thymus transplantation: outcome of 44 consecutive transplants.', *Blood, 109*(10): 4539–4547.

Maroteaux, P., Stanescu, R., Stanescu, V. and Rappaport, R. (1986) 'Acromicric dysplasia.', *American Journal of Medical Genetics, 24*: 447–459.

Marsh, D.J., Coulon, V., Lunetta, K.L., Rocca-Serra, P. *et al.* (1998) 'Mutation spectrum and genotype-phenotype analyses in Cowden disease and Bannayan-Zonana syndrome, two hamartoma syndromes with germline PTEN mutation.', *Human Molecular Genetics, 7*: 507–515.

Marsh, D.J., Kum, J.B., Lunetta, K.L., Bennett, M.J. *et al.* (1999) 'PTEN mutation spectrum and genotype-phenotype correlations in Bannayan-Riley-Ruvalcaba syndrome suggest a single entity with Cowden syndrome.' *Human Molecular Genetics, 8*(8): 1461–1472.

Marsh, R.W. and Cabaret, J.J. (1972) 'Down's syndrome treated with a low phenylalanine diet: case report.', *New Zealand Medical Journal, 75*(481): 364–365.

Marsh, S.E., Grattan-Smith, P., Pereira, J., Barkovich, A.J. and Gleeson, J.G. (2004) 'Neuroepithelial cysts in a patient with Joubert syndrome plus renal cysts.', *Journal of Child Neurology, 19*: 227–231.

Marshall, C.R., Noor, A., Vincent, J.B., Lionel, A.C. *et al.* (2008) 'Structural variation of chromosomes in autism spectrum disorder.', *American Journal of Human Genetics, 82*(2): 477–488.

Marshall, P.D. and Galasko, C.S. (1995) 'No improvement in delay in diagnosis of Duchenne muscular dystrophy.', [Letter] *Lancet, 345*: 590–591.

Marshall, W.F. (2008) 'The cell biological basis of ciliary disease.', *Journal of Cell Biology, 180*(1): 17–21.

Martanová, H., Krepelová, A., Baxová, A., Hansíková, H. et al. (2007) 'X-linked dominant chondrodysplasia punctata (CDPX2): multisystemic impact of the defect in cholesterol biosynthesis.', *Prague Medical Report*, *108*(3): 263–269.

Martin, C.L. and Ledbeter, D.H. (2007) 'Autism and cytogenetic abnormalities: solving autism one chromosome at a time.' *Current Psychiatry Reports*, *9*: 141–147.

Martin, D.M., Sheldon, S. and Gorski, J.L. (2001) 'CHARGE association with choanal atresia and inner ear hypoplasia in a child with a *de novo* chromosome translocation t(2;7)(p14;q21.11).', *American Journal of Medical Genetics*, *99*: 115–119.

Martin, J.P. and Bell, J. (1943) 'A pedigree of mental defect showing sex-linkage.', *Journal of Neurology and Psychiatry*, *6*: 154–157.

Martin, R.A., Grange, D.K., Zehnbauer, B. and DeBaun, M.R. (2005) 'LIT1 and H19 methylation defects in isolated hemihyperplasia.', *American Journal of Medical Genetics*, *134A*(2): 129–131.

Martin, S.C., Wolters, P.L. and Smith A.C. (2006) 'Adaptive and maladaptive behaviour in Children with Smith-Magenis syndrome.', *Journal of Autism and Developmental Disorders*, *36*: 541–552.

Martinelli, M., Scapoli, L., Pezzetti, F., Carinci, F. et al. (2001) 'C677T variant form at the MTHFR gene and CL/P: a risk factor for mothers?' *American Journal of Medical Genetics*, *98*: 357–360.

Martinho, P.S., Otto, P.G., Kok, F., Diament, A. et al. (1990) 'In search of a genetic basis for the Rett syndrome.', *Human Genetics*, *86*: 131–134.

Martins, S., Matama, T., Guimaraes, L., Vale, J. et al. (2003) 'Portuguese families with dentatorubropallidoluysian atrophy (DRPLA) share a common haplotype of Asian origin.', *European Journal of Human Genetics*, *11*: 808–811.

Marui, T., Hashimoto, O., Nanba, E., Kato, C. et al. (2004a) 'Association between the neurofibromatosis-1 (NF1) locus and autism in the Japanese population.', *American Journal of Medical Genetics B Neuropsychiatric Genetics*, *131*: 43–47.

Marui, T., Hashimoto, O., Nanba, E., Kato, C. et al. (2004b) 'Gastrin-releasing peptide receptor (GRPR) locus in Japanese subjects with autism.', *Brain and Development*, *26*(1): 5–7.

Marvit, J., DiLella, A.G., Brayton, K., Ledley, F.D. et al. (1987) 'GT to AT transition at a splice donor site causes skipping of the preceding exon in phenylketonuria.', *Nucleic Acids Research*, *15*: 5613–5628.

Masi, G., Favilla, L. and Millepiedi, S. (2000) 'The Kleine-Levin syndrome as a neuropsychiatric disorder: a case report.', *Psychiatry*, *63*(1): 93–100.

Maslen, C., Babcock, D., Robinson, S.W., Bean, L.J.H. et al. (2006) 'CRELD1 mutations contribute to the occurrence of cardiac atrioventricular septal defects in Down syndrome.', *American Journal of Medical Genetics*, *140A*: 2501–2505.

Mason, A., Banerjee, S., Eapen, V., Zeitlin, H. and Robertson, M.M. (1998) 'The prevalence of Tourette syndrome in a mainstream school population.', *Developmental Medicine and Child Neurology*, *40*(5): 292–296.

Matalon, R., Koch, R., Michals-Matalon, K., Moseley, K. et al. (2004) 'Biopterin responsive phenylalanine hydroxylase deficiency.', *Genetics in Medicine*, *6*: 27–32.

Matalon, R., Surendran, S., Matalon, K.M., Tyring, S. et al. (2003) 'Future role of large neutral amino acids in transport of phenylalanine into the brain.', *Pediatrics*, *112*: 1570–1574.

Matsuda, I., Matsuura, T., Nishiyori, A., Komaki, S. et al. (1996) 'Phenotypic variability in male patients carrying the mutant ornithine transcarbamylase (OTC) allele, arg40his, ranging from a child with an unfavourable prognosis to an asymptomatic older adult.', *Journal of Medical Genetics*, *33*: 645–648.

Matsuoka, R., Takao, A., Kimura, M., Imamura, S. et al. (1994) 'Confirmation that the conotruncal anomaly face syndrome is associated with a deletion within 22q11.2.', *American Journal of Medical Genetics*, *53*: 285–289.

Matsuura, K., Morimoto, Y., Sugimura, M., Taki, K. et al. (2009) ['Case report of dentatorubral pallidoluysian atrophy in a patient on a ketogenic diet.'] [Article in Japanese.] *Masui*, *58*(6): 762–764.

Matsuura, T., Sutcliffe, J.S., Fang, P., Galjaard, R-J. et al. (1997) '*De novo* truncating mutations in E6-AP ubiquitin-protein ligase gene (UBE3A) in Angelman syndrome.', *Nature Genetics*, *15*: 74–77.

Mattick, J.S. (2004) 'RNA regulation: a new genetics?' *Nature Reviews: Genetics*, *5*: 316–323.

Mattison, L.K., Fourie, J., Desmond, R.A., Modak, A. et al. (2006) 'Increased prevalence of dihydropyrimidine dehydrogenase deficiency in African-Americans compared with caucasians.', *Clinical Cancer Research*, *12*(18): 5491–5495.

Mattson, R., Gallagher, B.B., Reynolds, E.H. and Glass, D. (1973) 'Folate therapy in epilepsy, a controlled study.', *Archives of Neurology*, *29*: 78.

Matura, L.A., Sachdev, V., Bakalov, V.K., Rosing, D.R. and Bondy, C.A. (2007) 'Growth hormone treatment and left ventricular dimensions in Turner syndrome.', *Journal of Pediatrics*, *150*(6): 587–591.

Mautner, V.F., Kluwe, L., Thakker, S.D. and Leark, R.A. (2002) 'Treatment of ADHD in neurofibromatosis type 1.', *Developmental Medicine and Child Neurology*, *44*: 164–170.

Maynard, T.M., Haskell, G.T., Peters, A.Z., Sikich, L. et al. (2003) 'A comprehensive analysis of 22q11 gene expression in the developing and adult brain.', *Proceedings of the National Academy of Science*, *100*(24): 14433–14438.

Maynard, T.M., Meechan, D.W., Dudevoir, M.L., Gopalakrishna, D. et al. (2008) 'Mitochondrial localization and function of a subset of 22q11 deletion syndrome candidate genes.', *Molecular and Cellular Neuroscience*, *39*(3): 439–451.

Mazumdar, S., King, M., Liu, K-Y., Zerubavel, N. and Bearman, P. (2010) 'The spatial structure of autism in California, 1993–2001.', *Health and Place*, doi:10.1016/j.healthplace.2009.12.014.

Mazzoni, D.S., Ackley, R.S. and Nash, D.J. (1994) 'Abnormal pinna type and hearing loss correlations in Down's syndrome.', *Journal of Intellectual Disability Research*, *38*: 549–560.

Mbarek, O., Marouillat, S., Martineau, J., Barthélémy, C. et al. (2000) 'Association study of the NF1 gene and autistic disorder.', American Journal of Medical Genetics Part C: Seminars in Medical Genetics, 88(6): 729–732.

Medical Research Council (2001) MRC Review of Autism Research – Epidemiology and Causes. London: MRC. www.mrc.ac.uk/Utilities/Documentrecord/index.htm?d=MRC002394

Mefford, H., Sharp, A., Baker, C., Itsara, A. et al. (2008) 'Recurrent rearrangements of chromosome 1q21.1 and variable pediatric phenotypes.', New England Journal of Medicine, 359(16): 1685–1699.

Megson, M.N. (2000) 'Is autism a G-alpha protein defect reversible with natural vitamin A?' Medical Hypotheses, 54(6): 979–983.

Meguid, N.A., Atta, H.M., Gouda, A.S. and Khalil, R.O. (2008) 'Role of polyunsaturated fatty acids in the management of Egyptian children with autism.', Clinical Biochemistry, 41(13): 1044–1048.

Mehta, A.V. and Ambalavanan, S.K. (1997) 'Occurrence of congenital heart disease in children with Brachmann-de Lange syndrome.', American Journal of Medical Genetics, 71: 434–435.

Mehta, P.D., Capone, G., Jewell, A. and Freedland, R.L. (2007) 'Increased amyloid beta protein levels in children and adolescents with Down syndrome.', Journal of Neurological Science, 254(1–2): 22–27.

Meikle, L., Pollizzi, K., Egnor, A., Kramvis, I. et al. (2008) 'Response of a neuronal model of tuberous sclerosis to mammalian target of rapamycin (mTOR) inhibitors: effects on mTORC1 and Akt signaling lead to improved survival and function.' Journal of Neuroscience, 28: 5422–5432.

Meikle, L., Talos, D.M., Onda, H., Pollizzi, K. et al. (2007) 'A mouse model of tuberous sclerosis: neuronal loss of Tsc1 causes dysplastic and ectopic neurons, reduced myelination, seizure activity, and limited survival.', Journal of Neuroscience, 27: 5546–5558.

Melke, J., Goubran Botros, H., Chaste, P., Betancur, C. et al. (2007) 'Abnormal melatonin synthesis in autism spectrum disorders.', Molecular Psychiatry, 15th May 2007, doi:10.1038/sj.mp.4002016.

Meldrum B.S. and Rogawski M.A. (2007) 'Molecular targets for antiepileptic drug development.', Neurotherapeutics, 4(1): 18–61.

Melmed, R.D., Schneider, C.K., Fabes, R.A., Phillips, J. and Reichelt, K. (2000) 'Metabolic markers and gastrointestinal symptoms in children with autism and related disorders.', Journal of Pediatric Gastroenterology and Nutrition, 3: S31–S32.

Mencarelli, M.A., Kleefstra, T., Katzaki, E., Papa, F.T. et al. (2009) '14q12 Microdeletion syndrome and congenital variant of Rett syndrome.', European Journal of Medical Genetics, 52: 148–152.

Mencarelli, M.A., Spanhol-Rosseto, A., Artuso, R., Rondinella, D. et al. (2010) 'Novel FOXG1 mutations associated with the congenital variant of Rett syndrome.' Journal of Medical Genetics, 47: 49–53.

Mendell, J.R., Moxley, R.T., Griggs, R.C., Brooke, M.H. et al. (1989) 'Randomized, double-blind six-month trial of prednisone in Duchenne's muscular dystrophy.', New England Journal of Medicine, 320: 1592–1597.

Meng, X., Lu, X., Li, Z., Green, E.D. et al. (1998) 'Complete physical map of the common deletion region in Williams syndrome and identification and characterization of three novel genes.', Human Genetics, 103: 590–599.

Mensink, K.A., Ketterling, R.P., Flynn, H.C., Knudson, R.A. et al. (2006) 'Connective tissue dysplasia in five new patients with NF1 microdeletions: further expansion of phenotype and review of the literature.', Journal of Medical Genetics, 43: e8.

Mentzel, H.J., Dieckmann, A., Fitzek, C., Brandl, U. et al. (2005) 'Early diagnosis of cerebral involvement in Sturge-Weber syndrome using high-resolution BOLD MR venography.', Pediatric Radiology, 35: 85–90.

Mercimek-Mahmutoglu, S., Stoeckler-Ipsiroglu, S., Adami, A., Appleton, R. et al. (2006) 'GAMT deficiency: features, treatment, and outcome in an inborn error of creatine synthesis.' Neurology, 67: 480–484.

Merhar, S.L. and Manning-Courtney, P. (2007) 'Two boys with 47,XXY and autism.', Journal of Autism and Developmental Disorders, 37(5): 840–846.

Merlini, L., Cicognani, A., Malaspina, E., Gennari, M. et al. (2003) 'Early prednisone treatment in Duchenne muscular dystrophy.', Muscle and Nerve, 27: 222–227.

Merscher, S., Funke, B., Epstein, J.A., Heyer, J. et al. (2001) 'TBX1 is responsible for cardiovascular defects in velocardiofacial/DiGeorge syndrome.', Cell, 104: 619–629.

Mervis, C.B., Robinson, B.F. and Pani, J.R. (1999) 'Visuospatial construction.', American Journal of Human Genetics, 65: 1222–1229.

Meryash, D.L., Szymanski, L.S. and Gerald, P.S. (1982) 'Infantile autism associated with the fragile-X syndrome.', Journal of Autism and Developmental Disorders, 12(3): 295–301.

Mesa, L.E., Dubrovsky, A.L., Corderi, J., Marco, P. and Flores, D. (1991) 'Steroids in Duchenne muscular dystrophy – deflazacort trial.', Neuromuscular Disorders, 1: 261–266.

Messahel, S., Pheasant, A.E., Pall, H., Ahmed-Choudhury, J. et al. (1998) 'Urinary levels of neopterin and biopterin in autism.', Neuroscience Letters, 241(1): 17–20.

Messiaen, L.M., Callens, T., Mortier, G., Beysen, D. et al. (2000) 'Exhaustive mutation analysis of the NF1 gene allows identification of 95 per cent of mutations and reveals a high frequency of unusual splicing defects.', Human Mutation, 15: 541–555.

Messiaen, L.M., Callens, T., Mortier, G., Van Roy, N. et al. (2001) 'Towards an efficient and sensitive molecular genetic test for neurofibromatosis type 1 (NF1).', European Journal of Human Genetics, 9: 314.

Mestroni, L., Rocco, C., Gregori, D., Sinagra, G. et al. (1999) 'Familial dilated cardiomyopathy: evidence for genetic and phenotypic heterogeneity. Heart Muscle Disease Study Group.', Journal of the American College of Cardiology, 34: 181–190.

Meyer, G., Varoqueaux, F., Neeb, A., Oschlies, M. and Brose, N. (2004) 'The complexity of PDZ domain-mediated interactions at glutamatergic synapses: a case study on neuroligin.', Neuropharmacology, 47: 724–733.

Meyer-Lindenberg, A., Kohn, P., Mervis, C.B., Kippenhan, J.S. *et al.* (2004) 'Neural basis of genetically determined visuospatial construction deficit in Williams syndrome.', *Neuron*, 43: 623–631.

Meyer-Lindenberg, A., Mervis, C.B., Sarpal, D., Koch, P. *et al.* (2005) 'Functional, structural, and metabolic abnormalities of the hippocampal formation in Williams syndrome.', *Journal of Clinical Investigation*, 115: 1888–1895.

Meyers, R.L. and Grua, J.R. (2000) 'Bilateral laparoscopic adrenalectomy: a new treatment for difficult cases of congenital adrenal hyperplasia.', *Journal of Pediatric Surgery*, 35: 1586–1590.

Mikkelsen, M. (1977) 'Down's syndrome cytogenetic epidemiology.', *Hereditas*, 86: 45–59.

Mila, M., Castellvi-Bel, S., Gine, R., Vazquez, C. *et al.* (1996) 'A female compound heterozygote (pre- and full mutation) for the CGG FMR1 expansion.', *Human Genetics*, 98: 419–421.

Miladi, N., Larnaout, A., Kaabachi, N., Helayem, M. and Ben Hamida, M. (1992) 'Phenylketonuria: an underlying etiology of autistic syndrome. A case report.', *Journal of Child Neurology*, 7(1): 22–23.

Miles, J.H., Takahashi, T.N., Haber, A. and Hadden, L. (2003) 'Autism families with a high incidence of alcoholism.', *Journal of Autism and Developmental Disorders*, 33(4): 403–415.

Milewicz, D.M., Urbán, Z. and Boyd, C. (2000) 'Genetic disorders of the elastic fiber system.', *Matrix Biology*, 19(6): 471–480.

Miller, G. (2006) 'Fragile-X's unwelcome relative.' *Science*, 312: 518–521.

Miller, J.L., Goldstone, A.P., Couch, J.A., Shuster, J. *et al.* (2008) 'Pituitary abnormalities in Prader-Willi syndrome and early onset morbid obesity.', *American Journal of Medical Genetics A*, 146A(5): 570–575.

Miller, M.T., Strömland, K., Ventura, L., Johansson, M. *et al.* (2004) 'Autism with ophthalmologic malformations: the plot thickens.', *Transactions of the American Ophthalmologic Society*, 102: 107–121.

Miller, M.T., Stromland, K., Ventura, L., Johansson, M. *et al.* (2005) 'Autism associated with conditions characterized by developmental errors in early embryogenesis: a mini review.', *International Journal of Developmental Neuroscience*, 23: 201–219.

Mills, J.L., Kirke, P.N., Molloy, A.M., Burke, H. *et al.* (1999) 'Methylenetetrahydrofolate reductase thermolabile variant and oral clefts.' *American Journal of Medical Genetics*, 86: 71–74.

Mills, P.B., Surtees, R.A.H., Champion, M.P., Beesley, C.E. *et al.* (2005) 'Neonatal epileptic encephalopathy caused by mutations in the PNPO gene encoding pyridox(am)ine 50-phosphate oxidase.', *Human Molecular Genetics*, 14(8): 1077–1086.

Milner, K.M., Craig, E.E., Thompson, R.J., Veltman, M.W. *et al.* (2005) 'Prader-Willi syndrome: intellectual abilities and behavioural features by genetic subtype.', *Journal of Child Psychology and Psychiatry*, 46: 1089–1096.

Min, W.W., Yuskaitis, C.J., Yan, Q., Sikorski, C. *et al.* (2008) 'Elevated glycogen synthase kinase-3 activity in fragile-X mice: key metabolic regulator with evidence for treatment potential.', *Neuropharmacology*, xxx: 1–10, doi:10.1016/j.neuropharm.2008.09.017.

Minassian, B.A., DeLorey, T.M., Olsen, R.W., Philippart, M. *et al.* (1998) 'Angelman syndrome: correlations between epilepsy phenotypes and genotypes.', *Annals of Neurology*, 43: 485–493.

Ming, X., Stein, T.P., Brimacombe, M., Johnson, W.G. *et al.* (2005) 'Increased excretion of a lipid peroxidation biomarker in autism.', *Prostaglandins, Leukotrienes and Essential Fatty Acids*, 73: 379–384.

Mingroni-Netto, R.C., Angeli, C.B., Auricchio, M.T.B.M., Leal-Mesquita, E.R. *et al.* (2002) 'Distribution of CGG repeats and FRAXAC1/DXS548 alleles in South American populations.', *American Journal of Medical Genetics*, 111: 243–252.

Minshew, N.J. and Keller, T.A. (2010) 'The nature of brain dysfunction in autism: functional brain imaging studies.' *Current Opinion in Neurology*, 23(2): 124–130.

Mitchell, T.N., Free, S.L., Williamson, K.A., Stevens, J.M. *et al.* (2003) 'Polymicrogyria and absence of pineal gland due to PAX6 mutation.' *Annals of Neurology*, 53: 658–663.

Miura, H., Yanazawa, M., Kato, K. and Kitamura, K. (1997) 'Expression of a novel aristaless related homeobox gene "Arx" in the vertebrate telencephalon, diencephalon and floor plate.', *Mechanisms of Development*, 65: 99–110.

Mizugishi, K., Yamanaka, K., Kuwajima, K. and Kondo, I. (1998) 'Interstitial deletion of chromosome 7q in a patient with Williams syndrome and infantile spasms.', *Journal of Human Genetics*, 43(3): 178–181.

MMWR (2001) 'Racial disparities in median age at death of persons with Down syndrome – United States, 1968–1997.', *Morbidity and Mortality Weekly Reports*, 50(22): 463–465.

MMWR (2006) 'Deaths associated with hypocalcaemia from chelation therapy – Texas, Pennsylvania, and Oregon, 2003–2005.', *Morbidity and Mortality Weekly Report*, 55: 204–207.

MMWR (2007a) 'Prevalence of autism spectrum disorders – autism and developmental disabilities monitoring network, six sites, United States.', *Morbidity and Mortality Weekly Report*, 56: SS-1, 1–11.

MMWR (2007b) 'Prevalence of autism spectrum disorders – autism and developmental disabilities monitoring network, 14 sites, United States, 2002.', *Morbidity and Mortality Weekly Report*, 56: SS-1, 12–28.

MMWR (2007c) 'Evaluation of a methodology for a collaborative multiple source surveillance network for autism spectrum disorders – autism and developmental disabilities monitoring network, 14 sites, United States, 2002.', *Morbidity and Mortality Weekly Report*, 56: SS-1, 29–40.

Mobbs, D., Garrett, A.S., Menon, V., Rose, F.E. *et al.* (2004) 'Anomalous brain activation during face and gaze processing in Williams syndrome.', *Neurology*, 62: 2070–2076.

Mobius, F.F., Fitzky, B.U., Lee, J.N., Paik, Y-K. and Glossmann, H. (1998) 'Molecular cloning and expression of the human delta-7-sterol reductase.', *Proceedings of the National Academy of Science USA*, 95: 1899–1902.

Möbius, P.J. (1888) 'Über angeborene Facialis-Abducenslähmung.' *Münchener mediznische Wochenschrift*.

Mochizuki, H., Miyatake, S., Suzuki, M., Shigeyama, T. et al. (2008) 'Mental retardation and lifetime events of Duchenne muscular dystrophy in Japan.', *Internal Medicine, 47*(13): 1207–1210.

Modahl, C., Green, L., Fein, D., Morris, M. et al. (1998) 'Plasma oxytocin levels in autistic children.', *Biological Psychiatry, 43*: 270–277.

Moessner, R., Marshall, C.R., Sutcliffe, J.S., Skaug, J. et al. (2007) 'Contribution of SHANK3 mutations to autism spectrum disorder.', *American Journal of Human Genetics, 81*: 1289–1297.

Mogul, H.R., Lee, P.D., Whitman, B.Y., Zipf, W.B. et al. (2008) 'Growth hormone treatment of adults with Prader-Willi syndrome and growth hormone deficiency improves lean body mass, fractional body fat, and serum triiodothyronine without glucose impairment: results from the United States multicenter trial.', *Journal of Clinical Endocrinology and Metabolism, 93*(4): 1238–1245.

Mohammad, N.S., Jain, J.M.N., Chintakindi, K.P., Singh, R.P., Naik, U. and Akella, R.R.D. (2009) 'Aberrations in folate metabolic pathway and altered susceptibility to autism.', *Psychiatric Genetics, 19*: 171–176.

Moizard, M.P., Billard, C., Toutain, A., Berret, F. et al. (1998) 'Are Dp71 and Dp140 brain dystrophin isoforms related to cognitive impairment in Duchenne muscular dystrophy?' *American Journal of Medical Genetics, 80*: 32–41.

Mok, C.A., Héon, E. and Zhen, M. (2010) 'Ciliary dysfunction and obesity.' *Clinical Genetics, 77*: 18–27.

Moldrich, R.X., Dauphinot, L., Laffaire, J., Rossier, J. and Potier, M-C. (2007) 'Down syndrome gene dosage imbalance on cerebellum development.', *Progress in Neurobiology, 82*: 87–94.

Molfetta, G.A., Munoz, M.V.R., Santos, A.C., Silva, W.A. Jr. et al. (2004) 'Discordant phenotypes in first cousins with UBE3A frameshift mutation.', *American Journal of Medical Genetics, 127A*: 258–262.

Molloy, C.A., Keddache, M. and Martin, L.J. (2005) 'Evidence for linkage on 21q and 7q in a subset of autism characterized by developmental regression.', *Molecular Psychiatry, 10*: 741–746.

Molloy, C.A., Morrow, A.L., Meinzen-Derr, J., Dawson, G. et al. (2006) 'Familial autoimmune thyroid disease as a risk factor for regression in children with autism spectrum disorder: a CPEA study.', *Journal of Autism and Developmental Disorders, 36*(3): 317–324.

Moloney, D.M., Slaney, S.F., Oldridge, M., Wall, S.A. et al. (1996) 'Exclusive paternal origin of new mutations in Apert syndrome.', *Nature Genetics, 13*: 48–53.

Monaco, A.P., Bertelson, C.J., Liechti-Gallati, S., Moser, H. and Kunkel, L.M. (1988) 'An explanation for the phenotypic differences between patients bearing partial deletions of the DMD locus.', *Genomics, 2*: 90–95.

Moncla, A., Malzac, P., Voelckel, M-A., Auquier, P. et al. (1999) 'Phenotype-genotype correlation in 20 deletion and 20 non-deletion Angelman syndrome patients.', *European Journal of Human Genetics, 7*: 131–139.

Montagu, A. (1986) *Touching: The Human Significance of the Skin.* New York: Harper and Row.

Moog, U., Engelen, J.J., Weber, B.W., Van Gelderen, M. et al. (2004) 'Hereditary motor and sensory neuropathy (HMSN) IA, developmental delay and autism related disorder in a boy with duplication (17)(p11.2p12).' *Genetic Counselling, 15*: 73–80.

Moore, C.J., Daly, E.M., Schmitz, N., Tassone, F. et al. (2004) 'A neuropsychological investigation of male premutation carriers of fragile-X syndrome.', *Neuropsychologia, 42*: 1934–1947.

Moore, J.L. (2005) 'The significance of folic acid for epilepsy patients.', *Epilepsy and Behaviour, 7*: 172–181.

Moore, S.J., Green, J.S., Fan, Y., Bhogal, A.K. et al. (2005) 'Clinical and genetic epidemiology of Bardet-Biedl syndrome in Newfoundland: a 22-year prospective, population-based, cohort study.', *American Journal of Medical Genetics A, 132*: 352–360.

Moore, W.T. and Federman, D.D. (1965) 'Familial dwarfism and "stiff joints".' *Archives of Internal Medicine, 115*: 398–404.

Morales, J., Hiesinger, P.R., Schroeder, A.J., Kume, K. et al. (2002) 'Drosophila fragile-X protein, DFXR, regulates neuronal morphology and function in the brain.', *Neuron, 34*: 961–972.

Moran, C.N., Scott, R.A., Adams, S.M., Warrington, S.J. et al. (2004) 'Y chromosome haplotypes of elite Ethiopian endurance runners.', *Human Genetics, 115*: 492–497.

Morava, E., Cser, B., Karteszi, J., Huijben, K. et al. (2004) 'Screening for CDG type Ia in Joubert syndrome.', *Medical Science Monitor, 10*: 469–472.

Morell, P. and Jurevics, H. (1996) 'Origin of cholesterol in myelin.' *Neurochemical Research, 21*(4): 463–470.

Morey-Canellas, J., Sivagamasundari, U. and Barton, H. (2003) 'A case of autism in a child with Apert's syndrome.', *European Journal of Child and Adolescent Psychiatry, 12*: 100–102.

Morgagni, G.B. (1768) *Epistola anatomica medica.* XLVII, article 20.

Morgan, N.V., Gissen, P., Sharif, S.M., Baumber, L. et al. (2002) 'A novel locus for Meckel-Gruber syndrome, MKS3, maps to chromosome 8q24.', *Human Genetics, 111*: 456–461.

Morimoto, M., An, B., Ogami, A., Sin, N. et al. (2003) 'Infantile spasms in a patient with Williams syndrome and craniosynostosis.', *Epilepsia, 44*(11): 1459–1462.

Morita, H., Taguchi, J., Kurihara, H., Kitaoka, M. et al. (1997) 'Genetic polymorphism of 5,10-methylenetetrahydrofolate reductase (MTHFR) as a risk factor for coronary artery disease.', *Circulation, 95*: 2032–2036.

Mornet, E., Muller, F., Lenvoise-Furet, A., Delezoide, A-L. et al. (1997) 'Screening of the C677T mutation on the methylenetetrahydrofolate reductase gene in French patients with neural tube defects.' *Human Genetics, 100*: 512–514.

Moro, F., Pisano, T., Bernardina, B.D., Polli, R. et al. (2006) 'Periventricular heterotopia in fragile-X syndrome.', *Neurology, 67*(4): 713–715.

Morris, C.A., Thomas, I.T. and Greenberg, F. (1993) 'Williams syndrome: autosomal dominant inheritance.', *American Journal of Medical Genetics, 47*: 478–481.

Morris, J.K. and Alberman, E. (2009) 'Trends in Down's syndrome live births and antenatal diagnoses in England and Wales from 1989 to 2008: analysis of data from the National Down Syndrome Cytogenetic Register.', *BMJ*, *339*: b3794, doi:10.1136/bmj.b3794.

Morrison, G.B., Bastian, A., Dela Rosa, T., Diasio, R.B. and Takimoto, C.H. (1997) 'Dihydropyrimidine dehydrogenase deficiency: a pharmacogenetic defect causing severe adverse reactions to 5-fluorouracil-based chemotherapy.', *Oncology Nursing Forum*, *24*: 83–88.

Morrison, P.J., Mulholland, H.C., Craig, B.G. and Nevin, N.C. (1992) 'Cardiovascular abnormalities in the oculo-auriculo-vertebral spectrum (Goldenhar syndrome).', *American Journal of Medical Genetics*, *44*: 425–428.

Morrow, E.M., Yoo, S-Y., Flavell, S.W., Kim, T-K. *et al.* (2008) 'Identifying autism loci and genes by tracing recent shared ancestry.', *Science*, *321*(5886): 218–223.

Morrow, J.D., Whitman, B.Y. and Accardo, P.J. (1990) 'Autistic disorder in Sotos syndrome: a case report.', *European Journal of Pediatrics*, *149*(8): 567–569.

Moser, H.W., Loes, D.J., Melhem, E.R., Raymond, G.V. *et al.* (2000) 'X-linked adrenoleukodystrophy: overview and prognosis as a function of age and brain magnetic resonance imaging abnormality. A study involving 372 patients.', *Neuropediatrics*, *31*: 227–239.

Moser, H.W., Moser, A.B., Hollandsworth, K., Brereton N.H. and Raymond, G.V. (2007) "Lorenzo's oil" therapy for X-linked adrenoleukodystrophy: rationale and current assessment of efficacy.', *Journal of Molecular Neuroscience*, *33*(1): 105–113.

Moser, H.W., Moser, A.B., Smith, K.D., Bergin, A. *et al.* (1992) 'Adrenoleukodystrophy: phenotypic variability. Implications for therapy.', *Journal of Inherited Metabolic Disease*, *15*: 645–664.

Moser, H.W., Raymond, G.V., Lu, S-E., Muenz, L.R. *et al.* (2005) 'Follow-up of 89 asymptomatic patients with adrenoleukodystrophy treated with Lorenzo's oil.', *Archives of Neurology*, *62*: 1073–1080.

Mosher, D.S., Quignon, P., Bustamante, C.D., Sutter, N.B. *et al.* (2007) 'A mutation in the myostatin gene increases muscle mass and enhances racing performance in heterozygote dogs.', *PloS Genetics*, 3: e79, doi:10.1371/journal.pgen.0030079.

Moss, E., Wang, P.P., McDonald-McGinn, D.M., Gerdes, M. *et al.* (1995) 'Characteristic cognitive profile in patients with a 22q11.2 deletion: verbal IQ exceeds nonverbal IQ.', *American Journal of Human Genetics*, *57*(Supplement): A20.

Moss, J. and Howlin, P. (2009) 'Autism spectrum disorders in genetic syndromes: implications for diagnosis, intervention and understanding the wider autism spectrum disorder population.', *Journal of Intellectual Disability Research*, *53*(10): 852–873.

Moss, J.F., Oliver, C., Berg, K., Kaur, G. *et al.* (2008) 'Prevalence of autism spectrum phenomenology in Cornelia de Lange and cri du chat syndromes.', *American Journal of Mental Retardation*, *113*(4): 278–291.

Mostowska, A., Hozyasz, K.K. and Jagodzinski, P.P. (2006) 'Maternal MTR genotype contributes to the risk of non-syndromic cleft lip and palate in the Polish population.', *Clinical Genetics*, *69*: 512–517.

Motil, K.J., Schultz, R., Brown, B., Glaze, D.G. and Percy, A.K. (1994) 'Altered energy balance may account for growth failure in Rett syndrome.', *Journal of Child Neurology*, *9*: 315–319.

Moulin-Romsee, C., Verdonck, A., Schoenaers, J. and Carels, C. (2004) 'Treatment of hemifacial microsomia in a growing child: the importance of co-operation between the orthodontist and the maxillofacial surgeon.', *Journal of Orthodontics*, *31*(3): 190–200.

Mouridsen, S.E., Andersen, L.B., Sorensen, S.A., Rich, B. and Isager, T. (1992) 'Neurofibromatosis in infantile autism and other types of childhood psychoses.', *Acta Paedopsychiatrica*, *55*: 15–18.

Mouridsen, S.E. and Hansen, M-B. (2002) 'Neuropsychiatric aspects of Sotos syndrome: a review and two case illustrations.', *European Journal of Child and Adolescent Psychiatry*, *11*: 43–48.

Mouridsen, S.E., Rich, B. and Isager, T. (1993) 'Brief report: parental age in infantile autism, autistic-like conditions, and borderline childhood psychosis.', *Journal of Autism and Developmental Disorders*, *23*(2): 387–396.

Mouridsen, S.E., Rich, B., Isager, T. and Nedergaard, N.J. (2007) 'Autoimmune diseases in parents of children with infantile autism: a case-control study.', *Developmental Medicine and Child Neurology*, *49*: 429–432.

Mousain-Bosc, M., Roche, M., Polge, A., Pradal-Prat, D. *et al.* (2006a) 'Improvement of neurobehavioural disorders in children supplemented with magnesium-vitamin B6. I. Attention deficit hyperactivity disorders.', *Magnesium Research*, *19*(1): 46–52.

Mousain-Bosc, M., Roche, M., Polge, A., Pradal-Prat, D. *et al.* (2006b) 'Improvement of neurobehavioural disorders in children supplemented with magnesium-vitamin B6. II. Pervasive developmental disorder-autism. *Magnesium Research*, *19*(1): 53–62.

MRC (2001) *MRC Review of Autism Research: Epidemiology and Causes*. London: Medical Research Council. (www.mrc.ac.uk)

Mudd, S.H., Uhlendorf, B.W., Freeman, J.M., Finkelstein, J.D. and Shih, V.E. (1972) 'Homocystinuria associated with decreased methylenetetrahydrofolate reductase activity.' *Biochemical and Biophysical Research Communications*, *46*: 905–912.

Mueller, C., Patel, S., Irons, M., Antshel, K. *et al.* (2003) 'Normal cognition and behaviour in a Smith-Lemli-Opitz syndrome patient who presented with hirschsprung disease.', *American Journal of Medical Genetics A*, *123*(1): 100–106.

Muers, M.R., Sharpe, J.A., Garrick, D., Sloane-Stanley, J. *et al.* (2007) 'Defining the cause of skewed X-chromosome inactivation in X-linked mental retardation by use of a mouse model.', *American Journal of Human Genetics*, *80*: 1138–1149.

Muhle, R., Trentacoste, S.V. and Rapin, I. (2004) 'The genetics of autism.' *Pediatrics*, *113*: 472–486.

Mukaddes, N.M., Alyanak, B., Kora, M.E. and Polvan, O. (1999) 'The psychiatric symptomatology in Kleine-Levin syndrome.', *Child Psychiatry and Human Development*, *29*(3): 253–258.

Mukaddes, N.M., Fateh, R. and Kilincasian, A. (2008) 'Kleine-Levin syndrome in two subjects with diagnosis of autistic disorder.', *World Journal of Biological Psychiatry*, Feb. 6: 1–6.

Mukaddes, N.M. and Herguner, S. (2007) 'Autistic disorder and 22q11.2 duplication.', *World Journal of Biological Psychiatry*, 8(2): 127–130.

Mulley, J.C., Yu, S., Loesch, D.Z., Hay, D.A. *et al.* (1995) 'FRAXE and mental retardation.', *Journal of Medical Genetics*, 32: 162–169.

Mundschau, G., Gurbuxani, S., Gamis, A.S., Greene, M.E. *et al.* (2003) 'Mutagenesis of GATA1 is an initiating event in Down syndrome leukemogenesis.', *Blood*, 101: 4298–4300.

Munke, M., McDonald, D.M., Cronister, A., Stewart, J.M. *et al.* (1990) 'Oral-facial-digital syndrome type VI (Varadi syndrome): further clinical delineation.', *American Journal of Medical Genetics*, 35: 360–369.

Muñoz, E., Milà, M., Sánchez, A., Latorre, P. *et al.* (1999) 'Dentatorubropallidoluysian atrophy in a Spanish family: a clinical, radiological, pathological, and genetic study.', *Journal of Neurology, Neurosurgery and Psychiatry*, 67: 811–814.

Muntau, A.C., Roschinger, W., Habich, M., Demmelmair, H. *et al.* (2002) 'Tetrahydrobiopterin as an alternative treatment for mild phenylketonuria.', *New England Journal of Medicine*, 347: 2122–2132.

Muntoni, F., Torelli, S. and Ferlini, A. (2003) 'Dystrophin and mutations: one gene, several proteins, multiple phenotypes.', *Lancet Neurology*, 2(12): 731–740.

Muntoni, F. and Wells, D. (2007) 'Genetic treatments in muscular dystrophies.', *Current Opinion in Neurology*, 20: 590–594.

Muntoni, F. and Voit, T. (2004) 'The congenital muscular dystrophies in 2004: a century of exciting progress.' *Neuromuscular Disorders*, 14(10): 635–649.

Muratori, F., Bertini, N. and Masi, G. (2002) 'Efficacy of lithium treatment in Kleine-Levin syndrome.', *European Psychiatry*, 17: 232–233.

Murgatroyd, C., Patchev, A.V., Wu, Y., Micale, V. *et al.* (2009) 'Dynamic DNA methylation programs persistent adverse effects of early-life stress.', *Nature Neuroscience*, Nov 8. [Epub ahead of print], doi:10.1038/nn.2436.

Murphy, K.C., Jones, L.A. and Owen, M.J. (1999) 'High rates of schizophrenia in adults with velocardiofacial syndrome.', *Archives of General Psychiatry*, 56: 940–945.

Murphy, S.K. and Jirtle, R.L. (2000) 'Imprinted genes as potential genetic and epigenetic toxicologic targets.', *Environmental Health Perspectives*, 108: Supplement 1, 5–11.

Musio, A., Selicorni, A., Focarelli, M.L., Gervasini, C. *et al.* (2006) 'X-linked Cornelia de Lange syndrome owing to SMC1L1 mutations.', *Nature Genetics*, 38: 528–530.

Mutchinick, O.M., Lopez, M., Luna, L., Waxman, J. *et al.* (1999) 'High prevalence of the thermolabile methylenetetrahydrofolate reductase variant in mexico: a country with a very high prevalence of neural tube defects.', *Molecular Genetics and Metabolism*, 68: 461–467.

Muzugishi, K., Yamanaka, K., Kuwajima, K. and Kondo, I. (1998) 'Interstitial deletion of chromosome 7q in a patient with Williams syndrome and infantile spasms.', *Journal of Human Genetics*, 43(3): 178–181.

Muzzin, K.B. and Harper, L.F. (2003) 'Smith-Lemli-Opitz syndrome: a review, case report and dental implications.', *Special Care in Dentistry*, 23: 22–27.

Myers, A., Wavrant De-Vrieze, F., Holmans, P., Hamshere, M. *et al.* (2002) 'Full genome screen for Alzheimer disease: stage II analysis.', *American Journal of Medical Genetics*, 114: 235–244.

Myhre, S.A., Ruvalcaba, R.H.A. and Graham, C.B. (1981) 'A new growth deficiency syndrome.', *Clinical Genetics*, 20: 1–5.

Mykytyn, K., Mullins, R.F., Andrews, M., Chiang, A.P. *et al.* (2004) 'Bardet-Biedl syndrome type 4 (BBS4)-null mice implicate Bbs4 in flagella formation but not global cilia assembly.', *Proceedings of the National Academy of Science USA*, 101: 8664–8669.

Mykytyn, K. and Sheffield, V.C. (2004) 'Establishing a connection between cilia and Bardet-Biedl syndrome.', *Trends in Molecular Medicine*, 10: 106–109.

Nabi, R., Serajee, F.J., Chugani, D.C., Zhong, H. and Huq, A.H. (2004) 'Association of tryptophan 2,3 dioxygenase gene polymorphism with autism.', *American Journal of Medical Genetics B*, 125B(1): 63–68.

Nadeau, J.H. (2001) 'Modifier genes in mice and humans.', *Nature Review: Genetics*, 2: 165–174.

Nadesan, M.H. (2005) *Constructing Autism: Unravelling the 'Truth' and Understanding the Social.* Abongdon: Routledge.

Naito, H. and Oyanagi, S. (1982) 'Familial myoclonus epilepsy and choreoathetosis: hereditary dentatorubral-pallidoluysian atrophy.', *Neurology*, 32: 798–807.

Nakabayashi, K., Amann, D., Ren, Y., Saarialho-Kere, U. *et al.* (2005) 'Identification of C7orf11 (TTDN1) gene mutations and genetic heterogeneity in nonphotosensitive trichothiodystrophy.', *American Journal of Human Genetics*, 76: 510–516.

Nakamine, A., Ouchanov, L., Jimenez, P., Manghi, E.R. *et al.* (2008) 'Duplication of 17(p11.2p11.2) in a male child with autism and severe language delay. *American Journal of Medical Genetics A*, 146A(5): 636–643.

Nakamoto, M., Nalavadi, V., Epstein, M.P., Narayanan, U. *et al.* (2007) 'Fragile-X mental retardation protein deficiency leads to excessive mGluR5-dependent internalization of AMPA receptors.', *Proceedings of the National Academy of Science USA*, 104: 15537–15542.

Nakamura, A., Hattori, M. and Sakaki, Y. (1997a) 'A novel gene isolated from human placenta located in Down syndrome critical region on chromosome 21.', *DNA Research*, 4: 321–324.

Nakamura, A., Hattori, M. and Sakaki, Y. (1997b) 'Isolation of a novel human gene from the Down syndrome critical region of chromosome 21q22.2.', *Journal of Biochemistry*, 122: 872–877.

Nakamura, F., Sasaki, H., Kajihara, H. and Yamanoue, M. (1990) 'Laurence-Moon-Biedl syndrome accompanied by congenital hepatic fibrosis.', *Journal of Gastroenterology and Hepatology*, 5: 206–210.

Nakamura, T., Colbert, M., Krenz, M., Molkentin, J.D. *et al.* (2007) 'Mediating ERK1/2 signaling rescues congenital heart defects in a mouse model of Noonan syndrome.', *The Journal of Clinical Investigation*, 117(8): 2123–2132.

Nakane, T., Hayashibe, H. and Nakazawa, S. (2005) 'An MCA/MR syndrome with hypocholesterolemia due to familial hypobetalipoproteinemia: report of a second patient with Nguyen syndrome.', *American Journal of Medical Genetics A, 137A*(3): 305–307.

Nan, X., Hou, J., Maclean, A., Nasir, J. *et al.* (2007) 'Interaction between chromatin proteins MeCP2 and ATRX is disrupted by mutations that cause inherited mental retardation.', *Proceedings of the National Academy of Science, 104*(8): 2709–2714.

Nanba, Y., Oka, A. and Ohno, K. (2007) ['Severe diarrhea associated with X-linked lissencephaly with absent corpus callosum and abnormal genitalia: a case report of successful treatment with the somatostatin analogue octreotide.'] [Article in Japanese.] *No To Hattatsu, 39*(5): 379–382.

Naora, H., Kimura, M., Otani, H., Yokoyama, M. *et al.* (1994) 'Transgenic mouse model of hemifacial microsomia: cloning and characterization of insertional mutation region on chromosome 10.', *Genomics, 23*: 515–519.

Napolioni, V., Moavero, R. and Curatolo, P. (2009) 'Recent advances in neurobiology of tuberous sclerosis complex.', *Brain and Development, 31*(2): 104–113.

Napolitano, C., Bloise R. and Priori, S.G. (2006) 'Gene-specific therapy for inherited arrhythmogenic diseases.', *Pharmacology and Therapeutics, 110*: 1–13.

Naqvi, S., Cole, T. and Graham, J.M. Jr. (2000) 'Cole-Hughes macrocephaly syndrome and associated autistic manifestations.', *American Journal of Medical Genetics, 94*: 149–152.

Nash, K., Sheard, E., Rovet, J. and Koren, G. (2008) 'Understanding foetal alcohol spectrum disorders (FASDs): toward identification of a behavioural phenotype.', *Scientific World Journal, 8*: 873–882.

Nasrallah, F., Feki, M. and Kaabachi, N. (2010) 'Creatine and creatine deficiency syndromes: biochemical and clinical aspects.', *Pediatric Neurology, 42*: 163–171.

Nassogne, M-C., Henrot, B., Aubert, G., Bonnier, C. *et al.* (2000) 'Adenylsuccinase deficiency: an unusual cause of early-onset epilepsy associated with acquired microcephaly.', *Brain and Development, 22*: 383–386.

Nataf, R., Skorupka, C., Amet, L., Lam, A. *et al.* (2006) 'Porphyrinuria in childhood autistic disorder: implications for environmental toxicity.', *Toxicology and Applied Pharmacology, 214*: 99–108.

Naviaux, R.K. (2000) 'Mitochondrial DNA disorders.' *European Journal of Pediatrics, 159* (Supplement 3): S219–S226.

Neal, E.G., Chaffe, H., Schwartz, R.H., Lawson, M.S. *et al.* (2008) 'The ketogenic diet for the treatment of childhood epilepsy: a randomised controlled trial.', *Lancet Neurology, 7*(6): 500–506.

Nebesio, T.D., Ming, W., Chen, S., Clegg, T. *et al.* (2007) 'Neurofibromin-deficient Schwann cells have increased lysophosphatidic acid dependent survival and migration-implications for increased neurofibroma formation during pregnancy.', *Glia, 55*(5): 527–536.

Nectoux, J., Heron, D., Tallot, M., Chelly, J. and Bienvenu, T. (2006) 'Maternal origin of a novel C-terminal mutation in CDKL5 causing a atypical form of Rett syndrome.' *Clinical Genetics, 70*: 29–33.

Nee, L.E., Caine, E.D., Polinsky, R.J., Eldridge, R. and Ebert, M.H. (1980) 'Gilles de la Tourette syndrome: clinical and family study of 50 cases.', *Annals of Neurology, 7*: 41–49.

Need, A.C., Ge, D., Weale, M.E., Maia, J. *et al.* (2009) 'A genome-wide investigation of SNPs and CNVs in schizophrenia.', *PLoS Genetics*, February, *5*(2): e1000373.

Nehal, K.S., PeBenito, R. and Orlow, S.J. (1996) 'Analysis of 54 cases of hypopigmentation and hyperpigmentation along the lines of Blaschko.', *Archives of Dermatology, 132*(10): 1167–1170.

Neklason, D.W., Andrews, K.M., Kelley, R.I. and Metherall, J.E. (1999) 'Biochemical variants of Smith-Lemli-Opitz syndrome.', *American Journal of Medical Genetics, 85*: 517–523.

Nelen, M.R., Kremer, H., Konings, I.B., Schoute, F. *et al.* (1999) 'Novel PTEN mutations in patients with Cowden disease: absence of clear genotype-phenotype correlations.', *European Journal of Human Genetics, 7*: 267–273.

Nelson, E.C. and Pribor, E.F. (1993) 'A calendar savant with autism and Tourette syndrome: response to treatment and thoughts on the interrelationships of these conditions.', *Annals of Clinical Psychiatry, 5*(2): 135–140.

Nelson, K.B., Grether, J.K., Croen, L.A., Dambrosia, J.M. *et al.* (2001) 'Neuropeptides and neurotrophins in neonatal blood of children with autism or mental retardation.', *Annals of Neurology, 49*(5): 597–606.

Nelson, P.G., Kuddo, T., Song, E.Y., Dambrosia, J.M. *et al.* (2006) 'Selected neurotrophins, neuropeptides, and cytokines: developmental trajectory and concentrations in neonatal blood of children with autism or Down syndrome.' *International Journal of Developmental Neuroscience, 24*(1): 73–80.

Nelson, S.F., Crosbie, R.H., Miceli, M.C. and Spencer, M.J. (2009) 'Emerging genetic therapies to treat Duchenne muscular dystrophy.', *Current Opinion in Neurology, 22*(5): 532–538.

Nereo, N.E., Fee, R.J. and Hinton, V.J. (2003) 'Parental stress in mothers of boys with duchenne muscular dystrophy.', *Journal of Pediatric Psychology, 28*(7): 473–484.

Neri, G., Genuardi, M., Natoli, G., Costa, P. and Maggioni, G. (1987) 'A girl with G syndrome and agenesis of the corpus callosum.', *American Journal of Medical Genetics, 28*: 287–291.

Neri, G., Gurrieri, F., Zanni, G. and Lin, A. (1998) 'Clinical molecular aspects of the Simpson-Golabi-Behmel syndrome.' *American Journal of Medical Genetics, 79*: 279–283.

Neri, G., Marini, R., Cappa, M., Borrelli, P. and Opitz, J.M. (1988) 'Simpson-Golabi-Behmel syndrome: an X-linked encephalo-trophoschisis syndrome.', *American Journal of Medical Genetics, 30*: 287–299.

Neri, M., Torelli, S., Brown, S., Ugo, I. *et al.* (2007) 'Dystrophin levels as low as 30 per cent are sufficient to avoid muscular dystrophy in the human.' *Neuromuscular Disorders, 17*: 913–918.

Neshat, M.S., Mellinghoff, I.K., Tran, C., Stiles, B. *et al.* (2001) 'Enhanced sensitivity of PTEN-deficient tumors to inhibition of FRAP / mTOR.', *Proceedings of the National Academy of Science, 98*(18): 10314–10319.

Neves-Pereira, M., Müller, B., Massie, D., Williams, J.H. *et al.* (2009) 'Deregulation of EIF4E: a novel mechanism for autism.', *Journal of Medical Genetics, 46*(11): 759–765.

New, M.I. (2004) 'An update of congenital adrenal hyperplasia.', *Annals of the New York Academy of Science, 1038*: 14–43.

Nguyen, D., Turner, J.T., Olsen, C., Biesecker, L.G. and Darling, T.N. (2004) 'Cutaneous manifestations of Proteus syndrome: correlations with general clinical severity.', *Archives of Dermatology, 140*(8): 947–953.

NIASA (National Initiative for Autism: Screening and Assessment) (2003) *National Autism Plan for Children.* Report produced in collaboration with the Royal College of Paediatrics and Child Health, the Royal College of Psychiatrists, and the All-Party Parliamentary Group on Autism (APPGA). London: NAS.

Nicholls, A.C., Oliver, J.E., McCarron, S., Harrison, J.B. *et al.* (1996) 'An exon skipping mutation of a type V collagen gene (COL5A1) in Ehlers-Danlos syndrome.', *Journal of Medical Genetics, 33*: 940–946.

Nichols, J.C., Amato, J.E. and Chung, S.M. (2003) 'Characteristics of Lisch nodules in patients with neurofibromatosis type 1.', *Journal of Pediatric Ophthalmology and Strabismus, 40*(5): 293–296.

Nicholls, R.D., Saitoh, S. and Horsthemke, B. (1998) 'Imprinting in Prader–Willi and Angelman syndromes.' *Trends in Genetics, 14*: 194–200

Nickerson, E., Greenberg, F., Keating, M.T., McCaskill, C. and Shaffer, L.G. (1995) 'Deletions of the elastin gene at 7q11.23 occur in approximately 90 per cent of patients with Williams syndrome.', *American Journal of Human Genetics, 56*: 1156–1161.

Nicoletti, F., Bruno, V., Copani, A., Casabona, G. and Knöpfel, T. (1996) 'Metabotropic glutamate receptors: a new target for the therapy of neurodegenerative disorders?' *Trends in the Neurosciences, 19*: 267–271.

Nicolson, R., Bhalerao, S. and Sloman, L. (1998) '47,XYY karyotypes and pervasive developmental disorders.', *Canadian Journal of Psychiatry, 43*: 619–622.

Nicot, A., Otto, T., Brabet, P. and Dicicco-Bloom, E.M. (2004) 'Altered social behaviour in pituitary adenylate cyclase-activating polypeptide type I receptor-deficient mice.', *Journal of Neuroscience, 24(40)*: 8786–8795.

Niederhofer, H. (2007) 'Glutamate antagonists seem to be slightly effective in psychopharmacologic treatment of autism.' (Letter) *Journal of Clinical Psychopharmacology, 27*(3): 317.

Niedernhofer, L.J. (2008) 'Nucleotide excision repair deficient mouse models and neurological disease.', *DNA Repair, 7*: 1180–1189.

Nielsen, J., Pelsen, B. and Sorensen, K. (1988) 'Follow-up of 30 Klinefelter males treated with testosterone.', *Clinical Genetics, 33*: 262–269.

Nielsen, J. and Videbech, P. (1984) 'Diagnosing of chromosome abnormalities in Denmark.', *Clinican Genetics, 26*: 422–428.

Nielsen, J. and Wohlert, M. (1991) 'Chromosome abnormalities found among 34,910 newborn children: results from a 13-year incidence study in Arhus, Denmark.', *Human Genetics, 87*: 81–83.

Nienhuis, A.W., Dunbar, C.E. and Sorrentino, B.P. (2006) 'Genotoxicity of retroviral integration in hematopoietic cells.', *Molecular Therapy, 13*(6): 1031–1049.

Nigro, G., Comi, L.I., Politano, L. and Bain, R.J. (1990) 'The incidence and evolution of cardiomyopathy in Duchenne muscular dystrophy.', *International Journal of Cardiology, 26*: 271–277.

NIH Consensus Development Conference (1988) 'Neurofibromatosis. conference statement.', *Archives of Neurology. 45*: 575–578.

Niikawa, N. and Kajii, T. (1984) 'The origin of mosaic down syndrome: four cases with chromosome markers.', *American Journal of Human Genetics, 36*: 123–130.

Nijhawan, N., Morad, Y., Seigel-Bartelt, J. and Levin, A.V. (2002) 'Caruncle abnormalities in the oculo-auriculo-vertebral spectrum.' *American Journal of Medical Genetics, 113*: 320–325.

Niklasson, L. and Gillberg, C. (2010) 'The neuropsychology of 22q11 deletion syndrome: a neuropsychiatric study of 100 individuals.', *Research in Developmental Disabilities, 31*: 185–194.

Niklasson, L., Rasmussen, P., Oskarsdóttir, S. and Gillberg, C. (2001) 'Neuropsychiatric disorders in the 22q11 deletion syndrome.' *Genetics in Medicine, 3*: 79–84.

Niklasson, L., Rasmussen, P., Oskarsdottir, S. and Gillberg, C. (2002) 'Chromosome 22q11 deletion syndrome (CATCH 22): neuropsychiatric and neuropsychological aspects.' *Developmental Medicine and Child Neurology, 44*: 44–50.

Nilsson, M., Waters, S., Waters, N., Carlsson, A. and Carlsson, M.L. (2001) 'A behavioural pattern analysis of hypoglutamatergic mice – effects of four different antipsychotic agents.', *Journal of Neural Transmission, 108*: 1181–1196.

Nishi, A., Liu, F., Matsuyama, S., Hamada, M. *et al.* (2003) 'Metabotropic mGlu5 receptors regulate adenosine A2A receptor signaling.', *Proceedings of the National Academy of Science, 100*: 1322–1327.

Nishi, A., Watanabe, Y., Higashi, H., Tanaka, M., Nairn, A.C. and Greengard, P. (2005) 'Glutamate regulation of DARPP-32 phosphorylation in neostriatal neurons involves activation of multiple signaling cascades.' *Proceedings of the National Academy of Science, 102*: 1199–1204.

Nishimura, D.Y., Fath, M., Mullins, R.F., Searby, C. *et al.* (2004) 'Bbs2-null mice have neurosensory deficits, a defect in social dominance, and retinopathy associated with mislocalization of rhodopsin.', *Proceedings of the National Academy of Science USA, 101*: 16588–16593.

Nishimura, D.Y., Swiderski, R.E., Searby, C.C., Berg, E.M. *et al.* (2005) 'Comparative genomics and gene expression analysis identifies BBS9, a new Bardet-Biedl syndrome gene.', *American Journal of Human Genetics, 77*: 1021–1033.

Nishino, T., Okamoto, K., Kawaguchi, Y., Hori, H. *et al.* (2005) 'Mechanism of conversion of xanthine dehydrogenase to xanthine oxidase: identification of the two cysteine disulfide bonds and crystal structure of a non-convertible rat liver xanthine dehydrogenase mutant.', *Journal of Biological Chemistry, 280*: 24888–24894.

Nolan, M.A., Jones, O.D., Pedersen, R.L. and Johnston, H.M. (2003) 'Cardiac assessment in childhood carriers of Duchenne and Becker muscular dystrophies.', *Neuromuscular Disorders*. *13*(2): 129–132.

Nolin, S.L., Brown, W.T., Glicksman, A., Houck, G.E. Jr. *et al.* (2003) 'Expansion of the fragile-X CGG repeat in females with premutation or intermediate alleles.', *American Journal of Human Genetics*, *72*: 454–464.

Nolin, S.L., Glicksman, A., Houck, G.E. Jr., Brown, W.T. and Dobkin, C.S. (1994) 'Mosaicism in fragile-X affected males.' *American Journal of Medical Genetics*, *51*: 509–512.

Nonogaki, K., Ohashi-Nozue, K. and Oka, Y. (2006) 'A negative feedback system between brain serotonin systems and plasma active ghrelin levels in mice.' *Biochemical and Biophysical Research Communications*, *341*: 703–707.

Noonan, J.A. (2002) 'Noonan syndrome: a historical perspective.', *Heart Views*, *3*(2): 102–106.

Noonan, J.A., Raaijmakers, R. and Hall, B.D. (2003) 'Adult height in Noonan syndrome.', *American Journal of Medical Genetics A*, *123A*(1): 68–71.

Noordam, C., Peer, P.G., Francois, I., De Schepper, J. *et al.* (2008) 'Long-term GH treatment improves adult height in children with Noonan syndrome with and without mutations in protein tyrosine phosphatase, non-receptor-type 11.', *European Journal of Endocrinology*, *159*(3): 203–208.

Norio, R. (2003) 'The Finnish disease heritage. I. Characteristics, causes, background.', *Human Genetics*, *112*: 441–456.

Norremolle, A., Nielsen, J.E., Sorensen, S.A. and Hasholt, L. (1995) 'Elongated CAG repeats of the B37 gene in a Danish family with dentato-rubro-pallido-luysian atrophy.', *Human Genetics*, *95*: 313–318.

North, K. (1999) 'Cognitive function and academic performance.', In J.M. Friedman, D.H. Gutmann, M. MacCollin and V.M. Riccardi (eds.) *Neurofibromatosis: Phenotype, Natural History, and Pathogenesis.* Baltimore: Johns Hopkins University Press, pp. 162–189.

North, K.N., Riccardi, V., Samango-Sprouse, C., Ferner, R. *et al.* (1997) 'Cognitive function and academic performance in neurofibromatosis. 1: Consensus statement from the NF1 Cognitive Disorders Task Force.', *Neurology*, *48*(4): 1121–1127.

Nowacki, P., Byck, S., Prevost, L. and Scriver, C.R. (1997) 'The PAH mutation analysis consortium database: update 1996.', *Nucleic Acids Research*, *25*: 139–142.

Nowaczyk, M.J.M., Heshka, T., Eng, B., Feigenbaum, A.J. and Waye, J.S. (2001a) 'DHCR7 genotypes of cousins with Smith-Lemli-Opitz syndrome.', *American Journal of Medical Genetics*, *100*: 162–163.

Nowaczyk, M.J.M., Siu, V.M., Krakowiak, P.A. and Porter, F.D. (2001b) 'Adrenal insufficiency and hypertension in a newborn infant with Smith-Lemli-Opitz syndrome.', *American Journal of Medical Genetics*, *103*: 223–225.

Nowaczyk, M.J.M. and Waye, J.S. (2001) 'The Smith-Lemli-Opitz syndrome: a novel metabolic way of understanding developmental biology, embryogenesis, and dysmorphology. *Clinical Genetics*, *59*(6): 375–386.

Nowaczyk, M.J.M., Whelan, D.T. and Hill, R.E. (1998) 'Smith-Lemli-Opitz syndrome: phenotypic extreme with minimal clinical findings.', *American Journal of Medical Genetics*, *78*: 419–423.

Nowak, C.B. (2007) 'The phacomatoses: dermatologic clues to neurologic anomalies.', *Seminars in Pediatric Neurology*, *14*: 140–149.

Nowak, K.J. and Davies, K.E. (2004) 'Duchenne muscular dystrophy and dystrophin: pathogenesis and opportunities for treatment.', *EMBO Reports*, *5*: 872–876.

Nurmi, E.L., Bradford, Y., Chen, Y., Hall, J. *et al.* (2001) 'Linkage disequilibrium at the Angelman syndrome gene UBE3A in autism families.', *Genomics*, *77*(1–2): 105–113.

Nwokoro, N.A. and Mulvihill, J.J. (1997) 'Cholesterol and bile acid replacement therapy in children and adults with Smith-Lemli-Opitz (SLO/RSH) syndrome.', *American Journal of Medical Genetics*, *68*: 315–321.

Nyhan, W.L. (1987) 'Inborn errors of biotin metabolism.' *Archives of Dermatology*, *123*(12): 1696–1698.

Nylen, K., Velazquez, J.L., Sayed, V., Gibson, K.M. *et al.* (2009) 'The effects of a ketogenic diet on ATP concentrations and the number of hippocampal mitochondria in Aldh5a1(−/−) mice.', *Biochimica et Biophysica Acta*, *1790*(3): 208–212.

Obeid, R. and Herrmann, W. (2006) 'Priorities in the discovery of the implications of water channels in epilepsy and Duchenne muscular dystrophy.' *Cellular and Molecular Biology (Noisy-le-grand)*, *52*(5): 16–20.

Oberholzer, V.G., Levin, B., Burgess, E.A. and Young, W.F. (1967) 'Methylmalonic aciduria: an inborn error of metabolism leading to chronic metabolic acidosis.', *Archives of Diseases in Childhood*, *42*: 492–504.

O'Brien, G. and Yule, W. (eds.) (1996) *Behavioural Phenotypes*, Clinics in Developmental Medicine, *138*. Cambridge: Cambridge University Press.

O'Callaghan, F.J.K., Noakes, M. and Osborne, J.P. (2000) 'Renal angiomyolipomata and learning difficulties in tuberous sclerosis complex.', *Journal of Medical Genetics*, *37*: 156–157.

O'Donnell, L., Soileau, B., Patricia Heard, P., Carter, E. *et al.* (2010) 'Genetic determinants of autism in individuals with deletions of 18q.' *Human Genetics*, doi:10.1007/s00439-010-0839-y.

O'Dea, D., Parfrey, P.S., Harnett, J.D., Hefferton, D. *et al.* (1996) 'The importance of renal impairment in the natural history of Bardet-Biedl syndrome.', *American Journal of Kidney Disease*, *27*: 776–783.

O'Doherty, A., Ruf, S., Mulligan, C., Hildreth, V. *et al.* (2005) 'An aneuploid mouse strain carrying human chromosome 21 with Down syndrome phenotypes.', *Science*, *309*: 2033–2037.

O'Donovan, M.C., Craddock, N. and Owen, M.J. (2008) 'Schizophrenia: complex genetics, not fairy tales.', *Psychological Medicine*, *38*: 1697–1699.

Oexle, K., Thamm-Mucke, B., Mayer, T. and Tinschert, S. (2005) 'Macrocephalic mental retardation associated with a novel C-terminal MeCP2 frameshift deletion.', *European Journal of Pediatrics*, *164*: 154–157.

Ogawa, M., Moriya, N., Ikeda, H., Tanae, A. *et al.* (2004) 'Clinical evaluation of recombinant human growth hormone in Noonan syndrome.', *Endocrinology Journal, 51*: 61–68.

Ogier, M., Wang, H., Hong, E., Wang, Q. *et al.* (2007) 'Brain-derived neurotrophic factor expression and respiratory function improve after ampakine treatment in a mouse model of Rett syndrome.', *Journal of Neuroscience, 27*(40): 10912–10917.

Ogilvie, C.M., Crouch, N.S., Rumsby, G., Creighton, S.M. *et al.* (2006) 'Congenital adrenal hyperplasia in adults: a review of medical, surgical and psychological issues.', *Clinical Endocrinology (Oxford), 64*: 2–11.

Ogino, T., Ohtsuka, Y., Yamatogi, Y., Oka, E. and Ohtahara, S. (1989) 'The epileptic syndrome sharing common characteristics during early childhood with severe myoclonic epilepsy in infancy.', *Japanese Journal of Psychiatry and Neurology, 43*: 479–481.

Ogura, K. (2006) ['Dihydropyrimidine dehydrogenase activity and its genetic aberrations.'] [Article in Japanese.] *Gan To Kagaku Ryoho, 33*(8): 1041–1048.

Ohki, T., Watanabe, K., Negoro, T., Aso, K. *et al.* (1997) 'Severe myoclonic epilepsy in infancy: evolution of seizures.', *Seizure, 6*(3): 219–224.

Ohtsuka, Y., Maniwa, S., Ogino, T., Yamatogi, Y. and Ohtahara, S. (1991) 'Severe myoclonic epilepsy in infancy: a long-term follow-up study.', *Japanese Journal of Psychiatry and Neurology, 45*(2): 416–418.

Oikawa, H., Tun, Z., Young, D.R., Ozawa, H. *et al.* (2002) 'The specific mitochondrial DNA polymorphism found in Klinefelter's syndrome.', *Biochemical and Biophysical Research Communications, 297*: 341–345.

Oike, Y., Hata, A., Mamiya, T., Kaname, T. *et al.* (1999) 'Truncated CBP protein leads to classical Rubinstein-Taybi syndrome phenotypes in mice: implications for a dominant-negative mechanism.', *Human Molecular Genetics, 8*: 387–396.

Okano, M., Kitano, Y., Yoshikawa, K., Nakamura, T. *et al.* (1988) 'X-linked ichthyosis and ichthyosis vulgaris: comparison of their clinical features based on biochemical analysis.', *British Journal of Dermatology, 119*(6): 777–783.

Okten, A., Kalyoncu, M. and Yaris, N. (2002) 'The ratio of second- and fourth-digit lengths and congenital adrenal hyperplasia due to 21-hydroxylase deficiency.', *Early Human Development, 70*(1–2): 47–54.

Oldendorf, W.H. and Szabo, J. (1976) 'Amino acid assignment to one of three blood-brain barrier amino acid carriers.', *American Journal of Physiology, 230*: 94–98.

Oldridge, M., Zackai, E.H., McDonald-McGinn, D.M., Iseki, S. *et al.* (1999) '*De novo* Alu-element insertions in FGFR2 identify a distinct pathological basis for Apert syndrome.', *American Journal of Human Genetics, 64*: 446–461.

O'Leary, D.M., Movsesyan, V., Vicini, S. and Faden, A.I. (2000) 'Selective mGluR5 antagonists MPEP and SIB-1893 decrease NMDA or glutamate-mediated neuronal toxicity through actions that reflect NMDA receptor antagonism.', *British Journal of Pharmacology, 131*: 1429–1437.

Oliveira, G., Diogo, L., Grazina, M., Garcia, P. *et al.* (2005) 'Mitochondrial dysfunction in autism spectrum disorders: a population-based study.' *Developmental Medicine and Child Neurology. 47*: 185–189.

Oliveira, M.M., Conti, C., Saconato, H. and Fernandes do Prado, G. (2009) 'Pharmacological treatment for Kleine-Levin syndrome.', *Cochrane Database Systematic Reviews, 2*: CD006685.

Oliver, C., Moss, J., Petty, J., Arron, K. *et al.* (2003) *Self-injurious Behaviour in Cornelia de Lange Syndrome: A Guide for Parents and Carers.* Coventry: Trident Communications Ltd.

Oliveri, B., Mastaglia, S.R., Mautalen, C., Gravano, J.C. and Pardo Argerich, L. (2004) 'Long-term control of hypercalcaemia in an infant with Williams-Beuren syndrome after a single infusion of biphosphonate (Pamidronate).', *Acta Paediatrica, 93*(7): 1002–1003.

Olson, L.E., Richtsmeier, J.T., Leszl, J. and Reeves, R.H. (2004) 'A chromosome 21 critical region does not cause specific Down syndrome phenotypes.', *Science, 306*: 687–690.

Olsson, G.M., Montgomery, S.M. and Alm, J. (2007) 'Family conditions and dietary control in phenylketonuria.', *Journal of Inherited Metabolic Disease, 30*: doi:10.1007/s10545-007-0493-2.

O'Malley, M.R., Kaylie, D.M., Van Himbergen, D.J., Bennett, M.L. and Jackson, C.G. (2007) 'Chronic ear surgery in patients with syndromes and multiple congenital malformations.', *The Laryngoscope, 117*(111): 1993–1998.

Omerovic, J., Laude, A.J. and Prior, I.A. (2007) 'Ras proteins: paradigms for compartmentalised and isoform-specific signalling.', *Cellular and Molecular Life Sciences, 64*(19–20): 2575–2589.

Omgreen, M., Olsen, D. and Vissing, L. (2005) 'Aerobic training in patients with myotonic dystrophy type 1.', *Annals of Neurology, 57*: 754–757.

O'Neill, B.P., Vernino, S., Dogan, A. and Giannini, C. (2007) 'EBV-associated lymphoproliferative disorder of CNS associated with the use of mycophenolate mofetil.', *Neuro-Oncology, 9*: 364–369.

Onishi, A., Hasegawa, J., Imai, H., Chisaka, O. *et al.* (2005) 'Generation of knock-in mice carrying third cones with spectral sensitivity different from S and L cones.', *Zoological Science, 22*: 1145–1156.

Oostra, R.J., Baljet, B. and Hennekam, R.C. (1994) 'Brachmann-de Lange syndrome "avant la lettre".', *American Journal of Medical Genetics, 52*: 267–268.

Opitz, J.M. (1985) 'The Brachmann-de Lange syndrome.', *American Journal of Medical Genetics, 22*: 89–102.

Opitz, J.M. (1999) 'RSH (so-called Smith-Lemli-Opitz) syndrome.', *Current Opinion in Pediatrics, 11*: 353–362.

Opitz, J.M. and de la Cruz, F. (1994) 'Cholesterol metabolism in the RSH/Smith-Lemli-Opitz syndrome: summary of an NICHD conference.', *American Journal of Medical Genetics, 50*: 326–338.

Opitz, J.M., Gilbert-Barness, E., Ackerman, J. and Lowichik, A. (2002) 'Cholesterol and development: the RSH ("Smith-Lemli-Opitz") syndrome and related conditions.', *Pediatric Pathology and Molecular Medicine, 21*: 153–181.

Opitz, J.M., Penchaszadeh, V.B., Holt, M.C., Spano, L.M. and Smith, V.L. (1994) 'Smith-Lemli-Opitz (RSH) syndrome bibliography: 1964–1993.', *American Journal of Medical Genetics, 50*: 339–343.

Opitz, J.M., Summitt, R.L., Smith, D.W. and Sarto, G.E. (1965) 'Noonan's syndrome in girls: a genocopy of the Ullrich-Turner syndrome.', *Journal of Pediatrics, 5*(2): 968 (Abstract).

Opitz, J.M., Weaver, D.W. and Reynolds, J.F. Jr. (1998) 'The syndromes of Sotos and Weaver: reports and review.', *American Journal of Medical Genetics, 79*: 294–304.

Opitz, J.M., Westphal, J.M. and Daniel, A. (1984) 'Discovery of a connective tissue dysplasia in the Martin-Bell syndrome.' *American Journal of Medical Genetics, 17*: 101–109.

O'Riordan, S., Patton, M. and Schon, F. (2006) 'Treatment of drop episodes in Coffin-Lowry syndrome.', *Journal of Neurology, 253*: 109–110.

Ornitz, E.M. (1973) 'Childhood autism: a review of the clinical and experimental literature.', *California Medicine: The Western Journal of Medicine, 118*: 21–47.

Ornitz, E.M., Guthrie, D. and Farley, A.H. (1977) 'The early development of autistic children.', *Journal of Autism and Childhood Schizophrenia, 7*: 207–229.

Orphanet (2009) 'Prevalence of rare diseases: bibliographic data. 'www.orpha.net/orphacom/cahiers/docs/GB/Prevalence_of_rare_diseases_by_alphabetical_list.pdf

Orrico, A., Galli, L., Cavaliere, M.L., Garavelli, L. *et al.* (2004) 'Phenotypic and molecular characterisation of the Aarskog-Scott syndrome: a survey of the clinical variability in light of FGD1 mutation analysis in 46 patients.' *European Journal of Human Genetics, 12*: 16–23.

Orrico, A., Galli, L., Dotti, M.T., Plewnia, K. *et al.* (1998) 'Mosaicism for full mutation and normal-sized allele of the FMR1 gene: a new case.', *American Journal of Medical Genetics, 78*(4): 341–344.

Orrico, A., Hayek, G. and Burroni, L. (1999) 'Autosomal recessive syndrome of growth and mental retardation, seizures, retinal abnormalities, and osteodysplasia with similarity to the Gurrieri syndrome.', *American Journal of Medical Genetics, 82*(1): 84–87.

Orstavik, K.H., Eiklid, K., van der Hagen, C.B., Spetalen, S. *et al.* (2003) 'Another case of imprinting defect in a girl with Angelman syndrome who was conceived by intracytoplasmic sperm injection.', (Letter) *American Journal of Human Genetics, 72*: 218–219.

Orstavik, K.H., Stromme, P., Ek, J., Torvik, A. and Skjeldal, O.H. (1997) 'Macrocephaly, epilepsy, autism, dysmorphic features, and mental retardation in two sisters: a new autosomal recessive syndrome?' *Journal of Medical Genetics, 34*: 849–851.

Orth, M., Kirby, R., Richardson, M.P., Snijders, A.H. *et al.* (2005) 'Subthreshold rTMS over pre-motor cortex has no effect on tics in patients with Gilles de la Tourette syndrome.', *Clinical Neurophysiology, 116*(4): 764–768.

Orth, U., Gurrieri, F., Behmel, A., Genuardi, M. *et al.* (1994) 'Gene for Simpson-Golabi-Behmel syndrome is linked to HPRT in Xq26 in two European families.', *American Journal of Medical Genetics, 50*: 388–390.

Osborne, L.R., Martindale, D., Scherer, S.W., Shi, X-M. *et al.* (1996) 'Identification of genes from a 500 kb region at 7q11.23 that is commonly deleted in Williams syndrome.', *Genomics, 36*: 328–336.

Oskarsdóttir, S., Belfrage, M., Sandstedt, E., Viggedal, G. and Uvebrant, P. (2005) 'Disabilities and cognition in children and adolescents with 22q11 deletion syndrome.', *Developmental Medicine and Child Neurology, 47*: 177–184

Oskarsdóttir, S., Persson, C., Eriksson, B.O. and Fasth, A. (2005) 'Presenting phenotype in 100 children with the 22q11 deletion syndrome.', *European Journal of Pediatrics, 164*: 146–153.

Oskarsdóttir, S., Vujic, M. and Fasth, A. (2004) 'Incidence and prevalence of the 22q11 deletion syndrome: a population-based study in Western Sweden.', *Archives of Disease in Childhood, 89*(2): 148–151.

Ospina, M.B., Seida, J.K., Clark, B., Karkhaneh, M. *et al.* (2008) 'Behavioural and developmental interventions for autism spectrum disorder: a clinical systematic review.', *PLoS ONE, 3*(11): e3755. doi:10.1371/journal.pone.0003755.

Østergaard, J.R., Sunde, L. and Okkels, H. (2005) 'Neurofibromatosis von Recklinghausen type I phenotype and early onset of cancers in siblings compound heterozygous for mutations in MSH6.', *American Journal of Medical Genetics A, 139A*(2): 96–105.

Otani, H., Tanaka, O., Naora, H., Yokoyama, M. *et al.* (1991) 'Microtia as an autosomal dominant mutation in a transgenic mouse line: a possible animal model of branchial arch anomalies.', *Anaomischert Anzeiger, 172*: 1–9.

Otto, E.A., Loeys, B., Khanna, H., Hellemans, J. *et al.* (2005) 'Nephrocystin-5, a ciliary IQ domain protein, is mutated in Senior-Loken syndrome and interacts with RPGR and calmodulin.', *Nature Genetics, 37*: 282–288.

Otto, E.A., Schermer, B., Obara, T., O'Toole, J.F. *et al.* (2003) 'Mutations in INVS encoding inversin cause nephronophthisis type 2, linking renal cystic disease to the function of primary cilia and left-right axis determination.', *Nature Genetics, 34*: 413–420.

Otto, L.R., Boriack, R.L., Marsh, D.J., Kum, J.B. *et al.* (1999) 'Long-chain L 3-hydroxyacyl-CoA dehydrogenase (LCHAD) deficiency does not appear to be the primary cause of lipid myopathy in patients with Bannayan-Riley-Ruvalcaba syndrome (BRRS).', *American Journal of Medical Genetics, 83*(1): 3–5.

Ou, C.Y., Stevenson, R.E., Brown, V.K., Schwartz, C.E. *et al.* (1996) '5,10 methylenetetrahydrofolate reductase genetic polymorphism as a risk factor for neural tube defects.', *American Journal of Medical Genetics, 63*: 610–614.

Ouldim, K., Natiq, A., Jonveaux, P. and Sefiani, A. (2007) 'case report: tetrasomy 15q11–q13 diagnosed by FISH in a patient with autistic disorder.', *Journal of Biomedicine and Biotechnology*, Article ID 61538, doi:10.1155/2007/61538.

Ousley, O., Rockers, K., Dell, M.L., Coleman, K. and Cubells, J.F. (2007) 'A review of neurocognitive and behavioural profiles associated with 22q11 deletion syndrome: implications for clinical evaluation and treatment.', *Current Psychiatry Reports, 9*: 148–158.

Ozonoff, S., Iosif, A.M., Baguio, F., Cook, I.C. *et al.* (2010) 'A prospective study of the emergence of early behavioural signs of autism.', *Journal of the American Academy of Child and Adolescent Psychiatry, 49*(3): 258–268.

Ozonoff, S., Williams, B.J., Gale, S. and Miller, J.N. (1999) 'Autism and autistic behaviour in Joubert syndrome.', *Journal of Child Neurology, 14*: 636–641.

Pacher, P., Nivorozhkin, A., and Szabo, C. (2006) 'Therapeutic effects of xanthine oxidase inhibitors: renaissance half a century after the discovery of allopurinol.', *Pharmacological Reviews, 58*(1): 87–114.

Packer, R.J., Gutmann, D.H., Rubenstein, A., Viskochil, D. *et al.* (2002) 'Plexiform neurofibromas in NF1: toward biologic-based therapy.', *Neurology, 58*: 1461–1470.

Packer, R.J. and Rosser, T. (2002) 'Therapy for plexiform neurofibromas in children with neurofibromatosis 1: an overview.', *Journal of Child Neurology, 17*: 638–641.

Packham, E.A. and Brook, J.D. (2003) 'T-box genes in human disorders.', *Human Molecular Genetics, 12*(Review Issue 1): R37–R44.

Page, P.Z., Page, G.P., Ecosse, E., Korf, B.R. *et al.* (2006) 'Impact of neurofibromatosis 1 on quality of life: a cross-sectional study of 176 American cases.', *American Journal of Medical Genetics A, 140*: 1893–1898.

Page, T. (2000) 'Metabolic approaches to the treatment of autism spectrum disorders.', *Journal of Autism and Developmental Disorders, 30*: 463–469.

Page, T. and Coleman, M. (2000) 'Purine metabolism abnormalities in a hyperuricosuric subclass of autism.', *Biochimica et Biophysica Acta, 1500*: 291–296.

Page, T. and Moseley, C. (2002) 'Metabolic treatment of hyperuricosuric autism.', *Progress in Neuropsychopharmacology and Biological Psychiatry. 26*(2): 397–400.

Page, T., Yu, A., Fontanesi, J. and Nyhan, W.L. (1997) 'Developmental disorder associated with increased nucleotidase activity.', *Proceedings of the National Academy of Sciences USA, 94*: 11601–11606.

Pagliardini, S., Ren, J., Wevrick, R. and Greer, J.J. (2005) 'Developmental abnormalities of neuronal structure and function in prenatal mice lacking the Prader-Willi Syndrome gene necdin.', *American Journal of Pathology, 167*(1): 175–191.

Paine, R.S. (1957) 'The variability in manifestations of untreated patients with phenylketonuria (phenylpyruvic aciduria).', *Pediatrics, 20*(2): 290–302.

Palacios, J., Gamallo, C., Garcia, M. and Rodriguez, J.I. (1993) 'Decrease in thyrocalcitonin-containing cells and analysis of other congenital anomalies in 11 patients with DiGeorge anomaly.', *American Journal of Medical Genetics, 46*: 641–646.

Pallanti, S., Lassi, S., La Malfa, G., Campigli, M. *et al.* (2005) 'Short report. Autistic gastrointestinal and eating symptoms treated with secretin: a subtype of autism.', *Clinical Practice and Epidemiology in Mental Health, 1*: 24, doi:10.1186/1745-0179-1-24.

Palmer, S. (1978) 'Influence of vitamin A nutriture on the immune response: findings in children with Down's syndrome.', *International Journal of Vitamin and Nutrition Research, 48*(2): 188–216.

Palmini, A. and Luders, H.O. (2002) 'Classification issues in malformations caused by abnormalities of cortical development.', *Neurosurgical Clinics of North America, 13*: 1–16.

Palmucci, L., Mongini, T., Chiado-Piat, L., Doriguzzi, C. and Fubini, A. (2000) 'Dystrophinopathy expressing as either cardiomyopathy or Becker dystrophy in the same family.', *Neurology, 54*: 529–530.

Palomo, R., Belinchon, M. and Ozonoff, M. (2006) 'Autism and family home movies: a comprehensive review.' *Developmental and Behavioural Pediatrics, 27*: S59–S68.

Pan, L., Zhang, Y.Q., Woodruff, E. and Broadie, K. (2004) 'The drosophila fragile-X gene negatively regulates neuronal elaboration and synaptic differentiation.', *Current Biology, 14*: 1863–1870.

Pandi-Perumal, S., Srinivasan, V., Poeggeler, B., Hardeland, R. and Cardinali, D.P. (2007) 'Drug insight: the use of melatonergic agonists for the treatment of insomnia – focus on ramelteon.', *Nature Clinical Practice: Neurology, 3*(4): 221–228.

Pang, S. and Shook, M.K. (1997) 'Current status of neonatal screening for congenital adrenal hyperplasia.', *Current Opinion in Pediatrics, 9*: 419–423.

Pankau, R., Gosch, A., Simeon, E. and Wessel, A. (1993) 'Williams-Beuren syndrome in monozygotic twins with variable expression.', *American Journal of Medical Genetics, 47*: 475–477.

Pankau, R., Partsch, C-J., Gosch, A., Oppermann, H.C. and Wessel, A. (1992) 'Statural growth in Williams-Beuren syndrome.', *European Journal of Pediatrics, 151*: 751–755.

Pankau, R., Siebert, R., Kautza, M., Schneppenheim, R. *et al.* (2001) 'Familial Williams-Beuren syndrome showing varying clinical expression.', *American Journal of Medical Genetics, 98*: 324–329.

Panksepp, J. (2006) 'Emotional endophenotypes in evolutionary psychiatry.', *Progress in Neuro-Psychopharmacology and Biological Psychiatry, 30*: 774–784.

Papadimos, T.J. and Marco, A.P. (2003) 'Cornelia de Lange syndrome, hyperthermia and a difficult airway.', *Anaesthesia, 58*: 924–925.

Papapetrou, C., Lynch, S.A., Burn, J. and Edwards, Y.H. (1996) 'Methylenetetrahydrofolate reductase and neural tube defects.' (Letter) *Lancet, 348*: 58 only.

Parisi, M.A., Bennett, C.L., Eckert, M.L., Dobyns, W.B. *et al.* (2004) 'The NPHP1 gene deletion associated with juvenile nephronophthisis is present in a subset of individuals with Joubert syndrome.', *American Journal of Human Genetics, 75*: 82–91.

Parisi, M.A., Doherty, D., Chance, P.F. and Glass, I.A. (2007) 'Joubert syndrome (and related disorders).' *European Journal of Human Genetics, 15*(5): 511–521.

Parisi, M.A., Doherty, D., Eckert, M.L., Shaw, D.W.W. *et al.* (2006) 'AHI1 mutations cause both retinal dystrophy and renal cystic disease in Joubert syndrome.', *Journal of Medical Genetics, 43*: 334–339.

Parisi, M.A. and Glass, I.A. (2007) 'Joubert syndrome.', *GeneReviews*, web-based resource.

Park, B.K. and Kitteringham, N.R. (1988) 'Relevance and means of assessing induction and inhibition of drug metabolism in man.' In G.G. Gibson (ed.) *Progress in Drug Metabolism, 11*. New York: Taylor and Francis.

Park, W-J., Theda, C., Maestri, N.E., Meyers, G.A. *et al.* (1995) 'Analysis of phenotypic features and FGFR2 mutations in Apert syndrome.', *American Journal of Human Genetics*, *57*: 321–328.

Park, Y.D. (2003) 'The effects of vagus nerve stimulation therapy on patients with intractable seizures and either Landau-Kleffner syndrome or autism.', *Epilepsy and Behaviour*, *4*: 286–290.

Parkes, J.D. (1999) 'Genetic factors in human sleep disorders with special reference to Norrie disease, Prader±Willi syndrome and Moebius syndrome.', *Journal of Sleep Research*, *8*(Supp. 1): 14–22.

Parkes Weber, F. (1909) 'Cutaneous pigmentation as an incomplete form of Recklinghausen's disease with remarks on the classification of incomplete forms of the disease.', *British Journal of Dermatology*, *21*: 49–51.

Parry, G.J. and Bredesen, D.E. (1985) 'Sensory neuropathy with low-dose pyridoxine.' *Neurology*, *35*(10): 1466–1468.

Parsa, C.F., Hoyt, C.S., Lesser, R.L., Weinstein, J.M. *et al.* (2001) 'Spontaneous regression of optic gliomas: thirteen cases documented by serial neuroimaging.', *Archives of Ophthalmology*, *119*: 516–529.

Parsons, H.G., Jamal, R., Baylis, B., Dias, V.C. and Roncari, D. (1995) 'A marked and sustained reduction in LDL sterols by diet and cholestyramine in beta-sitosterolemia.', *Clinical and Investigative Medicine*, *18*(5): 389–400.

Parsons, S., Guldberg, K., MacLeod, A., Jones, G., Prunty, A. and Balfe, T. (2009) 'International review of the literature of evidence of best practice provision in the education of persons with autistic spectrum disorders.', *National Council for Special Education Research Reports*, *2*, University of Birmingham, downloadable from www.ncse.ie/uploads/1/Autism_Report.pdf.

Partington, M.W. (1988) 'Rett syndrome in monozygotic twins.', *American Journal of Medical Genetics*, *29*: 633–637.

Partington, M.W. and MacDonald, M.R. (1971) '5-hydroxytryptophan (5-HTP) in Down's syndrome.', *Developmental Medicine and Child Neurology*, *13*(3): 362–372.

Partington, M.W., Mulley, J.C., Sutherland, G.R., Hockey, A. *et al.* (1988) 'X-linked mental retardation with dystonic movements of the hands.', *American Journal of Medical Genetics*, *30*: 251–262.

Partington, M.W., Turner, G., Boyle, J. and Gecz, J. (2004) 'Three new families with X-linked mental retardation caused by the 428–451dup(24bp) mutation in ARX.', *Clinical Genetics*, *66*: 39–45.

Partsch, C-J., Japing, I., Siebert, R., Gosch, A. *et al.* (2002) 'Central precocious puberty in girls with Williams syndrome.', *Journal of Pediatrics*, *141*: 441–444.

Pascual-Castroviejo, I., Lopez-Rodriguez, L., de la Cruz Medina, M., Salamanca-Maesso, C. and Roche Herrero, C. (1988) 'Hypomelanosis of Ito: neurological complications in 34 cases.', *Canadian Journal of Neurological Science*, *15*(2): 124–129.

Pascual-Castroviejo, I., Pascual-Pascual, S.I., Quijano-Roy, S., Gutiérrez-Molina, M. *et al.* (2006) ['Cerebellar ataxia of Norman-Jaeken: presentation of seven Spanish patients'.] *Revista de Neurologia*, *42*(12): 723–728.

Pascual-Castroviejo, I., Roche, C., Martinez-Bermejo, A., Arcas, J. *et al.* (1998) 'Hypomelanosis of ITO: a study of 76 infantile cases.', *Brain and Development*, *20*(1): 36–43.

Pasterski, V., Hindmarsh, P., Geffner, M., Brook, C. *et al.* (2007) 'Increased aggression and activity level in 3- to 11-year-old girls with congenital adrenal hyperplasia.', *Hormones and Behaviour*, *52*(3): 368–374.

Patel, S. and Barkovich, A.J. (2002) 'Analysis and classification of cerebellar malformations.', *American Journal of Neuroradiology*, *23*: 1074–1087.

Patil, S.R. and Bartley, J.A. (1984) 'Interstitial deletion of the short arm of chromosome 17.' *Human Genetics*, *67*: 237–238.

Patrone, P.M., Chatten, J., Weinberg, P. (1990) 'Neuroblastoma and DiGeorge anomaly.' *Pediatric Pathology*, *10* (3): 425–430.

Patton, M.A. and Afzal, A.R. (2002) 'Robinow syndrome.', *Journal of Medical Genetics*, *39*(5): 305–310.

Patton, M.A., Goodship, J., Hayward, R. and Lansdown, R. (1988) 'Intellectual development in Apert's syndrome: a long term follow up of 29 patients.', *Journal of Medical Genetics*, *25*: 164–167.

Patwardhan, A.J., Brown, W.E., Bender, B.G., Linden, M.G. *et al.* (2002) 'Reduced size of the amygdala in individuals with 47,XXY and 47,XXX karyotypes.', *American Journal of Medical Genetics*, *114*(1): 93–98.

Paul, M. and Allington-Smith, P. (1997) 'Asperger syndrome associated with Steinert's myotonic dystrophy.', *Developmental Medicine and Child Neurology*, *39*: 280–281.

Paul, R., Cohen, D.J. and Volkmar, F.R. (1983) 'Autistic behaviours in a boy with Noonan syndrome.', *Journal of Autism and Developmental Disorders*, *13*(4): 433–434.

Pauls, D.L. and Leckman, J.F. (1986) 'The inheritance of Gilles de la Tourette's syndrome and associated behaviours: evidence for autosomal dominant transmission.', *New England Journal of Medicine*, *315*: 993–997.

Pauls, D.L., Leckman, J.F., Raymond, C.L., Hurst, C.R. and Stevenson, J.M. (1988) 'A family study of Tourette's syndrome: evidence against the hypothesis of association with a wide range of psychiatric phenotypes.', (Abstract) *American Journal of Human Genetics*, *43*: A64.

Pavol, M., Hiscock, M., Massman, P., Moore III, B. *et al.* (2006) 'Neuropsychological function in adults with von Recklinghausen's neurofibromatosis.', *Developmental Neuropsychology*, *29*: 509–526.

Pavone, P., Incorpora, G., Fiumara, A., Parano, E. *et al.* (2004) 'Epilepsy is not a prominent feature of primary autism.', *Neuropediatrics*, *35*(4): 207–210.

Pavone, P., Parano, E., Rizzo, R. and Trifiletti, R.R. (2006) 'Autoimmune neuropsychiatric disorders associated with streptococcal infection: sydenham chorea, PANDAS, and PANDAS variants.', *Journal of Child Neurology*, *21*: 727–736.

Paylor, R., Glaser, B., Mupo, A., Ataliotis, P. *et al.* (2006) 'Tbx1 haploinsufficiency is linked to behavioural disorders in mice and humans: implications for 22q11 deletion syndrome.', *Proceedings of the National Academy of Science USA*, *103*: 7729–7734.

Paz, M.F., Avila, S., Fraga, M.F., Pollan, M. *et al.* (2002) 'Germ-line variants in methyl-group metabolism genes and susceptibility to DNA methylation in normal tissues and human primary tumors.', *Cancer Research, 62*: 4519–4524.

Pazzaglia, S. (2006) 'Ptc1 heterozygous knockout mice as a model of multi-organ tumorigenesis.', *Cancer Letters, 234*: 124–134.

Peake, D., Notghi, L.M. and Philip, S. (2006) 'Management of epilepsy in children with autism.' *Current Paediatrics, 16*: 489–494.

Pearl, P.L., Capp, P.K., Novotny, E.J. and Gibson, K.M. (2005) 'Inherited disorders of neurotransmitters in children and adults.', *Clinical Biochemistry, 38*: 1051–1058.

Pearl, P.L. and Gibson, K.M. (2004) 'Clinical aspects of the disorders of GABA metabolism in children.', *Current Opinion in Neurology, 17*(2): 107–113.

Pearl, P.L., Gibson, K.M., Acosta, M.T., Vezina, L.G. *et al.* (2003) 'Clinical spectrum of succinic semialdehyde dehydrogenase deficiency.', *Neurology, 60*(9): 1413–1417.

Pearl, P.L., Gibson, K.M., Cortez, M.A., Wu, Y. *et al.* (2009) 'Succinic semialdehyde dehydrogenase deficiency: lessons from mice and men.', *Journal of Inherited Metabolic Disease*, doi:10.1007/s10545-009-1034-y.

Pearson, C.E., Edamura, K.N. and Cleary, J.D. (2005) 'Repeat instability: mechanisms of dynamic mutations.', *Nature Review: Genetics, 6*: 729–742.

Pedersen, C.B., Kølvraa, S., Kølvraa, A., Stenbroen, V. *et al.* (2008) 'The ACADS gene variation spectrum in 114 patients with short-chain acyl-CoA dehydrogenase (SCAD) deficiency is dominated by missense variations leading to protein misfolding at the cellular level.', *Human Genetics, 124*(1): 43–56.

Peek, F. (1997) *The Real Rainman: Kim Peek*. Ogden: Harkness Publishing Consultants.

Peek, F. and Hanson, L.L. (2007) *The Life and Message of the Real Rain Man: The Journey of a Mega-Savant*. Port Chester, New York: Dude Publishing.

Pelc, K., Cheron, G. and Dan, B. (2008) 'Behaviour and neuropsychiatric manifestations in Angelman syndrome.', *Neuropsychiatric Disease and Treatment, 4*(3): 577–584.

Pellegrino, J.E., Lensch, M.W., Muenke, M. and Chance, P.F. (1997) 'Clinical and molecular analysis in Joubert syndrome.', *American Journal of Medical Genetics A, 72*(1): 59–62.

Pellegrino, J.E., Schnur, R.E., Kline, R., Zackai, E.H. and Spinner, N.B. (1995) 'Mosaic loss of 15q11q13 in a patient with hypomelanosis of Ito: is there a role for the P gene?' *Human Genetics, 96*(4): 485–489.

Penderis, J., Calvin, J., Abramson, C., Jakobs, C. *et al.* (2007) 'L-2-hydroxyglutaric aciduria: characterisation of the molecular defect in a spontaneous canine model.', *Journal of Medical Genetics, 44*(5): 334–340.

Pennebaker, J.W. (1982) *The Psychology of Physical Symptoms*. New York: Springer.

Penrose, L.S. (1933) 'The relative effects of paternal and maternal age in mongolism.', *Journal of Genetics, 27*: 219–224.

Penrose, S.L. and Questel, J.H. (1937) 'Metabolic studies in phenylketonuria.', *Biochemical Journal, 31*: 266–274.

Peoples, R., Perez-Jurado, L., Wang, Y-K., Kaplan, P. and Francke, U. (1996) 'The gene for replication factor C subunit 2 (RFC2) is within the 7q11.23 Williams syndrome deletion.', *American Journal of Human Genetics, 58*: 1370–1373.

Peracchi, M., Bardella, M.T., Caprioli, F., Massironi, S. *et al.* (2006) 'Circulating ghrelin levels in patients with inflammatory bowel disease.' *Gut, 55*: 432–433.

Pérez-Dueñas, B., Pujol, J., Soriano-Mas, C., Ortiz, H. *et al.* (2006) 'Global and regional volume changes in the brains of patients with phenylketonuria.', *Neurology, 66*: 1074–1078.

Perez Jurado, L.A., Peoples, R., Kaplan, P., Hamel, B.C.J. and Francke, U. (1996) 'Molecular definition of the chromosome 7 deletion in Williams syndrome and parent-of-origin effects on growth.', *American Journal of Human Genetics, 59*: 781–792.

Pericak-Vance, M.A., Wolpert, C.M., Menold, M.M., Bass, M.P. *et al.* (1997) 'Linkage evidence supports the involvement of chromosome 15 in autistic disorder (AUT).', (Abstract) *American Journal of Human Genetics, 61* (supplement): A40 only.

Perilongo, G., Moras, P., Carollo, C., Battistella, A. *et al.* (1999) 'Spontaneous partial regression of low-grade glioma in children with neurofibromatosis-1: a real possibility.', *Journal of Child Neurology, 14*: 352–356.

Perlman, S.L. (2002) 'Spinocerebellar degenerations: an update.', *Current Neurology and Neuroscience Reports, 2*: 331–341.

Persaud, R. (2007) 'Failure to replicate gene-environment interactions in psychopathology.', (Letter to the Editor) *Biological Psychiatry*, doi:10.1016/j.biopsych.2006.10.032.

Petek, E., Kroisel, P.M., Schuster, M., Zierler, H. and Wagner, K. (1999) 'Mosaicism in a fragile-X male including a *de novo* deletion in the FMR1 gene.', *American Journal of Medical Genetics, 84*: 229–232.

Peters, S.U., Beaudet, A.L., Madduri, N. and Bacino, C.A. (2004) 'Autism in Angelman syndrome: implications for autism research.', *Clinical Genetics, 66*(6): 530–536.

Petersen, M.B., Adelsberger, P.A., Schinzel, A.A., Binkert, F. *et al.* (1991) 'Down syndrome due to *de novo* Robertsonian translocation t14;21: DNA polymorphism analysis suggests that the origin of the extra 21q is maternal.', *American Journal of Human Genetics, 49*: 529–536.

Petre–quadens, O. and de Lee, C. (1975) '5-hydroxytryptophan and sleep in Down's Syndrome.', *Journal of the Neurological Sciences, 26*: 443–453.

Petryk, A., Richton, S., Sy, J.P. and Blethen, S.L. (1999) 'The effect of growth hormone treatment on stature in Aarskog syndrome.', *Journal of Pediatric Endocrinology and Metabolism, 12*(2): 161–165.

Pey, A.L., Perez, B., Desviat, L.R., Martinez, M.A. *et al.* (2004) 'Mechanisms underlying responsiveness to tetrahydrobiopterin in mild phenylketonuria mutations.', *Human Mutation, 24*: 388–399.

Pfaendner, N.H., Reuner, G., Pietz, J., Jost, G. *et al.* (2005) 'MR imaging–based volumetry in patients with early-treated phenylketonuria.', *American Journal of Neuroradiology, 26*: 1681–1685.

Phelan, M.C. (2008) 'Deletion 22q13.3 syndrome.', *Orphanet Journal of Rare Diseases, 3*: 14, doi:10.1186/1750-1172-3-14.

Philip, M., Rich, P.M., Cox, T.C.S. and Hayward, R.D. (2003) 'The jugular foramen in complex and syndromic craniosynostosis and its relationship to raised intracranial pressure.', *American Journal of Neuroradiology*, 24: 45–51.

Philip, N., Chabrol, B., Lossi, A.M., Cardoso, C. *et al.* (2003) 'Mutations in the oligophrenin-1 gene (OPHN1) cause X linked congenital cerebellar hypoplasia.', *Journal of Medical Genetics*, 40: 441–446.

Philippart, M. (1990) 'The Rett syndrome in males.', *Brain and Development*, 12: 33–36.

Philippe, A., Boddaert, N., Vaivre-Douret, L., Robel, L. *et al.* (2008) 'Neurobehavioural profile and brain imaging study of the 22q13.3 deletion syndrome in childhood.', *Pediatrics*, 122: e376–e382.

Philippe, A., Martinez, M., Guilloud-Bataille, M., Gillberg, C. *et al.* (1999) 'Genome-wide scan for autism susceptibility genes: Paris Autism Research International Sibpair Study.' *Human Molecular Genetics*, 8: 805–812.

Philippe, C., Amsallem, D., Francannet, C., Lambert, L. *et al.* (2010) 'Phenotypic variability in Rett syndrome associated with FOXG1 mutations in females.' *Journal of Medical Genetics*, 47: 59–65.

Philippe, C., Amsallem, D., Francannet, C., Lambert, L. *et al.* (2010) 'Phenotypic variability in Rett syndrome associated with FOXG1 mutations in females.' *Journal of Medical Genetics*, 47: 59–65.

Phillips, L. and Appleton, R.E. (2004) 'Systematic review of melatonin treatment in children with neurodevelopmental disabilities and sleep impairment.', *Developmental Medicine and Child Neurology*, 46: 771–775.

Philofsky, A., Hepburn, S.L., Hayes, A., Hagerman, R. and Rogers, S.J. (2004) 'Linguistic and cognitive functioning and autism symptoms in young children with fragile-X syndrome.', *American Journal of Mental Retardation*, 109(3): 208–218.

Picketts, D.J., Higgs, D.R., Bachoo, S., Blake, D.J. *et al.* (1996) 'ATRX encodes a novel member of the SNF2 family of proteins: mutations point to a common mechanism underlying the ATR-X syndrome.' *Human Molecular Genetics*, 5(12): 1899–1907.

Pieretti, M., Zhang, F.P., Fu, Y.H., Warren, S.T. *et al.* (1991) 'Absence of expression of the FMR-1 gene in fragile-X syndrome.', *Cell*, 66: 817–822.

Pietrobono, R., Tabolacci, E., Zalfa, F., Zito, I. *et al.* (2005) 'Molecular dissection of the events leading to inactivation of the FMR1 gene.', *Human Molecular Genetics*, 14: 267–277.

Pietz, J., Rupp, A., Ebinger, F., Rating, D. *et al.* (2003) 'Cerebral energy metabolism in phenylketonuria: findings by quantitative in vivo (31)P MR spectroscopy.', *Pediatric Research*, 53: 654–662.

Pike, M.G., Hammerton, M., Edge, J., Atherton, D.J. and Grant, D.B. (1989) 'A family with X-linked ichthyosis and hypogonadism.', *European Journal of Pediatrics*, 148: 442–444.

Pilia, G., Hughes-Benzie, R.M., MacKenzie, A., Baybayan, P. *et al.* (1996) 'Mutations in GPC3, a glypican gene, cause the Simpson-Golabi-Behmel overgrowth syndrome.', *Nature Genetics*, 12: 241–247.

Pineles, S.L., Avery, R.A. and Liu, G.T. (2010) 'Vitamin B12 optic neuropathy in autism.', *Pediatrics, 126*(4): e967–970.

Pinsky, L. and DiGeorge, A.M. (1965) 'A familial syndrome of facial and skeletal anomalies associated with genital abnormality in the male and normal genitals in the female: another cause of male pseudohermaphroditism.', *Journal of Pediatrics*, 66: 1049–1054.

Pinter, J.D., Brown, W.E., Eliez, S., Schmitt, J.E. *et al.* (2001) 'Amygdala and hippocampal volumes in children with Down syndrome: a high-resolution MRI study.' *Neurology*, 56: 972–974.

Pinter, J.D., Eliez, S., Schmitt, J.E., Capone, G.T. and Reiss, A.L. (2001) 'Neuroanatomy of Down's syndrome: a high-resolution MRI study.', *American Journal of Psychiatry*, 158: 1659–1665.

Pinto, D., Pagnamenta, A.T., Klei, L., Anney, R. *et al.* (2010) 'Functional impact of global rare copy number variation in autism spectrum disorders.' *Nature*, 466 (7304) 368–372.

Piqueras, B., Lavenu-Bombled, C., Galicier, L., Bergeron-van der Cruyssen, F, *et al.* (2003) 'Common variable immunodeficiency patient classification based on impaired B cell memory differentiation correlates with clinical aspects.', *Journal of Clinical Immunology, 23*(5): 385–400.

Pithukpakorn, M. (2005) 'Disorders of pyruvate metabolism and the tricarboxylic acid cycle.', *Molecular Genetics and Metabolism*, 85: 243–246.

Plank, S.M., Copeland-Yates, S.A., Sossey-Alaoui, K., Bell, J.M. *et al.* (2001) 'Lack of association of the (AAAT)6 allele of the GXAlu tetranucleotide repeat in intron 27b of the NF1 gene with autism.', *American Journal of Medical Genetics*, 105(5): 404–405.

Platt, S.R. (2007) 'The role of glutamate in central nervous system health and disease – a review.', *The Veterinary Journal*, 173(2): 278–286.

Plenge, R.M., Stevenson, R.A., Lubs, H.A., Schwartz, C.E. and Willard, H.F. (2002) 'Skewed X-chromosome inactivation is a common feature of X-linked mental retardation disorders.' *American Journal of Human Genetics*, 71: 168–173.

Pletnikov, M.V., Moran, T.H. and Carbone, K. (2002) 'Borna disease virus infection of the neonatal rat: developmental brain injury model of autism spectrum disorders.' *Frontiers in Bioscience*, 7: d593–607.

Plissart, L., Borghgraef, M., Volcke, P., Van den Berghe, H. and Fryns, J.P. (1994) 'Adults with Williams-Beuren syndrome: evaluation of the medical, psychological and behavioural aspects.', *Clinical Genetics*, 46: 161–167.

Plomin, R. and Davis, O.S. (2009) 'The future of genetics in psychology and psychiatry: microarrays, genome-wide association, and non-coding RNA.', *Journal of Child Psychology and Psychiatry*, 50(1–2): 63–71.

Plotts, C.A. and Livermore, C.L. (2007) 'Russell-Silver syndrome and nonverbal learning disability: a case study.', *Applied Neuropsychology*, 14(2): 124–134.

Pober, B.R., Lacro, R.V., Rice, C., Mandell, V. and Teele, R.L. (1993) 'Renal findings in 40 individuals with Williams syndrome.', *American Journal of Medical Genetics*, 46: 271–274.

Pober, B.R. and Morris, C.A. (2007) 'Diagnosis and management of medical problems in adults with Williams-Beuren syndrome.', *American Journal of Medical Genetics C: Seminars in Medical Genetics, 145*(3): 280–290.

Podsypanina, K., Ellenson, L.H., Nemes, A., Gu, J. *et al.* (1999) 'Mutation of Pten/Mmac1 in mice causes neoplasia in multiple organ systems.', *Proceedings of the National Academy of Science USA, 96*: 1563–1568.

Poirier, K., Eisermann, M., Caubel, I., Kaminska, A. *et al.* (2008) 'Combination of infantile spasms, non-epileptic seizures and complex movement disorder: a new case of ARX-related epilepsy.', *Epilepsy Research, 80*: 224–228.

Poirier, K., Lacombe, D., Gilbert-Dussardier, B., Raynaud, M. *et al.* (2006) 'Screening of ARX in mental retardation families: consequences for the strategy of molecular diagnosis.', *Neurogenetics, 7*: 39–46.

Poirier, K., Van Esch, H. Friocourt, G. Saillour, Y. *et al.* (2004) 'Neuroanatomical distribution of Aex in brain and its localisation in GABAergic neurons.' *Brain Research: Molecular Brain Research, 122* (1: 35–46.

Poliak, S. and Peles, E. (2003) 'The local differentiation of myelinated axons at nodes of Ranvier.', *Nature Reviews Neuroscience, 4*(12): 968–980.

Poling, J.S., Frye, R.E., Shoffner, J. and Zimmerman, A.W. (2006) 'Developmental regression and mitochondrial dysfunction in a child with autism.', *Journal of Child Neurology, 21*(2): 170–172.

Polizzi, A., Pavone, P., Iannetti, P., Manfre, L. and Ruggieri, M. (2006) 'Septo-optic dysplasia complex: a heterogeneous malformation syndrome.', *Pediatric Neurology, 34*(1): 66–71.

Pollack, I.F., Shultz, B. and Mulvihill, J.J. (1996) 'The management of brainstem gliomas in patients with neurofibromatosis 1.', *Neurology, 46*(6): 1652–1660.

Pons, R., Andreu, A.L., Checcarelli, N., Vila, M.R. *et al.* (2004) 'Mitochondrial DNA abnormalities and autistic spectrum disorders.', *Journal of Pediatrics, 144*: 81–85.

Pons, R. and De Vivo, D.C. (1995) 'Primary and secondary carnitine deficiency syndromes.', *Journal of Child Neurology, 10* (Suppl 2): S8–S24.

Póo-Argüelles, P., Arias, A., Vilaseca, M.A., Ribes, A. *et al.* (2006) 'X-Linked creatine transporter deficiency in two patients with severe mental retardation and autism.', *Journal of Inherited Metabolic Disease, 29*(1): 220–223.

Poon, C.C., Meara, J.G. and Heggie, A.A. (2003) 'Hemifacial microsomia: use of the OMENS-Plus classification at the Royal Children's Hospital of Melbourne.', *Plastic and Reconstructive Surgery, 111*(3): 1011–1018.

Poot, M., Beyer, V., Schwaab, I., Damatova, N. *et al.* (2010) 'Disruption of CNTNAP2 and additional structural genome changes in a boy with speech delay and autism spectrum disorder.', *Neurogenetics, 11*(1): 81–89.

Popper, J.S., Hsia, Y.E., Rogers, T. and Yuen, J. (1980) 'Familial hibernation (Kleine-Levin) syndrome.', (Abstract) *American Journal of Human Genetics, 32*: 123A.

Poretti, A., Wolf, N. and Boltshauser, E. (2008) 'Differential diagnosis of cerebellar atrophy in childhood.', *European Journal of Paediatric Neurology, 12*: 155–167.

Porrini, G., Giovannini, A., Amato, G., Ioni, A. and Pantanetti, M. (2003) 'Photodynamic therapy of circumscribed choroidal hemangioma.', *Ophthalmology, 110*: 674–680.

Porter, F.D. (2000) 'RSH/Smith-Lemli-Opitz syndrome: a multiple congenital anomaly/mental retardation syndrome due to an inborn error of cholesterol biosynthesis.', *Molecular Genetics and Metabolism, 71*: 163–174.

Porter, F.D. (2002) 'Malformation syndromes due to inborn errors of cholesterol synthesis.', *The Journal of Clinical Investigation, 110*(6): 715–724.

Porter, F.D. (2003) 'Human malformation syndromes due to inborn errors of cholesterol synthesis.', *Current Opinion in Pediatrics, 15*(6): 607–613.

Porter, F.D. (2008) 'Smith-Lemli-Opitz syndrome: pathogenesis, diagnosis and management.', *European Journal of Human Genetics, 16*(5): 535–541.

Porter, J.A., Young, K.E. and Beachy, P.A. (1996) 'Cholesterol modification of hedgehog signaling proteins in animal development.', *Science, 274*: 255–258.

Potocki, L., Bi, W., Treadwell-Deering, D., Carvalho, C.M. *et al.* (2007) 'Characterization of Potocki-Lupski syndrome (dup(17)(p11.2p11.2)) and delineation of a dosage-sensitive critical interval that can convey an autism phenotype.', *American Journal of Human Genetics, 80*(4): 633–649.

Potocki, L., Chen, K-S., Park, S-S., Osterholm, D.E. *et al.* (2000a) 'Molecular mechanism for duplication 17p11.2 – the homologous recombination reciprocal of the Smith-Magenis microdeletion.', *Nature Genetics, 24*: 84–87.

Potocki, L., Glaze, D., Tan, D-X., Park, S-S. *et al.* (2000b) 'Circadian rhythm abnormalities of melatonin in Smith-Magenis syndrome.', *Journal of Medical Genetics, 37*: 428–433.

Pott, J.W. and Wong, K.H. (2006) 'Leber's hereditary optic neuropathy and vitamin B12 deficiency.', *Graefe's Archive for Clinical and Experimental Ophthalmology, 244*(10): 1357–1359.

Potter, C.J., Huang, H. and Xu, T. (2001) 'Drosophila Tsc1 functions with Tsc2 to antagonize insulin signaling in regulating cell growth, cell proliferation, and organ size.', *Cell, 105*: 357–368.

Potter, N.T. (1996) 'The relationship between (CAG) n repeat number and age of onset in a family with dentatorubral-pallidoluysian atrophy (DRPLA): diagnostic implications of confirmatory and predictive testing.', *Journal of Medical Genetics, 33*: 168–170.

Povey, S., Burley, M.W., Attwood, J., Benham, F. *et al.* (1994) 'Two loci for tuberous sclerosis: one on 9q34 and one on 16p13.', *Annals of Human Genetics, 58*: 107–127.

Powell, B.R., Budden, S.S. and Buist, N.R.M. (1993) 'Dominantly inherited megalencephaly, muscle weakness, and myoliposis: a carnitine-deficient myopathy within the spectrum of the Ruvalcaba-Myhre-Smith syndrome.', *Journal of Pediatrics, 123*: 70–75.

Powers, J.M., DeCiero, D.P., Ito, M., Moser, A.B. and Moser, H.W. (2000) 'Adrenomyeloneuropathy: a neuropathologic review featuring its noninflammatory myelopathy.', *Neuropathology and Experimental Neurology, 59*(2): 89–102.

Powers, J.M., Pei, Z., Heinzer, A.K., Deering, R. *et al.* (2005) 'Adreno-leukodystrophy: oxidative stress of mice and men.', *Journal of Neuropathology and Experimental Neurology*, 64(12): 1067–1079.

Poysky, J. (2007) 'Behaviour patterns in Duchenne muscular dystrophy: report on the Parent Project Muscular Dystrophy Behaviour Workshop 8–9 of December 2006, Philadelphia, USA.', *Neuromuscular Disorders*, 17: 986–994.

Prader, A., Labhart, A. and Willi, H. (1956) 'Ein Syndrome von Adipositas, Kleinwuchs, Kryptochismus und Oligophrenie nach myatonieartigem Zustand in Neugeborenenalter.', *Schweizerische Medizinische Wochenschrift*, 86: 1260–1261.

Prasad, C. and Galbraith, P.A. (2005) 'Sir Archibald Garrod and alkaptonuria – "story of metabolic genetics".' *Clinical Genetics*, 68: 199–203.

Prasad, C., Prasad, A.N., Chodirker, B.N., Lee, C. *et al.* (2000) 'Genetic evaluation of pervasive developmental disorders: the terminal 22q13 deletion syndrome may represent a recognizable phenotype.', *Clinical Genetics*, 57: 103–109.

Prasher, V.P. (1994) 'Screening for medical problems in adults with Down syndrome.', *Down Syndrome Research and Practice*, 2(2): 59–66.

Prasher, V.P. (1999) 'Down syndrome and thyroid disorders: a review.', *Down Syndrome Research and Practice*, 6(1): 25–42.

Prasher, V.P. (2004) 'Review of donepezil, rivastigmine, galantamine and memantine for the treatment of dementia in Alzheimer's disease in adults with Down syndrome: implications for the intellectual disability population.', *International Journal of Geriatric Psychiatry*, 19: 509–515.

Prasher, V.P. and Clarke, D.J. (1996) 'Case report: challenging behaviour in a young adult with Down's syndrome and autism.', *British Journal of Learning Disabilities*, 24: 167–169.

Preece, P.M. and Mott, J. (2006) 'Multidisciplinary assessment at a child development centre: do we conform to recommended standards?' *Child: Care, Health and Development*, 32: 559–563.

Preis, S., Majewski, F., Hantschmann, R., Schumacher, H. and Lenard, H.G. (1996) 'Goldenhar, Möbius and hypoglossia-hypodactyly anomalies in a patient: syndrome or association?' *European Journal of Pediatrics*, 155(5): 385–389.

Presti-Torres, J., de Lima, M.N., Scalco, F.S., Caldana, F. *et al.* (2007) 'Impairments of social behaviour and memory after neonatal gastrin-releasing peptide receptor blockade in rats: implications for an animal model of neurodevelopmental disorders.', *Neuropharmacology*, 52: 724–732.

Price, V.H., Odom, R.B., Ward, W.H. and Jones, F.T. (1980) 'Trichothiodystrophy: sulfur-deficient brittle hair as a marker for a neuroectodermal symptom complex.', *Archives of Dermatology*, 116: 1375–1384.

Pridjian, G., Gill, W.L. and Shapira, E. (1995) 'Goldenhar sequence and mosaic trisomy 22.', *American Journal of Medical Genetics*, 59(4): 411–413.

Probst, F.J., Cooper, M.L., Cheung, S.W. and Justice, M.J. (2008) 'Genotype, phenotype, and karyotype correlation in the XO mouse model of Turner syndrome.', *Journal of Heredity*, 99(5): 512–517.

Procopis, P.G. and Turner, B. (1972) 'Mental retardation, abnormal fingers, and skeletal anomalies: Coffin's syndrome.', *American Journal of Diseases of Childhood*, 124: 258–261.

Procter, M., Phillips, J.A. III and Cooper, S. (1998) 'The molecular genetics of growth hormone deficiency.', *Human Genetics*, 103: 255–272.

Proud, V.K., Levine, C. and Carpenter, N.J. (1992) 'New X-linked syndrome with seizures, acquired micrencephaly, and agenesis of the corpus callosum.', *American Journal of Medical Genetics*, 43: 458–466.

Pruszkowski, A., Bodemer, C., Fraitag, S., Teillac-Hamel, D. *et al.* (2000) 'Neonatal and infantile erythrodermas: a retrospective study of 51 patients.' *Archives of Dermatology*, 136: 875–880.

Puech, A., Saint-Jore, B., Merscher, S., Russell, R.G. *et al.* (2000) 'Normal cardiovascular development in mice deficient for 16 genes in 550 kb of the velocardiofacial/DiGeorge syndrome region.', *Proceedings of the National Academy of Science USA*, 97: 10090–10095.

Pueschel, S.M. (2006) 'The effect of acetyl-L-carnitine administration on persons with Down syndrome.', *Research in Developmental Disabilities*, 27: 599–604.

Pueschel, S.M., Reed, R.B., Cronk, C.E. and Goldstein, B.I. (1980) '5-hydroxytryptophan and pyridoxine: the effects in young children with Down's syndrome.', *American Journal of Diseases of Children*, 134: 838–844.

Purandare, K.N. and Markar, T.N. (2005) 'Psychiatric symptomatology of Lujan-Fryns syndrome: an X-linked syndrome displaying Marfanoid symptoms with autistic features, hyperactivity, shyness and schizophreniform symptoms.', *Psychiatric Genetics*, 15: 229–231.

Purcell, A.E., Jeon, O.H., Zimmerman, A.W., Blue, M.E. and Pevsner, J. (2001) 'Postmortem brain abnormalities of the glutamate neurotransmitter system in autism.', *Neurology*, 57: 1618–1628.

Purkinje, J.E. and Valentin, G. (1835) 'De phaenomeno generali et fundamentali motus vibratorii continui in membranis cum externis tum internis animalium plurimorum et superiorum et inferiorum ordinum obvii: commentatio physiologica.', In A. Schulz (ed.) *Commentatio Physiologica*. Wratislaviae: Sumptibus.

Purushottam, M., Ram Murthy, A., Shubha, G.N., Gayathri, N. and Nalini, A. (2008) 'Paternal inheritance or a *de novo* mutation in a Duchenne muscular dystrophy pedigree from South India.', *Journal of the Neurological Sciences*, 268(1–2): 179–182.

Puumala, S.E., Ross, J.A., Olshan, A.F., Robison, L.L. *et al.* (2007) 'Reproductive history, infertility treatment, and the risk of acute leukemia in children with Down syndrome: a report from the Children's Oncology Group.', *Cancer*, 110(9): 2067–2074.

Puvabanditsin, S., Garrow, E. and Augustin, G. (2005) 'Poland-Möbius syndrome and cocaine abuse: a relook at vascular etiology.', *Pediatric Neurology*, 32(4): 285–287.

Pyeritz, R.E., Stamberg, J., Thomas, G.H., Bell, B.B. *et al.* (1982) 'The marker Xq28 syndrome (fragile-X syndrome) in a retarded man with mitral valve prolapse.', *Johns Hopkins Medical Journal*, 151: 231–237.

Qin, M., Kang, J. and Smith, C.B. (2002) 'Increased rates of cerebral glucose metabolism in a mouse model of fragile-X mental retardation.', *Proceedings of the National Academy of Science USA*, 99: 15758–15763.

Quattrini, A., Ortenzi, A., Silvestri, R., Paggi, A. *et al.* (1986) 'Ichthyosis accompanied by neurological symptoms with special reference to epilepsy.', *Italian Journal of Neurological Science*, 7(2): 233–242.

Quinlivan, R., Ball, J., Dunckley, M., Thomas, D.J. *et al.* (1995) 'Becker muscular dystrophy presenting with complete heart block in the sixth decade.', *Journal of Neurology*, 242: 398–400.

Quintana-Murci, L. and Fellous, M. (2001) 'The human Y chromosome: the biological role of a "functional wasteland".', *Journal of Biomedicine and Biotechnology*, 1(1): 18–24.

Quintero-Rivera, F., Robson, C.D., Reiss, R.E., Levine, D. *et al.* (2006) 'Intracranial anomalies detected by imaging studies in 30 patients with Apert syndrome.', (Letter) *American Journal of Medical Genetics*, 140A: 1337–1338.

Quisling, R.G., Barkovich, A.J. and Maria, B.L. (1999) 'Magnetic resonance imaging features and classification of central nervous system malformations in Joubert syndrome.', *Journal of Child Neurology*, 14: 628–635.

Rabionet, R., Jaworski, J.M., Ashley-Koch, A.E., Martin, E.R. *et al.* (2004) 'Analysis of the autism chromosome 2 linkage region: GAD1 and other candidate genes.', *Neuroscience Letters*, 372: 209–214.

Race, V., Marie, S., Vincent, M-F. and van den Berghe, G. (2000) 'Clinical, biochemical and molecular genetic correlations in adenylosuccinate lyase deficiency.', *Human Molecular Genetics*, 9: 2159–2165.

Rae, C., Digney, A.L., McEwan, S.R. and Bates, T.C. (2003) 'Oral creatine monohydrate supplementation improves brain performance: a double-blind, placebo-controlled, cross-over trial.', *Proceedings of the Royal Society B: Biological Sciences*, 270: 2147–2150.

Rae, C., Karmiloff-Smith, A., Lee, M.A., Dixon, R.M. *et al.* (1998) 'Brain biochemistry in Williams syndrome: evidence for a role of the cerebellum in cognition?' *Neurology*, 51: 33–40.

Raevaara, T.E., Gerdes, A.M., Lonnqvist, K.E., Tybjaerg-Hansen, A. *et al.* (2004) 'HNPCC mutation MLH1 P648S makes the functional protein unstable, and homozygosity predisposes to mild neurofibromatosis type 1.', *Genes, Chromosomes and Cancer*, 40: 261–265.

Rahman, T., Ramanathan, R., Stroud, S., Sample, W. *et al.* (2001) 'Towards the control of a powered orthosis for people with muscular dystrophy.', *IMechE Journal of Engineering in Medicine*, 215(H): 267–274.

Rahmouni, K., Fath, M.A., Seo, S., Thedens, D.R. *et al.* (2008) 'Leptin resistance contributes to obesity and hypertension in mouse models of Bardet-Biedl syndrome.', *The Journal of Clinical Investigation*, 118(4): 1458–1467.

Rai, A.K., Singh, S., Mehta, S., Kumar, A. *et al.* (2006) 'MTHFR C677T and A1298C polymorphisms are risk factors for Down's syndrome in Indian mothers.', *Journal of Human Genetics*, 51: 278–283, doi:10.1007/s10038-005-0356-3.

Raja, M. and Azzoni, A. (2008) 'Comorbidity of Asperger's syndrome and bipolar disorder.', *Clinical Practice and Epidemiology in Mental Health*, 4: 26, doi:10.1186/1745-0179-4-26.

Rajesh, R. and Girija, A.S. (2003) 'Pyridoxine-dependent seizures: a review.' *Indian Pediatrics*, 40(7): 633–638.

Ramackers, G.J. (2002) 'Rho proteins, mental retardation and the cellular basis of cognition.' *Trends in the Neurosciences*, 25: 191–199.

Ramaekers, V.T., Heimann, G., Reul, J., Thron, A. and Jaeken, J. (1997) 'Genetic abnormalities and cerebellar structural abnormalities in childhood.' *Brain*, 120: 1739–1751.

Ramirez, N., Marrero, L., Carlo, S. and Cornier, A.S. (2004) 'Orthopaedic manifestations of Bardet-Biedl syndrome.', *Journal of Pediatric Orthopaedics*, 24: 92–96.

Rampazzo, C., Gallinaro, L., Milanesi, E., Frigimelica, E. *et al.* (2000) 'A deoxyribonucleotidase in mitochondria: involvement in regulation of dNTP pools and possible link to genetic disease.', *Proceedings of the National Academy of Science USA*, 97(15): 8239–8244.

Ramser, J., Ahearn, M.E., Lenski, C., Yariz, K.O. *et al.* (2008) 'Rare missense and synonymous variants in UBE1 are associated with X-linked infantile spinal muscular atrophy.', *American Journal of Human Genetics*, 82(1): 188–193.

Rao, P.N., Klinepeter, K., Stewart, W., Hayworth, R. *et al.* (1994) 'Molecular cytogenetic analysis of a duplication Xp in a male: further delineation of a possible sex influencing region on the X chromosome.', *Human Genetics*, 94: 149–153.

Rao, V.K., Dugan, F., Dale, J.K., Davis, J. *et al.* (2005) 'Use of mycophenolate mofetil for chronic, refractory immune cytopenias in children with autoimmune lymphoproliferative syndrome.' *British Journal of Haematology*, 129: 534–538.

Rapin, I. and Ruben, R.J. (1976) 'Patterns of anomalies in children with malformed ears.', *Laryngoscope*, 86(10): 1469–1502.

Rasmussen, P., Borjesson, O., Wentz, E. and Gillberg, C. (2001) 'Autistic disorders in Down syndrome: background factors and clinical correlates.', *Developmental Medicine and Child Neurology*, 43(11): 750–754.

Rasmussen, S.A. and Friedman, J.M. (2000) 'NF1 gene and neurofibromatosis 1.', *American Journal of Epidemiology*, 151(1): 33–40.

Rasmussen, S.A., Yang, Q. and Friedman, J.M. (2001) 'Mortality in neurofibromatosis 1: an analysis using U.S. death certificates.', *American Journal of Human Genetics*, 68: 1110–1118.

Ratcliffe, S.G., Butler, G.E. and Jones, M. (1990) 'Edinburgh study of growth and development of children with sex chromosome abnormalities. IV.', *Birth Defects Original Articles Series*, 26: 1–44.

Rau, M.J., Fischer, S. and Neumann, C.J. (2006) 'Zebrafish Trap230/Med12 is required as a coactivator for Sox9-dependent neural crest, cartilage and ear development.', *Developmental Biology*, 296: 83–93.

Raux, G., Bumsel, E., Hecketsweiler, B., van Amelsvoort, T. *et al.* (2007) 'Involvement of hyperprolinemia in cognitive and psychiatric features of the 22q11 deletion syndrome.', *Human Molecular Genetics*, 16(1): 83–91.

Rawls, J.M. Jr. (2006) 'Analysis of pyrimidine catabolism in drosophila melanogaster using epistatic interactions with mutations of pyrimidine biosynthesis and beta-alanine metabolism.', *Genetics*, *172*: 1665–1674.

Ray, J.G. and Laskin, C.A. (1999) 'Folic acid and homocyst(e)ine metabolic defects and the risk of placental abruption, pre-eclampsia and spontaneous pregnancy loss: a systematic review.' *Placenta, 20*(7): 519–529.

Rayasam, G.V., Wendling, O., Angrand, P.O., Mark, M. *et al.* (2003) 'NSD1 is essential for early post-implantation development and has a catalytically active SET domain.', *EMBO Journal, 22*: 3153–3163.

Raymond, G.V., Bauman, M.L. and Kemper, T.L. (1996) 'Hippocampus in autism: a Golgi analysis.', *Acta Neuropathologica (Berlin), 91*: 117–119.

Raynes, H.R., Shanske, A., Goldberg, S., Burde, R. and Rapin, I. (1999) 'Joubert syndrome: monozygotic twins with discordant phenotypes.', *Journal of Child Neurology, 14*: 649–654.

Reading, R. (2006) 'Prevalence of disorders of the autism spectrum in a population cohort of children in South Thames: the Special Needs and Autism Project (SNAP).', *Child Care Health and Development, 32*(6): 752–753.

Realmuto, G.M. and Main, B. (1982) 'Coincidence of Tourette's disorder and infantile autism.', *Journal of Autism and Developmental Disorders, 12*(4): 367–372.

Reardon, W., Gibbons, R.J., Winter, R.M. and Baraitser, M. (1995) 'Male pseudohermaphroditism in sibs with the alpha-thalassaemia/mental retardation (ATR-X) syndrome.', *American Journal of Medical Genetics, 55*: 285–287.

Reardon, W., Harbord, M.G., Hall-Craggs, M.A., Kendall, B. *et al.* (1989) 'Central nervous system malformations in Mohr's syndrome.', *Journal of Medical Genetics, 26*: 659–663.

Recklinghausen, F.D. von (1882) *Ueber die multiplen Fibrome der Haut und ihre Beziehung zu den multiplen Neuromen.* Berlin: Hirschwald.

Redcay, E. and Courchesne, E. (2005) 'When is the brain enlarged in autism? A meta-analysis of all brain size reports.', *Biological Psychiatry, 58*: 1–9.

Reddy, K.S. (2005) 'Cytogenetic abnormalities and fragile-X syndrome in autism spectrum disorder.' *BMC Medical Genetics, 6*: 3, doi:10.1186/1471-2350-6-3.

Reddy, S., Smith, D.B., Rich, M.M., Leferovich, J.M. *et al.* (1996) 'Mice lacking the myotonic dystrophy protein kinase develop a late onset progressive myopathy.', *Nature Genetics, 13*(3): 325–335.

Redon, R., Ishikawa, S., Fitch, K.R., Feuk, L. *et al.* (2006) 'Global variation in copy number in the human genome.', *Nature, 444*: 444–452, doi:10.1038/nature05329.

Reeves, R.H., Baxter, L.L. and Richtsmeier, J.T. (2001) 'Too much of a good thing: mechanisms of gene action in Down syndrome.', *Trends in Genetics, 17*(2): 83–88.

Regenbogen, L., Godel, V., Goya, V. and Goodman, R.M. (1982) 'Further evidence for an autosomal dominant form of oculoauriculovertebral dysplasia.', *Clinical Genetics, 21*: 161–167.

Reichelt, K.L. and Knivsberg, A.M. (2003) 'Can the pathophysiology of autism be explained by the nature of the discovered urine peptides?' *Nutritional Neuroscience, 6*: 19–28.

Reichenberg, A., Gross, R., Weiser, M., Bresnahan, M. *et al.* (2006) 'Advancing paternal age and autism.', *Archives of General Psychiatry, 63*(9): 1026–1032.

Reid, D.E., Maria, B.L., Drane, W.E., Quisling, R.G. *et al.* (1997) 'Central nervous system perfusion and metabolism abnormalities in Sturge-Weber syndrome.' *Journal of Child Neurology, 12*: 218–222.

Reilley, P.R. (2006) *The Strongest Boy in the World: How Genetic Information is Reshaping our Lives.* New York: Cold Spring Harbor Laboratory Press.

Reilly, C. (2009) 'Autism spectrum disorders in Down syndrome: a review.', *Research in Autism Spectrum Disorders, 3*: 829–839.

Reiner, D., Arnaud, E., Cinalli, G., Sebag, G. *et al.* (1996) 'Prognosis for mental function in Apert's syndrome.', *Journal of Neurosurgery, 85*, 66–72.

Reiner, O. and Coquelle, F.M. (2005) 'Missense mutations resulting in type 1 lissencephaly.', *Cellular and Molecular Life Sciences, 62*(4): 425–434.

Reiner, O., Coquelle, F.M., Peter, B., Levy, T. *et al.* (2006) 'The evolving doublecortin (DCX) superfamily.', *BMC Genomics, 7*: 188 doi:10.1186/1471-2164-7-188.

Reis, A., Dittrich, B., Greger, V., Buiting, K. *et al.* (1994) 'Imprinting mutations suggested by abnormal DNA methylation patterns in familial Angelman and Prader-Willi syndromes.', *American Journal of Human Genetics, 54*: 741–747.

Reiss, A.L. (2009) 'Childhood developmental disorders: an academic and clinical convergence point for psychiatry, neurology, psychology and pediatrics.', *Journal of Child Psychology and Psychiatry, 50*(1–2): 87–98

Reiss, A.L., Aylward, E., Freund, L.S., Joshi, P.K. and Bryan, R.N. (1991) 'Neuroanatomy of fragile-X syndrome: the posterior fossa.', *Annals of Neurology, 29*: 26–32.

Reiss, A.L., Eckert, M.A., Rose, F.E., Karchemskiy, A. *et al.* (2004) 'An experiment of nature: brain anatomy parallels cognition and behaviour in Williams syndrome.', *The Journal of Neuroscience, 24*(21): 5009–5015.

Reiss, A.L., Feinstein, C., Rosenbaum, K.N., Borengasser-Caruso, M.A. and Goldsmith, B.M. (1985) 'Autism associated with Williams syndrome.', *Journal of Pediatrics, 106*(2): 247–249.

Reiss, A.L. and Hall, S.S. (2007) 'Fragile-X syndrome: assessment and treatment implications.', *Child and Adolescent Psychiatric Clinics of North America, 16*: 663–675.

Reiss, A.L., Lee, J. and Freund, L. (1994) 'Neuroanatomy of fragile-X syndrome: the temporal lobe.', *Neurology, 44*: 1317–1324.

Reiter, R.J., Barlow-Walden, L., Poeggeler, B., Heiden, S.M. and Clayton, R.J. (1996) 'Twenty-four hour urinary excretion of 6-hydroxymelatonin sulfate in Down syndrome subjects.', *Journal of Pineal Research, 20*(1): 45–50.

Relling, M.V., Lin, J.S., Ayers, G.D. and Evans, W.E. (1992) 'Racial and gender differences in N-acetyltransferase, xanthine oxidase, and CYP1A2 activities.', *Clinical and Pharmacological Therapy, 52*: 643–658.

Renier, W.O. and Renkawek, K. (1990) 'Clinical and neuropathologic findings in a case of severe myoclonic epilepsy of infancy.', *Epilepsia, 31*: 287–291.

Renieri, A., Mari, F., Mencarelli, M.A., Scala, E. *et al.* (2009) 'Diagnostic criteria for the Zappella variant of Rett syndrome (the preserved speech variant).', *Brain and Development, 31*: 208–216.

Renner, E.D., Puck, J.M., Holland, S.M., Schmitt, M. *et al.* (2004) 'Autosomal recessive hyperimmunoglobulin E syndrome: a distinct disease entity.', *Journal of Pediatrics, 144*(1): 93–99.

Rett, A. (1966) 'Ueber ein eigenartiges hirnatrophisches Syndrom bei Hyperammoniamie in Kindesalter.' *Wiener Medizinische Wochenschrift, 116*: 723–738.

Rett, A. (1977) 'Cerebral atrophy associated with hyperammonaemia.' In P.J. Vinken and G.W. Bruyn (eds.) *Handbook of Clinical Neurology, 29*. Amsterdam: North Holland (pub.).

Rett, A. (1986) 'Rett syndrome: history and general overview.', *American Journal of Medical Genetics, Supplement, 1*: 21–25.

Reynolds, R., Burri, R. and Herschkowitz, N. (1993) 'Retarded development of neurons and oligodendroglia in rat forebrain produced by hyperphenylalaninemia results in permanent deficits in myelin despite long recovery periods.' *Experimental Neurology, 124*(2): 357–367.

Rhodes, L.E., de Rie, M.A., Leifsdottir, R., Yu, R.C. *et al.* (2007) 'Five-year follow-up of a randomized, prospective trial of topical methyl aminolevulinate photodynamic therapy vs surgery for nodular basal cell carcinoma.', *Archives of Dermatology, 143*(9): 1131–1136.

Riccardi, V.M. (1980) 'Pathophysiology of neurofibromatosis. IV. Dermatologic insights into heterogeneity and pathogenesis.', *Journal of the American Academy of Dermatology, 3*: 157–166.

Riccardi, V.M. (1999) 'Historical background and introduction.' In J.M. Friedman, D.H. Gutmann, M. MacCollin and V.M. Riccardi (eds.) *Neurofibromatosis: Phenotype, Natural History, and Pathogenesis*. Baltimore: Johns Hopkins University Press.

Riccardi, V.M. and Eichner, J.E. (1986) *Neurofibromatosis: Phenotype, Natural History, and Pathogenesis*. Baltimore: Johns Hopkins University Press,.

Ricchetti, E.T., States, L., Hosalkar, H.S., Tamai, J. *et al.* (2004) 'Radiographic study of the upper cervical spine in the 22q11.2 deletion syndrome.' *Journal of Bone and Joint Surgery, 86A*: 1751–1760.

Rich, P.M., Cox, T.S. and Hayward, R.D. (2003) 'The jugular foramen in complex and syndromic craniosynostosis and its relationship to raised intracranial pressure.', *American Journal of Neuroradiology, 24*: 45–51.

Richards, C.S., Watkins, S.C., Hoffman, E.P., Schneider, N.R. *et al.* (1990) 'Skewed X inactivation in a female MZ twin results in Duchenne muscular dystrophy.', *American Journal of Human Genetics, 46*: 672–681.

Richards, R.I., Holman, K., Friend, K., Kremer, E. *et al.* (1992) 'Evidence of founder chromosomes in fragile-X syndrome.', *Nature Genetics, 1*: 257–260.

Richieri-Costa, A., Monteleone-Neto, R. and Gonzales, M.L. (1986) 'Coffin-Siris syndrome in a Brazilian child with consanguineous parents.', *Revista brasileira de genética, IX*: 169–177.

Richter-Unruh, A., Knauer-Fischer, S., Kaspers, S., Albrecht, B. *et al.* (2004) 'Short stature in children with an apparently normal male phenotype can be caused by 45,X/46,XY mosaicism and is susceptible to growth hormone treatment.', *European Journal of Pediatrics, 163*(4–5): 251–256.

Riddle, J.E., Cheema, A., Sobesky, W.E., Gardner, S.C. *et al.* (1998) 'Phenotypic involvement in females with the FMR1 gene mutation.', *American Journal of Mental Retardation, 102*: 590–601.

Ridge, S.A., Sludden, J., Brown, O., Robertson, L. *et al.* (1998) 'Dihydropyrimidine dehydrogenase pharmacogenetics in Caucasian subjects.', *British Journal of Clinical Pharmacology, 46*(2): 151–156.

Riikonen, R. (2001) 'The PEHO syndrome.', *Brain & Development, 23*: 765–769.

Riikonen, R. (2003) 'Neurotrophic factors in the pathogenesis of Rett syndrome.', *Journal of Child Neurology, 18*(10): 693–697.

Riikonen, R. and Amnell, G. (1981) 'Psychiatric disorders in children with earlier infantile spasms.', *Developmental Medicine and Child Neurology, 23*: 747–760.

Riikonen, R. and Simell, O. (1990) 'Tuberous sclerosis and infantile spasms.', *Developmental Medicine and Child Neurology, 32*(3): 203–209.

Riise, R. (1996) 'The cause of death in Laurence-Moon-Bardet-Biedl syndrome.', *Acta Ophthalmologica Scandinavica Supplement, 219*: 45–47.

Riise, R., Andreasson, S., Wright, A.F. and Tornqvist, K. (1996) 'Ocular findings in the Laurence-Moon-Bardet-Biedl syndrome.', *Acta Ophthalmologica Scandinavica, 74*: 612–617.

Rimland, B. (1964) *Infantile Autism: The Syndrome and Its Implication for a Neural Theory of Behavior*. New York: Appleton-Century-Crofts.

Ringman, J.M. and Jankovic, J. (2000) 'Occurrence of tics in Asperger's syndrome and autistic disorder.', *Journal of Child Neurology, 15*(6): 394–400.

Rio, M., Clech, L., Amiel, J., Faivre, L. *et al.* (2003) 'Spectrum of NSD1 mutations in Sotos and Weaver syndromes.', *Journal of Medical Genetics, 40*(6): 436–440.

Rippon, G., Brock, J., Brown, C. and Boucher, J. (2007) 'Disordered connectivity in the autistic brain: challenges for the "new psychophysiology".', *International Journal of Psychophysiology, 63*: 164–172.

Ritvo, E.R., Mason-Brothers, A., Freeman, B.J., Pingree, C. *et al.* (1990) 'The UCLA-University of Utah epidemiologic survey of autism: the etiologic role of rare diseases.', *American Journal of Psychiatry, 147*: 1614–1621.

Rivera, S.M., Menon, V., White, C.D., Glaser, B. and Reiss, A.L. (2002) 'Functional brain activation during arithmetic processing in females with fragile-X syndrome is related to *FMR1* protein expression.', *Human Brain Mapping, 16*: 206–218.

Robb, S.A., Pohl, K.R.E., Baraitser, M., Wilson, J. and Brett, E.M. (1989) 'The "happy puppet" syndrome of Angelman: review of the clinical features.' *Archives of Diseases in Childhood*, 64: 83–86.

Roberts, K.B. and Hall, J.G. (1971) 'Apert's acrocephalosyndactyly in mother and daughter: cleft palate in the mother.', *Birth Defects Original Articles Series*, VII(7): 262–264.

Robertson, L., Hall, S.E., Jacoby, P., Ellaway, C. *et al.* (2006) 'The association between behaviour and genotype in Rett syndrome using the Australian Rett Syndrome Database.', *American Journal of Medical Genetics*, 141B: 177–183.

Robertson, M. and Cavanna, A. (2008) *Tourette Syndrome (The Facts)* (2nd Edn.) Oxford: Oxford University Press.

Robertson, M.M. (2000) 'Tourette syndrome, associated conditions and the complexities of treatment.', *Brain*, 123: 425–462.

Robin, N.H. (2006) 'It does matter: the importance of making the diagnosis of a genetic syndrome.', *Current Opinion in Pediatrics*, 18(6): 595–597.

Robin, N.H., Taylor, C.J., McDonald-McGinn, D.M., Zackai, E.H. *et al.* (2006) 'Polymicrogyria and deletion 22q11.2 syndrome: window to the etiology of a common cortical malformation.' *American Journal of Medical Genetics*, 140A: 2416–2425.

Robins, D.L., Fein, D., Barton, M.L. and Green, J.A. (2001) 'The Modified Checklist for Autism in Toddlers: an initial study investigating the early detection of autism and pervasive developmental disorders.', *Journal of Autism and Developmental Disorders*, 31(2): 131–144.

Robinson, A., Bender, B.G., Linden, M.G. and Salbenblatt, J.A. (1990) 'Sex chromosome aneuploidy: the Denver Prospective Study.', *Birth Defects Original Articles Series*, 26: 59–115.

Robinson, L.L. (1992) 'Down syndrome and leukemia.', *Leukemia*, 6: 5–7.

Rodenhiser, D. and Mann, M. (2006) 'Epigenetics and human disease: translating basic biology into clinical applications.', *Canadian Medical Association Journal*, 174: 341–348.

Rodier, P.M., Ingram, J.L., Tisdale, B., Nelson, S. and Romano, J. (1996) 'Embryological origin for autism: developmental anomalies of the cranial nerve motor nuclei.', *Journal of Comparative Neurology*, 370(2): 247–261.

Rodriguez, C., Mayo, J.C., Sainz, R.M., Antolin, I. *et al.* (2004) 'Regulation of antioxidant enzymes: a significant role for melatonin.', *Journal of Pineal Research*, 36: 1–9.

Rodríguez-Bujaldón, A.L., Vázquez-Bayo, C., Jiménez-Puya, R.J., Moreno-Giménez, J.C. (2008) 'Sturge-Weber syndrome and type 1 neurofibromatosis: a chance association?' (Article available in English and Spanish) *Actas Dermosifiliográficas*, 99(4): 313–314.

Rodriguez-Criado, G., Magano, L., Segovia, M., Gurrieri, F. *et al.* (2005) 'Clinical and molecular studies on two further families with Simpson-Golabi-Behmel syndrome.', *American Journal of Medical Genetics*, 138A: 272–277.

Rodriguez-Viciana, P., Tetsu, O., Tidyman, W.E., Estep, A.L. *et al.* (2006) 'Germline mutations in genes within the MAPK pathway cause cardio-facio-cutaneous syndrome.', *Science*, 311: 1287–1290.

Roecker, G.O. and Huethner, C.A. (1983) 'An analysis for paternal-age effect in Ohio's Down syndrome births, 1970–1980.', *American Journal of Human Genetics*, 35: 1297–1306.

Roelfsema, J.H., White, S.J., Ariyurek, Y., Bartholdi, D. *et al.* (2005) 'Genetic heterogeneity in Rubinstein-Taybi syndrome: mutations in both the CBP and EP300 genes cause disease.', *American Journal of Human Genetics*, 76: 572–580.

Roesch, C., Steinbicker, V., Korb, C., von Rohden, L. and Schmitt, J. (2001) 'Goldenhar anomaly in one triplet derived from intracytoplasmic sperm injection (ICSI).', *American Journal of Medical Genetics*, 101(1): 82–83.

Roesler, R., Henriques, J.A.P. and Schwartzmann, G. (2006a) 'Gastrin-releasing peptide receptor as a molecular target for psychiatric and neurological disorders.', *CNS and Neurological Disorders – Drug Targets*, 5: 197–204.

Roesler, R., Luft, T., Oliveira, S.H.S., Farias, C.B. *et al.* (2006b) 'Molecular mechanisms mediating gastrin-releasing peptide receptor modulation of memory consolidation in the hippocampus.', *Neuropharmacology*, 51: 350–357.

Rogawski, M.A., Funderburk, S.J. and Cederbaum, S.D. (1978) 'Oculocutaneous albinism and mental disorder: a report of two autistic boys.' *Human Heredity*, 28: 81–85.

Rogawski, M.A., Gryder, D., Castaneda, D., Yonekawa, W. *et al.* (2003) 'GluR5 kainate receptors, seizures and the amygdala.', *Annals of the New York Academy of Science*, 985: 150–162.

Roger, J., Bureau, M., Dravet, C., Genton, P. *et al.* (eds.). (2005) *Epileptic Syndromes in Infancy, Childhood and Adolescence.* (4th edn.) London: John Libbey.

Rogers, S.J. and Newhart-Larson, S. (1989) 'Characteristics of infantile autism in five children with Leber's congenital amaurosis.', *Developmental Medicine and Child Neurology*, 31(5): 598–608.

Rogers, S.J., Wehner, D.E. and Hagerman, R. (2001) 'The behavioural phenotype in fragile-X: symptoms of autism in very young children with fragile-X syndrome, idiopathic autism, and other developmental disorders.', *Journal of Developmental and Behavioural Pediatrics*, 22(6): 409–417.

Roizen, N.J. (2005) 'Complementary and alternative therapies for Down syndrome.', *Mental Retardation and Developmental Disabilities Research Reviews*, 11: 149–155.

Rollnick, B.R. (1988) 'Male transmission of Apert syndrome.', *Clinical Genetics*, 33: 87–90.

Rollnick, B.R. and Kaye, C.I. (1983) 'Hemifacial microsomia and variants: pedigree data.', *American Journal of Medical Genetics*, 15: 233–253.

Rollnick, B.R., Kaye, C.I., Nagatoshi, K., Hauck, W. and Martin, A.O. (1987) 'Oculoauriculovertebral dysplasia and variants: phenotypic characteristics of 294 patients.', *American Journal of Medical Genetics*, 26: 361–375.

Roman, E. and Beral, V. (1991) 'Possible aetiological factors in childhood leukaemia.' *Archives of Disease in Childhood*, 66: 179–180.

Román, G.C. (2007) 'Autism: transient in utero hypothyroxinemia related to maternal flavonoid ingestion during pregnancy and to other environmental antithyroid agents.', *Journal of Neurological Sciences*, 262(1–2): 15–26.

Romano, C., Smout, S., Miller, J.K. and O'Malley, K.L. (2002) 'Developmental regulation of metabotropic glutamate receptor 5b protein in rodent brain.', *Neuroscience*, 111: 693–698.

Romo, T. 3rd, Fozo, M.S. and Sclafani, A.P. (2000) 'Microtia reconstruction using a porous polyethylene framework.', *Facial Plastic Surgery*, 16(1): 15–22.

Romo, T. 3rd, Presti, P.M. and Yalamanchili, H.R. (2006) 'Medpor alternative for microtia repair.', *Facial Plastic Surgery Clinics of North America*, 14(2): 129–136.

Roohi, J., Montagna, C., Tegay, D.H., Palmer, L.E. *et al.* (2008) 'Disruption of contactin 4 in 3 subjects with autism spectrum disorder.', *Journal of Medical Genetics*, published online 18 Mar 2008, doi:10.1136/jmg.2008.057505.

Roper, R.J., Baxter, L.L., Saran, N.G., Klinedinst, D.K. *et al.* (2006) 'Defective cerebellar response to mitogenic Hedgehog signaling in Down's syndrome mice.', *Proceedings of the National Academy of Science USA*, 103: 1452–1456.

Ropers, H-H. (2006) 'X-linked mental retardation: many genes for a complex disorder.', *Current Opinion in Genetics and Development*, 16: 260–269.

Ropers, H-H. (2007) 'New perspectives for the elucidation of genetic disorders.', *American Journal of Human Genetics*, 81: 199–207.

Roposch, A., Bhaskar, A.R., Lee, F., Adedapo, S. *et al.* (2004) 'Orthopaedic manifestations of Brachmann-de Lange syndrome: a report of 34 patients.', *Journal of Pediatric Orthopedics B*, 13(2): 118–122.

Rosenblatt, D.S., Duschens, E.A., Hellstrom, F.V., Goldick, M.S. *et al.* (1985) 'Folic acid blinded trial in identical twins with fragile-X syndrome.', *American Journal of Human Genetics*, 37: 543–552.

Roses, A.D. (1996) 'From genes to mechanisms to therapies: lessons to be learned from neurological disorders.', *Nature Medicine*, 2: 267–269.

Ross, A.J. and Beales, P.L. (2007) 'Bardet-Biedl syndrome.', *GeneReviews*, web-based resource.

Ross, A.J., May-Simera, H., Eichers, E.R., Kai, M. *et al.* (2005) 'Disruption of Bardet-Biedl syndrome ciliary proteins perturbs planar cell polarity in vertebrates.', *Nature Genetics*, 37: 1135–1140.

Ross, J.A., Blair, C.K., Olshan, A.F., Robison, L.L. *et al.* (2005) 'Periconceptional vitamin use and leukemia risk in children with Down syndrome – a children's oncology group study.', *Cancer*, 104(2): 405–410.

Rosser, T. and Packer, R.J. (2002) 'Intracranial neoplasms in children with neurofibromatosis 1.', *Journal of Child Neurology*, 17: 630–637.

Rosser, T.L. and Packer, R.J. (2003) 'Neurocognitive dysfunction in children with neurofibromatosis type 1.', *Current Neurology and Neuroscience Reports*, 3: 129–136.

Rossi, A. and Cantisani, C. (2004) 'Trichothiodystrophy.', *Orphanet Encyclopaedia*, www.orpha.net/data/patho/GB/uk-trichothiodystrophy.pdf.

Rossi, E., Verri, A.P., Patricelli, M.G., Destefani, V. *et al.* (2008) 'A 12Mb deletion at 7q33–q35 associated with autism spectrum disorders and primary amenorrhea.', *European Journal of Medical Genetics*, 51(6): 631–638.

Roubertie, A., Semprino, M., Chaze, A.M., Rivier, F. *et al.* (2001) 'Neurological presentation of three patients with 22q11 deletion (CATCH 22 syndrome).', *Brain and Development*, 23: 810–814.

Rouse, B., Azen, C., Koch, R., Matalon, R. *et al.* (1997) 'Maternal phenylketonuria collaborative study (MPKUCS) offspring: facial anomalies, malformations, and early neurological sequelae.', *American Journal of Medical Genetics*, 69: 89–95.

Rouse, B., Matalon, R., Koch, R., Azen, C. *et al.* (2000) 'Maternal phenylketonuria syndrome: congenital heart defects, microcephaly, and developmental outcomes.', *Journal of Pediatrics*, 136: 57–61.

Rousseau, F., Heitz, D., Biancalana, V., Blumenfeld, S. *et al.* (1991) 'Direct diagnosis by DNA analysis of the fragile-X syndrome of mental retardation.', *New England Journal of Medicine*, 325: 1673–1681.

Rousseau, F., Heitz, D., Tarleton, J., MacPherson, J. *et al.* (1994a) 'A multicenter study on genotype-phenotype correlations in the fragile-X syndrome, using direct diagnosis with probe StB12.3: the first 2,253 cases.', *American Journal of Human Genetics*, 55: 225–237.

Rousseau, F., Robb, L.J., Rouillard, P. and Der Kaloustian, V.M. (1994b) 'No mental retardation in a man with 40 per cent abnormal methylation at the FMR-1 locus and transmission of sperm cell mutations as premutations.', *Human Molecular Genetics*, 3: 927–930.

Rousseau, F., Rouillard, P., Morel, M-L., Khandjian, E.W. and Morgan, K. (1995) 'Prevalence of carriers of premutation-size alleles of the FMRI gene and implications for the population genetics of the fragile X syndrome.' *American Journal of Human Genetics*, 57: 1006–1018.

Roux, C., Horvath, C. and Dupuis, R. (1979) 'Teratogenic action and embryo lethality of AY 9944R: prevention by a hypercholesterolemia-provoking diet.', *Teratology*, 19: 35–38.

Roze, E., Gervais, D., Demeret, S., de Baulny, H.O. *et al.* (2003) 'Neuropsychiatric disturbances in presumed late-onset cobalamin C disease.', *Archives of Neurology*, 60: 1457–1462.

Rubenstein, J.L.R. and Merzenich, M.M. (2003) 'Model of autism: increased ratio of excitation/inhibition in key neural systems.', *Genes, Brain and Behaviour*, 2: 255–267.

Rubinstein, J.H. and Taybi, H. (1963) 'Broad thumbs and toes and facial abnormalities.', *American Journal of Diseases in Childhood*, 105: 588–608.

Rubinsztein, D.C., Hon, J., Stevens, F., Pyrah, I., Tysoe, C. *et al.* (1999) 'Apo E genotypes and risk of dementia in Down syndrome.', *American Journal of Medical Genetics*, 88(4): 344–347.

Rubinsztein, D.C., Leggo, J., Chiano, M., Dodge, A. *et al.* (1997) 'Genotypes at the GluR6 kainate receptor locus are associated with variation in the age of onset of Huntington disease.', *Proceedings of the National Academy of Science USA*, 94: 3872–3876.

Rudling, O., Riise, R., Tornqvist, K. and Jonsson, K. (1996) 'Skeletal abnormalities of hands and feet in Laurence-Moon-Bardet-Biedl (LMBB) syndrome: a radiographic study.', *Skeletal Radiology*, 25: 655–660.

Rueda, J-R., Ballesteros, J. and Tejada, M-I. (2009) 'Systematic review of pharmacological treatments in fragile-X syndrome', *BMC Neurology*, 9: 53, doi:10.1186/1471-2377-9-53.

Rugarli, E.I. (1999) 'Kallmann syndrome and the link between olfactory and reproductive development.', *American Journal of Human Genetics*, 65(4): 943–948.

Ruggieri, M. and McShane, M.A. (1998) 'Parental view of epilepsy in Angelman syndrome: a questionnaire study.', *Archives of Disease in Childhood*, 79: 423–426.

Ruggieri, M. and Pavone, L. (2000) 'Hypomelanosis of Ito: clinical syndrome or just phenotype?' *Journal of Child Neurology*, 15: 635–644.

Rulli, I., Ferrero, G.B., Belligni, E., Delmonaco, A.G. *et al.* (2005) 'Myhre's syndrome in a girl with normal intelligence.', (Letter) *American Journal of Medical Genetics*, 134A: 100–102.

Rush, T., Hjelmhaug, J. and Lobner, D. (2008) 'Effects of chelators on mercury, iron, lead neurotoxicity in cortical cultire.', *Neurotoxicology*, 30(1): 47–51.

Russo, S., Briscioli, V., Cogliati, F., Macchi, M. *et al.* (1998) 'An unusual fragile-X sibship: female compound heterozygote and male with a partially methylated full mutation.', *Clinical Genetics*, 54: 309–314.

Rutter, M. (1968) 'Concepts of autism: review of research.', *Journal of Child Psychology and Psychiatry*, 9(1): 1–25.

Rutter, M. (1983) 'Low level lead exposure: sources, effects and implications.' In M. Rutter and R. Russell Jones (eds.) *Lead versus Health: Sources and Effects of Low Level Lead Exposure*. Chichester: John Wiley

Rutter, M. (1991) 'Nature, nurture and psychopathology: a new look at an old topic.', *Development and Psychopathology*, 3: 125–136.

Rutter, M. (2006) 'Autism: its recognition, early diagnosis, and service implications.', *Journal of Developmental and Behavioural Pediatrics*, 27(Supplement 2): S54–S58.

Rutter, M. (2010) 'Interview with Sir Michael Rutter: Interviewed by Normand Carrey, MD, June 9th 2010' *Journal of the Canadian Academy of Child and Adolescent Psychiatry*, 19(3): 212–217.

Rutter, M., Andersen-Wood, L., Beckett, C., Bredenkamp, D. *et al.* (1999) 'Quasi-autistic patterns following severe early global privation: English and Romanian Adoptees (ERA) Study Team.', *Journal of Child Psychology and Psychiatry*, 40(4): 537–549.

Rutter, M., Bailey, A. and Lord, C. (2003) *Social Communication Questionnaire*. Los Angeles: Western Psychological Services.

Rutter, M. and Schopler, E. (1988) 'Autism and pervasive developmental disorders.' In: M. Rutter, A. Hussain, I. Tuma and S. Lann (eds.) *Assessment and Diagnosis in Child Psychopathology*. London: David Fulton Publishers.

Rutter, S.C. and Cole, T.R. (1991) 'Psychological characteristics of Sotos syndrome.', *Developmental Medicine and Child Neurology*, 33(10): 898–902.

Ruvalcaba, R.H.A., Myhre, S. and Smith, D.W. (1980) 'Sotos syndrome with intestinal polyposis and pigmentary changes of the genitalia.', *Clinical Genetics*, 18: 413–416.

Ryall, R.G., Callen, D., Cocciolone, R., Duvnjak, A. *et al.* (2001) 'Karyotypes found in the population declared at increased risk of Down syndrome following maternal serum screening.', *Prenatal Diagnosis*, 21: 553–557.

Ryan, A.K., Bartlett, K., Clayton, P., Eaton, S. *et al.* (1998) 'Smith-Lemli-Opitz syndrome: a variable clinical and biochemical phenotype.', *Journal of Medical Genetics*, 35: 558–565.

Ryckman, K.K., Morken, N-H., White, M.J., Velez, D.R. *et al.* (2010) 'Maternal and foetal genetic associations of PTGER3 and PON1 with preterm birth.', *PLoS ONE*, 5(2): e9040, doi:10.1371/journal. pone.0009040.

Rzem, R., Veiga-da-Cunha, M., Noël, G., Goffette, S. *et al.* (2004) 'A gene encoding a putative FAD-dependent L-2-hydroxyglutarate dehydrogenase is mutated in L-2-hydroxyglutaric aciduria.', *Proceedings of the National Academy of Science USA.*, 101(48): 16849–16854.

Rzeski, M., Kuran, W., Mierzewska, H., Vreken, P. *et al.* (1999) 'Adrenomieloneuropatia – jedna z postaci adrenoleukodystrofii sprzezonej z chromosomem X – badania rodziny.' [Adrenomyeloneuropathy: a form of X-linked adrenoleukodystrophy. Report of a family] [Article in Polish], *Neurologia i Neurochirugia Polska*, 33(5): 1173–1185.

Saal, H.M., Samango-Sprouse, C.A., Rodnan, L.A., Rosenbaum, K.N. and Custer, D.A. (1993) 'Brachmann-de Lange syndrome with normal IQ.', *American Journal of Medical Genetics*, 47: 995–998.

Saar, K., Al-Gazali, L., Sztriha, L., Rueschendorf, F. *et al.* (1999) 'Homozygosity mapping in families with Joubert syndrome identifies a locus on chromosome 9q34.3 and evidence for genetic heterogeneity.', *American Journal of Human Genetics*, 65: 1666–1671.

Sacco, R., Militerni, R., Frolli, A., Bravaccio, C. *et al.* (2007a) 'Clinical, morphological, and biochemical correlates of head circumference in autism.', *Biological Psychiatry*, 62: 1038–1047.

Sacco, R., Papaleo, V., Hager, J., Rousseau, F. *et al.* (2007b) 'Case-control and family-based association studies of candidate genes in autistic disorder and its endophenotypes: TPH2 and GLO1.', *BMC Medical Genetics*, 8: 11, doi:10.1186/1471-2350-8-11.

Sacks, B. and Buckley, F. (1998) 'Multi-Nutrient Formulas and Other Substances as Therapies for Down Syndrome: An Overview.', *Down Syndrome News and Update*, 1(2): 70–83.

Sadamatsu, M., Kanai, H., Xu, X., Liu, Y. and Kato, N. (2006) 'Review of animal models for autism: implication of thyroid hormone.', *Congenital Anomalies (Kyoto)*, 46(1): 1–9.

Sadamatsu, M. and Watanabe, K. (2005) 'Is a neonatal hypothyroid rat useful as an animal model of autism?' *Neuroscience Research*, 52 (Supp 1): 28.

Sadler, L.S., Pober, B.R., Grandinetti, A., Scheiber, D. *et al.* (2001) 'Differences by sex in cardiovascular disease in Williams syndrome.', *Journal of Pediatrics*, 139: 849–853.

Saemundsen, E., Ludvigsson, P., Hilmarsdottir, I. and Rafnsson, V. (2007) 'Autism spectrum disorders in children with seizures in the first year of life – a population-based study.', *Epilepsia*, 48(9): 1724–1730.

Sagi, L., Zuckerman-Levin, N., Gawlik, A., Ghizzoni, L. *et al.* (2007) 'Clinical significance of the parental origin of the X chromosome in Turner syndrome.', *Journal of Clinical Endocrinology and Metabolism*, 92(3): 846–852.

Saher, G., Brugger, B., Lapper-Siefke, C., Mobius, W. *et al.* (2005) 'High cholesterol level is essential for myelin membrane growth.', *Nature Neuroscience*, 8: 468–475.

Saif, M.W., Mattison, L., Carollo, T., Ezzeldin, H. and Diasio, R.B. (2006) 'Dihydropyrimidine dehydrogenase deficiency in an Indian population.', *Cancer Chemotherapy and Pharmacology*, 58(3): 396–401.

Saitoh, S., Harada, N., Jinno, Y., Hashimoto, K. *et al.* (1994) 'Molecular and clinical study of 61 Angelman syndrome patients.', *American Journal of Medical Genetics*, 52: 158–163.

Saitoh, S., Kubota, T., Ohta, T., Jinno, Y. *et al.* (1992) 'Familial Angelman syndrome caused by imprinted submicroscopic deletion encompassing GABA-A receptor-3 subunit gene.', *The Lancet*, 339(8789): 366–367.

Saitoh, S., Momoi, M.Y., Yamagata, T., Miyao, M. and Suwa, K. (1998) 'Clinical and electroencephalographic findings in juvenile type DRPLA.', *Pediatric Neurology*, 18: 265–268.

Sajedi, E., Gaston-Massuet, C., Signore, M., Andoniadou, C.L. *et al.* (2008) 'Analysis of mouse models carrying the I26T and R160C substitutions in the transcriptional repressor HESX1 as models for septo-optic dysplasia and hypopituitarism.', *Disease Models and Mechanisms*, 1(4–5): 241–254.

Salama, G. and London, B. (2007) 'Mouse models of long QT syndrome.', *Journal of Physiology*, 578(1): 43–53.

Salen, G., Shefer, S., Batta, A.K., Tint, G.S. *et al.* (1996) 'Abnormal cholesterol biosynthesis in the Smith-Lemli-Opitz syndrome.', *Journal of Lipid Research*, 37: 1169–1180.

Salerno, C., D'Euphemia, P., Finocchiaro, R., Celli, M. *et al.* (1999) 'Effect of D-ribose on purine synthesis and neurological symptoms in a patient with adenylsuccinase deficiency.', *Biochimica et Biophysica Acta*, 1453: 135–140.

Salido, E.C., Li, X.M., Yen, P.H., Martin, N. *et al.* (1996) 'Cloning and expression of the mouse pseudoautosomal steroid sulphatase gene (Sts).', *Nature Genetics*, 13(1): 83–86.

Salman, M.S. (2002) 'Systematic review of the effect of therapeutic dietary supplements and drugs on cognitive function in subjects with Down syndrome.', *European Journal of Paediatric Neurology*, 6: 213–219.

Salomons, G.J., van Dooren, S.J.M., Verhoeven, N.M., Cecil, K.M. *et al.* (2001) 'X-linked creatine transporter (SLC6A8 gene) defect: a new creatine deficiency syndrome.', *American Journal of Human Genetics*, 68: 1497–1500.

Salonen, R., Somer, M., Haltia, M., Lorentz, M. and Norio, R. (1991) 'Progressive encephalopathy with oedema, hypsarrhythmia, and optic atrophy (PEHO syndrome).' *Clinical Genetics*, 39: 287–293.

Sampson, J.R., Scahill, S.J., Stephenson, J.B.P., Mann, L. and Connor, J.M. (1989) 'Genetic aspects of tuberous sclerosis in the west of Scotland.', *Journal of Medical Genetics*, 26: 28–31.

Samson, F., Mottron, L., Jemel, B., Belin, P. and Ciocca, V. (2006) 'Can spectro-temporal complexity explain the autistic pattern of performance on auditory tasks?' *Journal of Autism and Developmental Disorders*, 36(1): 65–76.

Samuraki, M., Komai, K., Hasegawa, Y., Kimura, M. *et al.* (2008) 'A successfully treated adult patient with L-2-hydroxyglutaric aciduria.', *Neurology*, 70(13): 1051–1052.

Sanaker, P.S., Nakkestad, H.L., Downham, E. and Bindoff, L.A. (2010) 'A novel mutation in the mitochondrial tRNA for tryptophan causing a late-onset mitochondrial encephalomyopathy.', *Acta Neurologica Scandinavica*, 121: 109–113.

Sanchez-Albisua, I., Borell-Kost, S., Mau-Holzmann, U.A., Licht, P. and Krägeloh-Mann, I. (2007) 'Increased frequency of severe major anomalies in children conceived by intracytoplasmic sperm injection.', *Developmental Medicine and Child Neurology*, 49(2): 129–134.

Sandanam, T., Beange, H., Robson, L., Woolnough, H. *et al.* (1997) 'Manifestations in institutionalised adults with Angelman syndrome due to deletion.', *American Journal of Medical Genetics*, 70: 415–420.

Sanklecha, M., Kher, A. and Bharucha, B.A. (1992) 'Asymmetric crying facies: the cardiofacial syndrome.', *Journal of Postgraduate Medicine*, 38: 147–150.

Sanlaville, D., Etchevers, H.C., Gonzales, M., Martinovic, J. *et al.* (2006) 'Phenotypic spectrum of CHARGE syndrome in fetuses with CHD7 truncating mutations correlates with expression during human development.' *Journal of Medical Genetics*, 43(3): 211–217.

Sanlaville, D. and Verloes, A. (2007) 'CHARGE syndrome: an update.', *European Journal of Human Genetics*, 15: 389–399.

Sano, M., Ernesto, C., Thomas, R.G., Klauber, M.R., Schafer, K. *et al.* (1997) 'A controlled trial of selegiline, alpha-tocopherol, or both as treatment for Alzheimer's disease.', *New England Journal of Medicine*, 336: 1216–1222.

Santos Dantas, A., Luft, T., Henriques, J.A.P., Schwartsmann, G. and Roesler, R. (2006) 'Opposite effects of low and high doses of the gastrin-releasing peptide receptor antagonist RC-3095 on memory consolidation in the hippocampus: possible involvement of the GABAergic system.', *Peptides*, 27: 2307–2312.

Saraiva, J.M. and Baraitser, M. (1992) 'Joubert syndrome: a review.', *American Journal of Medical Genetics*, 43: 726–731.

Saran, N.G., Pletcher, M.T., Natale, J.E., Cheng, Y. and Reeves, R.H. (2003) 'Global disruption of the cerebellar transcriptome in a Down syndrome mouse model.', *Human Molecular Genetics*, 12(16): 2013–2019.

Sargent, M.A., Poskitt, K.J. and Jan, J.E. (1997) 'Congenital ocular motor apraxia: imaging findings.' *AJNR. American Journal of Neuroradiology*, 18: 1915–1922.

Sarimski, K. (1997) 'Communication, social-emotional development and parenting stress in Cornelia-de-Lange syndrome.', *Journal of Intellectual Disability Research*, 41: 70–75.

Sarkar, P.S., Appukuttan, B., Han, J., Ito, Y., Ai, C., Tsai, W., Chai, Y., Stout, J.T. and Reddy, S. (2000) 'Heterozygous loss of Six5 in mice is sufficient to cause ocular cataracts.', *Nature Genetics*, 25: 110–114.

Sarkar, P.S., Paul, S., Han, J. and Reddy, S. (2004) 'Six5 is required for spermatogenic cell survival and spermiogenesis.', *Human Molecular Genetics*, 13: 1421–1431.

Sarkissian, C.N. and Gámez, A. (2005) 'Phenylalanine ammonia lyase, enzyme substitution therapy for phenylketonuria, where are we now?' *Molecular Genetics and Metabolism*, 86: S22–S26.

Sarkissian, C.N., Shao, Z., Blain, F., Peevers, R. *et al.* (1999) 'A different approach to treatment of phenylketonuria: phenylalanine degradation with recombinant phenylalanine ammonia lyase.', *Proceedings of the National Academy of Science*, 96: 2339–2344.

Sas, K., Robotka, H., Toldi, J. and Vécseia, L. (2007) 'Mitochondria, metabolic disturbances, oxidative stress and the kynurenine system, with focus on neurodegenerative disorders.', *Journal of the Neurological Sciences*, 257(1–2): 221–239.

Sasaki, N., Yamauchi, K., Sato, R., Masuda, T. *et al.* (2006) 'Klinefelter's syndrome associated with systemic lupus erythematosus and autoimmune hepatitis.', *Modern Rheumatology*, 16(5): 305–308.

Sataloff, R.T., Spiegel, J.R., Hawkshaw, M., Epstein, J.M. and Jackson, L. (1990) 'Cornelia de Lange syndrome: otolaryngologic manifestations.', *Archives of Otolaryngology, Head and Neck Surgery*, 116: 1044–1046.

Satir, P. and Christensen, S.T. (2008) 'Structure and function of mammalian cilia.', *Histochemistry and Cell Biology*, 129: 687–693.

Satran, D., Pierpont, M.E. and Dobyns, W.B. (1999) 'Cerebello-oculo-renal syndromes including Arima, Senior-Loken and COACH syndromes: more than just variants of Joubert syndrome.', *American Journal of Medical Genetics*, 86: 459–469.

Saucy, P., Eidus, L. and Keeley, F. (1980) 'Perforation of the colon in a 15-year-old girl with Ehlers-Danlos syndrome type IV.', *Journal of Pediatric Surgery*, 25(11): 1180–182.

Saugstad, L.F. (1975a) 'Anthropological significance of phenylketonuria.', *Clinical Genetics*, 7: 52–61.

Saugstad, L.F. (1975b) 'Frequency of phenylketonuria in Norway.', *Clinical Genetics*, 7: 40–51.

Saunier, S., Salomon, R. and Antignac, C. (2005) 'Nephronophthisis.', *Current Opinion in Genetics and Development*, 15: 324–331.

Sayer, J.A., Otto, E.A., O'Toole, J.F., Nurnberg, G. *et al.* (2006) 'The centrosomal protein nephrocystin-6 is mutated in Joubert syndrome and activates transcription factor ATF4.', *Nature Genetics*, 38: 674–681.

Scahill, L., Leckman, J.F., Schultz, R.T., Katsovich, L. and Peterson, B.S. (2003) 'A placebo-controlled trial of risperidone in Tourette syndrome.', *Neurology*, 60: 1130–1135.

Scala, E., Ariani, F., Mari, F., Caselli, R. *et al.* (2005) 'CDKL5/STK9 is mutated in Rett syndrome variant with infantile spasms.', *Journal of Medical Genetics*, 42: 103–107.

Scalco, F.B., Cruzes, V.M., Vendramini, R.C., Brunetti, I.L. and Moretti-Ferreira, D. (2003) 'Diagnosis of Smith-Lemli-Opitz syndrome by ultraviolet spectrophotometry.', *Brazilian Journal of Medical and Biological Research*, 36(10): 1327–1332.

Scambler, P.J. (2000) 'The 22q11 deletion syndromes.', *Human Molecular Genetics*, 9(16): 2421–2426.

Scambler, D.J., Hepburn, S.L. and Rogers, S.J. (2006) 'A two-year follow-up on risk status identified by the checklist for autism in toddlers.', *Journal of Developmental and Behavioural Pediatrics*, 27: 104–110.

Scarbrough, P.R., Huddleston, K. and Finley, S.C. (1986) 'An additional case of Smith-Lemli-Opitz syndrome in a 46,XY infant with female external genitalia.', *Journal of Medical Genetics*, 23: 174–175.

Scattone, A., Caruso, G., Marzullo, A., Piscitelli, D. *et al.* (2003) 'Neoplastic disease and deletion 22q11.2: a multicentric study and report of two cases.', *Pediatric Pathology and Molecular Medicine*, 22: 323–341.

Schaefer, G.B. and Lutz, R.E. (2006) 'Diagnostic yield in the clinical genetic evaluation of autism spectrum disorders.', *Genetics in Medicine*, 8(9): 549–556.

Schaefer, G.B. and Mendelsohn, N.J. (2008) 'Genetics evaluation for the etiologic diagnosis of autism spectrum disorders.', *Genetics in Medicine*, 10(1): 4–12.

Schaffer, J.V. and Bolognia, J.L. (2003) 'The treatment of hypopigmentation I children.', *Clinics in Dermatology*, 21: 296–310.

Schalkwijk, J., Zweers, M.C., Steijlen, P.M., Dean, W.B. *et al.* (2001) 'A recessive form of the Ehlers-Danlos syndrome caused by tenascin-X deficiency.', *New England Journal of Medicine*, 345: 1167–1175.

Schanen, C. and Francke, U. (1998) 'A severely affected male born into a Rett syndrome kindred supports X-linked inheritance and allows extension of the exclusion map.', (Letter) *American Journal of Human Genetics*, 63: 267–269.

Schanen, C., Houwink, E.J.F., Dorrani, N., Lane, J. *et al.* (2004) 'Phenotypic manifestations of MeCP2 mutations in classical and atypical Rett syndrome.', *American Journal of Medical Genetics*, 126A: 129–140.

Schanen, N.C., Kurczynski, T.W., Brunnelle, D., Woodcock, M.M., Dure, L.S. IV and Percy, A.K. (1998) 'Neonatal encephalopathy in two boys in families with recurrent Rett syndrome.', *Journal of Child Neurology*, 13: 229–231.

Schara, U., Benedikt, G.H. and Schoser, B.G.H. (2006) 'Myotonic dystrophies type 1 and 2: a summary on current aspects.', *Seminars in Pediatric Neurology*, 13: 71–79.

Schauerte, E.W. and St-Aubin, P.M. (1966) 'Progressive synosteosis in Apert's syndrome (acrocephalosyndactyly): with a description of roentgenographic changes in the feet.', *American Journal of Roentgenology*, 97: 67–73.

Schaumburg, H., Kaplan, J., Windebank, A., Vick, N. *et al.* (1983) 'Sensory neuropathy from pyridoxine abuse: a new megavitamin syndrome.', *New England Journal of Medicine*, 309(8): 445–448.

Scheffer, I., Brett, E.M., Wilson, J. and Baraitser, M. (1990) 'Angelman's syndrome.' (Letter) *Journal of Medical Genetics*, 27: 275–277.

Scheffer, I.E., Wallace, R.H., Phillips, F.L., Hewson, P. et al. (2002) 'X-linked myoclonic epilepsy with spasticity and intellectual disability: mutation in the homeobox gene ARX.', Neurology, 59(3): 348–356.

Schenck, C.H., Arnulf, I. and Mahowald, M.W. (2007) 'Sleep and sex: what can go wrong? A review of the literatures on sleep related disorders and abnormal sexual behaviours and experiences.', Sleep, 30(6): 683–702.

Schendel, D. and Bhasin, T.K. (2008) 'Birth weight and gestational age characteristics of children with autism, including a comparison with other developmental disabilities.', Pediatrics, 121(6): 1155–1164.

Schepis, C., Elia, M., Siragusa, M. and Barbareschi, M. (1997) 'A new case of trichothiodystrophy associated with autism, seizures, and mental retardation.', Pediatric Dermatology, 14: 125–128.

Scherer, S.W., Gripp, K.W., Lucena, J., Nicholson, L. et al. (2005) 'Observation of a parental inversion variant in a rare Williams-Beuren syndrome family with two affected children.', Human Genetics, 117: 383–388.

Schilling, G., Wood, J.D., Duan, K., Slunt, H.H. et al. (1999) 'Nuclear accumulation of truncated atrophin-1 fragments in a transgenic mouse model of DRPLA.', Neuron, 24(1): 275–286.

Schindler, D., Bishop, D.F., Wolfe, D.E., Wang, A.M. et al. (1989) 'Neuroaxonal dystrophy due to lysosomal alpha-N-acetylgalactosaminidase deficiency.', New England Journal of Medicine, 320: 1735–1740.

Schinke, M. and Izumo, S. (2001) 'Deconstructing DiGeorge syndrome.', Nature Genetics, 27(3): 238–240.

Schlesinger, B. (1931) 'Gigantism (acromegalic in type).', Proceedings of the Royal Society of Medicine, 24: 1352–1353.

Schmandt, S.M., Packer, R.J., Vezina, L.G. and Jane, J. (2000) 'Spontaneous regression of low-grade astrocytomas in childhood.', Pediatric Neurosurgery, 32: 132–136.

Schmidt, A., Marescau, B., Boehm, E.A., Renema, W.K.J. et al. (2004) 'Severely altered guanidino compound levels, disturbed body weight homeostasis and impaired fertility in a mouse model of guanidinoacetate N-methyltransferase (GAMT) deficiency.', Human Molecular Genetics, 13: 905–921.

Schmidt, C., Hofmann, U., Kohlmuller, D., Murdter, T. et al. (2005) 'Comprehensive analysis of pyrimidine metabolism in 450 children with unspecific neurological symptoms using high-pressure liquid chromatography–electrospray ionization tandem mass spectrometry.', Journal of Inherited Metabolic Disease, 28: 1109–1122.

Schmidt, H., Pozza, S.B., Bonfig, W., Schwarz, H.P. and Dokoupil, K. (2008) 'Successful early dietary intervention avoids obesity in patients with Prader-Willi syndrome: a ten-year follow-up.', Journal of Pediatric Endocrinology and Metabolism, 21(7): 651–655.

Schmitt, J.E., Eliez, S., Bellugi, U. and Reiss, A.L. (2001) 'Analysis of cerebral shape in Williams syndrome.', Archives of Neurology, 58: 283–287.

Schmucker, B. and Seidel, J. (1999) 'Mosaicism for a full mutation and a normal size allele in two fragile-X males.' American Journal of Medical Genetics, 84: 221–225.

Schneider, J.A., Rees, D.C., Liu Y-T. and Clegg, J.B. (1988) 'Worldwide distribution of a common methylenetetrahydrofolate reductase mutation.' American Journal of Human Genetics, 62: 1248–1252.

Schneider, J.E., Stork, L-A., Bell, J.T., Hove, M. et al. (2008) 'Cardiac structure and function during ageing in energetically compromised guanidinoacetate N-methyltransferase (GAMT)-knockout mice – a one year longitudinal MRI study.', Journal of Cardiovascular Magnetic Resonance, 10(1): 9 doi:10.1186/1532-429X-10-9, downloadable from www.pubmedcentral.nih.gov/articlerender.fcgi?artid=2254407.

Schoepp, D.D., Jane, D.E. and Monn, J.A. (1999) 'Pharmacological agents acting at subtypes of metabotropic glutamate receptors.', Neuropharmacology, 38: 1431–1476.

Schopler, E., Reichler, R.J., DeVellis, R. and Daly, K. (1980) 'Towards objective classification of childhood autism: Childhood Autism Rating Scale (CARS).', Journal of Autism and Developmental Disorders, 10: 91–103.

Schrager, C.A., Schneider, D., Gruener, A.C., Tsou, H.C. and Peacocke, M. (1998) 'Clinical and pathological features of breast disease in Cowden's syndrome: an underrecognized syndrome with an increased risk of breast cancer.', Human Pathology, 29: 47–53.

Schrander-Stumpel, C., Gerver, W-J., Meyer, H., Engelen, J. et al. (1994) 'Prader-Willi-like phenotype in fragile-X syndrome.', Clinical Genetics, 45: 175–180.

Schrander-Stumpel, C.T.R.M., de Die-Smulders, C.E.M., Hennekam, R.C.M., Fryns, J.P. et al. (1992) 'Oculoauriculovertebral spectrum and cerebral anomalies.', Journal of Medical Genetics, 29: 326–331.

Schrimsher, G.W., Billingsley, R.L., Slopis, J.M. and Moore, B.D. 3rd (2003) 'Visual-spatial performance deficits in children with neurofibromatosis type-1.', American Journal of Medical Genetics, 120A: 326–330.

Schroer, R.J., Phelan, M.C., Michaelis, R.C., Crawford, E.C. et al. (1998) 'Autism and maternally derived aberrations of chromosome 15q.', American Journal of Medical Genetics, 76: 327–336.

Schubbert, S., Zenker, M., Rowe, S.L., Boll, S. et al. (2006) 'Germline KRAS mutations cause Noonan syndrome.' Nature Genetics, 38: 331–336.

Schuelke, M., Wagner, K.R., Stolz, L.E., Hübner, C. et al. (2004) 'Myostatin mutation associated with gross muscle hypertrophy in a child.', New England Journal of Medicine, 350: 2682–2688.

Schuffenhauer, S., Lichtner, P., Peykar-Derakhshandeh, P., Murken, J. et al. (1998) 'Deletion mapping on chromosome 10p and definition of a critical region for the second DiGeorge syndrome locus (DGS2).', European Journal of Human Genetics, 6: 213–225.

Schulkin, J. (2007) 'Autism and the amygdala: an endocrine hypothesis.', Brain and Cognition, 65: 87–99.

Schultz, S.T., Klonoff-Cohen, H.S., Wingard, D.L., Akshoomoff, N.A. et al. (2006) 'Breastfeeding, infant formula supplementation, and autistic disorder: the results of a parent survey.', International Breastfeeding Journal, 1: 16–22.

Schulze, A. (2003) 'Creatine deficiency syndromes.', Molecular and Cellular Biochemistry, 244: 143–150.

Schulze, A. and Battini, R. (2007) 'Pre-symptomatic treatment of creatine biosynthesis defects.', *Subcellular Biochemistry, 46*: 167–181.

Schulze, A., Ebinger, F., Rating, D. and Mayatepek, E. (2001) 'Improving treatment of guanidinoacetate methyltransferase Schulze deficiency: reduction of guanidinoacetic acid in body fluids by arginine restriction and ornithine supplementation.', *Molecular Genetics and Metabolism, 74*(4): 413–419.

Schulze, A., Hess, T., Wevers, R., Mayatepek, E. *et al.* (1997) 'Creatine deficiency syndrome caused by guanidinoacetate methyltransferase deficiency: diagnostic tools for a new inborn error of metabolism.', *Journal of Pediatrics, 131*: 626–631.

Schulze, A., Mayatepek, E. and Rating, D. (2000) 'Improved treatment of guanidinoacetate methyltransferase (GAMT) deficiency.', *Journal of Inherited Metabolic Disease, 23*(Supp.1): 211.

Schumacher, A., Kapranov, P., Kaminsky, Z., Flanagan, J. *et al.* (2006) 'Microarray-based DNA methylation profiling: technology and applications.', *Nucleic Acids Research, 34*(2): 528–542.

Schumann, C.M. and Amaral, D.G. (2006) 'Stereological analysis of amygdala neuron number in autism.' *Journal of Neuroscience, 26*: 7674–7679.

Schwartz, C.E., Tarpey, P.S., Lubs, H.A., Verloes, A. *et al.* (2007) 'The original Lujan syndrome family has a novel missense mutation (p.N1007S) in the MED12 gene.', *Journal of Medical Genetics, 44*: 472–477.

Schwartz, S.M., Siscovick, D.S., Malinow, M.R., Rosendaal, F.R. *et al.* (1997) 'Myocardial infarction in young women in relation to plasma total homocysteine, folate, and a common variant in the methylenetetrahydrofolate reductase gene.', *Circulation, 96*: 412–417.

Schwartzman, J.S., Zatz, M., Vasquez, L.R., Gomes, R.R. *et al.* (1999) 'Rett syndrome in a boy with a 47,XXY karyotype.', (Letter) *American Journal of Human Genetics, 64*: 1781–1785.

Scothorn, D.J. and Butler, M.G. (1997) 'How common is precocious puberty in patients with Williams syndrome?' (Letter) *Clinical Dysmorphology, 6*: 91–93.

Scott, A., Micallef, C., Hale, S.L. and Watts, P. (2008) 'Cortical visual impairment in hypomelanosis of Ito.', *Journal of Pediatrics Ophthalmology and Strabismus, 45*(4): 240–241.

Scottish Intercollegiate Guideline Network (2007) *Assessment, Diagnosis And Clinical Interventions For Children and Young People with Autism Spectrum Disorders: A National Clinical Guideline.* Downloadable as PDF from: www.sign.ac.uk.

Scriver, C.R. (2001) 'Garrod's foresight: our hindsight.', *Journal of Inherited Metabolic Disease, 24*: 93–116.

Scriver, C.R., Eisensmith, R.C., Woo, S.L.C. and Kaufman, S. (1994) 'The hyperphenylalaninemias of man and mouse.', *Annual Review of Genetics, 28*: 141–165.

Searle, A.G., Edwards, J.H. and Hall, J.G. (1994) 'Mouse homologues of human hereditary disease.', *Journal of Medical Genetics, 31*: 1–19.

Sebat, J., Lakshmi, B., Malhotra, D., Troge, J. *et al.* (2007) 'Strong association of *de novo* copy number mutations with autism.', *Science, 316*(5823): 445–449.

Sebesta, I., Krijt, J., Kmoch, S., Hartmannova, H. *et al.* (1997) 'Adenylosuccinase deficiency: clinical and biochemical findings in 5 Czech patients.', *Journal of Inherited Metabolic Diseases, 20*: 343–344.

Sebire, N.J., Snijders, R.J., Brown, R., Southall, T. and Nicolaides, K.H. (1998) 'Detection of sex chromosome abnormalities by nuchal translucency screening at 10–14 weeks.', *Prenatal Diagnosis, 18*: 581–584.

Sedlackova, E. (1955) 'The syndrome of the congenital shortening of the soft palate.', [in Czech] *Cas Lek Ces, 94*: 1304–1307.

Seidl, R., Cairns, N., Singewald, N., Kaehler, S.T. and Lubec, G. (2001) 'Differences between GABA levels in Alzheimer's disease and Down syndrome with Alzheimer-like neuropathology.', *Naunyn Schmiedeberg's Archives of Pharmacology, 363*(2): 139–145.

Seifert, W., Holder-Espinasse, M., Spranger, S., Hoeltzenbein, M. *et al.* (2006) 'Mutational spectrum of COH1 and clinical heterogeneity in Cohen syndrome.', (Letter) *Journal of Medical Genetics, 43*: e22.

Seijo-Martínez, M., Navarro, C., Castro del Río, M., Vila, O. *et al.* (2005) 'L-2-hydroxyglutaric aciduria: clinical, neuroimaging, and neuropathological findings.' *Archives of Neurology, 62*(4): 666–670.

Sekul, E.A., Moak, J.P., Schultz, R.J., Glaze, D.G., *et al.* (1994) 'Electrocardiographic findings in Rett syndrome: an explanation for sudden death?' *Journal of Pediatrics, 125*: 80–82.

Selicorni, A., Fratoni, A., Pavesi, M.A., Bottigelli, M. *et al.* (2006) 'Thyroid anomalies in Williams syndrome: investigation of 95 patients.', *American Journal of Medical Genetics, 140A*: 1098–1101.

Selicorni, A., Russo, S., Gervasini, C., Castronovo, P. *et al.* (2007) 'Clinical score of 62 Italian patients with Cornelia de Lange syndrome and correlations with the presence and type of NIPBL mutation.', *Clinical Genetics, 72*(2): 98–108.

Seller, M.J., Flinter, F.A., Docherty, Z., Fagg, N. and Newbould, M. (1997) 'Phenotypic diversity in the Smith-Lemli-Opitz syndrome.', *Clinical Dysmorphology, 6*: 69–73.

Seller, M.J. and Wallace, M.E. (1993) 'Tail short variable: characterization of a new mouse mutant, and its possible analogy to certain human vascular disruption defects.', *Teratology, 48*(4): 383–391.

Sempere, A., Arias, A., Farré, G., García-Villoria, J. *et al.* (2010) 'Study of inborn errors of metabolism in urine from patients with unexplained mental retardation.', *Journal of Inherited Metabolic Disease, 33*(1): 1–7.

Senior, B., Friedmann, A.I. and Braudo, J.L. (1961) 'Juvenile familial nephropathy with tapetoretinal degeneration: a new oculorenal dystrophy.', *American Journal of Ophthalmology, 52*: 625–633.

Seracchioli, R., Bagnoli, A., Colombo, F.M., Missiroli, S. and Venturoli, S. (2001) 'Conservative treatment of recurrent ovarian fibromas in a young patient affected by Gorlin syndrome.', *Human Reproduction, 16*: 1261–1263.

Seragee, F.J., Zhong, H., Nabi, R. and Mahbubul Huq, A.H. (2003) 'The metabotropic glutamate receptor 8 gene at 7q31: partial duplication and possible association with autism.', *Journal of Medical Genetics, 40*: e42.

Serajee, F.J., Zhong, H. and Mahbubul Huq, A.H. (2006) 'Association of Reelin gene polymorphisms with autism.', *Genomics*, 87(1): 75–83.

Sergeyev, A.S. (1975) 'On the mutation rate of neurofibromatosis.', *Humangenetik*, 28(2): 129–138.

Seri, S., Cerquiglini, A., Pisani, F. and Curatolo, P. (1999) 'Autism in tuberous sclerosis: evoked potential evidence for a deficit in auditory sensory processing.' *Clinical Neurophysiology*, 110: 1825–1830.

Seroogy, C.M., Wara, D.W., Bluth, M.H., Dorenbaum, A. *et al.* (1999) 'Cytokine profile of a long-term pediatric HIV survivor with hyper-IgE syndrome and a normal CD4 T-cell count.', *Journal of Allergy and Clinical Immunology*, 104(5): 1045–1051.

Serra-Mestres, J., Ring, H.A., Costa, D.C., Gacinovic, S. *et al.* (2004) 'Dopamine transporter binding in Gilles de la Tourette syndrome: a [123I]FP-CIT/SPECT study.', *Acta Psychiatrica Scandinavica*, 109: 140–146.

Setzer, E.S., Ruiz-Castaneda, N., Severn, C., Ryden, S. and Frias, J.L. (1981) 'Etiologic heterogeneity in the oculoauriculovertebral syndrome.', *Journal of Pediatrics*, 98: 88–90.

Seven, M., Cengiz, M., Tüzgen, S. and Iscan, M.Y. (2001) 'Plasma carnitine levels in children with Down syndrome.', *American Journal of Human Biology*, 13(6): 721–725.

Sever, R.J., Frost, P. and Weinstein, G. (1968) 'Eye changes in ichthyosis.', *Journal of the American Medical Association*, 206: 2283–2286.

Shackleton, C.H.L., Roitman, E., Kratz, L.E. and Kelley, R.I. (1999) 'Equine type estrogens produced by a pregnant woman carrying a Smith-Lemli-Opitz syndrome fetus.', *Journal of Clinical Endocrinology and Metabolism*, 84: 1157–1159.

Shafeghati, Y., Vakili, G. and Entezari, A. (2006) 'L-2-hydroxyglutaric aciduria: a report of six cases and a review of the literature.', *Archives of Iranian Medicine*, 9(2): 165–169.

Shaffer, L.G., Jackson-Cook, C.K., Stasiowski, B.A., Spence, J.E. and Brown, J.A. (1992) 'Parental origin determination in 30 *de novo* Robertsonian translocations.', *American Journal of Medical Genetics*, 43: 957–963.

Shah, A. and Frith, U. (1993) 'Why do autistic individuals show superior performance on the block design task?' *Journal of Child Psychology and Psychiatry*, 34(8): 1351–1364.

Shah, A.S., Farmen, S.L., Moninger, T.O., Businga, T.R. *et al.* (2008) 'Loss of Bardet-Biedl syndrome proteins alters the morphology and function of motile cilia in airway epithelia.', *Proceedings of the National Academy of Science USA*, 105(9): 3380–3385.

Shahbazian, M.D., Young, J.I., Yuva-Paylor, L.A., Spencer, C.M. *et al.* (2002) 'Mice with truncated MeCP2 recapitulate many Rett syndrome features and display hyperacetylation of histone H3.', *Neuron*, 35: 243–254.

Shaikh, N.A. and Turner, D.T.L.T. (1988) 'Ehlers-Danlos syndrome presenting with infarction of stomach.', *Journal of the Royal Society of Medicine*, 81: 611.

Shamaly, H., Hartman, C., Pollack, S., Hujerat, M. *et al.* (2007) 'Tissue transglutaminase antibodies are a useful serological marker for the diagnosis of coeliac disease in patients with Down syndrome.', *Journal of Pediatric Gastroenterology and Nutrition*, 44(5): 583–586.

Shao, Y., Cuccaro, M.L., Hauser, E.R., Raiford, K.L. *et al.* (2003) 'Fine mapping of autistic disorder to chromosome 15q11–q13 by use of phenotypic subtypes.', *American Journal of Human Genetics*, 72: 539–548.

Shao, Y., Wolpert, C.M., Raiford, K.L., Menold, M.M. *et al.* (2002) 'Genomic screen and follow-up analysis for autistic disorder.', *American Journal of Medical Genetics*, 114: 99–105.

Shapiro, L.J., Weiss, R., Buxman, M.M., Vidgoff, J. and Dimond, R.L. (1978) 'Enzymatic basis of typical X-linked ichthyosis.', *Lancet* 312(8093): 756–757.

Shaposhnikov, A.M., Khal'chitskii, S.E. and Shvarts, E.I. (1979) '[Disorders of phenylalanine and tyrosine metabolism in Down's syndrome].', *Voprosy Meditsinskoi Khimii*, 25(1): 15–19.

Sharif, S., Ferner, R., Birch, J.M., Gillespie, J.E. *et al.* (2006) 'Second primary tumors in neurofibromatosis 1 patients treated for optic glioma: substantial risks after radiotherapy.', *Journal of Clinical Oncology*, 24: 2570–2575.

Sharland, M., Burch, M., McKenna, W.M. and Paton, M.A. (1992) 'A clinical study of Noonan syndrome.', *Archives of Disease in Childhood*, 67(2): 178–183.

Sharland, M., Patton, M.A., Talbot, S., Chitolie, A. and Bevan, D.H. (1992) 'Coagulation-factor deficiencies and abnormal bleeding in Noonan's syndrome.', *Lancet*, 339: 19–21.

Sharma, R., Chandrakantha, E.L. and Mold, B. (2007) 'National Autism Plan standards for assessment are achievable.', *Child: Care, Health and Development*, 33: 500–501.

Shashi, V., Keshaven, M.S., Howard, T.D., Berry, M.N. *et al.* (2006) 'Cognitive correlates of a functional COMT polymorphism in children with 22q11.2 deletion syndrome.', *Clinical Genetics*, 69: 234–238.

Shavelle, R.M., Strauss, D.J. and Pickett, J. (2001) 'Causes of death in autism.', *Journal of Autism and Developmental Disorders*, 31: 569–576.

Shaw-Smith, C. (2006) 'Oesophageal atresia, tracheo-oesophageal fistula, and the VACTERL association: review of genetics and epidemiology.', *Journal of Medical Genetics*, 43(7): 545–554.

Shear, C.S., Nyhan, W.L., Kirman, B.H. and Stern, J. (1971) 'Self-mutilative behaviour as a feature of the de Lange syndrome.', *Journal of Pediatrics*, 78: 506–509.

Sheen, V.L., Jansen, A., Chen, M.H., Parrini, E. *et al.* (2005) 'Mutations cause periventricular heterotopia with Ehlers-Danlos syndrome.', *Neurology*, 64: 254–262.

Sheen, V.L. and Walsh, C.A. (2006) 'Periventricular heterotopia: new insights into Ehlers-Danlos syndrome.', *Clinical Medicine and Research*, 3(4): 229–233.

Sheffield, V.C., Nishimura, D. and Stone, E.M. (2001) 'The molecular genetics of Bardet-Biedl syndrome.', *Current Opinion in Genetics and Development*, 11: 317–321.

Shelton, J.F., Tancredi, D.J. and Hertz-Picciotto, I. (2010) 'Independent and dependent contributions of advanced maternal and paternal ages to autism risk.', *Autism Research*, 3: 1–10.

Shen, J.X., Qiu, G.X., Wang, Y.P., Zhao, Y. *et al.* (2005) 'Surgical treatment of scoliosis caused by neurofibromatosis type 1.', *Chinese Medicine and Science Journal*, 20: 88–92.

Shenoy, S., Arnold, S. and Chatila, T. (2000) 'Response to steroid therapy in autism secondary to autoimmune lymphoproliferative syndrome.' *Journal of Pediatrics*, 136: 682–687.

Shereshevskii, N.A. (1925) 'In relation to the question of a connection between congenital abnormalities and endocrinopathies.', Lecture to the Russian Endocrinological Society, November 12th.

Sherman, S.L. (2000) 'Premature ovarian failure in the fragile-X syndrome.', *American Journal of Medical Genetics*, 97: 189–194.

Sherman, S.L., Allen, E.G., Bean, L.H. and Freeman, S.B. (2007) 'Epidemiology of Down syndrome.', *Mental Retardation and Developmental Disabilities Research Reviews*, 13(3): 221–227.

Sherr, E.H. (2003) 'The ARX story (epilepsy, mental retardation, autism, and cerebral malformations): one gene leads to many phenotypes.', *Current Opinion in Pediatrics*, 15: 567–571.

Sherr, E.H., Owen, R., Albertson, D.G., Pinkel, D. *et al.* (2005) 'Genomic microarray analysis identifies candidate loci in patients with corpus callosum anomalies.', *Neurology*, 65: 1496–1498.

Shervell, M.I., Colangelo, P., Treacy, E., Palomeno, R.C. and Rosenblatt, B. (1996) 'Progressive encephalopathy with oedema, hypsarrythmia and optic atrophy (PEHO syndrome).', *Pediatric Neurology*, 15: 337–339.

Shevell, M., Ashwal, S., Donley, D., Flint, J. *et al.* (2003) 'Practice parameter: evaluation of the child with global developmental delay. Report of the Quality Standards Subcommittee of the American Academy of Neurology and the Practice Committee of the Child Neurology Society.', *Neurology*, 60: 367–380.

Shimizu, T., Takao, A., Ando, M. and Hirayama, A. (1984) 'Conotruncal face syndrome: its heterogeneity and association with thymus involution.' In J.J. Nora and A. Takao (eds.) *Congenital Heart Disease: Causes and Processes.* Mount Kisco, New York: Futura Publishing.

Shimojo, Y., Osawa, Y., Fukumizu, M., Hanaoka, S. *et al.* (2001) 'Severe infantile dentatorubral pallidoluysian atrophy with extreme expansion of CAG repeats.', *Neurology*, 56: 277–278.

Singh, I., Khan, M., Key, L. and Pai, S. (1998) 'Lovastatin for X-linked adrenoleukodystrophy.' *New England Journal of Medicine*, 339(10): 702–703.

Shinohara, T., Tomizuka, K., Miyabara, S., Takehara, S. *et al.* (2001) 'Mice containing a human chromosome 21 model behavioural impairment and cardiac anomalies of Down's syndrome.', *Human Molecular Genetics*, 10: 1163–1175.

Shinohe, A., Hashimoto, K., Nakamura, K., Tsujii, M. *et al.* (2006) 'Increased serum levels of glutamate in adult patients with autism.' *Progress in Neuropsychopharmacology and Biological Psychiatry*, 30(8): 1472–1477.

Shonkoff, J.P. and Phillips, D.A. (eds.) (2000) *From Neurons to Neighborhoods: The Science of Early Childhood Development.* Washington, DC: National Academies Press.

Shprintzen, R.J. (1994) 'Velocardiofacial syndrome and DiGeorge sequence.' (Letter) *Journal of Medical Genetics*, 31: 423–424.

Shprintzen, R.J. (2008) 'Velocardiofacial syndrome – 30 years of study.', *Developmental Disabilities Research Reviews*, 14: 3–10.

Shprintzen, R.J., Goldberg, R.B., Young, D. and Wolford, L. (1981) 'The velocardiofacial syndrome: a clinical and genetic analysis.', *Pediatrics*, 67(2): 167–172.

Shuang, M., Liu, J., Jia, M.X., Yang, J.Z. *et al.* (2004) 'Family-based association study between autism and glutamate receptor 6 gene in Chinese Han trios.', *American Journal of Medical Genetics B Neuropsychiatric Genetics*, 131: 48–50.

Shuman, C., Smith, A.C., Steele, L., Ray, P.N. *et al.* (2006) 'Constitutional UPD for chromosome 11p15 in individuals with isolated hemihyperplasia is associated with high tumor risk and occurs following assisted reproductive technologies.', *American Journal of Medical Genetics*, 140A: 1497–1503.

Shumyatsky, G.P., Tsvetkov, E., Malleret, G., Vronskaya, S. *et al.* (2002) 'Identification of a signaling network in lateral nucleus of amygdala important for inhibiting memory specifically related to learned fear.', *Cell*, 111: 905–918.

Shusta, E.V. (2005) 'Blood-brain barrier genomics, proteomics, and new transporter discovery.', *NeuroRx*, 2(1): 151–161.

Shwayder, T. (2004) 'Disorders of keratinization: diagnosis and management.', *American Journal of Clinical Dermatology*, 5(1): 17–29.

Sicouri, S., Timothy, K.W., Zygmunt, A.C., Glass, A. *et al.* (2007) 'Cellular basis for the electrocardiographic and arrhythmic manifestations of Timothy syndrome: effects of ranolazine.', *Heart Rhythm*, 4(5): 638–647.

Sieg, K.G. (1992) 'Autism and Ehlers-Danlos syndrome.', *Journal of the American Academy of Child and Adolescent Psychiatry*, 31: 173.

Sieg, K.G. (2009) 'Co-occurrence of X-linked congenital adrenal hypoplasia and autistic disorder.', *Journal of Neuropsychiatry and Clinical Neurosciences*, 21(2): 227–228.

Sikora, D.M., Pettit-Kekel, K., Penfield, J., Merkens, L.S. and Steiner, R.D. (2006) 'The near universal presence of autism spectrum disorders in children with Smith-Lemli-Opitz syndrome.', *American Journal of Medical Genetics A*, 140: 1511–1518.

Sikora, D.M., Ruggiero, M., Petit-Kekel, K., Merkens, L.S. *et al.* (2004) 'Cholesterol supplementation does not improve developmental progress in Smith-Lemli-Opitz syndrome.', *Journal of Pediatrics*, 144(6): 783–791.

Silay, Y.S. and Jankovic, J. (2005) 'Emerging drugs in Tourette syndrome.', *Expert Opinion on Emerging Drugs*, 10(2): 365–380.

Simensen, R.J., Abidi, F., Collins, J.S., Schwartz, C.E. and Stevenson, R.E. (2002) 'Cognitive function in Coffin-Lowry syndrome.', *Clinical Genetics*, 61: 299–304.

Simmonds, H.A. (2003) 'Hereditary xanthinurea.', *Orphanet Encyclopaedia*, www.orpha.net/data/patho/GB/uk-XDH.pdf

Simon, T.J., Bearden, C.E., Moss, E.M., McDonald-McGinn, D. *et al.* (2002) 'Cognitive development in 22q11.2 deletion syndrome.', *Progress in Pediatric Cardiology*, 15: 109–117.

Simon Harvey, A., Leaper, P.M. and Bankier, A. (1991) 'CHARGE association: clinical manifestations and developmental outcome.', *American Journal of Medical Genetics*, 39: 351–356.

Simonyi, A., Schachtman, T.R. and Christoffersen, G.R.J. (2005) 'The role of metabotropic glutamate receptor 5 in learning and memory.', *Drug News Perspectives*, 18: 353–361.

Simpson, J.L., Landey, S., New, M. and German, J. (1975) 'A previously unrecognized X-linked syndrome of dysmorphia.', *Birth Defects Original Articles Series*, XI(2): 18–24.

Singer, H.S. (2005) 'Tourette's syndrome: from behaviour to biology.', *Lancet Neurology*, 4: 148–159.

Singer, H.S., Butler, I.J., Tune, L.E., Seifert, W.E. Jr. and Coyle, J.T. (1982) 'Dopaminergic dysfunction in Tourette syndrome.', *Annals of Neurology*, 12: 361–366.

Singhal, S., Birch, J.M., Kerr, B., Lashford, L. and Evans, D.G. (2002) 'Neurofibromatosis type 1 and sporadic optic gliomas.', *Archives of Disease in Childhood*, 87: 65–70.

Sinha, S., Mishra, S., Singh, V., Mittal, R.D. and Mittal, B. (1996) 'High frequency of new mutations in North Indian Duchenne/Becker muscular dystrophy patients.', *Clinical Genetics*, 50: 327–331.

Sinkkonen, S.T., Homanics, G.E. and Korpi, E.R. (2003) 'Mouse models of Angelman syndrome, a neurodevelopmental disorder, display different brain regional GABA(A) receptor alterations.', *Neuroscience Letters*, 340(3): 205–208.

Sisodiya, S.M. (2004) 'Malformations of cortical development: burdens and insights from important causes of human epilepsy.', *Lancet Neurology*, 3(1): 29–38.

Sivagamasundari, U., Fernando, H., Jardine, P., Rao, J.M. *et al.* (1994) 'The association between Coffin-Lowry syndrome and psychosis: a family study.', *Journal of Intellectual Disability Research*, 38: 469–473.

Skene, P.J., Illingworth, R.S., Webb, S., Kerr, A.R.W. *et al.* (2010) 'Neuronal MeCP2 is expressed at near histone-octamer levels and globally alters the chromatin state.', *Molecular Cell*, 37: 457–468.

Skidmore, F.M., Rodriguez, R.L., Fernandez, H.H., Goodman, W.K. *et al.* (2006) 'Lessons learned in deep brain stimulation for movement and neuropsychiatric disorders.', *CNS Spectrums*, 11(7): 521–537.

Skuk, D., Roy, B., Goulet, M., Chapdelaine, P. *et al.* (2004) 'Dystrophin expression in myofibers of Duchenne muscular dystrophy patients following intramuscular injections of normal myogenic cells.', *Molecular Therapeutics*, 9: 475–482.

Skuse, D.H. (2000) 'Imprinting, the X-chromosome, and the male brain: explaining sex differences in the liability to autism.', *Pediatric Research*, 47: 9–16.

Skuse, D.H. (2007) 'Rethinking the nature of genetic vulnerability to autistic spectrum disorders.', *Trends in Genetics*, 23(8): 387–395.

Skuse, D.H., James, R.S., Bishop, D.V., Coppin, B. *et al.* (1997) 'Evidence from Turner's syndrome of an imprinted X-linked locus affecting cognitive function.', *Nature*, 387(6634): 705–708.

Slack, J.M.W. (2002) 'Conrad Hal Waddington: the last Renaissance biologist?' *Nature Reviews: Genetics*, 3: 889–895.

Slager, R.E., Newton, T.L., Vlangos, C.N., Finucane, B. and Elsea, S.H. (2003) 'Mutations in RAI1 associated with Smith-Magenis syndrome.', *Nature Genetics*, 33: 466–468.

Slaney, S.F., Oldridge, M., Hurst, J.A., Morriss-Kay, G.M. *et al.* (1996) 'Differential effects of FGFR2 mutations on syndactyly and cleft palate in Apert syndrome.', *American Journal of Human Genetics*, 58: 923–932.

Slavotinek, A.M. and Biesecker, L.G. (2000) 'Phenotypic overlap of McKusick-Kaufman syndrome with Bardet-Biedl syndrome: a literature review.', *American Journal of Medical Genetics*, 95: 208–215.

Slavotinek, A.M. and Biesecker, L.G. (2003) 'Genetic modifiers in human development and malformation syndromes, including chaperone proteins.', *Human Molecular Genetics*, 12(Review Issue 1): R45–R50, doi:10.1093/hmg/ddg099.

Slavotinek, A.M., Stone, E.M., Mykytyn, K., Heckenlively, J.R. *et al.* (2000) 'Mutations in MKKS cause Bardet-Biedl syndrome.', *Nature Genetics*, 26(1): 15–16.

Slee, J.J., Smart, R.D. and Viljoen, D.L. (1991) 'Deletion of chromosome 13 in Möbius syndrome.', *Journal of Medical Genetics*, 28(6): 413–414.

Sleight, B.J., Prasad, V.S., DeLaat, C., Steele, P. *et al.* (1998) 'Correction of autoimmune lymphoproliferative syndrome by bone marrow transplantation.' *Bone Marrow Transplantation*, 22(4): 375–380.

Slor, H., Batko, S., Khan, S.G., Sobe, T. *et al.* (2000) 'Xeroderma pigmentosum family with a frameshift mutation in the xpc gene: sun protection prolongs life.', *Journal of Investigative Dermatology*, 115: 974–980.

Smalley, S. (1998) 'Autism and tuberous sclerosis.', *Journal of Autism and Developmental Disorders*, 28: 407–414.

Smalley, S.L. (1997) 'Genetic influences in childhood-onset psychiatric disorders: autism and attention-deficit/hyperactivity disorder.', *American Journal of Human Genetics*, 60: 1276–1282.

Smalley, S.L., Tanguay, P.E., Smith, M. and Gutierrez, G. (1992) 'Autism and tuberous sclerosis.', *Journal of Autism and Developmental Disorders*, 22(3): 339–355.

Smallwood, P.M., Olveczky, B.P., Williams, G.L., Jacobs, G.H. *et al.* (2003) 'Genetically engineered mice with an additional class of cone photoreceptors: implications for the evolution of color vision.', *Proceedings of the National Academy of Science*, 100(20): 11706–11711.

Smeets, H.J., Smits, A.P., Verheij, C.E., Theelen, J.P. *et al.* (1995) 'Normal phenotype in two brothers with a full FMR1 mutation.', *Human Molecular Genetics*, 4: 2103–2108.

Smets, K., Zecic, A. and Willems, J. (2004) 'Ergotamine as a possible cause of Möbius sequence: additional clinical observation.', *Journal of Child Neurology*, 19(5): 398.

Smith, A., Wiles, C., Haan, E., McGill, J. *et al.* (1996) 'Clinical features in 27 patients with Angelman syndrome resulting from DNA deletion.', *Journal of Medical Genetics, 33*: 107–112.

Smith, A.C.M., Allanson, J.E., Elsea, S.H., Finucane, B.M. *et al.* (2006 revision) 'Smith Magenis syndrome.', *GeneReviews*, web-based reaource.

Smith, A.C.M., Gropman, A.L., Bailey-Wilson, J.E., Goker-Alpan, O. *et al.* (2002) 'Hypercholesterolemia in children with Smith-Magenis syndrome: del(17)(p11.2p11.2).', *Genetics in Medicine, 4*: 118–125.

Smith, A.C.M., McGavran, L., Robinson, J., Waldstein, G. *et al.* (1986) 'Interstitial deletion of (17)(p11.2p11.2) in nine patients.', *American Journal of Medical Genetics, 24*: 393–414.

Smith, C.B. and Kang, J. (2000) 'Cerebral protein synthesis in a genetic mouse model of phenylketonuria.', *Proceedings of the National Academy of Science USA, 97*: 11014–11019.

Smith, D.W., Lemli, L. and Opitz, J.M. (1964) 'A newly recognized syndrome of multiple congenital anomalies.', *Journal of Pediatrics, 64*: 210–217.

Smith, G.F. (1966) 'A study of the dermatoglyphs in the de Lange syndrome.' *Journal of Mental Deficiency Research, 10*: 241–254.

Smith, I.M., Nichols, S.L., Issekutz, K. and Blake, K. (2005) 'Behavioural profiles and symptoms of autism in CHARGE syndrome: preliminary Canadian epidemiological data.', *American Journal of Medical Genetics A, 133*: 248–256.

Smith, J.C., Webb, T., Pembrey, M.E., Nichols, M. and Malcolm, S. (1992) 'Maternal origin of deletion 15q11–13 in 25/25 cases of Angelman syndrome.', *Human Genetics, 88*: 376–378.

Smith, J.K., Conda, V.E. and Malamud, N. (1958) 'Unusual form of cerebellar ataxia: combined dentato-rubral and pallido-Luysian degeneration.', *Neurology, 8*: 205–209.

Smith, J.M., (2003) *Seeds of Deception: Exposing Corporate and Government Lies about the Safety of the Genetically Engineered Foods You're Eating.* Totnes: Green Books.

Smith, J.M., Kirk, E.P.E., Theodosopoulos, G., Marshall, G.M. *et al.* (2002) 'Germline mutation of the tumour suppressor PTEN in Proteus syndrome.', *Journal of Medical Genetics, 39*: 937–940.

Smith, K.D., Kemp, S., Lelita, T., Braiterman, L.T. *et al.* (1999) 'X-linked adrenoleukodystrophy: genes, mutations, and phenotypes.', *Neurochemical Research, 24*(4): 521–535.

Smith, K.T., Coffee, B. and Reines, D. (2004) 'Occupancy and synergistic activation of the FMR1 promoter by Nrf-1 and Sp1 *in vivo*.', *Human Molecular Genetics, 13*: 1611–1621.

Smith, M. (2006) *Mental Retardation and Developmental Delay: Genetic and Epigenetic Factors.* Oxford: Oxford University Press.

Smith, M., Escamilla, J.R., Filipek, P., Bocian, M.E. *et al.* (2001) 'Molecular genetic delineation of 2q37.3 deletion in autism and osteodystrophy: report of a case and of new markers for deletion screening by PCR.', *Cytogenetics and Cell Genetics, 94*(1–2): 15–22.

Smith, M., Spence, M.A. and Flodman, P. (2009) 'Nuclear and mitochondrial genome defects in autisms.', *Annals of the New York Academy of Science, 1151*: 102–132.

Smith, M., Woodroffe, A., Smith, R., Holguin, S. *et al.* (2002) 'Molecular genetic delineation of a deletion of chromosome 13q12–q13 in a patient with autism and auditory processing deficits.', *Cytogenetics and Genome Research, 98*: 233–239.

Smith, P.F. (2005) 'Cannabinoids as potential anti-epileptic drugs.', *Current Opinion in Investigational Drugs, 6*(7): 680–685.

Smith, Q.R. (2000) 'Transport of glutamate and other amino acids at the blood-brain barrier.', *Journal of Nutrition, 130*: 1016S–1022S.

Smith, U.M., Consugar, M., Tee, L.J., McKee, B.M. *et al.* (2006b) 'The transmembrane protein meckelin (MKS3) is mutated in Meckel-Gruber syndrome and the wpk rat.', *Nature Genetics, 38*: 191–196.

Snape, K.M.G., Fahey, M.C., McGillivray, G., Gupta, P. *et al.* (2006) 'Long-term survival in a child with severe congenital contractural arachnodactyly, autism and severe intellectual disability.', *Clinical Dysmorphology, 15*: 95–99.

Sobin, C., Kiley-Brabeck, K., Daniels, S., Khuri, J. *et al.* (2005) 'Neuropsychological characteristics of children with the 22q11 deletion syndrome: a descriptive analysis.', *Child Neuropsychology, 11*: 39–53.

Soderpalm, A-C., Magnusson, P., Ahlander, A-C., Karlsson, J. *et al.* (2007) 'Low bone mineral density and decreased bone turnover in Duchenne muscular dystrophy.', *Neuromuscular Disorders, 17*: 919–928.

Sodhi, M.S. and Sanders-Bush, E. (2004) 'Serotonin and brain development.', *International Review of Neurobiology, 59*: 111–174.

Sohda, S., Arinami, T., Hamada, H., Yamada, N. *et al.* (1997) 'Methylenetetrahydrofolate reductase polymorphism and pre-eclampsia.', *Journal of Medical Genetics, 34*(6): 525–526.

Soljak, M.A., Aftimos, S. and Gluckman, P.D. (1983) 'A new syndrome of short stature, joint limitation and muscle hypertrophy.', *Clinical Genetics, 23*: 441–446.

Solomon, I.L. and Schoen, E.J. (1971) 'Sex-linked ichthyosis in XO gonadal dysgenesis.', (Letter) *Lancet, 297*(7712): 1304–1305.

Somer, M. (1993) 'Diagnostic criteria and genetics of the PEHO syndrome.', *Journal of Medical Genetics, 30*: 932–936.

Somerville, M.J., Mervis, C.B., Young, E.J., Seo, E-J. *et al.* (2005) 'Severe expressive-language delay related to duplication of the Williams-Beuren locus.', *New England Journal of Medicine, 353*, 1694–1701.

Sotos, J.F., Dodge, P.R., Muirhead, D., Crawford, J.D. and Talbot, N.B. (1964) 'Cerebral gigantism in childhood: a syndrome of excessively rapid growth with acromegalic features and a nonprogressive neurologic disorder.', *New England Journal of Medicine, 271*: 109–116.

Spaepen, A., Hellemans, H. and Fryns, J.P. (1994) 'X-linked mental retardation with Marfanoid habitus: the eye-catching psychiatric disorders.', *American Journal of Medical Genetics, 51*: 611.

Specchio, N., Balestri, M., Striano, P., Cilio, M.R. *et al.* (2009) 'Efficacy of levetiracetam in the treatment of drug-resistant Rett syndrome.', *Epilepsy Research*, doi:10.1016/j.eplepsyres.2009.10.005 (eprint ahead of publication).

Speiser, P.W., Dupont, B., Rubinstein, P., Piazza, A. *et al.* (1985) 'High frequency of nonclassical steroid 21-hydroxylase deficiency.', *American Journal of Human Genetics*, 37(4): 650–667.

Speiser, P.W. and White, P.C. (2003) 'Congenital adrenal hyperplasia.', *New England Journal of Medicine*, 349: 776–788.

Spence, S.J. (2004) 'The genetics of autism.', *Seminars in Pediatric Neurology*, 11: 196–204.

Spence, S.J. and Schneider, M.T. (2009) 'The role of epilepsy and epileptiform EEGs in autism spectrum disorders.', *Pediatric Research*, 65(6): 599–606.

Spencer, K., Tul, N. and Nicolaides, K.H. (2000) 'Maternal serum free beta-hCG and PAPP-A in foetal sex chromosome defects in the first trimester.', *Prenatal Diagnosis*, 20: 390–394.

Spiegel, E.K., Colman, R.F. and Patterson, D. (2006) 'Minireview: adenylsuccinate lyase deficiency.', *Molecular Genetics and Metabolism*, 89: 19–31, doi:10.1016/j.ymgme.2006.04.01.

Spiegel, M., Oexle, K., Horn, D., Windt, E. *et al.* (2005) 'Childhood overgrowth in patients with common NF1 microdeletions.', *European Journal of Human Genetics*, 13: 883–888.

Spirito, F., Meneguzzi, G., Danos, O. and Mezzina, M. (2001) 'Cutaneous gene transfer and therapy: the present and the future.', *Journal of Gene Medicine*, 3(1): 21–31.

Splawski, I., Shen, J., Timothy, K.W., Lehmann, M.H. *et al.* (2000) 'Spectrum of mutations in long-QT syndrome genes: KVLQT1, HERG, SCN5A, KCNE1, and KCNE2.' *Circulation*, 102(10): 1178–1185.

Splawski, I., Timothy, K.W., Decher, N., Kumar, P. *et al.* (2005) 'Severe arrhythmia disorder caused by cardiac L-type calcium channel mutations.', *Proceedings of the National Academy of Science USA*, 102(23): 8089–8096.

Splawski, I., Timothy, K.W., Sharpe, L.M., Decher, N. *et al.* (2004) 'CaV1.2 calcium channel dysfunction causes a multisystem disorder including arrhythmia and autism.', *Cell*, 119: 19–31.

Splawski, I., Yoo, D.S., Stotz, S.C., Cherry, A. *et al.* (2006) 'CACNA1H mutations in autism spectrum disorders.', *Journal of Biological Chemistry*, 281(31): 22085–22091.

Spritz, R.A., Fukai, K., Holmes, S.A. and Luande, J. (1995) 'Frequent intragenic deletion of the P gene in Tanzanian patients with type II oculocutaneous albinism (OCA2).', *American Journal of Human Genetics*, 56: 1320–1323.

Spurek, M., Taylor-Gjevre, R., Van Uum, S. and Khandwala, H.M. (2004) 'Adrenomyeloneuropathy as a cause of primary adrenal insufficiency and spastic paraparesis.', *Canadian Medical Association Journal*, 171(9): 1073–1077.

Stagi, S., Bindi, G., Neri, A.S., Lapi, E. *et al.* (2005) 'Thyroid function and morphology in patients affected by Williams syndrome.', *Clinical Endocrinology*, 63: 456–460.

Stalker, H.J. and Williams, C.A. (1998) 'Genetic counseling in Angelman syndrome: the challenges of multiple causes.', *American Journal of Medical Genetics*, 77: 54–59.

Stalmans, I., Lambrechts, D., De Smet, F., Jansen, S. *et al.* (2003) 'VEGF: a modifier of the del22q11 (DiGeorge) syndrome?' *Nature Medicine*, 9: 173–182.

Stanfield, A.C., McIntosh, A.M., Spencer, M.D., Philip, R. *et al.* (2007) 'Towards a neuroanatomy of autism: a systematic review and meta-analysis of structural magnetic resonance imaging studies.', *European Psychiatry*, 23(4): 289–299.

Stangle, D.E., Smith, D.R., Beaudin, S.A., Strawderman, M.S. *et al.* (2007) 'Succimer chelation improves learning, attention, and arousal regulation inlead-exposed rats but produces lasting cognitive impairment in the absence of lead exposure.', *Environmental Health Perspectives*, 115: 201–209.

Stanojevic, M., Stipoljev, F., Koprcina, B. and Kurjak, A. (2000) 'Oculoauriculo-vertebral (Goldenhar) spectrum associated with pericentric inversion 9: coincidental findings or etiologic factor?' *Journal of Craniofacial Genetics and Developmental Biology*, 20: 150–154.

Starck, L., Lovgren-Sandblom, A. and Bjorkhem, I. (2002a) 'Cholesterol treatment forever? The first Scandinavian trial of cholesterol supplementation in the cholesterol-synthesis defect Smith-Lemli-Opitz syndrome.', *Journal of Internal Medicine*, 252(4): 314–321.

Starck, L., Lovgren-Sandblom, A. and Bjorkhem, I. (2002b) 'Simvastatin treatment in the SLO syndrome: a safe approach?' *American Journal of Medical Genetics*, 113(2): 183–189.

Starink, T.M., van der Veen, J.P., Arwert, F., de Waal, L.P. *et al.* (1986) 'The Cowden syndrome: a clinical and genetic study in 21 patients.', *Clinical Genetics*, 29: 222–233.

Starr, E.M., Berument, S.K., Tomlins, M., Papanikolaou, K. and Rutter, M. (2005) 'Brief report: autism in individuals with Down syndrome.', *Journal of Autism and Developmental Disorders*, 35(5): 665–673.

Stathopulu, E., Ogilvie, C.M. and Flinter, F.A. (2003) 'Terminal deletion of chromosome 5p in a patient with phenotypical features of Lujan-Fryns syndrome.', *American Journal of Medical Genetics*, 119A: 363–366.

Stefan, M., Claiborn, K.C., Stasiek, E., Chai, J-H. *et al.* (2005) 'Genetic mapping of putative *Chrna7* and *Luzp2* neuronal transcriptional enhancers due to impact of a transgene-insertion and 6.8 Mb deletion in a mouse model of Prader-Willi and Angelman syndromes.', *BMC Genomics*, 6: 157, doi:1001186/1471-2164/6/157.

Stefanini, M., Vermeulen, W., Weeda, G., Giliani, S. *et al.* (1993) 'A new nucleotide-excision-repair gene associated with the disorder trichothiodystrophy.' *American Journal of Human Genetics*, 53: 817–821.

Stegink, L.D., Filer, L.J. Jr., Baker, G.L., Bell, E.F. *et al.* (1989) 'Repeated ingestion of aspartame-sweetened beverage: effect on plasma amino acid concentrations in individuals heterozygous for phenylketonuria.', *Metabolism*, 38: 78–84.

Stein, D., Weizman, A., Ring, A. and Barak, Y. (2006) 'Obstetric complications in individuals diagnosed with autism and in healthy controls.', *Comprehensive Psychiatry*, 47: 69–75.

Steinberg, H. (2005) 'Paul Julius Mobius (1853–1907).', *Journal of Neurology*, 252: 624–625.

Steiner, C.E., Guerreiro, M.M. and Marques-de-Faria, A.P. (2003) 'On macrocephaly, epilepsy, autism, specific facial features, and mental retardation.', *American Journal of Medical Genetics A*, 120(4): 564–565.

Steinert, H. (1910) 'Ein neuer fall von atrophischer myotonie: ein nachtag zu meiner arbeit in Bild 37.', *Deutsche Zeitschrift fur Nervenheilkunde*, 39: 168–173.

Steinlin, M., Schmid, M., Landau, K. and Boltshauser, E. (1997) 'Follow-up in children with Joubert syndrome.', *Neuropediatrics*, 28: 204–211.

Steinmann, B., Royce, P. and Superti-Furga, A. (1993) 'The Ehlers-Danlos syndrome.' In P. Royce and B. Steinmann (eds.) *Connective Tissue and its Heritable Disorders*. New York: Wiley-Liss.

Stephenson, J.B., Hoffman, M.C., Russell, A.J., Falconer, J. *et al.* (2005) 'The movement disorders of Coffin-Lowry syndrome.', *Brain and Development*, 27: 108–113.

Stern, J.S. and Robertson, M.M. (1997) 'Tics associated with autistic and pervasive developmental disorders.', *Neurologic Clinics*, 15(2): 345–355.

Stern, L., Francoeur, M.J., Primeau, M.N., Sommerville, W., Fombonne, E. and Mazer, B.D. (2005) 'Immune function in autistic children.', *Annals of Allergy, Asthma and Immunology*, 95: 558–565.

Stevens, G., Ramsay, M. and Jenkins, T. (1997) 'Oculocutaneous albinism (OCA2) in sub-Saharan Africa: distribution of the common 2.7-kb P gene deletion mutation.', *Human Genetics*, 99: 523–527.

Stevens, G., van Beukering, J., Jenkins, T. and Ramsay, M. (1995) 'An intragenic deletion of the P gene is the common mutation causing tyrosinase-positive oculocutaneous albinism in southern African Negroids.', *American Journal of Human Genetics*, 56: 586–591.

Stevens, L., Tartaglia, N., Hagerman, R. and Riley, K. (2010) 'Clinical report: a male with Down syndrome, fragile X syndrome, and autism.' *Journal of Developmental and Behavioral Pediatrics*, 31: 333–337.

Stevenson, R.E., Schroer, R.J., Skinner, C., Fender, D. and Simensen, R.J. (1997) 'Autism and macrocephaly.', *Lancet*, 349: 1744–1745.

Stevenson, R.E., Schwartz, C.E. and Schroer, R.J. (2000) *X-Linked Mental Retardation*. Oxford: Oxford University Press.

Stewart, T.L., Irons, M.B., Cowan, J.M. and Bianchi, D.W. (1999) 'Increased incidence of renal anomalies in patients with chromosome 22q11 microdeletion.', *Birth Defects Research A: Clinical and Molecular Teratology*, 59(1): 20–22.

Steyaert, J., Legius, E., Borghgraef, M. and Fryns, J.P. (2003) 'A distinct neurocognitive phenotype in female fragile-X premutation carriers assessed with visual attention tasks.', *American Journal of Medical Genetics A*, 116: 44–51.

Stiers, P., Swillen, A., De Smedt, B., Lagae, L. *et al.* (2005) 'Atypical neuropsychological profile in a boy with 22q11.2 deletion syndrome.', *Child Neuropsychology*, 11: 87–108.

Stirt, J.A. (1981) 'Anesthetic problems in Rubinstein-Taybi syndrome.', *Anesthesia and Analgesia*, 60(7): 534–536.

Stockfleth, E., Ulrich, C., Hauschild, A., Lischner, S. *et al.* (2002) 'Successful treatment of basal cell carcinomas in a nevoid basal cell carcinoma syndrome with topical 5 per cent imiquimod.', *European Journal of Dermatology*, 12: 569–572.

Stöckler, S., Hanefeld, F. and Frahm, J. (1996) 'Creatine replacement therapy in guanidinoacetate methyltransferase deficiency, a novel inborn error of metabolism.' *Lancet*, Sep 21, 348(9030): 789–790.

Stöckler, S., Holzbach, U., Hanefeld, F., Marquardt, I. *et al.* (1994) 'Creatine deficiency in the brain: a new, treatable inborn error of metabolism.', *Pediatric Research*, 36: 409–413.

Stöckler, S., Isbrandt, D., Hanefeld, F., Schmidt, B. and von Figura, K. (1996) 'Guanidinoacetate methyltransferase deficiency: the first inborn error of creatine metabolism in man.', *American Journal of Human Genetics*, 58: 914–922.

Stöckler, S., Schutz, P.W. and Salomons, G.S. (2007) 'Cerebral creatine deficiency syndromes: clinical aspects, treatment and pathophysiology.', *Subcellular Biochemistry*, 46: 149–166.

Stoetzel, C., Laurier, V., Davis, E.E., Muller, J. *et al.* (2006) 'BBS10 encodes a vertebrate-specific chaperonin-like protein and is a major BBS locus.', *Nature Genetics*, 38(5): 521–524.

Stoetzel, C., Muller, J., Laurier, V., Davis, E.E. *et al.* (2007) 'Identification of a novel BBS gene (BBS12) highlights the major role of a vertebrate-specific branch of chaperonin-related proteins in Bardet-Biedl syndrome.', *American Journal of Human Genetics*, 80(1): 1–11.

Stokke, O., Eldjarn, L., Norum, K., Steen-Johnsen, J. and Halvorsen, S. (1967) 'Methylmalonic acidemia: a new inborn error of metabolism which may cause fatal acidosis in the newborn period.', *Scandinavian Journal of Clinical Investigation*, 20: 213.

Stoler, J.M., Herrin, J.T. and Holmes, L.B. (1995) 'Genital abnormalities in females with Bardet-Biedl syndrome.', *American Journal of Medical Genetics*, 55: 276–278.

Stoll, C. (2001) 'Problems in the diagnosis of fragile-X syndrome in young children are still present.' *American Journal of Medical Genetics*, 100: 110–115.

Stoll, C., Viville, B., Treisser, A. and Gasser, B. (1998) 'A family with dominant oculoauriculovertebral spectrum.', *American Journal of Medical Genetics*, 78: 345–349.

Stone, J.L., Merriman, B., Cantor, R.M., Yonan, A.L. *et al.* (2004) 'Evidence for sex-specific risk alleles in autism spectrum disorder.', *American Journal of Human Genetics*, 75: 1117–1123.

Stone, R.L., Aimi, J., Barshop, B.A., Jaeken, J. *et al.* (1992) 'A mutation in adenylosuccinate lyase associated with mental retardation and autistic features.', *Nature Genetics*, 1: 59–63.

Stos, B., Dembour, G., Ovaert, C., Barrea, C. *et al.* (2004) 'Avantages et risques de la chirurgie cardiaque dans la trisomie 21.', [Risks and benefits of cardiac surgery in Down's syndrome with congenital heart disease.] *Archives de pédiatrie*, 11: 1197–1201.

Stover, P.J. (2006) 'Influence of human genetic variation on human nutritional requirements.', *American Journal of Clinical Nutrition*, 83(Supplement): 436S–442S.

Stover, P.J. and Garza, C. (2002) 'Bringing individuality to public health recommendations.', *Journal of Nutrition*, 132: 2476S–2480S.

Stratton, R.F., Dobyns, W.B., Greenberg, F., DeSana, J.B. *et al.* (1986) 'Report of six additional patients with new chromosome deletion syndrome.', *American Journal of Medical Genetics*, 24: 421–432.

Straus, S.E., Jaffe, E.S., Puck, J.M., Dale, J.K. *et al.* (2001) 'The development of lymphomas in families with autoimmune lymphoproliferative syndrome with germline Fas mutations and defective lymphocyte apoptosis.', *Blood*, 98: 194–200.

Straus, S.E., Lenardo, M. and Puck, J.M. (1997) 'The Canale-Smith syndrome.', (Letter) *New England Journal of Medicine*, 336: 1457.

Straus, S.E. Richardson, W.S., Glasziou, P. and Haynes, R.B. (2005) *Evidence Based Medicine*. Oxford: Churchill Livingstone.

Strauss, K.A., Puffenberger, E.G., Huentelman, M.J., Gottlieb, S. *et al.* (2006) 'Recessive symptomatic focal epilepsy and mutant contactin-associated protein-like 2.', *New England Journal of Medicine*, 354: 1370–1377.

Stromberger, C., Bodamer, O.A. and Stöckler-Ipsiroglu, S. (2003) 'Clinical characteristics and diagnostic clues in inborn errors of creatine metabolism.', *Journal of Inherited Metabolic Disease*, 26: 299–308.

Stromland, K., Miller, M., Sjogreen, L., Johansson, M. *et al.* (2007) 'Oculo-auriculo-vertebral spectrum: associated anomalies, functional deficits and possible developmental risk factors.', *American Journal of Medical Genetics A*, 143A(12): 1317–1325.

Strømme, P., Bjørnstad, P.G. and Ramstad, K. (2002a) 'Prevalence estimation of Williams syndrome.', *Journal of Child Neurology*, 17(4): 269–271.

Strømme, P., Mangelsdorf, M.E., Shaw, M.A., Lower, K.M. *et al.* (2002b) 'Mutations in the human ortholog of aristaless cause X-linked mental retardation and epilepsy.', *Nature Genetics*, 30: 441–445.

Strømme, P., Mangelsdorf, M.E., Scheffer, I.E. and Gecz, J. (2002c) 'Infantile spasms, dystonia, and other X-linked phenotypes caused by mutations in aristaless related homeobox gene, ARX.', *Brain and Development*, 24: 266–268.

Struthers, J.L., Carson, N., McGill, M. and Khalifa, M.M. (2002) 'Molecular screening for Smith-Magenis syndrome among patients with mental retardation of unknown cause.', (Electronic Letter) *Journal of Medical Genetics*, 39: e59, doi:10.1136/jmg.39.10.e5q.

Stuart, S.W., King, C.H. and Pai, G.S. (2007) 'Autism spectrum disorder, Klinefelter syndrome, and chromosome 3p21.31 duplication: a case report.', *Medscape General Medicine*, 9(4): 60.

Stuhrmann, M., Riess, O., Monch, E. and Kurdoglu, G. (1989) 'Haplotype analysis of the phenylalanine hydroxylase gene in Turkish phenylketonuria families.', *Clinical Genetics*, 36: 117–121.

Sturmey, P. (2005) 'Secretin is an ineffective treatment for pervasive developmental disabilities: a review of 15 double-blind randomized controlled trials.', *Research in Developmental Disability*, 26(1): 87–97.

Su, A.I., Cooke, M.P., Ching, K.A., Hakak, Y. *et al.* (2002) 'Large-scale analysis of the human and mouse transcriptomes.', *Proceedings of the National Academy of Science USA*, 99: 4465– 4470.

Sugarman, G.I., Katakia, M. and Menkes, J. (1971) 'See-saw winking in a familial oral-facial-digital syndrome.', *Clinical Genetics*, 2: 248–254.

Sujansky, E. and Conradi, S. (1995) 'Outcome of Sturge-Weber syndrome in 52 adults.', *American Journal of Medical Genetics*, 57: 35–45.

Sullivan, K.E. (2004) 'The clinical, immunological, and molecular spectrum of chromosome 22q11.2 deletion syndrome and DiGeorge syndrome.' *Current Opinion in Allergy and Clinical Immunology*, 4: 505–512.

Sullivan, K.E., McDonald-McGinn, D.M., Driscoll, D.A., Zmijewski, C.M. *et al.* (1997) 'Juvenile rheumatoid arthritis-like polyarthritis in chromosome 22q11.2 deletion syndrome (DiGeorge anomalad/velocardiofacial syndrome/conotruncal anomaly face syndrome).', *Arthritis and Rheumatology*, 40: 430–436.

Sullivan, P.B. (2008a) 'Gastrointestinal disorders in children with neurodevelopmental disabilities.', *Developmental Disabilities Research Reviews*, 14: 128–136.

Sullivan, P.F. (2008b) 'The dice are rolling for schizophrenia genetics.', *Psychological Medicine*, 38: 1693–1696.

Summar, M.L. and Tuchman, M. (2003) 'Urea cycle disorders overview.', *GeneReviews*, downloadable from http:// rarediseasesnetwork.epi.usf.edu/ucdc/documents/ucdreview.pdf.

Summitt, R.L. (1969) 'Familial Goldenhar syndrome.', *Birth Defects Original Articles Series*, V(2): 106–109.

Sun, X. and Allison, C. (2010) 'A review of the prevalence of autism spectrum disorder in Asia.', *Research in Autism Spectrum Disorders*, 4: 156–167.

Sunada, F., Rash, F.C. and Tam, D.A. (1998) 'MRI findings in a patient with partial monosomy 10p.', *Journal of Medical Genetics*, 35(2): 159–161.

Sutcliffe, J.S., Delahanty, R.J., Prasad, H.C., McCauley, J.L. *et al.* (2005) 'Allelic heterogeneity at the serotonin transporter locus (SLC6A4) confers susceptibility to autism and rigid-compulsive behaviours.', *American Journal of Human Genetics*, 77: 265–279.

Sutera, S., Pandey, J., Esser, E.L., Rosenthal, M.A. *et al.* (2007) 'Predictors of optimal outcome in toddlers diagnosed with autism spectrum disorders.', *Journal of Autism and Developmental Disorders*, 37: 98–107.

Sutherland, G.R. (1977) 'Fragile sites on human chromosomes: demonstration of their dependence on the type of tissue culture medium.', *Science*, 197: 265–266.

Sutherland, G.R., Gecz, J. and Mulley, J.C. (2002) 'Fragile-X and other causes of X-linked mental retardation.' in: D.I. Rimoin, J.M. O'Connor, R.E. Pyeritz and B.R. Korf (eds.) *Emery and Rimoin's Principles and Practice of Clinical Genetics*. New York: Churchill Livingstone.

Sutherland, G.R., Gedeon, A., Kornman, L., Donnelly, A. *et al.* (1991) 'Prenatal diagnosis of fragile-X syndrome by direct detection of the unstable DNA sequence.', *New England Journal of Medicine*, 325: 1720–1722.

Sutphen, R., Galan-Gomez, E., Cortada, X., Newkirk, P.N. and Kousseff, B.G. (1995) 'Tracheoesophageal anomalies in oculoauriculovertebral (Goldenhar) spectrum.', *Clinical Genetics, 48*: 66–71.

Sutton, E.J., McInerney-Leo, A., Bondy, C.A., Gollust, S.E., King, D. and Biesecker, B. (2005) 'Turner syndrome: four challenges across the lifespan.', *American Journal of Medical Genetics A, 139A*(2): 57–66.

Suzuki, H., Hirayama, Y. and Arima, M. (1989) 'Prevalence of Rett syndrome in Tokyo.', *No To Hattatsu, 21*: 430–433.

Suzuki, K. and De Paul, L.D. (1971) 'Cellular degeneration in developing central nervous system of rats produced by hypocholesteremic drug AY9944.', *Laboratory Investigation, 25*: 546–555.

Svensson, K., Mattsson, R., James, T.C., Wentzel, P. *et al.* (1998) 'The paternal allele of the H19 gene is progressively silenced during early mouse development: the acetylation status of histones may be involved in the generation of variegated expression patterns.', *Development, 125*: 61–69.

Sverd, J. (1991) 'Tourette syndrome and autistic disorder: a significant relationship.', *American Journal of Medical Genetics, 39*(2): 173–179.

Sverd, J., Montero, G. and Gurevich, N. (1993) 'Brief report: cases for an association between Tourette syndrome, autistic disorder, and schizophrenia-like disorder.', *Journal of Autism and Developmental Disorders, 23*(2): 407–413.

Swanson, C.J., Bures, M., Johnson, M.P., Linden, A-M. *et al.* (2005) 'Metabotropic glutamate receptors as novel target for anxiety and stress disorders.', *Nature Reviews: Drug Discovery, 4*: 131–146.

Swarts, L., Leisegang, F., Owen, E.P. and Henderson, H.E. (2007) 'An OTC deficiency "phenocopy" in association with Klinefelter syndrome.', *Journal of Inherited Metabolic Disease, 30*(1): 101.

Swedo, S. (2009) 'Report of the DSM-V Neurodevelopmental Disorders Work Group.', November, downloadable from: http://psychiatry.org/MainMenu/Research/DSMIV/DSMV/DSMRevisionActivities/DSMVWorkGroupReports/NeurodevelopmentalDisordersWorkGroupReport.aspx.

Sweeten, T.L., Bowyer, S.L., Posey, D.J., Halberstadt, G.M. and McDougle, C.J. (2003) 'Increased prevalence of familial autoimmunity in probands with pervasive developmental disorders.', *Pediatrics, 112*(5): e420.

Swerdlow, R.H. (2007) 'Treating neurodegeneration by modifying mitochondria: potential solutions to a "complex" problem.', *Antioxidants and Redox Signalling, 9*(10): 1591–1603.

Swigonski, N.L., Kuhlenschmidt, H.L., Bull, M.J., Corkins, M.R. and Downs, S.M. (2006) 'Screening for coeliac disease in asymptomatic children with Down syndrome: cost-effectiveness of preventing lymphoma.', *Pediatrics. 118*(2): 594–602.

Swillen, A., Glorieux, N., Peeters, M. and Fryns, J.P. (1995) 'The Coffin-Siris syndrome: data on mental development, language, behaviour and social skills in children.', *Clinical Genetics, 48*: 177–182.

Swillen, A., Hellemans, H., Steyaert, J. and Fryns, J.P. (1996) 'Autism and genetics: high incidence of specific genetic syndromes in 21 autistic adolescents and adults living in two residential homes in Belgium.' *American Journal of Medical Genetics, 67*: 315–316.

Swillen, A., Vandeputte, L., Cracco, J., Maes, B. *et al.* (1999) 'Neuropsychological, learning and psychosocial profile of primary school aged children with the velocardiofacial syndrome (22q11 deletion): evidence for a nonverbal learning disability?' *Neuropsychology Development and Cognition C Child Neuropsychology, 5*: 230–241.

Sykes, N.H. and Lamb, J.A. (2007) 'Autism: the quest for the genes.', *Expert Reviews in Molecular Medicine, 9*(24): 1–15, doi:10.1017/S1462399407000452.

Sykes, N.H., Toma, C., Wilson, N., Volpi, E.V. *et al.* (2009) 'Copy number variation and association analysis of SHANK3 as a candidate gene for autism in the IMGSAC collection.', *European Journal of Human Genetics*, doi:10.1038/ejhg.2009.47. [Epub ahead of print.]

Sykut-Cegielska, J., Gradowska, W., Mercimek-Mahmutoglu, S. and Stöckler-Ipsiroglu, S. (2004) 'Biochemical and clinical characteristics of creatine deficiency syndromes.', *Acta Biochimica Polonica, 51*: 875–882.

Sylvester, C.L., Drohan, L.A. and Sergott, R.C. (2006) 'Optic-nerve gliomas, chiasmal gliomas and neurofibromatosis type 1.', *Current Opinion in Ophthalmology, 17*: 7–11.

Symons, F.J., Clark, R.D., Hatton, D.D., Skinner, M. and Bailey, D.B. Jr. (2003) 'Self-injurious behaviour in young boys with fragile-X syndrome.', *American Journal of Medical Genetics A, 118*(2): 115–121.

Szatmari, P., Paterson, A.D., Zwaigenbaum, L., Roberts, W. *et al.* (2007) 'Mapping autism risk loci using genetic linkage and chromosomal rearrangements.', *Nature: Genetics*, On-line publication, 18th Feb 2007. doi:10.1038/ng1985

Szczaluba, K., Nawara, M., Poirier, K., Pilch, J. *et al.* (2006) 'Genotype-phenotype associations for ARX gene duplication in X-linked mental retardation.', *Neurology, 67*: 2073–2075.

Szeszko, P.R., Betensky, J.D., Mentschel, C., Gunduz-Bruce, H. *et al.* (2006) 'Increased stress and smaller anterior hippocampal volume.', *NeuroReport, 7*(17): 1825–1828.

Szudek, J., Birch, P. and Friedman, J.M. (2000) 'Growth in North American white children with neurofibromatosis 1 (NF1).', *Journal of Medical Genetics, 37*: 933–938.

Tabak, H.F., Braakman, I. and Distel, B. (1999) 'Peroxisomes: simple in function but complex in maintenance.', *Trends in Cell Biology, 9*(11): 447–453.

Tabin, C.J. and McMahon, A.P. (1997) 'Recent advances in hedgehog signalling.', *Trends in Cell Biology, 7*(11): 442–446.

Tabolacci, E., Pomponi, M.G., Pietrobono, R., Chiurazzi, P. and Neri, G. (2008) 'A unique case of reversion to normal size of a maternal premutation FMR1 allele in a normal boy.', *European Journal of Human Genetics, 16*(2): 209–214.

Takahashi, T.N., Farmer, J.E., Deidrick, K.K., Hsu, B.S., Miles, J.H. and Maria, B.L. (2005) 'Joubert syndrome is not a cause of classical autism.', *American Journal of Medical Genetics A, 132*: 347–351.

Takahashi, Y., Fujiwara, T., Yagi, K. and Seino, M. (1999) 'Photosensitive epilepsies and pathophysiologic mechanisms of the photoparoxysmal response.', *Neurology, 53*(5): 926–932.

Takami, Y., Takeshima, Y., Awano, H., Okizuka, Y. *et al.* (2008) 'High incidence of electrocardiogram abnormalities in young patients with Duchenne muscular dystrophy.', *Pediatric Neurology, 39*: 399–403.

Takano, H., Cancel, G., Ikeuchi, T., Lorenzetti, D. *et al.* (1998) 'Close associations between prevalences of dominantly inherited spinocerebellar ataxias with CAG-repeat expansions and frequencies of large normal CAG alleles in Japanese and Caucasian populations.', *American Journal of Human Genetics, 63*(4): 1060–1066.

Takano, K., Lyons, M., Moyes, C., Jones, J. and Schwartz, C. (2010) 'Two percent of patients suspected of having Angelman syndrome have TCF4 mutations.', *Clinical Genetics,* Feb 10. [Epub ahead of print]

Takesada, M., Naruse, H., Nagahata, A., Kazamatsuri, H. *et al.* (1992) 'An open clinical study of apropterinhydrochloride (R-tetrahydrobiopterin, R-THBP) in infantile autism – clinical effects and long-term followup.' In H. Naruse and E.M. Ornitz (eds.) *Neurobiology of Infantile Autism.* Exerpta Medica, International Congress Series, 965.

Takiyama, Y., Sakoe, K., Amaike, M., Soutome, M. *et al.* (1999) 'Single sperm analysis of the CAG repeats in the gene for dentatorubral-pallidoluysian atrophy (DRPLA): the instability of the CAG repeats in the DRPLA gene is prominent among the CAG repeat diseases.', *Human Molecular Genetics, 8*(3): 453–457.

Talebizadeh, Z., Bittel, D.C., Veatch, O.J., Kibiryeva, N. and Butler, M.G. (2005) 'Brief report: non-random X chromosome inactivation in females with autism.', *Journal of Autism and Developmental Disorders, 35*(5): 675–681.

Talebizadeh, Z., Lam, D.Y., Theodoro, M.F., Bittel, D.C. *et al.* (2006) 'Novel splice isoforms for NLGN3 and NLGN4 with possible implications in autism.', *Journal of Medical Genetics,* doi:10.1136/jmg.2005.036897.

Tan, W-H., Baris, H.N., Burrows, P.E., Robson, C.D. *et al.* (2007) 'The spectrum of vascular anomalies in patients with PTEN mutations: implications for diagnosis and management.', *Journal of Medical Genetics, 44*: 594–602.

Tang, P., Park, D.J., Marshall Graves, J.A. and Harley, V.R. (2004) 'ATRX and sex differentiation.', *Trends in Endocrinology and Metabolism, 15*: 339–344.

Tantam, D., Evered, C. and Hersov, L. (1990) 'Asperger's syndrome and ligamentous laxity.', *Journal of the American Academy of Child and Adolescent Psychiatry, 29*(6): 892–896.

Tao, J., Van Esch, H., Hagedorn-Greiwe, M., Hoffinann, K. *et al.* (2004) 'Mutations in the X-linked cyclin-dependent kinase-like 5 (CDKL5/STK9) gene are associated with severe neurodevelopmental retardation.', *American Journal of Human Genetics, 75*: 1149–1154.

Tariverdian, G., Kantner, G. and Vogel, F. (1987) 'A monozygotic twin pair with Rett syndrome.', *Human Genetics, 75*: 88–90.

Tarnopolsky, M.A., Mahoney, D.J., Vajsar, J., Rodriguez, C. *et al.* (2004) 'Creatine monohydrate enhances strength and body composition in Duchenne muscular dystrophy.', *Neurology, 62*: 1771–1777.

Tartaglia, M., Cordeddu, V., Chang, H., Shaw, A. *et al.* (2004) 'Paternal germline origin and sex-ratio distortion in transmission of PTPN11 mutations in Noonan syndrome.', *American Journal of Human Genetics, 75*: 492–497.

Tartaglia, M. and Gelb, B.D. (2005) 'Noonan syndrome and related disorders: genetics and pathogenesis.', *Annual Review of Genomics and Human Genetics, 6*: 45–68.

Tassabehji, M. (2003) 'Williams-Beuren syndrome: a challenge for genotype-phenotype correlations.', *Human Molecular Genetics, 12*: R229–R237.

Tassabehji, M., Metcalfe, K., Fergusson, W.D., Carette, M.J.A. *et al.* (1996) 'LIM-kinase deleted in Williams syndrome.', (Letter) *Nature Genetics, 13*: 272–273.

Tassabehji, M., Hammond, P., Karmiloff-Smith, A., Thompson, P. *et al.* (2005) 'GTF2IRD 1 in craniofacial development of humans and mice.', *Science, 310*(5751): 1184–1187.

Tassone, F., Hagerman, R.J., Ikle, D.N., Dyer, P.N. *et al.* (1999) 'FMRP expression as a potential prognostic indicator in fragile-X syndrome.', *American Journal of Medical Genetics, 84*: 250–261.

Tassone, F., Pan, R., Amiri, K., Taylor, A.K. and Hagerman, P.J. (2008) 'A rapid polymerase chain reaction-based screening method for identification of all expanded alleles of the fragile-X (*FMR1*) gene in newborn and high-risk populations.', *Journal of Molecular Diagnosis, 10*(1): 43–49.

Tatton-Brown, K., Douglas, J., Coleman, K., Baujat, G. *et al.* (2005) 'Genotype-phenotype associations in Sotos syndrome: an analysis of 266 individuals with NSD1 aberrations.', *American Journal of Human Genetics, 77*: 193–204.

Tatton-Brown, K. and Rahman, N. (2004) 'Clinical features of NSD1-positive Sotos syndrome.', *Clinical Dysmorphology, 13*: 199–204.

Tatton-Brown, K. and Rahman, N. (2007) 'Sotos syndrome.', *European Journal of Human Genetics, 15*: 264–271.

Tawil, R. (2008) 'Facioscapulohumeral muscular dystrophy.', *Neurotherapeutics, 5*: 601–606.

Tay, C.H. (1971) 'Ichthyosiform erythroderma, hair shaft abnormalities, and mental and growth retardation: a new recessive disorder.', *Archives of Dermatology, 104*: 4–13.

Taylor, D.C., Falconer, M.A., Bruton, C.J. and Corsellis, J.A. (1971) 'Focal dysplasia of the cerebral cortex in epilepsy.', *Journal of Neurology, Neurosurgery and Psychiatry, 34*: 369–387.

Teebi, A.S., Al-Awadi, S.A., Farag, T.I., Naguib, K.K. and El-Khalifa, M.Y. (1987) 'Phenylketonuria in Kuwait and Arab countries.', *European Journal of Pediatrics, 146*: 59–60.

Teebi, A.S., Rucquoi, J.K. and Meyn, M.S. (1993) 'Aarskog syndrome: report of a family with review and discussion of nosology.', *American Journal of Medical Genetics, 46*(5): 501–509.

Teitelbaum, P., Teitelbaum, O., Nye, J., Fryman, J. and Maurer, R.G. (1998) 'Movement analysis in infancy may be useful for early diagnosis of autism.', *Proceedings of the National Academy of Science USA, 95*: 13982–13987.

Teive, H.A., Chien, H.F., Munhoz, R.P. and Barbosa, E.R. (2008) 'Charcot's contribution to the study of Tourette's syndrome.', *Arquivos de Neuropsiquiatrica, 66*(4): 918–921.

Tellier, A-L., Lyonnet, S., Cormier-Daire, V., de Lonlay, P. *et al.* (1996) 'Increased paternal age in CHARGE association.', *Clinical Genetics, 50*: 548–550.

Telvi, L., Lebbar, A., Del Pino, O., Barbet, J.P. and Chaussain, J.L. (1999) '45,X/46,XY mosaicism: report of 27 cases.', *Pediatrics, 104*: 304–308.

Temple, C.M. and Sanfilippo, P.M. (2003) 'Executive skills in Klinefelter's syndrome.', *Neuropsychologia, 41*(11): 1547–1559.

Temtamy, S.A., Miller, J.D. and Hussels-Maumenee, I. (1975) 'The Coffin-Lowry syndrome: an inherited facio-digital mental retardation syndrome.', *Journal of Pediatrics, 86*: 724–731.

Terespolsky, D., Farrell, S.A., Siegel-Bartelt, J. and Weksberg, R. (1995) 'Infantile lethal variant of Simpson-Golabi-Behmel syndrome associated with hydrops fetalis.', *American Journal of Medical Genetics, 59*: 329–333.

Teriitehau, C., Adamsbaum, C., Merzoug, V., Kalifa, G. *et al.* (2007) 'Subtle brain abnormalities in adrenomyeloneuropathy.', *Journal de Radiologie, 88*(7–8): 957–961.

Tézenas du Montcel, S., Mendizabai, H., Aymé, S., Levy, A. *et al.* (1996) 'Prevalence of 22q11 microdeletion.', *Journal of Medical Genetics, 33*: 719.

Thacker, M.J., Hainline, B., St Dennis-Feezle, L., Johnson, N.B. and Pescovitz, O.H. (1998) 'Growth failure in Prader-Willi syndrome is secondary to growth hormone deficiency.', *Hormone Research, 49*(5): 216–220.

Thiagalingam, S., Flaherty, M., Billson, F. and North, K. (2004) 'Neurofibromatosis type 1 and optic pathway gliomas: follow-up of 54 patients.', *Ophthalmology, 111*: 568–577.

Thiel, R.J. and Fowkes, S.W. (2004) 'Down syndrome and epilepsy: a nutritional connection?' *Medical Hypotheses, 62*: 35–44.

Thiffault, I., Schwartz, C.E., Der Kaloustian, V. and Foulkes, W.D. (2004) 'Mutation analysis of the tumor suppressor PTEN and the glypican 3 (GPC3) gene in patients diagnosed with Proteus syndrome.', *American Journal of Medical Genetics A, 130*: 123–127.

Thomas, N.S., Roberts, S.E. and Browne, C.E. (2003) 'Estimate of the prevalence of chromosome 15q11–q13 duplications.', *American Journal of Medical Genetics A, 120A*(4): 596–598.

Thomas, N.S., Sharp, A.J., Browne, C.E., Skuse, D. *et al.* (1999) 'Xp deletions associated with autism in three females.' *Human Genetics, 104*(1): 43–48.

Thomas, P., Bossan, A., Lacour, J.P., Chanalet, S. *et al.* (1996) 'Ehlers-Danlos syndrome with subependymal periventricular heterotopias.', *Neurology, 46*: 1165–1167.

Thomas, P.Q., Dattani, M.T., Brickman, J.M., McNay, D. *et al.* (2001) 'Heterozygous HESX1 mutations associated with isolated congenital pituitary hypoplasia and septo-optic dysplasia.', *Human Molecular Genetics, 10*(1): 39–45.

Thompson, A.J., Tillotson, S., Smith, I., Kendall, B., Moore, S.G. and Brenton, D.P. (1993) 'Brain MRI changes in phenylketonuria: associations with dietary status.', *Brain, 116*: 811–821.

Thompson, P.M., Lee, A.D., Dutton, R.A., Geaga, J.A. *et al.* (2005) 'Abnormal cortical complexity and thickness profiles mapped in Williams syndrome.', *The Journal of Neuroscience, 25*(16): 4146–4158.

Thompson, B.L. and Levitt, P. (2010) 'The clinical-basic interface in defining pathogenesis in disorders of neurodevelopmental origin'. *Neuron, 67*: 702–712.

Thöny, B., Auerbach, G. and Blau, N. (2000) 'Tetrahydrobiopterin biosynthesis, regeneration and functions.', *The Biochemical Journal, 347*(1): 1–16.

Tibbles, J.A. and Cohen, M.M. Jr. (1986) 'The Proteus syndrome: the Elephant Man diagnosed.', *British Medical Journal, 293*: 683–685.

Tidball, J.G. and Spencer, M.J. (2003) 'Skipping to new gene therapies for muscular dystrophy.', *Nature Medicine, 9*: 997–998.

Tidyman, W.E. and Rauen, K.A. (2008) 'Noonan, Costello and cardio-facio-cutaneous syndromes: dysregulation of the Ras-MAPK pathway.', *Expert Reviews in Molecular Medicine, 10*:e37.

Tierney, E., Bukelis, I., Thompson, R.E., Ahmed, K. *et al.* (2006) 'Abnormalities of cholesterol metabolism in autism spectrum disorders.', *American Journal of Medical Genetics B Neuropsychiatric Genetics, 141*: 666–668.

Tierney, E., Nwokoro, N.A. and Kelley, R.I. (2000) 'The behavioural phenotype of RSH/Smith-Lemli-Opitz syndrome.', *Mental Retardation and Developmental Disabilities Research Reviews, 6*: 131–134.

Tierney, E., Nwokoro, N.A., Porter, F.D., Freund, L.S. *et al.* (2001) 'Behaviour phenotype in the RSH/Smith-Lemli-Opitz syndrome.', *American Journal of Medical Genetics, 98*: 191–200.

Tint, G.S., Irons, M., Elias, E.R., Batta, A.K. *et al.* (1994) 'Defective cholesterol biosynthesis associated with the Smith-Lemli-Opitz syndrome.', *New England Journal of Medicine, 330*: 107–113.

Tirosh, E. and Borochowitz, Z. (1992) 'Sleep apnoea in fragile-X syndrome.', *American Journal of Medical Genetics, 43*(1–2): 124–127.

Titomanlio, L., Marzano, M.G., Rossi, E., D'Armiento, M. *et al.* (2001) 'Case of Myhre syndrome with autism and peculiar skin histological findings.', *American Journal of Medical Genetics, 103*: 163–165.

Tobin, J.L. and Beales, P.L. (2008) 'Restoration of renal function in zebrafish models of ciliopathies.', *Pediatric Nephrology, 23*(11): 2095–2099.

Tognini, G., Ferrozzi, F., Garlaschi, G., Piazza, P. *et al.* (2005) 'Brain apparent diffusion coefficient evaluation in pediatric patients with neurofibromatosis type 1.', *Journal of Computer Assisted Tomography, 29*: 298–304.

Tolarova, M.M., Harris, J.A., Ordway, D.E. and Vargervik, K. (1997) 'Birth prevalence, mutation rate, sex ratio, parents' age, and ethnicity in Apert syndrome.', *American Journal of Medical Genetics, 72*: 394–398.

Toledano-Alhadef, H., Basel-Vanagaite, L., Magal, N., Davidov, B. *et al.* (2001) 'Fragile-X carrier screening and the prevalence of premutation and full-mutation carriers in Israel.', *American Journal of Human Genetics*, 69: 351–360.

Tomaiuolo, F., Di Paola, M., Caravale, B., Vicari, S. *et al.* (2002) 'Morphology and morphometry of the corpus callosum in Williams syndrome: a T1-weighted MRI study.', *Neuroreport*, 13(17): 2281–2284.

Tomas Vila, M. (2004) 'Rendimiento del estudio diagnostico del autismo. La aportacion de la neuroimagen, las pruebas metabolicas y los estudios geneticos.' ['Diagnostic yield in studies of autism. The contribution made by neuroimaging, metabolic tests and genetic studies.'] *Revista de Neurologia*, 38 (Supp 1): S15–S20.

Tomoda, A., Ikezawa, M., Ohtani, Y., Miike, T. and Kumamoto, T. (1991) 'Progressive myoclonus epilepsy: dentato-rubro-pallido-luysian atrophy (DRPLA) in childhood.', *Brain and Development*, 13: 266–269.

Tonkin, E.T., Wang, T.J., Lisgo, S., Bamshad, M.J. and Strachan, T. (2004) 'NIPBL, encoding a homolog of fungal Scc2-type sister chromatid cohesion proteins and fly Nipped-B, is mutated in Cornelia de Lange syndrome.', *Nature Genetics*, 36: 636–641.

Tonsgard, J.H., Kwak, S.M., Short, M.P. and Dachman, A.H. (1998) 'CT imaging in adults with neurofibromatosis-1: frequent asymptomatic plexiform lesions.', *Neurology*, 50: 1755–1760.

Tonsgard, J.H., Yelavarthi, K.K., Cushner, S., Short, M.P. and Lindgren, V. (1997) 'Do NF1 gene deletions result in a characteristic phenotype?' *American Journal of Medical Genetics*, 73: 80–86.

Topçu, M., Aydin, O.F., Yalçunkaya, C., Haliloglu, G. *et al.* (2005) 'L-2-hydroxyglutaric aciduria: a report of 29 patients.', *The Turkish Journal of Pediatrics*, 47: 1–7.

Tordjman, S., Anderson, G.M., Pichard, N., Charbuy, H. and Touitou, Y. (2005) 'Nocturnal excretion of 6-sulphatoxymelatonin in children and adolescents with autistic disorder.', *Biological Psychiatry*, 57(2): 134–138.

Toriello, H.V., Sharda, J.K. and Beaumont, E.J. (1985) 'Autosomal recessive syndrome of sacral and conotruncal developmental field defects (Kousseff syndrome).', *American Journal of Medical Genetics*, 22: 357–360.

Torniero, C., dalla Bernadina, B., Novara, F., Vetro, A. *et al.* (2007) 'Cortical dysplasia of the left temporal lobe might explain severe expressive-receptive language delay in patients with duplication of the Williams-Beuren locus.', *European Journal of Human Genetics*, 15(1): 62–67.

Torres, A.R. (2003) 'Is fever suppression involved in the etiology of autism and neurodevelopmental disorders?' *BMC Pediatrics*, 3: 9, doi:10.1186/1471-2431-3-9.

Torrey, E.F., Dhavale, D., Lawlor, J.P. and Yolken, R.H. (2004) 'Autism and head circumference in the first year of life.', *Biological Psychiatry*, 56: 892–894.

Tourette, G.A.E.B. de la (1885) 'Etude sur une affection nerveuse, characterisee par l'incoordination motrice accompagnee de l'echolalie et de coprolalie.', *Archives of Neurology*, 9: 158–200.

Towbin, J.A. (2003) 'A noninvasive means of detecting preclinical cardiomyopathy in Duchenne muscular dystrophy?' *Journal of the American College of Cardiology*, 42: 317–318.

Towbin, J.A., Hejtmancik, J.F., Brink, P., Gelb, B. *et al.* (1993) 'X-linked dilated cardiomyopathy: molecular genetic evidence of linkage to the Duchenne muscular dystrophy (dystrophin) gene at the Xp21 locus.', *Circulation*, 87: 1854–1865.

Towbin, K.E. (2003) 'Strategies for pharmacological treatment of high functioning autism and Asperger syndrome.', *Child and Adolescent Clinics of North America*, 12: 23–45.

Traboulsi, E.I., Koenekoop, R. and Stone, E.M. (2006) 'Lumpers or splitters? The role of molecular diagnosis in Leber congenital amaurosis.', *Ophthalmic Genetics*, 27(4): 113–115.

Traka, M., Goutebroze, L., Denisenko, N., Bessa, M. *et al.* (2003) 'Association of TAG-1 with Caspr2 is essential for the molecular organization of juxtaparanodal regions of myelinated fibers.', *The Journal of Cell Biology*, 162(6): 1161–1172.

Tranebjaerg, L., Baekmark, U.B., Dyhr-Nielsen, M. and Kreiborg, S. (1987) 'Partial trisomy 3q syndrome inherited from familial t(3;9)(q26.1; p23).', *Clinical Genetics*, 32: 137–143.

Treffert, D. (2006) *Extraordinary People: Understanding Savant Syndrome*. New York: Authors Guild Backprint.

Treffert, D.A. (2010) *Islands of Genius: The Bountiful Mind of the Autistic, Acquired and Sudden Savant*. London: Jessica Kingsley Publishers.

Trefz, F., de Sonneville, L., Matthis, P., Benninger, C., Lanz-Engelert, B. and Bickel, H. (1994) 'Neuropsychological and biochemical investigations in heterozygotes for phenylketonuria during ingestion of high-dose aspartame (a sweetener containing phenylalanine).', *Human Genetics*, 93(4): 369–374.

Trevarthen, C. and Aitken, K.J. (2001) 'Infant intersubjectivity: research, theory, and clinical applications.', Annual Research Review. *Journal of Child Psychology and Psychiatry*, 42: 3–48.

Trevarthen, C., Aitken, K.J., Vandekerckhove, M., Delafield-Butt, J. and Nagy, E. (2006) 'Collaborative regulations of vitality in early childhood: stress in intimate relationships and postnatal psychopathology.' In D. Cichetti and D.J. Cohen (eds.) *Developmental Psychopathology*, Vol.2, Ch.1. New York: John Wiley.

Trifilio, M. and Page, T. (2000) 'NAPDD patients exhibit altered electrophoretic mobility of cytosolic 5' nucleotidase.', *Advances in Experimental Medicine and Biology*, 486: 87–90.

Trillingsgaard, A. and Østergaard, O. Jr. (2004) 'Autism in Angelman syndrome: an exploration of comorbidity.', *Autism*, 8: 163–174.

Trip, J., Drost, G.G., van Engelen, B.G.M. and Faber, C.G. (2009) 'Drug treatment for myotonia (review).', *The Cochrane Library*, Issue 1, accessible at www.thecochranelibrary.com.

Tripi, G., Roux, S., Canziani, T., Brilhault, F.B., Barthélémy, C. and Canziani, F. (2007) 'Minor physical anomalies in children with autism spectrum disorder.' *Early Human Development*, 84: 217 – 223.

Tripodis, N., Palmer, S., Phillips, S., Milne, S., Beck, S. and Ragoussis, J. (2000) 'Construction of a high-resolution 2.5-Mb transcript map of the human 6p21.2–6p21.3 region immediately centromeric of the major histocompatibility complex.', *Genome Research*, 10(4): 454–472.

Troen, A.M. (2005) 'The central nervous system in animal models of hyperhomocysteinemia.' Progress in *Neuro-Psychopharmacology and Biological Psychiatry*, 29: 1140–1151.

Troger, B., Kutsche, K., Bolz, H., Luttgen, S. *et al.* (2003) 'No mutation in the gene for Noonan syndrome, PTPN11, in 18 patients with Costello syndrome.', *American Journal of Medical Genetics*, 121A: 82–84.

Tropea, D., Giacometti, E., Wilson, N.R., Beard, C. *et al.* (2009) 'Partial reversal of Rett syndrome-like symptoms in MeCP2 mutant mice.', *Proceedings of the National Academy of Science USA*, 106(6): 2029–2034.

Trovo-Marqui, A.B. and Tajara, E.H. (2006) 'Neurofibromin: a general outlook.', *Clinical Genetics*, 70: 1–13.

Tsankova, N., Renthal, W., Kumar, A. and Nestler, E.J. (2007) 'Epigenetic regulation in psychiatric disorders.', *Nature Reviews: Neuroscience*, 8: 355–367.

Tsao, C.Y. and Mendell, J.R. (2007) 'Autistic disorder in 2 children with mitochondrial disorders.', *Journal of Child Neurology*, 22(9): 1121–1123.

Tsao, C.Y. and Westman, J.A. (1997) 'Infantile spasms in two children with Williams syndrome.', *American Journal of Medical Genetics*, 71(1): 54–56.

Tsukahara, M., Okamoto, N., Ohashi, H., Kuwajima, K. *et al.* (1998) 'Brachmann-de Lange syndrome and congenital heart disease.', *American Journal of Medical Genetics*, 75: 441–442.

Tsukahara, M. and Opitz, J.M. (1996) 'Dubowitz syndrome: review of 141 cases including 36 previously unreported patients.', *American Journal of Medical Genetics*, 63(1): 277–289.

Tsukahara, M., Tanaka, S. and Kajii, T. (1984) 'A Weaver-like syndrome in a Japanese boy.', *Clinical Genetics*, 25: 73–78.

Tuchman, M., McCullough, B.A. and Yudkoff, M. (2000) 'The molecular basis of ornithine transcarbamylase deficiency.', *European Journal of Pediatrics*, 159 (Supp.3): S196–S198.

Tuchman, R. (2006) 'Autism and epilepsy: what has regression got to do with it?' *Epilepsy Currents*, 6(4): 107–111.

Tuchman, R. and Rapin, I. (2002a) 'Epilepsy in autism.', *Lancet Neurology*, 1(6): 352–358.

Tuchman, R. and Rapin, I. (eds.) (2002b) *Autism: A Neurological Disorder of Early Brain Development*. International Review of Child Neurology Series. Cambridge: MacKeith Press.

Tucker, A.S., Watson, R.P., Lettice, L.A., Yamada, G. and Hill, R.E. (2004) 'Bapx1 regulates patterning in the middle ear: altered regulatory role in the transition from the proximal jaw during vertebrate evolution.', *Development*, 131: 1235–1245.

Tunnessen, W.W., McMillan, J.A. and Levin, M.B. (1978) 'The Coffin-Siris syndrome.', *American Journal of Diseases of Childhood*, 132: 393–395.

Turic, D., Langley, K., Mills, S., Stephens, M. *et al.* (2004) 'Follow-up of genetic linkage findings on chromosome 16p13: evidence of association of N-methyl-D aspartate glutamate receptor 2A gene polymorphism with ADHD.', *Molecular Psychiatry*, 9: 169–173.

Turkel, H. (1975) 'Medical amelioration of Down's syndrome incorporating the orthomolecular approach.' *Journal of Orthomolecular Psychiatry*, 4: 102–115.

Turkel, H. and Nusbaum, I. (1985) *Medical Treatment of Down Syndrome and Genetic Diseases* (4th edn). Southfield, MA: Ubiotica.

Türkmen, S., Gillessen-Kaesbach, G., Meinecke, P., Albrecht, B. *et al.* (2003) 'Mutations in NSD1 are responsible for Sotos syndrome, but are not a frequent finding in other overgrowth phenotypes.', *European Journal of Human Genetics*. 11(11): 858–865.

Turner, G., Partington, M., Kerr, B., Mangelsdorf, M. and Gecz, J. (2002) 'Variable expression of mental retardation, autism, seizures, and dystonic hand movements in two families with an identical ARX gene mutation.', *American Journal of Medical Genetics*, 112(4): 405–411.

Turner, H.H. (1938) 'A syndrome of infantilism, congenital webbed neck, and cubitus valgus.', *Endocrinology*, 23: 566–574.

Turner, J.T., Cohen, M.M. Jr. and Biesecker, L.G. (2004) 'Reassessment of the Proteus syndrome literature: application of diagnostic criteria to published cases.', *American Journal of Medical Genetics A*, 130A(2): 111–122.

Tutor-Crespo, M.J., Hermida, J. and Tutor, J.C. (2005) 'Effect of antiepileptic drugs on the urinary excretion of porphyrins in non-porphyric subjects.', *Journal of Pharmacological Science*, 99: 323–328.

Twigg, S.J. and Cook, T.M. (2002) 'Anaesthesia in an adult with Rubenstein-Taybi syndrome using the ProSeal laryngeal mask airway.', *British Journal of Anaesthesiology*, 89(5): 786–787.

Tyagi, A. and Harrington, H. (2003) 'Cataplexy in association with Moebius syndrome.', *Journal of Neurology*, 250: 110–111.

Tyfield, L.A., Stephenson, A., Cockburn, F., Harvie, A. *et al.* (1997) 'Sequence variation at the phenylalanine hydroxylase gene in the British Isles.', *American Journal of Human Genetics*, 60: 388–396.

Tyler, C.V. Jr., Zyzanski, S.J. and Runser, L. (2004) 'Increased risk of symptomatic gallbladder disease in adults with Down syndrome.', *American Journal of Medical Genetics*, 130A: 351–353.

Tzeng, C.C., Tsai, L.P., Hwu, W.L., Lin, S.J. *et al.* (2005) 'Prevalence of the FMR1 mutation in Taiwan assessed by large-scale screening of newborn boys and analysis of DXS548-FRAXAC1 haplotype.', *American Journal of Medical Genetics A*, 133: 37–43.

Uhlmann, V., Martin, C.M., Sheils, O., Pilkington, L. *et al.* (2002) 'Potential viral pathogenic mechanism for new variant inflammatory bowel disease.', *Molecular Pathology*, 55(2): 84–90.

Ullrich, K., Weglage, J., Schuierer, G., Funders, B. *et al.* (1994) 'Cranial MRI in PKU: evaluation of a critical threshold for blood phenylalanine.', (Letter) *Neuropediatrics*, 25: 278–279.

Ullrich, O. (1930) 'Über typische Kombinationsbilder multipler Abartungen.', *Zeitschrift für Kinderheilkunde, Berlin, 49*: 271.

Unglaub, W.G. and Goldsmith, G.A. (1955) 'Oral vitamin B12 in the treatment of macrocytic anaemias.', *Southern Medical Journal, 48*: 261–269.

Unterrainer, G., Molzer, B., Forss-Petter, S. and Berger, J. (2000) 'Co-expression of mutated and normal adrenoleukodystrophy protein reduces protein function: implications for gene therapy of X-linked adrenoleukodystrophy.', *Human Molecular Genetics, 9*(18): 2609–2616.

Upadhyaya, M., Han, S., Consoli, C., Majounie, E. *et al.* (2004) 'Characterization of the somatic mutational spectrum of the neurofibromatosis type 1 (NF1) gene in neurofibromatosis patients with benign and malignant tumors.', *Human Mutation, 23*: 134–146.

Upadhyaya, M., Huson, S.M., Davies, M., Thomas, N. *et al.* (2007) 'An absence of cutaneous neurofibromas associated with a 3-bp inframe deletion in exon 17 of the NF1 gene (c.2970–2972 delAAT): evidence of a clinically significant NF1 genotype-phenotype correlation.', *American Journal of Human Genetics, 80*: 140–151.

Upadhyaya, M., Majounie, E., Thompson, P., Han, S. *et al.* (2003) 'Three different pathological lesions in the NF1 gene originating *de novo* in a family with neurofibromatosis type 1.', *Human Genetics, 112*: 12–17.

Upadhyaya, M., Ruggieri, M., Maynard, J., Osborn, M. *et al.* (1998) 'Gross deletions of the neurofibromatosis type 1 (NF1) gene are predominantly of maternal origin and commonly associated with a learning disability, dysmorphic features and developmental delay.', *Human Genetics, 102*: 591–597.

Urban, M. and Hartung, J. (2001) 'Ultrasonographic and clinical appearance of a 22-week-old fetus with Brachmann-de Lange syndrome.', *American Journal of Medical Genetics, 102*: 73–75.

Urban, Z., Helms, C., Fekete, G., Csiszar, K. *et al.* (1996) '7q11.23 deletions in Williams syndrome arise as a consequence of unequal meiotic crossover.', (Letter) *American Journal of Human Genetics, 59*: 958–962.

Utsch, B., Sayer, J.A., Attanasio, M., Rodrigues Pereira, R. *et al.* (2006) 'Identification of the first AHI1 gene mutations in nephronophthisis-associated Joubert syndrome.', *Pediatric Nephrology, 21*: 32–35.

Uyanik, G., Aigner, L., Martin, P., Gross, C. *et al.* (2003) 'ARX mutations in X-linked lissencephaly with abnormal genitalia.', *Neurology, 61*(2): 232–235.

Uyanik, O., Dogangun, B., Kayaalp, L., Korkmaz, B. and Dervent, A. (2006) 'Food faddism causing vision loss in an autistic child.' *Child: Care, Health And Development, 32*(5): 601–602.

Vaccarino, F.M. and Smith, K.M. (2009) 'Increased brain size in autism – what it will take to solve a mystery.', *Biological Psychiatry, 66*: 313–315.

Vajro, P., Strisciuglio, P., Houssin, D., Huault, G. *et al.* (1993) 'Correction of phenylketonuria after liver transplantation in a child with cirrhosis.', (Letter) *New England Journal of Medicine, 329*: 363 only.

Valdes-Flores, M., Kofman-Alfaro, S.H., Jimenez-Vaca, A.L. and Cuevas-Covarrubias, S.A. (2001) 'Carrier identification by FISH analysis in isolated cases of X-linked ichthyosis.', *American Journal of Medical Genetics, 102*: 146–148.

Valdovinos, M.G., Napolitano, D.A., Zarcone, J.R., Hellings, J.A. *et al.* (2002) 'Multimodal evaluation of risperidone for destructive behaviour: functional analysis, direct observations, rating scales, and psychiatric impressions.', *Experimental and Clinical Psychopharmacology, 10*: 268–275.

Valente, E.M., Brancati, F., Silhavy, J.L., Castori, M. *et al.* (2006a) 'AHI1 gene mutations cause specific forms of Joubert syndrome-related disorders.', *Annals of Neurology, 59*: 527–534.

Valente, E.M., Marsh, S.E., Castori, M., Dixon-Salazar, T. *et al.* (2005) 'Distinguishing the four genetic causes of Joubert syndrome-related disorders.', *Annals of Neurology, 57*: 513–519.

Valente E.M., Salpietro, D.C., Brancati, F., Bertini, E. *et al.* (2003) 'Description, nonmenclature, and mapping of a novel cerebello-renal syndrome with the molar tooth malformation.', *American Journal of Human Genetics, 73*(3): 663–670.

Valente, E.M., Silhavy, J.L., Brancati, F., Barrano, G. *et al.* (2006b) 'Mutations in CEP290, which encodes a centrosomal protein, cause pleiotropic forms of Joubert syndrome.', *Nature Genetics, 38*(6): 623–625.

Valente, K.D., Koiffmann, C.P., Fridman, C., Varella, M. *et al.* (2006c) 'Epilepsy in patients with Angelman syndrome caused by deletion of the chromosome 15q11–13.' *Archives of Neurology, 63*: 122–128.

Valicenti-McDermott, M.D., McVicar, K., Cohen, H.J., Wershil, B.K. and Shinnar, S. (2008) 'Gastrointestinal symptoms in children with an autism spectrum disorder and language regression.', *Pediatric Neurology, 39*: 392–398.

Valicenti-McDermott, M.D., McVicar, K., Rapin, I., Wershil, B.K. *et al.* (2006) 'Frequency of gastrointestinal symptoms in children with autistic spectrum disorders and association with family history of autoimmune disease.', *Journal of Developmental and Behavioural Pediatrics, 27*: 128–136.

Valle, D. (2004) '2003 (American Society for Human Genetics) Presidential Address: Genetics, Individuality, and Medicine in the 21st century.', *American Journal of Human Genetics, 74*: 374–381.

van Amelsvoort, T., Daly, E., Henry, J., Robertson, D. *et al.* (2004) 'Brain anatomy in adults with velocardiofacial syndrome with and without schizophrenia: preliminary results of a structural magnetic resonance imaging study.', *Archives of General Psychiatry, 61*(11): 1085–1096.

van Bockxmeer, F.M., Mamotte, C.D., Vasikaran, S.D. and Taylor, R.R. (1997) 'Methylenetetrahydrofolate reductase gene and coronary artery disease.', *Circulation, 95*(1): 21–23.

Van Buggenhout, G. and Fryns, J.P. (2006) 'Lujan-Fryns syndrome (mental retardation, X-linked, marfanoid habitus).', *Orphanet Journal of Rare Diseases, 1*: 26, doi:10.1186/1750-1172-1-26.

van Calcar, S.C., Gleason, L.A., Lindh, H., Hoffman, G. *et al.* (2007) '2-methylbutyryl-CoA dehydrogenase deficiency in hmong infants identified by expanded newborn screen.', *Wisconsin Medical Journal, 106*(1): 12–15.

van den Ouweland, A.M., de Vries, B.B., Bakker, P.L., Deelen, W.H. *et al.* (1994) 'DNA diagnosis of the fragile-X syndrome in a series of 236 mentally retarded subjects and evidence for a reversal of mutation in the FMR-1 gene.', *American Journal of Medical Genetics, 51*: 482–485.

van der Burgt, I., Thoonen, G., Roosenboom, N., Assman-Hulsmans, C. *et al.* (1999) 'Patterns of cognitive functioning in school-aged children with Noonan syndrome associated with variability in phenotypic expression.', *Journal of Pediatrics, 135*: 707–713.

van der Put, N.M.J., Eskes, T.K.A.B. and Blom, H.J. (1997) 'Is the common 677C-to-T mutation in the methylenetetrahydrofolate reductase gene a risk factor for neural tube defects? A meta-analysis.', *Quarterly Journal of Medicine, 90*: 111–115.

van Deutekom, J.C. and van Ommen, G.J. (2003) 'Advances in Duchenne muscular dystrophy gene therapy.', *Nature Reviews Genetics, 4*: 774–783.

van Diggelen, O.P., Schindler, D., Willemsen, R., Boer, M. *et al.* (1988) 'Alpha-N-acetylgalactosaminidase deficiency, a new lysosomal storage disorder.', *Journal of Inherited Metabolic Disease, 11*: 349–357.

Van Dyke, D.L. and Wiktor, A.E. (2006) 'Testing for sex chromosome mosaicism in Turner syndrome.', *International Congress Series, 1298*: 9–12.

van Esch, H., Groenen, P., Fryns, J.P., van de Ven, W. and Devriendt, K. (1999) 'The phenotypic spectrum of the 10p deletion syndrome versus the classical DiGeorge syndrome.', *Genetic Counselling, 10*(1): 59–65.

Van Esch, H., Groenen, P., Nesbit, M.A., Schuffenhauer, S. *et al.* (2000) 'GATA3 haplo-insufficiency causes human HDR syndrome.', *Nature, 406*(6794): 419–422.

van Essen, A.J., Abbs, S., Baiget, M., Bakker, E. *et al.* (1992) 'Parental origin and germline mosaicism of deletions and duplications of the dystrophin gene: a European study.', *Human Genetics, 88*(3): 249–257.

van Essen, A.J., Kneppers, A.L., van der Hout, A.H., Scheffer, H. *et al.* (1997) 'The clinical and molecular genetic approach to Duchenne and Becker muscular dystrophy: an updated protocol.', *Journal of Medical Genetics, 34*: 805–812.

van Essen, A.J., Mulder, I.M., van der Vlies, P., van der Hout, A.H. *et al.* (2003) 'Detection of point mutation in dystrophin gene reveals somatic and germline mosaicism in the mother of a patient with Duchenne muscular dystrophy.', *American Journal of Medical Genetics, 118A*: 296–298.

Van Essen, D.C., Dierker, D., Snyder, A.Z., Raichle, M.E. *et al.* (2006) 'Symmetry of cortical folding abnormalities in Williams syndrome revealed by surface-based analyses.', *Journal of Neuroscience, 26*(20): 5470–5483.

van Geel, B.M., Assies, J., Haverkort, E.B., Koelman, J.H.T.M. *et al.* (1999) 'Progression of abnormalities in adrenomyeloneuropathy and neurologically asymptomatic X-linked adrenoleukodystrophy despite treatment with "Lorenzo's oil".', *Journal of Neurology, Neurosurgery and Psychiatry, 67*: 290–299.

van Gennip, A.H., Abeling, N.G., Stroomer, A.E., van Lenthe, H. and Bakker, H.D. (1994) 'Clinical and biochemical findings in six patients with pyrimidine degradation defects.', *Journal of Inherited Metabolic Disease, 17*: 130–132.

van Gennip, A.H., Abeling, N.G.G.M., Vreken, P. and van Kuilenburg, A.B.P. (1997) 'Inborn errors of pyrimidine degradation: clinical, biochemical and molecular aspects.', *Journal of Inherited Metabolic Disease, 20*(2): 203–213.

van Haelst, M.M., Hoogeboom, J.J.M., Baujat, G., Bruggenwirth, H.T. *et al.* (2005) 'Familial gigantism caused by an NSD1 mutation.' *American Journal of Medical Genetics, 139A*: 40–44.

van Hagen, J.M., van der Geest, J.N., van der Giessen, R.S., Lagers-van Haselen, G.C. *et al.* (2007) 'Contribution of CYLN2 and GTF2IRD1 to neurological and cognitive symptoms in Williams syndrome.', *Neurobiology of Disease, 26*: 112–124.

van Kuilenburg, A.B. (2006) 'Screening for dihydropyrimidine dehydrogenase deficiency: to do or not to do, that's the question.', *Cancer Investigation, 24*(2): 215–217.

van Kuilenburg, A.B., Muller, E.W., Haasjes, J., Meinsma, R. *et al.* (2001) 'Lethal outcome of a patient with a complete dihydropyrimidine dehydrogenase (DPD) deficiency after the administration of 5-fluorouracil: frequency of the common IVS14 + 1G > A mutation causing DPD deficiency.', *Clinical Cancer Research, 7*: 1149–1153.

van Kuilenburg, A.B., Stroomer, A.E., Abeling, N.G. and van Gennip, A.H. (2006) 'A pivotal role for beta-aminoisobutyric acid and oxidative stress in dihydropyrimidine dehydrogenase deficiency?' *Nucleosides, Nucleotides and Nucleic Acids, 25*(9–11): 1103–1106.

van Kuilenburg, A.B., Stroomer, A.E., Van Lenthe, H., Abeling, N.G. and Van Gennip, A.H. (2004) 'New insights in dihydropyrimidine dehydrogenase deficiency: a pivotal role for beta-aminoisobutyric acid?' *Biochemical Journal, 379*(1): 119–124.

van Kuilenburg, A.B.P., Vreken, P., Abeling, N.G.G.M., Bakker, H.D. *et al.* (1999) 'Genotype and phenotype in patients with dihydropyrimidine dehydrogenase deficiency.', *Human Genetics, 104*(1): 1–9.

Van Meekeren, J.A. (1668) *Heel-en geneeskonstige aanmerkingen.* Amsterdam.

Van Meter, T.D. and Weaver, D.D. (1996) 'Oculo-auriculo-vertebral spectrum and the CHARGE association: clinical evidence for a common pathogenetic mechanism.', *Clinical Dysmorphology, 5*: 187–196.

van Rijn, S., Swaab, H., Aleman, A. and Kahn, R.S. (2006) 'X chromosomal effects on social cognitive processing and emotion regulation: a study with Klinefelter.', *Schizophrenia Research, 84*(2–3): 194–203.

van Rijn, S., Swaab, H., Aleman, A. and Kahn, R.S. (2008) 'Social behaviour and autism traits in a sex chromosomal disorder: Klinefelter (47XXY) syndrome.', *Journal of Autism and Developmental Disorders, 38*(9): 1634–1641.

Van Schaftingen, E., Rzem, R. and Veiga-da-Cunha, M. (2009) 'L-2-hydroxyglutaric aciduria, a disorder of metabolite repair.', *Journal of Inherited Metabolic Disease, 32*(2): 135–142.

Van Wyk, J.J., Gunther, D.F., Ritzen, E.M., Wedell, A. *et al.* (1996) 'The use of adrenalectomy as a treatment for congenital adrenal hyperplasia.', *Journal of Clinical Endocrinology and Metabolism, 81*: 3180–3190.

Vancassel, S., Durand, G., Barthélémy, C., Lejeune, B. *et al.* (2001) 'Plasma fatty acid levels in autistic children.', *Prostaglandins, Leukotrienes and Essential Fatty Acids, 65*(1): 1–7.

Vanderklish, P.W. and Edelman, G.M. (2005) 'Differential translation and fragile-X syndrome.' *Genes, Brain and Behaviour, 4*: 360–384.

Vanhanen, S-L., Raininko, R., Autti, T. and Santavuori, P. (1995) 'MRI evaluation of the brain in infantile neuronal ceroid-lipofuscinosis. Part 2: MRI findings in 21 patients.', *Journal of Child Neurology, 10*: 444–450.

Vanli, L., Yilmaz, E., Tokatli, A. and Anlar, B. (2006) 'Phenylketonuria in pediatric neurology practice: a series of 146 cases.', *Journal of Child Neurology, 21*: 987–990.

Vanthatalo, S., Somer, M. and Barth, P.G. (2002) 'Dutch patients with progressive encephalopathy, oedema, hypsarrhythmia, and optic atrophy (PEHO) syndrome.', *Neuropediatrics, 33*: 100–104.

Varela, M.C., Kok, F., Otto, P.A. and Koiffmann, C.P. (2004) 'Phenotypic variability in Angelman syndrome: comparison among different deletion classes and between deletion and UPD subjects.', *European Journal of Human Genetics, 12*: 987–992.

Vargas, L., Patino, P.J., Rodriguez, M.F., Forero, C. *et al.* (1999) 'Increase in granulocyte–macrophage-colony-stimulating factor secretion and the respiratory burst with decreased l-selectin expression in hyper-IgE syndrome patients.', *Annals of Allergy, Asthma and Immunology, 83*: 245–251.

Varghese, P.J., Izukawa, T. and Rowe, R.D. (1969) 'Supravalvular aortic stenosis as part of rubella syndrome, with discussion of pathogenesis.', *British Heart Journal, 31*: 59–62.

Varley, C.K. and Crnic, K. (1984) 'Emotional, behavioural, and cognitive status of children with cerebral gigantism.', *Journal of Developmental and Behavioural Pediatrics, 5*(3): 132–134.

Vatta, S., Cigui, I., Demori, E., Morgutti, M. *et al.* (1998) 'Fragile-X syndrome, mental retardation and macroorchidism.', *Clinical Genetics, 54*(4): 366–367.

Vaux, K.K., Wojtczak, H., Benirschke, K. and Lyons Jones, K. (2003) 'Vocal cord abnormalities in Williams syndrome: a further manifestation of elastin deficiency.', *American Journal of Medical Genetics, 119A*: 302–304.

Veenstra-Vanderweele, J., Christian, S.L. and Cook, E.H. Jr. (2004) 'Autism as a paradigmatic complex genetic disorder.', *Annual Review of Genomics and Human Genetics, 5*: 379–405.

Vega, A.I., Pérez-Cerdá, C., Desviat, L.R., Matthijs, G. *et al.* (2009) 'Functional analysis of three splicing mutations identified in the PMM2 gene: toward a new therapy for congenital disorder of glycosylation type Ia.', *Human Mutation, 30*(5): 795–803.

Veltman, M.W., Craig, E.E. and Bolton, P.F. (2005) 'Autism spectrum disorders in Prader–Willi and Angelman syndromes: a systematic review.', *Psychiatric Genetics, 15*(4): 243–254.

Veneselli, E., Biancheri, R., di Rocco, M. and Tortorelli, S. (1998) 'Neurophysiological findings in a case of carbohydrate-deficient glycoprotein (CDG) syndrome type I with phosphomannomutase deficiency.', *European Journal of Paediatric Neurology, 2*: 239–244.

Vento, A.R., LaBrie, R.A. and Mulliken, J.B. (1991) 'O.M.E.N.S. classification system.', *Cleft Palate-Craniofacial Journal, 28*(1): 68–77.

Venturin, M., Guarnieri, P., Natacci, F., Stabile, M. *et al.* (2004) 'Mental retardation and cardiovascular malformations in NF1 microdeleted patients point to candidate genes in 17q11.2.', *Journal of Medical Genetics, 41*: 35–41.

Vergine, G., Mencarelli, F., Diomedi-Camassei, F., Caridi, G. *et al.* (2008) 'Glomerulocystic kidney disease in hypomelanosis of Ito.', *Pediatric Nephrology, 23*(7): 1183–1187.

Verhage, J., Habbema, L., Vrensen, G.F., Roord, J.J. and Bleeker-Wagemakers, E.M. (1987) 'A patient with onychotrichodysplasia, neutropenia and normal intelligence.', *Clinical Genetics, 31*: 374–380.

Verhoeven, W.M. and Tuinier, S. (2006) 'Prader-Willi syndrome: atypical psychoses and motor dysfunctions.', *International Review of Neurobiology, 72*: 119–130.

Verkerk, A.J., Pieretti, M., Sutcliffe, J.S., Fu, Y.H. *et al.* (1991) 'Identification of a gene (FMR-1) containing a CGG repeat coincident with a breakpoint cluster region exhibiting length variation in fragile-X syndrome.' *Cell, 65*: 905–914.

Verkerk, A.J.M.H., Mathews, C.A., Joosse, M., Eussen, B.H.J. *et al.* (2003) 'The Tourette Syndrome Association International Consortium for Genetics: CNTNAP2 is disrupted in a family with Gilles de la Tourette syndrome and obsessive compulsive disorder.', *Genomics, 82*: 1–9.

Verkman, A.S., Binder, D.K., Bloch, O., Auguste, K. and Papadopoulos, M.C. (2006) 'Three distinct roles of aquaporin-4 in brain function revealed by knockout mice.' *Biochimica et Biophysica Acta, 1758*: 1085–1093.

Verloes, A., Massart, B., Dehalleux, I., Langhendries, J-P. and Koulischer, L. (1995) 'Clinical overlap of Beckwith-Wiedemann, Perlman and Simpson-Golabi-Behmel syndromes: a diagnostic pitfall.' *Clinical Genetics, 47*: 257–262.

Verloes, A., Sacré, J.P. and Geubelle, F. (1987) 'Sotos syndrome and fragile-X chromosomes.', *Lancet, 330*(8554): 329.

Vermeulen, W., Bergmann, E., Auriol, J., Rademakers, S. *et al.* (2000) 'Sublimiting concentration of TFIIH transcription/DNA repair factor causes TTD-A trichothiodystrophy disorder.' *Nature Genetics, 26*: 307–313.

Vermeulen, W., Rademakers, S., Jaspers, N.G.J., Appeldoorn, E. *et al.* (2001) 'A temperature-sensitive disorder in basal transcription and DNA repair in humans.', *Nature Genetics, 27*: 299–303.

Vermot, J., Niederreither, K., Garnier, J-M., Chambon, P. and Dolle, P. (2003) 'Decreased embryonic retinoic acid synthesis results in a DiGeorge syndrome phenotype in newborn mice.', *Proceedings of the National Academy of Science USA, 100*: 1763–1768.

Verri, A., Maraschio, P., Devriendt, K., Uggetti, C. *et al.* (2004) 'Chromosome 10p deletion in a patient with hypoparathyroidism, severe mental retardation, autism and basal ganglia calcifications.', *Annals of Genetics, 47*: 281–287.

Vervloed, M.P., Hoevenaars-van den Boom, M.A., Knoors, H., van Ravenswaaij, C.M. and Admiraal, R.J. (2006) 'CHARGE syndrome: relations between behavioural characteristics and medical conditions.', *American Journal of Medical Genetics A, 40*: 851–862.

Verzijl, H.T.F.M., Valk, J., de Vries, R. and Padberg, G.W. (2005) 'Radiologic evidence for absence of the facial nerve in Moebius syndrome.', *Neurology, 64*: 849–855.

Verzijl, H.T.F.M., van der Zwaag, B., Cruysberg, J.R.M. and Padberg, G.W. (2003) 'Möbius syndrome redefined: a syndrome of rhombencephalic maldevelopment.', *Neurology*, *61*: 327–333.

Viani, F., Romeo, A., Viri, M., Mastrangelo, M. *et al.* (1995) 'Seizure and EEG patterns in Angelman's syndrome.', *Journal of Child Neurology*, *10*: 467–471.

Vidal-Taboada, J.M., Sanz, S., Egeo, A., Scartezzini, P. and Oliva, R. (1998) 'Identification and characterization of a new gene from human chromosome 21 between markers D21S343 and D21S268 encoding a leucine-rich protein.', *Biochemical and Biophysical Research Communications*, *250*: 547–554.

Vieira, T.C., Boldarine, V.T. and Abucham, J. (2007) 'Molecular analysis of *PROP1*, *PIT1*, *HESX1*, *LHX3*, and *LHX4* shows high frequency of *PROP1* mutations in patients with familial forms of combined pituitary hormone deficiency.', *Arquivos Brasileiros de Endocrinologia and Metabologia*, *51*(7): 1097–1103.

Vijayakumar, S.T. and Kurup, P.A. (1974) 'Hypervitaminosis D and glycosaminoglycan metabolism in rats fed normal and high fat cholesterol diets.', *Journal of Nutrition*, *104*: 423–429.

Vilaseca, M.A., Briones, P., Ferrer, I., Campistol, J. *et al.* (1993) 'Controlled diet in phenylketonuria may cause serum carnitine deficiency.', *Journal of Inherited Metabolic Disease*, *16*(1): 101–104.

Villanueva, M.P., Aiyer, A.R., Muller, S., Pletcher, M.T. *et al.* (2002) 'Genetic and comparative mapping of genes dysregulated in mouse hearts lacking the Hand2 transcription factor gene.', *Genomics*, *80*: 593–600.

Villard, L., Bonino, M.C., Abidi, F., Ragusa, A. *et al.* (1999) 'Evaluation of a mutation screening strategy for sporadic cases of ATR-X syndrome.', *Journal of Medical Genetics*, *36*: 183–186.

Villard, L. and Fontes, M. (2002) 'Alpha-thalassemia/mental retardation syndrome, X-linked (ATR-X, MIM #301040, ATR-X/XNP/XH2 gene MIM #300032).' *European Journal of Human Genetics*, *10*(4): 223–225.

Villard, L., Gecz, J., Mattei, J.F., Fontes, M. *et al.* (1996) 'XNP mutation in a large family with Juberg-Marsidi syndrome.', [letter] *Nature Genetics*, *12*: 359–360.

Villard, L., Kpebe, A., Cardoso, C., Chelly, P.J. *et al.* (2000) 'Two affected boys in a Rett syndrome family: clinical and molecular findings.', *Neurology*, *55*(8): 1188–1193.

Villard, L., Levy, N., Xiang, F., Kpebe, A. *et al.* (2001) 'Segregation of a totally skewed pattern of X chromosome inactivation in four familial cases of Rett syndrome without MECP2 mutation: implications for the disease.', *Journal of Medical Genetics*, *38*: 435–442.

Villavicencio, E.H., Walterhouse, D.O. and Iannaccone, P.M. (2000) 'The sonic hedgehog-patched-gli pathway in human development and disease.', *American Journal of Human Genetics*, *67*: 1047–1054.

Vincent, J.B., Horike, S.I., Choufani, S., Paterson, A.D. *et al.* (2006) 'An inversion inv(4)(p12–p15.3) in autistic siblings implicates the 4p GABA receptor gene cluster.', *Journal of Medical Genetics*, *43*: 429–434.

Vincent, J.B., Kolozsvari, D., Roberts, W.S., Bolton, P.F. *et al.* (2004) 'Mutation screening of X-chromosomal neuroligin genes: no mutations in 196 autism probands.', *American Journal of Medical Genetics B Neuropsychiatric Genetics*, *129*(1): 82–84.

Vincent, M-C., Heitz, F., Tricoire, J., Bourrouillou, G. *et al.* (1999) '22q deletion in DGS/VCFS monozygotic twins with discordant phenotypes.', *Genetic Counselling*, *10*: 43–49.

Vinchon, M., Soto-Ares, G., Ruchoux, M.M. and Dhellemmes, P. (2000) 'Cerebellar gliomas in children with NF1: pathology and surgery.', *Child's Nervous System*, *16*: 417–420.

Vinken, P. and Bruyn, G. (eds.) (1975) *Handbook of Clinical Neurology.* North Holland: Elsevier.

Vinton, A., Fahey, M.C., O'Brien, T.J., Shaw, J. *et al.* (2005) 'Dentatorubral-pallidoluysian atrophy in three generations, with clinical courses from nearly asymptomatic elderly to severe juvenile, in an Australian family of Macedonian descent.', *American Journal of Medical Genetics*, *136A*: 201–204.

Virdis, R., Street, M.E., Bandello, M.A., Tripodi, C. *et al.* (2003) 'Growth and pubertal disorders in neurofibromatosis type 1.', *Journal of Pediatric Endocrinology and Metabolism*, *16*(Suppl 2): 289–292.

Viskochil, D., White, R. and Cawthon, R. (1993) 'The neurofibromatosis type 1 gene.', *Annual Review of Neuroscience*, *16*: 183–205.

Viskochil, D.H. (1999) 'The structure and function of the NF1 gene.' In J.M. Friedman, D.H. Gutmann, M. MacCollin and V.M. Riccardi (eds.) *Neurofibromatosis: Phenotype, Natural History, and Pathogenesis.* Baltimore: Johns Hopkins University Press.

Visootsak, J. and Graham, J.M. Jr. (2006) 'Review: Klinefelter syndrome and other sex chromosomal aneuploidies.', *Orphanet Journal of Rare Diseases*, *1*: 42, doi:10.1186/1750-1172-1-42, downloadable from: www.OJRD.com/content/1/1/42.

Vits, L., De Boulle, K., Reyniers, E., Handig, I. *et al.* (1994) 'Apparent regression of the CGG repeat in FMR1 to an allele of normal size.', *Human Genetics*, *94*: 523–526.

Vivarelli, R., Grosso, S., Calabrese, F., Farnetani, M. *et al.* (2003) 'Epilepsy in neurofibromatosis 1.', *Journal of Child Neurology*, *18*: 338–342.

Vockley, J., Rinaldo, P., Bennett, M.J., Matern, D. and Vladutiu, G.D. (2000) 'Synergistic heterozygosity: disease resulting from multiple partial defects in one or more metabolic pathways.', *Molecular Genetics and Metabolism*, *71*: 10–18.

Vogt, A., Chuang, P-T., Hebert, J., Hwang, J. *et al.* (2004) 'Immunoprevention of basal cell carcinomas with recombinant hedgehog-interacting protein.', *Journal of Experimental Medicine*, *199*(6): 753–761.

Voit, T., Kramer, H., Thomas, C., Wechsler, W. *et al.* (1991) 'Myopathy (sic) in Williams-Beuren syndrome.', *European Journal of Pediatrics*, *150*: 521–526.

Volkmar, F.R. and Nelson, D.S. (1990) 'Seizure disorders in autism.' *Journal of the American Academy of Child and Adolescent Psychiatry*, *29*(1): 127–129.

Vollind, Z.L., Xenophontos, S.L., Cariolou, M.A., Mokone, G.G. *et al.* (2004) 'The ACE gene and endurance performance during the South African ironman triathlons.', *Medicine and Science in Sports and Exercise*, *36*: 1314–1320.

von Aster, M., Zachmann, M., Brandeis, D., Wohlrab, G., Richner, M. and Steinhausen, H.C. (1997) 'Psychiatric, neuropediatric, and neuropsychological symptoms in a case of hypomelanosis of Ito.', *European Child and Adolescent Psychiatry, 6*(4): 227–233.

von Gernet, S., Golla, A., Ehrenfels, Y., Schuffenhauer, S. and Fairley, J.D. (2000) 'Genotype-phenotype analysis in Apert syndrome suggests opposite effects of the two recurrent mutations on syndactyly and outcome of craniofacial surgery.', *Clinical Genetics, 57*: 137–139.

von Tell, D., Bruder, C.E., Anderson, L.V., Anvret, M. and Ahlberg, G. (2003) 'Refined mapping of the Welander distal myopathy region on chromosome 2p13 positions the new candidate region telomeric of the DYSF locus.' *Neurogenetics, 4*(4): 173–177.

Von Neusser, E. and Wiesel, J. (1910) *Die Erkrankungen die Nebennieren.* Vienna: Holder.

Vostanis, P., Harrington, R., Prendergast, M. and Farndon, P. (1994) 'Case reports of autism with interstitial deletion of chromosome 17 (p11.2p11.2) and monosomy for chromosome 5 (5pter >5p153).', *Psychiatric Genetics, 4*: 109–111.

Vrolik, W. (1849) *Tabulae ad illustrandam embryogenesin hominis et mammalium, tam naturalem quam abnormem.* Amsterdam: G.M.P. Londinck.

Waage-Baudet, H., Dunty, W.C. Jr., Dehart, D.B., Hiller, S. and Sulik, K.K. (2005) 'Immunohistochemical and microarray analyses of a mouse model for the Smith-Lemli-Opitz syndrome.' *Developmental Neuroscience, 27*: 378–396.

Waage-Baudet, H., Lauder, J.M., Dehart, D.B., Kluckman, K. *et al.* (2003) 'Abnormal serotonergic development in a mouse model for the Smith-Lemli-Opitz syndrome: implications for autism.' *International Journal of Developmental Neuroscience, 21*: 451–459.

Wada, Y., Matsuoka, T., Imai, K., Taniike, M. *et al.* (1998) 'A case of juvenile-type DRPLA with psychomotor retardation since infancy.', *No To Hattatsu, 30*: 543–548.

Wadsby, M., Lindenhammer, H. and Eeg-Olofsson, O. (1989) 'Neurofibromatosis in childhood: neuropsychological aspects.', *Neurofibromatosis, 2*: 251–260.

Waggoner, D. (2007) 'Mechanisms of disease: epigenesis.', *Seminars in Pediatric Neurology, 14*: 7–14.

Wagner, K.R., Hamed, S., Hadley, D.W., Gropman, A.L. *et al.* (2001) 'Gentamicin treatment of Duchenne and Becker muscular dystrophy due to nonsense mutations.', *Annals of Neurology, 49*: 706–711.

Wagstaff, J., Knoll, J.H.M., Fleming, J., Kirkness, E.F. *et al.* (1991) 'Localization of the gene encoding the GABAA receptor β3 subunit to the Angelman/Prader-Willi region of human chromosome 15.', *American Journal of Human Genetics, 49*(2): 330–337.

Wagstaff, J., Knoll, J.H.M., Glatt, K.A., Shugart, Y.Y. *et al.* (1992) 'Maternal but not paternal transmission of 15q11–13-linked nondeletion Angelman syndrome leads to phenotypic expression.', *Nature Genetics, 1*: 291–294.

Wagstaff, J., Shugart, Y.Y. and Lalande, M. (1993) 'Linkage analysis in familial Angelman syndrome.', *American Journal of Human Genetics, 53*: 105–112.

Wainwright, P.E. (2002) 'Dietary essential fatty acids and brain function: a developmental perspective on mechanisms.' *Proceedings of the Nutrition Society, 61*: 61–69.

Waisbren, S.E., Hanley, W., Levy, H.L., Shifrin, H. *et al.* (2000) 'Outcome at age 4 years in offspring of women with maternal phenylketonuria: the maternal PKU collaborative study.', *Journal of the American Medical Association, 283*: 756–762.

Waite, K.A. and Eng, C. (2002) 'Protean PTEN: form and function.', *American Journal of Human Genetics, 70*: 829–844.

Wajner, M., Coelho Dde, M., Ingrassia, R., de Oliveira, A.B. *et al.* (2009) 'Selective screening for organic acidemias by urine organic acid GC-MS analysis in Brazil: fifteen-year experience.' *Clinica Chimica Acta. 400*(1-2): 77–81.

Wakabayashi, S. (1979) 'A case of infantile autism associated with Down's syndrome.', *Journal of Autism and Developmental Disorders, 9*(1): 31–36.

Waldman, M., Nicholson, S. and Adilov, N. (2006) 'Does television cause autism?' *National Bureau of Economic Research, Working Paper No.12632*, October 2006, www.nber.org/papers/w12632.pdf.

Walker, A. and Fitzgerald, M. (2006) *Unstoppable Brilliance.* Dublin: Liberties Press.

Walker, L., Thompson, D., Easton, D., Ponder, B. *et al.* (2006) 'A prospective study of neurofibromatosis type 1 cancer incidence in the UK.', *British Journal of Cancer, 95*: 233–238.

Walkup, J.T., LaBuda, M.C., Singer, H.S., Brown, J., Riddle, M.A. and Hurko, O. (1996) 'Family study and segregation analysis of Tourette syndrome: evidence for a mixed model of inheritance.', *American Journal of Human Genetics, 59*: 684–693.

Wallace, D.C. (2005) 'The mitochondrial genome in human adaptive radiation and disease: on the road to therapeutics and performance enhancement.', *Gene, 354*: 169–180.

Wallace, M.R., Marchuk, D.A., Andersen, L.B., Letcher, R. *et al.* (1990) 'Type 1 neurofibromatosis gene: identification of a large transcript disrupted in three NF1 patients.', *Science, 249*: 181–186.

Wallace, R.A. (2007) 'Clinical audit of gastrointestinal conditions occurring among adults with Down syndrome attending a specialist clinic.', *Journal of Intellectual and Developmental Disability, 32*(1): 45–50.

Wallace, R.H., Hodgson, B.L., Crinton, B.E., Gardiner, R.M. *et al.* (2003) 'Sodium channel 1-subunit mutations in severe myoclonic epilepsy of infancy and infantile spasms.', *Neurology, 61*: 765–769.

Wallace, S.J. (1998) 'Myoclonus and epilepsy in childhood: a review of treatment with valproate, ethosuximide, lamotrigine and zonisamide.', *Epilepsy Research, 29*: 147–154.

Wallace, S. and Farrell, K. (2004) *Epilepsy in Children* (2nd edn.). London: Hodder Arnold.

Walter, J.H., White, F.J., Hall, S.K., MacDonald, A. *et al.* (2002) 'How practical are recommendations for dietary control in phenylketonuria?' *Lancet, 360*: 55–57.

Walterfang, M.A., O'Donovan, J., Fahey, M.C. and Velakoulis, D. (2007) 'The neuropsychiatry of adrenomyeloneuropathy.', *CNS Spectrums, 12*(9): 696–701.

Walters, R.G., Jacquemont, S., Valsesia, A., de Smith, A.J. et al. (2010) 'A new highly penetrant form of obesity due to deletions on chromosome 16p11.2.', *Nature, 463*(7281): 671–675.

Walz, K., Caratini-Rivera, S., Bi, W., Fonseca, P. et al. (2003) 'Modeling del(17)(p11.2p11.2) and dup(17)(p11.2p11.2) contiguous gene syndromes by chromosome engineering in mice: phenotypic consequences of gene dosage imbalance.', *Molecular and Cellular Biology, 23*(10): 3646–3655.

Walz, K., Paylor, R., Yan, J., Bi, W. and Lupski, J.R. (2006) '*Rai1* duplication causes physical and behavioural phenotypes in a mouse model of dup(17)(p11.2p11.2).', *Journal of Clinical Investigation, 116*(11): 3035–3041.

Walz, K., Spencer, C., Kaasik, K., Lee, C.C. et al. (2004) 'Behavioural characterization of mouse models for Smith-Magenis syndrome and dup(17)(p11.2p11.2).' *Human Molecular Genetics, 13*: 367–378.

Walzer, S., Bashir, A.S. and Silbert, A.R. (1990) 'Cognitive and behavioural factors in the learning disabilities of 47,XXY and 47,XYY boys.', *Birth Defects Original Articles Series, 26*: 45–58.

Wanders, R.J.A. (1999) 'Peroxisomal disorders: clinical, biochemical, and molecular aspects.', *Neurochemical Research, 24*(4): 565–580.

Wanders, R.J.A., Vreken, P., Ferdinandusse, S., Jansen, G.A. et al. (2001) 'Peroxisomal fatty acid α- and β-oxidation in humans: enzymology, peroxisomal metabolite transporters and peroxisomal diseases.', *Biochemical Society Transactions, 29*(2): 250–267.

Wang, A.M., Schindler, D., Bishop, D.F., Lemieux, R.U. and Desnick, R.J. (1988) 'Schindler disease: biochemical and molecular characterization of a new neuroaxonal dystrophy due to alpha-N-acetylgalactosaminidase deficiency.', (Abstract) *American Journal of Human Genetics, 43*: A99 only.

Wang, G.S., Kearney, D.L., De Biasi, M., Taffet, G. et al. (2007) 'Elevation of RNA-binding protein CUGBP1 is an early event in an inducible heart-specific mouse model of myotonic dystrophy.', *Journal of Clinical Investigation, 117*(10): 2802–2811.

Wang, K., Zhang, H., Ma, D., Bucan, M. et al. (2009) 'Common genetic variants on 5p14.1 associate with autism spectrum disorders.' Nature, doi:10.1038/nature07999.

Wang, M.S., Schinzel, A., Kotzot, D., Balmer, D. et al. (1999) 'Molecular and clinical correlation study of Williams-Beuren syndrome: no evidence of molecular factors in the deletion region or imprinting affecting clinical outcome.', *American Journal of Medical Genetics, 86*: 34–43.

Wang, P.P., Hesselink, J.R., Jernigan, T.L., Doherty, S. and Bellugi, U. (1992) 'Specific neurobehavioural profile of Williams' syndrome is associated with neocerebellar hemispheric preservation.', *Neurology, 42*(10): 1999–2002.

Wang, P.P., Solot, C., Moss, E.M., Gerdes, M. et al. (1998) 'Developmental presentation of 22q11.2 deletion (DiGeorge/velocardiofacial syndrome).', *Journal of Developmental and Behavioural Pediatrics, 19*: 342–345.

Wang, R., Martinez-Frias, M.L. and Graham, J.M. Jr. (2002) 'Infants of diabetic mothers are at increased risk for the oculo-auriculo-vertebral sequence: a case-based and case-control approach.', *Journal of Pediatrics, 141*: 611–617.

Wang, X., Yang, N., Uno, E., Roeder, R.G. et al. (2006) 'A subunit of the mediator complex regulates vertebrate neuronal development.', *Proceedings of the National Academy Science USA, 103*(46): 17284–17289.

Wang, Y.C., Lin, M.L., Lin, S.J. et al. (1997) 'Novel point mutation within intron 10 of FMR-1 gene causing fragile-X syndrome.', *Human Mutation, 10*: 393–399.

Wardle, M., Majounie, E., Williams, N.M., Rosser, A.E. et al. (2007) 'Dentatorubral pallidoluysian atrophy in South Wales.', *Journal of Neurology, Neurosurgery and Psychiatry, 79*(7): 804–807.

Warner, T.T., Williams, L. and Harding, A.E. (1994) 'DRPLA in Europe.', (Letter) *Nature Genetics, 6*: 225.

Warwick, T.C., Griffith, J., Reyes, B., Legesse, B. and Evans, M. (2007) 'Case report. Effects of vagus nerve stimulation in a patient with temporal lobe epilepsy and Asperger syndrome: Case report and review of the literature.', *Epilepsy and Behaviour, 10*(2): 344–347, doi:10.1016/j.yebeh.2007.01.001.

Wasdell, M.B., Jan, J.E., Bomben, M.M., Freeman, R.D. et al. (2008) 'A randomized, placebo-controlled trial of controlled release melatonin treatment of delayed sleep phase syndrome and impaired sleep maintenance in children with neurodevelopmental disabilities.', *Journal of Pineal Research, 44*(1): 57–64.

Wassif, C.A., Maslen, C., Kachilele-Linjewile, S., Lin, D. et al. (1998) 'Mutations in the human sterol delta-7-reductase gene at 11q12–13 cause Smith-Lemli-Opitz syndrome.', *American Journal of Human Genetics, 63*: 55–62.

Wassif, C.A., Zhu, P., Kratz, L., Krakowiak, P.A. et al. (2001) 'Biochemical, phenotypic and neurophysiological characterization of a genetic mouse model of RSH/Smith-Lemli-Opitz syndrome.', *Human Molecular Genetics, 10*: 555–564.

Wassink, T.H., Piven, J., Vieland, V.J., Jenkins, L. et al. (2005) 'Evaluation of the chromosome 2q37.3 gene CENTG2 as an autism susceptibility gene.', *American Journal of Medical Genetics B Neuropsychiatric Genetics, 136*(1): 36–44.

Wasternack, C. (1980) 'Degradation of pyrimidines and pyrimidine analogs – pathways and mutual influences.', *Pharmacology and Therapeutics, 8*(3): 629–651.

Watanabe-Fukunaga, R., Brannan, C.I., Copeland, N.G., Jenkins, N.A. and Nagata, S. (1992) 'Lymphoproliferation disorder in mice explained by defects in Fas antigen that mediates apoptosis.', *Nature, 356*: 314–317.

Watson, L.R., Baranek, G.T., Crais, E.R., Reznick, J.S. et al. (2007) 'The first year inventory: retrospective parent responses to a questionnaire designed to identify one-year-olds at risk for autism.', *Journal of Autism and Developmental Disorders, 37*: 49–61.

Watson, P., Black, G., Ramsden, S., Barrow, M. et al. (2001) 'Angelman syndrome phenotype associated with mutations in MeCP2, a gene encoding a methyl CpG binding protein.', *Journal of Medical Genetics, 38*: 224–228.

Waye, J.S., Nakamura, L.M., Eng, B., Hunnisett, L. et al. (2002) 'Smith-Lemli-Opitz syndrome: carrier frequency and spectrum of DHCR7 mutations in Canada.', *Journal of Medical Genetics, 39*: E31.

Weaver, D.D., Graham, C.B., Thomas, I.T. and Smith, D.W. (1974) 'A new overgrowth syndrome with accelerated skeletal maturation, unusual facies, and camptodactyly.', *Journal of Pediatrics, 84*: 547–552.

Weaver, I.C.G., Meaney, M.J. and Szyf, M. (2006) 'Maternal care effects on the hippocampal transcriptome and anxiety-mediated behaviours in the offspring that are reversible in adulthood.', *Proceedings of the National Academy of Science USA, 103*(9): 3480–3485, www.pnas.org/cgi/doi/10.1073/pnas.0507526103.

Weaver, R.G. Jr., Martin, T. and Zanolli, M.D. (1991) 'The ocular changes of incontinentia pigmenti achromians (hypomelanosis of Ito).', *Journal of Pediatrics Ophthalmology and Strabismus, 28*(3): 160–163.

Weaving, L.S., Christodoulou, J., Williamson, S.L., Friend, K.L. *et al.* (2004) 'Mutations of CDKL5 cause a severe neurodevelopmental disorder with infantile spasms and mental retardation.', *American Journal of Human Genetics, 75*: 1079–1093.

Weaving, L.S., Ellaway, C.J., Gecz, J. and Christodoulou, J. (2005) 'Rett syndrome: clinical review and genetic update.', *Journal of Medical Genetics, 42*: 1–7.

Weaving, L.S., Williamson, S.L., Bennetts, B., Davis, M. *et al.* (2003) 'Effects of MeCP2 mutation type, location and X-inactivation in modulating Rett syndrome phenotype.', *American Journal of Medical Genetics, 118A*: 103–114.

Wechsler, J., Greene, M., McDevitt, M.A., Anastasi, J. *et al.* (2002) 'Acquired mutations in GATA 1 in the megakaryoblastic leukemia of Down syndrome.', *Nature Genetics, 32*: 148–152.

Weech, A.A. (1927) 'Combined acrocephaly and syndactylism occurring in mother and daughter: a case report.', *Bulletin of Johns Hopkins Hospital, 40*: 73–76.

Weeda, G., Eveno, E., Donker, I., Vermeulen, W. *et al.* (1997) 'A mutation in the XPB/ERCC3 DNA repair transcription gene, associated with trichothiodystrophy.' *American Journal of Human Genetics, 60*: 320–329.

Weger, M., Stanger, O., Deutschmann, H., Leitner, F.J. *et al.* (2002) 'The role of hyperhomocysteinemia and methylenetetrahydrofolate reductase (MTHFR) C677T mutation in patients with retinal artery occlusion.', *American Journal of Ophthalmology, 134*: 57–61.

Weglage, J., Pietsch, M., Denecke, J., Sprinz, A. *et al.* (1999) 'Regression of neuropsychological deficits in early-treated phenylketonurics during adolescence.', *Journal of Inherited Metabolic Disease, 22*: 693–705.

Wei, X., McLeod, H.L., McMurrough, J., Gonzalez, F.J. and Fernandez-Salguero, P. (1996) 'Molecular basis of the human dihydropyrimidine dehydrogenase deficiency and 5-fluorouracil toxicity.', *Journal of Clinical Investigation, 98*: 610–615.

Weiler, I.J. and Greenough, W.T. (1999) 'Synaptic synthesis of the fragile-X protein: possible involvement in synapse maturation and elimination.', *American Journal of Medical Genetics, 83*: 248–252.

Weinhausel, A. and Haas, O.A. (2001) 'Evaluation of the fragile-X (FRAXA) syndrome with methylation-sensitive PCR.', *Human Genetics, 108*: 450–458.

Weinzimer, S.A., McDonald-McGinn, D.M., Driscoll, D.A., Emanuel, B.S. *et al.* (1998) 'Growth hormone deficiency in patients with 22q11.2 deletion: expanding the phenotype.', *Pediatrics, 101*: 929–932.

Weise, P., Koch, R., Shaw, K.N. and Rosenfeld, M.J. (1974) 'The use of 5-HTP in the treatment of Down's syndrome.', *Pediatrics, 54*(2): 165–168.

Weiskop, S., Richdale, A. and Matthews, J. (2005) 'Behavioural treatment to reduce sleep problems in children with autism or fragile-X syndrome.', *Developmental Medicine and Child Neurology, 47*(2): 94–104.

Weiss, L.A., Arking, D.E., Daly, M.J. and Chakravarti, A. (2009) 'A genome-wide linkage and association scan reveals novel loci for autism.', *Nature, 461*(7265): 802–808.

Weiss, L.A., Escayg, A., Kearney, J.A., Trudeau, M. *et al.* (2003) 'Sodium channels SCN1A, SCN2A and SCN3A in familial autism.', *Molecular Psychiatry, 8*: 186–194.

Weiss, L.A., Shen, Y., Korn, J.M., Arking, D.E. *et al.* (2008) 'Association between microdeletion and microduplication at 16p11.2 and autism.', *New England Journal of Medicine, 358*: 667–675.

Weissman, J.R., Kelley, R.I., Bauman, M.L., Cohen, B.H. *et al.* (2008) 'Mitochondrial disease in autism spectrum disorder patients: a cohort analysis.', *PloS ONE, 3*(11): e3815. doi:10.1371/journal. pone.0003815.

Weissortel, R., Strom, T.M., Dorr, H.G., Rauch, A. and Meitinger, T. (1998) 'Analysis of an interstitial deletion in a patient with Kallmann syndrome, X-linked ichthyosis and mental retardation.', *Clinical Genetics, 54*(1): 45–51.

Welch, E.M., Barton, E.R., Zhuo, J., Tomizawa, Y. *et al.* (2007) 'PTC124 targets genetic disorders caused by nonsense mutations.' *Nature, 447*(7140): 87–91.

Welch, J.P. (1974) 'Elucidation of a "new" pleiotropic connective tissue disorder.' *Birth Defects Original Articles Series, X*(10): 138–146.

Welch, M.G., Ludwig, R.J., Opler, M. and Ruggiero, D.A. (2006) 'Secretin's role in the cerebellum: a larger biological context and implications for developmental disorders.', *The Cerebellum, 5*: 2–6.

Wells, R.S. and Jennings, M.C. (1967) 'X-linked ichthyosis and ichthyosis vulgaris: clinical and genetic distinctions in a second series of families.', *Journal of the American Medical Association, 202*: 485–488.

Wells, R.S. and Kerr, C.B. (1965) 'Genetic classification of ichthyosis.', *Archives of Dermatology, 92*(1): 1–6.

Welt, C.K., Smith, P.C. and Taylor, A.E. (2004) 'Evidence of early ovarian aging in fragile-X premutation carriers.' *Journal of Clinical Endocrinology and Metabolism, 89*: 4569–4574.

Wendel, U. and Bremer, H.J. (1984) 'Betaine in the treatment of homocystinuria due to 5,10-methylenetetrahydrofolate reductase deficiency.', *European Journal of Pediatrics, 142*: 147–150.

Werner, E. and Dawson, G. (2006) 'Validation of the phenomenon of autistic regression using home videotapes.', *Archives of General Psychiatry, 62*(8): 889–895.

Wessel, A., Pankau, R., Kececioglu, D., Ruschewski, W. and Bursch, J.H. (1994) 'Three decades of follow-up of aortic and pulmonary vascular lesions in the Williams-Beuren syndrome.', *American Journal of Medical Genetics, 52*: 297–301.

West, P.M.H., Love, D.R., Stapleton, P.M. and Winship, I.M. (2003) 'Paternal uniparental disomy in monozygotic twins discordant for hemihypertrophy.', *Journal of Medical Genetics, 40*: 223–226.

Westmark, C.J. and Malter, J.S. (2007) 'FMRP mediates mGluR5-dependent translation of amyloid precursor protein.', *PloS Biology*, 5(3): e52, doi:10.1371/journal.pbio.0050052.

Wheeler, P.G., Quigley, C.A., Sadeghi-Nejad, A. and Weaver, D.D. (2000) 'Hypogonadism and CHARGE association.', *American Journal of Medical Genetics*, 94(3): 228–231.

Wheeler, T.M., Lueck, J.D., Swanson, M.S., Dirksen, R.T. and Thornton, C.A. (2007) 'Correction of ClC-1 splicing eliminates chloride channelopathy and myotonia in mouse models of myotonic dystrophy.', *Journal of Clinical Investigation*, 117(12): 3952–3957.

White, J.F. (2003) 'Intestinal pathophysiology in autism.' *Experimental Biology and Medicine*, 228: 639–649.

Whiteford, M.L., Doig, W.B., Raine, P.A.M., Hollman, A.S. and Tolmie, J.L. (2001) 'A new case of Myhre syndrome.', *Clinical Dysmorphology*, 10: 135–140.

Whiteley, P., Dodou, K., Todd, L. and Shattock, P. (2004) 'Body mass index of children from the United Kingdom diagnosed with pervasive developmental disorders.', *Pediatrics International*, 46: 531–533.

Whiteley, P., Waring, R., Williams, L., Klovrza, L. *et al.* (2006) 'Spot urinary creatinine excretion in pervasive developmental disorders.' *Pediatrics International*, 48: 292–297.

Whitsel, E.A., Castillo, M. and D'Cruz, O. (1995) 'Cerebellar vermis and midbrain dysgenesis in oculomotor apraxia: MR findings.', *AJNR. American Journal of Neuroradiology*, 16: 831–834.

Whittington, J.E., Holland, A.J., Webb, T., Butler, J. *et al.* (2001) 'Population prevalence and estimated birth incidence and mortality rate for people with Prader-Willi syndrome in one UK health region.', *Journal of Medical Genetics*, 38(11): 792–798.

Wicksell, R.K., Kihlgren, M., Melin, L. and Eeg-Olofsson, O. (2004) 'Specific cognitive deficits are common in children with Duchenne muscular dystrophy.', *Developmental Medicine and Child Neurology*, 46: 154–159.

Widemann, B.C., Salzer, W.L., Arceci, R.J., Blaney, S.M. *et al.* (2006) 'Phase I trial and pharmacokinetic study of the farnesyltransferase inhibitor tipifarnib in children with refractory solid tumors or neurofibromatosis type I and plexiform neurofibromas.', *Journal of Clinical Oncology*, 24: 507–516.

Wieacker, P., Davies, K.E., Mevorah, B. and Ropers, H.H. (1983) 'Linkage studies in a family with X-linked recessive ichthyosis employing a cloned DNA sequence from the distal short arm of the X chromosome.', *Human Genetics*, 63: 113–116.

Wieczorek, D., Ludwig, M., Boehringer, S., Hein, P. *et al.* (2007) 'Reproduction abnormalities and twin pregnancies in parents of sporadic patients with oculo-auriculo-vertebral spectrum/Goldenhar syndrome.', *Human Genetics*, 121: 369–376.

Wiedemann, H.R., Burgio, G.R., Aldenhoff, P., Kunze, J. *et al.* (1983) 'The Proteus syndrome: partial gigantism of the hands and/or feet, nevi, hemihypertrophy, subcutaneous tumors, macrocephaly or other skull anomalies and possible accelerated growth and visceral affections.' *European Journal of Pediatrics*, 140(1): 5–12.

Wiemels, J.L., Smith, R.N., Taylor, G.M., Eden, O.B. *et al.* (2001) 'Methylenetetrahydrofolate reductase (MTHFR) polymorphisms and risk of molecularly defined subtypes of childhood acute leukemia.' *Proceedings of the National Academy of Science USA*, 98: 4004–4009.

Wier, M.L., Yoshida, C.K., Odouli, R., Grether, J.K. and Croen, L.A. (2006) 'Congenital anomalies associated with autism spectrum disorders.', *Developmental Medicine and Child Neurology*, 48: 500–507.

Wiggins, L.D., Baio, J. and Rice, C. (2006) 'Examination of the time between first evaluation and first autism spectrum diagnosis in a population-based sample.', *Developmental and Behavioural Pediatrics*, 27: s79–s87.

Wiley, S., Swayne, S., Rubinstein, J.H., Lanphear, N.E. and Stevens, C.A. (2003) 'Rubinstein-Taybi syndrome medical guidelines.', *American Journal of Medical Genetics A*, 119A(2): 101–110.

Wilkie, A.O.M., Slaney, S.F., Oldridge, M., Poole, M.D. *et al.* (1995) 'Apert syndrome results from localized mutations of FGFR2 and is allelic with Crouzon syndrome.', *Nature Genetics*, 9: 165–172.

Willems, P.J. (2008) 'Bottlenecks in molecular testing for rare genetic diseases.', *Human Mutation*, 29(6): 772–775.

Willemsen, R., Smits, A., Mohkamsing, S., van Beerendonk, H. *et al.* (1997) 'Rapid antibody test for diagnosing fragile-X syndrome: a validation of the technique.', *Human Genetics*, 99: 308–311.

Williams, C.A., Beaudet, A.L., Clayton-Smith, J., Knoll, J.H. *et al.* (2006) 'Angelman syndrome 2005: updated consensus for diagnostic criteria.', *American Journal of Medical Genetics*, 140A: 413–418.

Williams, C.A. and Frias, J.L. (1982) 'The Angelman ("happy puppet") syndrome.', *American Journal of Medical Genetics*, 11: 453–460.

Williams, C.A., Lossie, A. and Driscoll, D. (2001) 'Angelman syndrome: mimicking conditions and phenotypes.', *American Journal of Medical Genetics*, 101: 59–64.

Williams, J.C., Barratt-Boyes, B.G. and Lowe, J.B. (1961) 'Supravalvular aortic stenosis.', *Circulation*, 24: 1311–1318.

Williams, M.S. (2003) 'Can genomics deliver on the promise of improved outcomes and reduced costs? Background and recommendations for health insurers.', *Disease Management and Health Outcomes*, 11(5): 277–290.

Williams, M.S. (2006) 'Neuropsychological evaluation in Lujan-Fryns syndrome: commentary and clinical report.', *American Journal of Medical Genetics*, 140A: 2812–2815.

Williams, P.G. and Hersh, J.H. (1998) 'Brief report: the association of neurofibromatosis type 1 and autism.', *Journal of Autism and Developmental Disorders*, 28(6): 567–571.

Williams, R.A., Mamotte, C.D.S. and Burnett, J.R. (2008) 'Phenylketonuria: an inborn error of phenylalanine metabolism.', *The Clinical Biochemist Review*, 29: 31–41.

Williams, R.J. (1956) *Biochemical Individuality.* Chichester: John Wiley Publishing.

Williams, T.A., Mars, A.E., Buyske, S.G., Stenroos, E.S. et al. (2007) 'Risk of autistic disorder in affected offspring of mothers with a glutathione S-transferase P1 haplotype.', *Archives of Pediatric and Adolescent Medicine, 161*: 356–361.

Willmore, L.J., Abelson, M.B., Ben-Menachem, E., Pellock, J.M. and Shields, W.D. (2009) 'Vigabatrin: 2008 update.', *Epilepsia, 50*(2): 163–173,

Wilson, D.I., Burn, J., Scambler, P. and Goodship, J. (1993) 'DiGeorge syndrome, part of CATCH 22.', *Journal of Medical Genetics, 30*: 852–856.

Wilson, D.I., Cross, I.E., Goodship, J.A., Brown, J. et al. (1992) 'A prospective cytogenetic study of 36 cases of DiGeorge syndrome.', *American Journal of Human Genetics, 51*: 957–963.

Wilson, D.I., Cross, I.E., Goodship, J.A., Coulthard, S. et al. (1991) 'DiGeorge syndrome with isolated aortic coarctation and isolated ventricular septal defect in three sibs with a 22q11 deletion of maternal origin.', *British Heart Journal, 66*: 308–312.

Wilson, H.L., Wong, A.C.C., Shaw, S.R., Tse, W-Y. et al. (2003) 'Molecular characterization of the 22q13 deletion syndrome supports the role of haploinsufficiency of SHANK3/ PROSAP2 in the major neurological symptoms.', *Journal of Medical Genetics, 40*: 575–584.

Wilson, L.C., Leverton, K., Oude Luttikhuis, M.E.M., Oley, C.A. et al. (1995) 'Brachydactyly and mental retardation: an Albright hereditary osteodystrophy-like syndrome localized to 2q37.', *American Journal of Human Genetics, 56*: 400–407.

Wilson, R.G., Nimkarn, S., Dumic, M., Obeid, J. et al. (2007) 'Ethnic specific distribution of mutations in 716 patients with congenital adrenal hyperplasia owing to 21-hydroxylase deficiency.', *Molecular Genetics and Metabolism, 90*(4): 414–421.

Wimmer, K., Yao, S., Claes, K., Kehrer-Sawatzki, H. et al. (2006) 'Spectrum of genes chromosomes single- and multiexon NF1 copy number changes in a cohort of 1, 100 unselected NF1 patients.' *Cancer, 45*: 265–276.

Winship, I.M. (1985) 'Sotos syndrome – autosomal dominant inheritance substantiated.', *Clinical Genetics, 28*: 243–246.

Winter, M., Pankau, R., Amm, M., Gosch, A. and Wessel, A. (1996) 'The spectrum of ocular features in the Williams-Beuren syndrome.', *Clinical Genetics, 49*: 28–31.

Wintour, E.M. and Henry, B.A. (2006) 'Glycerol transport: an additional target for obesity therapy?' *TRENDS in Endocrinology and Metabolism, 17*(3): 77–78.

Wirojanan, J., Jacquemont, S., Diaz, R., Bacalman, S. et al. (2009) 'The efficacy of melatonin for sleep problems in Children with autism, fragile-X syndrome, or autism and fragile-X syndrome.', *Journal of Clinical Sleep Medicine, 5*(2): 145–150.

Wisbeck, J.M., Huffman, L.C., Freund, L., Gunnar, M.R. et al. (2000) 'Cortisol and social stressors in children with fragile-X: a pilot study.', *Journal of Developmental and Behavioural Pediatrics, 21*: 278–282.

Wisniewski, K.E., Kida, E., Connell, F. and Zhong, N. (2000) 'Neuronal ceroid lipofuscinoses: research update.', *Neurological Sciences, 21*(Supp 3): S49–56.

Wisniewski, K.E., Wisniewski, H.M. and Wen, G.Y. (1985) 'Occurrence of neuropathological changes and dementia of Alzheimer's disease in Down's syndrome.', *Annals of Neurology, 17*: 278–282.

Witkin, H.A., Mednick, S.A., Schulsinger, F., Bakkestrom, E. et al. (1976) 'Criminality in XYY and XXY men.', *Science, 193*(4253): 547–555.

Witsch-Baumgartner, M., Ciara, E., Loffler, J., Menzel, H.J. et al. (2001) 'Frequency gradients of DHCR7 mutations in patients with Smith-Lemli-Opitz syndrome in Europe: evidence for different origins of common mutations.', *European Journal of Human Genetics, 9*: 45–50.

Witsch-Baumgartner, M., Gruber, M., Kraft, H.G., Rossi, M. et al. (2004) 'Maternal apo E genotype is a modifier of the Smith-Lemli-Opitz syndrome.', *Journal of Medical Genetics, 41*(8): 577–584.

Witsch-Baumgartner, M., Schwentner, I., Gruber, M., Benlian, P. et al. (2008) 'Age and origin of major Smith-Lemli-Opitz syndrome (SLOS) mutations in European populations.', *Journal of Medical Genetics, 45*(4): 200–209.

Wittine, L.M., Josephson, K.D. and Williams, M.S. (1999) 'Aortic root dilation in apparent Lujan-Fryns syndrome.', *American Journal of Medical Genetics, 86*: 405–409.

Wiznitzer, M. (2004) 'Autism and tuberous sclerosis.', *Journal of Child Neurology, 19*: 675–679.

Wiznitzer, M., Rapin, I. and Van de Water, T.R. (1987) 'Neurologic findings in children with ear malformation.', *International Journal of Pediatric Otolaryngology, 13*: 41–55.

Wolfe, D.E., Schindler, D. and Desnick, R.J. (1995) 'Neuroaxonal dystrophy in infantile alpha-N-acetylgalactosaminidase deficiency.', *Journal of Neurological Science, 132*: 44–56.

Wolff, M., Casse-Perrot, C, and Dravet, C. (2006) 'Severe myoclonic epilepsy of infants (Dravet syndrome): natural history and neuropsychological findings.', *Epilepsia, 47*(Suppl. 2): 45–48.

Wolff, S. (2004) 'The history of autism.' *European Child and Adolescent Psychiatry, 13*(4): 201–208.

Wolkenstein, P., Durand-Zaleski, I., Moreno, J.C., Zeller, J. et al. (2000) 'Cost evaluation of the medical management of neurofibromatosis 1: a prospective study on 201 patients.', *British Journal of Dermatology, 142*: 1166–1170.

Wolkenstein, P., Freche, B., Zeller, J. and Revuz, J. (1996) 'Usefulness of screening investigations in neurofibromatosis type 1: a study of 152 patients.', *Archives of Dermatology, 132*: 1333–1336.

Wolkenstein, P., Rodriguez, D., Ferkal, S., Gravier, H. et al. (2008) 'Impact of neurofibromatosis 1 upon quality of life in childhood: a cross-sectional study of 79 cases.', *British Journal of Dermatology,* doi:10.1111/j.1365-2133.2008.08949.x.

Wolpert, C.M., Menold, M.M., Bass, M.P., Qumsiyeh, M.B. et al. (2000) 'Three probands with autistic disorder and isodicentric chromosome 15.', *American Journal of Medical Genetics (Neuropsychiatric Genetics), 96*: 365–372.

Wolters, P.L., Gropman, A.L., Martin, S.C., Smith, M.R et al. (2009) 'Neurodevelopment of children under 3 years of age with Smith-Magenis syndrome.', *Pediatric Neurology, 41*(4): 250–258.

Wong, D.F., Singer, H.S., Brandt, J., Shy, E. *et al.* (1997) 'D2-like dopamine receptor density in Tourette syndrome measured by PET.', *Journal of Nuclear Medicine*, 38: 1243–1247.

Wong, S-Y. and Roth, D.B. (2007) 'Murine models of Omenn syndrome.', *Journal of Clinical Investigation*, 117: 1213–1216.

Wong, V., Hui, L.H., Lee, W.C., Leung, L.S. *et al.* (2004) 'A modified screening tool for autism (Checklist for Autism in Toddlers [CHAT-23]) for Chinese children.' *Pediatrics*, 114(2): e166–176.

Wong, V. and Khong, P.L. (2006) 'Tuberous sclerosis complex: correlation of magnetic resonance imaging (MRI) findings with comorbidities.', *Journal of Child Neurology*, 21(2): 99–105.

Wong, W.S. and Nielsen, R. (2004) 'Detecting selection in non-coding regions of nucleotide sequences.', *Genetics*, 167: 949–958.

Woo, S.L.C., Lidsky, A.S., Guttler, F., Thirumalachary, C. and Robson, K.J.H. (1984) 'Prenatal diagnosis of classical phenylketonuria by gene mapping.', *Journal of the American Medical Association*, 251: 1998–2002.

Wood, J.D., Nucifora, F.C. Jr., Duan, K., Zhang, C. *et al.* (2000) 'Atrophin-1, the dentato-rubral and pallido-luysian atrophy gene product, interacts with ETO/MTG8 in the nuclear matrix and represses transcription.', *The Journal of Cell Biology*, 150(5): 939–948.

Woodin, M., Wang, P.P., Aleman, D., McDonald-McGinn, D. *et al.* (2001) 'Neuropsychological profile of children and adolescents with the 22q11.2 microdeletion.', *Genetics in Medicine*, 3(1): 34–39.

Wooten, N., Bakalov, V.K., Hill, S. and Bondy, C.A. (2008) 'Reduced abdominal adiposity and improved glucose tolerance in GH-treated girls with Turner syndrome.', *Journal of Clinical Endocrinology and Metabolism*, 93(6): 2109–2114.

Wraith, J.E. (2001) 'Ornithine carbamoyltransferase deficiency.', *Archives of Disease in Childhood*, 84(1): 84–88.

Wraith, J.E., Bankier, A., Chow, C.W., Danks, D.M. and Sardharwalla, I.B. (1990) 'Geleophysic dysplasia.', *American Journal of Medical Genetics*, 35: 153–156.

Wright, B., Brzozowski, A.M., Calvert, E., Farnworth, H. *et al.* (2005) 'Is the presence of urinary indolyl-3-acryloylglycine associated with autism spectrum disorder?' *Developmental Medicine and Child Neurology*, 47: 190–192.

Wu, B., Moulton, H.M., Iversen, P.L., Jiang, J. *et al.* (2008) 'Effective rescue of dystrophin improves cardiac function in dystrophin-deficient mice by a modified morpholino oligomer.', *Proceedings of the National Academy of Science*, 105(39): 14814–14819.

Wu, D.J., Wang, N.J., Driscoll, J., Dorrani, N., Liu, D., Sigman, M. and Schanen, N.C. (2009) 'Autistic disorder associated with a paternally derived unbalanced translocation leading to duplication of chromosome 15pter–q13.2: a case report.', *Molecular Cytogenetics*, 2: 27, doi:10.1186/1755-8166-2-27.

Wu, H.Y., Rusnack, S.L., Bellah, R.D., Plachter, N. *et al.* (2002) 'Genitourinary malformations in chromosome 22q11.2 deletion.', *Journal of Urology*, 168: 2564–2565.

Wu, J.Y., Kuban, K.C., Allred, E., Shapiro, F. and Darras, B.T. (2005) 'Association of Duchenne muscular dystrophy with autism spectrum disorder.', *Journal of Child Neurology*, 20: 790–795.

Wu, S., Jia, M., Ruan, Y., Liu, J. *et al.* (2005) 'Positive association of the oxytocin receptor gene (OXTR) with autism in the Chinese Han population.' *Biological Psychiatry*, 58: 74–77.

Wu, Y., Bolduc, F.V., Bell, K., Tully, T. *et al.* (2008) 'A drosophila model for Angelman syndrome.', *Proceedings of the National Academy of Science USA*, 105(34): 12399–12404.

Wu, Y–q., Sutton, V.R., Nickerson, E., Lupski, J.R. *et al.* (1998) 'Delineation of the common critical region in Williams syndrome and clinical correlation of growth, heart defects, ethnicity, and parental origin.', *American Journal of Medical Genetics*, 78: 82–89.

Wyrobek, A.J., Eskenaz, B., Young, S., Arnheim, N. *et al.* (2006) 'Advancing age has differential effects on DNA damage, chromatin integrity, gene mutations, and aneuploidies in sperm.', *Proceedings of the National Academy of Science*, 103(25): 9601–9606.

Wyse, R.K.H., Al-Mahdawi, S., Burn, J. and Blake, K. (1993) 'Congenital heart disease in CHARGE association.', *Pediatric Cardiology*, 14(2): 75–81.

Xekouki, P., Fryssira, H., Maniati-Christidi, M., Amenta, S. *et al.* (2005) 'Growth hormone deficiency in a child with Williams-Beuren syndrome: the response to growth hormone therapy.', *Journal of Pediatric Endocrinology and Metabolism*, 18(2): 205–207.

Xi, C.Y., Ma, H.W., Lu, Y., Zhao, Y.J. *et al.* (2007) 'MeCP2 gene mutation analysis in autistic boys with developmental regression.', *Psychiatric Genetics*, 17(2): 113–116.

Xiong, N., Ji, C., Li, Y., He, Z. *et al.* (2007) 'The physical status of children with autism in China.', *Research in Developmental Disabilities*, 30(1): 70–76.

Xuan, J.Y., Besner, A., Ireland, M., Hughes-Benzie, R.M. and MacKenzie, A.E. (1994) 'Mapping of Simpson-Golabi-Behmel syndrome to Xq25–q27.', *Human Molecular Genetics*, 3: 133–137.

Xuan, J.Y., Hughes-Benzie, R.M. and MacKenzie, A.E. (1999) 'A small interstitial deletion in the GPC3 gene causes Simpson-Golabi-Behmel syndrome in a Dutch-Canadian family.', *Journal of Medical Genetics*, 36: 57–58.

Yagi, H., Furutani, Y., Hamada, H., Sasaki, T. *et al.* (2003) 'Role of TBX1 in human del22q11.2 syndrome.', *Lancet*, 362: 1366–1373.

Yakoub, M., Dulac, O., Jambaqué, I., Chiron, C. and Plouin, P. (1992) 'Early diagnosis of severe myoclonic epilepsy in infancy.', *Brain and Development*, 14(5): 299–303.

Yam, W.K.L., Wu, N.S.P., Lo, I.F.M., Ko, C.H. *et al.* (2004) 'Dentatorubral-pallidoluysian atrophy in two Chinese families in Hong Kong.', *Hong Kong Medical Journal*, 10(4): 53–56.

Yamada, M., Sato, T., Tsuji, S. and Takahashi, H. (2002) 'Oligodendrocytic polyglutamine pathology in dentatorubral-pallidoluysian atrophy.', *Annals of Neurology*, 52: 670–674.

Yamagata, T., Aradhya, S., Mori, M., Inoue, K. *et al.* (2002) 'The human secretin gene: fine structure in 11p15.5 and sequence variation in patients with autism.', *Genome*, 80(2): 185–194.

Yamaguchi, S., Brailey, L.L., Morizono, H., Bale, A.E. and Tuchman, M. (2006) 'Mutations and polymorphisms in the human ornithine transcarbamylase (OTC) gene.', *Human Mutation, 27*: 626–632.

Yamakawa, K. (2006) 'Na channel gene mutations in epilepsy – the functional consequences.', *Epilepsy Research, 70*(Supp.): S218–S222.

Yamamoto, T., Kuramoto, H. and Kadowaki, M. (2007) 'Downregulation in aquaporin 4 and aquaporin 8 expression of the colon associated with the induction of allergic diarrhea in a mouse model of food allergy.' *Life Sciences, 81*: 115–120.

Yan, J., Bi, W. and Lupski, J.R. (2007) 'Penetrance of craniofacial anomalies in mouse models of Smith-Magenis syndrome is modified by genomic sequence surrounding Rai1: not all null alleles are alike.', *American Journal of Human Genetics, 80*: 518–525.

Yan, J., Feng, J., Schroer, R., Li, W. *et al.* (2008) 'Analysis of the neuroligin 4Y gene in patients with autism.', *Psychiatric Genetics, 18*(4): 204–207.

Yan, Q.J., Rammal, M., Tranfaglia, M. and Bauchwirtz, R.P. (2005) 'Suppression of two major fragile-X syndrome mouse model phenotypes by the mGluR5 antagonist MPEP.', *Neuropharmacology, 49*: 1053–1066.

Yang, F.C., Ingram, D.A., Chen, S., Zhu, Y. *et al.* (2008) 'Nf1-dependent tumors require a microenvironment containing Nf1+/− and c-kit-dependent bone marrow.', *Cell, 135*(3): 437–448.

Yang, M.S. and Gill, M. (2007) 'A review of gene linkage, association and expression studies in autism and an assessment of convergent evidence.', *International Journal of Developmental Neuroscience, 25*: 69–85.

Yang, P. and Tsai, J.H. (2004) 'Occurrence of priapism with risperidone-paroxetine combination in an autistic child.', *Journal of Child and Adolescent Psychopharmacology, 14*(3): 342–343.

Yang, Y., Guo, J., Liu, Z., Tang, S. *et al.* (2006a) 'A locus for autosomal dominant accessory auricular anomaly maps to 14q11.2–q12.', *Human Genetics, 120*: 144–147.

Yang, Y., Sun, F., Song, J., Hasegawa, Y. *et al.* (2006b) 'Clinical and biochemical studies on Chinese patients with methylmalonic aciduria.', *Journal of Child Neurology, 21*: 1020–1024.

Yasuda, S., Ishida, N., Higashiyama, A., Morinobu, S. and Kato, N. (2000) 'Characterization of audiogenic-like seizures in naive rats evoked by activation of AMPA and NMDA receptors in the inferior colliculus.', *Experimental Neurology, 164*: 396–406.

Yatsenko, S.A., Yatsenko, A.N., Szigeti, K., Craigen, W.J. *et al.* (2004) 'Interstitial deletion of 10p and atrial septal defect in DiGeorge 2 syndrome.', *Clinical Genetics, 66*(2): 128–136.

Yau, E.K.C., Shek, C.C., Chan, K.Y. and Chan, A.Y.W. (2004) 'Dihydropyrimidine dehydrogenase deficiency: a baby boy with ocular abnormalities, neonatal seizure and global developmental delay.', *Hong Kong Journal of Paediatrics (new series), 9*: 167–170.

Yazaki, M., Yoshida, K., Nakamura, A., Koyama, J. *et al.* (1999) 'Clinical characteristics of aged Becker muscular dystrophy patients with onset after 30 years.', *European Neurology, 42*: 145–149.

Yen, P.H., Marsh, B., Allen, E., Tsai, S.P. *et al.* (1988) 'The human X-linked steroid sulfatase gene and a Y-encoded pseudogene: evidence for an inversion of the Y chromosome during primate evolution.', *Cell, 55*: 1123–1135.

Yik, W.Y., Steinberg, S.J., Moser, A.B., Moser, H.W. and Hacia, J.G. (2009) 'Identification of novel mutations and sequence variation in the Zellweger syndrome spectrum of peroxisome biogenesis disorders.', *Human Mutation, 30*(3): E467–E480, doi:10.1002/humu.20932.

Yilmaz, K. (2009) 'Riboflavin treatment in a case with 1–2-hydroxyglutaric aciduria.', *European Journal of Pediatric Neurology, 13*: 57–60.

Ylisaukko-oja, T., Alarcon, M., Cantor, R.M., Auranen, M. *et al.* (2006) 'Search for autism loci by combined analysis of Autism Genetic Resource Exchange and Finnish families.', *Annals of Neurology, 59*(1): 145–155.

Ylisaukko-oja, T., Nieminen-von Wendt, T., Kempas, E., Sarenius, S. *et al.* (2004) 'Genome-wide scan for loci of Asperger syndrome.', *Molecular Psychiatry, 9*: 161–168.

Ylisaukko-oja, T., Rehnström, K., Auranen, M., Vanhala, R. *et al.* (2005) 'Analysis of four neuroligin genes as candidates for autism.', *European Journal of Human Genetics, 13*(12): 1285–1292.

Yntema, H.G., Poppelaars, F.A., Derksen, E., Oudakker, A.R. *et al.* (2002) 'Expanding phenotype of XNP mutations: mild to moderate mental retardation.' *American Journal of Medical Genetics, 110*: 243–247.

Yohay, K.H. (2006) 'The genetic and molecular pathogenesis of NF1 and NF2.', *Seminars in Pediatric Neurology, 13*: 21–26.

Yonan, A.L., Alarcon, M., Cheng, R., Magnusson, P.K. *et al.* (2003) 'A genomewide screen of 345 families for autism-susceptibility loci.', *American Journal of Human Genetics, 73*: 886–897.

Yorifuji, T., Muroi, J., Uematsu, A., Tanaka, K. *et al.* (1998) 'X-inactivation pattern in the liver of a manifesting female with ornithine transcarbamylase (OTC) deficiency.', *Clinical Genetics, 54*: 349–353.

Yoshihara, S., Omichi, K., Yanazawa, M., Kitamura, K. and Yoshihara, Y. (2005) 'Arx homeobox gene is essential for development of mouse olfactory system.', *Development, 132*(4): 751–762.

Yoshimura, I., Sasaki, A., Akimoto, H. and Yoshimura, N. (1989) ['A case of congenital myotonic dystrophy with infantile autism.'] *No To Hattatsu, 21*: 379–384.

Young, E.L., Wishnow, R. and Nigro, M.A. (2006) 'Expanding the clinical picture of Simpson-Golabi-Behmel syndrome.', *Pediatric Neurology, 34*: 139–142.

Yovich, J.L., Stanger, J.D., Grauaug, A.A., Lunay, G.G. *et al.* (1985) 'Foetal abnormality (Goldenhar syndrome) occurring in one of triplet infants derived from in vitro fertilization with possible monozygotic twinning.', *Journal of In Vitro Fertilization and Embryo Transfer, 2*: 27–32.

Yu, H. and Patel, S.B. (2005) 'Recent insights into the Smith-Lemli-Opitz syndrome.', *Clinical Genetics, 68*(5): 383–391.

Yussman, S.M., Ryan, S.A., Auinger, P. and Weitzman, M. (2004) 'Visits to complementary and alternative medicine providers by children and adolescents in the United States.', *Ambulatory Pediatrics, 4*(5): 429–435.

Zacharin, M. (2007) 'The spectrum of McCune Albright syndrome.', *Pediatric Endocrinology Reviews*, 4(Supplement 4): 412–418.

Zachor, D.A., Mroczek-Musulman, E. and Brown, P. (2000) 'Prevalence of coeliac disease in Down syndrome in the United States.', *Journal of Pediatric Gastroenterology and Nutrition*, 31(3): 275–279.

Zafeiriou, D.I., Ververi, A., Salomons, G.S., Vargiami, E. *et al.* (2007) 'L-2-hydroxyglutaric aciduria presenting with severe autistic features.', *Brain and Development*, 30(4): 305–307, doi:10.1016/j. braindev.2007.09.005.

Zafeiriou, D.I., Ververi, A. and Vargiami, E. (2006) 'Childhood autism and associated comorbidities.', *Brain and Development*, 29(5): 257–272.

Zaki, M.S., Abdel-Aleem, A., Abdel-Salam, G., Marsh, S.E. *et al.* (2008) 'The molar tooth sign: a new Joubert syndrome and related cerebellar disorders classification system tested in Egyptian families.', *Neurology*, 70: 556–565.

Zana, M., Janka, Z. and Kalman, J. (2007) 'Oxidative stress: a bridge between Down's syndrome and Alzheimer's disease.', *Neurobiology of Aging*, 28: 648–676.

Zannolli, R., Micheli, V., Mazzei, M.A., Sacco, P. *et al.* (2003) 'Hereditary xanthinuria type II associated with mental delay, autism, cortical renal cysts, nephrocalcinosis, osteopenia, and hair and teeth defects.', *Journal of Medical Genetics*, 40: 121 doi:10.1136/jmg.40.11.e121.

Zapella, M. (1990) 'Autistic features in children affected by cerebral gigantism.' *Brain Dysfunction, 3*: 241–244.

Zappella, M. (1993) 'Autism and hypomelanosis of Ito in twins.', *Developmental Medicine and Child Neurology*, 35: 826–832.

Zappella, M. (1997) 'The preserved speech variant of the Rett complex: a report of 8 cases.', *European Child and Adolescent Psychiatry*, 6(1): 23–25.

Zappella, M., Gillberg, C. and Ehlers, S. (1998) 'The preserved speech variant. A subgroup of the Rett complex: a clinical report of 30 cases.', *Journal of Autism and Developmental Disorders*, 28(6): 519–526.

Zappella, M., Meloni, I., Longo, I., Hayek, G. and Renieri, A. (2001) 'Preserved speech variants of the Rett syndrome: molecular and clinical analysis.', *American Journal of Medical Genetics*, 104: 14–22.

Zatz, M., Rapaport, D., Vainzof, M., Passos-Bueno, M.R. *et al.* (1991) 'Serum creatine-kinase (CK) and pyruvate-kinase (PK) activities in Duchenne (DMD) as compared with Becker (BMD) muscular dystrophy.', *Journal of Neurological Science*, 102: 190–196.

Zbuk, K.M., Stein, J.L. and Eng, C. (2006) '*PTEN* hamartoma tumor syndrome (PHTS).', *GeneReviews*, web-based resource.

Zecavati, N. and Spence, S.J. (2009) 'Neurometabolic disorders and dysfunction in autism spectrum disorders.' *Current Neurology and Neuroscience Reports*, 9: 129–136.

Zeev, B.B., Yaron, Y., Schanen, N.C., Wolf, H. *et al.* (2002) 'Rett syndrome: clinical manifestations in males with *MeCP2* mutations.', *Journal of Child Neurology*, 17: 20–24.

Zeng, L.-H., Bero, A.W., Zhang, B., Holtzman, D.M. and Wong, M. (2010) 'Modulation of astrocyte glutamate transporters decreases seizures in a mouse model of tuberous sclerosis complex.', *Neurobiology of Disease*, 37: 764–771.

Zeng, L.-H., Xu, L., Gutmann, D.H. and Wong, M. (2008) 'Rapamycin prevents epilepsy in a mouse model of tuberous sclerosis complex.', *Annals of Neurology*, 63: 444–453.

Zetterberg, H., Regland, B., Palmer, M., Ricksten, A. *et al.* (2002) 'Increased frequency of combined methylenetetrahydrofolate reductase C677T and A1298C mutated alleles in spontaneously aborted embryos.', *European Journal of Human Genetics*, 10: 113–118.

Zettersten, E., Man, M–Q., Sato, J., Denda, M. *et al.* (1998) 'Recessive X-linked ichthyosis: role of cholesterol-sulfate accumulation in the barrier abnormality.', *Journal of Investigative Dermatology*, 111: 784–790.

Zhang, Y.Q., Bailey, A.M., Matthies, H.J.G., Renden, R.B. *et al.* (2001) 'Drosophila fragile-X-related gene regulates the MAP1B homolog Futsch to control synaptic structure and function.', *Cell*, 107: 591–603.

Zhang, Y.Q. and Broadie, K. (2005) 'Fathoming fragile-X in fruit flies.', *Trends in Genetics*, 21(1): 37–45.

Zhou, J., Kong, H., Hua, X., Xiao, M. *et al.* (2008) 'Altered blood-brain barrier integrity in adult aquaporin-4 knockout mice.' *NeuroReport*, 19: 1–5.

Zhou, X., Hampel, H., Thiele, H., Gorlin, R.J. *et al.* (2001) 'Association of germline mutation in the PTEN tumour suppressor gene and Proteus and Proteus-like syndromes.', *Lancet*, 358: 210–211.

Zhou, X.P., Marsh, D.J., Hampel, H., Mulliken, J.B. *et al.* (2000) 'Germline and germline mosaic mutations associated with a Proteus-like syndrome of hemihypertrophy, lower limb asymmetry, arterio-venous malformations and lipomatosis.', *Human Molecular Genetics*, 9: 765–768.

Zhou, X.P., Waite, K.A., Pilarski, R., Hampel, H. *et al.* (2003) 'Germline PTEN promoter mutations and deletions in Cowden/Bannayan-Riley-Ruvalcaba syndrome result in aberrant PTEN protein and dysregulation of the phosphoinositol-3-kinase/Akt pathway.', *American Journal of Human Genetics*, 73: 404–411.

Zhu, Y. and Parada, L.F. (2001) 'Neurofibromin, a tumor suppressor in the nervous system.', *Experimental Cell Research*, 264: 19–28.

Zigman, A.F., Lavine, J.E., Jones, M.C., Boland, C.R. and Carethers, J.M. (1997) 'Localization of the Bannayan-Riley-Ruvalcaba syndrome gene to chromosome 10q23.', *Gastroenterology*, 113: 1433–1437.

Zikanova, M., Skopova, V., Hnizda, A., Krijt, J. and Kmoch, S. (2010) 'Biochemical and structural analysis of 14 mutant ADSL enzyme complexes and correlation to phenotypic heterogeneity of adenylosuccinate lyase deficiency.', *Human Mutation, 31*: 1–11.

Zimmerman, A.W., Jyonouchi, H., Comi, A.M., Connors, S.L. *et al.* (2005) 'Cerebrospinal fluid and serum markers of inflammation in autism.', *Pediatric Neurology, 33*: 195–201.

Zimmerman, A.W., Connors, S.L., Matteson, K.J., Lee, L-C. *et al.* (2007) 'Maternal antibrain antibodies in autism.', *Brain, Behaviour, and Immunity, 21*: 351–357.

Zimmermann, N., Acosta, A.M.B.F., Kohlhase, J. and Bartsch, O. (2007) 'Confirmation of EP300 gene mutations as a rare cause of Rubinstein-Taybi syndrome.', *European Journal of Human Genetics, 15*: 837–842.

Zingerevich, C., Greiss-Hess, L., Lemons-Chitwood, K., Harris, S.W. *et al.* (2009) 'Motor abilities of children diagnosed with fragile-X syndrome with and without autism.', *Journal of Intellectual Disability Research, 53*(1): 11–18.

Zinn, A.R., Roeltgen, D., Stefanatos, G., Ramos, P. *et al.* (2007) 'A Turner syndrome neurocognitive phenotype maps to Xp22.3.', *Behavioural and Brain Functions, 3*: 24, doi:10.1186/1744-9081-3-24.

Zipursky, A., Peeters, M. and Poon, A. (1987) 'Megakaryoblastic leukemia and Down syndrome – a review.', In E.E. McCoy and C.J. Epstein: *Oncology and Immunology of Down Syndrome.* New York: Alan R. Liss.

Ziter, F.A., Wiser, W.C. and Robinson, A. (1977) 'Three-generation pedigree of a Möbius syndrome variant with chromosome translocation.', *Archives of Neurology, 34*(7): 437–442.

Zittoun, J. (1995) 'Congenital errors of folate metabolism.', *Bailliere's Clinical Haematology, 8*(3): 603–616.

Zittoun, J. (2001) ['Biermer's disease.'] [Article in French.] *Revue Pratique, 51*(14): 1542–1546.

Zizka, J., Elias, P. and Jakubec, J. (2001) 'Spontaneous regression of low-grade astrocytomas: an underrecognized condition?' *European Radiology, 11*: 2638–2640.

Zoghbi, H.Y., Ledbetter, D.H., Schultz, R., Percy, A.K. and Glaze, D.G. (1990) 'A *de novo* X3 translocation in Rett syndrome.', *American Journal of Medical Genetics, 35*: 148–151.

Zoller, M.E., Rembeck, B. and Backman, L. (1997) 'Neuropsychological deficits in adults with neurofibromatosis type 1.', *Acta Neurologica Scandinavica, 95*: 225–232.

Zonana, J., Rimoin, D.L. and Davis, D.C. (1976) 'Macrocephaly with multiple lipomas and hemangiomas.', *Journal of Pediatrics, 89*: 600–603.

Zonana, J., Rimoin, D.L. and Fisher, D.A. (1976) 'Cerebral gigantism – apparent dominant inheritance.', *Birth Defects Original Articles Series, XII*(6): 63–69.

Zonana, J., Sotos, J.F., Romshe, C.A., Fisher, D.A. *et al.* (1977) 'Dominant inheritance of cerebral gigantism.', *Journal of Pediatrics, 91*: 251–256.

Zschocke, J., Graham, C.A., Stewart, F.J., Carson, D.J. and Nevin, N.C. (1994) 'Non-phenylketonuria hyperphenylalaninaemia in Northern Ireland: frequent mutation allows screening and early diagnosis.', *Human Mutation, 4*: 114–118.

Zschocke, J., Mallory, J.P., Eiken, H.G. and Nevin, N.C. (1997) 'Phenylketonuria and the peoples of Northern Ireland.', *Human Genetics, 100*: 189–194.

Zucconi, M., Ferini-Strambi, L., Erminio, C., Pestalozza, G. and Smirne, S. (1993) 'Obstructive sleep apnoea in the Rubinstein-Taybi syndrome.', *Respiration, 60*(2): 127–132.

Zwaigenbaum, L. (2010) 'Advances in the early detection of autism.', *Current Opinion in Neurology, 23*(2): 97–102.

Zwaigenbaum, L. and Tarnopolsky, M. (2003) 'Two children with muscular dystrophies ascertained due to referral for diagnosis of autism.', *Journal of Autism and Developmental Disorders, 33*(2): 193–199.

Zweier, C., Thiel, C.T., Dufke, A., Crow, Y.J. *et al.* (2005) 'Clinical and mutational spectrum of Mowat-Wilson syndrome.', *European Journal of Medical Genetics, 48*: 97–111.

INDEX